Routledge Handbook of Sustainable Development in Asia

In the present global context, some countries still face many challenges to bringing about inclusive, efficient, and environmentally sustainable development. Simultaneously, the stakes of survival are rising, as climate change exacerbates both environmental and social ills. Asia as a region is particularly vulnerable, as it is densely populated and includes both developed and developing countries.

The *Routledge Handbook of Sustainable Development in Asia* seeks to examine these issues in depth. Presenting a comprehensive literature review, as well as numerous case studies, this book examines sustainable development from economic and social perspectives, as well as from an environmental viewpoint. Divided into seven parts, the topics addressed include:

- Environmental challenges
- Energy dependence and transition
- Economic justice
- Social welfare
- Sustainable governance.

Providing comprehensive coverage of a wide variety of countries in the region, this handbook will be useful for students and scholars of sustainable development, environment and society, and Asian Studies in general.

Sara Hsu is an Associate Professor of Economics at the State University of New York at New Paltz. Her recent publications include *Development in China, India and Japan* (2016) and *Lessons in Sustainable Development from Malaysia and Indonesia* (2014).

Routledge Handbook of Sustainable Development in Asia

Edited by Sara Hsu

Routledge
Taylor & Francis Group
LONDON AND NEW YORK

First published 2018
by Routledge
2 Park Square, Milton Park, Abingdon, Oxon OX14 4RN

and by Routledge
52 Vanderbilt Avenue, New York, NY 10017

First issued in paperback 2020

Routledge is an imprint of the Taylor & Francis Group, an informa business

British Library Cataloguing-in-Publication Data
A catalogue record for this book is available from the British Library

Library of Congress Cataloging-in-Publication Data
Names: Hsu, Sara, editor.
Title: Routledge handbook of sustainable development in Asia/
edited by Sara Hsu.
Description: Abingdon, Oxon; New York, NY: Routledge, 2018. |
Includes bibliographical references and index.
Identifiers: LCCN 2017059113| ISBN 9781138182189 (hardback) |
ISBN 9781351008204 (ebook)
Subjects: LCSH: Sustainable development–Asia.
Classification: LCC HC415.E5 R684 2018 | DDC 338.95/07–dc23
LC record available at https://lccn.loc.gov/2017059113

ISBN 13: 978-0-367-58065-0 (pbk)
ISBN 13: 978-1-138-18218-9 (hbk)

Typeset in Bembo
by Sunrise Setting Ltd., Brixham, UK

Contents

Figures, tables and boxes

Figures

Tables

Boxes

Contributors

Ainul Jaria Maidin is a Professor at the Ahmad Ibrahim Kulliyyah of Laws, International Islamic University Malaysia.

Anil Markandya is an Honorary Professor of Economics at Bath University.

Ashiru Bello is a Lecturer in the Department of Urban and Regional Planning, Ahmadu Bello University Zaria, Nigeria.

Badri Narayanan Gopalakrishnan is a Visiting Scientist at the School of Environmental Sciences and Forestry, University of Washington.

Bijon Kumer Mitra is a Water Resource Specialist at the Institute for Global Environmental Strategies.

Carol Newman is an Associate Professor at the Department of Economics at Trinity College Dublin.

Choy Yee Keong is a Research Fellow at the Faculty of Economics, Keio University.

Christopher Dent is a Professor of East Asia's International Political Economy at the University of Leeds.

Cynthia Castillejos-Petalcorin is a Senior Economics Officer at the Economic Research and Regional Cooperation Department (ERCD), Asian Development Bank.

Dan Biller is Sector Manager of the Economics Unit in the Multilateral Investment Guarantee Agency at the World Bank.

Darrin Magee is an Associate Professor of Environmental Studies and Chair, Environmental Studies Program and Asian Studies Department at Hobart and William Smith Colleges.

Debashis Chakraborty is an Associate Professor at the Indian Institute of Foreign Trade.

Dennis Victor is an alumnus Research Scientist from the University of Malaya.

Donghyun Park is a Principal Economist at the Economic Research and Regional Cooperation Department (ERCD), Asian Development Bank.

Dulani Seneviratne is a Senior Research Officer at the IMF.

Edda Zoli is a Senior Economist in the Asia and Pacific Department at the IMF.

Edi Suharto is Deputy Minister for Social Rehabilitation, Ministry of Social Afffairs and senior lecturer at the Bandung College of Social Welfare, Indonesia.

Eunju Chi is a Research Professor at Peace and Democracy Institute at Korea University.

Farzad Taheripour is a Research Associate Professor of Agricultural Economics at Purdue University.

Gemma Estrada is a Senior Economics Officer at the Asian Development Bank.

Helen Cabalu is a Professor of Economics and Head of the School of Economics and Finance at Curtin University.

Hitomi Rankine is an Environmental Affairs Officer of the Environment and Development Division, UNESCAP.

Janice S.H. Lee is an Assistant Professor in the Asian School of the Environment at Nanyang Technological University.

John Fien is a Professor of Practice, School of Architecture and Urban Design, RMIT University, Melbourne.

John Rand is a Professor of Development Economics at the University of Copenhagen.

José A. Puppim de Oliveira is a Faculty Member at Fundação Getulio Vargas (FGV/EAESP and FGV/EBAPE), Brazil.

Kareff Limocon Rafisura is an Environment Affairs Officer of the Environment and Development Policy Section, UNESCAP.

Ken'ichi Matsumoto is an Associate Professor at Nagasaki University.

Lahiru S. Wijedasa is a researcher at the Theoretical Ecology & Modelling Lab, Department of Biological Sciences, National University of Singapore.

Lee Liu is a Professor of Geography at the University of Central Missouri.

Levan Lim is an Associate Professor and Head of Early Childhood & Special Needs Education at the National Institute of Education, Nanyang Technological University.

Luis Andrés is Lead Economist in the Water Global Practice at the World Bank.

Maizatun Mustafa is an Associate Professor of the Ahmad Ibrahim Kulliyyah of Laws, International Islamic University Malaysia.

Mark Elder is a Principal Researcher and Senior Coordinator in the Programme Management Office at the Institute for Global Environmental Strategies.

Mary Rose C. Posa is an Instructor in the Department of Biological Sciences at the National University of Singapore.

Matías Herrera Dappe is a Senior Economist in the Transport and ICT Global Practice at the World Bank.

Neda Trifkovic is a Postdoc at Department of Economics at the University of Copenhagen.

Peter Marcotullio is a Professor of Geography at Hunter College.

Rattan Lal is a Professor of Soil Science and Director of the Carbon Management and Sequestration Center at Ohio State University.

Reiji Takeishi is a Professor of Development Economics at Tokyo International University.

Riyana Miranti is an Associate Professor and Convenor of Indonesia Program, NATSEM, IGPA, at the University of Canberra.

Rupert Maclean is UNESCO Chair on Technical and Vocational Education and Training (TVET) and Sustainable Development at the College of The North Atlantic-Qatar.

Sacchidananda Mukherjee is an Associate Professor at the National Institute of Public Finance and Policy.

Sara Hsu is an Associate Professor of Economics at the State University of New York at New Paltz.

Sebnem Sahin is a Senior Environmental Economist at the World Bank.

Seck Tan is an Assistant Professor at the Singapore Institute of Technology.

Selim Elekdag is Deputy Division Chief of the Global Financial Stability Division at the IMF.

Shu Tian is an Economist at the Economic Research and Regional Cooperation Department (ERCD), Asian Development Bank.

Simi Mehta is a Fulbright-Nehru Doctoral Research Fellow at Ohio State University.

Soocheol Lee is a Professor of Economics at Meijo University.

Thana Thaver is a Senior Lecturer of Early Childhood & Special Needs Education at the National Institute of Education, Nanyang Technological University.

Thomas Markussen is an Associate Professor at the Department of Economics, University of Copenhagen.

Thomas W. Hertel is a Distinguished Professor of Agricultural Economics at Purdue University.

Vikash Kumar is an Assistant Professor at the Centre for Research in Rural and Industrial Development.

Vivek Prasad is Assistant Professor at George Mason University and World Bank Consultant.

Wenjie Zhang is an Associate Health Economist at Grey Health Group.

Yixiao Zhou is a Lecturer in Economics in the School of Economics and Finance at Curtin University.

Yu-Wai Vic Li is an Assistant Professor in the Department of Social Sciences at the Hong Kong Institute of Education.

Zeehan Jaafar is a Lecturer in the Department of Biological Sciences at the National University of Singapore.

1
Introduction

Darrin Magee

Sustainability

Sustainability. It's a word we often hear, an idea we rarely publicly question, and a goal we have yet to achieve. The notion of sustainable development first entered common parlance with the Brundtland Commission[1] report *Our Common Future* in 1987. Since then, its more slippery variant "sustainability" has proven harder to define, easier to co-opt, and – not surprisingly – more readily operationalized to justify countless policies and actions that are often at odds with each other and with the very ideals the Brundtland Commission report espoused. It is wise, then, at the start of any conversation about sustainable development, to ask three key questions:

Who is sustaining what for whom?
Why?
And finally, how?

At a glance, these queries may seem overly simplistic. Yet as this volume demonstrates, the subjects, objects, goals, and methods of sustainable development can vary widely depending on their geographic, political economic, and historical contexts. Indeed, given the vast complexity and rich diversity of Asia, the focal region of this volume, it should come as no surprise that the ways of understanding and implementing sustainable development in Asia should be as diverse as its inhabitants.

For the purposes of this volume, we understand sustainability as a goal, some sort of elusive steady state where humans manage to balance their own current needs and wants with those of the future, as well as with the non-human world. Sustainable development, then, represents the means – policies, technologies, behaviors, and most importantly, choices – for achieving that goal.

Framing sustainable development in Asia

Sustainable development has been a consideration for millennia, and this is most visible in Asia. For example, Western China's Sichuan province is home to perhaps the oldest example of sustainable development infrastructure in the world: the Dujiangyan flood control weir. The structure dates back to the first century BC, and was built to control and reduce the annual floods that had for centuries destroyed lives, homes, and livelihoods in one of the region's most agriculturally productive areas. Simple in design and elegant in function, the structure consists primarily of a weir, or an artificial divide in the river channel that was originally constructed by reed baskets filled with stones and placed in the river. The baskets were heavy and bulky enough that they remained in position despite the river's flow, allowing villagers time to gradually build up a solid and enduring underwater wall in the river channel. Under normal flow conditions, the weir allows water to flow in the main channel of the Min River, a left-bank tributary of the Yangtze (Chang) River. Yet during flood periods, a portion of the water spills over the weir and into the central Sichuan floodplains, bringing water and soil-enriching sediments to the floodplain without completely destroying it, all while relieving some of the pressure on the main channel to transport the volume of the full flood. Even though the structure has been reinforced many times over the centuries, including with concrete in recent times, its design and function have remained essentially the same, suggesting an early and sophisticated appreciation of the delicate balance between environmental stewardship and economic well-being among those who created and maintained the weir.

Now, some two millennia later, the origin of modern sustainability thinking can be traced to the 1972 United Nations Conference on the Human Environment. Held in Stockholm, Sweden, the conference marks the date when "the international community first explored the connection between quality of life and environmental quality" (Rogers, Jalal, and Boyd 2008, 42). The 1987 Brundtland Commission report defined sustainable development as "development that meets the needs of the present without compromising the ability of future generations to meet their own needs" (World Commission on Environment and Development 1987, Ch. 2.1). Perhaps the most enduring and noble aspect of that definition is the fact that development and its fruits – better health, cleaner air and water, greater educational outcomes, more reliable and resilient infrastructure, and so on – should be available across generations, not simply for those humans fortunate enough to inhabit the planet earlier than others. The Commission further identifies three pillars of sustainable development that, it argues, should be equally prioritized: economic growth, environmental protection, and social equality.

Unfortunately, leaders in most countries in Asia and around the world, from liberal democracies to autocratic regimes, have tended to prioritize economic development, most often measured in Gross Domestic Product (GDP). Yet that metric, while handy and relatively easy to calculate as a proxy for economic growth, is hopelessly flawed as a measure of the other two pillars indicated by the Brundtland Commission report. Many believe that alternative metrics such as the Human Development Index (HDI) – based on longevity, health, knowledge, and standard of living[2] – are more closely aligned with the priorities of sustainable development. Yet for the most part, GDP remains the gold standard for measuring development.

Commitments to sustainable development abound on the webpages of national governments, in the strategic plans of international non-governmental or inter-governmental organizations, and in the annual reports of multinational corporations doing business in Asia. The Asian Development Bank (ADB) website lists the 17 Sustainable Development Goals identified in the United Nations 2015 Sustainable Development Summit in New York, including putting an end to hunger and poverty, achieving gender equality, improving energy access and security, combating climate change, and working for peace and justice. None of the 17 would be easy to omit as frivolous or lower in priority than the others; yet many are mammoth in their scope and implications, making it difficult to imagine concrete steps that might result in the timely achievement of those goals by the stated target date of 2030, even when those 17 goals are accompanied by 169 targets designed to make them easier to operationalize and actualize. Similarly, the Association of Southeast Asian Nations (ASEAN) includes in its charter a commitment "to promote sustainable development so as to ensure the protection of the region's environment, the sustainability of its natural resources, the preservation of its cultural heritage and the high quality of life of its peoples" (ASEAN 2007, Art. 1.8). Petronas, Malaysia's largest oil company, touts its own commitment to "balancing the economic, environmental and social needs of [its] stakeholders" by "safeguarding people, assets, environment and [its] reputation" (Petronas 2017). Toyota, arguably an industry leader in lower-carbon transportation, showcases its vehicle recycling program, and hydrogen vehicle efforts (Toyota 2017).

At times, commitments on national, corporate, or organizational websites or other materials may appear as nothing more than hollow slogans designed to "greenwash" a business-as-usual approach to development premised on developing first and cleaning up later. At other times they may be more genuine, grounded in the realities of a particular country or region and reflecting a real commitment to blaze a new path forward, even if that commitment is motivated primarily out of leaders' concerns for social unrest in the face of looming socio-environmental catastrophes. Some of the chapters in this volume document commendable and well-intentioned sustainable development efforts led by governments, corporations, and NGOs in the region, many of which have produced real and tangible fruits for humans and their environments. Yet clear and significant roadblocks remain.

In keeping with the classic framework detailed in the Brundtland Commission report, this volume situates sustainable development at the nexus of various interrelated social, ecological, and economic dynamics. Individual chapters are organized into the six substantive sections of the volume, each of which fits under one of the three pillars noted above: sustainable development policy and sustainable governance comprise the social pillar; energy dependence and environmental issues comprise the ecology pillar; and economic justice and social welfare comprise the economic pillar. The lines separating the three pillars are, of course, rather arbitrary – indeed, one could argue that therein lies the crux of sustainability thinking – yet they are maintained here for analytical convenience. Figure 1.1 provides a schematic of the conceptual framework.

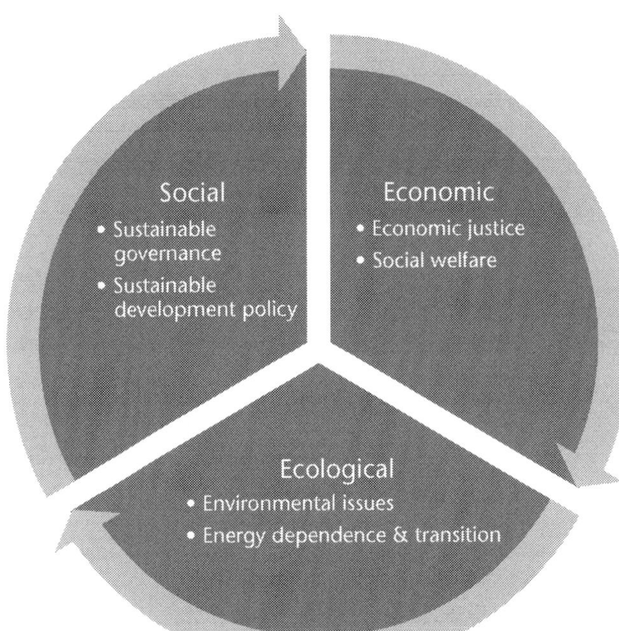

Figure 1.1 Conceptual framework for understanding sustainable development in Asia

Source: Author.

We intend readers to understand all three pillars, and their six sub-categories, to be equally important to the overall goal – elusive as it may seem – of pursuing sustainable development actions and policies that will enable humans to continue to thrive on the planet, in greater harmony with the non-human world, for centuries to come. On this point we follow Rogers, Jalal, and Boyd (2008, 46), who argue thus:

- Economic objectives cannot be maximized without satisfying environmental and social constraints.
- Environmental benefits cannot necessarily be maximized without satisfying economic and social constraints.
- Social benefits cannot be maximized without satisfying economic and environmental constraints.

Rogers et al. go on to provide a comprehensive and critical overview of various canonical definitions of sustainable development, along with different methods of assessing the social, economic, and ecological dimensions. In the remainder of this chapter, we examine in greater depth the six sub-categories of the sustainable development framework utilized in this volume, providing illustrative Asia-specific examples for each.

Economic pillar: economic justice and social welfare

Economics is about the efficient allocation of resources. Frequently used indicators of economic well-being include items such as rates of growth or expansion (usually measured in GDP growth); the number of jobs created; or the value of goods and services produced, consumed, imported, or exported. These things are all relatively easy to measure, and do indeed provide some insights into the state of economic activity in a country or region. Yet as is frequently the case, those indicators that are easiest to measure are not always reliable proxies of the actual things we care about and seek to measure. The corollary? If we fail to measure the things we value, we fail to account for them, and end up simply valuing the things we measure.

In a seminal work on the relationship between human societies and the natural world in which they are embedded, authors Hawken, Lovins, and Lovins (1999) argue that conventional economic development models have treated the Earth's productive *capital* assets (stocks) as if they were *income* (flows), consuming and degrading them and thereby reducing their ability to sustain human- and non-human life. More than just trees to be valued as lumber, for instance, a rainforest provides vital services such as oxygen production and carbon storage, services rarely valued in conventional economic accounting, but invaluable to our species' (and others') ability to survive, let alone thrive. Hawken et al. made a sobering but hopeful call to arms, now nearly two decades old, which focused on the need to shift our economic activities so that they restore and generate natural capital, thus creating more abundant assets on which future generations can depend. This perspective fits squarely with the Brundtland Commission's focus on intergenerational equity.

Economic justice and social welfare together comprise the economic pillar of our conceptual framework. Justice is about fairness, and economic justice is about envisioning – and creating – an economic system that produces fair outcomes for all involved. Given the current situation where a handful of global billionaires control the same wealth as the poorer half of the world's population, it is hard to imagine a more unjust system (OXFAM 2017). Perhaps the most readily apparent way of understanding economic justice is through measures of how income and wealth vary across different groups in a society: between women and men, immigrants and locals, rural and urban, and so on. The Gini coefficient is one such indicator, a widely used tool that captures the distribution of various income levels across society. Other indicators tally the number of people living at or below internationally accepted thresholds for poverty (e.g., $1.90 USD per day).

Closely related to economic justice, social welfare refers to government systems that provide some minimal level of well-being for their citizens. These services are especially vital for disadvantaged people who may not be able to attain that well-being by their own means, including those with mental or physical disabilities, children and the elderly, homeless families, immigrants, refugees, or others who have simply lost their job and having difficulty making ends meet. Often the costs of supporting these individuals falls to family members and friends who themselves may have limited financial means. While opponents of social welfare programs argue that they create unhealthy dependence on costly government services, harder to estimate (and far greater) are the cumulative long-term costs of *not* providing some form of a safety net for all citizens. Those long-term costs include not only mortality and morbidity due to inadequate health care, housing, or other basic needs assistance, but also the risk that children who grow up in impoverished conditions have a much more difficult time breaking out of those conditions as adults, and therefore risk extending the need for those services by a generation. Of particular concern are refugees leaving homes ravaged by war and, increasingly, the effects of climate change. Given that more developed countries (aka "The Global North") bear greater responsibility for cumulative climate greenhouse gas emissions responsible for climate change, those countries should shoulder more of the responsibility for helping those in need.

Ecological pillar: environmental issues and energy

Stewardship of the non-human world is the foundation of sustainability thinking and action. According to the editors of an earlier edited volume on environmental issues in East and Southeast Asia, "[t]he environment seldom degrades by itself and resources do not disappear of their own accord. It is human and social behavior that determines environmental health and, in turn, human and social vitality" (Harris and Lang 2014, 3). Should the life-support systems provided by the soils, waters, and atmosphere of our planet cease to function in a reliable and predictable fashion, humans will face enormous adaptive challenges. At that point, humans' ability to maintain the social and economic pillars of sustainable development would almost certainly deteriorate rapidly, and any discussion of sustainable development would, sadly, likely become moot.

Today, countries throughout Asia face serious environmental challenges that are intimately connected to the health of peoples and economies of the region, and indeed the world. The list is long, and while many of the environmental issues themselves are not unique to Asia, their connection to humans – either as *results* of human activities or as *causes* of human malady and suffering – are tighter than in many other parts in the world simply because population densities in many of Asia's most polluted places are so high. According to Harris and Lang (2014, 4), "the future of the global environment will be determined in Asia, where countries with very large populations are developing rapidly, in the process adopting many of the environmentally harmful practices of the Western world." Moreover, environmental issues such as pollution and lack of reliable and clean drinking water have measurable, tangible, and non-negligible costs in terms of economic productivity and social well-being.

It is important to note that we do not in this volume take environmental degradation – or progress toward reversing that – to be simply a function of population.[3] Instead, we recognize that while population and population growth rate do contribute to environmental, social, and economic challenges, it is only one variable in a more complex relationship, classically and presciently framed by Paul Ehrlich and John Holden as $\boldsymbol{I = P \cdot A \cdot T}$. Here, *I* represents impact, defined as the multiplicative product of *P* population, *A* affluence, and *T* technology, respectively. This relation characterizes a particular environmental impact such as deforestation or water pollution as a multiplicative product of not only the size of a population, but also the consumption habits and technologies employed by that population.[4]

Energy makes up the second component of the ecological pillar. While many of the environmental issues also considered here are directly related to energy – air pollution from coal combustion, for instance – the topic of energy is so crucial and complex that it merits, in our view, consideration on its own. Two focal concerns are the transition from conventional polluting energy sources to cleaner, renewable ones, and energy dependence. Both of these elements are closely linked to social and economic indicators. Renewable energy, for instance, is one of the fastest-growing sectors of many economies, providing employment opportunities, exports, and the chance for technology transfer that can then boost homegrown innovation. Dependence on other countries for energy resources, meanwhile, can bring geopolitical tensions or conflict, which in turn can skew government investment towards expensive military and security hardware and away from pro-poor programs at home that can improve the quality of life for the people of Asia. Some authors, as a consequence, have urged a rethinking of "energy security" to shift the focus away from traditional priorities of securing access to fossil fuels to a broader definition that recognizes the value of a more renewables-based energy system in providing real energy security (von Hippel et al. 2011).

Social pillar: sustainable governance and sustainable development policies

Sustainable governance takes the notion of good governance, long a priority in development circles, one step further to underscore the need for institutions – in government, the private sector, and the non-governmental and non-profit sector – that are sound, just, and durable. Rogers, Jalal, and Boyd (2008) note the four principles of good governance espoused by the World Bank and other multilateral lending agencies: accountability; participation and decentralization; predictability; and transparency. Good governance means that funds allocated for development reach the people and sectors that need it most, rather than line the pockets of corrupt officials. Equally important, it means that those who stand to be most affected by investments in particular projects should have a say in determining the nature and scope of those projects, should be able to independently verify that the investments are serving their intended purpose, and should not be surprised by investment priorities of the responsible agency or funder.

The Asian Development Bank was the first multilateral development bank to lay out a policy on good governance (Asian Development Bank 2017). That policy was first articulated in a 1995 report in which the Bank defined good governance essentially as effective management of economic and social resources (Asian Development Bank 1995, 3–4). A 2008 strategy document showed a continued commitment to essentially the same definition articulated in 1995, with good governance (and capacity building) seen as necessary to "improve the cost-effective delivery of public goods and services broaden inclusiveness" (Asian Development Bank 2008). Of course, a policy commitment does not always translate into actual outcomes "on the ground" in countries that host ADB-funded projects; this is where critical scholarship of the type showcased in this volume comes into play. ADB makes no pronouncement on which type of *government* system is best suited to foster good governance, noting on the one hand that rapid and sustained economic development has occurred under a variety of regime types across the region, and that governance is a function not only of governments, but also of non-governmental organizations, enterprises, and other entities. That said, it is difficult to imagine authoritarian regimes prioritizing the four principles of good governance noted above.

Sustainable development policies make up the second half of the social pillar. Just as there is great diversity of people across Asia, so, too, do we expect there to be a plurality of manners in which sustainable development priorities are articulated through policy throughout the region. Yet it is also reasonable to expect that those policies, diverse though they may be, will be science-based, humane, and equitable. Here, we do not intend for "science-based" to refer solely to knowledge derived using the scientific method; we also look for incorporation of place-based, traditional knowledge that is often overlooked during development interventions. This is a tall order; large-scale development projects such as dams have a particularly spotty track record for incorporating local and traditional knowledge about the impacts of major infrastructure on social, economic, and ecological systems (Magee 2014).

The United Nations Development Programme's Human Development Reports (HDR) rely on a range of indicators much broader than those comprising GDP to assess the level of *human* development – as opposed to the narrower *economic* development – of a country. Not surprisingly, some of those indicators are well suited for assessing sustainable development. Table 1.1 lists the indicators used by the HDR to determine a country's sustainable development profile and the units in which each indicator is measured. The data are complex and, appropriately, the HDR do not reduce a country's sustainable development profile to a single score or index; instead, values are given for each indicator, and on the web-based Dashboard (United Nations Development Programme 2016), high scores on indicators are highlighted by a bright green color.

Having sketched out the basic logic and justification of our framework for understanding sustainable development in Asia, we now turn to a high-level overview of the six sub-categories of the sustainable development framework. Each gives a snapshot of one or more key challenges to sustainable development that exist in Asia, challenges that, while significant, are not insurmountable. These snapshots are meant to be illustrative, not exhaustive; more detailed explorations come in the chapters that follow.

Table 1.1 Composition of UNDP Human Development Report's sustainable development profile

	Indicators	*Units*
Environmental sustainability	Renewable energy consumption	% of total final energy consumption
	CO_2 emissions	per capita (tons)
		Average annual change (%)
	Forest area	% of total land area
		Change (%)
	Fresh water withdrawals	% of total renewable water resources
Economic sustainability	Natural resource depletion	% of GNI
	Adjusted net savings	% of GNI
	External debt stock	% of GNI
	R&D expenditure	% of GDP
	Concentration index (exports)	–
Social sustainability	Income quintile ratio	Average annual change (%)
	Gender Inequality Index	Average annual change (%)
	Population in multidimensional poverty	Average annual change (%)
	Old age dependency ratio (ages 65 and over)	per 100 people ages 15–64

Source: Adapted from United Nations Development Programme (2016).

Sustainable development in Asia: challenges and opportunities

The three pillars of sustainable development – economic growth, social equality,[5] and environmental protection – are often referred to as the triple bottom line. This rhetorical device aims to shift the thinking of decision makers from prioritizing economic growth above all else (i.e., focusing only on the economic bottom line) to giving equal attention to all three pillars, recognizing that real and enduring progress on any one axis cannot be made without comparable progress on the other two. The chapters in this volume are organized into six sections reflecting the six categories of the conceptual framework outlined above. Each of those sections provides crucial insights into the challenges to and opportunities for more sustainable development practices and policies that await in the realms of Asia's environments, societies, and economies. In the paragraphs below, I draw on publicly available data from sources such as the United Nations and the World Bank to briefly highlight challenges in those six categories. The chapters ahead provide more detailed case studies and analysis.

Environmental challenges in Asia

Pressing environmental challenges in Asia are not hard to find, unfortunately. Perhaps among the most daunting are the quantity and quality challenges to fresh water for drinking, hygiene, agriculture, and industry that many countries in the region face. For instance, while continent-sized China is not water-scarce on average, certain areas of the country, particularly in the north and northwest, regularly face severe and persistent droughts even as other areas endure devastating floods. Still other parts of the country where water is abundant experience high levels of water pollution from point- and non-point contaminant sources, such as agricultural runoff and failing or non-existent wastewater treatment plants. Eutrophication of lakes due to nutrient loading is widespread, debilitating to aquatic ecosystems and drinking water facilities, and often prohibitively expensive to reverse. The toxins produced by many strains of the algae responsible for eutrophication can be quite toxic to humans and a range of other animal species.

At the other end of the geographic scale, tiny Singapore, with no real freshwater resources of its own, is forced to depend on neighboring Malaysia for all its freshwater resources, a situation that leaves the island in an unenviable position geopolitically. Other small island countries throughout Asia face similar freshwater challenges, as surface water sources often comprise swift rivers flowing down mountain slopes, while underground aquifers frequently contain high levels of salinity due their proximity to, and connectivity with, the surrounding ocean. Japan, Indonesia, Malaysia, Taiwan, Brunei, and the Philippines all face the problem of groundwater salinity to some degree, as do coastal areas of larger countries in continental Asia. Not surprisingly, some see desalination of virtual endless supplies of seawater as a promising solution to the problem. Yet desalination technology is expensive, highly energy-intensive, and produces highly concentrated salt brine as a byproduct, disposal of which can be problematic. China, meanwhile, takes an all-of-the-above approach to meeting localized freshwater scarcity, actively pursuing desalination options while at the same time working to complete the gargantuan South-North Water Diversion (SNWD) project. If completed, the SNWD will annually move some 44 billion cubic meters of water from water-rich areas in southern China's Yangtze basin to drier areas in the north. That volume, tiny in comparison to all of China's total renewable internal freshwater resources, equals roughly 10 percent of Japan's.[6]

Soil and air pollution are similarly alarming in some areas. Conversion – a misleadingly benign term – of tropical rain forests to oil palm plantations in tropical Indonesia through bulldozing and burning periodically brings smoke and haze to parts of the region hundreds of kilometers away, all while rendering formerly forested slopes vulnerable to topsoil loss in the seasonal heavy rains brought by the monsoons. Yet vital to agricultural or forest productivity as they are, those soils sometimes exhibit alarmingly high levels of contaminants whose toxicity is well understood, such as cadmium and mercury resulting from coal-fired power plants and factories, or of compounds whose effects on living organisms is less clear, such as the thousands of synthetic chemicals with endocrine disrupting effects. Still another form of conversion, this time rural or agricultural land to parking lots or industrial zones, occurs apace in rapidly industrializing countries around the world, and Asia is no exception. As pavement and rooftops overtake farms and forests, farmers are forced to feed an increasingly hungry population on smaller and smaller plots of land. The situation can be further exacerbated when the farmland that remains is of poor quality or on marginal land.

Energy dependence and transition in Asia

Energy demand in Asia is growing as industry makes up an increasingly large share of the region's economies. Demand for both primary energy[7] and electricity has risen steadily over the past two decades, showing only slight decreases in the annual rate of growth during the 1997 Asian financial crisis and at the onset of the more recent global economic slowdown that began in 2009. Such growth in energy demand is not a phenomenon peculiar to Asia; countries around the world that have undergone transitions from agrarian societies to modern industrialized societies have experienced similar energy use growth trajectories. What is, however, particular to much of Asia is the *rate* of that growth since around 2000, as China's manufacturing engines reached a fever pitch. A contributing dynamic has been the increase in the number of people in Asia with incomes to support middle-class lifestyles and the energy consumption choices – from automobiles to air conditioning – that those lifestyles imply. Figure 1.2 shows the growth in per capita primary energy consumption and electricity consumption for the period beginning roughly with the start of the so-called East Asian Economic Miracle (led by Hong Kong, Taiwan, Singapore, and South Korea), and including the height of China's economic boom.

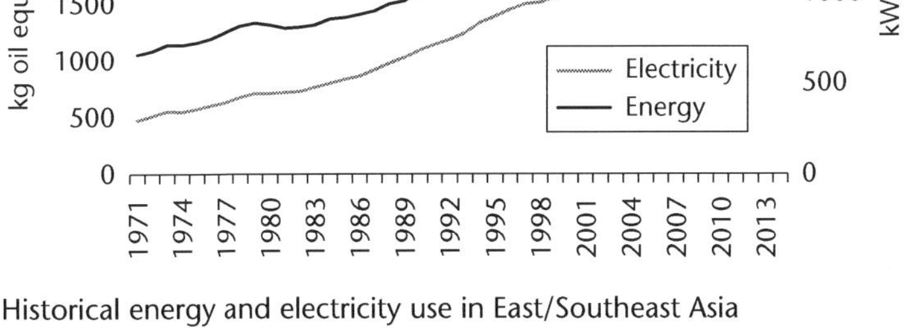

Figure 1.2 Historical energy and electricity use in East/Southeast Asia

Source: The World Bank. Available at http://data.worldbank.org/indicator/EG.USE.PCAP.KG.OE?locations=Z4&name_desc=false.

Energy transition in this volume refers to two types of transition. The first is a quantitative transition that accompanies the so-called economic transition, in which the prevalence of agriculture in a country's economy gives way to industry and then to services. Throughout that transition, and especially during the transition from agrarian to industrial economies, energy demand growth and GDP tend to be highly elastic, with the rate of growth in energy demand tending to mirror that of GDP. That said, as societies and economies mature and become more efficient, the energy intensity of GDP, or the amount of energy required to produce one unit of economic value, tends to shrink. This is particularly true as societies transition from economies that are heavily dependent on energy-intensive industries as the backbone of economic growth to ones that depend more heavily on services for that growth.

The second type of energy transition refers to that from conventional energy sources based heavily on fossil fuels such as coal, petroleum, and natural gas to renewable energy sources such as hydropower, solar power, biofuels, wind power, and efficiency. This transition has several benefits. First and most obvious, the global scientific community overwhelmingly agrees that human activities are magnifying the effects of and accelerating the pace of global climate change, primarily through the combustion of fossil fuels and consequent release of large amounts of carbon dioxide. Renewables help keep that carbon, the product of millions of years of sunshine photosynthesized by ancient plants, in the ground. Second, the cost of renewable energies is rapidly falling, spurred in large part by governments and private businesses around the world committing to large-scale purchases of renewable electricity, which then allows manufacturers to scale up their production of solar panels, wind turbines, and other renewable technologies, thereby driving down unit costs. Those cost declines have been so precipitous over the past decade that the cost of electricity generated by wind or solar farms is now essentially the same as coal-fired electricity, even without accounting for the cost of carbon emissions (which most countries continue to simply treat as an externality). In situations where carbon caps, carbon taxes, or other mechanisms to disincentivize fossil fuel combustion are implemented, renewables become even more cost-competitive with their fossil counterparts. As Figure 1.3 shows, however, the trend of renewables penetration in Asia does not match the trend worldwide, except perhaps in recent years where the two have ticked upward. This is somewhat troubling, and underscores the long

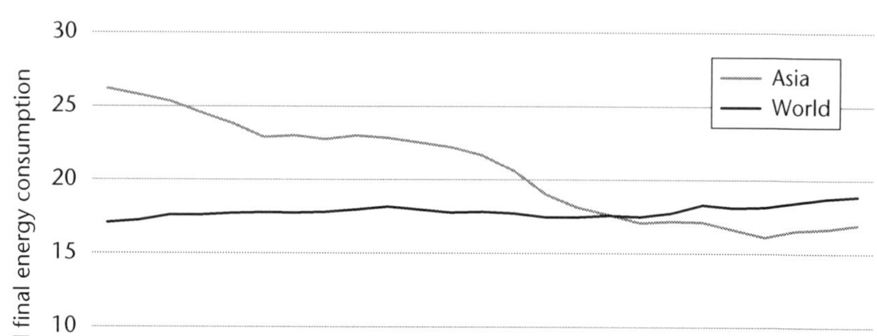

Figure 1.3 Percentage of renewable energy use in Asia and worldwide

Source: The World Bank. Available at http://data.worldbank.org/indicator/EG.FEC.RNEW.ZS?name_desc=false.

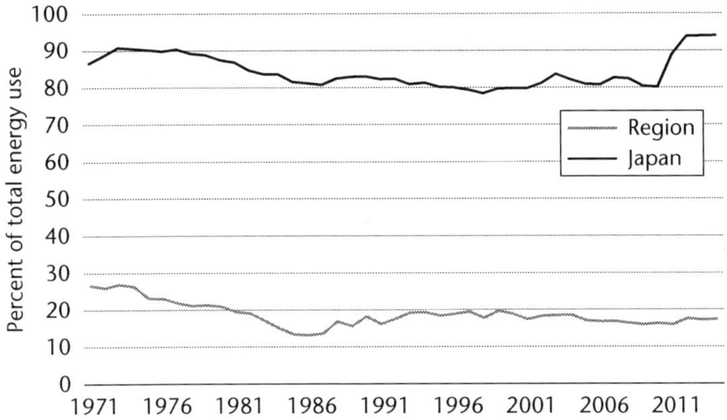

Figure 1.4 Energy imports in Asia (as a region) and Japan

Source: http://data.worldbank.org/indicator/EG.IMP.CONS.ZS?name_desc=false.

road ahead; dependence on fossil fuels in Asia remains high even as investments in renewables in countries like China outpace those in most places in the rest of the world.

A third important reason governments choose to invest in renewable energy is to reduce their energy dependence, or their dependence on other states for energy sources. In general, larger countries tend to have greater diversity of resources, and this usually holds true for energy resources. China, for instance, has massive reserves not only of fossil energy (most notably coal), but also of renewable energy (such as vast expanses of land suitable for utility-scale solar and wind power installations). Yet its supplies of petroleum and natural gas that are readily available are far less certain. Figure 1.4 shows the stark comparison between Asia's dependence on energy imports as a region to those of Japan, whose electricity sector was badly affected by the March 2011 earthquake and tsunami near Fukushima, which led to the meltdown of the Fukushima Daiichi nuclear plant and the subsequent shutdown of all the country's nuclear power plants. Most of these are now back online, but the country remains heavily dependent on imported energy.

In recent years, much has been made of the question of energy dependence in China as the country's economy has roared, and the South China Sea – and its expected treasure-trove of undersea petroleum and natural gas fields – has become a focal point of geopolitical conflict in Asia. This conflict is generally framed as motivated by competing attempts to control small islands and atolls whose sovereignty is contested and unresolved under the United Nations Convention on the Law of the Sea (UNCLOS). As the adage goes, possession is nine-tenths of the law, a truism that the Chinese government seems to have wholeheartedly adopted as it pursues a destructive and contentious campaign to shore up its presence and military force projection capability in the South China Sea through construction of artificial islands around and on top of contested atolls. From a realpolitik perspective, the state that controls these areas not only controls – de facto if not de jure – access to undersea hydrocarbon resources (not to mention fishing rights), but also gains the upper hand in preventing or ensuring passage of oceangoing vessels through the South China Sea and the Straits of Malacca. China (and much of the rest of the world) sees the Straits of Malacca as a shipping bottleneck critical for ensuring the steady flow of petroleum supplies to Asia from the Middle East and Africa. Thus despite an international tribunal's July 2016 ruling against China's claims, Beijing has vowed to continue to pursue what it sees as a sovereign right in developing its claims to the islands and surrounding waters (Kellogg 2016).

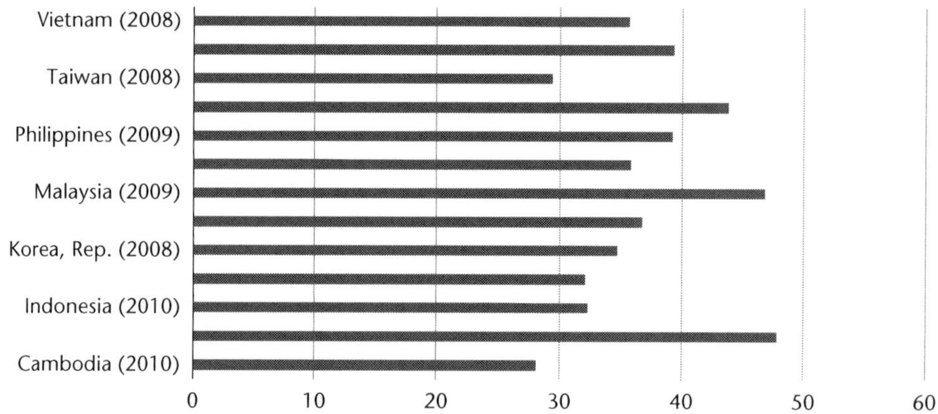

Figure 1.5 Normalized Gini coefficients for Asia

Source: The World Bank. Available at http://data.worldbank.org/data-catalog/all-the-ginis.

Economic justice in Asia

Economic justice is a difficult attribute to measure. As noted above, scholars and development professionals frequently use the Gini coefficient, a statistical tool designed to capture how scattered the income distribution is for individuals in a country, as a proxy for economic justice. The Gini coefficient is often interpreted as a measure of the income gap between a country's poorest and wealthiest individuals; a Gini of zero means that everyone in the country has the same income, whereas a Gini closer to 100 indicates that the highest incomes accrue to only a few individuals.[8] A Gini coefficient above 40 is generally considered to be a warning sign that income distribution in a country is skewed to a privileged elite.

The World Bank collects and reports income data, as do several other organizations, but comprehensive Gini data that are publicly available on an annual basis are not readily found. Figure 1.5 shows data for an incomplete set of East and Southeast Asian countries, with the numbers in parentheses on the vertical axis corresponding to the most recent year those data were available for that country. Clearly, data for different years are limited in their comparability, and the true picture of economic justice in many of these countries today is likely different from what is shown in the figure, but it is worth pointing out here that roughly half the countries shown have Gini coefficients in the mid-30s or higher, suggesting that the income gap between the richest and the poorest is rather high.

Another proxy for economic justice is poverty. The very first of the United Nation's eight Millennium Development Goals (MDGs), adopted in 2000, was to "eradicate extreme poverty and hunger" (United Nations 2016b). The UN's stated deadline for doing so was 2015. A 2016 UN report on progress toward the goals celebrated the decline in the proportion of people in extreme poverty, with one target – namely, halving between 1990 and 2015 the proportion of the population living on less than $1.25 a day (Target 1.A) – achieved by 2010. Progress on a second target related to poverty, "Achieving full and productive employment and decent work for all, including women and young people" (Target 1.B) has been more challenging, hampered in part by the global recession that began in 2008.

Social welfare in Asian nations

Social welfare, like economic justice, is somewhat difficult to measure. While countries publish data on volumes of goods produced, miles of road and railroad built, number of children

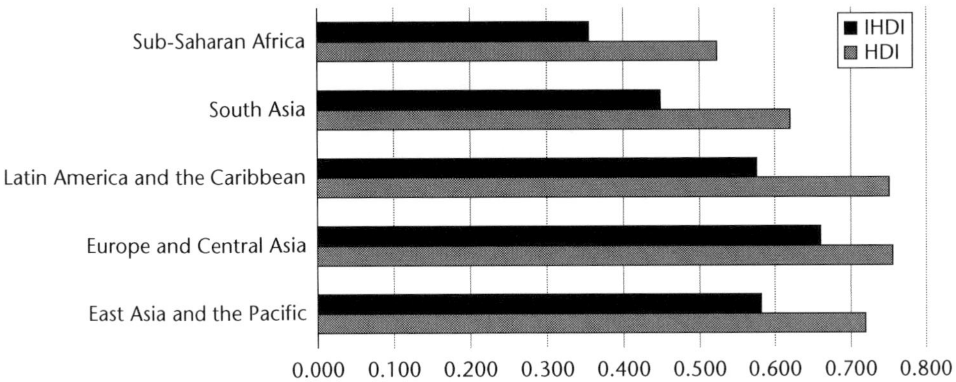

Figure 1.6 Human Development Index (HDI) by region

Source: United Nations Development Programme. Available at http://hdr.undp.org/en/composite/IHDI.

graduating from high school and so on, there is no single indicator for social welfare. As noted above, it is helpful to think of social welfare as a social safety net provided by government, a system that ensures that the state will be the guarantor of last resort that its citizens' basic needs are met. Education, health care access, and demographic measures can all be useful indicators of social welfare. So, too, can financial measures such as government expenditures and investments in those items, along with the number and specificity of policies designed to structure and direct those investments. Gross domestic product (GDP) per capita is often used as a crude measure of social welfare, despite its known limitations. Perhaps most important among those limitations, GDP per capita wholly fails to account for income distribution across a population, as indicated in the preceding section.

The World Bank's "Atlas of Social Protection: Indicators of Resilience and Equity (ASPIRE)" includes data on the adequacy of social insurance (welfare) programs, as measured "by the total transfer amount received by the population participating in social welfare programs as a share of their total welfare."[9] Yet the data are essentially non-existent for East and Southeast Asia, so the dataset's utility for analyzing social welfare in the region is extremely limited. The UNDP's Human Development Index (HDI) is more promising. As constructed, HDI is "a summary measure of average achievement in key dimensions of human development: a long and healthy life, being knowledgeable and having a decent standard of living" (United Nations Development Programme 2017). Clearly, such a measure is reflective of social welfare, even if it does not explicitly take into account actual government expenditures on social safety net programs. Figure 1.6 charts the 2015 HDI and IHDI, or the Inequality-adjusted HDI, for world regions. IHDI takes into account how evenly the HDI benefits are distributed across the population at various income levels, in this way capturing socioeconomic dynamics similar to those captured by the Gini coefficient.

Asia's sustainable development policies

The United Nations maintains an internet-based Sustainable Development Knowledge Platform[10] to track progress on the Sustainable Development Goals noted at the beginning of this chapter. Each year, the UN convenes a High-Level Political Forum (HLPF) on Sustainable Development, billed as the "central platform for follow-up and review of the 2030 Agenda for Sustainable Development and the Sustainable Development Goals" (United Nations 2017). Member countries are urged to submit annual Voluntary National Reviews documenting their progress toward the goals. The Voluntary National Reviews (VNR) highlight the priorities on which each country is acting at the moment, priorities that are reflective of each country's economic structure, population, and specific environmental and ecological conditions and challenges. The site provides a window into the sustainable development policies of member states, and how those policies vary from country to country. As an illustrative example, we briefly examine the 2017 report from China, which faces pressing challenges on all three pillars of sustainable development.

The Chinese VNR (United Nations 2016a) echoes many of the official buzzwords common in development discourse in China and reflects the Chinese government's priorities in domestic politics, foreign affairs, and trade. At times, such official statements can ring trite and hollow, as in "Coordinated development will be promoted to form a balanced structure of development." Further on, the author of the report notes that "[China] will make great efforts to deepen opening-up, thus realizing win–win cooperation." Other statements are almost tautological: "China will pursue green development by promoting a green and low-carbon development model and lifestyle, protecting ecological system (sic)." While the tongue-twisting "deepen opening-up" refers to China's "Open Up (Develop) the West" campaign (*xibu da kaifa*), officially underway since 2001, it is not clear who (or what) the two parties are in the "win–win" cooperation. The chapters in this volume dig beneath such sterilized official rhetoric to assess real progress and remaining challenges.

Domestically, China's National Development and Reform Commission (NDRC), ostensibly the most influential central government administration, is responsible for coordinating the priorities of various ministries and commissions and providing macroeconomic guidance for the country, primarily through the Five-Year Plans. Included in the main functions of the NDRC (number 10 of 15) is sustainable development, specifically:

> To promote the strategy of sustainable development; to undertake comprehensive coordination of energy saving and emission reduction; to organize the formulation and coordinate the implementation of plans and policy measures for recycling economy, national energy and resource conservation and comprehensive utilization; to participate in the formulation of plans for ecological improvement and environmental protection; to coordinate the solution of major issues concerning ecological building, energy and resource conservation and comprehensive utilization; to coordinate relevant work concerning environment-friendly industries and clean production promotion.
>
> *(National Development and Reform Commission n.d.)*

It is abundantly clear from the text that the NDRC's commitment to sustainable development, at least as articulated here, is exclusively focused on environmental issues. To some degree this is understandable, as the pollution threats to air, water, and soils in China are real and acute, and carry similarly real and acute human health and social stability implications. But the sole focus on the environmental pillar risks undermining the tight connection among the three pillars, and the simple truth that progress on one pillar may be offset or overshadowed by inattention to the other two.

Sustainable governance in Asia

Sustainable governance implies governance structures and practices that are durable and just, and which adhere to the principles of accountability, participation and decentralization,

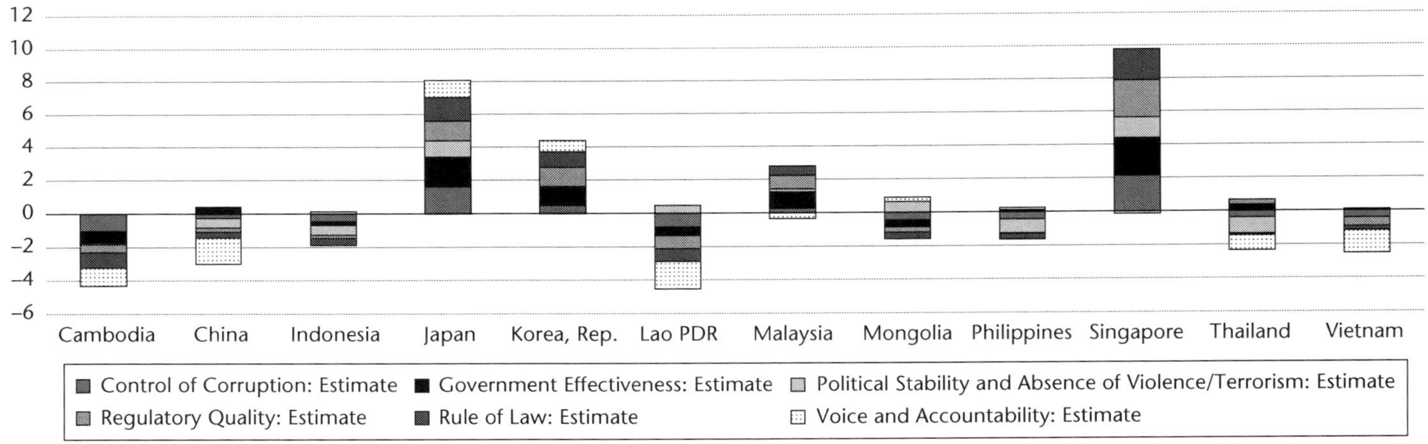

Figure 1.7 Governance Indicators for Selected Asian Countries

Source: World Bank, World Governance Indicators, available at http://data.worldbank.org/data-catalog/worldwide-governance-indicators.

predictability, and transparency. Sustainable governance indicates not only the structures and practices of governments, but also those of enterprises, non-governmental organizations, and inter-governmental and transboundary institutions such as ASEAN and the Mekong River Commission. Once more, it is a tall order to find ready indicators to quantitatively or qualitatively assess sustainable governance across such a wide variety of institutions and organizations.

Figure 1.7 is drawn from data in the World Bank's Worldwide Governance Indicators data series. As the chart shows, the data are estimates, and the metadata describing how the estimates were attained and the sources of supporting data are provided by the World Bank. While the indicators shown in the chart do not precisely reflect with the principles described in the preceding paragraph, they nevertheless reflect qualities most would agree are part and parcel of good governance. Not surprisingly, Asian states with low scores on indicators such as control of corruption and rule of law score poorly overall, with aggregate sums even in negative numbers. The cohort of countries scoring highly positive – Japan, Korea, and Singapore – is perhaps not surprising, and at the very least, the Bank's dissection of governance into these six quantifiable categories provides a starting point for further exploring the real hallmarks of and progress toward sustainable governance in Asia.

Conclusion

Asia, home to roughly half the world's population, is immense in geographic size, steeped in complex and interconnected histories, and endowed with exceedingly rich cultural and ecological diversity. It is to some extent, therefore, naïve and reductionist to speak of any one "Asia" or "Asian context." Nevertheless, I have endeavored to do just that in this chapter by first providing some background on the concept of sustainable development and then some thoughts on situating that concept in an Asian context (or, perhaps more appropriately, Asian *contexts*). In this volume, sustainable development broadly encapsulates the policies, technologies, behaviors, and choices that a country undertakes as a means of working toward a state of greater sustainability. Not surprisingly, many countries, enterprises, non-governmental organizations, and inter-governmental organizations operating in Asia, from the Asian Development Bank to United Airlines, all make some commitment to sustainable practices. At the very least, these commitments are little more than rhetorical and serve to normalize the discourse on sustainability, even while potentially diluting the potency of the concept. In the best case, commitments translate into changes in investment, spending, and behavioral practices that are better for the planet and its passengers.

The 1987 Brundtland Commission report prioritized intergenerational equity in development practices, in the hope that the decisions individuals and countries make today do not erode and degrade the planet's ability to provide ecosystem services so vital to human health and well-being, but rather restore and augment those systems. As in the Brundtland report, the conceptual framework that holds this volume together situates sustainable development at the nexus of ecological, social, and economic processes, a framing that demands a systems-thinking approach to complex problems such as climate change, water quality stewardship, and energy system transformation. We further refine the classic three-pillar approach to include six sub-categories: environmental issues and energy dependence constitute the ecology pillar; sustainable development policy and sustainable governance constitute the social pillar; and economic justice and social welfare constitute the economic pillar. The substantive chapters that follow offer detailed case studies from various Asian contexts that provide insights into the real progress made toward implementing more sustainable development models in Asia, along with the formidable challenges remaining.

Notes

1 Formally known as the World Commission on Environment and Development (WCED), with Gro Harlem Brundtland as its chair.
2 For more on HDI, see the United Nations Development Programme's Human Development Reports page at http://hdr.undp.org/en/content/human-development-index-hdi.
3 Nor, for that matter, do Harris and Lang (2014).
4 For a fuller discussion of the IPAT formula, see Rogers, Jalal, and Boyd (2008).
5 The concept is also framed by some as social equity.
6 Food and Agricultural Organization, AQUASTAT Data. Renewable internal freshwater resources, total (billion cubic meters). Retrieved from http://data.worldbank.org/indicator/ER.H2O.INTR.K3?name_desc=false&view=map.
7 Primary energy refers to energy resources used in their original form. Examples include fossil fuels such as coal, natural gas, and petroleum when used for heat as opposed to being converted to electricity. Some confusion often arises with nuclear power and hydropower, since their primary form is electricity.
8 Gini values may be presented as decimals ranging from 0 to 1 or they may be normalized to 100 for the sake of convenience.
9 See http://data.worldbank.org/indicator/per_si_allsi.adq_pop_tot. The quoted text is accessible via the Details link on the page.
10 The Platform is available at https://sustainabledevelopment.un.org/.

References

ASEAN. (2007) "Charter of the Association of Southeast Asian Nations." http://agreement.asean.org/media/download/20160509062115.pdf.

Asian Development Bank. (1995) "Governance: Sound Development Management." Asian Development Bank. www.adb.org/sites/default/files/institutional-document/32027/govpolicy.pdf.

Asian Development Bank. (2008) "STRATEGY2020: The Long-term Strategic Framework of the Asian Development Bank 2008–2020." www.adb.org/sites/default/files/institutional-document/32121/strategy2020-print.pdf.

Asian Development Bank. (2017) "ADB's Work on Governance and Development." Asian Development Bank. www.adb.org/sectors/governance/overview.

Harris, Paul G., and Graeme Lang. (2014) "East Asia and the Environment: A thematic introduction." In *Routledge Handbook of Environment and Society in Asia*, edited by Paul G. Harris and Graeme Lang, 3–18. London: Routledge.

Hawken, Paul, Amory B. Lovins, and L. Hunter Lovins. (1999) *Natural Capitalism: Creating the Next Industrial Revolution*. 1st ed. Boston: Little, Brown and Co.

Kellogg, Thomas E. (2016) "The South China Sea Ruling: China's International Law Dilemma." *The Diplomat*, July 14.

Magee, Darrin. (2014) "Dams in East Asia: Controlling Water but Creating Problems." In *Routledge Handbook of Environment and Society in Asia*, edited by Paul G. Harris and Graeme Lang, 216–236. London: Routledge.

National Development and Reform Commission. (n.d.) "Main Functions of the NDRC" [Government webpage]. http://en.ndrc.gov.cn/mfndrc/.

OXFAM. (2017) "An Economy for the 99 Percent." Last Modified January 15. www.oxfamamerica.org/explore/research-publications/an-economy-for-the-99-percent/.

Petronas. (2017) "Sustainability." www.petronas.com.my/sustainability/Pages/default.aspx.

Rogers, Peter P., Kazi F. Jalal, and John A. Boyd. (2008) *An Introduction to Sustainable Development*. London: Earthscan.

Toyota. (2017) "Environment" [Corporate webpage]. www.toyota-global.com/sustainability/environment/.

United Nations. (2016a) "China." https://sustainabledevelopment.un.org/hlpf/2016/china.

United Nations. (2016b) "We Can End Poverty: Millennium Development Goals and Beyond 2015." www.un.org/millenniumgoals/poverty.shtml.

United Nations. (2017) "Sustainable Development Knowledge Platform." https://sustainabledevelopment.un.org/hlpf.

United Nations Development Programme. (2016) "Dashboard 2: Sustainable Development." UNDP. http://hdr.undp.org/en/composite/Dashboard2.

United Nations Development Programme. (2017) "Human Development Reports." http://hdr.undp.org/en/content/human-development-index-hdi.

von Hippel, David, Tatsujiro Suzuki, James H. Williams, Timothy Savage, and Peter Hayes. (2011) "Energy security and sustainability in Northeast Asia." *Energy Policy* 39 (11):6719–6730. doi: 10.1016/j.enpol.2009.07.001.

World Commission on Environment and Development. (1987) "Our Common Future." United Nations. www.un-documents.net/our-common-future.pdf.

SECTION 1

Framework for understanding sustainable development

2

Framework for understanding sustainable development

Sara Hsu

Introduction

The *Handbook of Sustainable Development in Asia* highlights the important and relevant topic of sustainable development, which overlaps the fields of economics, environmental science, and social policy. At this stage in global development, countries face the challenge of bringing about development that is inclusive, efficient, and environmentally sound. Simultaneously, the stakes of survival are rising, as climate change exacerbates both environmental and social ills, threatening economic gains.

Asia as a region is particularly vulnerable, since it is the most densely populated region of the world and includes both developed and developing countries, some of which are growing at a rapid pace with limited concern for the environment and limited resources to provide social services. This volume focuses on sustainable development from a perspective of environmental challenges and energy dependence, economic justice and social welfare, and governance and policy making for sustainable development, specifically applied to Asia.

Sustainable development

As is well-discussed within this volume, sustainable development is associated with different definitions. The most common definition is that presented by the Brundtland Commission (1987, 16), which stated that sustainable development is the "ability to make development sustainable – to ensure that it meets the needs of the present without compromising the ability of future generations to meet their own needs." Robinson (2004) views sustainable development as a community-based process that integrates environmental, social, and economic aspects of development in a long-term perspective rather than a one-shot end goal. The World Conservation Union (IUCN) (1991, 10) defined sustainable development as a commitment to "to improve the quality of life while living within the carrying capacity of ecosystems."

Additional definitions have emphasized other aspects of development. Putnam (1993), for example, stresses the need to consider social capital, behavioral norms, trust, and social interactions. Conway and Barbier (1990) focused on the sustainability of economy, which they viewed as the ability to maintain productivity, or rate of consuming inputs to produce outputs.

Petkevičiūtė and Svirskaitė (2001) described sustainable development as the use of economic development and structural change to broaden human possibilities. We mention just a few here to provide an illustration of the breadth of sustainable development definitions, but we leave the full analysis of these myriad definitions to other works; indeed, there are entire volumes focused on defining sustainable development.

It is worth briefly mentioning that some researchers also make the distinction between strong versus weak sustainability. Strong sustainability emphasizes that the ability to substitute between natural and man-made capital is limited, whereas weak sustainability views these as substitutable, and unproblematic when the total capital stock remains constant over time (Daly 1994). As one can imagine, this broad difference has resulted in diverging policy implications.

In application, Atkinson et al. (1997) show that many countries fail the weak sustainability test, and would certainly fail the strong sustainability test. Many questions arise from the weak versus strong sustainability distinction. We can ask, for example, if natural capital stocks such as coal and oil can be directly substituted for by, say, renewable energy or other resources, why do they continue to play such an important role in the global economy? Why are water shortages so devastating? The answer seems to be that the natural resources we rely upon most are irreplaceable, or far less replaceable, than the weak sustainability requirements imply.

One may argue that definitions of sustainable development are of secondary importance to taking action toward sustainable development. In fact, at this critical juncture, in the face of impending irreversible climate change and lingering economic and social injustices, it is difficult not to view sustainable development as inseparable from development itself. Although the phrase has normative connotations, sustainable development is becoming an increasingly crucial policy mechanism to perpetuating life and human progress around the world, as well as a scientific field of study. If we continue to produce and consume in the same way in the future, humans will bring about rapid climate change, causing widespread suffering and even death for many. Rising sea levels will wipe out cities, violent storms will destroy homes, severe drought will result in rising hunger and water scarcity, hotter temperatures will result in increased vulnerability to disease and death, and destruction of ecosystems will result in dwindling sources of food and medicine. The good news is that we know enough about climate change and positive and negative impacts of various development trajectories to find a way forward, using a framework for sustainable development as a guide.

Sustainable development policies have risen to a level of global importance. In particular, it is significant that the United Nations has adopted Sustainable Development Goals as of September 2015. These goals augment the Millennium Development Goals by incorporating environmental and sustainability concerns, and can be applied not only to developing but also developed countries. These aim to:

- End poverty in all its forms everywhere;
- End hunger, achieve food security and improved nutrition and promote sustainable agriculture;
- Ensure healthy lives and promote well-being for all at all ages;
- Ensure inclusive and equitable quality education and promote lifelong learning opportunities for all;
- Achieve gender equality and empower all women and girls;
- Ensure availability and sustainable management of water and sanitation for all;
- Ensure access to affordable, reliable, sustainable and modern energy for all;
- Promote sustained, inclusive and sustainable economic growth, full and productive employment and decent work for all;
- Build resilient infrastructure, promote inclusive and sustainable industrialization and foster innovation;

- Reduce inequality within and among countries;
- Make cities and human settlements inclusive, safe, resilient and sustainable;
- Ensure sustainable consumption and production patterns;
- Take urgent action to combat climate change and its impacts;
- Conserve and sustainably use the oceans, seas and marine resources for sustainable development;
- Protect, restore and promote sustainable use of terrestrial ecosystems, sustainably manage forests, combat desertification, and halt and reverse land degradation and halt biodiversity loss;
- Promote peaceful and inclusive societies for sustainable development, provide access to justice for all and build effective, accountable and inclusive institutions at all levels; and
- Strengthen the means of implementation and revitalize the global partnership for sustainable development (United Nations (UN) 2015).

This is quite an agenda; it is one that seeks to address many aspects of sustainable development. Still, as Jabareen (2008) points out, there are inherent conflicts between growth and sustainability, and the way forward is not easy. Whereas economic growth stresses the environment in its deep use of natural resources, sustainability demands continued preservation of ecosystems over time, with little change. To this end, sustainable development has been dubbed by some as an oxymoron, but this appears to be an oversimplification. If anything, sustainable development should imply a wider discourse among environmental, economic, and social interest groups and policy makers, as well as more meaningful compromise. It should mean properly pricing natural resources and resource-intensive production processes. It should also include the use of innovations that reduce the need for resource-intensive production, changes in firm structures, movement away from industry-dependent growth to service-based or balanced growth, emphasis on better incorporating the rural sector into the development process, and creation of proper institutions to protect social and environmental interests.

Sustainable development has become increasingly important today, in contrast to past growth models and trajectories. Early growth models accounted only for the economic dimension of development, which was particularly emphasized after World War II through the late 1990s. In the wake of World War II, policy makers believed that international well-being could be achieved through trade and industry above all else. Focus on the environment mounted in the 1960s and 1970s, as the toxic effects of industrialization were sharply felt, but this movement remained segmented from the larger dialogue on development policy. At last, it was recognized with the Brundtland Report, produced for the UN in 1987, that economic development alone was insufficient in addressing the most pressing development-related issues. Gro Harlem Brundtland states in the report's introduction:

> The present decade has been marked by a retreat from social concerns. Scientists bring to our attention urgent but complex problems bearing on our very survival: a warming globe, threats to the Earth's ozone layer, deserts consuming agricultural land. We respond by demanding more details, and by assigning the problems to institutions ill-equipped to cope with them. Environmental degradation, first seen as mainly a problem of the rich nations and a side effect of industrial wealth, has become a survival issue for developing nations. It is part of the downward spiral of linked ecological and economic decline in which many of the poorest nations are trapped. Despite official hope expressed on all sides, no trends identifiable today, no programmes or policies, offer any real hope of narrowing the growing gap between rich and poor nations. And as part of our "development", we have amassed

> weapons arsenals capable of diverting the paths that evolution has followed for millions of years and of creating a planet our ancestors would not recognize.
>
> *(World Commission on Environment and Development (WCED) 1987)*

This is a significant statement, but the timing of its release was not ideal; it was around the time that the Brundtland Report was produced that unsustainable neoliberal development policies rose to the global forefront. These policies emphasized reduction in government participation in the economy and society and a robust strengthening of market forces, neither of which placed much focus on environmental sustainability or human well-being. The focus on private ownership of resources drew attention away from sustainable preservation of natural resources. It was not until the late 1990s or early 2000s, in the wake of a series of destructive financial crises and accelerating climate change (understood then as "global warming"), that neoliberalism lost traction and sustainable development gained credibility.

The acceleration of globalization, which has emphasized economic growth, particularly through trade, over all other objectives, has also increased public awareness of serious development issues around the world. The spread of internet usage and enhanced media coverage have highlighted pollution, poverty, health, inequality, and social issues. While globalization itself has resulted in greater inequality within and among nations, as well as severe environmental degradation, the exchange of people and ideas has provided a much richer picture of development challenges and potential solutions faced across societies.

Sustainable development in Asia

Sustainable development is especially important for Asia, which faces some of the worst social, economic and environmental problems on the planet. Poverty levels are high, especially in South Asia, second only to that in sub-Saharan Africa. Environmental issues such as air pollution, water pollution and scarcity, sharp reduction in biodiversity, and land degradation are particularly pressing in Asia, which is home to the majority of highest polluting cities and some of the most rapidly degrading ecosystems in the world. While Asia, particularly China and India, have focused on increasing growth over the past two decades, sustainability aspects of development have been largely overlooked.

The number of sustainable development issues in Asia is prodigious, as the region is home to some 48 countries. It would require hundreds of volumes to cover all of these issues for all Asian nations. Due to space constraints, we therefore rather focus on some key issues, particularly in East, South, and Southeast Asia. These countries can be found in different stages of development. While a few, such as Japan and Singapore, are developed, others, like China and Thailand, are at middle-income status, and others, like Indonesia, remain at low levels of development. All Asian countries experience challenges to sustainable development, but due to insufficient resources, low income countries face some of the most pressing needs.

The issues are diverse. For example, overcrowded urban areas have led to high levels of pollution, from vehicles, industrial and domestic activities, garbage, and waste. Urban slums in some countries, including India, Bangladesh, and Sri Lanka, are particularly polluted. Rising incomes in places like China have led to greater vehicle ownership, which has contributed to traffic congestion and air pollution. Polluted air has resulted in premature deaths in many locations. Coal burning in particular has brought about cases of chronic bronchitis and lung cancer, especially in China and India. Despite the adverse impact that air pollution in particular has had on Asian cities, many Asian nations are continuing to search for secure and diversified energy sources.

Overexploitation of land and natural resources in rural areas, home to about 50 percent of Asia's population, has led to pollution and reduction in the stock of natural resources. Improper irrigation and fertilization practices have brought about land degradation. About 70 percent of water throughout the region is used for agriculture, but water insecurity is high and water infrastructure low. Intensive farming has led to a decline in soil quality, especially in Thailand and Vietnam (Howes and Wyrwoll 2012). Flooding in Bangladesh may destroy hectares of crops, drought in Sri Lanka is likely to lead to declines in tea yields, and higher sea levels on farmlands of the Mekong Delta are likely to lead to food insecurity throughout Cambodia, the Lao PDR, and Vietnam (Sovacool 2014).

Other aspects of pollution, climate change, and land degradation can present problems in both urban and rural areas. Polluted water has led to a sharp decline in fish stocks, important food sources in Asia, and increased cost of access to clean water, essential to sustaining life. Much of the population resides in low-lying and coastal regions, which will become increasingly subject to rising waters as ocean levels rise. Deforestation for collection of fuel wood, biofuels, and palm oil eliminates carbon sinks and accelerates land erosion, worsening climate change and agricultural conditions. Deforestation in Southeast Asia has amounted to five times the global average.

This environmental degradation adversely impacts economic productivity. Due to the large population that continues to live in rural areas and depends on an agricultural livelihood, reduction in access to natural resources and arable land diminishes many livelihoods. Subsistence farmers, who are often mired in poverty to begin with, are particularly vulnerable to the negative effects of climate change. The disappearance of lowland and mangrove forests, which provide protection against soil and coastal erosion and preserve biodiversity, has led to decreased resilience against costly flooding and decline in fish stocks, resulting in a loss of GDP. Increases in temperature and loss of forest cover have led to higher incidences of disease outbreaks, raising health costs and reducing productivity.

Despite success in reducing the incidence of extreme poverty, poverty under slightly less extreme qualifications continues to pose challenges to the region. Poverty and lower levels of development in some Asian countries have resulted in low standards of living, insufficient access to health care or education, hunger and malnutrition, and job insecurity. State intervention in the form of social welfare in many parts of Asia is lower than that in Latin America and Central and Eastern Europe. Low levels of assistance to the elderly in the form of social pensions, low health assistance coverage, and low disability benefit coverage plague the region. Infant, maternal, and under-five mortality remain issues, especially in South Asia. Sustainable development implies that individuals are not only raised out of income poverty, but that their well-being is also improved, yet many aspects of well-being lag behind, even as industrialization advances in many Asian nations.

Furthermore, inequality has risen in Asia. As some individuals remain left behind in subsistence agriculture, others benefit from the processes of globalization and technological change. Economic inequality often translates also into inequality in access to education and health care. In some countries, for example, children in the poorest income quintile were three to five times as likely as those in the richest quintiles to be out of primary or secondary school (Asian Development Bank 2012). Infant mortality rates among poorest households are double or triple that of rich households.

Underdevelopment in some regions has led to insufficient or insecure employment. Youth unemployment is a problem, with 30 percent of individuals ages 15 to 24 remaining jobless across Asia (Packard and Van Nguyen 2014). Informal employment is common, and only increases insecurity of income and social protection. Gender bias also plays into less secure employment, as productive employment for women in child-bearing years is also often limited.

Asian governments have attempted to combat these challenges to sustainable development in different ways, and to various degrees. For example, Taiwan, Hong Kong, Singapore, Malaysia, Indonesia, Thailand and the Philippines all have work injury, health and old age social programs, but some are at low levels compared to GDP (Park 2007). Countries like South Korea and Japan have relatively sophisticated social welfare regimes as well as increasingly innovative climate change adaptation programs. Other countries, such as Indonesia and the Philippines, struggle with poverty and remain vulnerable to climate change.

Many of these issues are addressed in this handbook. Although full exploration of sustainable development issues would comprise many volumes, we attempt to examine some of the most salient and representative topics. In the next section, we discuss the structure of the handbook by section and chapter.

Structure of the handbook

In this handbook, we conceive of sustainable development as encompassing environmental issues, energy dependence, economic justice, social welfare, sustainable governance, and sustainable development policy. Darrin Magee of Hobart and William Smith Colleges provided an introduction to the volume, and Section 1 included a framework for understanding sustainable development by Sara Hsu of the State University of New York at New Paltz.

Section 2 examines the environmental challenges in Asian countries. In this section, Lee Liu, of the School of Environmental, Physical and Applied Sciences at the University of Central Missouri writes on air pollution and its threat to health in Asia; Debashis Chakraborty of the Indian Institute of Foreign Trade and Sacchidananda Mukherjee at the National Institute of Public Finance and Policy cover the topic of environmental challenges in Asia; Seck Tan, Singapore Institute of Technology, discusses environmental policies in Asia; and Farzad Taheripour and Thomas W. Hertel of Purdue University, Badri Narayanan Gopalakrishnan of the University of Washington, Sebnem Sahin of the World Bank, Anil Markandya of Bath University, and Bijon Kumer Mitra of Institute for Global Environmental Strategies discuss climate change and water scarcity in South Asia.

Section 3 addresses energy dependence and transition in Asia, with Reiji Takeishi, of Tokyo International University describing the energy situation in Asia; Helen Cabalu and Yixiao Zhou of Curtin University writing on indicators of energy security in Asia; Soocheol Lee in the Faculty of Economics at Meijo University, Japan examining energy systems and low-carbon policies in East Asia; and Peter Marcotullio in the Department of Geography at Hunter College covering the topic of urban energy systems in Asia.

Section 4 is about the topic of economic justice in Asia. In this section, Wenjie Zhang, Economist at Grey Health Group, discusses inequality in China; Eunju Chi at the Peace and Democracy Institute of Korea University lays out the issue of income inequality in East Asia; Dan Biller, Luis Andrés, and Matías Herrera Dappe of the World Bank analyze inequality in infrastructure access in South Asia; Riyana Miranti at the University of Canberra covers the topic of poverty, inequality and public health in Indonesia; and Simi Mehta, at the at the School of Environment and Natural Resources at Ohio State University, Vikash Kumar, at the Centre for Research in Rural and Industrial Development and Rattan Lal at the School of Environment and Natural Resources at Ohio State University write on climate change and food security in South Asia.

Section 5 contains perspectives on social welfare in Asian nations. Contributing to this section are Edi Suharto at the Bandung College of Social Welfare in Indonesia, writing on the topic of social welfare in Indonesia and conditional cash transfers; Selim Elekdag, Dulani Seneviratne,

Edda Zoli of the IMF, discussing social spending in Korea; Levan Lim and Thana Thaver of the National Institute of Education at Nanyang Technological University in Singapore analyzing inclusive education in Singapore; Donghyun Park and Gemma Estrada of the Asian Development Bank examining public pension programs in East Asia; and John Fien at RMIT University in Australia and Rupert Maclean at the College of The North Atlantic in Qatar writing on technical and vocational education for sustainable development in Asia.

Section 6 covers the issue of sustainable governance in Asia. In this section, Neda Trifkovicc and Thomas Markussen of the University of Copenhagen, Denmark, Carol Newman of Trinity College Dublin, and John Rand of the University of Copenhagen, Denmark, write about corporate social responsibility in Vietnam; Ashiru Bello of Ahmadu Bello University Zaria and Ainul Jaria Maidin of the International Islamic University Malaysia discuss sustainable development and the role of local governance in Malaysia; Mark Elder at the Institute for Global Environmental Strategies describes regional governance for environmental sustainability in Asia; and Christopher Dent at the University of Leeds analyzes the topic of renewable energy and developmentalism in East Asia.

Finally, Section 7 takes a look at Asia's sustainable development policy. Here, Dennis Victor, an alumnus Research Scientist from the University of Malaya, discusses policy trends on strategic environmental assessment in Asia; Choy Yee Keong of Keio University writes about sustainable development and environmental stewardship in Borneo; Yu-Wai Vic Li at the Hong Kong Institute of Education looks at green GDP in China; Maizatun Mustafa of the International Islamic University Malaysia describes legal solutions to air pollution control in Malaysia; Lahiru S. Wijedasa, Zeehan Jaafar, and Mary Rose C. Posa of the National University of Singapore and Janice S.H. Lee of Nanyang Technological University write on regulating transboundary haze in Southeast Asia; Ken'ici Matsumoto in the Graduate School of Fisheries and Environmental Sciences at Nagasaki University takes a look at energy security in Asia; and Hitomi Rankine, UNESCAP, Kareff Limocon Rafisura, UNESCAP, and José A. Puppim de Oliveira of the Fundação Getulio Vargas examine transformations in sustainable development in the Asia Pacific.

Following, we provide descriptions for each chapter contribution.

Darrin Magee provides an introduction to sustainability in Asia, providing a framework with which to understand the three pillars of sustainable development: the economic pillar, the ecological pillar, and the social pillar. Dr. Magee then discusses environmental challenges, energy dependence, economic justice, social welfare, sustainable development policies, and sustainable governance as these categories apply to Asia.

In Section 1, Sara Hsu writes in "Framework for understanding sustainable development," on sustainable development in general and sustainable development as it applies to Asia. Dr. Hsu then provides chapter summaries.

Section 2 begins with Lee Liu in "Air pollution and its threat to public health in Asia." Dr. Liu writes that air pollution presents a severe threat to environmental, social, and economic sustainability in Asia, and contributes to climate change, resulting in both desertification and rising sea levels in Asia. Access to clean air is essential to human life, but threatens sustainability in many parts of the world, especially Asia. In this chapter, Dr. Liu examines air pollution in Asian countries and then takes China as a case study on variations within a country. Liu explores how air pollution threatens sustainability in Asia in terms of its impact on human health and then uses Asia as an example to challenge the notion that developing countries cannot combat pollution at earlier stages.

Debashis Chakraborty and Sacchidananda Mukherjee discuss, in the following chapter, "Environmental challenges in Asia." They write that Asia contains great biological and environmental diversity, resulting in a diversity of challenges facing Asian countries. However,

Asian nations have in common dense population pressures and lower levels of development, which means that environmental objectives are often not a top priority. Asian nations have exploited natural resources, used greater amounts of power, and converted forests and wetlands to achieve growth targets. This chapter seeks to analyze environmental challenges in Asia and their economic drivers that often result in unsustainable development.

Seck Tan takes a close look at "Singapore's environmental policy." Due to the isolation and vulnerability of islands, climate change and its associated phenomena will generate greater environmental stress on island states. Seck Tan analyzes the potential impacts of climate change on island nations and especially on Singapore, and looks at how environmental policies can be crafted in response to observations associated with climate change. This chapter also outlines the progression of Singapore's environmental policy. One significant achievement which the island-state has demonstrated is to introduce a regulatory mechanism – namely, the Environmental Impact Assessment for developments and projects in Singapore. This serves to protect and create awareness for the environment as the island-state grows and develops. However, in light of less benign challenges ahead for Singapore, future policy directions and recommendations toward sustainable development will be critical as Singapore continues to balance economic performance and environmental protection.

Farzad Taheripour, Thomas W. Hertel, Badri Narayanan Gopalakrishnan, Sebnem Sahin, Anil Markandya, and Bijon Kumer Mitra contribute a chapter on "Climate change and water scarcity: growing risks for agricultural based economies in South Asia." Here, Taheripour, Hertel, Gopalakrishnan, Sahin, Markandya, and Mitra evaluate economic and environmental consequences of climate change and water scarcity on South Asian economies. The authors implement a computable general equilibrium (CGE) model using biophysical data on climate-induced crop yield changes, water scarcity measures, and land and water resources by Agro-Ecological Zone (AEZ) at the river basin level. They find that even when water supply for irrigation is not limited, climate-induced crop yield changes could generate negative economy-wide impacts and reduce food security across South Asia. Taheripour et al. then examine the combined impacts of the effects of climate-induced crop yield changes and water scarcity on the economies of South Asia, finding that water scarcity, induced by expansion in water demand in non-agricultural uses and lack of water infrastructure, will block the demand for irrigation, generating severe negative economic impacts, badly affecting food production and security, extending food imports and causing major land use changes in South Asia.

In Section Three, Reiji Takeishi takes a look at the "Energy situation in Asia." He shows that Asia's growth has resulted in a surge in energy demand, especially for power generation, particularly in the 2000s. Much of the rapid increase was caused by a rise in Chinese demand, but India and other developing Asian countries also contributed to this rise in energy consumption. Dr. Takeishi states that in the near future, approximately 80 to 90 percent of the projected increase of world energy demand will be due to Asian countries, based on forecasts such as that of the IEA International Energy Agency (IEA), such that most new facility construction for power generation, power transmission, refining, and gas transmission will occur in Asia. In this chapter, Dr. Takeishi describes energy demand in Asia and its challenges for the future.

Helen Cabalu and Yixiao Zhou, in "Evaluating indicators of energy security for sustainable development in Asia," examine the fossil fuel energy profile of selected Asian countries in terms of specific energy supply indicators, which include intensity, net import dependency, ratio of domestic energy production to total domestic energy consumption and geopolitical risk. Drs. Cabalu and Zhou discuss the indicators for selected countries in Asia in the period between 2002 and 2015. A composite supply security index for oil (OSSI), gas (GSSI) and coal (CSSI) are calculated to provide a quantitative measure of energy security for each of the fossil fuels, taking into account the dynamics among the identified set of energy supply indicators. The authors examine the energy profile of selected Asian countries, including China, India, Japan, Korea, Singapore and Thailand, then compile a supply security index for oil, gas and coal, analyzing and evaluating the index in order to draw policy conclusions.

Soocheol Lee takes a close look at the cases of East Asia especially in Japan and South Korea in "Energy systems and low-carbon policies in East Asia." Given that East Asian nations face different energy and carbon policies, institutional infrastructure-building, which is instrumental in developing a low-carbon society in the East Asia region, has been moving forward in recent years. In this chapter, Dr. Lee describes the progress and challenges mainly in Japan and South Korea, which have recently achieved some positive results toward reforming energy systems and enforcing low-carbon policies, then mentions briefly the recent development of energy and low carbon policies in China and Taiwan.

Peter Marcotullio examines, in his chapter contribution, "The Asian urban energy system." Asia's economic growth has been associated with the massive movement of people to the region's cities. From 1970 to 2010, approximately 1.36 billion people were added to urban areas across the region, bringing the urbanization level from 23.7 percent to 44.8 percent. Both economic growth and urbanization have driven and been driven by energy use and supply. With the expansion of economic activities and the building of cities in which much of this activity occurs, the region has increased its total energy supply from 4.4 to 12.7 gigatons oil equivalents (Gtoe), almost a threefold increase. All three of these factors are tightly interlinked, although the details of how each has changed together are as varied as the geographies and cultures of the region. This chapter explores the overall trends, patterns and dynamics among Asia's urbanization and energy supply and demand, using a systems approach in suggesting linkages between these patterns and those of economic progress. Peter Marcotullio first highlights both the overall dynamic change and the diversity among the region's nations and cities, then points out the sustainable development challenges ahead, including meeting the goals of lowering energy-related pollution, providing universal access to modern energy and reducing greenhouse gas (GHG) emissions.

Section 4 starts with Wenjie Zhang's chapter, "The evolution of China's pay inequality during the transitional period." This chapter provides new estimates of the evolution of pay inequality in China, overall and by region and sector, from 1987 to 2012, using the between-group component of Theil's T-statistic measured across regions and sectors. Dr. Zhang finds that China's overall pay inequality started to rise rapidly in the early 1990s, peaking in 2008, with the between-province component peaking as early as 2002. Zhang shows that since 2008, overall pay inequality has decreased, with between-province and between-sector inequality both showing steady declines. She argues that China's pay inequality during the reform period is not simply a matter of economic inequality; it is a joint product of both market forces and institutional forces. Zhang therefore argues that the recent decline of overall pay inequality after the crisis is not a temporary phenomenon triggered by the global economic downturn, but a long-term outcome driven by both economic and policy factors.

Eunju Chi focuses on economic and social well-being in "Income inequality and welfare in Korea and Taiwan." Dr. Chi states that deepening inequality is a trend that makes sustainable development difficult to attain. She writes that when a government actively responds to the deepening inequality by providing welfare, inequality is alleviated, and sustainable development is possible. In this chapter, Dr. Chi examines the causes and processes of deepening inequality in Korea and Taiwan, then turns to policies associated with improving economic distribution. Chi finds that democratization required measures to protect the victims of wealth polarization and, as a result, measures to tackle income inequality in Korea and Taiwan were introduced. However, these were implemented in an ad hoc fashion, rather than resulting from clear goals and plans.

Dan Biller, Luis Andrés, and Matías Herrera Dappe describe, in "Infrastructure gap in South Asia," the importance of access to basic infrastructure services with regard to welfare and the quality of life contrasted with the South Asia region's low rates of access to infrastructure. The challenge of increasing access to these services across the South Asian region is compounded by the unequal distribution of existing access for households. This study improves understanding of this inequality by evaluating access across the region's physical (location), poverty, and income considerations. The chapter also analyzes inequality of access across time-that is, across generations. It finds that while the regressivity of infrastructure services is clearly present in South Asia, the story that emerges is heterogeneous and complex. There is no simple explanation for these inequalities; although certainly geography matters, some household characteristics (such as living in a rural area with a head of household who lacks education) matter, and policy intent matters. If a poorer country or a poorer state can have better access to a given infrastructure service than a richer country or a richer state, then there is hope that policy makers can adopt measures that will improve access in a manner in which prosperity is more widely shared.

Riyana Miranti writes, in "Poverty, inequality and public health in Indonesia," that the rate of poverty reduction is slowing, while inequality has been increasing since 2000. Miranti focuses on the human development perspective of Indonesia's development story, taking into account the potential implications in the area of health. Dr. Miranti investigates the relationship between three economic variables: inequality, poverty and income level, and public health indicators during the development period in Indonesia. The focus on health has become very important in this nation, given the implementation of the Universal Health Insurance Scheme, starting in early 2014 and Indonesia's support toward the new Sustainable Development Goals (SDGs) to foster welfare and well-being for the next 15 years. In this chapter, Miranti analyzes the association between income, poverty, inequality and health in recent years prior to the implementation of the Universal Health Insurance Scheme, asking whether being wealthier is always associated with being healthier and whether the associations with poverty and inequality are different among various health indicators.

Simi Mehta, Vikash Kumar, and Rattan Lal write on "Climate change and food security in South Asia." South Asia (SA), home to around one-fourth of the world's population, has a unique geographical location on the world map, located entirely in the Northern and Eastern hemispheres. The constituent eight countries have a mix of climates, from equatorial to tropical savannah, and the coexistence of hot humid summers and mild to cold winters, with temperatures below the freezing points in some places. These climatic conditions lend to varieties of agricultural activities and vegetation practices. However, this region is amongst the most impoverished and food insecure part of the world. To add to the gravity of the situation, climate change increases the vulnerability of these low- or lower-middle income countries to weather-related shocks. This chapter establishes that the risk of food insecurity is directly linked to changes in climate, frequent occurrences of drought, flooding, and variability and extremes in rainfall. It elucidates the status of food security in the region as well as the levels of malnutrition and their socio-economic implications on the large section of people across the eight South Asian countries. The authors establish an interconnection between climate change and vulnerability of food production in SA and conclude with policy recommendations toward adapting and mitigating the negative implications of climate change, and contributing to the fulfillment of the Sustainable Development Goals (SDGs) of the United Nations (UN) by 2030 by ensuring a content and food-secure population in South Asia.

In Section 5, Edi Suharto discusses the "Development of social welfare in Indonesia: the rise of conditional cash transfer." The conditional cash transfer (CCT) is one of the most prominent social protection programs under the umbrella of social welfare policies. Focusing on the largest social assistance programs of CCT, namely Program Keluarga Harapan (PKH or The Family of Hope Program), Dr. Suharto discusses the management and impacts of CCT in improving the standard of living of the poor. While coverage of PKH continues to increase, it has impacts in the area of health and education as well as the level of household expenditure per capita. Suharto shows that as a national program, PKH has the opportunity to be integrated into a more comprehensive social protection system and hence can contribute to the development of social welfare in Indonesia.

Selim Elekdag, Dulani Seneviratne, and Edda Zoli write in "Social spending in Korea," that Korea faces two closely related challenges: sustaining economic growth against the backdrop of a rapidly aging population and ameliorating income inequality. Elekdag, Seneviratne and Zoli argue that a gradual increase in social spending could promote more sustainable and inclusive growth in Korea. In particular, simulation results suggest that social spending which supports labor market reforms can boost longer-term growth. However, despite rapid increases recently – albeit from a low base – there is still a social spending gap relative to Korea's OECD peers. They find that because of several fiscal challenges in the coming decades, increases in social spending should be incremental, and would be usefully guided by a longer-term fiscal framework.

Levan Lim and Thana Thaver next write on the "Inclusion of persons with disabilities in Singapore." Drs. Lim and Thaver show that although Singapore aspires to be an inclusive society, it struggles to explicitly address inclusive education as a significant agenda within its mainstream education initiatives and reforms. Singaporean schools often fail to sufficiently support students with special needs, with mainstream schools remaining separate from special education. This has had the effect of reinforcing societal prejudice against people with disabilities. In this chapter, Lim and Thaver provide a situated and contextual understanding of the evolution of Singapore's current attitudes and systemic structures regarding the construction and treatment of disability within society.

Donghyun Park and Gemma Estrada discuss social safety nets for the elderly in "Why does Asia need well-functioning pension systems?" Due to rapid population aging, Park and Estrada state, the number of retirees per worker is increasing. As such, economic security for the elderly looms on the horizon as one of the region's most significant strategic challenges, but the region is ill equipped to meet this challenge. In this chapter, Drs. Park and Estrada examine the pension systems of eight East Asian countries, namely China, Indonesia, Korea, Malaysia, the Philippines, Singapore, Thailand and Vietnam, all of which are witnessing a sustained rise in the share of the elderly relative to the labor force and total population. They show that extensive social and economic transformation is endangering the economic security of the elderly, and formal pension systems must fill the gap.

John Fien and Rupert Maclean discuss "Technical and vocational education (TVE) for sustainable and inclusive development in Asia" in the following chapter. Fien and Maclean write that the chapter has three goals. First, it describes the long-term interest in the "greening" of technical and vocational education and training (TVET) and the significance, scope and purpose of this according to international agencies concerned with balancing economic growth with sustainability, inclusiveness, and decent work. Drs. Fien and Maclean argue that the focus of TVET for sustainable development in Asia has had a decidedly social justice focus, for example in rural transformation, compared with the predominant concern with energy efficiency, resource conservation and pollution prevention in the Global North. Second, the chapter outlines the world-leading initiatives to reorient skills development toward green growth in the Republic of

Korea, despite the fact that a major research study found that such initiatives are not widespread in the region. This study, by the Asian Development Bank and the Education University of Hong Kong, on "kills development for inclusive growth, sustainable development and the greening of economies" in the Asia region found that the transition toward this goal is only occurring where the influence of government regulation and incentives is strong, in large firms, especially those with a foreign or export orientation, and where the perceived costs of change are low and perceived consumer demand is high. As a result, it is argued that there is currently a dispersed and disconnected narrative of skills training for sustainable and inclusive development in Asia.

Section 6 begins with a chapter by Neda Trifkovic, Thomas Markussen, Carol Newman and John Rand on "Corporate social responsibility in Vietnam." This chapter investigates the scope for corporate social responsibility (CSR) to play a role in advancing sustainable development. Trifkovic, Markussen, Newman and Rand focus on an empirical analysis of manufacturing firms in Vietnam. CSR is potentially a means for addressing market failures, such as environmental problems and under-provision of health services and infrastructure, although demand for some of the goods typically provided through CSR activities, such as environmental quality, may be increasing more than proportionally with per capita income. This chapter presents data on CSR activities from Vietnam's private manufacturing sector, which only started to emerge after the initiation of the Doi Moi reform program in 1986. The authors investigate to what extent firms undertake such activities, what characterizes the firms that are most engaged in CSR efforts, and how CSR is related to the financial performance (revenue and profits) of firms. The aim is to increase our understanding of the scope for CSR to a play a role in generating sustainable development in low and middle income countries in Asia.

Ashiru Bello and Ainul Jaria Maidin take a close look at Malaysia in "Sustainable development initiatives at the local government level in Malaysia." The authors write that land use planning and development control have been identified as essential tools in the prevention of many environmental problems, sustainable management of natural resources and management of the urban environment, and Malaysia supports initiatives that seek to achieve sustainable development. As part of this strategy, the Malaysian government promotes the incorporation of environmental protection measures into all the various national development plans. Sustainable development has contributed immensely to the array of issues considered in the efforts to balance between individual interest and common good. This being one of the focal points of Malaysia's planning system and also concords with international concerns. The argument that there is a firm adoption of sustainable development tenets in planning system as compared to other areas, does not guarantee the occurrence of a systematic transformation of the planning agenda itself. A number of cases particularly regarding spatial development and environmental conservation suggests that the planning system is still dominated by the crave for development which in a way contradicts the modest focus of sustainability. In order to develop a viable approach to environmental conservation and shape the spatial pattern of development at the local level, several strategies have been adopted in Malaysia. This chapter sets out the initiatives taken at the State and local government level in Malaysia guided by the Federal government policies adopted at the State and local authorities where they are entrusted with the task to plan and manage land use planning and development control processes for promoting sustainable development.

Mark Elder discusses in his chapter contribution "Regional governance for environmental sustainability in Asia in the context of sustainable development." Dr. Elder's chapter surveys the landscape of regional governance for sustainability in Asia, focusing on regional and sub-regional cooperation frameworks related to the environment. The survey covers not only frameworks specializing in environmental issues, but also broadly focused frameworks which include the environment and could help to mainstream the environment into other policy areas. Agenda

2030 calls on regional and sub-regional cooperation frameworks to facilitate the implementation of the Sustainable Development Goals. There are many cooperation frameworks in the region, and this chapter identifies and classifies the major ones. Elder finds that, although formal and large-scale international organizations and treaties exist in the region, the main trend has been toward smaller scale and looser, informal forms of international cooperation mechanisms. Another trend is increasing involvement of non-governmental stakeholders, which still work closely with governments, either as part of intergovernmental frameworks or in partnership with governments, often with financial support from governments. These frameworks have a wide variation in terms of their nature and structure, involving different levels of governance, and also a range of types of members. However, there are no supranational institutions like the EU, and most are voluntary. Overall, most are not very strong politically, with little authority and limited financial and human resources. Other challenges to regional sustainability governance include: overlaps and fragmentation, need for better coordination, insufficient coverage of issues by existing mechanisms, need for more emphasis on capacity building, and weak financial and human resource capacity. Some major institutions, particularly the ADB and APEC, are not formally focused on sustainability, so SDGs present a good opportunity for them to shift their focus more in that direction. Finally, regional governance for sustainability in Asia is characterized by key Earth System Governance concepts such as complex architecture, complex actors, multiple levels of governance.

Christopher Dent analyzes "Renewable energy and new developmentalism in East Asia." Prof. Dent's chapter examines renewable energy development in East Asia and the deeper sustainable and other development contexts in which this has been situated. East Asia comprises two sub-regions, Northeast Asia (China, Japan, South Korea, North Korea, Taiwan and Mongolia) and Southeast Asia (Brunei, Cambodia, East Timor, Indonesia, Laos, Malaysia, Myanmar, Philippines, Singapore, Thailand and Vietnam). Over the last five or six decades, East Asia has been the world's most dynamic and fastest growing economic region. Annual double-digit percent increases in economic growth have not been uncommon for many East Asia countries during this period. The region consists of a diverse set of economies that together accounted for around 30 percent of the global economy in 2014, a higher share than both the European Union and the United States. East Asia has also emerged as the world's most significant driver of renewable energy development over the last decade or so. It is argued that this can be broadly understood from the conflation of two influencing meta-factors, namely state capacity and ecological modernization that, combined, form the basis of the region's "new developmentalism." This concerns the pursuit of new "low-carbon economy" transformative objectives where renewables play a central role in various state strategies to realize these ends. However, this has not been without its conflicts, contradictions and controversies, as Prof. Dent lays out.

In Section 7, Dennis Victor evaluates the "Strategic environmental assessment as a policy framework for sustainable development in Asia." Dr. Victor provides an overview of the trends of Strategic Environmental Assessment (SEA) in Asia and explores it as a potential tool for sustainable development. Victor finds that SEA integration for sustainable development in Asia may require a paradigm shift from the current reliance on structured instruments such as legislation to unstructured instruments such as behavior based stakeholder and public engagements. SEA trends in Asia indicate that effective implementation of SEA as a tool for sustainable development requires an adaptable application of both structured and unstructured SEA instruments.

Choy Yee Keong writes about "Sustainable development and environmental stewardship," in the Heart of Borneo a 23-million-hectare tri-national and transboundary protected area in central Borneo, for conservation and sustainable management purposes. This area protects one of the most biological diverse habitats on Earth. However, this area is increasingly subjected to the threat of ecological destruction due to various unsustainable resource use practices that have prevailed in the region. Choy empirically assesses the drivers behind this environmental paradox and suggests ways to solve the present development-environmental dilemma, drawing from findings on the indigenous worldviews research conducted in Borneo Malaysia between 2007 and 2011.

Yu-Wai Vic Li writes on "China's green GDP and environmental accounting." Dr. Li notes that China's environmental conditions have deteriorated significantly as a result of rapid industrialization, massive urbanizations and shifting demographics that have resulted in resource depletion of unprecedented scale. The annual growth rates that surpass most of the developed and developing worlds invariably contain entail enormous costs to the natural environment and ecosystem. In the 2000s, Green GDP gained momentum when the country faced skyrocketing pollution in the 2000s and the top party and state leaders adopted a "scientific outlook" of development, endorsing the notion of green GDP and practices of environmental accounting. This galvanized the launch of China's green GDP accounting in March 2004 led by the State Environmental Protection Agency (SEPA; and upgraded to Ministry of Environmental Protection in 2008) and the National Bureau of Statistics (NBS). The joint-agency campaign centered on accounting of the abatement/treatment costs of, and the economic losses arising from air, water and solid waste pollution in ten provinces and municipalities and 42 industrial sectors. This herculean effort was accomplished in about two years, with the world's first official green GDP accounting report released in September 2006. However, behind the facade of the campaign's apparent success laid intractable methodological challenges and political resistance from the statistical bureau and local authorities involved. This not only undermined SEPA's lead in the accounting exercise, it also foreshadowed the unfortunate end in July 2007, when the NBS unilaterally announced the project's termination and local authorities quit the project. The research endeavor, however, was carried on by SEPA's affiliated research body, the Chinese Academy for Environmental Planning (CAEP), which published its own annual results. The central authorities did not extend their support again until 2013, when the new Chinese administration under Xi Jinping rallied for support of the "ecological civilization" campaign and the international framework of environmental economic accounting was finally well-developed. Blessed by the central authorities, the MEP resumed the green GDP study in early 2015, but this was rivaled by a different environmental accounting initiative championed by the NBS, which concerned stock-taking of natural capital that would expand the economy's asset/wealth level for long-term sustainable development. This added considerable uncertainties to the fate of China's green GDP survey.

Maizatun Mustafa discusses "Legal solutions to air pollution control in Malaysia." Despite the fact that air pollution presents the world's largest environmental health risk, for a developing country like Malaysia, the task of controlling air pollution can be a challenge, not only in understanding and dealing with complex interactions between emissions and resulting air quality, but in identifying and applying the most suitable pollution control strategies in order to achieve the overall targets of air quality enhancement and sustainable development. In Malaysia, most of the air pollution problems are associated with increased concentration of people and economic activities in urban and sub-urban areas, as well as growing numbers of agricultural areas and transportation. Maizatun Mustafa discusses the main sources of air pollution in Malaysia, and highlights existing environmental policy and law related to air pollution control as well as present regional air pollution problems facing Malaysia and its neighboring countries, mainly trans-boundary haze pollution.

Lahiru S. Wijedasa, Zeehan Jaafar, Mary Rose C. Posa and Janice S.H. Lee contribute a chapter on "Regulating trans-boundary haze in Southeast Asia." In this chapter, the authors describe the causes of and proposed regulations for trans-boundary haze. In particular, the tropical peat swamp forest ecosystem (TPSF) in Southeast Asia, covering over 200,000 km^2, represents a significant carbon pool. Over the past three decades, TPSF have been deforested at an alarming rate and converted to large and small-scale plantations. The loss of TPSF is strongly associated with fire, especially because anthropogenic disturbances adversely impact hydrological processes and make peat soils vulnerable to ignition. In addition to the globally significant amounts of carbon dioxide released, particulate matter from peat fires cause a persistent transboundary air pollution, also commonly referred to as "haze." The authors find that small wins against Southeast Asia's transboundary haze can be found in the penalization of companies for fire activity, consumer action to limit purchases from companies associated with burning and the successful engagement of local communities for fire prevention, but in the long run, clarifying land tenure procedures, ensuring peatland protection, and aligning agricultural development policies with ecosystem protection, hold the keys to a sustainable solution for the fire and haze problems in Southeast Asia.

Ken'ichi Matsumoto discusses "Energy security performance in Japan." Matsumoto shows that since Japan is poor in energy sources and because the energy situation in Japan will be tougher in the future, securing its energy supply will be a more important issue for Japan. Ken'ichi Matsumoto evaluates changes in the historical energy security performance and then analyzes energy security in the future under several scenarios for Japan. From the historical evaluation, it is shown that energy security performance evaluated by three energy security indicators improved over time, but energy security declined from 2011 due to the Fukushima nuclear disaster. This means that diversity of primary energy sources, including nuclear power, is important for high energy security performance, as measured by the three indicators introduced in this study. From the scenario analysis, energy security will improve under the future scenarios discussed in this chapter. It is suggested that energy balances mentioned above and also energy saving can improve the energy security performance of Japan compared to the historical situation.

Hitomi Rankine, Kareff Limocon Rafisura, and Jose Puppim de Oliveira write in "Transformations for sustainable development in the Asia and the Pacific" on how the 17 goals of the 2030 Agenda for Sustainable Development move beyond a vision to achievement in 15 years' time depends on whether we make use of the opportunities provided by regional megatrends, such as urbanization, rising incomes, changing consumption patterns and economic and trade integration. The authors note that aligning the megatrends with sustainable development requires changes in the structures and rules that mediate the relationship between the economy, society and nature. Transformations in social justice, investment flows, economic structures and resource efficiency are imperative. Drs. Rankine, Rafisura, and de Oliveira find that needed transformations are mutually supportive and essential for responding to the Sustainable Development Goals in a way that allows policy coherence and prevents trade-offs between goals.

An invitation

We invite you to read, in this volume, on a variety of topics related to the multifaceted aspects of sustainable development in Asia. The subject is timely, as we face many challenges to sustainable development in our world today.

References

Asian Development Bank. (2012) *Asian Development Outlook 2012: Confronting Rising Inequality in Asia.* Manila, Philippines: Asian Development Bank.

Atkinson, G., W.R. Dubourg, K. Hamilton, M. Munasinghe, D.W. Pearce, and C.E.F. Young. (1997) *Measuring Sustainable Development: Macroeconomics and the Environment.* Cheltenham: Edward Elgar.

Brundtland Commission. (1987) Report of the World Commission on Environment and Development: Our Common Future. UN Document A/42/427.

Conway, G.R. and E.B. Barbier. (1990) *After the Green Revolution: Sustainable Agriculture for Development*. London: Earthscan Publications.

Daly, H.E. (1994) "Operationalizing Sustainable Development by Investing in Natural Capital," in AnnMari Jansson et al. eds., *Investing in Natural Capital: The Ecological Economics Approach to Sustainability*. Washington, DC: Island Press.

Howes, S. and P. Wyrwoll. (2012) "Asia's Wicked Environmental Problems." ADBI Working Paper Series 348.

Jabareen, Y. (2008) "A New Concept Framework for Sustainable Development." *Environment, Development and Sustainability* 10: 179–192.

Packard, T.G. and T. Van Nguyen. (2014) *East Asia Pacific at Work*. Washington, DC: World Bank.

Park, C. (2007) "The Divergent Paths of the East Asian Welfare Regimes: The Effects of Production Regimes and Democratization." *Korean Social Science Journal* 34: 39–70.

Petkevičiūtė, N. and I. Svirskaitė. (2001) "Ekonominis vystymasis ir žmogaus socialinė raida." *Organizaciju vadyba: sisteminiai tyrimai* 17: 163–173.

Putnam, R.D. (1993) *Making Democracy Work: Civic Traditions in Modern Italy*. Princeton: Princeton University Press.

Robinson, J. (2004) "Squaring the Circle? Some Thoughts on the Idea of Sustainable Development." *Ecological Economics* 48: 369–384.

Sovacool, B.K. (2014) "Environmental Issues, Climate Changes, and Energy Security in Developing Asia." ADB Economics Working Paper 399.

The World Conservation Union (IUCN). (1991) *Caring for the Earth*. Gland: IUCN.

United Nations (UN). (2015) "Transforming our world: the 2030 Agenda for Sustainable Development." United Nations Resolution A/Res/70/1.

World Commission on Environment and Development (WCED). (1987) "Our Common Future." Report produced for UN General Assembly, Transmitted to the General Assembly as an Annex to document A/42/427.

SECTION 2

Environmental challenges in Asian countries

3

Air pollution and its threat to public health in Asia

Lee Liu

Introduction

Sustainable development is development that meets the needs of the present without sacrificing the ability of future generations to meet their own needs (World Commission on Environment and Development 1987). It has been illustrated as having three overlapping dimensions: the simultaneous pursuit of economic prosperity, environmental quality, and social equity, also known as the "three pillars" of sustainability (United Nations General Assembly 2005; Adams 2006; Liu 2009). Recent holistic and inclusive thinking of sustainability emphasizes overlapping dimensions and the interaction among them (Liu 2009). The question of how to achieve sustainability in Asia has long been contested, as different schools of thought exist in the interpretation of the relationship between economic development and environmental conditions. On the one hand, it is argued that the "grow (pollute) first, clean up later" path is unavoidable in some developing countries (Azadi et al. 2011). Some fast-growing Asian economies have followed that path, such as Japan, South Korea, Taiwan, and China (Rock 2002; Rock and Angel 2007). The theoretical support of the "grow first" path is provided by the environmental Kuznets curve (EKC). The EKC suggests that environmental quality first decreases and then improves with economic growth. The implication of the EKC is that economic growth is the key to achieve both economic and environmental goals (Beckerman 1992; Panayotou 1993; Ekins 2000; Weber and Allen 2010).

On the other hand, the "grow first, clean up later" approach has been long criticized and the applicability of the EKC disputed (Liu 2008, 2012, 2013a). EKC studies do not support the existence of a simple, predictable relationship between pollution and per capita income because multiple factors are involved (Stern 2004; Dasgupta et al. 2006). Harbaugh et al. (2002) conclude that there is little empirical support for an EKC relationship between important air pollutants and national income. However, governments in many Asian countries tend to promote rapid economic growth at the cost of the environment and social equity. The result is worsening environmental pollution and degradation in these countries.

Among the many environmental challenges, air pollution is a severe threat to environmental, social, and economic sustainability in Asia. Air pollution is a major cause of climate change that contributes to rising sea levels and intensification of extreme weather. Consequently, many Asian countries are losing their precious land due to desertification and rising sea levels. The loss of biodiversity has been disastrous to wildlife and ecosystems. It is the less developed countries or poorer parts of a country that are often affected the most by climate change. This causes worsening environmental injustice. Furthermore, environmental hazards threaten public health in both more and less developed countries. The World Health Organization (WHO 2014a, 2014b) estimated that indoor and outdoor air pollution exposure killed about 7 million people (one eighth of total deaths globally) in 2012. Of the 7 million deaths, 5.9 million were in the WHO's Southeast Asia and Western Pacific Regions. Lelieveld et al. (2015) estimated that outdoor air pollution (mainly PM2.5) was responsible for 3.3 million premature deaths globally, concentrated in Asia. PM2.5 refers to particulate matter (PM) 2.5 micrometers in diameter or smaller. PM2.5 can lodge deep into human lung and blood tissue. They may cause stroke, lung cancer, and even death, particularly among children and the elderly (WHO 2014c). Access to clean air is a basic human need and a human right, and comprises an important part of sustainability.

In recent years, there have been an increasing number of global and country-specific studies on air pollution and its impact on sustainability. However, Asia-specific studies are lacking. Such studies can potentially contribute to the understanding of global air pollution and sustainability. As the world's most populated region with diverse environmental, social, and economic processes, Asia is vitally important to global development and sustainability. This study will first provide an overview of air pollution in Asian countries, and its current situation with historical and regional comparison. It will provide an overview and comparison of all major countries in Asia. Variations within a country will be examined using China as a case study. The study will also explore how air pollution threatens sustainability in Asia in terms of its impact on human health. Furthermore, it will use the Asian experience to challenge the traditional approach to development such as the "grow first, clean up later" approach and the EKC, in order to promote sustainable policies.

Data and methods

Criteria for inclusion of countries/regions

This study intends to include all countries/regions in East, South, and Southeast Asia. However, some entities such as Macao, Fuji, and Brunei are small in size, and possess a unique economic structure, or incomplete data. These entities were excluded to enhance comparability among the countries/regions. Quantitative data were mainly from the WHO (2016a, 2016b, 2016c) and Yale University's Environmental Performance Index (EPI) Report (Yale University 2016a, 2016b, 2016c, 2016d, 2016e). We also note that the WHO and Yale's EPI Regions are a little different from the common geographic divisions. The Asian countries/regions included in this study belong to two different WHO and EPI Regions. The WHO classified Asia into a South-East Asia Region and a Western Pacific Region. The EPI categorizes Asian into an East Asia and Pacific Region and a South Asia Region, according to which EPI regional peer comparisons are conducted. In particular, this study excludes some Pacific countries such as Australia, New Zealand and some island countries in the western Pacific, which are in the EPI Regional comparison.

Data quality

The WHO data were based on reports by governments to the United Nations. In this case, the quality is variable because different countries/regions may use different data collection methods and guidelines. Air quality data from monitoring stations are regarded as accurate in the case of China (Rohde and Muller 2015). However, the placement of monitoring stations may be subject to various political considerations. The data quality is affected by the number of PM10 and PM2.5 stations and whether the data were measured or converted. The location of the stations in the cities matters. Some cities may place them near areas with the worst possible pollution so people will be alerted when pollution is at high levels. Chinese city officials tend to place them away from the most polluted spots because they want to use typical or representative spots for the city, or they may place some in highly polluted areas and others in less polluted areas so that the averages for the city may look "representative." This practice usually results in underestimated city averages.

Furthermore, the WHO city data on Indonesia and Sri Lanka were based on only a single station, while the number of stations for Nepal was unavailable (WHO 2016a). For Indonesia, data based on one station in the city of Bandung may not be representative of such a large country. Hong Kong uses 15 and Singapore uses 22 monitoring stations to directly measure both PM10 and PM2.5. Most cities in Bangladesh and Pakistan measure both PM10 and PM2.5 through monitoring stations. For other countries, one set of data is directly measured and the other is converted using the directly measured data. In India, Malaysia, South Korea, and Thailand, it is usually the case that PM10 is directly measured and PM2.5 is converted from PM10 measurements, In Japan and Taiwan, PM2.5 is directly measured while PM10 is converted from PM2.5 data. In China, PM2.5 is directly measured in all cities, while PM10 is directly measured in some and converted from PM2.5 measurements in other cities. Despite these variations and limitations, the data obtained were the best available for this study. Both the WHO and Yale University follow their own data collection standards and criteria and employ different methods to enhance data accuracy, completeness, and comparability across countries/regions in the published datasets.

Terminology

This study will focus on air pollution in terms of particulate matter (PM). PM is a complex mixture of extremely small particles and liquid droplets. Such a mixture may be made up of acids, organic chemicals, metals, soil, and dust. In addition to PM2.5 just discussed, another category is PM10, referring to particles larger than 2.5 micrometers and smaller than 10 micrometers in diameter. Such particles can pass through the throat and nose and enter the lungs. Thus they can cause heart and lung diseases.

PM2.5 guidelines (targets)

World organizations and countries have set different guidelines (targets) for small particulate pollution (Table 3.1). The guidelines by the WHO are the strictest. The WHO (2006) argues that small particulate pollution has health impacts even at very low concentrations – indeed no threshold has been identified below in which no damage to health is observed. Therefore, the WHO 2005 guideline limits aimed to achieve the lowest concentrations of PM possible. Few Asian countries/regions have set up these guidelines for annual averages and daily (24 hours) averages. Those published guidelines are compared to the WHO, USA, and European Union standards. Singapore, Japan, and Taiwan are quite compatible with such standards while other countries, such as China and India, have lower standards. Those Asian countries not listed in Table 3.1 do not yet have any official standards available, which are very important in fighting air pollution.

Current air pollution in Asian cities

The WHO (2016a, 2016b) just updated its urban air quality database, primarily based on government reporting. Annual mean concentrations of particulate matter (PM10 and/or PM2.5)

Table 3.1 Guidelines (targets) in Asian countries/regions for PM2.5 annual average and daily (24 hours) average ($\mu g/m^3$) as compared to the WHO, USA, and European Union standards

	Annual mean	*Daily average*
WHO	10	25
USA	12	35
European Union	25	na
Singapore	12	37.5
Japan	15	35
Taiwan	15	35
South Korea	25	50
Thailand	25	50
China	35	75
India	40	60

Sources: WHO: WHO (2006); USA: USEPA (2012); European Union: European Commission (2016); Singapore: National Environment Agency of Singapore (2016); Japan: Transport Policy Net (2016a); Taiwan: Environmental Protection Administration, ROC (2015); South Korea: Air Korea (2016); Thailand: Transport Policy Net (2016b); China: MEP (2012); India: IES (2016).

were based on daily measurements, or data which could be aggregated into annual means (WHO 2016a). The database includes PM10 and PM2.5 levels in selective monitored cities in 15 Asian countries or regions (Table 3.2). The number of cities in each country or region varied from just one to 194. The data indicate that South Asian countries, Pakistan, Bangladesh, and India, tend to have very high PM10 and PM2.5 levels. The highest annual average PM10 was 540 ug/m^3 in Peshawar, Pakistan. The highest annual average PM2.5 was 176 ug/m^3, which is 17.6 times the WHO limit, in Gwalior, India. China is fourth in terms of urban PM2.5 pollution with an annual average at 55 ug/m^3, 5.5 times the WHO limit. Urban Japan is the least polluted with an annual average PM2.5 at 15 ug/m^3 and PM10 at 28 ug/m^3. Malaysia, Singapore, Taiwan, South Korea, and Thailand are also among the least polluted. The means of PM10 and PM2.5 in Table 3.2 were derived by this study from averaging values among the cities regardless of city population size. WHO (2016c) also published country-wide urban PM2.5 means (Table 3.3). These means are higher than the means shown in Table 3.2 because larger urban areas tend to have higher PM2.5 pollution. Table 3.3 better reflects PM2.5 pollution in urban areas in a country than Table 3.2 does. It also shows that Asia was among the most PM2.5 polluted regions of the world. Table 3.4 presents Asia's most polluted cities in terms of PM2.5 levels 10 times the WHO limit. Of the 27 cities, 18 are found in India including the top four most polluted cities. China is a distant second with six cities, followed by Pakistan with two cities and Bangladesh with one. The top 14 most polluted cities include 10 from India and four from China.

Variations within a country: the case of Chinese cities

The national annual average of PM2.5 and PM10 levels is an important indicator of air pollution in a country. In addition, it is important to understand the regional variations within a country, which may be substantial for a large country such as China. While the annual average of PM2.5 is 55 ug/m^3 in China, there is a large variation among the provinces (Table 3.5). The following examines such variations at the province level in China. The WHO database covers 194 Chinese cities with a total population of 863.2 million. While air pollution in Beijing has been well known, 85.9 million people in nearby Hebei and Tianjin live in worse air pollution, with Hebei's

Table 3.2 Particulate matter (PM10 and PM2.5) levels in Asian cities

Country or region	*# of cities covered*	*Data*	*PM10 annual means (μg/m³)*			*PM2.5 annual means (μg/m³)*		
		Year	*Maximum*	*Minimum*	*Mean*	*Maximum*	*Minimum*	*Mean*
Bangladesh	8	2014	191	64	140	106	37	78
China	194	2014	305	23	89	128	15	55
Hong Kong	1	2014			49			29
India	122	2012	329	11	107	176	6	58
Indonesia	1	2014			59			33
Japan	15	2012	35	19	28	19	10	15
Malaysia	6	2014	47	20	31	25	10	16
Myanmar	14	2012*	140	31	95	78	17	53
Nepal	1	2013			88			49
Pakistan	5	2010*	540	217	339	111	66	88
South Korea	16	2014	54	38	47	28	22	25
Singapore	1	2014			30			18
Sri Lanka	1	2011			64			36
Taiwan	19	2014	51	16	31	34	11	24
Thailand	23	2014	57	23	46	32	13	25

Notes:
[#] of cities: Number of cities included in the WHO database.
*= mode year. The year when the data were measured in different cities was 2009, 2012, and 2013 in Myanmar and 2009-2011 in Pakistan. A mode year is used here for the two countries.

Source: Compiled from WHO (2016a). Means were derived by author from averaging values among the cities regardless of city population size.

Notes: Where only one city in a country was reported, only the mean of the city is included.

PM2.5 level being 8 percent higher than Beijing's. About 162.1 million or 19 percent Chinese live in PM2.5 pollution seven times or more of the WHO limit, 353.5 million or about 41 percent live in six times or more of the WHO limit, 656.4 or over 76 percent live in five times or more of the WHO limit, and 856.6 million or over 99 percent Chinese live in three times or more of the WHO limit. Only Tibet and Hainan with less than 1 percent of the Chinese population live in PM2.5 levels compatible to that of Japan. At the city level, variations are even greater. About 44.8 million Chinese in six cities live in PM2.5 levels 10 to 12.8 times the WHO limit (Table 3.6). Nearly 74.6 million people in nearby Hebei, Tianjin, and Henan cities live in air pollution worse than Beijing. Nearly 94.2 million or 11 percent of the Chinese population live in air quality at or worse than the air in Beijing. Xingtai with PM2.5 at 128 is 50 percent worse than Beijing. About 402.5 million or 47 percent of Chinese live in cities where PM2.5 levels are six to 12.8 times the WHO limit.

None of the 194 Chinese cities met the WHO guidelines for PM10 or PM2.5. Sanya, Hainan, had the lowest PM10 at 23 μg/m3 followed by Yifan, Heilongjiang, at 24 μg/m3. Both cities also had the lowest PM2.5 level at 15 μg/m3 and 16 μg/m3 respectively. The 17 worst cities had PM10 levels over seven to 15 times exceeding WHO limit ranging from 144 to 305 μg/m3 were Shijiangzhuan, Jinan, Xingtai, Baoding, Xi'an, Zhengzhou, Handan, Xining, Hengshui, Taiyuan, Tangshan, Lanzhou, Tianjin, Chengdu, Urumqi, Hohhot, and Langfang. In terms of PM2.5 air pollution, six cities had levels over 10 to 12 times exceeding the WHO limit. They were Xingtai, Baoding, Shijiangzhuan, Handan, Hengshui, and Tangshan. The PM2.5 levels in Langfang,

Table 3.3 Annual mean concentrations of fine particulate matter (PM2.5) in urban areas (μg/m3) in Asian countries and WHO regions, 2014

Country/WHO region	*PM2.5 ($\mu g/m^3$)*
Bangladesh	89.7
Nepal	75.7
India	73.6
Pakistan	68.7
China	61.8
Myanmar	56.7
Bhutan	39
Laos	33.6
Mongolia	33.5
North Korea	31.6
Viet Nam	28.7
Sri Lanka	28.6
South Korea	27.9
Philippines	27.6
Thailand	27.5
Cambodia	25
Indonesia	18.1
Singapore	17
Malaysia	16.7
Japan	13
African Region	36.7
Region of the Americas	14.5
South-East Asia Region	60.2
European Region	18.4
Eastern Mediterranean Region	62.9
Western Pacific Region	49.2
Global	38.4

Notes: Means were for all urban areas in the country.

Source: Compiled from WHO (2016a).

Cangzhou, Tianjin, Zhengzhou, Beijing, and Wuhan were from eight to nine times the WHO limit.

The most polluted tend to be lower and medium income manufacturing centers such as those in Hebei Province. This agrees with WHO findings that populations in less-developed cities are the most impacted by air pollution (WHO 2016b). On the other hand, less polluted areas tend to be more-developed cities such as those in Guangdong, Zhejiang, and Fujian. WHO (2016b) finds that 44 percent of cities in high-income countries meet the WHO air quality guidelines. However, none of the high-income Chinese cities do. Some of them are as wealthy as cities in high-income countries but severely polluted, such as Beijing, Tianjin, Wuhan, Tangshan, Zhengzhou, Nanjing, and Chengdu. Larger population centers also tend to be more likely to have higher pollution. However, there are many exceptions. Beijing and Tianjin more among the most developed and most polluted. Some of the least polluted Chinese cities are also less-developed, such as Zhanjiang, Sanya, Yilan, Haikou, Yuxi, Maoming, Yangjiang, Jiujiang, Chifeng, and Lhasa. Geographic factors also influence level of pollution. These factors include climate, particularly precipitation and wind direction and speed, topography, and distance to the coast.

Table 3.4 Most polluted Asian cities in terms of PM2.5 pollution 10 or more times the WHO limit

Country	*City*	*PM2.5 annual means ($\mu g/m^3$)*	*PM10 annual means ($\mu g/m^3$)*
India	Gwalior	176	329
India	Allahabad	170	317
India	Patna	149	167
India	Raipur	144	268
China	Xingtai	128	193
China	Baoding	126	190
India	Delhi	122	229
India	Ludhiana	122	228
China	Shijiazhuang	121	305
India	Kanpur	115	215
India	Khanna	114	213
India	Firozabad	113	212
India	Lucknow	113	211
China	Handan	112	169
Pakistan	Peshawar	111	540
India	Amritsar	108	202
India	Gobindgarh	108	201
Pakistan	Rawalpindi	107	448
China	Hengshui	107	161
Bangladesh	Narayangonj	106	191
India	Agra	105	196
China	Tangshan	102	153
India	Jodhpur	101	189
India	Dehradun	100	188
India	Ahmedabad	100	83
India	Jaipur	100	187
India	Howrah	100	186

Source: Compiled from WHO (2016a).

National air quality performance in Asian countries

The above discussion was based on outdoor air pollution data mainly from ground-based monitoring stations in selective spots in selective cities. Yale University (2016a) provides national level information on air quality including both urban and rural areas. It "ranks how well countries perform on protection of human health from environmental harm and protection of ecosystems." The Air Quality category is based on different indicators. They include average exposure to $PM_{2.5}$, health risk exposure to $PM_{2.5}$, percentage of the population exposed to $PM_{2.5}$ levels above WHO air quality guidelines, indoor solid fuel usage, and average concentration of NO_2 (Yale University 2016b). The Health Impacts indicator "assesses human health risks associated with unsafe water and sanitation as well as household and outdoor air quality" (Yale University 2016c). Different from the WHO data, the outdoor Air Quality indicators are mainly based on satellite-derived estimates (Yale University 2016d). Countries/regions are ranked by their performances and ten-year changes in each indicator as well as compared to their peers in terms of GDP per capita and their geographic neighbors.

Asian countries/regions tend to have lower rankings in air quality indicators (Table 3.7). Among the worst 21 countries/regions in PM2.5 exposure and exceedance, 12 are in Asia, with

Table 3.5 Population and particulate matter (PM2.5 and PM10) levels in Chinese provinces, 2014

Province level region	*Population*	*Number of stations*	*PM2.5 Annual mean ($\mu g/m^3$)*	*PM10 Annual mean ($\mu g/m^3$)*
Hebei	73	55	92	149
Tianjin	12.9	15	87	150
Beijing	19.6	14	85	108
Hubei	20.9	24	73	112
Henan	35.7	37	70	112
Subtotal	162.1			
Anhui	16.9	21	64	96
Shaanxi	33.1	51	64	120
Chongqing	28.8	17	61	106
Hunan	26.3	39	60	88
Jiangsu	86.1	92	60	92
Subtotal	353.5			
Jilin	12.1	17	57	103
Liaoning	35.2	62	56	86
Zhejiang	57.4	57	54	90
Guangxi	16.7	22	52	83
Shanghai	23	10	52	84
Shanxi	7.6	12	52	78
Sichuan	41.1	41	52	83
Xinjiang	4.1	15	52	94
Shandong	105.7	98	51	82
Subtotal	656.4			
Guizhou	10.4	15	49	80
Jiangxi	9.8	17	45	88
Ningxia	2.7	10	44	90
Heilongjiang	22.1	29	41	65
Gansu	5.8	10	40	83
Neimenggu	11.8	23	40	81
Guangdong	94	91	39	61
Shenzhen	10.4	11	34	61
Fujian	18.8	14	33	58
Yunnan	14.6	12	32	58
Subtotal	856.6			
Tibet	0.6	6	24	64
Hainan	2.7	7	19	35
Subtotal	3.3			
China	863.2			

Sources: PM10 and PM2.5 data were compiled from WHO (2016a). Population data are from National Bureau of Statistics of China (2012).

China, Bangladesh, India, Nepal, and Pakistan as the worst five. Other countries do not rank high except for Mongolia and the Philippines in PM2.5 exposure and Singapore and Mongolia being number one in PM2.5 exceedance. Asian countries/regions do not rank well in terms of exposure to NO_2 which tends to be associated with more developed economies. It is not surprising that South Korea, Japan, Singapore, and Taiwan were among the worst. However, it is a surprise that China as a developing country ranked 176, the fourth worst in the world and second only to

Table 3.6 Most polluted Chinese cities, 2014

Province level region	*City*	*2010 census population (million)*	*PM2.5 Annual mean, μg/m³*	*PM10 Annual mean, μg/m³*
Hebei	Xingtai	7.1	128	193
Hebei	Baoding	11.2	126	190
Hebei	Shijiazhuang	10.2	121	305
Hebei	Hengshui	4.3	112	169
Hebei	Tangshan	7.6	107	161
Hebei	Langfang	4.4	102	153
Subtotal		44.8		
Hebei	Cangzhou	7.1	96	144
Hebei	Shouguang	1.1	88	133
Tianjin	Tianjin	12.9	87	150
Henan	Zhengzhou	8.6	86	171
Subtotal		74.6		
Beijing	Beijing	19.6	85	108
Subtotal		94.2		
Hubei	Wuhan	9.8	80	124
Henan	Anyang	5.2	79	119
Anhui	Hefei	5.7	79	115
Hebei	Shouguang	1.1	78	117
Hubei	Jingzhou	5.7	74	112
Hunan	Changsha	7	74	94
Jiangsu	Nanjing	8	72	137
Liaoning	Shenyang	8.1	72	129
Sichuan	Chengdu	14	71	150
Jilin	Harbin	10.6	71	119
Henna	Kaifeng	4.7	70	106
Hubei	Yichang	4.1	70	106
Hubei	Yangquan	1.4	70	105
Henan	Pingdingshan	4.9	70	105
Hunan	Xiangtan	2.8	70	105
Shaanxi	Xi'an	8.5	70	189
Hunan	Zhuzhou	3.9	69	105
Shandong	Laiwu	1.3	68	103
Henan	Jiaozuo	3.5	68	103
Jiangsu	Jiangyin	1.6	68	102
Jiangsu	Suqian	4.7	68	102
Shaanxi	Weinan	5.3	68	102
Shaanxi	Changzhi	3.3	67	101
Shaanxi	Taiyuan	4.2	67	157
Jiangsu	Wuxi	6.4	67	101
Jiangsu	Xuzhou	8.6	66	100
Jiangsu	Zhenjiang	3.1	66	99
Jiangsu	Changzhou	4.6	65	99
Shaanxi	Xianyang	5.1	65	98
Guangxi	Liuzhou	3.8	65	98
Liaoning	Anshan	3.6	65	98
Jiangsu	Huai'an	4.8	65	98

(*Continued*)

Table 3.6 (continued)

Province level region	*City*	*2010 census population (million)*	*PM2.5 Annual mean, μg/m³*	*PM10 Annual mean, μg/m³*
Shaanxi	Baoji	3.7	65	98
Jiangsu	Jurong	0.6	65	97
Jiangsu	Yangzhou	4.5	65	97
Xinjiang	Urumqi	3.1	64	146
Sichuan	Zigong	2.7	64	97
Zhejiang	Shaoxing	4.9	64	105
Jiangsu	Suzhou	10.5	64	97
Shaanxi	Tongchuan	0.8	64	97
Henan	Sanmenxia	2.2	64	96
Liaoning	Changchun	7.7	64	130
Shandong	Liaocheng	5.8	63	96
Zhejiang	Jinhua	5.4	63	99
Zhejiang	Huzhou	2.9	63	111
Shanxi	Linfen	4.3	62	94
Qinghai	Xining	2.2	62	163
Chongqing	Chongqing	28.8	61	106
Zhejiang	Taizhou	6	61	82
Anhui	Wuhu	2.3	61	92
Jiangsu	Lianyungang	4.4	61	92
Zhejiang	Hangzhou	8.7	61	106
Shandong	Heze	8.3	60	91
Hebei	Qinhuangdao	3	60	91
Jiangsu	Zhangjiagang	1.2	60	91
Jiangsu	Nantong	7.3	60	90
Anhui	Fuyang	7.6	60	90
Total		402.5		

Sources: PM10 and PM2.5 data were compiled from WHO (2016a). Population data are from National Bureau of Statistics of China (2012).

South Korea in Asia. Myanmar and Bhutan had the highest ranking in Asia, in consistence with their level of economic development. Household air quality rankings are closely related to level of economic development. Japan, South Korea, and Singapore were the world best while most Asian countries rank poorly, with Laos, Myanmar, Cambodia, Bangladesh, Nepal, and Sri Lanka being the worst in Asia. The air quality category ranking was based on the above indicators. The world's worst eight countries in air quality are all in Asia. Thailand, Bhutan, and Taiwan are not doing well either with their rankings above 160. Only four of the 20 countries/regions were ranked above 100. Singapore, the Philippines, and Mongolia are better than their Asian neighbors but still ranked below the world's top 50. The poor air quality rankings reflect the low rankings in PM2.5 exposure and exceedance, except for exceedance in Singapore which is ranked number 1. Since the Health Impacts indicator refers to impacts by both air and water pollution, it may not agree with air pollution rankings. For example, Malaysia and Japan were ranked higher in water pollution performance so its Health Impacts ranking is better than its air quality ranking. The worst rankings are Bangladesh, Myanmar, Nepal, Cambodia, and India.

A country/region's level of economic development is commonly believed to be associated with certain level of air pollution. Such a belief calls for comparison among countries/regions at

Table 3.7 Air quality and health impacts rankings of selective Asian countries/regions among 180 countries/regions worldwide, 2014

Country or Region	*Exposure to PM2.5*	*PM2.5 Exceedance**	*Exposure to NO_2*	*Household Air Quality*	*Air Quality*	*Health Impacts***
China	180	179	176	116	179	95
Bangladesh	179	178	107	151	180	150
India	178	178	110	135	178	134
Nepal	177	177	61	146	177	141
Pakistan	176	176	105	125	175	123
South Korea	174	174	178	1	173	103
Laos	173	174	75	162	176	127
Viet Nam	170	165	103	119	170	93
Myanmar	168	168	40	156	174	143
Thailand	166	170	118	104	167	85
Taiwan	162	160	159	101	161	84
Bhutan	160	173	40	112	163	91
Cambodia	114	127	61	153	148	137
Malaysia	110	155	133	54	117	42
Sri Lanka	109	140	52	141	140	114
Japan	95	133	172	1	104	57
Singapore	93	1	163	1	54	63
Indonesia	74	122	101	113	92	78
Philippines	30	78	75	123	61	108
Mongolia	23	1	61	131	65	111

Notes:
*= the percentage of the population exposed to PM2.5 levels above the WHO limit. 179 was the worst ranking in 2016 Report.
**Impacts by both air and water pollution.

Source: Compiled from Yale University (2016c).

the same level of development in order to be fair. The result shows that majority Asian countries/regions compare rather unfavorably to their GDP peer set (Table 3.8). China appears to be the worst in the outdoor air quality comparison, followed by Bangladesh and India. In terms of Exposure to PM2.5, China and Bangladesh were 97.23 percent and 92.79 percent below their peers. India, Nepal, and Pakistan were all over 80 percent below their peers. On the other hand, six of the 20 countries/regions compare favorably with their GDP peers, such as Mongolia and the Philippines. In terms of PM2.5 exceedance, Bangladesh, China, and India were each 100 percent below their peers, followed by Nepal and Pakistan. Only three countries compared favorably to their GDP peers, including Singapore, Mongolia, and the Philippines. It was a surprise that Bhutan is compared unfavorably by 66.94 percent to its peers. The country has little manufacturing at low level of economic development. It is reasonable to assume that it has been affected by pollution from its southern neighbors such as India and Bangladesh. In the matter of Exposure to NO_2, South Korea was 100 percent below its GDP peers, followed by China at 80.68 percent. Six countries compared favorably including Myanmar, Bhutan, and Sri Lanka. With regard to Household Air Quality, half of the 20 countries/regions compared favorably to their GDP peers, with Nepal at 100 percent and Cambodia at 61.27 percent. On the other hand, Laos and Myanmar were over 50 percent below their peers. Pertaining to the Air Quality category, China and Bangladesh were over 70 percent worse than countries at the same economic development level. India, Laos, Nepal, and Pakistan were all over 50 percent below their peers in the comparison.

Table 3.8 Air quality and health impacts of selective Asian countries/regions as compared individually to countries/regions at the same level of GDP per capita (%), 2014

Country or Region	*Exposure to PM2.5*	*PM2.5 Exceedance*	*Exposure to NO_2*	*Household Air Quality*	*Air Quality*	*Health Impacts**
China	−97.23	−100	−80.68	−18.12	−71.65	−11.34
Bangladesh	−92.79	−100	−11.27	−37.24	−70.84	−28.8
India	−89.71	−100	−12.63	−8.72	−62.55	−12.89
Nepal	−83.49	−93.79	−1.35	100	−55.27	70.41
Pakistan	−81.7	−87.16	−10.61	−1.38	−53.88	−3.1
South Korea	−58.2	−73.52	−100	1.94	−44.26	−21.89
Laos	−52.13	−73.84	1.14	−67.17	−56.71	−7.02
Viet Nam	−41.56	−46.69	−9.95	5.94	−26.94	17.72
Thailand	−39.26	−60.65	−6.38	−8.54	−32.93	−6.39
Myanmar	−37.71	−53.32	6.78	−50.68	−40.85	−21.31
Taiwan	−28.31	−38.26	−18.13	−13.57	−25.31	−13.4
Bhutan	−20.25	−66.94	6.78	15.13	−22.57	19.51
Malaysia	−5.74	−34.56	−17.56	8.4	−11.07	11.63
Cambodia	−1.17	−17.28	−1.35	61.27	−0.68	78.38
Japan	1.51	−8.51	−54.13	1.94	−4.92	−2.69
Sri Lanka	2.17	−15.51	5.68	−16.53	−7.96	3.46
Singapore	2.45	27.55	−27.26	1.94	7.53	−4.91
Indonesia	17.83	−1.03	−8.65	12.08	7.21	27.56
Philippines	27.15	22.92	1.14	0.75	15.79	7.57
Mongolia	28.59	26.03	4	−6.39	15.65	5.54

Notes: *Impacts by both air and water pollution. The percentages range from positive 100 to negative 100.

Source: Compiled from Yale University (2016c).

The Philippines and Mongolia compared most favorably with their peers. In reference to the Health Impacts category, Bangladesh, South Korea, and Myanmar were the least favorably compared to their GDP peers while Cambodia and Nepal had the most favorably comparison.

With regard to PM2.5 exposure, 12 of the 20 countries/regions compared unfavorably to their neighbors in the same EPI Regions (Table 3.9). China was the worst, 97.13 percent below its neighbors. Bangladesh and India were over 80 percent worse than their neighbors. On the other hand, Sri Lanka, Bhutan, Mongolia, and the Philippines compared very favorably to their neighbors. The worst countries China, Bangladesh, and India were all 100 percent worse than their neighbors in the PM2.5 exceedance comparison. Nepal, South Korea, Laos, and Pakistan were over 70 percent worse than their neighbors. On the opposite side, Sri Lanka, Mongolia, Singapore, and the Philippines compared very favorably to their neighbors. South Korea was the worst when compared to its neighbors in Exposure to NO_2, followed by China, Japan, Singapore, and Taiwan. Half of the countries/regions, all of them less-developed, compared favorably to their neighbors. Yet, the less-developed economies tended to compare very unfavorably to their neighbors in Household Air Quality, except for Bhutan. More-developed economies tended to do better in Household Air Quality. In the overall Air Quality category, China was the worst, 68.28 percent worse than its neighbors, followed by Laos, Bangladesh, and India. On the other hand, Sri Lanka was nearly 37 percent higher compared to its neighbors. In terms of Health Impacts, most less-developed economies did not compare well with their neighbors. The exceptions were Bhutan, Malaysia, and Sri Lanka.

Table 3.9 Air quality and health impacts of selective Asian countries/regions as compared to their neighbors in the EPI Regions (%), 2014

Country or Region	*Exposure to PM2.5*	*PM2.5 Exceedance*	*Exposure to NO_2*	*Household Air Quality*	*Air Quality*	*Health Impacts**
China	−97.13	−100	−79.78	1.26	−68.28	−1.96
Bangladesh	−87.75	−100	−11.96	−28.92	−56.62	−25.59
India	−82.52	−100	−13.31	3.38	−44.3	−8.96
Nepal	−71.52	−84.44	3.19	−12.9	−40.79	−15.69
Pakistan	−68.92	−71.61	−11.31	11.71	−31.4	1.28
South Korea	−57.46	−72.43	−100	37.12	−39.38	−6.17
Laos	−54.23	−72.43	18.17	−69.59	−56.78	−21.75
Viet Nam	−44.12	−43.82	5.22	−1.88	−27.06	−0.93
Thailand	−37.06	−56.05	−1.99	13.12	−24.98	3.52
Taiwan	−27.03	−35.7	−41.29	16.25	−18.77	4.02
Cambodia	−4	−1.22	21.52	−43.28	−11.75	−28.94
Malaysia	−2.34	−26.91	−13.69	34.07	−0.52	23.45
Japan	3.32	−4.73	−67.1	37.12	3.41	16.89
Singapore	4.28	32.82	−47.83	37.12	16.95	14.23
Myanmar	5.81	3.21	5.95	−44.14	−12.01	−17.76
Indonesia	12.68	4.3	6.74	3.81	7.04	7.35
Philippines	21.59	29.54	18.17	−6.69	15.61	−9.47
Mongolia	22.97	32.82	21.52	−13.3	15.48	−11.18
Bhutan	35.47	−26.91	5.95	30.4	15.17	24.91
Sri Lanka	73.55	86.81	4.85	−5.46	36.9	8.14

Note: *Impacts by both air and water pollution.

Source: Compiled from Yale University (2016c).

Historical trends

From 2005 to 2014, PM2.5 Exposure increased in all countries/regions except for Japan and the Philippines (Table 3.10). The largest increases were by 68 percent to 84 percent in China, India, and Bangladesh. However, PM2.5 Exceedance increased in only five countries while most countries/regions experienced a declining trend in the 10 years. China's Exposure to NO_2 increased by 54.36 percent in ten years, the largest increase in Asia. The increases in other countries were small. Japan had a 58 percent decrease in ten years followed by Taiwan with a 45 percent decrease. Most countries improved their Household Air Quality by 90 percent to 100 percent in the 10 year period. The overall Air Quality increased in most countries/regions also, possibly benefiting from Household Air Quality improvement. Myanmar and Bangladesh experienced the largest decrease in overall Air Quality. The same trend also happened to Health Impacts with most countries/regions experienced improvement. Yet, Singapore, Malaysia, and Japan suffered some losses.

Historical data on pollution measurements from Yale University (2016e) reflect changing patterns in different countries/regions. Based on the data, means were derived for the historical periods (Table 3.11). With 78.4 percent of its population exposed to PM2.5 levels above the WHO limit, China is the highest in the world from 2000 to 2014. South Asian countries also had high levels except for Sri Lanka and Bhutan. Only six countries met the WHO annual limit. Furthermore, the worst seven countries in the world are in Asia, from China to North Korea. Again, South Asian countries also had a very depressing situation with Sri Lanka and

Table 3.10 Ten-year change (%) in air quality and health impacts of selective Asian countries/regions, 2014

Country or Region	*Exposure to PM2.5*	*PM2.5 Exceedance*	*Exposure to NO_2*	*Household Air Quality*	*Air Quality*	*Health Impacts**
Bangladesh	−83.57	0	−7.37	49.48	−18	−1.29
India	−72.84	0	−1.94	74.74	4.97	5.1
China	−67.79	0	−54.36	100	53.22	20
Nepal	−58.73	100	−0.77	95.82	13.98	30.36
Laos	−45.42	100	−1.97	−6.14	−9.38	14.73
Myanmar	−45.13	−36.18	−2.09	38.42	−25.73	12.45
Viet Nam	−36.51	83.51	−5.99	100	20.64	25.31
Thailand	−36.29	90.5	1.66	100	18.94	−0.63
Bhutan	−27.56	−42.64	−1.13	100	−1.04	15.93
Pakistan	−20.6	100	−4.92	100	51.36	20.99
Cambodia	−18.29	−2.27	−1.77	90.28	−0.02	24.61
Malaysia	−15.29	−0.7	3.49	98.56	15.71	−7.38
Sri Lanka	−15.18	−32.96	−0.19	87.64	−8.4	11.07
Taiwan	−10.86	100	44.97	−0.89	28.65	7.01
Singapore	−8.54	0	13.14	95	16.46	−13.66
South Korea	−6.1	100		95	77.15	−1.2
Indonesia	−3.93	15.5	7.21	100	20.7	6.86
Mongolia	−0.2	0	−2.28	96.28	11.28	18.56
Philippines	1.41	24.51	0.74	83.59	21.38	−0.45
Japan	5.03	56.86	57.9	95	45.1	−4.29

Note: *Impacts by both air and water pollution.

Source: Compiled from Yale University (2016e).

Bhutan as the exceptions. Singapore and Mongolia were very successful in dealing with this issue. Similar situation is true in regard to PM2.5 Exceedance, with Asian countries took the worst seven places. The situation is a little better with PM2.5 Health Risk Exposure from 1990 to 2013. China is the worst in Asia but the third worst in the world. South Asian countries followed, except for Sri Lanka and Bhutan. Mongolia and the Philippines had the lowest risk exposure. With regard to NO_2 Exposure, more-developed economies such as South Korea, Hong Kong, and Japan suffered high level of exposure from 1997 to 2011. The data again indicate that China experienced higher level of NO_2 pollution than would have been expected at its level of economic development. Most developing countries, such as Bhutan and Myanmar, had low levels of exposure, constant with their level of economic development.

Eight countries/regions were selected from Table 3.11 to illustrate the historical trends in each air quality indicator. In order to pay attention to the relationship between level of development and air quality, the figures included four more-developed economies: Japan, South Korea, Taiwan, and Hong Kong. In the case of PM2.5 Health Risk Exposure for which Hong Kong had no data, Singapore was used instead. They also include four less-developed economies: China, India, Pakistan, and Bangladesh. It should be noted that the more-developed economies are all Island countries/regions. Their air quality should have been favorably affected by their geographic location that is associated with stronger wind, ocean influence, and more precipitation.

Table 3.11 Asian countries/regions ranked in the world by their means of air pollution indicators

Country or region	*PM2.5 Exposure 2000–2014*	*Country or region*	*PM2.5 Exceedance 2000–2014*	*Country or region*	*PM2.5 Health Risk* 1990–2013*	*Country or region*	*NO_2 Exposure 1997–2011*
1. China	45.1	1. China	0.784	3. China	0.656	3. South Korea	7.06
2. India	28.4	2. Pakistan	0.686	7. Pakistan	0.621	4. Hong Kong	6.37
3. Pakistan	27.9	3. Nepal	0.656	10. Bangladesh	0.6	9. Japan	4.2
4. Nepal	27.3	4. India	0.642	15. India	0.579	16. China	3.29
5. Bangladesh	24.8	5. Bangladesh	0.614	16. Nepal	0.576	18. Taiwan	3.19
6. South Korea	21.5	6. South Korea	0.529	22. South Korea	0.527	59. Malaysia	1.03
7. North Korea	19.8	7. North Korea	0.482	40. North Korea	0.451	70. Thailand	0.71
10. Laos	16.7	10. Hong Kong	0.409	52. Bhutan	0.417	82. India	0.51
11. Hong Kong	16.6	15. Laos	0.379	59. Viet Nam	0.408	90. Bangladesh	0.41
14. Viet Nam	15.9	24. Taiwan	0.333	65. Singapore	0.397	91. Pakistan	0.4
26. Taiwan	14.5	28. Thailand	0.32	70. Taiwan	0.391	93. Viet Nam	0.38
32. Thailand	13.7	29. Viet Nam	0.319	73. Myanmar	0.388	101. Philippines	0.28
39. Bhutan	12.6	34. Bhutan	0.288	83. Laos	0.372	120. Laos	0.21
45. Japan	12.3	51. Japan	0.2	85. Thailand	0.367	123. Nepal	0.19
53. Myanmar	11.4	53. Myanmar	0.192	87. Japan	0.362	129. Cambodia	0.17
72. Malaysia	9.6	65. Malaysia	0.14	111. Sri Lanka	0.301	134. Sri Lanka	0.15
84. Indonesia	8.5	77. Indonesia	0.11	114. Cambodia	0.29	157. Myanmar	0.11
85. Cambodia	8.5	87. Cambodia	0.062	116. Indonesia	0.285	158. Bhutan	0.1
91. Sri Lanka	7.8	89. Sri Lanka	0.055	119. Malaysia	0.276		
113. Philippines	6.4	98. Philippines	0.035	149. Philippines	0.151		
153. Singapore	4.6	147. Mongolia	0.001	157. Mongolia	0.121		
		211. Singapore	0				

Note: *PM2.5 Health Risk Exposure is a unitless measurement from 0 to 1 with 1 being the highest risk.

Source: Compiled from Yale University (2016e).

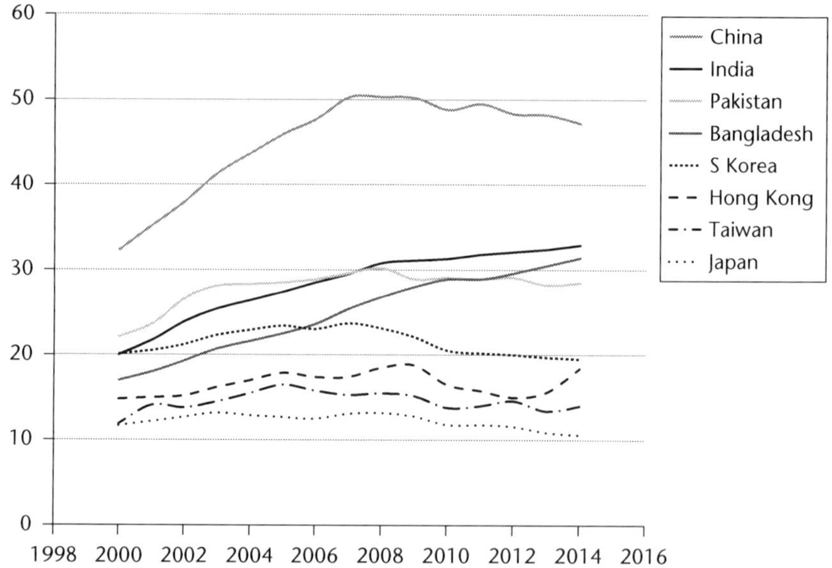

Figure 3.1 Annual mean PM2.5 Exposure in Asian countries/regions 2000–2014

Source: Compiled from Yale University (2016c).

Pertaining to annual PM2.5 Exposure, the less-developed economies all experienced an increasing trend from 2000 to 2014 (Figure 3.1). China experienced the fastest increasing trend with leveling off and slight decline in recent years. Leveling off and a slight decline also happened to Pakistan, while India and Bangladesh had a steady growing trend. The more-developed economies tend to have lower levels than the less-developed. South Korea, Taiwan, and to some lesser extent, Japan experienced a slight rise first, followed by a slight decline. Hong Kong was a little different with a recent rise. In regard to the proportion of population exposed to PM2.5 levels exceeding the WHO limit, the four less-developed countries had a higher rate than the more-developed (Figure 3.2). China and Pakistan had a leveling off while India and Bangladesh continue to rise. The more-developed economies experienced a rise and fall while maintaining low levels, with Hong Kong and South Korea having an increase in 2014. Japan's trend was rather flat, indicating a sustained low level. Comparing Figures 3.1 and 3.2, it may be argued that more proportion of Chinese suffered from PM2.5 pollution while the intensity of the pollution had leveled off in recent years. The pollution has become more widely spread while intensity slightly lowered.

In respect to PM2.5 Health Risk Exposure, the four less-developed countries had a high risk with a rising trend (Figure 3.3). The more-developed economies had a low risk with a slight declining trend, except for Singapore with an inverted shape. Its risk was higher than any other countries in the early 1990s but quickly bottomed to the lowest level and then increased again. Trends in NO_2 Exposure were very different among the countries/regions (Figure 3.4). China's NO_2 pollution caught up very quickly, overtaking Taiwan's in the early 2000 and Japan's in the late 2000s. The other less-developed countries all had very low level of NO_2 pollution with a slight increase. The more-developed economies experienced a declining trend starting in the late 1990s to mid-2000s. China was a less-developed country with NO_2 pollution at the level of more-developed economies. Its increasing trend leveled off from 2010 to 2011.

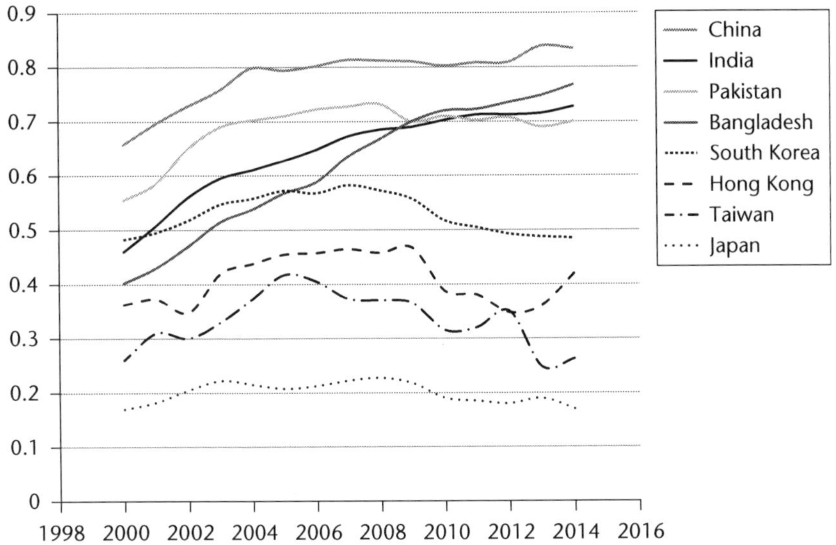

Figure 3.2 Annual mean PM2.5 Exceedance in Asian countries/regions 2000–2014

Source: Compiled from Yale University (2016c).

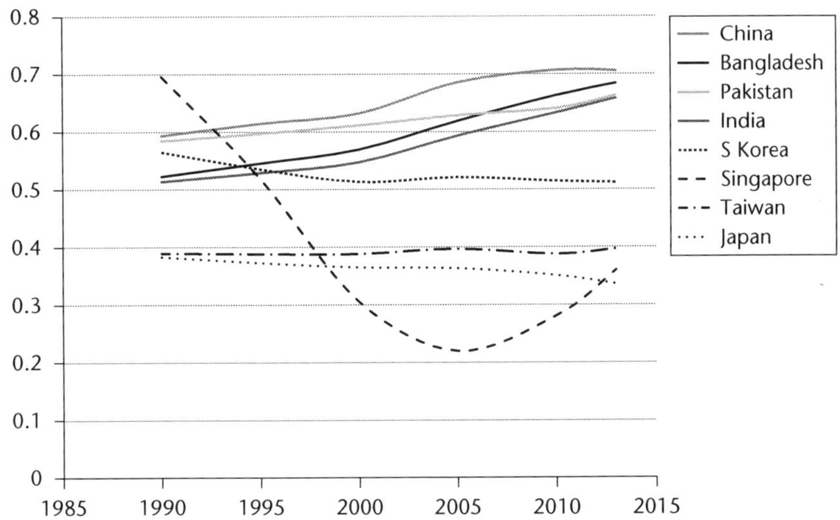

Figure 3.3 Annual mean PM2.5 Health Risk in Asian countries/regions 1990–2014

Source: Compiled from Yale University (2016c).

Air pollution in Asia may be the worst globally and historically

The above discussion indicates that the exact extent of pollution varies by sources of data, possibly due to different methods of measurement by the same or different organizations. For example, the WHO reported that annual mean PM2.5 for urban China was 61.8 $\mu g/m^3$ (Table 3.3). That was higher than what Rohde and Muller (2015) reported, noting 52 $\mu g/m^3$ as the population-weighted average based on station-measured data in 190 cities. Yale University

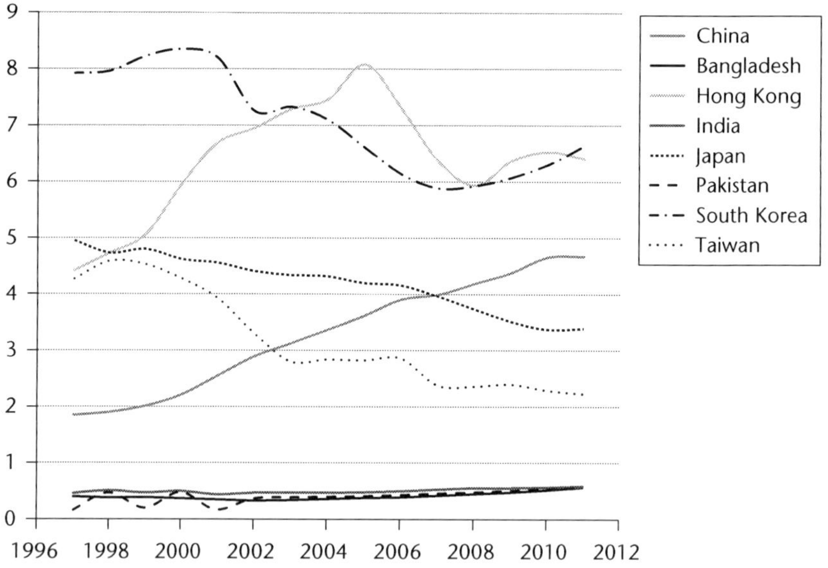

Figure 3.4 Annual mean NO_2 Exposure in Asian countries/regions 1997–2011

Source: Compiled from Yale University (2016c).

reported 45.13 $\mu g/m^3$ for both urban and rural areas. However, both the WHO and Yale University data suggested similar patterns and trends. Asia has been the worst hit by air pollution, particularly in terms of deadly PM2.5 exposure, despite the fact that some Asian countries such as Japan and Singapore have much lower levels of pollution. India, China, Pakistan, and Bangladesh are the worst in Asia. Furthermore, the country-wide averages may hide disparities in air pollution. Levels of pollution also varied greatly within large countries such as China, where about 44.8 million people live in PM2.5 polluted air 10 times or more the WHO limit. Eastern China, particularly areas around Beijing and Tianjin, has been the worst hit by PM2.5 pollution. Geographic factors such as climate and topography affect the level of air pollution, in addition to population and type of economy. Air pollution has also been reported to be the worst in the northern parts of India, Pakistan, and Bangladesh (WHO 2016d).

National level data from Yale University provided additional insight into air quality and pollution in Asia in a global context. Asian countries/regions tended to receive lower rankings in PM2.5 Exposure and Exceedance with China, Bangladesh, India, Nepal, and Pakistan ranked as the worst in the world. This generally coincides with the findings based on the WHO data. Furthermore, Asian countries/regions also ranked low in NO_2 Exposure, which tends to be associated with more-developed economies. This means that these countries/regions suffer more from NO_2 pollution than expected at their level of development. China is the worst in this aspect. Asia is also worst in terms of overall air quality based on outdoor and indoor pollution. Asia is home to the world's worst eight countries in terms of air quality. Asian countries/regions compare rather poorly to countries at similar levels of economic development, with China as the worst. As air pollution is not restricted by national borders, it is reasonable to assume that some less-developed countries such as Bhutan have been negatively affected by air pollution from their neighbors.

From 2005 to 2014, China, India, and Bangladesh led the increase in PM2.5 Exposure. Indeed, the worst seven countries in the world in terms of PM2.5 Exposure are located in Asia. There were also substantial increases in other Asian countries/regions except for Japan and the

Philippines. The good news is that most Asian countries/regions experienced a decrease in PM2.5 Exceedance. Historical data from 2000 to 2014 indicate that China is the worst in the world in PM2.5 Exceedance, as 78.4 percent of its population was exposed to PM2.5 above the WHO limit. The historical patterns appear to be different between more and less-developed economies. Less-developed economies tended to experience high levels and an increasing trend in PM2.5 Exposure while the more-developed economies tended to have lower levels with a rising and falling trend. Similar trends exist in terms of PM2.5 Exceedance and PM2.5 Health Risk Exposure.

Air pollution is a threat to public health in Asia

Air pollution is a threat to sustainability in several aspects, including its impact on climate change, human health, social justice, and economic equality and well-being. This study focuses on its threat to public health. The WHO just published its global assessment of disease burden due to environmental risks in 2012 (Prüss-Ustün et al. 2016). The WHO report and accompanying dataset provide a rare opportunity to compare environmental health in Asian countries. China and India each lost nearly three million people to environmental risks, contributing to 30 percent of all deaths in the two countries (Table 3.12). That was 30 percent higher than the world average

Table 3.12 Burden of disease from environmental risks, Asian countries, 2012

Country	*Total (000s)*	*% deaths*	*Total (000s)*	*% DALYs*	*Age-standardized deaths/100,000*	*Age-standardized DALYs/100,000*
Bangladesh	201.53	23	11346.44	22	189	8,520
Bhutan	1.26	26	70.26	25	225	10,574
Cambodia	21.01	25	1263.56	22	173	9,051
China	2986.68	30	95968.22	26	199	6,408
India	2911.67	30	133618.4	25	315	12,119
Indonesia	349.87	23	16163.07	21	198	7,479
Japan	131.28	11	4222.25	13	41	2,110
Laos	14.91	32	927.29	31	321	14,524
Malaysia	25.94	18	1427.05	19	123	5,504
Mongolia	5.17	27	238.72	24	309	10,665
Myanmar	109.24	25	5271.27	23	277	11,255
Nepal	46.69	25	2369.45	23	251	10,129
North Korea	70.45	31	2454.7	27	310	10,122
Pakistan	331.18	25	19468.4	23	258	11,385
Philippines	123.46	22	7024.14	21	206	8,809
Singapore	3.11	13	120.46	13	47	1,900
South Korea	37.96	14	1482.86	14	58	2,461
Sri Lanka	34.92	25	1337.63	22	169	6,265
Thailand	93.82	19	3941.21	18	124	5,389
Viet Nam	129.27	25	5748.16	23	158	6,764
Total	7629.42		596412.2			

Notes: DALY refers to Disability-Adjusted Life Year. One DALY can be thought of as one lost year of "healthy" life. The sum of these DALYs across the population, or the burden of disease, can be thought of as a measurement of the gap between current health status and an ideal health situation where the entire population lives to an advanced age, free of disease and disability. DALYs for a disease or health condition are calculated as the sum of the Years of Life Lost (YLL) due to premature mortality in the population and the Years Lost due to Disability (YLD) for people living with the health condition or its consequences (Prüss-Ustün et al. 2016).

Source: Compiled from Prüss-Ustün et al. (2016).

of 23 percent. Only a few Asian countries were below the world average, including Japan, Singapore, South Korea, Malaysia, Thailand, and the Philippines. Laos was the worst at 32 percent. In addition, environmental risks contributed to lost years of healthy life as indicated by Disability-Adjusted Life Years (DALYs). The percentages of DALYs varied among the Asian countries but were closely associated with percentages of deaths. The age-standardized death rates attributable to environmental risks were highest in Laos, India, North Korea, and Mongolia, with over 300 per 100,000. Japan, Singapore, and South Korea had the lowest rates of death due to environmental risks. The ratio of such deaths between Laos and Japan is nearly eight times, which could be used to argue for an association between economic development and environmental health. However, there is no justification to degrade environmental health in the name of development.

Environmental health risks include more than air pollution. Yet air pollution, especially PM2.5 pollution, is one of the most deadly risks to human health (Table 3.13). Beelen et al. (2014) found that naturally-caused mortality was associated with long-term exposure to PM2·5 in European countries, even if the air pollution level was well below the mean annual limit of 25 $\mu g/m^3$. Developing countries have been suffering from severe air pollution which is a major cause of health problems, resulting in between 1.2 to 2 million premature deaths a year in China alone (Yang et al. 2013; WHO 2014b). Rohde and Muller (2015) found that Eastern China, where most of the population resides, was the hardest hit by air pollution. They estimated that unhealthy air affected 92 percent of China's population, if US standards were applied.

Among the 21 countries for which data were available, air pollution is the most deadly in North Korea, contributing to 83.59 percent of all environment-attributed deaths (Table 3.13). China is second only to North Korea, with air pollution being responsible for 163.1 deaths per 100,000 population and over three-fourths of all environmentally-attributed deaths. Air pollution also causes over 70 percent of all environmentally attributed fatalities in Mongolia and Sri Lanka. On the other hand, four Asian countries, Singapore, Malaysia, South Korea, and Japan, are doing well, with air-pollution causing fewer than 25 deaths per 100,000 population and less than 37 percent of all environmentally attributed deaths. The total population for the 21 Asian countries is 3,931.8 million, about 54 percent of the global population. However, these countries contribute 4.917 million deaths, with 73 percent of the global deaths attributed to air pollution. China alone contributes 34 percent of the world deaths attributed to air pollution. The mortality rate of the 21 Asian countries is 125 per 100,000 population. That is 5.76 times the rate for the Americas, 2.1 times the rate for the Eastern Mediterranean Region, 93 percent higher than the rate for the European Region, and 61 percent higher than that of the African Region.

Is there an environmental Kuznets curve for air pollution in Asia?

Yale's 2016 EPI Report suggests that the relationship between Environmental Health and GDP per capita is strongly positive, possibly due to improvement in public health as countries develop (Yale University 2016a). It also pointed out that something other than economic development alone may also be critical in achieving environmental results. An EKC relationship was found in emissions in 14 Asian countries (Apergis and Ozturk 2015) and in NO_2 emissions in Indian cities (Sinha and Bhattacharya 2016). A few papers have attempted to explore if an EKC exists in PM2.5 pollution. Keene and Deller (2015) found such an EKC for the United States with the turning point occurring between US $27,100 and US $28,200 per capita income for PM2.5 emissions and US $24,000 and US $25,500 for PM2.5 concentration. However, Stern and van Dijk (2016) found that economic growth had relatively small effects on the variation in

Table 3.13 Mortality rate (per 100,000 population) and total deaths attributed to household and ambient air pollution versus total environment attributable deaths, Asian countries, WHO regions, and the world total, 2012

Country	*Deaths/100,000*	*Total deaths attributed to air pollution* (000s)*	*As % of total environment attributable deaths***
North Korea	234.1	58.89	83.59
China	163.1	2257.18	75.57
Mongolia	132.2	3.91	75.62
India	130	1704.37	58.54
Myanmar	127.4	68.66	62.86
Sri Lanka	119.4	24.73	70.84
Laos	107.6	7.32	49.08
Nepal	104.2	29.71	63.64
Pakistan	88.8	167.77	50.66
Viet Nam	84	78.5	60.72
Indonesia	83.9	216.1	61.76
Philippines	82.7	83.28	67.45
Cambodia	71.4	11.12	52.93
Bangladesh	68.2	109.8	54.48
Thailand	65.3	44.38	47.3
Bhutan	59.9	0.46	36.87
Japan	24.2	30.63	23.33
South Korea	23.7	11.92	31.4
Malaysia	22.4	6.79	26.19
Singapore	20.5	1.15	36.94
Subtotal	125	4916.67	64.44
African Region	77.4	765.62	
Region of the Americas	21.7	214.11	
South-East Asia Region	117.1	2257.89	
European Region	64.9	590.62	
Eastern Mediterranean Region	59.3	381.76	
Western Pacific Region	134.8	2500.71	
World	91.7	6706.03	53.12

Notes:
*Calculated by author based on the 2015 population published by WHO (2016c).
**Calculated by author based on Table 3.12.

Source: Compiled from WHO (2016c) and Prüss-Ustün et al. (2016).

PM2.5 pollution globally. Han et al. (2016) was unable to find such an EKC for Beijing, which they believed had not reached the turning point of an EKC.

To test the relationship between economic development and air pollution, the annual mean PM2.5 and PM10 measurements were plotted against GDP per capita in 131 cities in China. The results indicated no EKC or any relationship in either PM2.5 pollution (Figure 3.5) or PM10 pollution (Figure 3.6). The relationship was also tested using the EPI data for the Asian countries/regions in Table 3.11, with GDP per capita data for the Asian countries/regions obtained from the World Bank (2016) and CIA (2016). No associations were detected for the PM2.5 Exposure (Figure 3.7), PM2.5 Exceedance (Figure 3.8), or PM2.5 Health Risk (Figure 3.9). However, an EKC was found for NO_2 pollution (Figure 3.10).

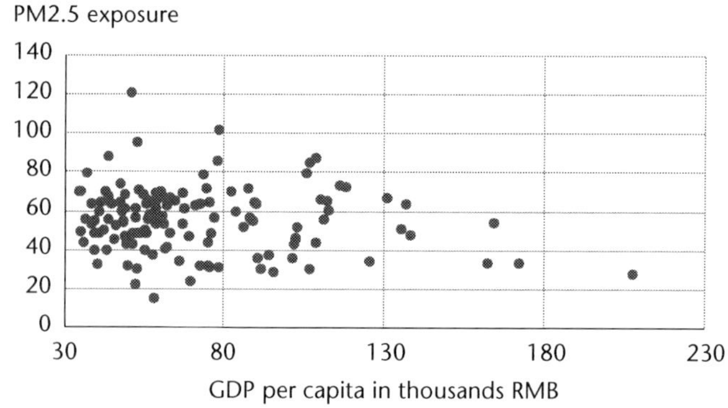

Figure 3.5 Annual mean PM2.5 Exposure and GDP per capita in Chinese cities, 2014

Source: Compiled from Yale University (2016e).

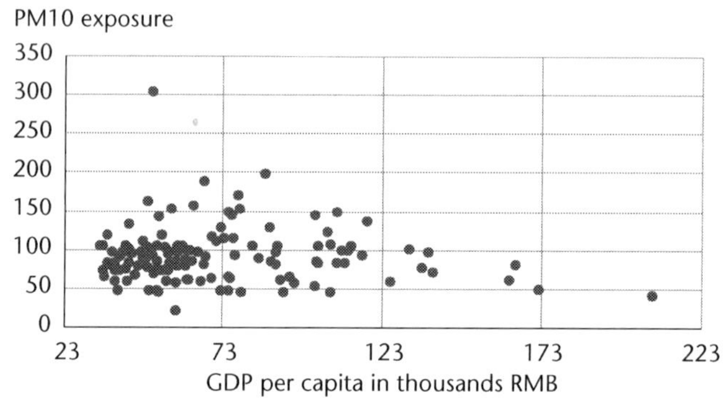

Figure 3.6 Annual mean PM210 exposure and GDP per capita in Chinese cities, 2014

Source: Compiled from Yale University (2016e).

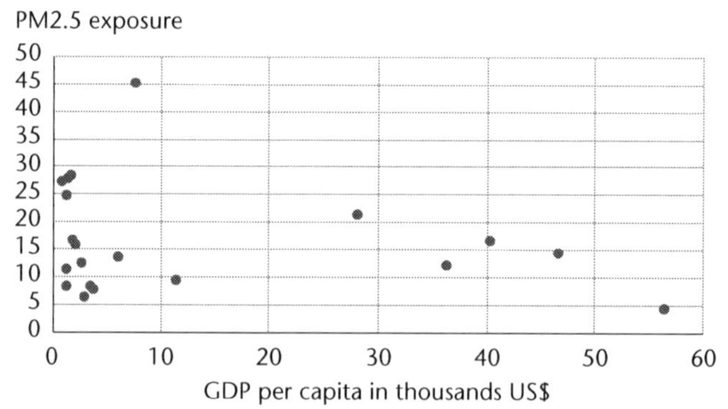

Figure 3.7 Annual mean PM2.5 Exposure and GDP per capita in Asian countries/regions, 2000–2014

Source: Compiled from Yale University (2016e).

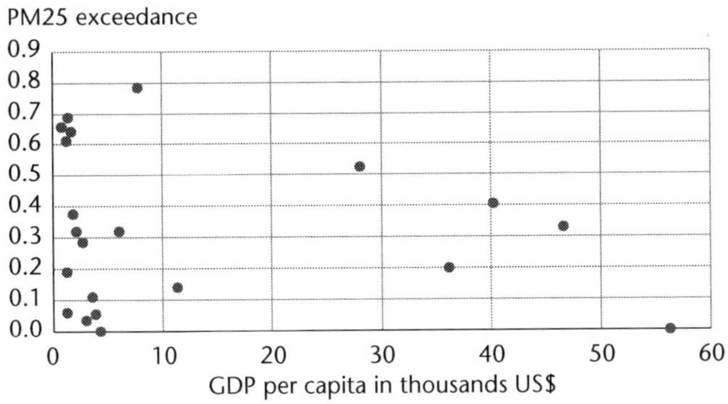

Figure 3.8 Annual mean PM2.5 Exceedance and GDP per capita in Asian countries/regions, 2000–2014

Source: Compiled from Yale University (2016e).

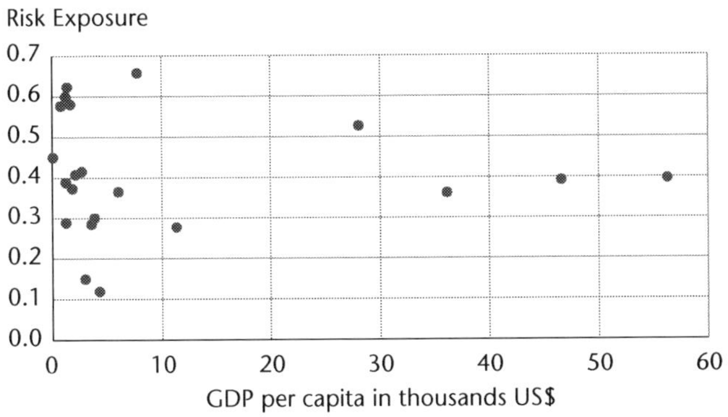

Figure 3.9 Annual mean PM2.5 Health Risk Exposure and GDP per capita in Asian countries/regions, 1990–2013

Source: Compiled from Yale University (2016e).

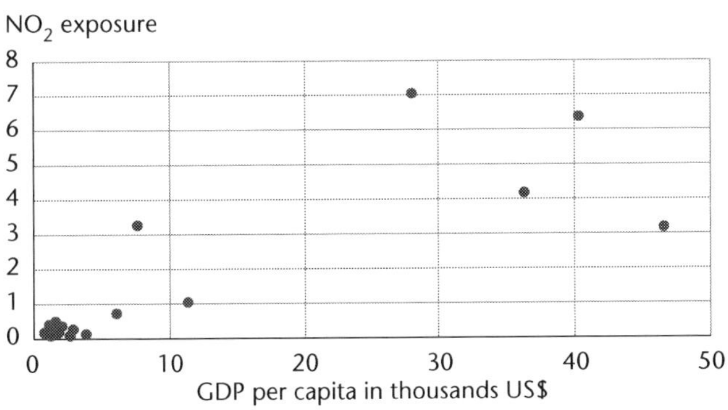

Figure 3.10 Annual mean NO_2 Exposure and GDP per capita in Asian countries/regions, 1997–2011

Source: Compiled from Yale University (2016e).

The literature is inconsistent in the existence of an EKC for air pollution in Asia. As pollution rises to dangerous levels, Asian governments are under pressure to take measures. This is true in almost all countries in Asia, including the most polluted countries such as China, India, Bangladesh, and Pakistan. Some progress has been reported. For example, a newly released UNEP (2015) review found that Beijing was effective in controlling air pollution from coal-fired plants and vehicle emissions. It is possible that major cities have made progress in controlling air pollution in their urban areas. However, it is important to note how this progress has been made in China. To avoid impacting economic growth, city governments often relocate polluting factories from the urban centers to nearby suburban and rural areas or to neighboring cities (Liu 2010, 2012, 2013a, 2013b). Some of these factories have caused severe pollution in their new locations. Some Model Cities have improved their environmental conditions at the expense of surrounding areas. This is supported by Yale's EPI data discussed earlier. Exposure to PM2.5 may have been leveled off or declined in recent years, but an increased proportion of the population has been exposed to PM2.5 pollution (Figures 3.1 and 3.2). Population in rural and suburban areas who benefit the least from polluting industries now suffer more from the pollution (Liu 2012, 2013a, 2013b).

Policy implications

The EKC and the "grow first, clean up later" approach may be extremely harmful to the powerless and poor (Liu 2012, 2013a, 2013b). Developed countries such as Japan took this path and were able to achieve better environmental conditions and some degree of sustainability. At that time, there was insufficient knowledge of the tremendous environmental, social, and economic costs of unsustainable development practices. Today, the importance of sustainability is common knowledge, and science and technology make sustainable practices possible. Political pressure, rather than economic growth, determines when the turning point of the EKC will occur. In an undemocratic political system such as China or some other Asian countries, political pressure may not be large enough to force governments and industries to switch to sustainable practices until much later. The turning point may be delayed if there even is one. Developing countries should avoid this approach and adopt a sustainable path to development and environmental management. Social determinants of health, such as poverty, access, and inequality, are the very determinants that make populations more vulnerable to environmental risk factors and environmental change (Kovats 2012). On the other hand, protecting the environment may bring health benefits and economic benefits from health-care savings, in addition to help with fighting global climate change (WHO 2014a).

Even if an EKC exists in PM2.5 concentration, less-developed countries in Asia are unlikely to be able to afford it, as the turning point requires such high income levels reported by Keene and Deller (2015). Irreversible damage to climactic conditions and human health would be disastrous. As populations in less-developed cities are the most impacted by air pollution (WHO 2016b), the poor in polluted countries suffer the most from air pollution because they do not have the resources to protect themselves and to treat their illnesses. To the millions of people who have died from air pollution, an EKC does not mean anything, even if there is one. Scientific evidence shows that air pollution poses greater risks to human health than we previously realized, particularly in causing strokes and heart diseases (WHO 2014a). In addition, it is projected that the impact on deaths from outdoor air pollution could double by 2050, if the current unsustainable practices continue (Lelieveld et al. 2015). That means the traditional unsustainable approach of "grow first, clean up later" must stop in order to avoid devastating the environment and people's livelihoods.

References

Adams, W.M. (2006) "The Future of Sustainability: Re-thinking Environment and Development in the Twenty-first Century," In *Proceedings of the IUCN Renowned Thinkers Meeting*, Gland, Switzerland, January 29–31.

Air Korea. (2016) "Air Quality Information," www.airkorea.or.kr/.

Apergis, N. and Ozturk, I. (2015) "Testing Environmental Kuznets Curve Hypothesis in Asian Countries," *Ecological Indicators*. 52:16–22.

Azadi, H., Verheijke, G., and Witlox, F. (2011) "Pollute First, Clean Up Later?" *Global & Planetary Change*. 78:77–82. www.dst.unipi.it/dst/rocchi/SR/GG_files/sdarticle.pdf.

Beckerman, W. (1992) "Economic Growth and the Environment," *World Development*. 20:481–496.

Beelen, R., Raaschou-Nielsen, O., Stafoggia, M., Andersen, Z.J.O., Weinmayr, G., Hoffmann, B., ... Hoek, G. (2014) "Effects of Long-term Exposure to Air Pollution on Natural-Cause Mortality: An Analysis of 22 European Cohorts within the Multicentre ESCAPE Project," *The Lancet*. 383:785–795. doi: 10.1016/S0140-67361362158-3

CIA (Central Intelligent Agency, USA). (2016) "World factbook. Taiwan," www.cia.gov/library/publications/the-world-factbook/geos/tw.html.

Dasgupta, S., Hamilton, K., Pandey, K.D., and Wheeler, D. (2006) "Environment During Growth: Accounting for Governance and Vulnerability," *World Development*. 34:1597–1611.

Ekins, P. (2000) *Economic Growth and Environmental Sustainability: The Prospects for Green Growth*. London/New York: Routledge.

Environmental Protection Administration, ROC. (2015) "PM2.5 Control (in Chinese)," http://air.epa.gov.tw/Public/suspended_particles.aspx.

European Commission. (2016) "Air Quality Standards," http://ec.europa.eu/environment/air/quality/standards.htm.

Han, L., Zhou, W., and Li, W. (2016) "Fine Particulate PM2.5 Dynamics During Rapid Urbanization in Beijing, 1973–2013," *Scientific Reports*. 6, Article number: 23604. doi: 10.1038/srep23604.

Harbaugh, W.T., Levinson, A., and Wilson, D.M. (2002) "Reexamining the Empirical Evidence for an Environmental Kuznets Curve," *The Review of Economics and Statistics* (MIT Press). 843:541–551.

IES. (2016) "Ambient Air Quality Standards in India," www.arthapedia.in/index.php?title=Ambient_Air_Quality_Standards_in_India.

Keene, A. and Deller, S. (2015) "Evidence of the Environmental Kuznets' Curve among US Counties and the Impact of Social Capital," *International Regional Science Review*. 38:358–387.

Kovats, R.S. (2012) "Global Health and Global Environmental Governance: Research for Policy," *Global Environmental Change*. 221:1–2. www.sciencedirect.com/science/article/pii/S0959378011001981.

Lelieveld, J., Evans, J.S., Fnais, M., Giannadaki, D., and Pozzer, A. (2015) "The Contribution of Outdoor Air Pollution Sources to Premature Mortality on a Global Scale," *Nature*. 525:367–371.

Liu, L. (2008) "Sustainability Efforts in China: Reflections on the Environmental Kuznets Curve Through a Locational Evaluation of 'Eco-Communities,'" *Annals of the Association of American Geographers*. 983:604–629.

Liu, L. (2009) "Sustainability: Living Within One's Own Ecological Means," *Sustainability*. 14:1412–1430.

Liu, L. (2010) "Made in China: Cancer Villages," *Environment: Science and Policy for Sustainable Development*. 522:8–21.

Liu, L. (2012) "Environmental Poverty, a Decomposed Environmental Kuznets Curve, and Alternatives: Sustainability Lessons from China," *Ecological Economics*. 73:86–92.

Liu, L. (2013a) "Geographic Approaches to Resolving Environmental Problems in Search of the Path to Sustainability: The Case of Polluting Plant Relocation in China," *Applied Geography*. 45:138–146. doi: 10.1016/j.apgeog.(2013)08.011.

Liu, L. (2013b) "Chinese Model Cities and Cancer Villages: Where Environmental Policy is Social Policy," In: Isidor Wallimann ed., *Environmental Policy is Social Policy – Social Policy is Environmental Policy: Toward Sustainability Policy*. pp. 121–134. New York: Springer.

MEP (Ministry of Environmental Protection of China). (2012) "Ambient Air Quality Standards (in Chinese)," GB 3095–(2012) http://210.72.1.216:8080/gzaqi/Document/gjzlbz.pdf.

National Bureau of Statistics of China. (2012) *Tabulation on the 2010 Population Census of Peoplès Republic of China by County*, compiled by the Population Census Office under the State Council and Department of Population and Employment Statistics. China Statistics Press, Beijing.

National Environment Agency of Singapore. (2016) "Air Quality and Targets," www.nea.gov.sg/anti-pollution-radiation-protection/air-pollution-control/air-quality-and-targets.

Panayotou, T. (1993) "Empirical Tests and Policy Analysis of Environmental Degradation at Different Stages of Economic Development," *World Employment Program Research Working Paper* WEP 2-22/WP 238 International Labour Office, Geneva.

Prüss-Ustün, A., Wolf, J., Corvalán, C., Bos, R., and Neira, M. (2016) *Preventing Disease through Healthy Environments: A Global Assessment of the Burden of Disease from Environmental Risks.* WHO. Report and age stand by country spreadsheet downloaded from www.who.int/quantifying_ehimpacts/publications/preventing-disease/en/.

Rock, M. (2002) *Pollution Control in East Asia.* Washington, DC: Resources for the Future.

Rock, M. and Angel, D. (2007) "Grow First, Clean Up Later? Industrial Transformation in East Asia," *Environment: Science and Policy for Sustainable Development.* 494:8–19.

Rohde, R.A. and Muller, R.A. (2015) "Air Pollution in China: Mapping of Concentrations and Sources," *PLoS ONE.* 108:e0135749.

Sinha, A. and Bhattacharya, J. (2016) "Environmental Kuznets Curve Estimation for NO_2 Emission: A Case of Indian Cities," *Ecological Indicators.* 67:1–11.

Stern, D.I. (2004) "The Rise and Fall of the Environmental Kuznets Curve," *World Development.* 32: 1419–1439.

Stern, D.I. and van Dijk, J. (2016) "Economic Growth and Global Particulate Pollution Concentrations," CCEP Working Paper 1604, Feb (2016) Crawford School of Public Policy. The Australian National University.

Transport Policy Net. (2016a) "Japan: Air Quality Standards," http://transportpolicy.net/index.php?title=Japan:_Air_Quality_Standards.

Transport Policy Net. (2016b) "Thailand: Air Quality Standards," http://transportpolicy.net/index.php?title=Thailand:_Air_Quality_Standards.

UNEP (United Nations Environment Program). (2015) "A Review of *Air Pollution* Control in *Beijing: 1998–2013,*" www.unep.org/roap/Portals/96/Documents/Air_Pollution.pdf.

United Nations General Assembly. (2005) World Summit Outcome, Resolution A/60/1, Adopted on September 15, 2005; New York, http://daccessdds.un.org/doc/UNDOC/GEN/N05/487/60/PDF/N0548760.pdfOpenElement/.

USEPA (United States Environmental Protection Agency). (2012) "The National Ambient Air Quality Standards for Particle Pollution. Revised Air Quality Standards for Particle Pollution and Updates to the Air Quality Index AQI," www3.epa.gov/airquality/particlepollution/2012/decfsstandards.pdf.

Weber, D.J. and Allen, D.O. (2010) Environmental Kuznets Curves: Mess or Meaning? *International Journal of Sustainable Development & World Ecology.* 173:198–207.

World Bank. (2016) "GDP Per Capita Current US $," http://data.worldbank.org/indicator/NY.GDP.PCAP.CD.

World Commission on Environment and Development. (1987) *Our Common Future.* Oxford: Oxford University Press.

World Health Organization (WHO). (2006) "WHO Air Quality Guidelines for Particulate Matter, Ozone, Nitrogen Dioxide and Sulfur Dioxide. Global Update 2005," http://apps.who.int/iris/bitstream/10665/69477/1/WHO_SDE_PHE_OEH_06.02_eng.pdf.

World Health Organization (WHO). (2014a) "7 Million Premature Deaths Annually Linked to Air Pollution," News release. www.who.int/mediacentre/news/releases/2014/air-pollution/en/.

World Health Organization (WHO). (2014b) *Burden of Disease from the Joint Effects of Household and Ambient Air Pollution for (2012).* WHO Technical Report. (2012) www.who.int/phe/health_topics/outdoorair/databases/AP_jointeffect_BoD_results_March(2014)pdf.

World Health Organization (WHO). (2014c) "Ambient Outdoor Air Quality and Health," www.who.int/mediacentre/factsheets/fs313/en/.

World Health Organization (WHO). (2016a) "WHO Global Urban Ambient Air Pollution Database update (2016)," www.who.int/phe/health_topics/outdoorair/databases/cities/en/.

World Health Organization (WHO). (2016b) "Air Pollution Levels Rising in Many of the World's Poorest Cities," News release. www.who.int/mediacentre/news/releases/2016/air-pollution-rising/en/.

World Health Organization (WHO). (2016c) "World Health Statistics 2016: Monitoring Health for the SDGs, Annex B: tables of health statistics by country, WHO region and globally," www.who.int/gho/publications/world_health_statistics/2016/Annex_B/en/.

World Health Organization (WHO). (2016d) "Global Ambient Air Pollution," http://maps.who.int/airpollution/

Yale University. (2016a) "Global Metrics for the Environment," www.epi.yale.edu/.
Yale University. (2016b) "Environmental Performance Index. Air Quality," http://epi.yale.edu/chapter/air-quality.
Yale University. (2016c) "Environmental Performance Index. Health Impacts," http://epi.yale.edu/chapter/health-impacts.
Yale University. (2016d) "Environmental Performance Index. Methods," http://epi.yale.edu/chapter/methods.
Yale University. (2016e) "Environmental Performance Index 2016 Report," 2016 EPI Raw Data. Air Quality. http://epi.yale.edu/downloads.
Yang, G., Wang, Y., Zeng, Y., Gao, G.F., Liang, X., Zhou, M., et al. (2013) "Rapid Health Transition in China, 1990–2010: Findings from the Global Burden of Disease Study 2010," *The Lancet.* 381: 1987–2015. doi: 10.1016/S0140-67361361097-1.pmid:23746901.

4

Environmental challenges in Asia

Debashis Chakraborty and Sacchidananda Mukherjee

Introduction

Asia as a continent is characterized by wide biological and environmental diversity, e.g., presence of various species, including threatened and endangered ones, across countries, the rainforests in Indonesia, deserts in the Arabian peninsula, cold deserts in the central Asian plateau, the Himalayan range in Nepal and India, extensive river networks in Indian and Chinese territories, and mangrove forests in the Bay of Bengal. Given the divergence, the challenges faced by Asian countries differ considerably, ranging from ice-melting in Nepal and Russia to rises in sea-level in the Maldives, Vietnam, the Philippines, Thailand and several other countries with coastlines.

Despite the diversity in the nature of the environmental challenges faced by Asian countries, there exists a degree of similarity among the drivers causing such challenges, particularly on the economic front. The continent is home to China and India, the two most populous countries, and several densely populated economies like Bangladesh. While around 60 percent of the world's population lives in Asia, the land area of the continent is a mere 30 percent of the global figure. By presence of Least Developed Countries (LDCs) in the continent, Asia ranks second to Africa. The population pressures in the face of development deficits often shift the focus on growth, with environmental objectives coming lower down in the priority list.

A number of countries located in East and Southeast Asia initiated economic liberalization programs during the 1970s, while their South Asian counterparts moved in that direction during the 1980s and 1990s. West Asia, on the other hand, continued to grow with an enhanced focus on energy product exports, although the management pattern of the resources evolved over time. The continuation of the growth engine and the increasing population pressures in several Asian countries necessitated exploitation of hitherto unutilized natural resources (e.g., intensification of primary activities, including agriculture, fishery and mining) and enhanced generation of power, conversion of forests and wetlands etc., with associated environmental repercussions (e.g., air and water pollution, land degradation, loss of biodiversity, climate change concerns). Given the presence of common land, river network and maritime borders, transboundary environmental challenges also emerged.

The present chapter looks into the major environmental challenges faced by Asian countries and their economic drivers. The chapter is arranged so that the major challenges faced by Asia are briefly discussed, along with the environmental scenario of key indicators and economic drivers. Following that, the policy conclusions on environmental governance are drawn.

Environmental challenges in Asia: issues and economic drivers

The journey to sustain growth in the Asian context often replicates the Environmental Kuznets Curve (EKC) hypothesis, which argues that diversification of economic activities by a low-income country (primarily agrarian) would initially result in environmental degradation (e.g., deforestation, land degradation, exploitation of natural resources). Conversely, when the country has reached middle-income status (primarily industry-based) and moves toward the tertiary sector, rising demand for a cleaner environment and emergence of better environmental governance mechanisms (e.g., enactment of stricter environmental standards) lead to an improvement in the sustainability scenario. In Asia, given the divergence in development stages, the EKC predictions are displayed in varied dimensions.

Table 4.1 summarizes the broad economic scenario prevailing in select Asian countries across sub-regions. It is observed that for almost all the countries, the proportional share of agriculture in the GDP is declining, while a reverse trend is noticed in the services sector over 1990–2000 and 2001–2015. Interestingly, the contribution of the manufacturing sector in GDP is shrinking in several economies (e.g., Japan, Malaysia, the Philippines). At the same time, the countries are witnessing a rising population pressure over 1990–2000 and 2001–2014, which underlines the potential overexploitation of resources.

As growing population pressure often fuels demand for conversion of forests to farmlands and space for cattle ranching, deforestation and associated challenges are quite common in the Asian context. In addition, growing focus on unsustainable agricultural practices, the conduct of mineral explorations in forests, shifting agriculture, etc., are enhancing the risk of soil erosion (Pimentel 2006). The resulting land degradation is likely to intensify the pressure on remaining land, degrading it at a faster rate, and creating a downward spiral. However, inclusion of the Land Use, Land Use Change and Forestry (LULUCF) sector in the Kyoto Protocol requires countries to report their carbon balance in forests as well as the changes in carbon stock through their domestic policies, including deforestation. Through the adoption of sustainable practices and growing awareness, as evident from Table 4.2, a number of Asian countries like Bhutan, China, Lao PDR and Vietnam have been able to expand the forest cover within their territories over the periods of 1990–2000 and 2011–2015. Several developed economies (Japan, Saudi Arabia), emerging economies (Kazakhstan, Russia), and LDCs (Afghanistan, Bangladesh) have been able to keep their forest cover almost constant. However, the scenario in several lower income countries (Nepal, North Korea, Myanmar) and middle-income countries (Cambodia, Indonesia, Pakistan) is alarming. The decline in forest cover lowers the rate of removal of greenhouse gases (GHGs) like CO_2. For instance, in South Asia, with reference to net GHGs emission from LULUCF, Afghanistan, Bangladesh, Nepal and Pakistan emerged as net source of GHGs, while Bhutan, India and Sri Lanka are net sinks of GHGs (Geekiyanage et al. 2015). The declining forest cover also underlines the evolving growth and urbanization dimension.

The challenges in arresting deforestation in Asia include both operational and developmental ones. Often the problems of illegal felling of tress are not adequately controlled, despite the presence of a punitive framework, either due to policy myopia or to deep-rooted corruption within the system (Kummer and Turner 1994; Howes and Wyrwoll 2012). For instance, in the face of chronic energy insecurity, North Korea facilitated a policy of felling trees for use as logs, which led to deforestation and land degradation in the long run (Chua 2013). In Southeast Asia on other hand, the drivers of deforestation include the rise in palm oil and other commercial crops cultivation. Over 1990–2005, in Malaysia and Indonesia the expansion of palm oil plantations led to the depletion of natural forest cover, with corresponding figures standing at 55–59 percent and over 56 percent, respectively (Koh and Wilcove 2008). In Myanmar, the renewed focus on agricultural exports resulted in increasing demand for farmlands and forest-clearing coupled with enhanced application of agro-chemicals, worsening the scenario even further (Simpson 2016). The methods applied for forest clearing often led to long-term consequences. For instance, the adoption of "Slash-and-Burn" method in Indonesia caused transboundary haze pollution in several Southeast Asian neighbors, including Singapore, Malaysia, Brunei and Thailand (Islam et al. 2016). In addition, the expansion of rice cultivation (e.g., Myanmar) and land conversion to palm oil plantations (e.g., Malaysia and Indonesia) resulted in the depletion of mangrove forests in Southeast Asia (Richards and Friess 2016). Contamination by intensified aquaculture activities (shrimp farming) is another major driver behind the destruction of mangroves and coastal areas in Vietnam and Thailand (Barker and Molle 2004). Similarly, in South Asia, forest cover in general and mangroves in particular are being threatened through multiple problems, including encroachment, erosion, other forms of land use including mining (e.g., sea salt extraction in Indus Delta), over-harvesting (e.g., intensified fruit cultivations in Sundarbans), pollution (waste disposal in Mumbai), and extreme climatic events (e.g., cyclones) (Giri et al. 2015).

Despite growing output of cereals, meat and dairy products, many Asian countries remain net importers of these commodities. It is reported that the estimated crop yields are likely to decline by 2.5 to 10 percent in various Asian countries during 2020–2030, with a predicted fall in both rice and wheat production (Gupta 2014). On the other hand, growing urbanization and emergence of high and middle-income households with refrigeration facilities in Asian cities are significantly enhancing demand (Satterthwaite et al. 2010). Therefore, there is greater pressure on land to produce higher yields, to reduce import dependence. Rising demographic pressures, growing demand from alternative uses of land (e.g., housing, infrastructure-building, urbanization) leave no option but to look for vertical expansion of agricultural output by increasing productivity through multiple-cropping. Commercialization of agriculture, land intensification and adoption of agro-chemicals (fertilizers and pesticides) and recourse to water-intensive crops often lead to substantial environmental consequences (Pingali 2001). For instance, over a two-decade period, pesticide use has increased by 489, 395, 246 and 129 percent in Bangladesh, Thailand, China and Pakistan, respectively (Pretty and Bharucha 2015). A similar trend is noted in other Asian economies characterized by high population density as well.

The environmental consequences of increasing chemical usage in agriculture include surface and ground water contamination, soil contamination, adverse impact on soil fertility (in turn requiring higher doses of chemicals in subsequent period), emission of GHGs as well as death of birds through sprays, and so on (Aktar et al. 2009). In addition, open storage of livestock waste and unbalanced and over-application of nitrogenous fertilizers are the major contributors of nonpoint source (NPS) pollution in Asia, the control of which is emerging as a major challenge (Mukherjee 2010). In China, the first national survey of pollution sources carried out by the Ministry of Environmental Protection concluded that between 2007 and 2010, NPS pollution accounted for about 44 percent of chemical oxygen demand (COD), 55 percent of nitrogen demand, and 67 percent of phosphorous discharges (Government of the People's Republic of China 2010). It also observed that runoff from farms and intensive animal husbandry, leading to nitrogen and phosphorous discharges respectively, contributed directly to pervasive eutrophication of water bodies in the PRC. Falling groundwater level (Richey et al. 2015), coupled with NPS groundwater pollution, pose serious challenges toward meeting demand for safe drinking water for those people who are not currently covered by organized drinking water supply networks (Mukherjee 2008). The extent of the challenge can be underlined from the fact that over 2012–

2030, East Asia and the Pacific and South Asian countries would be required to spend USD 304.9 and 208.6 billion respectively (in 2005 prices) to achieve universal access to water services and sanitation in their territories (Mukherjee and Chakraborty 2017).

Given the long coastline, marine fishing and related activities have emerged as professions for a significant proportion of the population in a number of Asian countries. However, over-exploitation of resources due to devolution of government subsidies on operational costs (e.g., fuel subsidy) to the fishing trawlers has emerged as a challenge. It is observed that several countries fishing in Asian waters, e.g., Japan, South Korea, Hong Kong SAR, Taiwan, etc. are receiving huge subsidies (Cox and Schmidt 2002). In particular, provisions of fuel subsidies are quite significant in the cases of China, Philippines, Russia and South Korea (Sumaila et al. 2006). Finally, through access right transfer payments, a higher-income country may secure subsidized fishing rights for its vessels in exclusive economic zones (EEZ) of lower-income economies. Given the poor operational framework in smaller economies to check whether foreign fishing vessels are abiding by the pre-agreed fishing quotas, access right transfer arrangements often leads to overfishing. Khan et al. (2006) estimated that among the 19 top access right subsidy-providing countries in the world, Japan, China, Russia, South Korea and Taiwan account for 20, 19, 7, 4 and 2 percent of the total transfers. The estimated high transfer of fisheries subsidies underlines the possibility of environmental risks through this channel.

As observed from Table 4.1, the manufacturing sector accounts for a sizable proportion of GDP in many Asian countries over 2001–2015, e.g., 45, 44, 43, 41, 38 and 37 percent for China, Indonesia, Iran, Malaysia, Thailand and South Korea, respectively. The industrialization in the Asian economies has been a result of both consolidation of the domestic manufacturing sector and technology transfer through foreign investment, often targeting export-oriented units. The urge to gain competitiveness vis-à-vis foreign players has often forced domestic firms to adopt a lax environmental standard. While the foreign investment augments domestic production capabilities through the technology spillover effect, the environmental repercussions of the same is ambiguous. The trade-investment-environment interrelationship can be explained using the Pollution Haven Hypothesis (PHH), which argues that FDI inflows in a lower income country often targets the polluting sectors, whose revitalization significantly worsens the sustainability scenario. The evidence in the Asian context reveals that FDI inflows have been significant in polluting industries in several South Asian countries (e.g., India), East Asian countries (e.g., China) and Southeast Asian countries (e.g., Malaysia, Thailand, the Philippines), leading to adverse environmental consequences (Chakraborty 2012; He 2006; Merican et al. 2007). To add to the worries, the rivers in the Southern, Central and Western Asian regions are already in poor condition and the discharge of industrial pollutants are further worsening the scenario (Viswanathan and Bahinipati 2016). However, the absence of PHH in the Asian context has been reported by several studies (Rock 2002).

The ambiguity in PHH evidence in the Asian context can be explained by the complex relationship between trade-investment flows, development dimensions, and climate change concerns, which function through three simultaneous channels (Zhang 2012). First, production and export growth fuels greater demand for energy products leading to higher emissions, i.e., *scale effect* (Cole and Elliott 2003). Second, short run focus on polluting sectors worsens environmental sustainability, i.e., *composition effect* (Honma and Yoshida 2011). Finally, with economic growth, environmental governance results in stricter emission standards and adoption of up-to-date pollution abatement technologies, i.e., *technique effect* (Dasgupta et al. 2001). In most of the Asian countries, given their urge to enhance per capita GDP, the *scale* and *composition effects* dominate. On the other hand, a country's ability to embrace the *technique effect* is slow, given the fact that the requisite technology often needs to be imported from abroad at a premium price. However, when a country crosses a threshold level of development, the pollution abatement technology adoption becomes easier. As a result, there exists a clear distinction in the manufacturing sector pollution tackling performance between advanced industrialized countries like Japan and Singapore and developing economies like Cambodia and Vietnam. The difference can be clearly observed from their Environmental Performance Index (*EPI*) rankings, presented in Table 4.2. While Singapore (ranked 14th) and Japan (39th) are among the better performers, Cambodia (ranked 146th) and Vietnam (131st) lie in the other extreme.

The EKC hypothesis argued that with development and a rise in per capita GDP, the countries will reduce dependence on the manufacturing sector and gradually move toward the services sector. With the growth in the services sector in most of the Asian countries, as evident from Table 4.1, it is therefore expected that the production pattern would move toward a more sustainable form. However, even in this sphere, sustainability challenges have surfaced. For instance, the tourism sector has emerged as a major contributor to service sector growth in many Asian countries, which bears significant implications on environmental sustainability. The concern is particularly serious in fragile environments, e.g., involving mountain-climbing in Nepal and water-sports and other forms of entertainments in Maldives. For instance, studies reveal that growth of the tourism sector in the Maldives has led to multiple concerns, e.g., beach erosion, sewage and waste disposal, groundwater contamination and so on (Kundur and Murthy 2013). Moreover, the extent of damage in the coral reefs in South and Southeast Asia are alarming (Wilkinson 2008). The study by the Mekong River Commission on the environmental impact of tourism in the lower Mekong basin across Cambodia, Vietnam, Lao PDR and Thailand revealed possible adverse impacts of tourist activities on water resources (i.e., rivers, streams and wetlands) through construction and waste management related activities (Mekong River Commission 2010). Disposal of plastic waste in tourist places is a concern in India as well (Chakraborty and Mukherjee 2013). The saving grace is that the Asian countries are increasingly acknowledging the need to ensure sustainability while retaining the economic benefits of tourism. This has led to greater focus on sustainable tourism in the recent period, with a goal to protect and conserve cultural heritage. For instance, the example of community participation in Nepal in protecting the nature and involvement of tourism and heritage managers and local communities at Nam Dee Waterfall in Laos in protecting the forest, endangered orchids and wildlife are worth mention (United Nations Educational, Scientific and Cultural Organization 2008).

Apart from the aforesaid limitations in the waste disposal system in tourist locations, solid waste management in Asian countries is a major source of pollution. Several countries have improved their waste management framework, e.g., in the development of "bio-organic soil enricher" plants in India, resource recovery and recycling framework in Sri Lanka, Thailand and China (Visvanathan and Trankler undated). The problem areas, however, abound: limited or no separation of waste at source, inadequate institutional facilities and financial resources, limitations in legal and administrative enforcement of environmental provisions, insufficient technical expertise in waste collection and transport, presence of open dump landfills, absence of standardized process of recovery, recycling, reuse and reduction of the solid waste, limited control on gas emissions and leachate in landfill (Visvanathan and Trankler undated; Dhokhikah and Trihadiningrum 2012). Given the absence of effective public waste removal services in the less developed regions, the burning of waste, leading to noxious GHGs emissions and release of toxic residues in environment and water bodies, is not uncommon (United Nations Educational, Scientific and Cultural Organization 2008). The wastewater treatment scenario is also poor, with only 19, 17, 12, 9 and 6 percent of the same being treated in Vietnam, Bangladesh, Tajikistan, Cambodia and Lao PDR, respectively (United Nations Economic and Social Commission for the Asia and the Pacific 2015). There is also considerable scope for securing semi-centralized to centralized treatment of fecal sludge in Asian cities (Ronteltap et al. 2014). Finally, with urbanization and rising medical tourism in several Asian countries, disposal of bio-medical wastes also poses a major challenge, given the load and contamination potential (Srividhya and Appasamy 2012).

Hazardous waste processing in Asia is also on the rise. With the growing volume of electronic waste, several Asian countries, particularly India (Das undated) and China (Wang et al. 2013) have emerged as major hubs for processing and recycling e-waste to extract various ferrous and non-ferrous metals. As most of the operations are carried out in informal sectors, environmental mitigation expenses in the e-waste processing sector often remains at a suboptimal level. In addition, given the cost advantages, Bangladesh, China, India and Pakistan have emerged as hubs for ship-breaking services, with obvious environmental repercussions (Greenpeace 2000).

Air pollution has emerged as another major challenge in Asia. The burning of crop residues and release of GHGs is a major driver of such pollution, particularly in South Asia. Estimates reveal that crop residue burning accounts for around 10 percent of South Asia's black carbon emissions, and the use of machines like the "Happy Seeder" is still limited (Irwin 2014). This releases harmful gases like carbon monoxide and nitrogen dioxide into the atmosphere, and the resulting smog leads to significant air pollution at source and, depending on the wind speed, in nearby urban centres (Singh and Kaskaoutis 2014). As many Asian cities are characterized by a high level of pollution, given the carbon monoxide emissions from the incomplete combustion of vehicle fuels, particulate matter from industrial activities, limited to moderate effectiveness of lead phase-out (in petrol) policies, and so on (Hirota 2010), the presence of smog poses a serious threat both to the environment and citizens' health. The transboundary nature of pollution often complicates the scenario, e.g., toxic smog of particulate matter (PM2.5) from China reaching South Korea and Japan during the winter (Choi 2017). A major concern is that many Asian cities, including several country capitals, lack even the capacity to estimate the trends in major pollutants and assess their environmental and health impacts (Schwela et al. 2006).

The concern over the emission of GHGs is further compounded by the growing energy demand in Asia. As most of the developing economies in Asia are in pursuit of a higher development plane, maintaining the level of economic activities keeps energy demand high. Comparing the energy use (kg of oil equivalent per capita) over 1990–2000 and 2001–2014 for select Asian countries, a general rising trend in energy demand can be identified, barring exceptions like Japan, North Korea and UAE (Table 4.1). The rising energy demand occurs across regions: China, South Korea (in East Asia), India, Maldives (in South Asia), Indonesia, Malaysia, Thailand (in Southeast Asia), Iran and Saudi Arabia (in West Asia). Future projections underline that around 55 percent of the rise in global energy consumption by 2040 will originate from China, India and the Association of Southeast Asian Nations (ASEAN) countries (IEA 2016). The other countries characterized by high energy demand include Japan, South Korea and Taiwan. The study also noted that the growing energy demand in Asia, primarily dependent on fossil fuel burning, comes from transport, power generation and industrial sectors. Though awareness on air pollution is on the rise and coal utilization rates are declining in Asian countries, including India and China, coal-based power generation plants still play a major role across the continent (Energy and Climate Intelligence Unit 2016).

As evident from Table 4.3, Asian countries are now participating in several crucial multilateral environment agreements: the protection of endangered species and biodiversity (CITES, CBD), GHGs emissions and climate change (Kyoto Protocol, Montreal Protocol on substances depleting ozone layer), combatting desertification and mitigating the adverse challenges of drought (UN Convention to Combat Desertification, 2017), persistent organic pollutants (Stockholm Convention), bio-safety (Cartagena Protocol) and so on. However, it is also observed from the timeline reported in Table 4.3 that several Asian countries have consented to the Kyoto Protocol, either in the late 1990s or in the new millennium, indicating a cautious approach toward the reduction of emissions. In addition, the time lag between signature or accession of these agreements and ratification or entry into force is telling for several countries.

Table 4.2 reveals that the cumulative effects of LULUCF, vehicular pollution, unsustainable practices like waste and crop residue burning, growing energy demand and so on in Asian countries, as reflected in their CO_2 emissions (metric tons per capita) pattern. Comparing the emission levels over 2001–2010 and 2011–2013, it is observed that the emission levels have gone up in several parts of the continent: in China, Mongolia, South Korea (East Asia), India, Maldives (South Asia), Indonesia, Malaysia, Singapore, Thailand, Vietnam (Southeast Asia), Iran, Saudi Arabia (West Asia) and Kazakhstan, Russia (Central Asia). The developmental aspect is evident from the fact that, apart from power generation and transport, residential segments and the manufacturing sector, particularly cement production, are major contributors to emission levels both in China (Liu 2015) and India (Sharma et al. 2011). Given the growing emissions of CO_2, SO_2, NO_2, suspended particulate matter (SPM), etc. and the role of the transport sector behind the same, recourse to road rationing has been witnessed, e.g., in China (Jie and Zuylen 2014) and India (Barik 2016).

One saving grace is that over the last decade, Asian countries are increasingly adopting cleaner forms of energy generation. The World Energy Outlook 2016 estimated that in 2040, around 60 percent of the power generated would come from renewables, with significant consequences for Asian power markets like China and India (International Energy Agency 2016). Presently, the growth potential of the renewable energy sector in Asian developing countries suffers from multiple drivers, including a lack of suitable materials, inadequate transmission capacity and financial constraints in bearing the additional burden of technology, which primarily needs to be imported (Shrestha et al. 2013). Moreover, it was estimated that over 2009–2050, global nuclear capacity would expand from 370 GW to 1200 GW (International Energy Agency 2010). Nuclear power generation received closer focus in the new millennium, but the Fukushima accident slowed the trend. The release of radioactive elements like Cesium, Strontium-90, Tritium etc. in the post-Fukushima period led not only to ocean contamination, but also produced abnormally high levels of these chemicals in freshwater fish, even in faraway places (Physicians for Social Responsibility 2013). As an immediate response, Japan's demand for fossil fuels increased, and other Asian countries became more cautious in their approval process, with a considerable rise in safety expenses for upcoming nuclear plants thereby prolonging the period of their economic non-viability (Hayashi and Hughes 2013). The incident also added fresh life to the ongoing protests against upscaling nuclear power generation capacities (Srikant 2009).

Given the importance of fossil fuels in power generation and the transport sector, oil and gas exploration continues to be a major economic activity in Asia, with obvious environmental repercussions. In the Arabian Gulf, the environmental effects include the impact on water and sediment quality, the burial of benthos, toxicity to flora and fauna and fish tainting, accidental oil spills, and so on (Qurban et al. undated). The other sustainability concerns relating to oil and gas exploration include drilling mud and other liquid wastes, disposal of drill cuttings, platform decommissioning, creating possible transboundary pollution through seawater, and so on (Lyons 2012; Madduri and Reddy 2003).

Apart from oil exploration, other mining activities also continue to threaten the sustainability scenario in Asia. For instance, the mining of gold, copper and other precious metals in Mongolia has led to significant environmental damage, including the excessive use of process water and the release of pumped water with impurities in water bodies, deterioration of surface and underground water qualities, dust, and other particulate matter pollution, exploration in protected areas, loss of biodiversity and so on (World Bank 2006). The near absence of environmental mitigation measures and the adoption of obsolete technologies in mining operations in Mongolia and Russia significantly impact sustainability in the Baikal watershed (Brunello et al. 2003). Sand mining, particularly from riverbeds, has led to serious threats to sustainability in terms of turbidity of streams, threat to habitat of birds, flora and fauna, contamination of water bodies with toxic metals, decline in groundwater tables, and so on, both in South (Saviour 2012) and Southeast (Ashraf et al. 2011; Earthworks and Oxfam America 2004) Asia. The demand for resources, coupled with weak enforcement scenarios, also create an informal market for small and illegal mining activities in several countries. Apart from organized large-scale mining, the pollution load is quite high in South Asian small mines and queries, given the weak enforcement mechanism (Lahiri-Dutt 2008).

The growing emission of CO_2 and other GHGs in Asia is significantly adding to global warming, and the consequent melting of ice caps is posing a serious environmental and health challenge in several regions. An OXFAM–WWF study underlined that with rising temperatures, warmer and shorter winters are leading to drastic shrinking of the iced area, erratic climate changes, change in lifestyle habits, infestation by newer and more irritating pests, and worsening quality of vegetation in Russia. The scenario reached an alarming level in 2007, when a record 4.3 million square km of iced area vanished (OXFAM and WWF Russia 2008). In Nepal the climate change effects are visible through vulnerability to unevenly distributed and erratic weather, snow melting and glacial retreat, greater risk of outburst flooding in glacial lakes, floods following glacial melt, and associated livelihood risks during the drought in the following period (Chaudhary and Aryal 2009). Tibet has witnessed a rise in temperatures by 0.4°C over the last five decades and a reduction in glacial area by 15 percent during the last three decades, leading to a greater risk of flash floods (Bradshaw 2016). On the other extreme, the rise in sea level due to global warming poses a serious challenge to several Asian countries like the Maldives, a major part of whose land might be inundated by 2100 (Asuncion and Lee 2017). This would deprive many LDCs from their tourism-related incomes, with the resulting poverty adding further pressure to the already fragile environment.

The skewness in water demand on the continent can be observed from the fact that seven countries, spread across East Asia (China, Japan), Southeast Asia (Indonesia, Philippines, Vietnam) and South Asia (India, Pakistan) accounted for around 88 percent of the regional total water withdrawals (United Nations Economic and Social Commission for the Asia and the Pacific 2016b). Water productivity in South Asia is the lowest among other continents (including SSA and MENA). Water productivity of East Asia and Pacific region was higher than world average, but declined in 2014 substantially (Figure 4.1). Inefficiencies in water management and the resulting consequences are major concerns for several Asian countries. Given deforestation and lower rainfall resulting from weather changes, drought is a major threat in several countries, and growing demand for food grains due to increasing population intensifies the focus on irrigation policy. In several South and Southeast Asian countries, inefficient groundwater mining due to over-reliance on deepwell irrigation has emerged as a serious threat (David 2004). Use of tubewells for irrigation purposes, on the other hand, leads to arsenic pollution in South Asia (Brammer and Ravenscroft 2009). The policy response of the countries often leads to even more complex outcomes. For instance, construction of large dams by China on the Tibetan Plateau has led to the displacement of local communities and biodiversity challenges, on use of the one hand, and major alteration of ecosystems, possibility of floods, and other livelihood challenges in countries located downstream, on the other (Bradshaw 2016). Similarly, interlinking of rivers in South Korea has led to several adverse environmental consequences, including fish kills, a 75 percent drop in wintering bird populations, worsened water quality, etc. (Kim 2015).

With declining forest cover, encroachment upon forest area for illegal logging, mining and other activities, the traditional separation of human settlements from the core forest area is fast receding and an increasing level of human–wildlife conflicts are being witnessed. For instance, in Russia, with the melting of ice, polar bears are forced to leave their natural habitat and hunt for food near human settlements, giving rise to major conflicts (OXFAM and WWF Russia 2008). In a similar vein, in South Asia, the wild animals like elephants and leopards are increasingly coming near human settlements in search of food (Acharya et al. 2016; Manral et al. 2016). Similar human-wildlife conflict (e.g., involving Sumatran Tigers) is witnessed in Southeast Asia as well (Nyhus and Tilson 2004). The loss of animals' natural habitats poses a direct threat to conservation of biodiversity, as many smaller birds and species face the risk of extinction (Brooks et al. 1997). While all the major Asian countries are members of the Convention on Biodiversity (Table 4.3), these instances indicate that priorities assigned to economic growth often take precedence over sustainability considerations.

The Asian animals are being threatened through another channel, poaching of exotic species and illegal cross-border trade in wildlife and wildlife products. As seen from Table 4.3, while all the Asian countries follow the CITES principles, illicit international trade is noticed involving several endangered animals found in their territories. For instance, Indian tigers are being killed by local poachers for illegally sending wildlife body parts to Southeast Asia for preparation of Traditional Chinese Medicines (TCM), popular in the East and Southeast Asian markets (Lee 1996). Apart from its application in preparing TCM, rhino horns are also used for the making of exotic items, such as Yemini dagger handles and hand-carved Asian bowls, thereby creating a strong illegal market (Sas-Rolfes 2012). Poaching is found to be an enforcement-related, rather than administrative, problem (Challender and MacMillan 2014). One practical challenge to effectively combatting poaching in Southeast and South Asia is the incidence of poverty, and the perverse incentives that illegal activities may offer to a wide section of population.

Given the poverty level, use of solid fuel for cooking has led to massive indoor air pollution in several Asian countries. The World Health Organization (WHO) identifies Southeast Asia as one of the regions having the highest share (32 percent in 2004) of the world's deaths attributable to solid fuel use (World Health Organization undated). Indoor air pollution from solid fuels accounted for 3.5 million deaths and 4.5 percent global loss of disability-adjusted life years (DALYs) in 2010 (Kankaria et al. 2014). South East Asia's share (30 percent in 2004) in the world's DALY lost due to solid fuel use is the second highest, after Africa (45 percent). In 2011–2012, 67.3 percent of rural households and 14 percent urban households in India used firewood and chips for cooking, and the practice of using dung cake (9.6 and 1.3 percent in rural and urban areas respectively) and coke and coal (1.1 and 2.1 percent in rural and urban areas respectively) is also rampant (Mukherjee and Chakraborty 2016a).

The resulting sustainability scenario in Asia can be observed from aggregate *EPI* scores of select countries during 2016, reported in Table 4.2. While Singapore (ranked 14th) and Japan (39th) are comfortably placed in the list, a number of developing countries, e.g., Malaysia (ranked 39th), Indonesia (107th), China (109th), India (141st) and LDCs like Lao PDR (148th), Myanmar (153rd), Bangladesh (173rd) and Afghanistan (176th) are located at the other extreme. Many of these middle and low income countries have witnessed a worsening of their *EPI* ranks over the last decade, signifying the environmental threat therein.

Kreft et al. (2016) measure climate-related extreme events and their impacts across countries for the period 1996–2015 based on four indicators – fatalities (annual average), fatalities per 0.1 million inhabitants (annual average), losses in millions (of USD, PPP), losses per unit of GDP (%). CRI indicates a level of exposure and vulnerability to extreme events, which countries should understand as warnings in order to be prepared for more frequent and/or more

Table 4.1 Key economic features of select Asian countries

Country	*GDP Group*	*Average Percentage Contribution to GDP (1990–2000)*			*Average Percentage Contribution to GDP (2001–2015)*			*Population density (people per sq. km of land area)*		*Energy use (kg of oil equivalent per capita)*	
		Agriculture	*Industry*	*Service*	*Agriculture*	*Industry*	*Service*	*1990–2000*	*2001–2014*	*1990–2000*	*2001–2014*
East Asia											
China	Middle	19.59	45.06	35.36	10.71	45.41	43.88	128.12	140.96	829.81	1638.39
Hong Kong, SAR, China	Upper	0.09	12.60	87.31	0.07	8.23	91.70	6048.38	6633.35	1800.29	1987.59
Japan	Upper	1.77	33.36	64.87	1.19	26.46	72.35	343.71	350.17	3848.02	3841.94
Macao, SAR China	Upper	0.00	16.17	83.83	0.00	12.67	87.33	19889.67	17596.69	–	–
Mongolia	Middle	29.19	31.64	39.17	18.42	34.00	47.58	1.48	1.71	1212.16	1369.68
North Korea	Lower	–	–	–	–	–	–	179.79	200.90	1088.03	748.40
South Korea	Upper	5.93	37.90	56.17	2.89	37.42	59.70	466.73	504.43	3114.64	4684.30
South Asia											
Afghanistan	Lower	–	–	–	28.50	24.35	47.15	24.90	40.70	–	–
Bangladesh	Lower	26.46	23.10	50.45	18.67	25.76	55.57	910.71	1136.71	129.15	181.54
Bhutan	Middle	31.74	31.25	37.01	20.57	41.70	37.73	12.57	17.92	104.53	317.88
India	Middle	26.97	26.09	46.94	19.07	30.06	50.87	323.36	401.86	383.90	510.45
Maldives	Middle	9.93	14.30	75.78	5.23	16.18	78.58	843.64	1169.37	233.47	805.95
Nepal	Lower	43.25	21.03	35.72	35.70	16.72	47.58	149.06	183.74	316.75	368.25
Pakistan	Middle	26.11	24.27	49.62	23.81	22.42	53.76	159.27	212.62	433.30	491.16
Sri Lanka	Middle	–	–	–	8.75	30.85	60.40	286.70	316.30	360.07	474.39
Southeast Asia											
Cambodia	Middle	45.53	16.81	37.65	33.39	25.55	41.06	60.35	79.15	277.16	320.82
Indonesia	Middle	18.09	42.29	39.62	14.06	44.67	41.27	108.61	130.08	639.55	813.63
Laos PDR	Middle	55.49	18.92	25.60	34.31	27.42	38.27	20.93	26.30	–	–
Malaysia	Middle	12.73	43.07	44.20	9.29	41.69	49.02	63.23	82.70	1705.26	2574.46
Myanmar	Lower	57.24	9.69	33.07	40.45	23.34	36.21	68.54	78.14	258.68	293.80

(*Continued*)

Table 4.1 (continued)

Country	*GDP Group*	*Average Percentage Contribution to GDP (1990–2000)*			*Average Percentage Contribution to GDP (2001–2015)*			*Population density (people per sq. km of land area)*		*Energy use (kg of oil equivalent per capita)*	
		Agriculture	*Industry*	*Service*	*Agriculture*	*Industry*	*Service*	*1990–2000*	*2001–2014*	*1990–2000*	*2001–2014*
Philippines	Middle	19.40	33.16	47.45	12.39	32.71	54.89	234.34	302.75	480.74	451.97
Singapore	Upper	0.18	33.62	66.20	0.05	29.03	70.92	5298.58	6856.78	5028.83	5223.22
Thailand	Middle	9.91	37.23	52.86	9.88	38.03	52.09	116.40	129.59	996.27	1612.11
Vietnam	Middle	–	–	–	20.50	36.87	42.63	222.02	274.47	312.17	550.13
West Asia											
Iran	Middle	11.06	37.98	50.96	7.50	43.50	49.00	37.30	44.66	1605.48	2564.50
Saudi Arabia	Upper	5.71	49.07	45.22	3.00	58.17	38.83	8.77	12.45	4374.00	5695.58
United Arab Emirates	Upper	–	–	–	–	–	–	28.48	77.98	11445.58	9076.79
Central Asia											
Kazakhstan	Middle	13.95	35.08	50.97	6.29	39.18	54.53	5.83	5.90	3425.39	3845.74
Russian Federation	Middle	8.49	41.32	50.19	4.78	34.57	60.65	9.04	8.77	4689.37	4705.87

Note: For individual country, sectoral shares may not add to 100, as these are average shares over 1990 to 2000 and 2001 to 2015.

Source: Constructed from World Bank (undated) by authors.

Table 4.2 Key environmental features of select Asian countries

Country	GDP Group	Forest Area (% of Land Area)			Overall Environment Performance Index 2016		CO_2 Emissions (metric tons per capita)			Climate Risk Index for 1996–2015 (average for 20 years)	
		1990–2000	2001–2010	2011–2015	Score	Rank	1990–2000	2001–2010	2011–2013	Score	Rank
East Asia											
China	Middle	17.796	20.462	21.861	65.1	109	2.562	4.540	7.402	52.00	34
Hong Kong, SAR, China	Upper	–	–	–	–	–	5.406	6.118	6.175	–	–
Japan	Upper	68.338	68.401	68.470	80.59	39	9.260	9.500	9.574	87.50	96
Macao, SAR China	Upper	–	–	–	–	–	3.313	3.822	4.068	–	–
Mongolia	Middle	7.806	7.666	8.205	64.39	114	3.850	4.362	12.066	60.17	48
North Korea	Lower	62.844	51.789	43.892	–	–	2.845	2.979	1.983	–	–
South Korea	Upper	65.613	64.507	63.646	70.61	80	7.801	10.080	11.773	76.83	75
Taiwan	Upper	–	–		74.88	60	–	–	–		
South Asia											
Afghanistan	Lower	2.068	2.068	2.068	37.5	176	0.093	0.108	0.602	36.17	12
Bangladesh	Lower	11.377	11.168	11.018	41.77	173	0.178	0.298	0.429	25.00	6
Bhutan	Middle	60.816	68.927	71.755	64.99	110	0.520	0.607	1.091	98.17	109
India	Middle	21.749	22.827	23.653	53.58	141	0.850	1.148	1.556	37.50	14
Maldives	Middle	3.333	3.333	3.333	57.1	137	1.043	2.101	2.666	–	–
Nepal	Lower	30.473	25.733	25.364	50.21	149	0.091	0.126	0.217	44.33	24
Pakistan	Middle	3.011	2.439	2.021	51.42	144	0.700	0.894	0.899	30.50	7
Sri Lanka	Middle	35.688	33.939	33.220	65.55	108	0.357	0.618	0.775	64.33	54
Southeast Asia											
Cambodia	Middle	69.369	60.633	55.018	51.24	146	0.155	0.237	0.365	36.50	13
Indonesia	Middle	60.156	53.622	50.994	65.85	107	1.125	1.579	2.222	70.83	67
Laos PDR	Middle	74.027	74.024	79.649	50.29	148	0.095	0.210	0.306	82.50	87

(Continued)

Table 4.2 (continued)

Country	*GDP Group*	*Forest Area (% of Land Area)*			*Overall Environment Performance Index 2016*		*CO_2 Emissions (metric tons per capita)*			*Climate Risk Index for 1996–2015 (average for 20 years)*	
		1990–2000	*2001–2010*	*2011–2015*	*Score*	*Rank*	*1990–2000*	*2001–2010*	*2011–2013*	*Score*	*Rank*
Malaysia	Middle	66.911	65.136	67.468	74.23	63	4.787	6.650	7.759	94.00	103
Myanmar	Lower	56.681	50.757	46.137	48.98	153	0.148	0.220	0.253	14.17	2
Philippines	Middle	22.776	23.458	25.355	73.7	66	0.832	0.859	0.955	21.33	5
Singapore	Upper	24.403	23.697	23.126	87.04	14	15.252	7.968	9.014	171.83	178
Thailand	Middle	30.355	31.958	31.981	69.54	91	2.453	3.719	4.459	34.83	10
Vietnam	Middle	32.549	42.302	46.812	58.5	131	0.462	1.208	1.775	31.33	8
West Asia											
Iran	Middle	5.649	6.397	6.564	66.32	105	4.542	7.039	8.229	77.17	76
Saudi Arabia	Upper	0.454	0.454	0.454	68.63	95	13.796	15.805	18.170	103.17	113
United Arab Emirates	Upper	3.319	3.746	3.833	69.35	92	27.965	25.077	18.744	154.67	167
Central Asia											
Kazakhstan	Middle	1.257	1.235	1.226	73.29	69	10.563	11.489	15.219	146.67	160
Russian Federation	Middle	49.384	49.501	49.766	83.52	32	11.315	11.296	12.551	48.17	31

Sources: Forest Area (% of Land Area) and CO_2 Emissions are constructed from World Bank (undated) by authors. Environment Performance Index is obtained from Hsu et al. (2016). Climate Risk Index is obtained from Kreft et al. (2016).

Table 4.3 Participation in key multilateral environmental agreements by select Asian countries

Country	*CITES*	*Montreal Protocol*	*Convention on Biodiversity*	*UN Convention to Combat Desertification*	*Stockholm Convention*	*Kyoto Protocol*	*Cartagena Protocol on Bio-safety*
Afghanistan	1985 (AC) 1986 (E)	2004 (AC)	1992 (S) 2002 (R)	1995 (AC)	2013 (AC)	2013 (AC) 2013 (E)	2013 (AC) 2013 (E)
Bangladesh	1981 (AC) 1982 (E)	1990 (AC)	1992 (S) 1994 (R)	1996 (R)	2001 (S) 2007 (R)	2001 (AC) 2005 (E)	2000 (S) 2004 (R) 2004 (E)
Bhutan	2002 (AC) 2002 (E)	2004 (AC)	1992 (S) 1995 (R)	2003 (AC)	–	2002 (AC) 2005 (E)	2002 (AC) 2005 (E)
Brunei Darussalam	1990 (AC) 1990 (E)	1993 (AC)	2008 (AC)	2002 (AC)	2002 (S)	2009 (AC) 2009 (E)	–
Cambodia	1997 (AC) 1997 (E)	2001 (AC)	1995 (AC)	1997 (R)	2001 (S) 2006 (R)	2002 (AC) 2005 (E)	2003 (AC) 2005 (E)
China	1981 (AC) 1981 (E)	1991 (AC)	1992 (S) 1993 (R)	1997 (R)	2001 (S) 2004 (R)	1998 (S) 2002 (APP) 2005 (E)	2000 (S) 2005 (APP)) 2004 (E)
India	1976 (AC) 1976 (E)	1992 (AC)	1992 (S) 1994 (R)	1996 (R)	2002 (S) 2006 (R)	2002 (AC) 2005 (E)	2001 (S) 2003 (R) 2003 (E)
Indonesia	1978 (AC) 1978 (E)	1992 (R)	1992 (S) 1994 (R)	1998 (R)	2001 (S) 2009 (R)	1998 (S) 2004 (R) 2005 (E)	2000 (S) 2004 (R) 2005 (E)
Iran	1976 (AC) 1976 (E)	1990 (AC)	1992 (S) 1996 (R) 1996 (E)	1997 (R)	2001 (S) 2006 (R) 2006 (E)	2005 (AC) 2005 (E)	2001 (S) 2003 (R) 2004 (E)
Japan	1980 (AC) 1980 (E)	1988 (ACP)	1992 (S) 1993 (ACP)	1998 (R)	2002 (AC)	1998 (S) 2002 (ACP) 2005 (E)	2003 (AC) 2004 (E)

(*Continued*)

Table 4.3 (continued)

Country	*CITES*	*Montreal Protocol*	*Convention on Biodiversity*	*UN Convention to Combat Desertification*	*Stockholm Convention*	*Kyoto Protocol*	*Cartagena Protocol on Bio-safety*
Kazakhstan	2000 (AC) 2000 (E)	1998 (AC)	1992 (S) 1994 (R)	1997 (R)	2001 (S) 2007 (R) 2008 (E)	1999 (S) 2009 (R) 2009 (E)	2008 (AC) 2008 (E)
Lao PDR	2004 (AC) 2004 (E)	1998 (AC)	1996 (AC)	1996 (R)	2002 (S) 2006 (R)	2003 (AC) 2005 (E)	2004 (AC) 2004 (E)
Malaysia	1977 (AC) 1978 (E)	1989 (AC)	1992 (S) 1994 (R)	1997 (R)	2002 (S)	1999 (S) 2002 (R) 2005 (E)	2000 (S) 2003 (R) 2003 (E)
Maldives	2012 (AC) 2013 (E)	1989 (R)	1992 (S) 1992 (R)	2002 (AC)	2006 (AC)	1998 (S) 1998 (R) 2005 (E)	2002 (AC) 2003 (E)
Mongolia	1996 (AC) 1996 (E)	1996 (AC)	1992 (S) 1993 (R) 1993 (E)	1996 (R)	2002 (S) 2004 (R) 2004 (E)	1999 (AC) 2005 (E)	2003 (AC) 2003 (E)
Myanmar	1997 (AC) 1997 (E)	1993 (AC)	1992 (S) 1994 (E)	1997 (AC)	2004 (AC)	2003 (AC) 2005 (E)	2001 (S) 2008 (E) 2008 (E)
Nepal	1975 (AC) 1975 (E)	1994 (AC)	1992 (S) 1993 (E)	1996 (E)	2002 (S) 2007 (E)	2005 (AC) 2005 (E)	–
North Korea	–	1995 (AC)	1992 (S) 1994 (APP)	2003 (AC)	2002 (AC)	2005 (AC) 2005 (E)	2001 (S) 2003 (R) 2003 (E)
Pakistan	1976 (AC) 1976 (E)	1994 (AC)	1992 (S) 1994 (E)	1997 (E)	2001 (S) 2008 (E)	2005 (AC) 2005 (E)	2001 (S) 2009 (R) 2009 (E)
Philippines	1981 (AC) 1981 (E)	1991 (E)	1992 (S) 1993 (E)	2000 (E)	2001 (S) 2004 (E)	1998 (S) 2003 (R) 2005 (E)	2000 (S) 2006 (R) 2007 (E)

Table 4.3 (continued)

Country	*CITES*	*Montreal Protocol*	*Convention on Biodiversity*	*UN Convention to Combat Desertification*	*Stockholm Convention*	*Kyoto Protocol*	*Cartagena Protocol on Bio-safety*
Russian Federation	1992 (C) 1992 (E)	1988 (ACP)	1992 (S) 1995 (R) 1995 (E)	2003 (R)	2002 (S) 2011 (R) 2011 (E)	1999 (S) 2004 (R) 2005 (E)	–
Saudi Arabia	1996 (AC) 1996 (E)	1993 (R)	2001 (AC)	1997 (R)	2002 (S) 2012 (R) 2012 (E)	2005 (AC) 2005 (E)	2007 (AC) 2007 (E)
Singapore	1986 (AC) 1987 (E)	1989 (AC)	1992 (S) 1995 (E)	1999 (AC)	2001 (S) 2005 (E)	2006 (AC) 2006 (E)	–
South Korea	1993 (AC) 1993 (E)	1992 (AC)	1992 (S) 1994 (E)	1999 (E)	2001 (S) 2007 (E)	1998 (S) 2002 (R) 2005 (E)	2000 (S) 2007 (R) 2008 (E)
Sri Lanka	1979 (AC) 1979 (E)	1989 (AC)	1992 (S) 1994 (E)	1998 (AC)	2001 (S) 2005 (E)	2002 (AC) 2005 (E)	2000 (S) 2004 (R) 2004 (E)
Thailand	1983 (AC) (1983)	1989 (AC)	1992 (S) 2004 (E)	2001 (AC)	2002 (S) 2005 (E)	1999 (S) 2002 (R) 2005 (E)	2005 (AC) 2006 (E)
United Arab Emirates	1990 (AC) 1990 (E)	1989 (AC)	1992 (S) 2000 (R)	1998 (R)	2001 (S) 2002 (R) 2004 (E)	2005 (AC) 2005 (E)	2014 (AC) 2014 (E)
Vietnam	1994 (AC) 1994 (E)	1994 (AC)	1993 (S) 1994 (R)	1998 (AC)	2001 (S) 2002 (R)	1998 (S) 2002 (R) 2005 (E)	2004 (AC) 2004 (E)

Note: AC – Accession; ACP – Acceptance; APP – Approval; C – Continuation; E – Entry into force; R – Ratified; S – Signed.

Source: Compiled by authors from Ratification Status of Respective Agreements.

Table 4.4 Government expenses for environmental protection in select Asian countries by support-type (% of GDP)

Country	*Income Group*	*2000–2005*	*2006–2010*	*2011–2014*
Afghanistan, Islamic Republic of	Lower	–	0.201	0.293
Australia	Upper	0.447	0.601	0.898
Bhutan	Middle	–	–	0.071
China, P.R.: Hong Kong SAR	Upper	0.694	0.580	0.642
China, P.R.: Macao SAR	Upper	0.449	0.535	0.214
China, P.R.: Mainland	Middle	0.788	0.566	0.563
Indonesia	Middle	–	0.292	0.243
Iran, Islamic Republic of	Middle	0.390	0.236	–
Israel	Upper	0.572	0.574	0.561
Japan	Upper	1.483	1.248	1.201
Korea, Republic of	Upper	–	0.212	–
Maldives	Middle	0.052	0.388	0.538
Russian Federation	Middle	0.083	0.064	0.064

Source: Constructed by authors from International Monetary Fund (IMF) (undated) data.

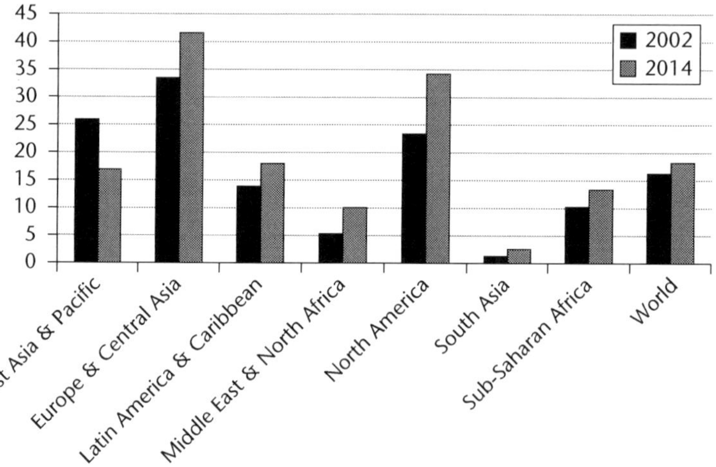

Figure 4.1 Water productivity, total (constant 2005 US$ GDP per cubic meter of total freshwater withdrawal)

Source: Constructed from World Bank (undated) data by authors.

severe events in the future. As seen from Table 4.2, many Asian countries are placed in the top in "Germanwatch Climate Risk Index (CRI) 2017" ranking, and the case of Myanmar (ranked 2nd), the Philippines (5th), Bangladesh (6th), Pakistan (7th), Vietnam (8th), Afghanistan (12th), Cambodia (13th) and India (14th) deserve mention as countries with the highest levels of risk. The existence of many middle and low-income Asian countries on the list is indeed a matter of grave concern.

Last but not least, an inclination toward the adoption of corrective measures through proactive engagement is not easily forthcoming in the Asian context. The present level of budgetary allocation of the general government to support environmental protection has been quite modest in several

Asian countries, as seen from Table 4.4. Japan stands out on the list, with barely above 1 percent of GDP set aside for this purpose. A substantial rise has been noted in Afghanistan, Hong Kong, SAR and Maldives over 2006–2010 and 2011–2014, as in all countries, climate change concerns play an important role. However, even in these economies, the amount spent is not adequate. On the other hand, the decline in budgetary transfers in the cases of China, Macao, SAR, Indonesia, Israel and Japan seems quite an alarming trend. Given the limited fiscal space of the governments of several South, East and Southeast Asian countries, it is unlikely that the government budgetary devolution will drastically increase in the coming years (Mukherjee and Chakraborty 2015a).

Lessons for the future

The environmental concerns in Asian countries are compounded by the prevailing poor environmental governance scenario (e.g., weak enforcement, susceptibility to corruption), the inclination to compromise on sustainability considerations in favor of growth prospects, and the exposure to livelihood-related challenges. Over the past decade, in addition to unilateral efforts, the Asian countries have also participated in the multilateral and regional forums for securing sustainability. However, as the earlier discussion indicates, there is considerable scope for further improvement, particularly with respect to the following aspects.

First, as most of the environmental challenges in Asia are direct results of certain development-determined activities (e.g., conversion of forests for commercialized agriculture, poor pollution abatement practices in the manufacturing sector), addressing these aspects are crucial. For instance, with a growing mismatch between the share of agriculture in GDP and the reliance of the population on the sector, in the presence of urbanization and growing food demand, the intensified application of agro-chemicals has emerged as a serious challenge (e.g., ground and surface water contamination). Through industrialization of agriculture and the associated enhancement of agricultural productivity, the pressure on land can be eased (United Nations Economic and Social Commission for the Asia and the Pacific 2016a). Moreover, encouraging the adoption of agricultural best management practices through public provision of agricultural extension services and spreading environmental awareness, education and training among farmers, are among other effective steps to tackle NPS pollution in Asia. Construction of a pan-Asian agri-environmental index to assess the long run risk of agricultural sustainability would be a crucial step in securing development while maintaining the growth momentum.

Similarly, tackling the concerns at source through strict monitoring and enforcement of environmental standards in pollution-intensive manufacturing (e.g., chemicals and petrochemicals) and services sectors (e.g., tourism services in ecologically fragile places) can play a crucial role. In addition, waste treatment and wastewater recycling, use of biogas from cattle and human waste for provision for cooking, etc. can significantly reduce environmental and health hazards (Mukherjee and Chakraborty 2016a).

One option for Asian countries would be to strictly comply with the ADB Safeguard Policy Statement (SPS), which is based on three broad objectives: (a) possible avoidance of adverse impacts of projects on the environment and on people, (b) in case avoidance is not possible, the adverse effects are to be minimized, mitigated and / or compensated, and (c) provision of support in borrower countries to strengthen their safeguard systems and enable them to manage environmental and social risks (Asian Development Bank 2009). There is a need for developing countries to strictly apply these criteria even to development projects that are financed internally, without the support of development banks.

Second, while environmental awareness across countries are on the rise, coordination among various government departments and agencies on growth and development repercussions of various economic activities is still lacking in many Asian countries. For instance, while the increased application of the agro-chemicals in the agriculture sector in a country can be objected to by the Ministry of the Environment from a sustainability perspective, the Ministry of Agriculture might hold a diametrically opposite view from the food security standpoint. Similarly, the idea of exploring minerals in forests areas might receive active support from the Ministry of Mining, the Ministry of Trade and the Ministry of Heavy Engineering, much to the chagrin of the Ministry of the Environment (Mukherjee and Chakraborty 2015b). There is an urgent need to formulate a national environmental policy at the country level for the sake of uniformity, guiding the responses of all the government departments while undertaking a cost-benefit analysis of any economic action.

Third, rather than creating an overbearing government monitoring framework, which might be susceptible to rent-seeking activities, internalization of environmental compliance may provide an efficient solution. Market based instruments (MBIs) are gaining acceptance in many Asian countries as environmental policy, since it is often impractical to follow the "First-Best" approach (Command-and-Control). Many Asian countries follow a "polluter-pays-principle" in their environmental management, and acceptance of economic instruments is increasingly favored (Gunatilake and De Guzman 2008). A careful design of economic instruments could help in securing environmental objectives, provided it could influence the behavior of consumers and producers to either adopt environmentally benign consumption and production practices or avoid practices which are detrimental for the environment. The adoption of MBIs like a discharge levy, sewage treatment fee, discharge permit trading, etc. in China are worth mentioning here (Wang and Wheeler 2000; Asian Development Bank 2011; Bluffstone 2003). Even economic instruments are gaining popularity to combat climate change in Asian countries (Matsumoto and Gao 2015).

Depending upon the fiscal space and competing demands for other public goods and services, governments allocate resources for environmental conservation. The urgency to devise suitable MBIs is all the more crucial due to the fact that the present level of budgetary allocation for environmental purposes in many Asian countries is not adequate, which creates a constraint for effective environmental governance. Lack of proper infrastructure and human resources to enforce environmental rules and regulations can be seen as an implicit subsidy for production or consumption ("race-to-the-bottom" phenomenon). Many Asian developing countries are often criticized for not implementing adequate mechanisms to enforce compliance, which has motivated several developed countries to explore the option of imposing "border adjustment tax" to target such implicit subsidies enjoyed by developing country exports (Mukherjee and Chakraborty 2016b). Improving environmental governance is therefore a priority for the Asian countries in their own interest.

Fourth, with the growing protectionism in developed countries, slowing global economic growth and low demand from oil producing countries, the economic prospects for Asian countries will remain at moderate levels for at least another 2–3 years. Growing political tensions in various parts of Asia and threats to maritime security could be detrimental to long-run economic prosperity for Asia. A larger focus on reviving domestic consumption demand and investment in infrastructure could be helpful to maintain the present growth rate. One of the strategies to cope with growing protectionism in developed countries could be secured through larger access to regional trade in Asia and mutual cooperation in access to technology and finance. Already a number of forums have emerged for financing cleaner energy technologies. For instance, in South Asia, the Indian Renewable Energy Development Agency (IREDA), Nepal's Alternative Energy Promotion Centre (AEPC), and Bangladesh's Infrastructure Development Company Limited (IDCOL) deserve mention here (Shrestha et al. 2013). There is a need to deepen national efforts on this front further.

Environmental cooperation among Asian countries are already deepening, e.g., through the South Asia Cooperative Environment Programme (SACEP), ASEAN Cooperation on Environment, and Protocol on Protection of the Marine Environment from Land-based Sources in South, Southeast and West Asia respectively. The need at the moment is to have a well-functioning pan-Asian institutional system to address environmental sustainability for facilitating mutual learning, both horizontal (countries having same socio-economic status) and vertical (having different socio-economic status), among Asian countries. This dialogue and mutual cooperation would be crucial in addressing problems associated with transboundary pollution and the sharing of natural resources (rivers, forests, groundwater). In addition, the forum would facilitate vertical learning for developing countries and LDCs from the countries ahead in the development ladder, enabling them to fulfil sustainability commitments in Multilateral Environmental forums. For instance, an ADB estimate showed that as per the Paris Climate Deal commitments, the Asian countries need to annually spend around $300 billion until 2050 by adopting a low-carbon growth path, and mutual learning can considerably facilitate the process (Yi 2016).

For effective management of the environment, availability of information is key. The most crucial challenge faced by Asian countries is their limitation in accurately projecting possible environmental challenges and formulating suitable corrective strategies. The underlying reason for this is that in the absence of an institutional framework to address environmental sustainability in many low-income Asian countries, an up-to-date database on the state of the environment is lacking. Moreover, in many Asian countries, multiple agencies and government departments are involved in monitoring the environment, and coordination among them in reporting and analysing of the information is lacking. In addition to regular monitoring of the environment by different government departments, a significant volume of project-related information is available which requires consolidation with the existing knowledge base. Consolidation of all these resources in a single platform could be the first step toward a larger consolidation of environmental information at the Asian level. Apart from consolidating the national environmental databases, taking a cue from OECD countries (Organisation for Economic Co-operation and Development undated), maintaining a comprehensive platform of environmental information for Asian countries could facilitate research on different aspects of transboundary environmental threats and their management.

Bibliography

Acharya, K.P., P.K. Paudel, P.R. Neupane and M. Köhl (2016) 'Human–Wildlife Conflicts in Nepal: Patterns of Human Fatalities and Injuries Caused by Large Mammals', *PLoS ONE*, 11(9): e0161717. doi: 10.1371/journal.pone.0161717.

Ashraf, M.A., M.J. Maah, I. Yusoff, A. Wajid and K. Mahmood (2011) 'Sand Mining Effects, Causes and Concerns: A Case Study from Bestari Jaya, Selangor, Peninsular Malaysia', *Scientific Research and Essays*, 6(6): 1216–1231.

Asian Development Bank (2009) 'Safeguard Policy Statement', Manila: Asian Development Bank.

Asian Development Bank (2011) 'Market-Based Instruments for Water Pollution Control in the People's Republic of China', Manila: Asian Development Bank.

Aktar, M.W., D. Sengupta and A. Chowdhury (2009) 'Impact of Pesticides Use in Agriculture: Their Benefits and Hazards', *Interdisciplinary Toxicology*, 2(1): 1–12.

Asuncion, R.C. and M. Lee (2017) 'Impacts of Sea Level Rise on Economic Growth in Developing Asia', ADB Economics Working Paper No. 507, Manila: ADB.

Barik, K. (2016) 'Road Rationing and Economic Gains: Assessing Delhi's Odd–Even Formula', *Economic and Political Weekly*, 51(2): 12–14.

Barker, R. and F. Molle (2004) 'Evolution of Irrigation in South and Southeast Asia', Colombo: International Water Management Institute.

Bluffstone, R.A. (2003) 'Environmental Taxes in Developing and Transition Economies', *Public Finance and Management*, 3(1): 143–175.

Bradshaw, S. (2016) 'Tibet: An Environmental Challenge', Darlinghurst: Australia Tibet Council.

Brammer, H. and P. Ravenscroft (2009) 'Arsenic in Groundwater: A Threat to Sustainable Agriculture in South and South-East Asia', *Environment International*, 35: 647–654.

Brooks, T.M., S.L. Pimm and N.J. Collar (1997) 'Deforestation Predicts the Number of Threatened Birds in Insular Southeast Asia', *Conservation Biology*, 11(2): 382–394.

Brunello, A.J., V.C. Molotov, B. Dugherkhuu, C. Goldman, E. Khamaganova, T. Strijhova and R. Sigman (2003) 'Lake Baikal', Paper Presented at the Lake Basin Management Initiative Regional Workshop for Europe, Central Asia and the Americas, Saint Michael's College, Vermont, USA, 18–21 June.

Chakraborty, D. (2012) 'Is India turning into a pollution haven? Evidences from trade and investment patterns', in S. Mukherjee and D. Chakraborty (Eds.), 'Environmental Scenario in India: Successes and Predicaments', pp. 243–266. London: Routledge.

Chakraborty, D. and S. Mukherjee (2013) 'How Does Trade Affect Environment? Some Exploratory Results', *Review of Glocal Studies*, 1(1): 45–51.

Challender, D.W.S. and D.C. MacMillan (2014) 'Poaching is More Than an Enforcement Problem', *Conservation Letters*, 7(5): 484–494.

Chaudhary, P. and K.P. Aryal (2009) 'Global Warming in Nepal: Challenges and Policy Imperatives', *Journal of Forest and Livelihood*, 8(1): 4–13.

Choi, Y. (2017) 'Sustainable Governance in Northeast Asia: Challenges for the Sustainable Frontier', *Sustainability*, 9. doi:10.3390/su9020191.

Chua, V. (2013) 'The Impossible State: North Korea, Past and Future', Vintage: London.

Cole, M.A. and R.J.R. Elliott. (2003) 'Do Environmental Regulations Influence Trade Patterns? Testing Old and New Trade Theories', *World Economy*, 26(8): 1163–1186.

Convention on Biological Diversity (2017) 'Parties to the Protocol and Signature and Ratification of the Supplementary Protocol'. Available online. HTTP: <www.cbd.int/information/parties.shtml> (accessed on March 17, 2017).

Convention on Biological Safety (2017) 'List of Parties'. Available online. HTTP: <www.cbd.int/information/parties.shtml#tab=1> (accessed on February 21, 2017).

Convention on International Trade in Endangered Species of Wild Fauna and Flora (CITES) (2017) 'List of Contracting Parties'. Available online. HTTP: <https://cites.org/eng/disc/parties/chronolo.php> (accessed on February 23, 2017).

Cox, A. and C. Schmidt (2002) 'Subsidies in the OECD Fisheries Sector: A Review of Recent Analysis and Future Directions', Background Paper for the FAO Expert Consultation on Identifying, Assessing and Reporting on Subsidies in the Fishing Industry, Rome, December 3–6.

Das, A.K. (undated) 'E-Waste Management in India: Current Scenario', Available online. HTTP: <www.epa.gov/sites/production/files/2014-05/documents/india.pdf> (accessed on March 19, 2017).

Dasgupta, S., A. Mody, S. Roy and D. Wheeler (2001) 'Environmental Regulation and Development: A Cross-country Empirical Analysis', *Oxford Development Studies*, 29(2): 173–187.

David, W.P. (2004) 'Water Resources and Irrigation Policy Issues in Asia', *Asian Journal of Agriculture and Development*, 1(1): 76–97.

Dhokhikah, Y. and Y. Trihadiningrum (2012) 'Solid Waste Management in Asian Developing Countries: Challenges and Opportunities', *Journal of Applied Environmental and Biological Sciences*, 2(7): 329–335.

Earthworks and Oxfam America (2004) 'Dirty Metals: Mining, Communities and the Environment', Washington, DC: Earthworks and Oxfam.

Energy and Climate Intelligence Unit (2016) 'Asia's Tigers: Reconciling Coal, Climate and Energy Demand', London: ECIU.

Geekiyanage, N., R.B. Bista, S. Nissanka and S. Mukherjee (2015) 'State of land use, land use change and forestry in South Asia', in M. P. McHenry, S. N. Kulshreshtha and S. Lac (Eds.), 'Land Use, Land Use Change and Forestry', pp. 1–14. New York: Nova Science Publishers.

Giri, C., J. Long, S. Abbas, R.M. Murali, F.M. Qamer, B. Pengra and D. Thau (2015) 'Distribution and Dynamics of Mangrove Forests of South Asia', *Journal of Environmental Management*, 148: 101–111.

Government of the People's Republic of China (2010) 'Census of the Pollution Sources in the PRC', Beijing: Ministry of Environment Protection.

Greenpeace (2000) 'Shipbreaking: A Global Environmental, Health and Labour Challenge', A Greenpeace Report for IMO MEPC 44th Session, Online. Available HTTP: <www.greenpeace.org/raw/content/international/press/reports/shipbreaking-a-global-environ.pdf (accessed May 20, 2011).

Gunatilake, H. and F.D. De Guzman (2008) 'Market-Based Approaches for Managing the Asian Environment: A Review', Economics Working Paper Series No. 124, Manila: Asian Development Bank.

Gupta, S. (2014) 'Future environmental challenges for Asia', in J. Huang and S. Gupta (Eds.), 'Environmental Policies in Asia: Perspectives from Seven Asian Countries', pp. 229–239. Singapore: World Scientific.

Hayashi, M. and L. Hughes (2013) 'The Fukushima Nuclear Accident and its Effect on Global Energy Security', *Energy Policy*, 59: 102–111.

He, J. (2006). 'Pollution Haven Hypothesis and Environmental Impacts of Foreign Direct Investment: The Case of Industrial Emission of Sulfur Dioxide (SO_2) in Chinese Provinces', *Ecological Economics*, 60(1): 228–245.

Hirota, K. (2010) 'Comparative Studies on Vehicle Related Policies for Air Pollution Reduction in Ten Asian Countries', *Sustainability*, 2: 145–162.

Honma, S. and Y. Yoshida (2011) 'Did International Trade Become Dirtier in Developing Countries? On the Composition Effect of International Trade on the Environment', Discussion Paper No. 52, Online. Available HTTP: <www.ip.kyusan-u.ac.jp/keizai-kiyo/dp52.pdf> (accessed March 21, 2017).

Howes, S. and P. Wyrwoll (2012) 'Asia's Wicked Environmental Problems', ADBI Working Paper Series No. 348, Tokyo: ADBI.

Hsu, A., et al. (2016) 'Environmental Performance Index 2016', New Haven: Yale University, Online. Available HTTP: <www.epi.yale.edu> (accessed March 26, 2017).

International Energy Agency (2010) 'Energy Technology Perspectives 2010: Blue Map Scenario', Paris: IEA.

International Energy Agency (2016) 'World Energy Outlook 2016', Paris: OECD-IEA.

International Monetary Fund (IMF) (undated) 'Government Finance Statistics', Online. Available HTTP: <http://data.imf.org/?sk=a0867067-d23c-4ebc-ad23-d3b015045405> (accessed February 17, 2017).

Irwin, A. (2014) 'Black Carbon Tackling: Crop-Residue Burning in South Asia', *Global Change*, 83: 8–11.

Islam, M.S., Y.H. Pei and S. Mangharam (2016) 'Trans-Boundary Haze Pollution in Southeast Asia: Sustainability through Plural Environmental Governance', *Sustainability*, 8: 1–13.

Jie, L. and H.J.V. Zuylen (2014) 'Road Traffic in China', *Procedia – Social and Behavioral Sciences*, 111: 107–116.

Kankaria, A., B. Nongkynrih and S.K. Gupta (2014) 'Indoor Air Pollution in India: Implications of Health and Its Control', *Indian Journal of Community Medicine*, 39(4): 203–207.

Khan, A., U.R. Sumaila, R. Watson, G. Munro and D. Pauly (2006) 'The nature and magnitude of global non-fuel fisheries subsidies', in U.R. Sumaila and D. Pauly (Eds.), '*Catching More Bait: A Bottom-Up Re-Estimation of Global Fisheries Subsidies*', Fisheries Centre Research Reports, pp. 5–37, Vancouver: Fisheries Centre, the University of British Columbia.

Kim, R.E. (2015) 'Green-blind growth: A critical appraisal of environmental governance in the Republic of Korea', in S. Mukherjee and D. Chakraborty (Eds.), 'Environmental Challenges and Governance: Diverse Perspectives from Asia', pp. 235–250, Abingdon: Routledge.

Koh, L.P. and D.S. Wilcove (2008) 'Is Oil Palm Agriculture Really Destroying Tropical Biodiversity?', *Conservation Letters*, 1: 60–64.

Kreft, S., D. Eckstein and I. Melchior (2016) 'Global Climate Risk Index 2017', Bonn: Germanwatch e.V.

Kummer, D.M. and B.L. Turner (1994) 'The Human Causes of Deforestation in Southeast Asia', *BioScience*, 44(5): 323–328.

Kundur, S.K. and K. Murthy (2013) 'Environmental Impacts of Tourism and Management in Maldives', *International Journal of Environmental Sciences*, 2(1): 44–50.

Lahiri-Dutt, K. (2008) 'Digging to Survive: Women's Livelihoods in South Asia's Small Mines and Quarries', *South Asian Survey*, 15(2): 217–244.

Lee, J. (1996) 'Poachers, Tigers and Bears . . . Oh My! Asia's Illegal Wildlife Trade', *Northwestern Journal of International Law and Business*, 16(3): 497–515.

Liu, Z. (2015) 'China's Carbon Emissions Report 2015', Cambridge: Belfer Center for Science and International Affairs Harvard Kennedy School.

Lyons, Y. (2012) 'Transboundary pollution from offshore oil and gas activities in the seas of Southeast Asia', in R. Warner and S. Marsden (Eds.), '*Transboundary Environmental Governance: Inland, Coastal and Marine Areas*', pp. 167–202. Abingdon: Routledge.

Madduri, S. and. E.M. Reddy (2003) 'An Environmental Assessment of Oil and Gas Exploration', Environmental Economics Research Committee Working Paper Series: IPP-8, Available online. HTTP: <http://coe.mse.ac.in/eercrep/fullrep/ipp/IPP_FR_Madduri.pdf> (accessed on May 8, 2017).

Manral, U., S. Sengupta, S.A. Hussain, S. Rana and R. Badola (2016) 'Human Wildlife Conflict in India: A Review of Economic Implication of Loss and Preventive Measures', *The Indian Forester*, 142(10): 928–940.

Matsumoto, K. and A.M. Gao (Eds.) (2015) 'Economic Instruments to Combat Climate Change in Asian Countries', Alphen aan den Rijn: Kluwer Law International.
Mekong River Commission (2010) 'An Assessment of Environmental Impacts of Tourism in the Lower Mekong Basin', MRC Technical Paper No. 28, Vientiane: Mekong River Commission.
Merican, Y., Z. Yusop, Z.M. Noor and L.S. Hook (2007) 'Foreign Direct Investment and the Pollution in Five ASEAN Nations', *International Journal of Economics and Management*, 1(2): 245–261.
Mukherjee, S. (2008) 'Economics of Agricultural Nonpoint Source Water Pollution: A Case Study of Groundwater Nitrate Pollution in the Lower Bhavani River Basin, Tamil Nadu', unpublished PhD thesis, University of Madras (Madras School of Economics).
Mukherjee, S. (2010) 'Nutrient-Based Fertiliser Subsidy: Will Farmers Adopt Agricultural Best Management Practices?', *Economic and Political Weekly*, 45(49): 66–72.
Mukherjee, S. and D. Chakraborty (2015a) 'Environmental governance scenario in Asia: lessons for the future', in S. Mukherjee and D. Chakraborty (Eds.), 'Environmental Challenges and Governance: Diverse Perspectives from Asia', pp. 251–268. Abingdon: Routledge.
Mukherjee, S. and D. Chakraborty (2015b) 'Walking a thin line between growth and development concerns? Environmental governance in India', in S. Mukherjee and D. Chakraborty (Eds.), 'Environmental Challenges and Governance: Diverse Perspectives from Asia', pp. 49–74. Abingdon: Routledge.
Mukherjee, S. and D. Chakraborty (2016a) 'Turning Human Waste into Renewable Energy: Opportunities and Policy Options for India', *Turkish Economic Review*, 3(4): 610–628.
Mukherjee, S. and D. Chakraborty (2016b) 'Environmental policy instruments for international trade: a review', in D. Chakraborty and J. Mukherjee (Eds.), 'Trade, Investment and Economic Development in Asia: Empirical and Policy Issues', pp. 249–262. Abingdon: Routledge.
Mukherjee, S. and D. Chakraborty (2017) 'Demand for infrastructure investment for water services: key features and assessment methods', in J. Chaisse (Ed.), 'Charting the Water Regulatory Future: Issues, Challenges and Directions', pp. 257–296. Cheltenham: Edward Elgar.
Nyhus, P.J. and R. Tilson (2004) 'Characterizing Human–Tiger Conflict in Sumatra, Indonesia: Implications for Conservation', Available online. HTTP: <http://digitalcommons.colby.edu/cgi/viewcontent.cgi?article=1052&context=faculty_scholarship> (accessed on January 15, 2017).
Organisation for Economic Co-operation and Development (undated) 'OECD Data: Environment', Available online. HTTP: https://data.oecd.org/environment.htm (accessed on March 20, 2017).
OXFAM and WWF Russia (2008), 'Russia and Neighbouring Countries: Environmental, Economic and Social Impacts of Climate Change', Moscow: OXFAM and WWF.
Physicians for Social Responsibility (2013) 'Fukushima Disaster: Impacts and Continuing Threats', Washington, DC: PSR.
Pimentel, D. (2006) 'Soil Erosion: A Food and Environmental Threat', *Environment, Development and Sustainability*, 8: 119–137.
Pingali, P.L. (2001) 'Environmental Consequences of Agricultural Commercialization in Asia', *Environment and Development Economics*, 6: 483–502.
Pretty, J. and Z.P. Bharucha (2015) 'Integrated Pest Management for Sustainable Intensification of Agriculture in Asia and Africa', *Insects*, 6: 152–182.
Qurban, M.A., T.V. Joydas, K.P. Manikandan, P.K. Krishnakumar and M. Wafar (undated) 'Oil-Related Activities and Environmental Concerns in the Gulf'. Available online. HTTP: <www.jccp.or.jp/international/conference/docs/hpe794a8_dr-mohammad-qurban-kfupm-abstract1.pdf> (accessed on March 23, 2017).
Richards, D.R. and D.A. Friess (2016) 'Rates and Drivers of Mangrove Deforestation in Southeast Asia, 2000–2012', *PNAS*, 113(2): 344–349.
Richey, A.S., B.F. Thomas, M.-H. Lo, J.T. Reager, J.S. Famiglietti, K. Voss, S. Swenson and M. Rodell (2015) 'Quantifying Renewable Groundwater Stress with GRACE', *Water Resources Research*, 51: 5217–5238.
Rock, M.T. (2002) 'Pollution Control in East Asia: Lessons from Newly Industrializing Economies', Washington, DC: Resources for the Future.
Ronteltap, M., P. Dodane and M. Bassan (2014), 'Overview of treatment technologies', in L. Strande, M. Ronteltap and D. Brdjanovic (Eds.), 'Faecal Sludge Management: Systems Approach for Implementation and Operation', pp. 97–122. London: IWA Publishing.
Sas-Rolfes, M. (2012) 'The Rhino Poaching Crisis: A Market Analysis'. Available online. HTTP: <www.rhino-economics.com/> (accessed on March 10, 2017).
Satterthwaite, D., G. McGranahan, and C. Tacoli (2010) 'Urbanization and Its Implications for Food and Farming', *Philosophical Transactions of Royal Society*, 365: 2809–2820.

Saviour, M.N. (2012) 'Environmental Impact of Soil and Sand Mining: A Review', *International Journal of Science, Environment and Technology*, 1(3): 125–134.

Schwela, D., G. Haq, C. Huizenga, W. Han, H. Fabian and M. Ajero (2006) 'Urban Air Pollution in Asian Cities: Status, Challenges and Management', London: Earthscan.

Sharma, S.K., A. Choudhury, P. Sarkar, S. Biswas, A. Singh, P.K. Dadhich, A.K. Singh, S. Majumdar, A. Bhatia, M. Mohini, R. Kumar, C.S. Jha, M.S.R. Murthy, N.H. Ravindranath, J.K. Bhattacharya, M. Karthik, S. Bhattacharya and R. Chauhan (2011) 'Greenhouse Gas Inventory Estimates for India', *Current Science*, 101(3): 405–415.

Shrestha, R.M., M. Ahmed, S. Suphachalasai and R. Lasco (2013) 'Economics of Reducing Greenhouse Gas Emissions in South Asia: Options and Costs', Manila: Asian Development Bank and Australia South Asia Development Partnership Facility.

Simpson, A. (2016) 'Starting from year zero: environmental governance in Myanmar', in S. Mukherjee and D. Chakraborty (Eds.), 'Environmental Challenges and Governance: Diverse Perspectives from Asia', pp. 152–165. Abingdon: Routledge.

Singh, R.P. and D.G. Kaskaoutis (2014) 'Crop Residue Burning: A Threat to South Asian Air Quality', *EOS*, 95(37): 333–340.

Srikant, P. (2009) 'Koodankulam Anti-Nuclear Movement: A Struggle for Alternative Development?', Working Paper No. 232, Bangalore: Institute for Social and Economic Change.

Srividhya, S. and P.P. Appasamy (2012) 'Environmental cost of biomedical waste management: a case study of Chennai city', in S. Mukherjee and D. Chakraborty (Eds.), 'Environmental Scenario in India: Successes and Predicaments', pp. 189–202. Abingdon: Routledge.

Sumaila, U.R., L. Teh, R. Watson, P. Tyedmers and D. Pauly (2006) 'Fuel subsidies to global fisheries: magnitude and impacts on resource sustainability', in U.R. Sumaila and D. Pauly (Eds.), 'Catching More Bait: A Bottom-Up Re-Estimation of Global Fisheries Subsidies', Fisheries Centre Research Reports, pp. 38–48. Vancouver: Fisheries Centre, the University of British Columbia.

United Nations Convention to Combat Desertification (2017) 'Update on Ratification of the UNCCD'. Available online. HTTP: www.unccd.int/Documents/Ratification%20list%20Dec2016.pdf (last accessed on March 7, 2017).

United Nations Economic and Social Commission for the Asia and the Pacific and United Nations Human Settlements Programme (2015) 'The State of Asian and Pacific Cities 2015: Urban Transformations – Shifting from Quantity to Quality', Bangkok: UNESCAP and UNHSP.

United Nations Economic and Social Commission for the Asia and the Pacific (2016a) 'Economic and Social Survey of Asia and the Pacific 2016', Bangkok: UNESCAP.

United Nations Economic and Social Commission for the Asia and the Pacific (2016b) 'Transformations for Sustainable Development Promoting Environmental Sustainability in Asia and the Pacific', Bangkok: UNESCAP.

United Nations Educational, Scientific and Cultural Organization (2008) 'Effects of Tourism on Culture and the Environment in Asia and the Pacific: Alleviating Poverty and Protecting Cultural and Natural Heritage through Community-Based Eco-tourism in Luang Namtha, Lao PDR', Bangkok: UNESCO.

United Nations Environment Programme Ozone Secretariat Montreal Protocol (2017) 'Status of Ratification'. Available online. HTTP: <http://ozone.unep.org/sites/ozone/modules/unep/ozone_treaties/inc/datasheet.php> (accessed on March 12, 2017).

United Nations Environment Programme Stockholm Convention (2017) 'Status of Ratification'. Available online. HTTP: <http://chm.pops.int/Countries/StatusofRatifications/PartiesandSignatories/tabid/252/Default.aspx> (accessed on February 25, 2017).

United Nations Framework Convention on Climate Change (2017) 'Status of Ratification of the Kyoto Protocol'. Available online. HTTP: <http://unfccc.int/kyoto_protocol/status_of_ratification/items/2613.php> (accessed on April 17, 2017).

Visvanathan, C. and J. Trankler (undated) 'Municipal Solid Waste Management in Asia: A Comparative Analysis', Available online. HTTP: <http://citeseerx.ist.psu.edu/viewdoc/download?doi=10.1.1.572.6735&rep=rep1&type=pdf> (accessed on March 23, 2017).

Viswanathan, P.K. and C.S. Bahinipati (2016) 'Water Security Challenges of South and South East Asia: Mainstreaming Local Governance Institutions', *Asian Profile*, 44(5): 405–416.

Wang, F., R. Kuehr, D. Ahlquist and J. Li (2013) 'E-Waste in China: A Country Report', StEP Green Paper Series, United Nations University.

Wang, H. and D. Wheeler (2000), 'Endogenous Enforcement and Effectiveness of China's Pollution Levy System', Policy Research Working Paper 2336, Washington, DC: World Bank.

Wilkinson, C. (Ed.) (2008) 'Status of Coral reefs of the World: 2008', Townsville: Reef and Rainforest Research Centre.

World Bank (undated) 'World Development Indicators', Available online. HTTP: <http://data.worldbank.org/data-catalog/world-development-indicators> (accessed on March 21, 2017).

World Bank (2006) 'Mongolia: A Review of Environmental and Social Impacts in the Mining Sector', Washington, DC: World Bank.

World Health Organization (undated) 'Regional Burden of Disease due to Indoor Air Pollution', Available online. HTTP: <www.who.int/indoorair/health_impacts/burden_regional/en/> (accessed on March 7, 2017).

Yi, B.L. (2016) 'Paris Climate Targets to Cost Asia $300 Billion a Year, Says Research', Live Mint E-paper, September 2016.

Zhang, Y. (2012) 'Scale, Technique and Composition Effects in Trade-Related Carbon Emissions in China', *Environmental and Resource Economics*, 51(3): 371–389.

5

Singapore's environmental policy: charting progression in the island-state

Seck Tan

Environmental challenges and weather phenomenon

Singapore is a small, nimble island-state in Southeast Asia nestled amongst a mix of Association of Southeast Asian Nations (ASEAN[1]) neighbors rich in culture, ethnicity and history and is part of the greater Asian[2] region. With proximity to her Southeast Asian neighbors, Singapore is highly susceptible to developments in the region. A regular feature on the environmental calendar is the Southeast Asian haze during the calendar months of July to September. This haze (suspension of dry, fine particles in the air) that is experienced by the region is a result of land clearing activities in Indonesia, primarily driven by growing palm oil demand. In Singapore, bad air quality has resulted in local schools reviewing their modus operandi, with the locals having to adjust their daily activities from outdoors to indoors. The haze in 2015 was more severe relative to earlier years, as it coincided with El Niño, in which the weather becomes dry due to reduced rainfall and rising temperatures. The warmth is experienced more over land than in oceans, and scientists have predicted that land temperatures will continue to rise to historic highs (Tyrrell and Dommenget 2015).

Singapore is not the only ASEAN member to feel the brunt of El Niño.[3] Indonesia experienced its worst drought in 18 years, with forest fires[4] causing poor air quality over the ASEAN region (particularly Malaysia, southern Thailand and southern Philippines), including Singapore (Soeriaatmadja 2015; Cook et al. 2016). Elsewhere, Thailand[5] and Vietnam experienced problems with rice production due to delayed rain (Cook et al. 2016); Thailand issued water rationing due to water shortages and reduced the number of SongKran 2016 festive days from four to three (Coconuts Bangkok 2016; Simmons 2016); and Vietnam experienced significant crop reductions. Now that El Niño has left its mark, it is left for La Niña to take over, with more rainfall and cooling expected at the equatorial Pacific Ocean region. Although La Niña (Agence France-Presse 2016) improves fishing conditions due to upwelling of cold nutrient rich waters, heavy monsoons in Southeast Asia are expected. The impact of a strong La Niña effect has been witnessed by severe floods in Germany and France;[6] wild storms on the east coast[7] of Australia and potentially flooded coal mines[8] after the worst floods happened in 2011.

It has been predicted by the Intergovernmental Panel on Climate Change (IPCC) that by 2100, the global average sea level rise (SLR) is expected to reach 0.26 to 0.55 meters under the best-case scenario [of 70 percent reduction of greenhouse gas (GHG) emissions], and nearly one meter under unabated increases in GHG emissions (IPCC 2013). Scholars have argued that it is important that the assumptions underpinning SLR projection models are clearly understood and disclosed to enable users a better grasp of the models, as the models are meant to be scientific and not merely statistical (Valentine 2015). Nevertheless, the threat of SLR is real after the loss of at least five reef islands in the remote Solomon Islands (Albert et al. 2016). There have been planned retreats for cities to move inland or to higher ground, and, as in the case of Fukushima after the nuclear disasters, for higher concrete walls to prevent future disasters such as tsunamis. However, these concrete barriers are likely to change marine ecology and the surrounding landscape, in addition to hindering fisheries development.

The Southeast Asian haze, El Niño and La Niña, and SLR are just some of the natural hazards presented by the environment. Although some may argue that these are natural observations, there is no doubt that both economic development and human activities play a role in aggravating the impacts of these weather phenomena. To counter these observations, Asia and the Pacific nations have crafted Sustainable Development Goals (SDGs) for implementation in 2016, which will address economic, social and environmental dimensions of the region (UN ESCAP et al. 2016). However, sustainable development means different things to different people; and for development to be truly sustainable, growth must be inclusive and garner equal attention to the tri-nexus of economy, society and the environment. Unfortunately, this is often not the case. In an effort to continue growing, the ASEAN region has given priority to economic integration and strengthening its institutional framework. Therefore, it is no surprise that attention is often skewed toward economic performance, with a lack of attention to the environment. A higher level of income from economic progress is likely to increase the utilization of the environment as a source of capital (Tan 2016a), with trade and economic development degrading the environment further (Tan 2016b).

As the region grows, ASEAN is projected to be the fourth largest single economy, behind the European Union, the USA, and China, with a GDP of USD $10 trillion (US-ASEAN Business Council 2014). In late 2015, the ASEAN Economic Community (AEC), founded on a regional common market, came into effect, allowing goods, services, capital and labor, particularly professional labor, free mobility to facilitate trade within ASEAN. The AEC is one of three pillars,[9] along with the Political-Security Community and the Socio-Cultural Community, aimed at building an economically competitive region. Singapore has offered her human capital services (Tan and Savchenko 2016) to the region and beyond in sectors such as engineering, sewerage and water treatment, but this transfer must include sustainable ways of development so that the island-state maintains its usefulness to the region. This chapter will evaluate what Singapore has achieved toward sustainable development and is structured as follows. First, a brief review of island states will be presented. This is followed by an overview of Singapore and her environmental policy. Thereafter, two cases of the use of Environmental Impact Assessment will be presented to trace the progress of this environmental measure, which has been undertaken on the island-state. A brief examination of future policy directions and recommendations for Singapore's sustainable development concludes this chapter.

Islands, Singapore as an island-state, and its environmental policy

Islands

When it comes to economic survival, there is no significance difference between island states and other global economies. Faced with an uncertain future from SLR and other natural environmental hazards, islanders are instinctively resilient, with strong migratory capabilities. But what render islands different from land-locked economies are their natural endowments like beaches, forests and mountains. Pristine forests and mountains, sandy white beaches, alluring atolls, crystal blue waters, and knee deep water are just some island attractions. For example, Aitutaki, amongst the group of Cook Islands, is a natural atoll with a cay known as the One Foot Island; and the archipelago Vanuatu boosts of the world's most accessible active volcanoes in Mount Yasur. There are also island nations which offer a mix between busy cities and laidback lifestyles such as the French Polynesia Tahiti and New Caledonia. Blessed with natural endowments but lacking in resources, tourism and international trade provide employment and are main economic drivers of island states.

However, beyond these natural luxuries lie the harsh realities of environmental issues, such as water crisis, poverty, health pandemics, financial crisis and challenges to economic growth, which are similar to those faced by most nations. Several island states are experiencing these depressing realities. Maldives (an Indian Ocean island) is facing a water crisis and could be submerged under water in the next two decades. The Pacific Islands, famed for their hospitality, are also facing a water crisis as well as economic and financial challenges. For instance, Fiji (with the largest population amongst the Pacific Islands and heavily dependent on tourism) faced a sharp decline in visitors after the 2007–2008 Global Financial Crisis (GFC). The European island-state of Iceland was not spared either by the GFC and had to rely on tourism for economic stability. Of late, there have been reports of Mauritius facing a probable Ponzi scheme that could threaten the financial system and lead to economic unrest (Arouff 2015) and Seychelles' escalating flood troubles are intensifying plans for a sanitation master blueprint (Lablache 2015).

Studies of small island states have been carried out by Nurse et al. (2001) and political economic reforms of islands were investigated by Duncan (2011). Singapore is no different from other island states in that she is not immune to extreme events. The impacts of extreme events are systemic and affect all aspects of Singaporean society; moreover, the island-state is more vulnerable to these shocks than is currently acknowledged (Tan and Lai 2016). Sustainable development points to the importance of economic, societal and environmental well-being, and ensures that they are factored into public policy formulation. For an island-state to attain the goals of sustainable development, a key ingredient is an agile and nimble bureaucracy. In addition, the state's reaction to and management of extreme events are just as critical. Singapore is both a country and an island-state alongside a limited land area and natural resources, with labor as its main source of capital.

Singapore as an island-state

Islands thrive on tourism[10] and international trade as economic drivers and sources of employment. Therefore, land[11] must be allocated for transport infrastructure such as airports, seaports, and rail networks. On land-scarce Singapore, this can only be achieved by adding more land. According to Sparke et al. (2004), land reclamation[12] in Singapore can be traced back to 1962 with 0.2 square kilometers of newly created usable land reserved for public housing[13] development along the east coast of the island leading to the International Airport. Larger areas of up to 11.6 square kilometers of land were reclaimed subsequently for infrastructure projects such as the Changi International Airport, and the joining of seven islands[14] off the island's southwest to form Jurong Island, for the petrochemical industry. Land reclamation in Singapore was viewed by her neighbors as an infringement on territorial boundaries in 2002; although this was amicably resolved in 2005 (see Koh and Lin 2006). One recent land reclamation project on Singapore's southern shore is the building of the Marina Coastal Expressway (officially opened in December 2013) and is the first under-sea road tunnel (420 meters) in Singapore. The building of this expressway serves to relieve congestion and facilitate expansion of the existing Central Business District.

There are smaller islands south of the main Singapore island where land reclamation has also taken place since the 1960s.[15] These include Sentosa,[16] Kusu Island, Lazerus Island, Pulau Renget (new island), Pulau Sebarok, Pulau Sudong, Pulau Hantu, Pulau Busing and Pulau Bukom. In the future, development plans by Singapore's Urban Redevelopment Authority are for Kusu Island, Lazarus Island, Pulau Tekukor and Pulau Renget to merge and become the Kusu Island group, while Pulau Bukom will be comprised of Pulau Hantu and Pulau Busing. Practices that move away from traditional landfill use waste as landfill, as experimented within Pulau Semakau (which sees Pulau Sakeng[17] as part of Pulau Semakau). As a result of land reclamation (Waller 1993), Singapore has grown from a land area of 580 square kilometers at independence (1965) to 680 square kilometers in 2002 (Lim 2002) and to 719[18] square kilometers in 2015. Further land reclamation is expected as per the Urban Redevelopment Authority's 2013 Land Use Plan[19] and 2014 Master Plan,[20] with The Economist (2015) forecasting that territorial expansion will grow by another 56 square kilometers by 2030.

Land is reclaimed by pouring sand and raw materials into the sea until new land is created. This has impacted marine life and their habitats, such as coral reefs[21] that used to surround the smaller islands in the early 1960s. Sand is poured over the reefs along the coastal areas, burying them as the seabed is raised to become dry land. The source of sand and raw materials for Singapore's reclamation[22] comes predominantly from Indonesian and Vietnamese territory and waters[23] where dredging[24] and mining have impacted the ability of the ecosystem to provide resources for the respective economies (see selected global studies from Boyd et al. (2005), Krause et al. (2010), and Desprez et al. (2010)). Coastlines are eroded and islands disappear when sand is being dredged from the surrounding seas. Although nature's adaptability (for instance, corals change shape and form) cannot be underestimated, this does not imply that using the environment as a source of capital should be further abused.

Coastal waters are full of life, containing food aplenty, with animal and plant remains carried into the sea by rivers. Currents bring food up from the sea floor close to the coasts, and this food is consumed by plankton, an important food source for fish and coral reefs. Dredging is done with special ships called dredgers to scoop sand up from the sea floor, and this process affects the water quality, as the water becomes cloudy for an extended period of time. There is a decrease in sunlight from the cloudiness, impacting the growth and reproduction of coral reefs, as well as food for the plankton. Without food, plankton die and the oxygen level in the water is reduced. This may result in the occurrence of red tides due to the boom of algae organisms named gymnodinium breve. The need to balance nutrients and plankton in the water further emphasize the precarious state of the ocean as a natural environmental source and sink.

As more land is cleared for urbanization on the island-state, there will be less of the natural flora such as mangrove forests. In a drive toward urbanization, the population of mangroves on Singapore has suffered significantly (see Turner 1994). Mangrove forests (or mangroves) are under stress from excessive urbanization and reduced resilience in light of SLR. This is because the resilience is conditioned by the composition and status of the stands and other factors such as tidal range and sediment supply (Woodroffe 1995; Ewel et al. 1998; Farnsworth 1998). More needs to be done to conserve Singapore's remaining mangroves (Hsiang 2000). Yang et al. (2011) suggests that conservation of mangroves in Singapore can be attained via: conserving existing habitats through holistic land use planning; conducting scientific studies to better understand mangrove plant growth; re-introducing extinct species; propagating endangered species, and applying creative inter-disciplinary solutions to protect and restore mangrove habitats.

There has been noticeable progress with mangrove conservation on the island-state. For example, marine life continues to thrive in the mangrove mudflats on the western shorelines of

Pulau Semakau, and conservation of mangroves is ongoing along the western coast of the main island and on offshore islands. Conservation and restoration of mangroves must continue as replanted mangroves provide added protection of coastlines against natural disasters (tsunamis and typhoons) and offer a carbon sequestration service. Friess (2015) echoed this view with regard to valuing Singapore's mangrove swamps on a convincing note, but there remain two challenges in how to value and measure them in a way that can be widely understood by the public; and how to ensure that policy makers embrace such valuations. These challenges do not pertain to valuation of mangroves alone but would also be relevant to valuation of environmental degradation and utilization. We now turn to Singapore's perspective on the environment as an island-state.

Environmental policy (or the lack of)

Singapore has been labeled an island-state with no alternative energy sources; this disadvantage has shaped environmental policies that are skewed in favor of economic development. The ease of evading environmental responsibility depends on how the message is communicated. The consistency in what is communicated about energy sources and the island-state's position on environmental policy suggests that there are major obstacles to a switch to renewables and a reduction in fossil fuel dependence. Coupled with traction from accumulated advancements in energy conservation, the scope of emissions reductions is further restricted for a relatively small economy. These set the trend for environmental policy which is unlikely to be sustainable. This is because island-states are susceptible to the natural hazards of the environment as well as to regional phenomena.

Environmental protection is secondary when economic development has been the priority over the past decades. The island-state cannot have it both ways, accepting that economic development impacts the environment but continuing to implement policies without any appreciation for the environment. For the ecosystem to play a functional role toward the well-being of both the economy and society, the rate of environmental degradation and utilization should not exceed that of economic growth. Environmental policies that are pro-development could negate Singapore's economic progress in the long run. To enable further sustainable economic development, policies must pay attention to the environment.

Further explanation on why environmental protection is overlooked with preference offered to economic development can be evaluated from two different angles, economics and regulation. In terms of economics, decision-making is bounded by costs and ruled by benefits (perceived), overriding any impacts on the environment. This is how assessing cost-effectiveness of alternative energy sources is carried out (Hamilton-Hart 2006). The second explanation is regulatory, which concerns the application of an Environmental Impact Assessment (EIA). Studies have found EIA to be a useful tool in administering environmental policies (Perry and Teng 1999) but its use in Singapore is limited, as it inconveniences the promotion of physical development (Chua 2005) and economic growth.

International trade has elevated the status of Singapore, but studies (Lopez 1994; Harris 2004; Frankel 2008) have found that trade can result in environmental degradation. Although Singapore's favorable geographic location offers a value proposition, it also leaves the island-nation at the mercy of an international system over which she has limited control (Connell 2013). In addition, Singapore's geographic location in the ASEAN region suggests that she can play no more than the role of a silent sufferer when environmental natural hazards such as the seasonal Southeast Asia haze occur. As Singapore explores alternative growth options, environmental mindfulness may offer prospects to promote a commercially viable green industry. This stewardship can provide further upstream employment, empower labor resources, and brand a unique island-state proposition.

The next section will attempt to discuss the EIA, which serves as a protection mechanism for the natural environment, and traces the path EIA has taken over the past decade on the island-state. Policy implications and recommendations stemming from the discussion will conclude the rest of this chapter.

Tracing Environmental Impact Assessment (EIA) on island-state Singapore

Environmental Impact Assessment (EIA)

An Environmental Impact Assessment (EIA) is a detailed analysis which assesses the type and extent of effects that a proposed project would have on the natural environment. An assessment of such would provide a holistic study on positive and negative consequences for the environment. It is typically undertaken before a decision to proceed with the project is made and the final decision is made by project stakeholders. The objective of this type of assessment is to ensure that decision makers are well-informed of the environmental impacts when the project proceeds. More specifically, an EIA serves to: (1) determine if the impacts can be accepted or need to be addressed; (2) propose mitigation measures; and (3) recommend options that incorporate the mitigation measures.

An EIA may underestimate the environmental impacts of a development as bias can skew the analysis. This is not uncommon, as third-party vendors (consultants) tend to be selected and employed by the EIA stakeholders. This presents a potential conflict of interest where the data collection and scenario analysis may not be autonomous; and it is uncertain if the investigation arrangement was correctly undertaken according to rule because all records are not publicly available. Therefore, an EIA should be carried out and drafted by an independent consultant offering the full facts and figures without prejudice nor influence if a project should proceed or not. It is expected that the consultant would engage subject matter experts with technical expertise to maintain a level of professionalism.

The case with Singapore

During the 1960s to the 1980s, developments on the island-state were excused from EIAs and decisions were made with loose assessments to ascertain if a project was appropriate for a particular location. Two decades ago, Hesp (1995) discussed the EIA process in Singapore suggesting that it was carried out in secret, or when the Government deems them necessary. It was not until 1989[25] when EIA was formalized and required for new projects. For instance, when a developer wishes to carry out a project, a proposal is forwarded to the Pollution Control Department for an initial assessment to determine if an EIA is required (Tan 1993). Chia (1998) had argued that Singapore practices discretionary EIA rather than mandatory EIA. In order not to adopt compulsory EIA, the island-state must show well-conceived physical plans to enable economic development and at the same time provide safeguards for the environment. Considering that the coastal zones of Singapore had undergone complete transformation through land reclamation, construction of air and sea-port, amalgamation of small islets into larger islands, and removal of coral reefs and mangroves, Chia (1998) had recommended that EIA be mandatory for environmentally fragile areas.

An EIA process should be invoked at the initial stage of any planning or development proposal with public participation and subsequent reviews (Hesp 1995). The purpose of public consultation serves to explain the nature of the proposal to the public, allowing stakeholders to understand the public's opinions of the proposal and incorporate these into the assessment.

Nonetheless, there remains no (or minimal) public consultation and EIAs are not freely available to the public in Singapore (Hesp 1995). There is reservation that even with public consultation, it is unlikely that the views of the public will be taken into consideration[26] and that EIA is merely a process to fulfil a requirement towards project advancement with informed decision-making. This reservation is unfounded because the development can still proceed with mitigation measures,[27] should there be strong opposition against a proposed development. There are two cases on the island-state which can highlight the contrasting engagement with the public and demonstrate EIA's progress over the years. They are namely, development of the integrated resort on Sentosa island, and the Cross Island Line (CIL).

Sentosa is one of the largest islands amongst the southern group of offshore islands with a land area of 1,236 hectares (five square kilometers); and it is the closest to the main island of Singapore accessible via cable car, ferry, monorail, and motorcar. In 2007, an integrated resort was planned on the western end of Sentosa that would occupy about 49 hectares of land. Wong (1998) had studied coastal tourism development in the region and proposed that EIA (with clear guidelines for the respective hotel operators) is critical for the sustainable development of island tourism as islands are vulnerable, with limited resources and size. EIA relates the development impacts to the coastal environment such as mangroves, seagrass,[28] and sandy beaches. However, public access[29] to the EIA analysis conducted by the resort was restricted on the premises of the resort management and during working hours. It is unclear if the public was consulted for their views and opinions prior development.

The development of the resort would contribute to Singapore's economy (during and post construction) but at the expense of habitat destruction, air-shed removal, soil erosion, and biodiversity losses.[30] The costs were clear: coral reefs were buried, and habitats along the coastal and marine areas were disturbed.[31] For instance, land cleared for construction was replaced with manicured landscape gardens. Coral reefs were buried to create a marine park, aquarium and artificial reefs. Coastal and marine areas were reclaimed only to be dug up subsequently to create waterways and promenades. The purpose of conducting an EIA is to minimize such environmental degradations and offer a resourceful way of alternative mitigation options.

By contrast, the case of public consultation on CIL was handled differently by the authorities in 2016. CIL is a Mass Rapid Transit (MRT) line that will cross the island from east to west when it is completed in 2030.[32] The CIL construction is expected to affect the catchment areas of the Central Catchment Nature Reserve (CCNR) and the MacRitchie Reservoir. A major infrastructure project of this scale calls for careful planning with minimal disturbance to both nature reserves and catchment areas. This project remains at the planning and evaluation stage with two available options. Even so, access of the EIA report was clearly communicated to the public and made available online.[33]

Phase 1 of the EIA report had commenced in August 2014 with strong support from the relevant ministries. The authorities had also provided timely updates with information that is easily understood by the public. This process resulted in two alignment options (direct or skirting) for the CIL construction; as well as supplemented measures. The ease of access to the EIA report for the CIL construction demonstrates public engagement and allows stakeholders to be cognizant of the potential environmental impacts. Although a decision on which of the two options to undertake has not been made, it is evident that the holistic approach to this construction project has been inclusive with utmost priority to environmental safeguard.

Singapore was ranked poorly on environmental protection (Bradshaw et al. 2010) but some measures have been taken to date to safeguard the environment. This has come in the form of EIA analysis where environmental impacts of a project or development are studied and the public is given an opportunity to provide feedback. In the case of the integrated resort on Sentosa island, the public was given access (by appointment) to the EIA analysis. For the CIL MRT line, not only was the public given open access (online), the public was offered the chance to provide their views and opinions on the infrastructure development. This is considered significant progress in environmental awareness from an island-state which has placed economic growth on a pedestal since independence. The next and final section discusses the policy implications and recommends future environmental policies for the island-state.

Conclusion with policy implications and recommendations

As an island-state, Singapore's basic requirement for survival is economic growth. Unfortunately, growth cannot be indefinite and more specifically, development must be sustainable. Islands are vulnerable as they are often isolated, have scarce resources and face significant constraints in terms of development potential. Singapore is not isolated as an island-state due to its geographic endowment in the ASEAN region; instead the island-state is confronted with the need to develop in a sustainable manner. The necessary policies to preserve biodiversity[34] will never be achieved unless the policy community first recognizes the fundamental conflict between economic growth and biodiversity (Mills and Waite 2009). This calls for development policies which appreciate and consider the environment. Good public policies must be crafted to safeguard the environment by treating the root cause. If policies are unable to protect the environment, it is preferable that help is not rendered as a matter of course, as treating symptoms is not good medicine.

Over the past decades since independence, Singapore has attained high economic status from trade and economic development. A higher level of income from economic progress is likely to increase the utilization of the environment as a source of capital (Tan 2016a), with trade and economic development further aggravating environmental degradation (Tan 2016b). Of late, Singapore's pattern of growth has borne some resemblance to the Kuznets curve[35] in terms of how the island-state has handled environmental issues, attempting to save the flora and fauna while they are still healthy. For instance, Pasir Ris Park (on the northeast of the main island) is built around a mangrove swamp in an attempt to preserve the biodiversity in the vicinity. There have also been significant efforts towards conservation on the Southern Island of Sisters' Islands (it was designated as Singapore's first marine park[36] in 2014 due to its coral reefs, sandy shores, and seagrass areas) where space has been earmarked for a coral nursery[37] (a coral can be adopted for as little as SGD200.00), turtle hatchery, forest trails, and intertidal pools for the public to know more about conservation efforts.

Singapore must continue to maintain this momentum of environmentally friendly practices. The first policy recommendation is to implement carbon pricing via emissions trading;[38] so that when trading is made in conjunction with achieving renewables targets, investments toward renewables will be encouraged. A second recommendation concerns environmental taxes, which is a permutation of carbon pricing with carbon taxes blanketed on all polluting goods and services. The key outcome from both recommended policies is to re-invest the tax revenues toward the maintenance of the environment as a source and sink function (Thampapillai et al. 2010). For example, the tax revenues can be channelled to environmental conservation in the form of forest and marine preservation. If and when regulations to effectively sanction excessive emissions are imposed, Singapore may well be on a firmer track to becoming an environment conscious economy.

The infatuation with rank in several aspects of the island-state should be redirected toward non-measurable assets such as the environment. The environment should be measured as a source of capital (Tan 2016a) and internalized as a component of national income (Tan 2015). There are other policy aspects which can be improved, such as integrating trade (which includes tourism) and regional development policies into environmental policies. Singapore has offered human capital services (Tan and Savchenko 2016) to the ASEAN region and beyond but the transfer should also include sustainable ways of development. To consolidate Singapore's role as a leading island-state, the nation can lead in sustainable initiatives[39] which allow economic development to occur within fragile environmental boundaries and the threat of extreme events. This will help maintain the competitive edge of the island-nation and ensure continued demand for technical know-how from regional nations. But first, Singapore must focus on getting the domestic house in order before making itself useful to the region. The evidence of EIA cases in Section 3 is clear indication that care is being bestowed to the environment in light of development (that drives economic growth).

Notes

1 The 10 ASEAN nations include: Brunei Darussalam, Cambodia, Indonesia, Laos, Malaysia, Myanmar, the Philippines, Singapore, Thailand and Vietnam.
2 Asia is made up of 50 countries www.countries-ofthe-world.com/countries-of-asia.html which includes the Southeast Asia region.
3 Together with El Niño, rising greenhouse gas (GHG) emissions from economic activities has resulted in warmer summers (Hesterman 2011) and summer temperatures will have an irreversible rise over the next 20 to 60 years. This has also affected fruit yields of wine growers in Australia and New Zealand.
4 The forest fires have indirectly impacted the dairy industry in New Zealand when the supplier IOI Group was suspended due to illegal clearing of protected peat land in Indonesia. Please see www.stuff.co.nz/business/industries/80176264/fonterra-pke-supplier-banned-after-forest-fires-dairy-feed-price-may-rise (accessed May 28, 2016).
5 The Thai rice industry is facing another challenge in succession planning with an aging group of rice farmers, urgent measures have been drawn to attract younger farmers. See Ghosh (2015).
6 Please see www.telegraph.co.uk/news/2016/06/05/france-floods-caused-one-billion-euros-worth-of-damage/ and english.cri.cn/12394/2016/06/05/2561s929920.htm (accessed June 24, 2016).
7 www.theguardian.com/australia-news/2016/jun/03/queensland-and-nsw-braced-for-gales-and-up-to-300mm-of-rainfall (accessed June 24, 2017).
8 www.reuters.com/article/coal-australia-lanina-idUSL3N17V3ES (accessed May 28, 2016).
9 asean.org/asean/asean-structure/asean-community-councils/ (accessed May 28, 2016).
10 Sustainable tourism has been explored by Savage et al. (2004) and applied to the Singapore River but the success of tourism sustainability faces challenges in light of continued economic growth.
11 Land was first allocated for housing with Mr. Lim Kim San spearheading the development of public housing in the 1960s to address the critical shortage of housing.
12 Land reclamation of up to 4 hectares was being authorized by the Law Minister with larger areas requiring Parliamentary approval (Wong 1992).
13 The eastern suburbs of Marina Bay, Kallang, Siglap, Bedok and Changi were a result of land reclamation since independence (1960s). Please see Wong (1992).
14 The seven islands were Pulau Merlimau, Pulau Seraya, Pulau Ayer Merbau, Pulau Sakra, Pulau Ayer Chawan, and Pulau Pesek. Please see Figure 4, Hesp (1995).
15 Please refer to Figures 3, 4, and 5 in Hesp (1995).
16 Sentosa island had housed the Exxon oil refinery during the early days of independence and relocated to Jurong Island thereafter.
17 Pulau Sakeng is home to the last village in Singapore's Southern Islands (Seah 2016).
18 According to the Department of Statistics, Singapore www.singstat.gov.sg/statistics/latest-data (accessed May 28, 2016).
19 www.mnd.gov.sg/landuseplan/e-book/index.html (accessed May 28, 2016).
20 www.ura.gov.sg/uol/master-plan/view-master-plan/master-plan-2014/master-plan/Introduction.aspxm (accessed May 28, 2016).
21 Some coral colonies have been moved to the Kusu Island group which were in the way of a port development in the western part of Singapore island. Please see www.straitstimes.com/singapore/environment/singapore-spends-6m-to-relocate-corals-that-were-in-the-way-of-tuas-port (accessed May 28, 2016).

22 Under the UN Convention on the Law of the Sea (UNCLOS), reclamation aids the sovereignty in rights to economic zones and claims to territorial waters with entitlement eligibility within a 22-kilometer radius and a distance of 322 kilometers.
23 UNEP and GEAS (2014) had reported that the source of sand is typically imported into Singapore from Cambodia, Malaysia, and Thailand.
24 Dutch companies provided much of the expertise in dredging and mining – the Dutch connection began in the 60s when a United Nations (UN) team led by Dr. Albert Winsemius (Dutch national) was responsible for the economic development of Singapore. See UNDP Global Centre for Public Service Excellence (2015).
25 The Clean Air Act of 1971 and Water Pollution Control and Drainage Act from 1975 allowed an EIA to be imposed.
26 Please see http://blog.nus.edu.sg/wildlifereverse/2015/03/18/environmental-impact-assessment-eia-for-developers/ (accessed May 28, 2016).
27 A Member of Parliament Mr. Chen Show Mao had raised a EIA debate on the March 11, 2015. Please see www.wp.sg/cos-2015-debate-mnd-environmental-impact-assessment-mp-chen-show-mao/ (accessed May 28, 2016).
28 Seagrass provides a habitat for marine fishes in the shallow and intertidal regions of the island.
29 Please see www.wildsingapore.com/news/20070708/070815-0.htm and http://wildfilms.blogspot.sg/2007/08/possibilities-of-truly-integrated.html (accessed May 28, 2016).
30 Please see http://thewip.net/2011/05/20/new-integrated-resorts-source-of-social-and-environmental-problems-in-singapore/ (accessed May 28, 2016).
31 Please see http://leafmonkey.blogspot.sg/2008/01/eia-of-sentosa-integrated-resort.html and http://developingsustainablyforabetterfuture.blogspot.sg/ (accessed May 28, 2016).
32 More information can be found here, www.lta.gov.sg/content/ltaweb/en/public-transport/projects/cross-island-line.html (accessed May 28. 2016).
33 Please see www.straitstimes.com/singapore/transport/ltas-environment-report-now-online and www.channelnewsasia.com/news/singapore/lta-releases-online/2532170.html (accessed May 28, 2016).
34 Cities are often developed around fertile soil and coincide with areas of high biodiversity.
35 The Kuznets curve depicts an inverted-U relationship between income per capita (development) and environmental degradation that is, degradation of the environment first rises then falls with increasing income per capita.
36 Please see www.straitstimes.com/singapore/sisters-islands-to-be-heart-of-marine-life-conservation (accessed May 28, 2016).
37 Please see www.straitstimes.com/singapore/environment/plant-a-coral-at-sisters-island-marine-park-for-200 (accessed May 28, 2016).
38 Buying and selling of carbon credits may be a quick and easy solution but it can give rise to a form of speculation which will not aid towards reduction of overall polluting gases' emissions. Classic equity markets are built on confidence and expectations for future cash flows. Financially, the market is designed for long-term financing, not short-term speculation. There must be mechanisms in the emissions trading market to police short-term speculations. In addition, what appears to be a certain commitment to the environment is not a radical change; hence, there must be procedures to balance consumption losses in selected sectors.
39 The objectives of emerging markets are boosting productivity and growth by lowering cost of transportation, improving energy availability, enhancing communications networks and distributing clean water. Singapore companies have taken the lead to address some of these as well as climate change, they are (selected) Sembcorp Industries, Banyan Tree Hotels and Resorts, Senoko Power, and Singtel.

References

Agence France-Presse. (2016). "El Niño's stormy sister La Nina looms," The Straits Times, Singapore, April 30, 2016, www.straitstimes.com/world/el-ninos-stormy-sister-la-nina-looms.

Albert, S., Grinham, A., Gibbes, B., Leon, J., and Church, J. (2016). "Sea-level rise has claimed five whole islands in the Pacific: First scientific evidence," The Conversation, May 7, 2016, http://theconversation.com/sea-level-rise-has-claimed-five-whole-islands-in-the-pacific-first-scientific-evidence-58511.

Arouff, J.P. (2015). "Mauritius revokes Bramer Bank licence, Prime Minister says Ponzi scheme found," Reuters, April 3, 2015, www.reuters.com/article/mauritius-banks-crime-idUSL6N0X00PA20150403.

Boyd, S.E., Limpenny, D.S., Rees, H.L., and Cooper, K.M. (2005). "The effects of marine sand and gravel extraction on the macrobenthos at a commercial dredging site (results 6 years post-dredging)," ICES Journal of Marine Science, Vol. 62, pp. 145–162.

Bradshaw, C.J.A., Giam, X., and Sodhi, N.S. (2010). "Evaluating the relative environmental impact of countries," PLoS ONE, Vol. 5, No. 5, p. e10440.

Chia, S.L. (1998). "Coastal management in Singapore: Institutional arrangements and implementation," Ocean & Coastal Management, Vol. 38, No. 2, pp. 111–118.

Chua, B.H. (2005). "Liberalization without democratization: Singapore in the next decade," *Southeast Asian responses to globalization: Restructuring governance and deepening democracy*, Loh, F.K.W and Ojendal, J. (Eds.), Singapore: Institute of Southeast Asian Studies and Nordic Institute of Asian Studies, pp. 57–82.

Coconuts Bangkok. (2016). "Drought desperation: Bangkok officially cuts Songkran short to save water," March 15, 2016, http://bangkok.coconuts.co/2016/03/15/drought-desperation-bangkok-officially-cuts-songkran-short-save-water.

Cook, A., Watkins, A.B., Trewin, B., and Ganter, C. (2016). "El Niño is over, but has left mark across the world," IFLScience, May 29, 2016, www.iflscience.com/environment/el-ni-o-over-has-left-its-mark-across-world.

Connell, J. (2013). Islands at risk? *Environments, economies and contemporary change*. Cheltenham: Edward Elgar.

Desprez, M., Pearce, B., and Le Bot, S. (2010). "The biological impact of overflowing sands around a marine aggregate extraction site: Dieppe (eastern English Channel)," ICES Journal of Marine Science, Vol. 67, No. 2, pp. 270–277.

Duncan, R. (Ed.) (2011). *The political economy of economic reform in the Pacific*. Mandaluyong City, Manila, Philippines: Asian Development Bank.

Ewel, K., John, B., Thomas, C., and Zheng, S. (1998). "Variation in environmental characteristics and vegetation in high-rainfall mangrove forests, Kosrae, Micronesia," Global Ecology & Biogeography Letters, Vol. 7, No. 1, pp. 49–56.

Farnsworth, E. (1998). "Issues of spatial, taxonomic and temporal scale in delineating links between mangrove diversity and ecosystem function," Global Ecology & Biogeography Letters, Vol. 7, No. 1, pp. 15–25.

Frankel, J. (2008). "Environmental Effects of International Trade," Expert Report No. 31 to Sweden's Globalisation Council, Sweden.

Friess, D. (2015). "Assessing the value of Singapore's mangrove swamps," Straits Times, February 21, 2015, www.straitstimes.com/opinion/assessing-the-value-of-singapores-mangrove-swamps.

Ghosh, N. (2015). "Empty rice bowl looms as Thai farmers grow older," The Straits Times, Singapore, August 15, 2015, www.straitstimes.com/opinion/empty-rice-bowl-looms-as-thai-farmers-grow-older.

Hamilton-Hart, N. (2006). "Singapore's climate change policy: The limits of learning," Contemporary Southeast Asia: A Journal of International and Strategic Affairs, Vol. 28, No. 3, pp. 363–384.

Harris, J.M. (2004). "Trade and the environment," *Environmental and natural resource economics: A contemporary approach*. Global Development and Environment Institute, Tufts University, Medford, US.

Hesp, P.A. (1995). "The Environmental impact assessment process in Singapore with particular respect to coastal environments and the role of NGOs," Journal of Coastal Conservation, Vol. 1, No. 2, pp. 135–144.

Hesterman, D. (2011). "Climate study: Permanently hotter summers predicted in 20 years," Stanford Report, June 6, 2011, http://news.stanford.edu/news/2011/june/permanent-hotter-summers-060611.html.

Hsiang, L.L. (2000). "Mangrove conservation in Singapore: A physical or a psychological impossibility?," Biodiversity & Conservation, Vol. 9, No. 3, pp. 309–332.

Intergovernmental Panel on Climate Change (IPCC). (2013). "Summary for Policymakers," *Climate change 2013: The physical science basis, Contribution of Working Group I to the Fifth Assessment Report of the Intergovernmental Panel on Climate Change*, Stocker, T.F., Qin, D., Plattner, G.-K., Tignor, M., Allen, S.K., Boschung, J., Nauels, A., Xia, Y., Bex, V., and Midgley, P.M. (Eds.), Cambridge and New York: Cambridge University Press, Chapter 3, pp. 257–259.

Koh, T., and Lin, J. (2006). "The land reclamation case: Thoughts and reflections," Singapore Year Book of International Law and Contributors, Vol. 10, pp. 1–7.

Krause, C., Diesing, M., and Arlt, G. (2010). "The physical and biological impact of sand extraction: A case study of the western Baltic Sea," Journal of Coastal Research, Vol. 51, pp. 215–226.

Lablache, J. (2015). "Towards a better management of waste water: Seychelles intensifies plan for a Sanitation master plan," Seychelles News Agency, April 6, 2015, www.seychellesnewsagency.com/

articles/2704/Towards+a+better+management+of+waste+water+Seychelles+intensifies+plan+for+a+Sanitation+master+plan.

Lim, L. (2002). "Bigger Singapore from sea and swamp," The Straits Times, Singapore, March 30, 2002.

Lopez, R. (1994). "The environment as a factor of production: The effects of economic growth and trade liberalization," Journal of Environmental Economics and Management, Vol. 27, No. 2, pp. 163–184.

Mills, J.H. and Waite, T.A. (2009) "Economic prosperity, biodiversity conservation, and the environmental Kuznets curve," Ecological Economics, Vol. 68, No. 7, pp. 2087–2095.

Nurse, L.A., Graham, S., Hay, J.E., Suarez, A.G., Wong, P.P., Briguglio, L., and Ragoonaden, S. (2001). "Small island states," Climate Change, pp. 843–875.

Perry, M. and Teng, T.S. (1999). "An overview of trends related to environmental reporting in Singapore," Environmental Management and Health, Vol. 10, No. 5, pp. 310–320.

Savage, V.R., Huang, S., and Chang, T.C. (2004) "The Singapore River thematic zone: Sustainable tourism in an urban context," The Geographical Journal, Vol. 170, No. 3, pp. 212–225.

Seah, P. (2016). "Preserving tangible links to the past," Institute of Policy Studies Commons, IPS, April 15, 2016.

Simmons, B. (2016). "Bangkok Songkran to be cut to 3 days per BMA," Thailand Discovery, March 15, 2016, www.thailanddiscovery.info/bangkok-songkran-cut-3-days-per-bma/.

Soeriaatmadja, W. (2015). "Indonesia correspondent in Jakarta Jakarta gears up for fight against forest blazes," The Straits Times, August 1, 2015, www.straitstimes.com/asia/se-asia/jakarta-gears-up-for-fight-against-forest-blazes.

Sparke, M., Sidaway, J.D., Bunnell, T., and Grundy-Warr, C. (2004). "Triangulating the borderless world: Geographies of power in the Indonesia–Malaysia–Singapore growth triangle," Transactions of the Institute of British Geographers, Vol. 29, No. 4, pp. 485–498.

Tan, P.N.S. (1993). "Environmental management and infrastructure-the Singapore experience," In: Proceedings Leadership Seminar on Environmental and Urban Management in South East Asia, August 10–13, Malaysia.

Tan, S. (2015). "Sustainable development: An empirical illustration for Saudi Arabia," The Journal of Developing Areas, Vol. 49, No. 6, pp. 517–529.

Tan, S. (2016a). "Framework for valuing the utilization of the environment," International Journal of Social Economics, Vol. 43, No. 6, pp. 1–26.

Tan, S. (2016b). "Potential environmental impacts of the Australia–South Korea free trade agreement and fiscal intervention," *Critical issues in environmental taxation, volume XVII, green fiscal reform for a sustainable future: Reform, innovation and renewable energy*, Stoianoff, N.P., Kreiser, L., Butcher, B., Milne, J.E., and Ashiabor, H. (Eds.), Cheltenham, UK and Northampton, MA: Edward Elgar, Chapter 7, pp. 109–123.

Tan, S. and Lai, A. (2016). "Economic repercussions of extreme events for an island nation: Case of Singapore," The Singapore Economic Review, Vol. 61, No. 1, pp. 1–19.

Tan, S. and Savchenko, A. (2016). "Understanding Singapore's development and its relevance to the free port of Vladivostok," *Fostering international cooperation in the development of Pacific Russia*, Huang, J., and Korolev, A. (Eds.), the Netherlands: Palgrave Macmillan, Chapter 9, pp. 223–242.

Thampapillai, D.J., Wu, X. and Tan, S. (2010). "Fiscal balance: Environmental taxes and investments," Journal of Natural Resources Policy Research, Vol. 2, No. 2, pp. 137–147.

The Economist. (2015). "Such quantities of sand," February 28, 2015, www.economist.com/news/asia/21645221-asias-mania-reclaiming-land-sea-spawns-mounting-problems-such-quantities-sand.

Turner, I.M. (1994). "Primary and secondary forest," *A first look at biodiversity in Singapore*, Wee, Y.C. and Ng, P.K.L. (Eds.), Singapore: National Council on the Environment, pp. 11–21.

Tyrrell, N. and Dommenget, D. (2015). "The tropical steam-engine: How does El Niño warm the entire globe?," The Conversation, September 30, 2015, http://theconversation.com/the-tropical-steam-engine-how-does-el-nino-warm-the-entire-globe-47865.

United Nations Economic and Social Commission for Asia and the Pacific (UN ESCAP), United Nations Environment Programme (UNEP), United Nations University (UNU), and Institute for Global and Environmental Strategies (IGES). (2016). Transformations for Sustainable Development: Promoting Environmental Sustainability in Asia and the Pacific, Bangkok, Thailand.

United Nations Environment Programme (UNEP) and Global Environment Alert Service (GEAS). (2014). "Sand, rarer than one thinks," March 2014, www.unep.org/pdf/UNEP_GEAS_March_2014.pdf.

UNDP Global Centre for Public Service Excellence. (2015). *UNDP and the making of Singapore's public service: Lessons from Albert Winsemius*. Singapore: Global Centre for Public Service Excellence.

US-ASEAN Business Council (2014). "ASEAN matters for America," East-West Centre and The Institute of Southeast Asian Studies, Asiamattersforamerica.org.
Valentine, S.V. (2015). "What lurks below the surface? Exploring the caveats of sea level rise economic impact assessments," Sustainability Science, Vol. 10, No. 1, pp. 139–147.
Waller, E. (1993). "Singapore's undeveloped offshore islands: How much land should be developed," Environmental Issues in Development and Conservation, Proceedings of a Conference, Vol. 12, pp. 63–86.
Woodroffe, C.D. (1995). "Response of tide-dominated mangrove shorelines in Northern Australia to anticipated sea-level rise," Earth Surface Processes and Landforms, Vol. 20, No. 1, pp. 65–85.
Wong, P.P. (1992). "The newly reclaimed land," *Physical adjustments in a changing landscape*, Gupta, A. and Pitts, J. (Eds.), Singapore: Singapore University Press, pp. 243–258.
Wong, P.P. (1998). "Coastal tourism development in Southeast Asia: Relevance and lessons for coastal zone management," Ocean & Coastal Management, Vol. 38, No. 2, pp. 89–109.
Yang, S., Lim, R.L., Sheue, C.R., and Yong, J.W. (2011). "The current status of mangrove forests in Singapore," In: Proceedings of the "Nature conservation for a sustainable Singapore" conference (Vol. 16) October 2011.

6

Climate change and water scarcity: growing risks for agricultural based economies in South Asia

Farzad Taheripour, Thomas W. Hertel, Badri Narayanan Gopalakrishnan, Sebnem Sahin, Anil Markandya, Bijon Kumer Mitra and Vivek Prasad

Introduction

Economies of South Asia have been growing relatively rapidly in recent years. The major economies of this region, including Bangladesh, India, Nepal, Pakistan, and Sri Lanka, have had average growth rates of 6 percent, 7.2 percent, 4.5 percent, 4.2 percent, and 5.6 percent, respectively between 2000 and 2015. During this period, the population has also continued to increase in these countries by 1.3 percent, 1.4 percent, 1.2 percent, 2.1 percent, and 0.8 percent on average per year, correspondingly. Population growth, coupled with economic growth, will translate into strong growth in food demand and hence in crop production in South Asia. Given that about 60 percent of crops produced in this region are irrigated, this will likely require a major expansion in demand for water for irrigation, assuming there is no major improvement in water use efficiency in irrigation.

Growing demand for irrigation, when coupled with industrial, residential, and commercial demands for water, is projected to result in intense competition for water in South Asia, particularly in India and Pakistan (UNESCO 2012, Rosegrant et al. 2013, and Rodriguez et al. 2013). However, the intensity of this competition will not be uniform across the different River Basins (RB) and Agro Ecological Zones (AEZs) of South Asia. In particular, in warmer and dryer AEZs, climate change may increase demand for irrigation as an adaptation strategy to higher temperatures and volatile weather conditions. On the other hand, in some AEZs, climate change may positively affect rain fed crop yields, and hence reduce demand for irrigation and weaken intensity of water scarcity. Therefore, while adoption of more irrigation is commonly suggested as an important alternative response to climate change, changes in water scarcity (either due to expansion in demand for water in non-agricultural uses, increase in population, higher demand for food, lack of water infrastructure, or induced by climate change itself) can affect, differentially, both the supply of water and the demand for additional irrigation in agriculture across AEZs.

This chapter uses an advanced computable general equilibrium (CGE) model in combination with biophysical data on land cover, harvested area, crop production, water used in irrigation, crop yield responses to climate change, and water scarcity measures to examine: (1) the consequences of climate change for South Asia's agricultural and food products; (2) the extent to which water scarcity can affect the irrigation adoption and demand for water across South Asia; and (3) how water scarcity, climate change, and trade jointly alter land use changes in this part of the world. This study covers the period from 2011 (base year) to 2050.

Many papers have studied the impacts of climate change on crop yields and food security (e.g., Lobell et al. 2008 and Nelson et al. 2010). These studies demonstrate how changes in climate variables affect food security across the world. However, they do not provide a clear picture on the interactions between climate change, crop yield, and water scarcity. More recent papers (e.g., Willis et al. 2014 and Marshall et al. 2014) have taken into account these interactions and shown that, while climate change can induce incentives for irrigation, water scarcity may limit the extent to which irrigation adoption can be implemented. Although these papers and the earlier work in this area provide valuable economic and biophysical analyses of the impacts of climate change for crop production and food security, they ignore the interplay between climate change and international trade. Some papers have examined the interaction between trade and climate change. For example, Reilly et al. (2002) have shown that trade can improve food security in regions in which crop production will be negatively affected by climate change factors. This paper and its successors (e.g., Baldos and Hertel 2015) usually ignore water scarcity induced by climate change and/or economic factors. In a recent paper, Liu et al. (2014) have shown that trade can mitigate the consequences of future irrigation shortfalls in regions where water scarcity threatens food security. However, this paper ignores the impacts of climate change on crop yields in the presence of water scarcity.

This chapter aims to enhance the existing literature by developing an analytical framework, allowing us to examine the interactions between climate change, crop yield, water scarcity, and trade, and their implications for South Asian economies. In what follows, we first introduce our modeling framework and the database used. Then, selected scenarios are analyzed and presented. The next section describes the numerical results, followed by the conclusion.

Modeling framework and its background

Many studies have developed and used CGE models to study the economic and environmental consequences of climate change, water scarcity, and water management. An early work in this area developed by Berck et al. (1991) explicitly introduced water in a small single-region CGE model to examine the economic impacts of water shortage in the San Joaquin Valley in California. Following this initial work, several authors included water into a number of CGE models to perform an economic analysis of water management and policy. Fadali et al. (2012) have listed many of these models. These models, which have been used in various applications, carry several common features including but not limited to: (1) incorporation of water as an input in the production functions of crop sectors;[1] (2) examination of water issues in a small region or a river basin;[2] (3) use of water supply as an exogenous variable in the CGE models;[3] (4) representation of water as a sluggish endowment with limited mobility;[4] and (5) lack of distinction between surface and ground water[5] in global models.

The CGE modeling framework developed and used in this research (GTA-BIO-W) extends the above common characteristics in several ways. The GTAP-BIO-W is an advanced version of the standard GTAP model originally developed by Hertel (1997). Several publications document the main features of the GTAP-BIO-W model and its background (Taheripour et al. 2013a, 2013b, Liu et al. 2014, 2016, and Taheripour et al. 2016). It is a static CGE model which combines economic and biophysical information on land and water. It is designed to examine the nexus between agricultural activities, industrial and energy sectors, and trade, in the presence of

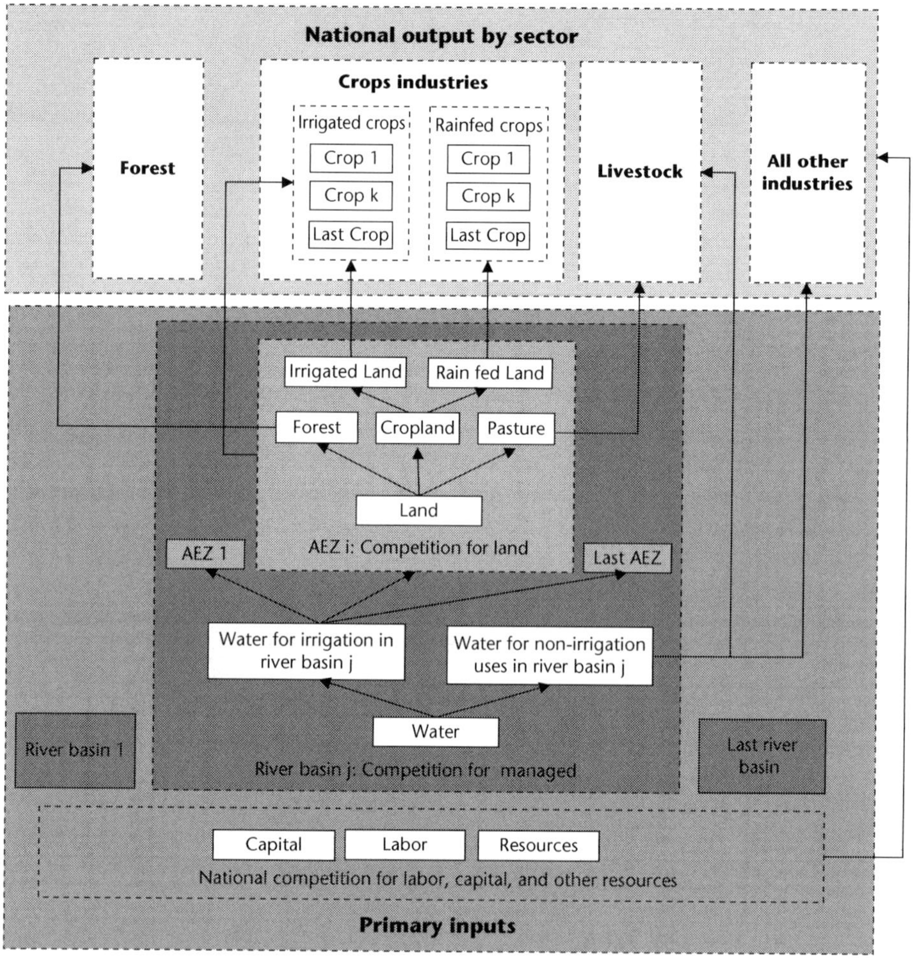

Figure 6.1 Structure of the GTAP-BIO-W static model

Source: Author.

climate change and water scarcity by region, at a global scale. The main structure of the GTAP-BIO-W model is presented in Figure 6.1. As shown in this figure, the GTAP-BIO-W model carries the following major advantages compared to the other existing global water-CGE models:

1 It is the first global CGE model that explicitly traces water by country at the river basin level and by Agro-Ecological Zones (AEZs). A large river basin could serve several AEZs.
2 It incorporates water into the production function of all economic activities, including crops, livestock, industries, and water utility services. Therefore, all economic activities compete for water.
3 Unlike all other existing CGE models, this model distinguishes between rain fed and irrigated crops to better capture the links between demands for irrigation and food.
4 The nested Constant Elasticity of Substitution (CES) production functions are used in this model.[6] Hence, it allows the user to examine alternative assumptions on substitution between water and other inputs, in particular for capital and land.

5 This model takes into account heterogeneity[7] in the price of water and traces demand for and supply of water by country at the river basin level, by AEZ. This means that the marginal value of water could be different at different places and across uses.

6 Unlike all other CGE models, it uses a nested Constant Elasticity of Transformation (CET) functional form to model the supply side of water. This is a consistent way to represent real world observations. As explained in this chapter, the data and modelling structure take into account the real world rigidities. While some adjustment of water use across sectors is possible, it is by no means freely mobile like other mobile inputs, such as labor or capital. The use of CET is a standard method to model a sluggish input like water, which cannot move freely across uses and across regions.

Benchmark database used

The database developed for this research is a modified version of the GTAP (Global Trade Analysis Project) database Release 9 which represents the world economy in 2011 (Narayanan et al. 2015). This database is a publicly available and fully documented economic dataset, which is constructed by balancing various data components from different sources across the world, including, but not limited to: (1) a bilateral trade dataset obtained from the United Nations Commodity Trade dataset; (2) a tariff dataset obtained from the MacMAP database developed by the International Trade Center; (3) a macro-economic dataset obtained from the World Bank; (4) a dataset on agricultural production and domestic support for several countries obtained from the Organisation for Economic Co-operation and Development; and finally (5) a dataset that includes national Input-Output (I-O) tables collected by several researchers across the world, usually constructed by their national statistical agencies. The GTAP database is the only available database that provides input-output tables for a wide range of countries and is utilized by thousands of researchers worldwide. It is a key input into many contemporary applied general equilibrium analyses of global economic issues.

Several modifications are made in this GTAP standard database to make it suitable for this research. The first major modification divides crop sectors into irrigated and rain fed categories according to the approach introduced by Taheripour et al. (2013a). The second important modification follows Taheripour et al. (2013b), Liu et al. (2016), and Taheripour et al. (2016) to enhance the standard GTAP database in representing the consumption of water in its alternative uses and supply of water by river basin. The third major modification divides the electricity sector of the standard GTAP database into two distinct electricity sectors: hydro and non-hydroelectric power. The last important modification, following Taheripour et al. (2007), brings biofuels into the database. In what follows we introduce some key aspects of this database with major attention to land, water, and crop production.

Land resources

Table 6.1 represents distribution of cropland in South Asia. It shows that cropland in South Asia is scattered across different AEZs. Croplands of Bangladesh are exclusively located only in AEZ4 and AEZ5, with rich moisture and long length of growing period. About 23 percent of India's cropland are distributed among dry AEZs, with short length of growing period (i.e., AEZs: 1, 2, 7, 8, 13, and 14). The rest of India's cropland (77 percent) is distributed among the rich, moist AEZs with long length of growing period. In Nepal, land is scattered across several non-dry AEZs. Land in Sri Lanka is divided among AEZ4, AEZ5, and AEZ6, which again are non-dry. Unlike Bangladesh, India, Nepal, and Sri Lanka, available cropland in Pakistan and the

Table 6.1 Distribution of cropland among AEZs in South Asia

AEZ	*Bangladesh*	*India*	*Nepal*	*Pakistan*	*Sri Lanka*	*Rest of South Asia*	*South Asia*
AEZ1	0.0	1.6	0.0	14.5	0.0	0.0	2.8
AEZ2	0.0	7.8	0.0	0.0	0.0	0.0	6.1
AEZ3	0.0	44.0	4.2	0.0	2.0	0.0	34.5
AEZ4	22.8	18.2	35.9	0.0	17.5	0.0	15.9
AEZ5	77.2	3.8	4.2	0.0	14.2	0.0	6.5
AEZ6	0.0	1.1	0.0	0.0	66.3	0.0	1.5
AEZ7	0.0	3.7	0.0	56.4	0.0	14.2	9.6
AEZ8	0.0	10.1	0.0	7.8	0.0	66.7	11.6
AEZ9	0.0	7.8	0.0	5.4	0.0	1.5	6.8
AEZ10	0.0	0.8	16.7	9.7	0.0	1.1	1.9
AEZ11	0.0	0.7	25.4	3.0	0.0	1.8	1.3
AEZ12	0.0	0.4	11.0	2.8	0.0	0.4	0.8
AEZ13	0.0	0.0	0.2	0.1	0.0	9.8	0.4
AEZ14	0.0	0.0	0.6	0.3	0.0	4.3	0.2
AEZ15	0.0	0.0	1.4	0.0	0.0	0.0	0.1
AEZ16	0.0	0.0	0.4	0.0	0.0	0.2	0.0
AEZ17	0.0	0.0	0.0	0.0	0.0	0.0	0.0
AEZ18	0.0	0.0	0.0	0.0	0.0	0.0	0.0
Total	100.0	100.0	100.0	100.0	100.0	100.0	100.0

Source: GTAP-BIO-W database version 11.

Rest of South Asia is distributed across dry AEZs (i.e., AEZs: 1, 2, 7, 8, 13, and 14). In Pakistan, 79 percent of the cropland is located in dry AEZs. The corresponding share in the Rest of South Asia is about 95 percent. Hence, Pakistan and the Rest South Asia will be faced with major challenges to produce food, if water is not available for irrigation.

In addition to the distribution of land resources by AEZ, our database represents the distribution of these resources by river basin. Three large river basins, including those of the Brahmaputra, Ganges, and Others (an aggregate of several basins), serve all of Bangladesh in our database. The shares of the first two basins in the total harvested area of Bangladesh were about 45.3 percent and 47.6 percent in 2011. Two river basins, those of the Ganges and the Indus, serve Nepal. About 99 percent of harvested area in Nepal belongs to the Ganges basin. Pakistan is divided among three river basins: the Indus, Western Asia, and Other basins. However, the Indus basin serves 98 percent of the total harvested area of Pakistan. Sri Lanka is served by its main river basin, named the Sri Lanka[8] basin. Several river basins, including the Amudarja, Brahmaputra, Indus and Western Asia basins, serve the Rest of South Asia. The only country which is supported by several river basins is India. Figure 6.2 represents these basins and their shares in total harvested area of India in 2011. As shown in this figure, the Ganges, Krishna, and Indus basins have the largest shares (34 percent, 11.4 percent and 11.2 percent, respectively) in total harvested area of India. Figure 6.3 represents distribution of available land (forest, pasture and cropland) in India by river basin.

Water resources

In 2011, water withdrawal from surface and underground sources in Bangladesh, India, Nepal, Pakistan, Sri Lanka, and the Rest of South Asia was about 38.4 billion cubic meters (BCM),

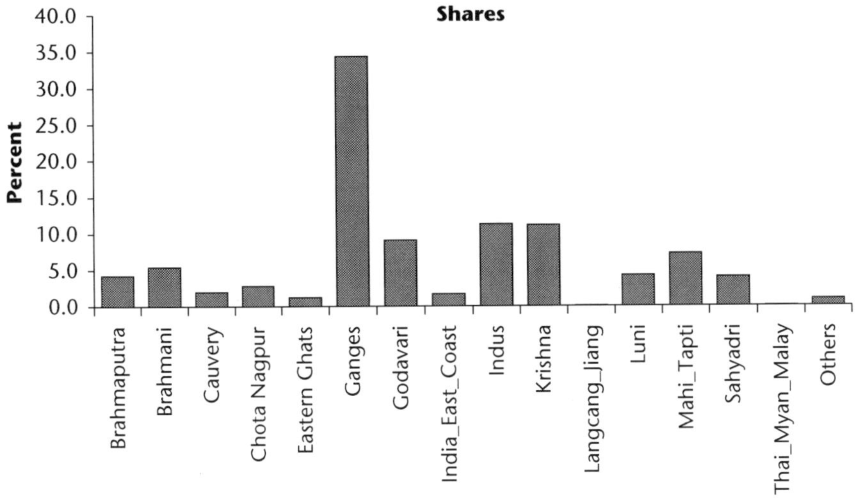

Figure 6.2 Distribution of India's harvested area by river basin.

Source: GTAP-BIO-W database version 11.

830 BCM, 8.3 BCM, 190.2 BCM, 7.8 BCM, and 17.4 BCM, respectively. Hence, India and Pakistan were the main users of water in South Asia. Water is used mainly in agricultural activities in South Asia, except for Sri Lanka. As shown in Figure 6.4, the share of agriculture in total water withdrawal was more than 80 percent everywhere in South Asia in 2011, except for Sri Lanka. In that country, the share of agriculture in water withdrawal was 51.3 percent. This is because Sri Lanka has limited irrigated cropland. In Bangladesh and Sri Lanka, water is used for rice. In other regions, water is mainly used to produce rice and wheat.

Figure 6.5 depicts two panels to show distribution of water used for irrigation by river basin in South Asia. The first panel represents this distribution in India. In India, the shares of the Ganges, Indus, Krishna, and Godavari in water withdrawal were about 40.4 percent, 17.7 percent, 8.6 percent and 8 percent in 2011. The second panel indicates distribution of water in other countries of South Asia by river basin. As shown in this panel, Bangladesh takes water mainly from the Ganges and Brahmaputra basins. Nepal relies on the Ganges and Pakistan on the Indus river basins.

Water withdrawal is divided into surface and underground categories in our database. Figure 6.6 represents the share of these two categories in total water withdrawal by river basin in South Asia. As shown in this figure, the share of underground water in some river basins in India is relatively large, for example, these include: 47 percent in Brahmari; 46 percent in Mahi Tapi; 40 percent in Sahyadri Ghats; 36 percent in Godavari; and 34 percent in Ganges. The share of underground water withdrawal in Pakistan and Bangladesh are 15 percent and 11 percent, respectively. The magnitude of this share is limited in other countries of South Asia.

Of global production in 2011, South Asia accounted for 31.2 percent of rice, 19.4 percent of sugar crops, and 16.9 percent of wheat. The shares of South Asia in other crop categories were less than 10 percent in this year. India is the largest crop producer in South Asia and is a relatively important crop producer at the global scale. It accounted for 69.6 percent of rice, 73.5 percent of wheat, 82.6 percent coarse grains, 91.6 percent of oilseeds, 84.3 percent of sugar crops, and 87.9 percent of other crops produced in South Asia in 2011. In general, the shares of other countries in crops produced in South Asia are not large. Bangladesh has only a large share in rice

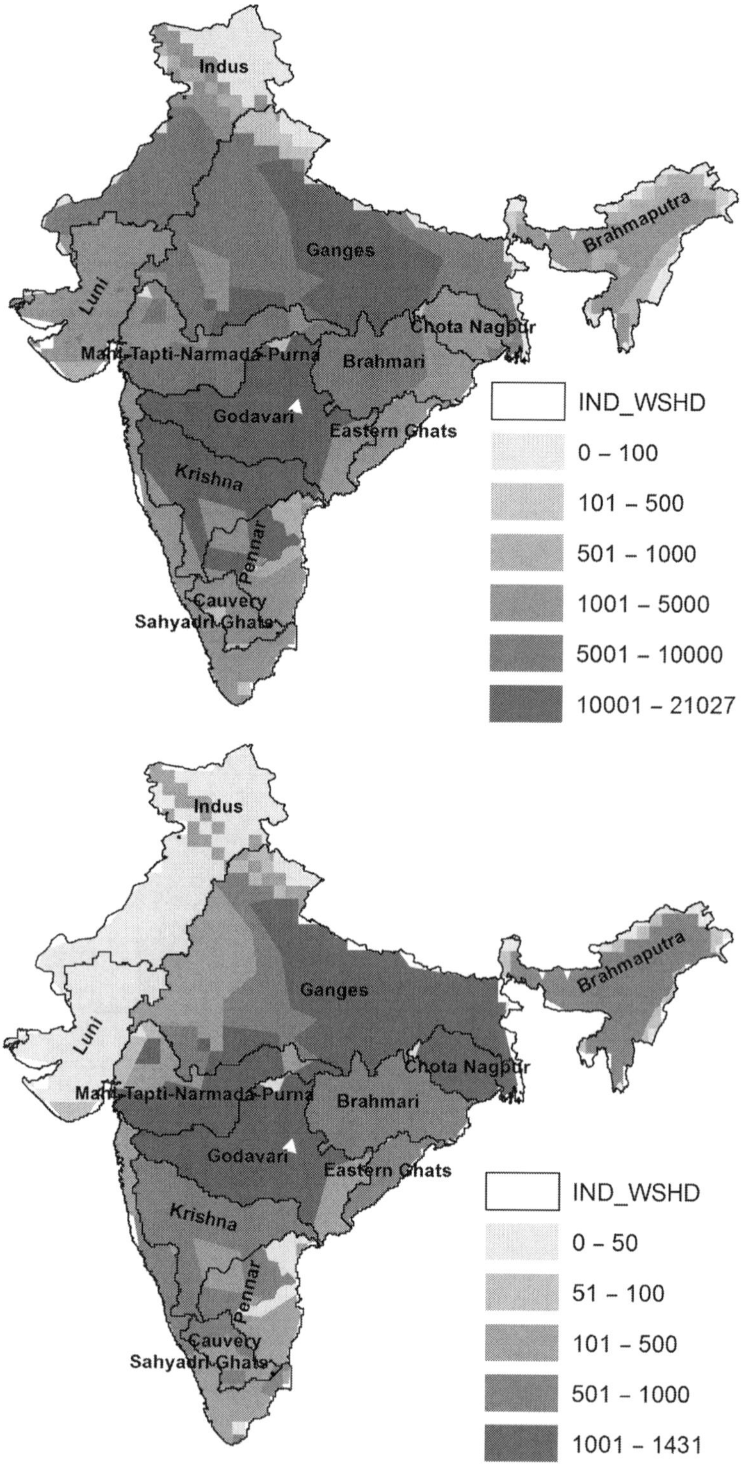

Figure 6.3 Distribution of available land in India by river basin

Source: GTAP-BIO-W database version 11.

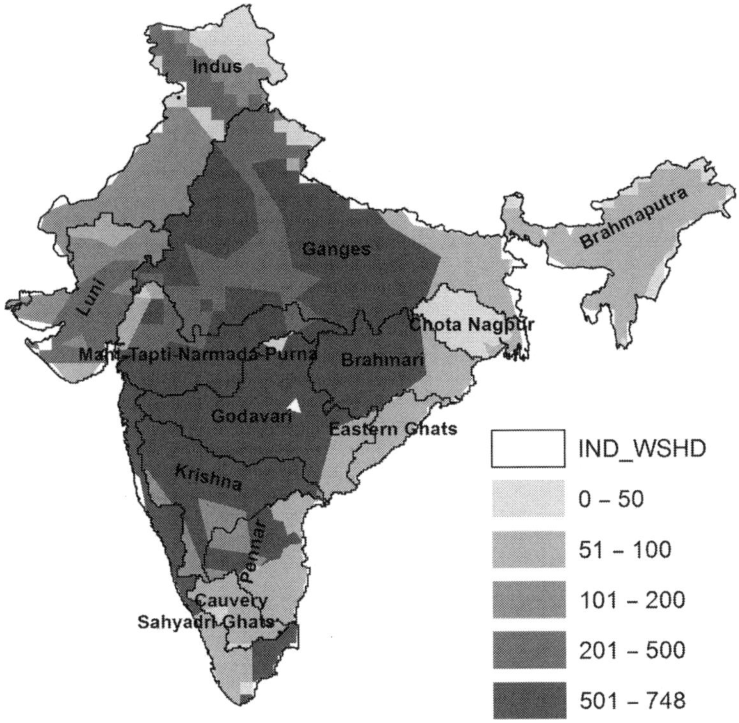

Figure 6.3 (Continued).

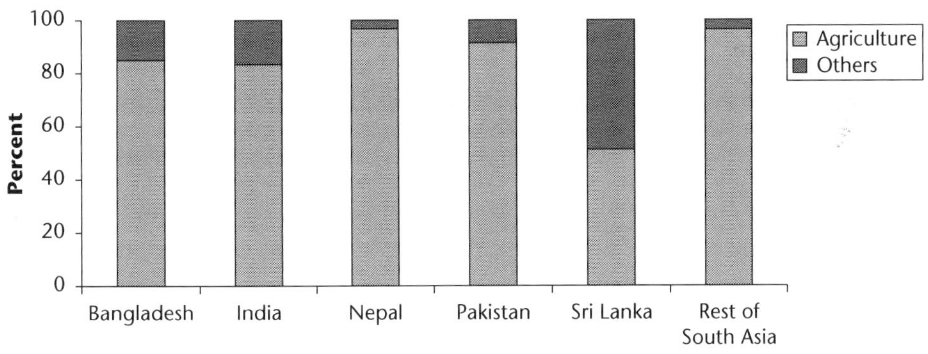

Figure 6.4 Shares of agricultural and non-agricultural uses in water withdrawal in South Asia in 2011

Source: GTAP-BIO-W database version 11.

(22.3 percent) and Pakistan has considerable shares in wheat (21.3 percent), coarse grains (9.2 percent), and oilseeds (13.6 percent).

While South Asia is a relatively large crop producer at the global scale, it does not trade crops extensively with the rest of the world. Crops produced in this region, except for rice, are mainly used locally. In other words, South Asia has a weak trade relationship with the rest of the world in commodity markets; even within the region, cross border linkages are relatively weak. This weak

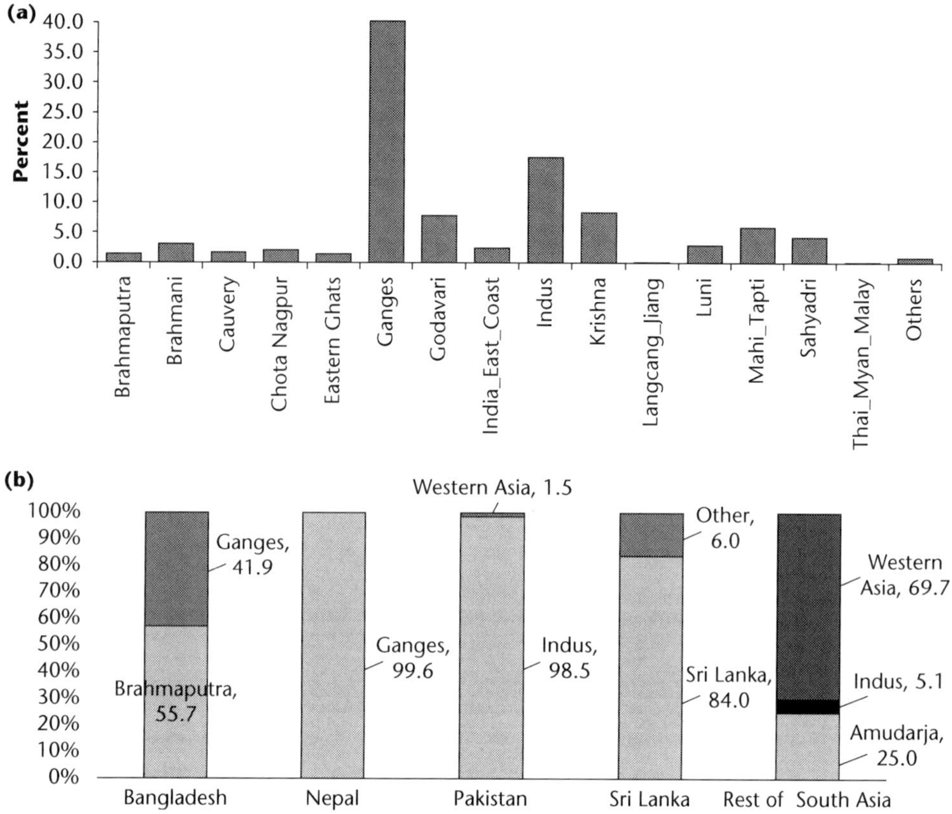

Figure 6.5 (a) Distribution of water withdrawal in India by river basin; (b) Distribution of water withdrawal in other countries of South Asia by river basin

Source: GTAP-BIO-W database version 11.

relationship could harm food security of South Asia in response to extreme climate events, as we will discuss later.

Crops are produced with relatively low yields in South Asia. In 2011, yields in this region were about: 3.7 tons per hectare (t/ha) for rice; 2.9 (t/ha) for wheat; 1.7 (t/ha) for coarse grains; 1.5 (t/ha) for oilseeds, 66.1 (t/ha) for sugar crops; and 5.3 (t/ha) for other crops. These yields were significantly lower than their corresponding figures (except for wheat and sugar crops) for the rest of the world in this year. For example, rice and coarse gain yields in South Asia were about 76 percent and 45 percent of their corresponding yields in the rest of the world. While yields are generally lower in South Asia compared with the rest of the world, some of them are far below the yields of advanced economies. For example, in 2011, yields in the USA over South Asia were about: 8.0 over 3.7 (t/ha) for rice; 8.7 over 1.7 (t/ha) for coarse grains; 2.8 (t/ha) over 1.5 for oilseeds; and 17 over 5.3 (t/ha) for other crops.

Key economy-wide factors

Finally, in this section we review some macro aspects of economies in South Asia, as shown in Table 6.2. This table shows that India is the largest economy of South Asia, with a GDP of

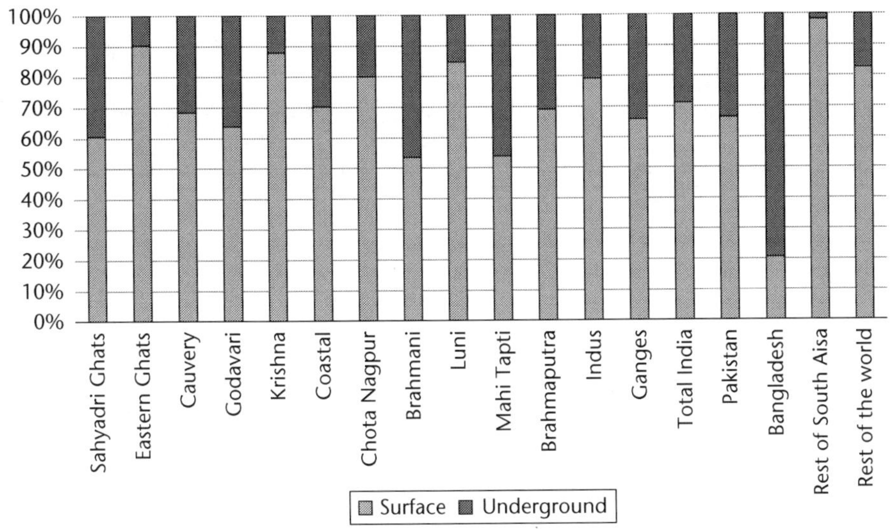

Figure 6.6 Shares of surface and underground water in total water withdrawal in South Asia by river basin

Source: GTAP-BIO-W database version 11.

Table 6.2 Major macro figures in 2011

Description	*Bangladesh*	*India*	*Nepal*	*Pakistan*	*Sri Lanka*	*Rest of South Asia*	*Rest of the World*
GDP (current US billion $)	**112**	**1,882**	**19**	**214**	**59**	**22**	**69,171**
Agriculture (% of GDP)	15.9	18.7	32.6	12.0	21.4	31.7	3.9
Industry (% of GDP)	34.9	29.3	16.5	33.2	32.1	15.1	33.3
Services (% of GDP)	49.2	52.0	50.9	54.8	46.5	53.2	62.8
Total of sectors	**100**	**100**	**100**	**100**	**100**	**100**	**100**
Household exp. (% of GDP)	75.8	62.4	87.2	88.0	73.5	101.5	58.7
Investment (% of GDP)	24.4	33.7	24.4	13.6	28.4	23.4	23.2
Government exp. (% of GDP)	5.6	12.1	10.9	10.6	15.5	15.0	17.8
Export (% of GDP)	25.2	19.9	7.6	14.5	20.9	17.1	28.5
Imports (% of GDP)	−31.0	−28.1	−30.1	−26.6	−38.3	−57.1	−28.2
Total of users	**100**	**100**	**100**	**100**	**100**	**100**	**100**

Source: GTAP database version 11.

$1.88 trillion in 2011. The second largest economy in this region is Pakistan with a GDP of $214 billion, followed by Bangladesh, with a GDP of $112 billion. Table 6.2 shows that Sri Lanka, Nepal, and the Rest of South Asia are very small economies with limited national incomes. The gross domestic products of these countries were about $59 billion, $19 billion, and $22 billion in 2011. This table also shows the distribution of GDP across major sectors (including agriculture, industry, and services), and the distribution of GDP among different expenditure groups (including private consumption, government expenditure, investment, and exports) across the world. Table 6.2 indicates that the economies of South Asia have relatively similar production structures, shown by the distribution of GDP between agriculture, industry, and service sectors. In these economies, agriculture has a relatively large share of GDP (ranging from 12 percent in Pakistan to 31.7 percent in the Rest of South Asia) in 2011. The share of agriculture in the rest of the world was about 3.9 percent in this year. These figures confirm that economies of South Asia still rely heavily on agricultural activities. In general, the share of industrial activities in GDP is around 30 percent to 34 percent in economies of South Asia. The only exceptions are Nepal and the Rest of South Asia, with 16.5 percent and 15.1 percent for the share of industrial activities in total GDP. The share of services in GDP is around 50 percent in South Asia. This share is about 63 percent for the rest of the world.

Table 6.2 represents distribution of GDP across private consumption, government expenditure, investment, and exports by region in 2011 as well. This figure indicates that Bangladesh and Nepal had the largest and smallest export shares (25.2 percent and 7.6 percent, respectively) in South Asia in 2011. This shows that Nepal is not an exporting country. India and Pakistan had the largest and smallest investment shares (33.4 percent and 13.6 percent) in South Asia in 2011. This reveals that India is preparing for faster growth. Table 6.2 shows that the share of household expenditures in GDP is high among all economies of South Asia compared to the rest of the world, amounting to about 88 percent of GDP of Pakistan consumed by households in 2011, while the corresponding rate for the rest of the world was 58.7 percent. On the other hand, investment as a share of GDP varies widely, with one country (Pakistan) being below the rest of the world average, three being close to the rest of the world average (Bangladesh, Nepal and Rest of South Asia), and one (India) being well above the rest of the world average. Finally, Table 6.2 shows that the share of government expenditure in GDP in economies of South Asia was around 6 percent to 16 percent in 2011, lower than the corresponding figure for the rest of the world (about 18 percent).

Experiments undertaken

Two experiments were undertaken in this chapter. The first studied the impacts of climate change on crop yields in South Asia and their implications for demand for irrigation. The second experiment investigated the extent to which water scarcity could alter the results of the first experiment and examined the joint impacts of climate change and water scarcity on food production, land use changes, demand for water and their consequences for the economies of South Asia. These two experiments are introduced in the rest of this section. Both experiments are examined using the modeling framework introduced in earlier in this chapter.

Experiment I: Impacts of climate change on crop yields and demand for irrigation when water supply is unlimited

Changes in climate variables have direct and indirect impacts on crop yields. Several studies have projected the long-run impacts of climate change on crop yields for many climate scenarios at the global scale and also for South Asia (Lobell et al. 2008, Nelson et al. 2010, Parry et al. 2007, Field et al. 2014, Rosenzweig et al. 2014, Rajeevan 2013 and Khan et al. 2009). These studies indicate that the impacts of climate variables on crop yields vary by region, AEZ, crop type, and time and are very uncertain.[9] While the literature recognizes that the climate change will affect crop yields, the studies argue that climate change could increase climate extremes, thereby increasing demand for irrigation as an important adaptation strategy (Marshall et al. 2014, Parry et al. 2007, Field et al. 2014, and Khan et al. 2009). Irrigation could eliminate a portion of vulnerability in crop yields induced by extreme weather events, thereby mitigating some of the risks associated with climate change. Farmers switch to irrigation when the expected gains due to irrigation are higher than the costs of irrigation (including initial investment and operation costs). When climate change affects the yields in favor of the irrigated crops, farmers switch to irrigation if the yield difference is large enough to cover the costs of irrigation. The first experiment developed in this section examines the impacts of climate change on crop yields and their consequences for demand for irrigation, during the time period of 2011–2050.

To examine the impacts of climate change on crop yields in South Asia, we rely on the database developed by Rosenzweig et al. (2014). These authors have evaluated the impacts of climate change on crop yields for a wide range of climate scenarios and several GCM and crop models at the global scale, at a 0.5 by 0.5 degree resolution. Villoria et al. (2014) have made these simulation results accessible to the public on the GOSHARE website under the AgMIP tool (https://mygeohub.org/tools/agmip). In what follows, we use this tool to assess the impacts of climate change on rain fed and irrigated crop yields in South Asia for a representative climate scenario. To avoid extreme scenarios, we concentrate on the RCP 4.5, which represents an average climate change scenario.[10] Among the existing crop models, we used the LPJml model (Rosenzweig et al. 2014 and Villoria et al. 2014) to evaluate impacts of climate change on irrigated and rain fed crop yields, separately. To focus on major crops, we concentrate on five key crops: rice, wheat, corn, and soybeans and sugarcane. The following steps are followed to evaluate the impacts of climate change on selected crop yields at AEZ level by country for the period of 2011–2050:

I Projected yields for the desired scenario and the selected crop model are downloaded at the grid cell level for annual rain fed and irrigated crop data. We denote the projected yields with Y^{w}_{irjt}, where w stands for irrigation type (rain fed or irrigated), i is the grid cell index, r indicates country, j represents crop type, and t is the time index.
II Yields are aggregated to the AEZ level by country using their corresponding harvested areas in the base year. We show the results of this stage with Y^{w}_{zrjt}, where z stands for 18 AEZs.
III Trend lines are estimated for each individual crop in each AEZ by country to summarize the findings of the second step.
IV Projected crop yields for 2011 and 2050 are obtained for the estimated trend lines for each individual crop by irrigation type, AEZ, and country. We show the results of this stage for these years with $Y^{w}_{irj2011}$ and $Y^{w}_{irj2050}$, respectively.
V The results of step IV are used to calculate percent changes in crop yields between 2011 and 2050 for each individual crop, by irrigation type, AEZ, and country. These figures measure impacts of climate change on crop yields by AEZ in each country.

To summarize the results of these steps, we further aggregated the percent changes in crop yields by country as shown in Table 6.3. Several conclusions can be made from this table: (1) climate change negatively affects crop yields across regions with few exceptions; (2) in some regions in India, climate change positively affects soybeans and sugarcane yields; (3) with some exceptions, rain fed crops suffer more than their irrigated counterparts. All of these observations confirm that climate change affects yields in favor of irrigated crops, which could lead to more irrigation to take advantage of the relative increase in favor of irrigation. However, the impacts of climate change on crop yields may vary across AEZ within a country. Figure 6.7, which represents percentage changes in crop yields due to climate change in India by AEZ, represents this important fact.

The first experiment examines the extent to which climate induced changes in crop yields affect demand for irrigation in South Asia and tests their economic consequences for this region by county. The approach we follow in this experiment isolates the impacts of climate change on crop yields from other factors, such as population growth, technological progress, and economic growth, which may affect crop yields over time. To highlight the impacts of the expected changes

Table 6.3 Projected percentage changes in crop yields in South Asia for 2011–2050 (%)

Country	*Crop Type*	*Rice*	*Wheat*	*Corn*	*Soybeans*	*Sugarcane*
Bangladesh	Irrigated	−10.7	−10.5	−6.0	−9.0	−8.1
	Rain fed	−9.2	−18.8	−5.0	−24.7	−9.9
	Total	−10.0	−14.8	−5.0	−21.5	−8.2
India	Irrigated	−8.3	−8.0	−5.7	−10.7	−4.6
	Rain fed	−13.1	−12.3	−4.4	10.7	10.7
	Total	−10.5	−8.6	−4.6	6.1	−3.1
Nepal	Irrigated	−7.5	−6.2	−2.4	−4.8	20.6
	Rain fed	−9.4	−5.5	−5.9	−6.9	22.4
	Total	−8.7	−6.2	−5.7	−6.7	21.3
Pakistan	Irrigated	−6.7	−7.4	−7.5	−9.0	−6.4
	Rain fed	−13.4	−17.7	−1.4	−3.3	37.0
	Total	−6.7	−8.1	−4.0	−5.9	1.5
Sri Lanka	Irrigated	−6.9	–	–	–	−5.6
	Rain fed	−12.3	–	−7.2	–	–
	Total	−8.1	–	–	–	–
Rest of South Asia	Irrigated	7.7	−7.2	−0.1	0.0	–
	Rain fed	−17.3	−0.4	11.5	−1.3	–
	Total	5.2	−3.2	2.3	−0.5	–

Source: Author, model projection.

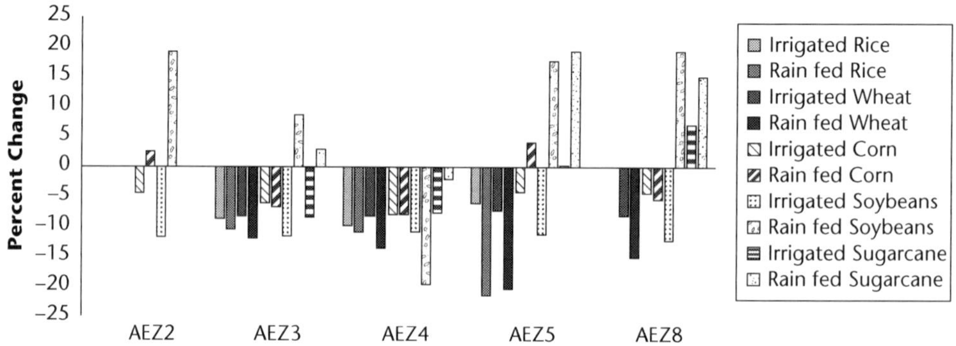

Figure 6.7 Projected percentage changes in crop yields in India by AEZ for 2011–2050 (AEZs with minor shares in harvested areas are intentionally ignored in this figure)

Source: Author, model projection.

in crop yields due to climate change on the demand for irrigation, we assume that there is no restriction on water supply (this assumption will be altered significantly in the subsequent experiments). Furthermore, given that the supply of unskilled labor is not a major constraint in South Asia, we assume that the real wage for this labor force remains constant due to the productivity shock. Finally, we exogenously impose the obtained productivity shocks on the economies of 2011 to examine how economies of South Asia react to these climate change impacts when we assume no water scarcity.

Experiment II: Impacts of climate change on crop yields and demand for irrigation when water supply is limited

As mentioned earlier, several studies confirm that many regions in South Asia will face water scarcity induced by rapid expansion in water demand in agricultural and non-agricultural uses, lack of proper water infrastructure, and/or climate change. However, only a few studies have quantified the magnitude of future water scarcity in South Asia. Rosegrant et al. (2013) have measured the Irrigation Water Supply Reliability (IWSR) index as a metric for irrigation water scarcity under several alternative scenarios, on a global scale, by river basin, for the period of 2000 to 2050, using the IMPACT-WATER model developed by IFPRI. This index measures the gap between demand and supply of water for irrigation. If this index equals one, there is no irrigation water shortage. For our study, following Liu et al. (2014), we use the Rosegrant et al. (2013) "business as usual" scenario to measure changes in irrigation water supply by river basin for the time period of 2011 to 2050. This scenario assumes that the current trends in population and economic growth, water use efficiency, and investment in water infrastructure, will continue into the future. Figure 6.8 represents expected changes in irrigation water supply by river basin in South Asia from 2011 to 2050. As shown in this figure, water supply for irrigation is expected to fall significantly in several river basins in South Asia.

In the first experiment, we examined a case where water supply is not limited, and hence crop producers could switch to irrigation in response to induced climate change yield losses. However, Figure 6.8 indicates that water supply for irrigation in many river basins is expected to fall. Hence, on one hand, climate change increases demand for irrigation in many river basins. On the other hand, if the economy of South Asia grows as usual, available water supply for irrigation will fall significantly in several river basins. In the second experiment, we analyze the joint impact of these two different forces on the economies of South Asia. To achieve this goal, we impose the projected changes in water supply by river basin (presented in Figure 6.8) and changes in productivities of rain fed and irrigated crops as an exogenous shock on the base year economies of South Asia, while we assume water supply in non-agricultural uses will remain unchanged.

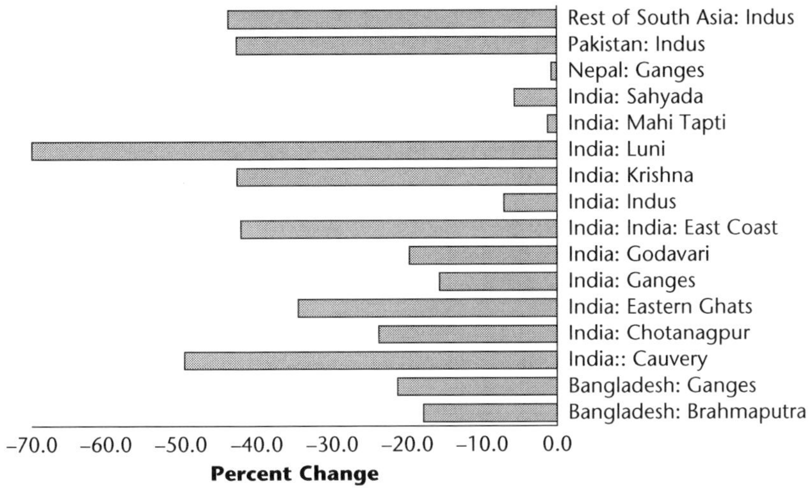

Figure 6.8 Projected percent changes in irrigation water supply in South Asia by river basin in 2011–2050

Source: Author, model projection.

Simulation results

Results of Experiment I

In what follows, we analyze some key selected results obtained from the first simulation. Changes in demand for irrigation, consequences for land use, impacts on crop and food production, impacts on food imports, and impacts at the macro level will be provided in this section.

Impacts on demand for water

When water supply is not limited, climate-induced crop yield changes significantly alter the demand for water in many river basins. As shown in Figure 6.9, increases in demand are observed in the following major river basins: the Brahmaputra (9.3 percent) and Ganges (15.4 percent) basins, in Bangladesh; the Brahmaputra (45.1), Brahmari (5.3 percent), Eastern Ghats (18.8 percent), East Coast (16.1 percent), Indus (17.6 percent), Sahyada (7.9 percent), and Thai Myan Malay (61.4 percent) basins in India; the Ganges (3.7 percent) and Indus (3.0 percent) basins in Nepal; the Western Asia (36.2 percent) basin in Pakistan; and the Brahmaputra basin in the Rest of South Asia (23.1 percent). Only in India does the demand for water drop slightly in a few basins including the Chotanagpui (−8.7 percent), Ganges (−5.4 percent), Krishna (−4.2 percent), Luni (−11.7 percent), and Mahi Tapti (−11.8 percent) river basins.

To understand the factors that affect these changes, consider two representative river basins of India: the Ganges and Indus basins. In India, climate-induced crop yield changes increase demand for water in the Indus basin by 17.6 percent (or 25.8 billion cubic meter) and reduce demand for water in the Ganges basin by 5.4 percent (18.1 billion cubic meters). The Indus river basin serves several relatively dry and semi dry AEZs, where the difference between irrigated and rain fed yields are large.[11] In these AEZs, reductions in rain fed crop yields are significantly larger than their corresponding changes for irrigated crops. Hence in these AEZs, when water supply is not limited, rain fed crop producers switch to irrigation to hedge against climate change and mitigate a portion of its negative impacts. In this river basin (and also other basins with similar conditions), demand for irrigation goes up. On the other hand, the Ganges serves several water-rich and humid AEZs where crops are mostly irrigated[12] and/or rain fed, irrigated yields are not very different, and climate change impacts on rain fed and irrigated yields are similar. In these AEZs, since both rain fed and irrigated crops suffer from climate change, crop production and hence demand for irrigation drops over time. As a result, we observe an overall reduction in demand for water in the Indus basin in India (and other basins with similar conditions). In the next experiment, we examine the extent to which water scarcity could alter these findings.

Impacts on crop production

When there is no water scarcity and additional water is available at a constant price, changes in the rain fed and irrigated yields due to climate change alter the mix of irrigated and rain fed crops on the market at the national level, as shown in Figure 6.10. This figure indicates that, if water is available, climate change will promote outputs of irrigated crops in most cases, and negatively affect their rain fed counterparts. As shown in Figure 6.11, the net of these changes is usually negative, except for sugarcane, which seems to perform better under climate change. This means that even if the water supply is not limited, climate change harmed the outputs of main staple crops in South Asia during 2011–2050. While moving towards irrigation could only partially mitigate some adverse impacts of climate change on agricultural outputs, it could not eliminate all

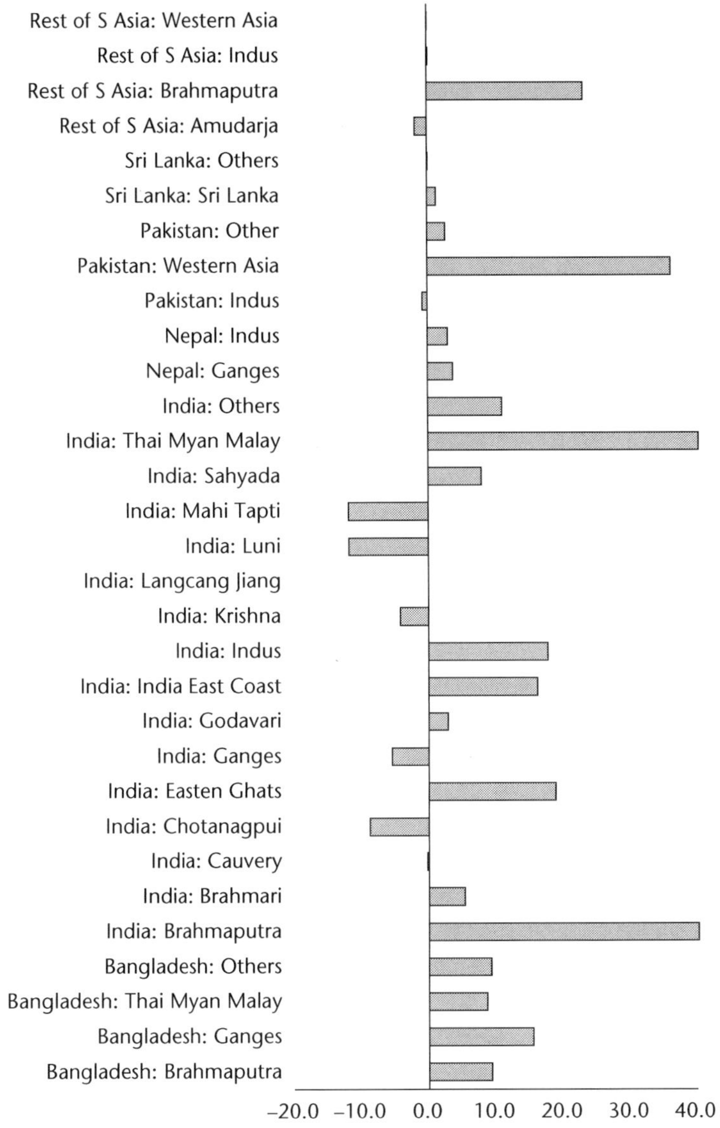

Figure 6.9 Percent change in demand for water for irrigation due to climate-induced crop yield changes, if water supply is unlimited

Source: Author, model projection.

the negative impacts. The next experiment shows that the impacts of climate change on crop yields worsen when we take into account the fact that the supply of water is limited.

Land use impacts

Here we only examine changes in the mix of irrigated and rain fed land, as presented in Figure 6.12. This figure confirms that, if water supply is unlimited, demand for irrigated cropland

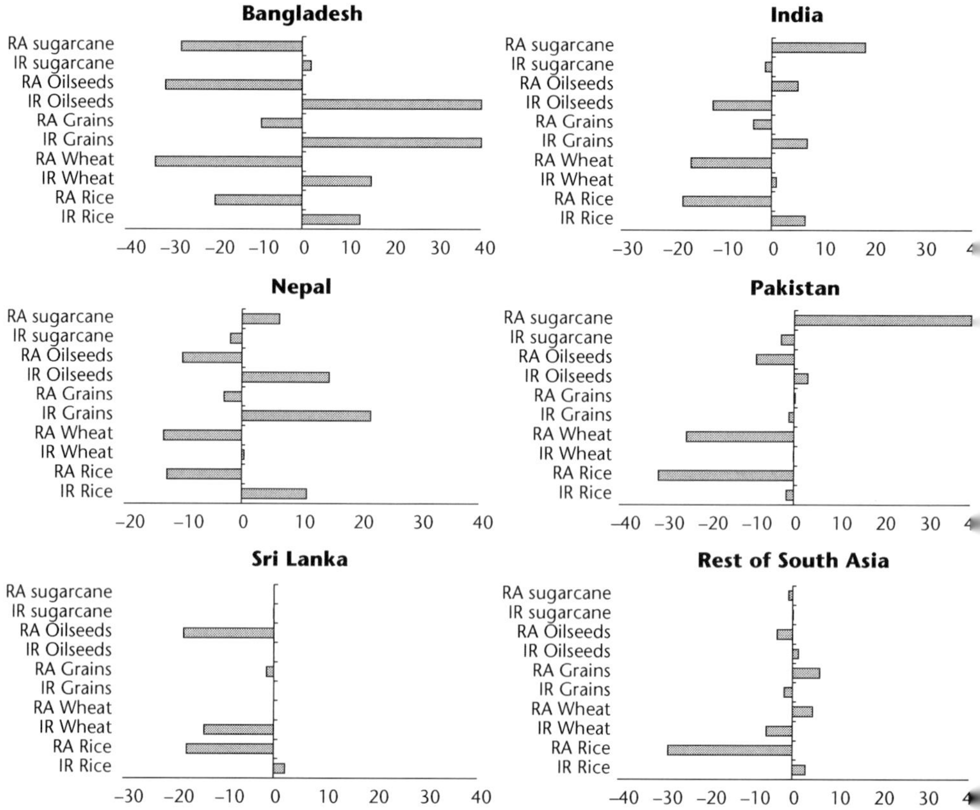

Figure 6.10 Percent change in irrigated and rain fed crop outputs due to climate-induced crop yield changes, if water supply is unlimited (IR and RA stand for irrigated and rain fed, respectively)

Source: Author, model projection.

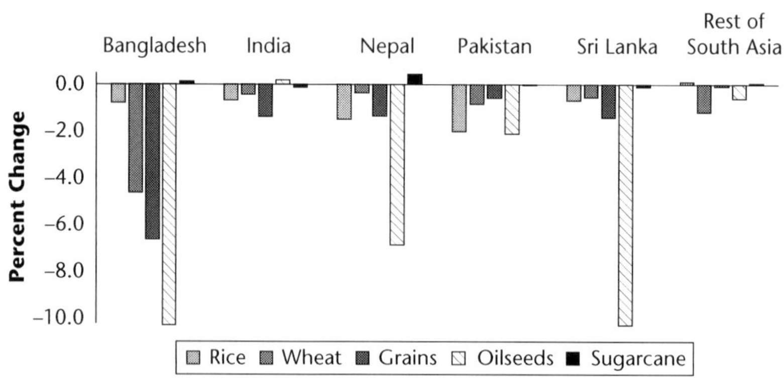

Figure 6.11 Percent change in crop outputs due to climate-induced crop yield changes, if water supply is unlimited

Source: Author, model projection.

will increase across almost all river basins in South Asia to mitigate the adverse impacts of climate-induced crop yield changes. The reverse is expected to happen for the case of rain fed cropland. Figure 6.12 shows that relatively large conversion from rain fed land to irrigated land could occur in several river basins such as: the Brahmaputra and Ganges basins in Bangladesh; the Brahmaputra, Brahmari, Eastern Ghats, Godavari, East Coast, Indus, and Sahyada basins in India;

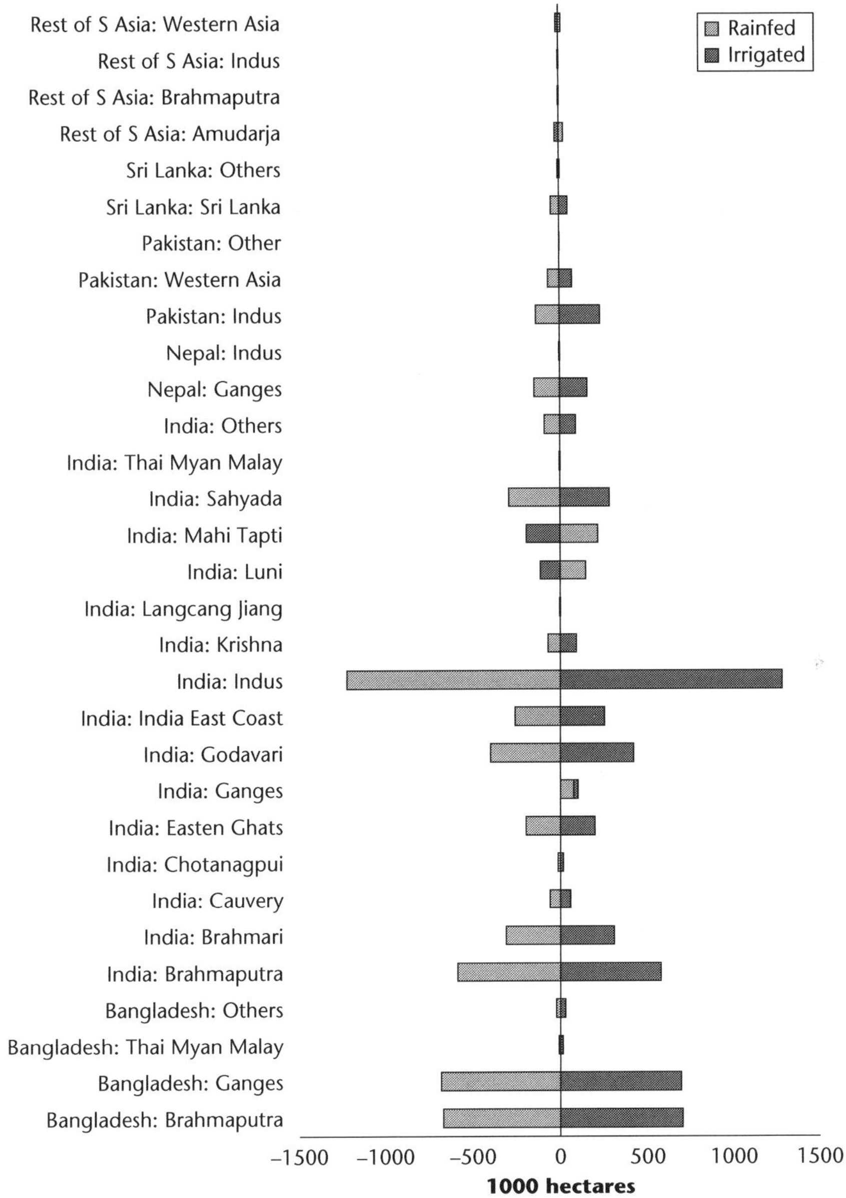

Figure 6.12 Percent change in the mix of irrigated and rain fed harvested areas due to climate-induced crop yield changes, if water supply is unlimited in South Asia

Source: Author, model projection.

the Ganges basin in Nepal; and the Indus basin in Pakistan. In short, if water supply is unlimited, total irrigated area could increase by 5.2 million hectares in South Asia to mitigate some adverse impacts of climate-induced crop yield changes. The corresponding reduction in rain fed areas is about 4.8 million hectares. Therefore, these changes could increase demand for cropland by about 0.4 million hectares, which of course generates deforestation.

Economy-wide impacts

We explained that if the supply of water is not limited, changes in irrigated and rain fed crop yields induced by climate change increase demand for irrigation, which in turn boosts irrigated crop outputs, partially mitigating some adverse impacts of climate change. Moving toward irrigation could generate new job opportunities and improve economic activities at the national level. However, the overall negative impacts of climate change on agricultural outputs are strong enough to harm the economies of South Asia, which are heavily dependent on agricultural activities. As shown in Figure 6.13, even when there is no restriction on water supply, economies of South Asia will lose a portion of their GDP due to climate-induced crop yield changes. The magnitudes of GDP losses are not large in terms of percentage changes in GDP, as shown in Figure 6.13. However, their monetary values are considerable, in particular when we take into account the losses over time between 2011 and 2015. The monetary values of losses at 2011 constant prices in 2050 are expected to be about \$394 million for Bangladesh, \$2.12 billion for India, \$60 million for Nepal, \$270 million for Pakistan, and \$135 million for Sri Lanka. The rest of South Asia does not lose out significantly, if water supply for irrigation is available. The next section shows that these results will change meaningfully when we take into account the fact that water supply will be limited and diminished in the future.

Results of Experiment II

Impacts on demand for water

In this experiment, at equilibrium, reduction in demand for irrigation water at the river basin level will be identical to the reduction in water supply for irrigation induced by water scarcity, as presented in Figure 6.8. In analyzing the first experiment, we mentioned that climate-induced crop yield changes increase demand for water used in irrigation, when water supply is not limited. However, in

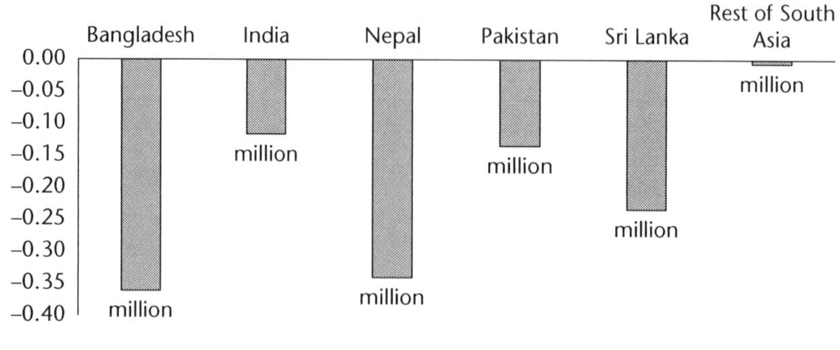

Figure 6.13 Percent change in GDP due to climate-induced crop yield changes, if water supply is unlimited (figures on the bars represent monetary values of changes at 2011 constant prices)

Source: Author, model projection.

the presence of water scarcity, the available water for irrigation will decline in many river basins, as projected in Figure 6.8. Hence, water scarcity blocks the demand for irrigation water, increasing the opportunity costs of water across South Asia everywhere, as presented in Figure 6.14. Since the intensity of water scarcity varies among river basins and water cannot move freely over them, the opportunity costs of using water in irrigation will increase at different rates across river basins.

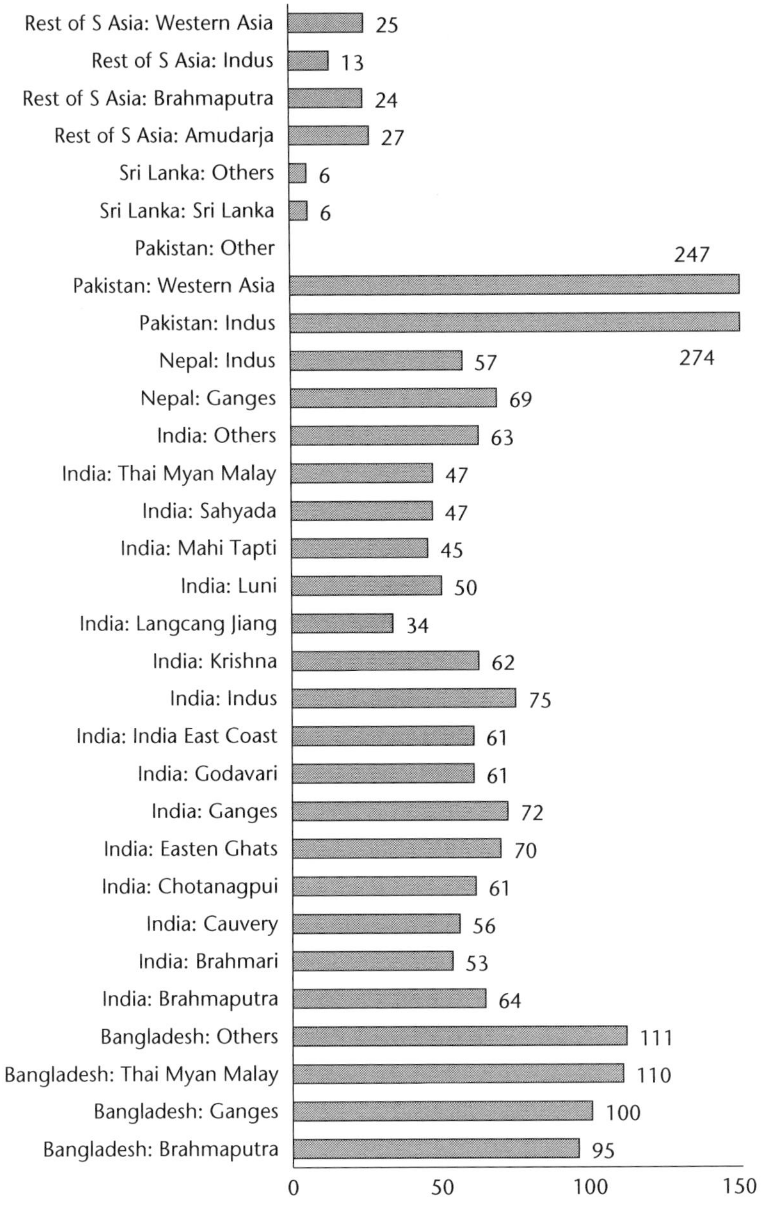

Figure 6.14 Percent change in shadow price of water across South Asia by river basin due to water scarcity and climate-induced crop yield changes (figures of Western Asia and Indus in Pakistan are out of scale)

Source: Author, model projection.

Figure 6.14 shows that increases are quite large in several basins. For example, in Bangladesh, the opportunity cost of water increases by around 100 percent across basins. In India, it goes up by more than 70 percent in the Eastern Ghats, Ganges, and Indus river basins. In Nepal, it rises by 50 percent to 70 percent. The opportunity cost of water for irrigation in Pakistan increases by three- to fourfold. The changes are not large in Sri Lanka. In the Rest of South Asia, it fluctuates around 20 percent to 30 percent. It is important to note that in South Asia, the actual price of water for irrigation is extremely low everywhere in the base year and may not reflect the opportunity cost (2011).

Impacts on food production and exports

Reduction in available water for irrigation, in combination with climate-induced crop yield changes, severely harms crop production in South Asia, in particular in drier regions as presented in the top panel of Table 6.4, if economies of this region continue to inefficiently use water in irrigation. In Bangladesh, crop outputs drop between 7 percent and 22 percent. In India, which is

Table 6.4 Changes in food production due to water scarcity and climate induced crop yield changes in South Asia: Projected for 2050 accumulation

	Crop	*Irrigation type*	*Bangladesh*	*India*	*Nepal*	*Pakistan*	*Sri Lanka*	*Rest of South Asia*
Changes in crop outputs (% change)	Rice	Irrigated	−4.8	−5.6	1.2	−14.8	1.5	−0.1
		Rain fed	−9.0	−5.0	−6.4	65.1	−17.7	−28.7
		Total	−6.6	−5.4	−2.8	−14.0	−1.4	−2.7
	Wheat	Irrigated	−13.0	−4.9	−1.5	−31.3	−56.0	−10.8
		Rain fed	−26.5	−0.9	−5.6	8.9	0.0	6.2
		Total	−18.6	−4.6	−1.7	−30.0	−2.2	−3.0
	Coarse Grains	Irrigated	−19.4	−28.4	8.9	−62.3	0.0	−3.9
		Rain fed	−12.7	1.6	−2.6	51.8	−1.5	8.2
		Total	−13.0	−4.6	−1.8	−17.8	−1.5	−1.2
	Oilseeds	Irrigated	0.2	−50.0	0.0	−56.7	0.0	−11.6
		Rain fed	−29.2	10.9	−8.7	36.6	−16.9	2.8
		Total	−21.6	−7.7	−7.6	−16.1	−16.8	−5.9
	Sugar crops	Irrigated	−5.0	−6.2	−9.7	−17.1	−0.4	−4.4
		Rain fed	−12.2	44.9	21.2	138.4	0.0	10.1
		Total	−5.4	−3.2	−0.8	−8.8	−0.4	−2.4
Changes in values of food items (million USD)	Crops		−1,978	−14,339	−105	−8,144	−96	−29
	Livestock		−259	−3,063	−24	−526	−15	−70
	Processed food		−1,127	−9,079	−38	−5,595	−125	−74
	Total		−3,364	−26,481	−168	−14,265	−237	−173
Changes in net exports of food items (million USD)	Crops		−1,078	−3,254	−58	−5,635	22	−28
	Livestock		12	−263	−12	343	−1	−36
	Processed food		−284	−3,505	−41	212	−38	−118
	Total		−1,350	−7,022	−111	−5,080	−17	−182

Source: Author, model projection.

a big crop producer, reductions range between 5 percent and 8 percent. In Pakistan, another big crop producer, crop outputs drop largely between 10 percent and 30 percent. In Nepal, Sri Lanka and the Rest of South Asia, crop outputs also decline, but at smaller rates. The top panel of Table 6.4 shows also these changes for irrigated and rain fed crops, separately.

The adverse joint impact of water scarcity and climate-induced crop yield changes on food production is not limited to the reduction in crop production. Reduction in crop outputs will also affect production of livestock and processed food industries. The second panel of Table 6.4 shows that water scarcity and climate-induced crop yield changes jointly push down the monetary values[13] of all food items (including crops, livestock, and processed food) produced in Bangladesh, India, Nepal, Pakistan, Sri Lanka, and the rest of South Asia in 2050, compared to 2011, by $3,364 million (6.2 percent), $26,481 million (4 percent), $168 million (2 percent), $14,265 million (10 percent), $237 million (1 percent), and $173 million (1.8 percent), at constant 2011 prices, respectively. These are significant losses, in particular when we take into account their accumulated values over time between 2011 and 2050.

Water scarcity and climate-induced crop yield changes also jointly reduce the net exports of food products from South Asia, particularly from India and Pakistan. As shown in the lowest panel of Table 6.4, these factors together push down the net exports of food products[14] from Bangladesh, India, Nepal, Pakistan, Sri Lanka, and rest of South Asia in 2050, compared to 2011, by $1,350 million, $7,022 million, $111 million, $5,080 million, $17 million, and $181 million, respectively. While these reductions in net exports (or increases in net imports) of food products help economies of South Asia to mitigate a portion of the negative impacts of water scarcity and climate-induced crop yield changes on food security, they put major pressure on the trade balances of these economies over time.

Impacts on crop price

Reductions in crop outputs due to water scarcity and climate-induced crop yield changes lead to higher crop prices across South Asia in 2050. Crop prices increase in Bangladesh, India and Nepal

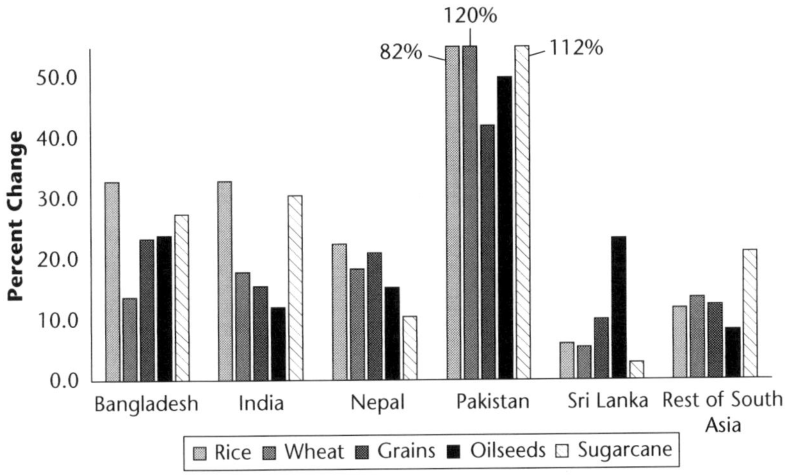

Figure 6.15 Percent change in crop price across South Asia due to water scarcity and climate-induced crop yield changes (figures of rice, wheat, sugar crops in Pakistan are out of scale)

Source: Author, model projection.

between 10 percent and 35 percent, as presented in Figure 6.15. In Pakistan, the crop price changes are large, between 45 percent and 120 percent. In Sri Lanka and the rest of South Asia, crop prices increases fall between 3 percent to 10 percent, with few exceptions. Of course, these higher crop prices will negatively affect everyone in South Asia, in particular low income and poor families.

Land use impacts

The mix of irrigated and rain fed land in the second experiment, where we introduce water scarcity into our analysis, moves in the opposite direction of the observed mix obtained from the

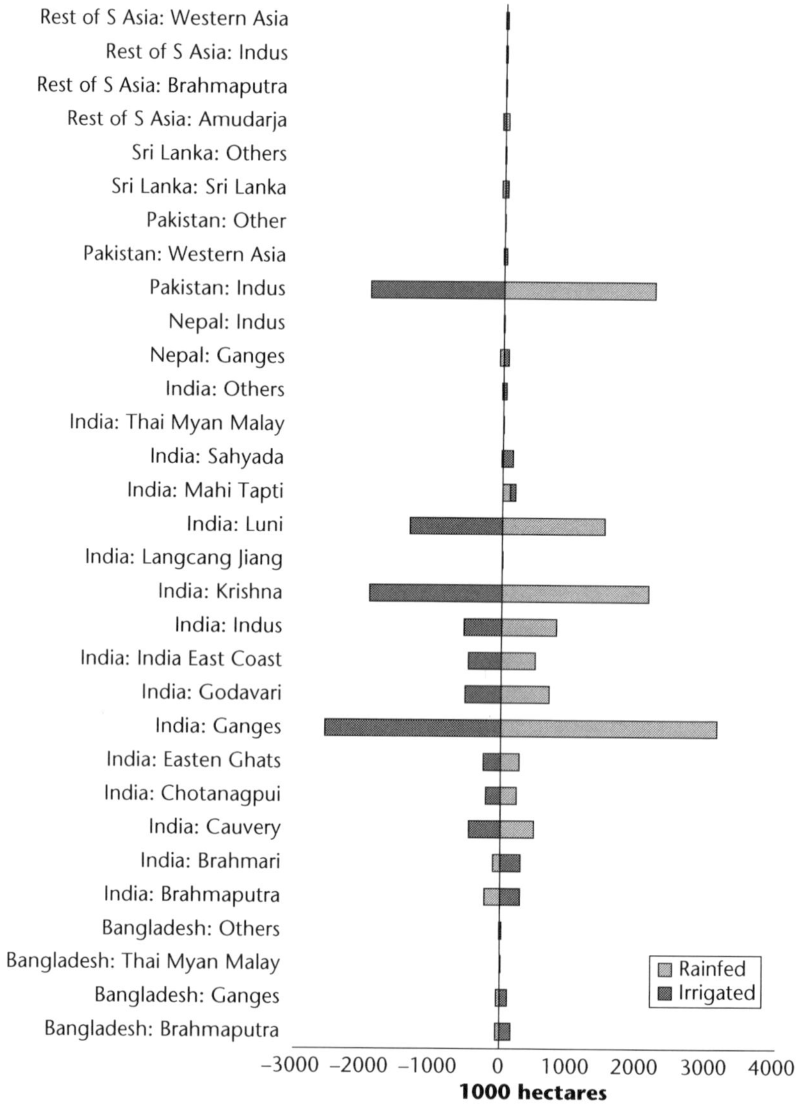

Figure 6.16 Percent change in the mix of irrigated and rain fed harvested areas due to climate-induced crop yield changes and water scarcity in South Asia

Source: Author, model projection.

first experiment. Unlike the first experiment, where the supply of water was not limited, in the second experiment, water scarcity eliminates irrigated areas in some river basins and extends rain fed areas in those basins, as shown in Figure 6.16. In the second experiment, the area of irrigated cropland in India goes down in several basins and largely in Chotanagpui (by −215,000 hectares), Eastern Ghats (by −250,000 hectares), Ganges, −2,559,000 hectares, Godavari (by −519,000 hectares), East Coast (by −473,000 hectares), Indus by (−541,000 hectares), Krishna (by −1,924,000 hectares), and Luni (by −1,346,000 hectares) basins. The area of irrigated cropland also drops greatly in Pakistan in the Indus basin, by −1,935,000 hectares. In short, in the presence of water shortages, total irrigated area decreases by 9 million hectares in South Asia. The corresponding increase in rain fed area is about 11.5 million hectares. Therefore, demand for cropland goes up by 2.5 million hectares, which of course generates more deforestation, compared with the results of the first experiment.

Economy-wide impacts

In analyzing the first experiment, we learned that even when supply of water is not limited and irrigation could be expanded in response to the adverse impacts of climate-induced crop yield changes, economies of South Asia suffer from these changes. These changes, in combination with water scarcity, extend the adverse impacts harshly. Figure 6.17 indicates that these factors jointly reduce the GDP of Bangladesh, India, Nepal, Pakistan, Sri Lanka, and rest of South Asia between 2011 and 2050 by 5.2 percent, 1.8 percent, 0.8 percent, 5.6 percent, 0.6 percent, and 0.5 percent, respectively. The corresponding monetary values of these losses at 2011 prices are −$5.67 billion, −$32.79 billion, −$138 million, −$11.22 billion, −$340 million, and −$117 million, as presented in Figure 6.17. These losses and their accumulation over time are massive.

To calculate the accumulated values of these loses over time, we provided two distinct but correlated measures for each country. The first one assumes a linear trend and calculates annual losses between 2011 and 2050, according to the monetary value of the reduction in GDP of 2050 versus 2011 for each country, and accumulates them for 2012–2050. The second measure represents the net present value of the first measure at a 3 percent social discount rate. We refer to these two measures as the "linear trend" and the "discounted trend." Figure 6.18 represents the results of these calculations for each individual country. The accumulated losses of the linear trends for Bangladesh, India, Nepal, Pakistan, Sri Lanka, and rest of South Asia between 2011 and 2050 are about −$113.4 billion, −$655.9 billion, −$2.8 billion, −$224.4 billion, −$6.8 billion, −$2.3 billion, respectively. The

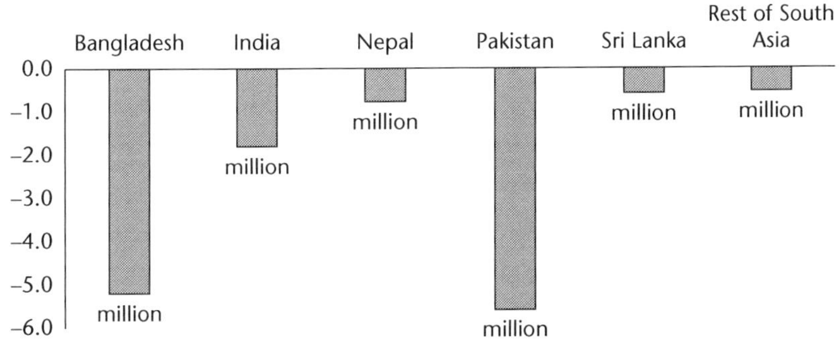

Figure 6.17 Percent change in GDP due to water scarcity and climate-induced crop yield changes (figures on the bars represent monetary values of changes at 2011 constant prices)

Source: Author, model projection.

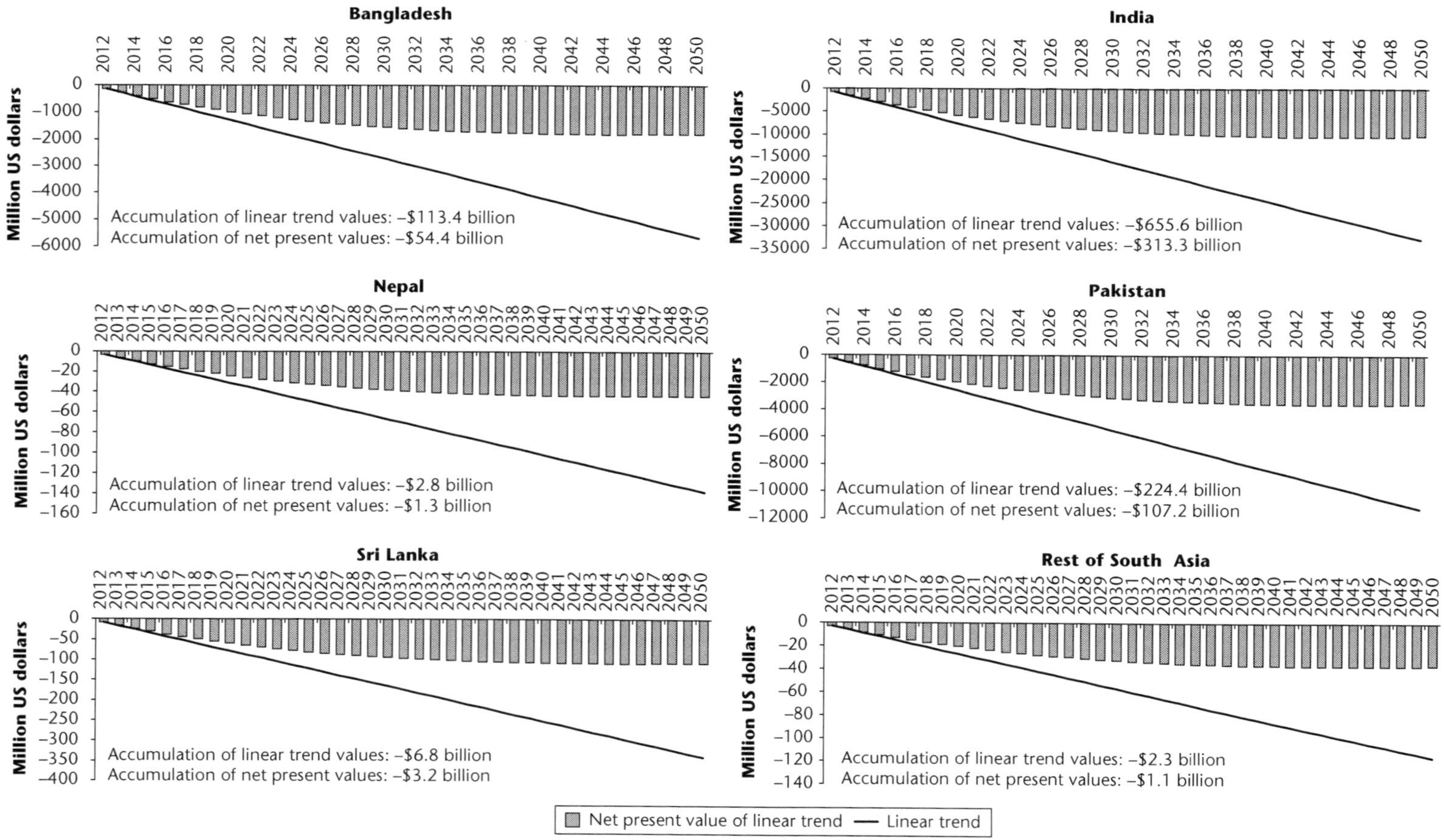

Figure 6.18 Percent change in GDP due to water scarcity and climate-induced crop yield changes (figures on the bars represent monetary values of changes at 2011 constant prices)

Source: Author, model projection.

corresponding discounted losses are about −\$54.2 billion, −\$313.3 billion, −\$1.3 billion, −\$107.2 billion, −\$3.2 billion, and −\$1.1 billion. These large losses indicate that climate-induced crop yield changes plus water scarcity could harm economies of South Asia seriously, if these economies do not take precautionary and aggressive mitigation approaches and policies against these factors.

Uncertainties

Three major items determine the magnitude of the simulation results provided in this chapter. These items are: impacts of climate change on crop yields; the extent of future water scarcity; and the assumption that skilled labor and capital remain at full employment in the presence of climate change and water scarcity. Here we explain these items briefly. The results provided in this chapter depend on the implemented shocks in crop yields due to climate change. We calculated these shocks for RCP 4.5, which represents a moderate, relatively optimistic climate scenario. Of course, under more pessimistic climate scenarios, with higher temperatures, crop yields may drop more, altering our results.

The extent to which economic growth could induce water scarcity is the next important item. In this chapter, we rely on the literature and use the results of a major research conducted at IFPRI on water scarcity for irrigation. Recent studies confirm that economies of South Asia will face major water scarcity issues as well. However, there is no consensus regarding the extent to which water scarcity will increase in the future in this region. If water scarcity occurs more intensively than what IFPRI has projected, then the economic implications will only worsen.

Finally, in this chapter, we assumed that climate change and water scarcity do not affect markets for skilled labor and capital. Several papers have shown that water scarcity and climate change could negatively affect markets for skilled and unskilled labor, reducing the productivity of labor, generating idled capacities, and damaging infrastructure. Due to limited space, our analysis ignored these adverse impacts.

Conclusions

In this chapter we first examined the impacts of changes in the irrigated and rain fed crops yields induced by climate change on the demand for water. We looked at the impacts of climate change on crop yields and found they vary across crops and agro ecological zones. In this experiment, we showed that, if water for irrigation is not limited, climate-induced crop yield changes increase the demand for irrigation, which could help partially mitigate the impacts of climate change on crop and food production. From the first experiment, we also learned that while changes in irrigated and rain fed crop yields induced by climate change generate surges in demand for irrigation in some river basins, we also noted that they reduce demand for irrigation in some other river basins. We also showed that, if water for irrigation is not limited, climate-induced crop yield changes could still generate negative economy-wide impacts across South Asia.

Next, we examined the combined impacts of the effect of climate-induced crop yield changes and water scarcity on the economies of South Asia. We showed that water scarcity, induced by expansion in water demand in non-agricultural uses and lack of water infrastructure, would block the demand for irrigation, generating severe negative economic impacts and causing major land use changes.

The authors are grateful for the generous funding by the World Bank, ESMAP and AUSAID.

Notes

1 A few small single region models take into account water used in non-agricultural sectors. As an example, Luckmann et al. (2016) developed a single region CGE model which takes into account water in non-agricultural uses.

2 A few CGE models have examined water issues at a global scale. For example, for the first time, Berrittella et al. (2007) introduced water into a global CGE model (GTAP-W) as an input in the production function of crops and the water utility sector at the national level. Galzadilla et al. (2011) extend this model by dividing value added of cropland into irrigated and rain fed.
3 Some CGE models were linked with hydrology models to better capture the link been economic and biophysical variables. Even in these hybrid models water supply remains exogenous in the CGE part. For example, Robinson and Gueneau (2013) combined a CGE model with a hydrology model. However, these authors run the CGE and the hydrology models separately in a sequence.
4 Usually a regional market clearing condition allocates water among its alternative uses. A few models use other techniques or ad hoc restrictions (or quotas) to allocate water among its alternative uses. For example, Berck et al. (1991) used linear programing to allocate water across crops.
5 Some single region or single river basin models distinguished between these two types of water resources. As an example, Diao et al. (2008) provided some economic analyses on using surface and ground water in Morocco.
6 A nested CES production function divides production inputs into several sub-groups and assigns different elasticity of substitution parameters between the inputs of each nest and among the nests.
7 In a competitive market, all users of a commodity pay the same price for that commodity. When there are rigidities in the market for an endowment (or a commodity), the users pay different prices for that endowment (or commodity). This represents heterogeneity in price paid by users. For example, when water cannot freely move from agricultural uses to non-agricultural uses due to the existing restrictions (e.g., quotas, water rights, or any other social restrictions), agricultural and non-agricultural users of water pay different prices for water. In this case, water is not a homogenous commodity across its alternative uses.
8 Sri Lanka has many small river basins. IFPRI has aggregated many of them under this name.
9 Crop models usually project the impacts of climate change on crop yields. These models project different yield trajectories for each crop for a given climate condition at fine spatial fine resolutions (e.g., a 0.5 by 0.5 degree resolution).
10 This RCP represents an intermediate mitigation scenario which assumes temperature will not exceed 2 degrees Celsius by 2100 relative to 1900 (Field et al. 2014).
11 About 75% of Indus cropland is distributed across dry AEZs.
12 About 79% of Ganges cropland is distributed across water rich AEZs.
13 Evaluated at 2011 constant prices.
14 Evaluated at 2011 constant prices.

References

Baldos, U. and Hertel, T. (2015). "The role of international trade in managing food security risks from climate change," Department of Agricultural Economics, Purdue University, 403 West State Street, West Lafayette, IN, USA.

Berck, P., Robinson, S., and Goldman, G. (1991). "The use of computable general equilibrium models to assess water policies," In: Dinar, A. and Zilberman, D. (eds.), *The economics and management of water and drainage in agriculture*. New York, NY: Springer, pp. 489–509.

Berrittella, M., Hoekstra, A., Roson, R., and Tol, R. (2007). "The economic impact of restricted water supply: A computable general equilibrium analysis," *Water Res.*, 41(8), 1799–1813.

Diao, X., Dinar, A., Roe, T., and Tsur, Y. (2008). "A general equilibrium analysis of conjunctive ground and surface water use with an application to Morocco," *Agric. Econ.*, 38(2), 117–135.

Fadali, E., Rollins, K., and Stoddard, S. (2012). "Determining water values with computable general equilibrium models," In *The Importance of Water to the U.S. Economy: Technical Workshop*. Washington, DC: National Academy of Public Administration.

Field, C.B., Barros, V.R., Mach, K. and Mastrandrea, M. (eds.) (2014). "Climate change 2014: impacts, adaptation, and vulnerability," *Contribution of Working Group II to the Fourth Assessment Report of the Intergovernmental Panel on Climate Change*. Cambridge, UK and New York, NY, USA: Cambridge University Press.

Galzadilla, A., Rehdanz, K., and Tol, R. (2011). "Water scarcity and the impact of improved irrigation management: A computable general equilibrium analysis," *Agric. Econ.*, 42(3), 305–323.

Hertel, T. (1997). "Global Trade Analysis, Modeling and Applications," Cambridge: Cambridge University Press.

Khan, A., Kumar, S., Hussain, M., and Kalra, N. (2009). "Climate change, climate variability and Indian agriculture: Impacts vulnerability and adaptation strategies," In: Singh, S.N. (ed.), Climate change and crops, environmental science and engineering. Berlin, Heidelberg: Springer-Verlag.

Liu, J., Hertel, T., and Taheripour, F. (2016). "Analyzing future water scarcity in computable general equilibrium model," *Water Econ. Policy*, 2, 1650006, pp. 30.

Liu, J., Hertel, T.W., Taheripour, F., Zhu, T., and Ringler, C. (2014). "International trade buffers the impact of future irrigation shortfalls," *Global Environ. Change*, 29, 22–31.

Lobell, D.B., Burke, M.B., Tebaldi, C., Mastrandrea, M.D., Falcon, W.P., and Naylor, R.L. (2008). "Prioritizing climate change adaptation needs for food security in 2030," *Science*, 319, 607–610.

Luckmann, J., Grethe, H., McDonald, S., Orlov, A., and Siddig, K. (2016). "An integrated economic model of multiple types and uses of water," *Water Resour. Res.*, 50, 3875–3892.

Marshall, E., Aillery, M., Malcolm, S., and Williams, R. (2014). "Agricultural production under climate change: The potential impacts of shifting regional water balances in the U.S.," AAEA Annual Meeting, Minneapolis, MN.

Narayanan, B.G., Aguiar, A., and McDougall, R. (2015). "Global Trade, Assistance, and Production: The GTAP 9 Database," West Lafayette, IN, USA: Center for Global Trade Analysis, Purdue University.

Nelson, G.C., Rosegrant, M.W., Palazzo, A., Gray, I., Ingersoll, C., Robertson, R., Tokgoz, S., et al. (2010). "Food Security, Farming, and Climate Change to 2050: Scenarios, Results, Policy Options," Washington, DC, USA: International Food Policy Research Institute.

Parry, M.L., Canziani, O.F., Palutikof, J.P., van der Linden, P.J. and Hanson, C.E. (eds.) (2007). "Climate change 2007: impacts, adaptation, and vulnerability," *Contribution of Working Group II to the Fourth Assessment Report of the Intergovernmental Panel on Climate Change*. Cambridge, UK and New York, NY, USA: Cambridge University Press.

Rajeevan, M. (2013). "Climate change and its impact on Indian agriculture," In: Shetty, P.K., Ayyappan, S., and Swaminathan, M.S. (eds.), Climate change and sustainable food security. Bangalore: National Institute of Advanced Studies, Indian Institute of Science Campus, pp. 1–13.

Reilly, J., Hrubovcak, J., Graham, J., Abler, D.G., Darwin, R., Hollinger, S.E., et al. *(2002)*. "Changing Climate and Changing Agriculture," New York, NY: Cambridge University Press.

Robinson, S. and Gueneau, A. (2013). "CGE-W: An Integrated Modeling Framework for Analyzing Water-Economy Links Applied to Pakistan," GTAP Conference Paper, International Food Policy Research Institute, Washington, DC.

Rodriguez, D.J., Delgado, A., DeLaquil, P., and Sohns, A. (2013). "Thirsty Energy," Water Partnership Program, World Bank, Washington, DC.

Rosegrant, M.W., Ringler, C., Zhu, T., Tokgoz, S., and Bhandary, P. (2013). "Water and food in the bioeconomy: Challenges and opportunities for development," *Agric. Econ.*, 44(s1), 139–150.

Rosenzweig, C., Elliott, J., Deryng, D., Ruane, A.C., Mueller, C., et al. (2014). "Assessing agricultural risks of climate change in the 21st century in a global gridded crop model intercomparison," *Proc. Natl. Acad. Sci. U.S.A.*, 111(9), 3268–3273.

Taheripour, F., Birur, D., Hertel, T., and Tyner, W. (2007). "Introducing Liquid Biofuels into the GTAP Database," GTAP Research Memorandum No. 11, Center for Global Trade Analysis, Purdue University, West Lafayette, IN, USA.

Taheripour, F., Hertel, T., and Liu, J. (2013a). "Introducing Water by River Basin into the GTAP Model: GTAP-BIO-W," GTAP Working Paper 77, Center for Global Trade Analysis, Purdue University, West Lafayette, IN, USA.

Taheripour, F., Hertel, T., and Liu, J. (2013b). "Role of irrigation in determining the global land use impacts of biofuels," *Energy Sustain. Soc.*, 3(4), 1–18.

Taheripour, F., Hertel, T., Narayanan, B., Sahin, S., Markandya, A., and Mitra, B. (2016). "Economic and land use impacts of improving water use efficiency in irrigation in South Asia," *J. Environ. Prot.*, 7, 1571–1591.

UNESCO. (2012). "Managing water under uncertainty and risk," The United Nations World Water Development Report 4.

Villoria, N., Elliott, J., Choi, H., and Zhao, L. (2014). "The AgMIP Tool: A GEOSHARE Tool for Aggregating Outputs from the AgMIPs Global Gridded Crop Model Intercomparison Project," West Lafayette, IN: Purdue University.

Willis, D.B., Rainwater, K., Tewari, R., Stovall, J., Hayhoe, K., Hernandez, A., and Johnson, J. (2014). "Projecting the economic impact and level of groundwater use in the Southern High Plains under alternative climate change forecasts using a coupled economic and hydrologic model," AAEA Annual Meeting, Minneapolis, MN.

SECTION 3

Energy dependence and transition in Asia

7

Energy situation in Asia

Reiji Takeishi

Energy supply and demand in Asia

World energy trend and Asia

Asia is the most dynamic region in the global economy, leading world economic growth. Due to the rapid expansion of its economy, Asia has shown efficient and overwhelming economic performance, especially in the 2000s. As a result, Asia's energy demand, especially for power generation, increased profoundly in the 2000s. Energy demand has often grown much more quickly than GDP. As shown in Figure 7.1, total energy demand in the Asia Pacific can be summarized in three stages: the first includes the period before the 1980s, the second includes the 1980s until the beginning of the 2000s, and the third includes the period after the 2000s. The increases in demand have been enormous, especially after the 2000s. Asia's total energy consumption exceeded that of Europe and Former Soviet Union countries (Here after FSU) combined in 2001 and that of North America in the following year. This rapid increase was caused primarily by a rise in Chinese demand, but India and other developing Asian countries also contributed to the exceptional surge in energy consumption.

Compared with other areas of the world, Asian countries have generally experienced higher GDP growth. From 1990 to 2014, countries such as China, Cambodia, India, Vietnam, Sri Lanka, and Singapore experienced annual average growth rates of over 6 percent. Compared with total GDP growth, the GDP growth rates of the industrial and service sectors in these countries were often much higher. Under strong economic conditions, energy demand had direct impacts on those sectors.

In the near future, approximately 80 to 90 percent of the projected increase of world energy demand will be due to Asian countries, based on forecasts such as that of the IEA International Energy Agency (IEA), which will be mentioned later. Therefore, most new facility construction for power generation, power transmission, refining, gas transmission, and so on will occur in Asia. Additionally, to dispatch fuels to Asia, facilities such as refineries and gas liquefaction plants will be constructed in energy-exporting regions such as the Middle East, Australia, and the Russian Far East. Some facilities to liquefy and export shale gas, which is produced in the US, will be constructed in that country, and some of the gas will be exported to Asian countries through the Panama Canal.

As shown in Figure 7.1, energy demand in Europe and Eurasia, as well as North America, has not increased after the 1990s. Compared with those two developed areas, where the demand for

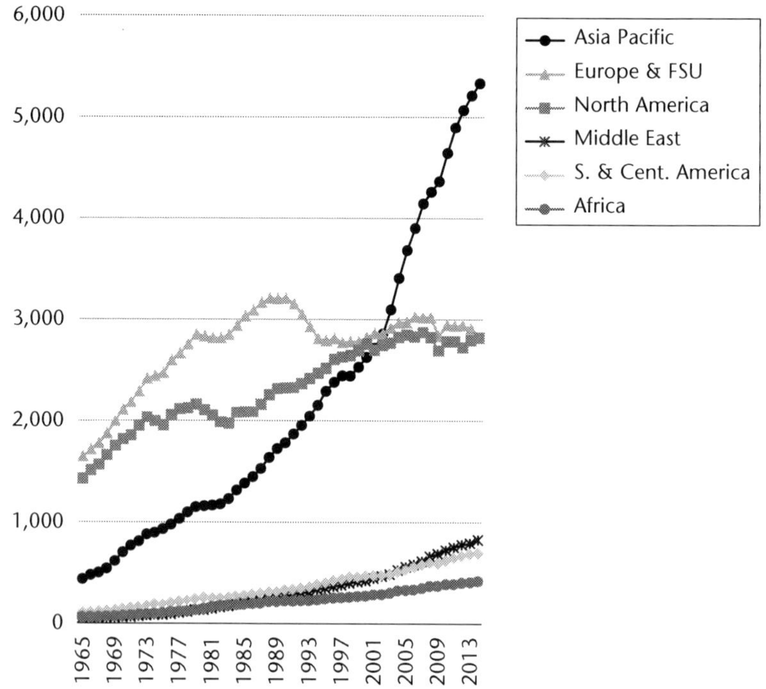

Figure 7.1 Energy demand in the world

Notes: Unit: million tons of oil equivalent. FSU means Former Soviet Union countries.

Source: Data from BP Statistics (2015).

energy has stagnated or even started to decrease, Asia continues to expand its energy demand. Therefore, Asian countries are very important to the energy industry as locations for business activities such as facility construction, transportation, engineering, and civil engineering.

Energy consumption by fuel type

Historically, each Asian country has a tradition of selecting different energy sources. Table 7.1 shows the composition of energy consumption by fuel type in Asian countries. China is heavily dependent on the supply of coal, with coal representing 66 percent of total energy consumption in 2014. Coal also represents over 50 percent of total energy consumption in India. No other countries in Asia are so heavily dependent on the supply of coal.

From a security perspective, a variety of fuels should be maintained to ensure a stable supply of energy. When accidents, natural disasters, or fighting occur, or if energy production shuts down in some area of the world, a diversified energy supply is crucially important for preventing a total stoppage of energy distribution.

As shown in Table 7.1, countries such as Japan, South Korea, and Taiwan maintain varied energy supplies. Note that Japan's 2014 figure shows no nuclear energy supply, causing increased dependence on fossil fuels, after the nuclear accident at the Fukushima Daiichi reactors in 2011.

Indonesia and Malaysia are highly dependent on the fossil fuel supply. Singapore is heavily dependent on oil utilization. Pakistan and Bangladesh depend primarily on the gas supply, because both countries produce gas domestically. Vietnam and the Philippines are also mainly

		Oil	*Natural Gas*	*Coal*	*Nuclear Energy*	*Hydro electric*	*Renewables*	*Total*
1	China	520.3	166.9	1,962.4	28.6	240.8	53.1	2,972.1
2	India	180.7	45.6	360.2	7.8	29.6	13.9	637.8
3	Japan	196.8	101.2	126.5	0.0	19.8	11.6	456.1
4	South Korea	108.0	43.0	84.8	35.4	0.8	1.1	273.2
5	Indonesia	73.9	34.5	60.8	0.0	3.4	2.2	174.8
6	Australia	45.5	26.3	43.8	0.0	3.3	4.1	122.9
7	Thailand	53.0	47.4	18.4	0.0	1.2	1.5	121.5
8	Taiwan	43.9	15.5	40.9	9.6	0.9	1.3	112.0
9	Malaysia	35.2	36.9	15.9	0.0	2.7	0.3	91.0
10	Singapore	66.2	9.7	0.0	0.0	0.0	0.2	76.1
11	Pakistan	22.6	37.8	4.9	1.1	7.2	0.1	73.6
12	Vietnam	18.7	9.2	19.1	0.0	12.3	0.1	59.3
13	Philippines	14.3	3.2	11.7	0.0	2.1	2.3	33.6
14	Bangladesh	5.7	21.2	1.0	0.0	0.1	0.1	28.2
15	China Hong Kong SAR	17.0	2.3	8.1	0.0	0.0	0.0	27.5
16	New Zealand	7.2	4.3	1.5	0.0	5.5	2.3	20.8
	Other Asia Pacific	19.7	5.6	16.7	0.0	12.0	0.2	54.2
	Total World	4,211.1	3,065.5	3,881.8	574.0	879.0	316.9	12,928.4
	Total Asia Pacific	1,428.9	610.7	2,776.6	82.5	341.6	94.2	5,334.6
	Total North America	1,024.4	866.3	488.9	216.1	153.5	73.6	2,822.8
	Total S. & Cent. America	326.5	153.1	31.6	4.7	155.4	21.5	692.8
	Total Europe & FSU	858.9	908.7	476.5	266.1	195.7	124.4	2,830.3
	Total Middle East	393.0	418.6	9.7	1.0	5.2	0.3	827.9
	Total Africa	179.4	108.1	98.6	3.6	27.5	2.9	420.1
	of which: OECD	2,032.3	1,432.6	1,052.5	449.8	315.7	215.9	5,498.8
	Non-OECD	2,178.9	1,632.9	2,829.3	124.2	563.3	101.1	7,429.6
	European Union	592.5	348.2	269.8	198.3	83.8	118.7	1,611.4
	Former Soviet Union	207.0	511.6	162.6	61.5	55.4	1.3	999.3

Note: Unit: Million tons oil equivalent.

Source: Data from BP Statistics (2015).

dependent on fossil fuels. However, Vietnam's hydropower capacity is rather extensive, representing over 12 percent of the country's total energy supply.

Oil consumption and production

Energy use in Asian countries is also influenced by the possibilities of domestic energy production. As shown in Figure 7.2, regarding oil consumption and production in Asian countries, China's oil consumption is skyrocketing and has continuously increased to over 10 million barrels per day from 2012 onward. Domestic oil production in China is also steadily increasing, but the increase in oil consumption has outstripped it such that the country's oil imports increased to almost 7 million barrels per day in 2014.

India's oil consumption is also increasing profoundly. In a few years, India's rate of oil consumption will likely outstrip that of Japan, and the nation will become Asia's second largest oil-consuming country, next to China. Compared with those two countries, Japan started to decrease its oil consumption in the 1990s. South Korea and Indonesia are both following India's trajectory and gradually increasing their consumption of oil.

Oil production is smaller than oil consumption in almost all Asian countries. Therefore, Asian countries must import oil from outside of the region, such as from the Middle East.

Vulnerability of oil supply in Asia is increasing year by year. Vehicle selling in Asia is increasing. In 2015, about 24 million passenger cars were sold in China and most of those cars were newly added to the existing number of 200 million vehicles in China. US's number of cars sold remained at around 17 million and most of them substituted oil ones. In Asia, India, Indonesia and other

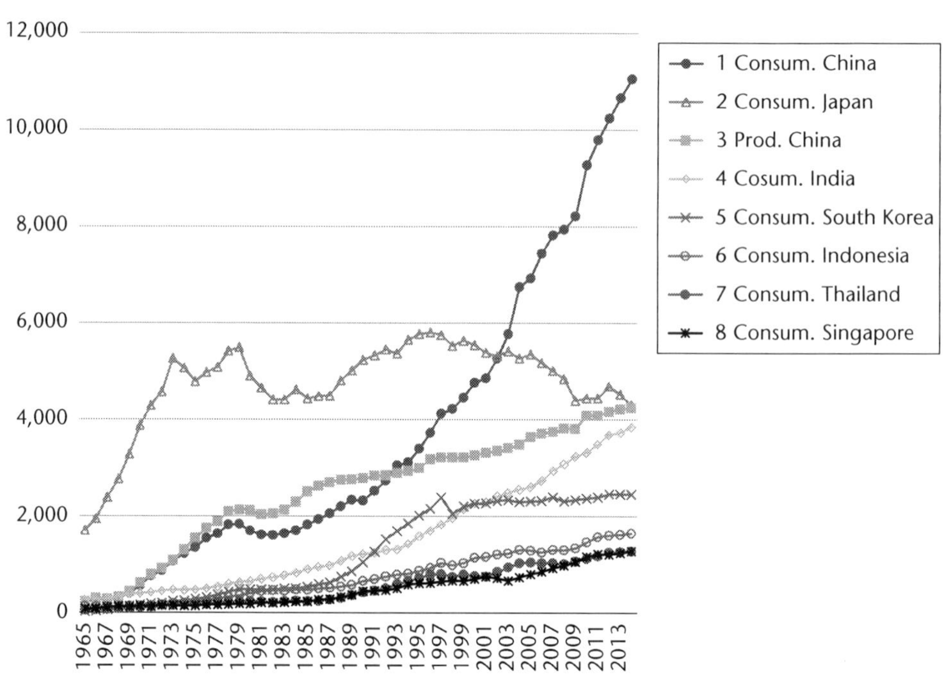

Figure 7.2 Oil consumption and production in Asian countries

Note: Unit: Thousand of barrels per day.

Source: Data from BP Statistics (2015).

countries, year by year and month by month, number of cars running in the cities are increasing. Therefore, oil consumption in Asia is inevitably increasing.

Oil refinery capacity

Due to the increase of oil consumption, oil refining capacity has expanded across Asia, except in several developed countries such as in Japan and Australia, as shown in Figure 7.3. Capacity has increased substantially in China: as of 2014, the country could refine 14 million barrels per day, 7 times its capacity in 1982.

India has also constructed several refineries, and in 2012, India's refining capacity exceeded that of Japan. India now possesses the second largest refining capacity in Asia. From the middle of 1990s, refining capacity in South Korea has been maintained at approximately 3 million barrels per day. As in Japan, and due to decreasing population and increasing energy efficiency, South Korea's oil consumption has remained almost flat.

Oil traded to Asia and within Asia

The amounts of oil traded to Asia and within Asia in 2014 are shown in Table 7.2. China's oil imports averaged 7.54 million barrels per day. Japan imported the second largest amount in Asia, at 4.333 million barrels per day. India's volume was slightly below Japan's, at 4.225 million barrels per day. Singapore is in a position to both import and export a great deal of crude oil and

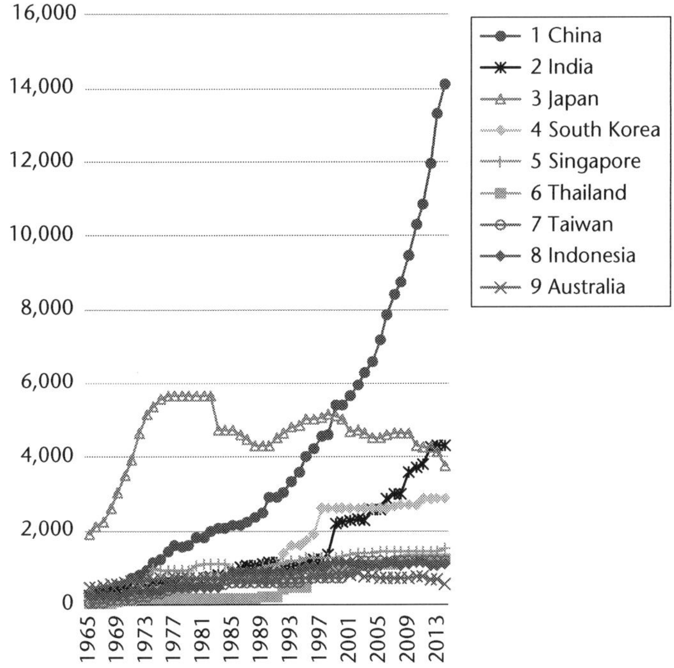

Figure 7.3 Oil refinery capacities in Asia

Note: Unit: Thousands of barrels per day.

Source: Data from BP Statistics (2015).

Table 7.2 Oil traded to Asia and within Asian in 2014

		Import							
		Australasia	*China*	*India*	*Japan*	*Singapore*	*Other Asia Pacific*	*Total Exports*	*% of Total*
Export	Middle East	121	3,457	2,440	3,166	1,082	4,796	19,761	34.8%
	North Africa	0	64	62	28	9	105	1,762	3.1%
	West Africa	89	1,153	581	60	5	296	4,431	7.8%
	East & Southern Africa	0	165	19	3	4	2	202	0.4%
	Former Soviet Union	40	926	41	314	247	557	8,932	15.7%
	Europe	12	74	43	18	154	195	2,293	4.0%
	US	14	118	96	137	113	86	4,099	7.2%
	Canada	0	17	12	11	1	4	3,535	6.2%
	Mexico	0	14	85	7	67	10	1,290	2.3%
	S. & Cent. America	1	751	691	56	229	80	3,929	6.9%
	Australasia	0	60	2	44	48	149	310	0.5%
	China	11	0	21	11	105	235	547	1.0%
	India	7	7	0	63	144	130	1,282	2.3%
	Japan	58	37	1	0	67	89	279	0.5%
	Singapore	207	140	13	4	0	991	1,495	2.6%
	Other Asia Pacific	465	557	117	410	780	0	2,589	4.6%
	Total imports	1,023	7,540	4,225	4,333	3,057	7,725	56,736	100.0%
	% of Total	1.8%	13.3%	7.4%	7.6%	5.4%	13.6%	49.2%	

Note: Unit: Thousands of barrels per day.

Source: Data from BP Statistics (2015).

petroleum products to Asia and Australia; its import amount in 2014 was 3.057 million barrels per day.

In 2014, Singapore exported 1.495 million barrels of oil per day, primarily to Australia, China, and other Asian countries such as Indonesia. India also exports more than 1 million barrels per day of petroleum products, with an average of 1.282 million barrels per day.

Gas consumption and production

Regarding gas consumption and production in Asian countries, as shown in Figure 7.4, production in China is increasing much more slowly than consumption. Therefore, China is importing larger quantities of gas from abroad. Japan's imports are also increasing, with an especially steep increase after the Fukushima accident in 2011. Gas production in Indonesia continuously increased until the year 2003, then decreased until 2007, and again increased to 2010 and then again decreased. Production from Malaysia is increasing and has nearly reached the format of Indonesia. After China and Japan, the greatest gas-consuming countries are Thailand, India, South Korea, Pakistan, Malaysia, and Indonesia. Most of Asia's gas consumption has continuously increased.

Coal consumption and production

Regarding coal consumption and production in Asian countries, as shown in Figure 7.5, China is the clear leader. China's figures for coal production and consumption have both drastically increased. In China, at the outset of reform, domestically produced coal had been consumed within the country, and coal import amounts were limited. Starting in the 2000s, however, coal consumption began to exceed coal production, and the balances had to be imported, mainly from Australia.

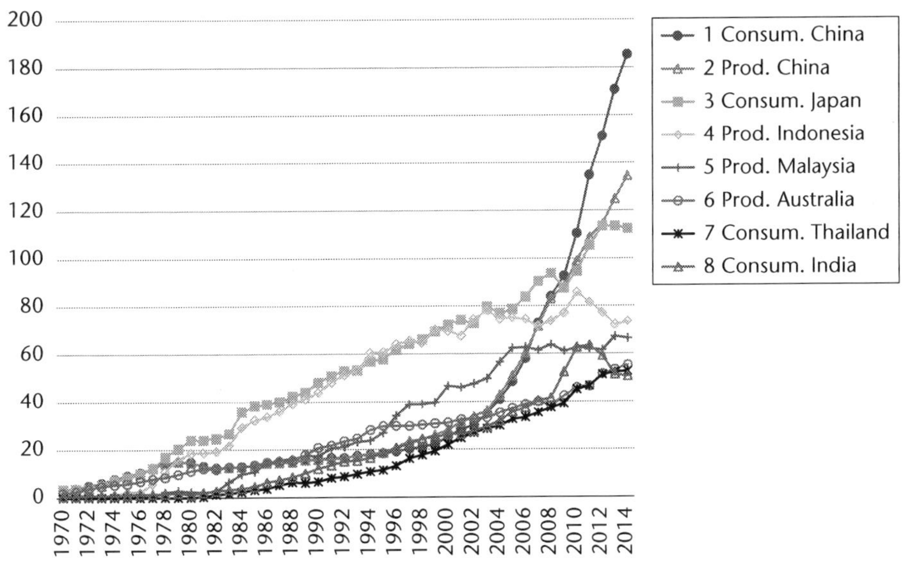

Figure 7.4 Gas consumption and production in Asian countries

Note: Unit: Billions of cubic meters.

Source: Data from BP Statistics (2015).

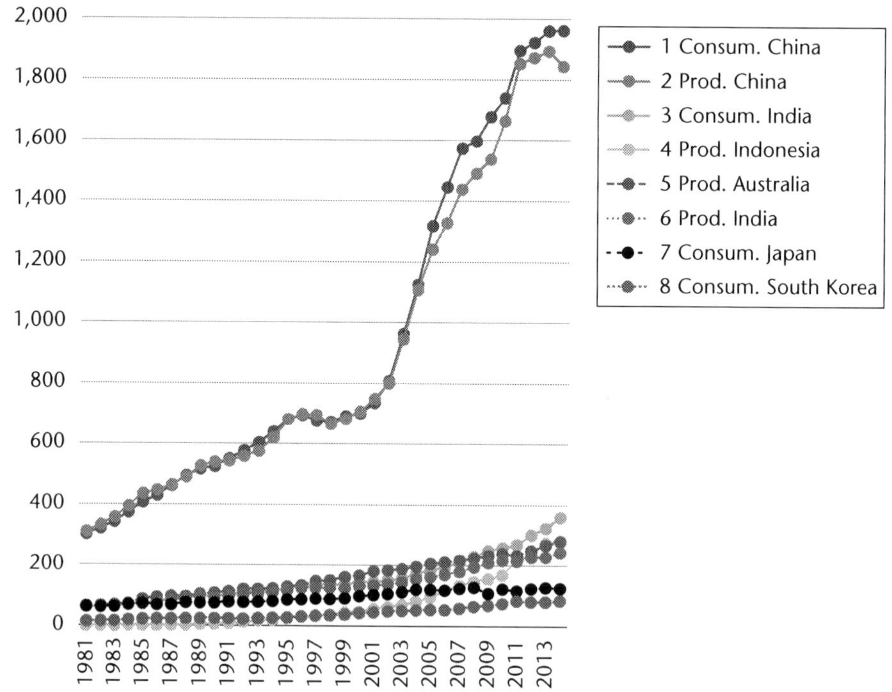

Figure 7.5 Coal consumption and production in Asian countries

Note: Unit: Million tons of oil equivalent.

Source: Data from BP Statistics (2015).

India consumes the next greatest amount of coal after China. India's ample coal supply supports its industrial development and protects it from energy shortages. As seen in Figure 7.5, India's coal consumption is followed by the production of Indonesia, Australia, and India. These figures show that India's rapid increase of coal consumption was largely supported by domestic production, with the balance of production and consumption covered by imports, mainly from Australia.

The next greatest coal-consuming country in Asia is Japan, followed by South Korea, Indonesia, Australia, and Taiwan. Only three Asia Pacific countries are net coal exporters: Indonesia, Australia, and Vietnam.

Figure 7.6 shows the trends of coal consumption and production in the Asia Pacific, excluding China, to demonstrate how rapidly Asian countries' coal consumption has increased. Indonesia has shown a rapid increase of coal production, while India has rapidly increased its coal consumption. The main Asia Pacific consumers and producers of coal are all increasing their amounts every year. Therefore, the necessity and importance of coal in the region is increasing.

Electricity generation

In Asia, the amount of electricity generated has expanded, due mainly to China's increased production, as shown in Figure 7.7. India's electricity generation has also increased very rapidly, overtaking Japan's production in 2013 and since remaining the second-highest generator in Asia next to China. South Korea follows Japan and is the fourth-largest electricity-generating country in Asia.

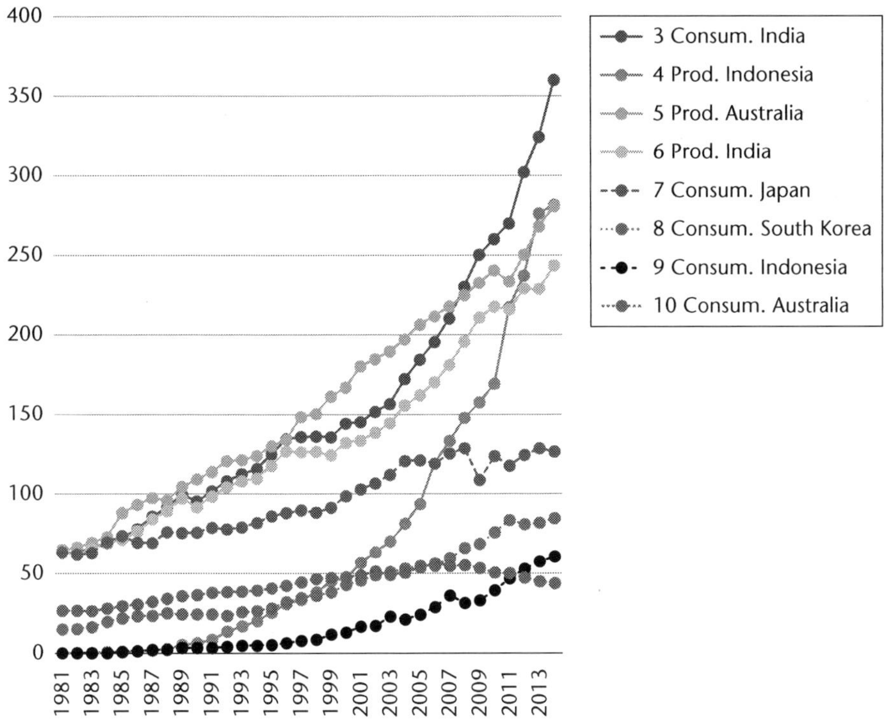

Figure 7.6 Trend of Asian coal consumption and production excluding China

Note: Unit: Million tons of oil equivalent.

Source: Data from BP Statistics (2015).

Hydroelectricity consumption

Regarding hydroelectricity consumption in Asian countries, as shown in Figure 7.8, China is overwhelmingly the biggest generator, followed by India and Japan. After 2010, Vietnam's amount has been increasing.

Nuclear power consumption

Regarding nuclear power consumption, as shown in Figure 7.9, Japan had been Asia's leader until the Fukushima Daiichi accident in 2011. After this event, Japan's nuclear power consumption dropped to zero at once. In 2016 the figurers of China were leading in nuclear power generation in Asia, followed by South Korea. China currently operates 30 nuclear power plants, with an additional 25 under construction as of April 2016. It is expected that China will become the third largest nuclear power–generating country in the world, surpassing Russia and next to US and France, when all the plants under construction completed (NDRC, China, 2016).

Consumption of renewables

As shown in Figure 7.10, the consumption of renewables other than hydroelectricity has increased in every Asian country, especially in China, which has experienced a rapid increase

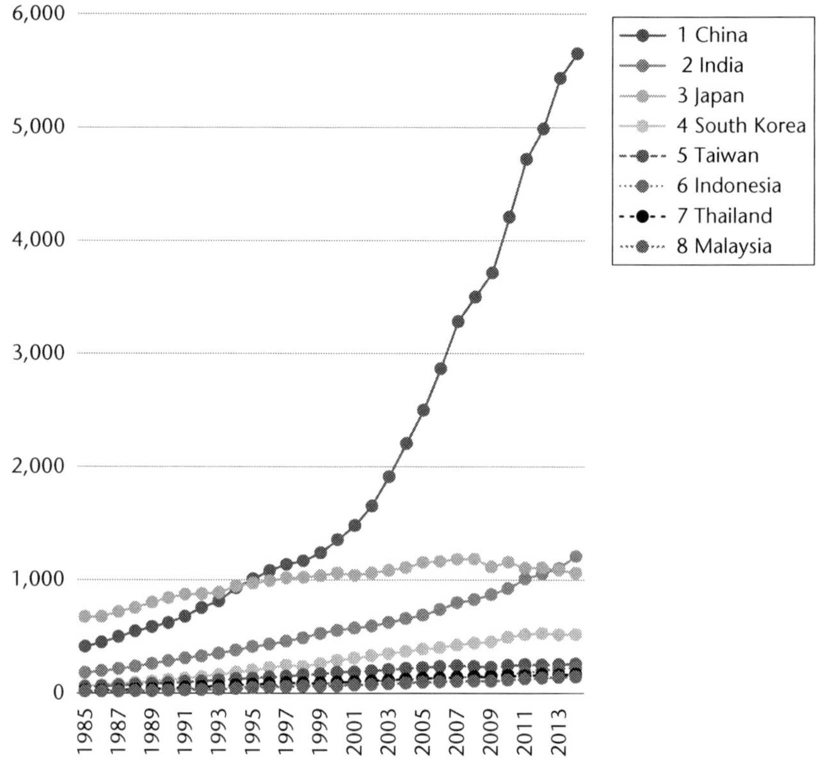

Figure 7.7 Electricity generation in Asia

Note: Unit: Terawatt-hours.

Source: Data from BP Statistics (2015).

from the 2000s onward. India is also enhancing its use of renewables. In 2010 India exceeded Japan, and India has been keeping the second position of renewable utilization in Asia.

Asian countries are trying to introduce and use renewable energy as much as possible and year on year the generation capacity of renewables has increased. But the share of power generation by renewables except hydroelectricity has remained low in most Asian countries. In the Philippines, the ratio of renewables to total energy sources occupies 13.0 percent and in India the ratio is 5.1 percent, but in Japan, Indonesia, and China it is 4–5 percent, and in Thailand between 3 and 4 percent. In other Asian nations, the ratio of renewables remains less than 3 percent.

Introduction of renewables in Asia Pacific countries

The use of renewables in Asia, excluding hydroelectricity, is shown in Table 7.3. This table also indicates how much electricity is generated using renewable sources in Asia as a whole, as well as other areas of the world.

OECD countries are advancing the introduction of renewables, including solar, wind, and biomass. But China is also enhancing the introduction of these sources, especially wind and solar. At the end of 2014, China's wind production represented 22.4 percent of the global share, and its solar production represented 15.7 percent. In total, China produced 16.7 percent of the world's renewable energy at that time.

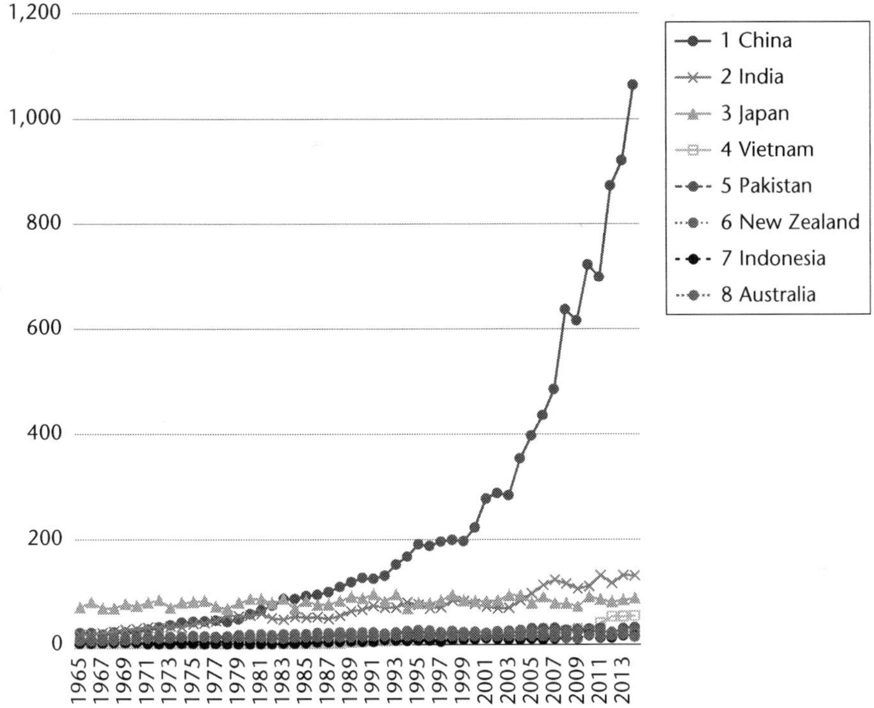

Figure 7.8 Hydroelectricity consumption in Asian countries

Note: Unit: Terawatt-hours.

Source: Data from BP Statistics (2015).

In total, the Asia Pacific region represented 29.7 percent of the world's renewable production. China accounted for over half of this production, followed by India and Japan.

In China 67 percent was occupied by wind power and solar was only 12 percent. In India, as in China, wind was the main contributing renewable power supply, at 62 percent.

In Japan solar occupies 38 percent and wind remained 10 percent.

After Japan, the Asia Pacific countries with the highest levels of renewable production were Australia, the Philippines, New Zealand, Indonesia, Thailand, Taiwan, South Korea, Malaysia, and Singapore. However, none of these countries produced more than 1.3 percent of the world share. Countries located in temperate zones or tropical zones are generally better for the introduction of renewables. Large, empty areas are suitable for wind and solar installations. Therefore, China and India are two main candidates for the further introduction of renewables.

The amounts of biofuels such as bioethanol and biodiesel produced in Asia in 2014 are shown in Table 7.4. Compared with Brazil and the US, Asian countries' production of biofuels is limited. In Asia, Indonesia is the leading producer of biofuels, followed by China and Thailand. India is expected to increase its production of biofuels based on its preferable climate conditions for growing biomass and its large possible growing areas.

Oil consumption in Indonesia was 1.6 million barrels per day, China was 11.1 million barrels per day, and Malaysia was 815 thousand barrels per day in 2014. Compared with those data, biofuel production remains small, so it is clear that substituting total oil consumption with bioenergy would be very difficult in Asia.

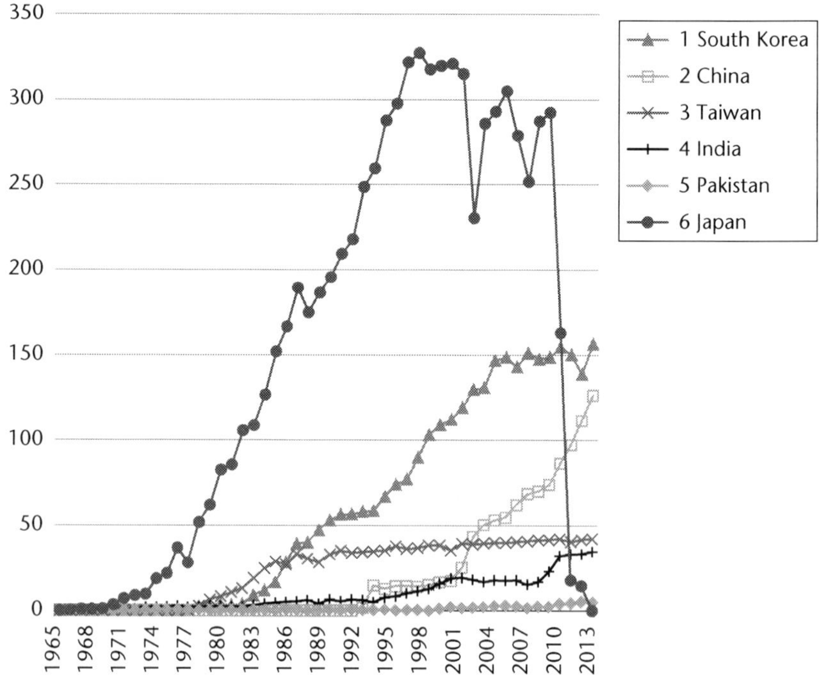

Figure 7.9 Nuclear power consumption in Asian countries

Note: Unit: Terawatt-hours.

Source: Data from BP Statistics (2015).

Asia's energy dependence on exterior sources

Asia's oil reserves are very important, because Asia is heavily dependent on oil imports. As shown in Table 7.5, the Asia Pacific region's total oil reserves are limited to 2.5 percent of the world total (as of 2014), and its reserves-to-production ratio (R/P) indicates there are only 14.1 years of remaining production.

Compared to other areas of the world, the Asia Pacific's R/P is very small. As shown in Table 7.5, the Middle East's R/P is 77.8 years, Africa's is 42.8 years, North America's is 34.0 years, and Europe and Eurasia's is 24.7 years. The R/P of South and Central America is over 100 years, due mainly to the existence of huge reserves of Venezuela.

The R/P values of individual Asian countries are limited. Vietnam's R/P is 33.0 years, and Brunei's is over 20 years, but the values of other oil-producing countries are generally just above 10 years.

The proven reserves of natural gas in Asia are shown in Table 7.6. Compared with oil reserves, gas reserves in Asia are slightly better and the average R/P of gas in Asia Pacific was 28.7 years as of 2014.

Australia, which is very important supplier of gas to Asia, had 67.7 years of reserves. Vietnam's R/P was 60.4 years. India's R/P was 45.0 years and Indonesia's and Papua New Guinea's R/P were over 30 years. China's and Brunei's R/P were over 30 years.

As shown in Table 7.7, the Asian proven reserves of coal represented 32.3 percent of the world total in 2014. The reserve ratio of coal in Asia is bigger than those of oil and gas. Indonesia is a major coal exporter, as is Australia, which is located in Oceania and exports mainly to Asian countries.

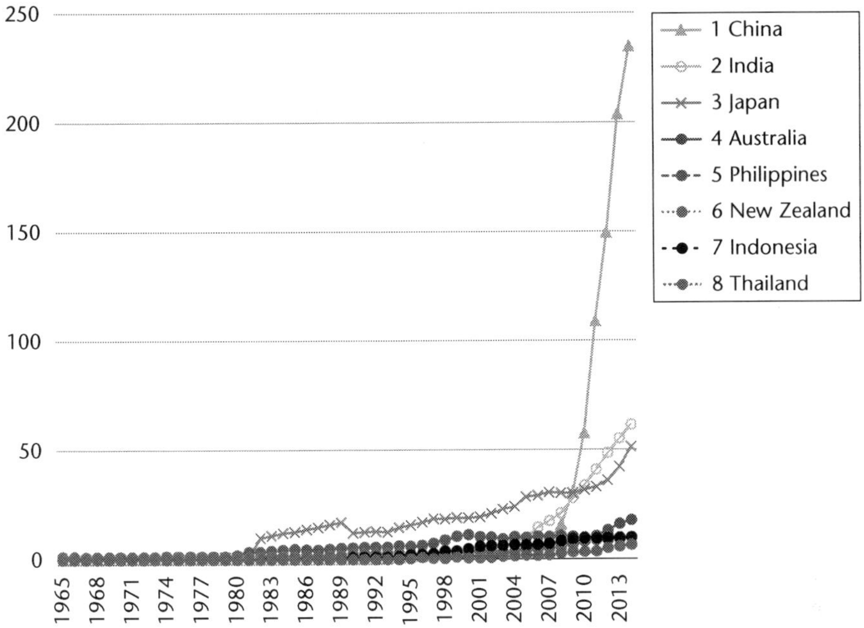

Figure 7.10 Consumption of renewables other than hydroelectricity in Asia

Note: Unit: Terawatt-hours.

Source: Data from BP Statistics (2015).

The basic condition of fossil fuel supplies in the Asia Pacific region can be analyzed based on the above data. Compared with production, consumption is very large in Asia, especially in oil. Asia's R/P for oil in 2014 was 14.1 years, as shown in Table 7.5; R/P for gas was 28.7 years, as shown in Table 7.6; and the R/P for oil was 51 years, as shown in Table 7.7. Therefore, Asian countries must increasingly rely on imports of oil and gas from foreign regions, such as the Middle East.

The total fossil fuel production and consumption of the Asia Pacific region is shown in Table 7.8. The figures for each fuel source are compared based on caloric conversion to tons of oil equivalent.

In the Asia Pacific region, oil, gas, and coal are all imported from outside the region, creating a negative balance for all three fossil fuels. Oil imports are particularly substantial: compared with the amount produced in the Asia Pacific, the region consumes 3.6 times more. Therefore, the Asia Pacific region is heavily dependent on oil imports, especially from the Middle East.

Asia Pacific coal production represents 76 percent of the region's total fossil fuel production. Coal reserves are larger than those of oil and other resources in the region. Regarding consumption, there is only a 2 percent difference between coal production and consumption in the Asia Pacific. Therefore, almost all the coal produced in the region is domestically consumed, and the remaining balance is imported from the outside.

When considering the Asia Pacific region, it is generally helpful to include Australia. When Australia is included, the self-sufficiency ratio of the regional fossil fuel supply dramatically improves, which enhances the security of the energy supply. Australia exports large amounts of coal and gas to Asian countries and also exports some oil.

Table 7.3 Introduction of renewables in Asia Pacific countries at the end of 2014

		Solar	*Share of total*	*Wind*	*Share of total*	*Geothermal Biomass*	*Share of total*	*Total*	*Share of total*
1	China	29.1	15.7%	158.4	22.4%	47.1	9.3%	234.6	16.7%
2	India	4.4	2.4%	38.4	5.4%	18.7	3.7%	61.5	4.4%
3	Japan	19.4	10.4%	5.1	0.7%	27.0	5.3%	51.5	3.7%
4	Australia	4.5	2.4%	10.2	1.5%	3.2	0.6%	17.9	1.3%
5	Philippines	^	♦	0.1	♦	10.0	2.0%	10.1	0.7%
6	New Zealand	^	♦	2.2	0.3%	7.8	1.5%	10.1	0.7%
7	Indonesia	^	♦	^	♦	9.9	1.9%	9.9	0.7%
8	Thailand	1.5	0.8%	0.5	0.1%	4.6	0.9%	6.6	0.5%
9	Taiwan	0.6	0.3%	1.5	0.2%	3.5	0.7%	5.6	0.4%
10	South Korea	2.5	1.3%	1.3	0.2%	1.3	0.3%	5.0	0.4%
11	Malaysia	0.2	0.1%	–	–	1.1	0.2%	1.3	0.1%
12	Singapore	^	♦	–	–	0.7	0.1%	0.7	♦
13	Bangladesh	0.2	0.1%	^	♦	^	♦	0.2	♦
14	Vietnam	^	♦	0.2	♦	0.1	♦	0.2	♦
15	Pakistan	0.1	0.1%	0.1	♦	–	–	0.2	♦
16	China Hong Kong SAR	^	♦	^	♦	0.1	♦	0.1	♦
	Other Asia Pacific	^	♦	0.3	♦	0.5	0.1%	0.8	0.1%
	Total Asia Pacific	62.6	33.7%	218.3	30.9%	135.4	26.6%	416.2	29.7%
	Total North America	19.3	10.4%	202.1	28.6%	103.7	20.4%	325.1	23.2%
	Total S. & Cent. America	1.1	0.6%	17.7	2.5%	76.2	15.0%	95.1	6.8%
	Total Europe & FSU	99.7	53.6%	261.6	37.0%	188.5	37.1%	549.8	39.3%
	Total Middle East	1.1	0.6%	0.3	♦	0.1	♦	1.5	0.1%
	Total Africa	2.1	1.1%	6.1	0.9%	4.7	0.9%	12.8	0.9%
	Total World	185.9	100.0%	706.2	100.0%	508.5	100.0%	1400.6	100.0%
	of which: OECD	143.6	77.3%	475.0	67.3%	335.3	65.9%	953.9	68.1%
	Non-OECD	42.3	22.7%	231.2	32.7%	173.2	34.1%	446.7	31.9%
	European Union	98.4	52.9%	249.7	35.4%	176.6	34.7%	524.6	37.5%
	Former Soviet Union	0.5	0.3%	2.4	0.3%	2.7	0.5%	5.6	0.4%

Note: Unit: Terawatt-hours.

^ Less than 0.05.

♦ Less than 0.05%.

Table 7.4 Biofuels production in Asia in 2014

1	Indonesia	49
2	China	42
3	Thailand	28
4	India	6
5	South Korea	6
6	Australia	3
	Other Asia Pacific	17
	Total Asia Pacific	151
1	Total North America	628
2	Total S. & Cent. America	408
3	Total Europe & FSU	235
4	Total Asia Pacific	151
5	Total Middle East	0
6	Total Africa	0
	Total World	1,422
	of which: OECD	864
	Non-OECD	557
	European Union	233
	Former Soviet Union	4

Note: Unit: Thousand barrel per day of oil equivalent.

Source: Data from BP Statistics (2015).

Table 7.5 Proven oil reserves in Asia Pacific

		Billion barrels	*Share of total*	*R/P ratio*
1	China	18.5	1.1%	11.9
2	India	5.7	0.3%	17.6
3	Vietnam	4.4	0.3%	33.0
4	Australia	4.0	0.2%	24.3
5	Malaysia	3.8	0.2%	15.4
6	Indonesia	3.7	0.2%	11.9
7	Brunei	1.1	0.1%	23.8
8	Thailand	0.5	♦	2.8
	Other Asia Pacific	1.1	0.1%	10.9
	Total Asia Pacific	42.7	2.5%	14.1
	Total Middle East	810.7	47.7%	77.8
	Total S. & Cent. America	330.2	19.4%	*
	Total North America	232.5	13.7%	34.0
	Total Europe & FSU	154.8	9.1%	24.7
	Total Africa	129.2	7.6%	42.8
	Total World	1,700.1	100.0%	52.5
	OPEC	1,216.5	71.6%	91.1
	Non-OPEC	341.7	20.1%	24.5

Note: Unit: Billion of barrels, %.

* More than 100 years.

♦ Less than 0.05%.

Source: Data from BP Statistics (2015).

Table 7.6 Proven reserves of natural gas in Asia Pacific

		Trillion cubic meters	*Share of world total*	*R/P ratio*
1	Australia	3.7	2.0%	67.6
2	China	3.5	1.8%	25.7
3	Indonesia	2.9	1.5%	39.2
4	India	1.4	0.8%	45.0
5	Malaysia	1.1	0.6%	16.2
6	Vietnam	0.6	0.3%	60.4
7	Pakistan	0.6	0.3%	13.8
8	Myanmar	0.3	0.2%	16.8
9	Brunei	0.3	0.1%	23.3
10	Bangladesh	0.3	0.1%	10.7
11	Thailand	0.2	0.1%	5.7
12	Papua New Guinea	0.2	0.1%	31.0
	Other Asia Pacific	0.3	0.2%	15.6
	Total World	187.1	100.0%	54.1
1	Total Middle East	79.8	42.7%	*
2	Total Europe & FSU	58.0	31.0%	57.9
3	Total Asia Pacific	15.3	8.2%	28.7
4	Total Africa	14.2	7.6%	69.8
5	Total North America	12.1	6.5%	12.8
6	Total S. & Cent. America	7.7	4.1%	43.8
	of which: OECD	19.5	10.4%	15.6
	Non-OECD	167.6	89.6%	75.8
	European Union	1.5	0.8%	11.3
	Former Soviet Union	54.6	29.2%	71.8

Note: Unit: Trillions of cubic meters, %. R/P means reserve-to-production ratio.
* More than 100 years.

Source: Data from BP Statistics (2015).

Future prospects for energy supply and demand in Asia

Issues of future energy supply and demand in Asia

The dialogue on climate change raised under the UNFCCC (United Nations Framework Convention on Climate Change) has often been critical of coal usage. In addition to the tendency to restrict the use of high CO_2-emission fuels such as coal, gas production in the US has increased due to technological innovations such as horizontal drilling, fracturing techniques, and three-dimensional analysis. With the addition of shale gas reserves to those of conventional gas, ample supplies of gas are now available in the US. US gas prices remain low, and power companies prefer to utilize low-cost gas as fuel. As coal generation decreases and gas power increases, CO_2 emissions in the US are starting to decrease. Based on this trend, US president Barack Obama declared that greenhouse gas emissions should be reduced by 26 to 28 percent by 2025 compared to 2005 levels, in observance of the Paris accord concluded at COP21 in 2015.

However, fossil fuel reserves are limited in Asian countries. While Asia contains large volumes of coal, these are located primarily in China and India. These countries are the world's two most

Table 7.7 Proven reserves of coal in Asia at the end of 2014

		Anthracite and bituminous	*Sub-bituminous and lignite*	*Total*	*Share of Total*	*R/P ratio*
1	China	62,200	52,300	114,500	12.8%	30
2	Australia	37,100	39,300	76,400	8.6%	155
3	India	56,100	4,500	60,600	6.8%	94
4	Indonesia	–	28,017	28,017	3.1%	61
5	Pakistan	–	2,070	2,070	0.2%	*
6	Thailand	–	1,239	1,239	0.1%	69
7	North Korea	300	300	600	0.1%	19
8	New Zealand	33	538	571	0.1%	143
9	Japan	337	10	347	♦	265
10	Vietnam	150	–	150	♦	4
11	South Korea	–	126	126	♦	72
	Other Asia Pacific	1,583	2,125	3,708	0.4%	97
	Total World	403,199	488,332	891,531	100.0%	110
1	Total Europe & FSU	92,557	217,981	310,538	34.8%	268
2	Total Asia Pacific	157,803	130,525	288,328	32.3%	51
3	Total North America	112,835	132,253	245,088	27.5%	248
4	Total Middle East & Africa	32,722	214	32,936	3.7%	122
5	Total S. & Cent. America	7,282	7,359	14,641	1.6%	142
	of which: OECD	155,494	229,321	384,815	43.2%	191
	Non-OECD	247,705	259,011	506,716	56.8%	83
	European Union	4,883	51,199	56,082	6.3%	111
	Former Soviet Union	86,725	141,309	228,034	25.6%	428

Note: Million tons of coal, %. R/P means reserve-to-production ratio.

* More than 100 years.

– Means less than millions of tons of coal.

♦ Means less than 0.05%.

Source: Data from BP Statistics (2015).

Table 7.8 Energy production, consumption, and balance in the Asia Pacific (at the end of 2014)

	Production	*Consmuption*	*Balance*
Oil	396.7	1,428.9	−1,032.2
Gas	478.1	610.7	−132.7
Coal	2,722.5	2,776.6	−54.0
Total	3,597.4	4,816.3	−1,218.9

Note: Unit: Million tons of oil equivalent.

populous, and domestic consumption of coal in each is substantial. Therefore, Asia as a region must rely on large imports of fossil fuels such as oil, gas, and coal. To decrease Asia's dependence on coal means enhancing its reliance on other fossil fuels. Oil is unevenly distributed across the world, especially in the Middle East and North Africa, which can export huge volumes of oil to other regions, especially Asia.

Table 7.9 Future prospects of energy demand and supply in OECD Asia and Oceania

	1990	*2013*	*2020*	*2025*	*2030*	*2035*	*2040*
Oil	335	351	306	281	258	237	221
Gas	66	189	177	179	186	188	186
Coal	138	246	233	217	207	192	175
Nuclear	66	39	104	130	141	149	158
Hydro	11	11	11	12	12	13	13
Bioenergy	10	23	28	31	33	36	39
Other renewables	4	10	24	34	47	60	74
Total	632	870	884	885	884	876	866

Note: Unit: Million tons oil equivalent.

Source: IEA "World Energy Outlook 2015."

Table 7.10 Future prospects of electricity generation in OECD Asia and Oceania

	1990	*2013*	*2020*	*2025*	*2030*	*2035*	*2040*
Nuclear	255	148	401	500	540	572	606
Coal	256	723	681	632	606	574	525
Hydro	133	124	134	138	143	148	154
Gas	208	607	504	494	504	505	493
Wind	0	16	44	68	93	122	152
Solar PV	0	20	79	93	104	115	127
Bioenergy	12	48	60	68	77	86	95
Geothermal	4	9	16	25	37	48	57
Oil	259	173	57	38	27	21	19
CSP	0	0	0	2	3	6	10
Marine	0	0	2	3	5	7	9
Total	1,127	1,868	1,975	2,060	2,138	2,202	2,247

Note: Unit: TWh. CSP: concentrated solar power.

Source: IEA "World Energy Outlook 2015."

Gas reserves are more evenly distributed, but the number of countries that can export gas through pipelines or liquefied natural gas transport to Asia is restricted. Therefore, Asia's energy supply could become highly vulnerable if coal utilization is restricted, even to a limited extent.

Future prospects of energy demand

The future prospects of energy demand in OECD Asia and Oceania are shown in Table 7.9. Japan and Australia are included in this figure. The total figure is expected to increase until 2025 and then will begin to decrease.

Coal and oil began to decrease in 2013, and gas is expected to peak around 2035. Total fossil fuel consumption shows a decline after 2013, due mainly to the decrease of oil. Nuclear, hydro, bioenergy, and other renewables show gradual and continuous increases through the year 2040.

Regarding the future prospects of electricity generation in OECD Asia and Oceania, total figures are expected to increase as shown on Table 7.10. Coal use will gradually decrease, while oil usage will be drastically reduced. Gas usage will also decrease, but nuclear usage is expected to increase. Hydro, bioenergy, geothermal, solar photovoltaics (PV), concentrated solar power

Table 7.11 Future prospects of energy demand in Japan

	1990	*2013*	*2020*	*2025*	*2030*	*2035*	*2040*
Oil	250	202	160	143	129	116	107
Gas	44	106	86	84	86	87	86
Coal	77	121	111	103	99	91	83
Nuclear	53	2	46	57	57	59	62
Bioenergy	5	11	13	14	16	17	18
Hydro	8	7	8	8	8	8	9
Other renewables	3	4	11	15	21	27	34
Total	439	455	434	424	414	406	399

Note: Unit: Million tons oil equivalent.

Source: IEA "World Energy Outlook 2015."

Table 7.12 Future prospects of electricity generation in Japan

	1990	*2013*	*2020*	*2025*	*2030*	*2035*	*2040*
Gas	179	402	305	290	295	296	284
Coal	116	337	306	290	290	275	254
Nuclear	202	9	175	218	218	228	239
Hydro	89	78	88	91	95	99	103
Solar PV	0	14	61	70	77	83	91
Bioenergy	11	41	48	51	55	60	64
Wind		5	9	15	22	32	44
Geothermal	2	3	5	7	12	17	22
Oil	237	150	45	29	20	15	14
Marine					0	1	2
Total	836	1,038	1,043	1,062	1,084	1,105	1,117

Note: Unit: TWh.

Source: IEA "World Energy Outlook 2015."

(CSP) and marine energy are all expected to increase through the year 2040. Wind and solar PV are estimated to experience especially substantial increases.

In Japan, the energy demand predicted until 2040 by the IEA is shown on Table 7.11. Total energy consumption will decrease gradually, and coal and oil are expected to decrease through 2040. Gas consumption is expected to level off after 2020. Nuclear generation is expected to remain relatively stable after 2025, but the figure will be lower than that planned before the Fukushima Daiichi accident. Regarding renewable energy sources, hydropower will remain at the same level, but other renewables such as bioenergy will increase gradually.

The future prospects of electricity generation in Japan, as predicted by IEA, are shown in Table 7.12. Total electricity generation is estimated to increase gradually. Generation by coal, oil, and gas is expected to decrease, while that by nuclear and hydropower is expected to increase. Generation from wind, geothermal, solar PV, and marine sources is also expected to increase gradually.

Non-OECD Asian countries' future prospects of energy demand, as predicted by IEA, are listed in Table 7.13. Total energy consumption is expected to increase substantially. Compared

Table 7.13 Future prospects of energy demand in non-OECD Asia

	1990	*2013*	*2020*	*2025*	*2030*	*2035*	*2040*
Coal	684	2,550	2,761	2,912	3,096	3,244	3,345
Oil	320	957	1,157	1,284	1,404	1,507	1,594
Gas	69	378	530	639	747	858	958
Nuclear	10	50	140	215	285	337	383
Hydro	24	106	138	158	178	194	205
Bioenergy	466	586	622	640	655	670	688
Other renewables	7	65	129	175	227	284	344
Total	1,579	4,693	5,478	6,023	6,592	7,094	7,518

Note: Unit: Million tons oil equivalent.

Source: IEA "World Energy Outlook 2015."

Table 7.14 Future prospects of electricity generation in non-OECD Asia

	1990	*2013*	*2020*	*2025*	*2030*	*2035*	*2040*
Coal	728	5,380	6,337	6,914	7,683	8,398	8,996
Hydro	274	1,237	1,605	1,839	2,072	2,259	2,388
Gas	59	659	971	1,282	1,567	1,900	2,221
Nuclear	39	192	538	824	1,092	1,292	1,471
Wind		175	513	746	971	1,206	1,445
Solar PV		21	181	307	442	584	731
Bioenergy	1	87	253	353	443	539	635
Geothermal	7	19	30	40	52	68	86
Oil	167	136	116	104	96	90	81
CSP			4	9	22	44	73
Marine					1	2	3
Total	1,274	7,906	10,547	12,419	14,441	16,380	18,132

Note: Unit: TWh.

Source: IEA "World Energy Outlook 2015."

with the total figure for 2013, consumption in 2040 is expected to increase by 60 percent, from 4,693 million tons to 7,518 million tons.

Coal will continue to be the dominant energy source in non-OECD Asia, followed by oil. Levels of gas, nuclear, hydro, bioenergy, and other renewable usage are all expected to increase through 2040.

The future prospects of electricity generation in non-OECD Asia are shown in Table 7.14. Coal will remain the most important energy source, accounting for approximately 50 percent of electricity production in non-OECD Asian countries. Oil consumption for power generation is expected to decrease, but the amount of gas consumed for power generation will continuously increase. New nuclear plants will also be installed to expand capacity, and by 2040, IEA projects that 8 percent of electricity will be generated by nuclear sources. Hydro, bioenergy, wind, geothermal, solar PV, CSP and marine renewables are all expected to continuously increase through the year 2040.

China's future prospects of energy demand are shown in Table 7.15. China's energy consumption is expected to increase annually. However, the Chinese government is trying to

Table 7.15 Future prospects of energy demand in China

	1990	*2013*	*2020*	*2025*	*2030*	*2035*	*2040*
Coal	533	2,053	2,060	2,070	2,078	2,053	1,978
Oil	122	483	590	647	685	702	710
Gas	13	142	252	317	375	422	456
Nuclear		29	104	167	217	255	287
Hydro	11	78	103	113	124	131	134
Bioenergy	200	216	222	227	234	244	258
Other renewables	0	37	81	108	136	165	197
Total	879	3,037	3,412	3,649	3,848	3,971	4,020

Note: Unit: Million tons oil equivalent.

Source: IEA "World Energy Outlook 2015."

Table 7.16 Future prospects of electricity generation in China

	1990	*2013*	*2020*	*2025*	*2030*	*2035*	*2040*
Coal	470	4,120	4,461	4,662	4,947	5,166	5,231
Oil	51	7	7	6	6	5	3
Gas	3	109	318	490	645	781	897
Nuclear		112	400	639	834	978	1,102
Hydro	127	909	1,193	1,317	1,438	1,518	1,559
Bioenergy		50	173	237	282	325	367
Wind		139	410	576	721	872	1,025
Geothermal			1	2	5	10	16
Solar PV		16	128	194	251	308	369
CSP			2	6	16	33	54
Marine					1	1	2
Total	650	5,462	7,093	8,128	9,146	9,998	10,626

Note: Unit: TWh.

Source: IEA "World Energy Outlook 2015."

decrease the consumption of coal after 2030 and compensate for this by using gas, nuclear, hydro, bioenergy and other renewables. Oil demand will also increase due to the introduction of more vehicles, including passenger cars and heavy-duty cars.

Electricity generation in China, as shown in Table 7.16, is expected to remain heavily dependent on coal and hydropower. Dependency on coal will continue through 2040, and nuclear, hydro, wind, and gas usage will increase, according to the IEA forecast. Other renewables, such as solar PV, bioenergy, geothermal, and CSP are expected to increase but remain a small share of China's overall energy consumption.

For India in 2013, as shown in Table 7.17, energy demand depends primarily on coal, followed by bioenergy and oil. In the future, the IEA predicts that India will rely more on coal while decreasing its oil demand. Gas supply and demand will also increase. Other energy sources, such as nuclear, hydro, and bioenergy, will slightly increase but remain small contributors to India's overall energy situation.

India's electricity generation, as shown in Table 7.18, is heavily dependent on coal, which accounted for over 70 percent of its production in 2013. Hydropower was the next most

Table 7.17 Future prospects of energy demand in India

	1990	*2013*	*2020*	*2025*	*2030*	*2035*	*2040*
Coal	94	341	476	568	690	814	934
Oil	63	176	229	273	239	393	458
Gas	11	45	58	81	103	126	149
Nuclear	2	9	17	28	43	57	70
Hydro	6	12	15	19	22	25	29
Bioenergy	133	188	209	215	217	213	209
Other renewables		4	13	23	35	47	60
Total	308	775	1,018	1,207	1,440	1,676	1,908

Note: Unit: Million tons oil equivalent.

Source: IEA "World Energy Outlook 2015."

Table 7.18 Future prospects of electricity generation in India

	1990	*2013*	*2020*	*2025*	*2030*	*2035*	*2040*
Coal	192	869	1,224	1,412	1,698	2,009	2,333
Oil	13	23	26	29	32	36	37
Gas	10	65	96	185	262	348	431
Nuclear	6	34	66	109	165	218	269
Hydro	72	142	174	215	253	293	333
Bioenergy		23	48	64	80	99	121
Wind		34	91	145	201	252	296
Geothermal				1	1	2	2
Solar PV		3	40	90	152	218	285
CSP			1	2	5	9	17
Marine							1
Total	293	1,193	1,766	2,251	2,848	3,485	4,124

Note: Unit: TWh.

Source: IEA "World Energy Outlook 2015."

important source, accounting for 12 percent of production in 2013. Gas and nuclear energy remain small contributors to power generation, accounting for 5 percent and 3 percent of the total, respectively, in 2013.

In the future, India must rely on coal for the bulk of its power generation. The IEA projection anticipates that coal will represent 56 percent of India's total production in 2040. Gas will be the next most important source, followed by hydropower, wind, solar PV, and nuclear energy. Based on this estimation, the contribution of bioenergy will remain small in India.

Summary and future of Asian energy supply and demand

China and India

Based on the expectations prepared by the IEA and discussed in the previous section, Asian energy consumption will continue to increase, except in Japan. But even in Japan, electricity consumption is expected to increase until 2040.

Importantly, each country's energy composition will be maintained through the future, to differing degrees. Each country tends to rely mainly on its domestic energy resources. Therefore, the market structure for the supply and demand of energy in each country will continue to depend on its energy resource availability.

Coal consumption in Asia is expected to increase under the IEA "World Energy Outlook 2015." Coal prices are preferable for developing Asian countries, and Banks (2000, 113) has written that "the age of coal has apparently come and gone, but many observers feel that it will return." His words are now becoming reality. From a security perspective, coal is essential because of its ample reserves in developed countries such as the US, Canada, and Australia.

Both China and India have substantial coal reserves and depend primarily on coal for their energy supplies, with other resources in supporting roles. However, the Chinese government has declared a plan to level off its coal consumption by 2030 and decrease it afterwards. Per capita energy consumption in China remains low compared with OECD countries, and as per capita GDP increases, energy consumption is also expected to increase. If the Chinese government plans to decrease coal consumption, it will be necessary to substitute coal with other kinds of energy, such as gas, nuclear, hydropower, and other renewable energy sources. China's energy consumption is massive; it is the world's leading consumer of coal, accounting for 50.6 percent of world total consumption in 2014. It would be highly difficult to substitute coal consumption through one energy source. All possible energy sources must be introduced to cover China's continuously increasing energy demand.

Banks (2015) writes that, in light of the future situation of energy scarcity in the world and the world's ample reserves of coal, this fuel must be used in the future. Drastic policies for decreasing coal consumption are therefore unrealistic. When necessary, coal may be used in the form of gasified methane gas.

Regarding renewables, Hanjalic et al. (2008) claims that renewable energy can partially substitute for other sources of electricity, but that the supply of renewables is insufficient for them to become the main source of energy. Renewables are sometimes called "distributed energy," which means that the production of each renewable source is limited.

Asia's position is weak regarding energy supplies, especially for oil. Although the region has rich reserves of coal in China and India, these countries are the world's two most populous. The per capita reserves of energy in these countries are therefore limited and less than the world average. The Chinese government endeavors to acquire energy and access foreign countries' energy reserves because its energy needs are enormous compared with those of less-populated countries.

India also has ample reserves of coal but, like China, is densely populated. Politically speaking, India is the world's largest democratic country, and its central government policy is decided by its assembly and legislative decisions. Therefore, India is relatively slow to implement regulations and introduce new policies, although the Indian people have more influence on these decisions. Compared with Chinese businesses, Indian companies experience less pressure from the central government and receive support from the local governments.

Energy issues in Asia

Huge differences in per capita income exist between Asian countries, and different countries are in different phases of development. Even among the Association of Southeast Asian Nations' (ASEAN) ten member countries, six countries are considered to play mentorship roles for the remaining four countries. In LCMV, Laos, Cambodia, Myanmar, and Vietnam, countries' per capita incomes are low compared with those of the other six countries, which comprise Singapore, Thailand, Malaysia,

Indonesia, the Philippines, and Brunei. Therefore, they have immense potential for development and could reach the level of the six economically advanced ASEAN countries.

When development levels differ between countries, it is sometimes difficult to adjust energy policies and come to a compromise that allows for mergers and acquisitions, in energy industries and mutual participation in business activities for each country. The governments of less-developed countries tend to protect their domestic companies, which are often fragile compared with foreign companies.

Therefore, each Asian country tends to compete for protecting its domestic industries and attracting the investment of foreign companies. Countries also compete to buy oil and gas from foreign regions, especially the Middle East, for as low a price as possible. The price of oil and gas destined for Asia thus tends to be higher than fuel destined for other regions, such as Europe and North America. This Asian premium, as well as possibilities for its reduction, is often discussed among Asian energy businesses and governments to reduce import expenditures and decrease national deficits.

Comparison of the EU with Asian countries

Compared to the EU, which has very actively proposed declarations and stressed its role as a single entity, Asian countries remain in more diverse developmental stages. In Asia, both the distribution of energy resources and the stage of development differ between countries. Therefore, it is difficult for Asian countries to compromise on energy policy issues.

In the EU, a political declaration called the International Energy Charter was prepared to encourage international cooperation in the field of energy. In advance, the EU declared the European Energy Charter to strengthen its energy security in 1991. Based on this the European Energy Charter, The Energy Charter Treaty was adopted in 1994 and entered into force in 1998.

Importantly, the EU welcomed participation in these treaties, not only from EU members and surrounding countries but also from the international community. For example, Japan ratified the European Energy Charter in 2002 and the International Energy Charter in 2015. Asian countries may follow the EU's progress in cooperating on energy issues. Promoting and signing these treaties would encourage mutual understanding, prevent conflict, and increase business opportunities. To prepare an Asian version of the Charter and Treaty will also contribute to stabilizing energy supply and demand in the Asian region.

Some Asian countries still operate under central governments that intervene in markets to some degree when prices fluctuate. The effects of governmental energy market intervention must be studied. Market-oriented reform and the opening of domestic markets have been welcomed in most of countries, but these steps have moved slowly.

The progress of IT communications has allowed global issues such as terrorism, war, public debt, and climate change to very easily impact world market conditions. Therefore, in Asia, as in the EU, it is crucial to promote and compile energy-related treaties. The process of negotiating energy-related issues and compiling energy treaties with countries that hold differences of opinion may be very useful for Asian countries.

Relationship with Middle Eastern countries

In 2016, the Saudi Arabian government assigned a new oil minister, Mr. Khalid A. Al-Falih, a change from the previous minister of roughly 20 years, Mr. Ali bin Ibrahim Al-Naimi. As Cordesman (2003) discusses, Saudi Arabia has gradually changed its governmental organization, introducing the Supreme Council for Petroleum and Minerals in 2000 to better shape its oil policy. However, the country is still shifting to dependence on market mechanisms.

Asian countries are approaching Middle Eastern countries on energy matters. Japan is negotiating a Gulf Cooperation Council (GCC) Free Trade Agreement (FTA). GCC includes six countries in the Middle East: Saudi Arabia, Kuwait, the United Arab Emirates, Qatar, Bahrain, and Oman. China and Korea are also approaching the GCC to negotiate an FTA. These countries are similar in that they are all importers of oil and gas, dependent on the Middle East or OPEC. These importers of energy share similar national interests. Therefore, cooperation among these energy-importing countries through information exchange, analysis, and amendment of the regulations and systems that enhance the efficiency of the energy markets could be very useful.

Future of energy supply and sustainability

As Yergin (2011) writes, world energy consumption must increase. How to cover this rising energy demand is the most important issue in the world. Does significant technological innovation remain in the future? How to pay energy costs and maintain efficiency and sustainability is also very important. New innovations will likely be developed, but as Yergin discusses, the timing of those innovations is uncertain. Therefore, steady trials to introduce environmentally friendly energy are necessary to secure the future prospects of countries that depend on energy imports from outside Asia. Lovins (2011) stresses the importance of energy conservation. Efforts to reduce energy consumption and introduce conservation will strengthen energy security, but forecasts by several research institutes and organizations suggest that it may be very difficult to decrease energy consumption.

The future scarcity of energy supplies such as oil, as mentioned long ago by Hoteling (1931), will cause prices of those supplies to fluctuate widely, as discussed by Laherrere (1995). Prices tend to depart from the trend line, and price fluctuations will extend several times more; for example, crude oil prices jumped from USD $50 per barrel to $100 per barrel in two to three years from 2005 to 2008, and from 2009 to 2011.

The price of energy may tend to increase, because global climate supporters have created strong pressure to reduce the use of fossil fuels. Every country must attempt to introduce renewables to the greatest possible extent. But the present analysis indicates that the substitution of fossil fuels by renewables will not be easy due to the limited availability and supply of renewables. Renewable energy generation is spread over wide areas, is comparatively difficult, and is often more expensive than comparative fossil fuels. For example, transmission lines are necessary for the distribution of wind power, but often there are insufficient transmission lines near suitable wind power installations because areas of heavy wind are not unsuitable agriculture and are sparsely populated.

Therefore, these energy shortages may occur due to the mismatching of supply and demand. This situation would cause an energy price hike. But when the prices of energy increase, global political will and grassroots activism on energy issues may lead to solutions (Hanjalic et al., 2008).

Regarding the possibility of renewables introduction, Randers (2012) is not optimistic. He writes that it will take approximately 40 years for solar PV to become fully competitive with other sources for power generation.

Hersh (2006) writes that as the world continues unsustainable development, further conflicts will occur over oil resources, as well as continual issues of poverty and hunger. It may be important to study again the necessity of sustainable development, reconstructing optimal markets, and composing cooperative ties in the Asian region.

Combarnous and Bonnet (2008) stress the importance of functional market mechanisms, especially for oil and gas. Both of these fuels are nonrenewable sources, so the market mechanisms may be disturbed by control of the market or distortion.

Afgan (2008) describes four main indicators for evaluating the sustainability of energy markets: technological efficiency, economical efficiency, ecological efficiency, and social efficiency. Banks (2015, 157) points out that on Wall Street, "the market knows more than any one player."

Energy prices often fluctuate due to conflicts, accidents, fighting, information bias, market distortion, governmental intervention, and other events. It is necessary to enhance the efficiency of energy trading and force market mechanisms to work optimally, thereby reducing the risks in the energy market.

As already analyzed, Asia's energy demand will continuously increase, so the market-oriented reform and the opening of domestic markets are essentially necessary for maintaining efficient energy use and enhancing stabilization of energy trade. For deepening mutual understanding in Asian countries, to promote the frequent exchange of ideas on energy-related issues and also to seek the way to compiling the Asian version of energy treaties seems to be significantly important.

References

Afgan, Naim Hamdia. (2008). "Sustainability Concept for Energy, Water and Environment Systems," Chapter 2, Hanjalic K., R. van de Krol, and A. Lekic, eds., *Sustainable Energy Technologies, Options and Prospects*. Dordrecht, the Netherlands: Springer.

Banks, Ferdinand E. (2000). *Energy Economics: A Modern Introduction*. Boston/Dordrecht/London: Kluwer Academic Publishers.

Banks, Ferdinand E. (2015). *Energy and Economic Theory*. New Jersey/London/Singapore: World Scientific.

Combarnous, Michel and Jean-Francois Bonnet. (2008). "World for Energy: How to Face the Challenge," Chapter 1, Hanjalic K., R. van de Krol, and A. Lekic, eds., *Sustainable Energy Technologies, Options and Prospects*. Dordrecht, the Netherlands: Springer.

Cordesman, Anthony H. (2003). *Saudi Arabia Enters the Twenty-First Century: The Political, Foreign Policy, Economic, and Energy Dimensions*. Westport, CT/London: Praeger Publishing.

Hanjalic K., R. van de Krol, and A. Lekic. eds. (2008). *Sustainable Energy Technologies, Options and Prospects*. Dordrecht, the Netherlands: Springer.

Hersh, Marion. (2006). *Mathematical Modelling for Sustainable Development*. Germany: Springer.

Hoteling, Harold. (1931). "The economics of exhaustible resources," *Journal of Political Economy*, 39: 137–175.

Laherrere, Jean. (1995). "World oil reserves," *OPEC Bulletin*, 14: 9–13.

Lovins, Amory. (2011). *Reinventing Fire: Bold Business Solutions for the New Energy Era*. White River Junction, VT: Chelsea Green Publishing Co.

NDRC (National Development and Reform Commission, Energy Research Institute). (2016). "13th Five-year plan and medium-and-long term energy development strategy of China," mimeo.

Randers, Jorgen. (2012). *2052: A Global Forecast for the Next Forty Years*. White River Junction, VT: Chelsea Green Publishing.

Yergin, Daniel. (2011). *The Quest: Energy, Security, and the Remaking of the Modern World*. New York: The Penguin Press.

Statistics

BP Statistical Review of World Energy, 2015.
www.ide.go.jp/Japanese/Event/Seminar/160607.html

IEA "World Energy Outlook 2015"
www.iea.org/

US DOE EIA
www.eia.gov/

8

Evaluating indicators of energy security for sustainable development in Asia

Helen Cabalu and Yixiao Zhou

Introduction

The energy sector is an important part of the global economy and underpins all forms of economic activity. It is of paramount importance that energy resources are managed to ensure a secure supply of energy that is essential to economic growth, jobs, and economic prosperity. Following three decades of strong economic and population growth accompanied by rapid urbanization and industrialization, the demand for energy in Asia has significantly increased, with many countries in the region becoming net importers of energy. Fossil fuels such as oil, gas and coal have remained the dominant energy sources in the region. From 1,162 mtoe (million tons of oil equivalent) in 1980 to 5,499 mtoe in 2015, energy consumption grew by 6.4 percent per year on average, more than twice as fast as the world average. In particular, oil consumption grew by 4.4 percent, natural gas consumption by 9.5 percent and coal consumption by 7.2 percent per year on average over the 1980–2015 period (BP 2016). These significant trends have led to energy security becoming a major concern, and the importance of maintaining secure energy supplies is well recognized by national governments. In Asia, governments are increasingly taking unilateral initiatives as well as making collective regional efforts to secure access to energy and satisfy regional energy demand (Hart 2016).

The IEA (2014) defines energy security as the availability of energy resource supply in a sustainable and timely manner at a competitive and stable price. This definition implicitly identifies four major factors that could potentially affect a country's vulnerability to supply disruptions: availability, accessibility, affordability and acceptability of energy. The prospects of fossil fuel supply remaining flat combined with a rising demand for energy, a growing reliance on imports, volatile energy prices, political instability in some major suppliers and a concerted effort to reduce CO_2 emissions all highlight the need to have a secure energy supply.

This chapter examines the energy profile of selected Asian countries in the context of a set of energy supply indicators, including intensity, net import dependency, ratio of domestic energy production to total domestic energy consumption and geopolitical risk. These indicators are evaluated for selected countries in Asia in the period between 2002 and 2015. The definition of "energy" in this chapter is restricted to the three major fossil fuels of oil, natural gas and coal. A composite supply security index for oil (OSSI), gas (GSSI) and coal (CSSI) are calculated following the methodology used in Cabalu (2010). The supply security indices calculated for each country provide a quantitative measure of energy security for each of the fossil fuels by taking into account the dynamics among the identified set of energy supply indicators. A higher supply security index indicates higher supply insecurity or vulnerability. This chapter is important in assessing energy supply security in oil, gas and coal in six Asian countries by providing metrics for future policy making particularly where security of supply is weak. The chapter is divided into five main sections. The next section examines the energy profile of selected Asian countries, including China, India, Japan, Korea, Singapore and Thailand. Section 3 constructs a separate composite supply security index for oil, gas and coal respectively. Section 4 evaluates these three indices for the six countries in our sample and presents the results and analysis. The final section concludes.

Asia's energy profile

In the past two and a half decades, Asia has scored strong economic growth. Despite the downturns during the 1997 Asian Financial Crisis and the 2008 Global Financial Crisis, economies in Asia have had great resilience and robust underlying growth momentum. The fastest growth was experienced by China, with the average annual growth rate of real GDP at 9.7 percent over the period 1980 to 2015. The second most rapidly growing economy was India, which recorded a 6.3 percent average annual growth in real GDP. The lowest growth in the region over that period was seen in Japan, which grew at 2 percent per annum on average (Figure 8.1). The strong growth was accompanied by increasing energy consumption in the region, causing a rise in the share in total consumption across fuels: the share in total world coal consumption rose from 27 percent in 1980 to 73 percent in 2015; that for oil grew from 17 percent in 1980 to 35 percent in 2015; and that for natural gas picked up from 5 percent in 1980 to 20 percent in 2015 (Figure 8.2).

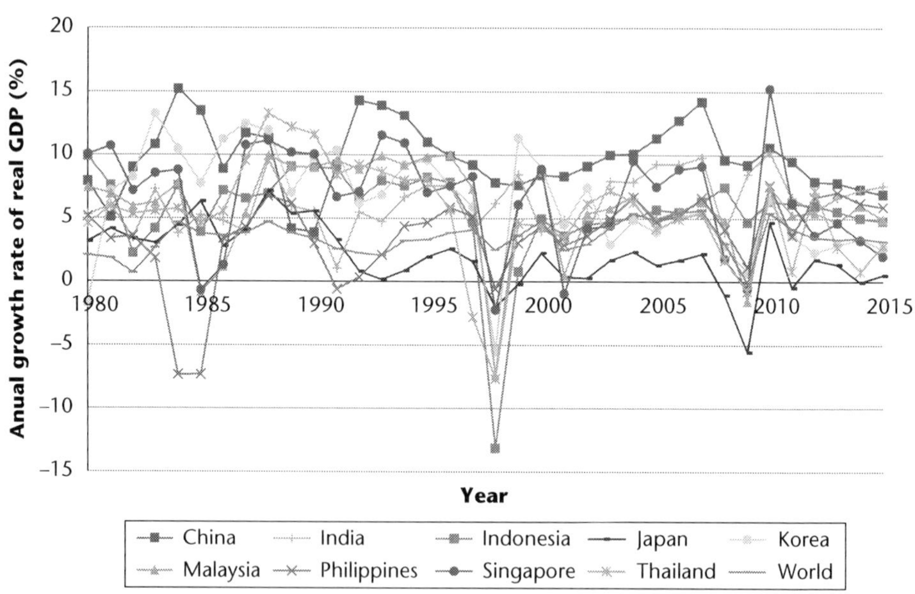

Figure 8.1 Annual growth rate of real GDP, 1980–2015

Source: IMF (2017).

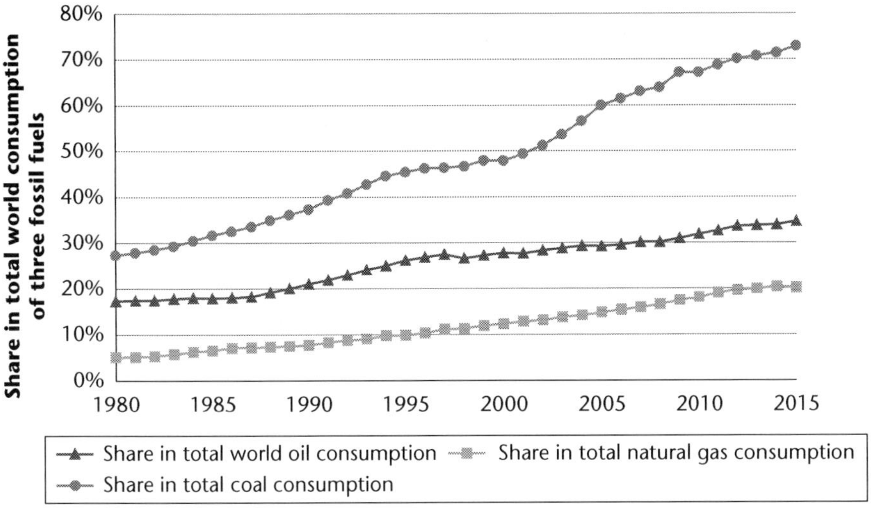

Figure 8.2 Asia Pacific's share in total world consumption of three fossil fuels, 1980–2015

Source: Authors' calculation based on BP (2016).

In line with the strong growth trends, increasing environmental concerns and technological improvements, energy needs were changing and the energy mix was shifting over this period. Natural gas has taken an increasing role in Asia's energy mix, being the fastest growing energy source while oil continues to grow, although at a slower pace than before. In 2015, about 13 percent of Asia's primary energy consumption was based on natural gas. In the past, gas has been used in the region where it is produced because of the relatively high costs of transport. With technological improvements leading to reduction in costs of gas liquefaction and transport, liquefied natural gas (LNG) has become competitive together with traditional pipeline gas. Natural gas markets have become more integrated with the growing importance of LNG where its cargoes can be redirected to different parts of the world in response to regional fluctuations in demand and supply (IEA 2015a). In 2015, Asia consumed 631 mtoe of natural gas but produced only 501 mtoe, with the rest being met by imports. As most major consumer countries become more reliant on imports, a greater share of gas is supplied via longer pipelines and longer liquefied natural gas (LNG) routes. Of Asia's total gas imports in 2015, 80 percent was LNG. Asia remains the largest destination for LNG. China, India and other Asian countries all increased their demand for LNG, resulting in a faster growth for gas than for either oil or coal in each of these economies.

There are significant variations in energy consumption among the Asian countries. In 2015, China had the highest energy consumption, accounting for 55 percent of the total energy consumed by the Asia Pacific region, followed by India at 13 percent and Japan at 8 percent (Figure 8.3). The dominance of consumption by China is strongest in coal: as high as 69 percent of coal consumption in the Asia Pacific regions is registered by the Chinese economy, despite the drop in its share in recent years (Figure 8.4). The consumption of natural gas is more equally distributed amongst the economies in the region. Japan's share in natural gas has been shrinking since 1980, decreasing from 33 percent in 1980 to 16 percent in 2015; and China's share has continuously dropped to a trough in the early 2000s and has been on the rise since then. In 1980, China's share in Asia' natural gas was 20 percent; it reached the trough in 1999 at 8 percent and then rose to 28 percent in 2015 (Figure 8.5). For oil, the shares taken up by China, India, Singapore, South Korea, Thailand, Indonesia and Malaysia expanded, with especially an strong

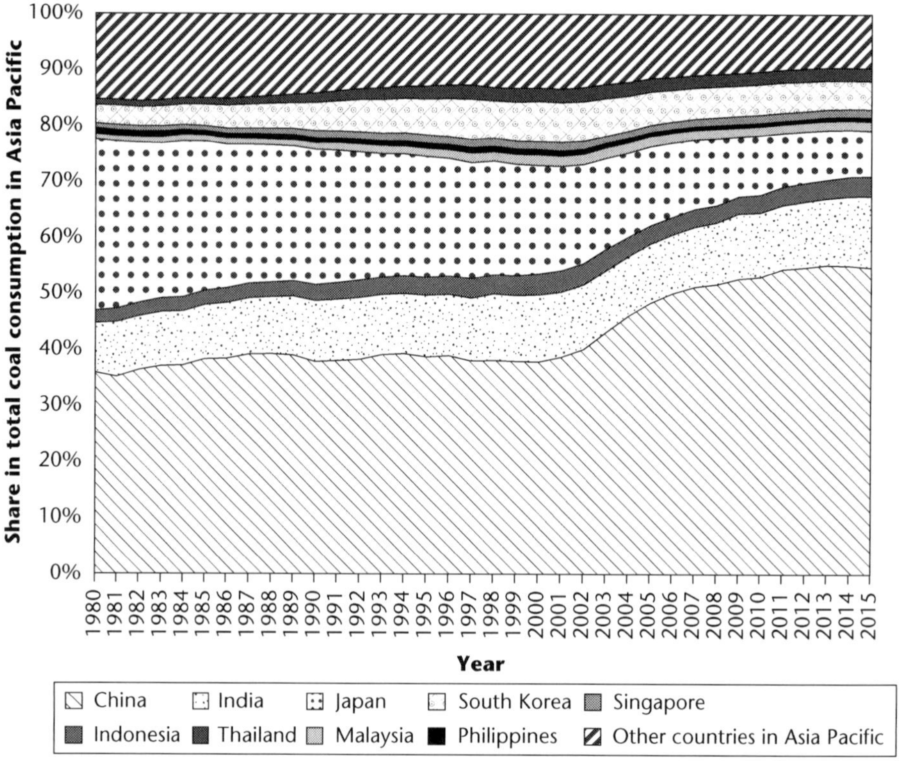

Figure 8.3 Share in primary energy consumption in Asia Pacific, 1980–2015

Source: Authors' calculation based on BP (2016).

rise seen in China and India; in contrast, significant drops in consumption took place in Japan and other countries in Asia (Figure 8.6).

The structure of energy consumption varies across countries in Asia. In 2015, around 64 percent of China's primary energy consumption consisted of coal while 19 percent was oil. Coal is also the dominant energy source in India (58 percent) and Indonesia (41 percent). In contrast, oil was the staple energy source in Singapore (87 percent), Thailand (45 percent), Japan (42 percent), Philippines (49 percent), and South Korea (41 percent). Natural gas plays a significant role in primary energy consumption in Malaysia (38 percent), Thailand (38 percent) and Japan (23 percent) (Table 8.1).

At the end of 2015, the Asia Pacific region had significant energy reserves: 5,700 mtoe of oil, 15.6 trillion cubic meters (tcm) of natural gas and 288,328 mtoe of coal. Coal is the most available source of energy in the region in terms of its share in the world's reserves, which stands at 32.3 percent in 2015. The Asia Pacific region is less endowed with natural gas and oil: in 2015, 8.4 percent of the world's natural gas reserves and 2.5 percent of the world's oil reserves were located in this region. Of the 288,328 mtoe of coal reserves in the region, around 39.7 percent is found in China and 26.5 percent in Australia. For natural gas, China, Australia, Indonesia, and Malaysia have the highest shares of the region's total gas reserves. Of the total regional oil reserves, 45 percent belongs to China, followed by India with 13.5 percent and Vietnam with 10.5 percent (BP 2016).

In 2015, China was the largest producer of all fuel types in the region. Out of world production, China accounted for 47.7 percent in coal, 3.9 percent in natural gas, and 4.9 percent in oil.

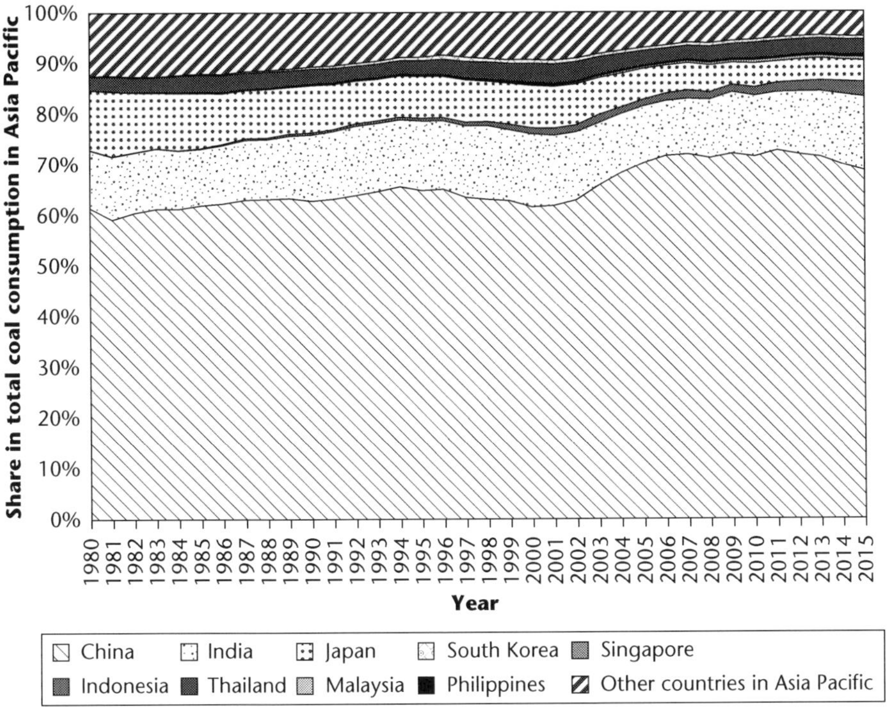

Figure 8.4 Share in total coal consumption in Asia Pacific, 1980–2015

Source: Authors' calculation based on BP (2016).

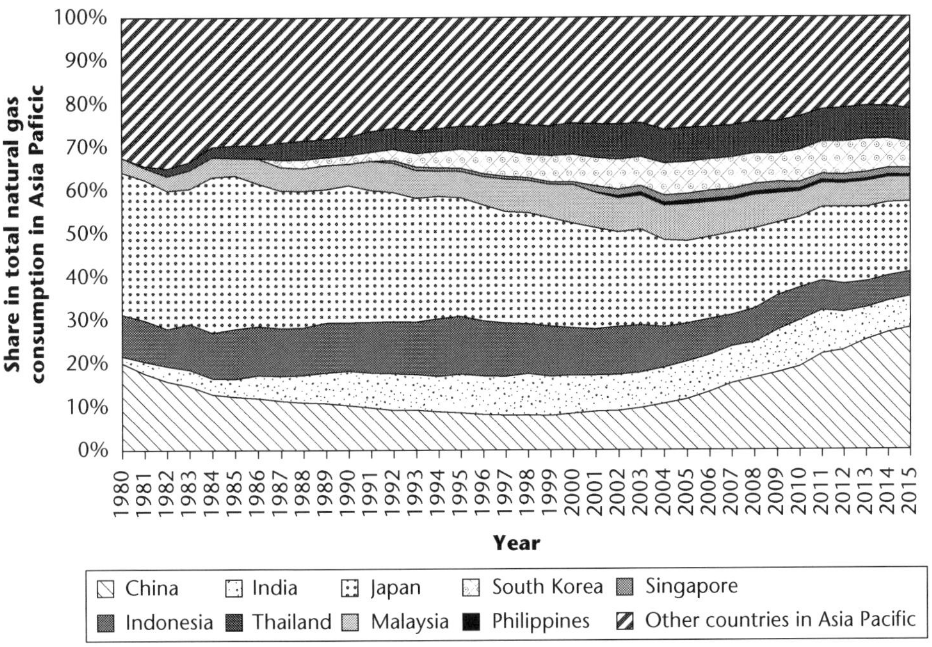

Figure 8.5 Share in total natural gas consumption in Asia Pacific, 1980–2015

Source: Authors' calculation based on BP (2016).

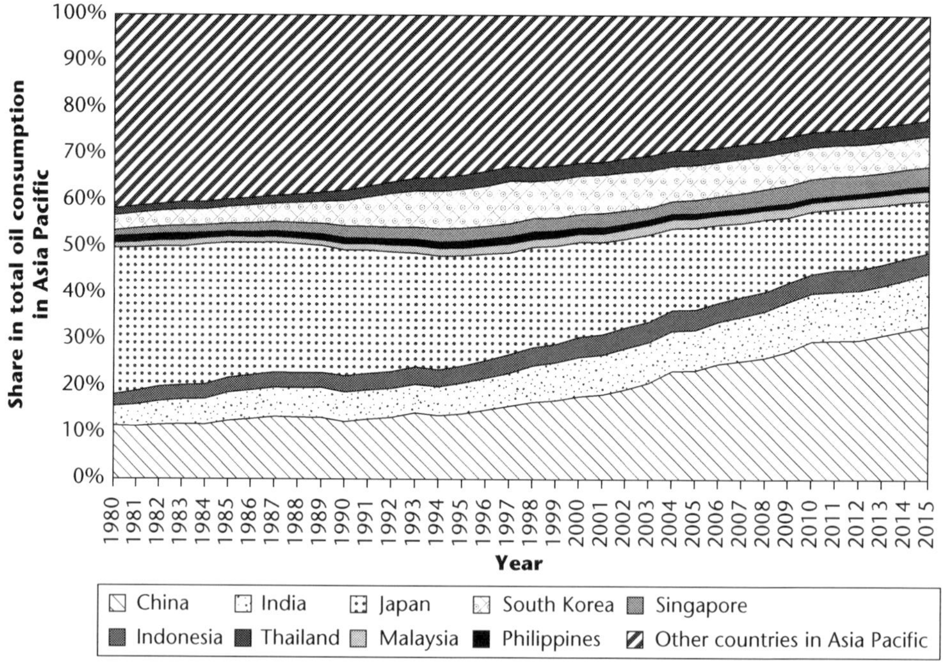

Figure 8.6 Share in total oil consumption in Asia Pacific, 1980–2015

Source: Authors' calculation based on BP (2016).

Table 8.1 Structure of primary energy consumption in selected Asian countries, 2015

	As percentage of primary energy consumption (%)					
	Oil	*Natural gas*	*Coal*	*Nuclear energy*	*Hydroelectric*	*Renewables*
China	19	6	64	1	8	2
Indonesia	38	18	41	0	2	1
Malaysia	39	38	19	0	4	0
Singapore	87	13	0	0	0	0
Thailand	45	38	14	0	1	2
India	28	7	58	1	4	2
Japan	42	23	27	0	5	3
Philippines	49	8	30	0	6	7
South Korea	41	14	30	13	0	1
Other Asia Pacific	34	11	31	0	23	0

Source: Authors' calculation based on BP (2016).

Coal production dominates in the region as well; coal produced in Asia Pacific also accounts for 70.6 percent of total world coal production, making the region, particularly China, one of the leading sources of coal in the world. Production of natural gas and oil in Asia Pacific has accounted for 15.7 percent and 9.1 percent of their respective levels of world production. Aside from China, other countries like India, Indonesia, Malaysia and Australia had strong production in natural gas and oil in 2015.

Table 8.2 Availability of energy supply in selected Asian countries: reserve to production (R/P) ratio, 2015

	Oil	*Natural gas*	*Coal*
Brunei	23.8	21.7	–
China	11.7	27.8	31
India	18	50.9	89
Indonesia	12	37.8	71
Japan	–	–	296
Malaysia	14.2	17.1	–
Mongolia	–	–	103
Myanmar	–	27	–
Singapore	–	–	–
South Korea	–	–	71
Thailand	2.3	5.5	82
Vietnam	33	57.9	4
Other Asia Pacific	12	15.8	37
Total Asia Pacific	14	28.1	53
Total World	50.7	52.8	114

Source: BP (2016).

Overall, average reserves to production (R/P) ratios for oil, natural gas and coal in the Asia Pacific have been below the world average in 2015. In oil production, Vietnam has the highest R/P ratio in the region, with 33 years, followed by Brunei (23.8 years), India (18 year) and Malaysia (14.2 years), all below the world average of 50.7 years. For natural gas, the reserves in the region have an estimated average of 28 years of supply. Reserves in India (50.9 year), Indonesia, and Vietnam (57.0 years) are above the regional average. Vietnam's R/P ratio is the highest, with 57.9 years, and India has around 50.9 years; and the world average of natural gas R/P ratio is 52.8 years. Coal reserves in the Asia Pacific are enough to supply, on average, 53 years at current production levels. Japan has a particularly large coal reserve to production ratio at 296, which is significantly above the world average and the average of the Asia Pacific region. Table 8.2 provides a summary of these R/P ratios.

Constructing the security of supply indices for the Asian energy market

Ensuring energy security is every government's concern, as the lack of it has been associated with negative economic and social impacts. The oil crisis of 1973–1974 demonstrated how vulnerable the majority of the world's economies were to supply unavailability and price volatility. Any energy infrastructure – oil, natural gas or coal, is often vulnerable to supply interruptions, accident or malice. The physical unavailability of supply has negative impacts primarily on energy markets where transmission systems need to be constantly working, as they are relied upon for uninterruptible supply. The economic damage caused by extreme price increases of energy imports contributes to inflationary pressures, displaces other consumption and investment because short-term energy demand is inelastic, and adversely affects the macroeconomic balance of payments (IEA 2014).

This chapter adopts the method developed in Cabalu (2010) and evaluates four distinct securities of supply indicators for oil, gas and coal: intensity (S_1), import dependency (S_2), ratio of domestic production to total domestic consumption (S_3) and geopolitical risk (S_4). S_1 is calculated as the ratio of energy (oil, gas or coal) consumed in an economy to gross domestic product (GDP). It is the amount of each type of energy needed to produce one dollar's worth of GDP and reflects the efficiency of the use of energy in producing the economy's output.

Intensity (S_1) is defined as:

$$S_{1i,j} = \frac{EC_{i,j}}{GDP_i} \quad (1)$$

The intensity of energy j (where j = oil, gas, coal) of GDP of country i ($S_{1i,j}$) is measured as the ratio of total energy j consumed in country i ($EC_{i,j}$) to real GDP of country i (GDP_i).[1] The relative indicator for country i associated with S_1 is ($\varphi_{1i,j}$) and this is constructed as:

$$\varphi_{1i,j} = \frac{S_{1i,j} - Min(S_{1j})}{Max(S_{1j}) - Min(S_{1j})} \quad (2)$$

The relative indicator normalizes $\varphi_{1i,j}$ in the interval [0, 1]. A low value of $\varphi_{1i,j}$ means that country i is less vulnerable to supply shocks compared with other countries in the sample.

The second indicator S_2 is expressed as the ratio of net imported energy j (oil, gas, coal) to total primary energy j consumption. Net energy j import dependency (S_2) is in percentage form:

$$S_{2i,j} = \frac{EM_{i,j}}{TPEC_i} \quad (3)$$

The import dependency of country i for energy j is expressed as the ratio of its net imports of energy j ($EM_{i,j}$) to total primary energy consumption in country i ($TPEC_i$). The relative indicator of country i associated with S_2 is ($\varphi_{2i,j}$) and is estimated as:

$$\varphi_{2i,j} = \frac{S_{2i,j} - Min(S_{2j})}{Max(S_{2j}) - Min(S_{2j})} \quad (4)$$

The above adjustment transforms the indicator $S_{2,j}$ to the [0, 1] interval with the value of 0 indicating lowest value of $S_{2,j}$ and least vulnerable in terms of the supply of energy j and the value of 1 representing highest value of $S_{2,j}$ and hence most vulnerable to the supply shock of energy j, as reflected by the security of indicator S_2.

S_3 is measured as the ratio of domestic production to total domestic consumption of energy j (oil, gas, coal) in country i.

$$S_{3i,j} = \frac{EP_{i,j}}{EC_{ij}} \quad (5)$$

where $EP_{i,j}$ is domestic production of energy j in country i and EC_{ij} is total consumption of energy j in country i. This indicator, different from the first two, is negatively related to supply vulnerability. A high value of $S_{3i,j}$ means that country i is less insecure to supply shocks to energy j compared with other countries in the sample. To take into account this negative relationship, the relative indicator for country i's security in energy j associated with S_3 is ($\varphi_{3i,\,j}$) and is estimated as:

$$\varphi_{3i,j} = \frac{Max(S_{3j}) - S_{3i,j}}{Max(S_{3j}) - Min(S_{3j})} \quad (6)$$

The relative indicator $\varphi_{3i,j}$ calculated in the above way transforms the indicator $S_{3i,j}$ into the interval [0, 1] with the value of 0 being assigned to the country with the highest value of S_3 for country *i* and therefore least vulnerable to supply shocks to energy *j* and the value 1 being assigned to the country with the lowest value of S_3 for energy *j* and hence most vulnerable to supply shocks to energy *j*.

S_4 captures the exposure of an economy to political risk and is largely determined by two aspects: diversification of energy *j* import sources and the associated political stability of these source countries. The measure of geopolitical risk (S_4) is calculated following the methodology suggested by ECN (2004), using the adjusted Shannon diversity index with the following steps:

$$S_{4i,j} = -\sum_{q}\left(h_q m_{i,j,q} \ln m_{i,j,q}\right) \tag{7}$$

Here h_q is the extent of political stability in exporting country *q*, with the range from 0 (most unstable) to 1 (most stable); and $m_{i,j,q}$ is the share of import of energy *j* from country *q* to country *i* in total import of energy *j* by country *i*. Therefore, the indicator $S_{4i,j}$ informs us about the geopolitical risk faced by country *i* in terms of energy *j*. If country *i* imports a larger share of energy *j* from countries with high political stability, then the value of $S_{4i,j}$ tends to be greater and vice versa. Therefore, a higher value of $S_{4i,j}$ indicates less vulnerability of country *i* in terms of energy *j*.

The relative indicator for country *i* in terms of energy *j* associated with S_4 is ($\varphi_{4i,j}$) and is estimated as:

$$\varphi_{4i,j} = \frac{Max\left(S_{4,j}\right) - S_{4i,j}}{Max\left(S_{4j}\right) - Min\left(S_{4j}\right)} \tag{8}$$

The relative indicator $\varphi_{4i,j}$ is positively related to supply vulnerability of energy *j* faced by country *i*, with the value of 0 indicating least vulnerability and the value of 1 the highest vulnerability.

Appendix Figure 8A.1 presents our calculations of the four relative indicators of security of supply for the three types of energy, i.e., oil, gas and coal in six countries in Asia. The relative indicators are scaled values of the four security of supply indicators for each country-energy combination. These relative indicators are calculated, as it is difficult to quantify a country's overall supply security for each of the fossil fuels using individual indicators expressed in different ways. The relative indicators are at least expressed in the same units and will facilitate comparison or aggregation of several indicators.

In order to quantify a country's overall supply security for each type of energy using individual relative indicators ($\varphi_{1i,j}, \varphi_{2i,j}$ $\varphi_{3i,j}$ and $\varphi_{4i,j}$), we develop a metric to synthesize the different indicators: a composite index for each type of energy – oil supply security index (OSSI), gas supply security index (GSSI) and coal supply security index (CSSI) for each country. To construct this composite index, we first estimate, for each of the four security indicators, a relative indicator by using the scaling technique discussed above. Under this scaling technique, the minimum value is set to 0 and the maximum to 1. The value of 0 is assigned to the country with the least vulnerability or insecurity to supply shocks and value 1 assigned to the country with the most vulnerability to supply disruptions. Following Cabalu (2010), the supply security index of country i in energy $j(SSI_{i,j})$ is derived as the root mean square of the four relative indicators or scaled values of the four security of supply indicators:

$$SSI_{i,j} = \sqrt{\frac{\Sigma_{m=1}^{4} \varphi_{mi,j}^{2}}{4}} \tag{9}$$

Data for real GDP are from the IMF World Economic Outlook database. Total primary energy consumption and individual consumption and production of oil, natural gas and coal are obtained from various issues of the BP Statistical Review. Net imports of natural gas, oil and coal are extracted from the Comtrade database. For the measure of political stability, we adopt the "political stability and absence of violence" component in the World Government Indicators.

Empirical results

This chapter estimated the OSSI, GSSI and CSSI (equivalent to $SSI_{i,j}$) for six selected Asian net energy-importing countries including China, India, Japan, Korea, Singapore and Thailand for the period 2002–2015. The final values calculated are plotted in Figure 8.7.

Of the countries in our sample, Singapore is the most vulnerable to oil shocks. Since 2003, it has registered the highest OSSI at approximately 0.87 over the period. This could be explained by Singapore's high oil intensity (S_{1O}), high import dependency (S_{2O}) and low oil production-consumption ratio (S_{3O}). Singapore has no indigenous sources of energy and limited alternative energy potential. Singapore relies on oil (87 percent) and natural gas (13 percent) for energy (EIA 2016a). As an indication of its high oil intensity, Singapore's 5.5 million people consumed about 1.3 million barrels of oil per day in 2014 while Thailand with its population of 67 million consumed only 1 million barrels per day. Singapore's demand for oil was largely channelled to industrial-related activities followed by the transport sector. In the absence of domestic sources of energy, Singapore is highly dependent on energy imports to meet its energy needs. Over 93 percent of Singapore's total energy imports were in the form of crude oil and petroleum products in 2014 and 2015. Although Singapore is a producer of oil, its consumption significantly exceeds its production, leading it to import. In recent times, however, Singapore has started to

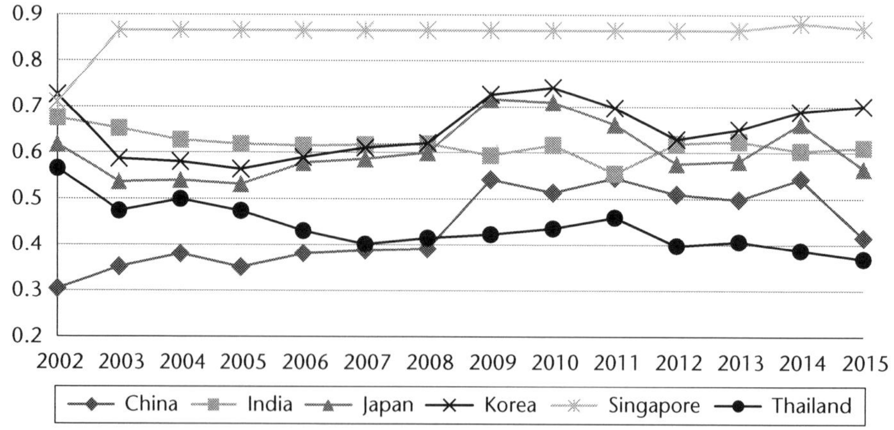

Figure 8.7 OSSI for selected Asian countries, 2002–2015

Source: Authors' calculations.

adopt cleaner energy sources to fuel electricity demand, moving away from petroleum products such as diesel and fuel oil to the more environmentally-friendly natural gas (EMA 2015, 2016).

Between 2002 and 2008, China is the least vulnerable to oil supply disruption among countries in our sample. It registered the lowest OSSI between 0.30 and 0.39 during that period. China's record of low oil supply insecurity can be explained by having the lowest oil import dependency (S_{2O}) and the highest ratio of domestic production to total domestic consumption of oil (S_{3O}) in the period 2002–2008. Oil is the second largest source of energy in China, supplying 19 percent of its total energy consumption. China was a net oil exporter until the early 1990s and its total oil production, which was the fourth largest in the world, has increased about 50 percent in the last two decades. In 2015, China held 24.6 billion barrels of proved oil reserves, up almost 0.3 billion barrels from the 2014 level and the highest in the Asia Pacific region (excluding Russia). However, this production growth has not kept pace with demand growth, as China became the world's largest net importer of crude oil and petroleum products in 2014 (EIA 2016b). Most of China's largest oil fields are mature and prone to declining production. China's recent energy policy aims to improve domestic production by developing new oil fields through production-sharing contracts and joint ventures with international oil companies. To strengthen its energy security, Chinese national oil companies have also expanded their purchases of international oil and natural gas assets since 2008 through direct acquisitions of equity and financial loans in exchange for oil supplies. To ensure adequate oil supply and reduce its exposure to geopolitical risks, China has diversified its import sources, increasing the import share of countries that are relatively politically stable such as Oman and the United Arab Emirates, and reducing the import share of countries that are unstable such as Sudan, Libya and Iran.

However, from 2009 to 2015 China was overtaken by Thailand as the least vulnerable to oil supply insecurity, with a declining OSSI, achieving 0.37 in 2015. Thailand's strength rests on its S_{4O} having the least exposure to geopolitical risks, particularly in relation to its import sources. Thailand's primary energy consumption is mostly from fossil fuels, accounting for 98 percent of the country's total energy consumption. Oil was 45 percent of total energy consumption in 2015, down from nearly half in 2000. Thailand consumes oil for transportation and industrial uses. Thailand is also an oil producer. However, with oil accounting for the majority of its primary energy consumption and domestic crude oil reserves declining, the country has imported a significant share of its total oil consumption. Thailand is a net importer of crude oil and a net exporter of petroleum products. The country imports over 60 percent of its total petroleum needs and almost 85 percent of its crude oil consumption, leaving Thailand highly dependent on world oil markets and volatile prices. About 78 percent of its crude imports originate from the Middle East, while an extra 7 percent are from other Asian suppliers. It is from these more diversified and relatively less risky sources of imports that Thailand surpasses China from the geopolitical risk perspective. Thailand's oil import dependency has spurred its government to promote the use of other fuels such as natural gas, renewable sources, and biofuels, including boosting crude oil and product stocks and encouraging investment in marginal field production (glObserver Asia 2015).

In terms of natural gas supply disruptions, a number of events have interrupted supply over the last decade, arising from weather-related catastrophes (e.g., hurricanes), accidents (e.g., fires, explosions) and contractual disputes. In our sample, between 2002 and 2011, Thailand was the most vulnerable to natural gas supply disruptions, with a GSSI that ranged from 0.73 to as high as 0.86 (see Figure 8.8). In the intervening years between 2012 and 2014, Singapore became the most vulnerable among the countries in the sample. In 2015, Thailand was back as most supply vulnerable with a GSSI of 0.73. Despite its strength on S_{3G}, Thailand's gas security of supply profile is weakest on S_{1G}, its gas intensity, and S_{4G}, geopolitical risk. Thailand is a natural gas producer and holds large proven reserves of natural gas. After a peak in 2006, natural gas reserves

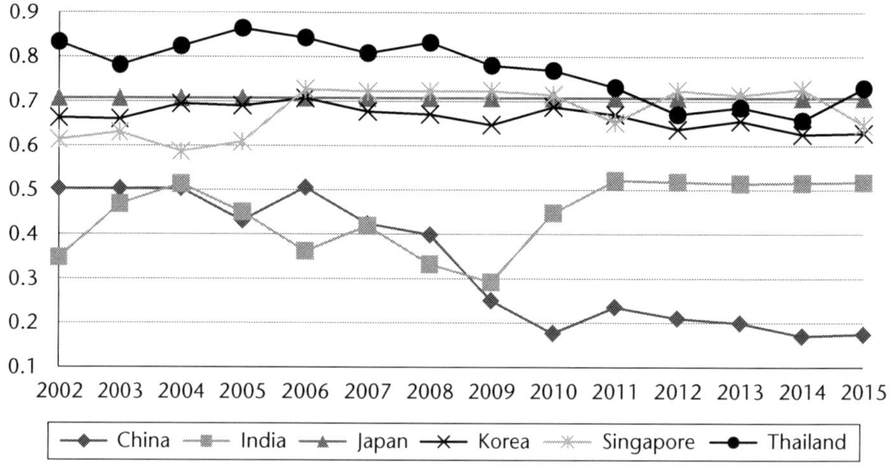

Figure 8.8 GSSI for selected Asian countries, 2002–2015

Source: Authors' calculation based on the method discussed in section 3.

have generally declined since then. Thailand has natural gas reserves of 255.9 billion cubic meters in 2015, with over 90 percent of these reserves located offshore; the Erawan and Bongkot fields as the largest natural gas fields located in the Gulf of Thailand.

In addition to joint ventures with foreign investors such as Chevron, Mitsui, Total and Shell in Thailand's natural gas fields, Thailand's partnership with Malaysia to develop the Malay Basin has increased Thailand's natural gas production since 2008. Its natural gas production has increased substantially over the last few years, but with high demand growth, the country became a net importer of natural gas in 2000. Intensity in gas use was further made possible when Thailand could import natural gas via pipeline from neighboring Myanmar. Aside from this pipeline gas, natural gas imports in the form of liquefied natural gas (LNG) commenced in 2011, mainly from Qatar. With undiversified import sources, Thailand is exposed to geopolitical risks and is vulnerable to supply disruptions. Thailand continues to be dependent on natural gas imports to meet domestic demand.

In 2015, production was estimated to be 41.8 billion cubic meters and consumption at 52.3 cubic meters (CIA 2016). Thailand utilizes natural gas for electricity generation. Natural gas-fired generation consisted of 68 percent of the capacity mix, with coal and renewable energy making up most of the remaining capacity. The industrial sector and natural gas processing plants also consume a significant amount of the country's gas supply. Another factor contributing to high gas intensity is Thailand's extensive natural gas transmission infrastructure, with the national gas pipeline system connecting onshore and offshore gas fields to several gas separation plants, power plants, and hundreds of industrial users (EIA 2017).

Singapore was most vulnerable to gas supply shocks between 2012 and 2014 with a GSSI of approximately 0.72. During this period in particular, Singapore's gas security of supply profile was relatively weak on S_{2G} and S_{4G} but more so on S_{3G}. The absence of domestic gas production, combined with high domestic gas consumption, makes Singapore relatively vulnerable to gas supply disruptions. Gas is a key energy resource for Singapore. About 95 percent of electricity is generated using natural gas. As a major step to reduce its carbon emissions, Singapore has switched from carbon-intensive oil to natural gas, which has lower carbon content per unit of electricity generated. Traditionally, most of Singapore's natural gas has been imported from four offshore natural gas pipelines linked to Indonesia and Malaysia. Since 2013, Singapore has started importing liquefied natural gas (LNG) to diversify and secure its energy sources.

From 2009 to 2015, China was consistently the least vulnerable to natural gas supply disruptions of the countries in the sample. The relative strengths of its natural gas security profile are on S_{3G} and S_{4G} but more so on S_{2G}. Although natural gas production and use has rapidly increased in the last decade, it accounted for only 6 percent of the country's total primary energy consumption in 2015. China was the world's sixth largest natural gas producer, with production of approximately 124 mtoe in 2015. Natural gas consumption in China is significantly lower than the other fossil fuels, and was primarily used as a local fuel and feedstock in chemical fertilizer in areas near production sites such as in Sichuan, Shaanxi, Gansu, Shanxi and Xinjiang provinces, where low cost gas is possible. The lack of gas transport infrastructure, particularly long distance pipelines from the major gas fields located in the western part of the country to eastern demand centers, has prevented the wide use of gas in China.

Although the majority of gas consumption stems from industrial users, the shares of gas consumption in the power and transportation sectors have been rising over the past decade. China was traditionally a net gas exporter until 2007, when it became a net natural gas importer for the first time (IEA 2009). Since then, gas imports via pipeline from Russia, Myanmar, Turkmenistan Uzbekistan and Kazakhstan, and in the form of LNG from Qatar, Australia, Malaysia, Indonesia, Yemen, Equatorial Guinea, Nigeria and Algeria have increased dramatically in line with China's desire to boost gas consumption instead of oil and coal to reduce high levels of pollution, and promote energy diversification and efficiency. Increased imports have been made possible with rapidly developing pipeline and natural gas processing infrastructure. LNG imports have been received in 13 LNG import terminals located in Guangdong, Fujian, Shanghai, Jiangsu, Dalian and Shenzhen (Clemente 2016).

It is interesting to note that in 2002, 2003, 2006 and 2008, that India was the least vulnerable to gas supply disruptions. It registered the lowest GSSI for these years primarily because of its relative strengths in S_{2G} and S_{3G} which indicate that India has a relatively low gas import dependency and relatively high production to consumption ratio during these years. India is endowed with large natural gas reserves. Since 1950, roughly 69 trillion cubic feet of proven and probable recoverable gas reserves have been discovered in India. Of this, only 42 trillion cubic feet have been developed and are currently under production. There remains a massive volume of reserves that is untapped. India's natural gas production comes from the western offshore regions, particularly the Mumbai High complex. The onshore fields in Assam, Andhra Pradesh, and Gujarat states are also major producers of natural gas. Natural gas is a minor source of fuel in India's energy mix, accounting for 7–8 percent of its total primary energy consumption, as the major source of energy is coal. Its imports represented just over 2 percent of its total primary energy consumption and India is hence not dependent on imports (EY 2016).

In terms of coal security of supply, Korea and Japan shared the position as most vulnerable to coal supply disruptions for a long time between 2002 and 2012. From 2013 to 2015, Korea was most vulnerable. Korea's CSSI was consistently high and peaked at 0.74 in 2004 together with Japan and registered 0.70 in 2015 together with Singapore (see Figure 8.9). Korea's weaknesses are primarily due to a relatively high import dependency (S_{2C}) and a low coal production to consumption ratio (S_{3C}). Korea's lack of domestic reserves has made it one of the top energy importers in the world. Rising coal consumption, amounting to 146 million short tons and negligible domestic production at 1.9 million short tons in 2015, resulted in Korea having to rely heavily on coal imports. Imports have increased substantially, from 131 million short tons in 2010 to 144 million short tons in 2015, as a result of forced shutdowns of some nuclear plants in late 2012 because of safety issues. In 2015, it was the fourth-largest coal importer in the world,

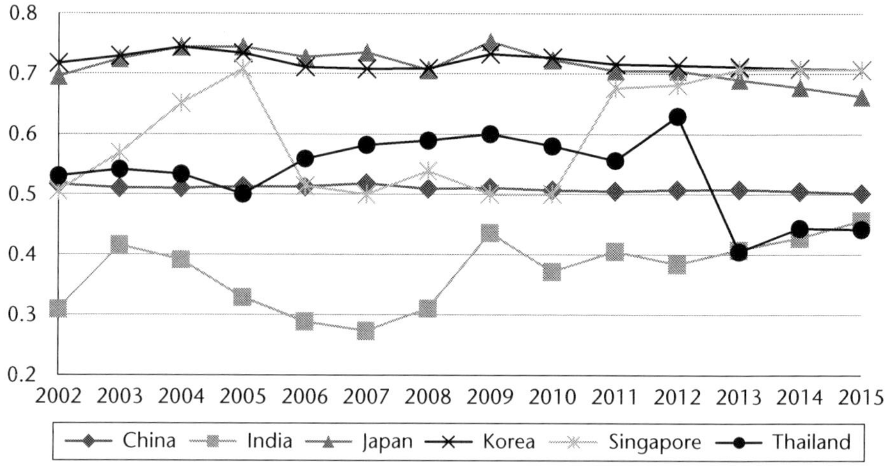

Figure 8.9 CSSI for selected Asian countries, 2002–2015

Source: Authors' calculation based on the method discussed in section 3.

following China, India and Japan. Coal consumption increased by 56 percent between 2005 and 2015, driven primarily by growing demand from the electric power sector. The electric power sector accounted for more than 60 percent of the country's coal consumption, while the industrial sector (primarily steel and cement) contributed to most of the remaining coal demand in 2015 (KEEI 2016).

Japan's vulnerability to coal supply disruption is associated with its relative weakness around high import dependency (S_{2C}) and low coal production to consumption ratio (S_{3C}). Japan's limited domestic energy resources have met less than 10 percent of the country's total primary energy consumption needs in the period of 2002–2012. It is a major importer of fossil fuels in the world, being the third-largest importer of oil behind the United States and China, and third-largest importer of coal, behind India and China, in 2015. Domestic coal production dwindled to virtually nothing by 2002, and Japan began importing all of its coal, primarily from Australia. Coal accounts for a significant share (27 percent) of total primary energy consumption. Coal is used as a baseload source for power generation, and it remains an important fuel source for generating electricity in Japan. Japan has the highest efficiency rate of coal-fired technology in the world. The country is installing new, clean coal plant technologies, such as ultra-supercritical units or integrated gasification combined-cycle technology, to meet environmental targets and to replace some of the decades-old coal power plants (FACTS Global Energy 2015). Japan's high level of investment in the R&D of energy technology since the 1970s has led to increased energy efficiency and the lowest energy intensities across all fossil fuels.

India is the least vulnerable to coal supply disruptions out of the countries in the sample for the entire period. Its CSSI was as low as 0.27 in 2007 and peaked at 0.45 in 2015. India's security of supply strength is mainly in having a relatively high coal production to consumption ratio (S_{3C}). Its net coal import dependency (S_{2C}) is also relatively low. Total proven coal reserves in India amount to 87 billion tons, which is roughly equivalent to 140 years of current output. Total coal resources, including deposits that are yet to be proven, are almost two-and-a-half-times larger, at 213 billion tons (EIA 2016c). Coal is not evenly dispersed across India. Most can be found in the east of the country, with two-thirds of Indian reserves located in the states of Jharkand, Odisha and Chhattisgarh (IEA 2015b). About 93 percent of India's total primary energy consumption is met by fossil fuels, with coal accounting for 58 percent of this in 2015. This is up from 33 percent in 2000. Increase in coal consumption is mainly because of the expansion of the coal-fired power generation fleet and the use of coking coal in India's steel industry. The availability and affordability of coal, relative to other fossil fuels, has also contributed to this increase, especially in the power sector. India is the third-largest coal producer in the world, but its coal is of inferior quality and it has to import high quality coal for meeting the needs of industries like steel plants and cement plants. India faces major obstacles in the form of poor availability of modern equipment and infrastructure, overreliance on surface mining, and low productivity from a very large workforce to enable it to develop its coal resources that would meet the quality requirements of an increasing domestic demand. India imports coal primarily from Indonesia, Australia and South Africa. In turn, India exports coal to Bangladesh and Nepal (Forest 2016).

Conclusion

Energy is a major input to all sectors of the economy. Energy demand, particularly in Asia, has been soaring. Its dominant role as the "engine" of economic growth and sustainable development justifies the growing concerns over energy supply security primarily focused on ensuring an uninterrupted supply of energy. A country's energy supply security in the fossil fuels (oil, natural gas and coal) is determined by a number of indicators which were measured in this chapter. Intensity (by energy source) is the ratio of oil, natural gas or coal consumed in an economy to GDP. This measure takes into account the degree of diversification of energy sources (oil, natural gas or coal) in energy supply. If a country has a diversified energy mix and is not overly dependent on one source of energy, then it is likely to be secure and not vulnerable to supply disruptions of a particular energy source. For instance, the oil price shocks of the 1970s have exposed a number of economies dependent on crude oil to economic risks. It was a period of limited economic growth, due in part to the energy crisis of that decade. Import dependency is another indicator that influences a country's energy security. It refers to the extent of dependency on imported energy source relative to the share of domestically-sourced energy. A country is more vulnerable to supply disruptions if it is highly dependent on imported energy sources where it does not have any control of external factors that could affect supply, such as mishaps, bottlenecks, environmental sensitivity and climatic conditions. A related indicator is geopolitical risk. Indeed, in measuring the exposure of an economy to geopolitical risks, we are concerned about how diversified import sources are and the political stability in these source countries. In general, the more politically-stable import sources an economy has, the better it is for energy security. The ratio of domestic production to domestic consumption is a good indicator of a country's capacity to cope with short-term supply disruption in case import supply is interrupted.

By identifying the major factors that determine a country's energy security, the indicators proposed in this study provide policymakers with a targeted approach to reduce the vulnerability of an economy to energy disruptions. Between 2002 and 2015, there was an overall decline in oil intensity in the six economies in our sample. It is interesting to note that when countries such as India increased their coal intensity between 2010 and 2015, their gas intensity declined at the same time. This indicates that there is some energy substitution or changing energy mix that occurs. To reduce energy intensity, governments could adopt policies to enhance technological innovation and technology transfer in the energy sector. The development of cleaner production technologies will reduce energy demand. New technologies are energy efficient. Governments could promote structural changes in the economy such as the need to promote growth in tradeable and services sectors that consume less electricity per unit of output.

In terms of import dependency, there was in general a fall in import dependency particularly for oil, with the strongest decline seen in Singapore; the rise in gas import dependency was significant in Japan, Korea and Singapore; and the import dependency for coal trended upward across most economies except China. As import dependency rises, better cooperation and freer trade among country partners would alleviate some of the supply risks. In order to reduce dependence on politically unstable source countries, some countries are beginning to look closer to home for new energy reserves. There is a general downward trend on production to consumption ratios. As economies grow, energy consumption increases. Meeting the increase in energy demand becomes a challenge and exerts a downward pressure on production to consumption ratios. Governments could help ramp up the production of renewable energy by designing policies to support solar, wind, biomass, and small-scale hydropower. The availability of renewable energies will diversify sources of energy supply and help alleviate the pressure on fossil fuel demand. The framework developed in this study will assist policymakers in measuring the progress of achieving energy security and identifying areas of further improvement.

Appendix

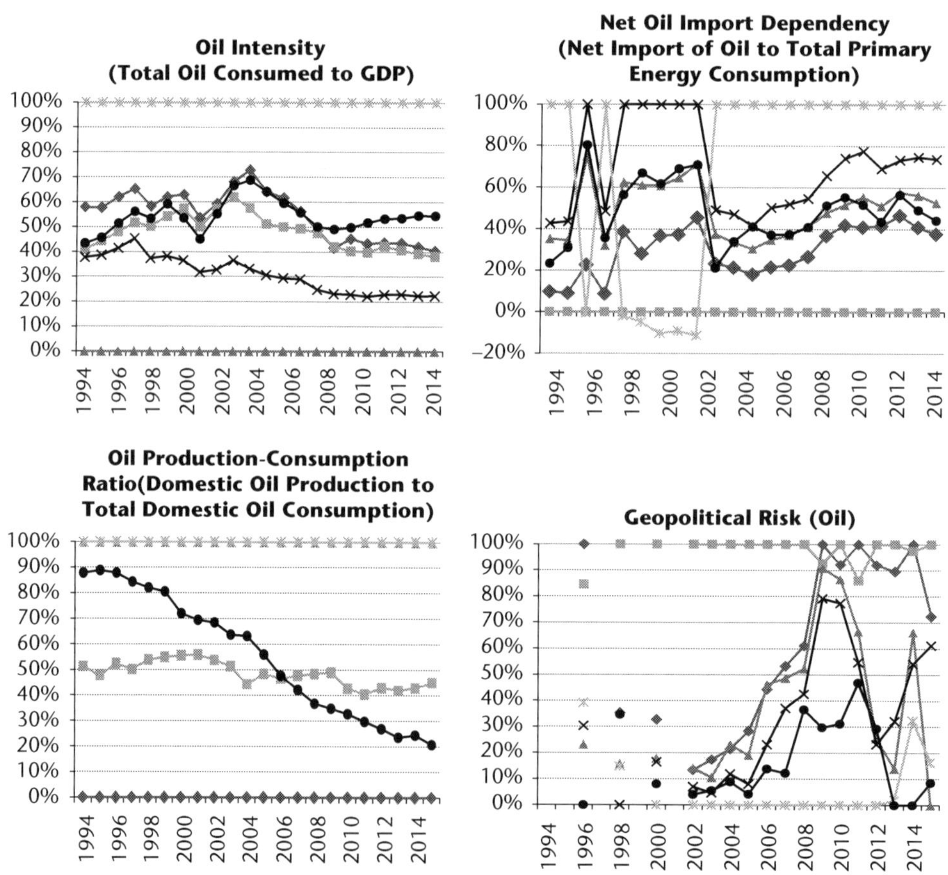

Figure 8A.1 Relative security of supply indicators ($\varphi_{i,j}$) for three types of energy (oil, gas and coal) in six countries in Asia from 2002 to 2015

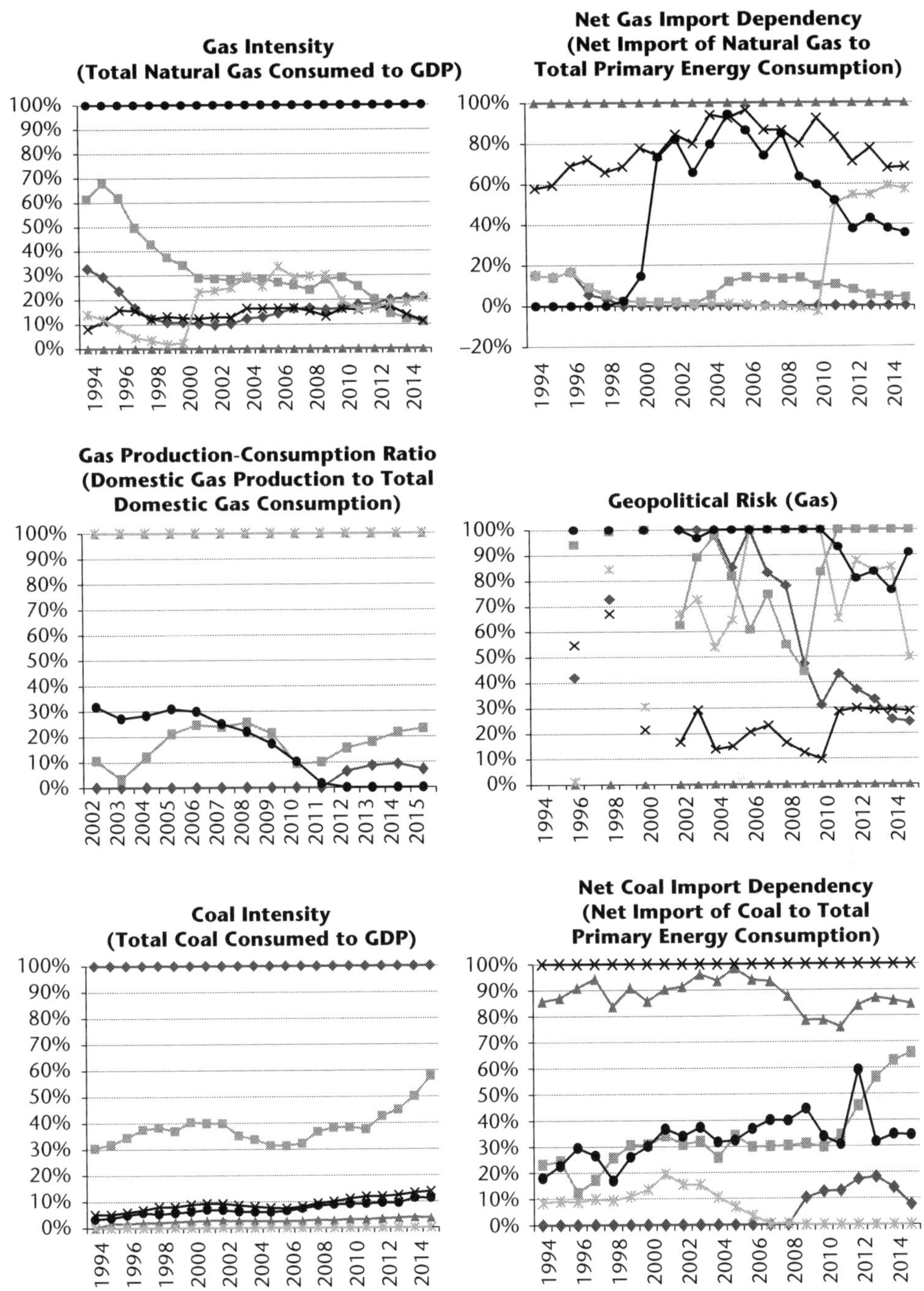

Figure 8A.1 (Continued).

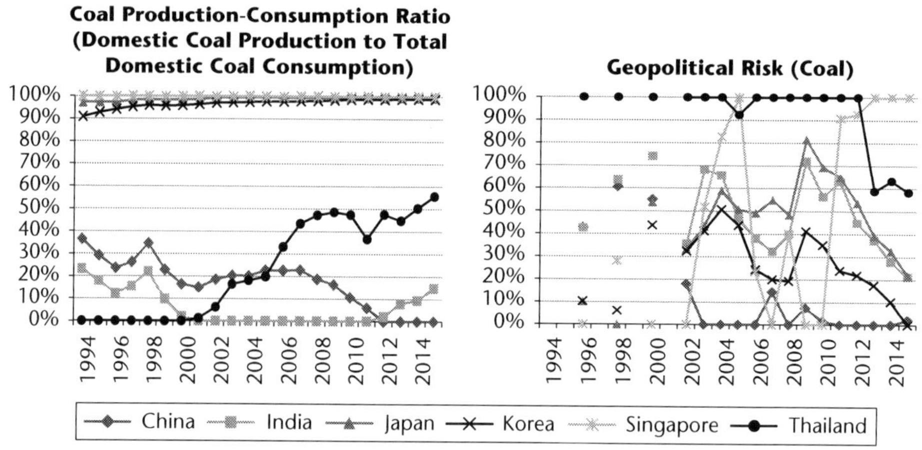

Figure 8A.1 (Continued).

Note

1 For gas, the unit of S_1 is cubic meter per unit of GDP; for oil, the unit of S_1 is kg per unit of GDP; for coal, the unit of S_1 is kg per unit of GDP.

References

British Petroleum (BP). (2016) *BP Statistical Review of World Energy 2016*. Accessed May 30, 2017. www.bp.com/content/dam/bp/pdf/energy-economics/statistical-review-2016/bp-statistical-review-of-world-energy-2016-full-report.pdf.

Cabalu, Helen. (2010) "Indicators of Security of Natural Gas Supply in Asia." *Energy Policy* 38:218–225.

Central Intelligence Agency (CIA). (2016) *The World Factbook*. October. Accessed May 23, 2017. www.indexmundi.com/thailand/energy_profile.html.

Clemente, Jude. (2016) "China's Rising Natural Gas Demand, Pipelines, and LNG." *Forbes*, April 24, 2016. Accessed May 24, 2017. www.forbes.com/sites/judeclemente/2016/04/24/chinas-rising-natural-gas-demand-pipelines-and-lng/2/#665bc43067d1.

Energy Research Centre of the Netherlands (ECN). (2004) *Designing Indicators of Long-Term Energy Supply Security*. ECN Policy Studies, the Netherlands.

Energy Information Administration (EIA). (2016a) *Singapore*. July. Accessed May 31, 2017. www.eia.gov/beta/international/analysis.cfm?iso=SGP.

Energy Information Administration (EIA). (2016b) *China: International Analysis*. April. Accessed May 24, 2017. https://energy.gov/sites/prod/files/2016/04/f30/China_International_Analysis_US.pdf.

Energy Information Administration (EIA). (2016c) *India*. June. Accessed May 23, 2017. www.eia.gov/beta/international/analysis.cfm?iso=IND&src=home-b6.

Energy Information Administration (EIA). (2017) *Thailand*. February. Accessed May 31, 2017. www.eia.gov/beta/international/analysis.cfm?iso=THA.

Energy Market Authority (EMA). (2015) *Singapore Energy Statistics 2015*. June. Accessed May 31, 2017. www.ema.gov.sg/cmsmedia/Publications_and_Statistics/Publications/SES2015_Final_website_2mb.pdf.

Energy Market Authority (EMA). (2016) *Singapore Energy Statistics 2016*. June. Accessed May 31, 2017. www.ema.gov.sg/cmsmedia/Publications_and_Statistics/Publications/SES/2016/Singapore%20Energy%20Statistics%202016.pdf.

Ernst and Young (EY). (2016) *Gas Market in India: Overview and Future Outlook*. Ernst and Young, New Delhi, India.

FACTS Global Energy. (2015) "Japan's Official Power Generation Mix Target for 2030." *Energy Insights* Issue No. 219, May 21.

Forest, Dave. (2016) *India is Changing the Global Coal Market*. July. Accessed May 23, 2017. www.businessinsider.com/india-is-changing-the-global-coal-market-2016-7?IR=T.

glObserver Asia. (2015) *Thailand Energy Profile*. February 16. Accessed May 15, 2017. http://globserver.cn/en/thailand/energy.

Hart, Michael. (2016) "East Asia' State-Led Search for Energy Security." *The Diplomat*, July 23. Accessed March 16, 2017. http://thediplomat.com/2016/07/east-asias-state-led-search-for-energy-security/.

International Energy Agency (IEA). (2009) *World Energy Outlook 2009*. International Energy Agency, Paris, France.

International Energy Agency (IEA). (2014) *Energy Supply Security: Emergency Response of IEA Countries*. International Energy Agency, Paris, France.

International Energy Agency (IEA). (2015a) *World Energy Outlook 2015*. International Energy Agency, Paris, France.

International Energy Agency (IEA). (2015b) *India Energy Outlook*. International Energy Agency, Paris, France.

International Monetary Fund (IMF). (2017) *World Economic Outlook Database*. Accessed March 3, 2017. www.imf.org/external/pubs/ft/weo/2017/01/weodata/index.aspx.

Korea Energy Economics Institute (KEEI). (2016) *Monthly Energy Statistics*. November 2016, pp. 61–64.

9

Energy systems and low-carbon policies in East Asia focusing on Japan and South Korea

Soocheol Lee

Recent situation and development of low-carbon policies in East Asia

East Asia consists of Japan, which is already in the mature stage of industrialization; South Korea and Taiwan, which are entering this mature stage; China, which is in the process of rapid industrialization; and, if Southeast Asian countries are included, countries and regions in a range of development stages, such as Indonesia and Vietnam, which are in the initial stages of industrialization. Consequently, the state and extent of progress of energy systems and related policies for a sustainable, low-carbon future in this region are not uniform (Lee et al., 2015).

Given this situation, institutional infrastructure-building, which is instrumental in developing a low-carbon society in the East Asia region, has been moving forward in recent years. For example, in Japan, this includes the "Environmental Model City" concept, begun in 2008, which selects cities and assists them as they pioneer approaches to wide-scale greenhouse gas reduction, such as feed-in-tariffs for renewable energy, which went into effect in July 2012; and a carbon tax (the so-called Global Warming Tax), which has been in effect since October 2012. In particular, Japan's carbon tax was the first such tax in Asia. However, the rate was low, at around 300 JPY per ton of CO_2, which is much lower than the level required to compare favorably with the environmental tax reform of Northern Europe.[1] Furthermore, the introduction of a scheme for trading greenhouse gas emissions, driven by the Ministry of the Environment (2013a), has not come to fruition. This delay is due to strong resistance from industry, largely from the Japan Business Federation. However, Asia's first greenhouse-gas emissions trading scheme has been in effect at the local government level in Tokyo since 2010. This scheme has influenced surrounding local governments, such as those in Saitama Prefecture (which introduced a scheme in 2011).

In South Korea, energy tax system reform, including the introduction of a carbon tax, has been put off without much discussion at the state level. Introducing a carbon tax was debated by multiple administrations in Taiwan as well, but met with strong political resistance from industry and never came to fruition. This speaks to the fact that low-carbon policies in this region have not overcome the barrier of real concerns about the possible reduction in industrial international competitiveness from introducing low-carbon policies. However, on fronts other than implementing a carbon tax, the state-led low-carbon green-growth policy pushed by South Korea under the previous government, the Lee Myung-Bak government, was a driving force from 2009 in significant development of South Korea's low-carbon economy, as will be discussed below (Lee, 2009). This symbolic policy can be considered the first emissions trading scheme to be introduced in Asia at the state level (related laws were enacted in 2012 and went into effect in 2015).

Climate policy in China took center stage with the finalization of the 12th FYP in March 2011. The plan is significant in its commitment to energy efficiency and emissions reduction, and is the first one to address climate change as a key issue. With regard to energy and climate change, the plan has four targets that are all designated as binding. They specify to decrease the energy intensity (energy consumption per unit of GDP) and CO_2 intensity (carbon emission per unit of GDP) by 16 percent and 17 percent, respectively, and to increase the share of non-fossil energy in primary energy consumption to 11.4 percent from the current level of 8.3 percent over the period 2010–2015.The purpose of a low-carbon system and associated policymaking in East Asia is to develop next-generation national strategic industries and guarantee energy security. Greenhouse-gas reduction and environmental improvement tend to be acknowledged as things that are obtained incidentally as a result (Lee, 2010).

Therefore, over the next decade there are likely to be quite profound changes to the ways in which energy is consumed in East Asia. Due to "lock-in" effects, the decisions made in the coming years could result in lasting consequences (Lee et al., 2015). It is important for East Asian countries to create an institutional system that properly assesses the social costs and benefits of different power sources in addition to conventional economic gains.

Table 9.1 summarizes the progress of East Asian economic growth, greenhouse gas levels and reduction targets, the status and targets of renewable energy and nuclear power, and the main low-carbon policies of China, Japan, South Korea, and Taiwan. In the next section, we consider in detail the progress and challenges mainly in Japan and South Korea, which have recently achieved some positive results toward reforming energy systems and enforcing low-carbon policies, and following South Korea, we mention the recent development of energy and low carbon policies in China.

Greenhouse-gas reduction and energy-planning and low-carbon policies

Japan

Japan emitted 1.365 billion tons of greenhouse gases in 2014, an increase of 7.5 percent from 1990 levels and a decrease of 3.1 percent from the previous year. According to the Kyoto Protocol, Japan is obligated to reduce its emissions so that they are 6 percent lower than 1990 levels, to be achieved during the first commitment period (2008 and 2012). Consequently, while greenhouse-gas emissions in 2009 were at a 1.6 percent decrease comparing to 1990 levels, they increased year-on-year by 9.5 percent increase in 2012 and 10.9 percent increase in 2013 comparing to 1990 levels because the operating rate of thermal power generation rose as part of the impact of the 2011 Fukushima nuclear disaster (Table 9.2).

By sector (CO_2 emissions from fuel combustion) for the period 1990–2013, the industrial sector decreased emissions by 15.1 percent, from 503 million tons in 1990 to 427 million tons; the transportation sector increased emissions by 5.3 percent, from 206 million tons to 217 million tons; and the business sector (commerce, office buildings, etc.) increased emissions by around 97.8 percent, from 134 million tons to 265 million tons, accounting for a majority of the increase in emissions in 2014.[2] The household sector increased emissions by 44.3 percent, from 131 million tons to 189 million tons. Considering this, in Japan, we see that there was a particularly significant increase in emissions from the business and household sectors.

Japan determined national targets and policy related to climate action in its "Outline for Promotion Effects to Prevent Global Warming," which was enacted in 1998. This outline asserted

Table 9.1 GDP, CO_2 emissions, GHG targets, energy systems and low-carbon policies in East Asia

		China (year)	*Japan (year)*	*Korea (year)*	*Taiwan (year)*
GDP	GDP (bn US$)	390 (1990), 9,181 (2013)	3,104 (1990), 4,902 (2013)	270 (1990), 1,222 (2013)	165 (1990), 489 (2013)
	GDP (per capita US$)	341 (1990), 6,747 (2013)	25,140 (1990), 38,491 (2013)	6,308 (1990), 24,329 (2013)	8,087 (1990), 20,930 (2013)
CO_2 emission and GHG targets	Energy related CO_2 emission (M CO_2ton)	2,461 (1990), 9,437 (2013)	1,095 (1990), 1,235 (2013)	247 (1990), 601(2013)	137 (1990), 271 (2012)
	INDC 2030 GHG target(%)	2030 would be peak year for CO_2 emission and 60~65% reduction per GDP unit	–18.0 (comparing to 1990) –25.4 (comparing to 2005) –26.0 (comparing to 2013)	–37.0% (BAU) –21% (comparing to 2010)	–50% (BAU) –20% (comparing to 2005)
Renewable energy and nuclear power target	Renewable (% of total electricity)	19.2% (including 17% hydro) (2012) 15% of primary energy (2020)	10.7% (2013), 13.5% (2020), 22~24.0% (2030)	3.7% (2012), 10% (2022), 20% (2035) 15% of primary energy (2035)	5.2% (2012), 15% (2025)
	Nuclear (% of total electricity)	1.8% (2010), 2.1% (2013), 11GW (2012), 200GW (2030)	29.2% (2010), 1.7% (2013), 20~22% (2030)	32.2% (2010), 27.6% (2013), 27.8% (2024), 29% (2035)	19.3% (2010), 19.1% (2013)
Low-carbon policy	Carbon tax	Not yet; under discussion	289 yen/tCO_2 from 2012	Not yet; under discussion	Not yet; tried but failed
	ETS	Nationally from 2019 (not fixed yet), piloting regional ETS from 2011	Not yet nationally but municipally from 2010 (Tokyo City), 2011 (Saitama Prefecture)	Nationally from 2015	Not yet
	Renewable energy policy	FIT (Feed-in-Tariff)	FIT	RPS(Renewable Portfolio Standard)	FIT

Note: Conventional hydropower is excluded from Korea's renewable targets for 2022 and 2035.

Sources: Websites of World Bank, IEA, IAEA, World Nuclear Association and Lee et al. (2015).

Table 9.2 Trend of Japan's national greenhouse gas emission

	1990	*2005*	*2009*	*2013*	*2014*	*2014/1990 (%)*
CO_2	1,156	1,306	1,163	1,312	1,265	9.4
CH_4	48.6	38.9	37.2	36.1	35.5	−27.0
N_2O	30.8	24.5	22.6	21.5	20.8	−32.5
HCFC,HFC	35.4	27.7	28.6	38.8	42.0	18.6
Total emission	1,271	1,397	1,251	1,408	1,364	7.3

Source: Ministry of Environment (2015).

the compatibility of caring for the environment and the economy, promoted staged action with cooperation in every area and on every level, and promoted partnerships with international society. Furthermore, it provided specific numeric targets for achieving targets set forth in the Kyoto Protocol.

In terms of medium- to long-term targets for greenhouse-gas reduction, at the 2008 Hokkaido Toyako Summit, then-Prime Minister Fukuda proposed cutting global emissions in half by 2050 and announced the so-called Fukuda Declaration that Japan would cut greenhouse gases by 60–80 percent of current (2008) levels. Furthermore, in June 2009, then-Prime Minister Aso established the medium-term target of reducing emissions to 5 percent below 2005 levels by 2020 (representing an 8 percent reduction below 1990 levels). However, after the Democratic Party of Japan (DPJ), which had been actively promoting the reduction of greenhouse gas emissions, came into power that year, then-Prime Minister Hatoyama officially declared at the Copenhagen Summit (CO15) in September 2009, a mere 3 months after Aso's announcement, that Japan would reduce greenhouse-gas emissions to 25 percent below 1990 levels by 2020, with a long-term target of an 80 percent reduction by 2050, despite resistance from the Japan Business Federation.[3]

However, when nuclear power generation ceased due to the Fukushima nuclear disaster that followed the Great East Japan Earthquake, the DPJ government at the time declared that it would repeal these medium-term targets. Then, after a national debate in 2012, the "Innovative Strategy for Energy and the Environment" was announced. This strategy aimed for complete non-reliance on nuclear energy by 2030, and dramatically revised the medium-term targets, striving to reduce greenhouse gases to 5–9 percent below 1990 levels by 2020 and to 20 percent below 1990 levels by 2030.

When Prime Minister Abe and the Liberal Democratic Party government came to power in December 2012, it was announced that energy policy and climate-change policy would be re-examined, and new emissions targets would be set. The declared target of no nuclear power by 2030, declared when the DPJ was in power, was repealed, and nuclear power was promoted as the main baseload power supply. We can see from this that the country's greenhouse-gas reduction targets changed considerably because of changes in the political and economic conditions. That is, Japan's targets for greenhouse-gas reduction and its energy plan were strongly influenced by political factors.

At COP21 (a summit of 21 signatory countries of the United Nations Framework Convention on Climate Change) in Paris, a new international framework for reducing greenhouse-gas emissions beyond the year 2020 was adopted. Consequently, in June 2015, the Abe government officially laid out "Japan's Intended Nationally Determined Contributions," which set Japan's greenhouse-gas reduction targets for 2030 at 26 percent below 2013 levels, and submitted it to the UN Framework Convention on Climate Change office.

Reducing emission of greenhouse gases requires coherence with national energy supply targets. In Japan, regulations contained in the "Basic Act on Energy Policy," enacted in 2002, require the government to formulate a basic plan on energy supply and demand (hereinafter referred to as the "Basic Energy Plan") in order to promote measures regarding energy supply and demand on a long-term, comprehensive, and systematic basis. Therefore, the "Basic National Energy Plan" called on governments to "pursue the best mix of assuring a stable energy supply, suitability for the environment, and economic efficiency." Consequently, the government established a target of 34 percent for so-called zero-emissions power supply through nuclear power and renewable energy as a percentage of total power supply in 2010, at near 50 percent in 2020, and near 70 percent in 2030.

After the Fukushima Daiichi nuclear accident, however, public trust in nuclear power wavered significantly, so the government had to revise the target to rely less on nuclear power and more on renewable energy. Consequently, the "New Basic Energy Plan," which centered on accelerating the introduction of renewable energy sources and rebuilding nuclear power generation capability, was officially announced in 2014. Under this New Basic Energy Plan, in April 2015 the Ministry of Economy, Trade and Industry published the "Long-term Energy Supply and Demand Outlook" (hereinafter, Outlook), which determined the energy mix until 2030. In promoting energy conservation in terms of BAU levels of 196.1 TWh from 2013 to 2030, this Outlook committed to lowering the thermal power ratio as a portion of gross generation to 60 percent or less by 2030, while expanding present policies to expand nuclear power to 20–22 percent and renewable energy to 22–24 percent (Figure 9.1).

Meanwhile, in Japan, renewable energy generation centered around solar power increased dramatically with the introduction of the feed-in-tariff scheme (Table 9.3). Under the feed-in-tariff scheme, the monthly renewable energy tariff per average family (families with average

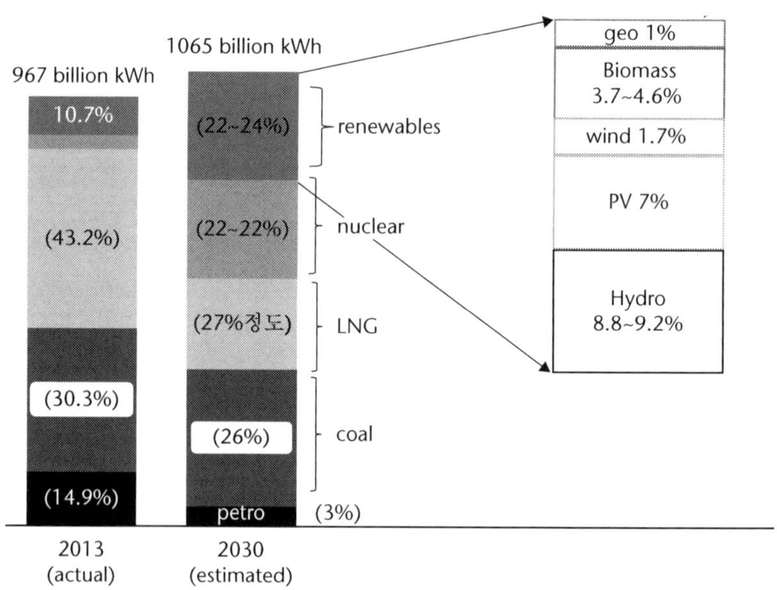

Figure 9.1 Japan's power generation mix in 2030 in long-term energy supply and demand outlook

Source: Ministry of Economy Trade and Industry (2015).

Table 9.3 FIT tariff and installed capacity of renewable energy in Japan

Technology	*Tariff (JPY/kWh)*						*Installed capacity (July 2012~December 2015) (MW)*
	Tariff years	*2012*	*2013*	*2014*	*2015*	*2016*	
PV (smaller than 10kW)	10	42	38	37	33~35	31~33	3740
PV (larger than 10kW)	20	40	36	32	29	24	21,430
Wind (smaller than 20kW)	20	55	55	55	55	55	430
Wind (larger than 20kW)	20	22	22	22	22	22	
Wind(off shore)	20	–	–	36	36	36	
Small hydro (smaller than 200kW)	20	34	34	34	34	34	140
Small hydro (200–1000kW)	20	29	29	29	29	29	
Geothermal (smaller than 15000kW)	15	40	40	40	40	40	10
Biogas	20	39	39	39	39	39	480
Solid biomass (unutilized wood)	20	32	32	32	32	32	
Solid biomass (wood and processed residue from agriculture)	20	24	24	24	24	24	
Waste	20	17	17	17	17	17	–

Source: Agency for Natural Resources and Energy, Japan, www.enecho.meti.go.jp/category/saving_and_new/saiene/kaitori/index.html (accessed June 2016).

monthly consumption of approximately 300 kWh) rose by 66 JPY in 2012, 105 in 2013, 225 in 2014, and 474 in 2015, and the cost to the general public has risen to a level that cannot be ignored. Consequently, the Ministry of Economy, Trade and Industry has launched a review of the renewable energy feed-in-tariff scheme. For example, they reduced the purchase price of solar each year for three years in a row (Table 9.3). As well, suspension of new purchases is being explored in the event that such purchases significantly exceed a specified amount.

South Korea and China

Korea emitted 694.5 million tons of greenhouse gases in 2013, an increase of 137.6 percent from 1990 levels. This exceeded the increase in Japan's emissions during the same period (10.9 percent) by a factor of more than 10. This can be attributed to the fact that while South Korea's GDP grew about 130 percent during this period, Japan's GDP grew by around 10 percent. The growing emissions from energy sectors such as electricity and gas, and from energy-derived fuel used by the manufacturing industry, are major contributors to this increase. Despite being an OECD country, the past rise in emissions on a cumulative basis in South Korea has been relatively low compared with that of other OECD member states, so it was not included among countries obligated to reduce emissions in the Kyoto Protocol. This, too, is one of the main factors behind why South Korea did not make active efforts to cut emissions of greenhouse gases during this time.

However, South Korea's low-carbon policy to reduce emissions of greenhouse gases has moved forward at a rapid pace since the inauguration of the (previous) Lee Myung-bak government, the success of which has been recognized even in international society. In 2008, one year after taking office, the president, as the chief executive of the South Korean government, revealed to the public the nation's new vision, "Low Carbon Green Growth." The main tenets of this are the development and proliferation of green technology and clean energy.

Seizing this opportunity, a concrete strategy for promoting cross-governmental low-carbon green growth was set. In February 2009, the "Green Growth Committee" was launched and designated as the organization responsible for formulating and reviewing this strategy. The committee is a collaboration between government and the public, spread across various government ministries, including the then Ministry of Environment; the Ministry of Transport and Maritime Affairs; the Ministry of Knowledge Economy; and the Ministry of Agriculture, Food and Rural Affairs.[4] This committee enabled the formulation of policy that tended to prioritize the interests of ministries and agencies within a vertical administration up to that time, as well as the formulation of policy that prioritized discussion and climate action that went beyond the barriers of ministries and agencies.

A legal system related to a green economy was rapidly developed, led by the Green Growth Committee. This included the National Strategy and 5-Year Plan for Green Growth (July 2009), establishment of the Framework Act for Low Carbon Green Growth (2009), establishment of the Smart Grid Promotion Act (2011), and establishment (2012) and enforcement (2015) of the Emissions Trading Act. Since the introduction of the Framework Act for Low Carbon Green Growth was revealed, because less than two years of debate had occurred, the effective period of the emissions trading scheme was extended (initially from 2013 to 2015) and the allocation of allowances was expanded in a way that broadly incorporated the views of industry (Table 9.4). This went into effect from 2015 in a friendlier form for business circles than the initial plan, with eased penalties and regulations (Lee, 2013b).[5]

As a concrete example of how systems related to the low-carbon economy improved, investment support for green industries was expanded and 27 key green technologies were selected (January 2009), the Green Product Certification System was established (April 2010), and the Renewable Portfolio Standard (RPS system) was introduced (January 2012). Along with these changes, since 2008, the average annual investment in green technology R&D has risen by approximately 26 percent in South Korea, and public investment in green growth businesses has reached 2 percent of GDP.[6] Furthermore, to activate the green market, actions are being taken to designate qualifying products as certified green products, to certify businesses as preferred green businesses, to mandate the installation of 60 percent LED lighting in public institutions by 2015, to expand green purchases by public institutions, and to provide assistance for installation of LED lighting for those with low incomes.

These results have achieved a degree of success in expanding products related to green business and have popularized the low-carbon economy in daily life. One typical example of this is the Green Card (Eco Money), which has been driven by the South Korean Ministry of the Environment (2013b). Eleven million people had already signed up for this system by the end of 2015. The system gives users points under the carbon point scheme, for using public transportation, and when purchasing eco products.

Among these, the carbon point scheme is a system in which the Ministry of the Environment, local governments, and card companies as well as power, gas, and water companies partner with customers to put a maximum of 70,000–100,000 points per year on the Green Card of families who visit the relevant website, enter their customer numbers for electricity, water, and gas, and reduce their six-month average carbon emissions by at least 5–10 percent from the previous two years.[7] In addition to carbon points, a total of 200,000 KRW in points in a year are accumulated on the Green Card, including a maximum of 70,000 KRW in points when public transportation is used and a maximum of 30,000 KRW in points when purchasing eco products in a green shop. These points can be exchanged for cash, to purchase products, or used to pay communication

Table 9.4 Summary of emissions trading scheme in Korea

	Phase one	*Phase 2*	*Phase 3*
Period	2015~2017	2018~2020	2021~2025
Greenhouse gas covered	Carbon Dioxide (CO_2), Methane (CH_4), Nitrous Oxide (N_2O), Hydrofluorocarbons (HFC), Perfluorocarbons (PFC), and Sulfur hexafluoride(SF6)	Same as left	Same as left
Sectors covered (Threshold)	23 sub-sectors from steel, cement, petro-chemistry, refinery, power, (Company >125,000 tCO2/year, or factory > 25,000tCO2e)	–	–
Target	By 2020: Unconditional, voluntary target of −30% below business as usual (BAU): 543 million tCO_2e. By 2030: 37% below BAU (536 $MtCO_2e$). This represents a 22% reduction below 2012 GHG levels.		
Allocation	100% free allocation, no auctioning.	97% free allowances, 3% auctioned	Less than 90% free allowances, more than 10% auctioned
	Only domestic credits from external reduction activities implemented by non-ETS entities Up to 10% of each entity's compliance obligation	Same as left	Up to 10% of each entity's compliance obligation with a maximum of 5% coming from international offset

Note: Banking is allowed without any restrictions. Borrowing is allowed only within a single trading phase (maximum of 10 percent of entity's obligation), not across phases.

Source: Ministry of the Environment (2015).

charges such as internet access charges. Half of the costs related to the Green Card are paid by the central government (on the Ministry of the Environment budget) and half by local governments.

South Korean Research, the South Korean public opinion polling body, surveyed 1,000 people from around the country in January 2013, and 97 percent of respondents reported that a low-carbon economy is the most important national issue to pursue even if the government changes in the future, and that the priorities of policy challenges to do so were developing and expanding new energy (54.6 percent), education and public relations for increasing national awareness of the low carbon economy (34.5 percent), greenhouse-gas regulatory policy (32.8 percent), and the development of green technologies (28.0 percent) (South Korean Research, 2013).

However, since the start of a new government in South Korea in December 2012, the function and role of the Green Growth Committee, which had led the country's low-carbon policy, has been severely curtailed. This is because the president of the new government did not show much interest in green growth, the eye-catching policy of the previous government. The ruling party of the current government actually amended the existing Framework Act for Low Carbon Green Growth in March 2013. This changed the oversight of the Green Growth Committee, which has been installed as the foundation of this act, from the president's office to the prime minister's office, thereby downgrading the committee. Furthermore, the authority and functionality of the committee was effectively slashed by abolishing the "Green Growth Planning Group," which had supported the committee's activities. It is unclear to what extent the new government will take over and develop the previous government's green growth strategy.

Meanwhile, China is working to solve a number of environmental issues associated with its recent rapid economic growth. As a staged outcome, they have decreased GDP per unit of energy use by nearly 20 percent under the 11th Five-Year Plan (2006–2010). China had not previously laid out a clear policy about institution building for greenhouse-gas reduction and a low-carbon society, but the situation has changed markedly since the beginning of the 2010s. For example, in 2010 in the "People's Republic of China National Economic and Social Development; Overview of the 12th Five-Year Plan (2011–2015)," a section on "green development, resource conservation, and building an environmentally friendly society" was set out, with a focus on an active response to global climate change and environmental protection. At the 18th National Congress of the Communist Party, held in November 2012, China announced the construction of an ecological civilization, Energy Department reform, and large-scale investment in green industries as the highest priority issues for the next five years. They also declared a goal of having greenhouse-gas emissions peak by 2030 as part of the agenda for greenhouse gas emissions reduction (which is an 80–100 percent increase from 2005 emissions).

While Chinese energy conservation and environmental measures still rely on administrative means, they have gradually begun to be examined and implemented in terms of economic policy. For example, in carrying out resource tax reform targeting oil and coal, the introduction of an environment tax, including a carbon tax, was discussed between relevant ministries and agencies. A greenhouse-gas emissions trading scheme had, by 2011, already been started in five cities and two provinces (Beijing, Tianjin, Shanghai, Chongqing, Guangdong Province, Hubei Province, and Shenzhen), with an aim to implement a scheme at the state level in 2019 similar to that in South Korea. Active support is also being given to expanding renewable energy, introducing energy-saving equipment, and expanding highly energy-efficient products.

Challenges to energy systems and low-carbon policy for a sustainable future in East Asia

As seen above, while Japan and South Korea have taken a general view toward promoting low-carbon policies in recent years, systemic reform related to low carbon in East Asian countries is significantly influenced by their mutual systems and policies. For example, after public opinion in Japan soured toward nuclear energy in the wake of the Fukushima Daiichi nuclear accident, Japan has chosen a scenario that reduces nuclear energy by the 2030s (a plan to reduce the target ratio of nuclear energy in 2030 from around 50 percent before the accident to 20–22 percent after the accident). Influenced by the accident in Japan, Taiwan is also examining whether to reduce or eliminate nuclear energy. The Taiwanese government published a New Energy Policy of Taiwan in June 2014 (Bureau of Energy, Taiwan, 2014). In the plan, a steady reduction of nuclear energy and full-scale promotion of renewable energy are anticipated. There would be no extension to the life span of existing nuclear plants, and no more new nuclear plants. In contrast, China and South Korea still position nuclear power as their primary source of power, firmly maintaining the existing nuclear course. Indonesia and Vietnam in Southeast Asia have clarified their intention to promote the use of nuclear energy.

When pushing low-carbon policy, a significant thing to be cautious about is whether the relevant policies in fact strengthen incentives to use nuclear power. In the future, it will be critical in East Asia to build systems to properly evaluate the costs of nuclear energy through tightening nuclear energy safety standards and reviewing nuclear risk calculations and laws on liability for damages. Furthermore, most of the countries in East Asia will need to depart from their reliance on fossil fuels by reviewing the various forms of direct and indirect subsidies for fossil fuels (Lee, 2013b).

The biggest barrier to accelerating low-carbon policies in East Asian countries is the lack of awareness about the damage caused to the environment by the use of fossil fuels and about the risks associated with nuclear energy. It is essential to understand approaches that attempt to have someone "internalize," that is, take responsibility for, environmental risk and pollution costs, such as by reflecting these in the market value of a product. This "external diseconomy" of environmental risk and environmental pollution (such as the risk that no one will take responsibility for environmental risk and pollution costs) could be addressed through economic means; that is, through environmental economics. The reason the environmental tax system reform in Europe has achieved a certain level of results is that the political leadership and institutional foundation exist to improve public awareness and thereby encourage those affected to accept the "pain" of higher energy costs so as to protect the environment and the welfare of future generations via actual policy (Lee et al., 2015).

Restructuring from the perspective of taxes, such as through environmental tax system reform, is important to progress toward a low-carbon society, but reform from the perspective of public finance expenditures (green reform of public finance) is also important. For example, Japan and South Korea have reduced the portion of government funds spent on public projects by way of subsidies for conventional fossil fuel energy (power plant construction) and road construction since the early 2000s and have increased the portion of funds spent on developing green technologies and expanding renewable energy. Both countries' governments have announced that they will develop these areas as strategic sectors that will lead future national growth.[8] China and Taiwan have also shown considerable interest in developing areas of key importance, including energy conservation. The Asian carbon market has enormous potential, and the sustainable economy will likely make significant headway in this region, such as through the efficient reduction of greenhouse gases and the innovation in and expansion of low-carbon technologies, if systems are built that lead to linkages with other regional markets and market activation.

The reality of low-carbon tax system reform is that it will be a difficult challenge in the short term. To make reform a reality, it is essential to present to the public a long-term vision for greening public finance and obtaining public consent by persuasion. To achieve this, governments will need to address economic reliance on fossil fuels and tackle pollution costs through effective and efficient policy. Also, they will need to steadily provide education and information on the risk of using nuclear energy. These will require strong leadership, with firm conviction that is not swayed by short-term economic conditions.

East Asia is deepening its interdependence along 3 lines: economy, environment, and energy. In this sense, East Asia must aim to create an environment and energy community. It is not easy to obtain consensus between countries involved in free trade agreements and economic integration in the region, because there are many areas with conflicting interests. This will require time and diligent negotiation (Lee, 2014).

Despite this, there are few areas in which their interests in the environment and energy clash, leaving ample room for mutual cooperation. As long as political and financial leaders have the will, it is more than feasible. We propose that political, industry, and academic leaders and intellectuals come together to launch the "East Asian Low Carbon Forum (provisional)" to discuss the future of energy and environment issues in Japan, China, and South Korea or all East Asia. From there it would be conceivable for it to develop into the "Organization for Cooperation in East Asian Energy and Environment (provisional)," which would have a legal foundation as the body responsible for implementing policy concerning the energy and environment community in this region.

In East Asia, a range of pending issues, including battery-related technology (which is expected to grow significantly in the future), construction of a supergrid and the development and expansion of renewable energy technology are being discussed. Progress is being made on a framework for designing and implementing systems and policies for solving these issues. There would be great significance for East Asia to work collaboratively to harmonize related policies, effectively save energy, and cut greenhouse gases as the driving force of low-carbon policy in the world moving forward.

Notes

1 Here environmental tax reform refers to efforts to introduce a fixed environmental tax (carbon tax or energy tax) and using this tax revenue towards reducing consumption tax, income tax, or corporate employment-related tax, while as a result of which concurrently improving the environment (reducing carbon dioxide, etc.) and activating the economy (increase GDP and employment).

2 Statistics on greenhouse-gas emissions by sector are basically allocated to and published by various sectors on the basis of emissions of the electricity sector.

3 However, Prime Minister Hatoyama had attached provisory clauses for when all major emitting countries participate to set enthusiastic reduction targets based on the principle of fairness.

4 See Lee (2009) and Yun et al. (2011) for more details on the structure and roles of the Green Growth Committee.

5 Lee (2013a) discusses South Korea's emissions trading scheme from a comparative perspective.

6 The change in overall investment has gone from 17.2 trillion KRW (2009) to 25.7 trillion KRW (2011) to 21.3 trillion KRW (planned for 2013).

7 40,000 points from electricity charges, 10,000 points from water charges, and 20,000 points from municipal gas charges. Here, 1 point is worth 1 KRW. Entities such as schools are given a maximum of 350,000 KRW per year.

8 For Japan, see website of the prime minister of Japan and his cabinet, https://japan.kantei.go.jp/index.html; for South Korea, see Green Growth Committee (2009, 2013) and Ministry of Trade, Industry and Energy (2013).

References

Green Growth Committee. (2009) *National strategy and 5-year plan for green growth*, Green Growth Committee, Seoul, South Korea (in Korean).

Green Growth Committee. (2013) *Results and future challenges of green growth*, Green Growth Committee, Seoul, South Korea (in Korean).

Lee, Soocheol. (2009) "Green growth and green new deal policy in Korea." *Sustainable Management*, 9(1): 1–17 (in Japanese).

Lee, Soocheol, eds. (2010) *Environmental charge system in East Asia: conditions and problems with institutional evolution*, Kyoto, Japan: Showado Press (in Japanese).

Lee, Soocheol. (2013a) "Comparative analysis of institutional designs and policy processes toward the introduction of emissions trading systems in Japan and Korea." *Journal of Meijo University*, 13(4): 159–172 (in Japanese).

Lee, Soocheol. (2013b) "Features and challenges of green growth strategy in East Asia." *Journal of Environmental Information Science*, 42(3): 20–24 (in Japanese).

Lee, Soocheol, eds. (2014) *Energy and environmental policy in East Asia: nuclear power/climate change/air and water pollution*, Kyoto, Japan: Showado Press (in Japanese).

Lee, Soocheol, Hector Pollitt and Park Seung-Joon, eds. (2015) *Low-carbon, sustainable future in East Asia: Improving energy system, taxation and policy cooperation*, London: Routledge.

Ministry of Economy Trade and Industry. (2015) *Long term outlook of energy supply and demand in Japan*, Tokyo, Japan: Ministry of Economy Trade and Industry (in Japanese).

Ministry of the Environment. (2013a) *Fiscal 2013 greenhouse gas and energy target management system*, Seoul, South Korea: Ministry of the Environment (in Korean).

Ministry of the Environment. (2013b) *Fiscal 2013 carbon rating certification mark system*, Seoul, South Korea: Ministry of the Environment (in Korean).

Ministry of the Environment. (2015) *Emission Trading Scheme in Korea*, Seoul, South Korea: Ministry of the Environment (in Korean).

Ministry of Trade, Industry and Energy. (2013) *Creating momentum for growth through financial diffusion*, Seoul, South Korea: Ministry of Trade, Industry and Energy (in Korean).

South Korean Research. (2013) *Public awareness survey on green growth strategy*, South Korean Research (in Korean).

Yun, Sunjin, Sungin Na Lee and Soocheol Lee. (2011) "Climate change policy governance of Korea." *Journal of Meijo University*, 10(4): 119–129 (in Japanese).

10

The Asian urban energy system: an overview of trends and challenges

Peter J. Marcotullio

Introduction

The Asia region includes over 40 nations stretching from Cyprus in the Mediterranean to the Philippines in the Pacific Ocean and northward to Japan and Mongolia (United Nations 2014). Included in this territory are vast deserts, extensive plains, the world's highest mountain ranges, tens of thousands of islands, lush jungles and magnificent river systems. Not only does this geography cover a range of biophysical systems, but it also includes a diverse set of cultures, political institutions and economies.

Two of the most impressive recent changes marking the region are its economic and urbanization growth. Over the past fifty years, the region has experienced spectacular increases in economic production. These increases have been underpinned by enormous inflows of foreign direct investment, trade, people and information. This economic growth has also been associated with the massive movement of people to the region's cities. From 1970 to 2010, approximately 1.36 billion people were added to urban areas across the region, bringing the urbanization level from 23.7 percent to 44.8 percent.

Both economic growth and urbanization have driven and been driven by energy use and supply. With the expansion of economic activities and the building of cities in which much of this activity occurs, the region has increased its total energy supply from 4.4 to 12.7 Gigatons oil equivalents (Gtoe), almost a threefold increase. All three of these factors are tightly interlinked, although the details of how each has changed together are as varied as the geographies and cultures of the region.

This chapter explores the overall trends, patterns and dynamics among Asia's urbanization and energy supply and use. We use a systems approach in suggesting linkages between these patterns and those of economic progress. The chapter's brief overview attempts to highlight both the overall dynamic change and the diversity among the region's nations and cities. It also points out the sustainable development challenges ahead, including meeting the goals of lowering energy-related pollution, providing universal access to modern energy and reducing greenhouse gas (GHG) emissions.

The chapter starts with an overview of contemporary urbanization across Asia, and then presents an overview of changes in Asia's energy systems. The fourth section examines linkages between energy trends and urbanization. The fifth section points out three major challenges related to urbanization and energy use in Asia. The final section concludes by summarizing the findings.

Urbanization in Asia

Researchers agree that urbanization trends in Asia are unique among world regions (UNESCAP and UN HABITAT 2010, Sheng and Thuzar 2012). This uniqueness stems from the historical context in which economies across the region developed, as well as from a contemporary development context. During the era of rapid economic growth in the second half of the twentieth century, the contemporary characteristics of Asian regional urbanization took shape. These qualities include: the rapid speed and large scale of urbanization and urban growth, the early timing of the urbanization process during development, the large size and density of the region's cities, and increasing heterogeneity of the inter-urban patterns and dynamics. All these trends have implications for energy demand.

Rapid speed of urbanization and urban growth

Asian urbanization and urban growth have been the fastest in human history. The speed of urban development can be measured in at least two ways. First, urban development is measured by changes in a nation's share of urban population. Second, the urban growth rate can also be indicated by population increase of individual urban centers. Asian countries have urbanized approximately 28 percent faster than Western countries. That is, when comparing the length of time it took to increase urbanization levels from 18 to 53 percent, Western economies took 74 years increasing by about 0.46 percent each year on average, while Asian countries took only 60 years with an average increase of 0.59 percent annually.

The growth of individual cities has also been rapid. Cho and Bauer (1987) demonstrate that during 1960–1980, Asian urban growth rates were much faster than the world average (except for Japan) and were also amongst the fastest in the developing world. Even today, there are over 135,000 people added to the Asian region's cities on a daily basis (United Nations 2014). Between 1950 and 2010, Asia had over 100 cities that grew by 100-fold during this period and 17 cities that grew by 200-fold (Table 10.1).

Large scale of urbanization

Asia is home to the largest human population of the world. Approximately three out of five people on the planet live in the region. If one includes the 40 economies defined by the UN as part of Asia, the region reached a total population of approximately 1.4 billion in 1950. Of this

Table 10.1 Number of cities and comparative growth rates between 1950 and 2010, by region

Region	*Total number of cities*	*Negative growth*	*Positive growth*	*Growth >=50 fold*	*Growth >= 100 fold*	*Growth >= 150 fold*	*Growth >= 200 fold*
Africa	179	0	179	25	6	4	1
Asia	880	0	880	182	102	38	17
Europe	253	13	240	2	1	1	0
South America	206	0	206	8	5	2	2
North America	151	1	150	11	5	4	4
Oceania	13	0	13	0	0	0	0
Total	1682	14	1668	228	119	49	24

Source: UN (2014).

total approximately 1.15 billion were rural residents. It is not surprising then that as the region urbanizes, the absolute numbers of people that are moving to cities dwarf any previous precedent. Indeed, the number of people moving to cities in Asia is astonishingly high. From 1950 to 2010, the urban population increased by 1.6 billion. When the region hits its 50 percent urban tipping point (approximately 2026), it will house 2.6 billion urban residents or approximately the size of the global urban population around 2000.

Early urbanization during development

Many scholars have emphasized the importance of economic activity for urban growth (see for example Satterthwaite 2007). This is largely because urbanization accompanies industrialization, which enhances economic activity. While industrialization was a motor of urban growth for Western cultures, in Asia industrialization has taken on new characteristics, as it is also associated with massive international trade, foreign investments and financial flows (Lo and Marcotullio 2000). Given the rapid globalization-driven economic development in the region, urbanization has occurred at increasingly lower levels of economic development than previously experienced (Figure 10.1). For example, for several Asian countries (Japan, Korea, Malaysia, China and Indonesia) urbanization levels are higher at similar levels of are occurring at GDP per capita levels than found in Western Countries (USA, Germany and France).

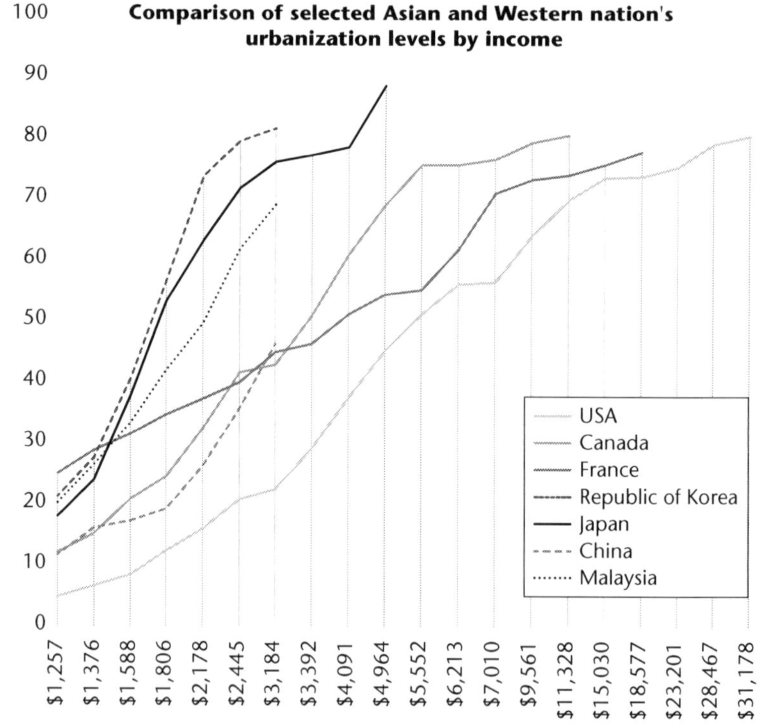

Figure 10.1 Comparison of selected Asian and Western nation's urbanization levels by GDP per capita

Sources: UN DESA (2014), Bolt and van Zanden (2014), UN (2014).

Large size and high density of cities

Asia houses the lion's share of the world's largest cities. By 2010, the region had 50 percent of all cities over 1 million and over 42 percent of all megacities. Indeed, Asia has increasingly dominated over other regions in terms of the emergence of large cities in all size categories (United Nations 2010).[1] Furthermore, the dominance of the largest city within Asian nations can be seen across the region. In 2010, approximately 21 Asian countries had major metropolitan centers that housed over 25 percent of all urban residents and 20 nations had an urban primacy index over 50 percent meaning that the urban national system was dominated by a single metropolitan center (Table 10.2).

Not only are cities now larger in population than during previous eras, but they are also expanding horizontally and vertically faster than previously experienced. Examples of rapidly expanding individual urban areas have been identified in China. Between 1973 and 2008, the average increase in urban land in a sample of 60 cities (4 municipalities, 28 provincial capitals,

Table 10.2 Urban Primacy Index, 1950–2030

Country	*1950*	*1980*	*2010*	*2030*
High primacy				
Dem. People's Republic of Korea	98.3	136.0	182.2	181.4
Afghanistan	50.9	75.0	84.6	86.6
Thailand	94.0	94.8	81.5	71.0
Philippines	78.7	80.4	79.1	77.7
Azerbaijan	87.5	78.4	76.6	79.2
Malaysia	54.9	55.7	74.6	75.8
Bangladesh	43.4	64.9	74.5	76.0
Primacy				
Myanmar	80.9	73.9	69.7	67.7
Iraq	61.8	74.1	65.3	64.1
Uzbekistan	66.6	66.0	64.6	62.3
Turkey	59.7	55.1	59.8	58.1
Israel	54.2	56.1	58.2	58.7
Iran (Islamic Republic of)	63.8	68.2	58.0	54.1
Vietnam	71.7	62.8	57.6	53.2
Indonesia	48.2	55.5	57.0	57.6
Yemen	34.4	39.3	56.0	59.3
Low primacy				
Pakistan	44.8	53.4	55.5	55.8
Republic of Korea	39.6	59.0	54.5	53.9
Jordan	65.9	62.0	52.4	47.8
Japan	51.4	49.2	51.8	51.8
No primacy				
United Arab Emirates	72.7	36.5	44.8	46.1
Kazakhstan	40.8	45.6	44.5	41.8
Syrian Arab Republic	42.1	44.7	39.8	39.1
China	40.6	32.2	35.0	32.9
India	44.1	32.9	22.3	19.7
Saudi Arabia	32.4	18.6	13.6	12.9

Source: UN (2014).

2 special administrative regions and 26 other well-known cities) was approximately 2.5 times (Wen 2010). Moreover, about 40 percent of the world's 200 tallest buildings have been completed since 2000 (Anon 2006) and most of them have been built in Asia. In 2012, of the world's buildings of 200 meters or more, over 75 percent were located in Asia (of this share only 3 percent were in Japan, 24 percent in Western Asia and the rest in developing parts of the region), 9 percent in North America, 6 percent in Central America, 5 percent in Australia and 3 percent in Europe (Anon 2013). Asia now houses approximately 57 percent of all skyscrapers in the world.

Asian cities are also well known for their high densities. According to the UN, average urban densities range from 10,000 to 20,000 population per square km, which is almost double the levels in Latin America, triple those in Europe and 10 times those found in US cities (UNESCAP and UN HABITAT 2010). The Asian Development Bank (2012), estimates that eight of the 10 densest cities in the world are located in the Asian region and Asian urban densities, are over 40 percent higher than those in Africa, the second highest urban density region.[2]

Increasing heterogeneity amongst and within cities

Given the strength and importance of regional urban integration processes operating across Asia, some have predicted convergence in form and function (Dick and Rimmer 1998, Hack 2000). These researchers note that Asian cities are known for their mix of people, traditions and customs, but argue that urbanization is a strong homogenizing force. While indeed, there are increasing numbers of global brands and similar cultural icons found in the region's major metropolitan centers, what is often missed is the increasing divergence in physical forms, environmental conditions, technologies and social conditions amongst cities compared to what was previously experienced. Some scholars have argued that what is unique among Asian cities is the high levels of heterogeneity in social and other factors, including environmental challenges (Marcotullio 2005, 2007). The argument in this case is that as the Asian urbanization process compresses and telescopes development processes with its speed and intensifies impacts creating a new range of urban experiences, as compared to what occurred in cities during previous eras. As a result of the time-space telescoping of development (Marcotullio 2005), we find an increasingly varied set of events, patterns and processes occurring across the region's cities.

Energy in Asia

Information on national energy statistics for most countries in the world has been collected since the 1970s (IEA 2016). These data suggest that Asia has undergone a profound and rapid energy transition. Prior to the1970s, many of the nations of the region possessed underdeveloped energy systems. Subsequently, the regional energy supply expanded dramatically, along with imports, energy use and electricity output. Today, Asia's total primary energy supply is the largest in the world, and more than doubles that of Europe and North America.

Total primary energy supply

Total primary energy supply (TPES) includes all energy sources used for both final energy use and the losses due to conversion to final energy use. The world's TPES exceeded 12.7 Gtoe in 2011, up from 4.4 Gtoe in 1971. Global TPES increased by more than 203 Mtoe annually from 1971 to 2011 translating into an annual change of 2.2 percent. The sources of supply did not change evenly. During this period, while all sources increased, the world experienced a disproportionate expansion of coal, natural gas, nuclear energy and renewable sources. By 2011, the fossil fuels, coal (29.8 percent), crude oil (33.1 percent) and natural gas (22.0 percent), remained the dominant sources, accounting for approximately 85 percent of the world TPES. Renewables (mainly hydropower and biofuels) accounted for 13 percent of world TPES.

Asia's expansive energy system has driven much of world change in TPES during the 1971–2011 period. For example, Asia experienced the largest increases in TPES among UN regions (Figure 10.2). In 1971, Asian TPES exceeded 1 Gtoe, but by 2011 it exceeded 6 Gtoe, increasing by 4.4 percent annually. As a result, Asia's share of total TPES rose from 23.3 percent in 1971 to 47.4 percent in 2011 (Table 10.3). Within Asia, coal (46.8 percent), crude oil (26.4 percent) and natural gas (18.8 percent) accounted for 91.9 percent of the change in the region's TPES. The increase in coal supply was particularly impressive. In 1971, Asian coal accounted for 28.2 percent of the global total, but by 2011, Asia used 69.5 percent of the coal used in global TPES. Another significant source of Asian energy supply that experienced rapid increases during the 1971–2011 period was nuclear power. During this period, nuclear supply increased by over 10 percent annual, rising from 2.4 Mtoe to over 108 Mtoe. This increase doubled Asia's global share of this energy supply, raising it from 8.9 percent in 1971 to 16.5 percent in 2011.

Much of the total supply and change in supply trends is influenced by three economies: China, India and Japan. Japan's share of total Asian TPES exceeded 25 percent in 1971, but dropped to less than 8 percent by 2011. The decrease in share was facilitated by the increases in China's share of Asian TPES (from 29 to 45.6 percent) during the same period. Over the 1971–2011 period, more than 45.6 percent of the increases in Asian TPES were driven by increases in China. Another 12 percent were driven by changes in India, while increases in Japan accounted for 4 percent of total TPES change in the region.

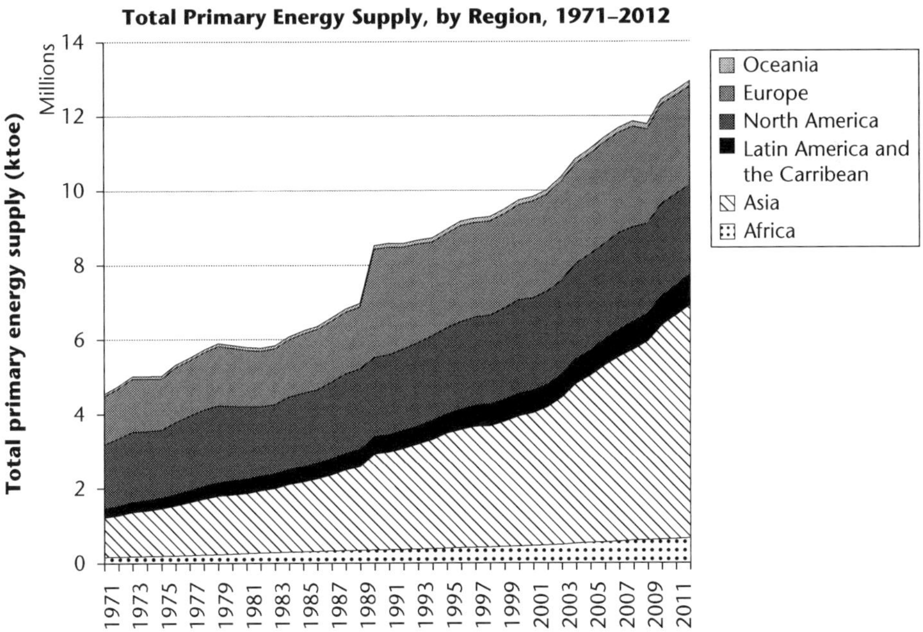

Figure 10.2 Total primary energy supply, by region, 1971–2012

Source: IEA (2016).

Table 10.3 Change in Asian total primary energy supply, by carrier, 1971–2011

	TPES total (ktoe)			*Annual percent change*			*Asia percent of global total*			*Asia percent of global change*
	1971	*1991*	*2011*	*1971–1991*	*1991–2011*	*1971–2011*	*1971*	*1991*	*2011*	*1971–2011*
Total TPES	1 058 373	2 614 331	6 001 875	4.6	4.2	4.4	23.3	30.5	47.4	60.8
Coal	316 647	847 555	2 627 937	5.0	5.8	5.4	28.2	39.2	69.5	87.0
Peat	0	0	1	NA	NA	NA	0.0	0.0	0.0	0.0
Crude, NGL and feedstocks	440 022	918 449	1 743 877	3.7	3.3	3.5	20.4	27.9	41.6	64.2
Natural gas	22 152	287 994	948 816	13.7	6.1	9.8	3.1	16.7	34.0	44.8
Nuclear	2 422	81 041	110 856	19.2	1.6	10.0	8.9	14.7	16.5	16.8
Hydropower	14 783	39 060	102 747	5.0	5.0	5.0	16.2	20.6	34.3	42.2
Geothermal	38	8 822	33 260	31.3	6.9	18.5	0.9	25.4	50.9	54.3
Solar/wind/other	0	1 718	23 755	NA	14.0	NA	0.0	70.2	38.8	38.8
Biofuels	335 688	482 758	587 478	1.8	1.0	1.4	58.7	55.0	46.9	37.0
Heat	0	0	90	NA	NA	NA	NA	0.0	8.1	8.1

Source: IEA (2016).

Energy imports

Associated with the expansion of global TPES is trade. Indeed, trade and total energy supply grew hand-in-hand. Global trade grew rapidly during the post-World War II era. Krugman (1995) calculates that in 1950, world exports amounted to 7 percent of world output, but rose gradually in the 1960s and more sharply in the early 1970s to reach 11.7 percent of global GDP. By the end of this period, levels of global trade was relatively equal to pre-World War I conditions. From 1980 to 2000 world trade increased by over 7 percent annually and much of this growth occurred in a spurt at the end of the century. The first decade of the twenty-first century has been extremely impressive, with world trade increasingly by more than 10 percent annually (UNCTAD 2015). The WTO (World Trade Organization 2015) calculates that global merchandise trade increased from $594 billion in 1973 to $18.6 trillion US dollars in 2014.

Growth in global energy trade expanded with the general trend. Total global energy imports increased from 1.7 Gtoe in 1971 to 5.0 Gtoe in 2011, translating into a 2.7 percent annual average change. The largest increases in trade were in natural gas (7.9 percent), coal (4.5 percent) and oil products (3.0 percent). Seaborne global oil movement alone, for example, increased from 1.3 billion tons in 1970 to 2.75 billion tons in 2010 (UNCTAD, various years).

Asia not only participated in the global expansion of trade, but was one of the driving forces of change. For example, from 1973 to 2014, Asia's share in global trade increased from 14.9 percent to 31.5 percent (World Trade Organization 2015). In terms of energy sources, from 1971 to 2011, Asian imports increased from 379 Mtoe to 2.2 Gtoe, translating into 4.5 annual average percentage change (Table 10.4). By 2011, the energy sources making up the largest shares of imports into the region were crude oil (43.4 percent), coal (22.1 percent), oil products (21.0 percent) and natural gas (13.5 percent). By 2011, imports of energy sources amounted to almost 37 percent of regional TPES. The imported sources with the highest annual increases were natural gas (14.8 percent), coal (7.0 percent) and oil products (5.3 percent). Imported electricity across the region also expanded, although the total amount by 2011 (6.6 Gtoe) was small in comparison to the other sources.

Eastern Asia, and in particular China, experienced the greatest increases in energy imports during the 1971–2011 period. China's total energy imports were only 124 ktoe in 1971, but rose to 451.3 Gtoe by 2011. This change accounted for 24.5 percent of total increases in the region during these 40 years. Japan's imports increased also, but at a much slower rate. In 1971 Japan's energy imports accounted for approximately 67 percent of total Asian energy imports, but by 2011 this percent share dropped to 19.7 percent. India also experienced large increases in energy imports, as it accounted for over 14.5 percent of the region's increase from 1971 to 2011. Many countries in Southeast Asia also experienced increases in energy imports. The entire sub-region accounted for over 16.3 percent of total increases in imports during the period.

These figures demonstrate that many Asian countries rely on energy imports, and this trend is predicted to increase through 2035. According to the Asian Development Outlook (2013), securing adequate energy is a serious challenge because Asia cannot rely solely on its endowment.

Energy end use

The world's energy use (or total final consumption – TFC) has increased annually on average from 1971 to 2011 at a rate of 2.2 percent, resulting in an increase in use from 3.5 to 8.4 Gtoe. Global energy end-uses experienced fairly even increases during this period. For example, average annual increases in energy use for commercial (2.4 percent), residential (1.7 percent) industry (1.9 percent), and transport (2.7 percent) do not vary as much as sources of TPES.

Table 10.4 Change in Asian energy imports, by carrier, 1971–2011

	Energy imports (ktoe)			*Annual percent change*			*Asian percent of global total*			*Asia percent of global change*
	1971	*1991*	*2011*	*1971–1991*	*1991–2011*	*1971–2011*	*1971*	*1991*	*2011*	*1971–2011*
Total energy imports	379 147	888 467	2 221 098	4.3	4.7	4.5	21.8	30.2	44.1	55.8
Coal	33 035	140 770	490 970	7.5	6.4	7.0	26.9	42.5	68.6	77.3
Peat	0	0	1	NA	NA	NA	NA	0.0	0.4	0.4
Crude, NGL and feedstocks	285 801	460 542	962 741	2.4	3.8	3.1	23.4	28.5	42.2	63.9
Oil products	59 080	197 492	466 177	6.2	4.4	5.3	17.2	35.7	42.3	53.6
Natural gas	1 169	83 828	294 203	23.8	6.5	14.8	2.8	21.0	33.9	35.4
Nuclear	0	0	0	NA	NA	NA	NA	NA	NA	NA
Hydropower	0	0	0	NA	NA	NA	NA	NA	NA	NA
Geothermal	0	0	0	NA	NA	NA	NA	NA	NA	NA
Solar/wind/other	0	0	0	NA	NA	NA	NA	NA	NA	NA
Biofuels and waste	59	78	331	1.4	7.5	4.4	67.0	97.8	2.2	1.8
Electricity	3	5 758	6 673	45.1	0.7	20.9	0.1	15.6	12.1	13.5
Heat	0	0	0	NA	NA	NA	NA	0.0	0.0	0.0

Source: IEA (2016).

By 2011, end use shares of global TFC include 23.8 percent for residential, 29.6 percent for industry, 24.9 percent for transport and 8.5 percent for commercial uses.

In Asia, TFC increased from 877 Mtoe to 3.8 Gtoe from 971 to 2011 amounting to a 3.8 percent annual average increase (Table 10.5). This change increased Asia's share of global TFC from 24.8 percent in 1971 to 45.6 percent in 2011. The energy end use sectors that experienced the highest annual average percentage changes include commercial (5.2 percent), industry (4.2 percent) and transport (5.2 percent).

In similar fashion to increases in TPES, China, India and Japan dominate the region for TFC. China accounted for over 43.5 percent of the total increase in Asian TFC, while India's share was 11.8 percent. Japan's TFC grew from 199.3 Gtoe in 1971 to 312.9 Gtoe in 2011, but this change accounted for less than 4 percent of the increase in the region during the time period. Interesting, Indonesia's TFC rose by a similar amount to that of Japan, but from a much lower level. From 1971 to 2011, the change in TFC in Indonesia accounted for over 4 percent of the Asian region's increase.

Space prohibits a larger exploration of all three trends, but both the dynamism and diversity of changes within Asia can be illustrated by the associated trends in transportation energy use. Vehicle usage, the main driver of transportation energy use, has increased dramatically in Asia, but not equally amongst nations. East, South and Southeast Asia's share of global automobiles on the road increased from 12.7 percent in 1985 to 21.8 percent in 2009 (an increase from 62.1 to 210.4 billion vehicles). Car ownership rates in China have been growing at 12 percent per annum and in India at 9 percent per annum (these growth rates include two and three wheeled vehicles). Annual car sales in China now exceed historical maximums of the US. Currently, Asia also produces 95 percent of global two- and three-wheeled vehicles, which constitutes 75 percent of the world's stocks and China is the fastest growing market for these vehicles (World Energy Council 2011).

Transportation fuel consumption patterns however, vary across the region. A study of transportation shifts over time suggest that different Asian nations are following distinctive paths (Barter 1999) with Hong Kong, Singapore and Japan on a low consumption path, Republic of Korea and Taiwan at the intermediate level, and Thailand and Malaysia following a more Western, high transport fuel consumption, trajectory (Marcotullio and Marshall 2007). The largest and most recent industrializing nations to embrace the automobile, such as China, India, Indonesia and Vietnam, may follow the high transport fuel consumption trend. From 2005 to 2009, India increased the number of cars on the road by 25 percent and the number of motor vehicles in China doubled. In 2009, car sales in China exceeded those in the USA (Ward's 2010). Some estimates suggest that by 2040, future automobile consumption in India and China alone will double the total number of vehicles currently on the road, adding an additional 800 million automobiles to the global car population (The Economist 2006, Wilson, Purushothaman and Fiotakis 2004). Because of the large size of these countries their transportation use patterns overwhelm those of smaller economies.

Electricity

Most economists and development specialists agree that electricity is the hallmark of advanced development and a basic condition for economic progress (see for example, Smil 1994). Electricity is considered secondary energy source, as electrical energy must be converted from primary sources. Usually around 30 percent of primary energy is lost in the transformation of the primary energy sources into electricity. There are a number of primary sources used in the conversion process, including fossil fuels, renewables and nuclear sources.

From 1971 to 2011, total global electricity output increased from 4.4 to 22 PWh. During this period, large annual average annual increases were in coal (4.2 percent), natural gas (5.6 percent)

Table 10.5 Change in Asian total final consumption, by end use, 1971–2011

	TFC total (ktoe)			*Annual percent change*			*Asia percent of global total*			*Asia percent of global change*
	1971	*1991*	*2011*	*1971–1991*	*1991–2011*	*1971–2011*	*1971*	*1991*	*2011*	*1971–2011*
Total final consumption	877 184	1 978 105	3 845 917	4.1	3.4	3.8	24.8	32.4	45.6	60.5
Commercial	31 386	102 879	231 113	6.1	4.1	5.1	11.2	21.6	32.4	46.1
Residential	383 230	638 004	920 550	2.6	1.9	2.2	37.9	41.9	45.8	53.9
Industry	286 879	642 903	1 430 845	4.1	4.1	4.1	24.8	35.9	57.2	85.2
Transport	90 967	281 326	687 505	5.8	4.6	5.2	12.5	20.3	32.7	43.4
Agriculture	18 552	62 415	86 115	6.3	1.6	3.9	28.8	37.9	47.5	57.8
Fishing	97	6 222	4 092	23.1	−2.1	9.8	17.7	76.8	53.3	56.0
Non-energy	43 288	152 213	404 535	6.5	5.0	5.7	21.4	30.6	49.7	59.0
Non-specified	22 785	92 144	81 162	7.2	−0.6	3.2	24.6	35.5	72.6	303.0

Source: IEA (2016).

and nuclear power (8.3 percent). In total, these sources amounted to 14.2 PWh of the total 17.7 PWh of increase during this period. The highest absolute annual increase, however, was experienced by renewable sources (geothermal, biofuels and solar, wind other sources). For example, geothermal increased by 7 percent, solar, wind and other 18.9 percent and biofuels by 10.3 percent. In 2011, the total renewable contribution (including hydropower, geothermal, solar, wind and other, and biofuels and waste) amounted to 20.2 percent of the total. Of these, hydropower (15.7 percent) had the largest share. Nuclear power contributed to about 11.7 percent of global electricity output.

In Asia, electricity output increased from 708 TWh to 9.9 PWh during the 1971 to 2011 period (Table 10.6). The largest significant increases in source contributions are from coal (8.8 percent), natural gas (12.8 percent) and nuclear (10.9 percent) primary sources.

The growth of nuclear energy in the Asia is reflected in the region's growing global share of thermonuclear power plants. For example, currently Asia has approximately 30 percent of the world's nuclear reactors and operates over 27 percent of the global nuclear MWh production (Nuclear Energy Institute 2016b). These facilities are shared between China, India, Iran, Japan, South Korea, Pakistan and Taiwan. Approximately 36 percent of the reactors responsible for 34 percent of the region's current nuclear capacity were built before 1990. Another 43 percent of the reactors with 44 percent of the electricity output capacity were built since 2000. The majority of the newest reactors have been built in China and India. For example, since 2010, 57 new nuclear reactors have come on line in Asia with a total capacity of 45,900 MW. Of these approximately 70 percent were built in China and India with a total capacity of 29,900 MW or 65 percent of the new capacity. Moreover, of the 68 thermonuclear generators currently under construction, 41 are slated for Asian economies, which will account for over 66 percent of the new global capacity. Of the 41 new reactors, 22 are being constructed in China and 6 in India (Nuclear Energy Institute 2016a).

As seen at the global scale, Asia also experienced dramatic increases in renewables. For example, hydropower average annual increases were 5.0 percent and annual increases in biofuels reached 17.7 percent. From 1991 to 2011, geothermal and solar, wind and other sources increased by 4.9 and 46 percent annually, respectively. By 2011, the contribution of total renewables to electricity output in Asia was 14.6 percent. Of the increases in renewable energy electric output, China alone was responsible for 64 percent of the increase in hydropower, 62 percent of the increase in solar and wind and 38 percent of the increase in biofuels and waste. India was responsible for 11 percent of the increase in hydropower, more than 21 percent of the increase in solar and wind and 16 percent of the increase in biofuels and waste. Several countries, such as Nepal, Tajikistan and Kyrgyzstan obtain over 905 of their electric energy from hydropower. Other countries such as Myanmar and Georgia obtain over 70 percent of their electricity from hydropower and the share of hydropower in electricity generation is over 30 percent for Sri Lanka, Vietnam and Armenia.

The connection between urbanization and energy use in Asia

How are the dramatic changes in urbanization and energy supply and use linked? As cities grow in size and complexity, the energy demands to keep them running smoothly increase. Recent surveys suggest that changes in many aspects of the urbanization process and city life, including land use (Seto et al. 2014), demographics (O'Neill et al. 2010), economic wealth (Ciccone and Hall 1996, Spence, Annez and Buckley 2009), behavior (Jackson 2005) urban form (Newman and Kenworthy 1999), geography and natural systems (Pataki et al. 2006) and political institutions (Romero-Lankao et al. 2014) affect energy demand. This section overviews selected drivers of

Table 10.6 Change in Asian electricity output, by carrier, 1971–2011

	Electricity output (GWh)			*Annual percent change*			*Asian percent of global total*			*Asia percent of global change*
	1971	*1991*	*2011*	*1971–1991*	*1991–2011*	*1971–2011*	*1971*	*1991*	*2011*	*1971–2011*
Total electricity output	708 139	2 898 849	9 889 035	7.3	6.3	6.8	16.1	24.1	44.8	52.0
Coal	188 644	1 058 464	5 505 732	9.0	8.6	8.8	10.9	23.5	60.4	72.0
Peat	0	0	0	NA	NA	NA	0.0	0.0	0.0	0.0
Crude, NGL and feedstocks	0	101 695	132 626	NA	1.3	NA	NA	96.0	94.2	94.2
Oil products	322 775	473 400	512 499	1.9	0.4	1.2	34.1	40.1	59.0	−247.5
Natural gas	15 371	479 635	1 867 624	18.8	7.0	12.7	2.8	26.8	38.3	42.8
Nuclear	9 294	310 971	425 377	19.2	1.6	10.0	8.9	14.8	16.5	16.8
Hydropower	171 893	454 190	1 194 742	5.0	5.0	5.0	16.3	20.7	34.5	42.4
Geothermal	0	8 721	22 809	NA	4.9	NA	0.0	23.3	32.9	35.2
Solar/wind/other	0	60	117 381	NA	46.1	NA	0.0	1.1	23.2	23.2
Biofuels and waste	162	11 617	110 048	23.8	11.9	17.7	2.0	142.1	26.9	27.4
Heat	0	0	152	NA	NA	NA	NA	0.0	8.4	8.4
Oil shale and oil sands	0	96	45	NA	-3.7	NA	NA	0.8	0.4	0.4

Source: IEA (2016).

energy demand linking these urban dynamics. The vast increases in energy supply, use and electricity output are driven by and in turn drive urban development in the region.

Urban land use

Approximately 3.7 million km^2 or 2.9 percent of the Earth's terrestrial ecosystems are covered with urban land uses (MA, 2005). This expansion of urban land use accompanies the growth of physical infrastructure, including the development of roads, bridges, buildings, commercial and governmental plants, ports and airports, etc. Building technologies are cement, metal (aluminum, iron and steel) and rock, gravel and sand intensive (Shen et al. 2005). Studies of material flows into urban areas demonstrate large material inputs for urbanization (Decker et al. 2000, Kennedy, Cuddihy and Engel-Yan 2007). For example, cement and heavy metal industries can account for a significant share of national energy use and GHG emissions. Aluminum, cement, iron and steel, and paper industries account for approximately 60 percent of China's CO_2 emissions from the industrial sector (Rock et al. 2013).

Recent estimates suggest that the urban land use in Asia may triple by 2030 (Angel, Sheppard and Civco 2005). Urban land use change in Asia is increasing at the fastest rates globally (Seto et al. 2011). Examples of rapidly expanding individual urban areas have been identified in China. Between 1973 and 2008, the average increase in urban land in a sample of 60 cities (four municipalities, 28 provincial capitals, two special administrative regions and 26 other well-known cities) throughout the country was approximately 2.5 times (Wen 2010). Some cities (such as Shenshen and Houkou) underwent spectacular growth, multiplying their land area by more than a factor of 20. From the 1980s to 2005, the urban lands of Beijing–Tianjin–Tangshan Region, Yangtze River Delta City Region and the Pearl River Delta City Region grew by factors of 1.15, 1.04 and 2.63, respectively (Liu 2011). Given these rapid and extensive urban land use changes (Seto, Guneralp and Hutyra 2012), the energy infrastructure used to support this city growth has become a key driver of GHG emissions across multiple scales (Davis, Caldeira and Matthews 2010).

Demographics

Studies that examine urban population at the urban scale demonstrate a positive relationship between size and energy use. This is not surprising, as a larger number of individuals translate into more activities and therefore higher energy demand and use, all else equal. For example, urban areas with the largest population size contribute the largest GHG emissions (Hoornweg et al. 2011, Marcotullio et al. 2013b). At the same time, however, there have been inconsistent findings when it comes to urban population scaling effects.

Given the massive urbanization that is predicted to occur over the next few decades, researchers have explored the role of urban population in energy use and GHG emissions levels (Seto et al. 2014). Will larger cities bring greater efficiencies and therefore lower energy use per capita than smaller cities? Scaling effects describe a variable's proportionality of impact on energy with increasing size. A more than proportionate effect means that with increasing variable size, the impact on energy increases. Scaling effects are described in detail by Bettencourt et al. (2007), who find that urban areas with larger population sizes have proportionately smaller energy infrastructures than smaller cities, suggesting that increasing efficiencies are gained in infrastructure provision with increasing population size. Studies on urban energy use and GHG emissions, however, are inconclusive. In both Germany for electricity consumption, and in the US for CO_2 emissions, it has been found that urban population size has near-proportionate impacts (Fragkias et al. 2013, Bettencourt et al. 2007). Alternatively, some studies find super-linear population effects on urban

GHG emissions, meaning that increases in population have a disproportionately larger impact on emissions in both developed and developing countries, although the effect is slightly smaller in the developed world (Marcotullio et al. 2012, 2013b). In a study of 225 cities across both Annex 1 and non-Annex 1 countries,[3] Grubler and Schulz (2013) find non-uniform scaling for urban final energy use within three different sets of urban areas. This study provides evidence of positive agglomeration economies of bigger cities (sub-linear effects) with respect to energy use and high elasticities in smaller urban areas with low current urban energy use (super-linear effects).

In developing Asia, the linkage between the scale of cities and energy use is further complicated by the concentration of energy infrastructure in the region's cities (see for example, Dhakal 2009). For example, industries, including heavy industries, are concentrated in rings around the industrial urban centers of the region (Lo and Yeung 1996). In general, residents of cities in developing Asia have higher energy demand and use than their counterparts in non-urban areas (see also Marcotullio et al. 2012). While there has not been a specific study on the scaling effects of energy use in Asian cities, it would not be surprising to find supra-linear effects across developing nations in the region, as this relationship has been found between city size and GHG emissions (Marcotullio et al. 2012).

Additional insight can be gleaned from current studies of household size. Recent evidence suggests that household size is decreasing globally (Liu et al. 2003). Worldwide, average household size has declined from 3.6 to 2.7 between 1950 and 1990, and this trend is occurring in both developed and developing countries, although at different rates (Mackellar et al. 1995). In terms of energy, larger households may be associated with lower energy use as households reap efficiency benefits. This notion is supported by macro-level, cross country analyses. For example, Liddle (2004) found that larger households were correlated with lower levels of per capita road energy use in OCED countries. Cole and Neumayer (2004) found that larger households were correlated with lower aggregate carbon emissions levels in developed and developing countries.

In household scale studies of developing Asian countries such as India, increasing household size is associated with lower energy use per capita (Pachauri 2004). In contrast in developed Asian countries such as Japan, larger household sizes correlate with slightly larger energy use (Lenzen et al. 2006). In all these studies, researchers find that urban populations typically have smaller household sizes than rural populations.

Economic wealth

Economic factors that correlate with urban energy use can be further broken down into income or general wealth influences, urban economic structure and urban economic function characteristics. All these categories are related, but research on each attempts to focus on a distinct area of economic influence. Perhaps the most important economic relationship is that of wealth or income and energy use. Researchers have long considered this relationship important at the national level (Kraft and Kraft 1978). These studies find a positive correlation between income and energy use at the national level, but results of decades of study have produced diverse and inconclusive directional results (for reviews see, Payne 2010a, 2010b, Ozturk 2010). No consensus has emerged from tests of four contending hypotheses, which find in turn that there is no causality that income growth causes increases in energy consumption, that energy consumption causes income growth, and that there is bi-directionality between energy consumption and economic growth. Notwithstanding the lack of understanding of dynamics, research consistently points to the positive relationship between income and energy demand and use.

Studies of cities find similar results to that of nations. Schulz (2010b) examines a number of different cities in Africa, Latin America, OECD and non-OECD nations and also finds a positive relationship between urban energy use and urban regional product. Housing size, automobile use, and heating and industrial fuel use are associated with income, suggesting that larger sizes for homes, modification of the levels of thermal comfort required by city residents, and mobile fuel use increase with income (Kennedy et al. 2009, Hu et al. 2010, Bannister, Watson and Wood 1997, Weisz and Steinberger 2010, Sahakian and Steinberger 2011). In Asia, cities of higher income typically have higher energy demand and energy use (Grubler et al. 2012). For example, Dhakal (2009) estimated and compared the per capita energy consumption (MJ per person) for 34 of the largest cities in China demonstrating an increasing trend in energy use with per capita gross regional product.

Studies also show a positive relationship between the speed of economic growth, urbanization and energy demand. For example, Poumanyvong and Kaneko (2010) demonstrate that the relationship between urbanization and GHG emissions is always positive, but varies across different levels of income. This study found, however, that nations with low incomes experience decreasing energy use with urbanization, which may be due to fuel switching in low-income societies. They find that urbanization in medium and high-income nations is associated with increasing energy use. In Asia, Jiang and Lin (2012) compare China's urbanization and industrialization process with that of the USA and Japan to highlight that energy demand is highest during the rapid phase of urbanization and industrialization (and economic growth), but thereafter drops off (see also, Shen et al. 2005).

Analysts suggest that urban economic structure is also important to urban energy use. For example, cities that are dependent on energy-intensive industries are likely to contribute to higher total and per capita energy uses than those whose economic base is in the service sector (Hoornweg et al. 2011). For example, UN-Habitat (2012) states that the industrial sector in Shanghai uses 80 percent of the total energy and Thane city, near Mumbai, industry that has only 2 percent of the users, consumes 44 percent of all energy supplied. This relationship is further strengthened if the energy supply mix is carbon intensive (Parikh and Shukla 1995, Sugar, Kennedy and Leman 2012). Dhakal (2009) demonstrates that trends in urban GHG emissions in China, amongst a select group of urban areas, can be divided into three energy intensive pathways: high, medium and low. Those in the high category have energy intensive industries. Those Chinese cities with lower energy intensive pathways have high service sector contributions to their economies.

Related to the urban economy, cities also assume different functional niches within larger regional and global urban systems (Lo and Yeung 1998, Sassen 2006). These functional roles, defined by the hierarchical space within the New International Division of Labor (NIDL), a notion that explains the shift in manufacturing from advanced economies to developing countries, have been associated with the variations in environmental impacts (Lo and Marcotullio 2001, Marcotullio 2003). Trade, FDI and the movement of people affect urban development. In Asia and the Pacific, for example, FDI investments have helped to create a ring of industrial firms surrounding urban core areas, affecting employment, transportation and housing demand (Lo and Marcotullio 2001). Cities often specialize within the global economic system, with some urban centers focusing on manufacturing and others on commercial or administrative functions. Some urban areas are important transport hubs, such as London for air transit, or Hong Kong, Cape Town and Rotterdam for shipping. The "global cities," largely concentrated in the developed world's largest economies, hold much of the command and control of the world economy, while industrial urban centers have moved from the developed world to the rapidly developing world, focused largely, but not solely, on a corridor from South Korea to Indonesia and across to South Asia. This new industrial belt is the center for the world's manufactured goods, and much of these activities take place within metropolitan or urban mega-regions (McGee and Robinson 1995).

Analysts have identified that industrial urban areas have specific carbon signatures which are typically higher than those of economic command and control cities. For example, GHG emissions from Shanghai and Beijing are higher than that of Tokyo (Dhakal and Imura 2004). Schulz (2010a) demonstrates the significance for Singapore's energy use associated with international trade in oil products. For example, Singapore's domestic and embodied energy use is 173 GJ per capita, but total energy imports to the city are in the order of 1,490 GJ per capita.

Behavior

Behavioral research seeks to understand the relationship between individual energy use and the factors that shape and constrain choices. Scholars argue that understanding consumer behavior is crucial to identifying and changing the impact that society has on the environment. For example, changing behavior is needed because technical efficiency gains resulting from energy efficiency (appliances, home insulation and water saving devices) can be overtaken by increasing use (Midden, Kaiser and McCalley 2007). While people are more likely to reduce their use when energy involves high costs (money, effort or convenience), researchers have also identified that well-being and ecologically responsible behavior are compatible (Brown and Kasser 2005).

In traditional energy studies, the role of behavioral factors was largely consigned to the notion that individuals maximize expected utility and that, therefore, as net costs of energy rise, use falls (for a review see, Scott 2000). For example, the three factors that the IEA examines in influencing energy are economic growth, demographics and energy cost and price (IEA 2016). More recently, research focusing on behavioral characteristics has moved beyond rational choice theory to integrated models (Stern 2000). For example, Jackson (2005) identifies over 20 different social psychological theories in this area, each with a rich background and different sets of empirical findings. Debates remains, however, on the extent to which and the processes by which different components of behavior shape environmental outcomes; research demonstrates that these micro-level variables are indeed important to motivating sustainable consumption (Spangenberg and Lorek 2002). These studies demonstrate that changing behavior reduces the overall human impact (Abrahamse et al. 2005).

Three new areas of behavioral studies include examining the role of social norms, mindfulness, and lifestyle choices. Social norms and values can induce people to change their behavior (Thøgersen and Olander 2002) and encourage them to, say, conserve energy (Schultz et al. 2007). In the Netherlands, researchers found that psychological factors (attitude, personal norm, awareness of consequences), such as higher levels of perceived behavioral control and lower levels of responsibility were associated with greater energy savings (Abrahamse and Steg 2009). Mindfulness is a quality of consciousness that denotes a receptive attention to and awareness of ongoing internal states and behavior (Brown and Ryan 2003). Research has found that mindfulness is associated with lower materialism and a tendency toward less consumption (spending) activity over time (Brown and Ryan 2004). Lifestyle choices include preferences for goods such as large homes, heated pools, good schools, etc. In a recent study, using geo-demographic (or analysis of people by where they live) consumer segmentation data, Baiocchi, Minx and Hubacek (2010) found that among 56 lifestyle groups in the UK, CO_2 emissions can vary by a factor of between 2 and 3. There is still a large debate on how environmental behavior is shaped and to what degree values and actions align, given the frequent gap found between intentions and behaviors (Thøgersen and Olander 2002).

In Asia, one of the most important behavior changes includes lifestyle. Lifestyle changes are experienced through consumption patterns with increasing income. Growing segments of the Asian population are experiencing 'well to do' lifestyles and are subsequently eager to obtain a quality life of nutrient-rich food, comfortable living, quality healthcare, and other quality services (Hubacek, Guan and Barua 2007). Researchers suggest that there are environmental gains to be made through targeting Asian lifestyle choices (UN-Habitat 2012), but few initiatives have been promulgated. One noteworthy attempt is by the government of Bhutan, which emphasizes a gross national happiness indicator as opposed to gross national production.[4] Most studies that examine resource consumption trends in the region note increasing patterns of consumption, many increasing at faster rates than seen in the now developed world (Marcotullio 2011).

Urban form

Researchers debate the linkage of urban population density to energy use. The arguments for higher densities suggest that higher density urban areas should have lower emissions per capita than more sprawled-out urban areas due to savings on transportation. The now classic studies of Newman and Kenworthy (1989, 1999), demonstrate that a negative relationship between density and transportation fuel use are supported by more recent research on transportation energy consumption (Liddle 2013), electricity consumption in buildings (Lariviere and Lafrance 1999) and urban GHG emissions (Marcotullio et al. 2012, 2013a, 2013b).

Despite these general results, however, scholars have found the urban population density – energy use relationship far from straightforward. Population density is only one way to measure compact settlements (Ewing and Cervero 2001, Transportation Research Board 2009). Recent work reviewing the large literature on the relationship between vehicle miles traveled and urban development find that destination accessibility is more important in explaining miles traveled in cars (and hence energy use by transportation) than the combination of density, design and diversity of land use indicators (Ewing and Cervero 2010). These relationships are further complicated in the developing world where many densely populated cities have large slum populations that lack access to electricity and modern fuels and are therefore likely to use less energy than more affluent populations with access to electricity modern fuels (Jorgenson, Rice and Clark 2010).

As mentioned above, cities in Asia are dense suggesting gains in energy use. Besides density, urban spatial patterns can also influence energy use. In a study of 5 urban areas within the Pearl River Delta, researchers found that fragmentation of urban land use patterns is positively correlated with energy use and that the increasing dominance of the largest urban patch is negatively correlated with energy use (Chen et al. 2011). Ultimately however, as pointed out by Grubler et al. (2012) it is by no means clear that there is an ideal urban form and morphology that can maximize energy performance and satisfy all other sustainability criteria.

Politics and institutions

Political conditions and institutional structures influence the energy use associated with urbanization in multiple ways. Arguably, cities are terrains of political struggle, which are influenced by local, regional, national and even global politics. At the same time, direct empirical results demonstrating causal linkages between urban political and institutional features and energy demand are few.

Growth politics can help to shape urban form, transportation patterns, and ultimately determine the levels and types of resources necessary to sustain urbanization processes. Growth politics refers to the conflict and contestation surrounding land use change and economic expansion in urban areas. Growth politics and conflicts are common in both developed and developing countries (Ju and Tang 2011, Aguilar and Santos 2011, Sager 2004). Given the association between urban form and transportation patterns, the outcome of these conflicts can influence energy use (Stone 2009). The political dynamics of urban growth even within neighborhoods can significantly structure alternative energy outcomes (Aylett 2013).

Governance includes institutional capacity, or the financial, scientific, legal, and human resources possessed by cities. Some cities have the institutional capacity to take steps to reduce the vehicle miles traveled within their territories through infrastructure design, pricing of various components of the transportation system, and availability of alternative transportation, while others cannot. In some cases, zoning laws help to control urban form. Building codes can influence energy demand. Whether urban decision makers decide to take such steps will depend on the institutions that are in place. Governance and institutional capacity are frequently scale and income dependent, meaning they tend to be weaker in smaller cities and in low-income settings (Grubler et al. 2012).

Energy use mitigation efforts have been implemented in Asia. These efforts have occurred across multiple scales. At the regional scale, for example, the Association for Southeast Asian Nations (ASEAN) has identified the need for improving energy efficiency, use of clean energy technologies and renewable energy sources (Yuen and Kong 2009). At the national level, several South, Southeast Asian and East Asian governments have addressed energy use and subsequent GHG emissions through national plans. Countries such as Bangladesh, China, India, Indonesia, Malaysia, Pakistan, the Philippines, Thailand and Vietnam have implemented national climate change mitigation plans and address energy use.

At the local level, the more wealthy cities in the region have higher environmental (including energy supply and use) performance (Economist Intelligence Unit 2011). Cities such as Tokyo, Seoul and Bangkok have developed energy use and GHG emission plans, but generally for most cities in the region, addressing these issues is only in the early stages (CAI-Asia and CDIA 2012).

Geography and natural systems

Local weather and climate can have significant impacts on energy use and therefore GHG emissions (Neumayer 2002). For urban areas, Toronto has cold winters and fairly warm summers, which could be linked to higher per capita energy use than London, Sydney, or Hong Kong, for example (Kennedy, Cuddihy and Engel-Yan 2007). Using US data, Glaeser and Kahn (2010) find that places with moderate temperatures, like coastal California, have significantly lower emissions than places in warmer climates. For example, they find that a standard household's carbon emissions are 78 percent higher in Memphis than in San Diego. Akbari et al. (1992) find that peak urban electric demand in five American cities (Los Angeles, CA; Washington, DC, Phoenix, AZ, Tucson, AZ; and Colorado Springs, CO) rises by 2–4 percent for each 1°C rise in daily maximum temperature above a threshold of 15-20°C. Thus, the additional air-conditioning use caused by this urban air temperature increase is responsible for 3–8 percent of urban peak electric demand.

Trees and generally green locations in urban settings are often planned and managed entities. They include urban farms, green roofs, blue landscape plans and other enhancements of ecosystem services. Studies have demonstrated that urban shade trees offer significant benefits in reducing building air-conditioning demand and improving urban air (Akbari 2002). In experiments in California, shade trees at two monitored houses yielded seasonal cooling energy savings of 30 percent, corresponding to an average daily savings of 3.6 and 4.8 kWh per day. Peak demand savings for the same houses were 0.6 and 0.8 kW (about 27 percent savings in one house and 4.2 percent in the other) (Akbari et al. 1997). While decreasing electricity use in the summer, tree shade, however, may increase electricity consumption in the wintertime due to lowering temperatures during winter mornings (Pandit and Laband 2010).

In Asia, average temperatures have been found to be associated with energy use. For example, in China, the average temperature during winter months is strongly negatively correlated with a city's household carbon footprint (Zheng et al. 2011). Given the range of latitude within the region, differential heating from the sun is an important factor in explaining differences in energy use (Kennedy et al. 2009).

In terms of urban public greenspace, outcomes vary in Asia. Some cities, such as Singapore and Hong Kong have 40 percent or more space devoted to open green space. Kuala Lumpur also has a large amount of green space. Others such as Istanbul, Mumbai, Shanghai and Tokyo have less than 5 percent of land use devoted to green space. Interestingly, urban farming has been a tradition in Asian cities (United Nations Development Programme 1996) although high densities, demand for land, and lack of local planning frameworks to protect these spaces have led to their decline (Asian Development Bank 2015). As a result, there is a decreasing amount of public greenspace in many Asian cities. This trend may contribute to increasing energy use in the future.

Energy-related urban sustainability challenges in Asia

This section identifies both the successes and sustainability challenges confronting Asian cities. While there have been major advances in the provision of and access to modern energy sources to and for residents, these gains have either not sufficiently address current needs or have led to other challenges. This section focuses on the success in providing electric energy to the region's cities, industry, and mobility and on the general increases in energy use.

Electricity output: equitable access

Many large cities appropriate energy in the form of electricity. As mentioned above, the electricity output for Asian nations has increased dramatically over the past decades. This increase has been accompanied by increased urban use of electricity and expansion of electric grids. For example, China's urban share increased from approximately 17 to 49 percent from 1971 to 2011. In total number of urban residents this translated into a 1.2 percent annual average increase. China's electricity output, however, increased by 9 percent during the period (IEA 2011). Much of the new electricity output went to servicing urban populations in the country. In India, the country's urban residents consume 87 percent of the nation's electricity (Sawin and Hughes 2007).

While there have been great strides in providing modern energy to urban residents across the world, however, the UN-Habitat (2003) estimates that large swaths of the world's urban populations, totaling approximately 800 million people globally, do not have access to adequate energy sources. This 'energy poverty' presents a significant challenge to poverty reduction generally (Practical Action 2014). It is also a real and present problem for the urban poor in high-income countries and in many former communist states (Weisz and Steinberger 2010). Asia houses about half of the global population without access to electricity (Asian Development Bank 2013).

In urban Asia, while electricity and modern fuel systems are growing, there remains a large population without access to electricity and non-solid fuels (Table 10.7). As of 2010, throughout Asia, approximately 54 million urban residents did not have access to electricity and over 222 million are using solid fuels (e.g. biomass) for cooking and heating. In India alone, 100,000 villages are yet to gain access to electricity (UN-Habitat 2012). This large population remains while the share of those without access to energy has dropped substantially. For example, in 1990, approximately 6.2 percent of the total Asian urban population was without electricity. By 2010, this value dropped by half to 2.9 percent. That is, the massive urban increases overwhelmed the efforts to provide modern energy to the region's urban residents. These figures demonstrate a

Table 10.7 Access to electricity and modern fuels in urban Asia

Sub-region	*Electricity*		*Non-solid fuels*
	1990	*2010*	*2010*
East	9.6	9.5	73
South	40.6	34.3	92.2
Southeast	8.8	6.1	52.8
Central	0.3	0	0.2
West	3.7	3.9	4.4
Asia	63	53.9	222.6

Share of urban population in Asia without access to energy, 1990–2010 (percent)

Asian sub-region	*Electricity*		*Non-solid Fuels*
	1990	*2010*	*2010*
East	2.1	1.1	8.6
South	12.8	6.2	16.8
Southeast	6.3	2.3	19.9
Central	1.3	0	1
West	4	2.5	2.8
Asia	6.2	2.9	12.1

Source: World Bank Indicators (2015) and UN (2014).

deficit within cities across the region, except in Central Asia, where the provision of this basic infrastructure has now reached all urban residents.

Industrialization and mobility: urban air pollution

Industry has acted as a driving force in economic growth and globalization across the region. Expanding manufacturing prowess has been manifested in rings of factories that encircle the region's industrial cities (Lo and Yeung 1996). Researchers identified selected industrial cities with high-energy use. For example, in Bangkok in 2005, industry accounted for 31 percent of total energy consumption (Phdungsilp 2010), while 25 percent of Thailand's carbon dioxide emissions came from manufacturing and construction (Corfield 2008), dominated by sectors in the Bangkok Metropolitan Region. In China, research demonstrates that industry has dominated energy use and carbon dioxide emissions in Beijing, Shanghai, Tianjin and Chongqing, although industrial emissions have been declining in share for Beijing (from 65 to 43 percent) and Shanghai (from 75 to 64 percent) over the past 20 years (Dhakal 2009).

With increasing industrial activities and growing employment in urban centers, citizens increasingly shift from non-motorized transport such as bicycling and walking to motorized passenger transport. As cities grow in size, more urban dwellers move to the city outskirts and employment areas also shift. Within this peri-urbanization, travel distance tends to lengthen, which has been occurring in Asia and the Pacific (APERC 2007).

Transportation accounts for a high level of energy use in many of the region's cities. For example, transportation accounted for 37 percent of Tokyo's energy consumption and 25 percent of Seoul's energy consumption in 1998 (Dhakal and Imura 2004). According to Phdungsilp (2010), in 2005 Bangkok's transportation sector accounted for 60 percent of energy demand.

Estimates suggest that for Dhaka, transportation accounts for 25-30 percent of total emissions (Alam and Rabbani 2007).

In the rapidly developing countries of the region, demand for private transportation far outstrips infrastructure supply, creating congestion, high levels of accidents, and increasing pollution (Vasconcellos 2001). With increasing infrastructure provision, transportation emissions in the region rise rapidly (Marcotullio and Marshall 2007).

Growing personal motor vehicle use, industrialization, and energy production have been associated with urban ambient air pollution (McGranahan and Murray 2003). Asian urban residents suffer from extremely high exposure to inhalation of micro particles (particles of 10 micrometers or less – $PM_{2.5}$ and PM_{10}) (UNESCAP and UN HABITAT 2010). A recent World Health Organization report (World Health Organization 2016) finds that the increase in mortality attributable to air pollution in cities has increased since 2004. This report also points out that, in general, cities in Asia have experienced increases in pollution levels. For example, the WHO attributed approximately 1.34 million premature deaths in 2008 to urban outdoor air pollution, an increase from the 1.15 million in 2004. Of the top 100 cities in the sample with the highest levels of PM_{10}, 89 percent are found in Asia. Cities in South, East and West Asian cities have annual means of over 150 ug/m^3. Citizens in China, Vietnam and the Philippines are exposed to an average of 93 micrograms. One can compare these values with those from urban areas in Latin America which have approximately 49 micrograms and cities in the US and Canada, which recorded approximately 21 micrograms. Urban air pollution is a significant burden on Asian residents and particularly on the poor.

Growing energy use: global GHG emissions

As argued above, growing urban populations are unambiguously associated with higher aggregate urban energy demand and associated greenhouse gas emissions (Hoornweg et al. 2011, Marcotullio et al. 2013b, Jones and Kammen 2014). This is theoretically the cumulative result of concentrated human and economic activity, which requires more energy-intensive processes in agriculture, transportation, buildings, industry, and waste management (Liddle 2013).

Few studies estimate the relative urban and rural shares of global GHG emissions (Dhakal 2010, Seto et al. 2014). Two estimates of the global picture on urban energy use have emerged recently (IEA 2008, Global Energy Assessment 2012).[5] While these studies examine different methods (bottom up and top down) to estimate urban shares, both examine urban energy-related sources and calculate carbon dioxide (CO_2) emissions. The shared findings of these studies put the global urban final energy use share at approximately three quarters of global final energy use (Grubler et al. 2012).[6]

Results of Grubler et al. (2012) are broken down by the 11 Global Energy Assessment (GEA) regions and for the global total (Table 10.8). While the central estimate for the global total is approximately 76 percent, this research also provides ranges of estimates. These results strongly suggest that urban energy use dominates global energy use and should, therefore, be a priority focus for energy sustainability challenges. Another study examined the range of urban GHG emissions for several compounds (including carbon dioxide, methane, nitrous oxide and sulfur hexafluoride) (Marcotullio et al. 2013b). This study's findings suggest that the share of emissions from all these compounds is lower than that of just energy-related CO_2 emissions. Hence, the total urban share of urban emissions was somewhere between 37 and 49 percent in the year 2000 (Table 10.9).

In Asia, studies of GHG emissions suggest growing urban shares (Marcotullio et al. 2012). The fact that energy use and GHG emissions are increasing faster in this region than any other region

Table 10.8 Range in urban final energy use and urban percent of total final energy use by region, 2005

Region	*Final energy use*	
	EJ	*Percent*
North America	51–63	69–87
Pacific OECD	11–16	59–92
Western Europe	31–41	64–83
Eastern Europe	4–6	51–72
Former USSR	14–20	54–78
Sub-Saharan Africa	5–10	35–71
Latin America	16–18	77–89
North Africa & Middle East	10–16	58–86
China and Central Pacific Asia	19–31	40–65
Pacific Asia	10–16	51–77
South Asia	5–10	29–51
World	176–246	56–78

Source: Grubler et al. (2012).

Table 10.9 Range in urban GHG emissions and urban percent of total GHG emissions by region, 2000

Region	*GHG emissions*	
	(million tons)	*Percent*
North America	3,688–5,450	49–73
Pacific OECD	1,045–1,283	51–62
Western Europe	2,072–2,573	44–55
Eastern Europe	312–549	29–50
Former USSR	1,540–1,746	44–50
Sub-Saharan Africa	174–299	15–26
Latin America	635–751	25–29
North Africa & Middle East	736–840	39–44
China and Central Pacific Asia	1,312–1,781	23–31
Pacific Asia	851–1,043	40–49
South Asia	433–612	18–25
World	12,798–16,926	37–49

Source: Marcotullio et al. (2013b) reallocated to GEA regions.

raises mitigation concerns, particularly in light of the recent Paris COP 21 agreements. For example, China and India now account for approximately 34 percent of global emissions, more than 4 times the levels of the USA and EU28 put together. Moreover, while the USA and EU28 emission levels have stabilized, the trends for both China and India are increasing (Le Quéré et al. 2015).

Marcotullio et al. (2013b) identify lower average per capita GHG emissions levels in urban areas of high-income countries as compared to national averages. Higher per capita emissions levels in areas outside urban cores are confirmed by case studies of individual cities such as Paris (Barles

2009). Other studies that examine the differences in per capita energy use and GHG emissions between urban and non-urban areas also find higher levels in the outer, low-density suburbs. For example, in Toronto, VandeWeghe and Kennedy (2008) find that beyond the transit-intensive central core, private auto emissions surpass the emissions from building operations.

Alternatively, in low- and middle-income countries, most of the energy consumption technologies are concentrated in urban areas along with industrial activities. Marcotullio et al. (2013b) note that in Asia, the average for emissions levels in cities is higher than national averages. These results confirm the findings in Grubler et al. (2012) for energy use patterns in some industrializing countries as well as differences in CO_2 emissions in several Chinese cities and national averages (Dhakal 2009). This is also due to the economic structure of cities in Asia, which are the manufacturing hubs of the country – if not the world – and the fact that energy use in non-urban areas in Asia tend to be low. In other words, the higher per capita emissions of urban dwellers in Asia are a reflection of both economic structural trends as well as low levels of development in rural areas.

Future trends portend that Asia's total emissions will soon swamp global targets (Asian Development Bank 2013). As the region continues to urbanize and grow economically, how it will address GHG emissions will remain an important regional, if not global, challenge. Without radical changes to the region's energy mix, Asia's increasing use of fossil fuels (especially coal, natural gas and oil) will result in almost 22 billion tons of CO_2 emissions by 2035 (Asian Development Bank 2013).

Conclusions

Asia is a vast region and includes a diverse set of nations, economics, culturally, demographically, and geo-physically. Over the past few decades, the region has experienced urbanization in unique and spectacular ways. With urbanization, the region has also experienced massive changes in its energy profile in terms of energy supply, energy use and electricity output. The trends between energy profile changes and urbanization are highly linked through a large number of factors including land use, demographic, economic, behavior, political-institutional, urban form and natural system and geography.

Given the tremendous diversity in the region, there remain large variation in trends and patterns of urbanization, economic growth and energy use. Arguably, trends in the region are dominated by Japan, China and India. In particular the increases in energy supply, use and electricity output have been largely driven by changes in China and India. For example, large shares of the increases in TPES, TFC, energy imports and electricity output is driven by the changes experiences in these countries. Given the extent and the importance of the factors linking urbanization and energy use in these countries (population size, growth, economic growth, behavioral change, etc.), this result isn't surprising.

Three important sustainability challenges for Asia have emerged over the past few decades in relation to urbanization and energy use. These include access to modern energy in the region's cities, energy related environmental pollution and the rise of GHG emissions. Given current trends, these challenges will grow in importance over the coming decades. How Asia will address these urban sustainability challenges will not only affect its cities, but the region if not the world.

Notes

1 Asia's dominance in large cities may seem new, but except for a brief historical period, Asia has always been the location for the majority of the world's largest cities. It was only the nineteenth and early to mid-twentieth century that this term trend experienced a fluctuation. At the beginning of the twenty-first century, the distribution of large cities began to shift back to the longer-term patterns.

2 Studies of global urbanization suggest that generally, urban population density or the number of people per unit of built land is decreasing. Certainly, while cities in Asia are dense, they are also becoming less dense over time.

3 Annex categories are defined by the United Nations Framework Convention on Climate Change. Annex 1 countries include the industrialized countries that were members of the OECD (Organisation for Economic Co-operation and Development) in 1992, plus countries with economies in transition (the EIT Parties), including the Russian Federation, the Baltic States, and several Central and Eastern European States. See http://unfccc.int/parties_and_observers/parties/annex_i/items/2774.php. Non-Annex I countries are mostly developing countries including groups of developing countries that are especially vulnerable to the adverse impacts of climate change and countries that rely heavily on income from fossil fuel production and commerce. See https://unfccc.int/parties_and_observers/parties/non_annex_i/items/2833.php.

4 The concept of gross national happiness was coined by the Former King of Bhutan, Jigme Wangchuck. The concept and importance of happiness has been increasingly used in social indicators. See www.gnhcentrebhutan.org/what-is-gnh/the-story-of-gnh/.

5 The Grubler et al. (2012) analysis is based upon spatially explicit urban data described in Grubler et al. (2007).

6 The IEA (2008) study results suggest that the urban share of primary energy use is approximately 67 percent of total primary energy use. According to Grubler et al. (2012), the IEA calculations for this category of energy are approximately the same as the 76 percent share of final energy use found in the IIASA/GEA 2012 study.

References

Abrahamse, W. & L. Steg (2009) "How do socio-demographic and pyschological factors related to households' direct and indirect energy use and savings?" *Journal of Economic Psychology*, 30, 711–720.

Abrahamse, W., L. Steg, C. Vlek & T. Rothengatter (2005) "A review of intervention studies aimed at household energy conservation." *Journal of Environmental Psychology*, 25, 273–291.

Aguilar, A.G. & C. Santos (2011) "Informal settlements' needs and environmental conservation in Mexico City: An unsolved challenge for land-use policy." *Land Use Policy*, 28, 649–662.

Akbari, H. (2002) "Shade trees reduce building energy use and CO_2 emission from power plants." *Environmental Pollution*, 116, S119–S126.

Akbari, H., S. Davis, S. Dorsano, J. Huang & S. Winnett (1992). *Cooling Our Communities, A Guidebook on Tree Planting and Light-Colored Surfacing*. Washington, DC: US EPA.

Akbari, H., D.M. Kurn, S.E. Bretz & J.W. Hanford (1997) "Peak power and cooling energy savings of shade trees." *Energy and Buildings*, 25, 139–148.

Alam, M. & M.D.G. Rabbani (2007) "Vulnerabilities and responses to climate change for Dhaka." *Environment and Urbanization*, 19, 81.

Angel, S., S.C. Sheppard & D.L. Civco (2005) *The Dynamics of Global Urban Expansion*. Washington, DC: Transport and Urban Development Department, The World Bank.

Anon (2006) "The skyscraper boom." *The Economist*, 379, 65–67.

Anon (2013) "Tall buildings in numbers 2013: a tall building review," *CTBUH Journal*, 2011 (II). www.ctbuh.org/LinkClick.aspx?fileticket=Bj14RQcNyis%3D&tabid=1108&language=en-US.

APERC (2007) *Urban Transport Energy Use in the APEC Region, Trends and Options*. Tokyo: Asia Pacific Energy Research Center (APERC).

Asian Development Bank (2012) *Key Indicators for Asia and the Pacific 2012: Green Urbanization in Asia*. Manila: ADB.

Asian Development Bank (2013) *Asian Development Outlook 2013: Asia's Energy Challenge*. Manila: ADB.

Asian Development Bank (2015) *Green City Development Tool Kit*. Manila: ADB.

Aylett, A. (2013) "The socio-institutional dynamics of urban climate governance: A comparative analysis of innovation and change in Durban (KZN, South Africa) and Portland (OR, USA)." *Urban Studies*, 50, 1386–1402.

Baiocchi, G., J. Minx & K. Hubacek (2010) "The impact of social factors and consumer behavior on carbon dioxide emissions in the United Kingdom." *Journal of Industrial Ecology*, 14, 50–72.

Bannister, D., S. Watson & C. Wood (1997) "Sustainable cities: Transport, energy and urban form." *Environment and Planning B*, 24, 125–143.

Barles, S. (2009) "Urban metabolism of Paris and its region." *Journal of Industrial Ecology*, 13, 898–913.

Barter, P. (1999) "An International Comparative Perspective on Urban Transport and Urban Form in Pacific Asia: The Challenge of Rapid Motorization in Dense Cities." PhD thesis, Murdoch University Perth.

Bettencourt, L.M.A., J. Lobo, D. Helbing, C. Kuhnert & G.B. West (2007) "Growth, innovation, scaling, and the pace of life in cities." *Proceedings of the National Academy of Sciences of the United States of America*, 104, 7301–7306.

Bolt, J. & J.L. van Zanden (2014) "The Maddison Project: collaborative research on historical national accounts." *The Economic History Review*, 67 (3), 627–651.

Brown, K.W. & T. Kasser (2005) "Are pyschological and ecological well-being compatible? The role of values, mindfulness and lifestyle." *Social Indicators Research*, 74, 349–368.

Brown, K.W. & R.M. Ryan (2003) "The benefits of being present: Mindfulness and its role in psychological well-being." *Journal of Personality and Social Psychology*, 84, 822–848.

Brown, K.W. & R.M. Ryan (2004) "Fostering healthy self-regulation from within and without: A self-determination theory perspective." In *Positive Psychology in Practice*, eds. P.A. Linley & S. Joseph, 105–124. Hoboken, NJ: Wiley.

CAI-Asia & CDIA (2012) *Climate Change and Infrastructure in Asian Cities*. Pasig City, Philippines: Clean Air Initiative for Asian Cities Center (CAI-Asia) and Cities Development Initiative for Asia (CDIA).

Chen, Y., X. Li, Y. Zheng, Y. Guan & X. Liu (2011) "Estimating the relationship between urban forms and energy consumption: A case study in the Pearl River Delta, 2005–2008." *Landscape and Urban Planning*, 102, 33–42.

Cho, L.-J. & J.G. Bauer (1987) "Population growth and urbanization: What does the future hold?" In *Urbanization and Urban Policies in Pacific Asia*, eds. R.J. Fuchs, G.W. Jones & E.M. Pernia, 15–37. Boulder and London: Westview Press.

Ciccone, A. & R.E. Hall (1996) "Productivity and the density of economic activity." *American Economic Review*, 86, 54–70.

Cole, M. & Neumayer, E. (2004) "Examining the impact of demographic factors on air pollution." *Population and Environment*, 26(1), 5–21.

Corfield, J. (2008) "Thailand." *Encyclopedia of Global Warming and Climate Change*, ed. S. George Philander, 961–962. Thousand Oaks, CA: Sage.

Davis, S.J., K. Caldeira & H.D. Matthews (2010) "Future CO_2 emissions and climate change from existing energy infrastructure." *Science*, 329, 1330–1333.

Decker, E.H., S. Elliott, F.A. Smith, D.R. Blake & F.S. Rowland (2000) "Energy and material flow through the urban ecosystem." *Annual Review of Energy and Environment*, 25, 685–740.

Dhakal, S. (2009) "Urban energy use and carbon emissions from cities in China and policy implications." *Energy Policy*, 37, 4208–4219.

Dhakal, S. (2010) "GHG emission from urbanization and opportunities for urban carbon mitigation." *Current Opinion in Environmental Sustainability*, 2, 277–283.

Dhakal, S. & H. Imura (2004) *Urban Energy Use and Greenhouse Gas Emissions in Asian Mega-cities, Policies for a Sustainable Future*. Tokyo: Institute for Global Environmental Strategies.

Dick, H.W. & P.J. Rimmer (1998) "Beyond the third world city: The new urban geography of South-east Asia." *Urban Studies*, 35, 2303–2321.

Economist Intelligence Unit (2011) *Asian Green City Index*. Munich, Germany: Siemens AG.

Ewing, R. & R. Cervero (2001) "Travel and the built environment." *Transportation Research Record*, 1780, 87–114.

Ewing, R. & R. Cervero (2010) "Travel and the built environment." *Journal of the American Planning Association*, 76, 265–294.

Fragkias, M., J. Lobo, D. Strumsky & K.C. Seto (2013) "Does size matter? Scaling of CO_2 emission and US urban areas." *PLoS ONE*, 8, e64727, DOI 10.1371/journal.pone.0064727.

Glaeser, E.L. & M.E. Kahn (2010) "The greenness of cities: Carbon dioxide emissions and urban development." *Journal of Urban Economics*, 67, 404–418.

Global Energy Assessment (2012) *Global Energy Assessment: Toward a Sustainable Future*. Cambridge, UK and New York, NY: Cambridge University Press.

Grubler, A. & N. Schulz (2013) "Urban energy use." In *Energizing Sustainable Cities: Assessing Urban Energy*, eds. A. Grubler and D. Fisk, 57–70. Oxford, UK and New York, NY: Routledge.

Grubler, A., B. O'Neill, K. Riahi, V. Chirkov, A. Goujon, P. Kolp, I. Prommer, S. Scherbov & E. Slentoe (2007) "Regional, national, and spatially explicit scenarios of demographic and economic change based on SRES." *Technological Forecasting and Social Change*, 74, 980–1029.

Grubler, A., X. Bai, T. Buettner, S. Dhakal, D.J. Fisk, T. Ichinose, J.E. Keirstead, G. Sammer, D. Satterthwaite, N.B. Schulz, N. Shah, J. Steinberger & H. Weisz (2012) "Chapter 18: Urban energy systems." In *Global Energy Assessment: Toward a Sustainable Future*, ed. Global Energy Assessment, 1307–1400. Cambridge, UK and New York, NY: Cambridge University Press.

Hack, G. 2000. "Infrastructure and regional form." In *Global City Regions, Their Emerging Forms*, eds. R. Simmonds & G. Hack, 183–192. London: Spon Press.

Hoornweg, D., L. Sugar, C. Lorena & T. Gomez (2011) "Cities and greenhouse gas emissions: Moving forward." *Environment and Urbanization*, 23, 207–227.

Hu, M., H. Bergsdal, E. van der Voet, G. Huppes & D.B. Muller (2010) "Dynamics of urban and rural housing stocks in China." *Building Research & Information*, 38, 301–317.

Hubacek, K., D. Guan & A. Barua (2007) "Changing lifestyles and consumption patterns in developing countries: A scenario analysis for China and India." *Futures*, 39, 1084–1096.

IEA (2008) *World Energy Outlook 2008*. Paris: OECD/IEA.

IEA (2011) *Electricity Information*. Paris: International Energy Administration.

IEA (2016) *World Energy Balances*. Paris: OECD-IEA.

Jackson, T. (2005) *Motivating Sustainable Consumption, A Review of Evidence on Consumer Behavior and Behavioral Change*. University of Surrey: Centre for Environmental Strategy, ESRC Sustaianble Technologies Programme & the Sustainable Development Reserach Network.

Jiang, Z. & B. Lin (2012) "China's energy demand and its characteristics in the industrialization and urbanization process." *Energy Policy*, 49, 608–615.

Jones, C. & D.M. Kammen (2014) "Spatial distribution of US household carbon footprints reveals suburbanization undermines greenhouse gas benefits of urban population density." *Environmental Science & Technology*, 48, 895–902.

Jorgenson, A.K., J. Rice & B. Clark (2010) "Cities, slums, and energy consumption in less developed countries, 1990 to 2005." *Organization & Environment*, 23, 189–204.

Ju, C.B. & S.-Y. Tang (2011) "External legitimacy, goal congruence and collective resistance environmental NGOs and land use politics in South Korea." *Urban Studies*, 48, 811–825.

Kennedy, C., J. Cuddihy & J. Engel-Yan (2007) "The changing metabolism of cities." *Journal of Industrial Ecology*, 11, 43–59.

Kennedy, C., J. Steinberger, B. Gason, Y. Hansen, T. Hillman, M. Havranck, D. Pataki, A. Phdungsilp, A. Ramaswami & G.V. Mendez (2009) "Greenhouse gas emissions from global cities." *Environmental Science & Technology*, 43, 7297–7302.

Kraft, J. & A. Kraft (1978) "On the relationship between energy and GNP." *Journal of Energy and Development*, 3, 401–403.

Krugman, P. (1995) "Growing world trade: Causes and consequences." In *Brookings Institute Working Paper on Economic Activity*, 327–377.

Lariviere, I. & G. Lafrance (1999) "Modelling the electricity consumption of cities: Effect of urban density." *Energy Economics*, 21, 53–66.

Lenzen, M., M. Wier, C. Cohen, H. Hayami, S. Pachauri & R. Schaeffer (2006) "A comparative multivariate analysis of household energy requirements in Australia, Brazil, Denmark, India and Japan." *Energy*, 31(2–3), 181–207.

Le Quéré, C., R. Moriarty, R.M. Andrew, J.G. Canadell, S. Sitch, J.I. Korsbakken, P. Friedlingstein, G.P. Peters, R.J. Andres, T.A. Boden, R.A. Houghton, J.I. House, R.F. Keeling, P. Tans, A. Arneth, D.C.E. Bakker, L. Barbero, L. Bopp, J. Chang, F. Chevallier, L.P. Chini, P. Ciais, M. Fader, R.A. Feely, T. Gkritzalis, I. Harris, J. Hauck, T. Ilyina, A.K. Jain, E. Kato, V. Kitidis, K. Klein Goldewijk, C. Koven, P. Landschützer, S.K. Lauvset, N. Lefèvre, A. Lenton, I.D. Lima, N. Metzl, F. Millero, D.R. Munro, A. Murata, J.E.M.S. Nabel, S. Nakaoka, Y. Nojiri, K. O'Brien, A. Olsen, T Ono, F.F. Pérez, B. Pfeil, D. Pierrot, B. Poulter, G. Rehder, C. Rödenbeck, S. Saito, U. Schuster, J. Schwinger, R. Séférian, T. Steinhoff, B.D. Stocker, A.J. Sutton,T. Takahashi, B. Tilbrook, I.T. van der Laan-Luijkx, G.R. van der Werf, S. van Heuven, D. Vandemark, N. Viovy, A. Wiltshire, S. Zaehle & N. Zeng (2015) "Global Carbon Budget 2015." *Earth Systems Science Data*, 7, 349–396.

Liddle, B. (2004) "Demographic dynamics and per capita environmental impact: Using panel regressions and household decompositions to examien population and transport." *Population and Environment*, 26, 23–39.

Liddle, B. (2013) "The energy economic growth, urbanization nexus across development: Evidence from heterogeneous panel estaimtes robust to cross-sectional dependence." *The Energy Journal*, 34, 223–244.

Liu, F. (2011) *Research on Urban Expansion and Its Forces of Typical Regions, China*. Beijing: Chinese Academy of Sciences.

Liu, J., G.C. Daily, P.R. Ehrlich & G.W. Luck (2003) "Effects of household dynamics on resource consumption and biodiversity." *Nature*, 421, 530–533.

Lo, F.-C. & P.J. Marcotullio (2000) "Globalization and urban transformations in the Asia Pacific region: A review." *Urban Studies*, 37, 77–111.

Lo, F.-C. & P.J. Marcotullio (2001) *Globalization and the Sustainability of Cities in the Asia Pacific Region.* Tokyo: United Nations University Press.

Lo, F.-C. & Y.-M. Yeung (Eds.) (1996) *Emerging World Cities in Pacific Asia.* Tokyo: UNU Press.

Lo, F.-C. & Y.-M. Yeung (1998) *Globalization and the World of Large Cities.* Tokyo: United Nations University.

Mackellar, L., W. Lutz, C. Prinz & A. Goujon (1995) "Population, households and CO_2 emissions." *Population and Development Review*, 21, 849–865.

Marcotullio, P.J. (2003) "Globalization, urban form and environmental conditions in Asia Pacific cities." *Urban Studies*, 40, 219–248.

Marcotullio, P.J. (2005) *Time-Space Telescoping and Urban Environmental Transitions in the Asia Pacific.* Yokohama: United Nations University Institute of Advanced Studies.

Marcotullio, P.J. (2007) "Variations of urban environmental transitions: The experiences of rapidly developing Asia Pacific cities." In *Scaling the Urban Environmental Transition: From Local to Global and Back*, eds. P.J. Marcotullio & G. McGranahan, 45–68. London: Earthscan, James & Janes Publishing.

Marcotullio, P.J. (2011) "Globalization and urban environmental conditions in the Asia Pacific region." In *Population Distribution, Urbanization, Internal Migration and Development: An International Perspective*, ed. United Nations, 205–242. New York: United Nations publication ESA/P/WP/223.

Marcotullio, P.J. & J.D. Marshall (2007) "Potential futures for road transportation CO_2 emissions in the Asia Pacific." *Asia Pacific Viewpoint*, 48, 355–377.

Marcotullio, P.J., A. Sarzynski, J. Albrecht & N. Schulz (2012) "The geography of urban greenhouse gas emissions in Asia: A regional analysis." *Global Environmental Change*, 22, 944–958.

Marcotullio, P.J., A. Sarzynski, J. Albrecht & N. Schulz (2013a) "A top-down regional assessment of urban greenhouse gas emissions in Europe." *Ambio: A Journal of the Human Environment*, 43 (7), 957–968.

Marcotullio, P.J., A. Sarzynski, J. Albrecht, N. Schulz & J. Garcia (2013b) "The geography of global urban greenhouse gas emissions: An exploratory analysis." *Climatic Change*, 121, 621–634.

McGee, T.G. & I.M. Robinson (1995) *The Mega-Urban Regions of Southeast Asia.* Vancouver: University of British Columbia Press.

McGranahan, G. & F. Murray (2003) *Air Pollution & Health in Rapidly Developing Countries.* London: Earthscan.

Midden, C.J.H., F.G. Kaiser & L.T. McCalley (2007) "Technology's four roles in understanding individuals' conservation of natural resources." *Journal of Social Issues*, 63, 155–174.

Neumayer, E. (2002) "Can natural factors explain any cross-country differences in carbon dioxide emissions?" *Energy Policy*, 30, 7–12.

Newman, P. & J. Kenworthy (1989) "Gasoline consumption and cities: A comparison of US cities with a global survey." *Journal of American Planning Association*, 55, 24–37.

Newman, P. & J. Kenworthy (1999) *Sustainability and Cities.* Washington, DC: Island Press.

Nuclear Energy Institute (2016a) "Nuclear units under construction worldwide." www.nei.org/Knowledge-Center/Nuclear-Statistics/World-Statistics/Nuclear-Units-Under-Construction-Worldwide.

Nuclear Energy Institute (2016b) "World nuclear power plants in operation." www.nei.org/Knowledge-Center/Nuclear-Statistics/World-Statistics/World-Nuclear-Power-Plants-in-Operation.

O'Neill, B.C., M. Dalton, R. Fuchs, L. Jiang, S. Pachauri & K. Zigova (2010) "Global demographic trends and future carbon emissions." *Proceedings of the National Academy of Science of the United States of America*, 107, 17521–17526.

Ozturk, I. (2010) "A literature survey on energy-growth nexus." *Energy Policy*, 38, 340–349.

Pachauri, S. (2004) "An analysis of cross-sectional variations in total household energy requirements in India using micro survey data." *Energy Policy*, 32(15), 1723–1735.

Pandit, R. & D.N. Laband (2010) "Energy savings from tree shade." *Ecological Economics*, 69, 1324–1329.

Parikh, J. & V. Shukla (1995) "Urbanization, energy use and greenhouse effects in economic development. " *Global Environmental Change*, 5, 87–103.

Pataki, D.E., R.J. Alig, A.S. Fung, N.E. Golubiewski, C.A. Kennedy, E.G. McPherson, D.J. Nowak, R.V. Pouyat & P. Romero-Lankao (2006) "Urban ecosystems and the North American carbon cycle." *Global Change Biology*, 12, 2092–2102.

Payne, J.E. (2010a) "Survey of the international evidence on the causal relationship between energy consumption and growth." *Journal of Economic Studies*, 37, 53–95.

Payne, J.E. (2010b) "A suvey of the electricity consumption-growth literature." *Applied Energy*, 87, 723–731.

Phdungsilp, A. (2010) "Integrated energy and carbon modeling with a decision support system: Policy scenarios for low-carbon city development in Bangkok." *Energy Policy*, 38, 4808–4817.

Poumanyvong, P. & S. Kaneko (2010) "Does urbanization lead to less energy use and lower CO_2 emissions? A cross-country analysis." *Ecological Economics*, 70, 434–444.

Practical Action (2014) *Poor People's Energy Outlook 2014: Key Messages on Energy for Poverty Alleviation*. Rugby, UK: Practical Action Publishing Ltd.

Rock, M.T., M. Toman, Y. Cui, K. Jiang, Y. Song & Y. Wang (2013) "Technological learning, energy efficiency, and CO_2 emissions in China's energy intensive industries." In *Policy Research Working Paper 6492*. Washington, DC: World Bank.

Romero-Lankao, P., K.R. Gurney, K.C. Seto, M. Chester, R.M. Duren, S. Hughes, L.R. Hutyra, P. Marcotullio, L. Baker, N.B. Grimm, C. Kennedy, E. Larson, S. Pincetl, D. Runfola, L. Sanchez, G. Shrestha, J. Feddema, A. Sarzynski, J. Sperling & E. Stokes (2014) "A critical knowledge pathway to low-carbon, sustainable futures: Integrated understanding of urbanization, urban areas, and carbon." *Earth's Future*, 2, 515–532.

Sager, F. (2004) "Metropolitan institutions and policy coordination: The integration of land use and transportation policies in Swiss urban areas." *Governance*, 18, 227–256.

Sahakian, M.D. & J.K. Steinberger (2011) "Energy reduction through a deeper understanding of household consumption." *Journal of Industrial Ecology*, 15, 31–48.

Sassen, S. (2006) *Cities in a World Economy*. Thousand Oaks: Sage Publications.

Satterthwaite, D. (2007) "The transition to a predominantly urban world and its underpinnings." In *Human Settlements Discussion Paper Series*. London: International Institute for Environment and Development (IIED).

Sawin, J.L. & K. Hughes. (2007) "Energizing cities." In *State of the World 2007, Our Urban Future*, ed. M. O'Meara Sheehan, 90–111. New York: W.W. Norton & Company.

Schultz, P.W., J.M. Nolan, R.B. Cialdini, N.J. Goldstein & V. Griskevicius (2007) "The constructive, destructive, and reconstructive power of social norms." *Psychological Science*, 18, 429–434.

Schulz, N. (2010a) "Delving into the carbon footprint of Singapore: Comparing direct and indirect greenhouse gas emissions of a small and open economic system." *Energy Policy*, 38, 4848–4855.

Schulz, N. (2010b) "Urban energy consumption database and estimations of urban energy intensities." In *GEA KM 18 Working Paper*. Vienna: IIASA.

Scott, J. (2000) "Rational choice theory." In *Understanding Contemporary Society: Theory of the Present*, eds. G. Browning, A. Halchi, N. Hewlett & F. Webster, 126–138. London: Sage.

Seto, K.C., S. Dhakal, A. Bigio, H. Blanco, G.C. Delgado, D. Dewar, L. Huang, A. Inaba, A. Kansal, S. Lwasa, J. McMahon, D. Mueller, J. Murakami, H. Nagendra & A. Ramaswami (2014) "Human settlements, infrastructure and spatial planning." In *Climate Change 2014: Mitigation of Climate Change, 5th Assessment Report*, 923–1000.

Seto, K.C., M. Fragkias, B. Guneralp & M.K. Reilly (2011) "A meta-analysis of global urban land expansion." *PLoS one*, 6, 1–9.

Seto, K.C., B. Guneralp & L. Hutyra (2012) "Global forecasts of urban expansion to 2030 and direct impacts on biodiversity and carbon ppools." *Proceedings of the National Academy of Sciences of the United States of America*, 109, 552–563.

Shen, L., S. Cheng, A.J. Gunson & H. Wan (2005) "Urbanization, sustainability and the utilization of energy and mineral resources in China." *Cities*, 22, 287–302.

Sheng, Y.K. & M. Thuzar (2012) *Urbanization in Southeast Asia, Issues and Impacts*. Singapore: Institute of Southeast Asian Studies.

Smil, V. (1994) *Energy in World History*. Boulder, CO: Westview Press.

Spangenberg, J.H. & S. Lorek (2002) "Environmentally sustainable household consumption: From aggregate environmental pressures to priority fields of action." *Ecological Economics*, 43, 127–140.

Spence, M., P.C. Annez & R.M. Buckley (2009) *Urbanization and Growth*. Washington, DC: Commission on Growth and Development, The World Bank.

Stern, P.C. (2000) "Toward a coherent theory of environmentally significant behavior." *Journal of Social Issues*, 56, 407–424.

Stone Jr., B. (2009) "Land use as climate change mitigation." *Environmental Science & Technology*, 43, 9052–9056.

Sugar, L., C. Kennedy & E. Leman (2012) "Greenhouse gas emisssion from Chinese cities." *Journal of Industrial Ecology*, 16, 552–563.

The Economist (2006) "More of everything." *The Economist*, 380, Survey "The new titans," 18–20.
Thøgersen, J. & F. Olander (2002) "Human values and the emergence of a sustainable consumption pattern: A panel study." *Journal of Economic Psychology*, 23, 605–630.
Transportation Research Board (2009) *Driving and the Built Environment, The Effects of Compact Development on Motorized Travel, Energy Use and CO_2 Emissions*. Washington, DC: National Research Council of the National Academies.
UN-Habitat (2003) *Water and Sanitation in the World's Cities*. London: Earthscan.
UN-Habitat (2012) *Sustainable Urban Energy: A Sourcebook for Asia*. Nairobi: UN-Habitat.
UNCTAD (2015) *World Investment Report 2015, Reforming International Investment Governance*. Geneva: United Nations Conference on Trade and Development.
UNESCAP & UN HABITAT (2010) *The State of Asian Cities 2010/11*. Fukuoka: UN HABITAT.
United Nations (2010) *World Urbanization Prospects: The 2009 Revisions*. New York: Department of Economic and Social Affairs.
United Nations (2014) *World Urbanization Prospects: The 2014 Revisions*. New York: Department of Economic and Social Affairs.
United Nations Development Programme (1996) *Urban Agriculture: Food, Jobs and Sustainable Cities*. New York: UNDP.
VandeWeghe, J.R. & C. Kennedy (2008) "A spatial analysis of residential greenhouse gas emissions in the Toronto census metropolitan area." *Journal of Industrial Ecology*, 11, 133–144.
Vasconcellos, E.A. (2001) *Urban Transportation, Environment and Equity; The Case for Developing Countries*. London: Earthscan Publications.
Ward's (2010) *World Motor Vehicle Data 2010*. Southfield, MI: Ward's Automotive Group.
Weisz, H. & J.K. Steinberger (2010) "Reducing energy and material flows in cities." *Current Opinion in Environmental Sustainability*, 2, 185–192.
Wen, Q. (2010) *Urban Expansion in China: Spatiotemporal Analysis Using Remote Sensing Data*. Beijing: Chinese Academy of Sciences.
Wilson, D., R. Purushothaman & T. Fiotakis. (2004) *The BRICS and Global Markets: Crude, Cars, and Capital*, 28. New York: Goldman Sachs.
World Bank (2015) World Development Indicators, Washington DC, World Bank, http://databank.worldbank.org/data/reports.aspx?source=world-development-indicators.
World Energy Council (2011) *Global Transportation Scenarios 2050*. London: WEC.
World Health Organization (2016) *WHO's Urban Ambient Air Pollution database: Update 2016*. Geneva: WHO.
World Trade Organization (2015) *International Trade Statistics 2015*. Geneva, Switzerland: WTO.
Yuen, B. & L. Kong (2009) "Climate change and urban planning in Southeast Asia." *S.A.P.I.EN.S.*, 2, 2–11.
Zheng, S., R. Wang, E.L. Glaeser & M.E. Kahn (2011) "The greenness of China: Household carbon dioxide emissions and urban development." *Journal of Economic Geography*, 11, 761–792.

SECTION 4
Economic justice in Asia

11

The evolution of China's pay inequality during the transitional period

Wenjie Zhang

Introduction

China has pursued economic reform since 1978. Favored by the Open-Door policy and special economic zones, a handful of coastal provinces and eastern municipalities have become the biggest beneficiaries of economic reform, while vast interior provinces remain relatively poor and underdeveloped. As Deng Xiaoping's favorite slogan described, some in China have to become rich first, but what was not stated was that the rest do not necessarily follow. Unbalanced economic development underlies a dramatic rise of economic inequality in China, especially since the early 1990s. From the 2000s, this rise has become both a focal point of public attention and a headache for the Chinese state.

In addition to impeding sustainable economic growth, the gap also challenges the foundation of the Chinese leadership by intensifying social tensions. Even though China's population has a high tolerance for inequality, public resentment of the rich has displaced the public's interest in or focus on their expectations for material prosperity through reform. Therefore, the Chinese policymakers have often reformed income distribution by raising individual property's income, increasing employment rates and minimum wage standards, expanding the middle class, improving the livelihood of the poor and enhancing the role of tax in income regulation.

Rising economic inequality in China is well-documented. Many studies have concentrated on rural–urban income inequality, its formation, direction and social and political effects (Tsui 1991; Kanbur and Zhang 1999; Gustafsson et al. 2010; Benjamin et al. 2005; Wu and Perloff 2005; Sicular et al. 2007; Luo and Zhu 2008; Gao and Riskin 2008). The well-accepted argument is that a rapidly rising trend in income inequality began in the early 1990s, which is mainly attributable to the widening gap between rural and urban regions. A variety of driving forces have been highlighted, ranging from endowments of household characteristics, such as location of residence and education (Luo and Zhu 2008; Sicular et al. 2007) to policy-related factors, such as economic restructuring and rural–urban reclassification (Benjamin et al. 2005), the revival of market forces (Gao and Riskin 2008), the degree of decentralization (Kanbur and Zhang 2005; Lin 1999), etc.

Rising interprovincial inequality is another well-covered topic (Tsui 1993, 2007; Gustafsson and Li 2002; Shorrocks and Wan 2005; Fan and Sun 2008; Gries and Redlin 2009; Hao and Wei 2010; Li and Wei 2010). Galbraith et al. (2004) show that much of the rise could be attributed to the relative gains of just a few provinces and municipalities, namely Guangdong, Shanghai and Beijing. Major losers in regional (and relative) terms included the NorthEast (Manchuria) and the SouthWest (Sichuan). Studying the household survey data of the Chinese Academy of Social Sciences (CASS), Gustafsson and Li (2002) also observe that the between-province inequality is more substantial than intra-province inequality at the county level. By decomposing inter-provincial inequality into between-and-within provincial inequality, Fan and Sun (2008) reveal the spatial dynamics of China's growing inequality. Using Theil's T Statistics and provincial GDP and population data from a number of issues of the Chinese Statistical Yearbooks, Akita (2003) reinforces the spatial characteristics of inequality in China during the 1990s. Applying Theil's L Index, Gustafsson et al. (2008) calculate inequality in three large geographical zones – East, Center and West, finding that the income gap between these three regions did not actually widen from 1995 to 2002 and that within East inequality even declined. Trade, government expenditures, foreign and domestic capital investments, globalization and marketization as well as human capital have been identified as key policy determinants of rising inequality (Kanbur and Zhang 1999; Tsui 2007; Gries and Redlin 2009).

While many studies discuss the rapid rise of China's economic inequality, very few studies suggest that inequality in China has peaked or is declining in recent years. Based upon survey data from the National Bureau of Statistics (NBS), Li (2013) found that China's overall income inequality started to decrease since 2008 with declines both in rural and urban areas. Does this finding truly reflect China's inequality trend? If it is true, is there any other evidence based upon different methodologies and different data sources?

In this study, we aim to answer these above-mentioned questions by investigating China's pay inequality, using between-group components of Theil's T statistics and wage data from official administrative yearbooks. Wage is one of the most important income sources for the Chinese population. According to the recent Global Wage Report 2014/2015, published by the International Labor Organization (ILO), wage income accounts for the largest share of household income in China, which is also the highest wage/income share among emerging markets and developing countries (Global Wage Report 2014/2015). As Gan (2013) found out, the contribution of wage income to the overall income inequality in China is around 40 percent, making it the largest contributor to the overall Gini coefficient compared to other sources of income, such as business income, investment income, and transfer income. The evolution of pay inequality across regions/sector categories is usually a good instrument for the evolution of inequality in other economic constructs, including household income. In general, the large changes of economic inequality that usually occur in relative income levels in any economy are those between separated regions (e.g., between the north and south in China, the West and Mid-West in the United States) and between disparate sectors (e.g., between farmers and bankers or between textile workers and petroleum engineers). While large inequalities exist within regions and within sectors, the changes in such inequalities, over time, tend to be comparatively smaller. And in any event, such changes do not usually differ in type from the between-group variations; there is self-similarity at different scales. Thus the between-group measure of pay inequality tends to capture the overall evolution of the distribution. Even though pay inequality is a good indicator of overall economic inequality, it has not been very much discussed in the literature. Therefore, we would like to fill this gap by providing new estimates of China's pay inequality, based upon Theil's T-statistic measured across regions and sectors. We are interested in exploring the main factors that may influence the trend of pay inequality in the context of economic development. We would also like to investigate whether the overall decline of China's pay inequality after the crisis is a temporary phenomenon or a long-term outcome driven by both economic and policy factors.

Methodology and data source

Two main inequality indices are commonly used to assess China's economic inequality: the Gini coefficient and the Generalized Entropy Index (Fan and Sun 2008; Hao and Wei 2009). Each index holds its own mathematical properties explaining inequality from different perspectives. For instance, the Gini coefficient is usually used to depict the panorama of inequality; it is also able to facilitate direct comparisons of two populations, regardless of size. Many researchers have calculated the Gini coefficients based upon different data sources (Khan and Riskin 1998; Ravallion and Chen 1999; Gustafsson and Li 2002; Benjamin et al. 2005; Wu and Perloff 2005; Kanbur and Zhang 2005; Chotikapanich et al. 2007; Wang et al. 2009; Chen et al. 2010). The major disadvantage of the Gini coefficient is that the index is difficult to decompose. So when exploring the contributions of various factors to overall inequality, researchers prefer to apply the technique of Generalized Entropy Index (namely, the Theil Index). In this study, we use the Theil Index to analyze the evolution of pay inequality.

The rationale for preferring the Theil index is that, compared to other inequality indices, this index not only allows inequality to be decomposed into the sum of a "between-group" component and a "within-group" component, but also has less stringent data requirements, which is a benefit when group data are easier to come by than individual survey data. There are two major data sources available to measure China's inequality: household survey data and grouped data (Chotikapanich et al. 2007). Although complete individual data would be preferable for analyzing trends in inequality, such data are rarely available. The existing datasets, such as the China Household Income Project (CHIP) survey data, the China Health and Nutrition Survey (CHNS), and the National Bureau of Statistics (NBS) household survey, only cover several isolated years and individual provinces. Therefore, researchers are left to compromise with aggregated data, which provide national coverage over continuous periods of time (Chotikapanich et al. 2007). A good data source alternative to the traditionally used household survey is found in annual statistical yearbooks.

The calculation of the Theil index requires two sets of data, each of which can be classified into mutually exclusive and completely exhaustive groupings. This requirement makes the annual state statistical yearbooks an attractive data source. Every year, China's National Bureau of Statistics (NBS) publishes a comprehensive yearbook, reflecting the country's economic and social development. The NBS yearbook chapter on "Employment and Wages" includes basic labor statistics, such as the number of employed persons, staff and workers, persons employed in different units, total wage bills, average wage bills, and registered unemployment rate in urban areas (National Bureau of Statistics [NBS] 2010). Wages and employment data on staff and workers were chosen for this study because they are disaggregated by economic sectors and provinces, and, have been consistently classified since 1988. In this study, the employment data refer to the total number of staff and workers at year-end by sector and province. The wage data are the total wage bills of staff and workers at year-end by sector and province. Total wage bills are the total remuneration to all staff and workers in all formal sectors during the reporting period. These bills include hourly-paid wages, piece-rate wages, bonuses, allowance and subsidies, overtime wages and wages paid under special circumstances. The wage bills are pre-tax and no social insurance premiums, utility bills, housing funds or subsidies are deducted (National Bureau of Statistics [NBS] 2012).

According to the editors' explanatory notes (National Bureau of Statistics [NBS] 2010), staff and workers are persons who work in and receive payment from units of state ownership, collective ownership, joint ownership, shareholding ownership, foreign ownership, and ownership by entrepreneurs from Hong Kong, Macao and Taiwan. Persons employed in township enterprises, persons employed in private enterprises, urban self-employed persons, foreigners and persons from Hong Kong, Macao and Taiwan who work in urban units are not included. Informal sectors are also excluded. However, this does not much change the moving pattern of inequality. The active element in the evolution of inequality tends to be captured by movements within the formal sector. This is due to the fact that inequalities in the informal sector, such as among peasant farmers or urban service workers, are inclined to be comparatively small and stable. There are no peasant farmers with the incomes of bankers or lawyers or doctors; there are no household domestics with the incomes of the professionals they work for. Thus while a measure based on the formal sector alone is necessarily incomplete, it is not for that reason misleading so far as the evolution of inequalities over time is concerned.

Another advantage of using statistical yearbooks is that yearbooks provide the most recent and standard official data on wage and employment over a continuous period of years, compared to household survey data. Payroll data are often available sooner than surveys, and the historical record is substantially more complete, so that this information source complements and extends the survey record while (generally) providing independent confirmation of general trends. Furthermore, the comparison between the results of this study and those of measurements based on data from household surveys also provides clear evidence that the data used here are reliable enough for drawing valid conclusions about the trend of China's pay inequality during the transitional period.

The evolution of pay inequality in China from 1987 to 2012

We present some original estimates of the evolution of pay inequality in China from 1987 to 2012. The metric is the between-provinces and between-sectors components of Theil's T-statistic; the underlying data are wage and employment records from the annual statistical yearbooks, for which consistent classification schemes exist (or can be constructed) going back to 1987. Figure 11.1 presents a broad overview of the evolution of pay inequality in China, both overall and by region and sector, from 1987 to 2012. As Figure 11.1 shows, pay inequality in China began rising in 1992, both between-provinces and between-sectors, as well as overall. However, in in the 2000s the behavior of these two dimensions of inequality diverged (Galbraith et al. 2009). Inequality between provinces peaked around 2002 and declined after 2003. In contrast, inequality between sectors continued rising and reached its apex in 2008. Combining the two factors, the growth of inequality overall slowed after 2002, peaked in 2008, and then began a pronounced decline.

Pay inequality between and within geographical regions

Figure 11.2 breaks out the changing inter-provincial dimensions of China's pay inequality in a stacked bar graph. Each bar represents a year, and each segment represents the contribution of a province to overall inequality in that year. Each segment reflects both the population weight of the province (measured by observed employment) and the ratio between average provincial wage and national average wage. Contributions greater than zero indicate provinces with mean wages above the national average. Contributions below zero indicate provinces with mean wages below the national average. The largest positive contribution (Beijing) is placed next to the zero line, while the largest negative (Henan) is placed at the bottom of the bar.

As the figure shows, the rise of between-province pay inequality was largely attributable to the surging relative wages in Guangdong, Shanghai, Beijing, Zhejiang, Jiangsu and Tianjin, while the low wages of interior provinces such as Henan, Heilongjiang, Hubei, Sichuan, Jiangxi, Shandong and Hunan did not change. The rapid development of rich provinces and municipal cities is clustered in eastern and coastal regions. These regions absorb the majority of foreign trade and

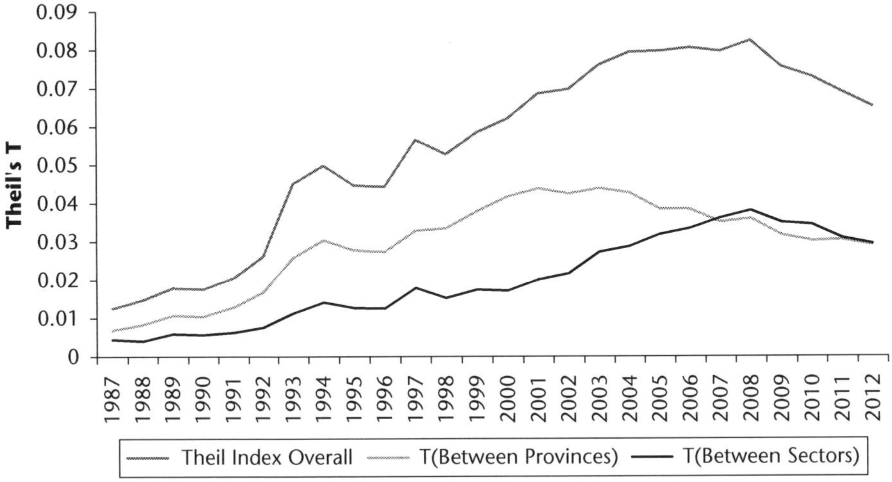

Figure 11.1 Inequality between and within provinces in China, 1987–2012

Source: Author's calculations.

receive investments both internally and externally. However, since 2003, between-province inequality has declined, as Zhejiang and Jiangsu started to catch up with Guangdong, becoming new important centers for manufacturing in China. After 2009, the decline of inter-provincial inequality accelerated, due mainly to loss of activity in Guangdong and Zhejiang, both of which were greatly affected by the global crisis.

Figure 11.3 confirms our observation by providing a clear chart of percent contribution of each province that has an average wage higher than the national average. As displayed in Figure 11.3, the contribution of Shanghai is relatively stable during the entire period. In contrast, Guangdong has switched its place with Beijing. During the eighties, both rose rapidly. However, the behavior of these two provinces has diverged since the mid-1990s. The contribution of Guangdong has gradually declined, while Beijing started to outshine all other provinces.

The rise of Beijing is not surprising. First, Beijing, as the capital of China, was given more opportunities to attract resources advantageous to its development. In particular, after Beijing won the right to host the 2008 Olympic Games in 2001, the total number of workers and staff in manufacturing and construction rose remarkably from 2001 to 2003. Second, wages in the financial and real estate sectors skyrocketed in Beijing from 2001 to the present, further widening the wage gap between the capital city and other locales. Third, Beijing has more jobs in high-wage sectors, including IT, social services, utilities, scientific research and education. In contrast, the contribution of Guangdong has shrunk dramatically since 2004. The decline of Guangdong is also not accidental. As one of the first economic special zones in China established in 1980, Guangdong has attracted huge amounts of foreign investment and capital in support of its economic development. Guangdong was known as the country's hub of manufacturing for export in the 1980s. The average pay in Guangdong province was much higher than the national average. However, with the rapid rise of Shanghai, Jiangsu, and Zhejiang in the 1990s, Guangdong has gradually lost its advantage in manufacturing, and the mean wage in Guangdong has also become less attractive. The decline of Guangdong and the rise of other provinces in the early 2000s has halted the growing tendency of between-province pay inequality, which it is observed in Figure 11.1.

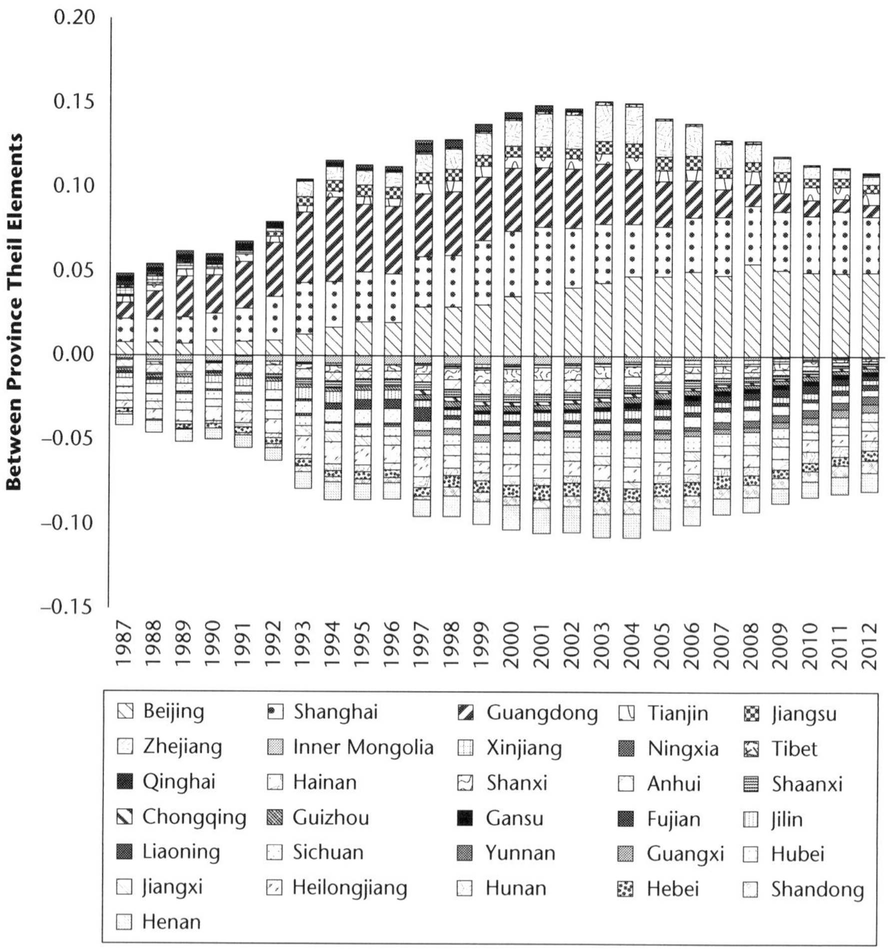

Figure 11.2 Contribution of provinces to inter-provincial inequality in China, 1987–2012

Source: Author's calculations.

However, not everyone gains in rich provinces and municipal cities. The pay gap within rich provinces is also dramatic. Figure 11.4 presents the contribution of each province to overall within-province pay inequality. Within-province inequality is measured as the pay difference between-sectors within a province. As is displayed in Figure 11.4, before the 2000s, most provinces shared a similar level of within-province pay inequality, indicating that the pay between sectors within most provinces was not dramatically different. However, since 1999, the situation has changed remarkably, with five provinces standing out. These include Zhejiang, Beijing, Guangdong, Shanghai, and Jiangsu. During the 1990s, the total contributions of these five regions were relatively small, fluctuating between 14 and 18 percent. Nevertheless, only within a decade from 1999, the total contribution of these five regions has jumped from 22 to 56 percent. This phenomenon implies that the wage difference between economic sectors in these rapidly developing regions is much higher than that in the rest of China. Not every economic sector gains in rich provinces. The underdeveloped economic sectors remain poor even in the rich regions.

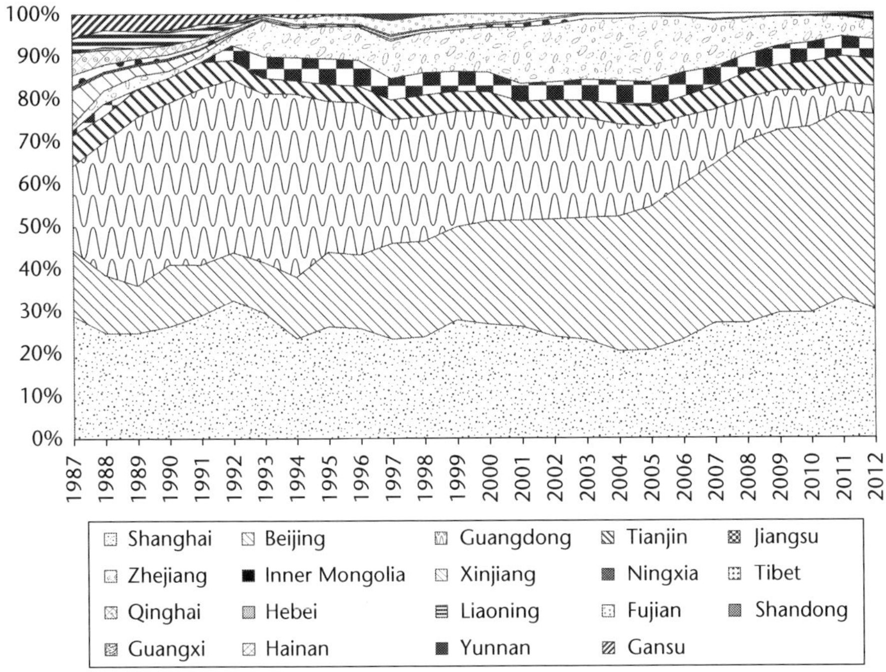

Figure 11.3 The percentage of contribution of the provinces from above (1987–2012)

Source: Author's calculations.

The sector-province Theil element is the smallest unit in our analysis; it represents the contribution of each sector, within each province, to pay inequality measured at the national scale. Figure 11.5 presents these elements ranked by size, for 1988, 1996, 2002 and 2009. Most sector-province cells contribute almost nothing to inequality, either because they are very small or because their pay is close to the national average. Thus, as shown in Figure 11.5, most of these Theil elements surround the 0 line, composing the horizontal portion of each curve. The figure also illustrates the importance of extreme cases, whose Theil elements are placed next to the Y-axis and compose the vertical portion of each curve. Just a few sectors (within a few provinces) drive the overall index. Note that China reclassified its industrial sector categorization twice, first in 1994 and again in 2004. The change of industrial classification is in fact not adding new sectors, but regrouping the original industries into more detailed classifications based upon global standards. Therefore, the analysis is still comparable while the length of each curve is different.

Tables 11.1 and 11.2 further explore these sector-province Theil elements by exemplifying the contribution of sector-province to overall inequality again in the single years 2009, 2002, 1996 and 1988. Positive numbers mean that the average wages in these cells are higher than the national average, while negative numbers stand for a lower mean wage. In each table, the top ten contributors and the last ten contributors are both listed. It is interesting to note that the forces pulling wages above and below the mean have changed significantly over two decades. In 1988, the farming sector in Hebei province was the biggest contributor to overall pay inequality, implying that the difference between the pay of people employed in the farming sector in Heibei province and the pay of people employed in the farming sector in other provinces was the largest in 1988. Correspondingly, the biggest losers were people working in the farming sector in

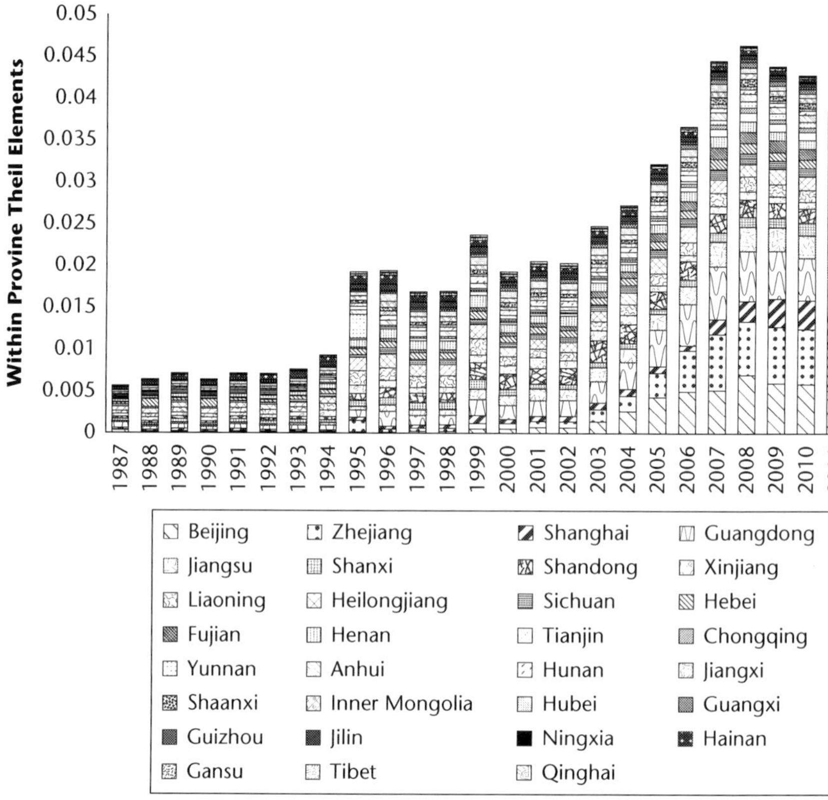

Figure 11.4 Contribution of provinces to between-sector inequality, 1987–2012

Source: Author's calculations.

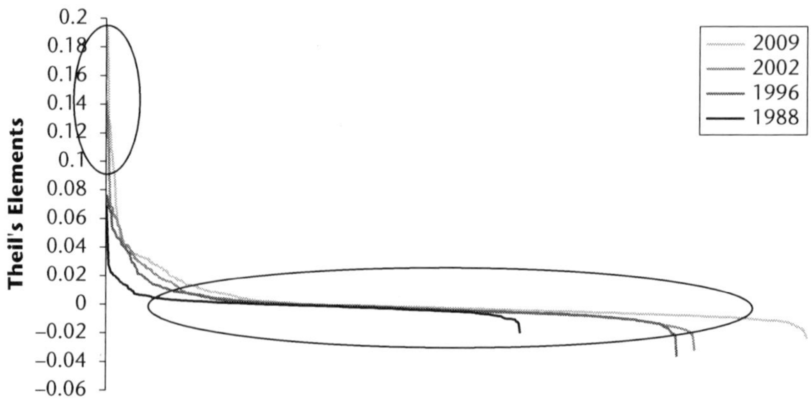

Figure 11.5 Contribution to inequality (sector-province cells) in 1988, 1996, 2002 and 2009

Source: Author's calculations.

Table 11.1 Province-sector contribution to overall pay inequality (1996 vs. 1988)

	1996			1988		
1	**Guangdong**	Bank and Insurance	0.0762	**Hebei**	Farming	0.0686
2	**Shanghai**	Bank and Insurance	0.0731	**Guangdong**	Real Estate	0.0478
3	**Guangdong**	Social welfare	0.0688	**Guangdong**	Wholesale and Retail Trade	0.0278
4	**Shanghai**	Others	0.0656	**Shanxi**	Real Estate	0.0251
5	**Beijing**	Social welfare	0.0646	**Xinjiang**	Mining	0.0224
6	**Shanghai**	Wholesale and Retail Trade	0.0531	**Guangdong**	Finance	0.0220
7	**Guangdong**	Real Estate	0.0522	**Beijing**	Real Estate	0.0203
8	**Guangdong**	Wholesale and Retail Trade	0.0510	**Guangdong**	Transportation	0.0202
9	**Beijing**	Bank and Insurance	0.0493	**Shanghai**	Transportation	0.0193
10	**Shanghai**	Social welfare	0.0466	**Shanghai**	Wholesale and Retail Trade	0.0184
471	**Heilongjiang**	Bank and Insurance	−0.0147	**Guizhou**	Real Estate	−0.0092
472	**Sichuan**	Utilities	−0.0153	**Heilongjiang**	Real Estate	−0.0092
473	**Sichuan**	Transportation	−0.0155	**Heilongjiang**	Wholesale and Retail Trade	−0.0092
474	**Henan**	Others	−0.0166	**Hubei**	Farming	−0.0094
475	**Heilongjiang**	Social Welfare	−0.0176	**Sichuan**	Farming	−0.0095
476	**Henan**	Wholesale and Retail Trade	−0.0188	**Guizhou**	Education	−0.0096
477	**Liaoning**	Bank and Insurance	−0.0191	**Guizhou**	Transportation	−0.0111
478	**Shandong**	Others	−0.0193	**Henan**	Healthcare	−0.0112
479	**Heilongjiang**	Farming	−0.0209	**Henan**	Wholesale and Retail Trade	−0.0123
480	**Heilongjiang**	Others	−0.0347	**Heilongjiang**	Farming	−0.0186

Source: China Statistical Yearbooks and author's calculations.

Heilongjiang province. As reform deepened, the top ten contributors became less diversified than they were in the 1980s.

In 1996, the biggest winners were workers and staff in the banking and insurance sectors in Guangdong. Meanwhile, Guangdong province and Shanghai each had four places among the top ten. The other two were taken by Beijing, but this situation has changed again since 2002, as Beijing has outshone all other provinces and municipal cities. In 2009, while Beijing took eight places among the top ten sectors with the highest average wages, Guangdong stepped down from the pinnacle ranking. Taking a look from below, we see that the poor are still poor. The populations of Henan and Heilongjiang, two interior and traditionally agricultural provinces, are not better off, even as the economies of other provinces take off. In addition, this observation confirms one of our hypotheses that not every economic sector gains in rich provinces. The dramatic rise of Beijing or Shanghai may only be attributed to the rapid development of a handful of sectors, such as high-tech related sectors, financial sectors and service sectors.

Pay inequality between and within larger geographical units

China can be roughly divided into three large geographical zones: East, West and Central. The East includes nine provinces and three municipal cities: Liaoning, Beijing, Tianjin, Hebei, Shandong, Jiangsu, Shanghai, Zhejiang, Fujian, Guangdong, Guangxi and Hainan. The West

Table 11.2 Province-sector contribution to overall wage inequality (2009 vs. 2002)

		2009				*2002*
1	**Beijing**	I.T. and Computer Science	0.1954	**Beijing**	Other	0.1418
2	**Beijing**	Leasing and Business Services	0.1878	**Beijing**	Social Welfare	0.1281
3	**Beijing**	Wholesale and Retail Trade	0.1287	**Beijing**	Scientific Research	0.1046
4	**Beijing**	Culture Sports and Entertainment	0.1272	**Beijing**	Wholesale and Retail Trade	0.0719
5	**Beijing**	Financial Intermediation	0.1085	**Beijing**	Real Estate	0.0683
6	**Beijing**	Scientific Research	0.1056	**Beijing**	Bank and Insurance	0.0678
7	**Heilongjiang**	Financial Intermediation	0.0927	**Shanghai**	Bank and Insurance	0.0631
8	**Shanghai**	Financial Intermediation	0.0927	**Shanghai**	Wholesale and Retail Trade	0.0617
9	**Beijing**	Real Estate	0.0711	**Shandong**	Excavation	0.0606
10	**Beijing**	Hotels and Restaurants	0.0648	**Guangdong**	Real Estate	0.0595
580	**Zhejiang**	Leasing and Business Services	−0.0138	**Henan**	Real Estate	−0.0161
581	**Henan**	Culture Sports and Entertainment	−0.0142	**Shandong**	Wholesale and Retail Trade	−0.0162
582	**Henan**	Financial Intermediation	−0.0142	**Hubei**	Farming	−0.0164
583	**Shandong**	Financial Intermediation	−0.0147	**Henan**	Construction	−0.0170
584	**Hebei**	Financial Intermediation	−0.0155	**Shandong**	Manufacturing	−0.0175
585	**Henan**	Public Management and Social Organizations	−0.0156	**Henan**	Healthcare	−0.0179
586	**Tianjin**	Services to Household and other Services	−0.0164	**Henan**	Education	−0.0188
587	**Shandong**	Wholesale and Retail Trade	−0.0178	**Henan**	Government	−0.0196
588	**Henan**	Wholesale and Retail Trade	−0.0202	**Henan**	Wholesale and Retail Trade	−0.0215
589	**Liaoning**	Farming Forestry Animal Husbandry Fishery	−0.0222	**Heilongjiang**	Excavation	−0.0302

Source: China Statistical Yearbooks and author's calculations.

region includes Xingjiang, Qinghai, Gansu, Ningxia, Shaanxi, Sichuan, Chongqing, Guizhou, Yunnan and Tibet. The central region consists of Heilongjiang, Jilin, Inner Mongolia, Shanxi, Henan, Anhui, Hubei, Hunan and Jiangxi. On the basis of this division, the Theil index for each region was recalculated, along with the measure of each region's contribution to overall inequality. The result is a new picture of pay inequality across China. Figure 11.6 presents the contributions of East, West and CentralWest China to overall pay inequality from 1987 to 2012. It is evident that the average pay in Eastern regions is much higher than in the rest of China.

Figures 11.7, 11.8 and 11.9 present profiles of pay inequality in these three large geographical units. As Figure 11.7 shows, the pattern of wage differences among eastern provinces follows the same trajectory as national pay inequality, within which between-province inequality is a larger contributor than the within-province inequality. However, this pattern did not occur in the

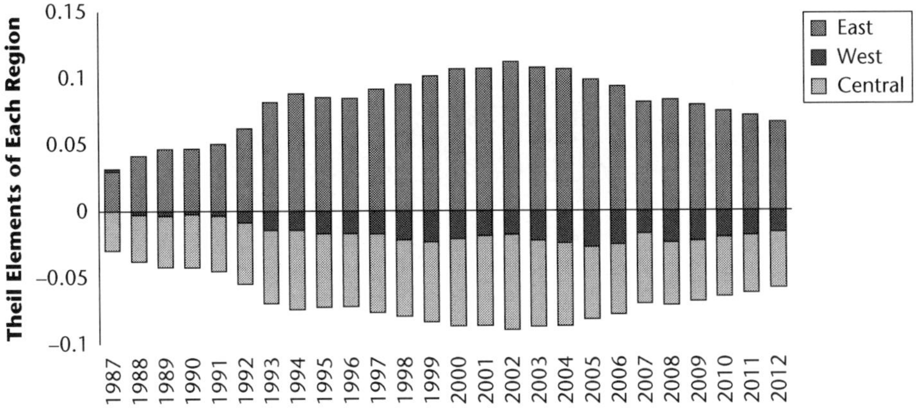

Figure 11.6 Contribution of East, West and Central to overall inequality (1987–2012)

Source: Author's calculations.

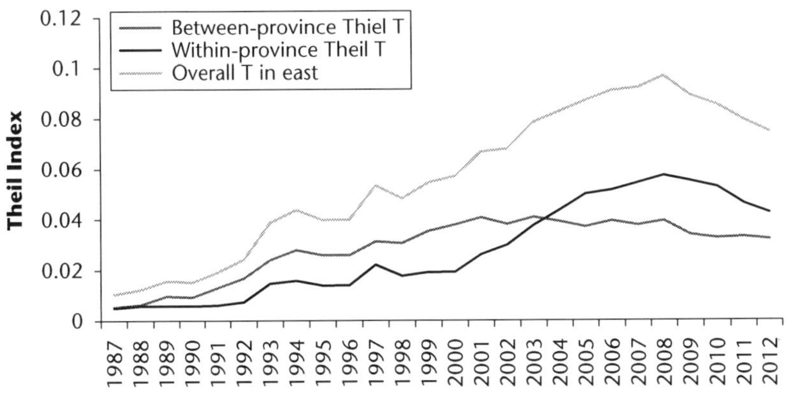

Figure 11.7 Inequality among Eastern Provinces (1987–2012)

Source: Author's calculations.

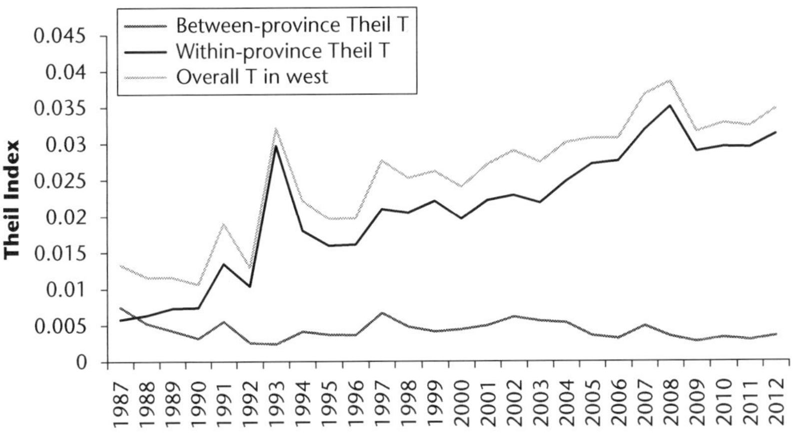

Figure 11.8 Inequality among Western Provinces (1987–2012)

Source: Author's calculations.

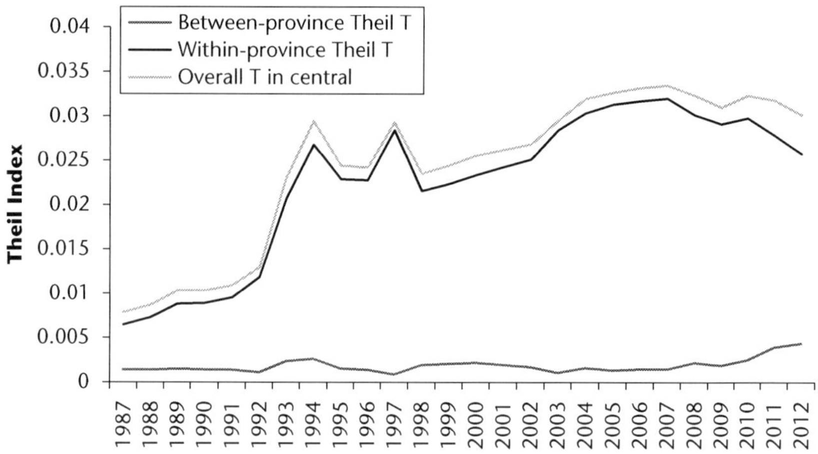

Figure 11.9 Inequality among Central Provinces (1987–2012)

Source: Author's calculations.

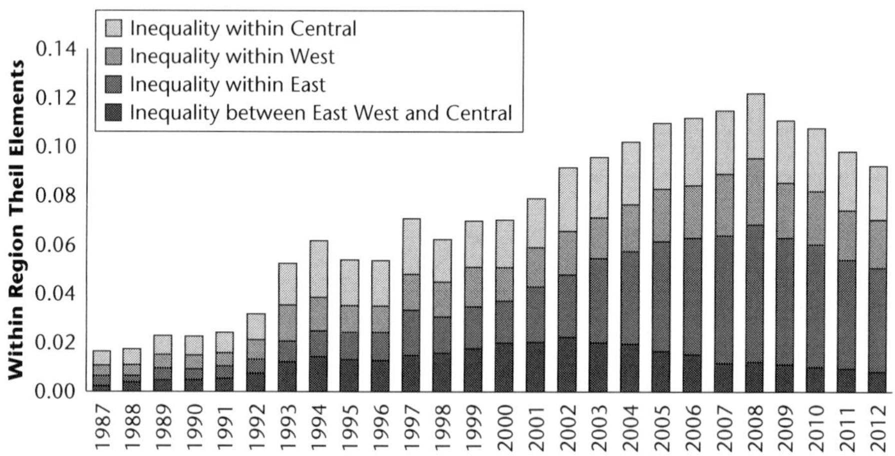

Figure 11.10 Income-weighted between-sector inequality within regions (1987–2012)

Source: Author's calculations.

western and Central regions. Within western and Central China, the variation between provinces is very small, whereas wage differences within provinces are substantial. This observation implies that there is no obvious difference in average pay between poor provinces. The poor provinces remain poor, but they are also internally unequal.

Figure 11.10 shows that variation within three different regions is getting larger, particularly in the East. This may be due to the fact the eastern region contains both the richest communities, such as Beijing and Shanghai, as well as some of the poorest provinces, such as Liaoning, where many ill-performing state-owned enterprises are concentrated. Moreover, there is a clearly narrowing gap between East, West and Central regions after 2002. This could be caused by several factors. First, rich provinces like Guangdong gradually lost their preeminent positions as the country's engine of the economy and export hub when some other eastern coastal provinces and municipal cities (e.g., Zhejiang, Jiangsu, Shanghai, and Beijing) rapidly caught up. Second,

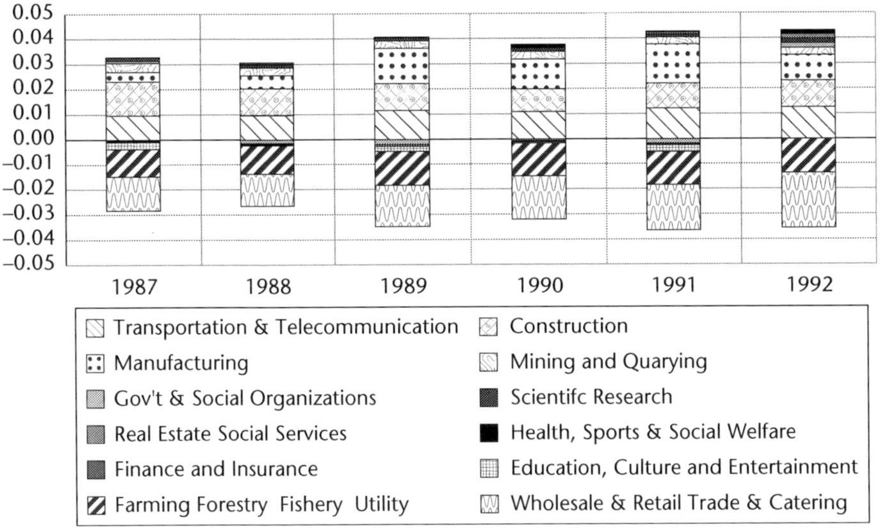

Figure 11.11 Theil elements for sectors in China, 1987–1992

Source: Author's calculations.

the government's development strategies focusing on the vast hinterland also started to take effect in terms of narrowing the between-region gap.

In 2001, the Chinese government embarked on the famous Great Western Development Campaign covering six provinces, five autonomous regions and one municipal city. This program was aimed at boosting economic development in the vast interior regions on the one hand and narrowing the gap between eastern and western regions on the other hand. In 2004, the government announced another campaign, The Rise of Central China Plan, aiming at accelerating the development of the central provinces including Shanxi, Henan, Anhui, Hubei, Hunan and Jiangxi. After a decade of development, positive effects are evident. Between-province wage inequality started to decline two years after the initiation of the Great Western Development Program; it continued declining since 2003, as displayed in Figures 11.1 and 11.10. Furthermore, a large number of labor migrants chose central and western China as their destination instead of eastern coastal regions, which greatly reduced the potential instability of previously receiving regions that have shown signs of saturation and diminished absorption capability.

Pay inequality between and within sectors

As indicated in Figure 11.1, between-sector pay inequality rose rapidly to a summit in 2008. The rapid increase of this pay inequality reflects a significant structural change of the Chinese economy during the transitional period. Figures 11.11, 11.12 and 11.13 display the contributions of each economic sector to the overall inter-sectoral inequality from 1987 to 2012. As is shown in Figure 11.11, from 1987 to 1992, the sectors, such as transportation & telecommunications, construction, manufacturing, mining and quarrying enjoyed relatively high wages and became the winners of the earlier economic reform period. In particular, the manufacturing sector saw the highest surge of average pay. The prosperity of manufacturing was largely caused by the export-led development strategy at the beginning of market-oriented economic reform.

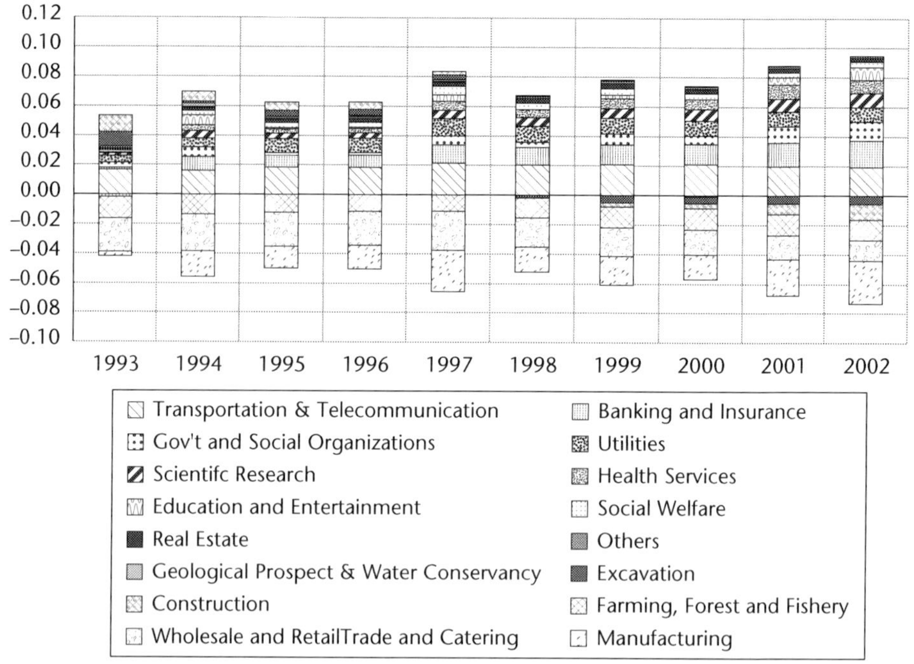

Figure 11.12 Theil elements for sectors in China, 1993–2002

Source: Author's calculations.

However, during the 1990s, the original high wage industries (i.e., manufacturing, construction, etc.) gradually lost their advantages and were soon replaced by other newly rising industries, including banking and insurance, utilities, government and social organizations, and scientific research. These new high-wage sectors began to drive up the inter-sectoral pay inequality since the early 1990s, as Figure 11.12 shows.

The rise of inter-sectoral pay inequality was a by-product of China's profound economic restructuring, which featured a financial boom and real property prosperity during the 1990s. Since the beginning of the decade, the government had promoted a series of important reforms in the financial sector, such as the launch of a stock market, the trade of government bonds on a secondary market, the mushrooming of shareholding companies, and the cleanup of massive non-performing loans of state-owned enterprises (SOEs). These reforms fundamentally restructured the country's financial system and stimulated a credit boom, which further enlarged the wage gap between the financial sector and other economic sectors. In the meantime, the urban housing system also underwent fundamental changes. The amendment of the Constitution in 1988 that allowed for land transactions eventually triggered a nationwide housing privatization. Starting from 1994, reforms including sales of public sector housing, provision of affordable housing, and the establishment of the Housing Provident Fund Scheme, took place everywhere in urban China. Until 1998, China had gradually transferred from a welfare housing system to a market housing system. These remarkable changes in the real estate sector greatly raised the average pay in the housing system. As is presented in Table 11.3, from 1993 to 2002, nine economic sectors, including banking and insurance, real estate, education, healthcare, and utilities, experienced remarkable growth in the relative wage and employment share. Among these sectors, the banking and insurance sector and the real estate sector achieved the most rapid growth in both dimensions.

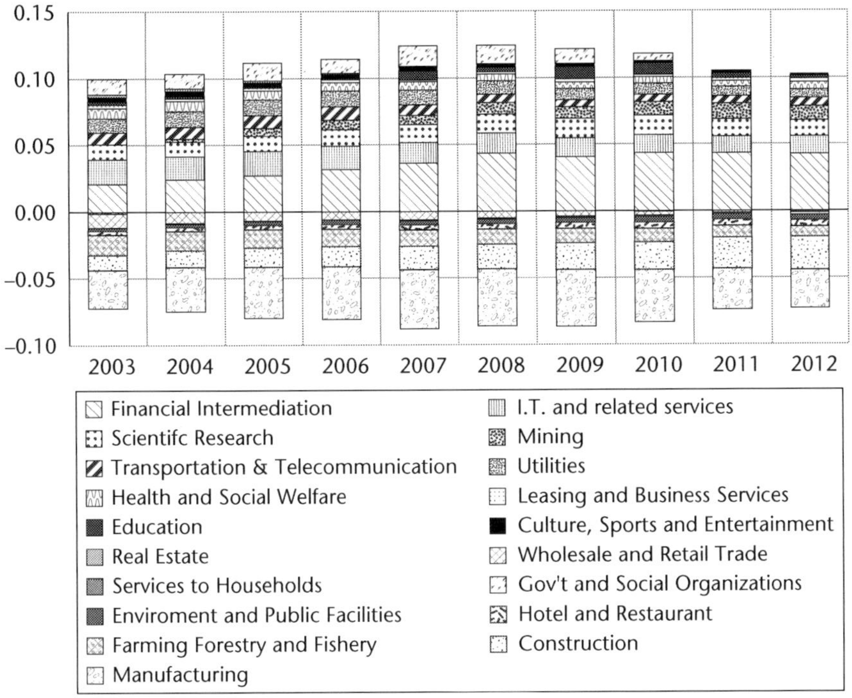

Figure 11.13 Theil elements for sectors in China, 2003–2012

Source: Author's calculations.

Table 11.3 The compositional change of relative wage and employment share of selected economic sectors (1993–2002)

	The change of relative wage	*The change of employment share*
High Wage Sector		
Banking and Insurance	141.62%	68.94%
Real Estate	127.27%	129.55%
Education and Entertainment	91.80%	76.97%
Healthcare and Sports	89.08%	62.50%
Social Welfare	89.08%	37.86%
Utilities	81.12%	73.08%
Scientific Research	70.54%	27.68%
Gov't and Social Organizations	53.85%	44.09%
Transportation & Telecommunication	6.675%	4.50%
Low Wage Sector		
Wholesale & Retail Trade and Food Services	−43.86%	−42.64%
Excavation	−34.35%	−18.30%
Manufacturing	−33.06%	−25.25%
Construction	−31.97%	−8.38%
Farming Forestry and Fishery	−37.91%	−7.73%
Geological Prospecting and Water Conservancy	−18.35%	−6.19%

Source: China Statistical Yearbooks and author's calculations.

Conversely, most low-wage sectors underwent a dramatic drop in their average pay due to the restructuring and the privatization of state-owned and urban collective-owned factories in the cities (Bannister, 2005). Sectors like manufacturing and construction, which were high-wage sectors in the previous period, had even turned into low-wage sectors, accompanied by an exodus of works. These compositional changes of wage and employment in both high-wage and low-wage sectors not only represent a deep structural change of the Chinese economy, with tertiary sectors playing an increasingly important role, but enlargements of the between-sector wage gap during the 1990s.

Entering the 2000s, the financial sectors remained the biggest winner of economic development, followed by other high wage sectors like I.T., government agencies, utilities, and scientific research. From 2003 to 2007, they all expanded rapidly with an increase in average pay. In contrast, low-wage sectors, such as agriculture and fishery, wholesale and retail trade, and hotels and restaurants, manufacturing kept worsening in terms of average pay and losing workers (see Table 11.4).

It is explicit in Figure 11.13 that the major increase of between-sector pay inequality before the 2008 global crisis was only attributable to the growth of two sectors, namely the financial intermediation and high-tech related sectors. However, the rising tendency of between-sector pay inequality has been halted since 2008. While finance still remained the top contributor to between-sector pay inequality, other high-wage sectors, such as government agencies and social organizations, and real estate, had stepped down from pinnacle.

As Table 11.5 presents, after 2008, almost half of the high-wage sectors, such as utilities, transportation and telecommunication, education, culture and entertainment, and mining, experienced wage reduction and depopulation. The real estate and government related sectors have even changed from being high-wage sectors in 2008 to being low-wage sectors in 2012. In contrast, the low-wage sectors, like construction, wholesale and retail trade, hotel and restaurants, gained momentum in both pay and employment. The diverging behaviors of high-wage sectors and low-wage sectors are mainly due to the joint forces of the global crisis and the state's 4-trillion

Table 11.4 The compositional change of relative wage and employment share of selected economic sectors (2003–2007)

	The change of relative wage	*The change of employment share*
High Wage Sector		
Financial intermediation	21.87%	−0.37%
Leasing and Business Services	12.05%	21.88%
Real Estate	11.02%	28.16%
Scientific Research	6.65%	1.02%
Gov't and Social Organizations	3.75%	0.91%
I.T. and related services	3.56%	21.21%
Education	0.37%	12.98%
Low Wage Sector		
Agriculture, Forestry and Fishing	−30.14%	−23.06%
Wholesale and Retail Trade	−21.43%	−25.53%
Hotel and Restaurants	−13.45%	−1.32%
Environment and Public Facilities	−10.45%	1.28%
Services to households	−7.32%	0.00%
Manufacturing	−0.12%	6.37%

Source: China's Annual Statistical Yearbooks and author's calculations.

Table 11.5 The compositional change of relative wage and employment share of selected economic sectors (2008–2012)

	The change of relative wage	*The change of employment share*
High wage sector		
Financial Intermediation	11.67%	22.20%
I.T. and related services	4.56%	1.46%
Health and Social Welfare	2.05%	1.38%
Utilities	−18.35%	−12.27%
Culture and Entertainment	−14.69%	−12.58%
Transportation and Telecommunication	−11.91%	−13.41%
Education	−16.07%	−16.18%
Leasing and Business Services	−6.21%	1.92%
Mining	−5.17%	−9.26%
Scientific Research	−1.66%	4.06%
Low wage sector		
Construction	63.65%	56.44%
Wholesale and Retail Trade	25.51%	10.46%
Hotels and Restaurants	13.62%	12.45%
Manufacturing	2.95%	−3.25%
Gov't and Social Organization	−20.50%	−9.82%
Real Estate	26.11%	31.76%

Source: China's Annual Statistical Yearbooks and author's calculations.

RMB stimulus package initiated right after the crisis. On one hand, the 2008 global crisis hit China's most prosperous sectors and regions extremely hard, directly leading to the withering of high flyers. On the other hand, the government promulgated its sweeping stimulus plan in order to minimize the negative impact of the global financial crisis. By providing funds for infrastructure projects and housing development, this stimulus package significantly drove up employment and pay in related economic sectors like construction. Furthermore, with government subsidies and support, low-wage sectors recovered more rapidly than high-wage sectors from the crisis. Therefore, it is observed from Table 11.5 that some low-wage sectors even enjoyed a relative wage gain and employment expansion during the downturn period. The increase of pay in low wage sectors with comparable employment growth and the withering of high-wage sectors contributed to a steady reduction in inter-sector inequality after crisis.

Conclusion

The rise in inequality within China has been, for decades, one of the most important and well-known features of Chinese development, and most observers believe that it is an ongoing phenomenon. The rapid growth of inequality has significantly challenged sustainable economic development in China in terms of intensifying social tensions, repressing productivity, exhausting and resources.

This chapter provides some new evidence of China's pay inequality from 1987 to 2012, using Theil's T statistics grouped by province and sector. As we observe, pay inequality in China started to rise in the early 1990s, and increased rapidly until it peaked in 2008, falling since then. With some provinces catching up in the early 2000s to the early leaders, the inter-province wage gap already began to narrow since 2002. However, the wage difference between sectors kept growing until 2008. Since 2009, the overall inequality has steadily decreased with both-provincial inequality and between-sector inequality showing declining tendencies. The decline of overall inequality after the crisis of 2008 could be attributed to many factors. One hypothesis is that the global financial crisis has hit China's most developed regions and sectors hardest, result in the narrowing wage gap between the rich provinces/sectors and the rest of the economy. But, is this the only force at work?

China's pay inequality is not simply a matter of economic inequality. It is a joint product of market forces and institutional forces and its changing pattern has been strongly influenced by both economic and policy factors. Economic factors, such as trade, foreign and domestic capital investments, marketization, are, without any doubt, the major forces at play. Government initiated development plans, state-dominated urbanization strategies and preferential policies for certain industries also have significant impacts on driving up and down the trend of China's pay inequality.

For instance, China's provincial pay inequality and regional disparity have been largely influenced by the country's urbanization strategies. Industrialization usually induces urbanization by generating more job opportunities that attract people to move to cities at in the early stage of economic reform. It is a long and generic process along with economic development. However, in China, this process could never occur without institutional forces. The *Hukou* household registration system is one of the main hurdle to this industrialization-induced urbanization, since it had greatly restricted the free flow of population and labor force across the country. As the government gradually lifted the *Hukou* system, the country saw its first wave of large-scale urbanization in the mid-1980s. Combining with opening-up policies that favored a handful of eastern coastal provinces and sectors, this urbanization trend had further led to the formation of several earliest megalopolises, such as Greater Beijing, Greater Shanghai and Greater Guangzhou. The rapid growth of these super-sized urban centers has, in turn, enlarged the wage gap both between regions and within regions. In 2001, the Chinese government initiated the famous Great Western Development Campaign, resulting in the establishment of megalopolises surrounding Chongqing, Chengdu, Kunming and Lanzhou. Three years later "The Rise of Central China Plan" was promulgated, triggering urbanization in central China. At the same time as boosting the economic development in vast interior regions, this type of campaign and development plan have tremendous impacts on narrowing the gap between eastern and western-central regions. Therefore, our findings indicate that both between-province wage inequality and between-region inequality began to drop after the initiation of these programs.

Sectoral inequality is also heavily affected by government's development strategies and policies. Since the late 1980s, China entered a new phase of economic reform that mainly focused on industrial restructuring and overhauling the financial sector. Thus, we observed significant changes in pay and employment among economic sectors, which completely changed the original picture of China's sectoral pay inequality. The between-sector inequality surged since the early 1990s, with the early leaders like manufacturing, construction being gradually replaced by a few newly rising high-wage sectors such as financial intermediation, real estate and IT related industries. This rising tendency ended by 2008. This was, on one hand, caused by the global crisis. On the other hand, the state's stimulus package that favored many low-wage economic sectors also contributed to narrowing the wage gap between sectors.

As Kuznets (1955) taught, economic inequality usually increases in the early stages of development. Urbanization induced by industrialization is a primary driver of inequality in developing countries in their early stage of development. As a country develops and urbanizes, inequality will grow until reaching a threshold and start to decline afterward. In this vein, we found that the urbanization initiated in the mid-1980s enormously increased China's regional disparity and led the formation of several megalopolises around eastern coastal areas. The rapid growth of the super-sized urban centers has further enlarged the wage gap both between regions and within regions. Although urbanization plays a significant role in rising inequality, accelerating mega-trend urbanization in underdeveloped regions has been repackaged by Chinese policymakers as one of main policy tools to combat inequality.

In March 2014, the government unveiled its landmark urbanization plan for 2014 to 2020, aiming at lessening inequality through better integrating migrant workers into cities and spreading urbanization out into less developed regions of the country. This new urbanization plan leads us to rethink the evolution of China's pay inequality, in particular, the recent declining tendency. Is the decline of pay inequality a temporary phenomenon that was only triggered by the global crisis? Our findings suggest that the inter-provincial pay inequality already declined a decade ago due to state-initiated development plans. Since then, the overall growing tendency of pay inequality had gradually slowed down and remained relatively stable until it finally dropped in 2009, as the global collapse compounded the inter-provincial decline. According to our findings, we argue that the declining tendency of pay inequality after the crisis is in fact a long-term outcome driven by both economic and policy factors over the past few decades. Combing various state's urbanization strategies, development plans and the deepening of economic reform, the overall pay inequality in China may continue dropping as the rest of the Chinese economy converges toward the standard of development and pay set initially in a very small part of this vast country. The declining trend of pay inequality will aid the Chinese government to maintain balanced and sustainable economic development towards a prosperous and stable society.

References

Akita, Takahiro (2003), "Decomposing Regional Income Inequality in China and Indonesia Using Two-Stage Nested Theil Decomposition Method" *Annals of Regional Science*, 37, 1, 55–77.

Bannister, Judith (2005), *Manufacturing Employment and Compensation in China*, November, Consultant's report to US Department of Labor, Bureau of Labor Statistics, online: <www.bls.gov/fls/chinareport.pdf> (January 6, 2016).

Benjamin, Dwayne, Loren Brandt, John Giles, and Sangui Wang (2005), *Income Inequality During China's Economic Transition*, Working Papers tecipa-238, Toronto: University of Toronto, Department of Economics, online: <www.economics.utoronto.ca/public/workingPapers/BBGW.pdf> (January 6, 2016).

Chen, J., et al. (2010). *The Trend of the Gini Coefficient of China*, Brooks World Poverty Institute. Working Paper 109.

Chotikapanich, Duangkamon, D. S. Rao, and Kam Ki Tang (2007), "Estimating Income Inequality in China Using Grouped Data and the Generalized Beta Distribution," *Review of Income and Wealth*, 53, 1, 127–147.

Fan, C. Cindy, and Mingjie Sun (2008), "Regional Inequality in China, 1978–2006," *Eurasian Geography and Economics*, 49, 1, 1–18.

Galbraith, James K., Sara Hsu, and Wenjie Zhang (2009), "Beijing Bubble, Beijing Bust: Inequality, Trade and Capital Inflow into China," *Journal of Current Chinese Affairs – China aktuell*, 38, 2, 3–26.

Galbraith, James K., Ludmila Krytynskaia, and Qifei Wang (2004), "The Experience of Rising Inequality in Russia and China during the Transition," *European Journal of Comparative Economics*, 1, 1, 87–106.

Gan, Li. (2013), *Income Inequality and Consumption in China*, Texas A&M University. Working Paper, online <http://international.uiowa.edu/files/international.uiowa.edu/files/file_uploads/incomeinequalityin-china.pdf> (February 10, 2016).

Gao, Qin, and Carl Riskin (2008), "Market versus Social Benefits: Explaining China's Changing Income Inequality," in: Deborah S. Davis and Feng Wang (eds), *Creating Wealth and Poverty in Postsocialist China*, Redwood, CA: Stanford University Press, 20–36.

Global Wage Report (2014/2015), *Wage and Income Inequality*, Geneva, Switzerland: International Labour Organization (December 5, 2014).

Gries, Thomas, and Margarethe Redlin (2009), "China's Provincial Disparities and the Determinants of Provincial Inequality," *Journal of Chinese Economic and Business Studies*, 7, 2, 259–281.
Gustafsson, Björn, and Shi Li (2002), "Income Inequality within and across Counties in Rural China 1988 and 1995," *Journal of Development Economics*, 69, 1, 179–204.
Gustafsson, Björn, and Shi Li (2001), "Economic Transformation and the Gender Earnings Gap in Urban China," *Journal of Population Economics*, 13, 2, 305–329.
Gustafsson, Björn, Shi Li, and Terry Sicular (2010), *Inequality and Public Policy in China*, New York, NY: Cambridge University Press.
Gustafsson, Björn, Shi Li, Terry Sicular, and Ximing Yue (2008), "Income Inequality and Spatial Differences in China, 1988, 1995 and 2002," in: Björn Gustafsson, Shi Li, and Terry Sicular (eds), *Inequality and Public Policy in China*, New York, NY: Cambridge University Press, 36–61.
Hao, Rui, and Zheng Wei (2009), "Measuring Inter-Provincial Income Inequality in China: A Sensitivity Analysis," *Journal of Chinese Economic & Business Studies*, 7, 1, 55–76.
Hao, Rui, and Zheng Wei (2010), "Fundamental Causes of Inland-Coastal Income Inequality in Post-Reform China," *Annals of Regional Science*, 45, 1, 181–206.
Kanbur, Ravi, and Xiaobo Zhang (1999), "Which Regional Inequality? The Evolution of Rural–Urban and Inland–Coastal Inequality in China from 1983 to 1995," *Journal of Comparative Economics*, 27, 4, 686–701.
Kanbur, Ravi, and Xiaobo Zhang (2005), "Fifty Years of Regional Inequality in China: A Journey through Central Planning, Reform, and Openness," *Review of Development Economics*, 9, 1, 87–106.
Khan, Azizur Rahman, and Carl Riskin (1998), "Income and Inequality in China: Composition, Distribution and Growth of Household Income, 1988 to 1995," *China Quarterly*, 154, 221–253.
Kuznets, Simon (1955), "Economic Growth and Income Inequality," *American Economic Review*, 45, 1, 1–28.
Li, Shi (2013), *Changes in Income Inequality in China in the Last Three Decades*, Working Paper, online: <http://uschinacenter.as.nyu.edu/docs/IO/32612/Li_shi_paper.pdf> (February 10, 2016).
Li, Yingru, and Y.H. Dennis Wei (2010), "The Spatial-Temporal Hierarchy of Regional Inequality of China," *Applied Geography*, 30, 3, 303–316.
Lin, George C.S. (1999), "State Policy and Spatial Restructuring in Post-Reform China, 1978–95," *International Journal of Urban and Regional Research*, 23, 4, 670–696.
Luo, Xubei, and Nong Zhu (2008), *Rising Income Inequality in China: A Race to the Top*, World Bank Policy Research Working Paper Series.
National Bureau of Statistics (NBS) (2010), (*Zhongguo Tongji Nianjian (中国统计年鉴), China Statistical Yearbook*), Beijing: Chinese Statistics Press (中国统计出版社).
National Bureau of Statistics (NBS) (2012), (*Zhongguo Tongji Nianjian* (中国统计年鉴), *China Statistical Yearbook*), Beijing: Chinese Statistics Press (中国统计出版社).
Ravallion, Martin, and Shaohua Chen (1999), "When Economic Reform is Faster than Statistical Reform: Measuring and Explaining Income Inequality in Rural China," *Oxford Bulletin of Economics and Statistics*, 61, 1, 33–56.
Shorrocks, Anthony, and Guanghua Wan (2005), "Spatial Decomposition of Inequality," *Journal of Economic Geography*, 5, 1, 59–81.
Sicular, Terry, Ximing Yue, Björn Gustafsson, and Shi Li (2007), "The Urban–Rural Income Gap and Inequality in China," *Review of Income and Wealth*, 53, 1, 93–126.
Tsui, Kai Yuen (1991), "China's Regional Inequality, 1952–1985," *Journal of Comparative Economics*, 15, 1, 1–21.
Tsui, Kai Yuen (1993), "Decomposition of China's Regional Inequalities," *Journal of Comparative Economics*, 17, 3, 600–627.
Tsui, Kai Yuen (2007), "Forces Shaping China's Interprovincial Inequality," *Review of Income and Wealth*, 53, 1, 60–92.
Wang, Z.X., et al. (2009), "A New Ordered Family of Lorenz Curves with an Application to Measuring Income Inequality and Poverty in Rural China," *China Economic Review* 20, 2, 218–235.
Wu, Ximing, and Jeffrey M. Perloff (2005), *China's Income Distribution, 1985–2001*, Institute for Research on Labor and Employment, Working Paper Series 55068, UC Berkeley: Institute of Industrial Relations.

12

Income inequality and welfare in Korea and Taiwan[1]

Eunju Chi

Introduction

Deepening inequality within countries is a worldwide trend. East Asia is no exception, where inequality has been increasing since the 1970s. Deepening inequality produces the marginalized groups and causes social conflicts that lead to division. Thus, it makes sustainable development difficult in the aspect of economy and society. Many countries face deepening inequality, but the responses to it are different. Among them, when a government actively responds to the deepening inequality by providing welfare, inequality is alleviated, and sustainable development is possible (Rueda 2008). In countries such as Korea and Taiwan, inequality began to increase as part of the process of globalization in the 1980s, and then increased further during the East Asian economic crisis in the 1990s and the global economic crisis in 2008 (Chi and Kwon 2012). Amidst the increase in inequality worldwide, the intensification of inequality in this region may be understood as simply a global trend. However, the causes and the processes of the deepening of inequality in East Asia and the countermeasures applied are significantly different from those in other regions, including Western countries.

In East Asia, Korea and Taiwan maintained equal societies before globalization. The Gini coefficients of Korea and Taiwan in 1990 were 0.2 and 0.3, respectively, and did not surpass 0.3 until 1988. This was a period in which Korea and Taiwan had high economic growth rates. Korea experienced its highest growth rates of 14.8 percent in the 1970s, and 13.2 percent in the early 1980s. Taiwan also experienced its highest growth rate of 12 percent in the 1980s. According to Kuznets, in an empirical case of the West, inequality intensifies in the early period of economic growth and then it tends to be alleviated after some degree of economic growth (Kuznets 1955). However, Korea and Taiwan have shown different trends. Both countries had the characteristic of "growth with equity;" that is, inequality did not intensify in the process of economic growth, but did so subsequent to this growth.

As a background to the intensification of income inequality, both countries experienced globalization and democratization. Globalization provided the cause that intensified the inequality. The market's destructive property that characterizes the free movement of capital (Polanyi 1944) demolished the characteristic of "growth with equity" maintained under the authoritarian regime. In the midst of an economic slowdown, inequality in both countries began to intensify. As income inequality began to increase after the 1990s, it emerged as the most pressing social and political issues. This thesis states that as income inequality deepened, "income disparity" (yag-guk-hwa) would increase in Korea (Kim 2008) and Taiwan would experience a "great U-turn" (Hung 1996). If labor flexibility due to globalization deepened income inequality as it brought increasing unemployment and a rise in the number of temporary jobs, democratization facilitated the growth of the labor force and contributed to the expansion of the welfare provision for disadvantaged victims of globalization (Ku 1997; Tang 2000). In Korea, the authoritarian military regime was replaced by a democratic competitive system in the late 1980s. Similarly, the authoritarian party in Taiwan also reformed to become a democratic and liberal government, which had free and fair elections during the 1990s. Democratized voices publicized the problems of inequality, and led to the respective governments providing solutions to these problems. That is, the two countries used their countermeasures and capabilities to determine their own income inequality levels.

Before globalization and democratization, Korea and Taiwan were characterized as "developmental states" (Johnson 1982; Wade 1990). Under the authoritarian regimes, developmental states achieved rapid economic growth, with clear goals and plans under strong state leadership. In addition, they maintained equal societies through fast economic growth and increased overall wealth (Gough 2008). However, as the economic strategy of developmental states reached its limits in the 1980s, they entered a process of seeking a new growth strategy. Taiwan turned to globalization in 1985, and Korea declared "sea-gae-wha" (globalization) in 1994. Even though globalization produced an unexpected increase in income inequality, the growth-oriented tendencies that were developed during the developmental state period facilitated strategies to sustain growth rather than distribution in the first stage. However, democratization required measures to protect the victims of wealth polarization and, as a result, measures to tackle income inequality in Korea and Taiwan were introduced. However, these were implemented in an ad hoc fashion, rather than resulting from clear goals and plans.

History

Developmental states and economic growth

In the 1960s and the 1970s, Korea and Taiwan achieved rapid economic growth by converting to export-oriented industrialization, acclaimed as the "East Asian economic miracle" (World Bank 1993). What made such economic growth possible was the role of the states. The developmental states in Korea and Taiwan had strong leadership and planned developmental strategies, which were fundamentally different to the Western economic development strategy of allowing a liberal market for economic development. While the growth of the market economy was facilitated by the role of the state, it was characterized as a "governed market," managed by the states in the developmental state model (Wade 1990).

The developmental state model, unique in East Asia and Southeast Asia, originated in Japan's economic model in the period of the Meiji restoration. Against the Western imperialist expansion, Japan promoted an economic growth strategy based on strong leadership. As such, the strategy was successful, and Japan was able to become a capitalist country on the basis of high economic growth. The successful developmental state is presented as an alternative form of capitalism to the Western model of laissez-faire capitalism (Johnson 1982). Korea and Taiwan's developmental state theory was derived from Japan's developmental model (Johnson 1987), and this model pursued economic growth through the nation's export-oriented industrialization. This was made possible based on outstanding human resources and a high saving rate. Rather than adopting policies that suppressed inflation, Korea and Taiwan implemented a pro-investment macroeconomic policy, strict controls on foreign direct investment, protection of infant industries, and an export promotion policy (Haggard and Kaufman 2008).

Korea's modernization and industrialization were promoted based on the developmental ideology of the 1960s. Before the developmental state, the Rhee Syng-man administration in the 1950s lacked the vision and concept of economic growth because it prioritized anti-Communism and unification with North Korea. During that time, the economic growth strategy was one of consumer-centered import-substitution industrialization, and relied on aid goods from the US. However, this strategy reached its limit due to a decrease in aid after a US policy change. Since then, the Park Chung-hee administration has criticized the anti-Communism stance of Rhee Syng-man, and has transformed the nation into a developmental state by prioritizing industrialization and economism. However, because the US aid policy changed during the period in which the full-fledged developmental state strategy was promoted, the government needed an independent economic growth strategy. In order to achieve this, the military government had to resolve the problem of a lack of capital and, thus, promoted policies to this effect; these included attracting foreign capital, encouraging savings, currency reform, and tax reform. In addition, the government controlled finance by nationalizing banks. Consequently, enormous amounts of foreign capital began to flow in, and economic growth began in earnest. However, the export-oriented light industry reached a limit to growth once again. Therefore, the authoritarian government in 1970 modified its developmental strategy to a heavy chemical industry, which enjoyed considerable success (Kim 2001).

Meanwhile, the Nationalistic government that withdrew to Taiwan in 1949 carried out economic reforms along with the state system modification, implementing currency reform and land reform. The original industrialization strategy was one of import-substitution industrialization, based on domestic demand. This strategy was initially successful. However, the import-substitution industry found consistent growth difficult due to the limited size of the domestic market based on the small population and the change in the US aid policy. Chiang Kai-Shek successfully modified the strategy to that of export-oriented industrialization in the 1960s. The government supported the export promotion policy through currency reforms, financial policy, a single exchange rate system, and export promotion. During the process, however, Chiang Kai-Shek still maintained partial protectionism to help major state enterprises, including intermediary goods, durable consumer goods, and transport equipment. Such growth was made possible by the intensification of the export promotion policy in the mid-1970s. During the recession in the early 1970s, developed countries regulated exports from Taiwan, a condition that was exacerbated by the oil crisis. The Taiwanese government needed a new strategy to resolve the vulnerability of its economic dependence on international markets. At that time, Taiwan was experiencing an external crisis. When Taiwan (the Republic of China) was removed from the UN in 1971, the nationalist government suffered serious damage to its legitimacy, and the number of countries maintaining diplomatic ties decreased rapidly. The KMT government needed a groundbreaking conceptual shift and power in order to maintain the growth. To achieve this, large-scale national projects were initiated in 1973, and the government attempted to promote heavy and chemical industrialization, based on shipbuilding and the expansion of social overhead capital. In addition, the government changed its private capital-based export strategy away from the existing labor-intensive industry to that of production, by adopting advanced technologies (Gold 1986).

During its development state era, Korea grew 10 percent in 1970, and maintained an annual average growth rate of around 10 percent during the 1970s. Then, despite negative growth in 1980, the economy recovered quickly. In addition, per capita income increased from USD $82 in 1961 to USD $1,647 in 1979. Taiwan experienced a serious trade deficit problem in 1975 due to the 1973–1974 oil crisis. However, it showed a growth rate of 5.4 percent in 1974, and maintained a high average annual growth rate of around 8 percent during the 1970s. Furthermore, the GNP per capita rose from USD $393 in 1970 to USD $2,391 in 1980.

Developmental welfare states and low social spending

Korea and Taiwan were successful economic models by the 1980s due to their high economic growth. Furthermore, in contrast to the Kuznets effect, Korea and Taiwan showed "growth with equity." That is, inequality did not intensify in the process of economic growth, and the developmental states were able to relieve inequality using their unique welfare models. After examining welfare states in the West and their developmental processes, Esping-Anderson suggested three types of welfare states: a liberal welfare regime; a corporatist welfare state; and a social democratic welfare state (Esping-Anderson 1990). However, welfare states in this period in Korea and Taiwan cannot be explained by Esping-Anderson's three types, which are based on the concepts of decommodification and social stratification. There are two reasons for this. First, welfare states in the West developed to resolve the problems of inequality that appeared during economic growth. However, welfare states in East Asia developed during economic growth in which inequality was not a serious concern. That is, these two have different historical origins and paths. Second, the role of the labor classes was important in the developmental stage of Western capitalism in relieving inequality. However, the development of labor classes was suppressed in Korea and Taiwan due to anti-Communism and security problems. Thus, the role of the labor classes aiming to improve labor conditions and welfare had to be minimized in Korea and Taiwan.

Therefore, a new framework was required to explain East Asia's unique welfare system that combines low inequality with growth. Above all, according to Esping-Anderson, it is essential to understand the major role of the state in order to understand the provision of the two countries' welfare schemes instead of the labor classes. While Korea and Taiwan had led economic growth in the area of social policy, the state had played a major role in introducing and expanding welfare schemes. In addition, this role of the state was not the result of pressure from the labor classes, and it did not face strong opposition from labor or capital during implementation (Kwon 1997, 479). During the developmental state period, Korea and Taiwan demanded considerable funds to foster their heavy chemical industries and, thus, could not afford welfare financially. Moreover, such a developmental welfare system was basically the welfare for economic growth, but not for redistribution (Gough 2001; Kwon 2007). The system had institutionalized conservative welfare financial management that aimed to minimize government spending on welfare for the sake of economic growth. Furthermore, it showed reciprocal characteristics for groups that supported the developmental state. Hence, only a small number of groups benefited from the social welfare program, excluding most vulnerable classes. Therefore, the "developmental welfare system" in Korea and Taiwan corresponds to the developmental strategy of "developmental states," and a welfare system in which expenditure on welfare is low and social policy is fundamentally dependent on an economic growth policy (Kwon 1997). In a similar vein, Holliday (2000, 2005) suggested the concept of "productivist welfare capitalism," while Gough (2008) used the term "productivist welfare regime" to describe developmental welfare system.

Welfare expenditure in a developmental welfare system was fundamentally different from being egalitarian. In Korea, the first social welfare framework was formed under the Park Chung-hee administration. The laws for social welfare, such as the Public Officials Pension Act and the Veterans Pension Act, were established between 1960 and 1963. However, they provided no substantive benefit due to the lack of budget. Although a national welfare pension system was introduced in 1974, it was more of a forced saving in order to supply financial resources for the heavy chemical industrialization at the time. During this process, the groups protected by the social welfare laws were the core labor manpower needed during the industrialization and the special groups needed for the management of the state, such as military servicemen, public servants, and teachers (Chung 2007, 283–289). The same was true in Taiwan. The social welfare system targets in Taiwan were the clients of the nationalist regime. Hence, military servicemen, government employees, veterans, and retired members of Parliament accounted for 75 percent of the overall welfare expense. Farmers and laborers took about only 9 percent and less than 1 percent, respectively (Ku 1997). Although it was fundamentally far from being egalitarian and was not intended to promote redistribution, Korea and Taiwan were able to realize a comparatively egalitarian society during the period of economic growth. This was due to their rapid economic growth, which increased their overall social wealth and, consequently, the substantive expense for welfare (Gough 2008). Although the government did not increase the proportion of welfare expenditure, the existing welfare expenditure increased as the state's wealth accumulated as a result of economic growth.

In fact, most members of society were excluded from the welfare benefit provided by the state, except special groups. However, the developmental welfare regime had a "residual form" of relying more on family support or livelihood protection than on the state's protection. In other words, in developmental welfare states, the role of the state as a welfare provider decreases, and the role of the family increases. In Korea and Taiwan, the family was the main provider of welfare during modernization. In this model, the man functions as the breadwinner, and the woman and children become dependents.[2] The provision of family-oriented welfare further reduces the role of the state in welfare provision. At the same time, the saving mobilization and tax policy of the developmental state became the foundation of guaranteeing a family's income, as well as the funding base for industrialization. The developmental state enforced savings in order to appropriate sufficient funds during the industrialization stage. These funds were also utilized for family education, housing funds, and old-age security. This saving mobilization, along with the low tax burden for households, contributed significantly to the formation of the developmental welfare system (Kim 2012).[3]

Thus, expenditure on welfare in Korea and Taiwan was low, which received much attention from researchers of East Asian welfare systems (Haggard and Kaufman 2008). This low rate of welfare expenditure was maintained during the rapid economic growth experienced by Korea and Taiwan. This trend continued after the end of the developmental state. Table 12.1 illustrates the public social spending after 1990 in Korea and net expenditure on social welfare after 1985 in

Table 12.1 Income inequality in Korea and Taiwan

	Public Social Spending (as of GDP)		*Net Expenditure on Social Welfare (as of GNI)*
	OECD	*Korea*	*Taiwan*
1985	17.0	n/a	1.4
1990	17.5	2.8	2.2
1995	19.3	3.2	3.1
2000	18.6	4.8	5.5
2005	19.4	6.5	3.1
2010	21.7	9.0	3.0
2012	21.6	9.6	3.6
2014	21.6	10.4	3.1

Source: Korea, OECD Social Expenditure Database (SOCX) http://www.oecd.org/social/expenditure.htm. Taiwan, Statistical Yearbook of the Republic of China 2013 (edited 2014).

Taiwan.[4] The OECD's average public social spending was 17.0 percent in 1985, 19.3 percent in 1995, 18.6 percent in 2000, and 21.6 percent in 2014. In comparison, Korea's public social spending was 2.8 percent in 1990, 3.2 percent in 1995, 4.8 percent in 2000, 9 percent in 2010, and 10.4 percent in 2014. The index in 2010 is about three times as much as that in 1990, illustrating that expenditure on welfare in Korea increased considerably. However, it is still far lower than the OECD average. For example, although public social spending in 2000, just after the financial crisis, was 4.8 percent, or 1.6 percent higher than in 1995, it was far below the OECD average of 18.6 percent. However, allowing for the difference of measurements, the discrepancy is more pronounced in Taiwan. Taiwan's net expenditure on welfare in 1985 was 1.4 percent, and increased to 3.1 percent in 1995 and 5.46 percent in 2000. However, it decreased at the beginning of the period of intensification in wealth inequality, falling to 2.92 percent in 2010, and remaining at 3.1 percent in 2014.

Globalization and the increase in income inequality

As the developmental economic strategy reached its limit after the mid-1980s, Korea and Taiwan started to seek new growth strategies. Both states chose a market liberalization strategy called "globalization," which allowed the opening of markets and the free flow of capital. In Korea, market liberalization began during the Chun Du-hwan authoritarian regime in the mid-1980s. As the export-oriented industrialization reached its limit, the military regime promoted passive enterprises via a new economic strategy so that they could compete in the global market through import liberalization and financial liberalization. The Kim Young-sam administration, which took office in 1993, officially pursued its "globalization" initiative and applied for admission to the OECD as part of its strategy. In addition, the Kim Youg-sam administration passed a new labor law to fulfill the global standard for labor, as requested by the OECD and the ILO, and to cope with the impact of globalization. The labor law in 1995 was unilaterally passed by the government, without consultation with or agreement from labor unions or the opposition party, and so had a considerable social impact at the time. The new labor law increased the flexibility of labor by introducing a layoff system, flexible working time, and a no-labor-no pay system. The financial crisis in 1997 led to enterprise restructuring and labor flexibility measures, as required by the IMF in exchange for its bailout. As a result, the number of low-wage temporary workers began to increase, which contributed to the deepening of income inequality in Korea.

In Taiwan, the economy was opening in a step-by-step manner. Taiwan's open trade and capital liquidity increased after the 1950s. However, until the 1980s, trade liberalization was passive, because it was limited to exports in order to protect the domestic market. After declaring a globalization policy in 1985, the government passed a new labor law that would meet the standards of globalization and reflect the reality of labor management. In contrast to the Korean case, Taiwan's labor law was a mechanism to mitigate income inequality by protecting the rights and interests of workers. However, the pro-labor law instead led to an increase in unemployment. After the 1980s, the expansion of foreign direct investment (FDI) as part of globalization resulted in an exodus of businesses that had lost profits under the strengthened labor law. As a result, the unemployment rate increased. Then, as wages later froze, this intensified the level of income inequality. In particular, the expansion of FDI had a negative effect on the bottom 20 percent of wage earners in Taiwan (Lue 2010, 9; Tsai and Huang 2007, 1864–1868).

Globalization in Korea and Taiwan introduced issues that they had not experienced under the developmental state. This resulted in the intensification of competition and an increase in inequality, which are regarded as characteristics of neoliberalism. As shown in Table 12.2, the Gini coefficients of Korea and Taiwan and the quintile ratios have increased since globalization.

Table 12.2 Income inequality in Korea and Taiwan

	Income inequality			
	Gini coefficient		*Quintile ratio*	
	Korea	*Taiwan*	*Korea*	*Taiwan*
1990	0.256	0.312	3.72	5.18
1992	0.245	0.312	3.52	5.24
1994	0.248	0.318	3.61	5.38
1996	0.257	0.317	3.79	5.38
1998	0.285	0.324	4.55	5.51
2000	0.266	0.326	4.05	5.55
2002	0.279	0.345	4.34	6.16
2004	0.277	0.338	4.41	6.03
2006	0.285	0.339	4.62	6.01
2008	0.294	0.341	5.75	6.05
2010	0.289	0.342	4.82	6.19
2012	0.307	0.338	5.54	6.13
2014	0.302	n/a	5.41	n/a

Source: Korea: http://kostat.go.kr/ Taiwan: http://www.cepd.gov.tw.

Korea's Gini coefficient rose from 0.256 in 1990 to 0.302 in 2014. Taiwan's Gini coefficient also increased, from 0.312 in 1990 to 0.338 in 2012. However, the change in the quintile ratio is more significant. Korea recorded an increase from 3.72 in 1990 to 4.55 in 1998, with a highest figure of 5.75 in 2008. Taiwan recorded a quintile ratio of 5.18 in 1990, 6.16 in 2002, and 6.19 in 2010. In the case of Korea and Taiwan, the similarity between the two indicators is evident. This shows a similar increase in inequality in both states, including in wages and income from the workplace and in household income (Chi and Kwon 2012).

At the same time, globalization resulted in increased unemployment. Korea and Taiwan both had achieved their goals of full employment under the developmental state. However, Korea's unemployment rate, which was around 2 percent before 1997, reached a peak of 7 percent immediately after the financial crisis in 1997. As the unemployment rate decreased again after 1999, it was maintained between 3 percent and 3.5 percent. Taiwan's unemployment rate was 1.7 percent in 1990 and 1.5 percent in 1992. It then increased to 2.6 percent in 1996 and 2.7 percent in 1998. And then, due to a serious economic downturn in exports and the decline of the economic growth rate, the unemployment rate suddenly increased to 5.2 percent in 2002. After that, it decreased to 3.9 percent in 2006, but increased again to 5.2 percent in 2010 (see Table 12.3). With regard to unemployment, Taiwan is in a more serious situation than is Korea, and it is known that the increase in unemployment is correlated with the increase in income inequality (Kenworthy and Pontusson 2005).

In sum, globalization has created social gaps in Korea and Taiwan, including income inequality and an increase in the unemployment rate. According to Rueda (2008), when facing market liberalization, states have two options. They can choose to protect victims by actively expanding social spending when economic openness leads to inequality, or they can protect businesses in order to become more competitive in the global market. In the latter case, expenditure on social welfare decreases, and income inequality intensifies. Most developing countries choose the second option, as did Korea and Taiwan, which did so in the early stage of

Table 12.3 Unemployment rate in Korea and Taiwan

	Unemployment rate	
	Korea	*Taiwan*
1990	2.4	1.7
1992	2.5	1.5
1994	2.5	1.6
1996	2.0	2.6
1998	7.0	2.7
2000	4.4	3.0
2002	3.3	5.2
2004	3.7	4.4
2006	3.5	3.9
2008	3.2	4.1
2010	3.0	5.2
2012	3.2	4.2
2014	3.5	4.0

Source: Korea: http://kostat.go.kr/ Taiwan: http://www.cepd.gov.tw.

globalization. Korea and Taiwan protected businesses and requested that workers make sacrifices for the sake of economic regeneration and development. A possible reason for this decision was the absence of a labor party in both countries. Political party activities were restricted under the authoritarian regime, and labor movements had been suppressed for security reasons. As a result, there was no labor party in the Legislature to support workers during the process of globalization in Korea and Taiwan. Consequently, the amendment of the labor law in Korea did not sufficiently secure laborers' rights and interests. In Taiwan, there were reviews of the ripple effect that an amendment of the labor law would bring about, but it was not conducted sufficiently well.

Democratization and the responses of governments

In the late 1980s, Korea and Taiwan experienced a democratic transition. A new democratic system was established, and the authoritarian military dictatorship fell. The democratic movements in Korea had been carried out by students and workers under the leadership of the opposition party. However, the process of democratization in Taiwan involved the interaction between the Kuomintang (KMT)'s liberalization policy and the demand for democratization by the Democratic Progressive Party (DPP), the opposition party. Democratization led to the following changes (Ku 2009).

First, democratization changed the power structure from vertical command relationships in the previous top-down command system to horizontal relationships of collaboration and governance. After democratization, opinions and requests were collected from the bottom and, at the same time, cooperation and the governance of various actors and states became important. Thus, the state's unilateral developmental strategy, which suggested and preceded the economic developmental strategy during the developmental state period, became impossible. Second, democratization revealed diverse social issues, such as environment, gender issues and inequality. Such a change was able to adapt to the dismantling of developmental states that had been growth oriented in the past. Furthermore, the gap between the rich and poor, the provision of welfare, and the issues of temporary workers and unemployment became important in the two new democracies.

During the process of democratization, the labor movement, which had been suppressed because of anti-Communism, erupted due to the change in the power structure in Korea and Taiwan. In the mid-1980s in Korea, labor movements began to develop as part of the pro-democracy movement, and emerged as a significant social force after democratization. The labor force organized the Korea Workers Council in 1990, and led a large-scale labor–management dispute in a relaxed social atmosphere. Subsequently, Korean workers formed the labor party and succeeded to have seats in National Assembly in 2001. At the same time, labor unions were organized in Taiwan during its democratization. The National Federation of Independent Trade Unions was organized in 1988, and the Labor Rights Association was organized in 1989. Although the labor force organized the labor party in 1989, it failed to have seats in the Legislative Yuan because it was unable to secure sufficient votes. The labor force that became highly active in Korea and Taiwan after democratization tried various ways of enhancing laborers' status, which had become disadvantageous under the developmental state's planned economy. At the same time, "the developmental welfare system" could no longer be maintained under the democratized society because welfare was provided to special groups for economic growth, and most of the disadvantaged were excluded from the provision. However, democratization features the universalization and inclusion of welfare. As a result, the democratization of Korea and Taiwan brought about the change in the developmental welfare system (Kwon 2007) and the expansion of welfare provision (Ku 2009).

Changes in the labor market

The labor market system is known to be the major determinant of wage levels, and can be largely divided into the American and English liberal market economy, the coordinated market economy of Europe, and the social market economy in northern Europe. While the liberal market economy is characterized by enterprise-specific bargaining, the coordinated market economy is characterized by industry-specific bargaining, and the social market economy is characterized by centralized bargaining (Hall and Soskice 2001; Esping-Anderson 1990). Given each case, the most important factor that creates economic inequality is related to the centralization of the labor market system (Rueda and Pontusson 2000; Wallerstein 1999). The wage gap reduces if wage bargaining takes place at a centralized level. But the wage gap increases when wage bargaining takes place in the market. In addition, when wage bargaining takes place within companies, the wage gap within these companies reduces, but a wage gap between companies increases. When wage bargaining takes place within an industry, the wage gap within that industry decreases, but a wage gap between industries increases (Wallerstein 1999). In the case of northern European countries, which have a system of Nordic corporatism, and where income inequality is low, most wage bargaining is centralized and, thus, these countries show a more equal distribution of income and wages.

Hence, under the triangular relation amongst the state, market, and labor, workers receive the most even wage when the state arbitrates for labor. The labor movement in Korea was highly active before democratization, and the most essential issue was a wage increase. However, labor was at a disadvantage in a labor market that featured a negative social atmosphere and a labor movement market type. Hence, the labor–management relations before democratization were of the market type, and wages were decided unilaterally by employers within each firm. Along with the growth of the labor force, the mechanism of determining wages changed around 1987. Although it generally featured the market type, the mechanism by which wages or working conditions were decided unilaterally by employers under the state of suppression of autonomous union movement changed, and began to reflect the opinions of workers. The Kim Young-sam administration in the 1990s guaranteed the neutrality of labor–management relations and legitimate labor–management activities. However, when the government realized that a wage increase could threaten its export-oriented growth model, it switched its attitude to determining wages through agreement between the representatives of labor and management (Park 2005, 235). As a result, after 1987, as the labor movement developed and large companies started to recognize trade unions, major working conditions began to be determined by collective bargaining between labor and management. However, such collective bargaining mostly took place within companies, and coordination between bargaining units was weak. Furthermore, as the ability of companies to make payments and the power relations between labor and management came to play important roles in the process of wage determination, large wage gaps between companies occurred. As this tendency expanded further after the financial crisis in 1997, wage gaps began to increase even between identical industries with similar working conditions and between companies of a similar size (Jung 2006, 126–127). The 1997 financial crisis aggravated the situation.

The labor–management relations in Taiwan featured the market type. However, the wage gap by firm size was smaller than that in Korea, and the gap did not increase much after the 1990s. Taiwan's social movements were completely suppressed for a long time under martial law. In addition, the small and medium-sized enterprise-oriented economic structure made it difficult for a labor class to form. However, the Taiwan Confederation of Trade Unions was formed by workers during democratization, and the number of labor disputes increased significantly. Moreover, the unionization rate increased; the industrial unionization rate reached 20.9 percent in 2000, and the craft unionization rate reached 49.2 percent in the same year. Still, unions did not grow into a force that could impact the labor market in terms of deciding labor conditions. The reasons are as follows. First, the revision of the labor law that influenced labor conditions was led mainly by the KMT after democratization. Taiwan's labor law was enacted in 1920, and did not practically reflect labor conditions. The KMT led the revision of the labor law for the necessity of globalization and for the welfare of workers (Lee 2007, 16). Second, the labor force in Taiwan was still vulnerable. Taiwan's industrial union was actually operated as the craft union. Most wage negotiations incorporated just the union representative's proposal to the employers. Moreover, those that practically concluded a collective agreement were few because the features of collective agreements were very weak. Third, and most importantly, the purpose of the labor movement in Taiwan was not to increase wages. After democratization, an average of 1,700 strikes occurred annually between 1987 and 1991 in Taiwan, but they were mostly related to individual labor–management relations, such as dismissal, unfair dismissal, delayed payment of wages, and accident compensation (Chu 1996, 501–504). Lastly, an occupation-specific labor union, formed in Taiwan, functioned as a gateway for workers to register for health insurance rather than as a labor union for collective bargaining. With regard to collective bargaining, agreements to improve wages and working conditions were few. Accordingly, Taiwan's labor–management relations are still close to being a market type, in which labor unions and collective bargaining do not have a significant effect in determining working conditions (Jung 2006, 127–128). However, industry-specific labor unions and globalization further intensified the dissimilarities between various industrial sectors and between company-specific divisions surrounding interests (Lue 2010).

Although the labor force grew considerably, the labor markets after democratization in Korea and Taiwan did not show a noticeable change. Korea and Taiwan could not escape the basic market-type labor market. In addition, wage decisions took place within individual firms in Korea. As a result, Korea witnessed its greatest overall inequality and the biggest wage gaps by company size (Jung 2006, 126–127). The market-type labor market in Taiwan before and after democratization meant that the labor force was vulnerable and fragmented compared to that in

Korea. Under such a structure, group action for wage improvement was impossible, and income inequality in Taiwan could not be relieved via the labor market. In Korea, there was an attempt to implement a Northern European social market economy, featuring centralized bargaining. Due to the financial crisis in 1997, Korea had to secure the restructuring of firms and labor flexibility in order to receive an IMF bailout program. For this, the Kim Dae-jung administration organized the Korea Tripartite Commission, in which a labor representative, firm representative, Minister of Labor, Minister of Finance, and party representative participated. However, the government, firm, and party representatives all took a hostile position against labor and, thus, labor left the Commission. As a result, the labor force, while its request was not accepted, had to accept the restructuring of firms and labor flexibility that were suggested by the government (Park 2005, 241). In Taiwan, under the market-type labor market structure, workers' welfare improved considerably during democratization. The government and political party were responsive to workers' demands, and labor conditions and welfare were reflected considerably in the process of democratization. However, a practical benefit to labor was not guaranteed with the reason that the labor market was fragmented. The minimum wage in Taiwan had stagnated between 1997 and 2006, during which income inequality intensified. In addition, real wages were stagnant. Hence, the labor market structures in Korea and Taiwan after democratization were still disadvantageous to labor.

Expansion of welfare provision

During the developmental state periods, the welfare regimes in Korea and Taiwan were weak. Welfare regimes remained subsidiary to economic and industrial development policies. Until the 1980s, Korean and Taiwanese social welfare focused on pensions and health care schemes for specific groups. Those who were excluded from this protection had no choice but to rely on family support or livelihood protection. The state's role in terms of welfare provision during the developmental state was vulnerable, which was well illustrated in the low government expenditure and lack of social programs. When the change to a horizontal power structure occurred and the welfare issue became important after democratization, the demand for the government's role and for expenditure on welfare began to increase. Moreover, the intensification of labor flexibility and the increase in unemployment caused by the economic crisis in East Asia produced the disadvantaged and, thus, the state emphasized protecting these groups. However, the development of social welfare programs in Korea and Taiwan were adapted mainly in response to immediate political and economic conditions, rather than as part of a coherent plan (Peng and Wong 2008, 200–208). This is well reflected in the introductory phases of the Korean and Taiwanese national health insurance systems and pension systems.

In introducing comprehensive national health insurance (NHI) systems, both countries extended the health care system to cover most people, and then integrated diverse social insurance schemes that had been present previously. The targets of health insurance during the developmental state were also restricted. In Korea, the first health insurance scheme introduced in 1974 was mostly for the recipients of livelihood programs, although the scope of the target expanded in 1977 to include workers from businesses with more than 500 people. The targets (i.e., major companies with more than 500 workers) were large companies in the heavy chemical industry based on the industrial policy of the developmental state. Then, health insurance was extended further in 1979 to include civil servants and private school teachers. There was demand in Korea to expand the provision of welfare during the process of democratization in 1986, and the Chun Doo-whan administration promised to expand the health insurance to cover rural areas in 1988. As a result, the first national health insurance was carried out in 1989. It was only after the opposition party seized power that health insurance was effectively expanded and applied. In 2000, the Kim Dae-jung administration integrated and applied the health insurance organizations that were previously fragmented. Finally, most of all citizens received health insurance and medical social security via medical care assistance.

Taiwan also introduced its national health insurance in 1995 which targeted all citizens after the democratic transition. After its introduction, about 97 percent of the population received medical treatment and health care equally. The important change was that the various types of insurance were integrated into a single system. In contrast to Korea, Taiwan provided health care insurance in the 1950s, with insurance for workers in 1950, and for civil servants in 1958. It was then extended as farmers' health insurance in 1985, and as a low-income household insurance in 1990. The reason for providing the insurance to small-income earners and farmers, along with special groups, during the developmental state period was the socialistic article specified in the Constitution of the Republic of China. However, most of the population, except special groups, small-income earners, and farmers, were excluded from the insurance. As a result of the demands of the DPP and of citizens after democratic transition, Taiwan introduced a universal health system in 1995, and increased insurance premiums to meet the increased demand. However, the fact that the national health insurance was operated by the state brought considerable controversy. In particular, the DPP was concerned that the system would cause moral laxity in recipients, and that it would further strengthen the government's power. Hence, a second-generation national health system was introduced in 2002. As the DPP came to power, a turning point seemed to have been reached; however, the basic form of the national health system was retained (Lue 2010, 30–32; Wong 2003).

Another axis of social security is the pension reform. Similar to the health care insurance, Korea's pension concentrated mainly on protecting the benefits of special groups under the developmental state. The civil servant pension scheme, introduced in 1960, is the oldest public pension scheme. In 1963, the military personnel pension was separated from the civil servant pension scheme. Then, the private school teacher pension scheme was introduced in 1973. The support for civil servants, soldiers, and teachers led them to being loyal to the developmental state. Although the National Pension Act, which targeted the whole population, was prepared in 1973, it was delayed indefinitely because of the economic recession caused by the first-world oil shock. However, due to the demand for democracy in 1986, the Chun Doo-whan administration promised to operate a national pension scheme, and did so effectively in 1988, just after the democratic transition. The national pension scheme is the most important public pension scheme, as well as the most significant social security program in Korea. However, numerous vulnerable groups are still excluded, although comprehensive coverage is possible through the national pension scheme by law.

In Korea, the national pension scheme that began just after democratization targeted workshops with more than 10 workers. In 1992, it expanded its coverage to workshops with more than five people, and then further included farmers, fishermen, and the self-employed in rural areas in 1995. The expanded policy struggled for a while because of the economic crisis in 1997, but it was expanded further to include the self-employed in urban areas in April 1999 (Chung 2007). One of the major changes related to the welfare policies is that political parties began to use welfare issues in election campaigns. In particular, as the number of temporary workers and low-income workers increased after the financial crisis in 1997, the provision of a social safety net became an important issue. Each party provided welfare issues competitively. During the presidential election in 2000, the National Congress for New Politics and the United Liberal Democrats, the opposition parties, suggested unifying the administration of the pension scheme and increasing the welfare budget. On the other hand, the Grand National Party, the ruling party, suggested expanding the coverage of existing insurance schemes and the substantiality of providing effective service. However, the pledge by the ruling party did not make a practical difference in terms of the welfare policy. In addition, a bigger problem was that, although securing the welfare budget was most urgent, political parties were not suggesting any specific plans to achieve this. Practically, a detailed proposal for pension reform does not exist in Korea, and there is no direction for pension reform. The ruling party is utilizing the welfare policy to maximize political votes.

While Korea's social insurance, which was fragmented based on the type of benefit, such as medical insurance, pension insurance, and unemployment insurance, was being independently introduced, Taiwan's insurance developed mainly in terms of jobs and their classifications. Taiwan's labor insurance is operated by securing medical treatment and pension, death, and disability insurance for laborers and the fund is managed in an integrated way. Just as in Korea, the most important part of Taiwan's social insurance under the developmental state was the government employee insurance that, until the late 1970s, targeted workers, including soldiers, civil servants, and teachers. The DPP strongly criticized the undeveloped pension scheme during the process of democratization. The DPP argued that the systematized pension scheme that targeted all citizens and the allowance programs that targeted the disadvantaged elderly must be implemented during the transition period. In particular, the area pointed out as being the most important during the process of pension reform was guaranteeing the economic security of the elderly. The most undeveloped part of Taiwan's social insurance system was the support for the elderly, most of whom needed private savings or family support after their retirement. The ruling Nationalist Party was very responsive to the DPP's demand, implementing the elderly living allowance for low-income families, welfare subsidies for elderly farmers, subsidies for the elderly, and living allowances for veterans. Moreover, the KMT integrated the fragmented pension schemes in 1994, and organized a task force for better systematic operation. However, it failed in its legalization due to the election failure in 2001. The DPP that won the election in 2000 then reorganized the social policies, although these were no more extensive or systematic than those of the KMT. The DPP's social policies focused more on providing a welfare service (e.g., a monthly living allowance for people older than 62, free medical care for children under three years old, interest rates as low as 3 percent for first-time home buyers, etc.) than on the institutionalization of a social security system. Along with the labor insurance and the civil servant insurance targeting soldiers, civil servants, and teachers, the private enterprise insurance currently provides retirement benefits as well (Lue 2010).

Consequently, in terms of health insurance and pension insurance in Korea and Taiwan, there was a demand to expand the provision of welfare during the process of democratic transition, which occurred as the government and the ruling party accommodated it. Hence, the democratization, which represented structural change, created the demand for welfare, and this resulted in the expanded provision of welfare. However, after democratization, rather than the role of labor, the role of the state was still important, as was that of the ruling party. Although the fact that the universal health care scheme was implemented in these two cases was a considerable achievement, this was the result of the ruling party's political maneuvering, rather than of accommodating the demands from the bottom. In Korea, the expansion of universal health security in 1989 was a result of a high economic growth rate in the late 1980s and the military regime's political calculation for securing political legitimacy. The case of Taiwan is similar to that of Korea. Here, the expansion of health security was promoted by the conservative KMT, whose social base became weak after democratization, and sought to build support through people-friendly health care policies.

After a considerable progress of democratization, the expansion of welfare provision became the foundation for gaining votes in party competition. Each party pledged to provide greater welfare in order to attract voters. Although the expansion of various types of welfare during this process was a positive aspect, the absence of clear goals and plans for welfare provision led them to be integrated. In addition, because parties' pledges in Korea and Taiwan were made without sufficient consideration of available funds, policies' sustainability was being questioned, even if a particular policy was selected. Furthermore, the support for special groups organized during the developmental state period, such as civil servants, soldiers, and teachers, continued, and the social security they receive is a burden on the overall welfare budget. This has caused problems in terms of support for other groups and fairness, and is a task that Korea and Taiwan must resolve.

Conclusion

When a government actively responds to the crippling effects of globalization, income inequality can be alleviated (Garrett 1998; Katzenstein 1985; Rodrik 1998). Complementing certain parts of inequality that occur as a result of market conditions is the role of the welfare state. If the market is a mechanism that creates inequality, the welfare state is the institutional and political realization of "politics against markets" (Kenworthy and Pontusson 2005; Moene and Wallerstein 2001, 2003; Rueda and Pontusson 2000; Wallerstein 1999). Korea and Taiwan chose to open their markets when the developmental state's economic growth strategy reached a limit, and this led to an intensification of income inequality that they had not experienced during economic growth. Although there was an attempt to protect the disadvantaged by popularizing welfare in the late period of the developmental state, Korea and Taiwan could not overcome the fundamental limitations of the developmental state. Democratization has highlighted income inequality as a social issue, and has laid a new milestone in resolving this issue by making the governance of various groups possible. However, the labor force that grew during the process of democratization did not play an important role in revising the labor laws and improving the labor market, and is still at a disadvantage in terms of wage negotiations. Although Korea and Taiwan's welfare provision, including health and pension insurance, is increasing under the social structure in which the state and the ruling party are still superior, the scale of support is still limited. Furthermore, the support for special groups that have been protected since the developmental state period and the relative gap have remained intact.

Notes

1 This research was supported by the National Research Foundation of Korea funded by the Korean government (NRF-2017S1A3A2066657).

2 This family-centered welfare system in East Asia is interpreted as the result of the influence of Confucianism, which is deeply rooted in society. As the "Confucian Welfare State" in East Asia actively draws the family into the welfare state, it is regarded as a cause that consequently introduced conservative corporatism without the participation of laborers, charity without church involvement, equality without solidarity, and laissez-faire without liberalism (Peng and Wong 2008; Jones 1990).

3 Kim (2012) further argued that this mobilization of savings in family units strengthened the importance of familism in terms of welfare provision.

4 Social Expenditure Database (SOCX) does not provide Taiwan index of public social spending. For a comparison, we use Net Expenditure on Social Welfare provided by Statistical Yearbook of the Republic of China. Net expenditure for social welfare covered social insurance, social relief, benefit service, nationwide employment service, medical care and community development, and environmental protection. But, since 1990, it excluded expenditure on community development, environmental protection and expenditures for pension and survivors' benefits.

References

Chi, Eunju and Hyeok Yong Kwon. (2012) "Unequal New Democracies in East Asia: Rising Inequality and Government Responses in South Korea and Taiwan." *Asian Survey* 52(5): 900–923.

Chu, Yin-wah (1996) "Democracy and Organized Labor in Taiwan." *Asian Survey* 36(5): 495–510.
Chung, MooKwon. (2007) "The Historical Formation of the Developmental Production and Welfare Regimes in Korea." *Korea Social Policy Review* 14(1): 256–307. [Korean]
Esping-Anderson, Gøsta. (1990) *The Three Worlds of Welfare Capitalism*. Princeton: Princeton University Press.
Garrett, Geoffrey. (1998) *Partisan Politics in Global Economy*. Cambridge: Cambridge University Press.
Gold, Thomas B. (1986) *State and Society in the Taiwan Miracle*. New York, NY: M.E. Sharpe.
Gough, Ian. (2001) "Globalization and Regional Welfare Regimes: The East Asian Case." *Global Social Policy* 1: 163–189.
Gough, Ian. (2008) "East Asia: The Limits of Productivist Regimes." In *Insecurity and Welfare Regimes in Asia, Africa, and Latin America: Social Policy in Development Context*, edited by Ian Gough, Geof Wood et al., 169–201. Cambridge: Cambridge University Press.
Haggard, Stephan and Robert Kaufman. (2008) *Development, Democracy, and Welfare States*. Princeton: Princeton University Press.
Hall, Peter A. and David Soskice. (2001) "An Introduction to Varieties of Capitalism." In *Varieties of Capitalism: The Institutional Foundations of Comparative Advantage*, edited by Peter A. Hall and David Soskice, 1–68. New York, NY: Oxford University Press.
Holliday, Ian. (2000) "Productivist Welfare Capitalism: Social Policy in East Asia." *Political Studies* 48(4): 706–723.
Holliday, Ian. (2005) "East Asian Social Policy in the Wake of the Financial Crisis: Farewell to Productivism?" *Policy and Politics* 33(1): 145–163.
Hung, Rundy. (1996) "The Great U-Turn in Taiwan." *Journal of Contemporary Asia* 26(2): 151–163.
Johnson, Chalmers. (1982) *MITI and the Japanese Miracle*. Stanford: Stanford University Press.
Johnson, Chalmers. (1987) "Political Institutions and Economic Performance: The Government–Business Relations in Japan, South Korea, and Taiwan." In *The Political Economy of the New Asian Industrialism*, edited by Fredric Deyo, 136–164. Ithaca: Cornell University Press.
Jones, Catherine. (1990) "Hong Kong, Singapore, South Korea, and Taiwan: Oikonomic Welfare States." *Government and Opposition* 25(4): 447–462.
Jung, EeHwan. (2006) "Industrial Relations and Wage Inequalities in East Asia." *Korean Journal of Sociology* 40(2): 118–48. [Korean]
Katzenstein, Peter. (1985) *Small States in World Market*. Cornell: Cornell University Press.
Kenworthy, Lane and Jonas Pontusson. (2005) "Rising Inequality and the Politics of Redistribution in Affluent Countries." *Perspectives on Politics* 3(3): 449–472.
Kim, Dokyun. (2012) "Mobilization through Saving and the Emergence of Developmental Welfare Regime: A Comparison of South Korea and Japan." *Korea Social Policy Review* 19(1): 163–198. [Korean]
Kim, Il Young. (2001) "Origin, Formation, Development, and Prospect of Developmental State in Korea." *Journal of Korean Political and Diplomatic History*, 23(1): 87–126. [Korean]
Kim, Mun Cho. (2008) *Class Disparity in Korea*. Paju: Gipmondang. [Korean]
Ku, Yeun Wen. (1997) *Welfare Capitalism in Taiwan*. New York, NY: Palgrave Macmillan.
Ku, Yeun Wen. (2009) "Comparative Welfare Policy Instrument in East Asia." In *Changing Governance and Public Policy in East Asia*, edited by Ka Ho Mok and Ray Forrest, 140–158. New York, NY: Routledge.
Kuznets, Simon. (1955) "Economic Growth and Income Inequality." *American Economic Review*, 83(2): 436–439.
Kwon, Huck-ju. (1997) "Beyond European Welfare Regimes; Comparative Perspectives on East Asian Welfare Systems." *Journal of Social Policy* 26: 467–484.
Kwon, Huck-ju. (2007) "Transforming the Developmental Welfare States in East Asia." DESA Working Paper No. 4. www.un.org/esa/desa/papers/2007/wp40_(2007)pdf.
Lee, Joseph S. (2007) "Labor Market Flexibility and Employment: An Overview." In *The Labor Market and Economic Development of Taiwan*, edited by Joseph S. Lee, 3–35. Northampton, MA: Edward Elgar.
Lue, Jen-Der. (2010) "Globalization and the Internal Segregation of Labor/Welfare regimes: The Analysis of Taiwan and China's Experience," Paper presented at the International Conference on 'Inequality' Organized by Department of Economics, Korea University, 28–29, May 2010, Seoul, Korea.
Moene, Karl Ove and Michael Wallerstein. (2001) "Inequality, Social Insurance, and Redistribution." *American Political Science Review* 95(4): 859–874.
Moene, Karl Ove and Michael Wallerstein. (2003) "Earnings Inequality and Welfare Spending: A Disaggregated Analysis." *World Politics* 55(4): 485–516.

Park, Chan Pyo. (2005) "Interest Representation Function in the National Assembly without Labor Party." *The Journal of Asiatic Studies* 48: 209–251. [Korean]

Peng, Ito and Joseph Wong. (2008) "Institutions and Institutional Purpose: Continuity and Change in East Asian Social Policy." *Politics & Society* 36(1): 61–88.

Polanyi, Karl. (1944) *The Great Transformation: the Political and Economic Origins of Our Time*. New York, NY: Amereon House.

Rodrik, Dani. (1998) "Why Do More Open Economies have Bigger Governments." *Journal of Political Economy* 106(5): 997–1032.

Rueda, David. (2008) "Left Government, Policy, and Corporatism: Explaining the Influence of Partisanship on Inequality." *World Politics* 60(2): 349–389.

Rueda, David and Jonas Pontusson. (2000) "Wage Inequality and Varieties of Capitalism." *World Politics* 5(3): 350–383.

Tang, Kong-leung. (2000) *Social Welfare Development in East Asia*. Basingstoke: Palgrave Macmillan.

Tsai, Pan-Long and Chao-His Huang. (2007) "Openness, Growth and Poverty: the Case of Taiwan." *World Development* 35(11): 1858–1872.

Wade, Robert. (1990) *Governing the Market: Economic Theory and Role of Government in East Asian Industrialization*. Princeton: Princeton University Press.

Wallerstein, Michael. (1999) "Wage-Setting Institutions and Pay Inequality in Advanced Industrial Societies." *American Journal of Political Science* 43(3): 649–80.

Wong, Joseph. (2003) "Resisting Reform: The Politics of Health Car in Democratizing Taiwan." *American Asian Review* 21(1): 57–90.

World Bank. (1993) *The East Asian Economic Miracle" Economic Growth and Public Policy*. New York, NY: Oxford University Press.

13

Infrastructure gap in South Asia: inequality of access to infrastructure services

Dan Biller, Luis Andrés and Matías Herrera Dappe

Introduction

The South Asia Region (SAR) is home to the largest pool of individuals living under the poverty line, coupled with some of the fastest demographic growth rates of any region in the world. Between 1990 and 2005, the number of people living on less than $1.25 a day in South Asia decreased by only 18 percent, while the population grew by 42 percent.[1] At the same time, over the past two decades, structural change has been slow, *with urbanization (around 31 percent) lower than in any other developing region*, despite economic growth rates that have exceeded most other regions. While the burst of economic growth has generated additional revenue and increased fiscal space to shift more funds to infrastructure, it has also put immense pressure on demands for infrastructure.

The challenges on the infrastructure front for SAR are monumental. For the past two decades, SAR and East Asia and the Pacific (EAP) have enjoyed similar growth rates, yet SAR lags significantly behind both EAP and Latin America and the Caribbean (LAC) when it comes to access to infrastructure services – with certain areas featuring access rates comparable only to sub-Saharan Africa (SSA). For example, Afghanistan, Nepal, and Bangladesh have access rates that resemble the average sub-Saharan country, while Sri Lanka and the Maldives are more similar to Latin American countries in terms of average rates of infrastructure services. At the same time, SAR features significant heterogeneities within and among countries in terms of access to infrastructure services. Districts with very low access to infrastructure can be found in rich Indian states and vice versa: some districts in poor Indian states fare better in terms of infrastructure than districts in rich states. Finally, heterogeneity across sectors is also found within districts. For example, high access rates to electricity coexist in the same district with low access rates to sanitation or other infrastructure services.

The importance of access to basic infrastructure services like clean water, adequate sanitation, and electricity to welfare and the quality of life is well established. Clean water and power services bring votes in democratic political processes, and individuals usually display high willingness to pay (WTP) as households benefit directly. These services are also associated with key health and environmental externalities. As a direct benefit to neighbors, individuals may have a lower WTP for adequate sanitation in their households, but the health and environmental externalities associated with it are even more important. There is a growing literature associating phone access to poverty reduction, and the rapid expansion of mobile access – largely driven by the private sector – reflects the fact that agglomeration effects and connectivity are important for the poor. In addition, cooking gas (LPG) as a source of fuel plays a vital role in diminishing indoor air pollution. Moreover, differences in access to infrastructure services could be a bottleneck not only in improving the well-being of current family members but also in breaking the inter-generational transmission of poverty.

It is commonly asserted that the poor have less access to infrastructure than the rich, just as in the case of private assets. In effect, a non-regressive access to infrastructure services would mean no correlation between actual access and different poverty related measures (such as number of households below poverty lines, and certain income and consumption levels). Whereas this may be desirable theoretically – especially for infrastructures with high public good characteristics – it is virtually impossible to achieve anywhere in the world. For example, location matters, and the choice between infrastructure access to all, regardless of where individual households are located, and quality access to where most households are located, is a real policy challenge illustrated in its extreme case. While literature on the topic is scant, it is clear that not all countries fare the same in their infrastructure service provision, and South Asian countries are not different. Yet, are there countries in South Asia that fare better with respect to providing infrastructure access to their poor? Are there infrastructure sectors that tend to be more regressive than others? Does geography matter? What is happening with access to infrastructure services in South Asian households? These are a few of the questions that we explore.

In this chapter we present three different views about the distribution of infrastructure services for selected countries in South Asia.[2] The chapter is organized as follows. We begin with the standard view of access to infrastructure services, a conceptual framework, and the relation between access deficit and the large infrastructure gap in South Asia. We then discuss inequality of access to infrastructure services across South Asia's spaces – namely physical space, poverty space, and income space. Next, we turn to inequality of access across time, focusing on the impact of the infrastructure gap across South Asian generations. Finally, we present policy suggestions on how to target the poor, while focusing on correcting market failures connected to infrastructure, and underscoring the importance of avoiding rent-seeking opportunities.[3]

Our conclusion is that while the regressivity of infrastructure services is clearly present in South Asia, the story that emerges is heterogeneous and complex. Countries with higher per capita income (like the Maldives and Sri Lanka) enjoy better access to infrastructure services both spatially and income wise, even though conflict areas are clearly worse off. Among sectors in SAR countries, some, such as water, tend to be more equally distributed than others, such as sanitation, energy, and telecommunications – with the widespread use of firewood for cooking, especially among the poor, somewhat surprising. Moreover, within SAR countries, some states and districts have better access to infrastructure than others. There is no simple explanation for these inequalities, although certainly geography matters, some household characteristics (like living in a rural area with a head of household who lacks education) matter, and policy intent matters. If a poorer country or a poorer state can have better access to a given infrastructure service than a richer country or a richer state, then there is hope that policy makers can adopt measures that will improve access in a manner that prosperity is more widely shared.

Access to infrastructure services and the infrastructure gap in South Asia

Consistent estimates of investment requirements across SAR are a prerequisite for developing a sound menu of policy and financial options to close the infrastructure gap.

Most governments in SAR have some estimates of the investments required to reach certain targets such as 24/7 electricity supply and the Millennium Development Goals in water and sanitation. However, those estimates are not consistent across the region. For that reason, Andres et al. (2013) have developed different methodologies for different sectors to have consistent estimates of physical investment needs and their costs across the region.

SAR needs to invest an estimated US $1.7 trillion to US $2.5 trillion in infrastructure until 2020.[4] These amounts are equivalent to US $1.4 trillion to US $2.1 trillion at 2010 prices. Going forward, a mix of investing in infrastructure stock and implementing supportive reforms will allow SAR to close its infrastructure gap. In GDP terms, if investments are spread evenly over the years until 2020, SAR needs to invest between 6.6 and 9.9 percent of 2010 GDP per year – an increase of up to 3 percentage points compared with the 6.9 percent of GDP invested in infrastructure by SAR countries in 2009.[5]

Regional benchmarking

SAR has a large infrastructure gap compared with other regions. Its access to infrastructure services closely resembles SSA, even though its economic growth rate is second only to EAP (Table 13.1).

- **Electricity access:** In SAR, only 71 percent of the population enjoys the benefits of electricity access, ahead of SSA at 35 percent, but way behind the rest of the regions at above 90 percent. According to businesses in South Asia, infrastructure is a major or severe hindrance to their growth, and electricity is the largest problem.
- **Improved sanitation access:** In this category, SAR (39 percent) is at the bottom, along with SSA (30 percent) – rates that are close to half the world average of 64 percent population access. Open defecation seems to be one of the most salient issues facing SAR, with 700 million people (i.e., 43 percent of the population) relying on it in 2010. This ranks South Asia as the region with the highest incidence of open defecation in the world.
- **Improved water access:** This is the only indicator where South Asia is about even with the rest of the world and EAP, averaging 90 percent population access. Yet the quality and quantity of improved water may be in question. Most of the access to water is through public stands; only 25 percent of the population has access to piped water, and 24/7 water supply is a rare exception in South Asian cities.
- **Telecom access:** Communication among people who are not in close proximity is inefficient. In terms of telecom access, SAR and SSA rank at the bottom (72 and 54 fixed and mobile lines per 100 people, respectively) with less than half the access found in ECA and LAC (157 and 125). This situation becomes even more dramatic given SAR's low level of urbanization.
- **Transport access:** This other form of connectivity is also poor, and is a problem that troubles much of the developing world. Using total road network per 1,000 people, SAR has 2.7 km, which is close to EAP (2.5 km), SSA (2.5 km), and MNA (2.8 km), but well below the world average (4.7 km), ECA (8 km), and North America (24 km). Furthermore, the transport infrastructure suffers from serious shortcomings, such as lack of intraregional connectivity between the national road networks, unrealized potential for rail and inland water freight transport, and inadequate road and rail connectivity of ports with hinterlands. These limitations turn transport infrastructure into a hindrance for regional and international trade, as investment climate surveys indicate.

Table 13.1 SAR lagging behind all but SSA in access to infrastructure services

	Avg GDP Growth (2000–2012)	*Urbanization Rate (2012)*	*Telecom Access (per 100 people) (2011)*[1]	*Electricity Access (% of pop.) (2010)*[2]	*Access to Improved Sanitation (% of pop.) (2011)*[3]	*Access to Improved Water (% of pop.) (2011)*[4]
EAP	8.9	50	98	92	67	91
ECA	4.4	60	157	100	94	95
LAC	3.1	79	125	94	81	94
MNA	4.2	60	105	94	89	89
SAR	6.7	31	72	71	39	90
SSA	4.7	37	54	35	30	63
World	2.5	53	103	78	64	89

Notes: 1. Telecom access is defined as the number of fixed and mobile lines; 2. World Energy Outlook 2010 by International Energy Association; 3. Improved sanitation is defined as connection to a public sewer, a septic system, pour-flush latrine, simple pit latrine, and ventilated improved pit latrine; 4. Improved water is defined as household connection, public standpipe, borehole, protected dug well, protected spring, rainwater collection.

Source: World Development Indicators (WDI 2013), except when noted otherwise.

Table 13.2 Big range among SAR countries in access to infrastructure services

	Avg. GDP growth (2000–2012)[1]	*Urbanization Rate (2012)*	*Telecom Access (per 100 people) (2011)*[2]	*Electricity Access (% of pop.) (2010)*[3]	*Access to Improved Sanitation (% of pop.) (2011)*[4]	*Access to Improved Water (% of pop.) (2011)*[5]	*Total Road Network (per 1000 people)*[6]	*% Paved Roads*[7,8]
SAR	6.7	31	72	71	39	91	2.9	51
AFG	8.7	24	54	30	29	61	1.6	29
BGD	5.9	29	58	47	55	83	0.1	10
BTN	8.7	36	69	65	45	97	9.7	40
IND	7.1	32	75	75	35	92	3.5	50
MDV	7.0	42	173	95	98	99	0.3	100
NPL	4.0	17	47	47	35	88	0.8	54
PAK	4.4	37	65	65	47	91	1.5	72
LKA	5.5	15	104	77	91	93	5.5	81
Brazil	3.3	85	145	99	81	97	8.1	14
China	10.2	52	94	100	65	92	3.0	54

Notes: 1. The average GDP growth for AFG is for the period 2002–2009; 2. Telecom access is defined as the number of fixed and mobile lines; 3. World Energy Outlook 2010 by International Energy Association, except BTN and MDV, which are based on authors' estimations; 4. Improved sanitation is defined as connection to a public sewer, a septic system, pour-flush latrine, simple pit latrine, and ventilated improved pit latrine; 5. Improved water is defined as household connection, public standpipe, borehole, protected dug well, protected spring, rainwater collection; 6. Varying data years: 2005 (MDV), 2006 (AFG), 2008 (IND, NPL), 2010 (BGD, BTN, PAK, LKA, Brazil, China); 7. Varying data years: 2003 (LKA), 2005 (MDV), 2006 (AFG), 2008 (IND, NPL, China), 2010 (BGD, BTN, PAK, Brazil).

Source: World Development Indicators, except when noted otherwise.

Within SAR benchmarking[6]

Sri Lanka and Maldives have the best access rates in the region. As Table 13.2 shows, more than 90 percent of the population in these two countries has access to improved sanitation, which is better than in LAC, at 81 percent. In terms of electrification, only Maldives (95 percent) and Sri Lanka (77 percent) are above the average rate for developing countries (76 percent).[7,8] On telecom, Sri Lanka and Maldives top the lists with 104 and 173 telephone lines per 100 people. This places Sri Lanka at the world average of 103 lines per 100 people and above EAP, at 98 lines per 100 people.

Afghanistan, Nepal, and Bangladesh have the worst access rates in the region. Nepal, with the lowest number of telephone lines per 100 people in SAR (47), is behind Afghanistan (54) – which matches SSA (54). For electrification, Afghanistan, not surprisingly, is the worst; a meager 30 percent of the population can rely on electricity-powered lighting at night. Moreover, Afghanistan and Bangladesh (47 percent) are closer to the 35 percent found in SSA than to the 71 percent found in SAR. Total road network (km) per 1,000 people is also low in Nepal, Afghanistan, and Bangladesh. Only 29 percent of Afghanistan's roads, and 10 percent of Bangladesh's roads, are paved.

The exception is high average access to improved water in SAR, and not just in a few countries. Five out of the eight countries in SAR (i.e., Bhutan, India, Maldives, Pakistan, and Sri Lanka) have access rates to improved water of at least 90 percent, similar to the 94 percent rate found in LAC.

Inequality of access to infrastructure across South Asia's Space

So *who* has access to each type of infrastructure? We begin with a look at inequality of access across South Asia's space, weighing physical, poverty, and income considerations – an assessment that gives an encompassing picture of the infrastructure gap effects in the region but has never been done before. Where data is available,[9] we use four different analytical methods:

- **Gini coefficients on access to infrastructure services and households are estimated for a sample of administrative regions for each country for all countries of the region.** As with any Gini coefficient, zero expresses perfect equality, which theoretically could mean equal access to service or no access to service. A coefficient of one expresses maximal inequality among values (for example, only one district has access to infrastructure service). The goal is to have a country level measure of spatial inequality of infrastructure access adjusted by household spatial distribution.
- **Individual access to infrastructure service provision is analyzed for Sri Lanka, Afghanistan, and India.** This method provides a clearer picture of each sector in these countries and potential spillovers across sectors. The correlation of individual infrastructure service provision and the poverty rate (head counting) is estimated to understand the income regressivity of access to these services by sector.
- **Infrastructure indexes are constructed via two different methods for Sri Lanka and India.**[10] These methods, chosen to ensure result robustness, include: (1) equal weights; and (2) a multi-criteria decision-making approach, assigning weights according to household level infrastructure service importance. The correlation of an infrastructure index and the poverty rate (head counting) is then presented visually. This analysis could be viewed as a proxy for how man-made capital, important in public services, is made available across space and income dimensions. The infrastructure index provides information about the overall service provision of key infrastructures across a country or group of countries. Yet, as a composite, it

overshadows information on specific infrastructures. Infrastructure service delivery may vary, owing to several factors, including characteristics inherent to the infrastructure (such as capital intensity), economic aspects (such as income), geography (such as proximity to source), and institutions (such as planning and implementation capacity, community cohesiveness).

- **Quintile analysis is carried out for Sri Lanka and Afghanistan.** The share of participation in total connections, that each quintile of income has for each type of infrastructure, is estimated where feasible, providing a very similar analysis to the classic Lorenz curve for income.[11]

Inequality of access to infrastructure: physical considerations

How (un)equal is access to infrastructure among different administrative areas of a country (such as a district or a province)? To analyze this, we estimate a Gini coefficient over the total of households that have access to a given type of infrastructure service, but differences in the distribution of the access could be determined by where the households are allocated in the country. Therefore, we estimate the Gini coefficient over the number of households of each administrative area. As the Gini can be a derivative from the Lorenz curve, we can subtract the Gini coefficient of population (H) from the Gini of connections (C). The intuition behind this estimation is to see if there are areas in a country that are not receiving a rate of access proportional to their population. Table 13.3 presents these measures of spatial inequality of infrastructure access, adjusted by household spatial distribution for each country in the region. Access to a particular infrastructure service is spatially evenly distributed if its Gini coefficient is equal to the Gini coefficient of households, although this could also mean an equal absence of services.

The snapshot of the spatial distribution of infrastructure services in South Asian countries is quite heterogeneous, with the Maldives having the lowest, and Afghanistan the highest, inequality of access to infrastructure services in the region (Table 13.3). These results are not surprising, especially in the case of Afghanistan, given its level of development, mountainous geography, and years of conflict. What is surprising, however, is Pakistan's adjusted Ginis, which show relatively low levels of spatial inequality. One possible explanation is the country's higher urbanization rate, with access to infrastructure services more skewed to its cities relative to other countries in the region.

In terms of infrastructure service, the picture is also heterogeneous, with cooking gas (LPG) the most unequally distributed in spatial terms. Given that cooking gas is mainly distributed by bottles, the high spatial inequality likely reflects LPG's reliance on transport connectivity and its capital-intensive nature. The alternative to LPG becomes biomass. The heavy use of biomass for cooking, rather than the cleaner LPG, implies an intergenerational and intra-gender trade-off, since the significant pollution risks via indoor air contamination affect mostly children and women.

Improved water is arguably the infrastructure that is most equally distributed in spatial terms, which is important in terms of welfare impacts, given that no one can survive without it, and in geographic terms, since proximity to water sources is fundamental, particularly in less developed countries.[12] The other sectors, improved sanitation, electricity, and telephones – have adjusted spatial Ginis indicating less equality. Households generally solve their own sanitation needs, appropriately or not, so the incentives to invest in adequate technologies are more limited than in the case of water. Lack of appropriate sanitation or lack of adequate sewage treatment becomes more of a locality problem, that is, a local public bad. This is in part implicit in the definition of unimproved versus improved sanitation.[13] Like water, electricity is a direct benefit to the household, as opposed to sanitation. One would expect that households are willing to pay more for power, but that adequate electricity services can be costly.

Table 13.3 Tremendous inequality of access across SAR's physical space

Gini Coefficients of Access to Infrastructure in South Asia

	AFG	*BGD*	*NPL*	*LKA*	*IND*	*BTN*	*PAK*	*MDV*
Access Gini Coefficients (C)								
Improved Water	0.49	0.32	0.41	0.34	0.15	0.36	0.47	0.13
Improved Sanitation	.	0.30	0.43	0.33	0.38	0.55	0.47	0.24
Electricity	0.86	0.42	0.41	0.36	0.25	0.46	.	0.23
Cooking Gas	0.86	0.80	0.61	0.66	0.44	0.58	0.45	0.24
Phone	0.65	0.46	0.42	0.36	0.30	0.55	0.48	0.23
Households Gini Coefficients (H)								
Population	0.37	0.31	0.37	0.32	0.10	0.36	0.45	0.23
Access Gini Coefficients Adjusted by Household Distribution (C–H)								
Improved Water	0.12	0.01	0.04	0.01	0.06	0.00	0.02	–0.10
Improved Sanitation	.	–0.01	0.06	0.01	0.29	0.18	0.02	0.01
Electricity	0.49	0.11	0.04	0.04	0.15	0.10	.	0.00
Cooking Gas	0.50	0.49	0.24	0.33	0.35	0.22	0.00	0.01
Phone	0.28	0.15	0.05	0.03	0.20	0.19	0.03	0.00

Note: The Gini coefficients are estimated over a sample of administrative subdivisions selected on each country.

Source: Authors' calculations based on surveys presented in Table 1 in Appendix B.

These sectoral results are influenced by the broad definitions used for improved water, sanitation, and electricity, which aggregate disparate type of services. The aggregation "penalizes" countries, provinces, and districts with good access to grid electricity because it incorporates other forms of service provision. For example, Sri Lanka's adjusted spatial Gini in electricity is low, reflecting the high connection to the grid across the island (Biller and Nabi, 2013). Pakistan's adjusted spatial Gini is also low, but so is its grid connectivity. The adjusted spatial Gini of phones is also variable across countries, probably reflecting topography and connectivity; that is, geography matters. This is true even for cooking gas, as cheaper alternatives like firewood are generally not available in an atoll like the Maldives. The aggregated numbers provide a broad sub-sectoral picture of service locations. Further analysis on poverty provides a more complete picture of regressivity in infrastructure service provision.

Inequality of access to infrastructure: poverty considerations

Another way to analyze spatial inequalities is by analyzing how pockets of poverty fit into the picture, in effect, introducing a socio-economic variable. Here, we correlate the district poverty rate (percentage of people of each district that live under the poverty line) with the district rate of access to infrastructure (percentage of households that have infrastructure in each district) in three countries. We assume that a country with a higher poverty rate will have worse access to infrastructure services than a country with a lower one. But how strong is that link? The results here show that it varies.

India shows strong regressivity of infrastructure service access except in water services (Figure 13.1) while Sri Lanka shows a relatively weak regressivity of infrastructure service access (Figure 13.2). In India, the water exception is similar to that in the other countries.

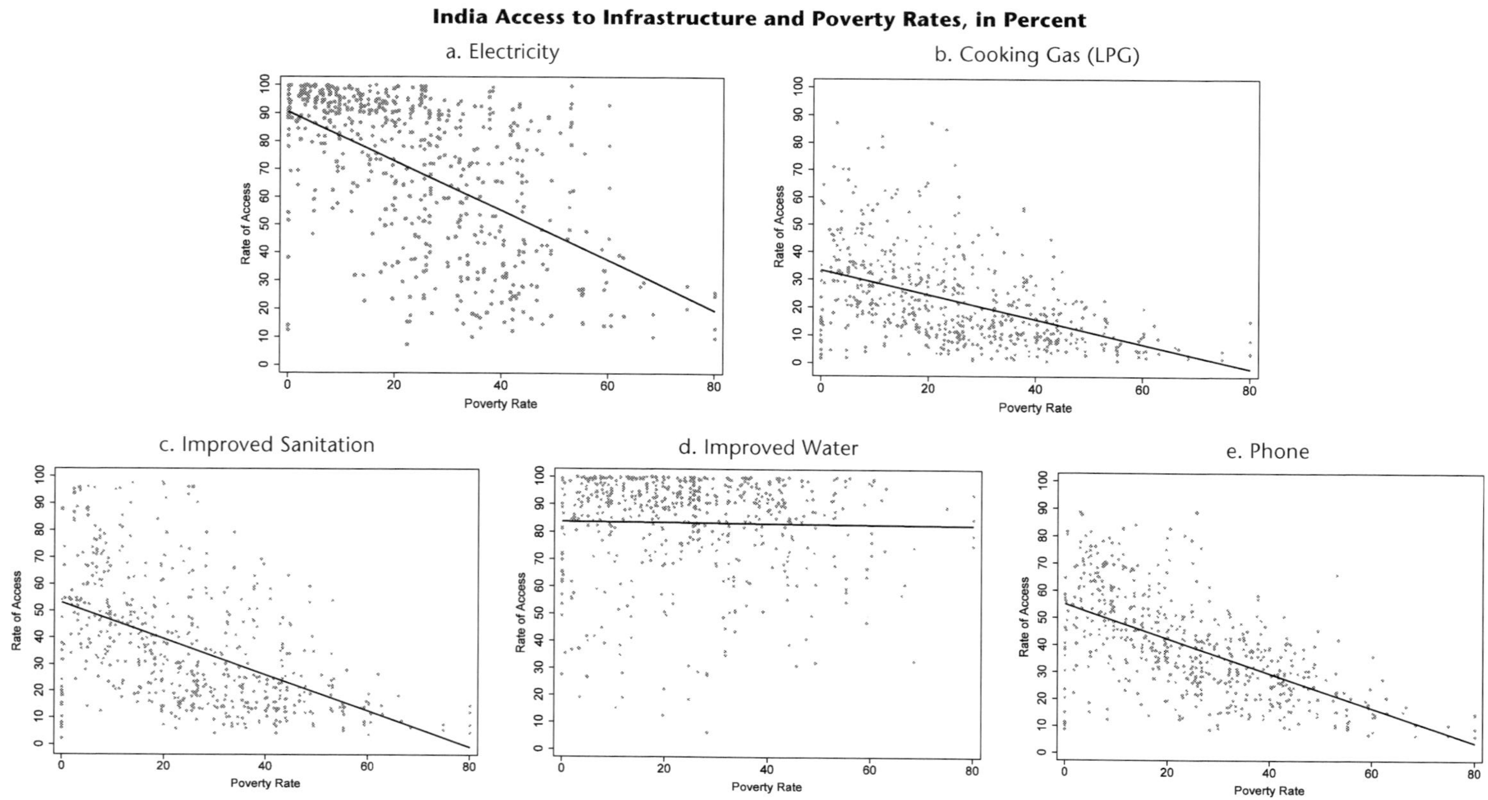

Figure 13.1 India's infrastructure services access is strongly regressive

Note: The size of each point is based on the population size. The coefficients associated with the scatter plots are –0.89 for electricity, –0.44 for cooking gas, –0.67 for improved sanitation, –0.02 for improved water, and –0.64 for phone. All (but improved water) these coefficients are significant at 99 percent confidence.

Source: Authors' calculations based in infrastructure access from India DHLS-3 and poverty rates from Debroy and Bhandari (2003).

Sri Lanka Access to Infrastructure and Poverty Rates, in Percent

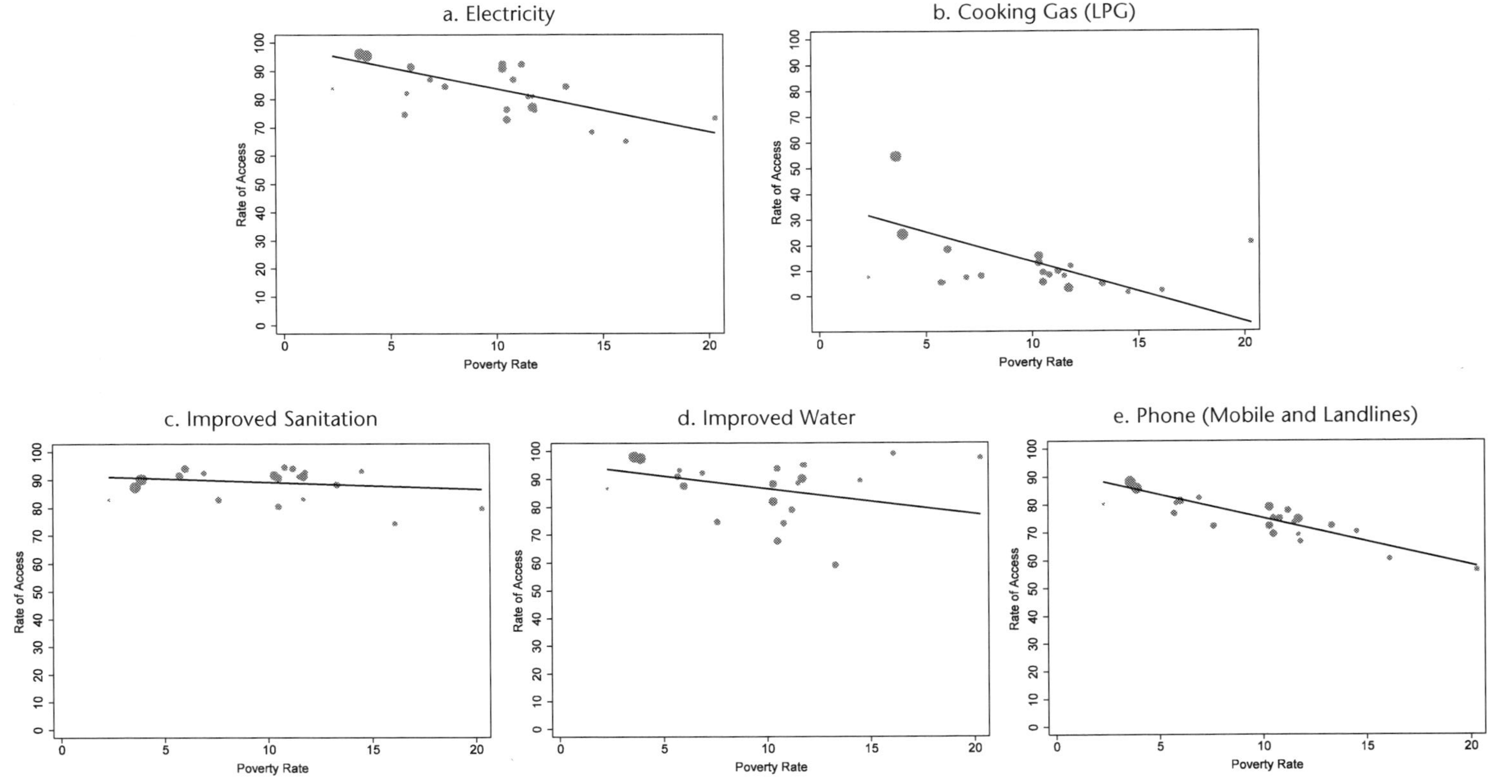

Figure 13.2 Sri Lanka's infrastructure services access is only weakly regressive

Note: The size of each point is based on the population size. The coefficients associated with the scatter plots are: –1.51 for electricity, –2.34 for cooking gas, –0.25 for improved sanitation, –0.9 for improved water, and for phone –1.69. All these coefficients (but improve sanitation and improved water) are significant at 99 percent confidence.

Source: Authors' calculations based in Sri Lanka HIES (2010).

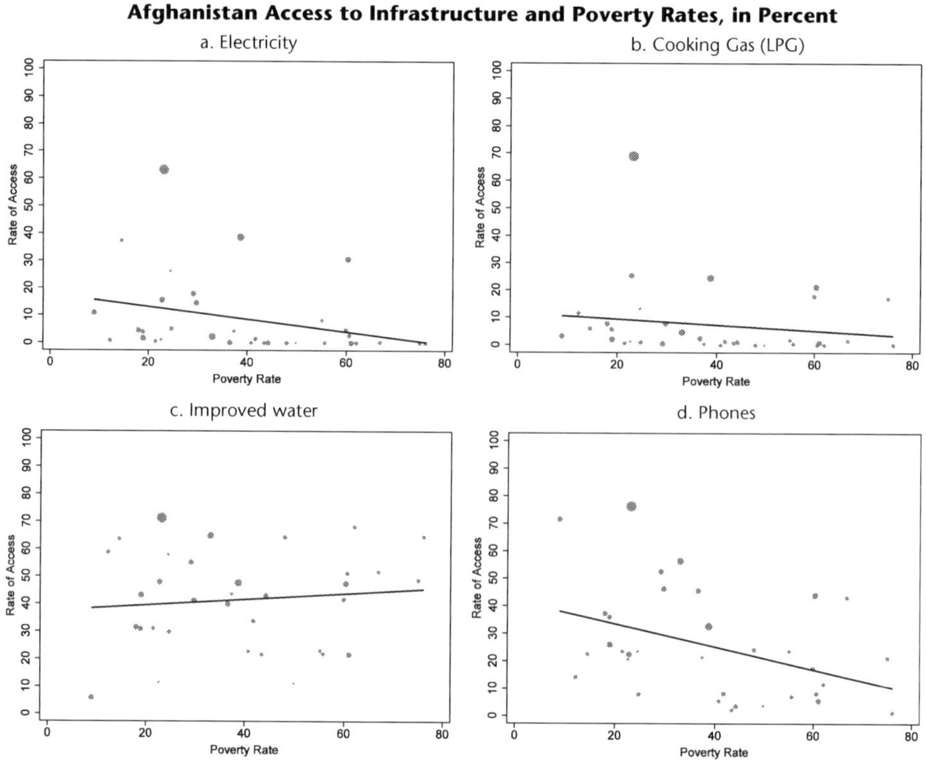

Figure 13.3 Afghanistan's infrastructure services access is regressive

Note: The size of each point is based on the population size. The coefficients associated with the scatter plots are –0.03 for improved water, –0.39 for electricity, –0.36 for cooking gas, and –0.66 for phone. The coefficients for electricity and phone are significant at 90 percent confidence.

Source: Authors' calculations based on Afghanistan NVRA (2008).

In Sri Lanka, the exceptions to this trend are cooking gas and telephones, which show a much stronger link. The overall low level of regressivity is a stark contrast to both Afghanistan and India, which show much stronger relationships, even for the most basic infrastructures.

Afghanistan shows a relatively strong regressivity, except in water, and also geographically, in its capital, as Kabul also has one of the lower poverty rates in the country (Figure 13.3). While most access to infrastructure services in the country is regressive in income, water stands out as non-regressive, even when the adjusted spatial Gini is much higher than in the other countries, illustrating the difference between a physical spatial measure and one involving socio-economic parameters. Yet, while sanitation appears more regressive in income then in other countries, cooking gas seems less regressive than in other South Asian countries.

Inequality of access to infrastructure: physical and poverty considerations

Yet another way to analyze spatial inequalities is by bringing poverty data together with access data. We do this for India and Sri Lanka. Using the infrastructure indexes described in Appendix C, maps overlaying the location of infrastructure services and poverty can be generated. The indexes encompass only the basic infrastructure services that have the highest impact on welfare (such as water, sanitation, and electricity).[14] Andres et al. (2013) present these maps using a multi-criteria decision-making approach to assign weights according to household level infrastructure service importance for India and Sri Lanka. Colors indicate access to infrastructure services; that is, gold and green represent better access. Height provides a relative poverty measure (a poverty rate); that is, it provides the number of poor individuals in each district /total headcount of each district.

Leading regions generally mean better access, but lagging regions do not necessarily mean worse access. As expected, the mountains of India are located in the lagging states (those with a higher poverty level) and the plains in the leading states (those with a lower poverty level). There is a clear dominance of reds and browns in lagging states as well, reflecting that states where poverty rates are higher have less access to basic infrastructure services. This is intuitively expected. The curious exception is the northeast area bordering Bangladesh, Bhutan, China, and Myanmar, where there is more green and gold.

The positive exception found in northeast India is more prevalent, generally, in Sri Lanka. Using the same technique, access to basic infrastructures seems to be more inclusive in Sri Lanka. Access is widely spread, and the quality of these services in the country is known to be generally good. It is clear that the leading region – the Western Province – enjoys better access and a lower poverty rate. Yet, for the lagging provinces, the story is more mixed, with some areas featuring both golden and green colors with poverty mountains. However, in areas where the country's 30-year conflict was more present, as expected, higher poverty mountains go hand in hand with red and brown colors.

Inequality of access to infrastructure: income considerations

One question that still remains is, among those who do have access to infrastructure services, how equitably is that access distributed? This matters if policy makers are concerned about providing access regardless of income levels, which is a common political assertion. To answer this question, we compared income quintiles and access rates for Afghanistan and Sri Lanka. Figures 13.4a and 13.4b display the share of total connections, which is the number of connections owned by a quintile of income over the total connections in the country, for each type of infrastructure.

In Sri Lanka and Afghanistan, the rich enjoy better access than the poor, but the countries differ greatly in how equal that access is across incomes. In Sri Lanka, the difference in access across quintiles is small – all quintiles are close to the mean – indicating that there is an almost equal share of access to infrastructure regardless of income quintile. The opposite story is true in Afghanistan.

However, some services (like water) are more equitably distributed than others (like cooking gas) among those with access. In Afghanistan, the equality of access across income quintiles is particularly striking for improved water. Whether poor or rich, the shares of quintile over the total connection in the country hardly deviate from the mean. This is particularly remarkable given that access to improved water is very low in the country, significantly lower than all other countries in South Asia and the region's average. Regardless of years of conflict and scarcity of service, it seems that the Afghani society has emphasized sharing household access to water. But for cooking gas, in both Sri Lanka and Afghanistan, its use is particularly prevalent for the highest quintile, making it the rich's form of cooking. The reason, as discussed, is the capital intensive nature of LPG, its reliance on network connectivity, and the easy available of cheaper, albeit inferior, alternatives.[15]

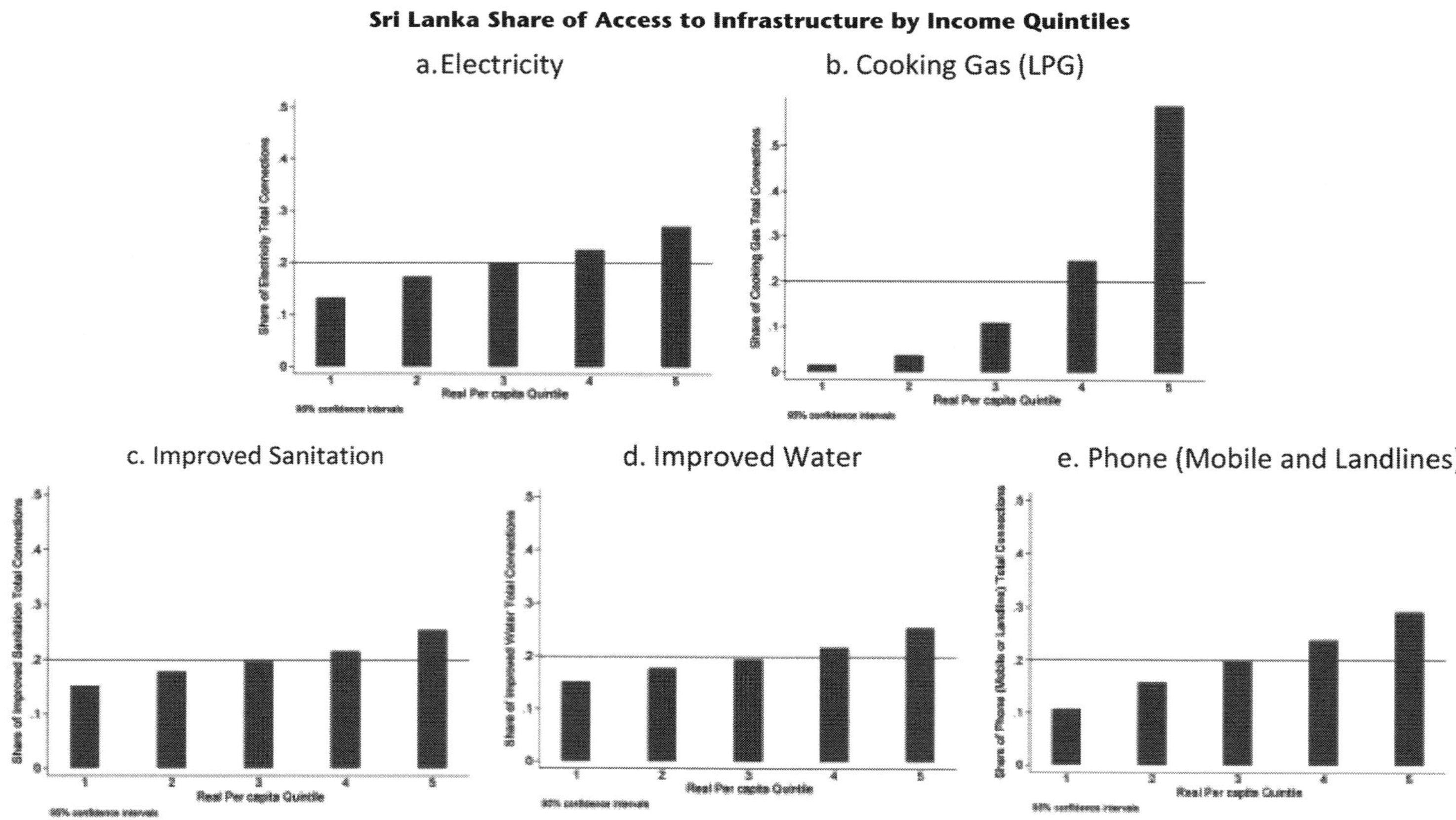

Figure 13.4a Once access is achieved, Sri Lanka's rich and poor have roughly equal shares ...

Source: Authors' calculations based in Sri Lanka HIES (2010).

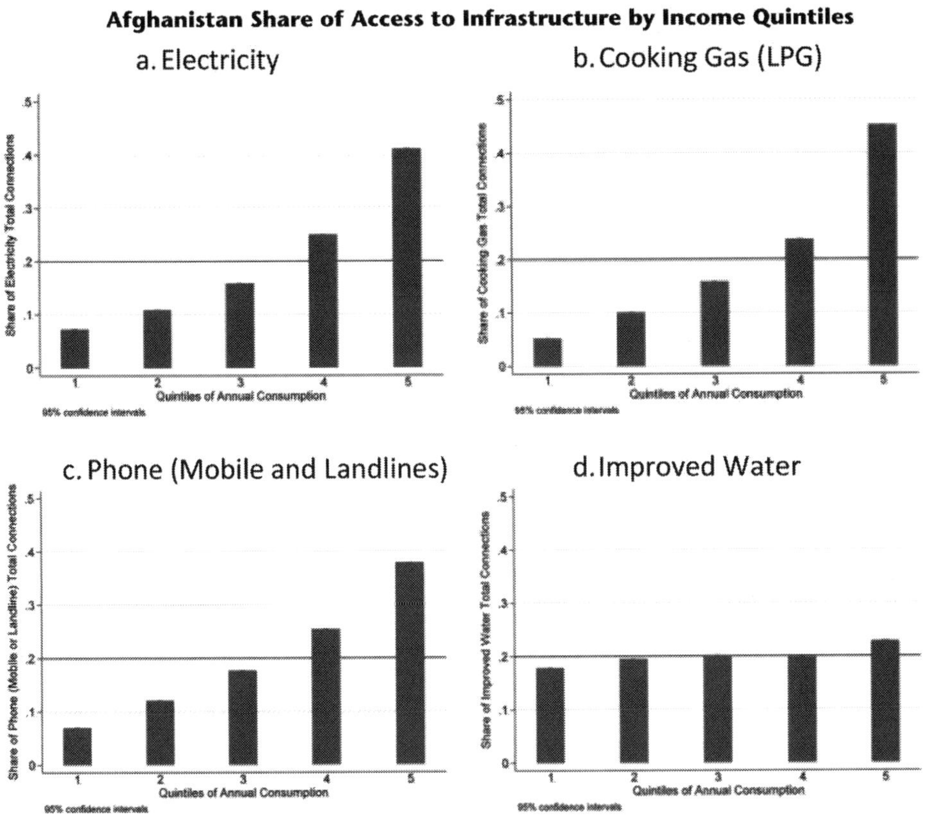

Figure 13.4b . . . unlike the rich and poor in Afghanistan

Note: The share of total connections correspond to the number of connections own by a quintile of income over the total connections in the country for each type of infrastructure.

Source: Authors' calculations based in Afghanistan NVRA (2008).

Inequality of access to infrastructure across South Asian generations

So how unequal is access to infrastructure across time, that is, across South Asian generations? After all, infrastructure investment choices to fill the infrastructure gap made today affect current and future generations. Moreover, not addressing the infrastructure gap threatens both welfare and economic growth in the medium and long term.

Access to infrastructure services is also weak in SAR when viewed in terms of how future generations will be affected. If we drill down further into the data and isolate access rates for households with at least one child under the age of 15, we see that future opportunities for children are being seriously undercut by limited access (Table 13.4).

The human opportunity index: access to infrastructure as opportunity

Our main instrument for measuring the inequality of access to infrastructure across time is the Human Opportunity Index (HOI), which was first published in 2008 and used to evaluate access in Latin America. It can be interpreted as a composite indicator of two elements:

Table 13.4 Better coverage typically goes with more equitable access and thus higher HOIs

Access to Infrastructure Services and Human Opportunity Index for household with children under 15 years old

Country	***AFG***	*BGD*	*BTN*	*IND*	*MDV*	*NPL*	*PAK*	*LKA*
Year	*2008*	*2006*	*2007*	*2007*	*2009*	*2011*	*2006*	*2010*
Sanitation								
Sewerage								
Coverage	0.01	0.02	.	0.06	0.41	0.03	0.28	.
Dissimilarity Index	0.81	0.68	.	0.60	0.40	0.56	0.38	.
HOI	0.00	0.01	.	0.02	0.24	0.01	0.17	.
Improved Sanitation								
Coverage	.	0.45	0.38	0.36	0.94	0.37	0.44	0.90
Dissimilarity Index	.	0.15	0.24	0.24	0.01	0.14	0.23	0.03
HOI	.	0.38	0.29	0.27	0.93	0.32	0.34	0.87
Water								
Piped Water								
Coverage	0.05	0.04	0.57	0.12	0.16	0.21	0.29	0.29
Dissimilarity Index	0.55	0.74	0.14	0.42	0.67	0.18	0.29	0.20
HOI	0.02	0.01	0.49	0.07	0.05	0.17	0.21	0.23
Improved Water								
Coverage	0.46	0.98	0.96	0.83	0.86	0.88	0.92	0.88
Dissimilarity Index	0.11	0.00	0.01	0.03	0.09	0.02	0.01	0.02
HOI	0.41	0.97	0.95	0.80	0.78	0.86	0.91	0.86
Energy Source								
Gas for Cooking								
Coverage	0.16	0.10	0.22	0.22	0.92	0.21	0.32	0.16
Dissimilarity Index	0.62	0.64	0.33	0.50	0.02	0.41	0.47	0.43
HOI	0.06	0.03	0.15	0.11	0.90	0.12	0.17	0.09
No Fossil for cooking								
Coverage	0.17	0.10	0.57	0.24	0.94	0.22	0.32	0.18
Dissimilarity Index	0.62	0.63	0.22	0.49	0.02	0.41	0.47	0.41
HOI	0.06	0.04	0.45	0.12	0.92	0.13	0.17	0.11

Table 13.4 (continued)

Access to Infrastructure Services and Human Opportunity Index for household with children under 15 years old								
Country	***AFG***	*BGD*	*BTN*	*IND*	*MDV*	*NPL*	*PAK*	*LKA*
Year	*2008*	*2006*	*2007*	*2007*	*2009*	*2011*	*2006*	*2010*
Electricity								
Coverage	0.17	0.50	0.72	0.68	1.00	0.75	.	0.85
Dissimilarity Index	0.58	0.20	0.12	0.12	0.00	0.08	.	0.05
HOI	0.07	0.40	0.63	0.60	1.00	0.69	.	0.81
Communications								
Mobile Phone								
Coverage	0.36	0.24	0.39	0.39	0.99	0.76	0.45	0.80
Dissimilarity Index	0.27	0.38	0.29	0.26	0.00	0.08	0.20	0.06
HOI	0.26	0.15	0.28	0.29	0.99	0.71	0.36	0.75
Phone (Landlines and Mobile)								
Coverage	0.36	0.23	0.39	0.37	0.99	0.76	.	0.63
Dissimilarity Index	0.27	0.38	0.29	0.27	0.00	0.08	.	0.09
HOI	0.26	0.15	0.28	0.27	0.99	0.70	.	0.57

Note: All piped water is restricted to piped water in the premises. We do not present the rate of access for Afghanistan because we cannot differentiate between latrines with and without slab. For Bangladesh improved water rate of access, we did not use the assumption made by JMP where they discard 20 percent of protected wells due to arsenic contamination. For Bangladesh improved sanitation data, in order to make rates comparable, we include JMP pit latrines without slab in the category of improved sanitation (when is categorized as unimproved). For further information about this changes in the JMP methodology, check JMP data by country (www.wssinfo.org/documents-links/documents/?tx_displaycontroller[type]=country_files). Given that there is no information about landlines in Bhutan, the definition of phone (mobile and landlines) is the same as mobile phones. Sri Lanka's sewerage connection is not presented because it is not identifiable in-the data. In Pakistan there is no information about the tenance of mobile of phones in the household. The lack of information about access to electricity in Nepal and Pakistan is caused by significant differences with the official data (World Energy Outlook,) which motivates us to think that they do not have comparable definitions of access to electricity.

Source: Authors calculation based on NVRA (2008) for Afghanistan, MICS (2006, in Bangladesh Bureau of Statistics and UNICEF 2007) for Bangladesh, LSMS (2007) for Bhutan, DLHS-3 for India (Institute for Population Sciences 2007–2008), DHS (2009, in Ministry of Health and Family (MOHF) [Maldives] and ICF Macro 2010), for Maldives, DHS (2011, in Ministry of Health and Population (MOHP) [Nepal], New ERA, and ICF International Inc. 2012) for Nepal, DHS (2006, in National Institute of Population Studies (NIPS) [Pakistan], and Macro International Inc. 2008) for Pakistan and HIES (2010) for Sri Lanka. All estimations represent the proportion of access in the sample of households with children under 15 years of age.

(1) the level of coverage of basic opportunities necessary for human development (such as access to primary education, water and sanitation, or electricity); and (2) the degree to which the distribution of those opportunities is conditional on circumstances children are born into (such as gender, income, or household characteristics). This study calculates an HOI that is focused on basic infrastructure as opportunities, and the importance of both improving overall access to it and ensuring its equitable allocation to achieve key socio-economic outcomes, such as early childhood development, education completion, good health, and access to information. So while in the previous sections, we delved into current realities of the lack of infrastructure service access and the disenfranchised, in the sections below we analyze how personal circumstances sustain this lack of access, thereby maintaining disenfranchisement across generations.

The HOI essentially measures how personal circumstances impact a child's probability of accessing the services that are necessary to succeed in life. This is critical because the opportunities a child gets throughout life are determined directly by the circumstances related to access to infrastructural services during the formative years, and not necessarily to the child's personal decisions or level of effort. People often do not choose to live in polluted environments devoid of adequate infrastructure services, especially those key to their well-being. This situation is more acute for children, as in their case, access defines opportunity, precisely because, "children are not expected to make an effort to access basic goods by themselves" (Paes de Barros et al., 2009). Moreover, empirical evidence indicates that the earlier the access in life, the more cost effective the results are in terms of final effects than having the access later in life (Heckman et al. 2010, among others). This is intuitively clear, given the long gestation periods of most appropriate infrastructure investments.

If societies aim for an equitable development process, then they need to ensure that as many children as possible have access to basic opportunities. Clean water, sanitation, and electricity are basic opportunities with important welfare benefits. Children in households without clean water and sanitation are more prone to certain illnesses. For example, excess mortality of girls during infancy and early childhood is rooted in the lack of clean water, sanitation, waste disposal, and drainage. The lack of electricity at home puts a heavy toll on a child's learning process by limiting the hours of study at home. For children in isolated rural areas, getting to school and to health care facilities are a challenge, and hence costlier than for children in areas well connected by transport services.

Choice of opportunities

Opportunities are defined as the access to or use of infrastructure services. The introduction of usage indicators is based on data availability, and rests on the observation of services that exist in the area of the household, but that are not utilized by household members due to habits, cultural traits, lack of information, or the need for additional conditions for use. Even among access indicators, we introduce measures that give a sense of quality of the service accessed by the household (compare, for example, access to improved water to access to piped water, and then to tap water in the household). These complementary indicators are selected based on relevance, but restricted by data availability, and thus are exploratory.

Water: The primary intent of water supply (and sanitation) interventions is to disrupt the transmission of water-related diseases to humans. The World Health Organization's current estimate of the impact of inadequate water and sanitation services is 58 percent of total diarrheal deaths. Together, inadequate services in low- and middle-income countries are estimated to be responsible for more than 800,000 deaths annually (WHO 2014). Water supply improvements can, in theory, affect development outcomes directly by providing sufficient water for basic hygiene to improve health, and indirectly through time saving, allowing for school attendance and employment. Health can improve as water-related diseases can infect people through the so-called "water washed" channel in which pathogens are incidentally ingested as a result of having insufficient water for bathing and basic hygiene (Zwane and Kremer, 2007). Secondly, a readily available water supply may lead to less need for household water storage – another opportunity for water contamination (Wright et al., 2004).

Sanitation: In terms of health and education outcomes, it makes a big difference having access to sanitation in general compared to not having it, but also makes a difference between having sanitation and a sewerage connection at home. If the benefits of sanitation are to be seized, there is still a long way to go in the sanitation ladder across South Asia. The lack of access to sanitation facilities either at households, school, or around places where people develop their economic activities, determines the prevalence of open defecation in some countries, particularly in India, where over 50 percent of households have members that practice open defecation.[16]

Energy use: The available indicators of energy access are used to assess two different sets of expected effects on development outcomes. Electricity affects the time available for school work and for school attendance, as well as access to information. Gas for cooking, on the other hand, is expected to also have effects on time, but is usually tracked, given its potential effects on health due to indoor air pollution.

Telephones: A recent study conducted by the UNDP places mobile phone penetration rates near 45 percent in low-income countries and 76 percent in lower-middle-income countries. The same study indicates that by 2015, ICTs should be accessible to everyone, resulting in the democratization of access to innovative ICT, with the potential to diminish barriers to access. The absorption rate of mobile phones by the world's poorest already indicates the incredible potential of cell phones in empowering developing communities to move up the socio-economic ladder. In developing countries, cell phones have taken on numerous roles, exceeding traditional uses of connectivity and browsing the internet. Rural communities and entrepreneurs use cell phones for making financial transactions, creating and managing client databases, and coordinating fundamental business responsibilities. By creatively transforming the cell phone into a small-business enabler, rural communities have successfully created and attracted small-businesses ventures that would typically not survive in such dire environments.

Choice of circumstances for the analysis: rationale

For this study, we have selected four circumstances: (1) household size, (2) location (urban versus rural), (3) education of household head, and (4) gender of household head. These circumstances reflect previous inequality of opportunities studies and are in line with similar analyses that are part of the SAR Regional Flagship Report on Inequality of Opportunities (World Bank, 2014).

Household size. This is a circumstance that is out of a child's control and that will mostly be linked to use of services. While the role of size is not expected to be significant for our choice of opportunity indicators, we keep it in the analysis for comparison purposes in further iterations of the HOI calculation, and to identify areas of the country where this circumstance seems to have a relatively higher prevalence in explaining the HOI. This approach also links with the previous spatial analysis undertaken earlier in the chapter.

Location (urban versus rural). This is key to understanding rural-urban migration patterns over time, given that services are concentrated in urban areas. The magnitude of location as a driver of inequality of opportunity is expected to be large in India, because 68 percent of the population (over 800 million people) still lives in rural areas, with about a 90 million rural population increase over the past 10 years.[17]

Education of the household head. Intuitively, one may expect households with heads that experienced higher education attainment would transmit the importance of education to their children. However, Azam and Bhatt's (2012) recent paper on intergenerational mobility in India using father-son data since 1940 finds that, "based on the estimated intergenerational elasticity, the transmission of educational attainment from father to son has decreased significantly across birth cohorts in the last 45 years," (p. 29). But when they looked at the estimated correlation between father-son educational attainments, there is no trend. According to the authors, the explanation is in the evolution of dispersion in educational attainment of both generations. So as to clarify the importance of household heads' education attainment, we keep this circumstance in the analysis.

Gender of the household head. South Asia gender data are particularly skewed against females. We thus choose this variable to understand if gender bias impacts children's opportunities in the region. This element is expected to be of relatively low importance, compared to the other three circumstances driving opportunity.[18] Even so, we will look at a variation of the relative weight of gender in inequality of opportunities across states and districts in India.

Calculation of HOI, dissimilarity index, penalties, and Shapley decompositions

The key to calculating the HOI is the dissimilarity index. This is originally a demographic measure of evenness, widely used in analysis of social mobility, sociology in general, and typically applied to dichotomous outcomes. Paes de Barros et al. (2009) define the dissimilarity index (D-index) as the weighted average of absolute differences of group-specific access rates (p_i) from the overall average access rate ($\bar{p}$), or:

$$D = \frac{1}{2\bar{p}}\sum_{i=1}^{n} \beta_i \left| p_i - \bar{p} \right| \tag{1}$$

The D-index will then be expressed in percentage terms, with a value between 0 and 1. A value of zero indicates that access rates for all groups considered are the same, while positive values indicate that certain groups of individuals have a lower probability of access to the infrastructure service considered.

In practical terms, the dissimilarity index that we calculate will reflect the percentage of the coverage rate of a particular opportunity that has to be discounted in order to obtain the HOI, i.e.:

$$HOI = \bar{p}(1 - D) \tag{2}$$

While the penalty (P) is the difference between coverage rates and the HOI:

$$P = \bar{p} - HOI \tag{3}$$

As equation (2) shows, the HOI can be improved either by an increase in coverage (which is still bounded at 100 percent universal access, and so the more people have access, the less likely is that a particular segment of population is being left behind), or by a closer to zero dissimilarity index. At higher levels of coverage for a service, there is less room for a dissimilar distribution of access across groups. However, the dissimilarity index, as we will see, varies across opportunities and units of analysis, even at similar levels of coverage.

Next, we calculate the contribution of each circumstance to observed inequality of opportunities across households, following Hoyos and Narayan (2010). This is done through Shapley decompositions on the dissimilarity index. These decompositions, originally proposed by Shorrocks (1999), show how much inequality changes as a consequence of adding an additional circumstance. Because circumstances are correlated with each other, the change in inequality when a circumstance is added depends on the initial set of circumstances to which it is added. To calculate the impact of each circumstance, the average of all possible changes to different combinations of other circumstances is found.

Finally, we calculate the total unique contribution of each circumstance to the dissimilarity index, along with a percentage of contribution that sums 100 percent. By construction, the closer access gets to 100 percent of households, the less room for inequality there is. Therefore, as coverage increases, we expect lower values of the dissimilarity index. However, coverage does not grow equally for different circumstance groups, and similar levels of coverage might present radically different levels of inequality of opportunity.

Inequality of opportunity in the access to infrastructure services in SAR

HOI across the region

The results show that the better a country's coverage, in sanitation, water, energy sources, and communications, the more equitable the access, and thus the higher the HOI (Table 13.4). In addition, in some cases, the HOI is lowered more by the problem of unequal access (measured by the dissimilarity index) than by insufficient coverage. Take the case of *improved sanitation*. As expected, countries with the highest coverage (the Maldives, Sri Lanka) feature the lowest dissimilarity index, and therefore, HOI is very close to the coverage. At the same time, countries with low levels of coverage (like Bangladesh) are associated with higher dissimilarity indexes. However, if we take two similar access rates, as in India (36 percent) and Nepal (37 percent), we see a significant difference in how that access to sanitation is distributed – with Nepal (0.14) more equal than India (0.24), which results in India having a lower HOI (0.27) than Nepal (0.32). This also reflects the spatial story told previously. Also, a country with higher coverage, like Pakistan, features virtually the same dissimilarity index as India, and a substantially higher HOI index than Nepal. In the case of access to *improved water*, rates are high enough to guarantee a low dissimilarity index. *Electricity* also follows the pattern of a decreasing dissimilarity index as coverage is higher, but in a less than proportional manner.

Contribution of circumstance to HOI in the region

Can we ascertain how much individual circumstances drive the HOIs for each type of infrastructure? We try to answer this question by looking at all nine types of infrastructure, then calculating the HOI (for each indicator (top panel), and then the contribution of each circumstance to the HOI (Figure 13.5).

A few patterns stand out, which point to better access for the most basic indicators than the more advanced ones, and to the importance of location and education of the household head together as the key explanatory variables, although location tends to dominate:

- Indicators of use (such as cooking fuels) and indicators linked to a higher quality of access (no fossil fuels for cooking, telephone, mobile phone, sewerage, and piped water) register a significantly higher inequality of opportunity than more basic access indicators (improved water source, improved sanitation, and access to electricity).
- Two factors, the location of the household (urban versus rural), and the education of the household head, explain over 70 percent of the HOIs across countries and across indicators (most of the time, in over 80 percent of cases).

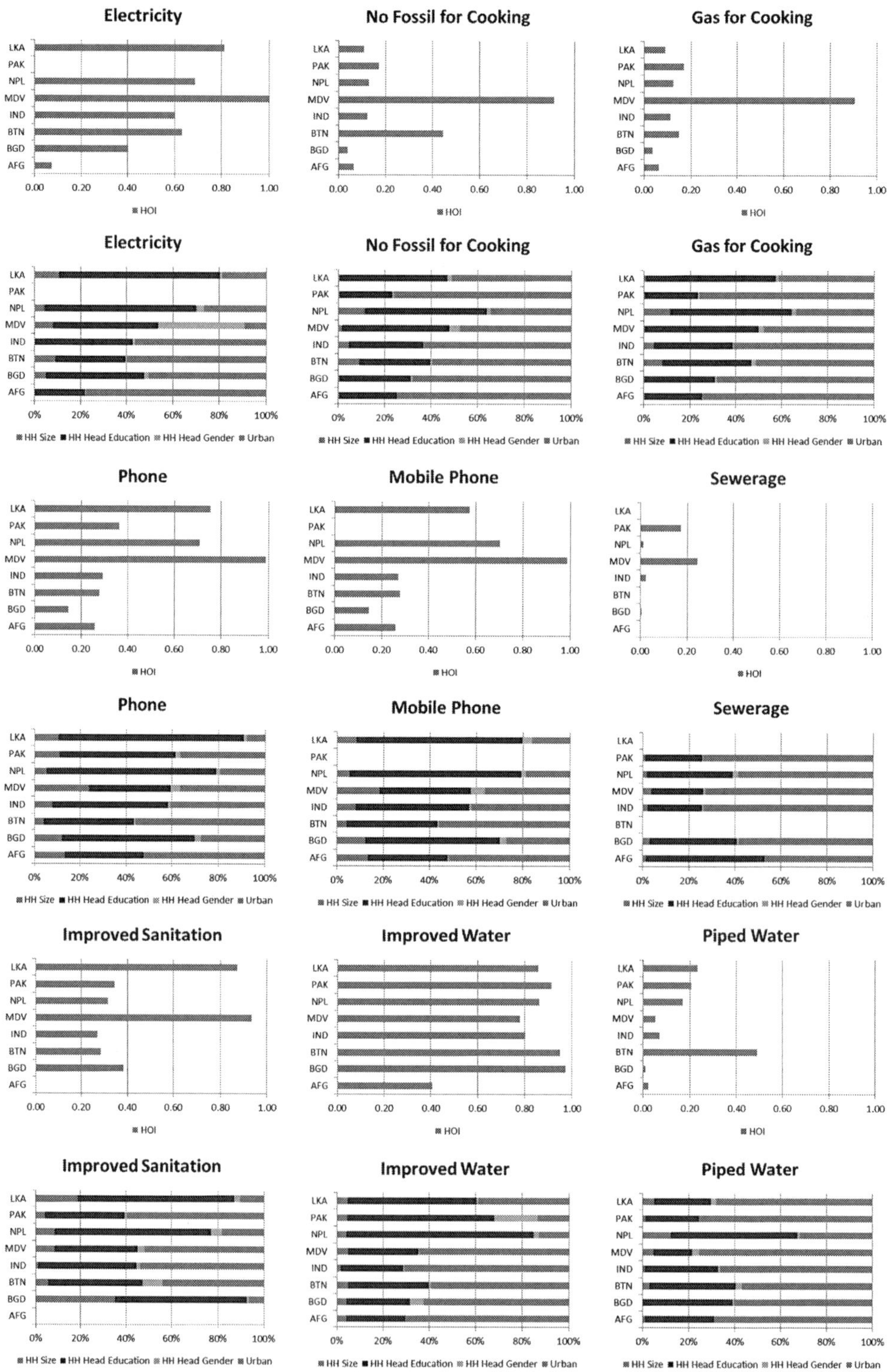

Figure 13.5 Location and education top circumstances explaining SAR's HOI outcomes

Source: Authors' calculation based on NVRA 2008 for Afghanistan, MICS 2006 for Bangladesh, LSMS 2007 for Bhutan, DLHS-3 for India, DHS 2009 for Maldives, DHS 2011 for Nepal, DHS 2006 for Pakistan and HIES 2010 for Sri Lanka.

A closer look at the three energy indicators (access to electricity, use of gas for cooking, and biomass for cooking), shows location and household head education to be the dominant factors. Among them, access to electricity features the most equitable access distribution, by far, although regrettably, we lack indicators of the quality of that access (in terms of number of hours of electricity each day, or information on shortages). With cooking fuels (the usage indicators), we see a close pattern between them, plus higher dissimilarity indexes than for electricity. As for circumstances explaining the HOI variations in access to energy sources, in Afghanistan, Bangladesh, Bhutan, and India, location (urban/rural divide) dominates, while the education of the household head dominates in Sri Lanka and the Maldives for electricity and cooking gas.

For the rest of the indicators, similar patterns emerge. The role of location can be easily understood, because improving access to infrastructure in urban areas allows governments and the private sector to reach higher concentrations of households, thereby reducing per capita costs. However, the role of education needs to be further scrutinized, given that it could be a proxy for access to information, for household income, or for location beyond the urban/rural category.

A sub-national look at inequality of opportunities

At the state or district level, Andres et al. (2013) presents regional maps with the inequality of opportunity for SAR in terms of access to water, sanitation, and electricity for all countries, suggesting that location is a dominant factor. But while there are areas notorious for low coverage rates (for example, Balochistan in Pakistan, Afghanistan's southwest, Sri Lanka's northeast, or parts of Bihar and Madhya Pradesh in India),[19] each of the three indicators seems to have a concentration of higher access rates across particular areas (such as the Ganges area for improved water sources; Kerala, Himachal Pradesh, and Punjab in India, together with areas around the capital cities of the region, for improved sanitation; and the latter together with Gujarat and north of Delhi for access to electricity). This observation calls for a more detailed look at sub-national level coverage and HOIs, which is what we do for four countries, including Afghanistan, Bangladesh, Bhutan, and India, comparing the national capital, where available, with other areas.

AFGHANISTAN[20]

Kabul has the highest coverage of households in the electric grid (62 percent), with an HOI of 53 percent. The capital also leads in access to improved water sources (71 percent), with an HOI of 66 percent. Location explains most of the HOI for electricity and access to water, but household size dominates for explaining the HOI for sanitation services.

Now consider Helmand province on the border with Balochistan (Pakistan), an area witnessing increased conflict, and where there is a large production of opium. Even having the Helmand River flowing across the province, the mainly desert area registers the lowest access to improved water sources (only 6 percent) of households, and highly unequal access to it, resulting in a HOI of 4 percent. It ranks 9th in access to electricity (11 percent coverage) and access is highly unequal within the province, with a dissimilarity index of 49 percent, for an HOI of 6 percent. Location is the key explanatory factor for all three coverage rates.

In Farah, a western province at the Iranian border, eminently rural and tribal, multiethnic, sparsely populated, but relatively conflict-free, with local authorities exerting local control, access to electricity is virtually null (1 percent). However, it has a 59 percent access to improved water sources, with an HOI of 57 percent. Here, education of household head is the chief explanatory factor.

BANGLADESH

Dhaka district has virtually universal access to improved water sources (100 percent), very high coverage rates of electricity (93 percent), and middling access to telephone (55 percent). However, the capital ranks 36th (out of 64) in access to improved sanitation, with 46 percent coverage, and 35 percent HOI. The key explanatory factor for all indicators is education of the household head.

Kurigram district in the far north is one of the poorest districts in Bangladesh. It has the lowest electricity access rate in the country (15 percent), with an HOI of 9 percent, and only 7 percent of households have access to a telephone, with a HOI of 3 percent. However, its HOI for improved sanitation is higher (45 percent) than in Dhaka, even though they have the same coverage rates. The key explanatory factor for the indicators is education of household head, followed by household size for sanitation, and location for electricity.

The industrial and business center of Narayanganj, on the other hand, has the highest electricity access rate of the country (93 percent) with an HOI of 91 percent, but one of the worst rates of access to improved sanitation at 28 percent, for an HOI of only 24 percent. The factors explaining HOI follow the exact same pattern as in the case of poor Kurigram.

BHUTAN

Thimpu is the district with the highest coverage rates for improved water, improved sanitation, and electricity. The largest inequality in access is registered for improved sanitation (58 percent coverage but a 49 percent HOI). The key explanatory factor for HOIs is education of the household head, except in the case of access to improved water sources, for which location equally matters.

The Zhemgang district hosts the poorest areas of the country, most of which are considered protected areas. Electricity access reaches 44 percent among households, but it is highly unequally distributed, featuring an HOI of 30 percent. The same applies to access to sanitation, as the access rate of 13 percent drops to an HOI of only 4 percent. Education of household head is the dominant circumstance.

INDIA

In Delhi, 93 percent of households have access to improved water sources, and 99 percent to electricity, at least for some time during the day. However, although access to improved sanitation is over the country average (63 percent), the HOI drops to 53 percent. For all indicators, the key explanatory factor is the education of the household head.

Bihar, one of the poorest states in India, has 93 percent access rates to improved water and a 92 percent HOI, but it has the worst access rates and high dissimilarity index for both improved sanitation (15 percent coverage, 8 percent HOI) and electricity (26 percent coverage, 17 percent HOI). Here, too, education of household head explains most HOIs.

Maharashtra, one of the richest states, underperforms Bihar in access to improved water (82 percent coverage, 76 percent HOI), and only ranks 25th and 23th in access to improved sanitation and electricity. In Maharashtra, however, location is the dominant factor explaining the HOIs.

KEY SUB-NATIONAL PATTERNS

At the state or district level, the role of education of the household head gains in importance, relative to the findings for the regional, compared to location, as the key

circumstance explaining the HOIs, although together they are still the dominant factors. In addition, household size also registers at a higher level than in the regional survey, primarily for sanitation.

An interesting pattern at the infrastructure sub-sector level emerges from this country-level analysis, which needs to be corroborated by further research. As discussed, urban environments provide the density needed to enable infrastructure services in a cost effective manner. The density factor is particularly important for grid type infrastructure, such as electricity and piped water, which are direct benefits to households. Extending a grid-based service like power to a nearby household is less expensive than bringing power to an isolated rural household. In the case of piped water, this is not even discussed by planners for being so prohibitive. Of course, this is limited by congestion and other public bads, but it is closely related to agglomeration benefits facilitated by urbanization, due to the importance of connectivity. As one expands the definition of adequate water services in urban environments to include these under improved water, the HOI analysis shows that rural areas become less penalized in terms of inequality.

Improved sanitation breaks the above pattern, and one can only theorize the reason at this stage. As discussed, individual households tend to solve their own sanitation problems by transferring their sewage to their neighbors, or by polluting their neighborhood or downstream areas; therefore, there is little incentive to invest in adequate sanitation from an individual household perspective beyond the gates of one's own property. Scarce household money is better invested in securing direct benefits, such as power and water, to one's household. It is less surprising to find out that size of household is an important explanatory factor in choosing improved sanitation facilities. In a sense, the density logic applied at urban environments applies in the case of individual households as well. Yet, the apparent inverse relationship between higher education and improved sanitation is quite surprising. Better education of household head is often linked to higher income, urban dwelling, and hence access to grid level infrastructure. It is interesting to realize that it can also be linked to a greater degree of public bads, like pollution. Several studies argue that education has few positive externalities. The lack of appropriate sanitation in urbanized environments may thus at least in part be explained by this lack of correlation between higher education and positive externalities.

A LOOK AT STATE-LEVEL RESULTS IN INDIA[21]

For India, these differences in access for certain households at the state level exacerbate the problem of low coverage rates of these services at the country level. The reality is that, despite significant improvements in access to water and electricity, access to infrastructure services in India remains mostly low in many areas with very heterogeneous results. While close to 70 percent of households (with children under 15 years old) in India have access to electricity, less than half of the households (with children under 15 years old) have access to improved sanitation, and only a fraction of those to a sewerage connection. Sanitation access data are heavily discounted, owing to inequality of access across circumstance groups; a similar pattern emerges for use of energy sources.

A look at coverage of infrastructure services across Indian states shows high variability and uneven performances. Take the cases of access to improved water, improved sanitation, electricity, and phones (Figure 13.6). We observe how a relatively high national coverage of access to improved water sources (83 percent) contrasts with the reality of two states (Manipur and Kerala) with less than a third of their households (with children under 15 years old) with access to it. In the case of sanitation, ten states have coverage rates lower than 33 percent.

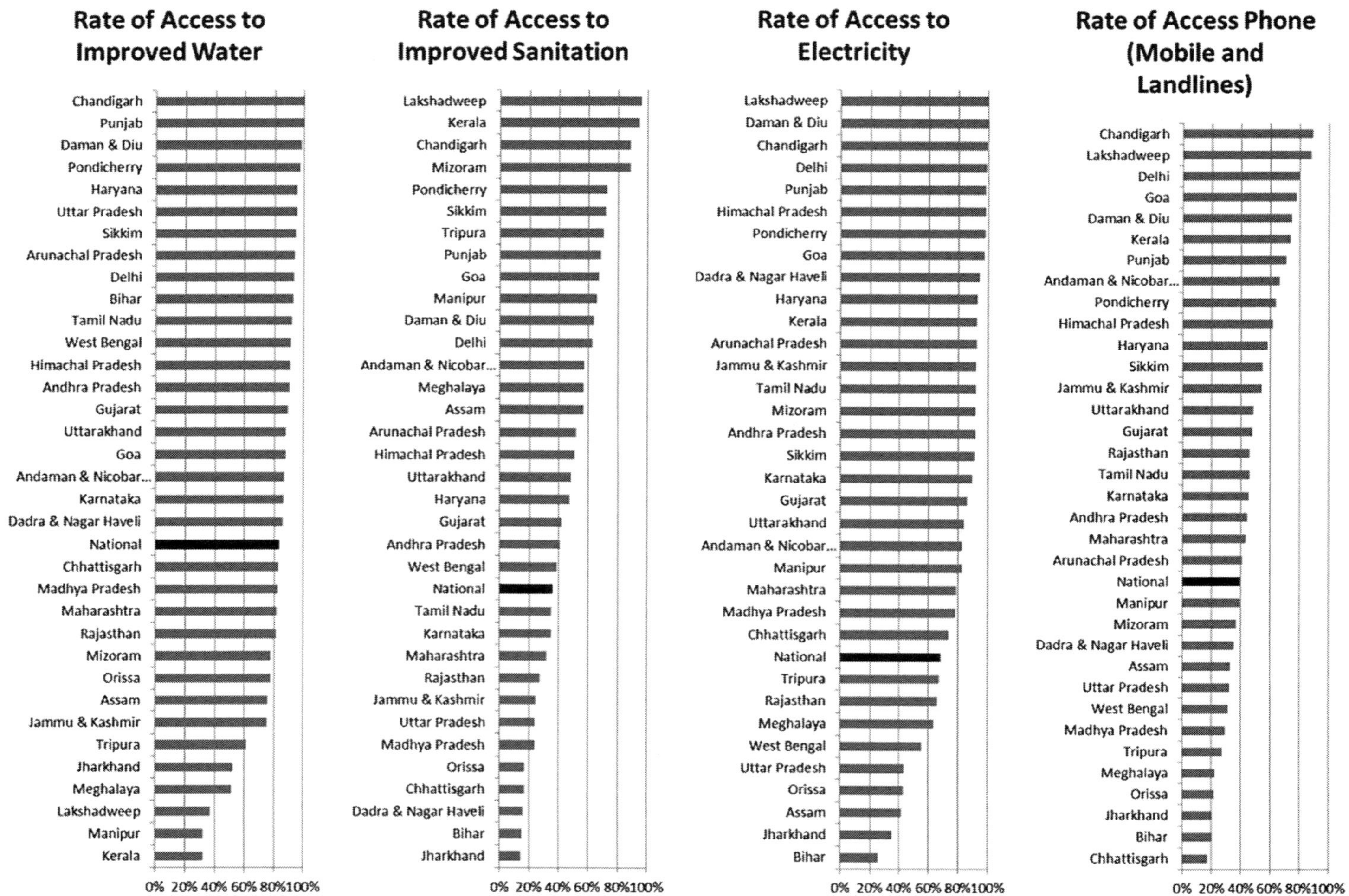

Figure 13.6 Access in India to key services varies greatly

Source: DHLS 3 India

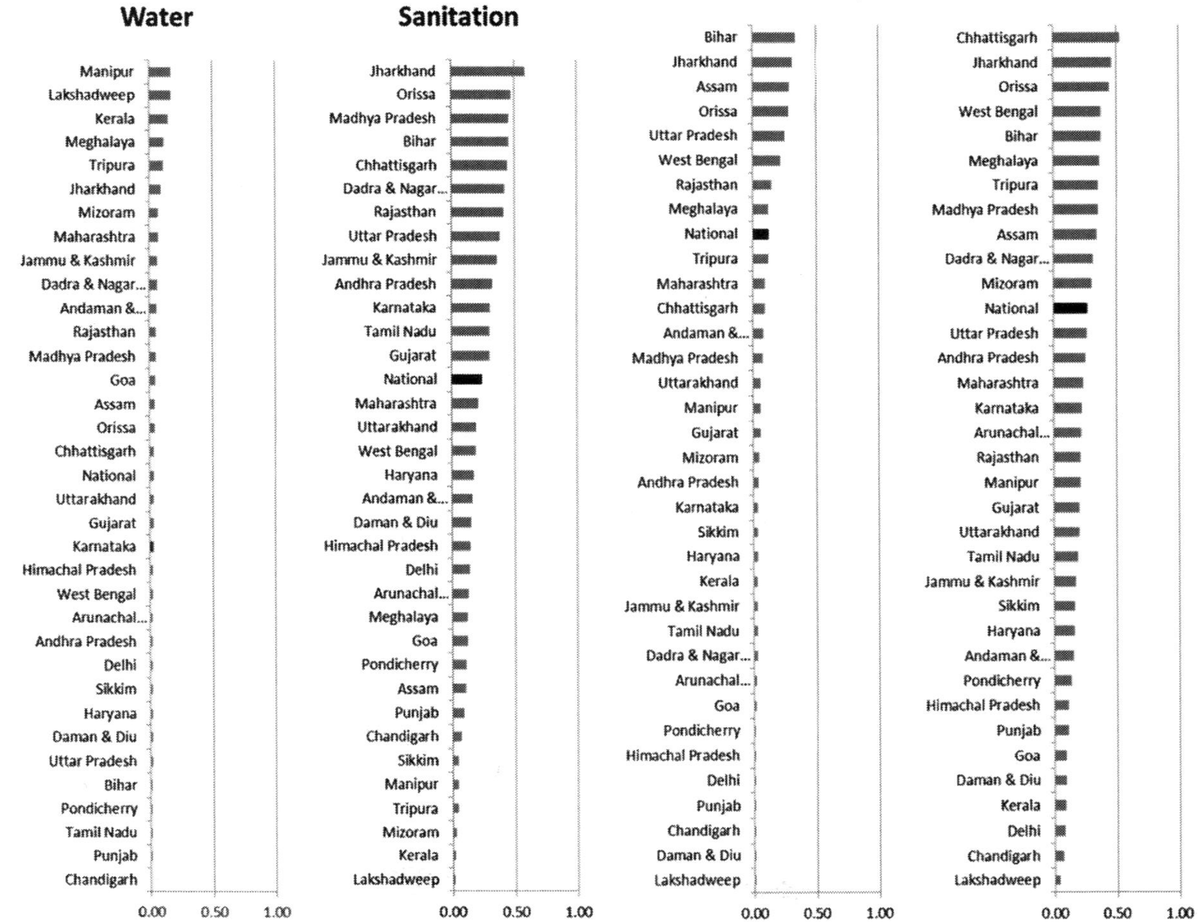

Figure 13.7 Dissimilarity index varies greatly across Indian states and among different services

Source: DHS (2010).

Another way to understand the presence of inequality of opportunities across states is by comparing the magnitude of the dissimilarity index (D-index) across states and the resulting HOI – in effect, permitting the identification of areas in the country where inequality of access can be targeted as a policy element. As Figure 13.7 shows, there is significant inequality in the access to improved sanitation services across states, compared to other services. Jharkhand, for example, with a coverage rate of 15 percent, receives a penalty of over 50 percent when the inequality of access across circumstance groups is considered. It also has the second largest D-index for access to electricity, while Manipur has the largest D-index for access to improved water sources. While this chapter does not discuss inequality of opportunities at the district level, it should be noted that the same variance in coverage and HOI values can be found among districts within the same state. For example, access to sanitation has its lowest coverage rate in Leh Ladakh district, Jammu and Kashmir state of the Himalayan region, at 2.5 percent.

CONTRIBUTION OF CIRCUMSTANCES TO INEQUALITY OF OPPORTUNITIES

Which circumstances contribute the most to inequality of opportunity at the state level? Education of the household head and location are the dominant ones (Figure 13.8). The location factor is to be expected, given that rural households are typically harder to reach with infrastructure services. However, the education factor is more difficult to explain, considering that this effect is net of location, caste, and other factors. A possible explanation is that even among rural areas, there are different levels of remoteness, which in turn are also correlated with lack of access to education services, more prevalent poverty, and by extension, less access to infrastructure services. In the case of indicators of use (use of fossil fuels, use of gas, open defecation), the question remains if the role of education of the head of household is linked to a lack of alternatives, the prevalence of habits, or lack of information.

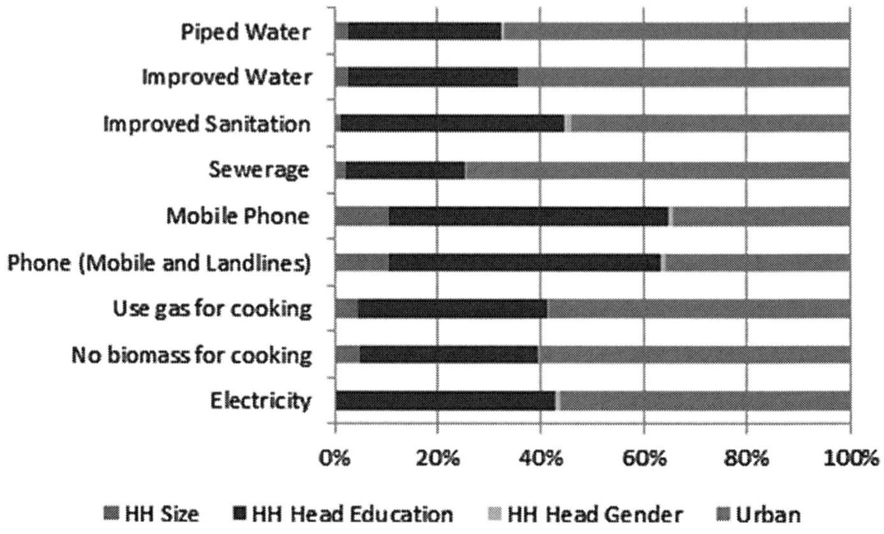

Figure 13.8 Household head education and location dominate India's HOI outcomes

Source: DHS (2010).

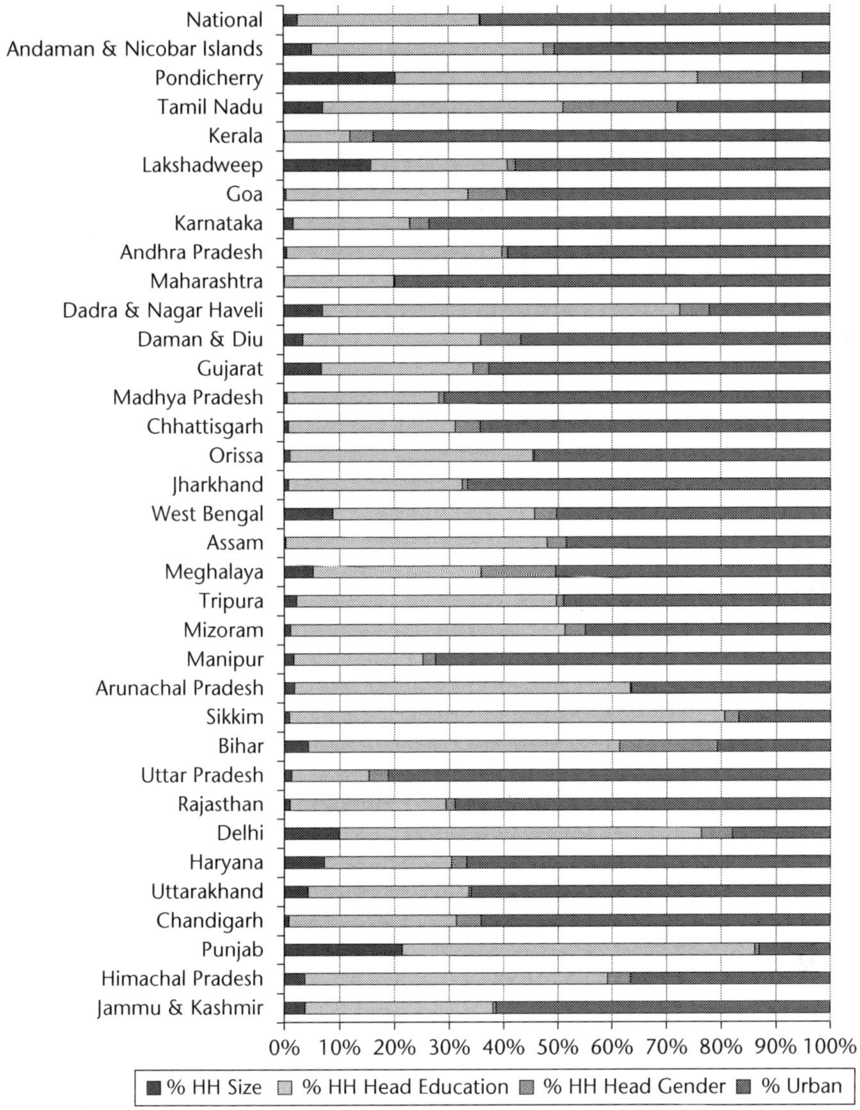

Figure 13.9 India, access to improved water: contribution of circumstances to inequality of opportunities

Source: Authors' calculations using the DLHS-3 (2007/2008).

The final step is to identify the relative contribution of each circumstance to the D-index in all Indian states, and through it, to inequality of opportunity (Figures 13.9–13.12). While location and education of the household head are also the dominant circumstances in explaining HOI across states, the analysis spotlights some finer variations.

- *First, gender appears to be a factor, unlike at the country level.* In particular, access to services is not evenly distributed among female and male headed households in a number of states. For those services with the highest coverage rates at the national level (water and sanitation), the highest contributions of gender to inequality tend to be clustered around states with high coverage of the service. In the case of access to water, gender contributes significantly to inequality in Bitar, Tamil Nadu, and Pondicherry (around 20 percent). For access to electricity, this is the case for Pondicherry, Lakshadweep, and Sikkim (around 10 percent). In the case of access to improved sanitation, the contribution of gender is consistently low, with the exception of a few states, such as Meghalaya (about 33 percent) and Goa (around 20 percent). The same lower access is found for phones, with the contribution of gender found in Pondicherry (about 8 percent).

- *Second, location plays a smaller role in inequality – and education of the head of household a larger role –* where higher access rates exist. This is consistent with the patterns of infrastructure expansion, which tend to serve population agglomerations first, and then progressively expand to the periphery.

Policy options to address inequality of access to infrastructure in South Asia

Key principles to guide policies

Access is fundamental, but usage determines impact. That is why policy makers should complement access to infrastructure with policies to incentivize the use of services, or make potential benefits more obvious or attainable. One way to do this is to focus on subsidizing (implicitly or explicitly, and with sunset clauses) the infrastructures that provide the greatest public benefit (public good), in contrast to those that provide large private benefits. This should be true across infrastructure sectors as well as within sectors.

- *For water*, rather than broadly subsidizing provision for which subsidies are often captured by richer groups in society, a municipal government would choose to subsidize flood control.
- *For energy*, a large country like India with a large energy gap may choose to subsidize cleaner sources like solar as opposed to coal fire plants. After all, if electricity is expected to be followed by the adoption of cleaner energy sources, there are several steps that need to occur in between.
- *For sanitation*, given the importance of the location of services, maintenance, and campaigns to promote use, a policy maker may choose to subsidize information provision to address open defecation, rather than subsidize off-site sewage system provision. If subsidies are provided for off-site sewage system provision, preference should be given to treatment and connection for poor households or a condominial type system rather than tariffs.

Ability-to-pay for access to infrastructure services cannot be the only instrument to determine provision. Infrastructure services have strong market failure characteristics, underscoring the need for adequate regulation. Some infrastructures are still close to natural monopolies (such as pipe water and off-site sanitation services). Many are associated with strong externalities (negative and positive) and public goods (and bads) characteristics, as in the case of a lack of sewage treatment or a lack of access to cooking gas. Information issues also abound. Moreover, since infrastructure may act as a spur to economic growth, relying on the ability-to-pay criterion might undercut efforts to reduce poverty.

Another way is to focus on improving women's access to services, as the improvement in household outcomes can be larger when women benefit fully from access. Still another way is to focus on enhancing quality and maintenance, which are major issues in South Asia, where there are on average 42 power shortages a month and 21 water shortages a month.

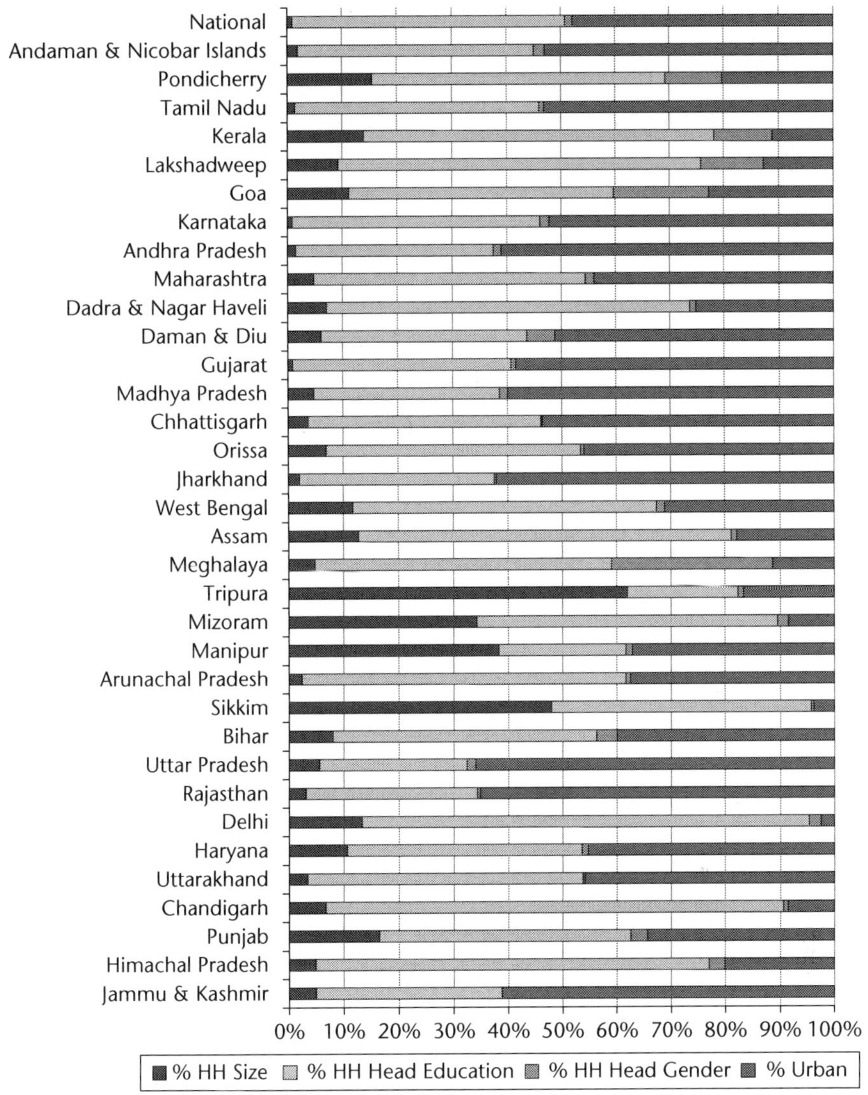

Figure 13.10 India, access to improved sanitation: contribution of circumstances to inequality of opportunities

Source: Authors' calculations using the DLHS-3 (2007/2008).

Yet, some infrastructure programs are too costly to be sustainably implemented without cost-recovery mechanisms that allow them to be self-supporting. The trade-off between providing access to infrastructure services and fully charging for these services is seldom an easy one to equate. It involves understanding the economic characteristics of particular infrastructure sectors and the technology available for provision under different physical, political, and socio-economic conditions. Take the case of piped water provision, which is a private good. It has important market failures associated with it, but essentially individual households have clear incentives to pay for a superior service, compared to other forms of getting water in an urban environment. Yet, piped water is seldom charged to attain full cost recovery, and often relies on

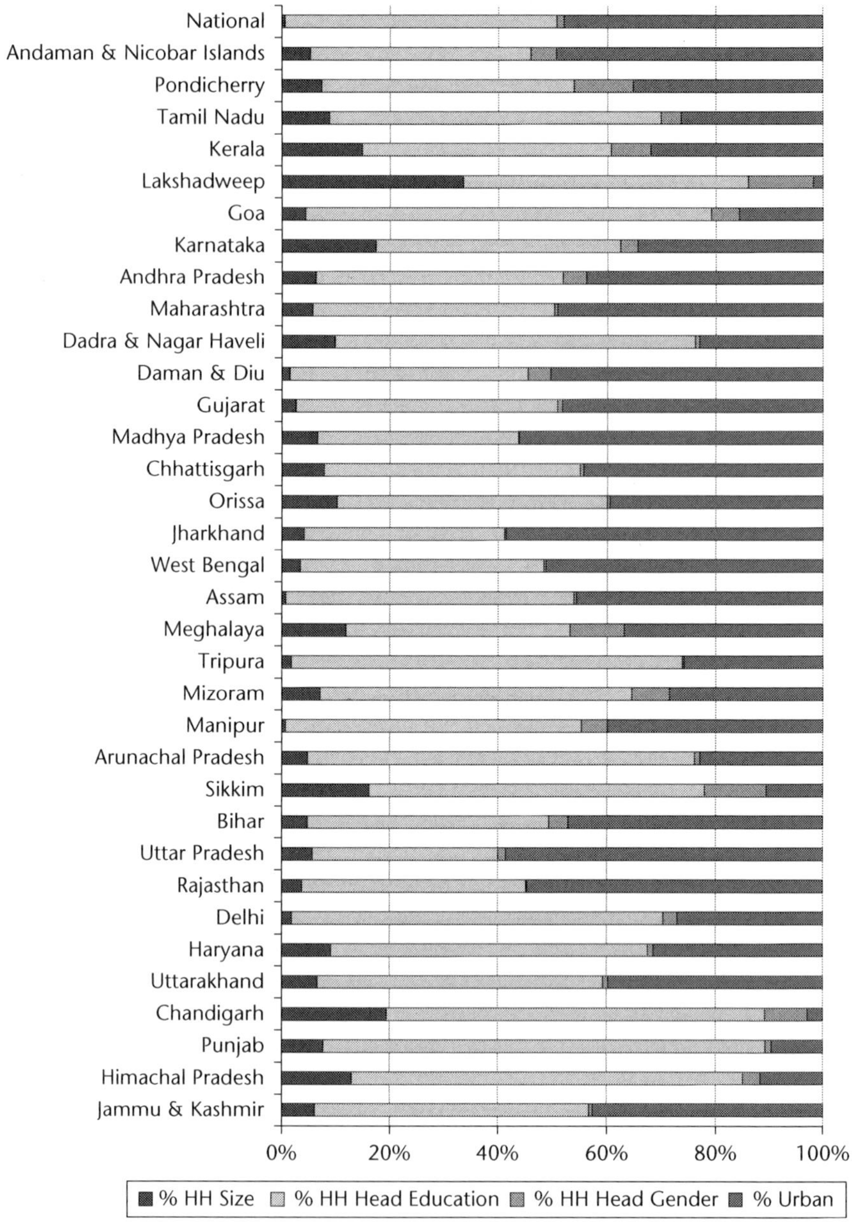

Figure 13.11 India, access to electricity: contribution of circumstances to inequality of opportunities

Source: Authors' calculations using the DLHS-3 (2007/2008).

direct or indirect subsidies that burden public budgets. Nonetheless, the expansion of piped water provision is often part of political manifestos during election campaigns. Now take the case of flood control, which is a public good. Direct cost recovery mechanisms like tariffs are difficult to design, but the lack of adequate flood control in a locality, for example, can cause substantial costs

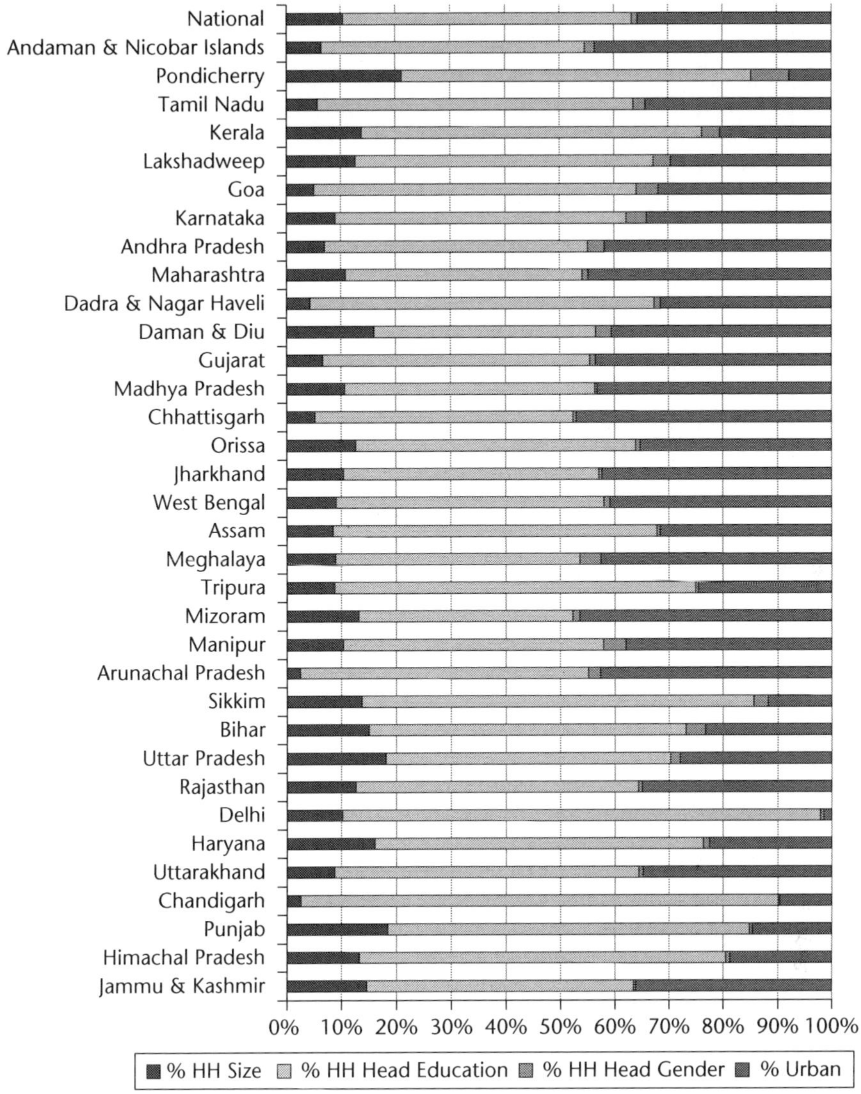

Figure 13.12 India, access to phone: contribution of circumstances to inequality of opportunities

Source: DLHS-3 (2007/2008).

to households via the loss of private assets and lives. Budgetary allocation for flood control is often inadequate, and the service is underprovided.

The likely aim of the policy maker is to attain a certain degree of balance in infrastructure access (especially basic infrastructure), while allowing for wealthier populations to shoulder most of the burden of improving coverage for all. Given the equality achieved in improved water in South Asia, one would be tempted to conclude that this objective is present as the service expands, but this conclusion might conceal rent-seeking behavior, where the wealthier capture proportionally larger amounts of rents that otherwise could be used for expansion and quality improvement for all and not just a few. The literature also argues that infrastructure service expansion is closely linked to rent seeking, since richer districts are better able to lobby the government for infrastructure provision (Cadot et al., 1999).

Although subsidies may improve affordability among underprivileged groups, they can also have the effect of increasing income inequality. Subsidies tend to be captured by those who have political connections, which, at least among unconnected households, tend to be the more middle class households. Ajwad and Wodon (2002) found that in Bolivia and Paraguay, the marginal benefit of improved access to a service tended to be two to three times higher among the upper two quartiles. Thus, while all income quartiles benefited from decentralization, the richer 50 percent benefited more than the poorer 50 percent, a net effect that would tend to increase income inequality. Estache (2005, 285) points out that in Latin America, "as much as 60 to 80 percent of cross-subsidies were aimed at households well above the poverty threshold, while as much as 80 percent of poor households failed to benefit." Thus, it is not surprising that even as absolute levels of connection increase, regressivity in access to infrastructure may still prevail.

Menu of instruments for poverty and access to infrastructure services

Subsidizing connection rather than service consumption may help target the poor. To avoid some of the drawbacks of subsidies, policy makers can adopt measures that reduce the cost of providing network services or improve the ability of poor households to pay for service at a given cost (Komives et al., 2005). These would be available only to unconnected households, reducing or eliminating the price customers have to pay to connect to the system. Alternatively, policy makers can subsidize lower service levels that the better-off find less attractive, such as social connections.

Another set of possible instruments is targeted interventions. Usually these instruments are centered narrowly on a certain district or group that is perceived as underserved. This approach has the advantage of fewer spillover effects; that is, there is less likelihood that the intervention ends up benefitting those who were not intended to be its beneficiaries. However, because these interventions are operating only within impoverished and underserved areas, they tend to face issues like inadequate staffing, funding, technical capacity, and political will (Menéndez, 1991).

A broader approach to address rent seeking could be institutional rather than infrastructure service specific. There are also a number of options to design programs to reduce elite capturing and increase the power of impoverished groups to allocate resources toward their priorities. These include:

- *Institutional re-centering.* Organizations can be created whose primary concern is to reduce poverty through providing infrastructure. For instance, Bolivia's Emergency Social Fund was a temporary organization that was created to finance infrastructure projects in underserved communities.
- *Community participation.* Incorporating transparent mechanisms for underserved people to easily provide input into the design and decision-making process behind infrastructure projects could potentially allow them to compete with the more informal mechanisms that richer populations use to influence decision-making (Menéndez, 1991).[22]

Innovative mechanisms are needed to make policies more effective. Service delivery mechanisms need to evolve to respond to the challenges of coverage, affordability, use, and sustainability. This is particularly important, given that poor households tend to pay more for services when they have to obtain them through non-network solutions. For example, community-based organizations and user groups can contribute to planning and operations; NGOs can help with monitoring and evaluation, promoting social accountability and raising awareness; and the private sector can get involved with investment and delivery (Andres and Naithani, 2013). These alternative mechanisms, which are context-specific, are becoming part of the policy toolkit as they are tested and mainstreamed.

Conclusions

If South Asia hopes to meet its development goals and not risk slowing down, or even halting, growth and poverty alleviation, it is essential to make closing its huge infrastructure gap a priority. Even though SAR's economic growth follows that of EAP, its access to infrastructure rates (sanitation, electricity, telecom, and transport) are closer to that of SSA, the one exception being water, where SAR is comparable to EAP and LAC. As discussed, this is closely related to SAR's urbanization level and the attractiveness cities may exert on people. A slow urbanization process also means, at least in part, forgoing agglomeration benefits at current technology levels.

While the regressivity of infrastructure services is clearly present in South Asia, the story that emerges is heterogeneous and complex. Countries with higher per capita income (like the Maldives and Sri Lanka) enjoy better access to infrastructure services both spatially (geographically within the country) and income wise, even though conflict areas are clearly worse off. That said, the widespread use of firewood for cooking, particularly among the poor, is somewhat surprising, although it may reflect a policy choice, which in turn may have dire consequences in the intergenerational transmission of poverty. Among infrastructure sectors, water is the most equally distributed in spatial terms, and sanitation, energy, and phones the least – although in countries like India, the telecom revolution has arrived, with phone access rising rapidly. Within a country, leading regions (those with a lower poverty level) generally mean better access, but lagging regions (those with a higher poverty level) do not necessarily mean worse access. Of course, the quality of the services also matters, and Sri Lanka, which has the best educated population in SAR and a benign geography, scores high in that regard, too.

The challenge of increasing access to infrastructure services across South Asia is compounded by the inequality in the distribution of existing access for households with certain characteristics, such as those that are: (1) located in rural areas; (2) with household heads that have not passed through the education system; (3) large households; and (4) with a female household head. Contribution, however, does not mean causality. The idea of the analysis is to identify what types of households seem particularly excluded from the way access has increased so far. At the country level, location and education together are the main explanatory factors. Location (which is actually a slightly stronger influence) seems obvious, but education does not, unless it is linked to income poverty and remoteness of household location (even among rural areas). At the Indian state level, education actually starts to become a bigger factor than at the country level. And while the contribution of gender as the household head seems negligible at the country level, there are a number of Indian states (and districts within them) where access is clearly biased toward male-headed households.

Policy choices should be aimed at increased shared prosperity. In effect, the widespread equality in the access to improved water, and to a lesser extent improved sanitation, may also reflect a policy choice. The expansion of water provision is a direct benefit to households, and providing water serves both politicians and households well. This does not mean that rent-seeking opportunities are not present or prevalent. Because of the widespread need to expand water services across income quintiles, improved water may hide rent-seeking opportunities, especially in tariff structures and different forms of explicit and implicit subsidies. Adequate access to improved water may also reflect geography, as implied by our maps on improved water access – for example, lagging states in India that happen to coincide with the presence of ample water sources. Alternatively, geography may be an insurmountable obstacle, as in the case of connective infrastructures in mountainous countries like Bhutan and Nepal. However, if a poorer country or a poorer state can have better access to a given infrastructure service than a richer country or a richer state, then there is hope that policy makers can adopt measures that will improve access in a manner that increases shared prosperity.

Infrastructure investments are no substitute for an income policy if the policy maker's objective is some sort of income redistribution. Yet, they are effective ways of empowering households either directly via innovative mechanisms of decision-making and implementation, or indirectly via welfare improvements, as in the "principle of inclusion," or through promoting economic growth, as in the "principle of connectivity" (Biller and Nabi, 2013). Policy makers should be cognizant *ex ante* that, because of the importance of infrastructure services in economic growth, poverty reduction, and improving quality of life, interventions in infrastructure services provision will likely generate some perverse incentives, regardless of the income quintiles that individual households belong to.

If shared prosperity is one of the ultimate goals of policy makers, it is important to get accurate infrastructure data. The analysis was constrained by the availability of data. The existing data allowed for a broad spatial analysis in physical terms and across time, looking at the impact on different generations. It created a baseline for tracking progress in closing the infrastructure gap, and on equality of opportunities across the region. It can be expanded and improved by considering more or less (opportunity and access) circumstances, exploring alternative indicators of access, and use and quality of infrastructure services. Yet, as specific economic questions were asked, the availability of consistent data across the board became scarcer. At different stages of the analysis, this constraint became more binding, restricting the number of countries and/or infrastructure sectors that could be studied. Some of the apparent inconsistencies in the data can only be clarified by in-depth field research. Without it, private and public investments may miss their targets of leveling the playing field and end up increasing inequality of infrastructure service provision.

Appendix A: Infrastructure definition

In order to have a comparable definition of access to infrastructure we will use:

a Improved Water: The definition of access to water is based on the WHO/UNICEF Joint Monitoring Programme for Water Supply and Sanitation (WHO and UNICEF 2013). This definition is based on differentiating the water sources that by nature or intervention are protected from outside contamination. In Table 13A.1 we can see how sources of water can be divided between improved and unimproved water.

b Improved Sanitation: The definition of access to sanitation is based on the WHO/UNICEF Joint Monitoring Programme (JMP) for Water Supply and Sanitation. This definition is based on the classification among sanitation facilities that hygienically separate human excreta from human contact, and it is for private use of the household. We can see in Table 13A.2 how to discriminate between facilities following JMP criteria for having a comparable sanitation infrastructure among countries of the region.

Table 13A.1 Improved water classification

Improved Water	*Unimproved Water*
Piped water into dwelling	Unprotected spring
Piped water to yard/plot	Unprotected dug well
Public tap or standpipe	Cart with small tank/drum
Tube well or borehole	Tanker-truck
Protected dug well	Surface water
Protected spring	Bottled water
Rainwater	

Source: WHO/UNICEF Joint Monitoring Programme for Water Supply and Sanitation.

Table 13A.2 Improved sanitation classification

Improved Sanitation	*Unimproved Sanitation*
Private flush toilet	All shared facilities
Private piped sewer system	Flush/pour flush to elsewhere
Private septic tank	Pit latrine without slab
Private flush/pour flush to pit latrine	Bucket
Private ventilated improved pit latrine (VIP)	Hanging toilet or hanging latrine
Private pit latrine with slab	No facilities or bush or field
Private composting toilet	

Source: WHO/UNICEF Joint Monitoring Programme for Water Supply and Sanitation.

c Electricity: A household with access to electricity is defined by asking the household which is the principal way of lighting the house.

d Phone: The definition of having access to phone includes two types of technologies: land-lines and mobile phones.

e Cooking gas: Bottled cooking gas – liquefied petroleum gas (LPG).

Appendix B: Data

Different data sources were used in the analysis. These sources are listed in Table 13B.1. To be part of the analysis on regressivity, each survey needs to satisfy two conditions: (a) Contain reliable information on most infrastructure services namely, improved sanitation, improved water, electricity, telephones, and cooking gas; and (b) Contain a sample design representative at the smallest administrative region in a given country. The infrastructure services chosen for detailed analysis needs to be comparable across countries (see Appendix A for details). Table 13B.1-Panel A lists all surveys with information on the infrastructure services and their level of representativeness.

On the poverty side, the analysis requires information about an income measure to estimate the poverty rate for each administrative region. Table 13B.1-Panel B displays a great level of country attrition. The lack of income measure at lower levels of representativeness restricts the analysis of regressivity primarily to India, Sri Lanka, and Afghanistan.[23] More in-depth analysis is feasible only for the latter two countries.

Table 13B.1 The Surveys

Country	*Survey*	*Year*	*Representativeness Level*
Panel A: Infrastructure Data Sources			
Afghanistan	National Risk and Vulnerability Assessment	2008	Province
Bangladesh	Multiple Indicator Cluster Survey	2006	District
Bhutan	Living Standard Measurement Study	2007	District
India	District Level Household Survey	2007	District
Maldives	Demographic Health Survey	2009	Region
Nepal	Demographic Health Survey	2011	Ecological zones
Pakistan	Demographic Health Survey	2006	Province
Sri Lanka	Household Income and Expenditure Survey	2010	District
Panel B: Poverty Rates Data Sources			
Afghanistan	National Risk and Vulnerability Assessment	2008	Province
Bangladesh			
Bhutan	Living Standard Measurement Study	2007	District
India	Debroy and Bhandari (2003) using NSS	2007	District
Maldives	–	–	–
Nepal	–	–	–
Pakistan	–	–	–
Sri Lanka	Household Income and Expenditure Survey	2010	District

Source: Authors' elaboration.

Appendix C: Infrastructure index

The idea of creating an infrastructure index is to be able to have a measure of average access.

The process followed to create the three indexes were:

1 For each type of infrastructure estimate in which the quartile of access is the administrative region, we use the quartiles instead of the rate of access because we try to see a relation between income differences and a relative position inside the country.
2 The first index is constructed as an equally weighted average of the quartiles.
3 The second index is constructed with an importance-weighted average. The weights used are 0.39 for improved water, 0.28 for improved sanitation, 0.33 for electricity, and zero for cooking gas and phone. These weights are selected to have a measure only for the principal basic need of the household.
4 The weights for the third index are created based on the data using a Principal Component Analysis (PCA). Using the elements of the first component eigenvector (the principal component that maximizes the variance of the score) we create a weight for each type of infrastructure.

For the colors in the three-dimensional maps, three scores were constructed. Score I: Simple average (sum of the points for each indicator divided by the number of indicators); Score II: Weighted average using predetermined weights to capture that WATSAN and Power are important direct benefits to households; and Score III: Weighted average using weights obtained from a Principal Component Analysis – a statistical procedure. They all yield similar results. Each district is then ranked between 1 and 4. This ranking is dependent on the quartile the aggregate scores fall into. If a district falls in the bottom quartile it ranks 1 (red in the map, which indicates poor accessibility to infrastructure, while a district that scores in the top quartile ranks 4 (gold in the map), which indicates highest accessibility.

Notes

1 The proportion of people living on less than $1.25 a day decreased from 54 percent to 31 percent (a 42 percent decrease), between 1990 and 2010, mainly due to the increase in population.
2 The selection of countries and infrastructures were based largely on data availability, data consistency across databases and consistencies within databases.
3 Additional information on methodology, models, background papers, stock taking reviews, and data used can be found in the Infrastructure Needs Regional Study webpage: http://go.worldbank.org/ZRTCA2AKR0.
4 The US$ 1.7 to US$ 2.5 trillion are at current prices, and they are equivalent to US$ 1.4 to US$ 2.1 trillion at 2010 prices.
5 These percentages are based on the investment requirements at 2010 prices.
6 It should be noted that in order to compare countries it is important to follow similar definitions of infrastructure services. Appendix A provides the definitions. Some countries may have higher than expected rates of access to a particular infrastructure, but this may come about because of the broad definition used for the particular infrastructure. The definitions are the basis of the household survey questionnaires commonly used and discussed in Appendix B.
7 It should be noted that data sources are kept the same for consistency purposes when comparing countries. The Ceylon Electricity Board (CEB) estimates for example that over 90 percent of Sri Lankan households were electrified in 2011.
8 World Energy Outlook, IEA: www.worldenergyoutlook.org/resources/energydevelopment/globalstatusofmodernenergyaccess/.
9 See Appendix B for a discussion on the available data.
10 See Appendix C for more details on how the indexes are constructed.
11 The Lorenz curve plots the percentage of total income earned by various portions of the population when the population is ordered by the size of their incomes.
12 Improved water is a noticeable outlier in the Maldives which may be explained by small atolls having more access in relative terms because of the inclusion of rain water in improved water.
13 An improved sanitation facility is defined as one that hygienically separates human excreta from human contact (see Appendix A).
14 Maps could be generated for each infrastructure service, but this analysis is easier done via other means as discussed later in the chapter.
15 This has been underscored in the literature as well (see Kojima et al., 2011; Kojima, 2011).
16 DLHS-3.
17 Census of India, 2011.
18 We settle for 'gender of the household head' as our proxy for gender weight in the HOI because the data available does not allow exploring restrictions in the access and use of services across household members. The low prevalence of female-headed households, however, contributes to a low weight of this variable in the HOI.
19 Coincidently or not, these are areas where conflict was or has been most intense.
20 In the case of electricity access, we have information for only 20 out of 34 provinces.
21 To keep the analysis of data manageable, we report state-level figures for only three indicators of opportunity: access to improved water sources, access to improved sanitation, and access to electricity.
22 The way incentives are designed play an important role in mitigating rent seeking. Community Driven Development Projects are particularly concern with elite capture even within poor communities.
23 Bhutan was excluded from the analysis due to data inconsistencies.

References

Ajwad, M.I., and Q. Wodon (2002). "Who Benefits from Increased Access to Public Services at the Local Level? A Marginal Benefit Incidence Analysis for Education and Basic Infrastructure." *World Bank Economists Forum*, *2*, 155–175.

Andres, L., D. Biller, and M. Herrera Dappe (2013). "Infrastructure Gap in South Asia: Infrastructure Needs, Prioritization, and Financing." Washington, DC: World Bank.

Andres, L., and S. Naithani (2013). "Mechanisms and Approaches in Basic Service Delivery for Access and Affordability." Washington, DC: World Bank.

Azam, M., and V. Bhatt (2012) "Like Father, Like Son? Intergenerational Education Mobility in India." *IZA Discussion Paper 6549*. Available at SSRN: http://ssrn.com/abstract=2062748.

Bangladesh Bureau of Statistics and UNICEF (2007). "Multiple Indicator Cluster Survey (MICS) 2006." Dhaka, Bangladesh: Ministry of Planning and UNICEF.

Biller, D., and I. Nabi (2013). "Investing in Infrastructure: Harnessing its Potential for Growth in Sri Lanka. " Washington, DC: World Bank.

Cadot, O., L.H. Röller, and A. Stephan (1999). "A Political Economy Model of Infrastructure Allocation: An Empirical Assessment." *(FS IV 99-15)*. Berlin: Wissenschaftszentrum Berlin für Sozialforschung.

Debroy, B., and L. Bhandari. (2003). "District Level Deprivation in the New Millennium." Delhi: Konark.

Estache, A. (2005). "On Latin America's Infrastructure Experience: Policy Caps and the Poor." In Nancy Birdsall and John Nellis (eds.) Reality Check: The Distributional Impact of Privatization in Developing Countries (pp. 281–296). Washington, DC: Center for Global Development.

Heckman, J.J., S.H. Moon, R. Pinto, P.A. Savelyev, and A. Yavitz (2010). "The Rate of Return to the High/Scope Perry Preschool Program." *Journal of Public Economics*, 94(1), 114–128.

Hoyos, A., and A. Narayan (2010). "Inequality of Opportunities Among Children: How Much Does Gender Matter?" *Working Paper: Background paper for the World Development Report 2012: Gender Equality and Development.*

Institute for Population Sciences (2007–2008). "District Level Household Survey (DLHS-3)." Delhi: Ministry of Health and Family and Welfare.

Kojima, M. (2011). "The Role of Liquefied Petroleum Gas in Reducing Energy Poverty." *Extractive Industries for Development Series #25.*

Kojima, M., R. Bacon, and X. Zhou. (2011). "Who Uses Bottled Gas? Evidence from Households in Developing Countries." *Policy Research Working Paper 5731*. Washington, DC: World Bank.

Komives, K., J. Halpern, V. Foster, Q. Wodon, and R. Abdullah (2005). "Water, Electricity, and the Poor: Who Benefits from Utility Subsidies?" Washington, DC: World Bank.

Menéndez, A. (1991). "Access to Basic Infrastructure by the Urban Poor." Washington, DC: World Bank.

Ministry of Health and Family (MOHF) [Maldives] and ICF Macro (2010). "Maldives Demographic and Health Survey (DHS) 2009." Calverton, MD: MOHF and ICF Macro.

Ministry of Health and Population (MOHP) [Nepal], New ERA, and ICF International Inc. (2012). "Nepal Demographic and Health Survey (DHS) 2011." Kathmandu, Nepal: Ministry of Health and Population, New ERA, and ICF International, Calverton, Maryland.

National Institute of Population Studies (NIPS) [Pakistan], and Macro International Inc. (2008). "Pakistan Demographic and Health Survey (DHS) 2006–07." Islamabad, Pakistan: National Institute of Population Studies and Macro International Inc.

Paes de Barros, R.P., F.H. Ferreira, J.R. Vega, and J.S. Chanduvi (2009). "Measuring Inequality of Opportunities in Latin America and the Caribbean." Washington, DC: World Bank.

Shorrocks, A.F. (1999). "A Decomposition Procedure for Distributional Analysis; a Unified Framework Based on Shapley Value." United Kingdom: University of Essex and Institute for Fiscal Studies (Mimeo).

World Bank (2014). "SAR Inequality of Opportunities." Washington, DC: World Bank (Forthcoming).

World Development Indicators (WDI) (2013). Retrieved from World Bank World Development Indicators Database website: http://data.worldbank.org/country.

World Health Organization (WHO) (2014). "Preventing Diarrhea through Better Water, Sanitation, and Hygiene: Exposures and Impacts in Low- and Middle-Income Countries." Geneva: World Health Organization.

World Health Organization (WHO) and United Nations Children's Fund (UNICEF) (2013). Retrieved from WHO/UNICEF Joint Monitoring Programme (JMP) for Water and Sanitation website: www.wssinfo.org/documents-links/documents/?tx_displaycontroller[type]=country_files.

Wright, J., S. Gundry, and R. Conroy (2004). "Household Drinking Water in Developing Countries: A Systematic Review of Microbiological Contamination Between Source and Point-of-Use." *Tropical Medicine & International Health*, *9*(1), 106–117.

Zwane, A.P., and M. Kremer (2007). "What Works in Fighting Diarrheal Diseases in Developing Countries? A Critical Review." *The World Bank Research Observer*, *22*(1), 1–24.

14

Poverty, inequality and public health in Indonesia: does wealthier mean healthier?

Riyana Miranti

Introduction

For the past several years, Indonesian economic development has been performing well, with the economy growing at 5.80 percent per annum during 2010–2014. The GDP per capita also has been increasing over time. The country's GDP per capita in 2010 was already 50 percent higher than its lowest point during the economic crisis in 1999 and was 70 percent higher in 2014.

One of the achievements of Indonesian development is that the poverty rate has been continuing to decline over time, both in rural and in urban areas. The World Bank (2015) has argued that sustained economic growth in Indonesia since the year 2000 has helped to reduce poverty. The latest data in 2014 shows the poverty rate is currently sitting at just under 11 percent. This is a level that had not been achievable earlier even during the pre-crisis period (based on the new BPS poverty calculation). Nevertheless, while the poverty rate declined at around 1 percentage point on average per annum in 2007–2010, it has declined by only 0.6 percentage points per annum since 2010. Furthermore, around 28 million people still live below the national poverty line.

On another spectrum, in terms of inequality, the Gini coefficient has been increasing since 2000 and has been stable at 0.41 since 2011, a level that has never been experienced by Indonesia before. Rising inequality in Indonesia is a national story, and has been rising in both urban and rural areas (Manning and Miranti, 2015; World Bank, 2015).

Manning and Miranti (2015), Miranti et al. (2013) and World Bank (2015) have identified several factors of increasing inequality, including high wealth concentration at the top 10 percent of consumption and wage, where the wealth of this group has been increasing; the issue of skill premium where there has been increasing demand for skilled workers in the labor market and slow growth in the labor intensive manufacturing sector; and fiscal policy in terms of expenditure, which has a less equalizing effect and low tax compliance and revenue. Furthermore, there have also been other exogenous factors, such as the resource boom in the 2000s (in coal and palm oil) which benefited certain regions in Indonesia over others. The World Bank (2015) has also proposed that inequality of opportunity, in which inequality has been present since birth, is one factor influencing Indonesia's increase in inequality.

Thus, from a welfare perspective, Indonesia is characterized by a sluggish rate of poverty reduction and high inequality, and these have been reflected at the regional level particularly in terms of inequality. Two-thirds of 33 provinces in 2014 experienced increasing inequality in the period of 2010–2014.

So, questions naturally emerge regarding the potential implications of these phenomena. Increasing inequality has been linked with many development impacts, including less secure property rights, increased uncertainty, and the negative impact on economic growth and reduction in investment opportunities especially in human capital development (Nissanke and Thorbecke, 2006). Interestingly, there has been limited discussion on this issue in general across countries or within single countries during the recent period in which increasing inequality has risen globally.

This chapter focuses on the human development perspective of Indonesia's development story, taking into account the potential implications in the area of health. We investigate the relationship between three economic variables: inequality, poverty and income level (using GDP per capita) and public health indicators during the development period in Indonesia, which is characterized by an increasing level of income, declining but sluggish poverty rates, and increasing inequality. Poverty rates and GDP per capita represent the level of wealth, while the inequality measures represent how well the wealth is distributed.

In the context of Indonesia, the focus on health has become very important, given the implementation of the Universal Health Insurance Scheme, starting in early 2014. Further, within national and international context this research topic is also important, since, following the Post 2015 Development Agenda, Indonesia has pledged its support toward the new Sustainable Development Goals (SDGs) as one of 150 economies adopting the ambitious post-2015 targets covering 17 goals to foster welfare and well-being for the next 15 years. One of goals is to ensure good health and well-being, for which this chapter is relevant.

Nevertheless, due to data availability particularly from the health indicators, this chapter analyzes the association between income, poverty, inequality and health in recent years prior to the implementation of the Universal Health Insurance Scheme. We aim to contribute to the policy debate by attempting to answer the following two research questions: first, is being wealthier always associated with being healthier? Second, are the associations with poverty and inequality different among various health indicators?

Literature has discussed the relationship between inequality and health with ambiguous results. Deaton (2003) has argued, critically, that there is no robust association between inequality and health, particularly in rich countries. Beckfield (2004) also suggests that the association between inequality and health becomes weaker when other control variables are included. Nevertheless, Wilkinson and Pickett (2006) in their comprehensive literature review covering 155 papers in this field of income inequality and population health, find that although this relationship has mixed results, more than half of the literature has suggested that health is worse in the economies where the income differential is bigger. This works out if inequality reflects social stratification in the country. Biggs et al. (2010) conclude that being wealthier is associated with being healthier, but the extent to which health is better depends on how the wealth has been distributed.

There are two strands of literature which summarize the mechanisms within the link between economic variables, particularly in the case of inequality and public health. First, as argued by Wilkinson and Pickett (2006), high inequality may lead to lower health through physiological effects of chronic stress due to low social status, and to low social esteem as the result of inequality. Another strand of literature mentions the potential implication of income inequality with voters' demand response for redistributions including on public health provisions through public spending on health (Meltzer and Richard, 1981). Most of the empirical literature in this field utilizes cross country data, although some apply single-country data, mostly for developed countries such as the US, Canada, UK, Spain, Brazil and Italy. The study on Italy finds that income inequality is negatively associated with life expectancy at birth, and that this association is robust, even after taking into account income per capita and educational attainment (De Vogli et al., 2005).

In addition to the literature on inequality and health, some studies have focused on the relationship between poverty and health. Benzeval et al. (1995, 2000) propose several factors with regard to the association between poverty and health outcomes, such as the concept that poverty may cause stress and anxiety that negatively affect health, and that poverty may limit people's choices and access to shelter, food and ability to participate in society, that may then have an adverse impact on health outcomes.

Biggs et al. (2010) have improved on this hypothesis by including not only inequality but also poverty, examining their associations with public health. Particularly, Biggs et al. (2010) examine whether the positive effects of economic development has been hampered by high inequality or poverty. This is a relevant issue for Indonesia, where many people still live in poor rural areas and have limited access to public health services.

Many previous studies tend to focus on the causes of increasing inequality, with limited discussion on the potential implications of inequality. Dabla-Norris et al. (2015) argue that inequality of health outcomes and access are issues in developing countries, including in Indonesia. These issues are also important, given the regional diversity within the country. with West Indonesia (the islands of Java, Sumatra and Bali) considered more advanced compared with its East Indonesia counterparts (Sulawesi, Kalimantan, Maluku and Papua islands).

The outline of the chapter is as follows. The next section discusses trends and patterns of poverty and inequality in Indonesia from a comparative and regional perspective. The third section analyzes recent health sector development and performance in Indonesia. The fourth section investigates empirically the evidence of the potential interplay between income, poverty and inequality, and its impact on the health performance of the country. The chapter concludes with a discussion of the lessons learned and policy implications.

Recent trends and patterns of poverty and inequality in Indonesia

International perspective

Poverty

Indonesia's international poverty status has been relatively better than that of other Asian countries. Indonesia has reduced the percentage of population below the international poverty line (<$1.25/day) from 21.4 percent in 2005 to 16.20 percent in 2011, and from 21.3 percent in 2008 to 15.9 percent in 2010 using the more recent $1.90 a day poverty line. Although the reduction of international poverty rates (by almost a quarter) is less than the reduction in the national poverty rate (by almost a third), this reduction is comparable to China and India, which also reduced their international poverty rates by more than 20 percent during the past decade. However, the picture is not so promising when the poverty headcount ratio at $3.10 a day is used, since around 42 percent of Indonesia's population live under this poverty line, more than in Cambodia, the Philippines and Thailand (Table 14.1).

That leads us to ask, how are poverty programs in Indonesia organized and implemented? The National Team for Acceleration of Poverty Reduction (*Tim Nasional Percepatan Penanggulangan Kemiskinan* or TNP2K) was constructed under Vice President Boediono's office during the Soesilo Bambang Yudhoyono Presidency, and manages poverty alleviation efforts in the country. TNP2K consists of a team comprised of academic scholars and bureaucrats who have developed various programs using strong research based evidence policies. These policies cover the following four

Table 14.1 Proportion of population living under the international poverty line $3.10 a day (%)

Country Name	*2006*	*2007*	*2008*	*2009*	*2010*	*2011*	*2012*
Cambodia		61.64	53.25	41.93	42.36	43.25	37
China			32.96		27.24		
India				67.92		58.01	
Indonesia			54.51		46.3		41.67
Malaysia		2.71		2.71			
Myanmar							
Philippines	40.66			36.45			37.61
Thailand	5.51	3.74	2.97	2.59	2.09	1.17	1.23
Vietnam	51.15		45.61		18.05		13.86

Note: Missing values mean data are not available.

Source: World Bank, World Development Indicators.

key strategies: improving social protection programs, providing access to the poor for basic services, empowering of community, and fostering development, which is inclusive to everybody. These strategies are then classified into four clusters (1) Integrated family-based social assistance programs, including *Jaminan Kesehatan Nasional* (Universal Health Insurance Program), *Program Keluarga Harapan* (Hopeful Family Program which is Conditional Cash Transfer program in Indonesia), *Raskin* (Rice for the Poor), (2) Community development poverty alleviation programs, (3) Micro and small enterprise empowerment poverty alleviation programs (*Kredit Usaha Rakyat*) and (4) improvement and expansion of pro poor programs.

Nevertheless, Miranti et al. (2013) argue that the poverty-targeting program has been fraught with leakages and exclusion errors. For example, as found in Miranti et al. (2013), 5.5 percent of total households who were the recipients of the rice for the poor program (RASKIN) in 2008, were the wealthier households who were at the top quantile of the SUSENAS consumption distribution.

To improve the targeting method, the government created an integrated database dedicated to the poor, called the Social Protection Card Database. This data contains information about the characteristics of the population that are likely to be the most appropriate beneficiaries of poverty alleviation programs, covering the population found in the lowest 40 percent (around 24.5 million households or 96 million of individuals) and listing their social and economic characteristics.

Recently, in the first cluster, our current President Joko Widodo (Jokowi) proposed the change of *Raskin* to the shopping voucher for varieties of staples, which aims to provide more options for the poor families so that they can shop for not only rice, the main staple for most of the Indonesian population, but also for other staples such as eggs, oil, sugar and other goods. The government under Jokowi also created a flagship program to create the Productive Families program, which covers three initiatives to improve the welfare level of the disadvantaged population. These initiatives include: (1) the Family Welfare Deposit program, which focuses on productive financial deposits for disadvantaged families; (2) the Smart Indonesia program, an education program which targets children from disadvantaged families who receive financial assistance for completing their education up of high school/vocational school, covering 12 years of education; and (3) the Healthy Indonesia program, which provides Healthy Indonesia cards for members of disadvantaged families, ensuring the families have access to the Universal Health Insurance Program.

Another initiative that has been intended to improve the welfare of the population, particularly for those who live in rural areas, while at the same time allowing the disadvantaged population to participate in the economic decision making process, is the implementation of

Indonesia's Village Law No.6/2014. The implementation of this law aims to ensure that intergovernmental transfers from central and local governments reach villages and communities to fulfil their basic necessities.

As explained earlier, within the international environment, Indonesia has continued its international commitment to accomplish the Millennium Development Goals (MDGs) by starting on efforts to achieve Sustainable Development Goals (SDGs).

Inequality

In terms of inequality, as shown in Figure 14.1, when comparing the lowest 20 percent among several neighboring countries, Indonesia performed relatively worse than India and Cambodia, but better than Malaysia, China, the Philippines and Vietnam. Nevertheless, the top 10 percent of the population with the highest expenditure in Indonesia still holds more wealth than 8.2 times the 10 percent of population with the lowest expenditure, indicating that a huge disparity still exists in this country.

As highlighted in Manning and Miranti (2015) and World Bank (2015), the government has been undertaking policies to tackle the issue of inequality in Indonesia through strong fiscal policy, covering both revenue and expenditure sides. From the revenue side, improving tax collection among the high income earners to increase the percentage of tax revenue to GDP is necessary, as it is still low. Improving tax compliance not only for personal income tax but also corporations, including multinational corporations, is important. From the expenditure side, the removal of Indonesia's fuel subsidies and addition of more productive programs, such as the development of infrastructure facilities to create better jobs, and social protection programs to improve living conditions for those who are poor and to providing them with protection from economic shock, are beneficial. As a response to the issue of the skill premium, providing training opportunities for improving skills required in the labor market is also necessary (Word Bank, 2015).

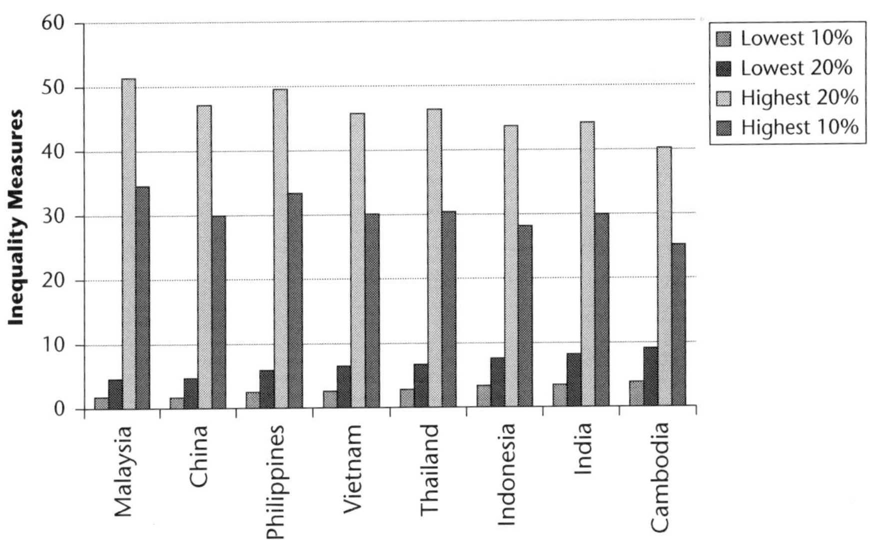

Figure 14.1 Composition of income or expenditure, Indonesia and selected countries

Note: Reference year refers to the latest data available.

Source: World Bank, World Development Indicators.

Regional perspective

Regional poverty

As discussed in Miranti (2011), as seen in Table 14.2, there are clear disparities in headcount poverty rates (calculated using expenditure data) among provinces in Indonesia.

However, in general, the headcount poverty was lower in 2014 than in 2010, except for Jakarta. Nevertheless, it can be seen that provinces such as West and East Nusa Tenggara, Maluku, Papua, West Papua, Bengkulu and Gorontalo persistently had high headcount poverty rates both in 2010 and 2014.

In terms of changes per annum, those provinces where the poverty rates had been low (such as Bali and South Kalimantan) experienced sluggish reduction in poverty rates per annum or even

Table 14.2 Provincial poverty rates, 2010 and 2014

Provinces	*2010*	*2014*	*Changes per annum (%)*
DKI Jakarta	3.48	4.09	4.35
Bali	4.88	4.76	–0.64
South Kalimantan	5.21	4.81	–1.91
Bangka Belitung	6.51	4.97	–5.93
Banten	7.16	5.51	–5.75
Central Kalimantan	6.77	6.07	–2.60
East Kalimantan	7.66	6.31	–4.41
Riau Islands	8.05	6.40	–5.12
West Sumatera	9.5	6.89	–6.87
North Maluku	9.42	7.41	–5.33
Riau	8.65	7.99	–1.90
West Kalimantan	9.02	8.07	–2.64
North Sulawesi	9.1	8.26	–2.31
Jambi	8.34	8.39	0.14
West Java	11.27	9.18	–4.65
South Sulawesi	11.6	9.54	–4.44
North Sumatera	11.31	9.85	–3.22
West Sulawesi	13.58	12.05	–2.82
East Java	15.26	12.28	–4.88
Southeast Sulawesi	17.05	12.77	–6.28
Central Java	16.56	13.58	–4.49
Central Sulawesi	18.07	13.61	–6.17
South Sumatera	15.47	13.62	–2.98
Lampung	18.94	14.21	–6.24
DI Yogyakarta	16.83	14.55	–3.39
Aceh	20.98	16.98	–4.76
West Nusa Tenggara	21.55	17.05	–5.22
Bengkulu	18.3	17.09	–1.65
Gorontalo	23.19	17.41	–6.23
Maluku	27.74	18.44	–8.38
East Nusa Tenggara	23.03	19.60	–3.72
West Papua	34.88	26.26	–6.18
Papua	36.8	27.80	–6.11
Indonesia	**13.33**	**10.96**	**–4.45**

Source: BPS.

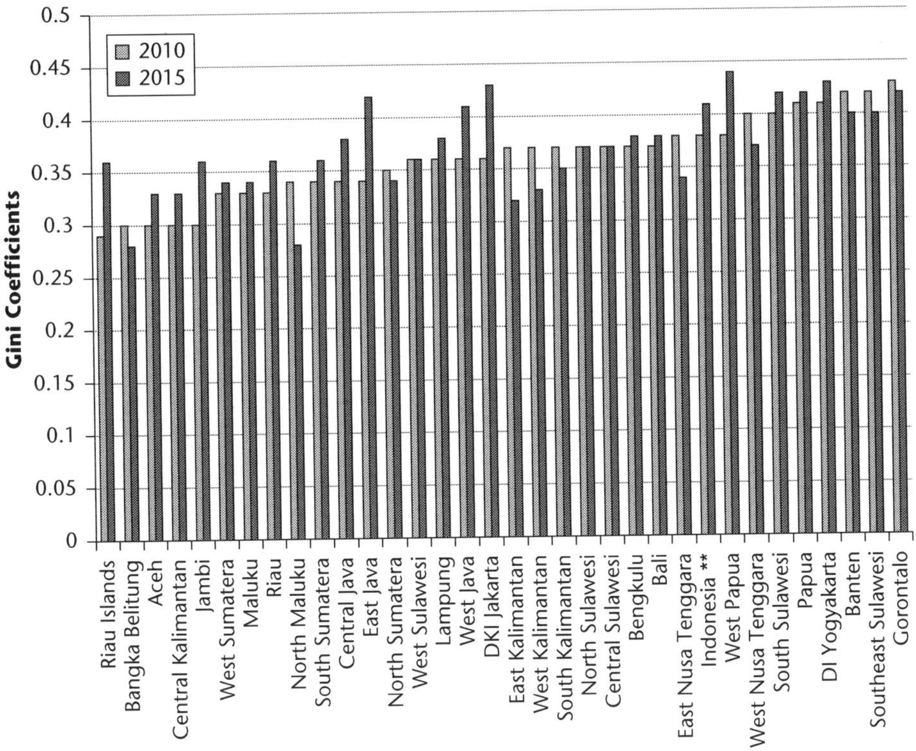

Figure 14.2 Provincial Gini coefficients, 2010 and 2015

Source: BPS.

increasing poverty rates, such as what was experienced by the capital city of Jakarta. By contrast, the poor provinces experienced a rapid reduction in poverty rates, as in West Nusa Tenggara, Papua, West Papua and Maluku.

Regional inequality

Using Gini coefficients calculated from expenditure data as the proxies for inequality, we find it interesting that only 11 provinces experienced a reduction in their inequality figures in 2015, in comparison to 2010. Those provinces are Bangka Belitung, North Maluku, East, West and South Kalimantan, North Sumatera, East and West Nusa Tenggara, Banten, Southeast Sulawesi, and Gorontalo, which means that two-thirds of provinces have experienced increases in inequality. Most provinces with high inequality are actually located in the most developed regions in Java, such as West and East Java, Yogyakarta and DKI Jakarta, and provinces with higher urbanization rates (Miranti, forthcoming). Nevertheless, poor provinces, such as Papua and West Papua are also among the provinces with high inequality (Figure 14.2).

Health sector development in Indonesia

The focus on the Indonesian National Health Development Program has been on primary health care, and the Ministry of Health is responsible for the overall national health policy.

Indonesian health policy has been part of the larger social assistance program. The Ministry's work is based on four pillars: community empowerment, health financing, access to health services, and, surveillance (World Bank, 2015). The role of Puskesmas as community health care centers has been significant in providing basic health services. The new development in Indonesia in the health sector has since commenced with the implementation of a Universal Health Insurance Scheme (*Jaminan Kesehatan Nasional* or JKN) since 2014; this is a subsidized health insurance program which covers everyone, including the poor. This scheme is organized by a new institution *Badan Penyelenggara Jaminan Kesehatan* (BPJS).

Health expenditure

The Indonesian health care system is primarily a public system (Gómez, 2015), with most funding coming from the central government, although decentralization has transferred some of the responsibilities to the local governments.

For this reason, local governments still consider the Indonesian Ministry of Health to be the provider of all health resources, not only in health but also other in health services/facilities, such as health personnel, equipment, medicines and vaccines/immunizations. Law No. 40/2004 on the National Social Security System provided the opportunity for local governments to develop their own local/district health insurance, called *Jaminan Kesehatan Daerah* (JAMKESDA). The aim of this local health insurance was to act as a complement to the National Health Insurance scheme, or *Jaminan Kesehatan Masyarakat* (JAMKESMAS) that was then run by the central government. During the period of 2008–2014, under the umbrella of Cluster 1 of the social assistance program that targeted households, the JAMKESMAS program targeted the poor and near-poor for a total of 86.4 million people which covered roughly around 35 percent of the Indonesian population. The local schemes were intended to provide protection for segments of the population who were not covered by JAMKESMAS. Many districts launched these local schemes, including districts of Kendal, Lebak, Tasikmalaya, Kutai Timur, Makassar and Balikpapan.

As indicated in Figure 14.3, the amount of health expenditure has been increasing over time. Nevertheless, when compared to other countries, Indonesia has spent less than half of what other East Asia and the Pacific developing countries spent. This amount was far below that of Malaysia and Thailand (in international PPP) as can be seen in Figure 14.4.

Patterns of health outcomes

The discussions above show that Indonesia has actively undertaken various policies and programs to improve the poverty and inequality situation in the country. Improvement on the health expenditure side is also underway. In this section, patterns of health outcomes are discussed. As discussed earlier, our analysis aims to investigate the potential impact of inequality and poverty on public health indicators. In general, Indonesia has made various improvements in terms of many of its health indicators at the national level. At the regional level, the picture is not so rosy, and there are still regional divides in various health outcome indicators, dividing those who have health complaints to those with serious health issues, such as tuberculosis prevalence and high infant mortality rates. The Indonesian Bureau Statistic Agency (BPS) defines health complaints as physical and mental health disturbances, including chronic health issues, health issues due to accidents and other reasons.

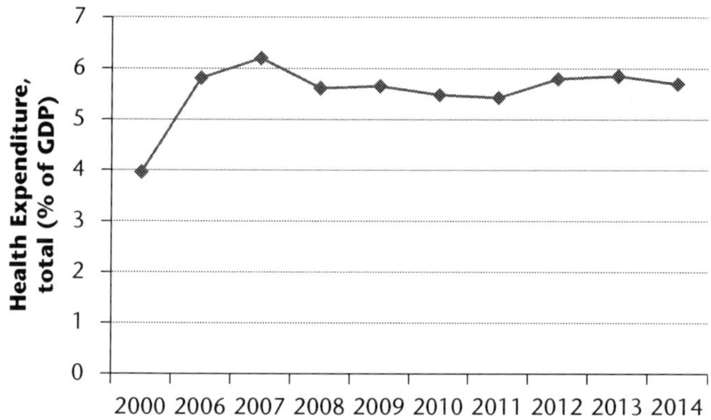

Figure 14.3 Health expenditure (% of GDP), 2000–2014

Source: World Bank, World Development Indicators.

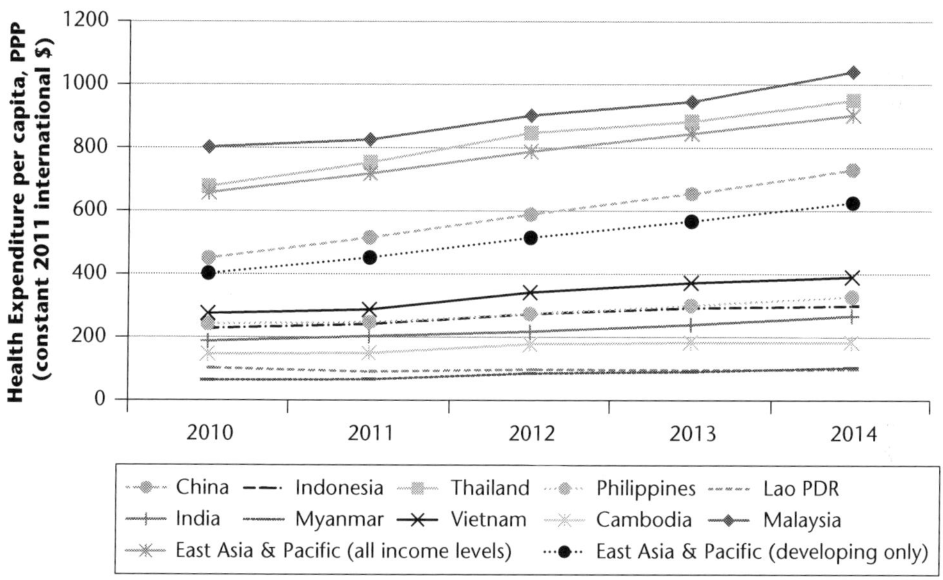

Figure 14.4 Health expenditure per capita, 2010–2014

Source: World Bank, World Development Indicators.

Population who have health complaints

In recent years, 2010–2015, around 29 percent of the Indonesian population experienced health complaints in the previous month. Nevertheless, more than half of the 33 provinces experienced higher rates of health complaints than the national average. Poor provinces such as West and East Nusa Tenggara experienced a high prevalence of health complaints among their populations, possibly due to still limited access to healthy and clean environments.

In comparison to 2010, in 2015, all provinces experienced improvements in terms of the proportion of those who have health complaints. Nationally, the proportion declined by only 0.62 percentage points during the period of 2010–2015 (see Figure 14.5).

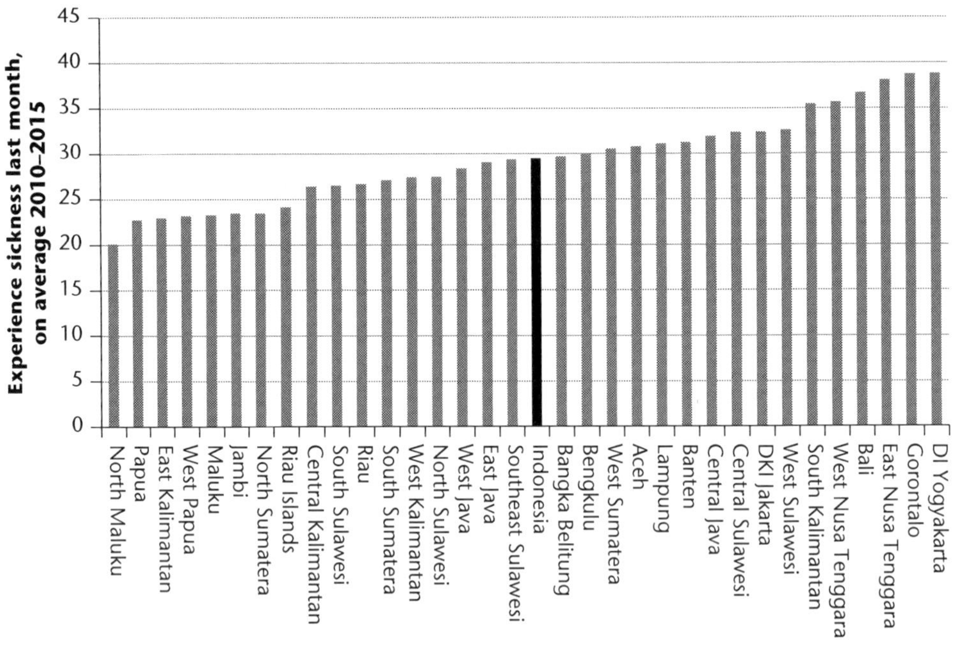

Figure 14.5 Proportion of population who have had health complaints last month on average (%) (2010–2015)

Note: North Kalimantan is included in East Kalimantan. Health complaints cover physical and mental health disturbances, including chronic health issues, health issues due to accidents and others (during last month).

Source: Author's calculation from BPS.

Life expectancy

There has been significant improvement in terms of life expectancy in Indonesia. The national life expectancy among males has increased by almost 1 percentage point during the recent five-year period, 2010–2014. For females, the increase was slightly lower, at 0.76 percentage points in the same period. Following the general trend, the life expectancy of females is higher than that of their male counterparts (Figure 14.6).

Figure 14.7 shows that regional divides still persist with only eight provinces out of 33 that have higher male life expectancy than the national average of 68.87 years, and unsurprisingly the majority of these provinces are located in West Indonesia the more advanced regions (Riau, Bali, West Java, DKI Jakarta, Central Java, DI Yogyakarta) with only two in East Indonesia (North Sulawesi and East Kalimantan).

The life expectancy of females also mirrors that of their male counterparts (see Figure 14.8).

There have been regional differences in this indicator. The poor provinces, again, are disadvantaged, with provinces such as Papua, West and East Nusa Tenggara located in the bottom group of life expectancy.

Prevalence in tuberculosis (TBC) infection

The World Health Organization (WHO) has designated Indonesia as a "high burden country" for tuberculosis. There are 22 high burden countries worldwide, and together they account for about

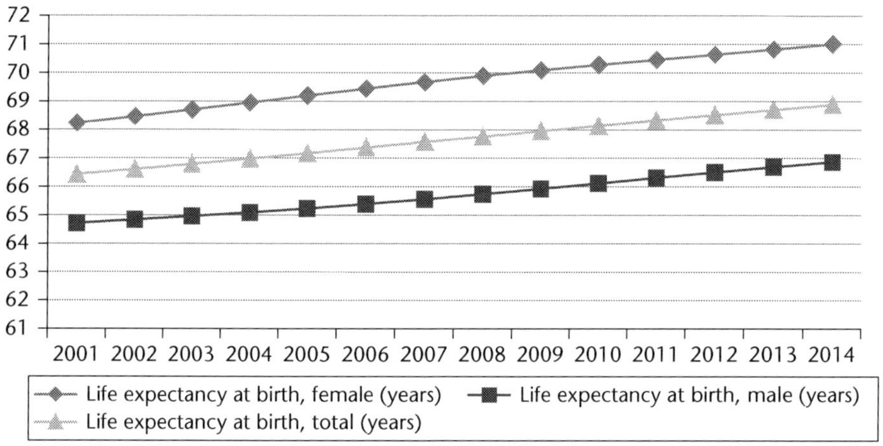

Figure 14.6 Life expectancy at birth, 2001–2014

Source: BPS.

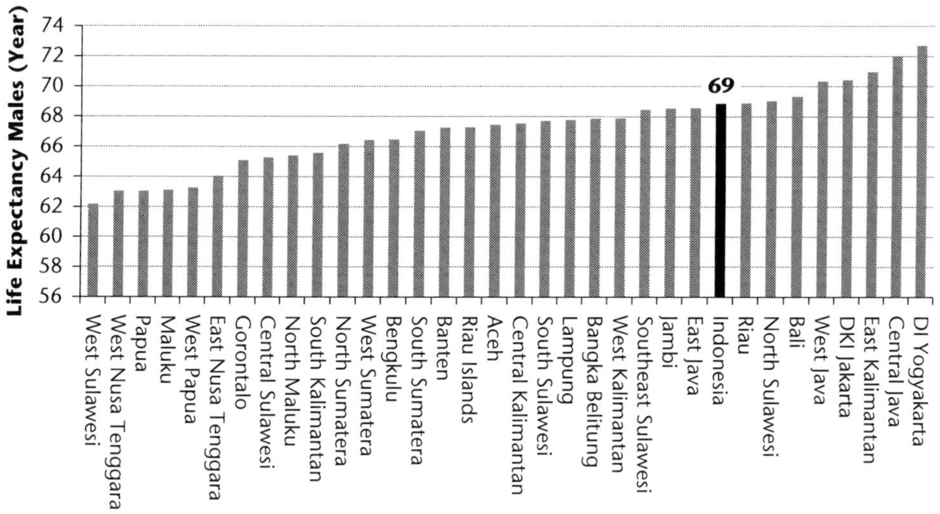

Figure 14.7 Provincial male life expectancy (year), 2014

Note: North Kalimantan is included in East Kalimantan.

Source: BPS.

80 percent of the world's tuberculosis infections. In Asia, these include other countries, such as Cambodia, China, India, Myanmar, the Philippines, Thailand and Vietnam. In comparison to average high burden countries, Indonesia's estimated TB mortality rate and prevalence are both relatively high, as can be seen in Table 14.3.

Despite achieving high success rates in the TBC treatment at around 90 percent nationwide, across regional Indonesia there are still disparities. The success rate of the TBC treatment in West Papua was still only 69.9 percent, although this has experienced more than a 21 percentage point improvement in comparison to its status in 2009 (Table 14.4).

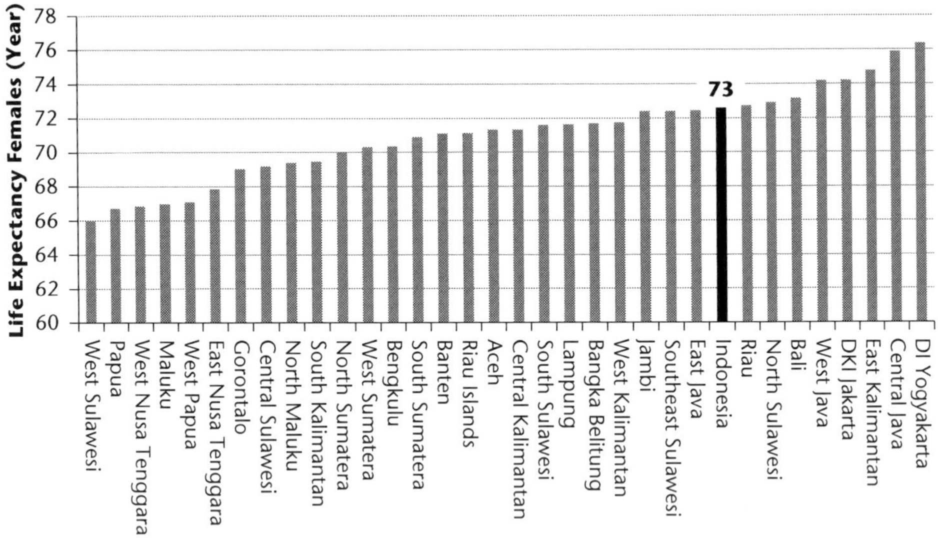

Figure 14.8 Provincial female life expectancy (year), 2014

Note: North Kalimantan is included in East Kalimantan.

Source: BPS.

Table 14.3 Estimated TB mortality rates and prevalence in selected high burden Asian countries, 2014

	Estimated TB mortality (rates per 100,000 population)	*TB prevalence*
Cambodia	58	668
China	2.8	89
India	17	195
Indonesia	41	647
Myanmar	53	457
Thailand	11	236
Vietnam	18	198
High burden countries	**21**	**227**

Source: Table 2.2. Global Tuberculosis Report (WHO, 2015).

Similarly, in the case of Papua, the success rate of the TBC medication has improved by 14.4 percentage points, reaching a 76.3 percent success rate in 2013. East Java, Banten, East Nusa Tenggara, West Kalimantan and Southeast Sulawesi are the other provinces which have experienced improvements in terms of the success rate of the TBC medication during the period 2009–2013.

It is also interesting to see that the number of positive cases has actually increased during this period by 15 percent, which indicates the need to continue focusing preventative efforts, including the need to better socialize the requirement for children to obtain Bacillus Calmette–Guérin (BCG) immunizations, a vaccine used against TBC and to contain active cases, to ensure that people do not pass TBC on to other people.

Table 14.4 TBC, number of positive cases and success rates, 2009–2013

No	*Provinces*	*Number of positive cases*		*Success rate of medication (%)*	
		2009	*2013*	*2009*	*2013*
1	Aceh	3065	2712	93.1	92.2
2	North Sumatera	13897	18095	96.1	94.6
3	West Sumatera	3732	4618	88.5	89.1
4	Riau	2880	3066	83.8	81.5
5	Jambi	2745	2938	94.2	90.2
6	South Sumatera	5181	5272	95.1	94.6
7	Bengkulu	1588	1498	94.8	95.2
8	Lampung	4943	6166	93.2	93.1
9	Bangka Belitung	951	1062	90.1	87.2
10	Riau Islands	784	1219	82	73.7
11	DKI Jakarta	7989	8878	85.8	81.1
12	West Java	31433	34194	92.2	92
13	Central Java	16906	20266	90.4	87.9
14	DI Yogyakarta	1155	1220	84.2	83.9
15	East Java	22598	25461	90.5	91.4
16	Banten	8134	8707	93.3	95
17	Bali	1517	1430	88.3	86.9
18	West Nusa Tenggara	3089	3834	94.1	91.3
19	East Nusa Tenggara	3369	4134	92	92.4
20	West Kalimantan	4156	2847	92.9	94.3
21	Central Kalimantan	1339	1382	94.8	88.4
22	South Kalimantan	2891	3378	93.9	93.5
23	East Kalimantan	2065	2618	85.3	83.9
24	North Sulawesi	3988	4942	96.1	93.8
25	Central Sulawesi	1918	2856	93.8	93.5
26	South Sulawesi	6428	9394	89.9	88
27	Southeast Sulawesi	2296	3672	94.3	94.6
28	Gorontalo	1370	1645	95.5	95.2
29	West Sulawesi	942	1381	92.4	88.9
30	Maluku	2014	2260	96.9	87.1
31	North Maluku	708	1028	84.6	78.8
32	West Papua	638	589	48.3	69.9
33	Papua	2504	2091	61.9	76.3
	Indonesia	**169213**	**194853**	**91.2**	**90.5**

Source: BPS.

Infant mortality rate (IMR) and under five mortality rate (U5MR)

Byrne et al. (2014) argue that Indonesia has experienced a decline both in the infant mortality rate (IMR) and under five mortality rate (UFMR) at the national level but not necessarily at the regional level. The disparities between Java-Bali and the most disadvantaged provinces persist. The figures are also still considered high in comparison to other countries. For example, the IMR in Indonesia is still relatively high in comparison with other Asian countries, including the neighboring countries (such as Thailand and Malaysia), due in particular to two issues: (1) many pregnant women are still malnourished while the baby is

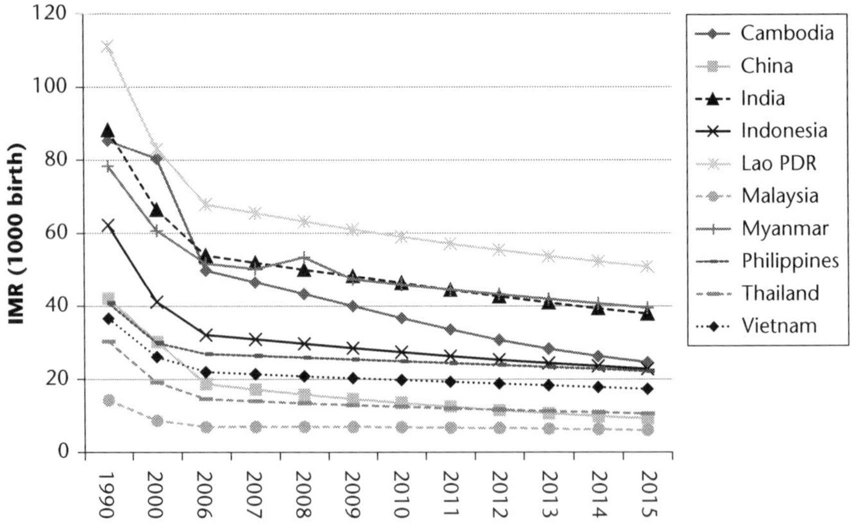

Figure 14.9 Infant mortality rate (IMR), Indonesia and selected countries, 1990–2015

Note: Infant mortality rate is the number of infants dying before reaching one year of age, per 1,000 live births in a given year.

Source: World Bank, World Development Indicators.

developing, so the newborns are not delivered healthy and (2) many pregnant women are giving birth without trained birth attendants and without proper health care facilities. These incidences are particularly relevant for those expectant mothers who live in remote and isolated areas in Indonesia (Figure 14.9).

Regionally, there has been a huge disparity in terms of the IMR, as West Sulawesi, North Maluku, Gorontalo and West Papua all recorded Infant Mortality Rates higher than 60 in 2012 (Figure 14.10).[1]

A similar phenomenon is also found in the Child Mortality Rate under 5 years old. Poor provinces such as Papua, West Papua, West and East Nusa Tenggara perform poorly in this indicator (Figure 14.11).

Measles, mumps and rubella (MMR) immunization

It is interesting to observe that West Nusa Tenggara is recorded as a province with the highest proportion of children with MMR immunizations. This is in contrast to the other indicators in which West Nusa Tenggara is left behind. This may reflect the success story of the immunization program in this poor province, although apparently this has not followed in other poor provinces such as East Nusa Tenggara or Papua (Figure 14.12).

Income, poverty, inequality and health indicators

Having discussed the trends and patterns of poverty and inequality, and also the health sector developments in Indonesia, this section provides an analysis on the relationship between these three main variables. In addition to poverty and inequality variables, GDP per capita is used to

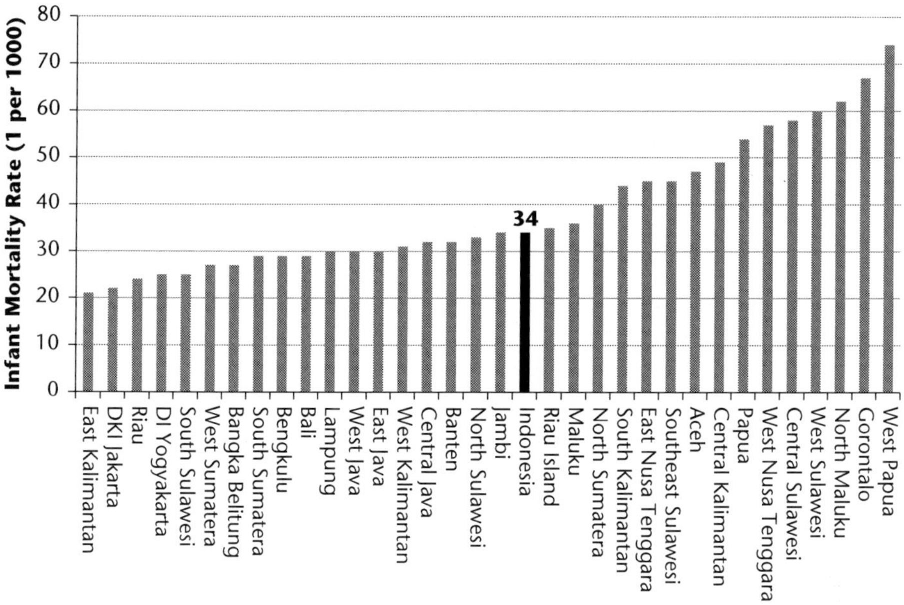

Figure 14.10 Infant mortality rate (in 1,000s), 2012

Source: BPS.

represent income level of the country. Poverty and GDP per capita represent wealth or lack of it, while inequality represents wealth distribution. There are six health indicators:

- Life expectancy at birth (which is divided into female and male)
- Infant mortality rate (IMR)
- Tuberculosis (TBC) success rate
- Proportion of population who have health complaints
- Measles, mumps and rubella (MMR) immunization rate
- *Puskesmas* availability (per 1,000 population), which represents supply in health facilities.

Table 14.5 presents the pairwise correlations between the three economic variables, poverty, inequality, and income per capita, with health indicators that are used in the analysis. Data are taken from the Indonesia Bureau of Statistics (BPS). Pairwise correlations are undertaken to understand the underlying relationship among the variables in raw data. As in Biggs et al. (2010), the correlations between poverty and health measures are strong and significant, with the expected negative sign, except for the correlation between poverty and proportion of population who have health complaints. It is interesting that the inequality variable that uses Gini coefficient as a proxy is only correlated significantly with the proportion of population who have health complaints. The correlations between income per capita and health measures are also strong and statistically significant, except for the MMR immunization rate which is a preventive activity. Poverty and income per capita seem to have stronger correlations with the health variables rather than the correlation between inequality and health variables. This makes sense knowing that poverty and income reflect more the availability of resources rather than the distribution of resources that is measured by income inequality.

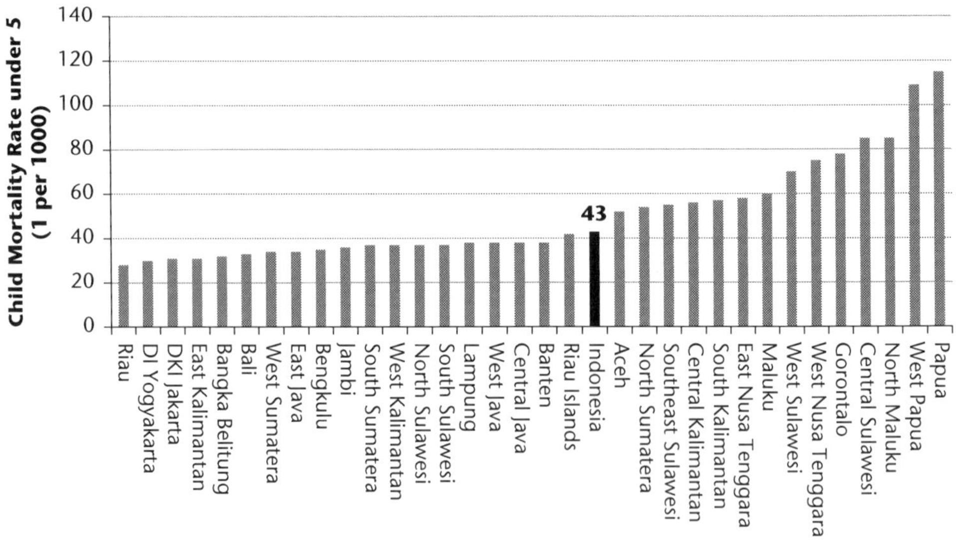

Figure 14.11 Under-five child mortality rate (in 1,000s), 2012

Source: BPS.

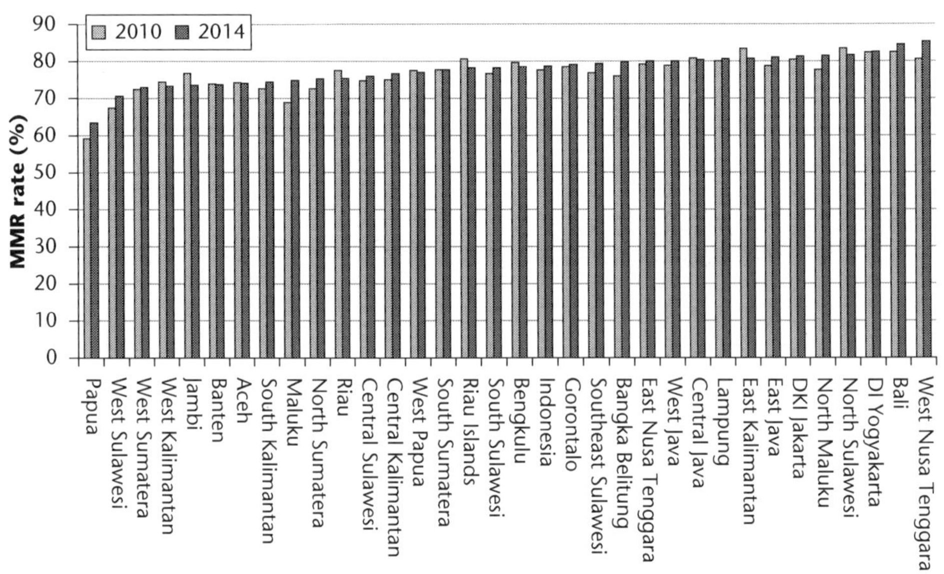

Figure 14.12 MMR immunization rate (%), 2010 and 2014

Source: BPS.

Many of the correlations between health variables are also significant. For example, the positive and significant correlation between availability of local health centers or *Puskesmas*, the pillar of the public health system in Indonesia, and services provided by health facilities to the communities, including basic health treatment for those who have health complaints, MMR and BCG immunizations to reduce TBC prevalence, and attendance of birth deliveries.

Table 14.5 Pairwise correlation coefficients

	Female life expectancy	*Male life expectancy*	*Inequality (Gini coefficient)*	*Poverty (Headcount rate)*	*Log Income per capita*	*Proportion that have health complaints (%)*	*MMR Immunization rate (%)*	*TB success rate %)*	*Log IMR per 1000 birth*	*Log Puskesmas* per 1000 population
Female life expectancy	1									
Male life expectancy	0.9997***	1								
Inequality (Gini coefficient)	0.097	0.101	1							
Poverty (Headcount rate)	–0.5259***	–0.5207***	0.2374***	1						
Log Income per capita	0.454***	0.4596***	0.019	–0.3988***	1					
Proportion who have health complaints (%)	–0.070	–0.068	0.1459*	0.108	–0.3147***	1				
MMR Immunization rate (%)	0.5289***	0.5256***	–0.014	–0.3243***	0.136	0.1548*	1			
TB success rate %)	0.1609*	0.1522*	–0.128	–0.3613***	–0.3424***	0.2737***	0.093	1		
Log IMR per 1000 birth	–0.6350***	–0.6401***	0.1384	0.3003**	–0.5038***	–0.0290	–0.2321*	–0.0250	1	0.4760***
Log *Puskesmas* per 1000 population	–0.5285	–0.5294	0.0475	0.4842***	–0.2773***	–0.2017**	–0.3414***	–0.3224***	0.4760***	1

Notes:

*Correlation is significant at $\alpha = 1\%$;

**Correlation is significant at $\alpha = 5\%$;

***Correlation is significant at $\alpha = 10\%$.

Source: Authors' calculation.

The success rates of TBC treatment and MMR immunizations also correlate positively with Female and Male Life Expectancy, while increasing IMR correlate negatively and significantly with the two genders' life expectancies.

Following Biggs et al. (2010), the associations between inequality, poverty and income with public health indicators are tested using multivariate regressions with provincial fixed effects, or provincial dummies and year dummies are included and capture the omitted variables. Panel data consisting of 33 provinces' data are used, covering the short time period 2010-2013, a period where inequality has been considered high and poverty reduction has been sluggish. The model is written as fixed effect estimators:

$$\widehat{H} = H_{i,t} - \bar{H}_i = \beta(ø_{i,t} - \bar{ø}_i) + (\mu_{i,t} - \bar{\mu}_i) \quad (1)$$

where $H_{i,t}$ is health variable; namely either female/male life expectancy, TB success rate, proportion of population who have health compaints, IMR, MMR immunization rate, and Puskemas availability for each i and t. $ø_{i,t}$ is an economic variable either the poverty rate, Gini coefficient which represents inequality or income per capita for each i and t. i refers to individual province while t refers to time (2010–2013). $\bar{H}_i$ refers to the average value of the health variables across time. $\bar{ø}_i$ refers to average value of the economic variable across time. $\mu_{i,t}$ refers to random errors for each i and t while $\bar{\mu}_i$ refers to average value of the random variable across time.

There are stronger and more significant relationships observed for the relationship between inequality and female/male life expectancy (negative relationship), and IMR (positive relationship) and MMR immunization rates (negative relationship) with the expected signs. Contrary to results of the correlation matrix, controlling for regional and time variables, inequality may be by far the most dominant out of the three economic variables. A one point increase in the Gini coefficient will lead in a decline in life expectancy by 1 year in women and 0.9 year in men.[2] A one point increase in the Gini coefficient will lead to an increase in infant mortality by 4.7 percent and a reduction in the MMR immunization rate by 15 percent.

Surprisingly, an increasing poverty rate is associated with a lower IMR, which may be due to the fact that the analysis was undertaken for the period in which poverty has been continuing to decline, although slowly. The associations between poverty rates and other variables are as expected. For example, an increase in poverty rate will potentially result in more people who experience health complaints. The findings on the relationship between poverty and MMR immunization rates and *Puskemas* may indicate limited access to immunization and to local health care as a result of poverty.

The association between income per capita and health is limited, with the coefficient only becoming significant in the regression with IMR (although with an unexpected sign) and the with density of the local community health center of *Puskesmas*. For the former, the unexpected result may reflect the same caveat as above, where income per capita continues to increase and poverty declines.

None of the economic variables has significant association with the success rate of tuberculosis medications, which means that this variable is determined by something else. Further examination on this issue will be warranted for future research.

To some extent, the results provide support for the earlier literature, which shows that wealthier is healthier (and, correspondingly, less wealthy is less healthy), but we also find here that the distribution of wealth matters (equity) more, which is not surprising, since the analysis is undertaken during the period which inequality has been increasing in this country. The results support Wilkinson and Pickett (2006) in the association between inequality and health indicators.

Table 14.6 Effect of poverty, inequality and income on health indicators

		Female life expectancy	*Male life expectancy*	*Log Infant Mortality Rate (IMR)*	*TB success rate (%)*	*Proportion who have health complaints (%)*	*MMR Immunization rate (%)*	*Log Puskesmas* per 1000 population
Inequality (Gini coefficient)	β	–1.004**	–0.857**	4.713***	–7.239	13.293	–15.384*	–0.156
	R^2	0.924	0.927	0.2068	0.057	0.671	0.189	0.170
Poverty (Headcount poverty rate)	β	–0.004	–0.001	–0.082***	–0.375	0.474**	–0.249*	–0.018***
	R^2	0.919	0.924	0.3743	0.068	0.687	0.186	0.441
Log Income per capita	β	–0.119	–0.1389	2.027***	5.673	–3.146	–2.768	0.239**
	R^2	0.919	0.924	0.3378	0.573	0.667	0.165	0.217
Year dummy		Yes	Yes	Yes	Yes	Yes	Yes	Yes
Provincial dummy		Yes	Yes	Yes	Yes	Yes	Yes	Yes

Notes:
*Correlation is significant at $\alpha = 1\%$;
**Correlation is significant at $\alpha = 5\%$;
***Correlation is significant at $\alpha = 10$.
Source: Authors' calculation.

The results show that lower health status due to low social status, and esteem as the results of inequality, may have an impact on life expectancy in the long term but impact infant mortality or immunization rates in the short term. It may be possible that when there is high inequality in the region, the population, including mothers, children, and infants become highly vulnerable, with limited access to immunization or limited access to health facilities for pregnant mothers, potentially causing an increase in the infant mortality rate. The results show that the impact of inequality on public health indicators is not significant, meaning that increasing inequality may not induce voters to demand more health spending for provision of public health. These findings are different from Chung (2004), who uses individual data to find that in general, there is no significant association between inequality and health indicators. The empirical results show that increasing inequality actually matters for public health (Table 14.6).

Conclusions and policy implications

This chapter examines the role that wealth indicators such as poverty and inequality play on the performance of health indicators of Indonesia, particularly in the period in which the income of the country remains high, but with creeping inequality and sluggish reduction in poverty rates.

So, does wealthier always mean healthier? The findings show that there have been mixed results on the impact between wealth variables and public health indicators, but inequality seems to be the most influential in terms of impacting the public health indicators.

The increasing inequality that has been experienced by Indonesia since the year 2000, peaking in 2011 onwards, has had some negative impacts on public health indicators. High poverty rates also have had detrimental effects on public health indicators and are positively associated with higher levels of health complaints. Poverty has likely prohibited some groups of the population from having access to basic necessities, such as nutrition or access to health facilities where needed, and has resulted in higher health complaints.

Where do we go from here? What are the policy implications of the findings? There are at least three policy implications.

First, both policy makers and public health professionals should not only pay attention to the issues of poverty and high income per capita but also to how wealth is distributed, since inequality has a potentially detrimental effect on health performance in a country.

Second, Universal Health Insurance should provide real social protection in health to everyone in Indonesia, including those who are at the bottom of the income distribution, since inequality has left some people behind, healthwise.

Third, general policies that do not directly focus on health, also matter in mediating the impact of inequality on health outcomes. For example, vocational training programs to overcome the issue of skills mismatch would be useful beyond labor market participation, as employment would provide financial resources that may be required to improve the health outcomes.

Many initiatives and policies have been launched to tackle the issues of poverty and inequality, and to improve the health performance of the country. Nevertheless, what is important is whether these programs have successful impacts to achieve the intended goals of the programs.

Notes

1 There has been limited recent data on the Infant Mortality Rates. The latest data available for this variable which has the regional component in it is for the year 2012.

2 Or one percentage point increase in Gini coefficient say from 0.32 to 0.33 will lead in a decline in life expectancy by 0.01 year in women and 0.009 year in men.

References

Beckfield, Jason. (2004) "Does income inequality harm health? New cross-national evidence." *Journal of Health and Social Behavior* 45, no. 3: 231–248.
Benzeval, Michaela, Ken Judge and Margaret Whitehead eds. (1995) *Tackling Inequalities in Health: An Agenda for Action*. London: King's Fund Centre.
Benzeval, Michaela, Jayne Taylor and Ken Judge. (2000) "Evidence on the relationship between low income and poor health: is the government doing enough?." *Fiscal Studies* 21, no. 3: 375–399.
Biggs, Brian, Lawrence King, Sanjay Basu and David Stuckler. (2010) "Is wealthier always healthier? The impact of national income level, inequality, and poverty on public health in Latin America." *Social Science & Medicine* 71, no. 2: 266–273.
Byrne, A., A. Hodge, E. Jimenez-Soto and A. Morgan (2014) "What works? Strategies to increase reproductive, maternal and child health in difficult to access mountainous locations: a systematic literature review." *PLoS One*, 9, no. 2: e87683.
Chung, W. (2004) "Income inequality and health: Evidence from Indonesia," Centre for Labour Market Research (CLMR) Discussion Paper Series 04/3. Crawley, WA: The University of Western Australia.
Dabla-Norris, Era, Kalpana Kochhar, Nujin Suphaphiphat, Frantisek Ricka and Evridiki Tsounta. (2015) *Causes and Consequences of Income Inequality: A Global Perspective*. Washington, DC: International Monetary Fund.
Deaton, Angus. (2003) "Health, inequality, and economic development." *Journal of Economic Literature* 41, no. 1: 113–158.
De Vogli, Roberto, Ritesh Mistry, Roberto Gnesotto and Giovanni Andrea Cornia. (2005) "Has the relation between income inequality and life expectancy disappeared? Evidence from Italy and top industrialised countries." *Journal of Epidemiology and Community Health* 59, no. 2: 158–162.
Gómez, Eduardo J. (2015) *Health Spending and Inequality in the Emerging Economies: India, China, Russia and Indonesian in Comparative Perspective*. Oxford: Oxfam Press.
Meltzer, Allan. H. and Scott. F. Richard. (1981) "A rational theory of the size of government." *Journal of Political Economy* 89, no. 5: 914–927.
Manning, Chris and Riyana Miranti. (2015) "The Yudhoyono Legacy on Jobs, Poverty and Income Distribution: A Mixed Record." In The Yudhoyono Years: An Assessment, E. Aspinall, M. Mietzner, D. Tomsa (eds.), pp. 303–324. Singapore: Institute of Southeast Asian Studies.
Miranti, Riyana. (2011) "Regional Patterns of Poverty in Indonesia: Why Do Some Provinces Perform Better Than Others." In Employment, Living Standards and Poverty in Contemporary Indonesia, C. Manning and S. Sumarto (eds.), pp. 90–110. Singapore: Institute of Southeast Asian Studies.
Miranti, R. (forthcoming) *Examining the Interdependencies between Urbanization, Internal Migration, Urban Poverty and Inequality: Evidence from Indonesia*. Manila: Asian Development Bank (ADB).
Miranti, Riyana, Yogi Vidyattama, Erick Hansnata, Rebecca Cassells and Alan Duncan. (2013) *Trends in Poverty and Inequality in Decentralising Indonesia* the OECD Social, Employment and Migration Working Papers, No. 148. OECD Publishing.
Nissanke, Machiko and Erik Thorbecke. (2006) "Channels and policy debate in the globalization–inequality–poverty nexus." *World Development* 34, no. 8: 1338–1360.
WHO (2015). Global Tuberculosis Report, 20th Ed, Geneva, Switzerland: www.bookdepository.com/publishers/World-Health-Organization"World Health Organization."
Wilkinson, Richard G. and Kate E. Pickett. (2006) "Income inequality and population health: a review and explanation of the evidence." *Social Science & Medicine* 62, no. 7: 1768–1784.
World Bank. (2015) *Indonesia's Rising Divide*. Washington, DC: The World Bank.

15

Climate change and food security in South Asia

Simi Mehta, Vikash Kumar and Rattan Lal

Background

South Asia (SA) is a region that is representative of the southern part of the continent of Asia. It lies entirely in the eastern and northern hemispheres and extends from 3.2° N to 34.53° N and 60.4° E 97.4° E and covers the countries of Afghanistan, Bangladesh, Bhutan, India, Maldives, Nepal, Pakistan and Sri Lanka. It stretches to about 5.1 million km^2 and occupies 3.4 percent of the world's land surface. The countries are a mix of small, medium and large with the population varying from 0.36 million in Maldives, to 20.71 million in Sri Lanka, to 1.31 billion in India in 2015 (United Nations, 2015). South Asia in general has six types of climate, where the southernmost parts of South Asia have two dominant climates – tropical wet or equatorial, which has heavy rainfall and rare dry seasons, and tropical wet and dry or tropical savannah, which has strongly pronounced wet and dry seasons. The tropical monsoon is a period of very heavy rain which covers much of Eastern South Asia and occurs between July and December. North and South Asia face hot humid summers and mild to cold winters.

Further north, there exists a highland climate where temperatures drop below the freezing point during October through March with cold winds and snow fall. In the north and west of South Asia, a desert type climate exists which experiences warm to high temperatures and little rainfall. Also, each country is characterized by diverse and distinct regions: for instance, the northern part of Bangladesh is geographically different from its coastal areas; India is divided in 15 distinct agro-ecological zones; Nepal has three demarcated zones of mountains, hills and Terai; Pakistan' Indus plains are in sharp contrast to the arid regions of Sindh or hilly and semi-arid areas of the northwest; Sri Lanka's landscape is clearly defined by its dry and wet zones.

Apart from the recognizable geographical proximity, these countries share a common culture and history. Judged by the criteria of food insecurity and poverty, SA has the dubious distinction of being the worst affected region in the world (World Bank, 2015a). In this region, the incidence of malnutrition is serious, with 78 million stunted children under the age of 5 years (UNICEF, 2014; Hatlebakk, 2012). The effects of climate change will be strong in South Asia, particularly because these are either low- or lower-middle income countries in which the rapidly growing populations continue to struggle with their daily needs. The poorer households spend a majority of their budgets on food, and are the most sensitive to the weather-related shocks that threaten to make daily staples unaffordable (IPCC, 2014; Bhatiya, 2014).

Thus, any effort of ensuring food security to the poor households should naturally look at the countries of this region. Also, the regional variations need to be taken into account when designing a meaningful program for food security, as the regions within the countries are distinct and subject to varying degrees of vulnerability. Furthermore, large areas in several of these countries are disaster-prone; for instance, Bangladesh and coastal parts of India, Sri Lanka and Maldives are threatened quite frequently by cyclones and floods. As a result of climate change, recurring droughts are a common feature in the arid and semi-arid parts of India and Pakistan. Low-lying Bangladesh and the whole of the Maldives are vulnerable to flooding and cyclones in the Indian Ocean, and scientific literature suggests that these uncertainties will become more intensive in coming decades (Bhatiya, 2014; IPCC, 2014). The incidence of natural calamities is more severe on food-insecure households. Extreme heat has begun disrupting the growing season for regions in Afghanistan, Pakistan, India, and Bangladesh. Wheat production in the fertile Indo-Gangetic Plains, is predicted to decrease by up to 50 percent by 2100, which would have disastrous effects on the hundreds of millions of people who rely on it for their sustenance and livelihood (Aggarwal, 2008). The respective governments thus must devote large resources to cope with frequent natural disasters (FAO, 1999).

As South Asia would have the largest numbers of food-insecure people in the world by 2050 (IPCC, 2014), this chapter seeks to establish that the risk of food insecurity is directly linked to changes in climate, frequent occurrences of drought, flooding, and variability and extremes in rainfall. At the same time, action programs in the area of poverty reduction and food security have to be grounded primarily within the countries, while regional collaboration may supplement country-level action. Some of the areas of cooperation will be identified in this chapter.

This chapter is broadly divided into two parts. The first part, through an elaborate review of literature from official documents and a host of studies carried out by scholars and international agencies, maps out the trends of food production and food distribution in SA. It also describes the status of food security in the region as well as the levels of malnutrition and their socio-economic implications on the large section of people across the eight South Asian countries. In the second section, an interconnection between climate change and vulnerability of food production in SA is established. Adverse impacts of abrupt climate change on the food system in SA, such as low agricultural yields and poor distribution system leading to food crisis and conflict are the central themes of the chapter.

Status of food security in south Asia

On January 13, 1996, the Rome Declaration on World Food Security and the World Food Summit Plan of Action laid out the various dimensions of food security. Food security exists when all people, at all times, have physical and economic access to sufficient, safe and nutritious food to meet their dietary needs and food preferences for an active and healthy life (FAO, 1996). The Food and Agricultural Organization of the United Nations (FAO) identified the four main elements of food security, namely, the physical availability of food, through sufficient supply; the economic and physical access to food and hence greater policy focus on incomes, expenditure, markets and prices in achieving food security objectives; utilization of the various nutrients of the food that determine the nutritional status of individuals; and stability of the first three elements, that is, ensuring food access is not at risk, the political and economic factors do not impact the food security and there is no deterioration of nutritional status (FAO, 2008a, 2003).

Equal and sustainable access to adequate nutritious food is essential for enjoyment of all other rights. The Universal Declaration of Human Rights recognizes fundamental human rights which are to be universally protected. Article 25 states, "everyone has the right to a standard of living adequate for the health and well-being of himself and of his family, including food, clothing, housing and medical care and necessary social services . . . " (United Nations, 1948). All the countries of SA except Bhutan are signatories to the International Covenant on Economic, Social and Cultural Rights (ICESCR), which has strong reference to food security. The covenant in Article 11 not only recognizes the state's responsibility to ensure adequate food security but also includes the method of improvement in "production, conservation and distribution of food by making full use of technical and scientific knowledge, by disseminating knowledge of the principles of nutrition and by developing or reforming agrarian systems in such a way as to achieve the most efficient development and utilization of natural resources" (United Nations, 1966). However, the Committee on Economic Social and Cultural Rights (CESCR) of respective South Asian countries has time and again expressed deep concerns over the high levels of food insecurity in these countries, as well as on the reports of corruption, inefficiency and discrimination in the food distribution system.[1]

The magnitude of food insecurity in SA is grim. The progress of the Strategy and Programme for Food Security (SPFS), developed by the South Asian Association for Regional Cooperation (SAARC) with technical assistance of the FAO, has been noted as being unsatisfactory. In order to mitigate the regional challenges, the Office for the South and South-West Asia of the UNESCAP organized SA Policy Dialogue on Regional Cooperation for Strengthening National Food Security Strategies in 2013, which was aimed at building upon existing networks to create a regional knowledge network of food security experts and policymakers (UNESCAP, 2013).

Hunger is direct evidence of lack of inclusive development in the region, and hence ensuring food security and eradicating hunger are development challenges. The 2015 Global Hunger Index (GHI) developed by the International Food Policy Research Institute (IFPRI) reflects the multi-dimensional nature of hunger by studying the percentage of the population that is undernourished; the percentage of children under the age of five who suffer from wasting (low weight for height); the percentage of children under the age of five who suffer from stunting (low height for age); and the percentage of children who die before the age of five (child mortality). Scores of 9.9 or lower denote low hunger; scores between 35.0 and 49.9 denote alarming hunger. While the overall situation of the region has been characterized as being 'serious' (29.4), the state of hunger in Afghanistan is 'alarming' (35.4).

Figure 15.1 shows temporal changes in the GHI score of South Asian region as a whole, from 1990 to 2015. While there has been a decline in the score from an alarming 47.7 percent in 1990, the problem of hunger and food security in 2015 still remains serious.

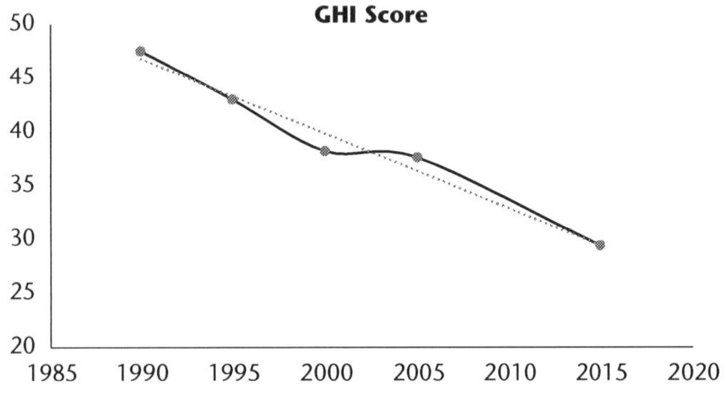

Figure 15.1 Temporal changes in the Global Hunger Index of South Asia between 1990 and 2015

Source: Redrawn from the data of Global Hunger Index, IFPRI 2015.

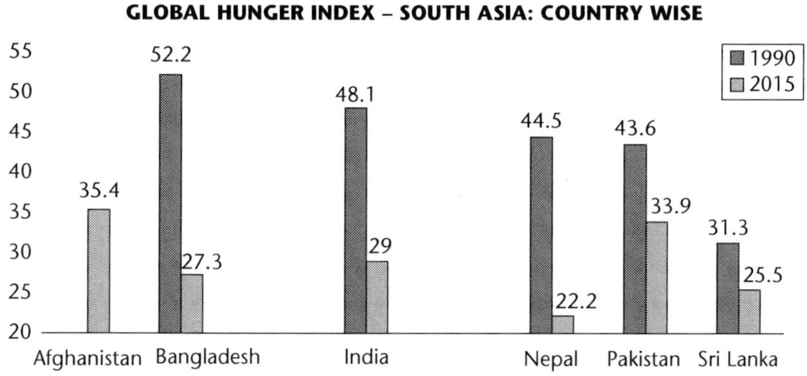

Figure 15.2 Country-wise differences in the Global Hunger Index in SA between 1991 and 2015

Source: Redrawn from the data of Global Hunger Index, IFPRI 2015.

The data in Figure 15.2 shows the GHI for all South Asian countries, except for Bhutan and Maldives, for which data were not available, and in the case of Afghanistan, 2015 is the first year for which the GHI could be calculated.

The above illustrations reveal that SA's GHI score is closely tied to that of India, where three-quarters of the South Asian population lives. Hunger has been dropping at a moderate rate both in India and in the region since 1990, with just a short stall between 2000 and 2005. Over the past decade, India has made some progress in fighting malnutrition.[2] Between 2005–2006 and 2013–2014, child wasting decreased from 20 to 15 percent, and stunting from 48 to 39 percent. The Indian government has scaled up nutrition-specific interventions over the past decade. Progress in reducing child malnutrition is uneven in India's states. One key factor that makes it more likely that babies are born underweight is the low social status of women, which affects women's health and nutrition (von Grebmer et al., 2015; United Nations, 2012a).

Prevailing and projected undernutrition[3] in SA

According to the South and South-West Asia Office, in 1992, SA was estimated to have 314 million people who were chronically undernourished, which by the latest available data of 2013 has been reduced to 294.7 million (FAO, 2013; Wickramasinghe, 2014). If the prevalence of undernutrition or food insecure population declines at this rate, countries in SA will still have 251 million undernourished people by 2050, distributed across the countries as follows: 22 million in Bangladesh, 191 million in India, 4.5 million in Nepal, 28 million in Pakistan, and 4.3 million in Sri Lanka (Wickramasinghe, 2014).

After that year, however, widespread declines in the extent and potential productivity of cropland could occur, with some of the severest impacts likely to be felt in the currently food-insecure areas of the world including SA (FAO, 2003). However, as the data in Figure 15.3 show, the countries have had enough food since 1990 until 2013, and produce sufficient food calories per person per day as stipulated by the basic dietary requirement of 1800 calories established by the FAO. Despite this progress, the available evidence suggests that there is 'serious' food insecurity and reduced calorie intake in the SA region.

The various causes of hunger range from deficiencies in macro and micro-nutrients, short-term to chronic shortages of food access; constraints on supply of sufficient quantity and quality of food; lack of purchasing power; and complex interactions of nutrition with poor sanitation

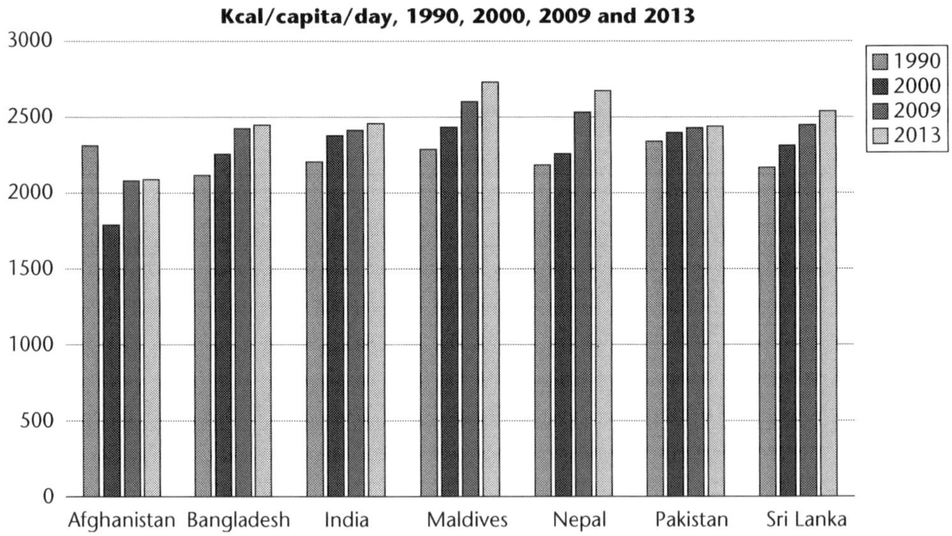

Figure 15.3 Production of food based on calories per person per day in South Asia

Source: Data adapted from the statistics from FAO in 1990, 2000, 2009 and 2013.

leading to infectious diseases and ill-health and high rates of micro-nutrient deficiencies, especially among women and children (Wheeler and von Braun, 2013). Additionally, the pressures of food price increases and extreme climatic events have led to reduced caloric intake and increased prevalence of undernutrition in SA. With the gradual increase in the population by 2030, the demand for agricultural products has been estimated to increase by 50 percent. Therefore, caloric intake in SA is likely to be reduced by 10 percent even if there is no significant climatic change (ADB, 2013; Bruinsma, 2003). Climate change will further worsen the global food equation, especially at the local levels, where small farm communities depend upon local or own production. Thus climate change could potentially slow down or reverse toward a world with hunger (HLPE, 2012).

Abrupt climate change (ACC) in SA

There are many definitions of climate change by international organizations. According to the World Meteorological Organization (WMO):

> [I]n the most general sense, this term encompasses all forms of climatic inconstancy (i.e., any differences from long-term statistics of the meteorological elements calculated for different periods but relating to the same area), regardless of their statistical nature or physical causes. Climate changes may result from such factors as changes in solar emission, long-term changes in the earth's orbital elements (eccentricity, obliquity of the ecliptic, precession of the equinoxes), natural internal processes of the climate system, or anthropogenic forcing (e.g., increasing atmospheric concentrations of carbon dioxide (CO_2) and other greenhouse gases).
>
> *(WMO, 1992)*

The United Nations Framework Convention on Climate Change (UNFCCC) defines climate change as "a change of climate which is attributed directly or indirectly to human activity that alters the composition of the global atmosphere and which is in addition to natural climate variability observed over comparable time periods" (UNFCCC, 1992). In its Climate Change and Food Security Framework, the FAO delineated the variables of climate change as:

> [T]he CO_2 fertilization effect of increased greenhouse gas concentrations in the atmosphere; increasing mean, maximum and minimum temperatures; gradual changes in precipitation-increase in the frequency, duration and intensity of dry spells and droughts; changes in the timing, duration, intensity and geographic location of rain and snowfall; increase in the frequency and intensity of storms and floods; and greater seasonal weather variability and changes in start/end of growing seasons.
>
> *(FAO, 2008b)*

Whatever cause to which climate change is attributed, the fact is that it is real and tangible. Its impact is of particular significance to SA because being composed of primarily agrarian economies, with a variety of climatic zones and in the stages of 'underdevelopment' or 'developing', even a mere increase in temperature of 1 degree Celsius has the potential of damaging the coastal and low-lying areas of the region. Bangladesh and the Maldives face the threat of complete inundation. In such a scenario, and amid high rates of poverty, with around 399 million people of the region living under $1.25 per day (World Bank, 2015b), ensuring food security for all becomes a challenge for each country. One major impact will arise from the melting of the Himalayan glaciers. In fact, it has been suggested that the food security implications of changes in the severity, frequency and extent of drought events will affect people in the future more than any other climate-related impact (Sheffield and Wood, 2008; Romm, 2011). These present disasters to human communities and cause substantial damage to economies and livelihoods, especially those related to agriculture.

SA has witnessed climate change trends that offer a perspective on the predictability of future trends. According to the Purdue University's Climate Change Research Center Report, the start of the summer monsoon in SA could be delayed by 15 days with the end of the century, which would significantly disturb the quantity and distribution of rainfall in most parts of the region, for instance more rainfall will occur in Indian Ocean, Myanmar and Bangladesh but India, Pakistan and Nepal will experience decreased and scattered rainfall (Mittal and Sethi, 2009).

Climate change impacts on food system of SA

Climate change has become highly heterogeneous in terms of severity and occurrence (World Health Organization, 2002). 'The Fourth Assessment Report: Climate Change' (IPCC, 2007a; Solomon et al., 2007) showed the trends and variability in climate in SA and the Fifth Assessment Report (IPCC, 2014) has elaborately discussed the impacts, adaptation, and vulnerability to climate change. The upstream glaciers are melting at a faster rate in monsoon seasons than in dry seasons, when water is needed more, thus substantially reducing the aggregate food production and yield, especially of wheat rather than rice (ADB, 2013).

In order to understand the impact of climate change on the food security in SA, it is important to recognize the underpinnings of the food system. The food system comprises of multiple food chains operating at the global, national and local levels. Some of these chains are short and simple, while others circle the globe in an intricate web of interconnecting processes and links. One simple chain, which is important for food security in many households, is practicing rain-fed agriculture. This begins with a staple cereal crop produced in a farmer's field, moves with the harvested grain through a local mill and back to the farmer's home as bags of flour, and finishes in the cooking pot and on the household members' plates (FAO, 2008a). Extreme weather events can damage or destroy food transport and distribution infrastructure and affect other non-agricultural parts of the food system adversely.

One of the greatest impacts of climate change that threatens food security and lives is the vulnerability to natural disasters, including flooding, droughts (OXFAM, 2007), fires, mudslides, tidal storms, cyclones and landslides, which threaten lives, leaving the population in food and water crisis. This adds to the huge economic burden upon the governments of the countries and stresses the food production and distribution systems (United Nations, 2012b; Earley, 2009). Evidence indicates that more frequent and more intense extreme weather events, rising sea levels, and increasing irregularities in seasonal rainfall patterns (including flooding) are already having immediate impacts on not only food production, but also food distribution infrastructure, incidence of food emergencies, livelihood assets and human health in both rural and urban areas. In addition, less immediate impacts are expected to result from gradual changes in mean temperatures and rainfall. These will affect the suitability of land for different types of crops and pasture; the health and productivity of forests; the distribution, productivity and community composition of marine resources; the incidence of different types of pests and diseases; the biodiversity and ecosystem functioning of natural habitats; and the availability of good-quality water for crop, livestock and inland fish production. Climate change will have multiple impacts on livestock, for instance heat stress would affect animal performance and productivity of dairy cows in all phases of production; livestock diseases will lead to a lowering of feed efficiency, milk production, and reproduction rates; and impact upon feed quality and availability. Further, environmental stress will reduce the productivity and health of livestock, resulting in significant economic losses (Thornton et al., 2013; Sejian et al., 2015; Balmaseda et al. 2013).

Arable land is likely to decline, owing to increased aridity (and associated salinity), groundwater depletion and sea-level rise. Food systems will be affected by internal and international migration, resource-based conflicts, and civil unrest, triggered by climate change (FAO, 2008a). Because of the tropical location of the Indian sub-continent, the impacts of mean temperature rise (that is, warming of more than 3°C) is expected to have negative effects on production (IPCC, 2007b). It is projected that by the end of the twenty-first century, the average annual temperatures will increase by 3 to 6°C and annual rainfall will increase by 15 to 40 percent (NATCOM, 2004), increasing particularly in northern parts of India (Aggarwal, 2007). Rising sea levels in the Maldives and Bangladesh and increasing incidence of extreme events pose new risks for the assets of people living in affected zones, threatening livelihoods and increasing vulnerability to future food insecurity because of loss of cropland due to rising sea levels. Major physical impacts of climate change on the marine system will be changes in ocean currents, a rise in average temperature, sharpening of gradient structures, and large and rapid increases of freshwater discharge. These often trigger an increase in chemical nutrients, typically compounds containing nitrogen or phosphorus, resulting in lack of oxygen and severe reductions in water quality, fish, and other animal populations (eutrophication). Such changes could result in a geographic redistribution of vulnerability and a relocalization of responsibility for food security (FAO, 2008a). There will also be substantial and far-reaching impacts on coastal fisheries and fishing communities. For climate variables such as rainfall, soil moisture, temperature and radiation, crops have thresholds beyond which growth and yield are compromised (Porter and Semenov, 2005). For example, cereals and fruit tree yields can be damaged by a few days of temperatures above or below a certain threshold (Wheeler et al., 2000).

Although precipitation is projected to increase at the global level, this will not necessarily lead to increased availability of water where it is needed. In fact, FAO's 2015/2030 projections, citing a 1999 Hadley Centre report, state that "substantial decreases are projected for Australia, India, southern Africa, the Near East/North Africa, much of Latin America and parts of Europe" (FAO, 2003).

Impact of climate change on agricultural productivity

The effectiveness of the agricultural sector is only one among many influences that determine whether an individual, community or population is food-secure. However, when considering the potential impacts of climate change on global food security, agriculture is a key sector because it is inherently sensitive to climate variability and change, whether attributable to natural causes or to human activities (Wheeler, 2015).

Negative impacts on crop productivity are expected in low-latitude and tropical regions. SA has made large gains in increasing food availability through higher output and crop yields over the last five decades. However, the growth in agricultural production has been declining steadily over the years since the 1960s (United Nations, 2012b). One of the main reasons for this is excessive reliance on water and ACC. Almost 40 percent of world food production comes from irrigated land, and large quantities of water are required for the production of SA's major cereals, especially paddy (rice). As a result of the ACC, the availability of water has become very uncertain. SA has witnessed a decline in the amount of water available for agriculture (World Bank, 2007). Agricultural irrigation and unsustainable uses of water supplies and electricity have caused huge wastage of the existing groundwater and freshwater resources (United Nations, 2012b). Added to this are the extreme weather events that have the potential to cause crop and livestock losses and also increase the difficulty in determining optimal investment options for future agricultural production (United Nations, 2012b).

It is estimated that cereal production could decrease by up to 10 percent by the year 2100 and countries like Bangladesh could see decreases in wheat production by 33 percent (UN-ESCAP, 2009). For countries like India, which are sensitive to temperature shifts, a 1°C rise in temperature could cause a 5 percent decrease in wheat and maize yield (UN-ESCAP, 2009). Thus, geographic patterns of food production are directly affected by climatic variables such as temperature and precipitation and the frequency and severity of extreme weather events (Rosenzweig and Tubiello, 2007; Aggarwal and Singh, 2010; Aggarwal et al., 2004). In the monsoon-affected regions of SA, high correlations are seen between seasonal rainfall and national crop yields. For instance, between 1966 to 1990, the average annual monsoon rainfall in India varied from 450 mm to 1200 mm, and during this period, the groundnut yield varied from an average of 600 kg/ha to over 1200 kg/ha. Within these country averages, considerable variation in rainfall existed from one place to another. It is estimated that over half of this variation in the crop yield during this time period and from one district to another could be attributed to rainfall alone (Challinor et al., 2004).

Agriculture, forestry and fisheries will not only be affected by climate change, but also contribute to it through emitting greenhouse gases (GHGs). These industries may potentially contribute to climate change mitigation through reducing emissions of GHGs by changing agricultural practices (Lal, 2010; FAO, 2008a). Conversion of natural lands for crop or livestock production on existing agricultural lands will negatively impact the environment, as there will create degradation of soil and water resources, increases in GHG emissions, and increased reduction of the critical soil organic carbon (SOC) due to typical farming practices (Lal, 2004). Thus, agriculture is sensitive to variability in weather and climate, mainly rainfall and temperature over a period of time, and as result will impact the prices of food grains.

Impact of climate change on the agricultural yields in relation to pest and pathogens

Pest-crop interactions play a crucial role in agro-ecosystems. Pest problems are likely to be exacerbated under changing climate conditions, as pests tend to thrive under warmer temperatures and wetter climates (Rosenzweig et al., 2001; Rosenzweig and Hillel, 2005). This is due to the lengthening of the frost-free seasons, allowing for increased generations of pests, the extension of overwintering ranges with warmer winters, and the potential for new pests to emerge and spread. Climate change may lead to the occurrence of plant pests like aphids during the early stages of crop growth and lead to tremendous loss of crop production. In addition, swarms of locusts fly eastward into Afghanistan, Pakistan and India during the summer season and reproduce during the monsoon season, and hence changes in rainfall, temperature, and wind speed patterns may influence the migratory behavior of these insects (Aggarwal and Singh, 2010). Thus, people who are already vulnerable and food insecure are likely to be the first affected. Agriculture-based livelihood systems that are already vulnerable to food insecurity face immediate risk of increased crop failure, new patterns of pests and diseases, lack of appropriate seeds and planting material, and loss of livestock. People living on the coasts and floodplains and in mountains, drylands and the Arctic are most at risk (FAO, 2008a).

Impact of climate change on food and nutritional security in SA

Non-availability of food and food insecurity and impact on human health

Adverse impacts of climate change on health through malnutrition, especially for the impoverished masses are increasingly becoming imminent. Higher CO_2 concentration is shown to lower the concentrations of zinc, iron and protein and raise the starch and sugar content in crop plants such as wheat, rice and soybeans. These findings exacerbate the malnutrition challenges, including obesity and nutrition deficits in poor communities (Elbehri, 2015).

In addition to adverse effects on food supply and adequate nutrition, climate change is likely to accentuate global health concerns such as: increased incidence of new influenza virus strains; decline of available seafood proteins due to warming up of the oceans, acidification and overfishing; and worsening freshwater shortages. Low income countries like Afghanistan, Bangladesh, Bhutan, Nepal and the remotely located populations of other South Asian countries are more vulnerable to physical hazards, undernutrition, diarrhea, and other infectious diseases (McMichael, 2013). Malaria in particular is expected to change its distribution as a result of climate change (IPCC, 2007a). In coastal areas, more people may be exposed to vector- and water-borne diseases through flooding linked to sea-level rise. Health risks can also be linked to changes in diseases from either increased or decreased precipitation, lowering people's capacity to utilize food effectively and often resulting in the need for improved nutritional intake (IPCC, 2007a, 2014).

Food insecurity is usually associated with malnutrition, since the diets of people who are unable to satisfy all of their food needs usually contain a high proportion of staple foods and lack the variety needed to satisfy nutritional requirements (FAO, 2008a). This has a long-term harmful impact on the physical and intellectual development, and on the immune system of children. Undernourishment and malnutrition result in reduced work capacities of adults who lack energy to carry out day-to-day work and less active, and less learning-engaged children. Women are particularly prone to anemia due to a lack of iron in their diets, often aggravated by soil degradation (Lal, 2011). The population as a whole becomes more susceptible to diseases (Pinstrup-Andersen and Schiøler, 2000).

In his message during the 39th Session of the Committee on World Food Security, held in Rome, the UN Secretary-General Ban Ki-moon said that tackling hunger constituted one of the greatest challenges of humankind at present (Ki-moon, 2012). Nutrient-rich diets are essential for the well-being and proper physical and mental development of people, especially children. It is important to build immunity against infections and diseases. Deficiencies in micronutrients are

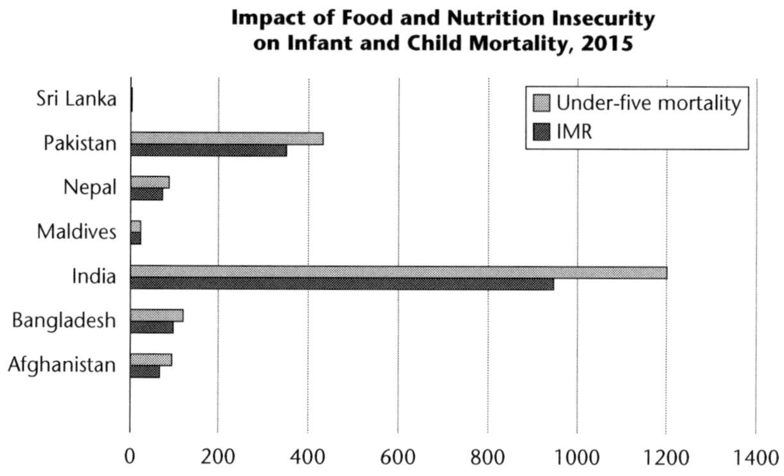

Figure 15.4 Impact of food and nutrition insecurity on infant and child mortality in South Asian countries in 2015

Source: Redrawn from Global Health Observatory data repository, World Health Organization (2015).

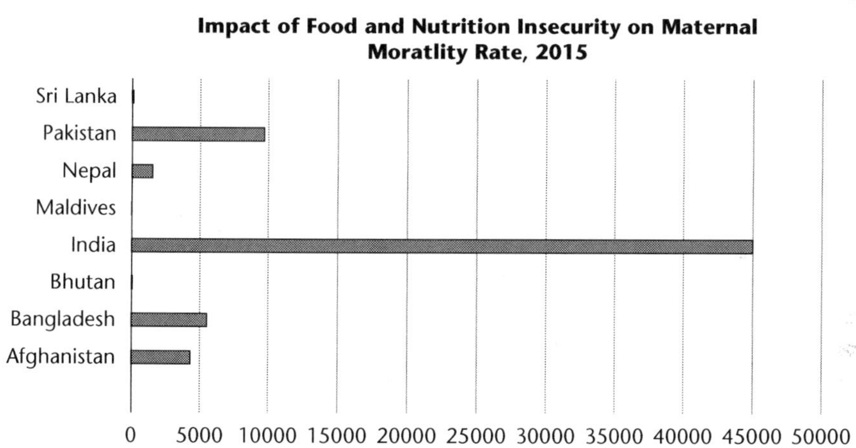

Figure 15.5 Impact of food and nutrition insecurity on maternal mortality rate in South Asian countries in 2015

Source: Redrawn from Global Health Observatory data repository, World Health Organization (2015).

evidence of food insecurity and are directly related to increases in mortality and morbidity. Caulfield et al. (2006) observed that 50 to 80 percent of children under the age of five in Bangladesh, Bhutan, India and Nepal were iron-deficient.

The data in Figures 15.4 and 15.5 show the Infant Mortality, Mortality under-five years and Maternal Mortality. A lack of a nutrient based diet is the reason for this (Data for the IMR and Child mortality for Bhutan was not available).

Adequate nutrition is necessary for achieving food security. Food utilization depends upon water and sanitation and will be affected by any impact of climate change on the health environment. Links with drinking water may be obvious, especially when climate variability stresses clean drinking water availability. Increasing degradation of drinking water quality due to climate change leads to an increase in health risks (Delpha et al., 2009). Hygiene may also be affected by extreme weather events, causing flooding or drought in environments where sound sanitation is absent (Kundzewicz et al., 2007). Hashizume et al. (2007) used hospital records in Dhaka, Bangladesh to show that diarrhea incidences increased by 5.1 percent and 3.9 percent for every 10 mm rainfall increase and decrease respectively around a threshold of 52 mm in the proceeding 0–8 weeks. They also found that a 1°C rise in temperature increases diarrhea rates by 5.6 percent. The temperature effect was higher for people with lower levels of education, poorly constructed houses and unsanitary toilets (Hashizume et al., 2007). Further, climate change can also impinge on diet quality, and increased costs may result from measures required to avoid food contamination stemming from ecological shifts of pests and diseases of stored crops or food (Wheeler and von Braun, 2013).

Food emergencies

Increasing instability of food supply, attributable to the consequences of climate change, have the capacity to lead to increases in the frequency and magnitude of food emergencies with an increase in human conflict, caused in part by migration and resource competition attributable to changing climatic conditions. Resource scarcity can also trigger conflict and could be driven by global environmental change (FAO, 2008a). SA has witnessed different types of conflicts, including prolonged, violent agrarian movements and protests leading to food insecurity in both pre and post-colonial eras. Such conflicts have generated a large number of refugees, weighing in at 21 percent of the global refugee population, as well as internally displaced people. In addition, in India and Nepal, the Maoist-Marxist movements have further complicated the food production and distribution system in areas of historical deprivation.

Impacts on the production of food will affect food supply at the global and local levels. Globally, higher yields in temperate regions could offset lower yields in tropical regions. However, in many low-income countries with limited financial capacity to trade and with high dependence on their own production to cover food requirements, it may not be possible to offset declines in local supply without increasing reliance on food aid (FAO, 2008a). Persistently high food prices force poor people to reduce consumption below the minimum required for a healthy and active life, and may lead to food riots and social unrest. Constraints on water availability are a growing concern, which climate change will exacerbate. Conflicts over water resources will have implications for both food production and people's access to food in conflict zones (Gleick, 1993).

Distribution depends on the reliability of import capacity, the presence of food stocks and, where necessary, access to food aid (Maxwell and Slater, 2003). These factors in turn often depend on the ability to store food. Storage is affected by strategies at the national level and by physical infrastructure at the local level. Frail transport infrastructure limits food distribution in SA. Where infrastructure is affected by climate, through either heat stress on roads or increased frequency of flood events that destroy infrastructure, there are impacts on food distribution, influencing people's access to markets to sell or purchase food (Abdulai and CroleRees, 2001).

Inequity across, gender aspects

While food insecurity is more prevalent among people living in poverty, it disproportionately affects women, rural populations, migrant workers and indigenous populations. Children are more likely to be undernourished, but there is also a gender difference as girls are more likely to go hungry than boys (United Nations, 2012b). This is more precarious in the male-dominated societies of SA. For the rural people in SA who produce a substantial part of their own food, climate change impacts on food production may reduce availability to the point that allocation choices have to be made within the household. A family might reduce the daily amount of food consumed equally among all household members, or allocate food preferentially to certain members, often the able-bodied male adults who are assumed to need it the most to stay fit and continue working to maintain the family. This has a particularly detrimental impact upon pregnant and nursing mothers who lack proper nutrition (FAO, 2008a).

In mechanized farming systems, shorter time windows result in increasing machinery investments. Where these are not possible, untimely operations can result in yield reductions and eventually result in crop failure or harvest loss. Where there is a shift from labor to mechanization, men and women whose livelihoods depend on employment can lose those livelihoods and consequently have less access to income, thereby reducing their capacity to buy food. In this process, women are likely to suffer disproportionately (FAO, 2007).

In non-mechanized farming systems, where women provide the bulk of farm labor, the increased burden of agricultural work during the shortened growing seasons could have adverse consequences on women's health and their ability to provide adequate care to their families, owing to a variety of factors such as lack of nutritious food and inadequate and inappropriate health care. In addition, women may not be able to produce enough to feed everyone in the family, so they will eat last, after the men and the boys. Agricultural mechanization and gender-appropriate machinery can provide some relief for this problem.

An International Federation of Red Cross and Red Crescent Societies (IFRC-RCS) case study of 2002 illustrated the importance of gender-sensitive participation in decision-making on cyclone preparedness. This study, carried out in Bangladesh, found that the highest proportions of cyclone victims came from sites where women were not involved in village-level disaster preparedness committees responsible for maintaining cyclone shelters and transmitting warnings. In Cox's Bazaar in East Bangladesh, women were fully involved in disaster preparedness and support activities (education, reproductive health, self-help groups, and small and medium-sized enterprises), and there have been enormous reductions in the numbers of persons affected by cyclones (Lambrou and Laub, 2004). Thus, the benefits of applying gender-sensitive participatory approaches for using information to avert loss of property and life during cyclones needs to be publicized.

As women are traditionally the carriers of local knowledge about the properties and uses of wild plants, and the keepers of seeds for cultivated varieties, they have an important role in protecting biodiversity. Providing appropriate compensation for this service could guarantee a sustainable livelihood to these women, many of whom belong to vulnerable and food-insecure groups.

Combating climate change and food insecurity – recommendations

i. Resolving the problem of food insecurity through committed governance and political leadership

The processes that contribute to the formulation of goals for food security are as important as the outcomes of food security. Together these help in the formulation of appropriate policies and future steps. Strengthening resilience for all vulnerable people involves adopting practices that enable them to protect existing livelihood systems; diversify their sources of food and income; change their livelihood strategies; and/or migrate if there is no other option (FAO, 2008a).

Political and social power relationships are key factors influencing allocation decisions in times of scarcity. If agricultural production declines and households find alternative livelihood activities, social processes and reciprocal relations in which locally produced food is given to other family members in exchange for their support may change or disappear altogether. Public and charitable food distribution schemes reallocate food to the neediest, but are subject to public perceptions about who needs help, and social values about what kind of help is incumbent on wealthier segments of society to provide. If climate change creates other, more urgent, claims on public resources, support for food distribution schemes may decline, with consequent increases in the incidence of food insecurity, hunger and famine related deaths.

ii. Need for sustainable agriculture and strengthening resilience

Safeguarding food security in the face of climate change also implies avoiding the disruptions or declines in global and local food supplies that could result from changes in temperature and precipitation regimes and new patterns of pests and diseases. Raised productivity from improved agricultural water management will be crucial to ensuring global food supply and global food security (Knox et al., 2012). Sustainable livestock management practices for adaptation and associated mitigation should also be given high priority. Conservation agriculture (CA) can make a significant difference to efficiency of water use, soil organic carbon (SOC) pool, capacity to withstand extreme events, and carbon sequestration (Lal, 2015a). It is precisely in these conditions that well-implemented CA can reverse soil degradation, restore soil quality, enhance productivity, and advance food and nutritional security (Lal, 2015a). Promoting agro-biodiversity is particularly important for local adaptation and resilience. Four basic components of CA (Lal, 2015b), including residue mulch, minimal soil disturbance, cover cropping and rotations, and integrated nutrient management, must be interconnected in order to replace the lost or removed nutrients and resources, respond rationally to changes in pedospheric processes, anticipate changes in soil/environment quality that may occur over time, and formulate an appropriate action plan.

iii. Need for climate risk management as a key to sustainable food security

Risk exists when there is uncertainty about the future outcomes of ongoing processes or about the occurrence of future events. Adaptation is about reducing and responding to the risks climate change poses to people's lives and livelihoods. Reducing uncertainty by improving the information base and devising innovative schemes for insuring against climate change hazards will both be important for successful adaptation. Adaptive management can be a particularly valuable tool for devising strategies that respond to the unique risks to which different ecosystems and livelihood groups are exposed (FAO, 2008a; Millennium Ecosystem Assessment, 2005).

Risk management focuses on preparing to deal with shocks. It focuses on modifying behaviors over the medium-to-long term to avoid disruptions or declines in global and local food supplies due to changes in temperature and precipitation regimes, and to protect ecosystems through providing environmental services. Adapting to climate change involves managing risk by improving the quality of information and its use, adopting known good practices to strengthen the resilience of vulnerable livelihood systems, and finding new institutional and technological solutions (FAO, 2008a).

iv. Need for increased investment in agricultural education, research and extension

A renewal of the agricultural sector and increased productivity in SA can be achieved through high commitments to increasing agricultural education, research and development capacity in agriculture and food production. A focus on technological innovations to improve agricultural productivity through best practices and techniques can maintain productivity gains. Such innovations include: addressing current agricultural methods and achieving yields and output improvements through greater efficiency in CA and rain-fed crop systems; application of technology in developing robust seed and plant varieties that are pest resistant, and requiring less fertilizer and less water. Another area of research and development that needs focus is strengthening the institutional capacity for better information and technologies to agricultural producers and educating them about nutrient management, water management and sustainable agriculture, thereby contributing to food security (FAO, 2008a).

SA countries would experience greater returns on agricultural investments by focusing on research and development strategies that maximize sustainable agricultural technologies. By adopting multi-sectoral approaches to food security, implementing policies that address food consumption, educating the farmers about the best practices of farming and reducing wastage, investing in basic infrastructure such as water, roads and electricity, intensifying agricultural output, increasing market access, targeting food assistance for consumption to the poor and the marginalized, including women and children, and ensuring adequate nutrient-rich diets SA countries can ensure faster gains in eradicating food and nutrition insecurity in the midst of the negative impacts of climate change.

v. *Investment in best practices*

Investing in wider adoption of best management practices (BMPs) for mitigation in the food and agriculture sector could therefore have multiple payoffs for food security, including contributing to the stability of global food markets and providing new employment opportunities in the commercial agriculture sector, as well enhancing the sustainability of vulnerable livelihood systems (ILO, 2007).

Some of these practices include:

- Reducing emissions of CO_2, such as through reduction in the rate of land conversion and deforestation, adoption of alternatives to the burning of crop residues after harvest, and use of more efficient energy by commercial agriculture and agro-industries. Good options exist for reducing the current level of agriculture-related emissions and, in the process, introducing more sustainable farming practices that strengthen ecosystem resilience and provide more security for agriculture-based livelihoods in the face of increased climatic variability.
- Sequestering carbon, such as through adoption of best management practices of SOC enhancement, with CA involving permanent organic soil cover, minimum mechanical soil disturbance and crop rotation (which also saves on fossil fuel usage); improved management of pastures and grazing practices on natural grasslands, through, for example, optimizing stock numbers and rotational grazing; introduction of integrated agroforestry systems that combine crops, grazing lands and trees in ecologically sustainable ways; use of degraded, marginal lands for productive planted forests or other cellulose biomass for alternative fuels; planting carbon sink trees; reforestation and afforestation, rehabilitation of degraded grasslands and cultivated soils, and promotion of conservation agriculture. Enhancing carbon sequestration in degraded drylands and mountain slopes through any of these methods could have direct environmental, economic and social benefits for local people, with consequent improvements in their food security status. The need of the hour is a "vigorous and a coordinated effort at a global scale towards desertification control, restoration of degraded ecosystems, conversion to appropriate land uses, and adoption of BMPs on cropland and grazing land" (Lal, 2004).

- Promoting CA, based on enhancing natural biological processes above and below ground. Interventions such as mechanical soil tillage are reduced to an absolute minimum, and external inputs such as agrochemicals and nutrients of mineral or organic origin are applied at optimum levels and in ways and quantities that do not interfere with or disrupt biological processes (Lal, 2015a, 2015b).
- Looking for opportunities as a result of ACC. There may be options to grow different crops and animals with higher productivity and adaptability to changing and uncertain climates.
- An illustration of adaptation to climate change impacts with simultaneous reduction in adverse effects comes from a study from Bangladesh that describes a sequenced framework, starting with raising awareness, scientific capacity building, generating evidence and conducting pilot studies to inform and engage the decision makers in policy planning (Ayers et al., 2014).

vi. Call for re-invigoration of South Asian Association for Regional Cooperation (SAARC)

Regional cooperation in SA through a re-invigoration of SAARC can provide numerous opportunities for the countries to achieve greater food productivity and availability as well as counter undernourishment among its population. Cooperation between countries across various regions of the world has known to bring several benefits to the populations. By collaborating in joint research, development and extension programs, sharing information, acquiring and maintaining advanced agricultural technology and equipment, countries of SA would be able to efficiently enhance their agricultural systems. Pooling of resources such as rain forecasting applications, remote sensing, geographic information systems (GIS), knowledge sharing on pests and diseases, and so on, through the SAARC Agricultural centers would exemplify further research and innovations to tackle the ill-effects of climate change in a concerted manner (United Nations, 2012b). Concrete actions in this regard would allow the countries to realize the gains of regional cooperation in agricultural development and achievement of food security.

Food reserve banks represent another area of increasing food security and regional cooperation. The SAARC Food Bank, which was established in 2007, should be further strengthened to supplement national efforts toward providing food security to the people of the region (Sekhar and Bhatt, 2012). The Public Distribution System (PDS) which has a long history in SA and all the countries of the region, have established a mechanism that should be linked to the SAARC Food Bank for intra-regional grain pooling (Wickramasinghe, 2014). Grains, seeds, fodder and tools can be utilized for borrowing and lending at pre-determined rates, for the larger benefit of the poor farmers. Grain banks can act as storehouses of food grains and complement the public distribution systems in cases of gaps in delivery or access. In order to utilize the tons of food grains in the warehouses of the countries, farmers can be provided with food grains instead of a food subsidy, which would not only act as an in-kind payment for ecosystem services for the restoration of degraded lands by providing them an alternative to shifting cultivation (prominent in North East India), but would also discourage the wastage of surplus food grains (Nath et al., 2015). The SAARC Food Bank should be re-launched, since a lack of food availability is influenced by different factors, including poverty, faulty economic and distribution systems, over-population, food and agriculture policies, and climate change (Hasina, 2015).

To foster greater understanding between people and governments, and to provide a stepping stone toward an integrated and prosperous South Asia, the following intra-regional initiatives could be undertaken:

> [The] harmonization of quality standards for food, animal and plant products and recognition of each other's sanitary and phyto-sanitary certification; mutual cooperation in physical

> infrastructure and human resource development for quality certification, particularly in view of the problems faced by relatively less developed countries like Nepal; improved regional connectivity to link the SAARC countries through the shortest routes and; removal of non-tariff barriers to cross-border trade in food including lifting of ban on import/export of food commodities within SAARC countries.
>
> *(Uddin and Haque, 2014, 14)*

SAARC could play an instrumental role in developing country-wise risk management policies for sustainable development. From a food security perspective, the objective of such frameworks is to protect local food supplies, assets and livelihoods against the effects of increasing weather variability and the increased frequency and intensity of extreme events. Frameworks should include pre-event preparedness, risk mitigating strategies, reliable and timely early warning and response systems, and innovative risk financing instruments to spread residual risks. Elements of such frameworks that are applicable for both rural and urban populations in all ecosystems include effective early warning systems; emergency shelters, provisions and evacuation procedures; and weather related insurance schemes (FAO, 2008a).

In implementing Article 4.9 of the Convention, the Conference of Parties (COP) of the UN Framework Convention on Climate Change (UNFCCC), in 2001, established a developing country work program that included National Adaptation Programmes of Action (NAPAs), to support these countries in addressing the challenge of climate change, given their particular vulnerability. Focus is placed on community-level input as an important source of information, recognizing that grassroots communities are the main stakeholders. Afghanistan, Bhutan, Bangladesh, Nepal are among the list of 50 countries on the list. The Maldives graduated from the list in the year 2011 (UNFCCC, 2014).

vii. Creating awareness about the environment and the dangers of climate change

Scientific work in response to the challenge of climate change includes development of tools and technologies for improved monitoring of weather and climate, incorporation of climate change variables and assessments into food security information and early warning systems, and observation and modeling of climate impacts on rural livelihoods. As already noted, it is critical that information generated by early warning systems and climate change models be packaged in ways that are accessible to vulnerable people, so it can assist them in making sound choices about how to adapt to climate change and other stressors. All actors in the food system need access to reliable information about climate change and its potential impacts, to avoid breakdowns in the system and adverse food security outcomes. Typically, these systems have focused on monitoring current weather and other socio-economic data to forecast the adequacy of food supplies and assess food aid needs in developing countries with high risks of drought. School education across elementary, primary and higher levels must have mandatory courses on environmental education, with a focus on greater awareness of ways to protect and preserve nature. Group activities like planting and caring for trees should be encouraged, in addition to engendering the responsibility of all children to be representatives of planet Earth and envisioning it as a common heritage.

The way forward

The growing threat of climate change to the global food supply, and the challenges it poses for food security and nutrition, requires urgent concerted policy responses and the deployment of all the scientific knowledge and accumulated evidence (Elbehri, 2015). The recent global food crisis of 2007–2009 reminds us about the vulnerability of the national and international food production and distribution systems (ADB, 2013). Robust development strategies and comprehensive yet multilayered policy frameworks are required. These include investments in infrastructure and prioritizing long-term resilience and holistic approaches to tackle the roots of risks associated with climate change. It also requires a greater focus on the important drivers of climate adaptation, including the potential role of trade to mitigate some of the negative impacts of climate change on the food production of South Asia.

Science and innovation have a role to play here, and in recent years there has been good progress made in improving food utilization through fortification and bio-fortification (Nestel et al., 2006). Vulnerability to food security shocks requires further research, as do ways to strengthen adaptive capacities under climate change, mainly related to agriculture, like the adoption of improved technologies to accommodate the effects of changes in temperature, precipitation patterns, and length of growing season (Ziervogel and Ericksen, 2010), as public policy responses depend on such insights. For example, appropriate design of programs transferring income to the poor, employment-related transfer programs, and early childhood nutrition actions (Rogers and Coates, 2002) may all need expansion to respond to climate-related volatilities.

A broad set of risks must be considered, of which climate change is an increasingly important one, that can ripple out to destabilize food systems, resulting in high and volatile food prices that temporarily limit poor people's food consumption (for instance, Torlesse et al. (2003) studied how changes in prices of rice in Bangladesh affected child nutrition), and risks that political disruptions and failed political systems cause food insecurity (Berazneva and Lee, 2013). This complex system of risks can assume a variety of patterns that could potentially collide in catastrophic combinations.

Some of the livelihood groups that warrant special attention in the context of climate change include: low-income groups in drought- and flood-prone areas with poor food distribution infrastructure and limited access to emergency response; low- to middle-income groups in flood-prone areas that may lose homes, stored food, personal possessions and means of obtaining their livelihood, particularly when water rises very quickly and with great force, as in sea surges or flash floods; farmers whose land becomes submerged or damaged by sea-level rise or saltwater intrusions; poor livestock keepers in dry lands where changes in rainfall patterns will affect forage availability and quality and others (Mehta and Nambiar, 2007).

As climate-related risks affect everybody, insurance against the consequences of catastrophic weather events needs to be globalized, and costs minimized through action to mitigate climate change. Innovative insurance schemes, such as a global reinsurance fund for climate change damage or expanded local coverage of weather-based insurance, are likely to be needed (Osgood, 2008).

Since water mediates much of the climate change impacts on agriculture, increased water scarcity in SA presents a major challenge for climate adaptation. Addressing the implications of future water availability for food security is critical and requires coherent regional and national strategies for management of water demand and supply. SAARC should institutionalize structures to ensure people's rightful access to this indispensable natural resource.

Conclusions

Global warming is the immediate consequence of increased GHG emissions with no offsetting increases in carbon storage. The current episode of human-induced global warming on the climate system will both cause additional stresses and create new opportunities for food systems, with consequent implications for food security.

From the above discussion it is evident that the net effect of climate change in SA is likely to be negative given the fragility of agricultural production to local climate trends and variations in temperature and rainfall (Hansen et al., 2010). The ability of countries to implement policies that increase effective long-term food security will be pivotal in determining if SA can maintain strong long-run growth and inclusive development (United Nations, 2012a).

The nutrition transition will unfold in parallel with climate change in coming decades (Wheeler and von Braun, 2013). The main cause of hunger across SA is not lack of food, but the economic and social distribution of that food which leaves populations undernourished and hungry. Thus it becomes imperative that governments, NGOs and other stakeholders improve the resilience of safe water systems in resource limited settings while also spreading novel technologies to purify water at the household level (Mellor et al., 2014).

There are various avenues through which countries can pursue cooperation not only for food security, but also for the improvement of mechanisms to increase food production, reduce excess demand and insulate against food price shocks. Regional cooperation would also help in accelerating the development gains in complementary areas like energy, related to the food demand–supply nexus and market management (United Nations, 2012b), as well as in positively harnessing women's capabilities in garnering attention toward mitigating the impacts of climate change. Since the adaptation and mitigation strategies of climate change in agriculture go hand in hand, adopting an integrated strategic approach represents the best way forward. This would go a long way in achieving food security for all and contribute towards the fulfillment of the SDGs of the UN by 2030, both in letter and in spirit.

Notes

1 For more detail on reports of CESCR visit the OHCHR country websites.
2 Malnutrition can be caused by eating too little, too much or an unbalanced diet that does not contain the right quantity and quality of nutrients necessary for adequate nutrition. Inadequate dietary intake and disease/infections which alter dietary requirements and the body's ability to, absorb and utilize nutrients effectively, are immediate causes of malnutrition (FAO, 2016).
3 Undernutrition exists when caloric intake is below the minimum dietary energy requirement (MDER) (FAO, 2016).

References

Abdulai, A. and A. CroleRees. (2001) "Constraints to Income Diversification Strategies: Evidence from Southern Mali." *Food Policy* 26(4): 437–452.

Aggarwal P.K. et al. (2004) "Adapting Food Systems of the Indo-Gangetic Plains to Global Environmental Change: Key Information Needs to Improve Policy Formulation." *Environmental Science Policy* 7: 487–498.

Aggarwal P.K. (2007) "Climate Change, Implications for Indian Agriculture." *Jalvigyan Sameeksha* 22: 37–46.

Aggarwal P.K. (2008) "Implications of Global Climate Change for Indian Agriculture," ISPRS Archives XXXVIII-8/W3 Workshop Proceedings: Impact of Climate Change on Agriculture.

Aggarwal, P.K. and A.K. Singh. (2010) "Implications of Global Climatic Change on Water and Food Security," in C. Ringler et al. (eds.) *Global Change: Impacts on Water and Food Security*. Berlin, Heidelberg: Springer-Verlag, pp. 49–63.

Asian Development Bank (ADB). (2013) *Food Security in Asia and the Pacific*. Manila, Philippines: ADB.

Ayers, Jessica et al. (2014) "Mainstreaming Climate Change Adaptation into Development in Bangladesh." *Climate and Development* 6(4): 293–305.

Balmaseda, M.A. et al. (2013) "Distinctive Climate Signals in Reanalysis of Global Ocean Heat Content." *Geophysical Research Letters* (40): 1754–1759.

Berazneva, J. and David R. Lee. (2013) "Explaining the African Food Riots of 2007–2008: An Empirical Analysis." *Food Policy* 39: 28–39.

Bhatiya, N. (2014) "Why South Asia Is So Vulnerable to Climate Change," The South Asia Channel, *Foreign Policy*, Washington, DC.

Bruinsma, Jelle (ed.) (2003) *World Agriculture: Towards 2015/2030: An FAO Perspective*. London: Earthscan.

Caulfield, L.E. et al. (2006) "Stunting, Wasting and Micronutrient Deficiency Disorders," in Dean T. Jamison et al. (eds.) *Disease Control Priorities in Developing Countries*. Washington, DC: Oxford University Press and The World Bank.

Challinor, A. et al. (2004) "Design and Optimisation of a Large-Area Process-Based Model for Annual Crops." *Agricultural and Forest Meterology* 124: 99–120.

Delpha, I. et al. (2009) "Impacts of Climate Change on Surface Water Quality in Relation to Drinking Water Production." *Environment International* 35(8): 1225–1233.

Earley, Jane. (2009) "Climate Change, Agriculture and International Trade: Potential Conflicts and Opportunities." *Biores, International Center for Trade and Sustainable Development* 3(3): 8–10.

Elbehri, Aziz (ed.). (2015) *Climate Change and Food Systems: Global Assessments and Implications for Food Security and Trade*. Rome: Food and Agricultural Organization of the United Nations.

FAO. (1996) "Rome Declaration on World Food Security," World Food Summit, November 13–17, 1996, Rome. Available at: www.fao.org/docrep/003/w3613e/w3613e00.HTM.

FAO. (1999) "Poverty Alleviation and Food Security in Asia: Lessons and Challenges." Food and Agriculture Organization of the United Nations Regional Office for Asia and the Pacific December 1998. RAP Publication 1999/1. Available at: www.fao.org/docrep/004/ab981e/ab981e0a.htm#bm10.

FAO. (2003) "World Agriculture: Toward 2015/2030," Chapter 13. Rome: Earthscan.

FAO. (2007) "The State of Food and Agriculture 2007. Paying Farmers for Environmental Services." Rome: FAO of the United Nations.

FAO. (2008a) "An Introduction to the Basic Concepts of Food Security," EC – FAO Food Security Programme, Rome, Italy. Available at: www.fao.org/docrep/013/al936e/al936e00.pdf.

FAO. (2008b) "Climate Change and Food Security: A Framework Document," Rome: FAO of the United Nations.

FAO. (2013) *Climate Smart Agriculture*, Sourcebook. Rome: FAO of the United Nations.

FAO. (2016) "Nutrition, Frequently Asked Questions." Available at: www.fao.org/food/nutrition-sensitive-agriculture-and-food-based-approaches/faq/en/.

Gleick, P.H. (1993) *Water in Crisis: A Guide to the World's Fresh Water Resources*. New York: Oxford University Press.

HLPE. (2012) *Food Security and Climate Change*. A report by the High Level Panel of Experts on Food Security and Nutrition of the Committee on World Food Security, Rome.

Hansen, J. et al. (2010) "Low Global Surface Temperature Change." *Reviews of Geophysics* 48: RG4004.

Hashizume, M. et al. (2007) "Association between Climate Variability and Hospital Visits for Non-Cholera Diarrhoea in Bangladesh: Effects and Vulnerable Groups," *International Journal of Epidemiology* 36(5): 1030–1037.

Hasina, Sheikh. (2015) *Inaugural Speech at the South Asia Right to Food Conference 2015*. Dhaka, Bangladesh: Krishibid Institution.

Hatlebakk, Magnus. (2012) "Malnutrition in South-Asia: Poverty, diet or lack of female empowerment?" Chr. Michelsen Institute (CMI), Working Paper 4, Norway.

ILO. (2007) "Chapter 4. Employment by sector," in *Key indicators of the labour market (KILM)*, 5th edition. Available at: www.ilo.org/public/english/employment/strat/kilm/download/kilm04.pdf.

IPCC. (2007a) *Climate Change 2007 Impacts, adaptation and vulnerability. Contribution of Working Group II to the Fourth Assessment Report of IPCC*. Cambridge, UK: Cambridge University Press.

IPCC. (2007b) *Climate Change 2007 the physical science basis. Contribution of Working Group I to the Fourth Assessment Report of IPCC*. Cambridge, UK: Cambridge University Press.

IPCC. (2014) "Summary for policymakers," in C.B. Field, V.R. Barros, D.J. Dokken, K.J. Mach, M.D. Mastrandrea, T.E. Bilir, M. Chatterjee, K.L. Ebi, Y.O. Estrada, R.C. Genova, B. Girma, E.S. Kissel, A.N. Levy, S. MacCracken, P.R. Mastrandrea, and L.L. White (eds.) *Climate Change 2014: Impacts, Adaptation, and Vulnerability. Part A: Global and Sectoral Aspects. Contribution of Working Group II to the Fifth Assessment Report of the Intergovernmental Panel on Climate Change*. Cambridge, UK and New York, NY, USA: Cambridge University Press.

Ki-Moon, Ban. (2012) "A video message at the opening session of the 39th Session of the Committee on World Food Security (CFS)." October 12, 2012, Rome. Available at: www.youtube.com/watch?v=kRYDeN3u7F8

Knox, J. et al. (2012) "Climate Change Impacts on Crop Productivity in Africa and South Asia." *Environmental Research Letters* 7(3): 034032.

Kundzewicz, Z.W. et al. (2007) "Freshwater resources and their management," in M.L. Parry, O.F. Canziani, J.P. Palutikof, P.J. van der Linden and C.E. Hanson (eds.) *Climate Change 2007: Impacts, Adaptation and Vulnerability, Contribution of Working Group II to the Fourth Assessment Report of the Intergovernmental Panel on Climate Change*. Cambridge, UK: Cambridge University Press.

Lal, R. (2004) "Soil Carbon Sequestration Impacts on Global Climate Change and Food Security." *Science* 304(5677): 1623–1627.

Lal, R. (2010) "Managing Soils and Ecosystems for Mitigating Anthropogenic Carbon Emissions and Advancing Global Food Security." *BioScience* 60(9): 708–721.

Lal, R. (2011) "Climate of South Asia and the Human Wellbeing," in R. Lal et al. (eds.), *Climate Change and Food Security in South Asia*. The Netherlands: Springer, pp. 3–12.

Lal, R. (2015a) "A System Approach to Conservation Agriculture." *Journal of Soil and Water Conservation* 70(4): 82A–88A.

Lal, R. (2015b) "Sequestering Carbon and Increasing Productivity by Conservation Agriculture." *Journal of Soil and Water Conservation* 70(3): 55A–62A.

Lambrou, Y. and R. Laub. (2004) "Gender perspectives on the conventions on biodiversity, climate change and desertification." Gender and Climate Change. Available at: www.gencc.interconnection.org/resources.htm.

Maxwell, S. and R. Slater. (2003) "Food policy old and new." *Development Policy Review* 21(5–6): 531–553.

McMichael, Anthony. (2013) "Globalization, Climate Change, and Human Health." *New England Journal of Medicine*, 368: 1335–1343.

Mehta, R. and R.G. Nambiar. (2007), "The Poultry Industry in India," FAO of the United Nations. Available at: www.fao.org/AG/againfo/home/events/bangkok2007/docs/part1/1_5.pdf.

Mellor, Jonathan, et al (2014) "Modeling the Sustainability of a Ceramic Water Filter Intervention." *Water Research*, 49: 286–299.

Millennium Ecosystem Assessment. (2005) *Ecosystems and Human Well-Being: Synthesis*. Washington DC: Island Press for WRI.

Mittal, S. and D. Sethi (2009) "Food Security in South Asia: Issues and Opportunities." Working Paper No. 240, Development Economics Working Papers 22917, East Asian Bureau of Economic Research. Available at: www.eaber.org/system/tdf/documents/ICRIER_Mittal_2009.pdf?file=1&type=node&id=22917&force=.

NATCOM. (2004) *India's Initial National Communication to the United Nations Framework Convention on Climate Change, National Communication Project (NATCOM)*. Ministry of Environment and Forests, Government of India.

Nath, A.J. et al. (2015) "Grains for Ecosystem Carbon Management in North East India." *Current Science* 109(8): 1387–1389.

Nestel, P. et al. (2006) "Biofortification of Staple Food Crops." *Journal of Nutrition* 136: 1064–1067.

Osgood, D. (2008) "Climate information, index insurance and climate risk management." Paper presented at the International Conference on Food Security and Environmental Change, April 24, 2008, Oxford, UK.

OXFAM. (2007) Report cited in BBC online weather disasters getting worse, November 25, 2007. Available at: www.bbc.com.UK.

Pinstrup-Andersen, P. and Ebbe Schiøler. (2000) *Seeds of Contention, World Hunger and the Global Controversy Over GM Crops*. Baltimore, MD: The Johns Hopkins University Press.

Porter, J.R. and M.A. Semenov (2005) "Crop Responses to Climatic Variation." *Philosophical Transactions of the Royal Society B: Biological Sciences* 360: 2021–2035.

Rogers, B.L. and J. Coates. (2002) "Food-Based Safety Nets and Related Programs," in The Gerald J. and Dorothy R. Friedman School of Nutrition Science and Policy (eds.), *Food Policy and Applied Nutrition Program Discussion Paper No. 12O*. Available at: www.nutrition.tufts.edu/documents/fpan/wp12-safety_nets.pdf.

Romm, J. (2011) "Desertification: The Next Dust Bowl." *Nature* 478(7370): 450–451.

Rosenzweig, C. and D. Hillel. (2005) "Climate Change, Agriculture and Sustainability," in R. Lal et al. (eds.), *Climate Change and Global Food Security*. Florida: Taylor and Francis Group.

Rosenzweig, Cynthia and Francesco Nicola Tubiello. (2007) "Adaptation and Mitigation Strategies in Agriculture: An Analysis of Potential Synergies." *NASA Publications*, Paper 25. Available at: http://digitalcommons.unl.edu/nasapub/25.

Rosenzweig, C. et al. (2001) "Climate Change and Extreme Weather Events: Implications for Food Production, Plant Diseases and Pests." *Global Change and Human Health* 2(2): 90–104. Available at: http://pubs.giss.nasa.gov/docs/2001/2001_Rosenzweig_etal_1.pdf.

Sejian, V. et al. (2015) "Introduction to Concepts of Climate Change Impact on Livestock and Its Adaptation and Mitigation," in V. Sejian et al. (eds.) *Climate Change Impact on Livestock: Adaptation and Mitigation*. New Delhi: Springer.

Sekhar, C.S.C. and Yogesh Bhatt. (2012) "Food Security in South Asia-Prospects for Regional Integration. " Background Paper no. RVC 6, New Delhi: Institute of Economic Growth.

Sheffield, J. and E. Wood. (2008) "Projected Changes in Drought Occurrence Under Future Global Warming from Multi-Model, Multi-Scenario, IPCC AR4 Simulations." *Climate Dynamics* 31(1): 79–105.

Solomon, S. et al. (eds.) (2007) *Climate Change 2007: The Physical Science Basis: Contribution of Working Group I to the Fourth Assessment Report of the IPCC*. New York: Cambridge University Press.

Torlesse, H. et al. (2003) "Association of Household Rice Expenditure with Child Nutritional Status Indicates a Role for Macroeconomic Food Policy in Combating Malnutrition." *Journal of Nutrition* 133: 1320–1325.

Thornton, P. et al. (2013) "The Livestock, Climate Change and Poverty Nexus." *Futures of Agriculture*. Brief No. 43 – English. Rome: Global Forum on Agricultural Research (GFAR).

Uddin, Md. Kamal and Md. Shahabul Haque. (2014) "The Challenges of Food Security in South Asia: Understanding it's dynamics with Reference to Bangladesh." *Developing Country Studies* 4(3): 7–15.

United Nations. (1948) The Universal Declaration of Human Rights, General Assembly resolution 217 A of 10 December 1948, Paris.

United Nations. (1966) *International Covenant on Economic, Social and Cultural Rights*, General Assembly resolution 2200A (XXI) of 16 December 1966, Geneva.

United Nations. (2012a) *Growing Together: Economic Integration for an Inclusive and Sustainable Asia-Pacific Century*. Thailand: United Nations Publications.

United Nations. (2012b) *Regional Cooperation for Inclusive and Sustainable Development, South and South West-Asia Development Report 2012–2013*. New Delhi: Routledge.

United Nations. (2015) Department of Economic and Social Affairs, Population Division. "World Population Prospects: The 2015 Revision," DVD Edition.

UN Economic and Social Commission for Asia and the Pacific (UN-ESCAP). (2009) "Sustainable Agriculture and Food Security in Asia and the Pacific," April 2009. Available at: www.refworld.org/docid/49f589db2.html.

UNESCAP. (2013) "South Asia Policy Dialogue on Regional Cooperation for Strengthening National Food Security Strategies," New Delhi: Office for the South and South-West Asia.

UNFCCC. (1992) "Article 1. Definitions," *UN Framework Convention on Climate Change*. Available at: https://unfccc.int/files/essential_background/background_publications_htmlpdf/application/pdf/conveng.pdf.

UNFCCC. (2014) "Background information on the NAPAs," *United Nations Framework Convention on Climate Change*. Available at: http://unfccc.int/adaptation/workstreams/national_adaptation_programmes_of_action/items/7572.php.

UNICEF. (2014) "Promoting Child Nutrition in Asia," presented by Christiane Rudert, Regional Advisor Nutrition UNICEF East Asia Pacific Regional Office, November 4–6, 2014, Vientiane

von Grebmer, Klaus et al. (2015) *2015 Global Hunger Index: Armed Conflict and the Challenge of Hunger*. Bonn, Germany, Washington, DC and Dublin, Ireland: Welthungerhilfe; International Food Policy Research Institute (IFPRI) and Concern Worldwide.

Wheeler, Tim (2015) "Climate Change Impacts on Food Systems and Implications for Climate-Compatible Food Policies," in Elbehri, Aziz (ed.), *Climate Change and Food Systems: Global Assessments and Implications for Food Security and Trade*. Rome: Food and Agricultural Organization of the United Nations.

Wheeler, Tim and Joachim von Braun. (2013) "Climate Change Impacts on Global Food Security." *Science* 341(6145): 508–513.

Wheeler, T.R. et al. (2000) "Temperature Variability and the Yield of Annual Crops." *Agriculture, Ecosystems and Environment* 82: 159–167.

Wickramasinghe, U. (2014) "Realizing Sustainable Food Security in the Post-2015 Development Era: South Asia's Progress, Challenges and Opportunities." Development Papers 1402. (South and South-West Asia Office, United Nations Economic and Social Commission for Asia and the Pacific (ESCAP), New Delhi.

WMO. (1992) *International meteorological vocabulary, 2nd edition*. Publication No. 182. Available at: http://meteoterm.wmo.int/meteoterm/ns?a=T_P1.start&u=&direct=yes&relog=yes#expanded.

World Bank. (2007) "Agriculture in South Asia." Available at: http://web.worldbank.org/WBSITE/EXTERNAL/COUNTRIES/SOUTHASIAEXT/0,,contentMDK:21571064~pagePK:146736~piPK:146830~theSitePK:223547,00.html#1analysis.

World Bank. (2015a) *South Asia Food and Nutrition Security Initiative (SAFANSI)*. Washington, DC: The World Bank.

World Bank. (2015b) "Overview: South Asia." Available at: www.worldbank.org/en/region/sar/overview#1.

World Health Organization. (2002) "Global and Regional Food Consumption Patterns and Trends." Available at: www.who.int/nutrition/topics/3_foodconsumption/en/.

Ziervogel, G. and P.J. Ericksen. (2010) "Adapting to Climate Change to Sustain Food Security." *WIREs Climate Change* 1: 525–540.

SECTION 5
Social welfare in Asian nations

16

Development of social welfare in Indonesia: the rise of conditional cash transfer

Edi Suharto

Introduction

In Indonesia, social welfare is associated with two meanings: first, social welfare as a condition in which material, spiritual and social needs of citizens are fulfilled, and second, social welfare as an organized activity of social services implemented in the form of social protection, social security, social rehabilitation and social empowerment programs (Suharto, 2009). While the first meaning refers to the condition of social well-being as the ultimate goal of social development, the second concept refers to the process of social development aimed at improving standard of living of a targeted population. This is known in the Law No.11 concerning "Social Welfare" as social welfare activities or *penyelenggaraan kesejahteraan sosial*. The main beneficiaries of social welfare are the poor such as homeless, beggars, neglected children, as well as the vulnerable people facing social problems such as street children, child labor, persons with disabilities, persons with HIV/AIDS, and domestic workers (Suharto, 2009).

Swedish scholar Esping-Andersen (1990) distinguishes three main regimes of social welfare model, namely the corporatist welfare regime, the liberal welfare regime and the social democratic welfare regime. The corporatist welfare model or known as social insurance model, is concerned with maintaining order and status and hence it accomplishes social insurance funds such as unemployment benefits, old age pension and health insurance designed to reward work performance and status. Such public insurance funds were established and operated either by the government (e.g., Germany, Austria) or run by labor associations (e.g., the miners' insurance fund).

Characterized by anti-state tradition and dominant position of the market, the liberal welfare model involves means-tested programs – a test to demonstrate need, and supports modest universal benefits which are based on public services or insurance scheme. This model usually covers beneficiaries from the low income working class with low level of services for the poor.

Often referred to as Scandinavian welfare regime, the social democratic welfare model relies on universalistic welfare state system that encompasses all aspects of people's lives. Since the enjoyment of benefits and services does not depend heavily on a person's performance in the market, and is, instead, corresponding to need, this model believes that social rights of citizens must be fully realized. Hence, countries adopt this model often provide extensive social security schemes and social services such as health care, day care, elder care, covering to even the most discriminating clusters of the middle class.

With reference to the above Esping-Andersen's (1990) social welfare models, Indonesia does not strictly fall into one of those three regimes. However, the closest model to Indonesia's social welfare orientation is the liberal since the government's responsibility is only to provide social services to such targeted beneficiaries as the poor and vulnerable people if the market fails (UK Essay, 2016). This so called "residual welfare" policy is characterized by low public expenditures for social protection and basic social provisions such as education, health and subsidies, compared to GDP.

The conditional cash transfer (CCT) is now among the most prominent social welfare programs under social protection initiatives implemented in Indonesia. The growing popularity of CCT programs in Latin America in the 1990s and early 2000s set a new trend of CCT adoption in many developing countries, including Indonesia. One widely known CCT program is PKH (*Program Keluarga Harapan*) or the Family of Hope Program, which was primarily designed using Mexico's Opportunidades and Brazil's Bolsa Familia as its model.

This chapter is aimed at exploring how Indonesia has developed CCT as part of its social welfare strategies to improve the standard of living of those categorized as poor and vulnerable. After reviewing the management of PKH, including the delivery system, coverage, benefits, and budget and financing, this chapter then looks at how PKH impacts the life of poor families as its beneficiaries.

An overview of social welfare and social protection

Social protection has been gaining importance in Indonesia's social welfare policies, especially after the financial crisis hit the country in 1997 (Suharto et al., 2006; Wetterberg et al., 1999). When the Asian financial crisis struck the ASEAN region in the 1990s, a heavy reliance on traditional family-based social protection systems and, in some cases, a poorly developed infrastructure for administering social protection programs, led to the failure of many governments to respond effectively to the needs of its citizens; and this inherent weakness within ASEAN countries has dramatically highlighted the vulnerability of the population to various sorts of shocks to their livelihoods. The economic crisis and the subsequent downturn in ASEAN "miracle" countries demonstrated that growth and sound macroeconomic policies alone are insufficient for sustained poverty reduction.

Social protection policies including safety nets, income support system for the elderly, and well-functioning labor markets with built in social safeguards are essential for reducing poverty over the long-term and protecting the gains already made during times of economic growth (Suharto et al., 2006). In the lead up to the financial crisis, the majority of the region's citizens, particularly those working in the shadow economy, were not covered by formal social protection schemes. While the traditional social protection systems in Indonesia are found to be poorly adapted to the demands of a liberal market economy, the gradual erosion of family and community networks undermined the very basis of those traditional safety nets.

In Indonesia, the initiative to strengthen social protection systems is paramount within the context of poverty reduction strategies. As part of its commitment, several laws and regulations highlighting the importance of social welfare and social protection have also been established by government of Indonesia. For example:

- The 1945 Constitution places high emphasis on social protection. Sub-section 2 of Article 34 states that the state shall develop a social security system for all citizens.

- Law No 40, 2004 about the National Social Security System (SJSN) states that social protection includes *pension and old-age benefits; health benefits; employment accident benefits; and death benefits.*
- Law No 11, 2009 about Social Welfare asserts that every citizen should have their minimum life needs and social services through social rehabilitation, social security, social protection and social empowerment.

The government of Indonesia plans to accelerate the pace of poverty reduction over the next five years. The government has declared that poverty reduction is the highest development priority of the current administration. The government plans to reach this goal by strengthening economic growth and job creation, as well as continuing its poverty reduction programs. The government strategy to alleviate poverty problems in Indonesia is articulated into three clusters based on the major group targeted by each one (Perdana, 2014: 4).

- **Cluster 1** includes programs targeting households. This cluster focuses on household-based social assistance programs. Some programs developed under this cluster include subsidized rice for the poor (*Raskin* or *Beras untuk Orang Miskin*), educational assistance for poor students (BSM or *Bantuan Siswa Miskin*), subsidized health care (*Jamkesmas*) and Conditional Cash Transfer (PKH or *Program Keluarga Harapan*). The objective of the cluster is to reduce poverty and improve the quality of human resources, especially among the poor.
- **Cluster 2** includes programs targeting communities. This cluster emphasizes community empowerment programs under the umbrella of *Program Nasional Pemberdayaan Masyarakat* or the National Program for Community Empowerment (PNPM) Mandiri. The aim of PNPM Mandiri is to improve communities' economic conditions and provide more employment opportunities for the poor.
- **Cluster 3** includes programs targeting micro, small-and medium-sized enterprises (MSME). This cluster seeks to expand economic opportunities for low-income households and to achieve economic and financial inclusion of the greater population in Indonesia. The program designed under this cluster is the Peoples' Business Credit program or *Kredit Usaha Rakyat* (KUR) in which the government offers a guarantee scheme for bank credit for the poor without collateral up to a certain amount.

Program Keluarga Harapan (PKH): management, benefits and impacts

Started in 2007, *Program Keluarga Harapan* (PKH) or Family of Hope Program is a CCT program aimed at improving the quality of human development, especially for children from chronically poor families. The specific objectives of PKH are to improve recipients' socio-economic conditions; education levels; improve the health and nutrition status of pregnant women, postnatal women, and children under five years of age in recipient households; and to improve recipients' access to and quality of education and health services. The CCT program has been chosen as the main income support program by two countries in Southeast Asia, the Philippines and Indonesia. Interest in and the scope of CCT programs have grown enormously in the last 10 years. The range of polities interested covers all continents, although the longest established and most evaluated programs are found predominantly in middle-income countries in Latin America (Fiszbein and Schady, 2009).

The role of CCT programs in social policy varies from place to place, as a consequence of differences in both their design and the context in which they operate. Most obviously, CCT programs vary with respect to the pertinent measures of size. In terms of absolute coverage, they range from millions of families (11 million in Brazil and almost 6 million in Indonesia in 2016) to 215,000 in Chile, to pilot programs with a few thousand families – such as in Kenya and Nicaragua.

In Indonesia, families are provided with an allowance conditional on their attention to their children's education and health. PKH offers transfers to chronically poor families through participation in health and nutrition programs as well as through children's school attendance. Cash transfers are made to households on the condition that certain health and education-related obligations are met. The transfers are given to women in the family because it is believed that they are more likely to focus spending on goods and services that are beneficial to children's well-being. There are no restrictions attached to the use of the money, but in order to improve the likelihood that it is put to the best use of the family, the benefit is primarily paid to the mother or another adult woman in the household.

Delivery system and governance

Involving three main ministries, the Ministry of Social Affairs (MOSA), the Ministry of Health, and the Ministry of Education and Culture, which are coordinated under Coordinating Ministry of Culture and Human Development, PKH has become one of the largest national programs fully supported by the government of Indonesia. Similar to other CCT programs, PKH provides social assistance to the beneficiaries, with the requirement of fulfilling the conditionalities to be met by beneficiaries.

Established at the national, provincial and regency levels, the Implementation Unit of PKH (IUPKH) is the working unit implementing the program policy and set up with the main objective of assuring that (1) PKH implementation works smoothly and in accordance with the plan of the program; (2) various existing problems may be resolved rapidly and accurately; and (3) all relevant parties are provided with sufficient information in order to implement and improve the program. The role and the responsibility of IUPKH at every administration level refer to the specific needs found at each level.

Central IUPKH at the national level is presided by the Chairman of IUPKH, who is also the Director of Social Security under the Directorate General of Social Protection and Security of the MOSA. In its operation, PKH is assisted by the Sub Directorate of Sustainable Cash Direct Transfer that also functions as the Vice-Chairman of IUPKH at the national level. The Chairman of central IUPKH is assisted by officials from MOSA and experts recruited from professional elements. The existing functions in IUPKH *Pusat* include administration, information systems, human resources and training, operations and socialization, and external relations (MOSA, 2012).

Coverage

PKH targeted 387,928 chronically poor households with incomes of less than IDR 480,000/month (USD 53/month) in 2007, increased the number to 816,000 in 2010, and covered 1.51 million in 2012. This means that PKH covered 43 percent of chronically poor households in Indonesia (3.5 million), 5.02 percent of the poor population (30.02 million, 2010), and 0.58 percent of the whole population (259 million in 2010). The number will continue to increase until 2016, reaching 6 million beneficiaries in all 34 provinces and more than 500 districts.[1]

The selection of beneficiary families is carried out by the Central Bureau of Statistics (CBS, 2012) using a three-step process. Families are identified based on a series of characteristics for chronically poor households derived from household surveys and on their potential to fulfill conditions (e.g., for pregnant women or children). Eligibility is validated in the field; and a final list is drawn up by the central IUPKH, usually in consultation with the central PKH technical team and provincial and local PKH coordinating teams. Until now, no beneficiaries have been determined on the basis of a self-selecting mechanism.

In terms of geographical selection, locations are first selected on the basis of several criteria: (1) poverty indicators based on the data of CBS – which include for instance, high incidence of poverty; high incidence of malnutrition; low transition rate from primary to secondary school education; and inadequate supply of health and education facilities; (2) supporting factors for the efficiency of PKH implementation such as work load of facilitators, operator, the performance of IUPKH districts/cities, as well regional coordinators; and (3) availability of health and education facilities to support PKH.

In addition, IUPKH highlights local governments' commitment to support the CCT program, for instance in the allocation of local budget funds in the form of provincial and district/city cost sharing in order to support PKH implementation. In the future, the CCT program is assumed to be carried out by local governments; therefore the readiness as well the commitment of local government is used as one criteria of the selection.

Benefits

As a CCT program, the updated data in PKH is required to ensure the accuracy of funds received by the beneficiaries. In one year, the payment period is scheduled to be carried out four times. Payment schedules in each sub-district are determined by the District/City UPPKH after coordination with the PT Pos; as the institution on which the agreement is based, it is responsible for carrying out the disbursement of PKH funds directly to the beneficiaries. One advance management information system has been developed to support the programs. The amount of money received by the beneficiaries is determined on the basis of their recent status – number of school children, pregnancy status, and the rate of school and health centers attendance. The cash transfer ranges from a minimum transfer of IDR 600,000 (USD 65) to a maximum transfer of IDR 2,200,000 (USD 235) per year and per household.

By practice, gender preference in benefit delivery is implemented. The withdrawal of the benefit payment can only be conducted by the women in the households (e.g., mothers, aunts, grandmothers or other women relatives in the family). When there is no woman available, under the supervision of PKH's facilitators, the head of the household (e.g., fathers or brothers) is able to withdraw the money. Facilitators are especially in charge of capturing any change in the eligibility status of beneficiaries, changes to the household structure of beneficiaries, changes in the educational and pregnancy status, address changes, as well as changes in the education and health centers beneficiaries are attending.

Home visits and crosschecks with the neighborhood are occasionally conducted to confirm the information as well as to prevent beneficiaries from manipulating the data. Teachers, in addition to monitoring conditionality, also verify the enrollment status of a child or attest to graduation. Health centers confirm pregnancies, births as well as death of children, in addition to monitoring conditionality. In 2011, IUPKH hired 4,823 facilitators – four times more than the 1,305 facilitators of 2007 (MOSA, 2012). Since PKH has covered all 34 provinces in Indonesia, in 2012 the number of facilitators has reached more than 6,000 people. Consisting of 44 percent male and 56 percent female, these paid facilitators mainly have bachelor degrees in social sciences (e.g., social work). The increase in the number of facilitators is a logical consequence of the enhancement of beneficiaries and coverage area of the program (Ayala, 2010).

As long as beneficiaries of PKH meet the criteria and conditionalities of the program, they will continually receive cash transfers for six years. Currently, households are supposed to be recertified after five years. All beneficiaries will be re-surveyed after five years of implementation to assess if the current beneficiaries are still entitled to the assistance (re-certification). In coordination with CBS, IUPKH Pusat is assumed to conduct an assessment through home visits to the beneficiaries and to carry out interviews similar to those used in the initial registration. The assessment is expected to identify numbers of household members who are eligible for the program in terms of economic conditions and educational and health status of family members. Data obtained from the assessment will be employed to identify the eligibility of the beneficiaries.

In every six years of implementation, PKH will assess whether or not the members are still eligible for the program, based on their poverty status, chronically poor and non-chronically poor (MOSA, 2012). The assessment is conducted to determine which transformation program the households belong to:

- *Transition*, is designed for households who are still eligible for PKH. The assistance will be extended for up to three years and the households will receive a "family/community development session." PKH shall ensure that the households will receive complimentary social programs (BSM, Jamkesmas, Raskin, etc.). The verification of conditionalities will continually be carried out.
- *Graduation*. Households which are ineligible for PKH will enter the graduation phase. In the graduation phase, households will receive no more cash transfer assistance. However, they are assured to receive other complementary social programs (such as the BSM, Jamkesmas, Raskin, etc.). Since the cash transfer in this stage is ended, verification does not need to be carried out.

Based on their poverty status, non-chronically poor households are automatically rendered ineligible for the program. These households will enter the phase of graduation. Further assessment however, will be carried out on chronically poor households. When the household members meet the categorical criteria, after six years they will enter the phase of transition. Those who are no longer eligible for the program based on the criteria will enter the graduation phase.

Budget and financing

In 2010, social expenditure[2] of the government reached IDR 130.4 trillion or approximately 31.1 percent of total expenditures distributed directly to citizens. Social expenditures in Indonesia are divided into two categories – social security (social assistance and insurance) and social services. In 2010, total expenditures on social security and social services amounted to IDR 86.8 trillion and 43.6 trillion respectively (Prakarsa, 2011). However, total expenditure for the social assistance component in 2010 decreased by 0.3 percent from 2009. Expenditure for social assistance in 2009 was IDR 77.9 trillion, compared to IDR 64.3 trillion in 2010 (ibid.). Under the social assistance component, the government allocates IDR 3 trillion for natural disaster assistance and IDR 61.3 trillion for distribution to citizens through various ministries and organizations.

Compared to other Asian countries, social security expenditures in Indonesia are relatively low. Nishino and Koehler (2011: 21–22) indicated that Indonesia's social security expenditure comprises only 2.3 percent of GDP – far below that of India (4 percent of GDP), Thailand (4.7 percent), Vietnam (4.9 percent) and Singapore (6.1 percent). In their report, the authors argue that social protection can be provided by developed as well as less developed countries – at a level of at least 1 percent to 5 percent of GDP.

While the World Bank study reveals that the total expenditure for such social assistance programs in Indonesia is relatively low, at about 0.5 percent of GDP, the PKH is the fourth largest among the existing programs after Raskin (Rice for the poor), *Jamkesmas* (subsidized health care), and BSM1 (assistance for poor students). In 2010, MOSA allocated IDR 1.3 trillion (approximately USD 1.45 million) for PKH, which comprises 3.34 percent of the total income support scheme (IDR 37.9 trillion) and 0.015 percent and 0.001 percent of social protection expenditure (IDR 86.8 trillion) and total social expenditure (IDR 130.4 trillion) respectively (Prakarsa, 2011).

Under PKH, two poverty alleviation programs are integrated, namely *Jamkesmas* and BSM. With the intention of increasing the performance of the program, the health and education sectors of PKH have strengthened and enlarged the coverage of services received by the beneficiaries in the past two years. In 2009, the Ministry of Education and Ministry of Health agreed to provide services of *Jamkesmas* and BSM for the beneficiaries of PKH. This initiative is exemplary but would benefit from smaller improvements in coordination as well as in the management of beneficiary information across Ministries.

Nevertheless, challenges appeared in the coordination and communication between these three programs managed by three different ministries during the implementation of PKH (Ayala, 2010). Regardless of the discussion of whether PKH beneficiaries should, for instance, enjoy priority in the allocation of scholarships from the Ministry of Education, it is also questionable to what extent it makes sense to give PKH beneficiaries a second scholarship from a different institution instead of combining the scholarship amounts and streamlining the processes all together. The Jamkesmas card is different in this regard, as it is not a monetary transfer but a fee-waiver. There is certainly scope for improving the communication between parents, health and education providers, and facilitators. When discussing, for instance, with beneficiaries their compliance with health and education conditions, it would make sense to invite the teacher(s) and health worker(s) so that they are equally aware of constraints to access.

The partly limited level of understanding of program rules and procedures among education and health stakeholders proves challenging. Some of the key personnel fail to identify the connection between PKH and other poverty alleviation programs. This incomplete understanding leads to PKH beneficiaries being considered ineligible. Additionally, the unclear description about the connection between PKH and other social and health programs, the high rate of rotation among government officials as well as the reluctance to read PKH implementation manuals have caused poor of understanding of program rules and procedures.

Coordination among different stakeholders is identified as the main issue, particularly at provincial and district level. This is also one of the reasons why the National Team for the Acceleration of Poverty Reduction (TNP2K) and their efforts to improve coordination across different ministries are so important. Although some policies have been launched at the national level, such as the official letter issued by the Ministry of Education, most of the facilitators believe that the level of coordination at provincial and district level is weak. This condition leads to inadequate quality of services provided at sub-district levels, where the core of PKH implementation takes place. Moreover, socialization of existing programs developed by different ministries should also be strengthened. As recalled by the facilitators in Bandung district, no information has been formally provided by education and health sectors regarding programs developed under their ministry that can be accessed by PKH beneficiaries. Such information is mostly gained by facilitators through informal meetings or personal contacts among staff from education and health sectors.

Impacts

Although CCT affects local markets by generating increased demand that can trigger a supply response from local producers, there is little evidence on the impact of cash transfers on the local economy and no evidence of cash transfer-induced increases in household welfare (Rawlings and Rubio, 2005). However, PKH provides impacts in the area of health and education as well as at the level of household expenditure per capita (Bappenas, 2009).

Evaluation on the impact of CCT programs in some countries indicates the positive impact on prevention health services. Similar conditions can also be found in the implementation of PKH. The evaluation of PKH (Bappenas, 2009) shows that PKH increases the number of health-care visits for under-three year old children up to 36 percent and enhances the number of health-care visits in general to 30 percent. PKH also raises the developmental detection of children and immunizations to 5 percent and 0.3 percent respectively.

Since the level of school attending of children aged 6-15 is relatively high, PKH manages to contribute a 1.79 percent increase to school attendance. Based on a follow-up survey in 2009, the level of household expenditure per capita of PKH's beneficiaries increased up to 44 percent compared to the baseline survey. Health care and education expenditure per capita also increase to 91 percent and 64 percent respectively (Bappenas, 2009).

Conclusions

At present, the formal Indonesian social welfare policies mainly consist of initially temporary and semi-permanent targeted food and health subsidies, and social assistance for education. PKH promotes a comprehensive strategy that offers both protection and promotion of human rights. It is important to ensure that PKH will not only be viewed as a social safety net program, but also as crucial element of longer term strategy of social welfare policy aimed at building a viable income support scheme that balances protection and opportunity in terms of assisting poor and vulnerable people to cope with the current condition of poverty and promoting the movement out of poverty. This is particularly carried out through encouragement of human capital formation and enhancement of economic opportunity among the poor.

PKH is a complex program that has faced many challenges in its implementation. Most of the program functions, which include data validation and update, payment, verification of compliance, service delivery, dissemination and capacity building, have been put in place. However, they must be strengthened. If it is not maintained and organized effectively, some of the challenges found may hinder the achievement of PKH goals.

PKH should take into account several areas of implementation that need to be improved. These areas include evaluation and dissemination, the complaint mechanism, as well as coordination among stakeholders. Evaluation and dissemination activities must become integrated parts of the program, on an ongoing basis. Dissemination plays an essential role, especially in improving the quality and impact of the processes and results of the program. Additionally, the complaint mechanism of the program acts as an important tool in providing feedback for the program. This area needs to be strengthened in order to ensure that an effective service has been delivered to the beneficiaries.

Improving the management of cross-sectoral and cross-level cooperation is essential in PKH. The existing relations between the central level structure as a steering committee and local structures is still challenging in terms of creating smooth cooperation, especially in the crucial field of service provision and verification of beneficiary commitment. Additionally, the sense of belonging to the program still needs to be encouraged among stakeholders and ministries involve in PKH. As the implementing agency, MOSA needs to strengthen the horizontal cooperation with other ministries and stakeholders that support the program, as well as the vertical coordination with local governments. In order to maintain an effective coordination, both a strategic opening of the process and working level streamlining of cooperation mechanism are required.

As a national program supported by well-trained social workers and an advanced management information system, PKH has the opportunity to initiate the development of a more comprehensive social protection system by for instance, linking the beneficiaries of PKH to another social assistance program available in the country. The idea is to develop a series of complementary interventions which target various poverty profiles throughout the country. The extensive coverage of PKH is strategic and therefore needs to be completed with other supporting elements, such as a well-designed program mechanism to target the most vulnerable people who are unlikely to benefit from economic growth; strong community development initiatives (and if possible, a temporary public works scheme) that build socio-economic opportunity; and established individual-based, direct, proactive micro-and small business promoting initiatives.

Notes

1 See www.kemsos.go.id/program-keluarga-harapan.
2 Social expenditure is commonly known as the expenditure allocated to social purposes. Social expenditure is often associated with the concept of social security and social welfare expenditure. Social welfare expenditure is usually understood to the arrangement in the payment of income – such as unemployment compensation to pension benefit; whilst social security usually refers to an additional expenditure of income payment arrangement system which includes spending for health care, education as well as housing (Prakarsa, 2011).

References

Ayala, Francisco. (2010), "Operational Assessment Report of Program Keluarga Harapan," Commissioned by GIZ/BAPPENAS, Unpublished Internal Working Document.
Bappenas. (2009), *Laporan Akhir Evaluasi Program Perlindungan Sosial: Program Keluarga Harapan 2009* (Final Report on the Evaluation of Social Protection Program: Program Keluarga Harapan 2009), Jakarta: Bappenas.
Central Bureau of Statistics (CBS). (2012), *Trends of Selected Socio-Economic Indicators of Indonesia*, Jakarta: CBS.
Esping-Andersen, Gøsta. (1990), *The Three Worlds of Welfare Capitalism*, Princeton: Princeton University Press.
Fiszbein, Ariel and Norbert Schady. (2009), *Conditional Cash Transfer: Reducing Present and Future Poverty*, Washington DC: World Bank.
MOSA (Ministry of Social Affairs). (2012), *PKH Work Book 2011*, Jakarta: MOSA.
Nishino, Yoshimi and Gabriele Koehler. (2011), "Social Protection in Myanmar: Making the Case for Holistic Policy Reform," IDS Working Paper Volume 2011 No 386. UK: IDS.
Perdana, Ari A. (2014), *The Future of Social Welfare Programs in Indonesia: From Fossil-Fuel Subsidies to Better Social Protection*, Geneva: The International Institute for Sustainable Development.
Prakarsa. (2011), *Belanja Sosial: Potret Buram Belanja Sosial APBN 2010*, Jakarta: Prakarsa.
Rawlings, L. and G. Rubio. (2005), "Evaluating the Impact of Conditional Cash Transfer Programs," *The World Bank Research Observer*, 20(1) (Spring), 29–55.
Suharto, Edi. (2009), "Development of Social Welfare in Indonesia: Situation Analysis and General Issues," Paper presented at International Conference on Building Capacity and Policy Networking for Effective Welfare Development, Center for International Administration Studies, National Institute of Public Administration, Jakarta November 18–19.
Suharto, Edi, Juni Thamrin, Michael Cuddy, and Eammon Moran. (2006), *Strengthening Social Protection Systems in ASEAN*, Galway: Galway Development Services International (GDSI).
UK Essay. (2016), *The Social Welfare Policy in Indonesia*, Nottingham: UK Essay.
Wetterberg, A., S. Sumarto, and L. Pritchett. (1999), "A National Snapshot of the Social Impact of Indonesia's Crisis," *Bulletin of Indonesian Economic Studies*, 35(3), 145–152.

17

Social spending in Korea: can it foster sustainable and inclusive growth?

Selim Elekdag, Dulani Seneviratne and Edda Zoli

Introduction

Korea has had a remarkable track record of economic growth. It embarked on a government-guided export promotion strategy that delivered average growth in excess of 7 percent for nearly half a century. Korea is now the 6th-largest exporter in the world and its national champions have entered the ranks of the globally most recognized companies.

However, growth has declined, and income converge may be constrained by structural headwinds. Although the fruits of success were widely shared, one byproduct of Korea's rapid export-oriented development was a dualist economy, characterized by large productivity gaps between manufacturing and services, large and small firms, and regular and non-regular workers. As described below, this dualist structure appears to be associated with income inequality. Indeed, due to the relatively insufficient social protection system, relative poverty rates remained high in certain groups of the population, especially the elderly. Likewise, the relative inadequacy of the pension benefits – only about one-quarter of the average wage in 2015 (Organisation for Economic Co-operation and Development [OECD], 2016) – seems to have elevated private sector precautionary savings and thereby depressed consumption and growth. Looking ahead, these structural challenges, compounded with a rapidly aging population, will weigh on growth prospects and most likely worsen income inequality (see also International Monetary Fund, 2016).

Against this backdrop, this chapter attempts to address the following question: can social spending reduce income inequality and, at the same time, increase longer-term growth? In particular, this chapter seeks to explore how social spending can (1) increase labor market participation, especially among women, (2) reduce labor market dualism, and (3) boost productivity in the service sector, thus supporting long-term growth. In this chapter social spending refers to a broad range of social welfare programs pertaining to healthcare, education, and social safety nets (for example, pension plans and income support for both the working-age and elderly population).

Social spending can foster more sustainable and inclusive growth in Korea (Elekdag, 2012). The argument that growth can help reduce income inequality is well known. However, social spending which improves income equality can also boost growth. As discussed in further detail below, social spending can address the issue of Korea's declining working-age population, help boost productivity (particularly in the services sector), and promote more inclusive growth. For example, investment in early childhood education and care would not only underpin future productivity gains, but also promote greater participation in the labor market by females, particularly after childbirth. This is one example of how well-designed and targeted social spending policies have the potential to catalyze virtuous cycles whereby lower inequality and stronger growth mutually reinforce each other.

Social spending and economic growth

Korea has been one of the fastest-growing countries in the world, allowing it to substantially narrow the per capita income gap with other advanced economies (Figure 17.1). Nonetheless, sustaining the convergence process will become increasingly challenging. This is because Korea, as an advanced industrialized economy, has moved closer to the global technology frontier and has a rapidly aging population. In fact, Korea's potential growth has already dropped from 7 percent in the early 1990s to below 3 percent now, reflecting slowing productivity growth and declining contributions from labor and capital inputs. Unless policies can help prevent the expected downtrend in productivity and labor supply going forward, the potential growth rate is expected to decline further.

Social spending can promote sustainable longer-term growth in Korea, by focusing on three interrelated challenges: (1) increasing labor market participation against the backdrop of a rapidly aging population, (2) reducing duality in the labor market, and (3) boosting productivity in the services sector.

Challenge 1: Increasing labor market participation

While estimates of the precise timing vary, the labor force is expected to peak within the coming decade in line with the population (Figure 17.2). The most important strategy to

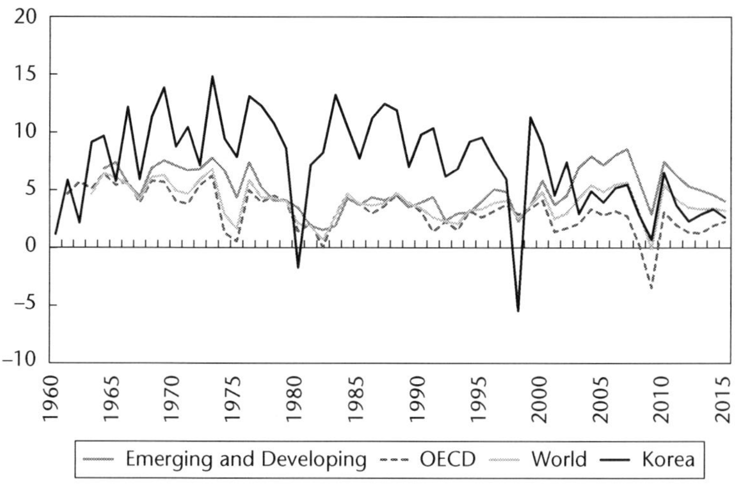

Figure 17.1 Real GDP growth (in percent)

Source: IMF, World Economic Outlook database.

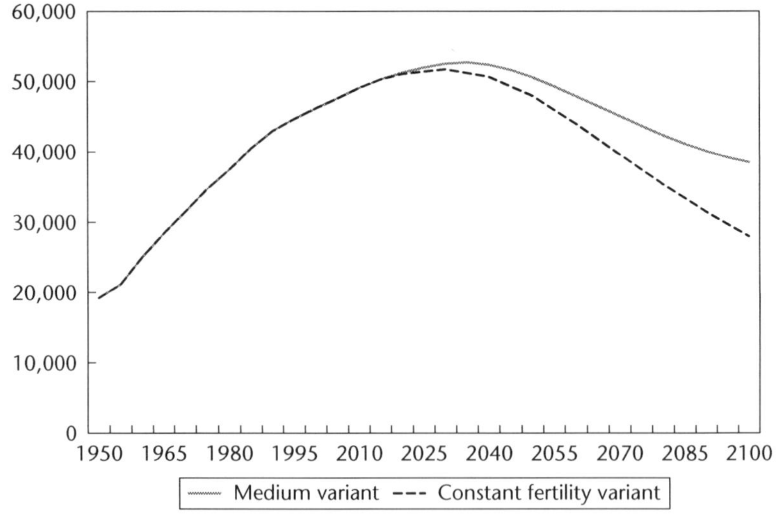

Figure 17.2 Korea: population projections (in thousands)

Source: United Nations.

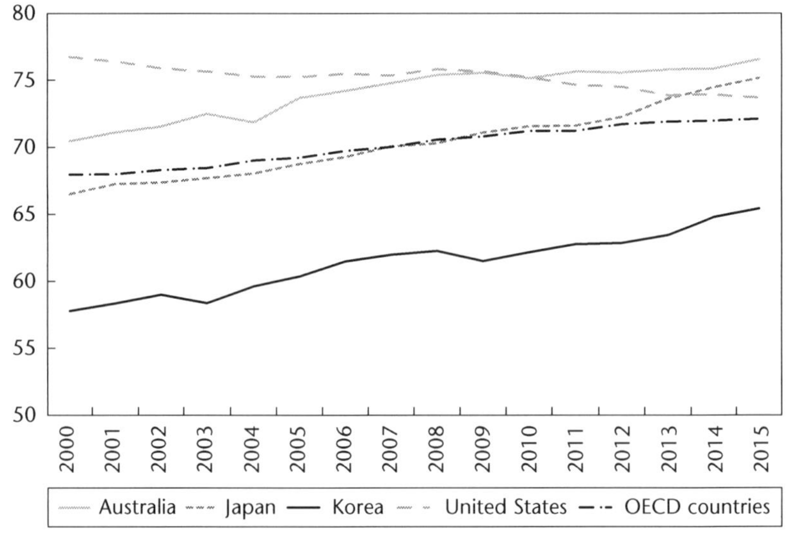

Figure 17.3 Female labor force participation rates

Source: OECD.

mitigate demographic change would be to increase the female labor force participation rate, which is low in international comparison Indeed, for women between the ages of 25 and 54, the labor force participation rate was 65 percent in 2015, the third lowest in the OECD area (Figure 17.3). Factors that hinder female labor market participation include, among others, a gender wage gap and the lack of affordable, high-quality childcare services (discussed further below).

Challenge 2: Reducing labor market dualism

Along with regular workers, Korean labor market duality stems from the elevated and rising share of non-regular workers – which include temporary workers (Figure 17.4), a major source of income inequality (Koske et al., 2011). Korea's rapid integration in a globalized economy, particularly after the mid-1990s, intensified competition, which prompted firms to reduce labor costs and increase temporary hiring, given the difficulty and cost of laying off regular workers (Koh, 2011). While regular workers are characterized by high wages, high employment protection, and broad coverage by the social safety net (and active labor market policies), non-regular workers face low wages, unstable employment, low employment protection, and weak coverage by the social safety net. As a group, non-regular workers tend to be older, less educated, employed in small- and medium-sized enterprises (SMEs), have shorter tenure, and work in the service sector. In addition, women are over-represented, with 42 percent of female employees in non-regular employment compared to 28 percent of males. Women's concentration in low-paid non-regular jobs is associated with a gender wage gap (thereby further reducing incentives to join the labor force).

Labor market duality also hinders productivity growth. The largest component of non-regular employment consists of temporary workers, and is associated with increased worker turnover and reduced firm-based training. This lack of firm-based training is compounded by low public spending on training, which is one of the lowest in the OECD area. Low productivity in the service sector translates into lower wages, and because of the disproportionate share of female employees in this sector, further aggravates the gender wage gap and increases in income inequality.

Challenge 3: Boosting productivity in the service sector

Increasing productivity in the services sector presents an opportunity that would underpin longer-term growth in Korea. Manufacturing has driven Korea's rapid economic development, making it a leading industrial power. In contrast, its service sector, which is dominated by SMEs, is much smaller and markedly less productive (Figure 17.5). The service sector is typically the

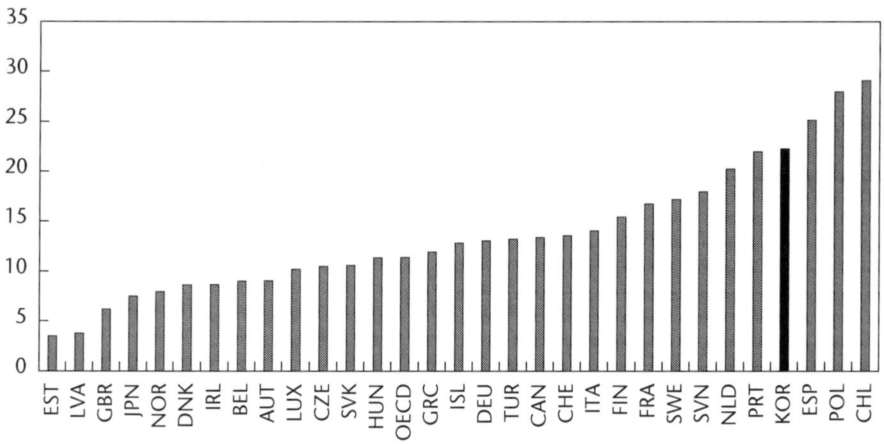

Figure 17.4 OECD: temporary employment (as a share of total employees in 2015)

Note: Temporary employees are defined as workers whose job has a predetermined termination date. For Korea, it includes only firms with a fixed-term contract of less than one year.

Source: OECD.

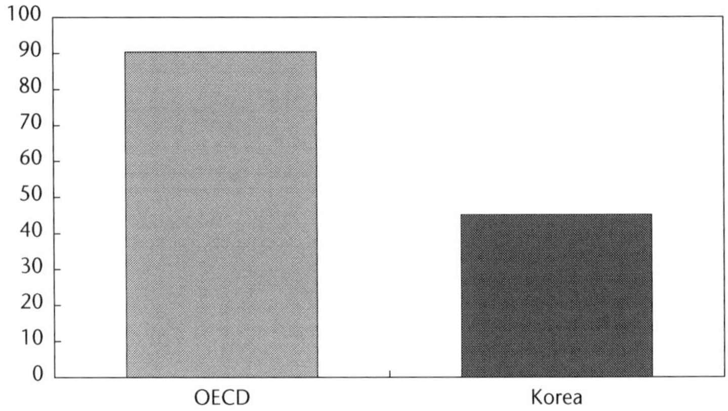

Figure 17.5 Productivity in the services sector relative to manufacturing, 2014 (manufacturing=100)

Sources: OECD National Accounts Database; OECD STI Database.

engine of growth in advanced economies – indeed over the past 25 years nearly 85 percent of GDP growth in high-income countries came from services (McKinsey and Company, 2010). Hence, Korea needs to enhance service sector productivity and growth to converge to the income levels of the most advanced countries.[1]

How can social spending promote sustainable growth?

Education and longer-term growth

Education has played a key role in Korea's rapid development. The emphasis on universal access to primary and secondary schools was a factor that contributed to Korea's early growth take-off, and promoted social mobility and income equality (Koh, 2011). Despite these advances, several aspects of the Korean education system raise equity issues, including low investment in pre-primary education and the heavy reliance on private tutoring, among others. Therefore, some aspects of the education system today should be improved, given that policies that promote equal access to education help reduce inequality (OECD, 2012, 2016).

Education reform can foster stronger growth over the longer term. For example, expanded vocational training and career consultation outside firms could enhance the employment prospects of non-regular workers and facilitate their transition to regular status. Along with reduced employment protection for regular workers, such reforms would promote a less rigid labor market, facilitate mobility and restructuring, thereby increasing the Korean economy's resilience to shocks.

Social spending and growth

Specific social spending policies can nurture growth in several dimensions. For example, investment in early childhood education and care (ECEC) offers a high return by boosting the later achievement of children. Central government spending on childcare and pre-primary education each rose from less than 0.1 percent of GDP in 2006 to 0.3 percent in 2013. Nevertheless, spending on pre-primary education per child in Korea in 2012 was 30 percent below the OECD average. The 2013 decision to provide 12 hours per day of free childcare for all children up to age five, regardless of the employment status of the mother and family income, may further push up government spending on childcare (OECD, 2016). Greater ECEC investment would provide a better educational foundation for children from low-income households, which would underpin future productivity gains. At the same time, the greater availability of affordable, high-quality childcare would promote greater participation in the labor market by females, particularly after childbirth. Taken together, targeted social spending policies, such as ECEC, would help increase labor market participation (by females especially), serve to boost productivity (especially in the services sector), and promote sustainable and inclusive growth going forward.

Social spending, labor market reforms, and growth: model-based insights

Model-based simulations indicate that social spending which encourages labor market reforms can boost longer-term growth. A general equilibrium model (described in the Appendix) is used to generate illustrative scenarios which show that a more competitive labor market associated with increased social spending implies a higher level of potential output. Social spending policies, which include high quality and affordable childcare, expanded maternity and paternity leave benefits, could help reduce duality in the labor market and, at the same time, increase female labor market participation. In turn, these developments would bring about a more competitive labor market with reduced inefficiencies and a greater supply of labor inputs, resulting in a higher potential output. As shown in Table 17.1 (row F, bottom panel), a less rigid and more competitive labor market could boost potential output by around 1 percent every year over the next decade. In other words, along with addressing inequality, social spending-induced labor market reforms can also boost longer-term growth.

Social spending and inclusive growth

Over the last decade, Korea's exceptionally high real GDP growth rates have not been sufficient to fully address income inequality. Between 1960 and the mid-1990s, Korea achieved one of the highest growth rates in the world. At the same time, Korea's Gini coefficient – a measure of income inequality – had fallen to among the lowest in the world in the mid-1990s[2]). Korea's outstanding performance was seen as supporting the hypothesis of a positive relationship between growth and equity (Alesina and Rodrik, 1994).

However, income inequality worsened first during the recession in the late 1990s and again in the first decade of this millennium. The Gini coefficient, the relative poverty ratio (defined as the share of the population that lives on less than half of the median income), and the LH ratio (measuring the share of income of the richest to the poorest quintiles) have been trending upward during the first decade since the early 2000s indicating deteriorating socio-economic conditions (Figure 17.6).

The Gini coefficient can range from 0 (perfect equality) to 1 (perfect inequality). Relative poverty is defined as the share of the population that lives on less than half of the median income. The LH ratio measures the share of income of the lowest quintile (richest) to the highest quintile (poorest).

Over the past five years, these unfavorable trends seem to have reversed. Additionally, after spiking in the late 1990s, the unemployment rate in Korea came back down, and remains at a low level, especially in contrast to the OECD average (Figure 17.7). The evolution of the unemployment rate in Korea, especially more recently, is a general indicator of improving social conditions, and could be taken as a sign that progress in reducing inequality is more enduring.

Table 17.1 Output gains from social spending-induced labor market reforms

Potential Ouput Gains Associated with Labor Market Reforms

λ	*Markup (In percent)*	*Steady-state level of output*				
		λ				
		1	*2*	*3*	*4*	*5*
3	50.0	0.8165	0.8736	0.9036	0.9221	0.9347
5	25.0	0.8944	0.9283	0.9457	0.9564	0.9635
6	20.0	0.9129	0.9410	0.9554	0.9642	0.9701
9	12.5	0.9428	0.9615	0.9710	0.9767	0.9806
11	10.0	0.9535	0.9687	0.9765	0.9811	0.9842
21	5.0	0.9759	0.9839	0.9879	0.9903	0.9919
51	2.0	0.9901	0.9934	0.9951	0.9960	0.9967
101	1.0	0.9950	0.9967	0.9975	0.9980	0.9983
	Change in wage markup (range)	*Range of potential output gains (In percent)*				
[A]	20–5	6.9	4.6	3.4	2.7	2.3
[B]	25–2	10.7	7.0	5.2	4.2	3.4
		Range of potential output gains over the next 5 years (In percent)				
[C]	20–5	1.4	0.9	0.7	0.5	0.5
[D]	25–2	2.1	1.4	1.0	0.8	0.7
		Range of potential output gains over the next 10 years				
[E]	20–5	0.7	0.5	0.3	0.3	0.2
[F]	25–2	1.1	0.7	0.5	0.4	0.3

Note: The value of 1.1 in row F, under column with parameter, η set to unity implies that a decrease in the wage markup from 25 percent to 2 percent could boost potential output by 1.1 percent per year over the next decade.

Source: Author's calculations.

Currently, Korea's Gini coefficient is near the OECD average, but the *relative* poverty rate (another measure of income inequality) is high compared to other OECD economies (Figure 17.8), especially among the elderly – for the population above 65 relative poverty is at 50 percent compared to the OECD average of 13 percent (OECD, 2016).[3]

Social spending trends

Social spending has increased rapidly, albeit from a low base. Public social spending share of GDP rose to around 10 percent in 2014 from 7.6 percent in 2007 and 2.8 percent in 1990 (Figure 17.9). Nevertheless, this upward trend has not been able to arrest the deterioration in the income distribution over most of the last decade. There are many potential factors responsible for rising inequality, including those related to technological progress and globalization. In the case of Korea, a key factor was the structural change in the economy, including a shift from high-paying jobs in manufacturing to lower-paying jobs in services. Labor market dualism, which results in large wage gaps between regular and non-regular workers, is another

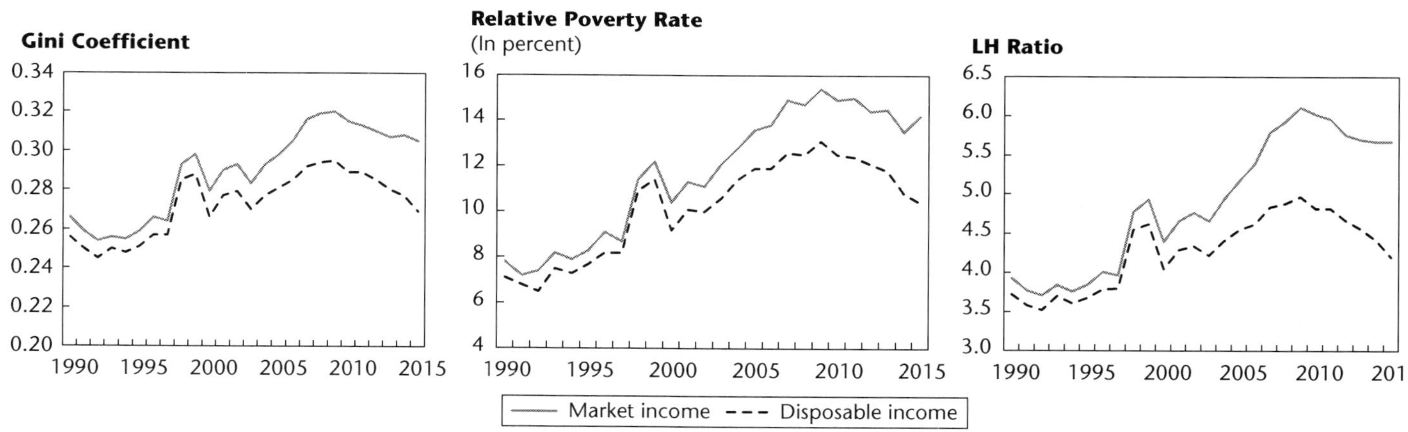

Figure 17.6 Korea: income inequality indicators

Source: CEIC Data Co. Ltd.

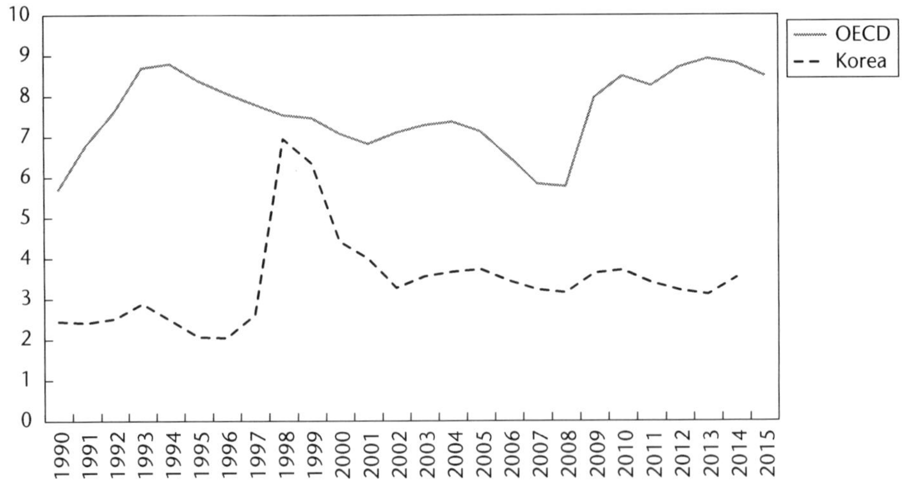

Figure 17.7 Unemployment rate (in percent)

Source: OECD.

contributing factor. These developments motivate the need to expand social spending programs and carry out labor market reforms.

Social spending in Korea is low when compared to its peers across the OECD. In 2013, Korea had the lowest ratio of public social spending to GDP (Figure 17.10). In particular, public social spending in Korea was lower than the OECD average in major areas such as healthcare and pensions (Figure 17.11). Within the OECD, also both family- and old age-related expenditures in Korea rank relatively low. In contrast, active labor market-related expenditures have increased markedly since 2007, and Korea is now close to the OECD average in this social spending category according to the 2013 data.

Mind the social spending gap

Part of the gap between public social spending in Korea and in other OECD economies may reflect some specific characteristics of Korea's economy. A crude comparison of public social spending indicates *spending gap* of about 12 percentage points of GDP between Korea and the OECD average. When compared to the OECD average, however, Korea has one of the lowest unemployment rates, *currently* has a younger population, and despite years of rapid growth, convergence in per capita income is ongoing (Figure 17.12).

Econometric analysis suggests that when these characteristics are factored in, Korea's *current* social spending gap may be relatively lower. Using the sample of OECD countries, the analysis relates social spending in 2007 to the unemployment rate, per capita income, and the dependency ratio.[4] When these characteristics are formally taken into account, regression analysis suggests that the social spending gap narrows to about 3.4 percentage points (Table 17.2). Indeed, in the first column, without any explanatory variables, the spending gap is 11.7 percentage points (of GDP). However, when the three main factors which differentiate Korea from the OECD average are taken explicitly into account, the spending gap decreases (as shown under the remaining columns). These results are generally quite robust; in fact, using quantile regressions which control for outliers (the last column) suggests an even smaller

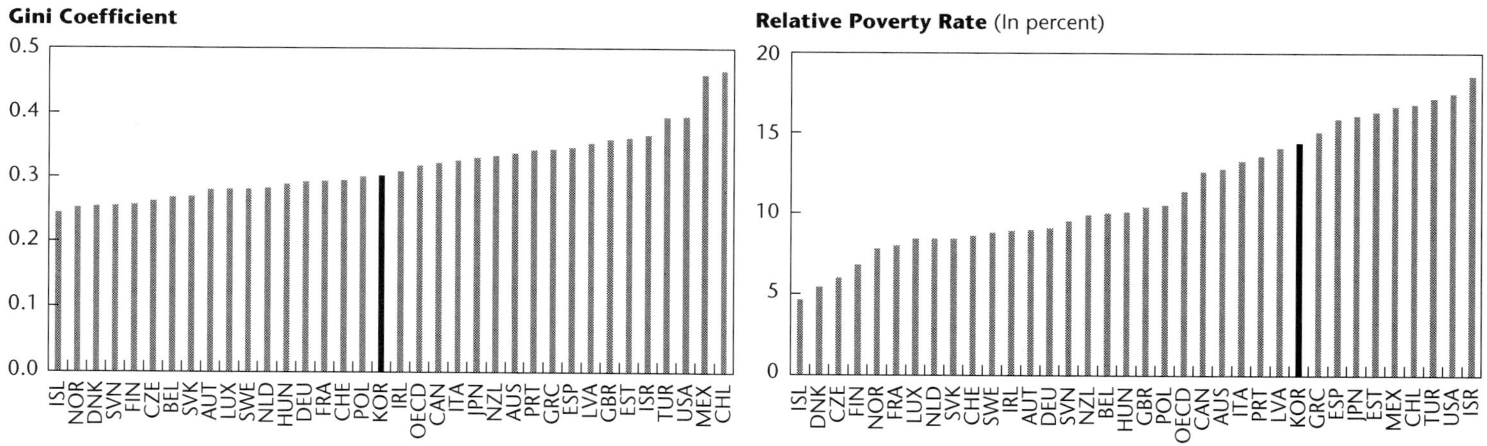

Figure 17.8 OECD: Gini coefficients and relative poverty rates

Note: Data as of 2014 or latest available. The Gini coefficient can range from 0 (perfect equality) to 1 (perfect inequality). Relative poverty is defined as the share of the population that lives on less than half of the median income.

Source: OECD.

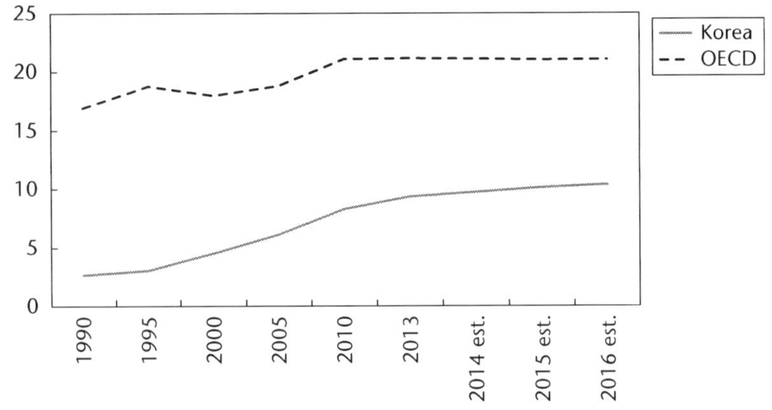

Figure 17.9 Social spending trends (in percent of GDP)

Source: OECD.

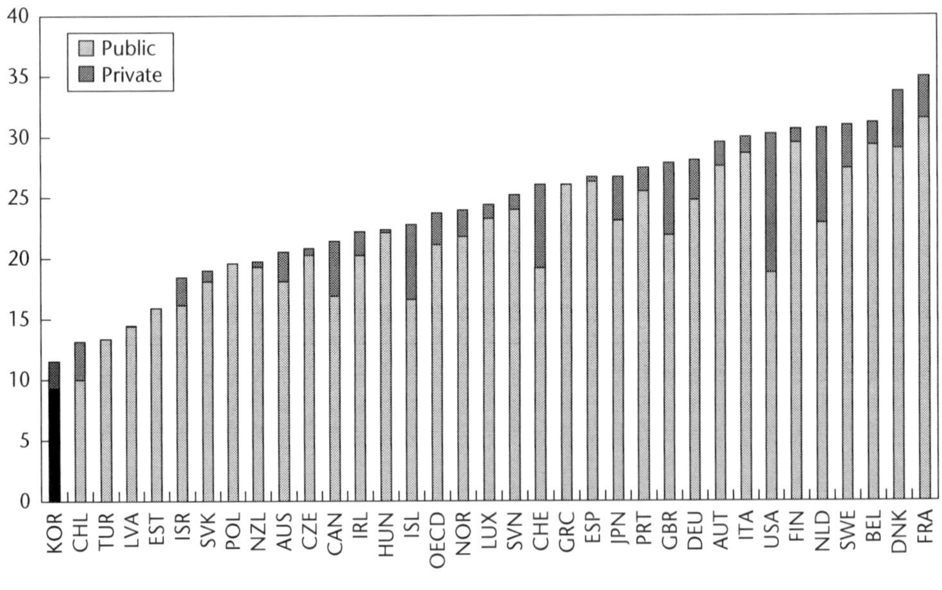

Figure 17.10 OECD: social spending in 2013 (in percent of GDP)

Source: OECD.

social spending gap. While the current gap may be smaller, projections of social spending are expected to reach 29 percent of GDP by 2060 (OECD, 2016). Nevertheless, regardless of the estimated amount of needs, there appears scope to improve targeting and the efficacy of social spending.

How to better target social spending?

To ensure more inclusive growth, social spending should be targeted to help those most in need.[5] Social spending is not well targeted on low-income households, with only a quarter of cash

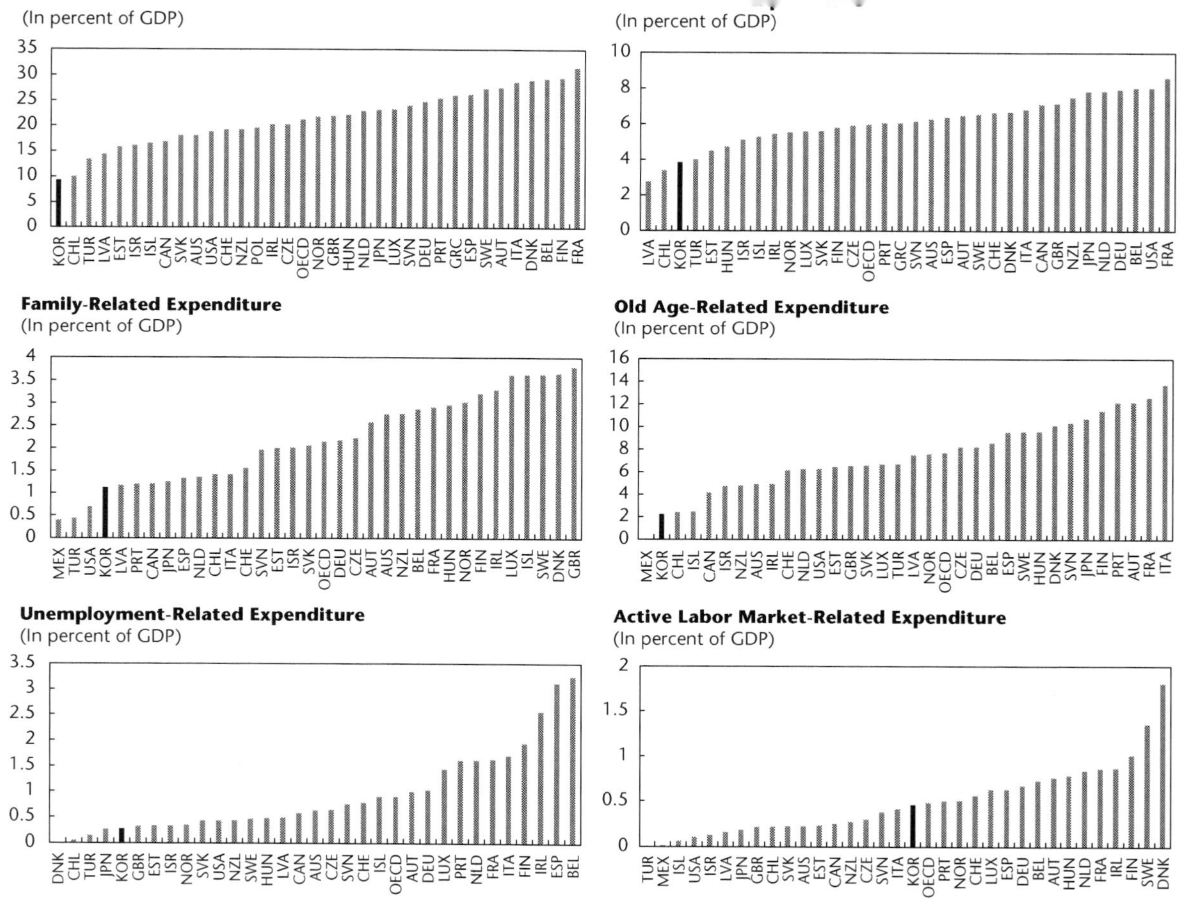

Figure 17.11 OECD: social spending categories in 2013

Source: OECD.

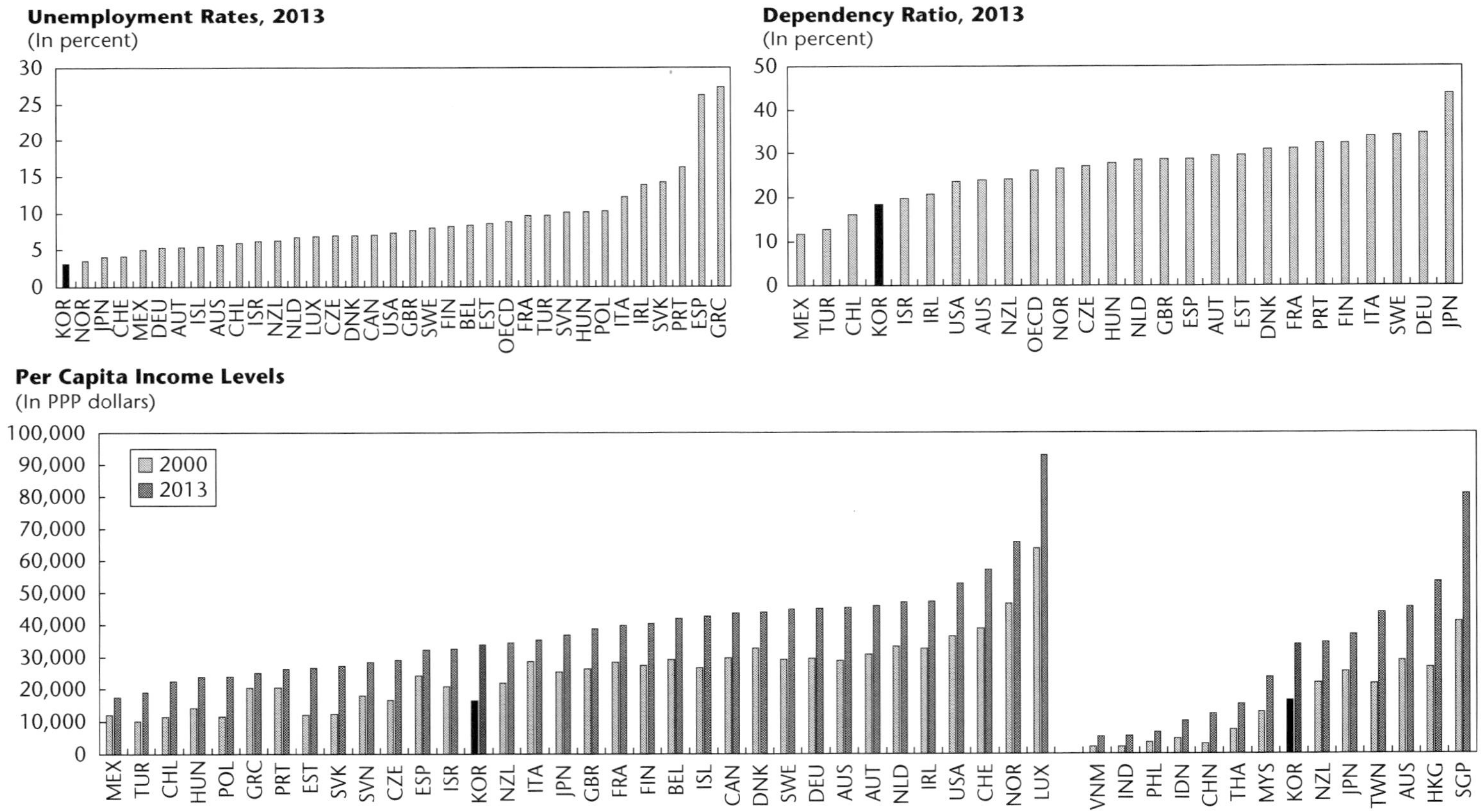

Figure 17.12 Selected indicators influencing the social spending gap

Note: Dependency ratio defined as the population 65 and over, divided by the population between 20 to 64. Per capita income levels in US dollars adjusted for purchasing power.

Sources: OECD; IMF, World Economic Outlook database.

Table 17.2 Korea: Social Spending Gap

Dependent variable: Social spending in 2007					
Explantory variables:	[1]	[2]	[3]	[4]	[5]
Constant	19.24	–0.29	6.22	–5.67	–5.35
	20.45	–0.10	1.51	–1.74	–1.32
Dependency ratio		63.66	0.95	56.40	64.13
		7.15	2.43	6.51	4.53
Per capital income			0.0002	0.0001	0.0001
			3.08	2.45	0.88
Unemployment rate				0.60	0.34
				2.30	1.14
Number of observations	34	34	34	34	34
R-squared		0.61	0.26	0.69	0.49
Social spending gap:	11.7	4.9	5.0	3.4	3.1

Note: p-values below regressions estimates.

Source: Author's calculations.

benefits from the government going to the poorest quintile of the population (OECD, 2012). In addition, as discussed below, spending on health could actually defray the costs associated with a rapidly aging population. Accordingly, reforms to most effectively promote inclusive growth should be directed to the following social protection programs:

- *National Health Insurance* (NHI): currently, although it aims at universal coverage, it is associated with high out-of-pocket payments which are inequitable and regressive because they do not depend on the income of patients. The NHI could therefore be reformed, to promote, among others, healthy ageing, which would limit future healthcare costs as the population ages. This is critical because, under current policies pension spending is projected to increase by nearly 5 percentage points of GDP between 2015 and 2015 (National Pension Research Institute, 2013) and public health spending is expected to increase by nearly 8 percent over the same period (International Monetary Fund, 2010).
- The *Basic Livelihood Security System* (BLSP): it is Korea's major welfare program, providing cash and a package of in-kind benefits, including housing, medical and educational benefits to the most vulnerable segments of society. But, under this program, benefits are provided to only 3 percent of the population, suggesting that there is scope for better targeting. In order to increase its effectiveness, BLSP eligibility conditions should be relaxed to cover a larger share of those in need.
- The *Basic Old-Age Pension System*: introduced in 2008, it provides assistance to elderly people who meet the income and asset criteria. At present, around 70 percent of the elderly receive the benefit, which is set at only 5 percent of the average wage, implying that the benefit spreads out resources very thinly over a large segment of the older population, while doing little to reduce income inequality among the elderly. Given that about 40 percent of the elderly have income below the minimum cost of living (Bae, 2011), larger benefits more targeted at low-income elderly would be more effective.
- The *earned income tax credit* (EITC): reduces taxes or provides a refund when the deduction is larger than the tax amount, raising take-home pay at the low end of the income distribution. The EITC is used in a number of OECD countries and is another important tool for reducing

income inequality. Therefore, to have a more significant effect on income distribution, the number of recipients and the amount of benefits provided by the EITC should be expanded. The EITC would also make any possible raises in the VAT more equitable.

Policy implications

A carefully targeted expansion of Korea's social spending could yield several benefits. First of all, it would alleviate relative poverty among vulnerable groups of the population, most notably the elderly. By increasing those groups' disposable income, it would also reduce the need for precautionary savings, thus contributing to boost consumption-led growth and lower the economy's reliance on volatile external demand. It could also reduce retirees' risky borrowing to open small businesses. Moreover, additional public spending on vocational training and career consultation outside firms could enhance the employment prospects of non-regular workers and facilitate their transition to regular status, thus reducing labor marker duality and inequality. Expanded spending on ECEC would strengthen educational foundation for children and support future productivity gains. In addition, more affordable high-quality childcare would promote female labor force participation, thus boosting labor supply and potential output.

However, over the longer term, costs owing to rapid population aging will put strains on the budget. While there may be room for expenditure reallocation (by squeezing non-age-related outlays), there are limits to how much other spending can be reduced. Hence, to preserve sustainability, revenue increases will likely be needed in the long term. Increases in social contributions and tax measures could be considered – currently, Korea's revenue is one of the lowest in the OECD. Fiscal rules could be introduced to enhance the commitment to fiscal sustainability.

Conclusion

There seems to be a need for a carefully targeted expansion of social spending, which would promote more inclusive and sustainable growth in Korea. While social spending in Korea is low when compared to OECD peers, any increase should be accompanied by strengthened revenue performance over the long-term term (including by base broadening). Measures should prioritize spending in areas that would increase labor market participation, reduce duality in the labor market, boost productivity, and alleviate poverty among vulnerable groups of the population. In sum, a combination of targeted social spending policies would further help reduce income inequality, but also boost potential growth over the longer term.

Appendix: Model overview

This section provides an outline of the general equilibrium model used for the illustrative scenarios relating labor market reforms, increased social spending, and longer-term potential growth. The model is a markedly simplified version of Alp, Elekdag, and Lall (2012) and conducts simulations similar to those presented in Chami, Elekdag, and Tchakarov (2004). In what follows, the goal here is to present the general intuition of the model, leaving the details to the indicated studies.

Using the model, it is argued that as duality in the labor market decreases, implying efficiency gains, lower deadweight losses, and an attendant increase in labor supply (including greater female labor market participation, especially because they account for a disproportionate share of temporary workers). In sum, along with addressing inequality, social spending-induced labor market reforms can also boost longer-term growth.

Firms

Output is generated using a linear production technology with labor inputs (L) augmented by total factor productivity (A):

$$Y_t = A_t L_t \tag{1}$$

Furthermore, the firm uses a CES combination of differentiated labor inputs. The idea is to capture the notion of labor market duality which is pervasive in the Korean economy. It is difficult and costly to lay off regular workers due to their intrinsic market power as they benefit from higher wages and higher employment protection, in marked contrast to temporary workers.

$$L_t = \left[\int_0^1 L_{i,t}^{\frac{\lambda - 1}{\lambda}} di \right]^{\frac{\lambda}{\lambda - 1}} \tag{2}$$

Here, L_i denotes the demand of a differentiated labor input, and the parameter, $\lambda > 1$, is the elasticity of substitution among labor inputs. Broadly speaking, the extent of labor input differentiation, and the degree of market power is captured by λ. In other words, the labor market is characterized by a monopolistically competitive environment. This lack of perfect competition is characterized by a markup, determined by the size of the parameter, λ, and drives a wedge between the real wage and the marginal rate of substitution between consumption and leisure. As this parameter approaches infinity, labor inputs can be thought of becoming increasingly similar, which erodes the monopolistic structure of the market. The loss of market power is associated with increased labor inputs, reduced deadweight losses, and the eventual perfectly competitive environment is thereby associated with a higher level of potential output.

Firms take the prices of labor inputs as given, and cost minimization implies that the demand for a certain type of labor input is a function of its relative wage:

$$L_{i,t} = \left(\frac{W_{i,t}}{W_t} \right)^{-\lambda} L_t \tag{3}$$

Where L_i, is the wage paid for labor input L_i, and the wage index, W, is defined as:

$$W_t = \left[\int_0^1 W_{i,t}^{1-\lambda} di \right]^{\frac{1}{\lambda - 1}} \tag{4}$$

Against this background, which will be useful below, note that cost minimization by the firm is a standard static problem implying that the real wage equals total factor productivity.

Households

Within the confines of their budget constraints, households maximize lifetime expected utility:

$$U_t = \mathbf{E}_0 \sum_{t=0}^{\infty} \beta^t \left[log C_t - \frac{1}{1+\eta} L_t^{1+\eta} \right] \tag{5}$$

where household preferences are additively separable in consumption, C, and labor effort, L, and the discount rate, β, is bounded by zero and unity. The flow budget constraint states that consumption is limited to the total wage bill, and any residual income, Π (for example, stemming from labor union premiums):

$$C_t = \frac{W_t}{P_t} L_t + \Pi_t \tag{6}$$

Because the focus is on comparative static simulations, borrowing and saving by the households was not necessary for the purposes here, and thus not modeled. As with other many features of this model, this is another dimension that could be readily developed.

As discussed above, each household is the monopolistic supplier of a differentiated labor input. Given their market power, households set the nominal wage for their specific labor input facing a downward-sloping demand curve.

Solution

Overall, in the steady state, the model boils down to four key equations: the production function, the budget constraint, the condition linking the real wage and total factor productivity, and equation stating that the real wage is equal to the marginal rate of substitution between consumption and leisure, but augmented with a markup. Note that with $\lambda = 11$, for example, the gross markup, $\lambda/(\lambda - 1)$, takes a value of 1.1 (implying real wages that are 10 percent higher than under a perfectly competitive labor market).

$$\begin{aligned} Y &= AL \\ C &= \frac{W}{P} L + \Pi \\ \frac{W}{P} &= A \\ \frac{W}{P} &= \frac{\lambda}{\lambda - 1} C L^{\eta} \end{aligned} \tag{7}$$

Because total factor productivity is exogenous, A, is essentially unity, and the system can be solved for output as follows:

$$Y = \left[\frac{\lambda - 1}{\lambda}\right]^{\frac{1}{1+\eta}} \tag{8}$$

In sum, the steady-state level of output, or for our purposes, potential output, depends on the calibration of two parameters, of which, the elasticity of substitution among labor inputs, the parameter, $\lambda > 1$, is most critical. Studies estimating structural model developed to capture salient features of the Korean economy by Elekdag, Justiniano, and Tchakarov (2006), and Alp, Elekdag, and Lall (2012) find that while the parameter, η, can range between 1.5 and 2.5, the substitution elasticity, λ, is typically in the 7 to 9 range, implying a wage markup of around 15 percent, in other words, the labor market is characterized by a notable degree of monopolistic competition.

Model simulations

Can lower labor market rigidity boost potential growth? Using the model, illustrative scenarios are generated which show that a more competitive labor market – brought on, in part, by higher social spending – implies a higher level of potential output. As duality in the labor market decreases, this implies efficiency gains, less deadweight losses, and a likely increase in female labor market participation (as they account for a disproportionate share of temporary workers). To do so, we start off with a high degree of monopolistic competition in the labor market as set the elasticity, λ, to three as shown in Table 17.1. Then the elasticity is increased, corresponding to a more competitive labor market (with an attendant decrease in duality). While the elasticity maybe a relatively abstract notion, the implied markups are also included in the table to facilitate intuition. Notice that as the elasticity increases (implying that labor inputs are more readily substitutable), the wage markup decreases as market power is eroded owing to labor market reforms.

A less rigid labor market implies a higher level of potential output. As shown in the table, if wage markups decrease from 25 percent (in line with the estimated values found in the studies cited above) to 2 percent, potential output could increase by 10.7 percent (row [B] in the bottom panel, with $\eta = 1$). These are gains over the long run, but if it is assumed that they could be materialized in the next decade, this implies a boost to potential output by around 1.1 percent every year (under same column with $\eta = 1$, in row [F]). Note that this main message is robust to other parameter choices. Taken together, social spending-induced labor market reforms can ameliorate income inequality and also boost longer-term growth.

Notes

1 Problems in services are linked to those of SMEs, which account for about 90 percent of service-sector employment. The weakness of SMEs prompted the government to ratchet up support, which has blunted competitive pressures, slowed reform, and reduced the efficiency of resource allocation. Supporting non-viable firms will act as a drag on Korea's growth potential, and should gradually be unwound.

2 The Gini coefficient can range from 0 (perfect equality) to 1 (perfect inequality).

3 The relative poverty ratio is defined as the share of the population that lives on less than half of the median income. For later reference, the LH ratio measures the share of income of the lowest quintile (richest) to the highest quintile (poorest).

4 Using the sample of OECD countries in 2007, public social spending (as a percent of GDP), the dependent variable, was regressed against a constant, the unemployment rate, PPP per capita income, and the dependency ratio (population 65 and over divided by population 30 to 64). Other specifications, including different variable choices, yield broadly similar results.

5 For additional perspective, see Balakrishnan, Steinberg, and Syed (2011).

References

Alesina, A. and D. Rodrik, (1994) "Distributive Politics and Economic Growth," *The Quarterly Journal of Economics*, Vol. 109, pp. 465–490.

Alp, H., S. Elekdag, and S. Lall, (2012) "Did Korean Monetary Policy Help Soften the Impact of the Global Financial Crisis of 2008–09?" IMF Working Paper, 12/5, Washington, DC: International Monetary Fund.

Bae, J., (2011) "Korean National Pensions: Facts and Functions in 2009," in Y. Kim and G. Szell (eds.), *Economic Crisis and Social Integration*, Peter Lang, Frankfurt, Germany, Vol. 1.

Balakrishnan, R., C. Steinberg, and M. Syed, (2011) "Asia's Quest for Inclusive Growth," Asia and Pacific Regional Economic Outlook, October, Washington, DC: International Monetary Fund.

Chami, S., S. Elekdag, and I. Tchakarov, (2004) "What are the Potential Economic Benefits of Enlarging the Gulf Cooperation Council?" IMF Working Paper, 04/152, Washington, DC: International Monetary Fund.

Elekdag, S., (2012) "Social Spending in Korea: Can It Foster Sustainable and Inclusive Growth?" IMF Working Paper, 12/250, Washington, DC: International Monetary Fund.

Elekdag, S., A. Justiniano, and I. Tchakarov, (2006) "An Estimated Small Open Economy Model of the Financial Accelerator," IMF Staff Papers, International Monetary Fund, Vol. 53, pp. 219–241.

International Monetary Fund (IMF), (2010) "Macro-Fiscal Implications of Health Care Reform in Advanced and Emerging Economies," Washington, DC: International Monetary Fund.

International Monetary Fund (IMF), (2016) Republic of Korea Article IV Consultation Report. IMF Country Report 16/278, Washington, DC: International Monetary Fund.

Koh, Y., (2011) *Social Safety Net in Korea: From Welfare to Workfare*, Korea Development Institute, Seoul, Korea, Mimeo.

Koske, I., J. Fournier and I. Wanner, (2011) "Less Income Inequality and More Growth – Are They Compatible?: Part 2, The Distribution of Labour Incomes," Organisation for Economic Co-operation and Development (OECD), Economics Department Working Papers, No. 925, OECD, Paris.

McKinsey and Company, (2010) "South Korea: Finding Its Place on the World Stage," *McKinsey Quarterly*, April.

National Pension Research Institute, (2013) *A Summary of the 2013 Actuarial Projection Result*, National Pension Research Institute, Seoul, Korea.

Organisation for Economic Co-operation and Development (OECD), (2012) *OECD Economic Survey of Korea*, OECD, Paris.

Organisation for Economic Co-operation and Development (OECD), (2016) *OECD Economic Survey of Korea*, OECD, Paris.

18

Inclusion of persons with disabilities in Singapore: an evolutionary perspective

Levan Lim and Thana Thaver

Introduction

The tiny island-state of Singapore had much to celebrate in 2015 to mark its fiftieth anniversary of independence since August 9, 1965. Without a hinterland, natural resources and tense race relations during its early years of independence, Singapore's spectacular ascent from a third world to a first world city par excellence in a few decades is an exceptional economic success story. To continue to flourish in its next fifty years, shortly after Singapore's fiftieth (SG50) birthday bash, the government began a new public engagement initiative for its citizens to stay united as a society and work together to shape the next fifty years of its future beyond SG50 to SG100 (Soon, 2015).

Such forward and pro-active planning for the future has been a hallmark of Singapore's approach to its sustainability and relevance in a rapidly changing and turbulent world. As a nation with a diverse multiracial, multicultural and multi-religious population, social cohesion, harmony and unity are paramount to Singapore's continuing success. Hence, sustainable development in Singapore has a very clear element of social and cultural sustainability as it is about building socially cohesive communities with a strong Singaporean identity. As highlighted by Kong (cited in Tng and Tan, 2012), "a socially sustainable Singapore is one which is socially inclusive, with strong bonds in the community, healthy social interaction, protection of the vulnerable, and respect for social diversity" (p. 24).

Over the past decade in Singapore, there has been an increasing reference by both the government and the public to the vision of an inclusive society for this cosmopolitan city-state. This aspiration toward an inclusive society underscores the important recognition that unless its people, made up of culturally, linguistically, racially and religiously diverse origins and backgrounds, unite to build a cohesive and inclusive society, Singapore's stellar track record as one of the world's most successful and wealthiest countries, and its future, will be compromised.

Against this backdrop of a resounding call to become an inclusive society, it can appear ironic, especially to inclusion advocates, that Singapore has yet to explicitly address inclusive education as a significant agenda within its mainstream education initiatives and reforms. In spite of the growing prominence of inclusive education and the rights of persons with disabilities worldwide over the past two decades (e.g., UNESCO, 1994; United Nations, 2006) and the many significant developments in Singapore to support students with special needs within its mainstream schools over the past decade, inclusive education remains elusive as an official educational policy to adopt on a national system-wide level – which is unlike and in contrast to the many countries in the Asia-Pacific region and beyond that have embraced inclusive education as national policy.

A recent survey (Lien Foundation, 2016) revealed that while the majority of Singaporeans (7 in 10) support the idea of inclusive education, only a third agree that Singapore is an inclusive society for children with special needs. Only one in 10 Singaporeans indicated confidence in interacting with children with special needs. Moreover, among parents surveyed, only half are comfortable with having their own children placed next to a child with special needs in the classroom. This survey highlights that Singaporeans "don't walk the talk" on accepting and including children with special needs (Tai, 2016b). Another recent survey found that six in 10 persons with disabilities do not feel that they are socially included, accepted or given opportunities to reach their potential. Of the general public polled, only 36 percent would be comfortable being close friends with a person with a disability (The Straits Times, 2016, p. B4; Tai, 2016c).

These survey findings are disappointing, especially in light of over a decade's worth of unprecedented attention and work by the government, disability voluntary welfare organizations, and charities to improve the lives of persons with disabilities (Tan, 2016b). Since Prime Minister Lee Hsien Loong announced in his inauguration speech in 2004 the vision of Singapore as an inclusive society where he explicitly mentioned including persons with disabilities, there have been two national blueprints (known as Enabling Masterplans) developed by the Ministry of Social and Family Development to create an inclusive society where persons with disabilities can maximize their potential and be embraced as equal citizens.

Generous amounts of funds have been afforded by the government to build hardware infrastructure to promote the physical and transport accessibility of persons with disabilities in living, school, work and community spaces across the island. A new, third masterplan to guide the development of policies and services has recently been announced (Tai, 2016a; Yi, 2016), following the previous two five-year masterplans (i.e., 2007–2011 and 2012–2016 respectively), coupled with the launch of a new national disability awareness and education campaign entitled "See The True Me" (Tai, 2016c) to cultivate more "heartware" among Singaporeans for their fellow citizens with disabilities.

In hindsight, the recent survey findings, though disappointing, are not surprising, considering that Singapore has long maintained a dual system of education where its mainstream education system has remained separate from its special education counterpart. These separate education systems have spawned the practice and perception that students with and without disabilities in Singapore do not belong together in the same education system. As a consequence, many Singaporeans have grown up with little or no personal knowledge and practical experience with fellow Singaporeans with disabilities; this has significantly contributed to the reproduction of past and current societal attitudes and beliefs about people with disabilities (Lim and Tan, 2004; Lim, Thaver and Poon, 2008; Lim, Thaver and Slee, 2008). Bereft of the "lived experience" of interacting and relating with persons with disabilities on a regular basis from a young age, it is unsurprising that many Singaporeans do not "walk the talk" on inclusion.

These current societal attitudes and beliefs about people with disabilities are attributable to Singapore's socio-historical and socio-political context where the relative lack of discourse and awareness of disability can be traced to economic and educational priorities during Singapore's growth as a nation since independence in 1965. The evolution of societies is a complex phenomenon, brought about by interconnected events, developments and tensions, which are time and context dependent. To add to the complexity and volatility of change, contexts are layered with inter-penetrations in an increasingly borderless world, where countries are increasingly affected and influenced by global forces and interdependence.

The purpose of this chapter is to provide a situated and contextual understanding of the evolution of Singapore's current attitudes and systemic structures regarding the construction and treatment of disability within society. The significance of understanding the emergence of disability from a peripheral to an increasingly conspicuous social issue, worthy of national attention through masterplans and government campaigns, highlights the key events, priorities and changes in Singapore over the past few decades that have contributed to its status quo on disability.

The next section of this chapter will therefore provide a historical portrait of salient developments within education and society during the past few decades of Singapore's growth as a nation, and their ramifications on disability. This historical account and analysis will help readers develop a clearer and more nuanced view of Singapore's challenges during its formative years, and its priorities as a nation charting its path into the future, bringing about both intended and unintended outcomes for its disability sector and society as a whole.

Historical development: from the 1960s to the new millennium

When the People's Action Party came into power in 1959, it faced the monumental task of rebuilding the country: one small in size, lacking in natural resources, fraught with socio-political and economic unrest, and unemployment problems. To ensure its economic survival, the Singapore government saw that it had to attract foreign investors and embark on the path toward industrialization. It realized quickly that what would enable it to succeed in this goal was an educated and skilled workforce. This goal became even more imperative when independence was suddenly thrust upon it in 1965 with its separation from Malaya. This signaled the start of the symbiotic relationship between education and economic planning and policy in Singapore, with the government determining what training was needed to progress economically, and educational institutions directed and supported to produce the skills and attitudes required of its workforce (Gopinathan, 1999).

The 1960s in Singapore, thus, saw the rapid building of schools to increase student enrollment, mass recruitment and training of teachers to staff these schools, the provision of free universal primary education for any child between ages six and fourteen, the creation of a centralized education system to provide basic education, and the cultivation within the Singapore workforce of skills and attitudes required to attract foreign investment for its industrialization plans (Ho and Gopinathan, 1999; Sharpe and Gopinathan, 2002). During this period, educational provisions for children with disabilities did not feature highly on the government's list of priorities given the urgent focus on harnessing all its resources to produce the workforce it needed for its economic survival. Thus, in Singapore, as in most countries, services for children with various disabilities were started and provided by religious bodies, voluntary welfare organizations (VWOs) and concerned philanthropists, or were part of the rehabilitation services provided by the health authorities as a follow-up to medical diagnoses of disabilities (Quah, 2004).

It must be noted that although the responsibility of the education of children with disabilities had been left to the VWOs, the government, through the Department of Social Welfare, which had been set up by the British Colonial Government in Singapore in 1946, did provide some financial assistance and offered land and buildings to set up their special schools at nominal rentals, and had agreed to the secondment of mainstream teachers to special schools teaching mainstream curriculum (Wong et al., 1974). In 1968, the Department of Social Welfare was subsumed under the Ministry of Social Affairs and a Rehabilitation Unit was formed and tasked with maintaining a central register of people with disabilities to plan programs. While this was a laudable move by the government, it was unfortunately insufficient to meet the needs of the disability sector.

The 1970s

The 1970s, thus, saw the disability sector in Singapore pressing for legislation to work toward equitable treatment in educational services for people with disabilities, and for these to be part of national policy and planning; however, this was a call that was not heeded (Wong et al., 1974). Even though the government was providing the special schools with infrastructure and financial and professional support, the sector was in straitened circumstances. The VWOs found themselves struggling with problems which included strained finances, a lack of trained teachers and specialist staff, frequent relocation because of short-term school leases and recurring structural costs due to the need to renovate the new premises to meet the needs of students (Advisory Council on the Disabled, 1988).

In 1972, at the First Regional Conference on Special Education and Mental Retardation held in Singapore, Wong et al. (1974) highlighted the dire situation faced by the disability sector with regard to the education of children with special needs. Of the number of children identified with special needs on the register of the various organizations in the special education sector, the VWOs who were providing educational services could only cater to about 31 percent of the children. The rest of the children were either on the waiting lists of special schools with few chances of being admitted or in mainstream schools where their needs were not being met. This number was not inclusive of children with mild intellectual disabilities, then termed as "educationally subnormal" (ESN), studying in mainstream schools. It was estimated at that point that there were 15,000 children with mild intellectual disabilities in the mainstream school population facing certain academic failure (Tan, 1974; Wong et al., 1974).

In contrast to the special education scene, the 1970s were to see almost universal primary education in the mainstream education system. A standardized common curriculum, with emphasis on being bilingual, in English and a second language, as well as on mathematics and science, was in place, and measures were taken to develop technical and vocational education to ensure a manpower base for industrialization (Ho and Gopinathan, 1999; Yip, Eng, and Yap, 1990). Cracks, however, were beginning to appear in the mainstream education system. Between the years 1966 to 1971, 41 to 47 percent of the students who sat for the Primary School Leaving Examination (PSLE) had failed the examinations. It was postulated that a proportion of this group who failed were children with mild intellectual disabilities who could not cope with the pace of the normal school curriculum (Tan, 1974). Figures from Singapore's Ministry of Education (MOE) indicated that from between 1975 to 1977, there was an average attrition rate of 29 percent at the primary school level and a further 36 percent at the secondary school level. Literacy levels were also low, with 66 percent of the student population failing either one or both their first and second language at the national examinations at secondary level, the General Certificate of Education (GCE) O'levels (Goh, 1979).

These problems of educational attrition, poor achievement and literacy levels in the mainstream education system, leading to unemployable school leavers, gained the immediate attention of the government as, left unchecked, the situation would jeopardize the creation of the educated and literate workforce which Singapore needed to fuel its newly industrializing economy. An indication of how seriously this was taken was the response it garnered from the then Prime Minister, Mr. Lee Kuan Yew. He raised this matter in his National Day Rally speech in 1978 and tasked the then-Deputy Prime Minister, Dr. Goh Keng Swee to lead a study team to identify problems in the Ministry of Education. In its "Report on the Ministry of Education 1978," the team pointed out that the high educational wastage and low achievement rates within the education system arose from an inflexible and rigid system that required all students to undergo the same curriculum and examinations irrespective of their capacities. It found the system to be one that tended to "favour the above-average pupils, penalizing the below-average and the slow learners" (Goh, 1979, p. 4). It was felt by the team that ability-based streaming and differentiation of courses and examinations according to ability at both primary and secondary levels would address the diversity of needs, and be the most viable alternative given the constraints of resources and manpower.

The 1980s

By 1980, the education system in Singapore was re-designed into what became known as the New Education System, with three ability streams at primary and secondary school levels. At the primary level, students would take a school-based streaming examination at primary 3 (age 9) and, depending on their performance in the examination, would be channeled to one of three streams, the Normal Bilingual, the Extended Bilingual, and the Monolingual. In the Normal Bilingual stream, students would take two languages and sit the national examination, the PSLE, in six years. The Extended Bilingual students would also take two languages but would study at a slower pace and sit the PSLE at the end of eight years, while the Monolingual stream students would be taught basic literacy and numeracy skills, and sit a different examination at the end of eight years, the Primary School Proficiency Examination. These students who were regarded as not academically inclined would go on to vocational training at the Vocational and Industrial Training Board.

At the secondary level, depending on their performance at the PSLE, students would be offered the Special Bilingual stream, where they would take English and Chinese at first language level (a more advanced level) or Express stream, taking English at first language level and mother tongue at second language level or the Normal stream, where students were taught a reduced curriculum. The first two streams would sit their GCE O-Levels at the end of four years, while students from the Normal stream would sit the GCE N-Level examination at the end of four years. If the students in the Normal stream did well at this national examination, they could proceed on to a fifth year of study and take their GCE O-Level examination.

This move to refine the education system can be seen as the first systemic attempt to provide for diverse needs within mainstream education. The stated intent of streaming was to provide "an opportunity for the less capable pupils to develop at a pace slower than that for the more capable pupils," and this was to be accompanied by "a properly organized implementation program, a realistic curriculum, competent teachers, sufficient teaching materials and facilities and a healthy social environment" (Goh, 1979, p. 6). The Report made it clear that the primary goal was to offer the pupil the most appropriate educational opportunity, rather than merely reducing attrition rates.

In hindsight, this would have been an opportune moment to expand the mainstream education community's awareness of how the principles of the reform of acknowledging diverse learning needs and using differentiation to cater to this diversity lay at the foundation of special education. With such awareness of the relevance of special education to catering to diverse learning needs within the mainstream education community, there could have been earlier recognition and validation of special education principles being embraced as part of the mainstream education system. Unfortunately, this opportunity did not eventuate since history has shown that special education had not evolved to be an integral part of mainstream education at that point because of the long-standing fissures between the special and mainstream education sectors. It appears that little heed was paid to the emergence of perspectives internationally in the 1960s and 1970s that special education should be treated as an integral part of an education system, and that its principles and pedagogies were just as pertinent as those of mainstream education (Jorgensen, 1974). This reform was not accompanied by provisions for training at the in-service and pre-service levels to increase mainstream teachers' knowledge of different types of learners, from the academically bright to those with learning disabilities, and how to provide for their different learning needs through instructional and curricular adaptations.

The 1980s was to prove to be an eventful decade for both the mainstream and special education sectors in Singapore. Within a year of the Report, in 1980, the New Education System was implemented within the mainstream education system and students were streamed into the various ability streams according to their performance in the examinations. The early 1980s witnessed the repercussions of the underlying assumptions made in the implementation of streaming within mainstream education: that mainstream teachers had the prerequisite knowledge and skills to teach not just the "below average" but also the "slow" learners, terms as used by Goh (1979) in the "Report on the Ministry of Education."

To evaluate the impact of the reform on primary schools, the then-Minister of State for Education in Singapore, Dr. Tay Eng Soon, commissioned the NIE to conduct a research study on the monolingual program and the problems faced by principals and teachers in its first year of implementation. The findings of the study revealed major difficulties and a great deal of frustration with catering to the students in the monolingual stream. Many issues raised could have been circumvented or addressed before the implementation if there had been greater knowledge of special education within the mainstream education community.

Most of the mainstream teachers interviewed in the study felt ill-prepared for this group of students, now streamed into one setting. They found them difficult to deal with because of their low intelligence, lack of motivation, and behavioral problems. Both principals and teachers in the study emphasized the need for smaller class sizes to be able to cater to the needs of the students, a differentiated curriculum, more specialized training for teachers in understanding and teaching slow learners, as well as knowledge and skills in making curricular adaptations, and more provision of teaching resources and professional support to schools (Eng et al., 1982). The report of the research team concluded with the need for greater dialogue and collaboration between schools, the MOE, the Curriculum Development Institute of Singapore (CDIS), which had been set up in 1980 to develop the curriculum materials for the different streams, and for the NIE to look into the provision of teacher training to cater to these students (Lim and Gopinathan, 1990).

A follow-up research study conducted by the NIE in 1983 to obtain a better understanding of the characteristics of the students in the monolingual stream and the factors that contributed to their learning problems revealed that there were 3 types of learners in the monolingual stream. In the sample of 38 monolingual students studied, 53 percent of the students were "slow learners" with IQs between 70–89, 39 percent were children with mild intellectual disabilities or termed as "ESN" (i.e., educationally subnormal) children, with IQs below 70, while 8 percent were students in the average IQ range (Eng et al., 1984). It was the conclusion of the researchers that each of these groups had different learning needs requiring differentiated approaches, and that mainstream teachers needed training in catering to this diversity of learning needs. They were also of the opinion that the "ESN" students, or children with mild intellectual disabilities found in the monolingual stream, needed specialized help that was not being provided in mainstream settings and were best educated in special schools.

Similar findings had also been found by Quah et al. (1982) in their study of 40 primary school students with learning and behavioral problems who had been referred to the Remedial Reading and Guidance Clinics at the NIE in Singapore. This situation had actually been raised by the Singapore Association for Retarded Children (SARC) in the early 1970s when it appealed for greater government assistance so that the VWOs could expand their services to include more children with disabilities, and in particular, those with intellectual disabilities. However, this appeal had not been given sufficient consideration until it became an issue within the mainstream education system (Tan, 1974; Wong et al., 1974).

For the special education sector, the 1980s were to herald changes as a result of what was occurring both locally and internationally. In 1980, the United Nations started worldwide efforts to encourage its member states to look into the rights of persons with disabilities, and to change the international discourse on disability from that of social welfare to one of human rights. It declared 1981 the International Year of Disabled Persons (IYDP) and called for plans of action at national, regional and international levels in the areas of prevention of disability, rehabilitation and the equalization of opportunities.

A major realization that emerged from the year was that unless social attitudes towards disability were addressed, the goal of full participation and equality in society for persons with disabilities would be difficult to attain (United Nations, 2008–2009). The United Nations followed up the IYDP with proclaiming 1983–1992 the United Nations Decade of Disabled Persons. It called upon its member states to implement the World Program of Action (WPA) concerning Disabled People, started during the IYDP in the three aforementioned areas, and to develop national policies and legislation to eliminate discrimination with regard to access to facilities, social security, education and employment (United Nations, 2008–2009).

Singapore's initial response to these international developments was promising. To commemorate the IYDP and kick-start the formation of self-help organizations in the disability sector, Singapore hosted the First Founding Congress of the Disabled Peoples International for international non-governmental organizations in November 1981. At its official opening, Dr. Ahmad Mattar, the Minister of Social Affairs, highlighted the need for all members of society, government, community and people with disabilities themselves, to work toward the equalization of opportunities for people with disabilities (Ministry of Social Affairs and Singapore Council of Social Service 1981; cited in Zhuang, 2007/2008).

A month later, in December 1981, the Singapore Council of Social Service (renamed the National Council of Social Service, NCSS, in 1985) sent a memorandum to the MOE stating the need for greater government involvement in special education because of the serious difficulties the VWOs were facing in providing sufficient places for the number of children who required special education (Advisory Council on the Disabled, 1988). To aid the disability sector, the NCSS launched the Community Chest of Singapore (CCS) in 1983 to coordinate their fund raising efforts, so that VWOs could then concentrate on the provision of their services and programs. This meant that the VWOs, once declared as charitable organizations, could apply for financial assistance from CCS (National Council of Social Service, 2008). SARC, in particular, was to benefit from a much-needed infusion of funds. With the financial assistance it obtained from CCS in 1984, and the help of the MOE in obtaining two more premises, it was finally able to open its next two new schools in the mid-1980s, after a period of more than 10 years, for the students with intellectual disabilities on its waiting list (Ong, 1985; Wong, 1990).

In 1987, perhaps in response to the appeals made by the disability sector and to resolve the issue of the presence of children with intellectual disabilities in mainstream schools due to a lack of options, the government increased its financial support of special education. The government offered a capitation grant of $1,500 to the NCSS to finance special education, equivalent to the cost of educating a student in a mainstream primary school. With this increased financial support, the disability sector was able to further expand its services, and at the end of the 1980s was to see the number of special schools increased to 11.

Another major event that occurred that was to have far-reaching consequences on provisions for children with disabilities was the establishment of the Advisory Council on the Disabled in February 1988, chaired by the then-Minister of Education, Dr. Tony Tan, to look into the situation of people with disabilities in Singapore. Based on data collected by the Ministry of Community Development, Youth and Sports (MCYS; reorganized in 2012 to become the Ministry of Social and Family Development, MSF) and various organizations, and from meetings with different interest groups, individuals and the public, the Council made its recommendations. These covered a broad spectrum of areas, from public education and awareness programs to address negative attitudes toward disability, prevention of disability in terms of early detection, assessment and intervention programs, special education, vocational rehabilitation, employment, accessibility to social services, and institutional care (Advisory Council on the Disabled, 1988).

In the area of special education, the Advisory Council made it clear that special education should be treated as an education matter rather than regarded as a welfare service, and that more had to be done for children with disabilities in both special and mainstream schools. In response to the recommendations of the Council, the MOE took over the disbursement of funds to the special schools, and began to work with the MCYS to supervise the sector in 1989. It increased the per capita grant to the special schools to twice the cost of education in a primary school to ease their financial difficulties. With an equivalent amount from the NCSS, special schools would obtain funding four times the cost of educating a child in normal primary school, the estimated cost of special education in Singapore according to the Advisory Council. Special schools not in the funding scheme were assured of the continued secondment of MOE teachers to their schools. To resolve the problem of frequent school relocation, all short-term leases were converted to long-term leases of 30 years, and land and funding were provided so that special schools could be purpose-built.

In the taking of special education under the government's aegis, the recommendation of the Council was to continue with the status quo. The Advisory Council felt that the special schools were better run by the VWOs because of their strong sense of mission and ability to respond more flexibly and quickly to changing needs. In time, this policy and approach to services and programs for people with disabilities became crystallized into a tripartite partnership between government, community and family, termed the "Many Helping Hands" approach (Tarmugi, 1995), and the segregation of the two education systems became further entrenched.

In the matter of educating students with disabilities in mainstream settings, the Advisory Council was of the opinion that whenever appropriate and feasible, special education should be provided within the regular mainstream educational system, and even recommended that integration efforts should progress to include students with disabilities besides those with sensory impairment. It also pointed out that the number of children with disabilities studying in the special schools only constituted 1 percent of the estimated 2.2 percent of children with disabilities in Singapore, and that there were probably many children within the regular education system who were experiencing mild to moderate learning difficulties as a result of undetected disabilities. To cater to the needs of these students, the Advisory Council recommended the setting up of a School Psychological Service to identify and help children with learning, behavior or speech difficulties, and those with problems arising from intellectual disabilities in mainstream schools. The MOE followed through on this recommendation in the 1990s.

Beyond these recommendations, the Council felt that integration of students with disabilities into mainstream settings should be left to the discretion of the particular mainstream school, which did not augur well for the future of integration, for by this time the mainstream education system had become increasingly focused on excellence. This emphasis on excellence was a goal that had been strongly supported by Dr. Tony Tan, the then-Minister of Education, in 1986 to create a workforce to catapult Singapore into its next stage of its economic development (Yip, Eng and Yap, 1990).

In retrospect, while the work of the Advisory Council was to bring significant improvement in the situation faced by the special education sector and greater support for students with certain disabilities in mainstream settings in the 1990s, the fundamental task of changing the attitudes of the mainstream education community toward people with disabilities was not explicitly addressed within the mainstream education system. The Council accurately stated in its Report that the successful integration of people with disabilities in Singapore was dependent upon society changing its attitude toward the disabled and accepting them as proper members of society (Advisory Council on the Disabled, 1988, p. D 2A). To achieve this, it recommended public education and awareness programs, specifically mentioning teachers and students, so that acceptance of children with disabilities in regular schools could be promoted. However, instead of suggesting that the MOE work on this recommendation with regard to students and teachers or that it work in concert with the NIE to address this through their teacher education programs, the report suggested that the MCYS (or MSF as it is currently known) and the NCSS take responsibility for the task.

The Council also proposed that moral education lessons in the mainstream curriculum could be the vehicle through which misconceptions of disability are dealt with and positive views of people with disabilities as contributing members of society nurtured. This recommendation was not taken up, since the moral education syllabus, re-conceptualized after the 1979 Report on Moral Education, showed no specific coverage of this area. There also seemed to be little realization of the magnitude of what was required in this proposal. To be able to teach this, mainstream teachers would themselves have to undergo a disability awareness course first, as most of them would not have the knowledge, skills, and experience with disability to deal with the topic, aside from the fact that there was no certainty that these teachers held inclusive beliefs.

The 1990s

The 1990s saw inclusive education gaining greater currency internationally, coming to prominence in 1994 with the Salamanca Conference on Special Needs Education organized by the United Nations Educational, Scientific and Cultural Organization (UNESCO) and the government of Spain. At this conference, attended by representatives from 92 governments and 25 international organizations, consensus was reached that there was a need for all countries to work toward inclusive education. Inclusion, it was felt, was "the most effective means of combating discriminatory attitudes, creating welcoming communities, building an inclusive society and achieving education for all" (UNESCO, 1994, p. ix).

Singapore did not participate in this conference nor become a signatory to the 1994 Salamanca Statement and Framework for Action on Special Needs Education, which sought to work toward "schools for all," institutions which include everybody, celebrate differences, support learning and respond to individual needs" (UNESCO, 1994, p. iii). Singapore, however, did become a signatory to the 1993–2002 Asia Pacific Decade of Disabled Persons, which required governments to look into enhancing the equality and full participation of people with disabilities in aspects such as education. It had also adopted the 1993 Standard Rules on the Equalization of Opportunities for Persons with Disabilities, of which Rule 6 asked governments to ensure equal educational opportunities and to take responsibility for educating persons with disabilities in integrated settings (United Nations, 2010).

In 1995, five years after the Convention on the Rights of the Child came into force, Singapore acceded to this legally binding instrument, which protected children's rights to healthcare, education and legal, civil and social services. This Convention was to prove an important instrument in propelling Singapore to review how it was protecting the rights of children with disabilities, as it was obligated to submit a report that would cover this aspect to the Committee on the Convention of the Rights of the Child within five years of its accession. The first report was sent to the UN in March 2003 (Singapore, 2002). It may be postulated that, aside from the recommendations of the 1988 Report of the Advisory Council on the Disabled, these developments on the international front encouraged more governmental attention to the educational needs of children with disabilities both within the special and mainstream education sectors. It was also found, in this decade, that whenever a new initiative was rolled out in mainstream education, there were efforts on the part of the MOE to include the special schools.

This period saw the rapid expansion of special schools, as the government actively aided the sector in acquiring land and school premises, and in the redevelopment costs and the recurrent expenditure of the special schools. In 1997, the MOE reviewed its funding formula for the recurrent expenditure to the SPED schools once more, and increased its proportion by 50 percent to a cap of 2.5 times the cost of primary education, with 1.5 times coming from the NCSS (Chan, 2004). By 1999, there were 17 special schools run by eight VWOs, catering to 3,900 children with intellectual, physical, sensory and multiple disabilities, and autism spectrum disorder (Report of the Committee on Compulsory Education in Singapore, 2000).

Within the mainstream education system, the 1990s found the MOE following through on the recommendations of the 1988 Advisory Council on the Disabled on integrating and creating greater support for students with sensory impairment, physical disability, and primary school students with learning difficulties. The MOE designated four mainstream secondary schools to integrate students with visual impairment from SAVH (renamed Lighthouse School in 2008) in 1990. These schools were equipped with special resource rooms in which specialist teachers, known as "resource teachers," would work to support these students. Students with hearing impairment from the Singapore School for the Deaf (SSD) trained in the Total Communication approach, which taught a variety of communicative methods from signing, finger-spelling, lip reading, speech, and the use of residual hearing, had the choice of two designated mainstream secondary schools if they were dependent on signing. While this was a step forward in terms of support, the path of the designated schools was to have the inadvertent effect of limiting the integration of these students to a small number of schools.

In response to the recommendation of the Advisory Council on the Disabled to look into the support of students with physical disabilities in mainstream settings and to address accessibility issues raised in the Agenda for Action for the 1993–2002 Asia Pacific Decade of Disabled Persons, the MOE began, in 1992, to retrofit mainstream schools it had designated to take in students with physical disabilities. In the interim period, concerned about the lack of support for students with physical disabilities who had been accepted into mainstream schools, a VWO, Asian Women's Welfare Association (AWWA), set up the TEACH ME (Therapy and Education Assistance for Children in Mainstream Education) program in 1991 to aid both students and schools in integration efforts. By 1996, 20 primary and secondary mainstream schools in different educational zones in Singapore had been equipped with handicap-friendly facilities for students with physical disabilities (Mathi, 1996).

To aid students with developmental delays in mainstream settings, the MOE set up the School Psychological Service (SPS) in 1991. The task of the SPS was to assist schools in identifying and helping students with learning difficulties so that they could remain in mainstream schools. It was to consist of four teams, one for each school zone in Singapore, with each team comprised of educational psychologists, social workers, counsellors, and a reading specialist led by a senior educational psychologist (Quah, 2004). A new position was also created in the primary school in 1992, the Learning Support Coordinator (LSC), to support students with learning difficulties in their first two years in the primary school, either through in-class support or withdrawal sessions of half an hour each day to learn in small groups (Chan, 2004). The LSCs, trained by both the NIE and SPS, worked closely with SPS to develop appropriate curriculum and teaching materials for these students with learning difficulties (Quah, 2004).

While this was a significant first step within the mainstream education system to meet the needs of students experiencing learning difficulties, it appeared lacking in two aspects. The first gap was the lack of a systematic program beyond the first two years to continue supporting students who were still experiencing difficulties. The second gap referred to the lack of preparation of all mainstream school teachers to cater to the needs of students with learning difficulties, a situation reminiscent of what occurred in an earlier decade with the monolingual stream students. There had been no call from the MOE in the 1990s for the NIE to include this as a compulsory component in the pre-service teacher education program for primary school teachers or to provide in-service training in this area. This training would have been crucial in supporting these students, as they would spend at most an hour per day with the LSC in a pull-out session, and were taught by their other primary school teachers the rest of the time. In addition, after the first two years in the LSP, these students would have to depend on these teachers for additional support.

Beyond these efforts, the integration of students with other types of disabilities in mainstream settings was not to progress much, partly because of the competitive educational climate in the 1990s, the origins of which resided in the economic downturn which Singapore suffered due to the global recession in 1985. An Economic Review Committee had been set up to study how economic growth could be stimulated (Singapore Economic Committee, 1986). The 1986 report of the Committee, "The Singapore economy: New directions: Report of the Economic Committee," suggesting how economic growth could be stimulated and the type of workforce needed to give Singapore a competitive edge, was to reinforce once again the close nexus between educational policy and economic planning. By 1987, in response to this report, mainstream schools were exhorted by the MOE to focus on excellence so that this competitive edge might be achieved (Yip, Eng and Yap, 1990).

The 1990s, thus, became a period primarily focused on competition and "being ahead of the pack." This competitive mindset was encouraged by Mr. Goh Chok Tong, the then Prime Minister of Singapore (Goh, 1979, p. 31, as cited in Lim and Tan, 1999) who saw a good education system as dependent on:

- students competing to do well in schools;
- schools competing against each other;
- good schools emerging to show other schools how they can improve.

This rivalry and focus on academic excellence was to intensify further with the annual ranking exercise of schools introduced by the MOE in 1992. The results of this exercise were made public by the MOE, with the rationale that stakeholders, parents and students could then make informed choices in selecting which schools to enter. This publicity escalated the jostling between schools to be in the upper reaches of the academic league table. Although the MOE did attempt to broaden the indicators in 1995, the ranking exercise was to continue unabated, despite criticism of its detrimental effects on the priorities of schools and its narrow focus on academic achievement (Ministry of Education, 1998, chapter 4, paras 11, 12 and 23).

The unrelenting competition and single-minded pursuit of academic excellence during this period led schools to become more selective in their student intake. Students who were high achievers were actively courted because of their ability to raise school rankings in the academic league table (Lim and Tan, 1999). One of the costs of this pursuit was the devaluation of students with disabilities in the eyes of the mainstream education community because their worth was measured by their ability to contribute to the academic standing of the school.

By 1998, this trend within the mainstream had become a cause for concern, and the MOE attempted to address this with the publication of the document on "The Desired Outcomes of Education." The then-Minister of Education, Rear Admiral (RADM) Teo Chee Hean, reminded the mainstream education community of the larger goals of education, stating that while academic achievement was important, it "should not be an all-consuming passion in itself, pursued to the exclusion of everything else. The goal of education was to nurture the whole person, not just the aspect of academic achievement but also that of high moral ideals and a caring community-minded spirit" (Teo, 1998, p. 2). While few in the education community would disagree with this, there seemed little, at that point, that could veer the education system from this "all-consuming passion."

However, the tide would turn, and the new millennium would see the MOE's attention being drawn back to special needs students within the mainstream. An early indication of the issues the MOE would need to deal with in the next decade came in the late 1990s, when it became aware of a growing number of students with autism spectrum disorder (ASD) who had been enrolling in mainstream schools. These students, while intellectually able, had been experiencing difficulties in school because of a lack of awareness and understanding of the disorder among mainstream teachers.

In an attempt to increase the knowledge and skills of its mainstream teachers, the MOE began to organize ad hoc workshops for mainstream teachers (Wong, 2000). This form of ad hoc training and dissemination of information on special needs through MOE publications was the general approach taken by the Ministry, during this period and the early years of the next decade, to equip its mainstream teachers for working with students with disabilities in mainstream settings. This, unfortunately, was inadequate and was to result in mainstream teachers being unprepared, both psychologically and professionally, for the official sanctioning of the initiative to integrate students with disabilities into mainstream settings in 2004 (Tam et al., 2006).

The 2000s

The millennium was to witness the education system experiencing the same challenges as in the 1970s; that is, the increasing presence of students with disabilities within mainstream schools, with a corresponding lack of adequate supports to help with their academic and social inclusion, and limited educational options available to them beyond the mainstream. MOE's response in the 2000s, however, was much quicker. It rapidly provided more funding to the disability sector (i.e., relevant VWOs) so that they could expand their services, and provided the funds to build new special schools. Thus, within the special education sector, these years were to see more special schools being set up to cater to students with mild intellectual disabilities and ASD.

Alongside the discovery of the growing numbers of students with ASD in mainstream settings in the late 1990s, a similar situation confronted the special education sector. There seemed to be a sudden spike in the cases of students diagnosed with autism seeking places in special schools. Unlike the slowness of its response to the special education sector in the 1970s with regard to students with intellectual disabilities, the MOE moved swiftly to address the problem of the long waiting list of students with ASD for places in special schools.

Working with the NCSS, the MOE provided a special grant to train special school teachers in autism so that these schools could expand their services to take in children with autism. By 2002, 11 special schools were able to offer programs for children with ASD, and the waiting list was reduced. In 2003, probably in an attempt to address the increasing numbers of students with ASD found in mainstream settings, the MOE invited a VWO, the Autism Resource Centre, to set up a special school offering the mainstream curriculum for students with ASD. As a result, Pathlight School officially opened its doors in January 2004 with 41 students on its rolls (Pathlight School, 2010).

The growing presence of students with disabilities within mainstream schools contributed to an increasingly diverse student population. This greater diversity in student profile in mainstream schools, however, was more likely due to the confluence of certain events and circumstances, rather than a clearly apparent national vision and intentional policy on the part of MOE to create more inclusive schools. In fact, what MOE had announced in 2000, that it was moving the mainstream education system toward an ability-driven education with greater streaming or "mass customization" to develop and harness the talents of its students to prepare them to meet the challenges of an increasingly competitive global world and the knowledge-based economy, seemed to contradict the ethos of inclusion.

A key element, which has witnessed more students with disabilities entering the mainstream school system, has been increasing parental aspirations for their children to be educated with their non-disabled peers. Several factors appear to have influenced parental decisions to enroll their children in mainstream schools. In Singapore, children enrolling in mainstream schools are not required to undergo a formal assessment for placement into schools, and parents are not obligated to inform schools if their children had any diagnosis of developmental delays. Lee (2002) reported that many parents having children with developmental delays or less discernible disabilities enrolled their children in mainstream schools, either because they wished their children to be educated in mainstream settings, or were unable to obtain a place in a special school. This situation has been further compounded by the Compulsory Education Act passed in October 2000 and implemented in 2003, which meant that no child of Singapore citizenship residing in Singapore could be denied a place in a national primary school (Compulsory Education Act, 2003).

Additional factors that could have contributed to the increasing presence of students with disabilities in mainstream schools were the developments in the preschool sector, as a result of the recommendation of the 1988 Advisory Council on the Disabled for an early identification and management program for children with developmental problems. The outcome was the setting up of the Development Assessment Clinic (DAC; subsequently renamed Child Development Unit, CDU, in 1997) at the Singapore General Hospital in 1991, to provide early diagnostic and intervention services to young children with developmental and behavioral problems. This became a health service program under the Ministry of Health (MOH) in 1995, and when more funding was received in 2002, two CDUs were established, one at Kandang Kerbau Hospital (KKH), and the other at National University Hospital (NUH). Diagnostic services were conducted at the two hospitals and intervention services at SingHealth Polyclinic under KKH and Jurong Polyclinic under NUH.

One of the primary objectives of the CDU was to detect young children with moderate- to low-severity developmental conditions (e.g., severe Attention Deficit Hyperactivity Disorder [ADHD], high-functioning ASD, severe/mild learning disability, attention problems, speech and language delays, motor, sensory or behavior problems, mild cerebral palsy), as well as those with developmental delays and behavioral problems early, so that appropriate early intervention and therapy could be provided. With this early identification and intervention, and close collaboration with the MCYS, the NCSS and the MOE, the CDU had hoped to ensure that these children, who made up 85 percent of its annual cases, could be integrated first into regular preschool centers and then into mainstream schools. It was estimated that the CDUs received between 1200–1400 referrals a year. The follow-up evaluation conducted on the children under the CDU had been consistently positive – between 85–90 percent of the children had shown improvement in their performance and functional skills, and thus had a greater chance of being educated in mainstream settings rather than in special schools (Ho, 2007).

Another event that could have led to the increasing presence of students with disabilities in mainstream schools was the decision made by the MCYS in 2003 to support the integration of students with disabilities in childcare centers run by welfare organizations. The Integrated Childcare Program (ICCP) sought to integrate preschoolers from ages two to six with mild to moderate disabilities into six childcare centers so that they could learn to interact with other children in a natural setting, and subsequently move on to be educated in a mainstream primary school. Plans had been made to offer the ICCP in six more centers in 2004 and more beyond (Clarke and Sharpe, 2004; Ministry of Community Development, Youth and Sports, 2010). As of 2016, there are fourteen ICCP centers (SG Enable, 2015).

By 2003, it was becoming apparent that more encompassing measures were needed to support the increasing number of students with disabilities within the mainstream education system, especially in the light of the strides made by the CDUs in their early detection and intervention programs, the preschool integration efforts, and the fact that children with disabilities or developmental delays, whether diagnosed or latent, were being enrolled in mainstream settings. While the government still remained strongly in favor of integrating only those students with disabilities who were able to cope with the rigorous pace of the mainstream setting, and did not require accommodation beyond what was present in the mainstream education system, by 2004, it found that this was not a stance that it could maintain, given the report that 20 percent of the school population entering mainstream schools had learning disabilities (Basu, 2006).

It also appeared that the special schools did not have the capacity to further expand their services to take in students with disabilities. One of the reasons cited then in the Report of the Committee on Compulsory Education in Singapore (2000, p. 19) for exempting children with special needs from the Compulsory Education Act was the inability of the special schools to take in all children with special needs because of a lack of resources. In 2010, special schools were able to admit only 5,214 children out of a possible number of 14,000 students, from primary one to secondary four (Mathi and Mohamed, 2011); it continues to be an issue even today.

Special schools, however, may not be an attractive option for parents and students with the social stigma attached to special education still prevalent in Singapore society (e.g., Tan, 2008) and the limited educational and employment opportunities facing students upon graduation from special schools. Apart from this, school fees are also higher in special schools if students are not entitled to financial subsidies. Pathlight School, for instance, charges $350 per month (Pathlight School, 2016) in comparison to the miscellaneous fees of $6.50 to $27 per month that Singaporean students at various levels (e.g., primary and secondary) in mainstream government schools pay (Ministry of Education, 2016).

Another reason that might have further encouraged the MOE to consider greater integration and support of students with disabilities within mainstream settings may have been the response it received in October 2003 from the United Nations Committee on the Rights of the Child, on the first report (Singapore, 2002) it submitted in March of that year. The Committee was concerned that there was no legislation prohibiting discrimination against people with disability in Singapore, and advised on the need to work on these aspects of legislation and install more proactive measures to combat societal discrimination, such as through public education and awareness campaigns.

The Committee also advised that children with disabilities be fully integrated into the education system. It recommended that measures, such as improvement of curricula and pedagogical practices, be taken to facilitate greater integration and participation of children with disabilities in mainstream schools and society, and the extension of compulsory education to cover all children with disabilities and special education. To enable Singapore to address the recommendations and provide specific information on the measures taken, the deadline for its next report to the Committee was extended to November 2007 (Committee on the Rights of a Child, 2003).

Toward the end of 2003, government rhetoric about disability began to take a slightly different slant. It had been customary in speeches given by government or MOE officials during events arranged by disability organizations to describe the extent of support provided by the government to the special education sector, the efforts made in mainstream schools to include students with sensory impairment and physical disabilities, and to highlight the importance and success of the "many helping hands" approach, an approach which had been criticized as being piecemeal (Mathi and Mohamed, 2011). In December 2003, at a fund-raising dinner organized by the Disabled People's Association, the then-Acting Minister for Education, Mr. Tharman Shanmugaratnam, declared that there was a need for a more civic-conscious society in Singapore where every person was valued, and that it should be the "collective aspiration [of society] to want people with disabilities to live full lives, integrated to the maximum extent possible in the workplace and in the community" (Shanmugaratnam, 2003, pp. 1–2).

This same hope was promulgated when Prime Minister Lee Hsien Loong shared his vision of a more inclusive society in August 2004 during his inauguration speech, when he proclaimed a "Government that will be open and inclusive in its approach towards all Singaporeans, young and old, disabled and able-bodied . . . " (Ibrahim, 2004, p. 10). About a month later, he committed his government to starting with education by calling for greater efforts to integrate people with disabilities into mainstream society, beginning with the integration of students with disabilities into mainstream schools (Teo, 2004). The recognition of the MOE that children with mild to moderate learning disabilities could benefit from being integrated into mainstream settings, with appropriate support, was to signal Singapore's increasing openness to inclusion. There was even a suggestion from the then-Minister of Education, Mr. Tharman Shanmugaratnam, at the official opening of Pathlight School for children with mild ASD in November 2004, that its students consider mainstream schooling as an option, given the new support structures (Shanmugaratnam, 2004).

To increase the likelihood of success of these efforts, the MOE promised schools additional teachers who could be deployed according to the needs of their students, and a considerable increase in their manpower grant to buy support services to ease teachers' workloads, aside from specialist support in the form of the Allied Educators, Learning and Behavioral Support (AED LBS). These measures were designed to give teachers more time to plan their lessons and try out new pedagogies, and to embark on professional development (Ministry of Education, 2004). In addition, the MOE also worked with the NIE on an initiative to start the compulsory training of a small proportion of its mainstream teachers in special education, 10 percent of its teaching force in the primary schools and 20 percent in the secondary school, Junior College, and Centralized Institute levels, to support students with other developmental problems such as ADHD and speech and language difficulties by 2012 (Shanmugaratnam, 2004). This training, as well as the training of AEDs (LBS), is still offered to teachers within the education service, provided by the Early Childhood and Special Needs Education Academic Group at the NIE.

In retrospect, 2004 proved to be the watershed year for disability in Singapore, with the explicit mention of persons with disabilities as part of the inclusive society vision, announced by the Prime Minister in his inauguration speech, followed by his call for better efforts to integrate students with disabilities within mainstream schools. Such rhetoric from the government and subsequent developments of greater system-wide educational supports for students with disabilities in mainstream schools in the form of specialist personnel and in-service professional development for mainstream teachers began to challenge the notion that special education in Singapore was equated with the special education system, VWOs, special schools, and the social welfare sector. The traditional lines of division between mainstream and special education were beginning to blur.

The greater involvement of the MOE over the past decade beyond 2004 in special education matters has continued in myriad areas, such as working with special schools in the areas of curriculum and pedagogy, setting up award schemes for students with disabilities, increasing financial assistance schemes for parents with children with disabilities, enhancing pathways and supports for students with special needs beyond the primary and secondary years into post-secondary levels, extended year schooling, and developing programs to prepare students while creating job opportunities to facilitate their entry people into supported or open employment. The MOE's greater involvement has also reinforced the integration of special and mainstream education, with greater opportunities for students with and without disabilities to interact during lessons and outside class, e.g., through the implementation of satellite special education classes in mainstream partner schools and the co-location of mainstream and special schools. Over the past decade, the MOE has also worked with many VWOs operating special schools to appoint school leaders from mainstream schools as principals of special schools.

In terms of media attention on disability, the past decade has seen an unparalleled explosion of media coverage, stories, reports, documentaries and the airing of public views about disability from both persons with and without disabilities. This proliferation of news coverage on disability in Singapore has certainly brought about greater societal awareness of the needs and views of persons with disabilities. The emphasis on the rights of Singaporeans with disabilities was given a boost when Singapore signed the United Nations Convention on the Rights of Persons with Disabilities (UNCRPD) in November 2012, which then came into effect for Singapore on August 2013 (Ministry of Social and Family Development, 2013). The ratification of this convention by Singapore is a momentous step toward the building of an inclusive society through efforts to remove all physical and attitudinal barriers that exclude persons with disabilities from being included within life in the community. What is heartening, more recently, is the government's decision to include students with special needs within the framework of the Compulsory Education Act in Singapore (Teng and Goy, 2016).

Conclusion

Within fifty years of its independence, Singapore has become one of the wealthiest and most successful countries in the world, a remarkable feat for a tiny city-state without natural resources. Clearly, the flourishing returns on having staunch priorities and focused efforts in educational, social, and national developments have sustained Singapore's rapid growth and exceptionality. However, in comparison with its long-standing trademarks of spectacular growth and global reputation such as economics, finance and mainstream academic excellence, the attention and focus on improving the lives of persons with disabilities has emerged as a significant priority only during the past decade. This is because there is an increasing realization across society that sustainable development in all spheres of Singaporean life has to revolve around putting the community and the well-being of its citizens at the core of development, and this focus on people has to sustain over time. There is a growing recognition that social bonds fostered through a socially inclusive society, when sustained through time, will be the best safeguard for all in Singapore, especially for the vulnerable and the to-be-vulnerable.

It is therefore very likely that this momentum on improving the lives of Singaporeans with disabilities will continue to sustain itself in years to come. Aside from the extensive media coverage, masterplans, public education, and the development of new policies and services related to disability and the envisioning of an inclusive society, the reality is that Singapore, as one of the most rapidly aging societies in the world, is witnessing an increase in its elderly population and hence the inevitable succumbing to loss of function and disabilities as it ages. Conversely, with greater awareness and better detection, there are now more children than ever before diagnosed with developmental problems in Singapore (Tan, 2016a). The growing presence of people with disabilities in Singaporean society, whether they exist in schools, homes, work environments and communities, will be the status quo for many years to come.

As revealed in the surveys shared in the beginning of this chapter, in spite of the campaigns, public education, masterplans, media coverage and new policies over the past decade, there is still much room for improvement in the attitudes of Singaporeans toward persons with disabilities and for people with disabilities to have a greater sense of belonging and inclusion within their communities and society. The change toward Singapore becoming an inclusive society for persons with disabilities will take time, and we strongly believe that inclusion begins with the young in schools, where they can learn the values, attitudes, beliefs and skills to support the inclusion of diverse others, including those with disabilities. For the young to learn inclusive values, beliefs and skills, and more importantly, sustain such attitudes over time in their youth and their transition to adulthood, the education and training of teachers come foremost to mind.

The education and training of teachers themselves requires learning and practicing inclusive attitudes, and must be a priority within teacher education in Singapore. There is still no clear and consistent priority in Singapore to mandate courses on disability awareness or special needs at pre-service and in-service teacher training levels. This has resulted in deeply entrenched and continued attitudes of discomfort, a sense of helplessness, and even resistance toward the inclusion of students with disabilities in mainstream settings (Eng et al., 1982; Lim and Thaver, 2008; Quah et al., 1982; Rao, Lim and Nam, 2001; Sharma, Ee and Desai, 2003; Sharma et al., 2006; Tam et al., 2006; West et al., 2004). There is a need for this position to change and to emphasize the examination of value systems, beliefs and practices, and how disability has been construed and treated in the context of Singapore within mainstream teacher education if attitudes are to change, and a more sustainable social-cultural shift in attitudes toward people with disabilities can occur.

Learning about the evolution of Singaporean society's position toward people with disabilities and how it has arrived at its current status, as narrated in this chapter, can help teachers situate and deconstruct their own (or lack of) experiences with disability within a larger historical and social contextual understanding relevant to their own lives. The personal deconstruction of their own positions toward disability can also facilitate their interrogation or questioning of larger and deeper systemic and institutionalized arrangements that have contributed toward their own and current societal attitudes regarding disability.

As this chapter has illustrated, the evolution toward the inclusion of persons with disabilities in Singapore has been a journey that has been shaped and influenced by directions and changes in educational, social and economic developments and priorities throughout the decades since Singapore's independence. Although there has been much ground gained in addressing the needs and aspirations of Singaporeans with disabilities within an inclusive society vision and operational framework, especially over the past decade, what is clear in reviewing past developments, events and outcomes is that the only sustainable path toward creating an inclusive society requires that both persons with and without disabilities are included in each other's lives through shared experiences, relationships and friendships afforded by inclusive spaces, opportunities, supports, services, and systems.

References

Advisory Council on the Disabled. (1988). *Opportunities for the disabled*. Singapore: Advisory Council on the Disabled.

Basu, R. (2006, November 17). "More kids with special needs attending MOE schools: Enrolment of kids with learning disabilities has seen 20% rise every year during past 3 years." *The Straits Times* (Singapore). Retrieved from http://web.lexis-nexis.com/scholastic/document?_m=a2b8f4764eece67b4c0b8 c0a6e3c93.

Chan, S.S. (2004, March 18). "Reply by Mr Chan Soo Sen, Minister of State, Ministry of Education on pre-school education, special education, compulsory education and family." Retrieved from www.moe.gov.sg/media/speeches/2004/sp20040318d.htm.

Clarke, C. and Sharpe, S. (2004). "Early intervention." In L. Lim and M.M. Quah (Eds.), *Educating learners with diverse abilities* (pp. 63–88). Singapore: McGraw-Hill.

Committee on the Rights of a Child. (2003, October 27). *Consideration of reports submitted by states parties under article 44 of the convention. Concluding observations: Singapore.* Geneva: United Nations. Retrieved from the Ministry of Social and Family development website: www.msf.gov.sg/policies/Children-and-Youth/Pages/Obligations-under-the-UN-Convention-on-the-Rights-of-the-Child.aspx.

Compulsory Education Act. (2003). "Singapore: Attorney-General's chambers." Retrieved from http://statutes.agc.gov.sg/aol/search/display/view.w3p;page=0;query=DocId%3A45ae5cd5-4eb4-41fd-a649-69cb72d46f55%20%20Status%3Ainforce%20Depth%3A0;rec=0.

Eng, S.P., Wong, L., Chew, J., Lui, E., Chuah, T.C., and Teo, S.K. (1982). *Principals' and teachers' views on teaching monolingual classes* (Occasional Paper No. 9). Singapore: Institute of Education.

Eng, S.P., Wong, L., Chua, E., Chuah, T.C., Lam, P.T.L., and Tan, E. (1984). *Report on case studies of 38 monolingual pupils* (Occasional Paper No. 22). Singapore: Institute of Education.

Goh, K.S. (1979). *Report on the Ministry of Education 1978*. Singapore: Singapore National Printers.

Gopinathan, S. (1999). "Preparing for the next rung: Economic restructuring and educational reform in Singapore." *Journal of Education and Work*, 12(3), 295–308.

Ho, L.Y. (2007). "Child development programme in Singapore 1988 to 2007." *Annals Academy of Medicine*, 36(11), 898–910.

Ho, W.K. and Gopinathan, S. (1999). "Recent developments in education in Singapore." *School Effectiveness and School Improvement: An International Journal of Research, Policy and Practice*, 10(1), 99–117.

Ibrahim, Z. (2004). "Let us shape our future together." *The Straits Times*, p. 10.

Jorgensen, S. (1974). "Philosophy and educational point of view of special education in Denmark." *Proceedings of the First Regional Conference on Special Education and Mental Retardation* (pp. 145–150). Singapore: Singapore Association for Retarded Children.

Lee, J. (2002, April 1). "Schools may be unaware of slow learners." *The Straits Times* (Singapore). Retrieved from http://web.lexis-nexis.com.libproxy.nie.edu.sg/scholastic/printdoc.

Lien Foundation. (2016). "Inclusive attitudes survey." Retrieved from www.lienfoundation.org/sites/default/files/FINAL%20-%20Inclusive%20Attitudes%20Survey%20Part%201_30May16.pdf.

Lim, S.T. and Gopinathan, S. (1990). "25 years of curriculum planning." In J.S.K. Yip and W.K. Sim (Eds.), *Evolution of educational excellence: 25 years of education in the Republic of Singapore* (pp. 59–105). Singapore: Longman Singapore Publishers.

Lim, L. and Tan, J. (1999). "The marketization of education in Singapore: Prospects for inclusive education." *International Journal of Inclusive Education*, 3(4), 339–351.

Lim, L. and Tan, J. (2004). "Learning and diversity." In L. Lim and M.M.L. Quah (Eds.), *Educating learners with diverse abilities* (pp. 1–28). Singapore: McGraw-Hill.

Lim, L. and Thaver, T. (2008). "Coping with diverse abilities in mainstream schools." Unpublished Technical Report. Singapore: National Institute of Education.

Lim, L., Thaver, T., and Poon, K. (2008). "Adapting disability studies within teacher education in Singapore." In S.L. Gabel and S. Danforth (Eds.), *Disability and the politics of education: An international reader* (pp. 583–597). New York: Peter Lang Publishing.

Lim, L., Thaver, T., and Slee, R. (2008). *Exploring disability in Singapore: A personal learning journey.* Singapore: McGraw-Hill Education (Asia).

Mathi, B. (1996, February 11). "20 schools have facilities for disabled." *The Straits Times* (Singapore). Retrieved from http://w3.nexis.com.libproxy.nie.edu.sg/new/results/docview/docview.do?docLinkInd=trueandrisb=21_T10108618444andformat=GNBFIandsort=BOOLEANandstartDocNo=1andresultsUrlKey=29_T10108618447andcisb=22_T10108618446andtreeMax=trueandtreeWidth=0andcsi=144965anddocNo=7.

Mathi, B., and Mohamed, S. (2011). *Unmet social needs in Singapore: Singapore's social structures and policies, and their impact on six vulnerable communities*. Singapore: Lien Centre for Social Innovation.

Ministry of Community Development, Youth and Sports. (2010). "The integrated childcare programme." Retrieved from http://app1.mcys.gov.sg/Publications/IntegratedChildcareProgramme.aspx.

Ministry of Education. (1998, March 21). "Learning, creating, communicating: A curriculum review." Retrieved from www.moe.gov.sg/media/speeches/1998/CurrRevueReport.htm.

Ministry of Education. (2004, September 29). "MOE gives more resources to support teaching." Retrieved from www.moe.gov.sg/media/press/2004/pr20040929.htm.

Ministry of Education. (2016). "General information on studying in Singapore." Retrieved from www.moe.gov.sg/admissions/international-students/general-info#monthly-school-fees.

Ministry of Social and Family Development. (2013, July 19). "Singapore ratifies UN Convention on the Rights of Persons with Disabilities (UNCRPD)." Retrieved from https://app.msf.gov.sg/Press-Room/Singapore-Ratifies-UNCRPD.

National Council of Social Service. (2008). *For all we care: 50 years of social service in Singapore 1958–2008*. Singapore: National Council of Social Service.

Ong, R. (1985). "Official opening of Towner Gardens School." *Special News*, 2(1), 2–4.

Pathlight School. (2010). "Milestones in the Pathlight story." Retrieved from www.pathlight.org.sg/aboutus/milestones.php.

Pathlight School. (2016). "Fees & subsidies." Retrieved from www.pathlight.org.sg/admissions/fees-and-subsidies.

Quah, M.M. (2004). "Special education in Singapore." In L. Lim and M.M. Quah (Eds.), *Educating learners with diverse abilities* (pp. 29–61). Singapore: McGraw-Hill.

Quah, M.L., Lui, E., Tan, E., and Yip, K. (1982). *Interdisciplinary approach in helping school pupils with learning problems* (IE Research Monograph 2). Singapore: Institute of Education.

Rao, S.M., Lim, L., and Nam, S.S. (2001). "Beliefs and attitudes of pre-service teachers towards teaching children with disabilities." In J. Tan, S. Gopinathan, and W.K. Ho (Eds.), *Challenges facing the Singapore education system today* (pp. 189–206). Singapore: Prentice Hall.

Report of the Committee on Compulsory Education in Singapore. (2000). Singapore: Committee on Compulsory Education.

SG Enable. (2015). "Integrated Child Care Programme (ICCP) FAQ." Retrieved from www.sgenable.sg/pages/content.aspx?path=/faq/services-for-children/integrated-child-care-programme-2/.

Shanmugaratnam, T. (2003, December 11). "Speech by Mr Tharman Shanmugaratnam, Acting Minister for Education, at the Disabled People's Association fund raising dinner on 10 December 2003." Retrieved from www.moe.gov.sg/media/speeches/2003/sp20031211.

Shanmugaratnam, T. (2004, November 13). "Speech by Mr Tharman Shanmugaratnam, Minister for Education, at the official opening of Pathlight School." Retrieved from www.moe.gov.sg/media/speeches/2004/sp20041113.htm.

Sharma, U., Ee, J., and Desai, I. (2003). "A comparison of Australian and Singaporean preservice teachers' attitudes and concerns about inclusive education." *Teaching and Learning*, 24(2), 207–217.

Sharma, U., Forlin, C., Loreman, T., and Earle, C. (2006). "Pre-service teachers' attitudes, concerns and sentiments about inclusive education: An international comparison of the novice pre-service teachers." *International Journal of Special Education*, 21(2), 80–93.

Sharpe, L. and Gopinathan, S. (2002). "After effectiveness: New directions in the Singapore school system?" *Journal of Education Policy*, 17(2), 151–166.

Singapore. (2002). "Committee on the rights of the child. Consideration of reports submitted by States Parties under Article 44 of the Convention: Initial reports of States parties due in 1997, Singapore." Retrieved from http://app1.mcys.gov.sg/Portals/0/Files/CRC_Initial_Report.pdf.

Singapore Economic Committee. (1986). *The Singapore economy: New directions: Report of the Economic Committee*. Singapore: Ministry of Trade and Industry.

Soon, W.L. (2015, November 30). "Singapore starts new public engagement initiative, looking at SG100." Retrieved from www.businesstimes.com.sg/government-economy/singapore-starts-new-public-engagement-initiative-looking-at-sg100.

Tai, J. (2016a, April 6). "Third edition of Enabling Masterplan: Inclusive push to improve lives." Retrieved from www.straitstimes.com/singapore/third-edition-of-enabling-masterplan-inclusive-push-to-improve-lives.

Tai, J. (2016b, May 31, A3). "S'poreans 'don't walk the talk on special needs kids." Retrieved from www.straitstimes.com/singapore/sporeans-dont-walk-the-talk-on-special-needs-kids.

Tai, J. (2016c, June 4). "If only Singaporeans stopped to think." Retrieved from http://ifonlysingaporeans.blogspot.sg/2016/06/see-true-me-disability-awareness.html.

Tam, K.-Y.B., Seevers, R., Gardner, R. III, and Heng, M.A. (2006). "Primary school teachers' concerns about the integration of students with disabilities in Singapore." *Teaching Exceptional Children Plus*, 3(2), Article 3. Retrieved from http://journals.cec.sped.org/cgi/viewcontent.cgi?article=1259andcontext=tecplus.

Tan, D. (1974). "Parental point of view." *Proceedings of the First Regional Conference on Special Education and Mental Retardation* (pp. 151–154). Singapore: Singapore Association for Retarded Children.

Tan, T. (2008). "Special schools renamed to avoid stigma." Retrieved from www.asiaone.com/print/News/Education/Story/ A1Story20081114-100677.html.

Tan, T. (2016a). "More children diagnosed with developmental problems." Retrieved from www.straitstimes.com/singapore/more-children-diagnosed-with-developmental-problems.

Tan, T. (2016b, June 9, A25). "The hard – and heart – part of inclusiveness for the disabled." *The Straits Times.*

Tarmugi, A. (1995). "Statement by Mr Abdullah Tarmugi, Acting Minister for Community Development at the World Summit for Social Development on 10 March 1995 in Copenhagen, Denmark." Retrieved from www.un.org/documents/ga/conf166/gov/950310074254.htm.

Teng, A. and Goy, P. (2016, November 4). "Children with moderate to severe special needs to be part of Compulsory Education Act." *The Straits Times* (Singapore). Retrieved from www.straitstimes.com/singapore/education/children-with-moderate-to-severe-special-needs-to-be-part-of-compulsory.

Teo, C.H. (1998, March 19). "Ministerial statement by the Minister for Education, RADM Teo Chee Hean at the budget debate on 19 Mar 1998." Retrieved from www.moe.gov.sg/media/speeches/1998/190398.

Teo, L. (2004, September 19). "$220m school aid for disabled kids." *The Straits Times* (Singapore). Retrieved from http://web.lexis-nexis.com/scholastic/document? m=d9c8b1a6dab3a7bd92dc9d94d450d054&.

The Straits Times. (2016). "People with disabilities in the spotlight." B4. Friday, June 3.

Tng, S. and Tan, S. (2012). "Designing our city: Planning for a sustainable Singapore." Retrieved from www.ura.gov.sg/skyline/skyline12/skyline12-03/special/URA_Designing%20our%20City%20Supplement_July12.pdf.

UNESCO. (1994). *The Salamanca statement and framework for action in special needs education.* World conference on special needs education: Access and quality. Paris: UNESCO. Retrieved from www.unesco.org/education/pdf/SALAMA_E.PDF.

United Nations. (2006). "Convention on the rights of persons with disabilities." Retrieved from www.un.org/disabilities/convention/conventionfull.shtml.

United Nations. (2008–2009). "The United Nations and persons with disabilities: 1980's–present." Retrieved from www.un.org/disabilities/ default.asp?id=125.

United Nations. (2010). "Standard rules on the equalisation of opportunities for persons with disabilities." Retrieved from http://daccess-dds-ny.un.org/doc/UNDOC/GEN/N94/119/96/PDF/N9411996.pdf?OpenElement.

West, J., Houghton, S., Taylor, M., and Phua, K.L. (2004). "The perspectives of Singapore secondary school students with vision impairments towards their inclusion in mainstream education." *Australasian Journal of Special Education*, 28(1), 18–27.

Wong, S.M. (1990). "Education of the ID in special education schools." In R. Ow (Ed.), *Intellectual disabilities: Issues and challenges* (pp. 28–34). Singapore: Tampines Home.

Wong, A. (2000, November 28). "Speech by Aline Wong, Senior Minister of State for Education, at the official opening of the 'We Can' worldwide conference on autism needs at PSB auditorium on 28 November 2000." Retrieved from www.moe.gov.sg/media/speeches/2000/sp28112000.htm.

Wong, M.K., Khoo, A.S.G., Lim, B., Medora, M., Ng, F.K., and Yeo, A. (1974). "Special education in Singapore." Proceedings of the First Regional Conference on Special Education and Mental Retardation (pp. 223–233). Singapore: Singapore Association for Retarded Children.

Yi, S.B. (2016, April 3). "New roadmap for people with disabilities." *The Straits Times*. Retrieved from www.straitstimes.com/singapore/new-roadmap-for-people-with-disabilities.

Yip, J.S.K., Eng, S.P., and Yap, J.Y.C. (1990). "25 years of educational reform." In J.S.K. Yip and W.K. Sim (Eds.), *Evolution of educational excellence: 25 years of education in the Republic of Singapore* (pp. 1–30). Singapore: Longman Singapore Publishers.

Zhuang, K.S. (2007/2008). "Enabling the Singapore Story: Writing a history of disability." Unpublished honours thesis, National University of Singapore, Singapore.

19

Why does Asia need well-functioning pension systems?

Gemma Estrada, Donghyun Park, Cynthia Castillejos-Petalcorin and Shu Tian

Asia's demographic transition toward older populations and economic security for the elderly

Asia has been undergoing a dramatic population aging process which is transforming the region's demographic landscape beyond recognition. A relatively young population with high ratio of workers to dependents – i.e., children and elderly – contributed substantially to the region's sustained rapid economic growth in the past. However, in recent years, as a result of rapid population aging, the number of retirees per worker is increasing. As such, economic security for the elderly looms on the horizon as one of the region's most significant strategic challenges. The problem is that Asia is currently ill equipped to meet this critical challenge. In particular, most Asian countries do not yet have sound and efficient pension systems.

In this chapter, we examine the pension systems of eight East Asian countries – China, Indonesia, Korea, Malaysia, the Philippines, Singapore, Thailand and Viet Nam. These countries span a broad spectrum of income and development levels, ranging from Viet Nam to Singapore (Figure 19.1). Population aging is more evident in East and Southeast Asia than in India and other countries in South Asia.

There is also a wide range of demographic diversity at the country level. For instance, in Korea and Singapore population aging is an immediate problem, in contrast to Indonesia and the Philippines, which are still young. But all eight countries are witnessing a sustained rise in the share of the elderly relative to the labor force (Figure 19.2) and total population (Figure 19.3). Asia as a whole will have a much older demographic profile by 2050. Falling fertility (Figure 19.4) and rising life expectancy (Figure 19.5) is driving Asia's population aging. Asians are living longer and having fewer children due to a number of socio-economic changes such as higher incomes, better educated women, and improved health care. A number of alternative indicators clearly confirm population aging (Table 19.1). Except in the Philippines, the median age will exceed the world average by 2050. In addition, life expectancy is already 60 and low fertility rates will jeopardize demographic stability by 2050.

Population aging is not the only reason why economic security for the elderly is an urgent priority in Asia. Above all, informal family-based support is weakening, strengthening the case for stronger pension systems across Asia. In the past, Asians relied extensively on family members for

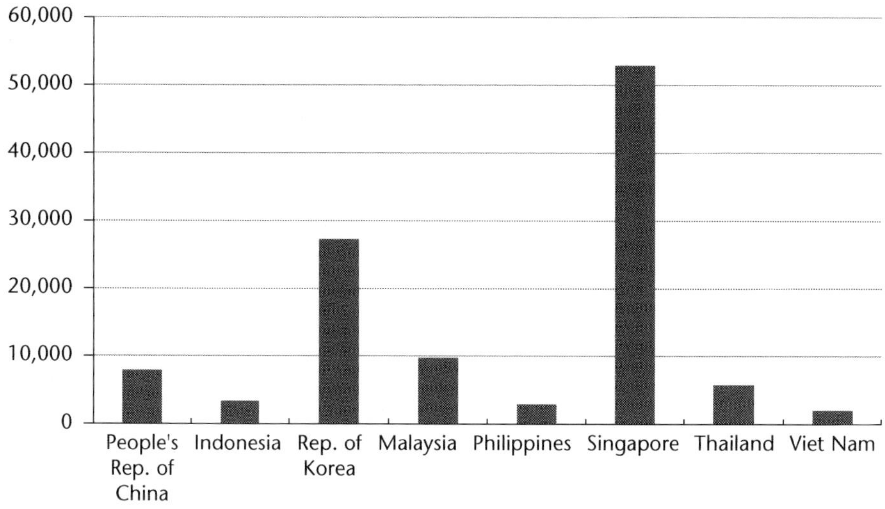

Figure 19.1 GDP per capita, 2015, current US$

Source: World Development Indicators online database, World Bank.

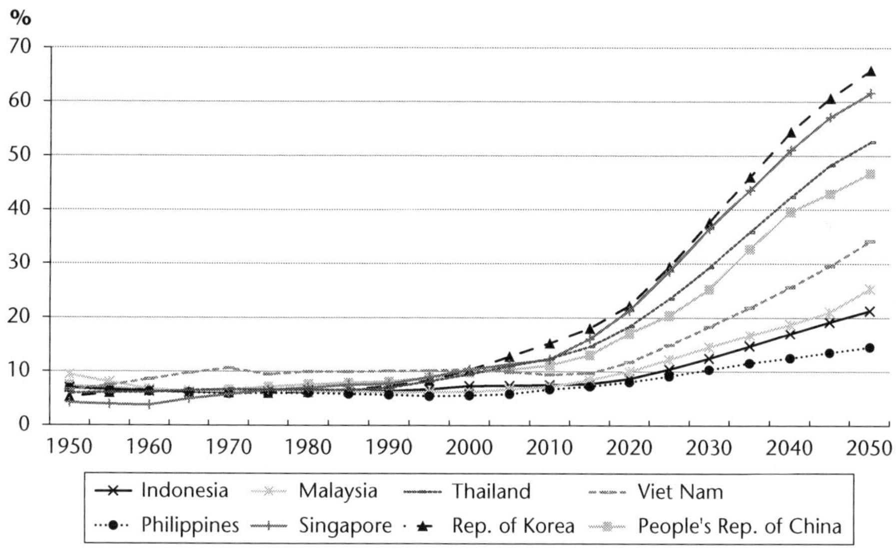

Figure 19.2 Ratio of population aged ≥65 to population aged 15–64, 1950–2050

Source: United Nations, Department of Economic and Social Affairs, Population Division (2015). World Population Prospects: The 2015 Revision, DVD Edition. https://esa.un.org/unpd/wpp/Download/Standard/Population.

old age support. Smaller nuclear families, which are less conducive to family-based support, are replacing larger extended families as a result of major social and economic changes, such as urbanization (Figure 19.6) and decline of agriculture (Figure 19.7). In short, extensive social and economic transformation is endangering the economic security of the elderly, and formal pension systems must fill the gap.

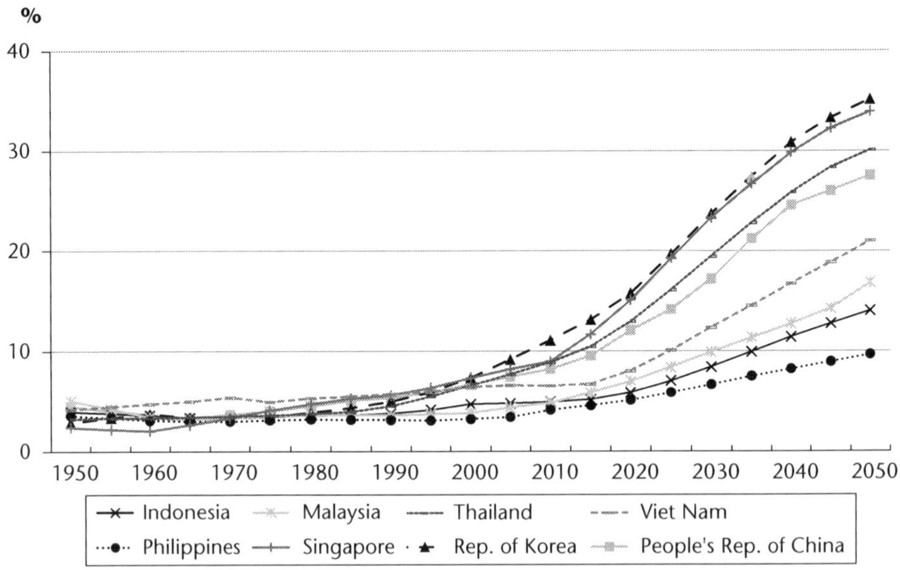

Figure 19.3 Ratio of population aged ≥65 to total population, 1950–2050

Source: United Nations, Department of Economic and Social Affairs, Population Division (2015). World Population Prospects: The 2015 Revision, DVD Edition. https://esa.un.org/unpd/wpp/Download/Standard/Population.

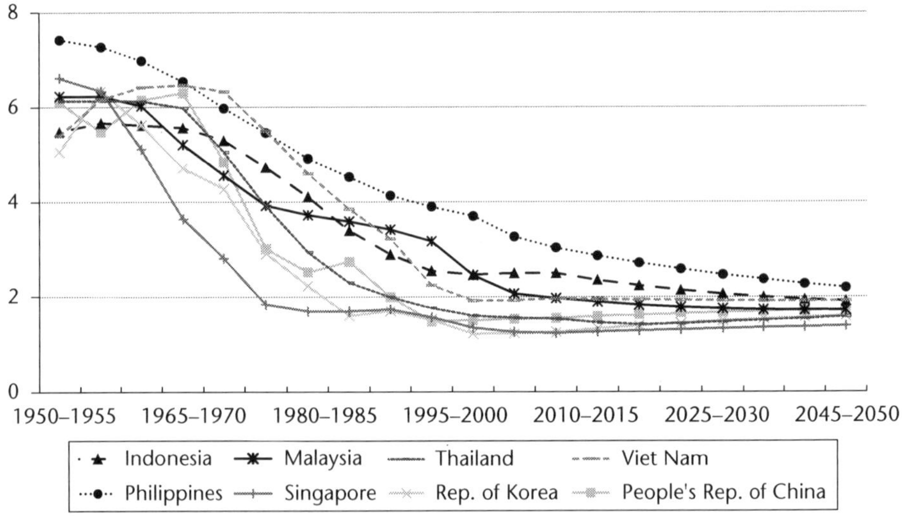

Figure 19.4 Total fertility rates (children per woman), 1950–2050

Source: United Nations, Department of Economic and Social Affairs, Population Division (2015). World Population Prospects: The 2015 Revision, DVD Edition. https://esa.un.org/unpd/wpp/Download/Standard/Population.

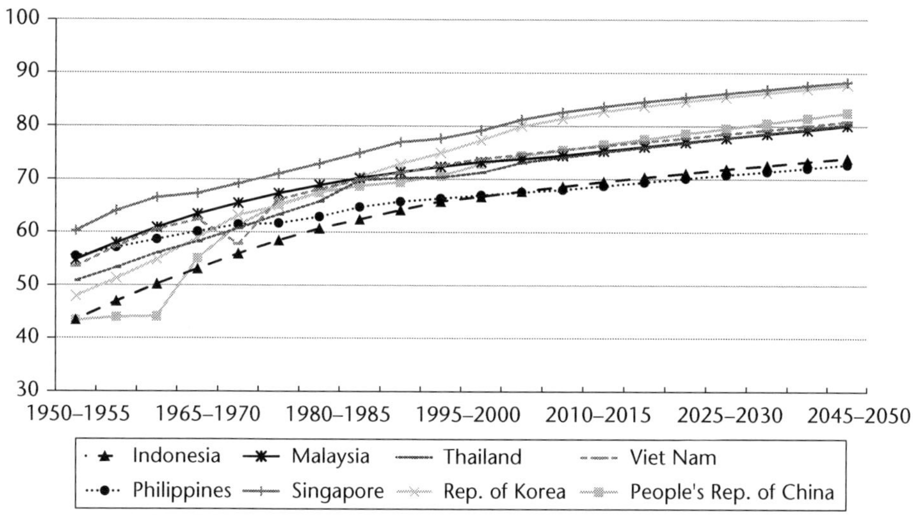

Figure 19.5 Life expectancy at birth (years), 1950–2050

Source: United Nations, Department of Economic and Social Affairs, Population Division (2015). World Population Prospects: The 2015 Revision, DVD Edition. https://esa.un.org/unpd/wpp/Download/Standard/Population.

Globalization further strengthens the case for stronger pension systems. Globalization is beneficial but it breeds a deep sense of insecurity, especially among those who lose from globalization. Well-functioning pension systems and social protection systems can ease insecurity and thus mobilize support for globalization among the general public. In Asia, insecurity related to globalization is exacerbated by a large informal sector (Figure 19.8). Those workers generally lack access to labor regulations and pensions. Rising labor mobility and extensive informal employment in Asia suggests the importance of improving pension coverage and pension portability.

This chapter is organized as follows. Section 2 'Basic concepts of pension systems' examines the key functions and objectives of pension systems. Section 3 'Anatomy of Asian pension systems' reviews the key features of the pension systems in Asia. Section 4 'Analysis of Asian pension systems' seeks to identify the main shortcomings of Asia's existing pension systems. Section 5 'Policy options for Asian pension reform' reviews the main directions for pension reform based on our analysis.

Basic concepts of pension systems

Defined broadly, pension refers to an annuity or lump sum of cash received by individuals upon their retirement. A narrower definition of a pension refers to an annuity or more generally, regular stream of income. Demographic transition toward older populations makes it imperative for Asia to develop well-functioning pension systems capable of protecting older Asians from poverty. A strong pension system should cover the largest possible share of population, provide adequate and affordable retirement income, and do both while remaining financially viable. All pension systems have four primary objectives: (1) even out consumption over time, (2) protect members against inflation risk, investment risk, longevity risk, and other risks, (3) transfer income from poor to rich, and (4) mitigate poverty. Such benefits will have to be weighed against economic growth, efficiency and flexibility of the labor market, and other fiscal priorities such as

Table 19.1 Demographic indicators of selected Asian countries

Country	*Total population (million)*		*Average annual population growth 9%*		*Total fertility rate (children per woman)*		*Median age (years)*	
	2015	*2050*	*2010–2015*	*2045–2050*	*2010–2015*	*2045–2050*	*2015*	*2050*
People's Rep. of China	1,376.0	1,348.1	0.52	0.39	1.6	1.7	37.0	49.6
Indonesia	257.6	322.2	1.28	0.25	2.5	1.9	28.4	36.5
Republic of Korea	50.3	50.6	0.48	0.41	1.3	1.6	40.6	53.9
Malaysia	30.3	40.7	1.51	0.43	2.0	1.7	28.5	40.5
Philippines	100.7	148.3	1.58	0.73	3.0	2.2	24.2	32.0
Singapore	5.6	6.7	1.97	0.01	1.2	1.4	40.0	53.0
Thailand	68.0	62.5	0.38	0.65	1.5	1.6	38.0	50.6
Viet Nam	93.4	112.8	1.12	0.20	2.0	1.9	30.4	41.9
World	**7,349.5**	**9,725.1**	**1.18**	**0.57**	**2.5**	**2.2**	**29.6**	**36.1**
Country	*Life expectancy at birth (years)*		*Life expectancy at 60 (years), 2010–2015*		*Percentage of population aged 60 & above*		*Population aged 60 & above (million)*	
	2010–2015	*2045–2050*	*Male*	*Female*	*2015*	*2050*	*2015*	*2050*
People's Rep. of China	75.4	82.5	18.3	20.6	15.2	36.5	209.2	491.5
Indonesia	68.6	73.9	15.2	17.8	8.2	19.2	21.2	61.9
Republic of Korea	81.4	87.7	21.5	26.5	18.5	41.5	9.3	21.0
Malaysia	74.5	80.1	18.4	20.1	9.2	23.6	2.8	9.6
Philippines	68.0	72.7	15.1	18.3	7.3	14.0	7.3	20.8
Singapore	82.6	88.3	22.5	27.5	17.9	40.4	1.0	2.7
Thailand	74.1	80.3	20.0	22.6	15.8	37.1	10.7	23.2
Viet Nam	75.6	80.9	19.3	24.8	10.3	27.9	9.6	31.4
World	**70.48**	**77.07**	**18.7**	**21.5**	**12.3**	**21.5**	**900.9**	**2,092.0**

Source: United Nations, Department of Economic and Social Affairs, Population Division (2015). World Population Prospects: The 2015 Revision, DVD Edition. https://esa.un.org/unpd/wpp/Download/Standard/Population.

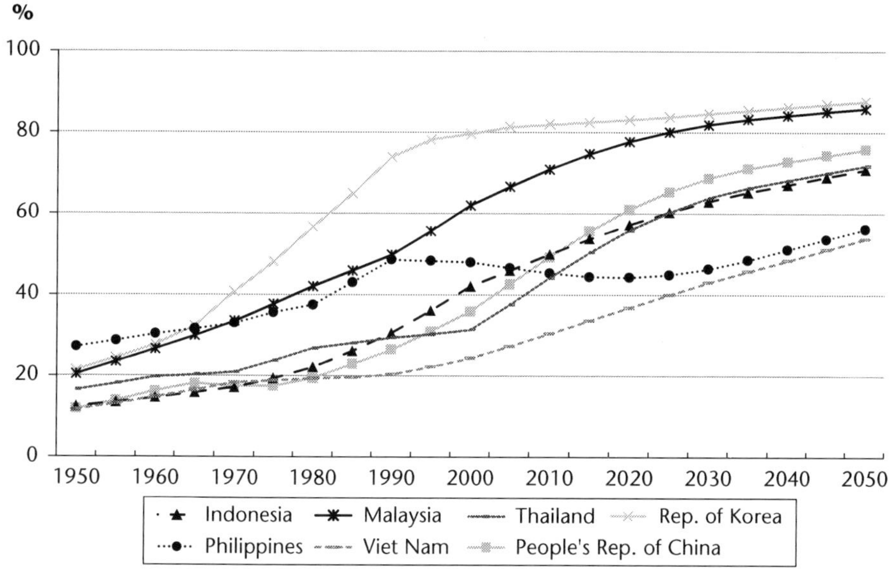

Figure 19.6 Urban population as share of total population, 1950–2050

Note: Singapore is not included since it does not have rural population.

Source: United Nations, Department of Economic and Social Affairs, Population Division (2014). World Urbanization Prospects: The 2014 Revision, CD-ROM Edition. https://esa.un.org/unpd/wup/CD-ROM/.

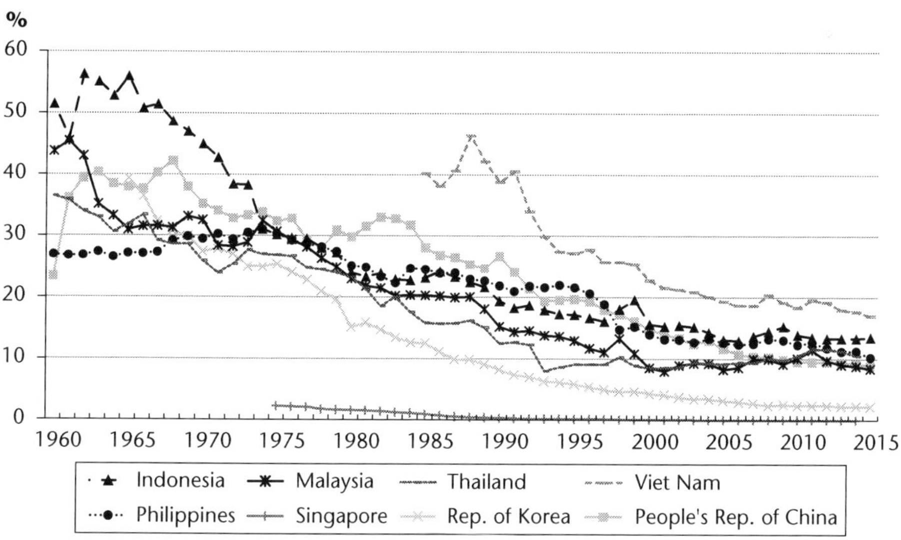

Figure 19.7 Agriculture value added as percent of GDP, 1960–2015

Source: World Development Indicators online database, World Bank.

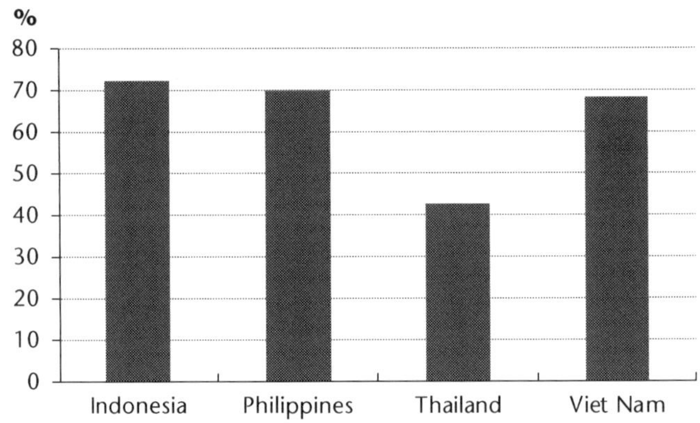

Figure 19.8 Share of informal sector employment in non-agricultural employment

Note: Data refer to 2008 for the Philippines, 2009 for Indonesia and Viet Nam, and 2013 for Thailand.

Source: World Development Indicators online database, World Bank.

health, education, and infrastructure. Pension system design should take into account individual, fiscal, and societal affordability. Benefits and affordability should grow in tandem.

Any pension system must perform five core functions (Ross, 2004). These are: (1) reliable collection of contributions; (2) timely and reliable payment of benefits; (3) sound financial management of pension assets; (4) effective communication network, accurate data and record keeping mechanisms; and (5) accurate financial statements and reports, which are indispensable for good governance. Any meaningful pension reform in emerging markets should contribute to improved performance of the five central functions. There are a number of characteristics of a well-designed pension system at the systemic level. These include ***adequately*** covering most of the population and most relevant risks; being ***affordable*** for employers, employees, the government and the economy as a whole; ensuring financial ***sustainability*** over time; achieving ***robustness*** against shocks; and offering a reasonable minimum income and ***safety-net*** for the elderly poor. Different societies will place different relative weights on the different attributes. Furthermore, a society may prioritize different attributes as its economy develops and population grows older.

At a broader level, there is a great deal of heterogeneity among pension systems even though they share universal core functions and goals. Different societies choose different types of pension systems depending on their needs and goals. For Asia, the biggest strategic choice in pension system design is how much risk individuals should bear and how much risk society should pool together. For example, under a defined contribution (DC) pension plan the individual must bear his own risks. In stark contrast, under a national defined benefit (DB) pension system, the government pools together individual risks and bears the risks on their behalf. There is a related but different distinction between fully funded and pay-as-you-go pension systems. DB schemes tend to be pay-as-you-go and DC schemes tend to be fully funded but there is a lot of overlap and the boundaries are not clear cut.

As a matter of fact, most pension systems are a mix of social risk pooling and individual risk taking. Some pension systems prioritize the former, others prioritize the latter, and yet others balance the two more or less evenly. According to the global benchmark multi-pillar model developed by the World Bank (see Appendix 1), the best retirement system consists of five different pillars with different degrees of individual risk taking. One pillar is DB pay-as-you-go pension schemes and another is involuntary DC pension schemes. The World Bank's multi-pillar framework had a great deal of impact on pension design and reform around the world. In fact, the framework has given rise to a firm consensus that economic security for the elderly requires a good mix of individual and social responsibilities. The concrete and specific challenge for each country in developing Asia is to develop a multi-pillar pension system that is most appropriate for its own circumstances.

Anatomy of Asian pension systems[1]

It would be impossible to identify pension reform directions without a good understanding of the anatomy of Asian pension systems. Such an understanding paves the way for understanding the key shortcomings and hence the key priority areas for reform. One central parameter of any pension system is the retirement age. At this age, pensioners are entitled to receive pension benefits. The retirement age varies greatly among Asian countries and is lower for women in some countries (Table 19.2). A pensioner receives pension payment from the time he retires until the time he passes away. The larger is this gap between life expectancy and retirement age, which varies substantially across Asian countries, the larger is the liabilities of the pension system. Due to rising living standards and improving medical care, life expectancy and retirement age are both expected to rise rapidly in the region.

While the national pension systems of all eight countries in this study are run by the government rather than the private sector, the basic framework of their pension systems varies greatly. Some countries have defined benefit systems while other have fully or partly defined contribution pension systems. DB systems are generally not pre-funded, in contrast to largely pre-funded DC systems. Only three of the eight countries explicitly seek to redistribute income from the rich to the poor.

The rules for calculating benefits vary widely across the four countries with DB pension systems [see Appendix 2]. Salary measures used to compute benefits vary, as does the indexation of benefits and pension eligibility requirements. Estimates from OECD show that for an average earner, the defined benefit replaces 67.3 percent of income in Viet Nam, 47.1 percent in Thailand, 39.6 percent in the Republic of Korea, and 37.7 percent in Philippines. The corresponding figure for China's basic pension is 77.9 percent. Under DC pension systems, the retiree receives a lump sum payment upon retirement. The lump sum consists of past accumulated contributions and the interest income on those contributions. Employer and employee contribution rates differ substantially among Asian countries (Figure 19.9). Employee contribution rate ranges from 3 percent of wages in Indonesia to 20 percent in Singapore. It should be pointed out that workers also make contributions under defined benefit systems. Singapore and Malaysia have the highest total contribution rates while Indonesia and Thailand have the lowest.

In terms of the strategic choice between individual risk taking and social risk pooling, the pension systems of Indonesia, Malaysia, and Singapore are skewed toward individual risk taking. The three countries are unique in the region for explicitly rejecting the social insurance principle. Malaysia and Singapore have mandatory savings schemes or provident funds. The mandatory contributions of employers and employees are managed by government organizations on behalf of employees, and each employee has an individual account. Singapore's Central Provident Fund (CPF) and Malaysia's Employee Provident Fund (EPF) were set up to encourage savings for retirement. Nevertheless, members can use their balances for health, housing, education, and other purposes. Both countries have high national savings rates due to the provident funds. Indonesia's pension system pays accumulated savings as a lump sum payment.

The pension systems of the five other countries are characterized by significantly more social risk pooling. In particular, their main pension systems are primarily defined benefit systems. The capacity to effectively implement a social insurance system varies greatly among the five countries. At one end, Korea offers its citizens a comprehensive social security system similar to those of Western countries.

Table 19.2 Pension age and basic structure of pension systems, 2012

Economy	*Pension Age (Years)*	*Difference between Life Expectancy and Pension Age (Years)*		*Defined Benefit or Defined Contribution*	*Element of Income Redistribution*
		Male	*Female*		
China, People's Rep. of	60 (55)	14	22	Defined Benefit, Defined Contribution (funded or notional)	Yes
Indonesia	56	11	15	Defined Contribution	No
Korea, Rep. of	65	13	20	Defined Benefit	Yes
Malaysia	55	17	22	Defined Contribution	No
Philippines	65	0	7	Defined Benefit	Yes
Singapore	65	15	21	Defined Contribution	No
Thailand	55	16	23	Defined Benefit	No
Viet Nam	60 (55)	11	25	Defined Benefit	No

Note: The pension age in parentheses refers to the pension age for women, where different from men. Life expectancy refers to life expectancy at birth. Defined benefit: value of benefits is relative to individual earnings. Defined contribution: value of benefit depends on contributions.

Sources: Organisation for Economic Co-operation and Development (OECD) (2013). Pensions at a Glance Asia-Pacific. Paris; United Nations, Department of Economic and Social Affairs, Population Division (2015). World Population Prospects: The 2015 Revision, DVD Edition. https://esa.un.org/unpd/wpp/Download/Standard/Population.

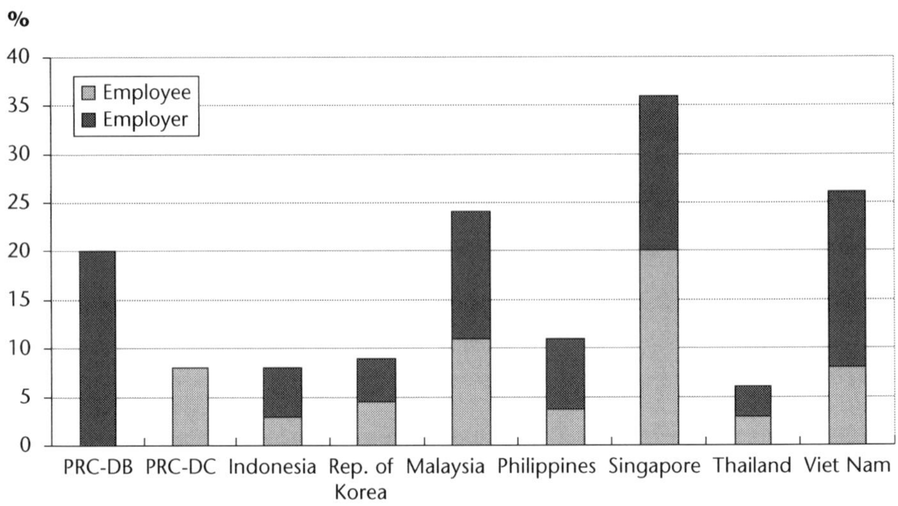

Figure 19.9 Employee, employer and total contribution rates of pension systems

Source: Authors' compilation.

In contrast, Indonesia has only recently instituted a social insurance scheme to complement its defined contribution pension system.[2] China has a redistributive basic pension in its defined benefit system while Indonesia is in the midst of a shift from a DC system to a mixed system with greater role for social insurance principle. None of the region's DB pension systems, which are predominantly pay-as-you-go (PAYG), has substantial pre-funding, with the sole exception of Korea.

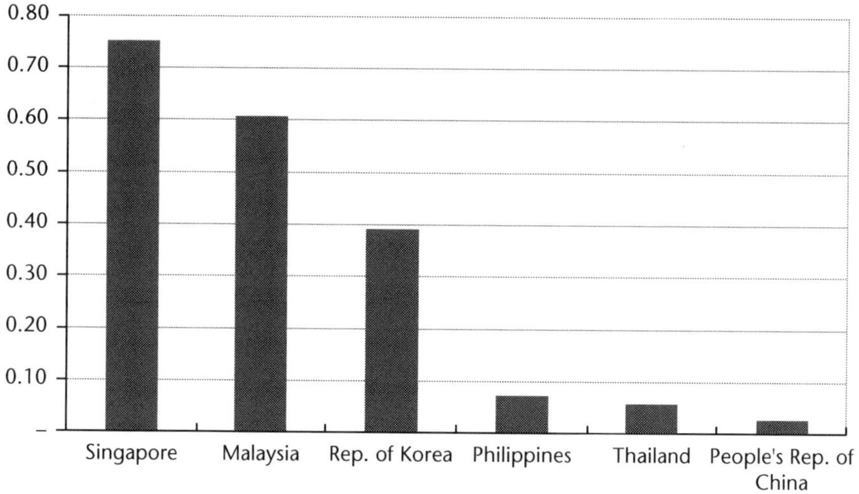

Figure 19.10 The ratio of total pension assets to GDP

Note: Assets of the People's Rep. of China refer to those of National Social Security Fund (NSSF). The assets of Philippines and Thailand refer to those of the pension systems for government workers. Data for the Philippines refer to 2014

Source: Authors' compilation.

Interestingly and significantly, the region's national pension systems are relatively new and far from settled. The most mature systems can be found in Malaysia, Philippines, and Singapore, and those are continuously evolving. Surprisingly, Korea's pension system, which is relatively advanced in the regional context, was set up in 1988. It is still in a state of flux and experiencing significant reforms such as the introduction of minimum basic pension for the elderly poor. Similarly, other countries such as Thailand and Viet Nam are reforming their pension systems to expand coverage and enhance benefits. China is systemically consolidating its pension system from a fragmented and disorganized system to a well-organized and orderly two-pillar state system.

Total pension assets are rapidly growing across the region and exerting a significant macroeconomic impact. In some countries, most notably Malaysia and Singapore, provident fund assets account for much of national savings. Due to their sheer size, the investment of pension assets can have an outsized effect on domestic financial markets. In particular, Korea, Malaysia, and Singapore have set up large funds to manage the large amount of contributions in their funded pension systems. The Philippines and Thailand have funds which manage the contributions of their civil serve pension plans. In 2000, China set up a pension reserve fund – the National Social Security Fund – to cope with the effect of population aging on pension liabilities. Asian pension funds and reserve funds manage substantial amounts of assets but their size varies greatly across countries. The ratio of state pension assets to GDP is highest in Singapore, followed by Malaysia and Korea (Figure 19.10). Asia's pension funds are moving toward greater diversification in terms of both asset classes and increasing share of overseas investments.

Analysis of Asian pension systems

Reforming pension systems requires a diagnosis of their main weaknesses, which hinder their ability to fulfill their basic objectives. Identifying the core areas of pension system that needed to be improved and strengthened will help policymakers map out strategic directions for pension reform. In general, the challenges facing Asian pension systems fall into two areas: (1) difficulty in performing the five core functions of pension systems, and (2) inadequate coverage and benefits of its pension systems. Asian pension systems thus have to improve greatly if they are to achieve their strategic objective of delivering affordable, adequate yet sustainable old-age income support for the region's burgeoning elderly population.

Performance of five core functions

Pension reform in developing and developed countries differs fundamentally. Above all, developing countries have lower institutional capacity than developed countries. Therefore, pension reform based on the experience of developed countries with more mature and well-established pensions systems will be counterproductive. Instead, developing countries must design public pension policies based on their own specific needs and limited institutional capacity. Inefficiency in administration and high transaction costs in developing countries in Asia, excluding Korea and Singapore, can be significantly reduced. The existence of pension-related transaction costs, either in the form of time or money, ultimately reduces the amount of pension benefits received by pensioners. China, Indonesia, Malaysia, the Philippines, Thailand, and Viet Nam all suffer from high administrative and transactions costs that compromise the ability of their pension systems to implement the five core functions to different degrees. A case in point is inefficient administrative and political interference making it difficult to collect contributions from and pay benefits to mainly rural and informal sector workers and other vulnerable groups. The fact that many Asian pension systems are constantly evolving further complicates matters and thus adds to administrative and transaction costs.

A large number of Asian countries are adversely affected by excessive compliance costs in their pension systems. Compliance cost is a specific transaction cost that refers to the costs that employers and the employees incur because they adhere to the provisions of pension systems. For instance, employee pension contributions are collected by employers, who then remit them to relevant authorities. In addition, they have to contribute their own share. For their part, pensioners incur high compliance costs when they do not get their benefits on time, or have to make multiple trips to the pension offices to follow up on their claims for benefits. In some countries, employees are forced to bribe pension officials just to receive their rightful benefits. In a pension system saddled with very high compliance costs, employers and employees may rationally elect not to participate at all. Moreover, if the government has weak compliance enforcement policy, employers may choose to avoid contributing payments. An example is the Philippines, which has a fairly comprehensive pension system. Due to weak governance, the pension system suffers from widespread non-compliance, which opened up a large gap between nominal and effective old-age income support.[3]

The generally weak governance and regulation of Asian pension systems seem to be the root cause of the lack of institutional capacity. Improved performance of the five core functions of pension systems requires improved governance, management, and regulation. Furthermore, for pre-funded pension systems, governance and regulation are needed to foster sound financial management of these funds and productive investment of pension assets. In well-developed financial markets such as the US and the EU, there are explicit regulatory structures and laws governing pension funds. In contrast, Asian banks and insurance companies are regulated but there are no dedicated regulatory authorities for pension funds. The absence of strong governance and regulation causes overall lack of public confidence and trust in pension systems, which consequently reduces compliance and active participation. Unless the general public has full confidence that they will receive their pension benefits when they retire, it will be difficult to mobilize grassroots political support for pension systems in Asia.

Improper design of the pension system

While high transaction costs and weak governance limit the performance of the five core functions by Asian pension systems, other design issues also contribute to less efficient pension systems in the region. In general, Asian pension systems perform poorly in terms of coverage, equity, adequacy, sustainability, and affordability.

Asian pension systems suffer from generally lower coverage ratio compared to advanced economies. In major advanced economies like the US, Germany, and Japan, pension systems cover about 90 percent of the labor force and 70 percent of the working-age population. While the pension coverage ratio in Asia varies significantly across countries, it is generally low, with a ratio ranging between 11 percent and 80 percent of the workforce and between 8 percent and 64 percent of the working age population (Figure 19.11).

In addition to limited coverage, Asia's pension system also lacks equity. Pension systems are highly skewed towards urban and formal sector workers. Weak institutional capacity and high administrative costs constrain the extension of coverage to rural and informal sector workers. For instance, according to estimates, the coverage ratio of pension systems is less than 10 percent in rural China. Given the large size of the rural workforce, this limited rural pension coverage lowers China's pension coverage ratio to 34 percent of the labor force and 28 percent of the working age population. Moreover, the immobility of pension systems weakens pension coverage for workers who migrate from rural to urban areas. In economies such as China and Viet Nam, which experience large-scale rural-to-urban migration of informal-sector workers, this is a major problem. At the other end, public sector workers generally enjoy better coverage and net benefits than their private sector peers. In fact, in many Asian economies, the pension system was initially designed to cover workers only.

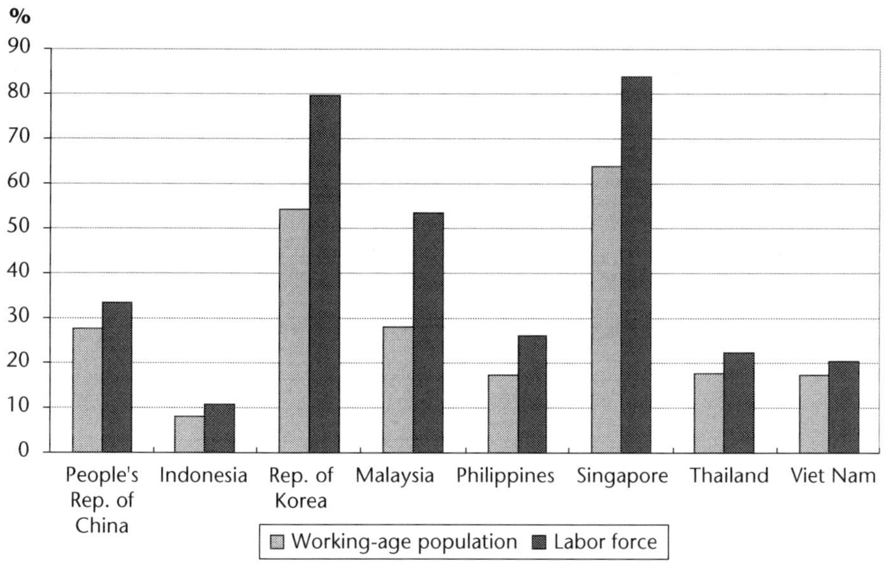

Figure 19.11 Share of labor force covered by mandatory pension systems and share of population aged 15–65 covered by pension systems

Note: Data are for 2009 for Thailand; 2010 for People's Rep. of China, Indonesia, Malaysia, and Viet Nam; 2011 for Rep. of Korea and Philippines; and 2012 for Singapore.

Source: OECD (2013). Pensions at a Glance. Paris.

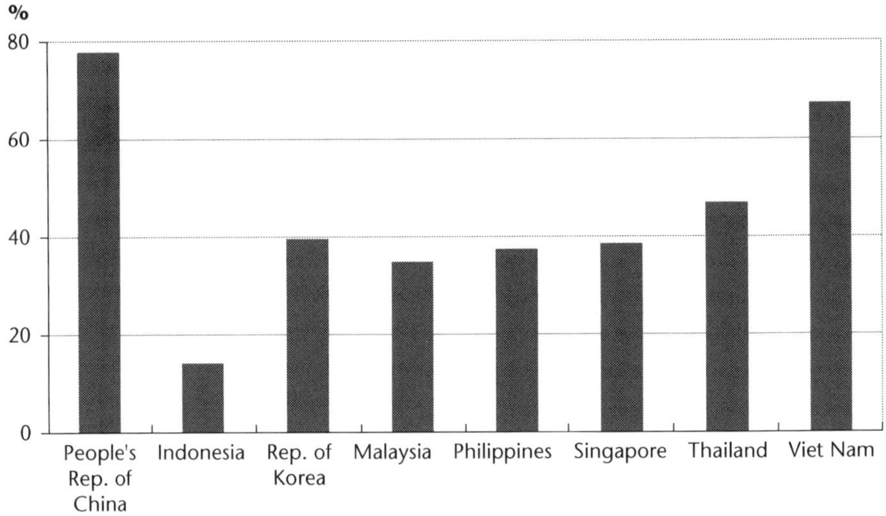

Figure 19.12 Replacement rate – ratio of retirement income to pre-retirement income

Note: Refers to gross replacement rate of average earners.

Source: OECD (2013). Pensions at a Glance. Paris.

Another key issue pertaining to Asia's pension design is adequacy. The replacement rate, i.e., the ratio of post-retirement to pre-retirement income, is commonly used to gauge pension adequacy. A higher replacement rate implies a higher post-retirement income and hence higher old-age quality of life. It is commonly acknowledged by pension experts that a sound longevity and inflation risk adjusted replacement rate ranges between 60 percent and 75 percent. Among the eight Asian economies, only China and Viet Nam are in this range (Figure 19.12). This suggests that Asian pension systems in general do not provide retirees with adequate income. Improved pension design, for example, a more diversified pension system, may complement the public pension system to increase the level of benefits.

Sustainability also needs to be improved in Asian pension systems. A widely employed measure of sustainability is the difference between present value of all future pension obligations and the amount of pre-funding. This gap is known as implicit pension debt. According to World Bank research, in particular Holzmann et al. (2004) and Sin (2005), three Asian economies – China, Korea and the Philippines – have substantially higher implicit pension debt than their public debt. The relative size of pension benefits has challenged the pension system's capacity to repay its future liabilities. Facing high implicit debt, Korea started to reduce pension benefits in 2008. The situation in China and Philippines may be even more serious given their even larger implicit debts. When pension systems are unsustainable, they pose serious risks to fiscal sustainability, which is why financial sustainability must be at the front and center of any meaningful pension reform process.

Last but not least, pension contribution in some Asian economies may be unaffordably high. The contribution rates in many Asian pension plans might superficially seem affordable for employers and employees, but the lack of compliance renders the real pension contribution rate much higher and thus less affordable. On the other hand, pension costs do not significantly distort the incentives of employers and workers, even in Asian countries where pension contribution rates are relatively high. Nevertheless, reforming Asian pension systems must take affordability into account.

As Asian economies grow and develop, their pension systems continuously evolve, consolidate and improve. During this relatively early phase of pension system development in the region, it might be too early to evaluate whether Asian pension systems are resilient enough to withstand large shocks such as the Asian financial crisis of 1997–1998 and the global financial crisis of 2008–2009. Given the risk of widespread old-age poverty due to rapid population aging, some Asian economies have made efforts to protect elderly people with inadequate income, for example, safety net practices, such as minimum basic social pension for the elderly poor in China, Korea, and the Philippines.[4] However, Asian countries need to do much more to ensure that their elderly poor populations enjoy adequate protection from the risk of old-age poverty.

Policy options for Asian pension reform

Our analysis of Asian pension systems confirms an urgent case for pension reform across the region. There is a lot of room for improving the pension system's effectiveness in performing the five core functions of pension systems. A lot of work still lies ahead for Asian countries if they are to achieve sound pension systems that satisfy adequacy, sustainability, and other systemic properties. Failures in both function performance and system design compromise performance. Therefore, pension reform requires addressing both types of failures. Given the huge diversity in pension needs and capacities among Asian countries, there are no universal, one-size-fits-all paths to pension reform in Asia. Nevertheless, some common themes emerge from our diagnosis, and those themes will help to set the broader common contours of pension reform in Asia.

An Asia-wide reform direction is to strengthen the ***institutional and administrative capacity*** of Asian pension systems so that they can better perform the five core functions. Improving institutional capacity is the first step of Asian pension reform since adequate institutional capacity is a prerequisite of a well-functioning pension system. The lack of capacity affects most Asian countries. Developing accurate data and record keeping systems are mundane functions but that should not detract from their significance. Capacity-strengthening organizational reform must be completed before broader systemic reform.

Another related reform direction is strengthening the ***governance and regulation*** of Asian pension systems. The operational efficiency and transparency of *any* pension system requires sound governance and regulation, as does building up the institutional capacity for the effective performance of the five core functions. Better accounting, tougher financial controls, and use of information technology are among the measures that can improve governance. In light of the generally weak regulatory structures in the region, a dedicated regulator can help to ensure professionalism in performing the core functions, promote the pension fund industry, expand financial education, and give rise to a systematic framework that integrates the diverse components of the pension system.

A third direction for reform is ***expanding coverage***. Even in high-income countries like Korea and Malaysia, there remains significant scope for expanding coverage. Asian pension systems often cover only a limited segment of the population due to administrative inefficiency. Coverage expansion should extend to the informal sector only after first covering the formal sector. Lack of pension portability hampers coverage given the growing mobility of Asian workers. One way to improve portability is to promote defined contribution occupational pension plans for individuals. Better coordination of fragmented pension plans also enhances portability.

Improving financial sustainability is another area of pension reform. This is an urgent priority for defined contribution pension systems. Promoting sustainability requires painful but necessary reforms which adjust key parameters such as retirement age. Asia's demographic transition to older populations strengthens the case for fully funded defined contribution pension systems, which renders the payment of benefits less dependent on ratio of workers to retirees.

It is critical for pre-funded Asian pension funds to ***improve the returns*** from the assets they manage. The Chilean experience suggests that even developing countries can do so.[5] Asian governments are moving to deregulate and liberalize pension fund management. For instance, the pension funds of Korea, Malaysia, the Philippines, and Thailand are purchasing relatively more foreign assets. Higher returns allow for more adequate benefits and enhance sustainability.

Given the looming risk of widespread old-age poverty, Asian pension systems must ***protect the elderly poor***. In some Asian countries, the lifetime poor may constitute as much as 30 percent of the workforce. The best way to tackle old age poverty is to build a universal social pension system that delivers basic sustenance to everybody. Limiting the number of beneficiaries through means-testing is an alternative to universal coverage. General budgetary revenues rather than contributions would fund the basic social pension. A social pension system which has the explicit objective of poverty relief can prevent ad hoc uses of the main pension system's funds to fight old age poverty.

Asian policymakers may also need to ***think outside the box***. The parameters of the pension system can change over time. For instance, government policies could arrest the decline in fertility and delay retirement, which, in turn, would reshape the financial and demographic constraints confronting Asian pension systems. To tackle rapid population aging, Korea has shifted course from population control policies to fiscal incentives to encourage more births. Tax breaks for children who support their parents is another example of thinking outside the box. Box-changing policies often entail their own fiscal costs so these must be weighed against benefits.

After sustained rapid economic growth which has dramatically lifted general living standards and massively reduced poverty, Asia is turning its attention to social protection which can foster more inclusive growth. Asia's demographic transition toward older populations means that helping the old achieve an adequate income is a vital component of social protection. A growth pattern which leaves a large and growing population group – the elderly – poor and marginalized is, by definition, not inclusive. At a deeper level, Asia's population aging implies that the social and political barriers to growth may eventually turn unsustainable without sound and effective pension systems. Therefore, the urgent argument for pension reform in Asia is not only social but also economic.

The eight countries we examined are extremely diverse in income and development levels, as well as the soundness and effectiveness of their pension systems. At a broader level, the constraints and preferences of old-age income support systems differ a lot. In light of the country-specific challenges of establishing well-functioning pension systems, each country must pursue its own unique policies and reforms, within the broad contours of reform directions outlined in this chapter.

Appendix 1: World Bank's multi-pillar model of old age income support (World Bank, 1994, 2005)

There is no consensus in developing Asia about what constitutes the best or optimal pension system despite substantial experience and extensive discussions. Nevertheless, there is growing agreement that a single-pillar system is less effective than a multi-pillar system in tackling the risks stemming from the region's demographic change. In its groundbreaking 1994 report *Averting the Old Age Crisis*, the World Bank spelled out a three-pillar model, which has become a universal benchmark for pension design and reform.

The first pillar is pay-as-you-go, defined benefit pension schemes. These are managed by the government and based on social insurance principles, and funded by general taxes. The second pillar consists of mandatory defined contribution pension schemes. These tend to be based on individual accounts, privately managed, and are funded. The 1994 World Bank report highlighted the second pillar while downplaying the first pillar. There is also a third pillar of voluntary savings that are privately managed which complements the first two pillars.

The World Bank's 2005 report *Old-Age Income Support in the 21st Century* refined and extended the three-pillar model. Two more pillars were added to create a five-pillar model. Zero pillar provides a minimum level of economic security for the elderly poor by providing them with a basic non-contributory social pension funded from the government's general fiscal revenues. Given that the lifetime poor account for almost one third of the workforce in some countries in the region, zero pillar is vital for social stability. The fourth pillar refers to family support, which has traditionally been the main source of old-age income support in Asian countries. While the fourth pillar is weakening due to social, economic, and cultural forces, it remains a critical source of old age income support. The World Bank's multi-pillar model provides the intellectual underpinnings of the now widely accepted notion that a mixture of defined benefit (DB) and defined contribution (DC) schemes, with varying degrees of social risk pooling, is required for a well-functioning pension system.

Appendix 2: Benefit rules of Asian pension systems

China: China's defined contribution pension scheme provides a lump sum payment of accumulated contributions plus interest earned on those contributions to the retiree. The defined benefit basic pension scheme is redistributive and pays 1 percent of the average earnings in the city where the individual resides, and individual earnings for each year of coverage, subject to a minimum of 15 years of service. The basic pension is indexed to a mix of wages and prices.

Indonesia: Employees in private sectors are covered by defined-contribution pension plans, which in 1993 to 2013 was referred to as the Employees Social Security Programmes (Jamsostek). The defined contribution pension pays a lump sum consisting of accumulated contributions, net of pre-retirement withdrawals, and interest income upon retirement. The pension can also be paid monthly up to a maximum of five years. In June 2015, the country introduced a new social security plan with the passage of Regulation No. 45/2015. This is expected to operate alongside the existing BP JS Employment (formerly Jamsostek) retirement provisions. Under the new defined benefit plan, monthly pension is calculated as 1 percent of average revalued wages of each year of contribution. Minimum and maximum retirement pension amounts are set for those with at least 15 years of contribution and will be adjusted for inflation, while lump sum payments will be payable to those with fewer than 15 years of contributions.

Korea: Until 2007, pension benefits were designed to replace 60 percent of earnings for workers who worked for more than 40 years. To improve financial sustainability, the pension reform reduced the replacement rate to 50 percent in 2008, and will reduce it further by 0.5 percent every year until it reaches 40 percent in 2028. The earnings basis is a weighted average of individual lifetime earnings and economy-wide earnings over the previous three years. The first variable is adjusted for wage inflation while the second variable is adjusted for price inflation. Pension benefits are indexed to price inflation.

Malaysia: The defined contribution pension of the provident fund can be received in lump sum, monthly installments, or a combination of both. Upon retirement, the scheme pays the provident fund member a lump sum which is the sum of net accumulated contributions, excluding withdrawals prior to retirement, and interest income earned on those contributions.

Philippines: A component unrelated to earnings is the monthly basic pension of 300 pesos. The main component of monthly pension is related to earnings. The main component is the greater of (1) the sum of 20 percent of average monthly earnings and, for each year of service exceeding ten years, 2 percent of average monthly earnings, or (2) 40 percent of average monthly earnings. The basis for computing earnings which determines the pension benefit is the greater of: (1) average earnings for the period during which the worker made contributions or (2) average earnings of the five-year period prior to receiving pension benefits. Benefits are changed from time to time to account for price and wage inflation. The minimum pension for the poorest workers is 1,200 pesos for 10 years minimum of service and 2,400 pesos for 20 years of minimum service. The elderly poor have been given a monthly allowance of 500 pesos since 2010.

Singapore: The lump sum paid out by the defined contribution pension system, a provident fund, consists of accumulated contributions excluding withdrawals for housing, education and other purposes and interest income above a minimum sum. Since 2013, the minimum sum must be used by the provident fund member to purchase deferred annuity.

Thailand: Subject to a maximum of 35 years, workers accrue 1 percent of their earnings each year. For instance, a worker who worked for 15 years is paid a pension benefit which is equal to 15 percent of the base wage. The average wage over the final five pre-retirement working years is the base wage for computing benefits. There are rules for indexing benefits to price and wage inflation but these are discretionary.

Viet Nam: The monthly pension comprises three components: (1) 45 percent of average earnings for a minimum 15 years of service, (2) 2 percent of the average earnings in the final five pre-retirement working years for each year of service above the minimum 15 years, and (3) a lump sum equal to 50 percent of average earnings in the final five pre-retirement working years for workers who contributed for more than 30 years. Pension benefits are indexed to the minimum wage.

Notes

1 The analysis of the features and weaknesses of Asian pension systems is largely drawn from Park (2009, 2011).

2 See Muliati (2013) for a review of the key features and potential issues for implementation of Indonesia's new social security system.

3 Regardless of the form of government, public confidence and trust plays a key role in an effective pension system. A pension is, after all, a promise of benefits in the distant future in exchange for contributions made today.

4 These safe net practices still need to be further improved to provide enough funding to give the elderly a minimum living standard. For instance, in the Philippines the minimum monthly pension level for the elderly is only 1,200 pesos (or approximately US$24), while in the Republic of Korea a means-tested benefit is only about 5% of the average wage level.

5 However, the Chilean system's investment returns have not been as impressive in more recent years, prompting major reforms such as strengthening the zero pillar financed out of the government budget.

References

Holzmann, R., Palacios, R. and Zviniene, A. 2004. "Implicit Pension Debt: Issues, Measurement and Scope in International Perspective." Social Protection Discussion Paper Series No. 0403. Washington, DC: World Bank.

Muliati, I. 2013. "Pension Reform Experience in Indonesia." Paper prepared for the IMF Conference for Designing Equitable and Sustainable Pension Post Crisis World, Tokyo, 9–10 January.

Organisation for Economic Co-operation and Development (OECD). 2013. *Pensions at a Glance: Asia/Pacific Edition.* Paris: OECD.

Park, D. 2009. "Developing Asia's Pension Systems: Overview and Reform Directions." ADB Economics Working Paper no.165. Manila: Asian Development Bank.

Park, D., ed. 2011. *Pension Systems and Old-Age Income Support in East and Southeast Asia: Overview and Reform Directions.* New York and Oxon: Asian Development Bank and Routledge.

Ross, S. 2004. "Collection of Social Contributions: Current Practice and Critical Issues." Presented at the International Conference on Changes in the Structure and Organization of Social Security Administration, Cracow, Poland, June 3–4, 2004.

Sin, Y. 2005. "China Pension Liabilities and Reform Options for Old Age Insurance." Working Paper Series No. 2005-1. Washington, DC: World Bank.

United Nations, Department of Economic and Social Affairs, Population Division. 2014. World Urbanization Prospects: The 2014 Revision, CD-ROM Edition. https://esa.un.org/unpd/wup/CD-ROM/.

World Bank. 1994. *Averting the Old Age Crisis*. Washington, DC: World Bank.

World Bank. 2005. *Old Age Income Support in the 21st Century*. Washington, DC: World Bank.

20

Technical and vocational education (TVE) for sustainable and inclusive development in Asia

John Fien and Rupert Maclean

A number of facts about urbanization, industrialization, and resource consumption in Asia point to the priority that needs to be given to re-orienting business and industry toward sustainability and the development of skills that can catalyze this goal. These are as follows:

- Sixty percent of world's population lives in Asia and the Pacific;
- The region's population density is 1.5 times higher than global average;
- Ten of the world's 25 largest and fastest-growing cities are in Asia;
- Asia's urban population is projected to increase by 44 million annually over the next 20 years;
- Air pollution in most Asian cities exceeds the World Health Organization standard limits;
- Indoor air pollution is high in most Asian cities;
- Net forest loss is 1.4 million hectares/year in the last 10 years;
- Deforestation and other land use changes are responsible for 75 percent of total GHG emission in Southeast Asia;
- Demand for food in Asia is projected to increase by 40 percent by 2050;
- About 70 percent of freshwater withdrawals in the region are for irrigation for food; and
- The region accounts for 25 percent of the world GDP but consumes 50 percent of world's raw material consumption (Asian Development Bank, 2011).

The need to address the significant role of the world of work in contributing to these patterns has been on the international agenda for nearly three decades. The 1992 Earth Summit, the 2002 World Summit on Sustainable Development and the 2012 Rio+20 World Conference on Sustainable Development, all stressed the importance of growing employment through the transition to a more environmentally-attuned economy and the significance of:

> [T]raining, technical know-how and strengthening national institutions in . . . economically viable, socially acceptable and environmentally sound development – with the goal of improving human health and access to safe water and hygienic sanitation, conserving the natural resource base upon which social and economic development depends, and fostering the use of technologies for cleaner production and renewable energy.
>
> *(World Summit on Sustainable Development, 2002)*

Technical and Vocational Education for Sustainable Development (TVET for SD) has become a common, but key, policy recommendation for addressing the economic, social and environmental challenges of our times.

The global "Agenda for Development" produced for the Rio + 5 Special Assembly of the United Nations, which gave rise to the Millennium Development Goals (MDGs), identified several closely interlinked dimensions that permeate all aspects of development (United Nations, 2008). One of these is the realization of a just society, which includes the principle of responsibility between generations, social equity within generations, and the just distribution of work, income and opportunities in life. Replacing the MDGs with a new set of Sustainable Development Goals (SDGs) for 2030, the world's nations have agreed to "by 2030, upgrade infrastructure and retrofit industries to make them sustainable, with increased resource-use efficiency and greater adoption of clean and environmentally sound technologies and industrial processes, with all countries taking action in accordance with their respective capabilities" (United Nations, 2015, Goal 9.4; see also Robinson and Anderson, 2013).

Education plays a key role in this by providing access to knowledge and skills for the twenty-first century through pathways of learning that widen opportunities for future workers and entrepreneurs. Indeed, education is the key to the labor market and the citizenship skills that enable participation in the social and economic life of society. Accordingly, as far back as 2000, Goal 3 of the Dakar Framework of Action in Achieving Education for All (EFA) stressed the significance of life skills, citizenship education, and skills for employability in this (UNESCO, 2000).

> This EFA goal represented a reassertion of international calls for vocational education and training to contribute to sustainable development. For example, Agenda 21, the statement of agreements at the 1992 Rio Earth Summit, identified training as a key strategy for developing human resources and facilitating the transition to a more sustainable world. It called for vocational training programs "that meet the needs of environment and development," and the promotion of a "flexible and adaptable workforce of various ages equipped to meet growing environment and development problems and changes arising from the transition to a sustainable society."
>
> *(United Nations Commission for Sustainable Development (UNCSD), 1992, Ch. 36)*

The International Implementation Scheme for the United Nations Decade of Education for Sustainable Development (DESD) (UNDESD, 2005–2014) similarly stressed the importance of educating for sustainability skills for employability:

> Every workplace should consider how daily working practices and relationships are related to sustainable development and an explicit commitment to positive practices should be included in the procedures and manuals of the institution .... The DESD should work with vocational training institutes networks to establish a common framework for making sustainable development a foundational theme of such training.
>
> *(UNESCO, 2006)*

The global environmental movement of the last decades of the 20th Century prepared the way for TVET to respond to these wider social and economic (as well as environmental) dimensions of sustainable development. For example, in Australia, "training for a better environment" was being promoted (Guthrie and Cesnich, 1995) and case studies of training for green industries were featuring in discussions of the skill needs for "the new economy" (Ferrier, 2001). In Germany, a Congress on "Learning and Structuring the Future: Training for Sustainable Development" prompted the formation of a "Vocational Education and Training for Sustainable Development" program and a Sustainability Portal for documenting and disseminating examples of good practice (Haertel, 2008). In the United Kingdom, *Towards Sustainability: A Guide for Colleges* was published in 1999 (Ali Khan, 1999) while a "Sustainable Development Action Plan for Education and Skills" was released by the Department for Education and Skills (DfES, 2003) to provide funding for campus greening projects and the revision of courses to emphasize green skills (Taylor, 2003; Martin, Martin and Cohen, 2008). Canada was also an early innovator in TVET for SD. For example, *Green Guide* was published in 1992 by the Association of Canadian Community Colleges (1992). *Green Guide* contained ten case studies of innovative TVET for SD as well as a "model program" for review and adaptation. By 2004, expert consultations with industry had produced a Sustainable Development Skills Profile (SDSP) for the Canadian workforce (Chinien, Boutin, McDonald and Searcy, 2004).

However, these developments in OECD countries tended to be predominantly environmental in focus, with little attention to the social, economic and cultural dimensions, which are integral to sustainable development. This was not the case in Asia, where the pressures of urbanization and the decline in rural livelihoods meant that social and economic factors were influential. Indeed, a key driver of the early adoption of sustainability thinking in vocational education in Asia was the education for rural transformation movement, which was led jointly by UNESCO and the United Nations Food and Agricultural Organization (FAO) (UNESCO-INRULED, 2001; Atchoarena and Gasperini, 2003; Cavanagh, Shaw and Wan, 2013). Key skill needs for rural transformation identified by these partners included:

- Improving the overall environment of rural areas with improved basic amenities and services;
- Improving capacity of poor rural people to manage many risks arising from personal circumstances, national and global factors and natural hazards;
- Strengthening individual capabilities through improved education and skills development; and
- Strengthening the collective capabilities of rural people, building social capital, improving governance, promoting participatory practices, and expanding their own membership-based organizations.

(International Fund for Agricultural Development (IFAD), 2010)

Meeting all four of these skill needs requires significant contributions from TVET. Community-based approaches to training for sustainable livelihoods in the rapidly burgeoning informal urban settlements of Asia (as well as Africa, and Latin America) have also been important outcomes of sustainability thinking in skills development in Asia. Training for employment in recycling has been particularly significant in this, with the "waste" of affluent urbanites being transformed into sustainable products and processes to support many thousands of families. Together with education for rural transformation, such programs have been described as "an antidote to urban-biased elite education," as they promote equity by catering to the learning and livelihoods of relatively poor people (Tilak, 2002).

The legacy of Seoul, 1999

The implications of these global trends for TVET were identified at a Ministerial-level International Conference on Technical and Vocational Education held in Seoul, Korea, in 1999. The Final Report of the conference stated:

> We have concluded that Technical and Vocational Education (TVE), as an integral component of lifelong learning, has a crucial role to play in this new era as an effective tool

> to realize the objectives of a culture of peace, environmentally sound sustainable development, social cohesion, and international citizenship.
>
> *(UNESCO, 1999)*

Reflecting such imperatives, the Seoul conference looked to an innovative paradigm of technical and vocational education based upon "a learning culture" that encourages and educates people "to be productive and competitive, and to care for the well-being of its people" (p. 54). This represents a broadening of TVET from the narrow task of providing training for industry and occupation-specific skills to the comprehensive task of workforce development and lifelong learning. A related initiative that impacted TVET thinking in a similar way was the International Labor Organization's (ILO) (2001) Decent Work Agenda:

> Decent work means productive work in which rights are protected, which generates an adequate income with adequate social protection .... Decent work also means a way out of poverty, allowing economic growth to benefit from competition, and workers from economic growth.

As a result, the joint ILO and UNESCO Recommendations on Technical and Vocational Education for the Twenty-First Century states that, as "a vital aspect of the educational process in all countries" TVET should:

a Contribute to the achievement of the societal goals of greater democratization and social, cultural and economic development;
b Lead to a ... critical view of the social, political and environmental implications of scientific and technological change;
c Empower people to contribute to environmentally sound sustainable development through their occupations and other areas of their lives.

(UNESCO and ILO, 2002, p. 9)

These three goals are central to orienting TVET for sustainable and inclusive development, and framed discussion at the 2004 (Seoul + 5) International Experts' Meeting on "Learning for Work, Citizenship and Sustainability" (UNESCO, 2005), which issued a UNESCO Bonn Declaration that recognized vocational education as the "master key" to sustainable development (UNESCO-UNEVOC, 2004; Fien and Wilson, 2005). UNESCO-UNEVOC convened several workshops around the world to disseminate this significant new vision for TVET and to build capacity in senior policy makers and industry representatives to contextualize it for their countries and TVET systems. Four such workshops were held in Asia between 2006 and 2011 where, among a wide range of interesting examples of TVET for sustainable development were model programs, such as: rebuilding fishing boats in southern Thailand after the 2004 Indian Ocean Tsunami; developing confidence and communication skills amongst workers in Thai steel mills, so that flaws in the smelting process (which would lead to extensive molten ore wastage) could be quickly brought to the attention of supervisors; and a textile and garment company in Vietnam ensuring that preserving water quality was a compulsory module in its own TVET colleges.

However, these examples remain the exception rather than the rule. Thus, questions about the impact of normative prescriptions (such as governments "ought to do ... " while TVET systems "should do ... ") must be asked. Indeed, little overt diversion of TVET from its economic steerage can be reported in most countries of Asia. The challenge to change has not been sufficient

Table 20.1 Employment and growth in the European Union, 2000–2014 (2000 = 100)

Employment and Growth Indicators	*2000*	*2005*	*2010*	*2014*
Overall economy: Employment	100	103	105	106
Environmental economy: Employment	100	113	141	149
Overall economy (GDP)	100	110	115	118
Environmental economy	100	124	163	175

Source: Eurostat (2017).

to galvanize significant short-term action toward the "Green Economy" that will support the demand for "green skills."

The 2012 Rio+20 World Conference on Sustainable Development prioritized the transition toward a green economy as the key, not only to eradicating poverty, but also to promoting economic stability. Coming at the tail of the worst economic depression since the 1930s, the conference recognized that "economic stability, social justice and resource efficiency were prerequisites to addressing the interrelated crises of rising global unemployment and global warming as well as the financial crisis." Taking the example of the European Union, Table 20.1 illustrates this connection through data on the way economic and employment growth in green industries has outstripped the overall economy.

The Republic of Korea (South Korea) is a leading example of a country that has recognized this potential of energy efficiency and other environmental measures, not only to achieve conservation goals but also to redress economic recession and unemployment. Thus, its 2008 Economic Stimulus Package, which was designed as a social and economic safeguard during the Global Financial Crisis, allocated 83 percent of the US $38 billion package to green measures, the highest percentage in the world. This represented an investment equal to 3 percent of GDP and involved creating nearly one million green jobs. The package included:

- US $7 billion investment in mass transit and railways – 138,000 jobs.
- $5.8 billion on energy conservation in villages and schools – 170,000 jobs.
- $1.7 billion on forest restoration stimulus – over 130,000 jobs.
- $690 million on water resource management stimulus – over 16,000 jobs.
- $10 billion investment on river restoration – 200,000 jobs.

(Ban, 2009)

There was also substantial investment in preparing workers to take up such jobs. This investment was based upon a wide range of measures for green job creation and training at various levels and sectors, covering young students to professionals. Aligned to the National Green Growth Strategy and the Five Year Plan (2009–2014), the Plan for Green Job Creation and Capacity Building focused both on high-skilled "new generation" occupations in green technology industries, such as renewable energy, as well as lower-skilled work in existing industries such as transportation and construction which benefitted from a greening of existing skills (ILO and CEDEFOP, 2011). The aim was to train a pipeline of green-skilled workers and, at the same time, generate sufficient green jobs by investing in green industries. Korea's labor policies on green job creation focused on:

- *Information management* to develop systems for needs assessment and workforce monitoring to ensure a sustained match between demand and supply of labor. This is integrated into the existing economy-wide forecasting by the Ministry of Labor and the Ministry of Education, and has also been addressed through a project by the Korean Research Institute for Vocational Education and Training to design and conduct a new national survey specifically focused on skill needs.

- *Green workforce development* by vocational training. Some of the examples include training technical workers for new green industries, reskilling the workforce to improve environmental standards of existing industries, developing targeted green skilled workers for SMEs and localities, and developing a national certification system for green industry.
- *Development of green professionals* by investing in green to create demand for highly-skilled professionals, investing in higher education to increase capabilities for R&D and the green service industry (Wang and Ha, 2015).

From the policy design to implementation, the government has consulted or partnered with private sectors and academia. The government established MoUs with industrial associations, such as the Korea New and Renewable Energy Association, Korean Financial Investment Association, and Korea Ubiquitous City Association to provide green training programs. New national certification programs, such as for the Emissions Trainings Expert and Solar Energy Technician programs, were introduced. Some of the existing certifications were also reformed, such as by adding energy- and environment-related modules. The government also encouraged industry-college partnerships in the provision of skills development. One example is the "Meister" schools (vocational high schools) where industries are involved in designing the curriculum, managing school boards, and recruiting graduates. Another example is the Industry-Vocational College/University Cooperation (LINC) Project where the industry invests in courses or projects that provide practical skills required by the industry. (For further details, see Wang and Ha, 2015.)

The situation is quite dissimilar in other countries of Asia.

Opportunities and impediments to TVET for sustainable and inclusive development in Asia: a case study

The Asian Development Bank (ADB) in Manila commissioned the Education University of Hong Kong (EduHK) to undertake a major research study (2012 to 2014) on "skills development for inclusive growth, sustainable development and the greening of economies" in the Asia region, for which the joint author of this article, Professor Rupert Maclean, was Team Leader. This large-scale study involved case studies of India, Indonesia, Sri Lanka and Vietnam. Interest in this area by the ADB and its Member States in the Asia-Pacific occurs due to the growing body of empirical evidence identifying the green economy as a potential source of employment, as a model to halt further productivity loss, and as a method to address climate change and environmental degradation in support of sustainable development.

This ADB-EduHK research study is unique in the sense that the findings, conclusions and recommendations reported on are based on primary data that were specifically collected for the study. Other studies conducted in Asia on the same topic have largely relied on secondary sources of data, reporting on the research and related literature already in existence on the topic examined. By comparison, the ADB study, in addition to reporting on existing research and related literature, for each of the four countries examined, surveyed TVET providers and business enterprises, both policy makers and practitioners, through questionnaires and on a face-to-face basis through interviews, in order to ascertain their views on key aspects of education and skills for inclusive growth and the greening of economies. In addition, in-country workshops were held in each of the four countries to ascertain the views of key stakeholders in government, non-government organizations, members of the international development community, TVET providers, and members of the business sector. These workshops were organized to discuss face-to-face, in an interactive setting, key aspects of green growth, green jobs, inclusive growth and the greening of economies, and to discuss with participants main findings emerging from the ADB-EduHK research study.

It is beyond the scope of this chapter to fully summarize the results of the ADB case study, with regard to such matters as the main findings and recommendations arising out of the study, and the key issues, concerns and prospects, both for individual countries (India, Indonesia, Sri Lanka and Vietnam) and across these countries. Instead, the purpose here is to convey the essential flavor of the ADB-EduHK study, since the full country studies and the regional report are available elsewhere (Maclean, Jagannathan and Panth, 2017).

Critical themes in the selected industry sectors

The pace of development in India, Indonesia, Sri Lanka, and Vietnam demonstrates that growth and industry respond to the demands of the society and progressive policies, rather than to different forms of government. While India is the largest democracy, the presidential democracy in Sri Lanka is being driven by a visionary leadership after a difficult war-torn past. Vietnam, on the other hand, had been a single party socialist republic, while Indonesia was dealing with a relatively recent democracy. Despite such differences, in all the cases, the pace of economic growth has exceeded expectations, and has mainly been due to a positive response to the growth of the world economy, global trade, and high domestic demand.

Industry sectors such as construction, energy, transportation, and hospitality have experienced high growth in all four countries; however, each of these sectors, despite their dynamism, are facing constraints in the form of:

- the informal nature of activities in these sectors;
- unorganized human employment;
- low penetration of new technologies and innovation in the various industries;
- poor implementation of policies related to environment in these sectors; and
- low productivity due to poor human capital development.

The ADB-EduHK study has systematically evaluated the legislation, standards, and social demand in each of these sectors in the four countries, and has sought to understand the ways in which industry sectors are trying to respond to emerging needs and key issues, including areas impeding a transition from traditional practices to green practices. The study also examined various innovations in terms of policies and exemplar practices, in both government and the private sector.

Key issues in the selected industry sectors triggering a demand for green jobs and how industry is responding to those demands

Strong regulation acts both as a deterrent as well as a motivator toward sustainable practices

Rising regulatory requirements have an impact on all industry sectors, and many of the companies surveyed believed that being strongly regulated through government interventions was both a deterrent as well as an opportunity to instill environmentally sustainable practices. Forty-one percent of industry respondents in the ADB-EduHK survey in India, and 51 percent of survey respondents in Sri Lanka, agreed that government regulation has an impact on their businesses. Nearly 80 percent of construction sector and energy sector respondents in Indonesia also agreed with this proposition; however, respondents from hospitality, transport and manufacturing believed that other reasons, more than government regulation, have been impacted, thereby bringing the overall proportion in Indonesia to nearly 20 percent.

Some regulatory requirements, such as impact assessments, are the norm in larger enterprises, where they have dedicated staff to manage such assessments; however, in smaller enterprises. such assessment is usually out-sourced, and ways and means are sought to cut corners in the process so that additional requirements do not impact the cost of production. Similarly, waste management is often a costly process in both large and small enterprises, forcing them to manage these matters more casually and cheaply. However, when enterprises come to realize the longer-term benefits of such practices, find incentives for investment in practices to adopt green practices, and find skilled human resources to implement the programs, acceptability is much higher, particularly in the larger enterprises and less so in smaller enterprises. The adoption of such practices can inter-alia give rise to green jobs and, subsequently, a requirement for green skills.

While at one level, there exists policy challenges for industries and businesses, such as a need to integrate economic, industrial, environmental, and skills development policies, at another level, institutional bottlenecks exist to balance multiple efforts, ranging from compliance related matters, to ensuring productivity enhancement, to saving costs, managing innovations to be competitive, and developing human capital.

Increasing costs of production push back the importance of sustainable practices

Short-term targets often overshadow long-term outcomes, both in government and the private sector. Rising costs, increased competition, and low profitability outweigh the efforts of technological innovations, skill development, and sustainable practices. Almost 60 percent of respondents in Sri Lanka, and over 40 percent of industry respondents in India, feel the adverse impact of rising costs. Though the overall response rate in Indonesia and Vietnam is relatively lower, sectoral response rates, such as 70 percent in construction (in Indonesia) or approximately 60 percent in manufacturing (in Vietnam), confirm that the increasing costs of production are a serious issue.

In addition, there is a strong realization amongst industries that the best way to manage increasing costs is to adopt sustainable practices. However, the dilemma persists that adopting sustainable practices adds up to increasing costs. While an institutional approach to sustainability is yet to evolve, individual motivation remains high amongst survey respondents across the four countries.

Small and medium enterprises have less motivation to adopt sustainable practices. Larger corporations are more sensitive to meeting green demands

The burden of existing issues often overshadows the importance of emerging issues in both public and private institutions. In addition, institutions are more responsive to complying with policy directions and regulatory provisions than they are to developing priorities for themselves. The urgency to deliver targets or exhaust budgets often results in institutions neglecting issues that may have a long-term impact, and may go past a point of no return where no future action is likely to occur.

While it is difficult for government institutions to move out of the framework of their constitution to address emerging issues quickly, small and medium enterprises are primarily focused on achieving profits, and although they may superficially agree with emerging issues such as the green growth agenda, they may find it difficult to accommodate this agenda in a highly competitive market. For example, almost 50 percent of respondents in Sri Lanka and in India agreed that they are influenced by industry standards and competition; and 80 percent of construction and 100 percent of transport respondents in Indonesia felt the pressure of industry standards over their businesses.

Fortunately, every country has a combination of large public and private corporations where an awareness of the importance of sustainable practices and green skills is high. In addition, the idea that green skills are appropriate for all jobs is more widely understood than is the concept of green jobs, and companies that have strong international linkages tend to be more appreciative of the importance of sustainable practices. They also possess international and national environmental accreditations of one kind or another, and value customer demands for green products, and compliance across supply chains. In many large corporations, mandates for Corporate Social Responsibility (CSR) and import–export requirements are key drivers toward developing green jobs and green skills.

Strong social demand and/or customer demand is a big incentive for encouraging change toward sustainable practices and the requirement of green skills

National and international standards for products and services are highly dependent on the changing preferences and choices of consumers. Awareness about the involvement of child-laborers in production activities has dissuaded many customers to move away from products where child-labor is involved. Sensitivity toward greener production has attracted customers to buy more "green products" even if these products are more expensive. Such buying behavior, and pressure for rights-based groups, has influenced the structuring or restructuring of the standards set for different industry sectors. Thirty-four percent of respondents in India, 29 percent in Indonesia, and nearly 20 percent in Vietnam and Indonesia regard rising consumer demand for green products and services as being important.

In addition to changing customer demand, industry standards have also influenced global climate change mandates, competitive pressures, and government regulations, which inadvertently get reflected in skill demands by industry. For example, cleaner technology processes in power plants trigger the need for corresponding training and education. The introduction of compressed natural gas (CNG) has triggered the need for training about clean and green fuels.

While most industry respondents, across industry sectors, recognized the importance of green jobs, a smaller percentage agreed that the absence of green skills is impacting their businesses. Only 23 percent in India, 18 percent in Indonesia and 17 percent of businesses in Vietnam agreed that there was an impact on their businesses due to a demand for green skills.

Expectations from downstream members of the supply chains vary, but compliance with upstream supply chains remains high

Industry sectors such as hospitality or apparel, which have a strong dependence on raw materials from downstream members of the supply chain, also have strong expectations regarding sustainable practices from their vendors. This may also be because the customers are closer to industry and so there is a direct interface between the two parties. However, this situation is not as strong in other sectors, such as construction, energy or transport, because supply chain products are less likely to have a direct interface with customers. When it comes to upstream supply chain mandates, enterprises across sectors are robust in managing international standards, client demands, and global trade treaties and mandates.

Industry and TVET linkages are weak and cosmetic giving rise to parallel training provision

The low level of engagement between industry and TVET institutions continues to be a deterrent to improving courses and developing industry-relevant curricula. Although the nature of linkages may differ across the four countries, with a few institutions doing extremely well in terms of industry linkages (such as the Central Institute of Plastics Engineering and Technology Micro Small and Medium Enterprises (CIPET, MSME) tool room in India or UNIVOTEC or the National Apprenticeship and Industrial Training Authority (NAITA) in Sri Lanka, or some of the vocational schools (SMK) in Indonesia), the majority of training providers work in isolation and continue to do traditional training as mandated by archaic government content and curriculum. Often, the faculty designing and teaching courses remain complacent and not updated about new technologies and developments in the industry concerned.

As a result, several large, formal corporations have made provisions for in-house training in order to develop customized training programs for employees to facilitate a smooth transition into their respective jobs. For example, Infosys Technologies in India has invested more than US $450 million in building its own training center. Wipro Technologies in India allocates 1 percent of its revenue every year to the specific purpose of training fresh graduates (Technopak, 2009). The Hayleys group in Sri Lanka has identified "sustainability champions" from the 12 sectors of the Hayleys group, and each group organizes sustainable skills training in areas such as promoting energy efficiency, waste reduction, and meeting Global Reporting Initiative requirements. Even smaller companies such as Vo Trong Nghia Architects in Vietnam have developed a niche in sustainable practices by promoting the use of natural and local materials in construction.

Apart from apprenticeships and other traditional in-house training mechanisms, internships have recently gained popularity. By providing internships, enterprises effectively address the issue of a lack of practical and up-to-date knowledge imparted by the technical and vocational training institutions. It also proves to be a potential way of recruiting good employees.

Given the large and burgeoning shortage of skilled workers, coupled with poor training and accreditation mechanisms, a number of large corporations, for-profit institutions, voluntary organizations, and NGOs have also started working in the area of human resource development and training. For example, in India, out of approximately 10,000 Industrial Training Institutes (ITI), nearly 7,300 are private. Similarly, nearly 73 percent of TVET institutions in Indonesia are private. There are also efforts by industry associations such as the Confederation of Indian Industries (CII), Federation of Indian Chambers of Commerce and Industry (FICCI) in India, or the Vietnam Business Council for Sustainable Development (VBCSD) and the Vietnam Environmental Industry Association (VEIA), in and through the work of international development agencies, such as the World Bank, International Labor Organization, and Asian Development Bank, as an important way to bring in new perspectives and models, flexible funding, high quality research, best practices, and to develop individual and institutional capacities to deliver large scale programs. Although global experience may not provide a solution to all the challenges being faced in these countries, the experience can generate an array of options that could be leveraged and contextualized to meet field level conditions and realities.

The green narrative: both dispersed and disconnected

The concept of green workplaces, green jobs, and green skills is relatively new in most countries. There is not yet a proven set of methods, policies, or approaches to successfully implement green initiatives. While each country has strong environmental policy frameworks that seek to meet global standards, implementation mechanisms at the grassroots level continue to be weak. There is a lack of punitive measures to encourage defaulters to behave differently, and weak incentives exist to dissuade enterprises from compliance. For example, the *Vietnam National Green Growth Strategy* 2012 seeks to promote green thinking by aiming to reduce greenhouse gas emissions and increase clean and renewable energy. Similarly, the presidential orders in Indonesia regulate CO_2 emissions, waste management, and renewable energy. Although such initiatives are cutting-edge and progressive, in both cases implementation is yet to happen on a large scale.

The actual green practices required in agriculture, industry, and the services sector are quite different. The agriculture sector has connotations of "green," such as water conservation, minimum use of fertilizers, and adoption of appropriate cropping patterns. The services sector is concerned more with conserving energy, while the industry sector is interested in processes such as pollution control, recycling, waste management, procurement, and energy audits. The demand for green skills in traditional industries mostly arises out of the need to comply with regulations. Green skills demands in new industries, such as renewable energy production, arise out of the need to conserve resources and to comply with global sustainability agreements. Within the industrial sector, there are different "shades of green" between the sectors that need to be considered when developing strategies.

Conclusion

This chapter has set out to accomplish three goals. First, it has described the long-term interest in the "greening" of TVET and the significance, scope and purposes of this, according to important United Nations agencies concerned with economic growth balanced with sustainability and decent work. It also outlined that TVET for sustainable development in Asia has a decidedly social justice focus on inclusive growth, compared with the predominant concern with energy efficiency, resource conservation, and pollution prevention in the Global North. Second, the chapter identified the many world-leading initiatives to promote green growth in the Republic of Korea through a reorientation of skills development. However, it was explained that these initiatives were not widespread in the region. Thus, third, the chapter provided a thematic analysis of the results of the ADB-EduHK research study of "skills development for inclusive growth, sustainable development, and the greening of economies" in the Asia region. This large-scale study involved quantitative analyses of industry and labor force trends and qualitative case studies of government, industry and TVET initiatives in this area in India, Indonesia, Sri Lanka and Vietnam. It also systematically evaluated the legislation, standards, and social demand in key economic sectors (such as construction, tourism, etc.) in the four countries, and has sought to understand the ways in which different industrial sectors are trying to respond to emerging needs and key issues, including areas impeding a transition from traditional practices to green practices. The influence of government regulation and incentives, the size and foreign orientation of firms, and the perceived cost versus perceived consumer demand have all played a role in creating what was found to be a both a dispersed but disconnected narrative of skills training for sustainable and inclusive development in Asia.

References

Ali Khan, S. (1999) *Towards Sustainability: A Guide for Colleges*. FEDA (later Learning and Skills Development Agency), London.

Asian Development Bank (2011) Sustainability Report. Asian Development Bank, Manila.

Association of Canadian Community Colleges (1992) *Green Guide*. National Roundtable on the Environment and the Economy, Ottawa.

Atchoarena, D. and Gasperini, L. (ed.) (2003) *Education for Rural Development: Towards New Policy Responses*. Rome and Paris: FAO and UNESCO.

Ban, K. (2009) *Korea Herald, 14 April*. Accessed online December 21, 2013 from http://huwu.org/sg.

Cavanagh, D., Shaw, G. and Wang, L. (2013) Technical and vocational education and training and skills development for rural transformation. In UNESCO-UNEVOC, *Revisiting Global Trends in TVET: Reflections on Theory and Practice*. UNESCO-UNEVOC, Bonn, pp. 309–340.

Chinien, C., Boutin, F., McDonald, C. and Searcy, C. (2004) *Skills to Last. Broadly Transferable Sustainable Development Literacy for the Canadian Workforce*. Human Resources Development Canada, Ottawa.

Department for Education and Skills (UK) (DfES) (2003) *Sustainable Development Action Plan for Education and Skills*. Accessed online May 14, 2014 from www.dfes.gov.uk/sd/action.shtml.

Eurostat (2017) Environmental economy – employment and growth. Accessed online December 14, 2017 from http://ec.europa.eu/eurostat/statistics-explained/index.php/Environmental_economy_-_employment_and_growth.

Ferrier, F. (2001) Can VET meet the skill needs of new industries? Case studies of two 'green' industries. In F. Beven, C. Kanes, and D. Roebuck (eds), *Knowledge Demands for the New Economy*. CLWR, Brisbane, pp. 223–230.

Fien, J. and Wilson, D. (2005) Promoting sustainable development in TVET: The Bonn declaration. *Prospects*, 3, pp. 273–288.

Guthrie, H. and Cesnich, J. (1995) *Training for a Better Environment*. National Centre for Vocational Education Research, Adelaide.

Haertel, M. (2008) Germany: Policy-making strategies and project experiences. In J. Fien, R. Maclean, and M.-G. Park (eds), *Work, Learning and Sustainable Development: Opportunities and Challenges*. Springer, Dordrecht, pp. 261–278.

International Labor Organization (ILO) (2001) 89th Session, Geneva. Accessed online December 10, 2013 from www.ilo.org/public/english/standards/relm/ilc/ilc89/.

ILO and CEDEFOP (2011) *Skills for Green Jobs: A Global View: Synthesis Report Based upon 21 Case Studies*. Accessed online July 23, 2012 from www.ilo.org/wcmsp5/groups/public/@dgreports/@dcomm/@publ/documents/publication/wcms_159585.pdf.

International Fund for Agricultural Development (IFAD) (2010) *Rural Poverty Report 2011*. Accessed online November 19, 2013 from www.ifad.org/rpr2011/report/e/rpr2011.pdf.

Maclean, R., Jagannathan, S. and Panth, B. (2017) *Education and Skills for Inclusive Growth, Green Jobs and the Greening of Economies in Asia: Case Studies of India, Indonesia, Sri Lanka and Vietnam*. Springer, Dordrecht.

Martin, J., Martin, M. and Cohen, J. (2008) UK: Developing the strategy for sustainable development in TVET. In J. Fien, R. Maclean, and M-G. Park (eds), *Work, Learning and Sustainable Development: Opportunities and Challenges*. Springer, Dordrecht, pp. 261–278.

Robinson, J.P. and Anderson, I. (2013) *How the Post-2015 Agenda can have a Transformative Impact on Life Skills and Livelihoods*. Accessed online October 25, 2013 from www.brookings.edu/blogs/education-plus-development/posts/2013/02/08-post-2015-agenda-robinson-anderson.

Taylor, S. (2003) *Learning and Skills for Neighbourhood Renewal*. Learning and Skills Development Agency, London.

Technopak (2009) *Case Study for Setting up Sector Skills Councils in India*. Technopark, New Delhi.

Tilak, J. (2002) Vocational Education and Training in Asia. Accessed online August 10, 2016 from www.eldis.org/go/topics/resource-guides/education/key-issues/education-and-growth/vocational-educationandid=23469andtype=Document.

UNESCO (1999) *Final Report, Second International Conference on Technical and Vocational Education*. UNESCO, Paris.

UNESCO (2000) *The Dakar Framework for Action. Education or All: Meeting our Collective Commitments*. UNESCO, Paris. Accessed online October 24, 2013 from http://unesdoc.unesco.org/images/0012/001211/121147e.pdf.

UNESCO (2005) *Learning for Work, Citizenship and Sustainability: Final Report*. UNESCO International Experts' Meeting, Bonn. Accessed online November 29, 2015 from www.unevoc.unesco.org/fileadmin/user_upload/pubs/SD_FinalReport_e.pdf.

UNESCO (2006) *Framework for the UN DESD International Implementation Scheme*. Section for Education for Sustainable Development (ED/PEQ/ESD). UNESCO, Paris. Accessed online October 23, 2013 from http://unesdoc.unesco.org/images/0014/001486/148650E.pdf.

UNESCO and ILO (2002) *Technical and Vocational Education for the Twenty-First Century: ILO and UNESCO Recommendations*. UNESCO, Paris and ILO, Geneva.

UNESCO-INRULED (2001) *Education for Rural Transformation: Towards a Policy Framework*. International Research and Training Centre for Rural Education. UNESCO-INRULED, Beijing.

UNESCO-UNEVOC (2004) Learning for Work, Citizenship and Sustainability: The Bonn Declaration. Accessed online November 29, 2015 from www.unevoc.unesco.org/fileadmin/user_upload/pubs/SD_BonnDeclaration_e.pdf.

United Nations (2008) *Encyclopaedia of the United Nations*. Vol. 1. Infobase Publishing, New York.

United Nations (2015) *Transforming our World: The 2030 Agenda for Sustainable Development*. Accessed online June 12, 2016 from https://sustainabledevelopment.un.org/content/documents/21252030%20Agenda%20for%20Sustainable%20Development%20web.pdf.

United Nations Commission for Sustainable Development (UNCSD) (1992) *Agenda 21*. UNCSD, New York. Chapter 36.

Wang, S. and Ha, S. (2015) *Policies for Green Skills and Job Creation in Korea*. Accessed May 14, 2016 from www.ggbp.org/case-studies/korea/policies-green-skills-and-job-creation-korea.

World Summit on Sustainable Development (2002) *Plan of Implementation*. United Nations, New York.

SECTION 6
Sustainable governance in Asia

21

Corporate social responsibility in Vietnam

Neda Trifkovic, Thomas Markussen, Carol Newman and John Rand

Introduction

This chapter investigates the scope for *corporate social responsibility* (CSR) to play a role in advancing sustainable development. We focus on an empirical analysis of manufacturing firms in Vietnam. CSR refers to actions taken by firms to advance some social good, which is beyond the direct interests of the firm (McWilliams and Siegel 2001).[1] Examples include efforts to secure the health and safety of workers, supply community infrastructure or combat pollution.

A precondition for the emergence of CSR is that some agents have "social preferences," i.e., that they care not only about their own and the welfare of their immediate relatives, but also about others (Crifo and Forget 2015). Note, however, that it is not necessary to assume that the owners or managers of firms have such preferences in order to explain CSR activities. If other stakeholders, such as customers, suppliers or employers have social preferences, they may induce purely profit maximizing owners and managers to pursue a CSR strategy. The psychological and behavioral economics literature provides ample evidence that many people do indeed have social preferences (e.g., Fehr and Schmidt 1999; Charness and Rabin 2002). This provides scope for CSR to arise even in competitive environments.

CSR is potentially a means for addressing market failures, such as environmental problems and under-provision of health services and infrastructure. Since such failures are an important barrier to economic and social progress, CSR may have role to play in generating sustainable development. Of course, the textbook solution to market failures is state intervention, but the state may suffer from failures of its own (lack of incentives, corruption, limited fiscal capacity, etc.) and CSR might therefore be a useful, or even necessary, complement to government regulation and public goods production. This is especially true in developing countries, where the capacity of governments to address market failures is often low.

On the other hand, demand for some of the goods typically provided through CSR activities, such as environmental quality, may be increasing more than proportionally with per capita income. This is part of the explanation for the "environmental Kuznets curves," i.e., the finding that pollution first increases and then decreases during the process of economic development (Grossman and Krueger 1995). This would suggest that CSR might be less important in poor than in rich countries.

This chapter presents data on CSR activities from an emerging economy, namely Vietnam. The main reason for focusing on Vietnam is the availability of high-quality data. Vietnam is most readily comparable to other countries with a history of communist rule, such as China, Cambodia and Laos. It is unclear, though, whether the past and present influence of communism leads to more of less CSR activity. On the one hand, communist authorities may be less restrained than authorities in other countries in terms of putting pressure on firms to pursue CSR activities. On the other hand, there is some evidence that communism undermines people's propensity for voluntary, pro-social activities (Ockenfels and Weimann 1999).

A private manufacturing sector only started to emerge in unified, Communist-led Vietnam after the initiation of the Doi Moi reform program in 1986. The Vietnamese government has displayed considerable capacity for supplying public goods, such as infrastructure, schooling and health care facilities, but there is nevertheless increasing pressure on private firms to provide some types of public goods through CSR activities.

We investigate to what extent firms undertake such activities, what characterizes the firms that are most engaged in CSR efforts, and how CSR is related to the financial performance (revenue and profits) of firms. The aim is to increase our understanding of the scope for CSR to play a role in generating sustainable development in low and middle income countries in Asia.

We distinguish between three categories of CSR activities, namely "compliance," "management" and "community" CSR activities. Compliance activities are mandated by law. Since they are not strictly voluntary, some people may not regard them as genuine CSR activities. However, they fit the definition, stated above, of "advancing some social good, which is beyond the direct interest of the firm," and we find it interesting to compare the prevalence, determinants and effect of mandatory and voluntary CSR activities, respectively. "Management" CSR refers to voluntary procedures, internal to the firm, which increase its focus on CSR activities. "Community" CSR is comprised of specific activities that contribute to public goods production outside the firm. Our measures of CSR activities are self-reported by firms, but national and international certificates are checked during the enumeration process.

Our main conclusions are, first, that mandatory CSR activities are unsurprisingly more prevalent than voluntary ones. However, a significant share of firms also reports that they engage in voluntary CSR activities. For example, 75 percent of firms have a written down CSR policy, and 26 percent engage in voluntary activities to protect the environment. Second, larger and more technologically sophisticated firms are more likely than other firms to engage in CSR activities. Firms that sell final rather than intermediate goods are also more engaged in CSR, suggesting that the social preferences of private consumers are important drivers of CSR. Finally, we find no evidence that CSR activities are associated with declining revenue or profits. Correlations between CSR activities and financial performance are generally positive, and often statistically significant. The positive correlation is mostly driven by community CSR, i.e., by voluntary public goods production outside the firm. This suggests that engagement in CSR activities is far from incompatible with commercial success, perhaps even the contrary is true. From a theoretical perspective, this suggests that CSR is driven more by the social preferences of consumers and employees than by such preferences on the part of managers and owners, indicating that firms engage in CSR for strategic reasons. From a practical point of view, the results suggest significant scope for CSR to play a role in generating sustainable development in poor and middle income countries.

Background and literature

Murphy and Poist (2002, 24) emphasize that firms can "seek socially beneficial results along with economically beneficial ones." Further, Kitzmueller and Shimshack (2012) conclude that profit maximization and philanthropy, such as improving environmental and social (e.g., diversity, philanthropy, human rights and safety) responsibility, can simultaneously be reasons for adopting CSR. For example, firms invest in community-based activities to improve relationships with the local community, public reputation or efficiency by providing additional motivation to the employees (Bagnoli and Watts 2003). In our analysis, we embrace the emphasis on economic sustainability and investigate how social and environmental activities affect firm performance. In a perfect competition setting (without externalities), only economically efficient social and environmental responsibility will be sustainable. A socially and environmentally friendly firm that is not economically successful will sooner or later disappear from the market and so will its socio-environmental activities.[2]

We focus on the relationship between CSR practices and firm performance, as it is not known a priori which direction this relationship will take. There can be several reasons for a positive association between CSR and firm performance. By adopting CSR, firms are likely to improve their reputations and attract more customers, which in turn can influence firm performance. CSR activities can also be appealing to employees and improve their motivation and productivity (Delmas and Pekovic 2013; Levine and Toffel 2010). Firms can experience efficiency gains and attract investors by introducing new, CSR-compatible production strategies with higher sensitivity to sustainability issues. Finally, firms can benefit from CSR by managing CSR-related risks such as the avoidance of negative press coverage (Hamilton 1995). CSR activities, however, do not necessarily improve firm performance, since they are costly. A recent meta-study shows that CSR in some cases affects firm profits negatively (Margolis et al. 2009). This is most likely to occur if shareholders prefer social or environmental goods over profits (Kitzmueller and Shimshack 2012).

The CSR discourse in Asia during the 2000s focused mostly on the environment (Chapple and Moon 2007), but it has since progressed to include issues such as fair governance, business and labor practices, human rights, and community engagement (UNIDO 2011). Overtime, hazardous working conditions, worker safety, as well as the use of child labor have been a major concern (GCNV 2010).

Vietnamese SMEs are growing increasingly aware of different aspects of CSR (UNIDO 2013). The first formal requirements for socially and environmentally responsible practices in Vietnam came through codes of conduct developed by customers in foreign markets or multinational companies. After that, several initiatives started encouraging domestic firms to follow global trends within human rights, labor standards, environment protection practices, and anti-corruption policies. For example, the Global Compact Network Vietnam was launched in 2007 as cooperation between the United Nations, the Vietnam Chamber of Commerce and Industry, the Spanish Agency for International Cooperation, and Unilever Viet Nam (UNGC 2015). Furthermore, the United Nations Industrial Development Organization encourages integration of Vietnamese SMEs into global supply chains through the adoption of CSR (UNIDO 2011).

The Vietnamese government currently aims to enhance CSR through regulation, such as the labor code and the reform of the union law. The labor code (10/2012/QH13) regulates the length of working hours, the content of contracts, the rules for hiring, the payment of social and medical insurance, and the minimum salary level that is established at the region level. Vietnam has ratified most international labor conventions and working conditions have been improving slowly as a result of changes in social health insurance regulation (Lee and Torm 2015). Enforcement of such regulation is still relatively weak, which has led to several initiatives, especially in the garment and footwear industry. For example, Fair Labor Association, an international NGO, supports a project of improving working conditions and social compliance programs in 50 garment and footwear factories (Fair Labor Association 2015). Better Work, a global partnership program between the International Labour Organization (ILO) and the

International Finance Corporation (IFC), performs independent assessments of working conditions in around 200 Vietnamese apparel factories. After inspections, Better Work advises factories on how to implement continuous improvements to their working conditions (ILO and IPC 2015).

Some authors argue that the main proponents for spreading CSR in Vietnam are multinational companies. Toyota launched a Go Green campaign in 2010, followed by an educational program on television that provides basic knowledge about various environmental issues, together with Go Green student club and many public events (Toyota 2010). Additionally, Panasonic has been focusing on environmental protection programs with the Eco Ideas campaign (Panasonic 2015). Canon has been helping the less fortunate in the community; upgrading learning conditions and school infrastructure, and engaging in environmental protection activities (Canon 2014). ACE Life insurance company has committed VND2.2 billion to support construction of a primary school in Hue province (VBN 2016a), while Samsung has helped to upgrade classrooms, electrical systems, and school yard, and donated books and gifts worth VND200 million to children at Lam Son school in Dong Nai province (VBN 2016b). General Motors Vietnam has donated two vehicles and 10 sets of engines and transmissions to 12 universities and vocational training schools across the country (VBN 2016c). Cargill facilitates access to education for low-income students in Vietnam since 1995. The company has built more than 70 schools in 44 provinces under the umbrella of "Cargill Cares" program (Cargill 2016). According to Hamm (2012) and Jeppesen et al. (2012), domestic firms are still not able to match these activities due to resource constraints or the inability to hire qualified personnel to overlook CSR activities.

Data and summary statistics

The analysis is based on the Technology and Competitiveness Survey (TCS) and the Vietnam Enterprise Survey (VES), both of which are administered yearly by the General Statistics Office (GSO). We use the most recent data available, 2010 to 2013. TCS is a representative subset of manufacturing firms from the VES, which includes around 50,000 manufacturing enterprises. We match the TCS data for the sampled firms with information on the activities of firms and their financial accounts gathered using the main VES instrument. This leaves us with around 7,000 manufacturing firms in the unbalanced panel and around 5,000 firms in the balanced panel.

Both TCS and VES are administered at the same time and under the same conditions. Firms receive questionnaires by mail and return them to the Provincial Statistics Office after completion. The Law on Statistics obligates all firms to comply with the survey request. Provincial authorities contact firms that do not respond by mail, phone or visits in person. Data validity is checked by the GSO for internal consistencies and cross-checked with the administrative provincial data before being made available. Additional details about the data can be found in CIEM, GSO and DERG (2015, 5).

CSR measures

Firms can engage in socially responsible activities that can be internal and/or external to the firm. Internal activities include relations with employees, such as provision of written contacts, insurance or organization of local trade unions. We term such activities *compliance CSR*, because they are mandated by the official regulatory framework. Internal activities can also be voluntary (beyond compliance) and relate to management activities, such as appointing a CSR committee in the firm, declaring CSR policy, joining CSR-promoting groups or obtaining CSR certificates. We term such activities *management CSR*, as they reflect strategic aspects of CSR. External CSR activities are those directed toward the local community and are voluntary in nature. The indicator *community CSR* captures engagement of firms in local contexts, such as environment protection, education, infrastructure development, health care services, youth programs, poverty alleviation, local heritage protection and sporting events. We give scores to firms for each of these three groups of activities and construct separate indicators of compliance, management and community CSR. Compliance and management CSR range from 0 to 4, while community CSR ranges from 0 to 8. Summing all scores produces the overall CSR index on a scale of 0–16.

Summary statistics

Table 21.1 shows the prevalence of CSR activities among manufacturing firms in Vietnam in the period from 2010 to 2013, disaggregated by the indicators described above. We also show summary statistics for the unbalanced and balanced panels with 29,244 and 21,688 observations, respectively.[3] As expected, results show that firms in Vietnam engage in compliance CSR more often than in voluntary CSR. Around 80 percent of firms provide social and health insurance and 96 percent of firms have written labor contracts for all employees. Just over half of firms have a local trade union.[4] These figures indicate high adherence with current labor regulation. However, a sizeable share of firms also reports engaging in voluntary CSR. Around two-thirds of surveyed firms have a CSR policy and around 10 percent have CSR certification. One quarter of firms contributes to environmental protection and around 20 percent contribute to poverty alleviation projects in their local communities. Other community activities, such as youth support and local heritage protection are rare. Engagement in different CSR activities has not changed a lot over time. A few exceptions are a higher prevalence of social and health insurance contributions and increased establishment of committees that oversee CSR practices.

Table 21.2 shows average values of the CSR index for firms of different ownership type and size, measured by number of full-time regular employees. We see that firms on average engage in five out of 16 CSR activities. Private domestic firms represent the average, while state-owned firms engage on average in seven out of 16 activities. Foreign firms have only a slightly larger than average score. Clear size effects can be observed, as the CSR index increases in firm size. Large firms have a larger score than the full sample of firms, engaging in on average 6.5 out of 16 CSR activities.

Empirical approach

The impact of CSR practices on firm performance is investigated through a fixed effects panel regression as described in equation (1):

$$y_{ijt} = \alpha_i + +\beta CSR_{ijt-1} + \delta X_{ijt} + \varphi_j + \tau_t + e_{ijt} \tag{1}$$

where i denotes firm, j denotes sector and t denotes time period. The dependent variable, y_{ijt}, is firm revenue in the first set of estimations and firm profit in the second set of estimations. CSR_{ijt-1} is the firm-level measure of engagement in CSR practices from period t–1. We also estimate a contemporaneous model, with the CSR index from period t. We consider four different CSR indicators: the overall CSR index, the compliance CSR index, the management CSR index and community CSR index, constructed as described in Table 21.1. The vector X_{ijt} comprises time-varying firm-level control variables, such as firm size, value of assets, ownership type, production of final or intermediate goods and engagement in research and development activities, all of which have been identified previously as significant predictors of firm performance. α_i, φ_i and τ_i are, respectively, firm, sector and time fixed effects,[5] while e_{ijt} denotes the statistical noise term.

Table 21.1 Summary statistics for Corporate Social Responsibility (CSR) indicators and other key variables

CSR indicator	*2010 (%)*	*2011 (%)*	*2012 (%)*	*2013 (%)*	*Unbalanced (%)*	*Balanced (%)*
Labor (compliance)						
1. All permanent employees have a written labor contract	100[a]	93.6	95.5	94.1	95.8	96.4
2. Enterprise has a local/plant level trade union	47.3	50.7	50.4	55.0	50.8	56.0
3. Enterprise pays contribution to social insurance for employees	70.9	73.7	73.4	79.0	74.2	78.3
4. Enterprise pays contribution to health insurance for employees	71.6	74.2	73.6	79.0	74.6	78.3
Management (beyond compliance)						
1. Has committee/board over-seeing CSR practices	35.8	36.3	47.7	45.2	41.1	43.3
2. Has written down CSR policy	72.0	71.8	74.8	75.5	73.5	74.6
3. Member of groups or has agreements that promote CSR standards	2.5	2.4	3.3	2.1	2.6	3.0
4. Has been awarded CSR type certifications or awards	10.3	10.2	9.7	10.4	10.2	11.3
Community (beyond compliance)						
1. Environmental protection	25.4	26.8	24.3	23.7	25.1	25.7
2. Education	7.7	8.9	8.4	8.5	8.4	8.9
3. Infrastructure development	7.6	7.8	7.2	7.2	7.5	7.9
4. Health care services	4.6	5.0	5.0	4.4	4.8	5.1
5. Youth development	3.0	3.3	3.3	3.2	3.2	3.4
6. Poverty alleviation	19.6	21.6	19.5	18.6	19.9	20.9
7. Local heritage	2.8	3.5	3.2	3.3	3.2	3.2
8. Sporting events	5.0	5.3	5.3	5.5	5.3	5.3
Control variables						
Firm size	213.8	209.5	218.9	221.9	215.9	248.5
Assets (ln)	9.8	9.9	10.0	10.1	10.0	10.1
Firm engages in R&D activities (%)	11.4	10.6	6.6	6.1	8.7	9.2
Final goods in total output (%)	81.2	82.2	82.4	83.0	82.2	82.1
State firm (%)	3.3	3.5	3.3	3.1	3.3	3.2
Foreign firm (%)	19.2	19.6	20.5	20.3	19.9	22.3
Number of observations	7,348	7,604	7,048	7,185	29,244	21,688

Note: [a] The question about labor contracts was asked in a slightly different way in 2010. Firm size is the number of full-time regular employees.

Source: Author's compilation based on data obtained from the Vietnam Technology and Competitiveness Survey (CIEM, GSO, and DERG 2015).

Table 21.2 Average score of the CSR index

CSR index	*2010*	*2011*	*2012*	*2013*	*Unbalanced*	*Balanced*
Private	4.8	4.9	4.9	5.1	4.7	4.9
State	7.0	7.2	7.4	7.4	7.1	7.2
Foreign	5.5	5.6	5.7	5.7	5.6	5.6
Micro	2.9	3.4	3.5	3.7	3.3	3.4
Small	4.1	4.3	4.3	4.5	4.2	4.3
Medium	5.5	5.6	5.7	5.8	5.6	5.7
Large	6.3	6.5	6.6	6.6	6.5	6.5
All	4.9	5.0	5.1	5.2	5.0	5.2
Number of observations	7,348	7,604	7,048	7,185	29,244	21,688

Source: Author's compilation based on data obtained from the Vietnam Technology and Competitiveness Survey (CIEM, GSO, and DERG 2015).

Firm size has been found to positively predict CSR adoption (McWilliams and Siegel 2001). It can be easier for larger firms to finance CSR-related activities, such as, for instance, adjustments in the production process to comply with environmental regulation or investments in community projects. We use the number of full-time employees as a measure of firm size. Table 21.1 shows that the average firm in the full sample employs around 215 employees. The average for the balanced panel is around 250. Some types of production may be more compatible with CSR (McWilliams and Siegel 2001), so we control for the type of technology with the value of assets. Table 21.1 shows that the average value of assets has increased in the observed four-year period. The value of assets is measured as the deflated value of the total assets of the firm at the end of the year. Following Siegel and Vitaliano (2007), we include a variable that captures whether a firm engages in R&D activities to control for the possibility that CSR is related to product innovation and differentiation. Earlier studies have found a positive effect of R&D intensity on CSR adoption in manufacturing industries (Padgett and Galan 2009). Table 21.1 shows that around nine percent of firms conduct in-house R&D and that the trend is declining. We also control for production of intermediates or goods for final use (indicator variable taking the value one if final goods are produced and zero otherwise) and see from Table 21.1 that firms from the sample mostly produce goods for final use (around 80 percent). This is an important control variable because private customers may care more about CSR activities than corporate customers. We control for firm ownership as foreign-invested firms and state-owned firms are found to be more likely to engage in CSR (Earnhart et al. 2014; Kolk et al. 2010; Hettige et al. 1996; Pargal and Wheeler 1996). Around three percent of the sample are state-owned firms and around 20 percent are foreign firms, as shown in Table 21.1.

We now turn to describing our approach to analyzing the relationship between CSR and the financial performance of firms. Identifying a causal relationship between CSR activity and firm performance is challenging for several reasons. Potential bias could arise if, for example, firms with higher revenue and profit engage in CSR in order to increase revenue and profit. A robustness check, including incorporation of the CSR adoption variable at a lag, may go some way toward alleviating concerns regarding reverse causality, but does not eliminate the endogeneity problem entirely. There may also be unobserved firm-specific characteristics that influence the firm's CSR policy that are also correlated with firm performance. For example, a manager of a firm may have access to specific information or experience, which could both lead to adoption of CSR and better firm performance. Including firm fixed effects addresses this issue to some extent, given that it allows us to control directly for all time-invariant unobserved firm specific factors, such as manager characteristics. In addition, sector indicator variables help control for sector switchers, while time dummies control for general trends affecting all firms and sectors. In the OLS estimations we also control for the province in which the firm is located (time-invariant), using Ho Chi Minh City as a baseline. This accounts, among other things, for relative autonomy in implementing government initiatives in different provinces in Vietnam (Nguyen et al. 2007).

There could, however, also be omitted time-varying unobservable factors that impact both firm performance and the decision to adopt CSR activities, such as, for example, a change in management. The bias due to time-varying unobservable factors could be both positive and negative. For example, a change in management could lead a firm to be both more profitable and to engage in more CSR in which case OLS estimates will have a positive bias. It may also be that new management reduces investment in CSR in order to increase profit. Similarly, regulations at the sector level may change in such a way as to force firms to engage in more CSR, which could reduce profit.[6] This could negatively bias the estimates. These examples illustrate that the direction of causality between CSR and financial performance may be difficult to disentangle, implying that causal interpretations of correlations must be treated with some caution.[7]

Results

Determinants of CSR activities

To see which firms engage in CSR, we estimate CSR adoption as a function of observable firm characteristics, such as size, asset ownership, research and development, production of final goods, and state or foreign ownership, as described in the previous section. Table 21.3 shows the determinants of firm engagement in CSR activities using pooled OLS and fixed effects estimations on the unbalanced and balanced panel, respectively. All OLS specifications control for province in which a firm is located, sector in which it operates, and survey year.

We see from column (1) that firm size is a strong predictor of the adoption of CSR. The subsequent columns show that other firm characteristics also matter for the decision to adopt CSR, as the firm size coefficient declines when variables measuring these characteristics are entered in regressions. Table 21A.1 in the Appendix shows that firm size positively predicts all types of CSR activities (described earlier in Table 21.1), while Table 21A.2 shows a more nuanced picture where a fixed effects estimator is used on the balanced panel. Looking at Table 21A.2, we see that firm size is an important predictor of whether a firm has a written CSR policy, written labor contracts, a trade union, paid social and health insurance for employees, and whether a firm will invest in community health care and youth development projects.

Firms who are endowed with more capital are more likely to adopt CSR activities, although this effect is imprecisely estimated in the fixed effects estimation using the balanced panel in column (4), perhaps because capital stocks change slowly over time. Firms with in-house research and development and state-owned firms are more likely to adopt CSR. This is confirmed in all specifications. Producing final as opposed to intermediate goods is also a positive predictor of engagement in CSR activities. This suggests that CSR activities are in part pursued because they are valued by private customers.

In column (5) we remove location fixed effects and investigate if being located in the northern or the southern part of Vietnam is associated with a different attitude towards CSR adoption. The estimates show a higher likelihood of CSR adoption in the north. This could be due to a higher prevalence of state-owned organizations in the north. State-owned corporate customers are likely to request CSR activities to a higher extent than privately owned corporate customers (note that while we control for state ownership of the companies in the sample, we do not observe the ownership status of corporate customers).

Table 21.3 Determinants of CSR

	(1) OLS	(2) OLS	(3) FE	(4) FE, balanced	(5) OLS	(6) OLS
Firm size (ln)	0.735***	0.411***	0.165***	0.148***	0.419***	0.395***
	(0.014)	(0.019)	(0.028)	(0.033)	(0.020)	(0.026)
Assets (ln)		0.295***	0.065*	0.041	0.289***	0.269***
		(0.016)	(0.037)	(0.042)	(0.016)	(0.021)
Firm engages in R&D activities		1.114***	0.418***	0.388***	1.157***	1.163***
		(0.067)	(0.060)	(0.066)	(0.068)	(0.080)
Final goods		0.173***	0.074*	0.042	0.275***	0.292***
		(0.038)	(0.039)	(0.043)	(0.040)	(0.048)
State firm		0.554***	0.463***	0.356*	0.699***	0.743***
		(0.113)	(0.178)	(0.198)	(0.115)	(0.148)
Foreign firm		–0.108**	0.279	0.161	–0.148***	–0.292***
		(0.046)	(0.195)	(0.226)	(0.044)	(0.054)
South					–0.161***	
Main market:					(0.039)	
Same province						0.001
						(0.001)
Same region						0.000
						(0.001)
Country						0.001**
						(0.001)
Export						0.020***
						(0.004)
Location	Yes	Yes	No	No	No	No
Sector	Yes	Yes	No	No	Yes	Yes
Year controls	Yes	Yes	Yes	Yes	Yes	Yes
Constant	2.263***	0.617***	3.877***	4.487***	0.250*	0.500***
	(0.099)	(0.145)	(0.718)	(0.784)	(0.135)	(0.179)
Observations	29,244	29,244	29,244	21,688	29,244	21,688
R^2	0.265	0.306	0.015	0.015	0.260	0.247

Note: Dependent variable is CSR index (0-16). OLS and FE in column (3) based on the unbalanced panel. Standard errors in parentheses;

*p<0.10, **p<0.05, ***p<0.01.

Source: Author's compilation based on data obtained from the Vietnam Technology and Competitiveness Survey (CIEM, GSO, and DERG 2015).

In column (6) we investigate how CSR adoption varies by the type of market in which main products are sold. The motivation for this analysis is that Newman et al. (2018) have demonstrated that engagement in international trade positively affects CSR behavior. We observe shares of goods sold in, respectively, the same province, region, country, and in foreign markets. The estimates show that the likelihood of CSR adoption increases with trading distance, illustrated by positive coefficients for trading beyond the same region and exporting. This suggests that CSR is not driven by relationships with customers that are geographically close to the firm.

Table 21.4 looks separately at compliance, management and community CSR correlates. This enables us to understand how important different types of CSR activities are for overall CSR performance. The positive effect of firm size, and of research and development, is confirmed for all CSR categories. Selling final goods matters for management CSR, but not for compliance and

Table 21.4 CSR determinants (disaggregated)

	(1) Compliance CSR OLS	(2) Compliance CSR FE, balanced	(3) Management CSR OLS	(4) Management CSR FE, balanced	(5) Community CSR OLS	(6) Community CSR FE, balanced
Firm size (ln)	0.094***	0.029**	0.226***	0.062***	0.091***	0.057**
	(0.008)	(0.014)	(0.010)	(0.016)	(0.012)	(0.023)
Assets (ln)	0.081***	–0.005	0.168***	0.013	0.047***	0.033
	(0.007)	(0.018)	(0.008)	(0.020)	(0.010)	(0.027)
R&D	0.415***	0.180***	0.251***	0.057***	0.448***	0.151***
	(0.025)	(0.028)	(0.023)	(0.022)	(0.045)	(0.049)
Final goods	0.035**	0.039*	0.083***	0.002	0.055**	0.002
	(0.017)	(0.020)	(0.019)	(0.018)	(0.022)	(0.029)
State firm	0.129***	0.225**	0.231***	0.153***	0.194**	–0.022
	(0.041)	(0.104)	(0.039)	(0.059)	(0.086)	(0.176)
Foreign firm	0.069***	0.046	0.227***	–0.014	–0.404***	0.130
	(0.023)	(0.098)	(0.022)	(0.108)	(0.028)	(0.179)
Sector	Yes	Yes	Yes	Yes	Yes	Yes
Location	Yes	Yes	Yes	Yes	Yes	Yes
Year controls	Yes	Yes	Yes	Yes	Yes	Yes
Constant	0.157**	1.305***	0.572***	3.026***	–0.112	0.156
	(0.061)	(0.337)	(0.072)	(0.363)	(0.092)	(0.343)
Observations	29,244	21,688	29,244	21,688	29,244	21,688
R^2	0.169	0.022	0.440	0.019	0.136	0.004

Note: OLS based on the unbalanced panel. Standard errors in parentheses;

*p<0.10, **p<0.05, ***p<0.01.

Source: Author's compilation based on data obtained from the Vietnam Technology and Competitiveness Survey (CIEM, GSO, and DERG 2015).

community CSR, reconfirming the message that CSR plays a role in the market visibility of firms. We also see that foreign firms tend not to focus on CSR beyond compliance CSR. Hence, the anecdotal evidence of a positive effect on CSR activities from being multinational company, discussed in the section above, seems largely to be driven by firm size. Large firms are more likely to engage in CSR activities, regardless of whether they are Vietnamese or multinationals.

In sum, mandatory CSR activities are, as expected, more prevalent than voluntary ones but a fairly large share of firms also engage in voluntary CSR activities. For example, 75 percent of firms have a written down CSR policy, and 26 percent engage in voluntary activities to protect the environment. Larger and more technologically sophisticated firms are more likely than other firms to engage in CSR activities. Firms that sell final rather than intermediate goods are also more engaged in CSR, suggesting that the social preferences of private consumers are important drivers of CSR.

CSR activities and firm performance

We now turn to analyzing the relationship between CSR activities and financial performance. Table 21.5 presents our first analysis of CSR and firm performance, measured by firm revenue and profit. Columns (1) to (4) show results of revenue estimates and columns (5) to (8) show results of profit estimates. All specifications show a positive association between the aggregate CSR index and firm revenue and profit. Adding one additional CSR activity gives on average a one percent increase in firm revenue and 4.5 percent increase in profit. These results are robust to the use of location, sector and time fixed effects. Control variables, such as firm size, assets and state ownership also correlate positively with firm revenue. Notice that in both the revenue and profit specifications, fixed effects results are lower than the OLS estimates, indicating that the unobserved heterogeneity correlates positively with CSR incidence. This suggests that more productive firms are more likely to self-select into CSR adoption and that fixed effects correct for the upward bias in OLS estimation.

Table 21.6 shows that the overall positive association between CSR and revenue is driven by community and, to a lesser extent, management CSR. At the same time, the link between CSR and firm profit goes through community CSR, that is, corporate activities focused on servicing local society (e.g., environmental protection activities, participation in local poverty alleviation programs, community based education and health programs). Our results are in line with Newman et al. (2016) who found a positive effect of community CSR on firm efficiency. Moreover, our results corroborate earlier findings on commercial reasons for emerging market companies to take action on sustainability (Thorpe and Prakash-Mani 2003). This indicates that firms may benefit from engaging in activities that advance social goods. Our results support the view that strategic, profit-seeking motivations on the part of firm managers may play a significant role in driving CSR adoption (McWilliams and Siegel 2001). In other words, CSR is driven by the social preference of *customers*, rather than owners and managers.

Using lagged CSR variables confirms the positive association between CSR and revenue, as shown in Table 21.7. The size of the coefficient decreases slightly compared to contemporaneous estimation presented in Table 21.6, from 0.009 to 0.007. As shown in Table 21.7, the positive association between CSR and revenue appears to be driven by community CSR. This is in line with Liu (2009), who found that Chinese firms are more likely to show socially responsible behavior when influenced by the local community and NGOs. Moreover, local stakeholders (customers, suppliers, employees, etc.) are found to reciprocate socially responsible actions by local firms over time (Crifo and Forget 2015). Firms who are most likely to experience such reciprocity are firms with a stronger financial engagement with local community actors. This is

Table 21.5 Revenue, profit and CSR

	Revenue (ln)				*Profit (ln)*			
	OLS	*OLS*	*FE*	*FE*	*OLS*	*OLS*	*FE*	*FE*
	(1)	*(2)*	*(3)*	*(4)*	*(5)*	*(6)*	*(7)*	*(8)*
CSR all categories	0.072***	0.014***	0.008***	0.009***	0.075***	0.026**	0.035***	0.046***
	(0.005)	(0.004)	(0.003)	(0.003)	(0.011)	(0.011)	(0.012)	(0.014)
Firm size (ln)	1.095***	0.478***	0.475***	0.456***	1.138***	0.696***	0.653***	0.663***
	(0.009)	(0.011)	(0.018)	(0.020)	(0.023)	(0.029)	(0.044)	(0.053)
Assets (ln)		0.702***	0.409***	0.398***		0.478***	0.468***	0.497***
		(0.009)	(0.022)	(0.023)		(0.025)	(0.073)	(0.088)
R&D		–0.063***	–0.004	–0.003		0.108	0.066	0.026
		(0.021)	(0.015)	(0.015)		(0.080)	(0.078)	(0.084)
Final goods		–0.106***	0.004	0.003		–0.147**	–0.022	–0.002
		(0.019)	(0.013)	(0.013)		(0.060)	(0.061)	(0.069)
State firm		–0.020	0.072**	0.107***		1.087***	0.411*	0.337
		(0.042)	(0.035)	(0.039)		(0.155)	(0.246)	(0.257)
Foreign firm		–0.096***	0.092	0.108		–0.114	0.963***	1.289***
		(0.023)	(0.057)	(0.066)		(0.092)	(0.325)	(0.401)
Sector	Yes	Yes	Yes	Yes	Yes	Yes	Yes	Yes
Location	Yes	Yes	Yes	Yes	Yes	Yes	Yes	Yes
Year controls	Yes	Yes	Yes	Yes	Yes	Yes	Yes	Yes
Constant	5.826***	1.562***	3.651***	3.854***	–0.967***	–3.238***	–4.374***	–3.907***
	(0.067)	(0.072)	(0.352)	(0.355)	(0.134)	(0.220)	(0.851)	(0.981)
Observations	29,244	29,244	29,244	21,688	29,244	29,244	29,244	21,688
R^2	0.699	0.827	0.239	0.246	0.264	0.289	0.037	0.035

Note: Columns (4) and (8) based on the balanced panel. All other estimations based on the unbalanced panel. Robust standard errors clustered at firm level in parentheses.

*p<0.10, **p<0.05, ***p<0.01.

Source: Author's compilation based on data obtained from the Vietnam Technology and Competitiveness Survey (CIEM, GSO, and DERG 2015).

Table 21.6 Revenue, profit and CSR categories

	Revenue (ln)				*Profit (ln)*			
	OLS	*OLS*	*FE*	*FE*	*OLS*	*OLS*	*FE*	*FE*
	(1)	*(2)*	*(3)*	*(4)*	*(5)*	*(6)*	*(7)*	*(8)*
Compliance CSR	0.198***	0.050***	0.011	0.007	0.123***	0.009	0.012	0.017
	(0.011)	(0.008)	(0.008)	(0.008)	(0.022)	(0.022)	(0.026)	(0.030)
Management CSR	0.099***	0.002	0.007	0.010*	0.099***	0.017	0.025	0.047
	(0.011)	(0.008)	(0.005)	(0.005)	(0.027)	(0.027)	(0.028)	(0.031)
Community CSR	0.027***	0.006	0.010***	0.011***	0.077***	0.051***	0.058***	0.068***
	(0.007)	(0.005)	(0.004)	(0.004)	(0.018)	(0.017)	(0.018)	(0.020)
Observations	29,244	29,244	29,244	21,688	29,244	29,244	29,244	21,688

Note: Columns (4) and (8) based on the balanced panel. All other estimations based on the unbalanced panel. Coefficients from separate estimations for each CSR variable. Control variables: firm size, assets, R&D, final goods, state firm, foreign firm, sector, location and year. Robust standard errors clustered at firm level in parentheses.

*p<0.10, **p<0.05, ***p<0.01.

Source: Author's compilation based on data obtained from the Vietnam Technology and Competitiveness Survey (CIEM, GSO, and DERG 2015).

Table 21.7 Revenue, profit and CSR (lagged)

	Revenue (ln)				*Profit (ln)*			
	OLS	*OLS*	*FE*	*FE*	*OLS*	*OLS*	*FE*	*FE*
	(1)	*(2)*	*(3)*	*(4)*	*(5)*	*(6)*	*(7)*	*(8)*
CSR all categories	0.072***	0.012***	0.006*	0.007**	0.050***	0.001	0.013	0.016
	(0.005)	(0.004)	(0.003)	(0.003)	(0.012)	(0.012)	(0.014)	(0.015)
Compliance CSR	0.191***	0.045***	0.006	0.010	0.102***	0.088***	0.045	0.067**
	(0.012)	(0.009)	(0.008)	(0.008)	(0.027)	(0.027)	(0.032)	(0.034)
Management CSR	0.094***	–0.004	0.005	0.007	0.080**	–0.000	–0.002	–0.002
	(0.012)	(0.008)	(0.006)	(0.006)	(0.031)	(0.031)	(0.033)	(0.035)
Community CSR	0.033***	0.007	0.007*	0.008*	0.035*	0.009	0.013	0.009
	(0.008)	(0.006)	(0.004)	(0.005)	(0.020)	(0.020)	(0.019)	(0.021)
Observations	20,299	20,299	20,299	16,266	20,299	20,299	20,299	16,266

Note: Columns (4) and (8) based on the balanced panel. All other estimations based on the unbalanced panel. Coefficients from separate estimations for each CSR variable. Coefficients from separate estimations for each CSR variable. Control variables: firm size, R&D, final goods, state firm, foreign firm, sector, location and year. Robust standard errors clustered at firm level in parentheses.

*p<0.10, **p<0.05, ***p<0.01.

Source: Author's compilation based on data obtained from the Vietnam Technology and Competitiveness Survey (CIEM, GSO, and DERG 2015).

Table 21.8 Revenue, profit and CSR by market

	Revenue (ln)				*Profit (ln)*			
	Same province (1)	*Same region (2)*	*Country (3)*	*Export (4)*	*Same province (5)*	*Same region (6)*	*Country (7)*	*Export (8)*
CSR all categories	0.023***	0.014	0.013**	0.006	0.003	0.053	0.048*	0.033**
	(0.006)	(0.011)	(0.005)	(0.004)	(0.021)	(0.041)	(0.027)	(0.015)
Compliance CSR	0.015	0.012	0.009	0.018*	0.030	0.041	–0.008	0.065
	(0.014)	(0.022)	(0.010)	(0.009)	(0.053)	(0.095)	(0.062)	(0.041)
Management CSR	0.073***	0.042	0.026*	0.019*	–0.038	0.047	0.109*	0.035
	(0.015)	(0.027)	(0.015)	(0.010)	(0.043)	(0.083)	(0.061)	(0.032)
Community CSR	0.012	0.005	0.014*	–0.002	0.014	0.080	0.070*	0.038
	(0.008)	(0.015)	(0.008)	(0.006)	(0.032)	(0.059)	(0.042)	(0.024)
Observations	4,701	1,846	4,408	6,088	4,701	1,846	4,408	6,088

Note: Fixed effects estimation on balanced panel. Coefficients from separate estimations for each CSR variable. Control variables: firm size, assets, R&D, final goods, state firm, foreign firm, sector, location and year. Robust standard errors clustered at firm level in parentheses.

*$p<0.10$,** $p<0.05$, ***$p<0.01$.

Source: Author's compilation based on data obtained from the Vietnam Technology and Competitiveness Survey (CIEM, GSO, and DERG 2015).

Table 21.9 Revenue, profit and CSR by firm location (North or South)

	Revenue (ln)		*Profit (ln)*	
	North *(1)*	*South* *(2)*	*North* *(3)*	*South* *(4)*
CSR all (lagged)	0.006	0.007*	–0.010	0.043*
	(0.005)	(0.004)	(0.020)	(0.022)
Compliance CSR (lagged)	0.002	0.015	0.073*	0.075
	(0.012)	(0.011)	(0.043)	(0.054)
Management CSR (lagged)	0.006	0.007	–0.042	0.024
	(0.012)	(0.007)	(0.053)	(0.047)
Community CSR (lagged)	0.009	0.007	–0.033	0.055*
	(0.007)	(0.006)	(0.030)	(0.030)
Observations	6,579	9,687	6,579	9,687

Note: All other estimations based on the balanced panel. Coefficients from separate estimations for each CSR variable. Control variables: firm size, assets, R&D, final goods, state firm, foreign firm, sector, location and year. Robust standard errors clustered at firm level in parentheses.

*p<0.10, **p<0.05, ***p<0.01.

Source: Author's compilation based on data obtained from the Vietnam Technology and Competitiveness Survey (CIEM, GSO, and DERG 2015).

corroborated in Table 21.8, which shows a positive effect of CSR for firms selling primarily in the domestic market. Table 21.7 further reveals a positive association between compliance CSR and next-period firm profit. There is, however, no clear pattern in terms of the location of a firm's main customers and profits (Tables 21.8 and 21.9).

In sum, we find no evidence that CSR activities are associated with declining revenue or profits. Correlations between CSR activities and financial performance are generally positive, and often statistically significant. The positive correlation is mostly driven by community CSR, i.e., by voluntary public goods production outside the firm. The results suggest that engagement in CSR activities is far from incompatible with commercial success, perhaps even the contrary is true. From a theoretical perspective, this indicates that CSR is driven by the social preferences of consumers and employees, more than it is driven by such preferences on the part of managers and owners. The implication is that owners and managers engage in CSR for strategic reasons.

Conclusion

This chapter has examined the relationship between CSR and firm performance, measured as revenue and profit, in a sample of manufacturing firms in Vietnam. We measured CSR by 16 indicators and constructed an overall aggregate index of CSR activities and three separate indices, for (1) the extent to which the firm complies with national labor regulations ("compliance CSR"), (2) the management commitment to acting beyond immediate regulatory requirements ("management CSR") and (3) the engagement in community-level activities outside direct firm operations ("community CSR").

We find that a sizeable share of firms report that they engage in voluntary CSR activities. Larger and more technologically sophisticated firms are more likely than others to engage in CSR. Final goods producers are more likely than intermediate goods producers to be involved in CSR activities. The number of CSR activities undertaken by firms is in general positively correlated with firm revenue and profits. This association is mostly driven by the effect of "community CSR."

Whether and to what extent these results generalize to other Asian countries is an issue for further research. As explained, the results presented here are generally in line with results from other studies on CSR and as such there is no reason to expect that Vietnam is an outlier.

The results show that there is significant scope for corporate social responsibility to play a role in promoting sustainable development. Many firms are already engaged in CSR activities and this behavior appears to be financially sustainable (i.e., not costly for firms). Our data do not allow us to investigate whether and to what extent CSR activities are socially beneficial, and this is an important topic for further research.[8] However, it seems reasonable to assume that they have at least some effect on, for example, working conditions, environmental quality and local infrastructure, all of which are important ingredients in recipes for sustainable development.

If so, our results contribute to justifying increased focus on stimulating CSR activities. While many companies do engage in voluntary CSR activities, most do not, even though our results suggest that such activities are not in general costly in terms of revenue and profits. Governments that seek to encourage CSR may consider policy initiatives, such as tax deductions for a part of CSR expenditures and information campaigns on how to deduct some of the CSR costs. This could presumably encourage firms in Vietnam and other countries to increase investments in CSR and thereby contribute to sustainable economic growth.

An important complement to CSR activities is free and independent media. If CSR activities are driven by strategic concerns on the part of managers and owners, as our results suggest, then it is crucial that workers and customers can hold managers and owners to account for (alleged) CSR initiatives. For example, it is difficult for consumers to observe how environment-friendly the activities of a given company are. This is an area where the media can play an important role in generating transparency.

Appendix

Table 21A.1 Determinants of CSR (OLS)

	Management CSR					*Compliance CSR*						*Community CSR*				
	CSR 1	*CSR 2*	*CSR 3*	*CSR 4*	*CSR 5*	*CSR 6*	*CSR 7*	*CSR 8*	*CSR 9*	*CSR 10*	*CSR 11*	*CSR 12*	*CSR 13*	*CSR 14*	*CSR 15*	*CSR 16*
Firm size (ln)	0.04***	0.03***	0.01***	0.02***	0.00	0.11***	0.06***	0.06***	0.02***	0.02***	0.01***	0.01***	0.01***	0.02***	0.00*	0.01***
	(0.00)	(0.00)	(0.00)	(0.00)	(0.00)	(0.00)	(0.00)	(0.00)	(0.00)	(0.00)	(0.00)	(0.00)	(0.00)	(0.00)	(0.00)	(0.00)
Assets (ln)	0.04***	0.02***	0.01***	0.02***	0.00**	0.05***	0.06***	0.06***	0.01***	0.01***	0.00	0.00**	0.00**	0.01***	0.00	0.01***
	(0.00)	(0.00)	(0.00)	(0.00)	(0.00)	(0.00)	(0.00)	(0.00)	(0.00)	(0.00)	(0.00)	(0.00)	(0.00)	(0.00)	(0.00)	(0.00)
R&D	0.17***	0.09***	0.05***	0.10***	–0.00	0.12***	0.07***	0.06***	0.07***	0.07***	0.05***	0.05***	0.04***	0.09***	0.03***	0.05***
	(0.01)	(0.01)	(0.01)	(0.01)	(0.00)	(0.01)	(0.01)	(0.01)	(0.01)	(0.01)	(0.01)	(0.01)	(0.01)	(0.01)	(0.01)	(0.01)
Final goods	0.05***	–0.01	–0.00	0.00	–0.00	0.02**	0.04***	0.03***	0.01	0.01**	0.00	0.01**	0.00	0.01**	0.00	0.00
	(0.01)	(0.01)	(0.00)	(0.01)	(0.00)	(0.01)	(0.01)	(0.01)	(0.01)	(0.00)	(0.00)	(0.00)	(0.00)	(0.01)	(0.00)	(0.00)
State firm	0.06***	0.03**	0.02	0.02	–0.01	0.17***	0.03**	0.03***	–0.01	0.03*	0.01	0.03**	0.04***	0.05**	0.00	0.04**
	(0.02)	(0.02)	(0.01)	(0.02)	(0.01)	(0.02)	(0.01)	(0.01)	(0.02)	(0.02)	(0.01)	(0.01)	(0.01)	(0.02)	(0.01)	(0.02)
Foreign firm	0.03**	0.02**	–0.00	0.02**	–0.01**	0.12***	0.06***	0.06***	–0.08***	–0.04***	–0.04***	–0.02***	–0.03***	–0.15***	–0.02***	–0.03***
	(0.01)	(0.01)	(0.00)	(0.01)	(0.00)	(0.01)	(0.01)	(0.01)	(0.01)	(0.01)	(0.01)	(0.01)	(0.00)	(0.01)	(0.00)	(0.01)
Constant	–0.13***	0.51***	–0.08***	–0.13***	0.92***	–0.34***	–0.01	0.01	0.07**	–0.11***	0.02	–0.03**	–0.04***	0.11***	–0.02*	–0.11***
	(0.04)	(0.03)	(0.01)	(0.02)	(0.01)	(0.03)	(0.03)	(0.03)	(0.03)	(0.02)	(0.02)	(0.01)	(0.01)	(0.03)	(0.01)	(0.02)
Obs.	29,244	29,244	29,244	29,244	29,244	29,244	29,244	29,244	29,244	29,244	29,244	29,244	29,244	29,244	29,244	29,244
R^2	0.118	0.071	0.046	0.098	0.127	0.395	0.344	0.345	0.130	0.064	0.054	0.044	0.041	0.119	0.042	0.045

Note: All estimations include province and sector controls. Robust standard errors clustered at firm level in parentheses.

*p < 0.10, **p < 0.05, ***p < 0.01.

Source: Author's compilation based on data obtained from the Vietnam Technology and Competitiveness Survey (CIEM, GSO, and DERG 2015).

Table 21A.2 Determinants of CSR (FE, balanced)

	Management CSR					*Compliance CSR*						*Community CSR*				
	CSR 1	*CSR 2*	*CSR 3*	*CSR 4*	*CSR 5*	*CSR 6*	*CSR 7*	*CSR 8*	*CSR 9*	*CSR 10*	*CSR 11*	*CSR 12*	*CSR 13*	*CSR 14*	*CSR 15*	*CSR 16*
Firm size (ln)	0.01	0.02**	0.00	–0.00	0.01*	0.03***	0.01*	0.02**	0.01	0.01	0.00	0.01**	0.01***	0.01	–0.00	0.01
	(0.01)	(0.01)	(0.00)	(0.00)	(0.00)	(0.01)	(0.01)	(0.01)	(0.01)	(0.00)	(0.01)	(0.00)	(0.00)	(0.01)	(0.00)	(0.00)
Assets (ln)	–0.00	–0.01	–0.00	0.01	0.00	–0.01	0.01	0.01	0.01	0.01	0.00	–0.00	–0.00	0.01	0.00	0.00
	(0.01)	(0.01)	(0.00)	(0.01)	(0.00)	(0.01)	(0.01)	(0.01)	(0.01)	(0.01)	(0.01)	(0.01)	(0.00)	(0.01)	(0.00)	(0.00)
R&D	0.06***	0.04***	0.02**	0.07***	0.00	0.04***	0.02**	0.00	0.02	0.03***	0.01	0.02**	0.00	0.03**	0.02**	0.02
	(0.01)	(0.01)	(0.01)	(0.01)	(0.01)	(0.01)	(0.01)	(0.01)	(0.02)	(0.01)	(0.01)	(0.01)	(0.01)	(0.01)	(0.01)	(0.01)
Final goods	0.04***	–0.01	0.00	0.01	0.00	0.01	–0.00	–0.01	0.01	0.01	–0.01	0.00	0.00	–0.00	–0.00	–0.01
	(0.01)	(0.01)	(0.00)	(0.01)	(0.01)	(0.01)	(0.01)	(0.01)	(0.01)	(0.01)	(0.01)	(0.01)	(0.00)	(0.01)	(0.00)	(0.01)
State firm	0.06	0.03	0.04	0.09*	0.03	0.05**	0.03*	0.04	0.03	–0.02	–0.00	–0.03	–0.01	–0.02	0.00	0.02
	(0.06)	(0.04)	(0.03)	(0.05)	(0.03)	(0.02)	(0.02)	(0.02)	(0.06)	(0.04)	(0.03)	(0.02)	(0.04)	(0.06)	(0.02)	(0.03)
Foreign firm	0.07	–0.02	0.01	–0.01	0.01	0.01	–0.01	–0.03	–0.01	0.05	0.02	0.06	–0.01	0.00	0.00	0.03
	(0.06)	(0.04)	(0.01)	(0.07)	(0.03)	(0.04)	(0.03)	(0.04)	(0.06)	(0.05)	(0.03)	(0.04)	(0.02)	(0.04)	(0.02)	(0.03)
Constant	0.57***	0.70***	0.01	0.03	0.89***	0.48***	0.83***	0.83***	0.04	–0.06	0.05	0.03	–0.06	0.19*	–0.01	–0.01
	(0.17)	(0.18)	(0.04)	(0.12)	(0.06)	(0.13)	(0.16)	(0.15)	(0.15)	(0.07)	(0.07)	(0.06)	(0.05)	(0.10)	(0.04)	(0.06)
Observations	21,688	21,688	21,688	21,688	21,688	21,688	21,688	21,688	21,688	21,688	21,688	21,688	21,688	21,688	21,688	21,688
R^2	0.038	0.004	0.005	0.007	0.022	0.023	0.014	0.013	0.003	0.003	0.002	0.002	0.003	0.004	0.002	0.002

Note: All estimations include province and sector controls. Robust standard errors clustered at firm level in parentheses.

*p < 0.10, **p < 0.05, ***p < 0.01.

Source: Author's compilation based on data obtained from the Vietnam Technology and Competitiveness Survey (CIEM, GSO, and DERG 2015).

Notes

1 Many authors have offered definitions and characterizations of CSR. The OECD describes CSR as "business's contribution to sustainable development" (OECD 2001). Carroll (1979) treats social responsibility as a four-part concept comprising legal, economic, ethical and philanthropic responsibilities of companies. The UN Global Compact has set the foundation of core CSR values in its ten principles for ensuring responsible supply chain management through practices such as respecting basic labor rights and working against corruption. Immediately after, the CSR Compass expressed a view of CSR as a set of voluntary initiatives for businesses to integrate social and environmental considerations into their operations and stakeholder relationships (CSR Compass 2010). International Organization for Standardization (ISO) has developed ISO 26000, an international standard for social responsibility, which helps organizations to address social responsibilities that are relevant to their operations (ISO 2010). We integrate these different views in the analysis of CSR practices among the Vietnamese manufacturing firms.
2 We add social responsibility to the concept of environmental sustainability and economic success proposed by Schaltegger and Synnestvedt (2002).
3 Balanced panel includes only firms that appear in all four survey rounds.
4 According to the Trade Union Law of 1994 enterprises are obligated to establish a local trade union if the firm employs 10 or more workers. In practice local trade unions are established under the auspices of the Vietnam Confederation of Labour, which is overseen by the Communist Party.
5 Sectors are identified at two-digit level according to Vietnam Standard Industrial Classification from 2007. Around 3 percent of firms from the sample change the main sector in the considered four-year period. We do not report the statistics, but they are available from authors upon request.
6 We do not have access to detailed information about changes in regulations at the sector level.
7 An instrumental variables approach could potentially be pursued in order to determine direction of causality with more certainty, but a valid instrument for CSR activities is unfortunately not available.
8 cf. Kitzmueller and Shimshack (2012).

References

Bagnoli, M. and Watts, S.G. (2003) "Selling to Socially Responsible Consumers: Competition and the Private Provision of Public Goods," *Journal of Economics & Management Strategy*. 12(3), 419–445
Canon (2014) "Corporate Social Responsibility." Canon. Available at: www.canon.com.vn/business/web/company/about/csr?languageCode=EN (Accessed: October 27, 2016).
Cargill (2016) "Building schools in rural Vietnam." Cargill. Available at: www.cargill.com/150/en/VIETNAM-SCHOOLS.jsp (Accessed October 27, 2016).
Carroll, A.B. (1979) "A Three-Dimensional Conceptual Model of Corporate Social Performance," *Academy of Management Review*. 4 (4), 497–505.
Chapple, W. and Moon, J. (2007) "CSR Agendas for Asia," *Corporate Social Responsibility and Environmental Management*. 14 (4), 183–188.
Charness, G. and Rabin, M. (2002) "Understanding Social Preferences with Simple Tests," *Quarterly Journal of Economics*. 117(3): 817–869.
CIEM, GSO and DERG. (2015) Firm-level Technology and Competitiveness in Vietnam: Evidence from 2010–2014 Surveys. Hanoi: Central Institute of Economic Management (CIEM). Available at: www.ciem.org.vn/en/hoptacquocte/duanciem/tabid/303/articletype/ArticleView/articleld/1508/default.aspx (Accessed June 18, 2015).
Crifo, P. and Forget, V.D. (2015) "The Economics of Corporate Social Responsibility: A Firm-Level Perspective Survey," *Journal of Economic Surveys*. 29 (1), 112–130.
CSR Compass (2010) "CSR Compass Guidelines." CSR Compass. Available at: www.csrcompass.com/guidelines (Accessed: June 23, 2016).
Delmas, M.A. and Pekovic, S. (2013) "Environmental Standards and Labor Productivity: Understanding the Mechanisms that Sustain Sustainability," *Journal of Organizational Behavior*. 34 (2), 230–252.
Earnhart, D.H., Khanna, M. and Lyon, T.P. (2014) "Corporate Environmental Strategies in Emerging Economies," *Review of Environmental Economics and Policy*. 8 (2), 164–185.
Fair Labor Association (2015) "Promoting Sustainable Compliance in Vietnam." Fair Labor Association. Available at: www.fairlabor.org/our-work/special-projects/project/promoting-sustainable-corporate-social-responsibility-vietnam (Accessed September 24, 2016).

Fehr, E. and Schmidt, K. (1999) "A Theory of Fairness, Competition, and Cooperation," *Quarterly Journal of Economics*. 104 (3): 817–868.

GCNV (2010) "A review of the social and environmental conditions of industries in Vietnam against the Global Compact Principles." Available at: www.globalcompactvietnam.org/detail.asp?id=83 (Accessed October 27, 2016).

Grossman, G.M. and Krueger, A. (1995). "Economic Growth and the Environment," *The Quarterly Journal of Economics*. 110(2), 353–377.

Hamilton, J.T. (1995) "Pollution as News: Media and Stock Market Reactions to the Toxics Release Inventory Data," *Journal of Environmental Economics and Management*. 28 (1), 98–113.

Hamm, B. (2012) "Corporate Social Responsibility in Vietnam: Integration or Mere Adaptation?" *Pacific News*. (38), 4–8.

Hettige, H., Huq, M., Pargal, S. and Wheeler, D. (1996) "Determinants of Pollution Abatement in Developing Countries: Evidence from South and Southeast Asia," *World Development*. 24 (12), 1891–1904.

ILO and IFC (2015) *Better Work Vietnam: Garment Industry 8th Compliance Synthesis Report*. International Labour Organization (ILO) and International Finance Corporation (IFC). Available at: http://better-work.org/vietnam/?p=3882 (Accessed October 27, 2016).

ISO (2010) *ISO 26000 – Social Responsibility*. 2010. International Organization for Standardization (ISO). Available at: www.iso.org/iso/home/standards/iso26000.htm (Accessed: June 23, 2016).

Jeppesen, S., Kothuis, B. and Ngoc Tran, A. (2012) *Corporate Social Responsibility and Competitiveness for SMEs in Developing Countries*. Focales 16. Paris: Agence Française de Développement.

Kitzmueller, M. and Shimshack, J. (2012) "Economic Perspectives on Corporate Social Responsibility," *Journal of Economic Literature*. 50 (1), 51–84.

Kolk, A., Hong, P. and van Dolen, W. (2010) "Corporate Social Responsibility in China: An Analysis of Domestic and Foreign Retailers' Sustainability Dimensions," *Business Strategy and the Environment*. 19 (5), 289–303.

Lee, S. and Torm, N. (2015) "Social Security and Firm Performance: The Case of Vietnamese SMEs." *International Labour Review*. 156 (2), 185–212.

Levine, D.I. and Toffel, M.W. (2010) "Quality Management and Job Quality: How the ISO 9001 Standard for Quality Management Systems Affects Employees and Employers," *Management Science*. 56 (6), 978–996.

Liu, Y. (2009) "Investigating External Environmental Pressure on Firms and their Behavior in Yangtze River Delta of China," *Journal of Cleaner Production*. 17 (16), 1480–1486.

Margolis, J.D., Elfenbein, H.A. and Walsh, J.P. (2009) "Does it Pay to Be Good … And Does it Matter? *A Meta-Analysis of the Relationship between Corporate Social and Financial Performance*." Available at: http://ssrn.com/abstract=1866371 (Accessed: June 3, 2016).

McWilliams, A. and Siegel, D. (2001) "Corporate Social Responsibility: A Theory of the Firm Perspective," *The Academy of Management Review*. 26 (1), 117–127.

Murphy, P.R. and Poist, R.F. (2002) "Socially Responsible Logistics: An Exploratory Study," *Transportation Journal*. 41 (4), 23–35.

Newman, C., Rand, J., Tarp, F. and Trifkovic, N. (2016) "The Transmission of Socially Responsible Behaviour Through International Trade." UNU-WIDER Working Paper 68/2016. Helsinki: UNU-WIDER.

Newman, C., Rand, J., Tarp, F. and Trifkovic, N. (2018) "Corporate Social Responsibility in a Competitive Business Environment." UNU-WIDER Working Paper 7/2016. Helsinki: UNU-WIDER.

Nguyen, B.T., Albrecht, J.W., Vroman, S.B. and Westbrook, M.D. (2007) "A Quantile Regression Decomposition of Urban–Rural Inequality in Vietnam," *Journal of Development Economics*. 83 (2), 466–490.

Ockenfels, A. and Weimann, J. (1999) "Types and Patterns: An Experimental East–West-German Comparison of Cooperation and Solidarity," *Journal of Public Economics*. 71 (2), 175–287.

OECD (2001) *Corporate Social Responsibility: Partners for Progress*. Paris: Organisation for Economic Co-operation and Development.

Padgett, R.C. and Galan, J.I. (2009) "The Effect of R&D Intensity on Corporate Social Responsibility," *Journal of Business Ethics*. 93 (3), 407–418.

Panasonic (2015) "Sustainability Initiatives – About Us – Panasonic Vietnam." Panasonic. Available at: www.panasonic.com/vn/en/corporate/sustainability.html (Accessed October 27, 2016).

Pargal, S. and Wheeler, D. (1996) "Informal Regulation of Industrial Pollution in Developing Countries: Evidence from Indonesia." *Journal of Political Economy*. 104 (6), 1314–1327.

Schaltegger, S. and Synnestvedt, T. (2002) "The Link between 'Green' and Economic Success: Environmental Management as the Crucial Trigger between Environmental and Economic Performance," *Journal of Environmental Management*. 65 (4), 339–346.

Siegel, D.S. and Vitaliano, D.F. (2007) "An Empirical Analysis of the Strategic Use of Corporate Social Responsibility." *Journal of Economics & Management Strategy*. 16 (3), 773–792.

Thorpe, J. and Prakash-Mani, K. (2003) "Developing Value: The Business Case for Sustainability in Emerging Markets," *Greener Management International*. (44), 17–32.

Toyota (2010) "Go Green Program." Toyota. Available at: www.toyotavn.com.vn/en/social-contribution/environment/go-green-program (Accessed October 27, 2016).

UNGC (2015) *Viet Nam UN Global Compact*. United Nations Global Compact. Available at: www.unglobalcompact.org/engage-locally/asia/viet%20nam (Accessed: June 3, 2016).

UNIDO (2011) *Baseline Survey Report 2010: Awareness, Understanding and Usage of Social Corporate Responsibility (CSR) among Vietnam's Small and Medium Enterprises*. Vienna: United Nations Industrial Development Organization.

UNIDO (2013) *End of Action Survey 2013 Helping Vietnamese SMEs to Adapt and Adopt CSR for Improved Linkages in Global Supply Chains in Sustainable Production*. Vienna: United Nations Industrial Development Organization.

VBN (2016a) "ACE Life Funds School Building in Central Vietnam." Viet Nam Breaking News. Available at: www.vietnambreakingnews.com/2016/10/ace-life-funds-school-building-in-central-vietnam (Accessed October 27, 2016).

VBN (2016b) "Samsung Staff with Community." Viet Nam Breaking News. Available at: www.vietnambreakingnews.com/2016/10/samsung-staff-with-community (Accessed October 27, 2016).

VBN (2016c). "GM Vietnam Donated Vehicles, Engines and Transmissions to Support Automotive Education." Viet Nam Breaking News. Available at: www.vietnambreakingnews.com/2016/06/gm-vietnam-donated-vehicles-engines-and-transmissions-to-support-automotive-education (Accessed October 27, 2016).

22

Sustainable development initiatives at the local government level in Malaysia

Ashiru Bello and Ainul Jaria Maidin

Introduction

Rapid economic growth to meet the needs of society usually leads to extensive land development, exploitation of natural resources and urbanization that naturally lead to a multiplicity of environmental problems. Land use planning and development control have been identified as essential tools in the prevention of many environmental problems, sustainable management of natural resources, and management of the urban environment. Strengthening the integration of environmental considerations in development planning is likely to have a considerable impact over time as development is controlled and directed in ways that are environmentally neutral or at least minimize negative impacts.

Malaysia supports initiatives that seek to achieve sustainable development. As part of this strategy, the Malaysian government promotes the incorporation of environmental protection measures into all the various national development plans. Sustainable development has contributed immensely to the array of issues considered in the efforts to balance individual interest and common good. This is one of the focal points of Malaysia's planning system and also concords with international concerns. The argument that there is a firm adoption of sustainable development tenets in planning systems, as compared to other areas, does not guarantee the occurrence of a systematic transformation of the planning agenda itself. A number of cases, particularly regarding spatial development and environmental conservation (such as in Maruani, 2011), suggests that the planning system is still dominated by the desire for development, which in a way contradicts the modest focus of sustainability. In order to develop a viable approach to environmental conservation and shape the spatial pattern of development at the local level, several strategies have been adopted in Malaysia. This chapter sets out the initiatives taken at the state and local government level in Malaysia, guided by the federal government policies adopted at the state and local authorities, where they are entrusted with the task to plan and manage land use planning and development control processes for promoting sustainable development.

Necessity for promoting environmental protection

Global warming and climate change are worsening and can cause adverse impacts on the capacity of man to carry on his livelihood universally. Sustainable development is a concept that is derived from the Brundtland Report of 1987, when the nations around the world gathered to identify the root causes of environmental degradation and the methods for balancing the developmental needs. In its process of conceptual evolution, sustainable development has broadened its focus to cover issues of environmental protection alongside social and economic development. Sustainable development is the phrase used to refer to the various processes involved in balancing the exploitation of the non-renewable resources necessary for the future generation to sustain human livelihoods on earth for many generations to come. It is often summarized as a process that ensures enough resources for all and forever. This is of course without undermining the integrity and stability of the natural ecosystem. The concept of sustainable development has now evolved to include the incorporation of principles of resilience and disaster management.

Tracing back to the factors giving rise to desperate poverty and weak or non-existent social safety nets in Europe and the United States during the Great Depression period, it has been shown that the policies developed in these countries were not driven by the needs of the majority population but by the affluent few (Harris, 2000). It should be asserted that positive changes in development and governance patterns are actually difficult to realize, owing to the prioritization of the demand of the majority for progress and development. Efforts of a committed minority are usually very significant in producing open and transparent governance systems. In several societies however, the lay majority often lacks support, and their voices are usually dismissed.

The conflict between environment and development goals which still exist today has provided the principal basis for the evolution of the traditional concept of sustainable development, and gave rise to the 1987 definition of the term by the World Commission on Environment and Development as "development which meets the needs of the present without compromising the ability of future generations to meet their own needs" (Brundtland, 1987, p. 44). The three components or dimensions of sustainable development – the economic, social and environmental dimension – were thus recognized. However, efforts to balance the three components or dimensions have made the simple definition of sustainable development to be very complex. Questions at this juncture are, do we consider the three dimensions as separate but related entities; or, do we view the environment as the host for the two other components of social and economic; or is there one dimension contained within the others, from economic, social to the environment? (See Figure 22.1 for a description of these varying relationships.)

According to Bell and Cheung (2009), the first scenario in the diagram (first from the left) signifies the traditional view of sustainable development which is focused on environmental management. The second diagram depicts the present dynamics while the last diagram is said to present the idealistic perspective of sustainable development where the economy, society and

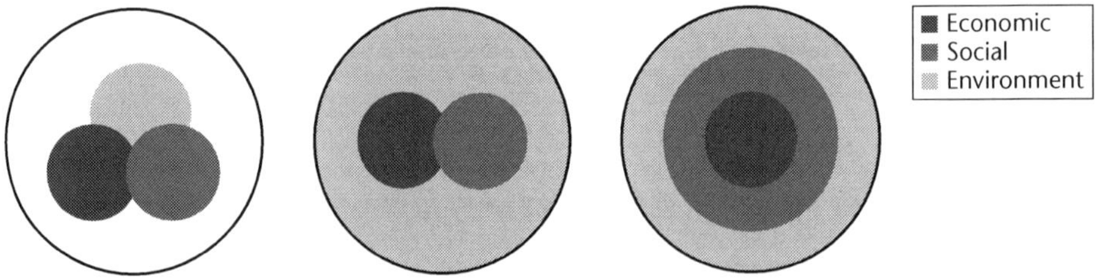

Figure 22.1 Dimensions of relationships between the three components of sustainable development

Source: Adapted from Bell and Cheung (2009).

environment are given independent existence with interaction. Harris (2000, p. 6) is concerned and wondered:

> ... what if provision of adequate food and water supplies appears to require changes in land use which will decrease biodiversity? What if non-polluting energy sources are more expensive, thus increasing the burden on the poor, for whom they represent a larger proportion of daily expenditure? Which goal will take precedence?

Harris suggested that the conflict between development and environment can never be resolved as the balance can never be achieved when the needs of the people for development are imminent and unavoidable. Form the economic perspective, the production and consumption aspects are related to the environment in two ways. First, the renewable and non-renewable resources are taken from the environment for the production of goods and services, and second, waste is emitted into the environment in the production and consumption processes. This is a vicious cycle that cannot be stopped so long as mankind exists.

Men fail to appreciate the importance of preserving the environment, as they often detach themselves from nature despite the fact that they are created as part of nature. Men are under the fallacy that they are above natural resources, and are thus entitled to exploit and manage the resources. Men fail to realize the need to preserve resources for the benefit of future generations, whose prosperity will be threatened without them. The need to preserve the environmental resources and protect them from over-extraction and waste is therefore obvious.

Governments of the countries around the world have come together year after year to promote the importance of sustainable development to ensure the global wellbeing. The role of the local government is undeniably important, as this is the level where policies and laws are implemented to promote sustainable development.

Local governance

World Bank (1992, p. 1) defined governance as "the manner in which power is exercised in the management of a country's economic and social resources for development." According to Bello and Dola (2014, p. 270), governance "traditionally connotes the act or process of governing" in which several contemporary theories attempt to incorporate into it, the "notion of providing balance between the (economically) rational human trait and that of irrationality (which has the potential to promote sustainability)." In recent times, the connotation of governance has been expanded to involve variety of instruments designed to alter and channel the behavior of individual and collective actors (Kardos 2012; Loorbach, 2007; Pierre and Peters, 2000; Adger and Jordan, 2009). Adapting the World Bank's definition, local governance is concerned with the "manner in which power is exercised in the management of economic and social resources for development" in a local context, a context that is usually lower in terms of administrative hierarchy than a state or region.

The governance structure in East Asia for example, varies significantly by nations. While Indonesia, Malaysia and Vietnam exhibit a three tier system (national, state and local), China (in spite of the constitutional provisions for the three tiers) at present exhibits up to five local governance levels. They include the provincial, prefecture, county, township and village levels. The province may be a municipality, autonomous or a special administrative region. The Philippines has provinces and independent cities; component cities and municipalities; as well as barangays. Thailand adopted a four tier system. In contrast, Cambodia exhibits a structure with two levels operating in two parallel systems (provinces and municipalities). The East Asian experience in local governance generally is largely surrounded by struggles for sharing of economic and political power

Table 22.1 Comparison of local expenditure between East Asia and other large countries

Countries	*% of national expenditure at the lower tier of government*
China	50
Indonesia	28
Philippines	14
Thailand	5
Vietnam	15
Other large countries:	
Australia	6
New Zealand	9
North America	17.8

Source: Blane and Bob (2010).

and authority between the local governments on one hand and the other tiers (state and national or federal) on the other. As we shall see later in the discourse, Malaysia is not an exception.

According to White and Smoke (2005), the responsibilities of local governments are not clear in many of the East Asian countries. This is usually reflected in the overlap of functions and responsibilities between the local governments and other tiers (federal and state) that are usually more powerful constitutionally. Where mayors are appointed by the state or national government rather than being elected, as is the case with Malaysian major cities, the autonomy of such local authorities is greatly compromised. In some cases, where responsibilities are clear, the corresponding resources and authority are either absent or poorly matched with the assignments. As such, the local governments cannot be held accountable for nonperformance, thereby making the evolution of institutions for managing expenditures focused on effective and responsive service delivery unlikely. Table 22.1 sets out the comparative subnational spending of some East Asian countries with the larger economies.

Considering the status of local governments as being the closest tiers to the public, the role they can play in the realization of sustainable development goals is increasingly being recognized. This is reflected equally in the quest of cities to become resilient by equipping their residents with the capacity to live with their unavoidable challenges.

Urban resilience in the context of sustainable development

Cities' resilience is measured as a function of the degree to which they are able to adapt and continue to cope with different shocks and stresses. Being resilient does not mean sailing in an ocean with no waves. Rather, it connotes a situation whereby a city sails in a ship that no waves can sink. Urban resilience has four essential dimensions, including Health and Wellbeing; Economy and Society; Infrastructure and Environment; and Leadership Strategy. As a subset of sustainable development, urban resilience has become a common slogan across local authorities and municipalities in Malaysia. As we shall see in the sections that follow, some of the local governance initiatives in Malaysia during the last two to three years lists urban resilience as one of the principal targets. The objectives of urban resilience as targeted by a number of municipalities and even national and municipal programs in Malaysia are listed below:

1 Minimization of human vulnerability
2 Diversification of livelihood and employment

3 Safeguarding human health
4 Optimization of financial resources
5 Reduction of physical exposure
6 Achieving collective mutual support
7 Attainment of social stability and security
8 Continuity of social services
9 Fostering reliable communications
10 Effective leadership
11 Empowered stakeholders, and
12 Integrated development planning.

Local governance in Malaysia: reflecting the tenets of sustainable development

This part discusses the system of local governance and how sustainable development indicators are addressed at all levels, from policies, legal framework and institutional arrangements, and various other related initiatives.

Local government structure in Malaysia

Malaysia has adopted a three tier system, including the federal government, the state governments, and the local governments. Local governments, despite being placed at the lowest level of the administration, handle most administration of the land use planning and development activities. With the exception of local governments in the Federal Territories, the Malaysian constitution placed local governments under the umbrella of their respective states. At the federal level, the Ministry of Housing and Local Government provides a coordinating role and promotes uniformity in the practice of local governance across the country. Paragraphs 4 and 5 of the Federal Constitution of Malaysia vested the responsibility of local governance under the jurisdiction of the state governments.

Rural district councils and urban councils are the two main divisions of local governments and perform the same functions. The urban councils are further classified into municipalities and city councils. Municipalities can be upgraded to cities once they satisfy the required criteria. There are 12 city councils, 39 municipal councils and 109 district councils. However, cities are led by mayors, while municipalities and districts are led by presidents. Constitutionally, mayors, presidents, and councilors are appointed by the state governments. State government elections are conducted every five years, while local council's appointments last for three years. Councilors and mayors may, however, be reappointed. This is practiced uniformly across Malaysia.

A committee structure that is usually determined by the local authority is responsible for the decision making process. At the city councils, the executive powers lie with the mayor, while at the municipal and district councils, the power lies with the president. Respective state governments are responsible for the appointment of local executives on either a full- or a part-time basis and also decide on their remuneration. Although local councils are empowered to form some committees on general and specific matters, executive committees which are usually presided over by mayors, or presidents are established by the state governments. As is a common characteristic of the national–subnational government relationship in other East Asian countries, the federal government in Malaysia exercises considerable power and influence over the local governments (Nooi, 2008). Concentration of power at the central government level, according to Nooi (2008), suggests that the local governments in Malaysia accounts for only 1 percent of its GDP.

The 1976 report by Royal Commission of Inquiry in Malaysia outlined the following factors as the key characteristics of local governments:

i They represent the third and lower level of governance.
ii They are administered and have their councilors or mayors appointed by the state.
iii They constitute a geographical portion of the country.
iv They possess partial sovereignty.
v They have limited powers in terms of financial and administration issues – largely governed by the state.
vi They are legal administrative entities different from other tiers of government.
vii They are empowered to sue and be sued.
viii They are obliged to provide goods and services and sometimes do so at their discretion.

In addition to general maintenance of urban infrastructure, local governments in Malaysia are charged with the responsibility for public health and management of waste and sanitation, as well as environmental protection, town planning and local socio-economic development. Table 22.2 summarizes the different categories of local governments in Malaysia.

We now examine the role of the institutions and agencies involved in promoting the achievement of sustainable development at the local government level.

Institutional framework

The institutions involved as key drivers of sustainable development are primarily the Ministry of Urban Well-being, Housing and Local Government, the Federal Department of Town and Country Planning (FDTCP), the Ministry of Energy, Green Technology and Water (KeTTHA) as well as the respective City Halls and local authorities. In addition to such areas statutorily granted city status by law, other densely populated and urbanized areas are often referred to as cities, even though they do not officially have city status. In any case, however, status of a city is granted to places within local government areas. Other populated areas than those with city status are usually classified as municipalities or towns. Professional institutions such as the Malaysian Institute of Planners, Malaysian Institute of Architects, Real Estate and Housing Developer's Association (REHDA), and others also assume an important role in promoting sustainable development.

Table 22.2 Categories of local governments in Malaysia

CATEGORY	*NUMBER*	*EXAMPLE*
City Halls	12	Kuala Lumpur City Hall Johor Bahru City Council George Town Petaling Jaya Kuala Trengganu
Municipal Councils	39	
District Councils for Rural Areas	109	Cameron Highland, Semporna
Special or Modified LGs	5	Putrajaya, Kulim Hi-Tech Park

Source: FDTCP (2005); Bello and Dola (2014).

Land use planning and development control regime

Rapid economic growth to meet the needs of society usually leads to extensive land development, exploitation of natural resources and urbanization that naturally lead to a multiplicity of environmental problems. Land use planning and development control have been identified as essential tools in the prevention of many environmental problems, sustainable management of natural resources and management of the urban environment. Strengthening the integration of environmental considerations in development planning is likely to have a considerable impact over time, as development is controlled and directed in ways that are environmentally neutral or at least minimize negative impacts. Malaysia supports initiatives that seek to achieve sustainable development. As part of this strategy, the Malaysian government promotes the incorporation of environmental protection measures into all the various national development plans. In consonance with international concerns, the Malaysian government has included sustainable development issues in the wide range of thematic areas of national interest. The issues of environmental conservation and resilience have been integrated into national development strategies to address the various concerns of sustainability in development.

Development policies for balancing land development and environmental protection

Malaysia faces an issue often encountered in federal systems of government. Regarding land use, local governance, town and country planning, as well as management of natural resources, state governments are given substantial powers by the Malaysian constitution. This is clearly outlined in Article 74 of the constitution concerning the jurisdictional powers of state authorities. Under this constitutional provision, the constitution has vested enormous powers on the state legislative assemblies to enact laws on items in the state list. However, uniformity is lacking on various state laws related to soil water or forestry development and conservation. There are little or no incentives for state governments to allow the federal government to control forest and mineral resources even when such needs arise. This also undermines the potential of the federal government to set uniform standards for conservation across the states. Even where the federal parliament is allowed to legislate on regulations for environmental issues regarding forest, wildlife and development of offshore hydrocarbon, the powers are subject to clear restrictions applied by the constitutional powers within states' jurisdiction. Environmental planning and management have been rendered cumbersome as a result of the power sharing pattern between the states and national government. The central governments' ability to implement such policies on environmental protection is dependent to some extent upon the nature of its relationship with the host state.

The federal government, realizing the importance of promoting environmental protection, incorporated into the Malaysian National Development Plans, policies for promoting environmental management since the Third Malaysia Plan. This plan sets out the need to balance the goals of socio-economic development with environmental protection, with a special focus on land development.[1] A National Policy on Environmental Protection was only formulated in 2002, with the objectives of achieving (a) safe and healthy environment for present and future generations; (b) conserved natural and cultural heritage of the country with active societal engagement; and a (c) pattern of lifestyle, production and consumption that is sustainable. The three elements of sustainable development (economic, socio-cultural development and environmental conservation) are integrated by the National Policy on Environment. The objectives of the policy include sustained socio-cultural and economic progress as well as enhancement of citizens' quality of life. These objectives are supposed to be achieved through sustainable development that is environmentally sound. The eight interrelated principles based on which economic development is harmonized with environmental concerns in pursuance of the policy's objectives are listed below.

1 Environmental stewardship
2 Conservation of eco-system diversity
3 Improving environmental quality
4 Sustainable resource use
5 Integrated decision making
6 Private sector participation
7 Commitment and accountability
8 Active participation in the international community.

The National Development Policy, Vision 2020, Five-yearly Development Plans, National Urbanization Policy formulated in 2006 and the National Environmental Policy have become the cornerstone for national development planning laying the policy directions for implementation of environmental protection measures in land development activities. These plans have embodied in them certain objectives of environmental policies which are supported by various international concerns reflected in international agreements and soft law instruments, such as the Brundtland Report in 1987, the United Nations General Assembly Resolution 44/228 and the Rio Declaration.

The National Urbanization Policy provides for the creation of cities with a vision which supports harmonious communities and living conditions, and aspects relating to disaster risk reduction and climate change to ensure urban development is carried out within the limited and permissible capacity.

In addition, to all the policy initiatives, the Federal Town and Country Planning Department introduced the Integrated Resource Planning and Management (IRPM) system, which is ideally aimed at assessing (at the planning stage) the potential environmental impacts of proposed land use projects; Strategic Environmental Assessments (SEA) that are required to be conducted during the policy formulation stage. Information and relevance of SEA is incorporated in the Ninth Malaysia Plan (2006–2010, p. 453), where it provides that:

> [E]nvironmental planning tools such as environmental impact assessments (EIA), strategic environmental assessments (SEA), analysis of costs and benefits, environmental and instruments auditing that is market based shall all be adopted in the evaluation of potential impacts of development activities and also mitigating them.

Figure 22.2 illustrates the interaction between various policies, development plans that makes up the National Development Planning Framework, and the authorities responsible to implement these policies.

The Federal Department of Town and Country Planning also formulated various Physical Planning Guidelines to provide guidance for the local planning authorities in implementing the policy directions for environmental protection set out in the National Physical Plan. The local planning authorities have been using the guidelines where requests for development permits on coasts and other ecologically sensitive areas such as retention ponds are processed. This notwithstanding, encroachments are now observable on such delicate areas as forest reserves and headwaters of major watersheds. This causes periodic scarcity of water, incessant flash floods, and landslides. Weak implementation of the physical development plans at the national and state level has resulted in unplanned development of the urban fringes. This has actually compelled the introduction of a much more coordinated and comprehensive strategy to manage land use planning particularly at local levels.

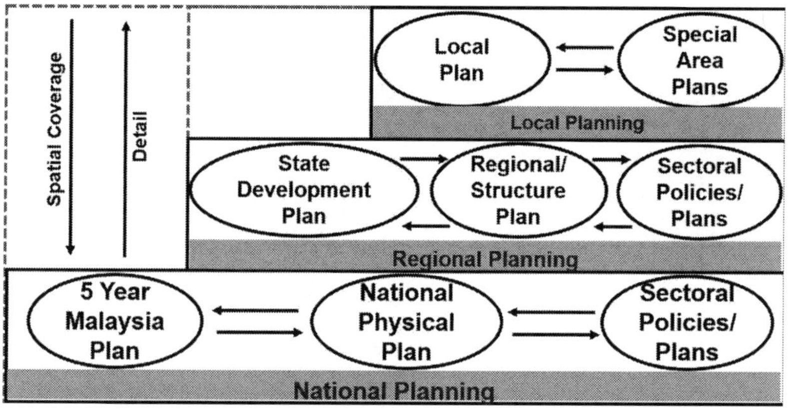

Figure 22.2 National Development Planning Framework and responsible authorities

Source: Federal Department of Town and Country Planning.

The fourth thrust of the tenth Malaysia Plan (2011–2015) is thus concerned with "improving the standard and sustainability of quality of life." Chapters 3 and 6 of the thrust outlined the objectives as, ensuring effective sourcing and delivery of energy, as well as developing a climate resilient growth strategy respectively. The eleventh Malaysia Plan (2016–2020) on the other hand, has as its theme 'Anchoring Growth on People.' This reflects Malaysia's attempt to integrate as much as possible the principles of inclusiveness in the planning process through active and meaningful participation. One of the key focus areas of the eleventh Malaysia plan is adopting the sustainable consumption and production concept through creation of green markets, increasing share of renewables in the energy mix, enhancing demand side management (DSM), encouraging low carbon mobility, and promoting holistic waste management. In addition to this focus area, the other three are:

- Strengthening resilience against climate change and natural disasters,
- Conserving natural resources for present and future generations, and
- Strengthening the enabling environment for green growth.

A holistic look at all the key focus areas of the eleventh Malaysia Plan is suggestive of Malaysia's efforts to incorporate sustainable development tenets into its planning. Regarding disaster reduction at the national and local level for instance, since the year 2005 or even earlier, local initiatives have been incorporating these ideas in their development planning. The Federal Department of Town and Country Planning Peninsular Malaysia (FDTCP) has prepared various planning guidelines and manuals as key reference materials for planners and other professionals to incorporate in their disaster risk reduction agenda. One of such manuals highlights the role of local authorities, hospitals and schools. Additionally, the Land Use Planning Appraisal for Risk areas (LUPAr) by the FDTCP in 2005, aimed at providing effective disaster mitigation strategies and general guidelines for development control and mitigation measures in hazard prone areas (Ahmad, 2008). Figure 22.3 shows how disaster risk reduction has been captured in Malaysia's development plans at the local level using two development plan sectors of commercial city centers and transportation as examples.

The same details are provided for other plan sectors of housing, public facilities, rural area development, industry, population and employment, drainage and irrigation as well as natural resource management.

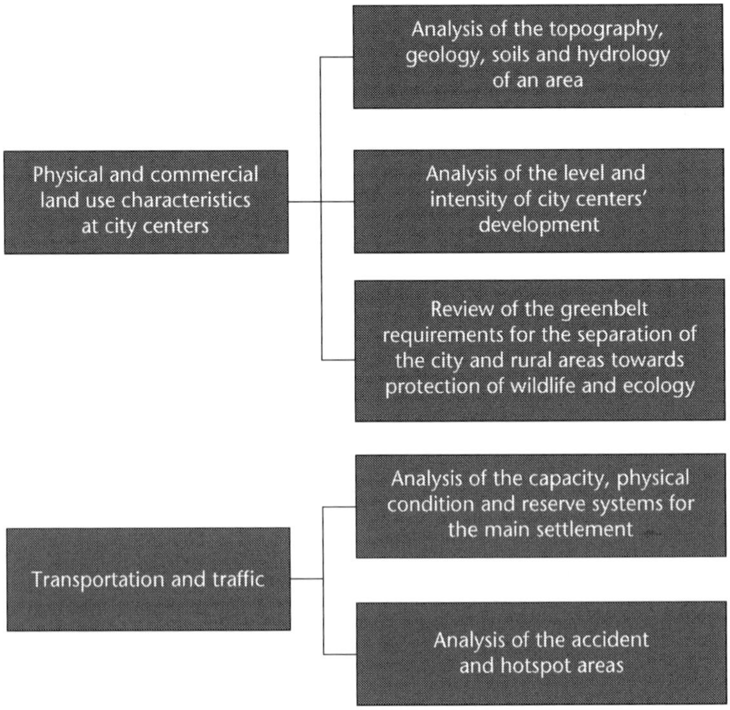

Figure 22.3 Disaster risk reduction in some sectors of Malaysia's development plans

Source: Mohamad-Amin and Hashim (2014).

The Kota Tinggi District Plan 2020 and National Coastal Zone Physical Plans are some other development plans where the aspects relating to flood risks are emphasized and incorporated into the land use planning process. Flood Risk maps were developed through consultations with local communities and technical agencies, taking into account the needs of the local flood governance aimed at promoting sustainable development. These plans are developed using the following considerations to ensure usefulness in promoting sustainable development.

- To prevent and avoid inappropriate development in areas where there is imminent risk of flooding;
- Plan new developments taking into consideration the factors that will cause flood risk, especially arising from surface water run-off;
- Ensure the requirements of the prevailing policies and law in relation to the natural environment and nature conservation are taken into account and complied with at all stages of flood risk management.

I-Plan application

The I-Plan application is an online interface developed to enhance the sustainability in local and regional planning and development control activities through the creation of an integrated land use database for storing, managing and updating land use planning database; using open source technology to ease data sharing and create a user friendly system that will facilitate the monitoring of land use changes. This is a good initiative that enables the local government to monitor the land development projects that might adversely impact the environment.

World class sustainable city initiative

The World Class Sustainable City initiative is one of the ways in which Malaysia's readiness to learn from elsewhere is manifested. Under this initiative, the World Class Sustainable City Conference (WCSC) is organized annually by the Real Estate and Housing Developers' Association (REHDA), the Malaysian Institute of Planners (MIP) and Malaysian Institute of Architects (*Pertubuhan Arkitek Malaysia* – PAM) supported by the Kuala Lumpur City Hall (DBKL – *Dewan Bandaraya Kuala Lumpur*). Since 2009, the WCSC has been an annual event with the sole objective of learning from the experiences of other successful cities to identify the factors that can make Kuala Lumpur a world class sustainable city. Since its inception in 2009, the conference has been gathering experts from around the globe to discuss issues of sustainable development and challenges. The lessons from the WCSC conferences are expected to serve as pointers for future development and management of Kuala Lumpur and its environs (largely the Klang valley or Greater KL).

The Malaysian local governance has been strongly influenced by the state government, which acts as the central government for all the local authorities within a particular state. Thus, the success of the implementation of the principles of sustainable development is very much dependent on the ideology of the state government as well the political will to implement the principles.

Multimedia super corridor

According to Yigitcanlar et al. (2008a, 2008b), the modern production system is largely promoting the creation, distribution, and consumption of intangible goods and services, particularly in the information and communications technology sector. In this sector, a highly skilled manpower is produced whose activities do not necessarily respond to space and time needs as indicated by classical urban economic theories. Malaysia's attempt to harvest the utility of this modern sector is reflected in the establishment of the multimedia super corridor around the city of Cyberjaya through a number of government policies and actions. The establishment of the Multimedia University is one of such efforts. The usefulness of this "virtual" production and consumption system according to Jaffee (1998) is manifested in the provision of information infrastructure providing enormous support to science and technology investments. It has also helped in promoting equity, transparency and community participation in governance and financial matters.

Putrajaya and Iskandar region

The National Urbanization Policy (NUP), created in 2006, has set the promotion of sustainable urbanization and effective governance as one of its policy trusts. As laid out in the earlier part of this chapter, the planning process at various levels delineates the practical actions to be taken to ensure the integration of the principles of sustainable development. The NUP's objective to promote strict adherence to the provisions of the development plans is a good mechanism for ensuring the incorporation of the principles of sustainable development at all levels of the planning process. According to Bello and Dola (2014, p. 274):

> [I]n spite of the administrative weaknesses of local governments in Malaysia, adhering to other good governance principles outlined in the Local Agenda 21 (LA21) such as effective community involvement [as part of the implementation strategies of the NUP] will aid the formulation of sustainable plans at the local levels.

Putrajaya and Iskandar Malaysia are two of the municipalities as well as regional development authorities where the incorporation of elements to foster economic growth by balancing sustainable development are exemplified.

With the implementation of the green building index, green technology, efficient public transportation system, urban farming and centralized cooling center in Putrajaya, the per-capita greenhouse gas emissions are likely to stabilize between 2007 and 2025 even under normal circumstances (BaU) scenario according to Ho et al. (2012).

The cluster concept conurbation proposal of the NUP provided an avenue to establish regional growth centers such as the Iskandar region (see Figure 22.4). The Iskandar region's development is governed by the Iskandar Malaysia Comprehensive Development Plan (CDP) comprising the five flagship zones.

The Iskandar Regional Development Authority (IRDA) is the regulatory authority entrusted with the function of planning for the region and facilitation of its sustainable development. The comparative advantages of the Iskandar Region as a regional growth center, according to IRDA (2016), include the following aspects:

- Less than ten hours of flight from other key regional growth centers such as Dubai, Shaghai and Bangalore;
- Accessible to a large global market;
- Strong spatial connectivity by air, land and sea;
- Endowed with three major ports for effectiveness and efficiency in commerce.

The IRDA have signed memoranda of understanding (MoUs) with a number of partners to collaborate in the establishment of the smart city component as envisaged in the comprehensive development plan. A MoU between the Country Garden Pacific View, Huawei Malaysia and Celcom Axiata has aimed at developing Forest City with the Smart City criteria such as, Smart Utilities, Safe City, Smart Traffic and Transportation, Smart Building, Connected City, Smart City Intelligence, Smart Home, Smart Healthcare, and Smart Education.

The core elements of Iskandar's Comprehensive Development Plan II was comprised of wealth generation, wealth sharing inclusiveness, as well as resources optimization and low carbon as set out in Figure 22.5.

Under each of the core elements, other specific sub-elements are identified. For example, the wealth generation core element is composed of the promotion of a green economy, deepening of cluster linkages, as well as the creation of job opportunities and workforce productivity. The wealth sharing core element consists of the promotion of economic participation, social connectedness and equity in wealth sharing. The resource optimization and low carbon core elements include integration of infrastructure resources, enhancing urban connectivity and mobility, planning and management of built environment, promotion of natural ecology and green areas as well as enhancing balanced regional growth.

With regard to resource optimization and low carbon emission, the carbon emission intensity for the Iskandar region as reported by Ho et al. (2013) suggests a 27 percent reduction in carbon emissions by 2025 under the business as usual scenario.

Legal framework for promoting environmental protection in the development control system

The role of land use planning in promoting sustainable development was reaffirmed at the Rio Earth Summit in 1992. Amongst the 27 principles of the Rio Declaration, many can be linked to

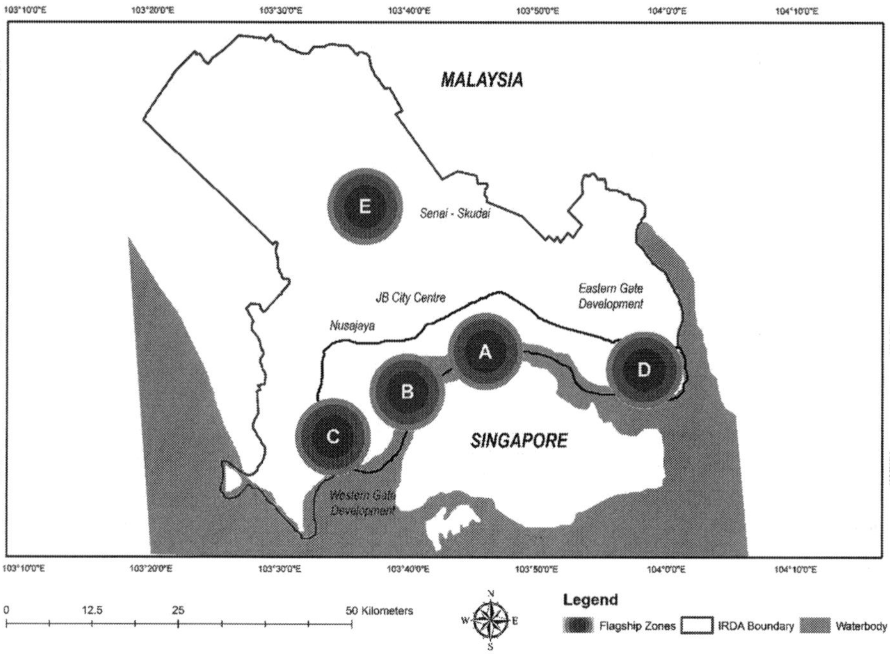

Figure 22.4 The Iskandar region's flagship zones

Source: Iskandar Regional Development Authority (IRDA).

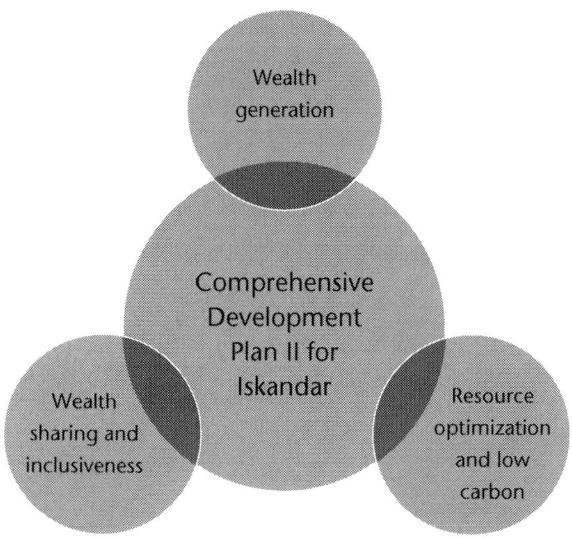

Figure 22.5 Core elements of the Iskandar Comprehensive Development Plan II

Source: IRDA (2016).

Table 22.3 Key planning principles from the Rio Declaration

Principles	*Principles for land use planning*
Principle 3: right of development must equitably meet the needs of the present and future generations	Land use planning must address the meaning and spirit of sustainable development
Principle 4: environmental protection to play an integral part of the development process	Development plans must be 'environment-led' and sustainable
Principle 10: participation of all concerned citizens at all levels	Public participation as an integral component in planning processes
Principle 11: effective environmental legislation	A strong and comprehensive planning law that is able to integrate the current legislation with the whole environment
Principle 17: environmental impact assessment	Environmental assessments should be integrated with the present planning control mechanism

Source: LA21 (1992).

land use planning. Five important principles set out in the Rio Declaration relating to land planning are set out in Table 22.3.

The land use planning process in Malaysia as regulated by the Town and Country Planning Act 1976 (Act 172) incorporates the above-mentioned five principles. Act 172 provides for the establishment of the planning machinery, preparation of development plans, and development planning, taking into account the national development plans. The interaction between the planning authorities and the national development policies guiding the preparation of development plans in promoting sustainable development in the land use planning system is achieved through the National Physical Planning Council, which is anchored by the Prime Minister as the chairman and the Director General of the Town and Country Planning, and the council's secretary is responsible for the National Physical Plan. The State Planning Committee and the State Planning Committee – Local Planning Authority which are anchored by the Chief Minister as the chairman and Senior Director Town and Country Planning as the secretary of the two committees are responsible for State Structure Plan and Local Plan, respectively. The Regional Growth, Development Area and Special Area Plans are the responsibilities of the State Planning Committee, Local Planning Authority or Town and Country Planning Department.

The government, recognizing that the characteristics and quality of the urban environment were major determinants of the quality of life of the urban population, introduced environmental protection measures into the town and country planning system. Act 172 was amended in 1995 and 2001 to address the lack of priority granted to environmental conservation considerations in the development approval process, especially with respect to hill lands and the preservation of the natural topography. The amendment was made for the following purposes:

- To strengthen the planning controls process by requiring all applications for planning permission to be accompanied by a development proposal report containing the relevant information on land use and proposed development to assist the local planning authority in making decisions;
- To create special provisions for control of trees in the local planning authority areas. It makes it a duty for every local planning authority to ensure that when granting planning permission for development, adequate conditions are attached for the protection of trees, and preservation of open spaces; and as a further requirement, to impose a duty on the local planning authority to ensure that when granting planning permission for development, adequate conditions are

made for the preservation of the natural topography of the land to which the development relates. In this manner, the natural land conditions would be protected from excessive disturbances caused by earthworks carried out without proper plans and specifications.

The establishment of the National Physical Planning Council to ensure effectiveness and efficiency in the improvement of environmental quality toward sustainable development through coherent town and country planning was a good move. The National Physical Planning Council provides:

- spatial focus to social and economic policies of the nation, which in turn strengthens national planning;
- spatial view to sectoral policies which in turn coordinates sectoral agencies responsible for such policies;
- provides regional as well as state and local planning frameworks.

Section 6B of Act 172 requires the Council to prepare the National Physical Plan as a policy document providing guidance to the state and local governments in preparing development plans (the blueprint for development planning and control activities). The hierarchy of the development plans in Malaysia begins with the National Physical Plan at the federal level, the Regional Plans involving two or more states to tackle common issues, the State Structure Plan, the Local Plan, and at the bottom-most level, the Special Area Plan.

The first National Physical Plan (NPP) was prepared in 2005, pursuant to section 6B of the Town and Country Planning Act 1975, and it was reviewed in 2010 in tandem with the Five year Malaysian Plans. The NPP sets out broad policies for the development of a spatial framework which is efficient and sustainable enough to anchor Malaysia's national development, one of the objectives of this spatial framework being the attainment of high income nation status by the year 2020. Briefly, the NPP outlines the foundational direction for national spatial development in Malaysia. According to Gee (2012), the NPP provides the basis for the National Spatial Framework 2020 focusing on the following:

- Achieving an integrated and sustainable land use planning, coordinated with various other sectoral policies and development plans;
- Providing the general directions of physical development for the nation;
- Forming the basis for preparing detailed development plans at regional, state and local levels; and
- Ensuring resources are optimally used, avoid duplication of infrastructure investments and strive for sustainable development.

In addition to the amendment to Act 172, various other related laws that were amended to incorporate environmental concerns have been implemented. The Federal Department of Town and Country Planning introduced non-legal measures to promote incorporation of environmental protection measures in the land use planning system by using the MURNInets as a mechanism to measure the sustainability and well-being of the local authority areas.

Other local initiatives

Measuring sustainability and well-being of local authority areas using MURNInets

Sustainability assessment as an evaluation process for ensuring that a particular plan strives to achieve the objectives of sustainable development strategies set out in proposals for development.

In the long run, this helps planners and communities better embed sustainability into policy processes (Holman, 2009). In the context of the Local Plans, the evaluation is carried out in the following preparation stages:

- Local plan objectives and proposals;
- Preliminary proposals;
- Development strategies.

The Federal Department of Town and Country Planning, a department under the Ministry of Housing, Local Government and Urban Wellness, developed the Malaysian Urban Indicator Network (MURNInets), comprising a set of indicators for measuring the sustainability of urban development activities, and the minimum quality and living standard that need to be achieved by each town or city. It is the first assessment approach introduced in Malaysia, incorporating six dimensions, comprised of economic development, optimum use of land and resources, infrastructure and transportation, environmental quality, livable community, and effective governance, in order to promote sustainable development at the local government level to ensure the effective implementation of the National Development Policies prepared by the federal government.

MURNInets, according to Shamsuddin and Abdulrashid (2013), is an application system designed to analyze urban conditions, effects of development, survey temporary changes and formulate urban scenarios based on fixed standards. The objectives of MURNInets are to assist the federal, states and local governments to:

- Determine the level of sustainability for each town in the country based on the Malaysian Urban Indicators;
- Identify the strength and weaknesses of cities in promoting sustainable development based on the indicators;
- Suggest improvements to upgrade the level of sustainability based on the data collected. It addresses the gap between the policies and actual implementation of sustainable practices;
- Implement a survey mechanism for assisting administrative and technical staff in formulating policy directions, promote public participation and monitoring the implementation of development plans;
- Evaluate the performance of cities;
- Improve public services;
- Indicators can provide basic information to upgrade the status of urban areas (e.g., from town to cities);
- Help government to assess the budget needed to improve the sustainability of a town or city;
- Help provide feedback on social and environmental commitments at local government levels to the federal and state governments.

The MURNInet has assumed an important role at the local government level to help promote sustainability and is being accepted by nearly all local authorities. This to a certain extent has been able to promote effective compliance with the federal government policies which were initially not given serious attention in the pursuit of economic development at state and local authority levels.

Sustainable town award

Besides MURNInets, the Bandar Lestari (Sustainable Town) Environment Award was introduced by the Department of Environment to recognize the Local Authorities that make the most effort to keep abreast of innovations and practices in creating and maintaining a healthy environment for human habitation. This award was developed to promote the sharing of environment-development information expertise and construction of inter-agency partnerships; building of environmental planning and management capacity; and leveraging of environmental resources and managing risks for achieving sustainable development. The award requires the local authorities to take into account aspects such as physical conditions, ecological well-being, urban environmental services, good governance, and active community participation in planning and implementing the development activities at the local government level. This is an ongoing initiative to motivate the local authorities to compete with each other in promoting sustainable development and promote effective implementation of the related policies.

The Malaysia's Green Building Index (GBI)

The Malaysia's Green Building Index (GBI) was developed by the Malaysian Institute of Architects and the Association of Consulting Engineers, which is an initiative from the private sector to assist in meeting the increasing demand from building end-users for green-rated buildings to reduce adverse effects of buildings on the environment. The GBI is the first attempt by Malaysia to develop a system of rating that is comprehensive for evaluating Malaysian buildings in terms of environmental design and performance, based on six main criteria, namely: energy efficiency, sustainability in materials and resource use, water efficiency, air quality, site planning and innovation. Points will be awarded for each criterion fulfilled, and property developers have adopted the Index as part of their corporate social responsibility index. Malaysia's GBI has been developed with the aim of saving energy and resources through material recycling and harmonization of buildings with local culture and climate. This is hoped to ultimately support the maintenance of the ecosystem's capacity at global and local levels. GBI has been successful in influencing sustainability in the development of the built environment and raises awareness among professionals in planning, design and construction industries as well as other stakeholders regarding sustainable development.

Conclusion

The pronouncement of the Malaysian government makes it clear that the 11th Malaysia Plan (2016–2020) will continue to elevate a sustainable development agenda as its prime target and that inclusiveness will be one of the thrusts of the Plan that is launched in 2015. The National consultations on the post-2015 Development Agenda have marked the beginning of the process that is hoped to direct Malaysia's move to achieve a developed nation status by 2020. These consultations focused on the driving and restraining forces associated with the implementation of inclusiveness and sustainability in governance.

This is also reflected in the indication of willingness and commitment of the national government to adopt a policy of inclusiveness and openness; the Prime Minister stated that "the era of the government knows all is over" (Bernama, 2009) and wants people from all walks of life to contribute towards promoting sustainable and inclusive development. Inclusiveness and civic commitment are necessary ingredients for the achievement of sustainable development. The emphasis here should not only be on promoting growth that creates economic opportunities but also social cohesion in which all the segments of society have a feeling of importance (including the poor). This will ultimately promote political stability as well. As new programs are developed in order to achieve resilience and sustainability in development, coherent efforts are required to integrate realistic measures of social inclusiveness in them. Incidentally, the post-2015 agenda concords with the sustainable development goals as promoted by the United Nations. It is imperative, therefore, that local governments in Malaysia work in a good synergy with the state authorities to promote sustainable development.

Note

1 Abu Bakar Jaafar (1994) "Malaysia Country Report," in *Environmental and Urban Management in SEA*, Azman Awang, Mahboob Salim, and Halldance, J.F. (eds.), Malaysia, Sultan Iskandar Institute of Urban Habitat and High-Rise, pp. 87–109.

References

Adger, W.N., and Jordan, A. (2009). "Sustainability: Exploring the Processes and Outcomes of Governance," in Adger, N.W. and Jordan, A. (eds.), *Governing Sustainability* (3–31). Cambridge: Cambridge University Press.

Ahmad, M.J. (2008). Management of Geohazards Through Spatial Planning. Paper presented at Second National conference on Extreme Weather and Climate Change Understanding Science and Risk Reduction, 14–15 October 2008, Putrajaya International Convention Centre, Putrajaya.

Bell, D.V., and Cheung, Y.K.A. (eds.) (2009). *Introduction to Sustainable Development-Volume I.* Oxford, UK: EOLSS Publications.

Bello, A., and Dola, K. (2014). Sustainable development and the role of local governance: experience from Malaysian model regions. *International Journal of Humanities and Social Science*, 4(1), 268–280.

Bernama. (2009, April 9). Accessed from www.bernama.com/bernama/v5/index.php on January 24, 2018.

Blane, L., and Bob, S. (2010). "Asia Pacific," in Jorge, M., and Smoke, P. (eds.), *Local Government Finance: The Challenges of the 21st Century. Second Global Report on Decentralization and Local Democracy* (27–34). Barcelona: United Cities and Local Governments.

Brundtland, G.H. (1987). *Report of the World Commission on Environment and Development: Our Common Future.* Geneva: United Nations.

FDTCP. (2005). *National Physical Plan.* Kuala Lumpur: Federal Department of Town and Country Planning, Peninsular Malaysia.

Gee, L.T. (2012). National Green Technology Policy and Its Implementation Challenges. Accessed from www.akademisains.gov.my/download/2ga/GT%20POLICY%20AND%20IMPLEMENTATION%20CHALLENGES.pdf on November 26, 2013.

Harris, J.M. (2000). Basic Principles of Sustainable Development. Global Development and Environment Institute, Working Paper 00-04, Tufts University.

Ho, C.S., Matsuoka, Y., and Hashim, O. (2012). *Putrajaya Green City 2025. Baseline and Preliminary Study.* Revised edition. UTM, Johor Bahru, Malaysia. Accessed from http://2050.nies.go.jp/report/file/lcs_asialocal/Putrajaya_2012.pdf May 14, 2016.

Ho, C.S., Matsuoka, Y., Simson, J., and Gomi, K. (2013). Low carbon urban development strategy in Malaysia: The case of Iskandar Malaysia development corridor. *Habitat International*, 37, 43–51.

Holman, N. (2009). Incorporating local sustainability indicators into structures of local governance: A review of the literature. *Local Environment*, 14(4), 365–375.

IRDA (Iskandar Regional Development Authority) (2016). Our Development Plan. Accessed from http://iskandarmalaysia.com.my/our-development-plan/ on June 26, 2016.

Jaffee, D. (1998). *Levels of Socio-economic Development Theory.* London: Praeger.

Kardos, M. (2012). The reflection of good governance in sustainable development strategies. *Procedia-Social and Behavioral Sciences*, 58, 1166–1173.

LA21 (Local Agenda 21). (1992). Earth Summit. *The United Nations programme for action from Rio.* Geneva: United Nations.

Loorbach, D. (2007). *Transition Management: New Mode of Governance for Sustainable Development.* Utrecht: International Books.

Maruani, T. (2011). The role of courts in open space conservation: Lessons from the Israeli experience. *Landscape and Urban Planning*, 100(4), 364–368.

Mohamad-Amin, I.A., and Hashim, H.S. (2014). Disaster risk reduction in Malaysian urban planning. *Planning Malaysia (Journal of the Malaysian Institute of Planners)*, 12(1), 35–58.

Ninth Malaysia Plan (2006–2010). *Thrust four, chapter 22: Promoting Environmental Stewardship*. Kuala Lumpur: Government Printers, Malaysia.

Nooi, P.S. (2008). Decentralisation or recentralisation? Trends in local government in Malaysia. *Commonwealth Journal of Local Government*, 1, 126–132.

Pierre, J., and Peters, G.B. (2000). *Governance, Politics and the State*. London: Palgrave Macmillan.

Shamsuddin, S., and Abdulrashid, A. (2013). Malaysian Urban–Rural National Indicators on Sustainable Development (MURNInets). 43rd UAA conference, San-Francisco, California. April 3–6, 2013.

White, R., and Smoke, P. (2005). *East Asia Decentralizes*. Washington: The World Bank.

World Bank. (1992). Governance and Development. Report no. 10650. Washington: The World Bank.

Yigitcanlar, T., Velibeyoglu, K., and Baum, S. (eds.) (2008a). *Creative Urban Regions: Harnessing Urban Technologies to Support Knowledge City Initiatives*. Hershey, PA: Information Science Reference.

Yigitcanlar, T., Velibeyoglu, K., and Baum, S. (eds.). (2008b). *Knowledge-based Urban Development: Planning and Applications in the Information Era*. Hershey, PA: Information Science Reference.

23

Regional governance for environmental sustainability in Asia in the context of sustainable development: a survey of regional cooperation frameworks

Mark Elder

Introduction

This chapter surveys the landscape of regional governance for sustainability in Asia, focusing on government-related regional and sub-regional institutions and cooperation frameworks related to the environment. Many of these frameworks include exclusively multi-stakeholder participation of non-governmental actors, but this chapter does not survey non-governmental organizations or frameworks. This chapter examines more broadly focused frameworks which include environmental issues, and could perform an integrating role as well as frameworks which specialize in environmental issues. There are many cooperation frameworks in the region, and this chapter endeavors to identify and classify the major ones. This chapter also discusses challenges facing these institutions and frameworks.

Agenda 2030 calls on regional and sub-regional cooperation frameworks to facilitate the implementation of the Sustainable Development Goals (SDGs), although the main responsibility still lies with governments and other stakeholders. Overall monitoring and follow up of SDGs are planned at the global level under the United Nations (UN) General Assembly, the Economic and Social Council (ECOSOC), and the High Level Political Forum (HLPF). The UN's regional and sub-regional commissions and other bodies are also mandated to contribute to the implementation of Agenda 2030, but the wide scope of the SDGs is expected to involve a great variety of regional institutions, organizations, and frameworks relating to various areas of sustainable development.

Despite the importance of regional cooperation, a recent survey found that regional environmental governance "has been a neglected topic in the scholarly literature on international relations and international environmental politics" (Balsiger and VanDeveer 2012[1]). Up to Rio+20, many studies of global environmental governance and international environmental cooperation focused on comprehensive global issues (Najam, Papa, and Taiyab 2006), multilateral environmental agreements (Mitchell 2003; Andresen and Hey 2005; Young 2011), the role of international organizations such as the United Nations Environment Programme (UNEP) (Biermann 2007; Ivanova 2010; Elder and Olsen 2012), and linkages (or insufficient linkages) between environmental regimes and regimes in other policy areas such as trade (IISD and UNEP-DTIE 2005). These studies generally do not emphasize regional governance.

There is some literature on regional environmental governance institutions and frameworks in Asia. This has mainly addressed specific cooperation areas such as air pollution (Kim 2007; Yoon 2007; Takahashi 2002); specific institutions or frameworks such as the Association of South East Asian Nations (ASEAN) (Elder and Miyazawa 2015; Koh 2013; Elliott 2012; Robinson and Koh 2002) or the Tripartite Environment Ministers Meeting (TEMM) (PRCEE, IGES, and KEI 2009); sub-regional cooperation (Yoshimatsu 2010); or regional integration (IGES 2015; Asian Development Bank 2010). The author is not aware of any surveys with a broad scope; one study made a preliminary effort to explore institutions and frameworks (Elder and Olsen 2012), and one study addressed more general issues of regional environmental cooperation without addressing the range of specific institutions and frameworks (Mori 2013).

The earth system governance (ESG) perspective has identified a variety of new trends, especially, "the emergence of new types of agency and of actors in addition to national governments," "the emergence of new mechanisms and institutions of global environmental governance that go beyond traditional forms of state-led, treaty-based regimes," the "increasing segmentation and fragmentation of the overall governance system across levels and functional spheres" (Biermann and Pattberg 2008[2]), and the focus on "governance architectures," particularly their fragmentation (Biermann et al. 2009). There is also a desire to move beyond the traditional social science focus on explaining existing phenomena to make a greater effort to contribute to promoting political change in order to improve the condition of the earth system (Nicholson and Jinnah 2016).

The cases of regional governance surveyed here can be interpreted as part of the segmentation and fragmentation of governance architectures as explained by the ESG perspective, as the regional level, between the national and global levels, becomes more active. Moreover, this survey finds that many of the other general trends identified by the ESG perspective can also generally be seen at the regional level in the Asia-Pacific. Many multilateral environmental agreements are global, and many countries in the region are signatories of many of them. In the Asia-Pacific region, the number of regional multilateral environment agreements does not seem to be large. There are also not many large international organizations. This chapter shows that new types of cooperation mechanisms have emerged in the region over the past two decades beyond traditional multilateral agreements and international organizations. International cooperation on the environment in the region is characterized by a substantial number and wide variety of voluntary forums, frameworks, and networks with a wide variety governance and implementation structures.

This survey does not claim to be comprehensive, and it is possible that some cooperation frameworks deserving of mention may have been overlooked. There is no single repository of information on environmental cooperation efforts in the region, and many of these efforts are small scale and not well-known beyond their members and participants. This survey also includes frameworks with a broader focus on sustainability which also have some environmental components. Moreover, because of their broader scope, these broader frameworks could potentially help to facilitate the integration of the environment into other policy areas. Regarding the geographic scope, this survey attempts to achieve some balance among sub-regions, though some may be over or under represented.

There are three main reasons why this chapter focuses on frameworks which involve governments and excludes frameworks comprised exclusively of non-governmental actors. First, it is already a major task simply to survey the ones involving governments. Second, it is often easier to find information on frameworks which involve governments. Third, despite many studies arguing about the declining power of nation-states, much international cooperation is still organized by national governments, which still have the power to raise revenue through taxes as well as make laws and regulations, even though these powers may be eroding over time.

A common pattern found in the frameworks surveyed here is cooperation between national governments and other actors, such as NGOs, on joint actions. Sometimes the initiative is from the NGO side, and a common strategy of many NGOs and research institutes is to work through national (and sometimes local) governments, and attempt to persuade governments to create or join a cooperation framework, contribute funding, and participate in the development and implementation of the framework's ideas. But sometimes, the initiative still comes from the government side, and it is also common for one or more governments to jointly form a cooperation framework, provide it with funding, and invite NGOs or research institutes to help develop and implement the framework's ideas. NGOs or research institutes may serve as secretariats for some of these frameworks. So the role of national governments remains important.

The organization of the rest of this chapter is as follows. Section 2 surveys existing regional cooperation frameworks. Section 3 addresses challenges faced by these frameworks. Section 4 discusses the results and concludes.

Survey of existing regional cooperation frameworks

Sorting out the noodle bowl

Asia's complex, intricately intertwined regional integration initiatives have been described as a spaghetti or noodle bowl (Kawai and Wignaraja 2009). This chapter argues that the region's international cooperation frameworks and programs for environment and sustainability are just as complex and overlapping as the ones related to regional integration, or even more. There is a wide variety of frameworks which this chapter tries to sort out.

A survey of regional cooperation mechanisms should begin with those which could be considered as institutions or international organizations, but there is no generally agreed definition of these terms. Typical examples, such as the UN and its agencies, and multilateral development banks, operationally speaking, are usually based on a treaty or formal agreement, clear criteria for membership, and they have rules and procedures, a regular budget, and a regular secretariat. The common examples are also not time-limited, suggesting an expectation for an indefinite, or at least relatively long term existence. Members are typically nation states, though there is increasing scope for other kinds of members and participation by non-members.[3]

Most frameworks reviewed here have most of these characteristics, but in many cases, one or more of these characteristics may apply only to a small extent, or may be missing. Budgets and secretariats may be regular but small, and some frameworks' continued existence may be uncertain. There may be an agreement among member governments, but the nature and status of these agreements can vary widely. Some intergovernmental agreements may be between ministries and not at a higher political level. Agreements between ministries may also be at various levels, including at the minister, director-general, or director levels. Many cooperation mechanisms have the feeling of a program or collection of projects rather than an international organization. Many describe themselves as networks or forums, not as international organizations. Overall, the impression is that governments in Asia are reluctant to make major, permanent, long term commitments that characterize traditional international organizations such as UN agencies or multilateral development banks (MDBs). Therefore, many of these frameworks seem difficult to classify as international organizations or institutions, so this chapter uses the broader label of "cooperation framework" to classify these mechanisms.

There are also some peculiarities in how various mechanisms and frameworks are officially named by the member governments. On one hand, some, like APEC (Asia-Pacific Economic

Cooperation), have achieved a certain level of institutionalization, but its members do not want to call it an international organization, instead calling it a "forum," while its official name, ending in "cooperation" deliberately avoids any label hinting at an organizational structure. On the other hand, others, like the Global Green Growth Institute (GGGI), have the formal structure and label of an international organization, but the scope and scale of its actual activities were not very large when research for this chapter was begun (although its size increased rapidly by 2017), and it seemed to be more like the smaller frameworks instead. The Asia-Europe Meeting (ASEM) does not have a secretariat, but it has a foundation to implement activities, which in practice may perform many of the functions of a secretariat.

This chapter divides international cooperation frameworks into three main types, based on whether their scope is broad or specific, and whether government involvement is mainly at the national or local level. These are outlined in Table 23.1. Frameworks of the first type have a fairly broad scope, and they are mainly led by national governments. Here, broad includes not only frameworks which address a broad range of policy areas beyond just the environment, but also those which focus on a broad range of issues within the environmental field. The second type is more narrowly focused on the environment or a specific environmental issue. Some are mainly led by national governments, while in others, a larger role is played by non-governmental actors, although national governments are also involved and typically provide funding. The third type is centered on local governments. The local government frameworks considered here are mainly related to environmental issues. Most frameworks have at least some level of multi-stakeholder participation, especially for project implementation, but the nature and degree of participation varies widely.

Another issue is how to distinguish between cooperation frameworks on one hand and programs or projects on the other hand. A framework suggests some kind of membership, regular meetings, agreed procedures, common activities, and continued existence (not ad hoc or time-limited). Some cooperation frameworks which are mainly led and funded by one country or organization may seem more like a program or project, which is often used to describe an initiative sponsored by a single government with beneficiaries who do not directly participate in a formal decision making process as members, even if it is also supported by an international organization such as the Asian Development Bank (ADB) or the United Nations Environment Programme (UNEP). In order to be classified as a cooperation framework for this survey, several criteria were considered. The first is the name of the initiative, and whether it suggests some kind of membership rather than just participation, such as forum or network, although this is not necessarily definitive since some regularized frameworks use the word "program" in their name. These terms are not used with consistent meanings by the various frameworks or organizations. The second is other evidence of membership as described in the website or official documents. Third is reference to an intergovernmental meeting or official agreement among countries. Fourth is whether the governance structure suggests an indefinite existence (not specifically time-limited), for example, with a governing board and/or bylaws. Fifth is whether members are contributing at least some of their own resources. These criteria are sometimes not easy to assess,

Table 23.1 Classification of international cooperation frameworks

	National governments	*Local governments*
Broad	Type 1: Broad scope	
Specific	Type 2: Focused on the environment or a specific environmental issue	Type 3: City-focused

Source: Author.

especially financial arrangements, since public information is not often available. A network could still be classified as a cooperation framework even if it was mainly funded by one country, if it has a formal membership structure with a variety of members represented on a governing board. A project or program funded by a few donor countries and implemented by a few international organizations for a group of developing country beneficiaries would not be counted as a cooperation framework if it did not have a regular governing board or intergovernmental meeting including representatives from the beneficiary countries.

Type 1: Broad scope international cooperation frameworks

Broad scope international cooperation frameworks centered on national governments are summarized in Table 23.2, which identifies nine different types, plus formal treaties. There are three varieties of international organizations addressed here. The most prominent are probably the regional offices or branches of UN organizations such as the Economic and Social Commission for Asia and the Pacific (ESCAP), UNEP, and United Nations Development Programme (UNDP). MDBs are also very prominent since they often provide significant funding. There are three global international organizations which are based in Asia, the Global Green Growth Institute (GGGI) and the Green Climate Fund (GCF) in Korea, and the United Nations Commission on Regional Development (UNCRD) based in Japan. Other than international organizations, there are two forums with a broad scope which link Asia-Pacific countries with other countries outside of the region: APEC (Asia Pacific Economic Cooperation) and the Asia Europe Meeting (ASEM). They do not call themselves international organizations, although they have built up a certain degree of institutionalization. There are several sub-regional, broad focused forums/programs which include important environmental components in Northeast Asia, South Asia, the Himalayan Mountain region, and the Pacific. In Southeast Asia, there is ASEAN, which has more extensive cooperation with a higher diplomatic profile compared to the other sub-regions. Other sub-regional frameworks are more directly focused on environment-related issues. Several frameworks have meetings of environment ministers, as well as ministers of other related areas. Then, there are regional seas agreements (some under the umbrella of UNEP) as well as river basin organizations; there are similar frameworks in other regions, particularly Europe, such as the Mediterranean Action Plan, Baltic Marine Environment Protection Commission – Helsinki Commission, and the Convention on the Protection of the Rhine. Finally, this survey mentions three formal treaties which include some kind of regional cooperation mechanism. The rest of this section contains summary descriptions of the frameworks.

International organizations

Regional offices of UN organizations are, of course, international organizations in the traditional sense. They play a major role in international cooperation on sustainability in Asia. ESCAP, which has a broad mandate spanning a range of areas, plays the major coordinating role at the regional level for implementing the SDGs. ESCAP has also convened major regional preparatory meetings for other global sustainability discussions including Rio+20. One special characteristic is that it is coordinated by foreign ministries, not tied to specific sectoral ministries, and it has considerable convening powers. Therefore, it has the potential to play a coordinating role in promoting more integrated implementation of SDGs. UNEP-ROAP plays the major coordinating role in the environmental area, and it is overseen by environment ministers. In 2015, it organized the first Forum of Ministers and Environment Authorities of Asia Pacific, which in turn reports to the United Nations Environment Assembly in Nairobi. UNEP-ROAP plays a role in

Table 23.2 International cooperation frameworks centered on national governments

Category	*Major Examples*
International Organizations: UN (including regional offices)	• ESCAP (Economic and Social Commission for Asia and the Pacific) • UNEP-ROAP (Regional Office for Asia Pacific) • UNDP (United Nations Development Programme) • GEF (Global Environment Fund) • WHO (World Health Organization) • FAO (Food and Agriculture Organization)
International Organizations: Multilateral Development Banks	• ADB (Asian Development Bank) (1966) • AIIB (Asian Infrastructure Investment Bank) (2016) • World Bank (regional presence) • NDB (New Development Bank) (2015)
Global International Organizations Based in Asia	• GGGI (Global Green Growth Institute) (2010) • Green Climate Fund (2013) • UNCRD (United Nations Centre for Regional Development) (1971)
Broad-scope Forums Linking with Outside Regions	• APEC (Asia Pacific Economic Cooperation) (1989) • ASEM (Asia-Europe Meeting) (1996)
Broad Sub-regional Frameworks with Environmental Activities/Programs	• ASEAN (Association of Southeast Asian Nations) (1967) • Other ASEAN-related groups (ASEAN+3, ASEAN+6, etc.) • Trilateral Summit (China, Japan, Korea) (1999) • SPC (the Pacific Community) (1947) • SAARC (South Asian Association for Regional Cooperation) (1985) • GTI (Greater Tumen Initiative) (1991) • GMS (Greater Mekong Sub-region) (1992) • BIMP-EAGA (Brunei Darussalam-Indonesia-Malaysia-Philippines East ASEAN Growth Area) (1994) • Indonesia-Malaysia-Thailand Growth Triangle (IMT-GT) (1993) • BIMSTEC (Bay of Bengal Initiative for Multi-Sectoral Technical and Economic Cooperation) (1997) • LMI (Lower Mekong Initiative) (2009)
Sub-regional Environment-related Frameworks	• NEASPEC (Northeast Asian Subregional Programme on Environmental Cooperation) (1993) • SPREP (Secretariat of the Pacific Regional Environment Programme) (1993) • SACEP (South Asia Co-operative Environment Programme) (1982) • ICIMOD (International Centre for Integrated Mountain Development) (1983)
Environment Ministers Meetings	• EAS-EMM (East Asian Summit – Environment Ministers Meeting) • AMME (ASEAN Ministerial Meeting on the Environment) (1981) • TEMM (Tripartite Environment Ministers Meeting among China, Japan, and Korea) (1999) • MCED (Ministerial Conference on Environment & Development) (1985) • APEC (Asia Pacific Economic Cooperation) (1994) • ASEM (2002) • Forum of Ministers and Environment Authorities of Asia Pacific (2015)

(Continued)

Table 23.2 (continued)

Category	*Major Examples*
Regional and Sub-regional Seas Frameworks	• COBSEA (Coordinating Body on the Seas of East Asia) (1981) • PEMSEA (Partnerships in Environmental Management for the Seas of East Asia) (1993) • NOWPAP (Northwest Pacific Action Plan) (1994)
River Basin Organizations	• NARBO (Network of Asian River Basin Organizations) (2004) • Mekong River Commission (1995)
Formal Treaties	• ASEAN Haze Agreement (Asian-regional) (2002) • Basel Convention Regional Centre for Asia and the Pacific (regional arm of global agreement) • Stockholm Convention on POPs (regional centers)

Note: Date indicates date of establishment, where relevant or available.

Source: Author.

many cooperation frameworks, including serving as the secretariat, and sometimes provides modest levels of funding. UNDP plays a key role in development issues, and one of its distinguishing characteristics is that it has national offices, in contrast to UNEP, which mainly has regional offices. GEF plays an important role in funding, and according to UNEP-ROAP, supports a total of 52 projects totaling USD 530 million, including co-funding, in the region, mostly implemented through external partners.[4] The WHO, FAO, and others also have an important regional presence, and their work is connected to sustainability issues, through specific sectors like health and agriculture. UNCRD's environment-related work in the region focuses on transport and waste management.

Multilateral development banks (MDBs) are also considered traditional international organizations. The Asian Development Bank has long played a key role in the region, and over time, its operations have gradually but steadily incorporated more concerns about the environment and broader issues of sustainability. ADB's Strategy 2020, issued in 2008, identified environmentally sustainable growth as one of its three priority agendas. ADB appears to intend to move further in this direction in its next long-term strategy, Strategy 2030, which is currently under development. ADB conducted an independent evaluation to solicit advice on concrete ways to further enhance its focus on sustainability issues (Asian Development Bank 2016). China recently played the lead role in establishing a new multilateral development bank, the Asian Infrastructure Investment Bank (AIIB) in 2015. AIIB adopted its "Energy Sector Strategy: Sustainable Energy for Asia" (Asian Infrastructure Investment Bank 2017) in support of SDGs, the Paris Agreement on climate change, and Sustainable Energy for All (SEforALL). Its "Environmental and Social Framework" is intended to "ensure the environmental and social soundness and sustainability of projects"(Asian Infrastructure Investment Bank 2016). China, in cooperation with the other BRICS countries, was also one of the leading founding members of the New Development Bank, which was established in 2015, with its headquarters in Shanghai. It is not clear yet to what extent it will focus on sustainability issues or the Asian region. The World Bank, a global multilateral development bank, also has extensive operations and offices in the Asian region.

GGGI is a self-styled "new kind of international organization" which promotes "a new model of economic growth – green growth – founded on principles of social inclusivity and environmental sustainability" which is "interdisciplinary" and "multi-stakeholder" in character.[5] GGGI was created in 2010 as a Korean non-profit foundation, and it was launched as an international organization in 2012 at the Rio+20 conference. Its membership is global in scope, but it is included in this survey since the founding country and host is South Korea, and 11 of its 24 member countries are located in East Asia or the Pacific. GGGI conducts significant activities in the Asia-Pacific. Member types include contributing (5), participating (6), and the host country, South Korea. Major types of activities are country green growth planning and implementation, producing policy relevant knowledge products and services, technical knowledge, and promoting a global dialogue on green growth.

Broad scope intergovernmental forums linking with outside regions

There are two broad scope intergovernmental forums linking Asian countries with outside regions. These focus on a wide range of issues, particularly related to overall economic cooperation, but cooperation on the environment is a part of their activities. APEC (Asia Pacific Economic Cooperation) links some Asia-Pacific countries with some countries in North and South America. It mainly focuses on trade-related issues, and its environment-related activities are not very extensive. In contrast, the Asia Europe Meeting (ASEM) has more extensive activities related to sustainable development and the environment which are implemented by the Asia-Europe Environment Forum (ASEF).

APEC, established in 1989, does not indicate what kind of entity it is in its name, which ends vaguely with the word "cooperation," although its website calls it a "forum." Thus, its members clearly do not call it an international organization. Still, it has some elements of the form of an international organization, including a small secretariat, and it conducts a variety of activities. It also aims at economic integration, although the linkages may not be as deep as ASEAN. According to its mission statement, its purpose is primarily economic, "to support sustainable economic growth and prosperity in the Asia-Pacific region," mainly through promoting economic integration and free and open trade and investment, and its brochure clarifies this objective to include "balanced, inclusive, sustainable, innovative and secure growth" (APEC Secretariat 2014). Nevertheless, its mission statement also includes promoting human security, and its activities include a broad range of areas with broad influence on the economy. Member countries develop their own Individual Action Plans based on the Osaka Action Plan adopted in 1995. Most of these activities are related to economic integration and trade liberalization, but APEC also has a section on its website specifically related to sustainability. The Economic Leaders' Declaration in Canada in November 1997 stated that "achieving sustainable development is at the heart of APEC's mandate." The APEC environment ministers endorsed three activities in 1997: the Action Plan for Sustainability of the Marine Environment, the APEC Sustainable Cities Program of Action, and the APEC Cleaner Production Strategy, although there has been no formal meeting of the Senior Environment Officials Group since 1997. APEC's website explains that "since sustainable development is a cross-cutting issue, implementation of the related initiatives have [sic] been carried out by the relevant sectoral fora."[6]

ASEM is also considered an informal intergovernmental forum by its members, and its distinguishing characteristic is its cross-regional nature related to its purpose of promoting cooperation between Europe and Asia. ASEM began in 1996 and its membership has expanded to include 28 EU member states, 20 other European countries, and 21 Asian countries, plus the EU and the ASEAN Secretariat.[7] The Asia-Europe Foundation was established as ASEF's only "institution" in 1997. Since its establishment, it has implemented about 700 projects with over 750 organizations. Sustainable development is one of its six major work areas, although the other five areas (economy, governance, culture, education, and public health) are also broadly related to sustainable development.[8] ASEM launched the Asia-Europe Environment Forum (ASEF) in

2003 as a multi-stakeholder forum "to foster inter-regional cooperation between Europe and Asia on sustainable development and its environmental dimensions," and recently it has been working on the SDGs.[9]

Broad sub-regional frameworks with environmental activities/programs

There are a number of broad sub-regional frameworks with environmental activities and programs. Their main focus is generally on economic, development, and trade cooperation. There is also a very wide variation in the geographic scope, nature of cooperation, and organizational structure. ASEAN is the most advanced one, with a comprehensive focus beyond economic development, and a steady development of its institutional structure to include a range of ministers meetings, senior officials meetings, and working groups. It has other variations including other countries, ASEAN+3 and ASEAN+6, which extend its geographic scope beyond Southeast Asia to a broader regional scope. At the other end of the spectrum are smaller regional groupings linked to major donors such as ADB or the US. The promotion of economic development and economic integration are common themes of all of these frameworks.

ASEAN is also an international organization. It is not as advanced as the EU in terms of policy integration and supranational institutions, but it is also more comprehensive and institutionalized compared to other sub-regional frameworks in the region. ASEAN is a long term effort aiming at regional integration in a broad sense. In 2015, it launched the ASEAN community, which cooperates on a broad range of issue areas. It includes not only the ASEAN Economic Community, but also the Political and Security Community and the Social and Cultural Community. The environmental field is included in the Social and Cultural Community. ASEAN has a modest but permanent secretariat. The ASEAN Ministerial Meeting on the Environment (AMME) coordinates ASEAN's cooperation on the environment, and under it, the ASEAN Senior Officials on the Environment (ASOEN) have established several working groups to address environmental issues. In addition to the core ASEAN countries, ASEAN has special relationships with groups of its neighbors, forming two larger regional groupings. ASEAN+3 includes Japan, China, and South Korea, while ASEAN+6 adds three additional countries, Australia, New Zealand, and India. ASEAN+3 holds ministerial meetings in a variety of areas including the environment, and has work plans on climate change and sustainable development cooperation.[10]

The Trilateral Summit among China, Japan, and Korea was first held in 1999 at the ASEAN+3 Summit, but an independent summit was initiated in 2008. It is quite sensitive to geopolitical considerations, and no summit was held in 2013 or 2014, until the 6th summit was held in 2015. Nevertheless, the countries agreed to establish a permanent Trilateral Secretariat in 2011. Environment-related cooperation activities are implemented through the Tripartite Environment Ministers Meeting (TEMM) as described elsewhere in this chapter.[11]

The Pacific Community (SPC) focuses broadly on well-being and sustainable development "through the effective and innovative application of science and knowledge." It was established in 1947 and has 26 country and territory members.[12] Its headquarters, with about 200 staff, is located in New Caledonia. Environment related elements in the Pacific Community Strategic Plan 2016 2020 include sustainable management of natural resources, sustainable transport and energy security, and multi-sectoral responses to climate change and disasters (Pacific Community 2015).

The South Asian Association for Regional Cooperation (SAARC), established in 1985 and mainly focused on economic and social cooperation, has eight members: Afghanistan, Bangladesh, Bhutan, India, Maldives, Nepal, Pakistan and Sri Lanka, and its secretariat is located in Nepal. The institutional structure includes a leaders summit, council of ministers, and various technical committees, working groups, and expert groups. "Environment, natural disasters, and biotechnology" is one of SAARC's eight areas of cooperation. Its Environment Action Plan was adopted in 1997, and the SAARC Convention on Cooperation on Environment was ratified by all member countries and went into effect in 2013. In 2008, the SAARC Ministerial Meeting on Climate Change adopted a three-year Action Plan on Climate Change. The environment ministers met nine times after 1992, but the last meeting was in 2011.[13]

The Greater Tumen Initiative (GTI) has four members: China, South Korea, Mongolia, and Russia. GTI is supported by UNDP. It was initiated in 1991 as the Greater Tumen Area Development Programme, and it adopted its current name in 2005. GTI focuses broadly on development, but environment is one of its main work areas, and environment is also related to other work areas such as energy and transport.[14]

ADB began an initiative to promote regional cooperation in 1994 which facilitated the creation of several sub-regional cooperation frameworks to promote economic development involving national governments as members. One of them, the Greater Mekong Subregion (GMS), discussed in more detail below, has undergone extensive institutional development with summit and ministerial meetings as well as working groups. It also has a significant environmental component. Two of ADB's other sub-regional frameworks, BIMP-EAGA and IMT-GT, have more modest environmental components, so they are also briefly discussed below. However, two others, CAREC (Central Asia Regional Economic Cooperation) and SASEC (South Asia Subregional Economic Cooperation), do not appear to have any significant environmental activities as described on their websites, and even their energy and transport-related activities mainly do not appear to have major focuses on environmental aspects, so they are not discussed here.[15]

The Greater Mekong Subregion (GMS) is broadly focused on economic development and regional integration, but it also has a major environmental component. Established in 1992 with the assistance of the Asian Development Bank, which serves as the secretariat, the GMS has five member countries – Cambodia, China (specifically Yunnan Province and Guangxi Zhuang Autonomous Region), Laos, Myanmar, Thailand, and Vietnam. GMS holds a leaders' summit every three years and a Ministerial Conference annually. Priority sectors are coordinated by working groups and forums.[16] Environment ("Protecting the Environment and Promoting Sustainable Use of Shared Natural Resources") is one of the five "thrusts" of the Greater Mekong Subregion Economic Cooperation Program Strategic Framework 2012–2022. The sector priorities in the Framework also include environmental elements, including "promoting competitive, climate friendly, and sustainable agriculture," "enhancing environmental performance in the GMS," incorporating climate change considerations in transport development, "developing and utilizing more efficiently indigenous, low carbon, and renewable resources, while reducing the sub-region's dependence on imported fossil fuels," improving energy efficiency, promoting renewable energy, and promoting sustainable tourism. The Core Environment Program and Biodiversity Conservation Corridors Initiative (CEP–BCI) is included in the Framework. GMS holds an environment ministers meeting, and the GMS Working Group on the Environment has steering and umbrella functions and receives progress reports from the GMS Environment Operations Centre (EOC) (Asian Development Bank 2011). Regarding the scale of its work, "as of September 2011, the program had implemented 55 investment projects with a total project cost of about USD 14 billion" (Asian Development Bank 2011).

The Brunei Darussalam–Indonesia–Malaysia–Philippines East ASEAN Growth Area (BIMP-EAGA) initiative, according to ADB, "was launched in 1994 as a cooperation initiative by the four BIMP-EAGA nations to accelerate economic development in areas that are geographically distant from their national capitals." Its members include the "entire sultanate of Brunei Darussalam; the provinces of Kalimantan, Sulawesi, Maluku and West Papua of Indonesia; the states of Sabah and Sarawak and the federal territory of Labuan in Malaysia; and Mindanao and the province of Palawan in the Philippines." It does not appear to have its own website independent of the ADB webpage.[17] Most of the BIMP-EGA Vision 25 focuses on economic development, but one of the Vision's five "pillars" is the "environment pillar." The "Environment Strategy's" four "strategic priorities" are climate change adaptation and mitigation, promotion of clean and green technologies, sustainable management of natural resources and ecosystems, and public awareness and capacity building for environmental awareness and sustainability. The Vision also explains the initiative's governance structure, which, like other similar frameworks, includes summits of leaders, ministerial meetings, and senior officials meetings. State and local governments as well as businesses are involved (BIMP-EAGA n.d.).

The Indonesia-Malaysia-Thailand Growth Triangle (IMT-GT), established in 1993, is similar in many ways to BIMP-EAGA in terms of its structure and contents. Unlike BIMP-EAGA, it has its own website, but there is very little information on it. Most publicly available information seems to be on the ADB website.[18] Most of the IMT-GT's Vision 2036 focuses on economic development, but one of its seven "pillars" is on the environment. The Vision's environmental focus areas include a low carbon economy, sustainable management of natural resources, a green city initiative, and ecosystem management and restoration. It also has similar institutional governance structures including the leaders' summit, ministerial meetings, senior officials meetings, working groups, and a forum for chief ministers and governors of local governments. Other stakeholders such as businesses and local governments are involved (IMT-GT 2017).

The Bay of Bengal Initiative for Multi-Sectoral Technical and Economic Cooperation (BIMSTEC) was established in 1997 with seven member countries from two sub-regions around the Bay of Bengal, South Asia (Bangladesh, Bhutan, India, Nepal, and Sri Lanka) and Southeast Asia (Myanmar and Thailand). Its secretariat is located in Dhaka, Bangladesh. Its institutional structure is similar to other frameworks, including a leaders summit, ministerial meetings, a senior officials meeting, working groups, and task forces. Two out of its 16 priority sectors are related to the environment, "environment and natural disaster management," and climate change. Detailed information about its environment-related activities is not available on its website.[19]

The Lower Mekong Initiative (LMI), established in 2009, "is a multinational partnership among Cambodia, Laos, Myanmar, Thailand, Vietnam, and the United States to create integrated sub-regional cooperation among the five Lower Mekong Countries" according to its website. Regarding funding, its website explains that "the United States has provided significant funds to LMI projects and activities" and highlights the major contributions made by ADB and the World Bank. Moreover, the Friends of the Lower Mekong (FMI) is a platform to facilitate donor coordination and policy dialogue, and includes Australia, the European Union, Japan, New Zealand, the Republic of Korea, the Asian Development Bank, and the World Bank in addition to the main LMI members. Regarding the governance structure, the website explains that "the LMI official calendar includes Regional Working Group, Senior Officials', and Ministerial Meetings." "Environment and water" is one of its six "pillars" of activities.[20]

Sub-regional environment-related frameworks

There are at least four sub-regional frameworks with a focus on environmental issues. NEASPEC focuses on Northeast Asia, SPREP focuses on the Pacific, SACEP focuses on South Asia, and ICIMOD focuses on a group of countries related to the Hindu-Kush Himalayan Mountains.

NEASPEC was established in 1993 and has six member countries (China, Japan, South Korea, North Korea, Mongolia, and Russia). One of its distinctive features is that it includes North Korea, although North Korea does not attend the meetings when they are held in South Korea or

Japan. Another feature is that member countries do not necessarily participate in all of the programs; they can just participate in the ones that interest them. In 2010, ESCAP's East and Northeast Asia Office (ENEA) became the permanent secretariat. NEASPEC is governed by the Senior Officials Meeting, and member countries are represented by both foreign and environment ministries. Its main work areas include nature conservation in transboundary areas, transboundary air pollution mitigation, prevention of dust and sandstorms, eco-efficiency partnership, and marine protected areas.[21]

SACEP was established in 1982 and has eight member countries (Afghanistan, Bangladesh, Bhutan, India, Maldives, Nepal, Pakistan, and Sri Lanka). Its mission focuses on environment in the context of sustainable development. Its programs mainly focus on six areas: the Post 2015 South Asian Development Agenda, biodiversity conservation, sustainable consumption and production (SCP), waste management, climate, and the South Asian Seas Program. The Secretariat is located in Colombo, Sri Lanka, and it has 10 staff including the Director General.[22]

SPREP focuses on both environment and sustainable development. It achieved autonomy as an international organization in 1993. It has 19 members including 14 Pacific island countries, four countries from outside the region with Pacific island possessions (US, UK, France, New Zealand) and Australia. SPREP has four major priorities: biodiversity and ecosystem management, climate change, waste management and pollution control, and environmental monitoring and governance. Each of these areas is associated with a network. SPREP is based in Apia, Samoa, with over 90 staff.[23]

ICIMOD, based in Kathmandu, Nepal and established in 1983, has eight member countries: Afghanistan, Bangladesh, Bhutan, China, India, Myanmar, Nepal, and Pakistan. ICIMOD's activities span a broad range of issues related to environment and development including agriculture; air, snow, and glaciers; climate change; ecosystems, gender, mountain livelihoods, remote sensing and GIS, and water. Core donors include not only the regional member countries, but also five non-regional countries (Australia, Austria, Norway, Switzerland, UK), and others.[24]

Ministers meetings

Environment ministers meetings are another important type of international cooperation framework in the region. The Tripartite Environment Ministers Meeting among China, Japan, and Korea (TEMM), which began in 1999, is one of the most active ones (TEMM 2010). TEMM's second five-year Tripartite Joint Action Plan, with over 30 activities covering nine priority areas, was adopted in 2015.[25] ASEAN also has regular meetings of environment ministers (AMME), as well as other ministers, as a part of ASEAN's governance structure (Elder and Miyazawa 2015). The newest meeting with the broadest geographic membership is the Forum of Ministers and Environment Authorities of Asia Pacific. Its first meeting was organized by UNEP in 2015 to discuss implementation of resolutions and decisions adopted at the first UN Environmental Assembly (UNEA-1) and identify "regional priorities and recommendations to promote environmental sustainability for the post-2015 Sustainable Development Agenda, and priority issues for consideration at UNEA-2, and for UNEP's Medium Term Strategy (MTS) for 2018 2021" (UNEP 2015). This meeting was held back-to-back with the third Asia Pacific Forum on Sustainable Development organized by ESCAP, which aimed to discuss regional priorities for the implementation of Agenda 2030 in the region.[26] APEC has also held meetings of environment ministers, but not regularly. The APEC environment ministers have only met three times, in 1994, 1997, and 2012. The ASEM Environment Ministers Meeting has been held four times, first in 2002 and most recently in 2014. The Asia Pacific Ministerial Conference on Environment and

Development (MCED) has been held every five years since 1985, organized by ESCAP in cooperation with UNEP and ADB. ECOASIA was a meeting of the region's environment ministers organized by and held in Japan from 1991 to 2008.[27] Finally, Japan hosted the G7/G8 environment ministers meeting twice, in 2008 in Kobe (G8), and in 2016 in Toyama (G7).

Ministries related to other aspects of sustainable development have also held ministerial meetings in the context of these frameworks. These ministries include finance, trade, energy, transport, health, and others. Reviewing these is beyond the scope of this chapter.

Regional and sub-regional seas frameworks

Globally, there are 18 Regional Seas Programmes which aim to "promote the sustainable management and use of coastal and marine environments" according to UNEP. Seven of these are administered by UNEP. Four are in the Asia-Pacific region, and two of these, COBSEA and NOWPAP, are directly administered by UNEP, while the other two, the South Asian Seas Programme and the Pacific Environment Programme, are not administered by UNEP, but instead by SACEP and SPREP, respectively.[28]

COBSEA's members include nine countries: Cambodia, China, Indonesia, South Korea, Malaysia, Philippines, Singapore, Thailand, and Vietnam. The East Asian Seas Action Plan was approved in 1981 with five participating countries. Another five countries joined in 1994 when the Plan was revised, but Australia was no longer a member. COBSEA's secretariat only has four staff members.[29]

NOWPAP's Northwest Pacific Action Plan was adopted in 1994. There are four member countries: China, Japan, South Korea, and Russia, and four staff members in the coordinating unit.[30]

PEMSEA is not listed under UNEP regional seas webpage. It has 11 member countries including Cambodia, China, Indonesia, Japan, North Korea, South Korea, Lao, Philippines, Singapore, Timor Leste, and Vietnam. PEMSEA's website explains that it was created in 1993 based on an intervention by the GEF, "implemented" by UNDP, "executed" by the International Maritime Organization (IMO). Based in the Philippines, PEMSEA's secretariat only has seven staff members. PEMSEA's network also includes 20 NGOs. The Sustainable Development Strategy for Seas of East Asia (SDS-SEA) is the main basis for PEMSEA's activities.[31]

River basin frameworks

The Network of Asian River Basin Organizations (NARBO) was established in 2004 in order to promote integrated water resources management in Asia through strengthening capacity, exchange of information and experience, and improving water governance. NARBO works with a variety of actors including national river basin organizations, sectoral agencies, and knowledge partners. NARBO also provides technical advice and promotes regional cooperation. The 86 member organizations include government agencies from 13 countries (Bangladesh, Cambodia, Indonesia, Japan, Laos, Malaysia, Philippines, Thailand, Vietnam, Nepal, India, Thailand, and Pakistan) and river basin organizations from a slightly different list of 12 countries (China, Indonesia, Japan, Korea, Laos, Malaysia, Myanmar, Pakistan, Philippines, Sri Lanka, Thailand, Vietnam) and the Mekong River Commission. It has a variety of knowledge partners such as other sub-regional and national water partnerships, universities, research institutes, and other NGOs, giving NARBO a multi-stakeholder character. Regarding the secretariat role, NARBO's website states that the Secretary-General and one of the three Vice Secretaries General are from the Japan Water Agency, and the two others are from the Asian Development Bank (Philippines), and the Asian Development Bank Institute (Japan). NARBO's location is not specifically stated, but its website url suggests a location in Japan.[32]

The Mekong River Commission was established in 1995, succeeding the Mekong River Committee. It has four member countries, Cambodia, Lao PDR, Thailand, and Vietnam. The Secretariat has about 150 staff members in two offices – one in Phnom Penh, Cambodia, and the other in Vientiane, Lao PDR. The Commission has two dialogue partners, China and Myanmar, and there is a Donor Consultative Group. Each member country has a National Mekong Committee. Main programs include agriculture and irrigation, basin development, climate change and adaptation, drought management, environment, fisheries, flood management and mitigation, information and knowledge management, sustainable hydropower, integrated capacity building, integrated water resources management, and navigation.[33]

Treaties

There are few formal regional treaties or environmental agreements in Asia. The most prominent one is the ASEAN Agreement on Transboundary Haze Pollution (ASEAN Haze Agreement). It was signed in 2002, and has been ratified by all 10 ASEAN member states after Indonesia ratified it in 2015. Indonesia effectively cooperated with the Agreement's implementation before its ratification in 2015 (Jerger 2014). In terms of institutionalization, the ASEAN Coordinating Centre for Transboundary Haze Pollution Control (ACC) was created, and the ASEAN Secretariat serves as the interim ACC.[34]

The Basel Convention is an example of a global agreement which has regional coordinating centers. Four of them are in Asia and the Pacific. The center for the Asia-Pacific region is located in China (Tsinghua University), the center for Southeast Asia is located in Indonesia (Ministry of the Environment), the center for technology transfer and training in the South Pacific is located in Samoa (SPREP), and another regional center is in Tehran (Ministry of the Environment). Funding comes from the host countries, project-related funding, and voluntary contributions. Their functions include training, information dissemination, consulting, and awareness raising.[35]

The Stockholm Convention on Persistent Organic Pollutants (POPs) has also established five regional centers in the Asia-Pacific region in China, India, Indonesia, Iran, and Kuwait. These regional centers are intended to provide technical assistance and promote technology transfer.[36]

Type 2: Focused environment-related forums/programs/networks

There is a large number and wide variety of environment-related forums/ programs/ networks in the region focused more narrowly on specific environment-related issues. Some examples are highlighted in Table 23.3. These are also characterized by a range of institutional arrangements. Governments are involved in a range of ways, but most of these also have some kind of multi-stakeholder involvement. This wide range is exemplified by the case of regional air pollution frameworks. Some are mainly intergovernmental in character, or are at least mainly led by governments; EANET's "legal instrument" clarifies its intergovernmental character. At the other end of the spectrum is Clean Air Asia (CAA), where initiative is mainly taken by the staff who work very hard to engage governments, other donor organizations, and various stakeholders. Some initiatives originated from the leadership of one country, and some remain mainly centered around one or a small number of leading countries. In all of these initiatives, participation is voluntary, although participation is generally motivated by the expected benefits of participation, and often most of the costs are paid by the initiating country.

The remainder of this section classifies these forums/ programs/ networks into government-led and multi-stakeholder-oriented. Some government-led ones are intergovernmental, based on an agreement among several governments. Others are based on the initiative of

Table 23.3 Focused, environment-related forums/programs/networks

Name	*Founded*	*Members**	*Focus*	*Nature*
EANET	1998	13	Air pollution	Government-led
Male Declaration	1998	8	Air pollution	Government-led
CAA	2001	250**	Air pollution	Multi-stakeholder
LTP	1995	3	Air pollution	Formally multi-stakeholder; government-led in practice
WEPA	2004	13	Water	Government-led
AECEN	2005	19	Compliance & enforcement	Government-led
Regional Forum on Environment & Health	2005	13	Environment and health	Government-led
3R Forum	2009	39	Resource efficiency	Government-led
APCAP	NA	NA	Sustainable consumption and production	Multi-stakeholder
APAN	2009	NA	Climate adaptation	Multi-stakeholder
ACP	2009	NA	Co-benefits (multi sector)	Government-led
AP-Bon	2009	NA	Biodiversity	Government-led
ESABII	2009	14	Biodiversity	Government-led

Notes: * Government members; ** Includes non-government members. NA = not available.

Source: Author.

mainly one government, or take the form of a partnership among a few governments. Generally, these involve non-governmental stakeholders, but decision making and funding is largely directed by governments. In the case of arrangements classified as multi-stakeholder, typically the initiative is taken by non-governmental stakeholders, especially the secretariat, although governments are certainly involved. Nevertheless, often, the situation is that the non-governmental stakeholders try to persuade governments to take some kind of action and/or provide funding.

Government-led

EANET (Acid Deposition Monitoring Network in East Asia) was created in 1998 in order to "create a common understanding on the state of acid deposition problems in East Asia, provide useful inputs for decision making at various levels with the aim of preventing or reducing the adverse impacts on the environment, and promote cooperation." It has 13 member countries, its secretariat is the Regional Resource Centre for Asia and the Pacific (RRC.AP) at the Asian Institute of Technology – A UNEP Collaborating Centre, and it has a network center, the Asia Center for Air Pollution Research (ACAP), located in Japan.[37]

The Male Declaration is focused on air pollution issues, like EANET, but it is geographically focused on South Asia instead of East Asia. Established in 1998, it has eight member countries: Bangladesh, Bhutan, India, Iran, Maldives, Nepal, Pakistan, and Sri Lanka. Also like EANET, its secretariat is RRC.AP.[38] This initiative published a report on its progress from 1998 to 2013 which indicated that in addition to RRC.AP, its activities were also supported by the government of Sweden, SIDA, SEI, UNEP, SWEREA/KIMAB, and the Swedish Environmental Research Institute (IVL) (Male Declaration 2013).

ACP (Asian Co-benefits Partnership) was created in 2009 in order to "support the mainstreaming of co-benefits into sectoral development plans, policies and projects in Asia," particularly for climate change measures which can simultaneously address other environmental issues such as air pollution, water pollution, and waste management. This is an example of a relatively small initiative, initiated by the Ministry of Environment of Japan, with the participation of two other countries, the Ministry of Environment of Indonesia, and the Pollution Control Department of Thailand. A research institute affiliated with the Ministry of Environmental Protection of China, the Policy Research Centre for Environment and Economy (PRCEE), also participates in the Advisory Group, along with representatives of other international organizations (UNEP and ESCAP) and other air pollution networks (CAA and the Global Atmospheric Pollution Forum). The Institute for Global Environmental Strategies (IGES) serves as the secretariat.[39]

The Regional Forum on Environment and Health in Southeast and East Asian Countries was established in 2005 and has 13 member countries. The ministers of health and environment have met once every three years since 2007. The secretariat role is jointly shared by WHO and UNEP. The distinguishing feature of this Forum is to connect two sets of ministries, health and environment, to work on common issues.[40]

WEPA (Water Environment Partnership in Asia) "aims to promote good governance in water environment management by providing necessary, relevant information and knowledge, through a series of databases." WEPA, established in 2004, has 13 member countries: Cambodia, China, Indonesia, Japan, South Korea, Lao PDR, Malaysia, Myanmar, Nepal, Philippines, Sri Lanka, Thailand, and Vietnam. The organization diagram on WEPA's website shows WEPA as a partnership between Japan and the other countries, governed by an annual workshop, and implemented through two working groups. It states that WEPA is an initiative of the Ministry of Environment of Japan. WEPA's third phase began in 2014.[41]

The Regional 3R Forum in Asia and the Pacific is an initiative of the UN Centre for Regional Development (UNCRD), based in Nagoya, Japan, and 39 countries are participating. It was established in 2009 in order to promote national governments to mainstream the 3Rs into overall policy, planning, and development, as part of the 3R Initiative, which was launched in 2005. The Regional 3R Forum also has a related knowledge platform.[42]

The regional Environmentally Sustainable Transport (EST) Forum in Asia, also coordinated by UNCRD, implements the Asian Environmentally Sustainable Transport Initiative, which was started in 2004, also as an initiative of the Ministry of Environment, Japan. As of 2013, there were 21 members of the Forum which included representatives from ministries of environment, transport, and health as well as experts and representatives from international organizations, donor agencies, and NGOs.[43]

ESABII (East and Southeast Asia Biodiversity Information Initiative) was established in 2009, and its members as of 2012 included 14 countries (Brunei, Cambodia, China, Indonesia, Japan, Korea, Lao PDR, Malaysia, Mongolia, Myanmar, Philippines, Singapore, Thailand, and Vietnam), three organizations (Secretariat of the CBD, ASEAN Centre for Biodiversity, and the Global Biodiversity Information Facility), and two networks (AP-BON and BioNET-International). The Biodiversity Center of Japan, Nature Conservation Bureau, Ministry of the Environment of Japan, serves as the secretariat. It focuses on capacity building for taxonomy and building an information system on biodiversity in the region (ESABII Secretariat 2012).[44]

AP-BON (Asia Pacific Biodiversity Observation Network) was established in 2009 as a regional network related to the Global Earth Observation Network (GEO BON). "AP-BON's approaches for biodiversity observation are on three levels: remote sensing, ecological process research and species/genetic research." Its organization has a Steering Committee and five working groups. The

Secretariat is the Biodiversity Center of Japan, Nature Conservation Bureau, of the Ministry of Environment Japan. Members and partners are not listed on the website.[45]

The mission of AECEN (Asian Environmental Compliance and Enforcement Network), established in 2005, is to "promote improved compliance with environmental legal requirements in Asia through regional exchange of innovative policies and practices." There are 18 member countries. Members include environmental agencies from Cambodia, India, Indonesia, Japan, Korea, People's Republic of China, Lao PDR, Malaysia, Maldives, Mongolia, Myanmar, Nepal, Pakistan, Philippines, Singapore, Sri Lanka, Thailand, and Vietnam. Additional partners include USAID, ADB, and the US Environmental Protection Agency. The Executive Committee has no more than nine members, including geographically balanced representatives from six member countries and three international development agencies. The Institute for Global Environmental Strategies (IGES) serves as the secretariat.[46]

Multi-stakeholder-oriented

CAA (Clean Air Asia) was established in 2001 by the ADB, World Bank, and USAID, and it is governed by a Board of Trustees. Since 2007, it has been a UN-recognized partnership with almost 250 member organizations. Unlike the government-led frameworks described above, CAA is not governed as an intergovernmental framework, although some governments are members and contribute to its activities. Government agencies contributing in 2014 included the Environmental Protection Administration of Taiwan, Guangdong Province (China) Department of Transport, Hanoi Urban Transport Development (Vietnam), Ministry of Environment (Japan), USAID, and the US Environmental Protection Agency. Donors also included corporations, foundations, several UN organizations, research institutes, and related networks. CAA clearly involves a very wide range of stakeholders. The website solicits paid memberships. Revenues for 2014 totaled about USD 2.3 million, and 33 staff are listed on the website (Clean Air Asia 2014).[47]

APAN (Asia Pacific Adaptation Network), a self-styled "network of networks," was created in 2009, launched by the Prime Minister of Thailand. In 2011, it merged with the Regional Climate Change Adaptation Knowledge Platform (AKP) which was launched in 2008 as a partnership between UNEP, Regional Resource Centre for Asia Pacific (RRC.AP), and the Stockholm Environment Institute. APAN is facilitated by UNEP-ROAP, and operates through a Regional Hub, jointly hosted by IGES and the Regional Resource Centre for Asia Pacific (RRC.AP), in partnership with key "centers of excellences" [sic] and actors. The Ministry of Environment Japan, Asian Development Bank, and the Swedish International Development Cooperation Agency (SIDA) provided financial support from its inception. Regarding governance, APAN's brochure explains that it:

> [I]s governed by a Steering Committee that comprises renowned climate change scientists and senior government officials and representatives from donor agencies. APAN is supported by the Ministry of the Environment, Japan, the Asian Development Bank, the USAID funded ADAPT Asia-Pacific project and others.[48]

LTP (Long-Range Transboundary Air Pollutants in North East Asia), according to its website, is an international joint research project among China, Korea, and Japan, focusing on the long range transport of air pollutants in Northeast Asia. It was established in 1995. Its secretariat is Korea's National Institute of Environmental Research (NIER). Officially it is not an intergovernmental organization, but the researchers from the three countries are funded by their respective environment ministries. Environment ministry officials from the three countries typically attend the meetings. Technically, China considers LTP to be a combination of two bilateral research projects (China–Korea and Japan–Korea) rather than a multilateral initiative.[49]

The Asia Pacific Roundtable on Sustainable Consumption and Production (APRSCP), according to its website, is an "Asia-focused international, nongovernmental, non-profit, network institution" and "multi-stakeholder dialogue" which promotes sustainable consumption and production in the region. Seven national governments are listed as "host countries" (Thailand, Australia, Philippines, Indonesia, Malaysia, Vietnam, Sri Lanka), but there is also participation from a wide variety of stakeholders including international organizations, NGOs, NPOs, other research organizations and businesses. Most of the officers and members of the Board of Trustees are not described as government officials. The website highlights four main supporting partners: UNEP, UNIDO, GIZ, and the EU.[50]

Type 3: City-related networks

Cities have also created various networks of different types, varying widely in terms of their geographic scope, membership, and partnerships. Table 23.4 highlights three major examples. One is global, one is regional, and one is global with regional and national branches. CityNet has closer relations with UN organizations and other stakeholders such as NGOs and private companies, while the others are more focused on their member cities.

CityNet is an example of a region-focused network covering the Asia-Pacific region. According to its website, it was "established in 1987 with the support of ESCAP, UNDP and UN-Habitat. The network has grown to include 131 municipalities, NGOs, private companies and research centers." The Secretariat was established in 1992 with the support of the City of Yokohama, Japan, and was moved to Seoul, South Korea, in 2013, although a Project Office remains in Yokohama. CityNet has a broad focus on a wide range of issues related to sustainable development.[51]

ICLEI (ICLEI-Local Governments for Sustainability), in contrast, is a global network, but it also has regional and country offices. Of its nine regions, four are in the Asia-Pacific (East Asia, South Asia, Southeast Asia, and Oceania). The East Asia region, which includes China, Chinese Taipei, South and North Korea, and Japan, has over 70 city members, and it has offices in Korea, Japan, and Taiwan, in addition to its secretariat in Seoul (established in 2012). The South Asian region, with over 60 city members, has an office in India, while ICLEI Southeast Asia, which was established in 1999 and covers the countries of the Philippines, Indonesia, Thailand, and Malaysia, has a project office in Indonesia in addition to its base in the Philippines. The office for the Oceania region, serving Australia, New Zealand and the Pacific islands, was established in 1999 and is located in Australia. The Oceania region has over 45 members, mostly in Australia, but also in New Zealand, Solomon Islands, and Vanuatu. ICLEI has a broad focus on a wide range

Table 23.4 International cooperation frameworks focusing on local governments

Name	*Type*
CityNet	Asia-Pacific (regional) network
ICLEI	Global network with formal regional and national divisions in Asia
C40	Global network with significant Asian membership

Source: Author.

of issues related to sustainability, although many are related to the environment. Moreover, each region may focus on issues of particular interest to its members.[52]

C40, established in 2005, is a global initiative focused more specifically on climate change issues, not sustainable development more broadly. Of the 85 member cities, over one-third are in Asia, including 13 in East Asia (mostly China, but also Korea and Japan), nine in South or West Asia, and nine in Oceania or Southeast Asia.[53]

Some international cooperation frameworks mentioned earlier mixed national and local cooperation, such as NARBO, BIMP-EAGA, and IMT-GT, but these have not been led by cities. Although international cooperation is not generally within cities' mandates, the Japanese national government has encouraged international cooperation by cities in the field of environment (Nakamura, Elder, and Mori 2011), and city awards programs have been established by ASEAN and the EMM (Teoh and Maeda 2014), but it seems difficult to classify these as distinct regional cooperation frameworks.

Challenges for regional cooperation frameworks and initiatives

There are many initiatives and frameworks in the region, but they have a number of challenges. This chapter did not conduct a systematic study of effectiveness, which would be a good topic for future research, since their effectiveness has not been well studied. Nevertheless, several points can be readily observed from the examples presented in this chapter.

First, many initiatives are small in scale in terms of the nature and scope of their activities, and funding is generally modest. Small scale and modest funding do not necessarily mean that they are ineffective, but it does mean that their impact is not likely to be large.

Second, some issues, like environmental problems caused by mining, may not be addressed well by these frameworks despite their large number. Moreover, even in the case of air pollution, which is addressed by several frameworks, the efforts of the existing frameworks are not considered to be sufficient (Elder and Shimizu 2013; Elder and Matsumoto 2014).

Third, the large number of frameworks raises the question about the potential burden of their management and coordination on national governments. Before Rio+20, the large number of multilateral environmental agreements was said to be one of the salient features of international environmental governance, which caused a variety of problems such as straining the human resource capacity of governments to coordinate these agreements, especially for small countries with severe human resource as well as financial constraints (Kanie 2007; Najam, Papa, and Taiyab 2006; Inomata 2008). To this may be added the potential burden of cooperating with partnerships; over 3000 partnership initiatives and commitments were registered on the Partnerships for SDGs online platform as of June 2017.[54] On one hand, the rise of these new cooperation frameworks seems to add to the coordination burden of governments in the region, especially environment ministries. On the other hand, many of these frameworks are of small or modest size, and governments' financial and human resource commitments to them are usually not very large. In some cases, frameworks are organized by a one or more lead countries, sometimes in cooperation with MDBs, in order to provide assistance to developing countries. The relatively small size of these frameworks means that they might not be a large burden to the leading countries, while the beneficiary countries are expected to gain capacity.

Thus, these kinds of frameworks could be seen as a way to address issues in a more flexible and targeted way compared to formal multilateral agreements, which often require a long time to negotiate and need costly secretariats. Still, although this chapter does not conduct a formal assessment of their effectiveness, the overall scale of most of these efforts is generally quite small in relation to the scale of the problems they are trying to address. They tend to focus on information sharing, capacity building, research, or at most, pilot projects, and the pace of their work is generally not very fast. Although these frameworks are voluntary and tend not to have complicated structures or decision making processes, nevertheless, the intergovernmental nature of many of them still may prevent quick decision making, and governments are often slow to promise budgets and even slower to actually transmit the promised funds. Frameworks which are mainly led by non-governmental stakeholders may have quicker decision making processes, but the process of gaining cooperation and support from governments, especially funding, can still be slow. Government decision making procedures can also be unstable, especially after major transitions to new governments or political leaders, or even routine rotations of ministry officials.

Fourth, there is often some degree of overlap among different frameworks, with air pollution as a major example. Of course, each framework strives to identify its niche, so there is no exact duplication. However, in some areas, several existing frameworks are doing similar work, so there could be scope for rationalization or increased coordination.

Fifth, policy coordination among different policy areas and difficulties in mainstreaming environmental considerations into sustainable development more broadly remain as challenges. Some of the frameworks and initiatives described in this chapter include a broad range of issues and promote integrated approaches to sustainability. However, others are mainly related to environmental issues. There may be other frameworks and initiatives that are related to other areas of sustainability and SDGs such as agriculture, health, energy, and transportation. Various regional periodic ministerial meetings are held in many areas, for example, environment, energy, finance, or trade ministers meetings, and it is not clear to what extent they address issues related to sustainability in an integrated way.

Sixth, mainstreaming sustainability into regional economic integration is a major challenge for the most important cooperation frameworks, especially ASEAN, APEC, and ADB. The ASEAN Community was launched in 2015. Its organization is divided into three communities – Economic, Political-Security, and Socio-Cultural. These are partly based on the traditional three-pillar approach to sustainable development, with environment included in the Socio-Cultural Community, but sustainability was not established as the core principle of ASEAN. The ASEAN Community may need to take a more integrated approach in order to achieve the SDGs (Olsen, Teoh, and Miyazawa 2015). It was also difficult to assess whether APEC is expanding its efforts on sustainability and SDGs, since they were not highlighted on its website. ADB appeared to be making more efforts to orient its activities towards a greater emphasis on sustainability, as mentioned above. In addition, of the 17 focus areas highlighted on its home page, several are devoted directly to sustainability topics including environment and climate change, health, social development and poverty, and sustainable development goals. All of the other focus areas, such as energy, transport, agriculture and food security, could include sustainability elements.[55]

Seventh, the Trans Pacific Partnership (TPP), if it comes into force, could generate momentum for greater economic integration in the region.[56] However, it is not mainly focused on sustainability. TPP does not mention either the SDGs or the Paris Agreement on climate change. Instead, its main focus is on trade and investment liberalization and promoting traditional economic growth. Some have suggested that the emphasis on enforceable investor-state dispute settlement procedures could endanger countries' environmental policies and regulations, potentially offsetting the various vague safeguard clauses for environment and labor which lack concrete enforcement mechanisms (Sachs 2015). It has also been observed that the TPP is a step back, in some ways, by specifically recognizing fewer multilateral environment agreements compared to previous trade agreements (Mann 2016; Solomon and Beachy 2015).

Moreover, TPP would create new institutional mechanisms, for example relating to investor–state dispute settlement, apart from the standard dispute settlement system. Some TPP articles, including those on trade in goods, agriculture, environment, labor, and regulatory coherence, call for the establishment of councils related to that area which are to meet at least once after the agreement comes into force, which may carry out functions such as review priorities, review reports, guide cooperation and capacity building activities, and establish work programs. Functions may differ according to the area, and new ones may be added later if countries agree, and the frequency of meetings differs by article and may be changed later if countries agree.[57] Article 27 would establish a Trans-Pacific Partnership Commission to supervise the activities of all committees and working groups (and merge or dissolve them if desirable), periodically review the "economic relationship and partnership among the parties," and consider proposals for amendment or modification. It is not clear how these institutional arrangements might function in practice, but it represents a much greater degree of institutional development compared to most trade agreements, and if implemented, it would likely have a significant influence on sustainability issues in the region.

Discussion and conclusion

A major finding of this chapter is that there is a large number and wide variety of international cooperation frameworks in the region, with a variety of types of organization, membership, and activities. Moreover, this survey is not comprehensive, and it is likely that there are many more, especially smaller initiatives led by individual countries. This suggests a need to think more deeply about the different forms of international cooperation.

This large number of frameworks and initiatives reflects the wide range of environment and sustainability issues being addressed in the region as well as the large number of countries in the region and the broad range of their interests. According to (Matsuoka 2014), this may partly reflect some competition between different countries in establishing these frameworks. For example, in the area of air pollution, EANET was initiated by Japan while LTP was initiated by Korea, and there is some competition among the two frameworks even though both Japan and Korea are members of both frameworks. Overlaps among frameworks and initiatives are sometimes due to differences in their membership, as different groups of countries prefer to work in different ways. The challenge is that the large number of frameworks and initiatives places a large burden on governments for their management. This management is especially challenging for environment ministries, which have limited capacity.

These frameworks are characterized by an increasing degree of multi-stakeholder participation, as suggested by the ESG perspective. Governments in the region are increasingly working with other stakeholders, particularly from NGOs, research institutes, and the scientific community, but also business and others, while providing some support.

UN organizations and MDBs, especially UNEP, ESCAP, and ADB, are involved in many of the cooperation frameworks. ESCAP has considerable convening power to assemble governments together to discuss broad sustainability issues, such as Rio+20 and Sustainable Development Goals. UNEP coordinates a broad range of initiatives and serves as the secretariat for some frameworks. UNDP is involved in many country-based projects. ADB is an important source of funding as well as project coordination; it also supports a number of cooperation frameworks. In some cases, UNEP, ESCAP, or other international organizations may provide small amounts of funding, but ultimately, these international organizations themselves receive most of their funding from governments.

There are not very many frameworks specifically focused on cities, although cities do participate in some of the broader and specific cooperation frameworks which are managed mainly by national governments. Generally, cities have little capacity to engage in international cooperation since it is generally not part of their mandate, and they have limited ability to raise funds for it. Nevertheless, many Asian cities have shown a strong interest in participating in various international cooperation frameworks. In some cases, such as Japan, city involvement in international cooperation is encouraged and supported by national governments (Nakamura, Elder, and Mori 2011), especially for specific projects.

Many of the frameworks discussed in this chapter are small and/or weakly resourced. This raises questions about their effectiveness. Some frameworks resulted from initiatives of particular governments or NGOs. NGOs sometimes try to persuade governments, international organizations, and MDBs to establish new frameworks. In other cases, governments, international organizations, and/or MDBs work with NGOs or other stakeholders to establish a new framework to promote a particular issue. Sometimes, this results in a degree of overlap or duplication. It is difficult for one government or a few governments to bear most of the burden of funding a framework. Moreover, it is difficult for many governments to support such a large number of frameworks.

Nevertheless, this chapter's survey of regional cooperation does not suggest that national governments are being largely eclipsed, as they play key roles in most of the frameworks discussed in this chapter. National governments, sometimes working through larger international organizations and MDBs, have created a large number of frameworks. National governments are the main members and provide most of the financing, so they have the ability to set agendas and put projects and programs in motion by creating, supporting, and participating in these frameworks. Even though their ability or willingness to fund frameworks may be limited or insufficient, national governments are still the main funding source for many frameworks. Even in cases where funding is provided by MDBs, most of the funding for the MDBs is provided or authorized by national governments. NGOs often target national governments for funding for new frameworks or programs, and compete for funding from national governments to help governments to implement existing frameworks. In many cases, the stakeholders in these frameworks, particularly from the scientific community, would not be able to sustain the activities on their own without support from national governments.

The experience of the regional frameworks in Asia does provide additional evidence for the hypothesis that fragmentation in governance is increasing. Existing literature has observed governance for particular areas becoming more complex, overarching institutional complexity, and greater linkages among issue areas (Zelli and van Asselt 2013). This study illustrates another dimension, that there may also be an expansion in the type and nature of frameworks which do not fit the traditional image of international organizations.

Overall, these findings are generally along the lines of the trends identified by the ESG perspective, but there are some differences. The ESG literature related to architectures generally has a global focus, while this chapter highlights the regional aspect of architecture, particularly from the perspective of Asia, which may get less attention compared to other regions like Europe.

Finally, this survey is selective, not comprehensive, so there is plenty of room for further research. One possibility would be to undertake a more comprehensive survey, and possibly expand the focus to other areas of sustainability besides the environment. Perhaps more important would be to attempt to assess the effectiveness of some of these frameworks to understand the factors influencing effectiveness, especially in a comparative context rather than focusing separately on individual frameworks.

Acknowledgments

I wish to thank my colleagues Peter King and Hidefumi Imura for their comments, which were very helpful to improve this chapter. Hironori Hamanaka and Hideyuki Mori provided generous institutional support at IGES. I also wish to thank the editor of this book, Sara Hsu, for kindly inviting me to participate in this project and for her effective editorial direction. Any errors or omissions remain the responsibility of the author.

Notes

1 Quotation is taken from the abstract, available at www.mitpressjournals.org/doi/abs/10.1162/GLEP_e_00120 (accessed January 29, 2018).
2 Quotation is taken from the abstract, available at www.annualreviews.org/doi/pdf/10.1146/annurev.environ.33.050707.085733 (accessed January 29, 2018).
3 For a short discussion of the definition of international organizations see Martin and Simmons (2012). Also see the discussion in the *Yearbook of the International Law Commission 2003* Vol. II, Part 2, Report of the Commission to the General Assembly on the Work of Its Fifty-fifth Session, pp. 2022, available at http://legal.un.org/ilc/publications/yearbooks/english/ilc_2003_v2_p2.pdf (accessed June 25, 2017).
4 See UNEP-ROAP's website at http://web.unep.org/regions/roap/regional-initiatives-and-partnerships/ecosystem-management (accessed July 27, 2016).
5 GGGI's website is available at http://gggi.org/ (accessed July 18, 2016).
6 The sustainability-related section on APEC's website is located at www.apec.org/Home/Groups/Other-Groups/Sustainable-Development.aspx (accessed July 13, 2016).
7 Basic information about ASEM can be found at its website, www.aseminfoboard.org/ (accessed July 15, 2016).
8 Basic information about ASEF can be found at its website, www.asef.org/ (accessed July 15, 2016).
9 Basic information about the Asia-Europe Environmental Forum is available at its website, http://asef.org/projects/programmes/517-asia-europe-environment-forum-(envforum) (accessed July 15, 2016).
10 ASEAN's website has information on its external cooperation in all areas, at http://asean.org/asean/external-relations/ (accessed July 31, 2016).
11 Basic information about the Trilateral Secretariat can be found at its website, www.tcs-asia.org/index.php (accessed July 13, 2016).
12 SPC's website is available at www.spc.int/about-us/ (accessed June 20, 2017).
13 SAARC's website is available at http://saarc-sec.org/ (accessed June 22, 2017).
14 GTI's website is available at www.tumenprogramme.org/ (accessed July 16, 2016).
15 CAREC's website is available at www.carecprogram.org/, and SASEC's website is available at http://sasec.asia/ (accessed June 26, 2017).
16 Basic information about the Greater Mekong Subregion can be found at its website, http://greatermekong.org/ (accessed June 21, 2017).
17 Basic information on BIMP-EAGA is available on ADB's website at www.adb.org/countries/subregional-programs/bimp-eaga (accessed June 21, 2017).
18 The IMT-GT website can be accessed at http://imtgt.org/. ADB's webpage for IMT-GT is available at www.adb.org/countries/subregional-programs/imt-gt (accessed June 21, 2017).
19 BIMSTEC's website is available at http://bimstec.org/ (accessed June 21, 2017).
20 LMI's website is available at http://lowermekong.org/ (accessed June 21, 2017).
21 NEASPEC's website is available at www.neaspec.org/ (accessed July 16, 2016).
22 SACEP's website is available at www.sacep.org/ (accessed July 16, 2016).
23 SPREP's website is available at www.sprep.org/ (accessed July 16, 2016).
24 ICIMOD's website is available at www.icimod.org/ (accessed July 16, 2016).
25 The Plan is available at www.env.go.jp/press/files/jp/26974.pdf (accessed July 20, 2016).
26 The meeting's website is available here, www.unescap.org/events/apfsd3 (accessed July 16, 2016).
27 ECOASIA's website is available from the Ministry of Environment of Japan at www.env.go.jp/en/earth/ecoasia/index.html (accessed June 19, 2017).
28 UNEP's Regional Seas Programme is described at http://drustage.unep.org/regionalseas/who-we-are/regional-seas-programmes (accessed June 24, 2017).
29 COBSEA's website is available at www.cobsea.org/index.html (accessed July 16, 2016).
30 NOWPAP's website is available at www.nowpap.org/ (accessed June 21, 2017).
31 PEMSEA's website is available at www.pemsea.org/ (accessed July 16, 2016).
32 NARBO's website is available at www.narbo.jp/index.html (accessed July 18, 2016).

33 The Mekong River Commission's website is available at www.mrcmekong.org/ (accessed July 18, 2016).
34 The ASEAN Haze Agreement's website is available at http://haze.asean.org/ (accessed July 18, 2016).
35 Information about the Basel Convention Regional and Coordinating Centers can be found at www.basel.int/Partners/RegionalCentres/Overview/tabid/2334/Default.aspx (accessed July 18, 2016).
36 Information on the Stockholm Convention Regional Centres is available at http://chm.pops.int/Partners/RegionalCentres/Overview/tabid/425/Default.aspx (accessed July 18, 2016).
37 Information on EANET is available from its website at www.eanet.asia/ (accessed July 19, 2016).
38 Information on the Male Declaration is available from the website of its secretariat, RRC.AP at www.rrcap.ait.asia/male (accessed July 19, 2016).
39 Information on ACP is available from its website at www.cobenefit.org/index.html (accessed July 19, 2016).
40 Information about the Regional Forum on Environment and Health in Southeast and East Asian Countries is available from its website at www.environment-health.asia/rfeh/ (accessed July 26, 2016).
41 Information on WEPA is available from its website at www.wepa-db.net/index.htm (accessed July 18, 2016).
42 Information about the Regional 3R Forum in Asia and the Pacific is available from its website at www.uncrd.or.jp/index.php?menu=389, and more information is available from the related website managed by Japan's Ministry of Environment, www.env.go.jp/recycle/3r/en/index.html (accessed July 18, 2016). The 3R concept refers to reduce, reuse, and recycle.
43 Information on the Regional Environmentally Sustainable Transport (EST) Forum in Asia is available from its website at www.uncrd.or.jp/index.php?menu=384 (accessed July 18, 2016).
44 Information on ESABII is available from its website at www.esabii.biodic.go.jp/index.html (accessed July 19, 2016).
45 Information on AP-BON is available from its website at www.esabii.biodic.go.jp/ap-bon/index.html and its brochure www.esabii.biodic.go.jp/ap-bon/documents/AP-BON_Brochure.pdf (accessed July 19, 2016).
46 Information on AECEN is available from its website at www.aecen.org/ (accessed July 19, 2016).
47 Information on CAA is available from its website at http://cleanairasia.org/ (accessed July 19, 2016).
48 Information on APAN is available from its website at www.asiapacificadapt.net/ and its brochure at www.asiapacificadapt.net/sites/default/files/pdfs/APAN%20Brochure%20Oct2013.pdf (accessed July 19, 2016).
49 Information on LTP is available from its website at https://ltp.nier.go.kr/cmmn/main.ltp (accessed July 19, 2016). Information through discussions with participants was also collected directly by the author who attended several meetings of LTP and related air pollution frameworks during 2011 and 2012.
50 Information about APRSCP is available from its website at www.aprscp.net/index.html (accessed July 26, 2016).
51 Information on CityNet is available from its website at http://citynet-ap.org/ and its brochure at http://citynet-ap.org/wp-content/uploads/2016/04/CityNet-Booklet-2016.pdf (accessed July 19, 2016).
52 Information on ICLEI and its regions is available from its website at www.iclei.org/ (accessed July 19, 2016). According to its website, "ICLEI originally stood for the "International Council for Local Environmental Initiatives," but the full phrase was dropped in 2003 ... to reflect a broader focus on sustainability."
53 Information on C40 is available from its website at www.c40.org/ (accessed July 19, 2016).
54 The platform's website is available at https://sustainabledevelopment.un.org/partnerships/ (accessed June 20, 2017).
55 ADB's home page is available at www.adb.org/.
56 The text of the TPP is available on the website of the Office of the US Trade Representative, https://ustr.gov/tpp/ (accessed July 21, 2016).
57 For example, Article 2.17 for the Committee on Trade in Goods, 2.27 on agriculture, 19.15 on labor and 20.19 on environment, and 25.6 on regulatory coherence.

References

Andresen, Steinar, and Ellen Hey. (2005) "The Effectiveness and Legitimacy of International Environmental Institutions." *International Environmental Agreements: Politics, Law and Economics* 5 (3): 211–226. doi: 10.1007/s10784-005-3804-9.

APEC Secretariat. (2014) *APEC at a Glance*. Singapore: Asia Pacific Economic Cooperation (APEC). www.apec.org/Publications/2013/10/APEC-at-a-Glance-2014.

Asian Development Bank. (2010) *Institutions for Regional Integration*. Manila: Asian Development Bank. https://aric.adb.org/pdf/Institutions_for_Regionalization_Web.pdf.

Asian Development Bank. (2011) *The Greater Mekong Subregion Economic Cooperation Program Strategic Framework 2012–2022*. Manila, Philippines: Asian Development Bank. www.greatermekong.org/sites/default/files/gms-ec-framework-2012-2022.pdf.

Asian Development Bank. (2016) "Environmentally Sustainable Growth: A Strategic Review." www.adb.org/sites/default/files/evaluation-document/177137/files/in119-16.pdf.

Asian Infrastructure Investment Bank. (2016) "Environmental and Social Framework." www.aiib.org/en/policies-strategies/_download/environment-framework/20160226043633542.pdf.

Asian Infrastructure Investment Bank. (2017) "Energy Sector Strategy: Sustainable Energy for Asia." www.aiib.org/en/policies-strategies/strategies/.content/index/_download/aiib-energy-sector-Strategy-(2017)pdf.

Balsiger, Jörg, and Stacy D. VanDeveer. (2012) "Navigating Regional Environmental Governance." *Global Environmental Politics* 12 (3): 1–17. doi: 10.1162/GLEP_e_00120.

Biermann, Frank. (2007) "Reforming Global Environmental Governance: From UNEP Towards a World Environment Organization." In *Global Environmental Governance: Perspectives On The Current Debate*, edited by L. Swart and E. Perry, 103–123. New York: Center for UN Reform Education.

Biermann, Frank, and Philipp Pattberg. (2008) "Global Environmental Governance: Taking Stock, Moving Forward." *Annual Review of Environment and Resources* 33 (1): 277–294. doi: 10.1146/annurev.environ.33.050707.085733.

Biermann, Frank, Philipp Pattberg, Harro van Asselt, and Fariborz Zelli. (2009) "The Fragmentation of Global Governance Architectures: A Framework for Analysis." *Global Environmental Politics* 9 (4): 14–40. doi: 10.1162/glep.(2009)9.4.14.

BIMP-EAGA. (n.d.) *BIMP-EAGA Vision*. Brunei Darussalam-Indonesia-Malaysia-Philippines East ASEAN Growth Area (BIMP-EAGA). www.adb.org/sites/default/files/related/72256/bimp-eaga-vision-2025.pdf.

Clean Air Asia. (2014) *Clean Air Asia Annual Report (2014)*. Pasig City, Philippines: Clean Air Asia. http://cleanairasia.org/wp-content/uploads/2015/12/CAA-Annual-report-folded-122315.pdf.

Elder, Mark, and Naoko Matsumoto, eds. (2014) *International Workshop on Strengthening the International Cooperation Framework and Science-Policy Interface to Promote Air Pollution Control in East Asia: Proceedings*. Hayama, Japan: Institute for Global Environmental Strategies. http://pub.iges.or.jp/modules/envirolib/view.php?docid=5300.

Elder, Mark, and Ikuho Miyazawa. (2015) *A Survey of ASEAN's Organizational Structure and Decision Making Process for Regional Environmental Cooperation and Recommendations for Potential External Assistance*. Hayama, Japan: Institute for Global Environmental Strategies. http://pub.iges.or.jp/modules/envirolib/view.php?docid=5694.

Elder, Mark, and Simon Olsen. (2012) "Strengthening Governance for Environment and Sustainable Development: The Potential for a Capacity and Information Exchange Platform in Asia-Pacific." In *Greening Governance in Asia-Pacific*, edited by IGES, 17–34. Hayama, Japan: Institute for Global Environmental Strategies. http://pub.iges.or.jp/modules/envirolib/view.php?docid=4011.

Elder, Mark, and Mika Shimizu, eds. (2013) *International Workshop on Strengthening the International Cooperation Framework and Science-Policy Interface to Promote Air Pollution Control in East Asia 2013: Proceedings*. Hayama, Japan: Institute for Global Environmental Strategies. http://pub.iges.or.jp/modules/envirolib/view.php?docid=4521.

Elliott, Lorraine. (2012) "ASEAN and Environmental Governance: Strategies of Regionalism in Southeast Asia." *Global Environmental Politics* 12 (3): 38–57. doi: 10.1162/GLEP_a_00122.

ESABII Secretariat. (2012) *EASABII East and Southeast Asia Biodiversity Information Initiative*. Tokyo: ESABII Secretariat.

IGES. (2015) *Greening Integration in Asia: How Regional Integration Can Benefit People and the Environment*. Hayama, Japan: Institute for Global Environmental Strategies. www.iges.or.jp/en/pmo/wp5.html.

IISD, and UNEP-DTIE. (2005) *Environment and Trade: A Handbook*, 2nd Edition. United Nations Environment Programme and the International Institute for Sustainable Development. IISD: Winnipeg, Manitoba, Canada and UNEP-DTIE: Geneva, Switzerland. www.iisd.org/sites/default/files/pdf/2005/envirotrade_handbook_(2005)pdf.

IMT-GT. (2017) *IMT-GT Vision 2036*. Indonesia Malaysia Thailand Growth Triangle (IMT-GT). www.adb.org/sites/default/files/related/72271/imt-gt-vision-2036.pdf.

Inomata, Tadanori. (2008) *Management Review of Environmental Governance within the United Nations System.* Geneva: United Nations Joint Inspection Unit (JIU).
Ivanova, Maria. (2010) "UNEP in Global Environmental Governance: Design, Leadership, Location." *Global Environmental Politics* 10 (1): 30–59. doi: 10.1162/glep.(2010)10.1.30.
Jerger, David B. (2014) "Indonesia's Role in Realizing the Goals of ASEAN's Agreement on Transboundary Haze Pollution." *Sustainable Development Law and Policy* 14 (1): 35–45, 70–74. http://digitalcommons.wcl.american.edu/cgi/viewcontent.cgi?article=1545&context=sdlp.
Kanie, Norichika. (2007) "Governance with Multilateral Agreements: A Healthy or Ill-Equipped Fragmentation." In *Global Environmental Governance*, edited by Lydia Swart and Estelle Perry, 67–86. New York: Center for UN Reform Education. www.centerforunreform.org/?q=node/251.
Kawai, Masahiro, and Ganeshan Wignaraja. (2009) "The Asian 'Noodle Bowl': Is It Serious for Business?" *Asian Development Bank Institute Working Paper*, April. www.adb.org/sites/default/files/publication/155991/adbi-wp136.pdf.
Kim, Inkyoung. (2007) "Environmental Cooperation of Northeast Asia: Transboundary Air Pollution." *International Relations of the Asia-Pacific* 7:439–462. doi: 10.1093/irap/lcm008.
Koh, Kheng-Lian, ed. (2013) *ASEAN Environmental Law, Policy and Governance: Selected Documents.* Vol. 2. Singapore: World Scientific Publishing.
Male Declaration. (2013) "Male Declaration 1998–2013: A Synthesis – Progress and Opportunitites." www.rrcap.ait.asia/Publications/Synthesis Report.pdf.
Mann, Howard. (2016) "The TPP, Part I: A Deal Too Far." *IISD Commentary*, January. www.iisd.org/sites/default/files/publications/tpp-part-i-deal-too-far-commentary_1.pdf.
Martin, Lisa, and Beth Simmons. (2012) "International Organization and Institutions." *Handbook of International Relations*, edited by Walter Carlsnaes, Thomas Risse, and Beth A. Simmons, 326–351. London: Sage.
Matsuoka, Shunji. (2014) "Japan's Asian Environmental Strategy and a Soft Power of the 21st Century." *Public Policy Review* 10 (1): 189–226. doi: 10.11126/stanford/9780804785259.003.0009.
Mitchell, Ronald B. (2003) "International Environmental Agreements: A Survey of Their Features, Formation, and Effects." *Annual Review of Environment and Resources* 28: 429–461. doi: 10.1146/annurev.energy.28.050302.105603.
Mori, Akihisa, ed. (2013) *Environmental Governance for Sustainable Development: East Asian Perspectives.* Tokyo: United Nations University Press.
Najam, Adil, Mihaela Papa, and Nadaa Taiyab. (2006) *Global Environmental Governance: A Reform Agenda.* Winnipeg, Manitoba: International Institute for Sustainable Development and Ministry of Foreign Affairs of Denmark. www.iisd.org/library/global-environmental-governance-reform-agenda.
Nakamura, Hidenori, Mark Elder, and Hideyuki Mori. (2011) "The Surprising Role of Local Governments in International Environmental Cooperation." *The Journal of Environment & Development* 20: 219–250. doi: 10.1177/1070496511415644.
Nicholson, Simon, and Sikina Jinnah, eds. (2016) *New Earth Politics: Essays from the Anthropocene.* Cambridge, MA: MIT Press.
Olsen, Simon Høiberg, Shom Teoh, and Ikuho Miyazawa. (2015) "ASEAN Community and the Sustainable Development Goals: Positioning Sustainability at the Heart of Regional Integration." In *Greening Integration in Asia: How Regional Integration Can Benefit People and the Environment*, edited by Institute for Global Environmental Strategies, 59–78. Hayama, Japan: Institute for Global Environmental Strategies. http://pub.iges.or.jp/modules/envirolib/view.php?docid=6051.
Pacific Community. (2015) "Pacific Community Strategic Plan 2016–2020." www.spc.int/wp-content/uploads/2016/11/Strategic-Plan-2016-2020.pdf.
PRCEE, IGES, and KEI. (2009) *Tripartite Joint Research on Environmental Management in Northeast Asia.* Policy Research Center for Environment and Economy (PRCEE), Institute for Global Environmental Srategies (IGES), Hayama, Japan, and Korea Environmental Institute (KEI), Seoul, South Korea. http://enviroscope.iges.or.jp/modules/envirolib/upload/2253/attach/nea_report_final.pdf.
Robinson, Nicholas A., and Kheng-Lian Koh. (2002) "Strengthening Sustainable Development in Regional Inter-Governmental Governance: Lessons from the 'ASEAN Way.'" *Singapore Journal of International & Comparative Law* 6: 640–682. http://digitalcommons.pace.edu/cgi/viewcontent.cgi?article=1370&context=lawfaculty.
Sachs, Jeffrey D. (2015) "TPP Is Too Flawed for a Simple 'Yes' Vote." *Boston Globe*, November 8. www.bostonglobe.com/opinion/2015/11/08/jeffrey-sachs-tpp-too-flawed-for-simple-yes-vote/sZd0nlnCr18RurX1n549GI/story.html.

Solomon, Ilena, and Ben Beachy. (2015) *A Dirty Deal: How the Trans Pacific Partnership Threatens Our Climate*. Washington, DC: Sierra Club. www.sierraclub.org/sites/www.sierraclub.org/files/uploads-wysiwig/dirty-deal.pdf.

Takahashi, Wakana. (2002) "Problems of Environmental Cooperation in Norhteast Asia: The Case of Acid Rain." In *International Environmental Cooperation: Politics and Diplomacy in Pacific Asia*, edited by Paul Harris, 222–247. Boulder: University Press of Colorado.

TEMM. (2010) "Footprints of TEMM: Historical Development of Cooperation among Korea, China, and Japan from 1999 to (2010)." http://pub.iges.or.jp/modules/envirolib/view.php?docid=3237.

Teoh, Chin Shom Wei, and Toshizo Maeda. (2014) "National City Awards As a Practical Approach to Encourage Local Government Initiatives For Sustainable Cities." *IGES Policy Report*, March.

UNEP. (2015) "Chair's Summary: The First Forum of Ministers and Environment Authorities of Asia Pacific." www.unep.org/roap/Portals/96/forumdocuments/Chair's summary_22 May (2015)pdf.

Yoon, Esook. (2007) "Cooperation for Transboundary Pollution in Northeast Asia: Non-Binding Agreements and Regional Countries' Policy Interests." *Pacific Focus* 22 (2): 77–112.

Yoshimatsu, Hidetaka. (2010) "Regional Governance and Cooperation in Northeast Asia: The Cases of the Environment and IT." *RCAPS Working Paper*.

Young, Oran R. (2011) "Effectiveness of International Environmental Regimes: Existing Knowledge, Cutting-Edge Themes, and Research Strategies." *Proceedings of the National Academy of Sciences of the United States of America* 108 (50): 19853–19860. doi: 10.1073/pnas.1111690108.

Zelli, Fariborz, and Harro van Asselt. (2013) "The Institutional Fragmentation of Global Environmental Governance: Causes, Consequences, and Responses." *Global Environmental Politics* 13 (3): 1–14. doi: 10.1162/GLEP.

24

Renewable energy and new developmentalism in East Asia

Christopher M. Dent

Introduction

This chapter examines renewable energy development in East Asia and the deeper sustainable and other development contexts in which this has been situated. East Asia comprises two sub-regions, Northeast Asia (China, Japan, South Korea, North Korea, Taiwan and Mongolia) and Southeast Asia (Brunei, Cambodia, East Timor, Indonesia, Laos, Malaysia, Myanmar, Philippines, Singapore, Thailand and Vietnam). Over the last five or six decades, East Asia has been the world's most dynamic and fastest growing economic region. Annual double-digit percent increases in economic growth have not been uncommon for many East Asia countries during this period. The region consists of a diverse set of economies that together accounted for around 30 percent of the global economy in 2014, a higher share than both the European Union and the United States. East Asia has also emerged as the world's most significant driver of renewable energy development over the last decade or so. It is argued that this can be broadly understood from the conflation of two influencing meta-factors, namely state capacity and ecological modernization that, combined, form the basis of the region's 'new developmentalism'. This concerns the pursuit of new 'low-carbon economy' transformative objectives where renewables play a central role in various state strategies to realize these ends. However, this has not been without its conflicts, contradictions and controversies, as we shall discuss.

Renewable energy and East Asia

East Asia is the world's most energy-intensive and carbon-intensive region. Its demand for energy has increased over sevenfold over the last four decades, from around 600 million tons of oil equivalent (mtoe) in 1970 to 4,334 mtoe by 2012: this was three times faster than the global average (Dent 2016). The region's electricity grid capacity has expanded almost fivefold in the last 20 years, from 391.7 gigawatts (GW) in 1990 to 1,824GW by 2012, over doubling the region's global share from 14.7 percent to 32.9 percent (Table 24.1). This is primarily due to East Asia's industrialization driven economic development, and corresponding rapid urbanization. Both connected processes have required huge energy inputs, primarily fossil fuels. Through a combination of domestic and foreign investment, East Asian nations make manufactured products for the rest of world, and have increased their import demand for energy in order to do so. As the premier global production hub, the region's carbon emissions – and thereby impact on climate change – is greater than any other. Table 24.1 shows that its total carbon emissions have well over doubled from 1990 to 2012, from 4.6 billion tons CO_2 per annum to 11.6 billion, and its global share from 20.8 percent to 36.5 percent accordingly.

East Asia's burgeoning urban-industrial development has also created many of the world's most polluted cities and a variety of other notable environmental problems locally and transnationally. The World Health Organization (WHO 2012) estimates that every year 1.3 million people in China are prematurely dying from air pollution. The region is furthermore highly susceptible to climate change risks at every level. Large swathes of its population are concentrated in low-lying river basins and deltas, and coastal areas. Rising sea-levels and extreme weather cycles pose a real threat. The imperatives to move toward environmentally sustainable energy paradigms in East Asia are arguably greater than in any other part of the world. Renewable energy has a vitally important part to play in this process, being derived from replenishable natural processes, sources or phenomena, such as wind, solar, hydropower, geothermal, waves, tides, and biological matter. They are 'renewable' in actual or theoretical terms because they can provide inexhaustible supplies of significantly cleaner energy to meet the needs of humankind. In contrast, fossil fuels (oil, natural gas, coal – sometimes collectively known as hydrocarbons) and nuclear energy (based on uranium) are non-renewable because they essentially derive from depletable mineral resources.

Today, we often refer to renewables in terms of their technological applications, among the most common being wind turbines, solar modules or panels, tidal barrages, biofuels, and so on. These can vary enormously in terms of scale, for example from small solar photovoltaic cells generating a few watts of electricity to power electronic devices such as calculators to large hydropower dams that provide power to millions of households through national power grid systems. Renewable energy (RE) technologies can hence be deployed on a *micro-scale*, where individuals and local communities own installations and are both producer and consumer, and on a *macro-scale* in which RE plants and products serve the energy needs of large parts of the country, or indeed the whole country. In addition to the environmental virtues of renewable energy, its micro-scale applications are also making an important contribution to reducing global energy poverty (IPCC 2011). Roughly 1.2 billion people currently do not have access to electricity, and many more only have access to unstable supplies of it (REN21 2016). Wind, solar, bioenergy and small-hydro in particular have scope for deployment in remote areas located far from national grid infrastructure, thus helping improve livelihoods by sustainable methods by providing power for schools, hospitals, small enterprises, communications and other utility services. Renewables have played an important part in the rural electrification programs of many East Asian countries.

Renewable energy is arguably the main element of a broader 'clean energy' cluster of technologies that additionally includes energy efficiency and saving, electric vehicles, fuel cells and other eco-industry sectors. The ability of renewables to produce cleaner forms of energy makes them crucial to decarbonizing economic activity, achieving sustainable development and tackling climate change. Around three-quarters of aggregated greenhouse gases derive from energy use (IPCC 2011). It is helpful to use an illustrative example to help explain the relevance of renewable energy in combating historic increases in carbon emissions. Based on average power ratings, wind energy typically generates around 2.5 gigawatt hours (GWh)[1] per megawatt (MW) installed capacity[2] over the course of a year. Using also a generalized world average, each GWh of clean energy produced yields an estimated 600 tons reduction in CO_2 emissions (GWEC 2009). Thus, electricity generated by a 100MW wind farm would annually lead to a nominal average of 150,000 tons CO_2 saving, or the equivalent emissions produced on a yearly average basis in 2010 by 24,194 individuals collectively in China, 20,000 in the EU, or 8,523 people in the US (Dent 2014).

Table 24.1 East Asia's energy and carbon emissions profile

	Energy use (million tons of oil equivalent)*		*Electricity grid capacity (gigawatts)*		*Renewable energy installed electricity capacity (gigawatts)*		*Carbon dioxide (CO_2) emissions (million tons)*		*CO_2 emissions per capita (tons)*	
	1990	*2012*	*1990*	*2012*	*2012*	*% total*	*1990*	*2012*	*1990*	*2012*
China	872	2,894	126.6	1,174.3	320.7	27.9	2,461	8,205	2.2	6.1
Japan	439	452	169.2	293.3	35.4	12.3	1,095	1,223	8.9	9.6
South Korea	93	263	20.0	94.4	3.8	4.2	247	593	5.8	11.9
Taiwan	55	105	17.9	48.4	3.5	7.2	129	257	6.2	11.0
Hong Kong SAR	9	15	7.5	12.6	0.0	0.0	28	45	4.8	6.3
Macau SAR	2	3	0.2	0.5	0.0	0.0	1	1	2.9	1.9
North Korea	33	15	9.5	9.5	5.0	52.6	244	45	12.2	1.8
Mongolia	3	4	0.9	0.8	0.0	0.0	10	14	4.6	5.1
Northeast Asia	1,506	3,751	351.8	1,633.8	368.4	22.5	4,214	10,383	–	–
Brunei	2	4	0.4	0.8	0.0	0.0	6	8	25.0	20.4
Cambodia	0.6	5	0.0	0.6	0.02	4.9	0.5	4	0.1	0.3
Indonesia	99	214	12.7	47.8	6.2	16.7	150	435	0.8	1.8
Laos	0.8	4	0.2	3.0	3.0	97.7	0.2	2	0.1	0.3
Malaysia	22	81	5.0	28.5	2.1	8.0	57	196	3.1	6.7
Myanmar	11	15	1.1	3.6	0.8	46.7	4	12	0.1	0.2
Philippines	29	43	6.8	16.9	5.4	31.2	42	79	0.7	0.8
Singapore	12	25	3.4	10.8	0.02	0.2	47	50	15.4	9.4
Thailand	42	127	8.3	53.9	4.8	8.9	96	257	1.7	3.8
Vietnam	18	65	2.0	24.5	10.0	45.2	21	143	0.3	1.6
Southeast Asia	236	583	39.9	190.4	32.3	17.0	424	1,186	–	–
EAST ASIA	**1,739**	**4,334**	**391.7**	**1,824.2**	**400.7**	**22.0**	**4,638**	**11,569**	–	–
% world total	*20.3*	*32.4*	*14.7*	*32.9*	*27.8*	–	*20.8*	*36.5*	–	–

(*Continued*)

Table 24.1. (continued)

	Energy use (million tons of oil equivalent)*		*Electricity grid capacity (gigawatts)*		*Renewable energy installed electricity capacity (gigawatts)*		*Carbon dioxide (CO_2) emissions (million tons)*		*CO_2 emissions per capita (tons)*	
	1990	*2012*	*1990*	*2012*	*2012*	*% total*	*1990*	*2012*	*1990*	*2012*
United States	1,915	2,141	714.7	1,063.0	157.6	14.8	4,879	5,074	19.5	16.2
% world total	*22.3*	*16.0*	26.9	*19.2*	11.0	–	*21.9*	*16.0*	–	–
European Union	1,275	1,644	669.3	948.4	317.1	33.4	3,236	3,505	8.6	6.9
% world total	*14.9*	*12.3*	25.2	*17.1*	22.0	–	*14.5*	*11.0*	–	–
India	317	788	71.8	254.7	66.0	25.9	691	1,954	0.8	1.6
% world total	*3.7*	*5.6*	*2.7*	*4.6*	*4.6*	–	*3.1*	*6.2*	–	–
World	**8,575**	**13,371**	**2,658.3**	**5,549.6**	**1,438.8**	**25.9**	**22,274**	**31,734**	**4.2**	4.5

Notes: * Use of primary energy before transformation to other end-use fuels, which is equal to indigenous production plus imports and stock changes, minus exports and fuels supplied to ships and aircraft engaged in international transport; 2. Minus figure indicates net exporting position; 3. To quote the data source: "The ratio of GDP to energy use indicates energy efficiency. To produce comparable and consistent estimates of real GDP across economies relative to physical inputs to GDP – that is, units of energy use - GDP is converted to 2005 international dollars using purchasing power parity (PPP) rates" (data.worldbank.org).

Sources: World Bank (2015), International Energy Agency (2015), Energy Information Administration (2015).

East Asia's push on renewable energy development

Key drivers

There are three key inter-related drivers or motives behind renewable energy development in the region. The first are a set of *environmental and sustainable development imperatives*. High carbon economic activity is causing acute pollution and other environmental problems in East Asia and correspondingly adverse social welfare effects on its societies. When compared to other parts of the world, its energy-intensive development structures appear especially unsustainable. In addition to local and national pressures to establish cleaner energy systems, many governments in the region are under increasing international pressure on this front due to East Asia's growing impact on global climate change.

The second key driver is *energy security*, which can be understood in simple conceptual terms as addressing supply risk (securing reliable sources of energy fuels), price risk (maintaining predictable or at least stable energy prices) and environmental risk (mitigating the adverse environmental impacts of energy use), as discussed under the first main driver. The promotion of renewable energy in East Asia can also be explained in relation to the first two risk types. Sustained high growth rates in energy demand have led to a rapid depletion of the region's own fossil fuel deposits, and many of its countries have moved to or are moving toward a net energy importing position. East Asia's most advanced economies (Japan, South Korea, Taiwan and Singapore – these also being among the largest) have chronically high energy import dependency ratios, making them especially susceptible to the vicissitudes of foreign supply sources (Dent 2013). This is potentially further compounded by volatility in international prices for oil, gas and coal. Renewables have the advantage of being inherently indigenous energy sources, hence providing a long-term solution to foreign energy supply risks. Although some RE sectors are prone to occasional commodity price spikes (e.g., polysilicon and solar PV cell manufacturing), they have been historically less exposed to price risk than fossil fuel sectors.

The third key driver relates to the promotion of renewables as *emerging strategic industries*. Much of East Asia's contemporary economic success has been based on fostering strategic industries through exercises of state capacity aimed at forging developmental relationships between government and business. This is a core theme of this chapter. Strategic industries can be any or all of the following: (1) new or emerging sectors having substantial growth potential and therefore important to generating future prosperity, income and welfare; (2) sectors performing essential functions in the economy such energy and material supply; (3) industries providing a material or other kind of foundation on which other sectors are based, for example steel and chemicals for various manufactured products. Most RE sectors possess the first general attribute, while wind, solar and bioenergy are perhaps the most relevant in this respect. Although the core technological foundations of many modern renewables can be traced back some decades, their rates of techno-innovatory advance have substantially quickened since the mid-2000s, corresponding with their rapid sector growth generally. Hence they may still be considered to be 'emerging'. Renewables are also being increasingly viewed in the region as possessing the second attribute, particularly as a long-term prospect to resolve the aforementioned energy security and environmental predicaments of over-reliance on fossil fuels. Renewables may not yet be seen as strategic industries regarding the third attribute but could possibly be in the future.

Regional and global growth in renewables

Renewable energy technologies have existed for centuries and in some cases millennia. Human societies around the world have devised ingenious and different ways to harness natural

Table 24.2 Renewable energy development, sector overview (2005–2015)

	Electricity generation (GW installed capacity, world)			*East Asian producers, 2015 (installed capacity level, Top 10 world ranking)*
	2005	*2015*	*added*	
Hydropower	770.5	1,064.0	293.5	China 296.0GW (1)
Wind	59.0	443.0	384.0	China 145.4GW (1)
Solar Photovoltaic	5.4	227.0	221.6	China 43.5GW (1) Japan 34.4GW (3)
Biomass	44.0	106.0	62.0	China 8.5GW (4) Japan 3.3GW (5)
Concentrating Solar Power	0.4	4.8	4.4	China 10MW (9) Thailand 5MW (10)
Geothermal	9.3	13.2	3.9	Philippines 1.9GW (2) Indonesia 1.4GW (3) Japan 0.5GW (8)
Ocean	0.3	0.5	0.2	South Korea 0.25GW (1)
Renewables total	**889**	**1,849**	**960**	China 496GW (1), Japan 65GW (4)
Bioethanol	33bn liters	98bn liters	65bn liters	China 2.8bn (3); Thailand 1.2bn (5)
Biodiesel	4bn liters	30bn liters	26bn liters	Indonesia 1.7bn (5); Thailand 1.2bn (7)

Sources: REN21 (2006, 2016).

phenomena as sources of energy. In China, Japan, Korea and Taiwan, hydropower was the prime electricity power source that enabled their early industrialization in the first half of the twentieth century (Dent 2014). The 1973/74 oil crisis helped spur the development of modern renewables but far more investment went into the nuclear power industry in the immediate years and decades that followed. It was not until the early or mid-2000s that significant growth and development in renewables began as new RE technologies became scaled up and approached commercialization. Wind, solar and bioenergy deserve special mention here, and electricity generation is arguably where renewables have made the biggest impact on global energy systems. As Table 24.2 shows, worldwide renewables' power generation capacity has risen from 889GW in 2005 to 1,849GW by 2015, which according to REN21 (2016) represents 23.7 percent of total global generation,[3] up from 15.6 percent in 2005. There has been steady growth also in the biofuels sector, and traditional biomass still accounts for a large share of energy use for cooking and heating purposes in developing countries.

East Asia has been at the forefront of this recent global expansion of renewable energy, accounting for now well over a third of world total for power generation from RE sources. China has been the region's prime source of this development. Its installed renewables capacity has expanded on various fronts in recent years, rising from 106GW in 2006 to 496GW by 2015. The country's ambitious hydropower sector policy accounts for much of this expansion but since the early 2010s it has been the wind and solar PV sectors that have provided the main momentum. China's wind energy capacity has grown from 0.8GW in 2004 to 145.4GW by 2015, and solar PV from a few megawatts to 43.5GW over the same period, consequently taking the global lead in both sectors. Japan, once the world leader of the solar PV industry in the 1990s, has returned as a heavy investor here after the 2011 Fukushima nuclear disaster. Meanwhile in smaller sectors, the Philippines and Indonesia are ranked second and third globally, respectively, in geothermal power, and South Korea is the world's largest investor in tidal energy. Furthermore, China is now the world's largest manufacturer of renewable energy products, and has helped make them more affordable worldwide: the price of solar PV panels has fallen dramatically since 2010. Japan, South Korea, Taiwan and some Southeast Asian countries are also significant producers across the spectrum of RE industries. Seven out of the global top ten solar PV panel manufacturers and five of the world's largest wind turbine makers are from the region. In 2005, China accounted for 5 percent of total global solar PV manufacturing but by the mid-2010s this had risen to 65 percent. Japanese companies are world leaders in geothermal equipment production.

Controversies and challenges

However, the impressive growth of renewables in East Asia has not been without notable controversy and challenges, such as the environmental and also socio-economic problems arising from hydropower development. For example, construction of China's Three Gorges Dam, the world's largest power station, involved relocating up to an estimated two million people. On the technical side, many key RE sectors such as wind and solar also face the intermittent power constraints regarding the dependability and unpredictability of atmospheric conditions, combined with the fact that we still lack the technology to store electricity at the utility-scale generation levels required by mass populations. This presently makes depending on wind and solar for even up to just half a national grid's power generation a very difficult challenge. Moving from a fossil fuel thermal power generation system to a renewable energy based one where installation scales are much more varied and 'distributed' (i.e., from household solar PV panels, local community micro-hydro plants to large wind farms) necessitates new kinds of 'smart' electricity grid infrastructures. The same applies in transport energy infrastructures to accommodate the expanded use of electric vehicles and biofuels. Renewable energy sectors are also industries, with their own dependability on depletable materials, such as steel in the manufacture of wind turbines and lithium for making solar panels.

From country-level perspectives, RE shares of total electricity generation are not that high in East Asia's most developed economies: in Japan, South Korea, Taiwan and Singapore they are still at single digit or small double digit levels (Table 24.1). Moreover, the relatively high share figures for many of the region's developing countries often depend heavily on singular sectors (e.g., Laos, Myanmar and North Korea on hydropower; Indonesia and Philippines on geothermal) while some smaller economies (Brunei, Hong Kong and Macau) have virtually or actually no renewable power generation capacity. From a sector-specific perspective, the patterns and stages of renewable energy development vary considerably across the different sectors. Some are well established and relatively unchanged in their current technical form (hydropower, traditional bioenergy), some have experienced strong techno-innovatory development leading to scaled up commercialization and impressive growth (solar PV, wind energy and biomass power generation), others have conversely remained relatively static (geothermal and tidal energy), or have achieved comparatively modest advances (biofuels), and some are still micro-sectors (concentrated solar power, ocean energy) or at the experimental stages of development such as wave energy and solar cooling technologies.

Fossil fuels are still persistently dominant in the region's energy mix, and may remain so for some time to come. China may have recently scaled back its earlier ambitious plans to expand its coal-fired power stations due mainly to acute urban air pollution problems but, even so, will still invest heavily in this sector and the gas industry by international comparison.[4] Japan's post-Fukushima energy policy has involved a vast increase in its fossil fuel imports to compensate for the shutdown of nuclear power plants, on which the nation once depended for a third of its electricity.[5] While China, South Korea, India and some other countries have plans to construct a number of new nuclear plants, and Japan will re-start most of its established ones after its safety check program, the nuclear power industry globally has been steady declining for the last decade. Installed capacity and generation levels were already falling well before the 2011 Fukushima disaster.

Despite the structural dominance of fossil fuels in the world energy industry, there have been signs of renewable energy gaining ground and challenging this position held so long by hydrocarbons. Since 2008, renewables in aggregate have accounted for at least half of all investment as well as additional capacity in new power generation facilities worldwide (REN21 2014, REN21 2016). This share is also rising: in 2015, global investment in RE power generation capacity[6] was US$265.8 billion (around 80 percent of this in solar and wind energy combined), more than double the US$130 billion directed towards coal and gas-fired power stations. Total investment in all renewable energy applications that year was a record US$328.9 billion, and also for the first time in 2015 developing countries collectively invested more in renewables than developed countries (REN21 2016). An increasing number of nations are implementing RE policies and strategies, and there are growing international co-ordinated efforts in both the public and private sectors to promote the advance of renewables as part of tackling climate change, as most recently demonstrated at the COP21 Paris meeting of the UNFCCC in December 2015. The COP21 agreement commits signatory states to embark on faster paced transitions to a low carbon global economy, and fossil fuel combustion accounts for over 80 percent of total greenhouse gas emissions. Although the COP21 agreement does not explicitly state so, its signatory states cannot fulfill their treaty obligations without further promoting renewables. There is thus now clear evidence that renewable energy is gathering momentum regarding investment in future energy infrastructures and systems worldwide, with East Asia playing a vitally important role.

East Asia, renewable energy and 'new developmentalism'

State capacity

So how did East Asia become the world's leading consumer and producer region on renewable energy? There are now an estimated 146 countries worldwide as well as dozens of sub-national jurisdictions (e.g., cities, provinces) that operate policy support measures for RE development (REN21 2016). Over time, these countries have mutually learned best practice measures among themselves and a certain degree of international convergence is evident on policy instrument application, e.g., use of feed-in tariffs, renewables portfolio standards. East Asian nations have been part of this process but what makes them quite unique is the incorporation of renewable energy into national strategic 'macro-development' plans, and the depth of strategization on RE development itself. This is consistent with the region's predilection for state-directed development. East Asia hosts a number of successful developmental states (e.g., Japan, South Korea, Taiwan, Singapore and Malaysia) and socialist market economies such as China and Vietnam, both examples of 'state capacity' practice. Understanding East Asia's development political economy is vital when examining the recent growth of renewable energy industries in the region.

Theories on developmental statism have roots in both 'late industrialization' theory and the German Historic School (Gerschenkron 1962, Polanyi 1944, Weber 1947), being first directly applied to Japan (Johnson 1982) and thereafter to other East Asian economies, especially South Korea, Taiwan and Singapore (Amsden 1989, Evans 1995, Low 2001, Pereira 2008, Weiss 1998, Woo-Cumings 1999, World Bank 1993). Developmental states are fundamentally capitalist economies with three general attributes:

- *state institutions* with the capacity to strategize and plan a transformative economic development path, with institutional and planning coordination led by a 'pilot agency'.

- *strategic policies* to operationalize these plans and realize their transformative economic goals that change over time in accordance with developmental progress. Multiple-year economic plans have been adopted across the whole East Asia region.
- *developmental partnerships* forged by the state primarily with the business sector but also with society, whereby non-state actors are co-opted into transformative economic projects through various institutionalized consultative mechanisms.

Meanwhile, the socialist market concept has been applied to China, Vietnam and other countries where the state too has strategic economic planning institutions and policies but where the state plays a substantial interventionist role in the economy through more direct control of markets and the means of production where state-owned enterprises (SOEs) are highly active (Suliman 1998). At the same time these states still harness the power of private enterprise to help realize strategic economic objectives. The state's capacity to bring about prosperity-generating transformative change is a core issue that links both concepts, and the notion of 'state capacity' has been deployed more commonly to examine the effective role played by governments in economic management (Beeson and Pham 2012, Weiss 2010).

However, from the late 1980s onward, globalization and ascendant neo-liberalism created critical pressures and challenging conditions for both developmental state practices in East Asia. The combination of globalizing forces, technological developments and strengthening neo-liberal orthodoxy made national economic spaces more permeable through the growth of transnational systemic linkages (e.g., production networks and supply chains), and more liberalized and integrated national markets. This presented certain challenges for governments when defining and controlling national development projects at both macro-plan (i.e., whole economy) and industry sector levels. Moreover, the stronger adoption of neo-liberal oriented policies in East Asia led to less proactive state economic management and a corresponding greater faith placed in purely market mechanisms (Radice 2008). The concurrent rise in the influence of business and civil society over economic policy formation also compelled the region's governments to adapt and re-balance their developmental partnerships accordingly (Holden and Derneritt 2008, Lee and Park 2009, Pirie 2008).

As the 2000s progressed, though, the increasingly evident risks associated with globalization and neo-liberalism, culminating in the 2008/09 global financial crisis, its prime cause being generally attributed to mismanaged deregulation, combined with the emergent global challenges of climate change and deepening energy security predicaments worldwide. This resulted in reinvigorations of state capacity in East Asia and elsewhere, or at least refocused state capacity in response to these risks (Dittmer 2007, Gills 2010, Holden and Derneritt 2008, Karagiannis and Madjd-Sadjadi 2007, Weiss 2010). Emphasis was placed on the stronger institutionalization of market order in the Weberian and Polyanian sense where states seek to make markets work better rather than supplant them (Khan and Christiansen 2010, Mok and Yep 2008). This was, in many senses, a market-oriented developmental partnership between government and business but, additionally, a situation in which the state was engaged in developing new or emerging markets and industries through the implementation of strategic plans and their associated policy instruments. Both the substance of these plans and the proportionate state funding to support them were generally greater in East Asia than in any other region. Strategic plans themselves are more than just target-setting: they entail structured, multi-layered policy frameworks that comprise a series of instruments and programs backed up by public finance and often mechanisms for leveraging private investment. They also normally set staged development steps that progress toward defined medium to long-term goals or targets on installed capacity and production, advances in techno-innovation and industrial capacity-building. Strategic planning locks in policy commitment to developing renewables and, in principle, brings greater coherence to RE policy overall (Dent 2014). We examine later how this has worked in the East Asian context.

Ecological modernization

In the meantime, ideas on 'ecological modernization' that were first developed in Europe during the 1980s were beginning to gain influence in East Asia. Briefly defined, ecological modernization prescribes the reform, modification and improvement of existing economic, business and social structures to realize environmental objectives through the application of new technologies, policies and practices. It may be considered an evolved form of economic modernization, which seeks to reconcile the conventional aims of economic growth with sustainable development, and essentially prescribes gradual, adaptive change rather than radical or revolutionary change to economic and societal structures (Huber 1982, Jänicke 1985, Weale 1992, Hajer 1995, Mol 1995, Dryzek 1997). As York and Rosa (2003: 274) succinctly summarize:

> Central to [ecological modernization theory] EMT is the view that the era of late modernity offers promise that industrialization, technological development, economic growth, and capitalism are not only potentially compatible with ecological sustainability but also may be key drivers of environmental reform ... It argues for the potential of attaining sustainability from within – a greening of business as usual – thereby avoiding such challenging alternatives as radical structural or value changes in society.

From this perspective, renewable energy is viewed as providing important technical solutions to key problems facing modern human society.

EMT has become the dominant discourse among government and business decision-makers on environmental sustainability issues. An important reason for this is the appealing economic case EMT makes on how companies can increase profitability by pursuing green corporate strategies, through for instance improving material efficiency and waste management, and exploiting the emerging market potential of environmentally friendly products such as renewables (Christoff 1996, Jänicke 1988). Ecological modernization is thus not viewed as a threat to existing business structures and interests, but rather as a commercial opportunity. It hence postulates that economic and business growth is reconcilable with resolving environmental problems, and firms can generate financial gains through adopting new environmental technologies and practices (Buttel 2000, Langhelle 2000). Unlike later evolved understandings of sustainable development, which took on a stronger social dimension by tacking issues of global economic inequity between rich developed and poor developing nations, ecological modernization has remained largely preoccupied with economic, business and technological related challenges.

Ecological modernization's main protagonists have long stressed its applications to policy, and more generally contended the state and other institutions have a crucial role to play in achieving ecological modernization aims (Andersen and Massa 2000, Huber 1982, Jänicke 1985, Murphy and Gouldson 2000, Seippel 2000). This constitutes important common ground with state capacity theory. Over time, EMT thinking has spread from advanced industrial countries to developing economy regions like East Asia, first to its more advanced economies of Japan, South Korea, Taiwan and Singapore in the late 1980s and 1990s, and then to lesser developed nations in Southeast Asia and also China.

Chinese views on ecological modernization are largely representative of, as well as crucially important to, how developing East Asia has approached its ideas and principles. Like many other emerging economies from the region, it began to examine the applicability of EMT to its national context in the early 2000s, and subsequently incorporating it into policy discourses and planning thereafter (Huan 2007, Lai et al. 2012, Li and Lang 2010, Yee et al. 2013, Zhang et al. 2007). The 'scientific development concept', first formally proclaimed by then President Hu Jintao around this time, then became the official ideological basis for China's future economic and social development when it was ratified into the national constitution in October 2007. Guided by this concept, China was to foster a more resource-saving and environment-friendly 'harmonious society', and "developing the economy in a more balanced manner, paying less attention to gross domestic product (GDP) growth per se and more attention to such things as the ecological costs of the headlong rush for development" (Fewsmith 2008: 88). In the same year, the Chinese Academy of Sciences published the *China Modernization Report 2007: Study on Ecological Modernization*, when the government also launched its Medium and Long-Term Development Plan for Renewable Energy as well as its National Climate Change Strategy, where the EMT thinking was clearly evident in each case (NDRC 2007a, 2007b).

The scientific development concept was more broadly and systematically applied to China's five-year plans (FYPs) and associated strategic development program, such as on energy. The 11th FYP (2006–2010) accordingly reflected a shift toward more qualitative development objectives, and this relative change in thinking was evidently stronger in the design of the 12th FYP (2011–2015). Ecological modernization has had a clear influence on these FYPs and related development policies, with renewable energy forming an integral part of the state's recent low(er) carbon, 'clean industry' strategies. Yet as in other developing East Asia, EMT's influence on development has manifested itself in a rather top-down and technocratic manner, primarily through state policies and strategies. Most elements of East Asian society have yet to be strongly imbued with ideas of ecological modernization. Yee et al. (2013) argue that while certain elements of China's domestic business community are aligned with EMT thinking, Chinese society generally is only just beginning to assimilate EMT's ideas and afford more serious priority to environmental goals.

New developmentalism

The 'new developmentalism' concept combines state capacity theory (SCT) and ecological modernization theory (EMT), and was first introduced and fully explained in my earlier works (Dent 2012, 2014) for understanding the broad political economy context of renewable energy development in East Asia. New developmentalism can be simply defined as revitalized and refocused forms of state capacity aimed at realizing the transformative economic objectives associated with low carbon development. Renewables are often referred to as modern technologies and modern industries, where 'modern' infers that they are at current or new frontiers of economic development. This raises the question of whether the expansion of RE systems may be considered part of a long-term modernization process or alternatively a means of helping to establish a new kind of post-modern development paradigm or philosophy in the early twenty-first century. Thus, does East Asian states' strong promotion of renewables represent a break from their past development models, or more of a continuation?

With specific reference to fellow EMT thinkers Leroy and van Tatenhove (1999), Mol (1995) and others, Buttel (2000: 62) further observed that, "the core thinkers of ecological modernization share very similar ideas about state effectiveness and state-civil society ties." We have seen more broadly how SCT is principally concerned with the state playing an effective positive role in transforming the economy toward more advanced development ends. It was contended that both past exercises of state capacity as well as recent revitalized forms of it have been especially evident in East Asia, compared to other regions. Ecological modernization, meanwhile, highlights the importance of state policies and institutions in helping shape markets and paths of economic development toward more environmentally friendly outcomes, and EMT's influence on East Asian policy-makers has grown, as is evident in their ambitious renewable energy plans and strategies. Both SCT and EMT are thus essentially concerned with transformative economic development, where the state has a key contributing role to play in partnership with business and society, and new developmentalism focuses on how this specifically applies to realizing low carbon development. There is also an apparent conflation of SCT and EMT ideas on the aforementioned drivers or motives behind the promotion of renewable energy development and low carbon development generally in East Asia, namely: environmental and sustainable development imperatives, energy security, and emerging strategic industries.

Empirically speaking, East Asian state strategies on RE development constitute one of three main policy domains of the region's new developmentalism, the other two being climate change strategies and strategic macro-development plans on decarbonizing the economy. Table 24.3 shows that many East Asian states have introduced all three elements from the mid-2000s onward, and a good majority at least two elements. There are close inter-linkages among them, as earlier shown with in the example of China. Governments from the region normally explicitly state in their renewable energy strategies how these contribute to meeting national climate change strategy targets on carbon emission reduction targets, where set. Renewable energy strategies also tend to be embedded within strategic macro-plans on low carbon development. East Asia 'first-phase' of multi-sector strategic planning on renewables began in the early 2000s, starting with South Korea, Malaysia and Vietnam from 2001 onward:

- *South Korea*: 2001 Basic Plan for New and Renewable Energy Development.
- *Malaysia*: 2001 Small Renewable Energy Programme was integrated into the 8th Malaysia Plan (2001–2005) and devised to also complement the Five Fuel Policy introduced in the same year.
- *Vietnam*: 2001 Renewable Energy Action Plan was part of its broader 2001–2010 Master Plan of Power Development.
- *Philippines*: 2003 Renewable Energy Policy Framework (2003–2013).
- *Thailand*: 2004 Strategic Plan for Renewable Energy Development.
- *Indonesia*: 2005 National Energy Blueprint (2005–2025) that included RE elements, and 2006 National Biofuel Roadmap.
- *China*: 2007 Medium and Long-Term Development Plan for Renewable Energy.
- *Singapore*: 2007 Comprehensive Blueprint for Clean Energy.
- *Taiwan*: 2008 Green Energy Industry Sunrise Plan.
- *Japan*: 2008 Cool Earth 50 Energy Innovative Technology Plan.

These were later superseded or followed by a 'second-phase' of more coherent, ambitious and substantive renewable energy strategy-making in the late 2000s and early 2010s, as shown under the RE plan column in Table 24.3. This can be mainly understood in the context of the 2008/09 global financial crisis and its impacts, when ecological modernization and state capacity approaches to economic development further converged around the introduction of various 'green growth' initiatives and strategies in different parts of the world. This has been substantively evident in East Asia and which has provided an important impetus to the region's new developmentalism and renewable energy development more specifically. Although originating ideas and debates on green growth long pre-dated 2008, the global financial crisis brought it into the mainstream policy arena. According to Jacobs (2013), the new green growth discourse has succeeded for similar reasons that the discourse on ecological modernization did, namely by

Table 24.3 East Asia's new developmentalist plans and carbon mitigation commitments by 2015

		Renewable Energy Plan	National Climate Change Action Plan	Macro-Plan on Low Carbon (Green Growth) Development	Kyoto Protocol of UNFCCC				Carbon Emission Reduction Targets
					Ratified	In force	Status	Targets	
Northeast Asia	China	Medium to Long-Term Development Plan for Renewable Energy to 2020	National Climate Change Programme (2007)	12th Five-Year Plan 2011–2015 (elements of)	August 2002	February 2005	non-Annex member		Energy consumption per GDP unit: 16% (2011–2015). CO2 emission per GDP unit: 17% (2011–2015), 40 to 45% (2011–2020)
	Japan	Innovative Strategy for Energy and Environment (2012)		New Growth Strategy (2010)	June 2002	February 2005	Annex I, II	[6%: 2008–2012]. 2013–2020 not set	3.8% below 2005 emission levels by 2020
	Mongolia				December 1999	February 2005	non-Annex member		
	South Korea	New Renewable Energy Medium-Term Plan 2010–2015	[integrated into Green Growth Strategy (2009)]	Green Growth Strategy (2009)	November 2002	February 2005	non-Annex member		30% reduction compared to 'business as usual' scenario by 2020
	North Korea				April 2005	July 2005	non-Annex member		
	Taiwan	New Energy Policy to 2030	Adaptation Strategy to Climate Change (2012)	Green Energy Industry Sunrise Plan (2009)			non-signatory		Return to 2005 emission level (2020, 45% business as usual reduction), return to 2000 level (2025)

(Continued)

Table 24.3. (continued)

		Renewable Energy Plan	*National Climate Change Action Plan*	*Macro-Plan on Low Carbon (Green Growth) Development*	*Kyoto Protocol of UNFCCC*				*Carbon Emission Reduction Targets*
					Ratified	*In force*	*Status*	*Targets*	
Southeast Asia	Brunei				August 2009	November 2009	non-Annex member		
	Cambodia		National Adaptation Programme of Action to Climate Change (2007)	National Strategic Plan on Green Development 2013–2030	August 2002	February 2005	non-Annex member		
	Indonesia	National Energy Blueprint 2005–2025, National Biofuel Roadmap 2006–2025	National Action Plan Addressing Climate Change (2007)	Mid-Term Development Plan 2010–2014	December 2004	March 2005	non-Annex member		26% from business-as-usual level by 2020 based on domestic funding, or 41% by 2020 based on international funding (US $18.2 billion)
	Laos			7th Five-Year National Socioeconomic Development Plan 2011–2015	February 2003	February 2005	non-Annex member		
	Malaysia	National Renewable Energy Policy and Action Plan, 2011–2015	National Policy on Climate Change (2009)	Green Technology Strategy (2009), 10th Malaysia Plan 2011–2015	September 2002	February 2005	non-Annex member		
	Myanmar				August 2003	February 2005	non-Annex member		

Table 24.3. (continued)

	Renewable Energy Plan	*National Climate Change Action Plan*	*Macro-Plan on Low Carbon (Green Growth) Development*	*Kyoto Protocol of UNFCCC*				*Carbon Emission Reduction Targets*
				Ratified	*In force*	*Status*	*Targets*	
Philippines	National Renewable Energy Programme 2011–2030	National Framework Strategy on Climate Change (2007)		November 2003	February 2005	non-Annex member		
Singapore		National Climate Change Strategy (2008)	Sustainable Singapore Blueprint (2007)	April 2006	July 2006	non-Annex member		16% from projected 2020 'business-as-usual' level
Thailand	Alternative Energy Development Plan 2012–2021	National Strategy on Climate Change (2008)	11th National Economic and Social Development Plan 2012–2016	August 2002	February 2005	non-Annex member		30% from 2009 level by 2020, 42 million tons CO_2 equivalent in 2020
Vietnam	Renewable Energy Master Plan 2011–2015	National Climate Change Strategy (2011)	Vietnam Green Growth Strategy (2012)	September 2002	February 2005	non-Annex member		

Sources: Asian Development Bank database on national climate change action plans (www.aric.adb.org/climate-change.php), UNFCCC website on Kyoto Protocol (http://unfccc.int/essential_background/kyoto_protocol/items/6034.php), authors research.

attracting support from powerful economic interests. Indeed, green growth policies and strategies may be viewed as the latest phase of ecological modernization as well as a major basis for reinvigorated state capacity in East Asia in particular, thus establishing stronger common empirical ground between SCT and EMT.

This phase of new developmentalism in East Asia thus combined counter-cyclical fiscal stimulus funding with highly structured strategies on renewable energy development. South Korea's Green Growth Strategy (GGS) for example – implemented from 2009 onward and based on an US$87 billion (2 percent GDP equivalent) stimulus package – reinstalled the nation's Five-Year Plan framework that had run from 1962 to 1993. The First GGS Five-Year Plan (2009–2013) introduced by President Lee Myun-bak was followed by a Second Five-Year Plan for Green Growth (2014–2018) under his successor, Park Geun-hye (Global Green Growth Institute 2015). South Korea launched a New Renewable Energy Medium-Term Plan 2010–2015 as an extension of the new plan framework.

The Chinese government's own fiscal stimulus package categorized US$219 billion of initiatives under green growth. As with South Korea's macro-development plans, China's 12th Five-Year Plan (2011–2015) placed a heavy concentration on renewables, and complementary sector-specific plans on RE development (n.b. on solar PV, wind, hydropower and biomass) that further built on the above noted 2007 medium to long-term plan. Three of the seven selected sectors of the US$610 billion Strategic Emerging Industries program for 'clean' development and a new industry base, as part of the 12th Plan, were clean energy industries: renewables plus energy efficiency technologies and 'new energy' vehicles.

Meanwhile, in response to the 2008/09 financial crisis, the Japanese government launched its New Growth Strategy (NGS) and Industrial Structure Vision (ISV) initiatives in 2010 (METI 2010a, 2010b). The NGS's main goal was the "creation of a low-carbon society through a comprehensive policy package including new systems design, systems changes, new regulations, and regulatory reform, and to support the rapid spread and expansion of environmental technologies and products" (METI 2010a: 20). This transformation would include "measures to support the spread and expansion of renewable energies (solar, wind, small-scale hydropower, biomass, geothermal, etc.) by expanding the electric power feed-in tariff system" (METI 2010a: 21–22). A core element of the NGS strategy is to strengthen Japan's industrial-technological capabilities in seven strategic areas up to 2030, environment and energy ('green innovation') being the first listed, the other six being medical/health care, finance, science and technology nation, tourism/local revitalization, human resources, and Asian regional economic integration (Jones and Yoo 2011). These are underpinned by 21 national strategic projects, one of which under 'green innovation' is the expansion of renewables sector into a JPY10 trillion (US$110 billion) market by 2020.

Over the late 2000s and early 2010s, Taiwan, Cambodia, Indonesia, Laos, Malaysia, Thailand and Vietnam all instigated new renewable energy strategies, and many their own versions of green growth plans (see Table 24.3). In the ecological modernization context, we can see the combination of environmental and strategic industry development drivers or motives with counter-cyclical economic policy factors working together, where renewables formed a core element in the push toward realizing new transformative, low-carbon development objectives. This is turn can be understood in the deeper historical context of Kondratiev's (1935) 'long wave' theory on the relationship between techno-innovation and economic development. According to Kondratiev and other long wave theorists such as Perez (2010) and Warner (2010), world economic development has been driven forward in spurts based on the emergence of certain technology clusters, which arise every few decades (typically every 50 to 60 years) and lead to the creation of new techno-economic paradigms that have transformative effects across industry and society. A new techno-economic paradigm arose in the late nineteenth century based on electrical power and chemical industries, another in the early twentieth century founded on mass production techniques and petrochemicals, and then later in the late twentieth century based on the information technology revolution. Green energy, with renewables at its center, is certainly among the strongest contenders as one of the new technology clusters on which the next 'long wave' of world development in the early twenty-first century could be based. East Asia will have arguably played the most significant role in establishing it.

It is evident that while low carbon development forms an important and often core goal of East Asia's new developmentalism, it also vies with other strategic imperatives, such as strengthening national economic competitiveness. Furthermore, the region's new strategic macro-development plans contain programs or promote industries strongly associated with 'old developmentalism'. For example, the expansion of physical infrastructures, export-oriented manufacturing, and an emphasis on state directed financial support remain defining characteristics of China's 12th FYP, while its promotion of higher levels of domestic consumption somewhat contradict the plan's sustainable development objectives. Meanwhile, conventional energy and chemicals are amongst the 20 strategic areas that comprise the Singapore Economic Development Board's industrial master-plan, which includes the further expansion of the city-state's already huge petrochemical complex and the construction of a large new liquefied natural gas terminal. In South Korea, the First GGS Five-Year Plan simultaneously contended with the government's strategic industry policy for upgrading the traditional 'flagship industries', including the energy-intensive sectors of shipbuilding and steel.

More generally, East Asia's national energy strategies and systems are still heavily dependent on securing fossil fuel resources. This is indicative of the broader problem of how many of East Asia's core industrial structures, policies and practices remain geared toward carbon-intensive development. In Indonesia, for instance, the continued heavy subsidization of fossil fuel prices makes it difficult for the nation's geothermal sector to seriously compete in the electricity generation market. Furthermore, many countries persist with old industrial policies involving mass-scale ecological damage (e.g., Indonesia and Malaysia's palm oil industries) whilst rolling out low carbon development strategies (Gunningham 2011). Despite the 2011 Fukushima disaster, many East Asian countries may still maintain blueprints on nuclear power development, and moreover include nuclear under the policy rubric of green or clean energy. While the inclusion of nuclear power in low carbon strategies may be defensible, it remains highly contentious, given the very serious environmental risks associated with nuclear fission's by-products. East Asia's 'modernist' industrialized development may remain entrenched for some considerable time, given the enormity of the structural change required to establish the broad foundations of low carbon development. As discussed earlier, the influence of ecological modernization ideas and theories is growing within East Asia and has evidently had a positive effect on greening state policies and exercises of state capacity studied in this chapter, yet this influence still remains somewhat limited in both depth and scale. Furthermore, EMT itself has limitations in bringing about the profound structural changes required to secure humanity's low carbon future. In addition, many Southeast Asian governments still lack sufficient state capacity to implement coherent low carbon development and renewable energy policies technocratically and institutionally, as shown by the lack of RE policy definition and detail, and poor co-ordination of RE policy across their state bureaucracies (IEA 2013, Olz and Beerepoot 2010, REEEP 2016).

East Asia's developing countries face especially difficult challenges moving toward low carbon development given both the high proportionate GDP costs of replacing old or rudimentary equipment and infrastructure, and their relative lack of indigenous techno-innovatory capacity. Furthermore, there are domestic political pressures to meet more immediate socio-economic needs (e.g., poverty alleviation, provision of basic welfare and utility services) than to prioritize environmental-related goals. This being said, socio-economic and environmental problems are increasingly conflating in developing country regions. Many of East Asia's major cities (most notably China's) are now subject to acute levels of pollution, causing chronic health problems on a mass scale and palpably deteriorating societal welfare. Even in relatively poor and authoritarian states there has been mounting civil unrest regarding pollution and a growing acknowledgement of problems caused by pursuing economic growth whatever the costs. Worsening environmental conditions and tensions at the local, national, regional and global level will only create stronger imperatives for expanding and developing the use of renewable energy technologies in East Asia and worldwide.

Conclusion

The remarkable growth of renewable energy in East Asia raises a number of questions concerning the region's future economic and social development, and how this can also be understood in its longer-term historic paths of development, especially with regard to whether the switch to renewables will help establish new sustainable development paradigms. It has been argued that the meta-factors of state capacity and ecological modernization have conflated to form a new developmentalism in East Asia, where renewable energy forms a core element in the region's push to realize low(er) carbon transformative economic objectives. This has been, however, critiqued as a generally top-down, state-driven process, where government strategies could arguably be categorized as much industrial policies as environmental or climate policies. It is certainly the case that the region's more authoritarian governments have often exhibited little regard for local community consultation or involvement in the siting of RE plants whereas in the region's more open democratic societies local and environmental impact assessments and consultations have become an integral part of RE policy. Although the ambitious top-down approaches of East Asian governments for expanding renewables have helped scale them up, the long-run future of renewables ultimately relies on society's willingness to accept and use them.

Furthermore, the impressive growth of renewables in East Asia has been asymmetric from a country perspective (e.g., China's dominance of the regional record generally) and a sectoral perspective (e.g., dominance of hydropower, wind and solar), making for skewed patterns of development across the region. Future development will entail considerable structural changes to incumbent systems of energy production, distribution and consumption. As energy underpins many if not most forms of economic activity, the greater use of renewables would also shape key aspects of the economy, as well as relationships between economic agents in East Asia. Renewables not only offer cleaner and more sustainable methods of producing energy, but also a much wider variety of energy technology options for society. Most importantly, many RE applications can operate on a small enough scale to allow individuals, households and communities to take greater control of their own energy needs. In this sense, renewables have the potential to bring about a systemic revolution in energy production and consumption. Solar modules, very small wind turbines, pico-hydro machines, geothermal heat pumps, biogas digesters and other micro-level devices are helping expand 'distributed' energy in East Asia and elsewhere, thereby increasing the number of energy *prosumers*: those who both produce and consume their own electricity and thermal power. In East Asia's case, it would mean a shift from a state-centric to a more society-centric approach to energy development, at least regarding power and heat generation, although for scale economy reasons utility-scale forms of generation (e.g., wind farms and hydropower dams) will remain crucially important if the broader structural and systemic transformations in energy practice noted earlier are to be realized.

Notes

1 Gigawatt hour (GWh) is a common unit used to measure energy produced by a generating source over set time periods.
2 This is based on around a 28–30 percent average operational efficiency rating of a typical wind turbine.
3 Nuclear accounted for around 3 percent that year, and fossil fuels the remaining 73 percent.
4 *New Year Times*, April 26, 2016, 'China Curbs Plans for More Coal-Fired Power Plants'. Although the Chinese government announced a clamp down in April 2016 on most new proposed coal-fired plants across the nation's provinces, China was still continuing with the construction of existing coal plant projects with a collective total 190GW capacity, the equivalent of twice Britain's total national power grid capacity.
5 *East Asia Forum*, November 23, 2015, 'Japan's Post-Fukushima Energy Challenge'.
6 Not including hydropower projects larger than 50MW. If this category was included the share of renewables would be around another 10 percent higher.

References

Amsden, A. (1989) *Asia's Next Giant: South Korea and Late Industrialisation*, Oxford: Oxford University Press.

Andersen, M.S. and Massa, I. (2000) "Ecological Modernization: Origins, Dilemmas and Future Directions," *Journal of Environment and Policy Planning*, Vol. 2, pp. 337–345.

Beeson, M. and Pham, H.H. (2012) "Developmentalism with Vietnamese Characteristics: The Persistence of State-led Development in East Asia," *Journal of Contemporary Asia*, Vol. 42(4), pp. 539–559.

Buttel, F.H. (2000) "Ecological Modernization as Social Theory," *Geoforum*, Vol. 31(1), pp. 57–65.

Christoff, P. (1996) "Ecological Modernisation, Ecological Modernities," *Environmental Politics*, Vol. 5(3), pp. 476–500.

Dent, C.M. (2012) "Renewable Energy and East Asia's New Developmentalism: Towards a Low Carbon Future?," *The Pacific Review*, Vol. 25(5), pp. 561–587.

Dent, C.M. (2013) "Understanding the Energy Diplomacies of East Asian States," *Modern Asian Studies*, Vol. 47(3), pp. 935–967.

Dent, C.M. (2014) *Renewable Energy Development in East Asia: Towards a New Developmentalism*, London: Routledge.

Dent, C.M. (2016) *East Asian Regionalism: 2nd Edition*, London: Routledge.

Dittmer, L. (2007) "The Asian Financial Crisis and the Asian Developmental State," *Asian Survey*, Vol. 47(6), pp. 829–833.

Dryzek, J.S. (1997) *The Politics of the Earth: Environmental Discourses*, Oxford: Oxford University Press.

Energy Information Administration (2015) *International Energy Statistics Database*, Washington DC: EIA, available at: www.eia.gov.

Evans, P. (1995) *Embedded Autonomy: States and Industrial Transformation*, Princeton: Princeton University Press.

Fewsmith, J. (2008) "China in 2007: The Politics of Leadership Transition," *Asian Survey*, Vol. 48(1), pp. 82–96.

Gerschenkron, A. (1962) *Economic Backwardness in Historical Perspective*, Cambridge, MA: Harvard University Press.

Gills, B. (ed.) (2010) *Globalisation in Crisis*, London: Routledge.

Global Green Growth Institute (2015) *Korea's Green Growth Experience: Process, Outcomes and Lessons Learned*, Seoul: GGGI.

Global Wind Energy Council / GWEC (2009) *Wind Power is Crucial for Combating Climate Change*, Brussels: GWEC Secretariat.

Gunningham, N. (2011) "Energy Governance in Asia: Beyond the Market," *East Asia Forum Quarterly*, Vol. 3(1), pp. 29–30.

Hajer, M.A. (1995) *The Politics of Environmental Discourse: Ecological Modernisation and the Policy Process*, Oxford: Oxford University Press.

Holden, K. and Demeritt, D. (2008) "Democratising Science? The Politics of Promoting Biomedicine in Singapore's Developmental State," *Environment and Planning D*, Vol. 26(1), pp. 68–86.

Huan, Q. (2007) "Ecological Modernisation: A Realistic Green Road For China?," *Environmental Politics*, Vol. 16(4), pp. 683–687.

Huber, J. (1982) *Die Verlorene Unschuld der Okologie*, Frankfurt am Main: Fischer Verlag.
Intergovernmental Panel on Climate Change / IPCC (2011) *Special Report on Renewable Energy Sources and Climate Change*, Geneva: IPCC Secretariat.
International Energy Agency / IEA (2013) *Southeast Asia Energy Outlook*, Paris: IEA.
International Energy Agency / IEA (2015) *Global Renewable Energy: Policy and Measures Database*, Paris: IEA.
Jacobs, M. (2013) "Green Growth," in R. Falkner (ed.) *Handbook of Global Climate and Environmental Policy*, Oxford: Wiley Blackwell.
Jänicke, M. (1985) *Umweltpolitische Pravention als Okologische Modernisierung und Strukturpolitik*, Berlin: Wissenschaftszentrum.
Jänicke, M. (1988) "Okologische Modernisierung: Optionen und Restriktionen Praventiver Umweltpolitik," in U. Simonis (ed.) *Praventive Umweltpolitik*, Frankfurt am Main: Campus.
Johnson, C. (1982) *MITI and the Japanese Miracle*, Stanford: Stanford University Press.
Jones, R.S. and Yoo, B. (2011) "Japan's New Growth Strategy to Create Demand and Jobs," OECD Economics Department Working Papers, No. 890, Paris: OECD.
Karagiannis, N. and Madjd-Sadjadi, Z. (2007) *Modern State Intervention in the Era of Globalisation*, Cheltenham: Edward Elgar.
Khan, S.R. and Christiansen, J. (eds.) (2010) *Towards New Developmentalism: Market as Means Rather than Master*, London: Routledge.
Kondratiev, N.D. (1935) "The Long Waves in Economic Life," *Review of Economic Statistics*, (17), pp. 105–115.
Lai, K.H., Wong, C.W.Y. and Cheng, T.C.E. (2012) "Ecological Modernisation of Chinese Export Manufacturing via Green Logistics Management and its Regional Implications," *Technological Forecasting and Social Change*, Vol. 79, pp. 766–770.
Langhelle, O. (2000) "Why Ecological Modernization and Sustainable Development Should Not Be Conflated," *Journal of Environmental Policy and Planning*, Vol. 2(4), pp. 303–322.
Lee, Y.H. and Park, T.Y. (2009) "Civil Participation in the Making of a New Regulatory State in Korea: 1998–2008," *Korea Observer*, Vol. 40(3), pp. 461–493.
Leroy, P. and van Tatenhove, J. (1999) "Political Modernization Theory and Environmental Politics," in F. Buttel, G. Spaargaren and A.P.J. Mol (eds.) *Environment and Global Modernities*, London: Sage Publishers.
Li, V. and Lang, G. (2010) "China's "Green GDP" Experiment and the Struggle for Ecological Modernisation," *Journal of Contemporary Asia*, Vol. 40(1), pp. 44–62.
Low, L. (2001) "The Singapore Developmental State in the New Economy and Polity," *The Pacific Review*, Vol. 14(3), pp. 411–441.
Ministry of Economy, Trade and Industry / METI (2010a) *The New Growth Strategy: Blueprint for Revitalising Japan*, Tokyo: METI.
Ministry of Economy, Trade and Industry / METI (2010b) *The Industrial Structure Vision 2010 (Outline)*, Tokyo: METI.
Mok, K.H. and Yep, R. (2008) "Globalisation and State Capacity in Asia," *The Pacific Review*, Vol. 21(2), pp. 109–120.
Mol, A.J.P. (1995) *The Refinement of Production*, Utrecht: Van Arkel.
Murphy, J. and Gouldson, A. (2000) "Environmental Policy and Industrial Innovation: Integrating Environment and Economy through Ecological Modernisation," *Geoforum*, Vol. 31(1), pp. 33–44.
National Development and Reform Commission / NDRC (2007a) *Medium and Long-Term Development Plan for Renewable Energy in China*, Beijing: NDRC.
National Development and Reform Commission / NDRC (2007b) *China's National Climate Change Programme*, Beijing: NDRC.
Olz, S. and Beerepoot, M. (2010) *Deploying Renewables in Southeast Asia*, Paris: IEA.
Pereira, A.A. (2008) "Whither the Developmental State? Explaining Singapore's Continued Developmentalism," *Third World Quarterly*, Vol. 29(6), pp. 1189–1203.
Perez, C. (2010) "Technological Revolutions and Techno-Economic Paradigms," *Cambridge Journal of Economics*, Vol. 34, pp. 185–202.
Pirie, I. (2008) *The Korean Developmental State: From Dirigisme To Neo-Liberalism*, London: Routledge.
Polanyi, K. (1944) *The Great Transformation*, Boston, MA: Beacon Press.
Radice, H. (2008) "The Developmental State under Global Neoliberalism," *Third World Quarterly*, Vol. 29(6), pp. 1153–1174.
Renewable Energy and Energy Efficiency Partnership / REEEP (2016) *Policy and Regulation Review Database*, Vienna: REEEP (www.reeep.org).
REN21 (2006) *Global Status Report on Renewable Energy 2006*, Paris: REN21.

REN21 (2014) *Global Status Report on Renewable Energy 2014*, Paris: REN21.
REN21 (2016) *Global Status Report on Renewable Energy 2016*, Paris: REN21.
Seippel, Ø. (2000) "Ecological Modernization as a Theoretical Device: Strengths and Weaknesses," *Journal of Environment and Policy Planning*, Vol. 2, pp. 287–302.
Suliman, O. (ed.) (1998) *China's Transition to a Socialist Market Economy*, London: Praeger.
Warner, R. (2010) "Ecological Modernisation Theory: Towards a Critical Ecopolitics of Change?," *Environmental Politics*, Vol. 19(4), pp. 538–556.
Weale, A. (1992) *The New Politics of Pollution*, Manchester: Manchester University Press.
Weber, M. (1947) *The Theory of Social and Economic Organisation*, New York: Oxford University Press.
Weiss, L. (1998) *The Myth of the Powerless State: Governing the Economy in a Global Era*, London: Polity.
Weiss, L. (2010) "The State in the Economy: Neoliberal or Neoactivist?," in J. Campbell, C. Crouch, P. Hull Kristensen, O.K. Pedersen, and R. Whitley (eds.) *Oxford Handbook of Comparative Institutional Analysis*, Oxford: Oxford University Press.
Woo-Cumings, M. (ed.) (1999) *The Developmental State*, Ithaca: Cornell University Press.
World Bank (1993) *The East Asian Miracle: Economic Growth and Public Policy*, Oxford: Oxford University Press.
World Bank (2015) *Statistics Database*, Washington DC: World Bank.
World Health Organisation / WHO (2012) *Global Burden of Disease Report 2011*, Geneva: WHO.
Yee, W.H., Lo, C.W.H. and Tang, S.Y. (2013) "Assessing Ecological Modernization in China: Stakeholder Demands and Corporate Environmental Management Practices in Guangdong Province," *The China Quarterly*, Vol. 213, pp. 101–129.
York, R. and Rosa, E. (2003) "Key Challenges to Ecological Modernization Theory," *Organization and Environment*, Vol. 16(3), pp. 273–287.
Zhang, L., Mol, A.P.J. and Sonnenfeld, D.A. (2007) "The Interpretation of Ecological Modernisation in China," *Environmental Politics*, Vol. 16(4), pp. 659–668.

SECTION 7

Asia's sustainable development policy

25

Strategic environmental assessment as a policy framework for sustainable development in Asia

Dennis Victor

Introduction

Strategic Environmental Assessment (SEA) is promoted as a system of incorporating environmental considerations into policies, plans and programs (PPP) (Figure 25.1). SEA is the evaluation of the potential environmental effects of PPP and the carrying out of public participation and consultations (United Nations, 2012). SEA was initially promoted to address the gaps in project-based environmental impact assessment (EIA) principles and practice. This was due to the limited ability of the EIA to address environmental and sustainable aspects at the strategic levels, especially during the policy planning stage. Consequently, SEA provided the opportunity to integrate environmental and sustainable development principles during the planning stage (Victor & Agamuthu, 2014).

SEA is evolving from a project based environmental impact assessment (EIA) tool to a strategic sustainable development instrument in national policy planning. The current proliferation of SEA legislation around the world emphasizes the role of SEA as an essential sustainable development tool, used to integrate environmental considerations as well as to complement EIA in environmental protection. SEA can potentially satisfy the emerging need for environmental policy integration (EPI) and sustainable development at a more strategic level. This enables governments to integrate sustainable development environmental objectives in national policy planning (Lafferty & Hovden, 2003).

International trends in SEA are increasingly exploring the potential for SEA as a sustainable development instrument (Sadler et al., 2011; Tetlow & Hanusch, 2012). Consequently, this chapter aims to critically review, analyze and synthesize SEA trends in Asia and to evaluate its potential as a tool for sustainable development. Ultimately, this may enable SEA to fulfil its full potential as a strategic environmental governance instrument in Asia.

Overview of SEA in Asia

A review of ten countries in Asia is presented below in terms of problems, progress and prospects for SEA implementation.

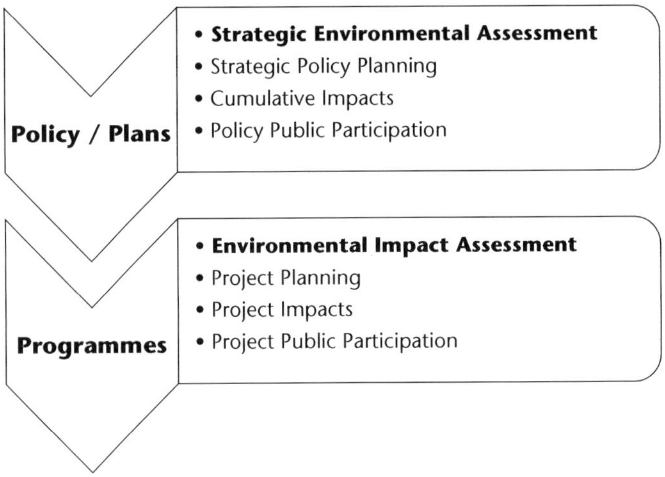

Figure 25.1 SEA and EIA in PPP

Source: Adapted from OECD (2006).

China

China has transposed its SEA requirements into its national planning framework via its regional environmental impact assessment (R-EIA) practices. This is required for its EIA Law which requires SEA for strategic planning at national, provincial and sector levels (Dalal-Clayton & Sadler, 2004). A primary problem for SEA implementation for China has been the limited public participation and the isolated nature of its policies and strategies. This has been intensified by the opinion of government agencies that SEA is not timely for a country like China (Bao et al., 2004a; Che et al., 2002; Zhu et al., 2005). The trends in SEA implementation may indicate that China is still battling its socio-political dynamics of engaging in a policy planning tool, such as SEA, that requires access to information and public participation in decision making (Zhu & Ru, 2008). Meanwhile, notable progress of SEA implementation in China has been the distribution of SEA principles, procedures, technical guidelines, environmental indicators and reporting formats for various planning sectors. Finally, SEA prospects seem to be in the development of sector specific technical guidelines and capacity building for SEA professionals and government agencies (Bina, 2008; Chang & Wu, 2013; Tao et al., 2007).

Hong Kong

Hong Kong has integrated its SEA requirements into its national planning framework via a government directive. A primary problem for SEA implementation in Hong Kong has been the lack of a macro environmental planning policy framework, which has been compounded by the lack of SEA implementation for significant PPPs. The trends in SEA implementation may indicate that Hong Kong is at a crossroads of SEA development from its EIA roots, which may result in SEA evolving into a strategic planning framework for sustainable development (Au, 1998; Au et al. 2004; Ng, 1993; Ross et al., 2006). Meanwhile, notable progress of SEA implementation in Hong Kong has been its potent integration of public participation within the SEA process. Finally, SEA prospects seem to be in the development of sustainability centric SEA application where the shift toward increased public participation is viewed as the foundation for a transparent and multi-tiered inclusive environmental governance system, in line with a sustainability focused society (Ng & Obbard, 2005).

India

India has not transposed its SEA requirements into national legislation. Nevertheless, India has conducted SEA for irrigation projects in Central India, the Indian eco-development project, the Gujerat State Highway Programme and the Gujerat National Dairy Support Project (Garcia et al., 2011; Hirji & Davis, 2009; Singh & Singh, 2011). A primary problem identified in SEA implementation for India has been the low prioritization of SEA as compared to EIA in the environmental assessment process. Furthermore, India also encounters low accountability and transparency from environmental agencies and professionals in disclosing environmental findings. The trends in SEA implementation may indicate that India is restricted by excessive bureaucratic, inefficient and potentially corrupt administrative barriers to sustainable environmental governance (Banham & Brew, 1996; Paliwal, 2006; Valappil et al., 1994; Vyas & Reddy, 1998). Meanwhile, notable progress of SEA implementation in India has been the internalization of environmental considerations for a common vision through a systematic participatory process involving multiple stakeholder engagements. Finally, SEA prospects seem to be in the updating of environmental policy guidelines to augment the accountability of environmental professionals (Rajvanshi, 2001, 2003, 2005).

Indonesia

Indonesia has transposed its SEA requirements into national legislation which requires mandatory SEA for spatial and development plans at all levels. A primary problem identified in SEA implementation for Indonesia is the adaptability and efficacy of the newly formulated SEA legislation in the policy planning process. Furthermore, there is also the potential for economic concerns to supersede SEA implementation and adoption of SEA findings (Dusik & Xie, 2009). The trends in SEA implementation may indicate that Indonesia has evolved from its EIA approach to a SEA framework (Purnama, 2003; Spaling & Vroom, 2007). Meanwhile, notable progress of SEA implementation in Indonesia has been made in the establishment of its SEA legislative framework which includes provisions for public participation, a relatively novel initiative in the region. Finally, SEA prospects seem to be in the development of integrated SEA frameworks that provides for multi-plan assessment within a single assessment process (Dusik et al., 2010; Dusik & Kappiantari, 2010; Ministry of Environment, Indonesia, 2007).

Japan

Japan has not incorporated its SEA requirements into national legislation, though it is currently establishing the groundwork for a SEA system. A primary problem identified in SEA implementation for Japan has been a lack of legislative framework for SEA. The trends in SEA implementation may indicate that Japan does not perceive the need for SEA as part of its national policy planning process where existing environmental systems may be deemed adequate for addressing environmental issues at a strategic level (Barrett & Therivel, 1989; Harashina, 1998). Meanwhile, notable progress of SEA implementation in Japan has been the initiation of a public involvement (PI) system which considers environmental, social and economic aspects as part of sustainable development initiatives. Finally, SEA prospects seem to be in the development of a SEA legislative framework (Imura & Schreurs, 2005; Sachihiko, 2001; Uesaka et al., 2000).

Philippines

The Philippines has not transposed its SEA requirements into national legislation, though it has implemented it in an ad hoc manner via its para-SEA elements. A primary problem identified in SEA implementation for the Philippines has been the piecemeal manner of SEA implementation. The trends in SEA implementation may indicate that the Philippines is still hesitant in evolving from EIA to SEA in a comprehensive manner (Abracosa & Ortolano, 1987; Lim, 1985; Smith & Van der Wansem, 1995). Meanwhile, notable progress of SEA implementation in the Philippines has been the inclusion of SEA elements within its process for the formulation of the Palawan Sustainable Development Act. Finally, SEA prospects seem to be in the development of a SEA framework within the Environmental Assessment Act that would require SEA for PPPs involving multi-component, multi-sector projects and activities (Gilbuena et al., 2013; Mercado, 2007).

South Korea

South Korea has transposed its SEA requirements into national legislation, including the Prior Environmental Review System, which is designed to realize environmentally sustainable growth. A primary problem identified in SEA implementation for South Korea has been the limited scope of SEA application for the final plan or program (Hayashi, 2007; Hayashi et al., 2011; Song & Glasson, 2010). The trends in SEA implementation may indicate that South Korea is resolutely though practically proceeding forward in its SEA implementation (Ahn et al., 2008). Meanwhile, notable progress of SEA implementation in South Korea has been visible in the major improvements to the SEA process by expanding the scope of application, integration timing and stakeholder engagement. Finally, SEA prospects seem to be in the expansion of sustainable development indicators and capacity building from the local governments (Volkery, 2004).

Taiwan

Taiwan has transposed its SEA requirements into national legislation, including the EIA Act, SEA manual and SEA PPP list. A primary problem identified in SEA implementation for Taiwan has been the lack of a comprehensive SEA scoping process, consensus and prioritization of environmental aspects. An additional problem has been the negligible public participation in SEA implementation, which is characteristically limited to government agencies and approving bodies. The trends in SEA implementation may indicate that Taiwan is still limited in its political will and stakeholder engagement, with a bureaucratic top-down policy planning system. Meanwhile, in the notable progress of SEA implementation, Taiwan has been early adopter of a SEA legislative framework, relative to other Asian countries (Chen et al., 2011; Kuo & Chiu, 2006; Kuo et al., 2005). Finally, SEA prospects seem to be in the introduction of sustainability concepts within the SEA framework via the Taiwan Sustainable Development Indicators (Liou et al., 2003, 2006; Wang et al., 2012).

Malaysia

Malaysia has not transposed its SEA requirements into national legislation, though it has introduced EIA through its Environmental Quality Act. The current application of SEA in Malaysia is mainly focused on land use development plans via the Town and Country Planning Department (Briffett et al., 2004; Memon, 2000). A primary problem identified in SEA implementation in Malaysia has been that it has not been widely adopted as a policy planning tool, even though it has been explicitly stated in the National Policy on the Environment and the Ninth Malaysia Plan 2006–2010. An additional problem is the existing low level of awareness on SEA and its potential for the super-streaming of environmental considerations among environmental agencies and the public. The trends in SEA implementation may indicate that Malaysia is still experimenting with the use of SEA as a policy planning mechanism and is hesitant in embracing SEA. This may be due to its traditional top-down policy planning with minimal public participation and cross-sectoral integration as well as its conventional reliance on EIA as its environmental planning mechanism. Meanwhile, notable progress of SEA implementation in Malaysia has been made in the recommendation by the Ministry of Natural Resources and Environmental for SEA to be implemented in mainstreaming biodiversity. Finally, SEA prospects seem to be in the development of public participation initiatives of national legislation and policies. This includes the Malaysian government circular on the online public engagement on new or revised legislation as well as the utilization of sustainability assessments in land use planning (Government of Malaysia, 2012; Halimaton, 2007; Marzuki, 2009; Moi, 2007).

Vietnam

Vietnam has adopted its SEA requirements into national legislation including the Law on Environmental Protection, which includes mandatory SEA requirements for national, provincial

Table 25.1 SEA problems, progress and prospects in Asia

Country	*Problem*	*Progress*	*Prospect*
China	Restrictive public participation.	SEA guidelines and indicators.	Expansion of SEA scope.
Hong Kong	Development centric SEA.	Heightened SEA public participation.	Sustainability centric SEA.
India	Bureaucratic restrictions.	Systematic participatory process.	Augmenting accountability of environmental professionals.
Indonesia	Perception of SEA as a burden by planning agencies.	SEA legislative provisions for public participation.	SEA multi-plan assessments.
Japan	Lack of SEA legislation.	Public involvement system.	SEA legislation.
Philippines	Reactive approach to SEA implementation.	SEA application in regional planning.	SEA inclusion in environmental legislation.
South Korea	Problematic legislative cohesion.	Down-streaming SEA findings to EIA.	SEA sustainable development indicators.
Taiwan	Limited political will with top-down planning.	SEA systems.	SEA capacity building.
Malaysia	Top-down policy planning with conventional reliance on EIA.	Promotion of SEA in mainstreaming biodiversity and in land use plans.	Public participation initiatives on new legislation.
Vietnam	Limited influence on strategic decision making.	Synchronized SEA implementation with policies.	Inter-sectoral coordination.

Source: Author's own calculations.

and local strategies, programs and plans. A primary problem identified in SEA implementation for Vietnam has been the lack of SEA knowledge, experience and skills at the ministerial and local levels. An additional problem is the limited influence of the SEA on strategic decisions. The trends in SEA implementation may indicate that Vietnam is implementing SEA at a disconnected rate with its SEA capacity building (Clausen et al., 2011; Doberstein, 2004). Meanwhile, notable progress of SEA implementation in Vietnam has been made in creation of the requirements for a synchronized implementation and integration of SEA with national development strategies on a temporal scale. Finally, SEA prospects seem to be in the development of inter-sectoral coordination and harmonization on SEA for various policy planning processes, including urban development strategies (Obbard et al., 2002; Partidário et al., 2008; Sekhar, 2005).

SEA problems, progress, and prospects

SEA trends in Asia indicate a proliferation of SEA legislation, possibly a mimicking of trends in Europe due to the EU SEA Directive (Briffett et al., 2003; Dusik & Xie, 2009; Hayashi et al., 2011). Meanwhile, SEA implementation also ranges from the use of a non-regulatory framework, including the use of existing EIA systems to resistance to SEA. The primary problem of SEA implementation in Asia has been its limited integration and pragmatic implementation in strategic decision making. This is due to the highly political and sensitive nature of policy planning, even in developed countries with a SEA legislative framework. These trends indicate that SEA in Asia is still in an evolutionary pathway. Meanwhile notable progress in SEA implementation in Asia has been made toward invoking the global awareness on the need for SEA as a complementary environmental planning mechanism for sustainable development. Finally, SEA prospects in Asia seem to be present in the integration of sustainability assessments within the SEA framework (see Table 25.1) (White & Noble, 2013).

SEA sustainable development analysis

A SEA sustainable development analysis was conducted to determine the potential of SEA to be used as an instrument in integrating sustainable development principles in Asia, using two main approaches:

- Strength, Weaknesses, Opportunities and Threats (SWOT) Analysis. The SWOT analysis involved identifying the internal and external factors that are supportive and unsupportive for sustainable development implementation (Ghazinoory et al., 2011). Strengths are internal elements that enable facilitation of policy goals while weaknesses are internal elements that obstruct policy goals. Finally, opportunities are external elements that have the potential to facilitate policy goals while threats are external elements that have the potential to obstruct policy goals.
- SEA Matrix Analysis. The SEA Matrix analysis involved ranking the potential for SEA as a sustainable development instrument by identifying the implementation of SEA legislation and SEA public/stakeholder engagement. The ranking of SEA legislation refers to the extent of the implementation of SEA legislation in policy planning, while the SEA public/stakeholder engagement refers to the extent of public/stakeholder engagements as part of the SEA process. The combined score of SEA legislation implementation and SEA public/stakeholder engagement provides a combined ranking of "high," "moderate" or "low" for the potential of SEA to be used as a sustainable development integration instrument.

SEA SWOT analysis

Strengths

The SWOT analysis indicates that the strengths for SEA sustainable development policy integration are in the formulation of SEA legislation, especially in China, Hong Kong, Indonesia, South Korea and Taiwan. The existence of a SEA legislative framework is considered a high enabler for sustainable development policy integration.

Weaknesses

The SWOT analysis indicates that the weaknesses for SEA sustainable development policy integration are in the area of public/stakeholder engagement, especially in China, Indonesia, the Philippines, Taiwan and Vietnam. The lack of public/stakeholder engagement in countries with SEA legislation such as China, Indonesia and Taiwan gives the impression that the provision is more of a public relations exercise rather than a consultation engagement as part of the decision making process. This may be indicative of a root-cause problem where countries in Asia may still be reliant on a top-down policy planning process in Asia where the Power Distance Index (PDI) is relatively high. PDI is a measure of how much lower ranking individuals of a society comply and submit to high ranking individuals (Hofstede, 2010). The potential lack of public participation is considered a high barrier for sustainable development policy integration.

Opportunities

The SWOT analysis indicates that the opportunities for SEA sustainable development policy integration are in the introduction of sustainable development principles and indicators within the SEA framework, especially in Hong Kong, Japan, India and the Philippines. These trends indicate the potential of SEA as platform for mainstream sustainable development within the policy process as the next logical stage after implementing SEA. The progression of SEA to integrating sustainable development principles that is observed in Asia is considered a high enabler for sustainable development policy integration.

Threats

The SWOT analysis indicates that the threats for SEA sustainable development policy integration are in the gap between theory and practice of SEA implementation, especially in China, Indonesia, Taiwan and Vietnam. These countries have formulated SEA legislation, but seem to lack SEA public/stakeholder engagement. Implementing a theoretical SEA based solely on developed countries without taking into consideration local socio-economic cultural issues may result in SEA with limited influence (Axelsson et al., 2012; Bina, 2007). This also implies that SEA is a not a "silver bullet" that can be mimicked from developed countries but has to be customized based on national environmental conditions (Agamuthu & Dennis, 2013). Theoretical implementation of SEA is considered a high barrier for sustainable development policy integration.

SEA matrix analysis

SEA Legislation (L) x SEA Public/Stakeholder Engagement (E) = SEA Sustainable Development Integration Potential (see Tables 25.2, 25.3, 25.4 & 25.5).

Table 25.2 SEA legislation implementation

Description	*Rank*	*Score*
No SEA Legislation or Administrative Implementation	Low	1
No SEA Legislation but Administrative Implementation	Moderate	2
Formulated SEA Legislation	High	3

Source: Author's own calculations.

Table 25.3 SEA public/stakeholder engagement

Description	*Rank*	*Score*
Minor Implementation of SEA Public/Stakeholder Engagement	Low	1
Moderate Implementation of SEA Public/Stakeholder Engagement	Moderate	2
High Implementation of SEA Public/Stakeholder Engagement	High	3

Source: Author's own calculations.

Table 25.4 SEA sustainable development integration potential

	SEA Public/Stakeholder Engagement		
SEA Legislation	*Low (1)*	*Moderate (2)*	*High (3)*
Low (1)	1	2	3
Moderate (2)	2	4	6
High (3)	3	6	9

Low Potential (1&2) Moderate Potential (4&6) High Potential (6&9).

Source: Author's own calculations.

SEA for sustainable development policy implications

SEA policy trends in Asia indicate that SEA legislation formulations in Asian countries may provide the legal and institutional framework for mainstreaming sustainable development in national policy planning. This potentially may result in environmental and social considerations addressed in the early stages of national policy planning, thus balancing the typically high emphasis on economic development. Nevertheless, SEA legislation formulations without effective public/stakeholder engagement implementation in Asia may limit the effectiveness of SEA's role in promoting sustainable development in integrating social considerations in national policy planning. This is particularly noticeable in countries such as China, Indonesia, Philippines, Taiwan and Vietnam that have SEA legislation or have translated SEA requirements in national policy planning but have limited SEA public/stakeholder engagement.

The dichotomy of SEA legislation formulations without SEA public/stakeholder implementation may indicate a greater systemic policy formulation and governance challenge in Asia. This

Table 25.5 Ranking of SEA sustainable development integration potential in Asia

No	*Countries*	*Legislation*	*Engagement*	*Ranking*
1	Hong Kong	3	3	9
2	Japan	2	3	6
3	South Korea	3	2	6
4	India	2	2	4
5	China	3	1	3
6	Indonesia	3	1	3
7	Taiwan	3	1	3
8	Vietnam	3	1	3
9	Malaysia	1	2	2
10	Philippines	2	1	2

Source: Author's own calculations.

may relate to the existing overreliance on legislation as the main driving force for policy implementation as well as the top-down decision-making process (Partidário, 1996; Wallington et al., 2007). Thus, SEA integration to promote sustainable development in Asia may require a paradigm shift to balance the legislative aspects of SEA with behavioral policy instruments. This finding highlighting the emphasis on legislation in Asia is consistent with SEA trends observed in the literature (Dusik & Xie, 2009; Hayashi et al., 2011; Sadler et al., 2011). The common prevailing mindset is that SEA implementation will take care of itself once SEA legislation is formulated. Nevertheless, SEA trends in Asia indicate a complex policy planning dynamic between policy makers and the public/stakeholders that is influenced by each countries' socio-cultural background (Axelsson et al., 2012; Bina, 2007). SEA experiences in China, Taiwan and Indonesia demonstrate that SEA implementation can be highly multi-dimensional, due to differing environmental and social contexts (Bao et al., 2004b; Liou & Yu, 2004; Ministry of Environment, Indonesia, 2007). This may simply imply that SEA legislation is a not a "silver bullet" that can be mimicked by other countries but must be complemented with a locally customized and validated SEA framework.

Conclusion

SEA implementation in Asia is currently at a crossroads in Asia where it can either be implemented as a public relations exercise without integration of sustainable development considerations or it can realize its full potential of integrating environmental and social considerations to balance the current economic emphasis in national policy planning. Thus, SEA is advocated as a framework and a potential pathway for sustainable development in Asia. One point of view is that SEA should be linked to the sustainable development agenda while others contend that SEA should be focused on its core function of environmental protection to ensure its viability (Gao et al., 2013; Lafferty & Hovden, 2003; Sadler et al., 2011). However, the SEA value proposition is when SEA functions as a stepping stone for sustainable development. This can only be achieved when SEA demonstrates its strategic value by integrating both environmental and social considerations in policy planning. Consequently, the policy implication of these trends is that countries considering SEA as a framework for sustainable development integration require a paradigm shift toward SEA legislative and public/stakeholder engagement policy instruments, thus ensuring SEA mainstreams sustainable development in national policy planning.

References

Abracosa, R., & Ortolano, L. (1987). "Environmental impact assessment in the Philippines: 1977–1985." *Environmental Impact Assessment Review*, 7(4), 293–310.

Agamuthu, P., & Dennis, V. (2013). "Policy trends of e-waste management in Asia." *Journal of Material Cycles and Waste Management*, 15(4), 411–419. https://doi.org/10.1007/s10163-013-0136-7.

Ahn, K., Han, S.-W., Han, Y.-H., Jung, J., Jung, J.-G., Kim, I.-S., ... Ryu, J.-G. (2008). "Method development for the integrated impact assessment in Korea – a case study for the construction of great Korean waterway." In IAIA Conference Proceedings, The Art and Science of Impact Assessment 28th Annual Conference of the International Association for Impact Assessment. Perth, Australia.

Au, E. (1998). "Status and progress of environmental assessment in Hong Kong: facing the challenges in the 21st century." *Impact Assessment and Project Appraisal*, 16(2), 162–166.

Au, E., Hui, S., Morrison-Saunders, A., & Arts, J. (2004). "Learning by doing: EIA follow-up in Hong Kong." In A. Morrison-Saunders and J. Arts (eds), *Assessing Impact: Handbook of EIA and SEA Follow-up*. London: Routledge, Chapter 9.

Axelsson, A., Annandale, D., Cashmore, M., Slunge, D., Ekbom, A., Loayza, F., & Verheem, R. (2012). "Policy SEA: lessons from development co-operation." *Impact Assessment and Project Appraisal*, 30(2), 124–129.

Banham, W., & Brew, D. (1996). "A review of the development of environmental impact assessment in India." *Project Appraisal*, 11(3), 195–202.

Bao, C., Lu, Y., & Shang, J.-C. (2004a). "Framework and operational procedure for implementing strategic environmental assessment in China." *Environmental Impact Assessment Review*, 24(1), 27–46.

Bao, C., Lu, Y., & Shang, J.-C. (2004b). "Framework and operational procedure for implementing strategic environmental assessment in China." *Environmental Impact Assessment Review*, 24(1), 27–46. https://doi.org/10.1016/S0195-9255(03)00137-9.

Barrett, B., & Therivel, R. (1989). "EIA in Japan: environmental protection v economic growth." *Land Use Policy*, 6(3), 217–231.

Bina, O. (2007). "A critical review of the dominant lines of argumentation on the need for strategic environmental assessment." *Environmental Impact Assessment Review*, 27(7), 585–606. https://doi.org/10.1016/j.eiar.2007.05.003.

Bina, O. (2008). "Context and systems: thinking more broadly about effectiveness in strategic environmental assessment in China." *Environmental Management*, 42(4), 717–733.

Briffett, C., Obbard, J. P., & Mackee, J. (2003). "Towards SEA for the developing nations of Asia." *Environmental Impact Assessment Review*, 23(2), 171–196. https://doi.org/10.1016/S0195-9255(02)00100-2.

Briffett, C., Obbard, J., & Mackee, J. (2004). "Environmental assessment in Malaysia: a means to an end or a new beginning?" *Impact Assessment and Project Appraisal*, 22(3), 221–233. https://doi.org/10.3152/147154604781765923.

Chang, I.-S., & Wu, J. (2013). "Integration of climate change considerations into environmental impact assessment—implementation, problems and recommendations for China." *Frontiers of Environmental Science & Engineering*, 7, 1–10. https://doi.org/10.1007/s11783-013-0496-1.

Che, X., Shang, J., & Wang, J. (2002). "Strategic environmental assessment and its development in China." *Environmental Impact Assessment Review*, 22(2), 101–109.

Chen, C.-H., Liu, W.-L., & Liaw, S.-L. (2011). "Integrated dynamic policy management methodology and system for strategic environmental assessment of golf course installation policy in Taiwan." *Environmental Impact Assessment Review*, 31(1), 66–76.

Clausen, A., Vu, H.H., & Pedrono, M. (2011). "An evaluation of the environmental impact assessment system in Vietnam: the gap between theory and practice." *Environmental Impact Assessment Review*, 31(2), 136–143.

Dalal-Clayton, B., & Sadler, B. (2004). *Strategic environmental assessment: an international review*. London: International Institute for Environment and Development. Retrieved from http://pubs.iied.org/pdfs/G02207.pdf.

Doberstein, B. (2004). "EIA models and capacity building in Viet Nam: an analysis of development aid programs." *Environmental Impact Assessment Review*, 24(3), 283–318.

Dusik, J., & Kappiantari, M. (2010). *Customizing strategic environmental assessment for Indonesian decision making context: Initial lessons learnt*. Internal report on lessons learnt, Unpublished.

Dusik, J., Setiawan, B., Kappiantari, M., Argo, T., Nawangsidi, H., Wibowo, S. A., ... Djoekardi, A. (2010). "Making SEA fit for political culture of strategic decision-making in Indonesia: recommendations for MOE general guidance on SEA. Indonesia–Denmark Environmental Support Programme, Phase 2, Component 1." Retrieved from www.esp2indonesia.org/.

Dusik, J., & Xie, J. (2009). "Strategic environmental assessment in East and Southeast Asia." In J. Dusik and J. Xie (eds), *A progress review and comparison of country systems and cases*. Washington, DC: World Bank, pp. 23–50.

Gao, J., Kørnøv, L., & Christensen, P. (2013). "The politics of strategic environmental assessment indicators: weak recognition found in Chinese guidelines." *Impact Assessment and Project Appraisal* (ahead-of-print), 31, 1–6.

Garcia, K., de Brigard, J.C.G., Holm, T., le Maitre, D., Mathur, V., Muhamad, S., ... Slater, M. (2011). "SEA as a tool for the conservation and sustainable use of biodiversity in developing countries 1." In B. Sadler, R. Ashemann and J. Dusik (eds), *Handbook of Strategic Environmental Assessment*. London: Earthscan, Chapter 8, p. 274.

Ghazinoory, S., Abdi, M., & Azadegan-Mehr, M. (2011). "SWOT methodology: a state-of-the-art review for the past, a framework for the future." *Journal of Business Economics and Management*, 12(1), 24–48. https://doi.org/10.3846/16111699.2011.555358.

Gilbuena Jr., R., Kawamura, A., Medina, R., Amaguchi, H., Nakagawa, N., & Bui, D.D. (2013). "Environmental impact assessment of structural flood mitigation measures by a rapid impact assessment matrix (RIAM) technique: a case study in Metro Manila, Philippines." *Science of the Total Environment*, 456–457, 137–147. https://doi.org/10.1016/j.scitotenv.2013.03.063.

Government of Malaysia. (2012). *Malaysian government circular on online public participation for new or revised legislation*. Putrajaya, Malaysia: Government of Malaysia.

Halimaton, S.H. (2007). "A Malaysian Experience in Strategic Environmental Assessment (SEA)," Presentation at a Workshop "Understanding Strategic Environmental Assessment." Putrajaya, August.

Harashina, S. (1998). "EIA in Japan: creating a more transparent society?" *Environmental Impact Assessment Review*, 18(4), 309–311.

Hayashi, K. (2007). "Comparative study on strategic environmental assessment system in selected countries. " In *International Symposium on EcoTopia Science (ISETS 2007)*, Nagoya, Japan, pp. 23–25.

Hayashi, K., Song, Y., Au, E., & Dusik, J. (2011). "SEA in the Asia region." In B. Sadler, R. Aschemann and J. Dusik (eds), *Handbook of Strategic Environmental Assessment*, London: Earthscan, pp. 89–107.

Hirji, R., & Davis, R. (2009). Strategic environmental assessment: improving water resources governance and decision making. Water Sector Board Discussion Paper No 12, Washington, DC: World Bank.

Hofstede, G. (2010). *Cultures and Organizations: Software of The Mind; Intercultural Cooperation And Its Importance For Survival*. New York, NY, USA: McGraw-Hill.

Imura, H., & Schreurs, M. A. (2005). *Environmental policy in Japan*. Cheltenham, UK: Edward Elgar Publishing.

Kuo, N.-W., & Chiu, Y.-T. (2006). "The assessment of agritourism policy based on SEA combination with HIA." *Land Use Policy*, 23(4), 560–570.

Kuo, N.-W., Hsiao, T.-Y., & Yu, Y.-H. (2005). "A Delphi–matrix approach to SEA and its application within the tourism sector in Taiwan." *Environmental Impact Assessment Review*, 25(3), 259–280.

Lafferty, W., & Hovden, E. (2003). "Environmental policy integration: towards an analytical framework." *Environmental Politics*, 12(3), 1–22. https://doi.org/10.1080/09644010412331308254

Lim, G.-C. (1985). "Theory and practice of EIA implementation: a comparative study of three developing countries." *Environmental Impact Assessment Review*, 5(2), 133–153.

Liou, M., Kuo, N.-W., & Yu, Y.-H. (2003). "Sustainable indicators for strategic environmental assessment in Taiwan." *Ecosystems and Sustainable Development*, I, 623–634.

Liou, M., Yeh, S.-C., & Yu, Y.-H. (2006). "Reconstruction and systemization of the methodologies for strategic environmental assessment in Taiwan." *Environmental Impact Assessment Review*, 26(2), 170–184. https://doi.org/10.1016/j.eiar.2005.08.003.

Liou, M., & Yu, Y.-H. (2004). "Development and implementation of strategic environmental assessment in Taiwan." *Environmental Impact Assessment Review*, 24(3), 337–350. https://doi.org/10.1016/j.eiar.2003.10.018.

Marzuki, A. (2009). "A review on public participation in environmental impact assessment in Malaysia." *Theoretical and Empirical Researches in Urban Management*, 3(12), 126–136.

Memon, P.A. (2000). "Devolution of environmental regulation: environmental impact assessment in Malaysia." *Impact Assessment and Project Appraisal*, 18(4), 283–293. https://doi.org/10.3152/147154600781767295.

Mercado, E. (2007). "A discussion paper for a strategic environmental assessment (SEA) policy in the Philippines." *CIDA Manila*, September.

Ministry of Environment, Indonesia. (2007). "A brief overview on environmental impact assessment and strategic environmental assessment in Indonesia," Presentation by the State Ministry of Environment of the Republic of Indonesia, ASEAN-China Workshop on EIA. SEA, Beijing, 15–20.

Moi, T.K. (2007). "An overview of SEA in Malaysia," Presentation by the ASEAN-China Workshop on EIA. SEA, Beijing, October.

Ng, K.L., & Obbard, J.P. (2005). "Strategic environmental assessment in Hong Kong." *Environment International*, 31(4), 483–492. https://doi.org/10.1016/j.envint.2004.09.023.

Ng, M.K. (1993). "Strategic planning in Hong Kong: lessons from TDS (territorial development strategy) and PADS (port and development strategy)." *Town Planning Review*, 64(3), 287.

Obbard, J.P., Lai, Y.C., & Briffett, C. (2002). "Environmental assessment in Vietnam: theory and practice." *Journal of Environmental Assessment Policy and Management*, 4(3), 267–295.

OECD (2006). "Applying strategic environmental assessment. Good practice guidance for development co-operation." Paris: Organisation for Economic Co-operation and Development.

Paliwal, R. (2006). "EIA practice in India and its evaluation using SWOT analysis." *Environmental Impact Assessment Review*, 26(5), 492–510. https://doi.org/10.1016/j.eiar.2006.01.004.

Partidário, M. (1996). "Strategic environmental assessment: key issues emerging from recent practice." *Environmental Impact Assessment Review*, 16(1), 31–55.

Partidário, M., Paddon, M., Eggenberger, M., Chau, D.M., & Van Duyen, N. (2008). "Linking strategic environmental assessment (SEA) and city development strategy in Vietnam." *Impact Assessment and Project Appraisal*, 26(3), 219–227.

Purnama, D. (2003). "Reform of the EIA process in Indonesia: improving the role of public involvement." *Environmental Impact Assessment Review*, 23(4), 415–439.

Rajvanshi, A. (2001). "Strategic environmental assessment of the India ecodevelopment project: experiences, prospects and lessons learnt." *Journal of Environmental Assessment Policy and Management*, 3(3), 373–393.

Rajvanshi, A. (2003). "Promoting public participation for integrating sustainability issues in environmental decision-making: the Indian experience." *Journal of Environmental Assessment Policy and Management*, 5(3), 295–319.

Rajvanshi, A. (2005). "Strengthening biodiversity conservation through community-oriented development projects: environmental review of the India ecodevelopment project." *Journal of Environmental Assessment Policy and Management*, 7(2), 299–325.

Ross, W.A., Morrison-Saunders, A., Marshall, R., Sanchez, L.E., Weston, J., Au, E., … Sadler, B. (2006). "Round table: common sense in environmental impact assessment: it is not as common as it should be (with responses and a riposte)." *Impact Assessment and Project Appraisal*, 24(1), 3–22.

Sachihiko, H. (2001). "A new stage of EIA in Japan: towards strategic environmental assessment." *Built Environment*, 27(1), 8–15.

Sadler, B., Aschemann, R., & Dusik, J. (2011). *Handbook of Strategic Environmental Assessment*. London: Earthscan.

Sekhar, N.U. (2005). "Integrated coastal zone management in Vietnam: present potentials and future challenges." *Ocean & Coastal Management*, 48(9), 813–827.

Singh, M., & Singh, N. (2011). *Strategic Environment and Social Assessment (SESA) for National Dairy Support Project* (NDSP). Anand, Gujarat, India: ERM India Private Ltd.

Smith, D. B., & Van der Wansem, M. (1995). *Strengthening EIA Capacity in Asia: Environmental Impact Assessment in the Philippines, Indonesia, and Sri Lanka*. Washington, DC: World Resources Institute.

Song, Y.-I., & Glasson, J. (2010). "A new paradigm for Environmental Assessment (EA) in Korea." *Environmental Impact Assessment Review*, 30(2), 90–99.

Spaling, H., & Vroom, B. (2007). "Environmental assessment after the 2004 tsunami: a case study, lessons and prospects." *Impact Assessment and Project Appraisal*, 25(1), 43–52.

Tao, T., Tan, Z., & He, X. (2007). "Integrating environment into land-use planning through strategic environmental assessment in China: towards legal frameworks and operational procedures." *Environmental Impact Assessment Review*, 27(3), 243–265.

Tetlow, M., & Hanusch, M. (2012). "Strategic environmental assessment: the state of the art." *Impact Assessment and Project Appraisal*, 30(1), 15–24. https://doi.org/10.1080/14615517.2012.666400.

Uesaka, K., Ohnishi, H., & Tachibana, H. (2000). "New environmental impact assessment method for road traffic noise in Japan." In *Proceedings Of The 29th International Congress on Noise Control Engineering in Internoise 2000, Held August 27–31, 2000*, Nice, France, Vol. 3.

United Nations. (2012). *Resource Manual to Support Application of the Protocol on Strategic Environmental Assessment*. New York: United Nations.

Valappil, M., Devuyst, D., & Hens, L. (1994). "Evaluation of the environmental impact assessment procedure in India." *Impact Assessment*, 12(1), 75–88.
Victor, D., & Agamuthu, P. (2014). "Policy trends of strategic environmental assessment in Asia." *Environmental Science & Policy*, 41, 63–76. https://doi.org/10.1016/j.envsci.2014.03.005.
Volkery, A. (2004). "Republic of Korea Case Study." IISD Unedited Working Paper.
Vyas, V.S., & Reddy, V.R. (1998). "Assessment of environmental policies and policy implementation in India." *Economic and Political Weekly*, 33, 48–54.
Wallington, T., Bina, O., & Thissen, W. (2007). "Theorising strategic environmental assessment: fresh perspectives and future challenges." *Environmental Impact Assessment Review*, 27(7), 569–584. https://doi.org/10.1016/j.eiar.2007.05.007.
Wang, H., Bai, H., Liu, J., & Xu, H. (2012). "Measurement indicators and an evaluation approach for assessing strategic environmental assessment effectiveness." *Ecological Indicators*, 23, 413–420. https://doi.org/10.1016/j.ecolind.2012.04.021.
White, L., & Noble, B.F. (2013). "Strategic environmental assessment for sustainability: a review of a decade of academic research." *Environmental Impact Assessment Review*, 42, 60–66. https://doi.org/10.1016/j.eiar.2012.10.003.
Zhu, D., & Ru, J. (2008). "Strategic environmental assessment in China: motivations, politics, and effectiveness." *Journal of Environmental Management*, 88(4), 615–626. https://doi.org/10.1016/j.jenvman.2007.03.040.
Zhu, T., Wu, J., & Chang, I.-S. (2005). "Requirements for strategic environmental assessment in China." *Journal of Environmental Assessment Policy and Management*, 7(1), 81–97.

26

Sustainable development and environmental stewardship: the Heart of Borneo paradox and its implications on green economic transformation in Asia

Choy Yee Keong

Introduction

The island of Borneo, shared by Indonesia (Kalimantan), Borneo Malaysia (comprising the states of Sarawak and Sabah) and Brunei Darussalam, is the third largest island in the world covering an area of 74 million hectares (ha). Its forest covers which evolved between 100 and 150 million years ago are among the most biologically diverse on Earth. The island is home to roughly four million indigenous people whose socio-economic fabrics, cultures and traditions are intimately associated with the earthly systems. Agriculture, mining, timber harvesting, tourism and recently, the promotion of energy-intensive industries, are some of the important economic activities in the region.

Following the publication of the Brundtland Report in 1987 which popularized the concept of sustainable development defined as "*development that meets the needs of the present without compromising the ability of future generations to meet their own needs*," each country in Borneo have committed to promote environmental sustainability while enhancing economic growth (WCED 1987, p. 43). Environmental sustainability is associated with human responsible decisions and action when interacting with the natural environment. Its main focus is to preserve the ecological resilience and productive capacity of the natural environment which underpin long-term socio-economic progress. It is one of the three main components of sustainable development. The other two are economic sustainability and social sustainability.

Environmental sustainability may be distinguished from ecological sustainability. Environmental suitability is defined as the ability to maintain the ecological health of ecosystems expressed in terms of diversity, resiliency and productive capacity. This is to ensure that their controlling mechanisms and functions are sustained over time. Ecological sustainability is a conservation concept and is concerned about the dualistic relationship between human beings and ecosystems. While ecological sustainability places great emphasis on protecting the ecological health of ecosystems, environmental sustainability is more concerned with the wiser use of the natural environment to support human socioeconomic development (Choy 2015a). It may thus be claimed that ecological sustainability is a strong form of environmental sustainability. However, within the present analysis, these two overlapping concepts may be used interchangeably to refer to sustainable resource management and environmental conservation.

In responding to the above environmental sustainability challenges, regional leaders in Borneo have created a large tri-national protected area known as the Heart of Borneo (HoB) for environmental conservation and sustainable management purposes. A wide range of environmental protection policies has been designed to strengthen conservation efforts of the HoB. Despite this, however, an empirical assessment of the conservation progress in the HoB in general has revealed that they have failed to protect the regional ecosystems from persistent ecological impoverishment.

The chapter posits that the driver behind this HoB environmental paradox is attributed to the regional approach to environmental sustainability, which is heavily skewed toward economic maximization vis-à-vis environmental conservation. Presenting a basic non-anthropocentric narration of the value of nature, the chapter suggests ways to solve the present development-environmental dilemma. The analysis is expected to shed light onto the ultimate factors that contribute to environmental degradations across the Asia-Pacific region, and the ways to address them.

Forests of Borneo: some basic facts

Borneo which covers an area of 74 million hectares (ha) is the third largest island in the world next to Greenland and New Guinea. For millions of years, Borneo had been a pristine tropical paradise with dense and uninterrupted tracts of a wide variety of forest habitats, including lowland forests such as dipterocarp rainforests, peat swamp forests and freshwater swamp forests. These forests are predominantly found near the coastal areas of Borneo, especially in West Kalimantan and the state of Sarawak in Borneo Malaysia. Mangrove forests are found mostly on river deltas and along most of Borneo's coastline while Montane rainforests are mainly seen in the mountainous areas in central and north-eastern parts of Borneo. The lowland forests are the most biologically diverse habitats in Borneo (WWF 2005a).

The island, which accounts for just one percent of the world's landmass, houses roughly six percent of global biodiversity. Its rainforests are also characterized by exceptionally high concentrations of unique, endemic and threatened plant and animal species. The flora of Borneo alone consists of roughly 15,000 species of which over 5,000 species or 34 percent are endemic, that is, they are found only in the region and nowhere else in the world. It is noteworthy that its diversity is richer than that the entire continent of Africa, which is 40 times larger than the island. For example, it has been found that the Lambir Hills National Park in Sarawak has the highest plant diversity in the world, with a record of 1,175 species in a 52-hectare plot (MacKinnon et al. 1996; Schithuizen 2007; WWF 2007). It is estimated that about 620 species of birds and 221 species of mammals are found in the park (ASEAN Secretariat 2009).

There are about 100 amphibian species, over 420 bird species (37 endemic), around 210 mammal species (44 endemic) and 394 fish species (19 endemic) found in Borneo as a whole (WWF 2017). It may be noted in passing that the forests in Borneo also serve as a life-support system for food and water security and for the livelihoods of various tribal communities including the Iban, Penan, and Kenyah, among others (Choy 2014).

Environmental protection of the Heart of Borneo: the institutional framework

In an attempt to protect the HoB ecological treasure, the governments of Indonesia, Malaysia and Brunei (hereafter the HoB member countries) with the cooperation and advocacy efforts of the

World Wildlife Fund (WWF) formally signed the Heart of Borneo Declaration (hereafter the Declaration) in 2007 and established a regional environmental protection framework known as the Heart of Boneo Initiative (HoBI). The HoBI was officially endorsed by all ASEAN Heads of Government.[1] It was further adopted as a flagship project of the Brunei Darussalam–Indonesia–Malaysia–The Philippines East ASEAN Growth Area (BIMP-EAGA) sub-regional cooperation program established in 1994 (WWF 2012).

The formal adoption of HoBI led to the mapping of a 23-million-hectare of tri-national and transboundary protected area (almost a third of Borneo Island) in central Borneo known as the Heart of Borneo (HoB) for conservation and sustainable management purposes. Respectively, Indonesia, Malaysia and Brunei contributed roughly 16.8 million, 6 million and 570,000 ha to its formation (WWF 2010a). The HoB is the last great Asian rainforest and a unique global ecological treasure which houses roughly 10,000 out of the 15,000 plant species found in Borneo Island as a whole, 10 primate species, 150 reptile and amphibian species, 100 mammal species and over 350 bird species. In addition, new species continued to be discovered in the region. In 2006 alone, 52 new species were identified, and between 2007 and 2009, a total of 123 new species were discovered (WWF 2007, 2010b).

The HoBI is one of most important regional cooperative environmental arrangements to promote sustainable development in the HoB region. It is in part governed by the ASEAN Agreement on the Conservation of Nature and Natural Resources (the ASEAN Agreement). The ASEAN Agreement, which was adopted in 1985 and formally came into force in 1995, is a legally binding instrument. It provides some of the most holistic guidelines for the design of a sustainable environmental management framework to ensure that the regional rich biological diversity is sustainably managed toward enhancing social, economic and environmental sustainability as emphasized under the Brundtland Report.

In particular, Article 1 of the ASEAN Agreement explicitly stipulates that each member country is required to adopt measures in accordance with its national laws to ensure sustainable use of natural resources and to protect the ecological resilience and genetic diversity of ecosystems. It further asserts that each member country should undertake to integrate environmental protection measures into development policies. The ASEAN Agreement which covers every area of environmental management represents one of the most comprehensive regional legal frameworks for environmental planning and management in Asia (Choy 2015a). Apart from the regional environmental initiative, each HoB member country has also put in place various national environmental laws and instruments to reinforce environmental protection (Table 26.1).

The above regional cooperative efforts and national legal enactments and environmental instruments reflect that the HoB member countries are committed to protecting the regional environment while pursuing socio-economic progress by transforming the HoB region into a green economy. The "green economy" concepts proposed by the United Nations Environment Program (UNEP) in its paper entitled *Towards a Green Economy–Pathways to Sustainable Development and Poverty Eradication* (2011), which set the agendas for Rio+20, call on the international community to move away from a "brown economy" to a "green economy" (UNEP 2011, p. 2). "Brown economy" refers to environmentally unsustainable or harmful modes production and consumption patterns. In contrast, "green economy" refers to development that "improves human well-being and social equity, while significantly reducing environmental risks and ecological scarcities" (UNEP 2011, p. 2).

The green economy within the HoB perspective may be defined as the decoupling of economic growth from overexploitation of natural resources, environmental impairment, biodiversity degradation and biospheric disruption. In this regard, economic growth means "sustained and inclusive growth," that is, economic growth in perpetuity and for the benefit of

Table 26.1 Legal and environmental instruments in HoB member countries

Indonesia	*Malaysia*		*Brunei*
	Sarawak	*Sabah*	
Environmental Management Act (1997, revised 1982; 1990)	Statement of Forest Policy (1954)	Forest Enactment (1968)	Forest Act (1934, amended 2007)
Forestry Law (1999)	Natural Resources and Environment (Amendment) Ordinance (1993)	Forest Rules (1969)	The Wildlife Protection Act (1978, revised 1984)
Conservation Law (1990)	Forest Ordinance (1958, amended 1997)	Wildlife Conservation Enactment (1997)	National Forest Policy (1989)
Environmental Protection Law (2009)	Sarawak Forestry Corporation Ordinance (1995)	Cultural Heritage (Conservation) Enactment (1997)	The Wild Fauna and Flora Order (2007)
Cultivation Law (1992)	The National Park and Nature Reserves Ordinance (1998)	Park Enactment (1984)	The Fisheries Order (2009)
Plantation Law (2004)	Wildlife Protection Ordinance (1998)	Biodiversity Enactment (2000)	The Brunei Darussalam Long-term development Plan – Wawasan 2035
Ministry of Agriculture Regulation (2007)	Sarawak Biodiversity Centre Ordinance (1998)	Environment Protection Enactment (2002)	Marine Protected Area Network (2012)

Source: Sabah Biodiversity Centre, http://ww2.sabah.gov.my/sabc/index.php?option=com_content&view=article&id=49&Itemid=57.

everyone in term of improved human well-being and social equity. The green economic transformation in this context necessarily involves the creation of a low carbon economy by limiting greenhouse gases, especially carbon dioxide emissions, improvement of social well-being and promotion of poverty alleviation, efficient use of natural resources, sustainable consumption, and other green development initiatives (WWF and PWC 2011; UNEP 2011).

In addressing the green economic transformation challenges, the HoB member countries have jointly developed a Trilateral Strategic Plan of Action to put policies into action. Accordingly, five sustainability programs have been identified under the trilateral action plan, namely, Transboundary Management, Protected Areas Management, Sustainable Natural Resource Management, Ecotourism Development, and Capacity Building (Table 26.2) (Sabah Forestry Department 2009). Each country has also formulated its own specific HoB Strategic Plan of Action or Project Implementation Framework to reinforce the green implementation processes (WWF and PWC 2011). The green implementation processes are further enhanced by the establishment of national environmental governance to address environmental sustainability challenges. These include the HoB National Council in Brunei; the HoB Working Group in Indonesia; and the National Expert Group and Steering Committee in Malaysia (Sarawak and Sabah) (WWF 2012).

Table 26.2 Trilateral strategic plan of action programs

Program	*aim*
Transboundary management:	To address issues of management off natural resources and socio-economic welfare of the local communities on the border areas
Protected area management	To enhance and promote effective management of protected areas especially those located on the common border
Sustainable resource management	To enhance sustainable management of natural resources outside the protected areas
Ecotourism development	To recognize and protect natural assets of special natural or cultural values within the HoB area
Capacity building	To ensure effective implementation of HoB initiative at all levels, both public and private sectors as well as the local community level

Source: Sabah Forestry Department (2009).

It seems that the above all-encompassing institutional evolution paves the way for an effective green economic transformation in the region. In Indonesia, for example, its HoB area is legally recognized as an area of National Strategic Importance through the enactment of the Government Regulation No.26 of 2008. Furthermore, Presidential Decree No.2 of 2012 was also created to prevent activities that may be ecologically destructive to the HoB while Presidential Decree No.3 of 2012 recognized the HoB as the "lungs of the world." The latter environmental initiative aims to achieve the national target of reducing greenhouse gases emissions by 26 percent by 2020 (Ariaini 2013). Furthermore, nature conservation is enhanced due to the legal creation of Nature Reserves, National Parks, Game Reserves, Recreation Parks and Grand Forest Parks based on various legal instruments as listed in Table 26.1 (Ministry of Forestry, Indonesia 2009).

In Sarawak, the HoB protection initiatives are fundamentally guided by the state's Sustainable Forest Management (SFM) framework. The framework places great emphasis on sustainable utilization and conservation of forests and their genetic resources, and the maintenance of the ecological health of ecosystems based on nature conservation. Nature conservation takes the form of legal creation of Totally Protected Areas (TPAs) under various legislations as indicated in Table 26.1. These include National Park, Nature Reserve and Wildlife Sanctuary as well as Transboundary Conservation Areas (TBCAs) (WWF 2010a; Sarawak Monitor 2013; Spence 2013).

Since the adoption of HoBI in 2007, the land areas of national parks, nature reserves and wildlife sanctuaries in Sarawak have increased from 301,000 ha, 945 ha and 192,000 ha to 417,000 ha, 1,900 ha and 206,000 ha, respectively (Sarawak Forestry Corporation 2014). Also, the state government is planning to expand the area of TPAs in the HoB region to enhance forest connectivity between the landscapes and biodiversity corridor for wildlife (Chia 2015). It is noteworthy that various important TBCA projects have been implemented to reinforce biodiversity conservation of HoB. They are the Lanjak-Entimau Wildlife Sanctuary in the state of Sarawak and the Bentuang-Karimun National Park in Indonesian Kalimantan. The state government of Sarawak has also taken the initiative to create a large transboundary conservation area by linking its Pulong Tau National Park located in Kalabit Highland to Kayan Mentarang National Park located in Indonesia (Eaton 2005; ITTO et al. 2006; Hitchner 2010).

Similarly, in Sabah, in enhancing HoB green development, the state government has increased its Totally Protected Areas (TPA) from 800,000 ha to 1.55 million ha or about 21 percent of the total state land area. The state has further pledged to increase its TPA to 30 percent or 2.1 million ha of its total land area over the next 10 years (Chong 2015). The current TPA expansion has contributed to the widening of buffer zones in the Maliau Basin and Imbak Canyon conservation areas (WWF 2014). To reinforce conservation efforts, the state government has also institutionalized the application of multiple-use forest landscape planning and management models to establish forest connectivity among the protected forest islands. A case in point is the proposed 261,264 ha of landscaping area which forms an important connecting landmass to three renowned protected areas in Sabah, namely, the Maliau Basin Conservation Area (58,840 ha) to the West, the Danum Valley Conservation Areas (43,800 ha) to the East, and the Imbak Canyon Conservation Areas (16,750 ha) to the North (UNDP 2012). The state government has also established 19 field outposts within HoB landscapes for wildlife monitoring and forest-encroachment-reduction (Chong 2015).

Similarly, in response to the HoBI, the Government of Brunei Darussalam has committed 58 percent (about 576,400 ha) of its total landmass as protected areas for sustainable management and conservation purposes (WWF 2010a). Logging activities are banned in these areas. The management of biodiversity within the delineated HoB landscape is guided by the National Biological Resources (Biodiversity) Policy and Strategic Plan of Action (2012) The plan outlines the strategic objectives and actions to conserve the biological richness in the HoB region (Ministry of Development, Brunei 2015). The Brunei government has also established a transboundary peatland project and a new species discovery scientific expedition program to enhance environmental conservation efforts (UNDP 2012). In addition, the Brunei Heart of Borneo Project Implementation Framework (PIF) was developed to serve as a launchpad for a transition to a green economy (Ministry of Industry and Primary Resources of Negara Brunei Darussalam 2008).

It is increasingly clear from the above that since the adoption of the HoB Declaration in 2007, the HoB environmental stewardship has grown in strength and sophistication. Environmental stewardship may be defined as the act of undertaking responsibility for the ecological health of the environment and taking action to achieve that aim. Here, action refers to green action, that is, steps undertaken to promote a green economy, which entail balancing economic growth with environmental sustainability by determining the full extent of the adverse impacts on the environment, when optimizing its economic use.

Yet, ironically, despite decades of environmental efforts, it seems that most initiatives have failed to stem the tide of environmental decline in the HoB region. In fact, the ecological health of the HoB has worsened. It seems that the HoB canonical green formula for greater environmental sustainability still sounds hollow. In what follows is an attempt to examine this environmental paradox based on a quantitative investigation of the changes in the HoB ecological state over the past few decades, amid increasing legal and regional environmental controlling efforts.

The Heart of Borneo paradox: an overview

Casual observation on the ground reveals that the dynamics of the market economy is increasingly exposing the HoB region to heighten risks of commodification and the threat of irreversible destruction. For example, the gradual depletion of natural forests and the upsetting of the HoB ecological systems caused by illegal logging activities spurred by cross border timber trade between Indonesia Kalimantan and Borneo Malaysia, uncontrolled oil palm plantation expansions which involved clear cutting of natural forests, and dam infrastructure development within or in the vicinity of HoB, which has involved extensive habitat transformation, are some of the cases in point (Choy 2005; Obidzinski et al. 2007; WWF 2007).

To wit, each year, an estimated one million cubic meters of timber are being smuggled out of the HoB area, leaving destroyed forests and threatened biodiversity behind (ADP 2013). The opening up of new roads and logging tracts in the smuggling process also provides easy access to the commercially valuable trees in the once-inaccessible areas surrounding the HoB region (Obidzinski et al. 2007). Analysis of satellite imagery collected between 1990 and 2009 shows that approximately 226,000 miles (364,000 kilometer) of roads were constructed throughout the forests in Borneo Malaysia (Bryan et al. 2013). This poses further threats to the long-term ecological health of the HoB ecosystems as easy accessibility often leads to unrestrained logging activities. Easy accessibility also encourages poaching, illegal wildlife trading and smuggling, adversely affecting the continued survival of many of the endangered and rare species of animals thriving in the HoB habitats (JEC 2005; Felbab-Brown 2011). It is noteworthy that the HoB has lost 10 percent (2 million ha) of its forest cover since 2007, despite putting in place various all-encompassing environmental conservation policies and measures as discussed above (Denton 2014; Wulffraat et al. 2014).

Also, despite the Indonesian government's call for a paradigmatic shift of development discourse toward a green economy, new areas of extensive forest cover in the HoB have been designated for infrastructure and economic development in the Indonesian HoB region. The HoB environmental paradox will be the main subject for discussion in the following section with specific reference to Indonesia Kalimantan and Borneo Malaysia. A brief discussion will be made in the case of Brunei, the smallest country involved in the HoB initiative.

Indonesia Kalimantan environmental paradox

In Indonesia, in the hope to realize its overarching goal of becoming a developed country by 2025, the government has unveiled an ambitious plan, the Master Plan for the Acceleration and Expansion of Indonesian Economic Development (MP3EI) to direct the future course of Indonesia's development. The plan focuses on the development of eight main targets, namely, agriculture, mining, energy, industrial, marine, tourism, telecommunication and the development of strategic areas (CMEA 2011). Under this master plan, six economic corridors have been identified, out of which one is linked to the sustainable future of HoB – the "Center for Production and Processing of National Mining and Energy Reserves" in Kalimantan.[2] One of the potential projects designated under this specific economic corridor is the IndoMet Coal Project (ICP). The project aims to exploit coal deposits found in East and Central Kalimantan, covering a combined area of 350,000 ha – over four-and-a-half times the size of Greater Jakarta or more than twice the size of Greater London (Denton 2014).

The coal project itself is located within the HoB especially in the heavily forested Upper Barito Basin, which is home to large populations of orangutans and many unknown scientific biological species (CMD 2014). The planned open-cut coal mining method as proposed under the coal project involves extensive habitat destruction and is environmentally destructive. It will not only contribute directly to erosion and heavy metals leaching into waterways, producing an adverse impact on the aquatic ecosystem but also, will be detrimental to the ecological health of the HoB. The construction of a coal railway infrastructure to improve extraction and production process will aggravate the environmental quagmire in the form of clear cutting of forests.

The master plan also aims to transform Kalimantan into an agricultural hub in Asia with specific focus on oil palm plantation development. This "green transformation" which necessarily involves extensive and irreversible rainforest destruction further worsens the environmental condition in the HoB region. In this connection, it may be revealed that currently, Indonesia is the world's largest palm oil producer and oil palm grower (Erik and Douglas 2013).

Demonstrably, between 2009 and 2011, about 296,000 ha (24 percent of the country's forested area) and 95,000 ha (eight percent) of forests in central and west Kalimantan respectively have been cleared for various economic activities especially oil palm plantation development. In 2008, the government has also lifted a year-long ban on new oil palm plantation development in the carbon-rich peat land area in order to expand its palm oil industry further (Hitchner 2010). Oil palm plantation is currently the largest single driver of deforestation in Kalimantan as well as in Indonesia as a whole (Green Peace International 2013). In reflection, between 2000 and 2012, Indonesia has cleared more than six million ha of forest mostly for agricultural development, especially for oil palm plantation expansion (Margono et al. 2014).

It may be of interest to note that the Indonesian government had in 2005 proposed a mega agricultural project, the Kalimantan Border Oil Palm Project which aimed to convert 1.8 million has of forests along the 850 kilometer Indonesia–Malaysia border in Kalimantan. However, the launch of the HoB project in 2006 spelled out the end of this world's largest palm oil plantation scheme which would have had irreversible and destructive ecological consequences on the HoB if it were to materialize (Oetami 2013). Despite this, the Indonesian government has never officially canceled the project and oil palm expansion is still taking place in the border area, leaving the option to revive the plan when the time is ripe (Oetami 2013).

The Indonesian palm oil industry and its resultant massive scale of habitat fragmentation is threatening the continued existence of some of the world's iconic and endangered species such as the Sumatran tiger, the Sumatran elephant, the Javan rhinoceros and the orangutan (Choy 2015a, 2015b). The unsustainable land use patterns in the name of a "green economy" have also resulted in extensive greenhouse gas emissions and regional warming caused by forest burning for oil palm plantation conversion. For example, in 2010 alone, land-clearing for oil palm plantations in Kalimantan emitted more than 140 million tons of carbon dioxide – an amount equivalent to annual emissions from about 28 million vehicles (Jordan 2012). To be sure, this greenhouse effect is detrimental to the health of the HoB forest biota (Scriven et al. 2015).

Borneo Malaysia environmental paradox

The state of Sarawak

In the state of Sarawak, nearly 80 percent of its rainforests have been degraded by logging activities (Bryan et al. 2013; Straumann 2014). Today, very little rainforest and ecosystems remain undisturbed by logging activities and only three percent of the land area in the state is covered with intact forests in isolated patches, spreading haphazardly across the region (Global Witness 2014). The logging industry, which is dominated by the "Big-6" firms, namely, Samling, Shin Yang, Rimbunan Hijau, Ta Ann, WTK, and KTS, is now expanding its timber harvesting activities into the last frontiers of the intact rainforest. For example, by the end of 2014, one of the Big-6 timber giants, Shin Yang, was decimating the proposed Danum Linau National Park located within the HoB conservation area at a rate of nine square kilometer a month, causing damage to the once intact rainforest canopy.

Indeed, the uncontrolled logging activities of these timber giants are threatening the continued existence of the proposed Sungai Moh Wildlife Sanctuary, which lies in the HoB (Global Witness 2015). Furthermore, satellite imagery reveals that logging operations in river buffer zones and severe erosion and landslides from road construction, and severe canopy destruction caused by unrestrained timber extraction were observed in or near the HoB region. Large scale logging activities have also been observed in the totally protected forests, the Usun Apau National Park (Global Witness 2015).

Forest concessions have also been allocated to logging companies to extract timber logs from the Danum Linau National Park and two extension areas within the HoB region (Global Witness 2015). Thousands of ha of logging concessions lie within the HoB, including those areas adjacent to the Indonesian Bentuang Karimun National Park to the south, and bordering the Lanjak Entimau Wildlife Sanctuary (Sarawak) to the west, which have also been given out to various logging companies for timber harvesting. These forests are home to a wide range of critically endangered species totally protected under Sarawak Laws and include orangutans, Clouded Leopard, The Bornean Gibbon, Hose's Langur, Western Tarsier, Slow Loris, and Giant Squirrel (Council on Ethics for the Government Pension Fund Global 2013). The logging of these pristine rainforests has also resulted in a series of catastrophic landslides that blocked Sarawak's largest river for a 50 kilometer stretch in 2010 (Global Witness 2012).

The construction of mega-dam infrastructure is also one of the major factors that hinders the progress of HoB stewardship efforts. For example, the construction of the Bakun and Murum dams adjacent to the HoB region, which involved an irreversible destruction of roughly 94,000 ha of rainforests, has destroyed the forest corridors leading toward the HoB territory, impacting the ecological health of HoB biodiversity (Choy 2005). In this regard, it is relevant to note in passing that in an attempt to transform Sarawak into a developed state by 2020, the government has launched its long-term development strategy, the SCORE (Sarawak Corridor of Renewable Energy), in 2008. Underlying the core of this strategy is the state's plan to construct 12 dams in the forest interiors with a total generation capacity of 7,000 megawatts to promote heavy or energy-intensive industries. The realization of this mega-dam infrastructure blueprint necessarily involves a complete and irreversible destruction of approximately 230,000 ha of rainforests, which is equivalent to one-and-a-half times the size of Greater London. Its environmental impact on the health of HoB will be undoubtedly far reaching.

Added to this is the expansion of the environmentally destructive oil palm industry in the state spurred by the exhaustion of land banks in Peninsular Malaysia. Between 1990 and 2010, about 500,000 ha of intact forests in the interior have been cleared for commercial scale oil palm plantation expansion, leading to extensive habitat fragmentation (Tsuyuki et al. 2011). Overall, for the past few decades, oil palm plantations have expanded substantially from 23,000 ha in 1980 to 1.4 million ha in 2015, exerting an immense ecological impact on the HoB flora and fauna (Lyddon 2014; MPOB 2016).

The state of Sabah

Similarly, in the state of Sabah, about 80 percent of its rainforests have been heavily impacted by logging activities or oil palm plantation development. The rapid rate of deforestation is further accelerated by the presence of a dense pattern of logging roads which penetrate almost the entire area of the remaining forests in the state (Bryan et al. 2013). Indeed, during the period between 1973 and 2010, Sabah had the highest deforestation rate in Borneo at 39.5 percent, compared to Sarawak (23.1 percent) and Kalimantan (30.7 percent). It also has the second lowest proportion of intact forest in Borneo at 19.1 percent compared to Brunei (56.9 percent) and Kalimantan (32.6 percent). The state of Sarawak has the lowest proportion at 14.6 percent (Gaveau et al. 2014). The logging industry in the state has also penetrated right into the HoB region and today, very little rainforest remains untouched by logging (Bryan et al. 2013).

Currently, Sabah is Malaysia's largest palm oil producing state with a total plantation area of 1.5 million ha as of 2015 (Sabah Times 2015). The oil palm plantation development, which cut across the rainforest landscape in Sabah, is taking a heavy toll on its natural environment and its biodiversity. For instance, despite the fact that conserving the mega-diverse pockets of rainforest in Danum Valley, Maliau Basin and Imbak Canyon conservation areas is instrumental in connecting the biodiversity "crown jewels" of the HoB, they are not spared from human economic intervention (Butler 2012a). What aggravates the environmental condition is that about 82,000 ha of forest reserve in this region have been approved for oil palm plantation development (Butler 2012b; Rayat Post 2014).

The above commercial agricultural activity has generally contributed to the dramatic decline in orangutan populations in Sabah, which decreased by 50 percent from 22,000 to 11,000 in 50 years due to extensive habitat destruction (Hance 2009; Butler 2010). Indeed, aerial surveys showed large numbers of orangutans were forced to move to the oil-palm plantations, especially in small forest patches within the oil-palm matrix due to the destruction of their original habitats (Erik and Douglas 2013). Also, the agricultural development has resulted in severe river pollution in the state (Butler 2012a).

Brunei Darussalam's HoB status quo

Brunei Darussalam offers an interesting counterexample to Indonesia Kalimantan and Borneo Malaysia in forest conservation. Unlike these two regions whose economies are skewed toward the economic exploitation of land and forests, Brunei Darussalam, a tiny oil-rich nation with a total area of 5,265 sq km and a small population of about 412,000 as of 2012, relies on petroleum and natural gas export and associated energy resource services to support its economy (Bryan et al. 2013).

Thus, this small nation-state can afford to avoid extensive logging or oil palm plantation development in favor of forest conservation. As a matter of fact, Brunei's forest policy is oriented toward the production of wood for local needs and it prohibits timber export completely (Collins et al. 1991). The difference in policy offers a stark contrast in term of forest cover where about 54 percent of Brunei's forest remains relatively intact with only 15 percent degraded and six percent severely degraded (Bryan et al. 2013).

Despite this, however, based on the Brunei Forest Reserve Report (2010), while 17 percent of its forest is classified as Protected Area, the rest (38 percent) is categorized as Production Forest. This means that the Production Forest is subject to exploitation. Given that Brunei limits its annual timber extraction to 100,000 cubic meters, it is estimated that the rest Production Forest will be disturbed by logging around 2040 (Engbers 2010). This may threaten the ecological integrity of the HoB caused by environmental degradation. In fact, it has been reported that the Brunei HoB area has been partially damaged due to various housing infrastructure projects like dam and road construction, including logging road construction (Engbers 2010).

The HoB paradox and its implications on green economic transformation in Asia

The above analysis provides incontrovertible evidence that the HoB regions in Indonesia Kalimantan and Borneo Malaysia have increasingly been exposed to the threat of ecological destruction. This is despite having in place an all-encompassing Trilateral Strategic Plan of Action Programs and national environmental protection initiatives, local action plans, and legal instruments to reinforce conservation efforts while providing opportunities for various economic activities in the region. The analysis reveals succinctly that policy makers in these two regions have failed to give equal weight to the promotion of environmental sustainability when optimizing the economic use of nature.

It may well be remarked that when it comes to the policy implementation stage, the concept of sustainable development or green economic transformation exhibits a perceptual shift from environmental sustainability to economic sustainability. Put otherwise, the locus of sustainability in the regions has shifted from conservation of nature, to sustaining long-term economic growth or material progress. This HoB environmental paradox generally bespeaks the real meaning of "sustainable development" or "green economy" not only in Southeast Asia but also, in the Asian developing region at large.

To be sure, since the United Nations convened its first world conference on the human environment (Stockholm Conference) in 1972 to call on the international community to promote environmental conservation while pursuing economic growth, world leaders, especially those in the fast Asian emerging economies, including China, have responded positively. They were committed to streamlining their development path for a wiser use of nature that is critical to the well-being and livelihood of present and future generations (Choy 2015a, 2015b).

Subsequent international environmental meetings and conferences convened by the United Nations, including (1) the Rio Earth Summit (1992), (2) the Johannesburg World Summit on Sustainable Development (2002),(3) the Rio+20 Summit (2012), (4) the High-Level Summit on the Millennium Development Goals (2013), and (5) the United Nations Framework Convention on Climate Change (UNFCC) Conferences ranging from the first Conference of the Parties (COP 1) held in Berlin 1995 to COP 21 held in Paris in 2015, have provided further impetus for the Asian leaders to reinforce their commitment to green economic transformation toward a low carbon, environmentally friendly and socially sustainable economy.

However, as it has turned out, the overall state of the global environment has hardly improved and new environmental threats and challenges continue to emerge. In China, for instance, in affirming its commitment to achieving sustainable development as emphasized in the Brundtland Report (1987), it has elevated its State Environmental Protection Commission established in 1984 to the State Environmental Protection Administration in 1998, which finally became the Ministry of Environmental Protection in 2008 (Choy 2016a). At the same time, it has enacted and revised various environmental laws, some of which are indicated below in order to strengthen its environmental protection efforts:

(i) Environmental Protection Law (1979, amended 1989),
(ii) Wildlife Protection Law (1986, amended in 2000 and 2004),
(iii) Fisheries Law (1986, amended in 2000 and 2004),
(iv) Water Pollution Prevention Law (1984, revised in 1996),
(v) Protection of Terrestrial Wildlife Law (1992), and
(vi) Regulation of Aquatic Wild Animals (1993).

Despite this, nonetheless, the above far-reaching environmental protection framework and legal instruments have generally failed to halt further environmental decline. Cases in point are, for example (1) up to 70 percent of China's rivers are seriously polluted and out of the world's 20 most polluted river, 16 are found in China, (2) annual discharge of industrial wastes including toxic wastes, heavy metals and chemical effluents into the Yangtze river has increased at an alarming rate from 15 billion tons in the 1980s to 33.9 billion tons in 2010, causing extensive destructive impacts on the Yangtze aquatic ecosystem (Choy 2015a, 2015b, 2016a).

Similarly, for the rest of the Southeast Asian countries including Thailand, the Philippines and Vietnam, institutional improvement and legal enactment have failed to arrest extensive environmental destruction in the region. This is mainly due to the regional leaders' overwhelming emphasis placed on achieving economic growth over environmental sustainability (Choy 2015a, 2015b, 2016a).

On the whole, the ecological footprint which measures humanity's demands on Earth's natural resources including forest, cropland, atmosphere and oceans as carbon sinks, and fishing grounds, have increased to an unsustainable level across the Southeast Asian region, as indicated by the widening bio-capacity deficit in the region (WWF 2005b; WWF et al. 2012; UNEP 2014; Choy 2016b). Indeed, in Asia and the Pacific, the per capita ecological footprint measured at 1.6 global ha (gha) far exceeds the per capita biocapacity at 0.9 gha in the Asian Pacific region, leaving a bio-capacity deficit of 0.8 gha per capita (WWF et al. 2012). This is despite decades of the United Nations' continuous and unrelenting efforts to promote environmental conservation and sustainable resource use in the region. If current environmental issues are left unaddressed with stronger commitment to sustainable development, this could lead to abrupt or irreversible damage of the earth's ecosystems, threatening human survival.

In addressing the environmental sustainability challenges, the way forward is for us to dismantle our unrestrained capitalist mode of resource exploitation and to build a common future in harmony with the environment via a moral and ethical engagement with nature. It may well be that thinking morally or ethically about the natural environment *can* influence human beings' attitudes and aid environmental conservation. The rationale behind this argument is that environmental conservation and environmental ethics go hand in hand, and it is only by extending environmental ethics to nature that can we avoid crossing the planetary tipping point that could lead to abrupt or irreversible ecological destruction. This will be briefly discussed in the following section.

The HoB paradox and the green economic transformation in Asia: the ethical implications

It is increasingly clear that the HoB environmental paradox is mainly attributed to the lack of ethical considerations in resource use decision-making or planning processes. That said, many of the environmental protective policies often involve ethical questions. In other words, in our economic use of nature, human environmental value judgments directly influence our distinct moral stance toward nature. The question is how we see ourselves with respect to nature, and what ethical principles should shape humans' environmental attitudes and decision-making for the benefit of humans and the natural system. In passing, environmental attitude is defined as a collection of beliefs or behavioral intentions an individual holds in association with environmentally related activities or issues while environmental values underlying determinants of more specific environmental attitudes or behaviors (Schultz et al. 2005). Implicitly, resource use decision-making aiming at promoting a genuine course of sustainable development or green economy must express values based on a "non-anthropocentric moral system."

To begin with, the anthropocentric value system is human-centered and censures behavior that threatens human social well-being (Shrader-Frechette 1981). Accordingly, human beings are ends-in-themselves and the sole bearers of intrinsic value and all other living things including animals and plants have no intrinsic value (MacKinnon and Fiala 2015) They are targeted for protection only if they are useful to serve human interest. That is to say, nature can only be of instrumental value and is not deemed worthy of direct moral concern. Under the anthropocentric worldview, human beings exercise dominance over nature.

By contrast, the biocentric (life-centered) ethic recognizes the moral relations between humans and all other living things. It holds the belief that all life, including plants and animals, has intrinsic value and moral consideration and that, human beings are members of the larger ecological communities (Taylor 1986; Rolston 2003). Put differently, humans are not considered to be inherently superior to other living things as in anthropocentrism. Biocentric ethics is a type of individualistic environmental ethics in that it only extends moral consideration to the individual organism. Thus it may not be adequate to serve as an ethical foundation or a persuasive moral justification for developing a more respectful relationship to the earth as a whole.

In addressing the above shortcomings, an alternative is to embrace the ecocentrism which incorporates biocentrism into its nature-centered value system. Ecocentrism, sometimes referred to as deep ecological ethics, holds that moral concern and ethical protection should be extended to a spectrum of holistic natural entities such as species, ecosystems, landscapes or even the entire biosphere rather than individual entity as in biocentrism (Callicot 1989). The hallmark of ecocentrism may be traced back to Aldo Leopold's classic land ethics, which focused on protecting the integrated community of life or the biotic community, which includes plants, animals, rocks, lands, soils and water, or more simply the ecosystem as a whole. The golden rule of Leopold's land ethics is "a thing is right when it tends to preserve the integrity, stability, and beauty of the biotic community. It is wrong when it tends otherwise" (Leopold 1949, pp. 224–225). Leopold environmental moral maxim removes completely the anthropocentric view of the human race toward nature. As he claims further, "land is a community to which we belong" not "a commodity belonging to us" and that, human beings are but "plain members and citizens of the biotic community" (Leopold 1949, pp. viii, 204). That is to say, ecocentrics necessarily see themselves as a part of nature, rather than being in control of it, and assume moral responsibility toward nature, focusing on how to preserve its ecological integrity and stability. The positive relationship between the ethical norms that guide human environmental behaviors and sustainable resource use has been verified based on extensive field studies conducted between 2007 and 2011 with the indigenous people in the Borneo state of Sarawak in Malaysia (Choy 2014).

As has been extensively discussed in Choy (2014), suffice it to state briefly that five years of field research conducted with indigenous people in the forest interiors in Sarawak in Borneo Malaysia revealed that the local communities have traditionally seen themselves as an inherent part of nature Choy (2014). Also, their centuries-old custom known as "adat" required them to adopt a morality of care when optimizing the instrumental use of nature for socio-economic sustenance. The "adat" also required the local communities to ascribe the moral beliefs of environmental justice toward future generations by protecting the surrounding environment from degradation. This is to ensure that the future generations can inherit a healthy environment as enjoyed by the present generation. For the past few centuries the indigenous people have built up their cultural relationship with nature through their ethical behavior and moral concern for land and forests. Based on field observation, the ethical norm of behavior has been able to help the local communities to protect the ecological integrity of their environment for the past few centuries.

The HoB environmental paradox and the indigenous environmental worldviews shed immense insights into the reality that many of today's environmental problems are basically caused not because of the lack of institutional arrangements or environmental laws, but due to the lack of ethics on the part of economic agents when optimizing the economic use of nature. To put it starkly, sustainable development from the Asian perspective in general still solidly rests on an anthropocentric foundation. Its main concern is to sustain long-term growth and material progress through the commodification and liquidation of natural assets in the name of a "green economy" rather than the promotion of environmental sustainability.

The upshot is that the man-nature relationship in the Asian region is, to a large extent, dominated by economic motives, entailing little obligation for environmental protection. It is only through the cultivation of the kind of ethics that aims at a harmonious coexistence between humanity and nature that can we hope to halt further environmental degradation across the Asian region. This necessarily involves a basic change in our value systems based on the holistic focus of ecocentrism. In summary, the integration of the three pillars of sustainable development, namely, economic growth, environmental sustainability and social development must be guided by environmental ethics.

Concluding remarks

The HoB environmental paradox bespeaks the fact that the regional environmental problems are not due to the deficiency of regional cooperative efforts, institutional arrangements or environmental laws but basically owe to the lack of an ethical commitment to sustainable resource use and environmental protection. To put it bluntly, the HoB environmental problem is a behavioral problem – a moral failure that has led to collective stewardship collapse. To be sure, environmental problems facing us today are not exclusively physical, biological, economical, political or social problems. They are a mixture of these. But one thing is for sure, that the lack of a moral philosophy for sustainable resource use has resulted in continued human transgressions of the biophysical limits of growth across the planet.

It may well be that viewed from the Asian perspective; the moral concern for environmental protection under the sustainable development or green economy framework is often eclipsed by the economic concern for long-term growth expressed in terms of expanding capital accumulation or material progress. This pervasive "sustainability" logic necessarily entails extensive commodification and liquidation of nature in the name of "sustainable development." Thus, the implicit promises for a green Asian world cease to command credibility. This self-interested pursuit of capitalist expansion has been the status quo for the past few decades in the Asian region since the publication of the Brundtland Report in 1987.

It must be admitted that the HoB ecological irrationality which succinctly mirrors the Asian green failure has ethical dimensions not typically considered during green transformation processes. However, the green economy as proposed by the United Nations has very little to say about the ethical imperative of sustainable development. Within this perspective, it may well be noted that human beings are arguably the most powerful force of environmental modification and ecological impoverishment, and only we are capable of solving the problems facing our planet.

It thus follows that green economic transformation cannot be disentangled from the ethical dimension of sustainable development. That said, the real solution to the HoB environmental problems or many of the Asian unsustainable development issues lies in a specific transformation of values – the transcendence toward a human-based value system based on right and wrong in our actions toward nature. More specifically, policies that ensure the protection of the holistic natural entities such as endangered species, critical ecosystems such as watersheds, forest green lungs, and land, ocean and atmospheric carbon sinks, which underpin human long-term socio-economic progress, must express values based on a non-anthropocentric moral system.

Indeed, the indigenous case study conducted in Borneo Malaysia shows clearly that environmental sustainability and the ethics of human-nature relations are inextricably connected, and it is only through the extension of environmental ethics to nature that we can avoid crossing the planetary tipping point that could lead to abrupt or irreversible ecological destruction. Under the conditions of finitude governing our planet, the finishing line to the racetrack of sustainable development is to integrate environmental ethics into green development discourse, as this will help to build a sustainable relationship between humans and the natural environment. This will discourage humans from tapping into the patrimony of nature beyond its biophysical limits, thus, leading to a genuine course of green economic transformation.

Acknowledgement

This work was in part supported by the MEXT* – Supported Program for the Strategic Research Foundation at Private University, 2014–2018 (*Ministry of Education, Culture, Sports, Science and Technology, Japan).

Notes

1 ASEAN (the Association of Southeast Asian Nations) comprised 10 member countries, namely, Brunei Darussalam, Cambodia, Indonesia, Laos, Malaysia, Myanmar, Philippines, Singapore, Thailand and Vietnam.

2 The rest of the five corridors are Center for Production and Processing of Natural Resources and the Nation's Energy Reserves in Sumatra, Driver for National Industry and Service Provision in Java, Center for Production and Processing of National Agricultural, Plantation, Fishery, Oil & Gas, and Mining in Sulawesi, Gateway for Tourism and National Food Support in Bali-Nusa Tenggara, and Center for Development of Food, Fisheries, Energy, and National Mining in Papua – Moluccas.

References

ADP (Asian Development Bank). (2013) "Heart of Borneo: saving forests in southeast Asia." The Philippines: Asian Development Bank, www.adb.org/features/heart-borneo-saving-lungs-southeast-asia.

Ariaini, Nancy. (2013) "Focus Group Discussion on Heart of Borneo Green Economy in Indonesia." Washington, DC: World Wildlife Fund.

ASEAN Secretariat. (2009) *Fourth ASEAN State of the Environment Report (2009)*. Jakarta: ASEAN Secretariat.

Bryan, Jane E., Philip L. Shearman; Gregory P. Asner; David E. Knapp; G. Aoro and B. Lokes. (2013) "Extreme differences in forest degradation in Borneo: comparing practices in Sarawak, Sabah, and Brunei." *PLOS ONE (Public Library of Science)* 8(7): e69679/1–7.

Butler, Rhett A. (2010) "Orangutans vs palm oil in Malaysia: setting the record straight." Mongay.com (January 16), https://news.mongabay.com/2010/01/orangutans-vs-palm-oil-in-malaysia-setting-the-record-straight/.

Butler, Rhett A. (2012a) "Industrial logging leaves a poor legacy in Borneo's rainforests." Mongay.com (July 17), http://news.mongabay.com/2012/07/industrial-logging-leaves-a-poor-legacy-in-borneos-rainforests/.

Butler, Rhett A. (2012b) "In pictures: rainforests to palm oil." Mongay.com (July 2), http://news.mongabay.com/2012/07/in-pictures-rainforests-to-palm-oil/.

Callicot, Baird J. (1989) *In Defense of the Land Ethics: Essays in Environmental Philosophy*. Albany, NY: State University of New York Press.

Chia, Jonathan. (2015) "Sarawak to have more, bigger TPAs under HoB – Adenan." Sarawak, Malaysia: Borneo Post (November 4), www.theborneopost.com/2015/11/04/sarawak-to-have-more-bigger-tpas-under-hob-adenan/.

Chong, Rebecca. (2015) "Sabah doubles protected areas to 1.55 mln." Sarawak, Malaysia: Borneo Post (August 12), www.theborneopost.com/2015/08/12/sabah-doubles-protected-areas-to-1-55-mln/.

Choy, Yee Keong. (2005) "Sustainable development – an institutional enclave (with special reference to the Bakun Dam-induced Development Strategy in Malaysia." *Journal of Economic Issues* 39(4): 951–971.

Choy, Yee Keong. (2014) "Land ethic from the Borneo tropical rainforests in Sarawak, Malaysia: an empirical and conceptual analysis." *Environmental Ethics* 36(4): 861–874.

Choy, Yee Keong. (2015a) "From Stockholm to Rio+20: the ASEAN environmental paradox, environmental sustainability and environmental ethics." *The International Journal of Environmental Sustainability* 12(1): 1–25.

Choy, Yee Keong. (2015b) "Sustainable resource management and ecological conservation of mega-biodiversity: the southeast Asian Big-3 Reality." *Journal of Environmental Science and Development* 6(11): 876–882.

Choy, Yee Keong. (2016a) "Economic Growth, Sustainable Development and Ecological Conservation in the Asian Developing Countries: The Way Forward," in, *Naturalists, Explorers and Field Scientists in South-East Asia and Australasia*. Topics in Biodiversity and Conservation Series, Indraneil Das and Andrew Alek Tuen (eds.). Springer Cham Heidelberg, New York, Dordrecht, London: Springer International Publishing Switzerland, pp. 239–283.

Choy, Yee Keong. (2016b) "Ecosystem health, human existence, and bio-capacity deficit: the ethical relationship." *International Journal of Sustainable Development Planning* 11(6): 1004–1016.

Choy, Yee Keong. (2018) "Cost–benefit analysis, values, wellbeing and ethics: an indigenous worldview analysis." *Ecological Economics* 145: 1–9.

CMD (Center for Media and Democracy). (2014) *IndoMet Coal Project*. Madison, Wisconsin: Center for Media and Democracy.

CMEA (Coordinating Ministry for Economic Affairs). (2011) *Masterplan for Acceleration and Expansion of Indonesia Economic Development 2011–2025*. Republic of Indonesia: Coordinating Ministry for Economic Affairs.

Collins, N. Mark., J.A. Sayer, and T.C. Whitmore (eds). (1991) *The Conservation Atlas of Tropical Forests: Asia and the Pacific*. Morges, Switzerland: International Union for the Conservation of Nature and Natural Resources, New York: Simon & Schuster.

Council on Ethics for the Government Pension Fund Global. (2013) *Annual Report*. Norway: Council on Ethics for the Government Pension Fund Global.

Denton, Jenney. (2014) "Asia's last great rainforest." Indonesia: The Jakarta Post (May 20), www.thejakartapost.com/news/2014/05/20/asia-s-last-great-rainforest.html.

Eaton, Peter. (2005) *Land Tenure, Conservation and Development in Southeast Asia*. New York, NY: RoutledgeCurzon.

Engbers, Peter. (2010) "Forest cover of Borneo and Brunei." Panaga Natural History Society, http://pnhsbrunei.blogspot.jp/2010/12/forest-cover-of-borneo-and-brunei.html.

Erik, Meijaard and Sheil Douglas. (2013) "Oil-Palm Plantations in the Context of Biodiversity Conservation," in *Encyclopedia of Biodiversity* (2nd edition, vol. 5). Simon A. Levin (ed.). Waltham, MA: Academic Press, pp. 600–612.

Felbab-Brown, Vanda. (2011) *The Disappearing Act. The Illicit Trade in Wildlife in Asia*. Foreign Policy at Brooking. Massachusetts, Washington DC: The Brooking Institution, www.brookings.edu/~/media/research/files/papers/2011/6/illegal-wildlife-trade-felbabbrown/06_illegal_wildlife_trade_felbabbrown.pdf.

Gaveau, David L. A., Sean Sloan, Elis Molidena, Husna Yaen, Doug Sheil, Nicola K. Abram, Marc Ancrenaz, Robert Nasi, Marcela Quinones, Niels Wielaard, and Erik Meijaard. (2014) "Four Decades of Forest Persistence, Clearance and Logging on Borneo." *PLOS One* (Public Library of Science) 9(7): e101654. doi:10.1371/journal.pone.0101654.

Global Witness. (2012) *In the Future, There Will Be No Forests Left*. United Kingdom: Global Witness.

Global Witness. (2014) *Japan's Timber Imports Fuelling Rainforest Destruction in Sarawak and Violation of Indigenous land Rights: New Findings from Recent Research and Field Investigations*. United Kingdom: Global Witness.

Global Witness. (2015) *The Threat to a Sustainable 2020 Tokyo Olympics Games Posed by Illegal and Unsustainable Logging in Sarawak, Malaysia*. United Kingdom: Global Witness.

Green Peace International. (2013) *Certifying Destruction*. Amsterdam, the Netherlands: Greenpeace International.

Hance, Jeremy. (2009) "Emotional call for palm oil industry to address environmental problems." Mongay.com (October 21), http://news.mongabay.com/2009/10/emotional-call-for-palm-oil-industry-to-address-environmental-problems.

Hitchner, Sarah L. (2010) "Heart of Borneo as a '*Jalan Tikus*': exploring the links between indigenous rights, extractive and exploitative industries, and conservation at the World Conservation Congress 2008." *Conservation and Society* 8(4): 320–330.

Jordan, Rob. (2012) "Stanford researchers show oil palm plantations are clearing carbon-rich tropical forests in Borneo." Stanford, California: Stanford Woods Institute for the Environment, Stanford University (October 8), http://news.stanford.edu/news/2012/october/oil-palm-plantation.html.

ITTO (International Tropical Timber Organization), Sarawak Forest Department, and Sarawak Forestry Corporation. (2006) *The Flora of Pulong Tau National Park. TITTO Project PD 224/30 Rev.1(F). Transboundary Biodiversity Conservation – The Pulong Tau National Park, Sarawak, Malaysia*. Japan: ITTO; Sarawak, Malaysia: Sarawak Forestry Department and Sarawak Forestry Department.

JEC (Japan Environmental Council). (2005) *The State of Environment in Asia: 2005/2006*. Tokyo: Springer-Verlag.

Leopold, Aldo. (1949) *A Sand County Almanac*. New York: Oxford University Press.

Lyddon, Chris. (2014) "Focus on Malaysia," WORLD-GRAIN.com. Kansas City: Sosland Publishing Co, www.world-grain.com/Departments/Countrypercent20Focus/Countrypercent20Focuspercent20Home/Focuspercent20onpercent20Malaysia.aspx?cck=1.

MacKinnon, Barbara and Andrew Fiala. (2015) *Ethics: Theory and Contemporary Issues*. (8th edition). Stamford, CT: Cengage Learning.

MacKinnon, Kathy, Arthur Mangalik, and Gusti Hatta. (1996) *The Ecology of Kalimantan*. Hong Kong: Periplus Editions.

Margono, Belinda A., Peter V. Potapov, Svetlana Turubanova, Fred Stolle, and Matthew C. Hansen. (2014) "Primary forest cover loss in Indonesia over 2000–2012." *Nature Climate Change* 4: 730–735.

Ministry of Development, Brunei. (2015) *Brunei Darussalam's Intended Nationally Determined Contribution (INDC)*. Brunei Darussalam: Ministry of Development. http://www4.unfccc.int/submissions/INDC/Publishedpercent20Documents/Brunei/1/Bruneipercent20Darussalampercent20INDC_FINAL_30percent20Novemberpercent20(2015)pdf.

Ministry of Forestry, Indonesia. (2009) *National Strategic Plan of Action. Bridging Conservation and Sustainable Development in Three Countries. Heart of Borneo National Working Group*. Indonesia: Ministry of Forestry of Indonesia.

Ministry of Industry and Primary Resources of Negara Brunei Darussalam. (2008) *Heart of Borneo. Project Implementation Framework Negara Brunei Darussalam. Final Report 2008*. Brunei Darussalam: Ministry of Industry and Primary Resources, www.hobgreeneconomy.org/downloads/Brunei_heartofborneo_projectimplementationframework.pdf.

MPOB (Malaysia Palm Oil Board). (2016) "Statistics. Oil palm planted area by state as at December 2015 (hectare)," Malaysia: MPOB, Economics and Industry Development Division, http://bepi.mpob.gov.my/images/area/2015/Area_summary.pdf.

Obidzinski, K., A. Andrianto, and C. Wijaya. (2007) "Cross-border timber trade in Indonesia: critical or overstated problem? Forest governance lessons from Kalimantan." *International Forestry Review* 9(1): 526–535.

Oetami, Devi. (2013) "Reconciling development, conservation, and social justice in Western Kalimantan," in *The Palm Oil Controversy in Southeast Asia: A Transnational Perspective*, Oliver Pye and Jayati Bhattacharya (eds.). Singapore: ISEAS Publishing, pp. 164–178.

Rayat Post. (2014) "DAP: why was oil palm project approved in forest reserve in Sabah?" Malaysia: The Rayat Post, www.therakyatpost.com/news/2014/11/27/dap-oil-palm-project-approved-forest-reserve-sabah/.

Rolston, Holmes. (2003) "Environmental Ethics," in *The Blackwell Companion to Philosophy* (2nd edition). N. Bunnin and E. Tsui-James (eds.). Oxford: Blackwell Publishing, pp. 517–530.

Sabah Forestry Department. (2009) *Strategic Plan of Action (Sabah). The Heart of Borneo Initiative*. Sabah, Malaysia: Sabah Forestry Department.

Sabah Times. (2015) "Oil palm council hailed, but Sabah needs to go downstream." Sabah: Sabah Times (November 24), www.newsabahtimes.com.my/nstweb/fullstory/1282.

Sarawak Forestry Corporation. (2014) "Sarawak National Parks: National Parks and Reserves." Sarawak, Malaysia: Sarawak Forestry Corporation, www.sarawakforestry.com/htm/snp-np.html.

Sarawak Monitor. (2013) "Heart of Borneo. A joint commitment to conserve, protect diverse world ecosystem." Sarawak, Malaysia: Sarawak Monitor. http://sarawakmonitor.blogspot.jp/2013/12/heart-of-borneo-joint-commitment-to.html.

Schithuizen, Menno. (2007) *Biodiscoveries. Borneo's Botanical Secret*. Indonesia: World Wildlife Fund.

Schultz, P. Wesley, Valdiney V. Gouveia, Linda D. Cameron, Geetika Tankha, Peter Schmuck, and Marek Franek. (2005) "Values and their relationship to environmental concern and environmental behavior." *Journal of Cross-Cultural Psychology* 36(4): 457–475.

Scriven, Sarah A., Jenny A. Hodgson, Colin J. McClean, and Jane K. Hill. (2015) "Protected areas in Borneo may fail to conserve tropical forest biodiversity under climate change." *Biological Conservation* 184: 414–442.

Shrader-Frechette, Kristin S. (1981) *Environmental Ethics*. Pacific Grove, CA: Boxwood Press.

Spence, Jane. (2013) *Heart of Borneo Seminar: The Living Treasure of Sarawak*. Washington, DC: World Wildlife Fund, http://wwf.panda.org/wwf_news/?209728/Heart-of-Borneo-Seminar-The-Living-Treasure-of-Sarawak.

Straumann, Lukas. (2014) *Money Logging. On the Trail of the Asian Timber Mafia*. Switzerland: Bergli Books.

Taylor, Paul W. (1986) *Respect for Nature: A Theory of Environmental Ethics*. Princeton, NJ: Princeton University Press.

Tsuyuki, Satoshi, Mia H. Goh, Stephen Teo, Kamlun U. Kamlun, and Mui H. Phua. (2011) "Monitoring deforestation in Sarawak, Malaysia using multitemporal Landsat data." *Kanto Forest Research Journal* 61: 87–90.

UNDP (United Nations Development Programme). (2012) *Project Document: Biodiversity Conservation in Multiple-use Forest Landscapes in Sabah, Malaysia*. New York, NY: United Nations Development Programme.

UNEP (United Nations Environment Program). (2011) *Towards a Green Economy: Pathways to Sustainable Development and Poverty Eradication – A Synthesis for Policy Makers*. Nairobi, Kenya: United Nations Environment Program.

UNEP (United Nations Environment Program). (2014) *Keeping Track of our Changing Environment in Asia and the Pacific. From Rio to Rio+20 (1992–2012)*. Bangkok, Thailand: United Nations Environment Program.

WCED (World Commission on Environment and Development). (1987) *Our Common Future*. Oxford: Oxford University Press.

Wulffraat, Stephan et al. (2014) *The Environmental Status of the Heart of Borneo*. Switzerland: WWF's HoB Initiative: World Wildlife Fund.

WWF (World Wildlife Fund). (2017) *Borneo's Wildlife*. Australia: World Wildlife Fund, www.wwf.org.au/our_work/saving_the_natural_world/forests/forests_work/heart_of_borneo/borneo_wildlife/o.

WWF (World Wildlife Fund). (2005a) *Borneo: Treasure Island at Risk*. Frankfurt am Main, Germany: World Wildlife Fund.

WWF (World Wildlife Fund). (2005b) *Asia-Pacific Region 2005: The Ecological Footprint and Natural Wealth*. Gland, Switzerland: World Wildlife Fund.

WWF (World Wildlife Fund). (2007) *Forests of Borneo. Forest Area Key Facts & Carbon Emissions from Deforestation*. Indonesia: World Wildlife Fund.

WWF (World Wildlife Fund). (2010a) *Feasibility Assessment for Financing the Heart of Borneo Landscape. Malaysia (Sabah and Sarawak)*. Malaysia: World Wildlife Fund, www.hobgreeneconomy.org/downloads/heartofborneo_malaysia_financial_feasibility_assessment_report.pdf.

WWF (World Wildlife Fund). (2010b) *Borneo's New World. Newly Discovered Species in the Heart of Borneo*. Washington, DC: World Wildlife Fund.

WWF (World Wildlife Fund). (2012) *Building a Green Economy in the Heart of Borneo: South-South Cooperation between Brunei Darussalam, Indonesia, and Malaysia*. Malaysia: World Wildlife Fund, www.unep.org/south-south-cooperation/case/casefiles.aspx?csno=69.

WWF (World Wildlife Fund). (2014) "WWF-Malaysia commends Sabah Forestry Department for setting aside more forests for protection and restoration." Malaysia: World Wildlife Fund.

WWF (World Wildlife Fund), ADP (Asian Development Bank) (ADB) and Global Footprint Network. (2012) *Ecological footprint and investment in natural capital in Asia and the Pacific*. Gland, Switzerland: WWF; Manila, Philippines: ADB; Oakland, CA: Global Footprint Network.

WWF (World Wildlife Fund) and PWC (Pricewaterhouse). (2011) *Roadmap for a Green Economy in the Heart of Borneo: A Scoping Study*. United Kingdom: World Wildlife Fund–Pricewaterhouse, http://awsassets.panda.org/downloads/pwc_report_green_economy_roadmap_1.pdf.

27

China's green GDP and environmental accounting

Yu-Wai Vic Li

Introduction

The environmental issues of no other nation command the enormous global attention paid to those of China. The world's second largest economy by gross domestic product (GDP) has experienced annual economic growth rates that have surpassed most of the rest of the world for nearly four decades. Now, however, China not only faces the challenges associated with an economy losing steam and switching gears to a "new normal" of slower expansion rates, but also faces those brought about by significantly deteriorating environmental conditions caused by rapid industrialization, massive urbanization, shifting demographics, and resource depletion on an unprecedented scale.

Well before the notion of sustainable development entered official discourse in the early 1990s, Chinese environmental researchers had proposed the use of a "green GDP" to gauge the ecological costs of development. Successive and disparate local experiments did not generate any strong political momentum until the country faced the skyrocketing pollution of the 2000s, when the top party and state leaders adopted a "scientific outlook" towards development and endorsed the notion of green GDP and other practices of environmental accounting. This galvanized the launch of China's green GDP accounting in March 2004, led by the State Environmental Protection Agency (SEPA, which was upgraded to Ministry of Environmental Protection in 2008) and the National Bureau of Statistics (NBS). The joint-agency campaign centered on accounting for the abatement and treatment costs of, and the economic losses arising from, air, water and solid waste pollutions in ten provinces and municipalities over 42 industry sectors. This herculean effort was accomplished in about two years, and the world's first official green GDP accounting report was released in September 2006. The survey was also expected to cover all of China's provinces and municipalities in its second round.

However, behind the facade of the campaign's apparent success lay intractable methodological challenges and political resistance from the statistical bureau and involved local authorities. This not only undermined SEPA's lead in the accounting exercise, it also foreshadowed the unfortunate end of July 2007, when NBS unilaterally announced the project's termination and the local authorities quit the project. Left with little choice, the environment agency was forced to end its support, and the second report never reached the public. Research endeavors, however, were carried on by SEPA's affiliated research body, the Chinese Academy for Environmental Planning (CAEP), which published its own results annually.

While these results contributed to some advances in accounting methodologies and did spur the interest of some local authorities enough to made them re-consider green GDP, the central authorities did not extend support again until 2013, when the new Chinese administration under Xi Jinping rallied support for an "ecological civilization" campaign and an agreed international framework of environmental economic accounting had been developed. With the blessing of the central authorities, the MEP resumed study of green GDP in early 2015 (UNEP, 2016). However, this was rivaled by a different environmental accounting initiative championed by NBS, which concerned the stock-taking of natural capitals in order to expand the economy's assets and wealth levels to allow for long-term sustainable development. This led China's green GDP survey to be surrounded by an atmosphere of considerable uncertainty.

Environmental accounting and its global context

There are four primary approaches used within environmental accounting to assess the progress of sustainable development. These include the use of a dashboard of indicators, expressed in varying units, being associated with social, economic and environmental domains in order to provide a general assessment of how the various aspects of sustainability are faring, without implying relationships between individual indicators and assigning importance of some over others. Prominent examples of this category include the OECD Green Growth Indicators and the Eurostat Sustainable Development Indicators (Narloch et al., 2016: 8–14).

Unlike this inherently multi-dimensional endeavor, the other three approaches attempt to consolidate diverse measures into a few "synthetic" metrics. Calculations of the environmental footprints of human economic activities are derived from condensing a selected group of measures concerned with resource consumption and production patterns. Similarly, the development of composite indicators that rank countries according to progress in sustainable development, such as the UNEP Green Economy Progress Index, has involved aggregating indicators of different units into a single measure. While these methods ease comparison between economies and over time, the inevitable re-scaling and re-weighing of data is often arbitrary and can generate multiple and sometimes conflicting interpretations. Finally, computation of adjusted economic measures seeks to generate a single monetary metric through adjusting an economic variable already in use. Instead of simply integrating specific indicators into a composite measure, monetary values are assigned and summed and, in turn, used to adjust the economic variable concerned (Narloch et al., 2016).

The last two approaches have generated the most policy and research interest, especially since the concept of sustainable social and economic development was popularized by the World Commission on Environment and Development, and by the global environmental conferences of the early 1990s that included the June 1992 United Nations Conference on Environment and Development (UNCED) in Rio de Janeiro. Agenda 21, the landmark document endorsed by UNCED, made explicit that an essential step towards integrating the concepts of sustainability and economic management was to establish:

> [B]etter measurement of the crucial role of the environment as a source of natural capital and as a sink for by-products generated during the production of man-made capital and other human activities ... (and) that national accounting procedures are not restricted to measuring the production of goods and services that are conventionally remunerated.
>
> *(UNCED, 1993: 41–42)*

To facilitate implementation of these goals, the UN assigned its statistics division to serve as the focal point of action that would develop the appropriate methodologies in environmental accounting. Soon, the division proposed the concept of Environmentally Adjusted Domestic Product (EDP), also known colorfully as "Eco Domestic Product" or green GDP in the interim version of *Integrated Environmental and Economic Accounting*. As an adjusted economic measure, EDP was defined as an environmental accounting aggregate obtained by "subtracting the cost of natural resource depletion and environmental degradation from net domestic product (NDP)" (United Nations Statistics Division, 1993: 98). However, in the same publication in 2003, the UN conceded that methodological problems surrounding green GDP remained unresolved, and cautioned:

> [C]an we calculate a measure of GDP that adequately accounts for demands placed on the environment? The simplest and most honest answer is that there is no consensus on how green GDP could be calculated and . . . still less consensus on whether it should be attempted at all.
>
> *(United Nations et al., 2003: 415)*

Some countries have also engaged in developing specific national level accounting frameworks that might help value natural resources in monetary terms. The Nordic states, the Netherlands, Germany, Mexico and the Philippines all implemented similar initiatives. Norway, for example, has experimented with resource and energy accounting since its Economic and Environmental Accounting Project (NOREEA) of 1978. It sought to develop a nationally integrated account that referenced all pertinent environmental information and, in doing so, helped evaluate the stocks and flows of natural resources (Wang et al., 2016b).

But decades of experience did not transform Norway into a leading auditor of green GDP. On the contrary, the Norwegian government concluded that it is highly problematic to assign numerical values to environmental assets that do not trade on the market, such as air and water, and that the notion of adjusting the conventional GDP figure to reflect problems of pollution and environmental damage was not practical. According to an official report:

> A green GDP will in many contexts do more to obscure problems than resolve them . . . a one-sided focus on aggregated indicators (for sustainable development or in the green GDP tradition) without a theoretical framework and a solid statistical underpinning is likely to lead to little policy-relevant information.
>
> *(Alfsen et al., 2006: 15)*

For these reasons, Australia, Italy, Germany, France and the UK chose to conduct their environmental accounting without trying to come up with adjusted economic measures such as green GDP. Rather, they tended to opt for developing composite indicators, or counting multiple metrics related to the different dimensions of sustainability. These untoward international experiences, however, did not seem to have deterred the Chinese authorities from pursuing the world's first official green GDP accounting in the early 2000s. Indeed, both the green GDP and the recent focus on natural capital accounting (NCA) are leading examples of the use of adjusted economic measures in the face of international experiments yet to attain clear success. In the case of green GDP, the social-economic impacts of pollutions are expressed in monetary terms and subtracted from headline growth figures. NCA, by contrast, regards natural resources as an extended form of assets and wealth, and thus adds value to the overall capital stock of an economy. The successive local experiences within China that began in the 1980s arguably paved the way for subsequent national initiatives.

Local antecedents of green GDP accounting in China

Since the early reform years, Chinese academics have explored the possibilities of environmental accounting to estimate economic losses due to industrial pollution. These efforts have been typically carried out by individual researchers and did not typically receive much high-level official attention. For example, Chinese researchers at the Chinese Academy of Science investigated the burden of "ecological deficit" to the country's long-term development. Angang Hu, now a close advisor to top governmental and party officials, was reportedly one of the first scholars to advocate the use of green GDP to assess development at the provincial level in the mid-1980s (Li, 2011). The official research center of the State Council also looked at how resource accounting could be integrated with the GDP framework, and SPEA hosted training workshops on environmental accounting with the World Health Organization (Wang et al., 2016b).

It was only in the 1990s the theoretical and methodological bases of environmental accounting were further developed with official endorsement and financial support that made possible empirical studies of various scales throughout China (for details, see Wang et al., 2004: 4–5; see also Green GDP Technical Working Group, 2004). A study assessing the green GDP in Beijing was conducted by city authorities in 1997. The concept was defined in a similar fashion to the later definition of national green GDP by SEPA and NBS, possibly indicating the influence of the city government on the national agencies, or more likely their common sources of learning – the various United Nations (UN) statistical documents and guidelines.

The municipal survey suggested that green GDP was roughly 75 percent of the city's total GDP, implying that there was about 25 percent of the headline growth figure attributable to various forms of pollutions resulting from the capital's rapid development. Beijing's officials, however, were hesitant to continue the environmental cost survey as an effort to gauge the "actual" economic growth and evaluate the performance of officials in promoting sustainable development (Beijing Planning Office of Philosophy and Social Sciences, 2003). Huzhou of Zhejiang Province also launched a green GDP study in 2004 led by a research team from Beijing Normal University. SEPA and NBS were also involved in the local pilot that hoped to obtain data for refining the measurement methodologies of the subsequent joint national green GDP survey (Xinhua Net, 2006). Zhejiang's leading role in green GDP development was in part attributable to the support of Xi Jinping, the then provincial secretary general, who resurrected the green GDP scheme in his tenure as China's top leader.

Other than initiatives in these well-developed coastal provinces and municipalities, small-scale projects were rolled out in landlocked localities like Datong (Shanxi Province) and Yaan (Sichuan Province) that built on collaborations between local authorities and research institutes. Although they helped test the feasibility of using green GDP as a new accounting metric, the local authorities concerned also saw the pilots as a means of introducing some elements of "scientific outlook on development" to policy making. Through adjusting the local growth figures to take into account environmental costs, the practice showed compliance with the ideological line advanced in 2003 by Hu Jintao, the then President and General Secretary of China's Communist Party, which featured sustainable development (however nominally defined) and emphasized harmony between man and nature (Chan, 2010).

Results of these studies, however, were reported almost exclusively in mainland academic journals. In Yaan, for example, green GDP was estimated to be 20 percent smaller than headline GDP figures (Yang and Zhang, 2005). The 2002 study in Datong revealed that green or net GDP was only about 60 percent of total GDP, suggesting that remarkable environmental costs accrued from the local economy (Wang and Ren, 2005). These surveys, however, provided few insights relevant to environmental planning and policy making, since there were significant discrepancies in the accounting scopes and procedures employed by the researchers (Wang et al., 2016b). This perhaps drove the central government, and NBS in particular, to look for ways to standardize the practice of environmental accounting in order to bring some degree of consistency in data collection, computation and reporting.

In 1998, with help from Statistics Norway, NBS developed rudimentary energy accounts that documented China's production and consumption of energy. Water, industrial pollution and forest resources accountings were carried out in Chongqing, Heilongjiang and Hainan Provinces in the late 1990s, both in physical and monetary terms (Alfsen et al., 2006: 32–33). The Norwegian officials also partnered with counterparts in NBS and Chongqing for a green GDP study that lasted from 2001 to 2004. At the global level, delegations of Chinese statistical officials were involved in some of the international discussions at the London Group of Environmental Accounting, the expert platform that has met every year to date since 1994 in order to share and develop international best-practices on environment-related accounting methods (Chan et al., 2001).[1] Inputs from these transnational initiatives provided plausibly important lessons to NBS and motivated it to work with SPEA in a later national exercise launched in March 2004.

National green GDP survey, 2004–2007

Despite the lack of international consensus on how green GDP accounting was to proceed and the largely exploratory nature of previous studies within China, Beijing was determined to introduce green GDP accounting on an extensive scale in 2004. This was catalyzed by the nationwide campaign that promoted Hu Jintao's scientific outlook of development, as well as the emerging discourse of "ecological modernization" of the early 2000s, promoted by the Chinese Academy of Sciences, a top government-affiliated think tank (Zhang et al., 2007; Chinese Academy of Sciences, 2007). More importantly, Hu himself also endorsed the notion of green GDP, which significantly boosted the legitimacy of a SEPA-led campaign commencing in March 2004.

SEPA, in collaboration with NBS, CAEP, and units from Renmin University, took the lead in the project and designated ten provinces and municipalities (Beijing, Chongqing and Tianjin; Anhui, Guangdong, Hainan, Heibei, Liaoning, Sichuan, Zhejiang Provinces) as the pilot sites for the first round of a green GDP audit. In an October 2004 notice, SEPA invited all eligible EPBs and statistics bureaus to participate in the green GDP survey. It cited the order by Hu Jintao in a state-level meeting on population and natural resources management that "the country has to develop a green GDP methodology in order to fully grasp the extent of natural resources depletion, environmental damage, and energy efficiency in the course of the country's economic growth" and planned to develop a comprehensive green GDP audit system within a time span of three to five years (SEPA, 2004). To ensure local cadres possessed the technical know-how for the undertaking, CAEP was tasked with the mission of providing technical training and guidance and environmental accounting systems were also crafted to fit each area's specific conditions. Three major rounds of training were delivered by SEPA, NBS and CAEP's representatives to local cadres throughout 2005 in the form of lectures and seminars.

Calculation of China's green growth figures involved the manipulation of different "tiers" of environmental accounting. It started with physical quantification of air, water and solid waste pollutions, through which the hypothetical cost of abating their impacts and the cost of environmental degradation were calculated. Resources depletion costs were also appraised by estimating the hypothetical amount of investment needed to recover exploited resources, such as fisheries, forestry, minerals, and farmlands. GDP figures of provinces and municipalities participating in the project were then adjusted respectively, taking into account these cost metrics. The adjusted growth figures of 42 industry sectors were also computed, allowing for a comparison of the environmental costs of different types of production activities. It should be noted, however, that SEPA's environmental accounting portfolio was deliberately made very selective. It focused exclusively on the environmental costs of the three major sources of pollution and their associated ecological damage. Largely omitted in the accounting portfolios were hard-to-quantify items, like the impact of pollution on public health and workforce productivity, depletion of underground water resources, and loss of arable farmland (and agricultural productivity) as a result of soil erosion (SEPA and NBS, 2006; see also UNEP and Tongji Institute of Environment for Sustainable Development, 2008).

The result of the first green GDP study was due to be released in early 2006, but was delayed to September 2006 due to the complicated accounting procedures and the resistance from local authorities discussed below. The final report, officially known as "China Green National Accounting Study Report 2004" (SEPA and NBS, 2006), estimated that the cost of containing and managing the environmental impacts in 2004 (that is, the virtual abatement cost) constituted 1.8 percent of the annual GDP (about 287.4 billion yuan), and economic losses from various kinds of pollution totaled an additional 3.05 percent of GDP (about 511.8 billion yuan). This added up to nearly 5 percent of the economic output of 2004. Geographically, the eastern, middle and western parts of the country had respectively 1.13 percent, 2.17 percent and 3.12 percent of GDP adjustment. Industry sectors also yielded markedly different scores; primary industry had 1.58 percent of GDP attributable to pollution and abatement, whereas the secondary and tertiary industries had 2.42 percent and 1.16 percent of their outputs deducted. Among all sectors, paper-making and non-ferrous metallurgy sectors had the highest reductions (30.13 percent and 11.63 percent) (SEPA and NBS, 2006: 7–10).

These results drew considerable public attention and interest, and in late 2006 the green GDP research group was honored as "China's Green Warrior" by the central authorities. The green GDP survey, however, gradually lost support from the local authorities, the cooperation of which in sharing data and staying committed was vital to the project's success. After 2006, participating local governments began to complain about the soundness of the measurement scheme devised by the green GDP project team – some even threatened to withdraw from the pilot study, or asked SEPA and NBS not to report their results publicly. Even though SEPA's senior leaders like Pan Yue, the Deputy Director, were determined to complete the project even if there was only one city/province participating, officials at the green GDP's technical working group confessed that local officials were increasingly hesitant to disclose pollution related data and compile them in accordance within the standardized format SEPA and NBS expected (Li and Lang, 2010: 51–52).

For these reasons, it was not surprising that the front cover of the 2004 green GDP report was labeled "Public Version," clearly indicative of the fact that the national survey result had only been partially reported – due largely to the opposition of local governments and other government agencies. NBS, concerned about the rigor of the results, was reportedly reserved about putting its name on the report (Li and Higgins, 2013). Details which would allow comparison across provinces and municipalities, except for general discussion about the variation between central, western and eastern China, were entirely excised. Some informed sources suggested that in the "internal" edition of the report detailed breakdowns of the green GDP of provinces were included, with Hebei being the worst case and recording a discount of 6 percent from their 2004 GDP figure, followed by Shanxi and other provinces with heavy concentrations of industry (Biganzi, 2006, 2007).

This tension between local governments and SEPA officials committed to carrying on the green GDP audit further escalated in the preparatory stage of the second report that was supposed to estimate the 2005 figures for 31 provinces and municipalities in China. After the summer of 2006, Inner Mongolia, Ningxia, Hebei, and Shanxi became vocal in resisting participation in the exercise. Worse still, provinces like Guangdong, which were initially receptive to the exercise, became aloof to SEPA's researchers. As a result, despite its much expanded coverage, the report of the second exercise was never made available to the public. Researchers in the green GDP Group, however, divulged some figures that provided at least a glimpse of the extent of environmental challenges facing the country and some basis for speculation about the divergent attitudes toward the environmental survey within the bureaucracy.

Some provinces with double-digit GDP growth in 2005 had accrued an equally large share of environmental externalities, implying that their economies were not making any progress at all in the year (Qiu, 2007). In fact, in a few unnamed cases their growth rates after adjustment were found to be negative. Nationwide, two-thirds of cities and provinces had their GDP reduced by more than 1.8 percent after ecological costs were included. The average discount percentages for cities in middle and western China were 2.14 percent and 3.16 percent respectively, showing that geography and underlying local industry structures did affect accounting for the variations in green GDP (Qiu, 2007; Shanghai Securities News, 2007).

This drove a wedge between the central government and SEPA, and culminated in Beijing's decision to indefinitely postpone the release of the second green GDP report. In May 2007, SEPA and NBS each submitted position papers to the State Council detailing their views about how to handle the second report. SEPA restated their recommendation to make the study publicly available. NBS, by contrast, questioned the relevance of the green GDP exercise, and preferred to effectively shelve the 2005 report as an internal reference document for the government. In the end, NBS's view prevailed within the administration. In a press conference hosted only by NBS in July 2007, the agency announced their decision and argued that green GDP was only "shorthand" for promoting public discussion about the environmental impact of economic growth, and that neither the Chinese government nor the UN had ever come up with any agreed standard for environmental audits (Li and Lang, 2010: 53). In response, CAEP held a separate media event to defend the project (and to some extent SEPA) and blamed the disagreements between the two central agencies as the primary reason for the withholding of the 2005 results from the public (Qiu, 2007). Although SEPA pressed on with the initiative counting on the technical supports from the devoted CAEP researchers, the ten provinces and municipalities involved in the two rounds of the survey decided to quit the scheme (Li and Higgins, 2013), leaving SEPA with little choice but to acknowledge that the green GDP project was officially terminated in March 2009 (Steinhardt and Jiang, 2007; Rauch and Chi, 2010).

Assessing the downfall of the national exercise

The dramatic downfall of the national green GDP survey not only revealed the fluidity of China's policy making, in which seemingly bold and politically-backed initiatives were enacted but subsequently retracted, it also made evident the split within the central government over environmental accounting, and the enduring political tension between the environmental bureaucracy and local counterparts.

This did not shield the agency from the many challenges arising from its counterparts at NBS, even though it was clear that SEPA had successfully obtained some blessing from the central's leaders during the early stage of the green GDP survey. In the words of Wang Jinnan, a leading SEPA engineer and member of the green GDP technical working group, the once "covert struggle (between the two agencies) has become a public standoff" (cited in Li and Lang, 2010: 54). The inter-agency discord became so pronounced that, even though SEPA maintained a higher bureaucratic standing relative to NBS (as an "administration" – a similar ranking to a ministry, as opposed to NBS being a bureau), it was unable to ward off criticisms from within government, or prevent the unilateral withdrawal of NBS from the project in 2007. Indeed, as the survey went on, NBS and provincial level statistical bureaucracies became increasingly cautious about releasing data, and were wary of the uncertain and controversial methodological grounding of the green accounting procedures.

Several leading statisticians in China had questioned the validity of green GDP as a sound measurement of environmental impacts on the economy. They contended that SEPA had underestimated the daunting methodological challenges of computing and obtaining reliable data from local governments. In addition to the difficulties of quantifying and estimating the economic costs of air, water and solid waste pollutions, many of the important socio-economic impacts, like public health and long-term ecosystem degradation, were overlooked in the exercise due to the ambitious and tight timeframe of the SEPA-led project. Indeed, although green GDP was a catchy notion that attracted public attention, as an adjusted economic indicator, its calculations could be seen to have inappropriately blended together various distinct and incommensurable environmental benchmarks and measures (UNEP and Tongji Institute of Environment for Sustainable Development, 2008, chapter 4).

Moreover, NBS statisticians also cast doubt over the relevance of green GDP in national accounting. They argued that, although a GDP calculation based largely on the UN System of National Accounts (SNA) needed to be adjusted to provide an updated understanding of the impacts of economic growth on the environment, GDP remained the cornerstone and indispensable element of SNA. Attempts to "loosen" the SNA and replace the conventionality of GDP with its green counterpart not only gave rise to an inaccurate estimate of reality, but also subverted the lasting and proven paradigm of GDP in understanding the scale and progress of a market economy (Li and Lang, 2010: 51–52).[2]

On the other hand, local authorities, worrying that their vested and potential interests might be compromised by the hard and quantifiable measure of local environmental costs, had worked through personal connections with the central party and state apparatus and through vertical relationships with central government bureaus, to undercut the green GDP survey (Steinhardt and Jiang, 2007). In such situations, the local officials found NBS a natural ally that shared a similar position of sidetracking and watering down the green GDP exercise, and the two parties essentially had no qualms about withholding data essential for the computation of green GDP. By contrast, environmental officials experienced much more pervasive tension with local authorities during the green GDP survey. Unlike the statistical bureaucrats, SEPA and its local bureaus gave little weight to local economic, investment and planning affairs at odds with SEPA's mandate to enforce environmental regulations and ensure compliance from local parties. As a result, it was not uncommon for local EPBs and statistical bureaus to find it difficult to coordinate their work throughout the survey (Wu, 2005).

Further, with growth-related benchmarks (e.g., level of GDP, foreign direct investment flow, taxation, and fiscal capacity) remaining the dominant pillars of assessing the performance of local cadres (provincial governors, mayors and party secretaries), being too proactive in environmental performance at the expense of economic achievement went against the interests of most local authorities (Tsui and Wang, 2004: 77–78). Indeed, although many people had developed a high degree of environmental awareness, this did not necessarily translate into policy preferences. Often, green actions would come forth only after economic stakes were secured and realized (Tong, 2007). As a result, despite the blessings and rhetorical support from the highest party and state leader, the green GDP survey did not survive the strong resistance of the statistical bureaucracy and local leaders that skillfully employed "scientific" reasoning that challenged the technical worthiness of green accounting and supported adherence to traditional methods of GDP computation and reporting.

Green GDP 2.0: the revival yet to come

Despite the technical challenges and adverse political circumstances surrounding the 2004 green GDP exercise, environmental scientists and the policy makers of SEPA did not entirely give up their initiatives. They continued to press forward with the idea on a limited scale. Leading scientists such as Wang Jinnan, for example, became a central figure supporting research endeavors within the CAEP community.

For years after 2004, Wang and his collaborators continued to publish *China Environmental and Economic Accounting Report* as an internal reference. Full details of the assessments, however, were never entirely disclosed even the "public version" caveat was attached to the report. As with SEPA's green GDP report, this suggested the political sensitivity of the findings and the severe degree to which China's natural environment was being exploited. The 2005 and 2006 studies, for example, showed continuing increases of economic losses arising from pollution. The two years' figures, compared with the official 2004 figure (of 511.8 billion yuan), recorded pollution-related losses of 578.79 and 650.77 billion yuan respectively. There was also a dramatic rise in hypothetical treatment costs from 287.4 billion yuan in 2004 to 411.26 billion yuan in 2006, roughly equal to 2 percent of the nation's economic output. The 2010 study (completed in late 2012) warned off a surge of environmental degradation costs during the eleventh five-year planning period (2006–2010), upped 89.6 percent from the previous planning cycle. In monetary terms, ecological damages amounted to 1.53 trillion yuan, doubling the 2004 measure revealed in SEPA's official green GDP report and equivalent to 3.5 percent of the country's GDP in 2010 (Wang et al., 2016b).

Other than these SEPA sponsored initiatives, local governments employed the "greening of GDP" rhetoric for their own pursuits after the late 2000s. In what appears to be a blatant irony after the national green GDP setback, several provincial governments demonstrated strong interest in the green GDP notion as part of their strategies to facilitate socio-economic reforms. In December 2007, Hubei and Hunan secured approval from the National Development and Reform Commission, the central planning body, to launch a "national experimental zone for comprehensive reform," with emphasis on building resource-conserving and environmentally friendly metropolises (NDRC, 2007). To translate the central mandate into practice, the Hubei authorities sought in late 2012 to incorporate green GDP as one of the metrics benchmarking local economic development of the entire province. Hunan pioneered a pilot initiative built on a locally devised indicator system in 2011, bringing a range of green GDP related measures into the performance review system for officials of the Greater Changsha region, consisting of three local economic hubs.[3]

Similarly, in late 2012, 16 cities of Anhui linked their mayoral performance to a set of ecological indicators made up of nearly two dozen specific measures. The island province, Hainan, also outlined its plan to evaluate officials with reference to the environmental costs of economic growth. Although these local efforts were in many ways different from SEPA's green GDP methodology and appeared to emulate existing sustainability indicator systems, they seemed to signal a changing outlook among local cadres about the ways in which economic growth could be realized, and suggested a more receptive stance for using quantifiable measures to assess associated ecological impacts.

These disparate experiments of environmental accounting within China, however, did not culminate in a political momentum strong enough to rekindle central-level support for another national green GDP exercise. Technical complexity remained a lingering obstacle to the environmental bureaucracy, even though there were considerable methodological advances in the subject within China during the late 2000s. The real breakthrough that helped pry open the policy window arrived when the UN released the System of Environmental Economic Accounting (SEEA2012) in

March 2014. As the first global environmental-economic accounting framework, the SEEA2012 presented detailed operational guidelines for how stocks and flows of natural resources could be measured by statistical indicators, how specific environmental assets could be valued and, in turn, aggregated into composite indexes important to policy making. In addition to the master document, two supplementary volumes on experimental ecosystem accounting applications and extensions of SEEA2012 were completed (United Nations et al., 2014). These provided the knowledge base for green GDP advocates within MEP and CAEP to push forward their agendas.

On the domestic front, the new leadership lineup of the Chinese state and party provided the necessary political catalyst to the MEP. After taking full power in 2013, the Xi Jinping and Li Keqiang administration ratcheted up the discussion of "ecological civilization," first proposed by their predecessors Hu Jintao and Wen Jiabao, in order to "green-wash" Xi's China Dream (Xinhua Net, 2015; UNEP, 2016). In addition to the strengthening of China's environmental protection law in 2014, a dozen quantifiable goals and hundreds of policy objectives were promulgated by the State Council and are slated to be attained nationwide by 2020. These include, for example, slashing carbon dioxide intensity (i.e., CO_2 per unit of GDP) to 40–45 percent below the 2005 level, and promoting renewable energy uses to about 15 percent of total primary energy consumption. Perhaps more importantly, the State Council also called for the building up of a comprehensive ecological accounting system and the incorporation of environmental damages into the political accountability system for officials at all administrative levels (State Council of China, 2015a).

These elements provided the requisite policy basis for the MPE to re-engage the green GDP exercise after eight years of hiatus. Extensively citing the mandates provided by Xi, a MEP press release of March 2015 formally announced that the ministry would resume *research* into green GDP in two phases, taking into account of the "costs of resource depletion, environmental degradation, ecological damage as well as pollution control" when calculating the GDP, and would include "an index of ecological condition in evaluation of the social-economic development" (Zhang et al., 2017: 466). In its first stage, the MEP was to assess the applicability of the SEEA2012 framework and other environmental accounting methodologies to the country, and develop a China-specific approach of appraising the country's green GDP (due to be completed by the end of 2015). This would be followed by policy pilots running through 2016–2017 in seven localities to generate lessons for MEP decision making. The ministry deliberately designated the exercise as "green GDP 2.0" to distinguish it from the previous failure ("green GDP 1.0"). It also maintained that there would be no binding timeframe to re-launch the new measurement nationwide, given the trailblazing nature of the research (MEP, 2015). As such, the program's revival advocated by China's environmentalists would remain an unlikely possibility for some time to come (Wang et al., 2016a).

A turn to natural capital and wealth accounting

In addition to the difficulties of aggregating environmental costs into an adjusted economic measure, MEP's green GDP was rivaled by "natural capital accounting" (NCA) (Costanza et al., 1997, 2014b). Instead of focusing on the ecological costs of production activities as when computing green GDP, NCA tries to gauge the values of natural resources and ecosystem services. It is based on more sophisticated methodological grounds and has won broad support within China since 2013 (Feng et al., 2015). Since parting company with the SPEA in the green GDP project, National Statistics has partnered with the State Forestry Administration in leading the audit exercise of forest resources. With the support of industrial groups and local governments, the two agencies were keen to develop a framework crucial to a monetary valuation of China's forest and woodlands.

A preliminary 2004 study was re-launched a decade later and became an integral part of a nationwide NCA investigation spearheaded by multiple government agencies, including NBS, and the Ministries of Finance, Agriculture, and Land and Resources, and covering additional natural resources like water and minerals (NBS, 2016; Wang et al., 2016b: 221–224).

The ambitious exercise sought to develop a "natural capital balance sheet" that would reveal the stock level of natural resources and ecosystem services gained (or lost) during economic growth. Several cities undertook the stock-taking exercise with technical support from private environmental consultancies. Sanya, the provincial capital of Hainan, completed China's first city-level NCA with assistance of top environmental research institutes. The collaborative study attempted to monetize the economic potential of the tropical city's natural resources and identified industries that received the most added value from natural capital stocks. According to the project team, the city was in possession of natural resources worth 5.6 times the city's 2013 GDP, but the ecosystem services values did not grow as much as the headline growth figures (DeTao Institute of Green Investment, 2015). With proper restructuring of local economic activities, the ecosystem values could be boosted substantially, adding considerable gains to the city's GDP.

These findings from the initially little-known local initiative elicited tremendous interest from other local governments that were striving to devise action plans in response to the central government's green transition mandates, and to find niches of sustainable growth beyond manufacturing and polluting production activities. In addition to the five cities joining the central NCA pilot in November 2015, dozens of local authorities of differing administrative statuses (some counties and other prefectural cities) started their own exercises after 2014 in an effort to fully gauge the total natural resource assets within their jurisdictions (State Council of China, 2015b; Sun et al., 2016). However, the motivations of local authorities implementing the NCA framework (and whether the framework might help promote a genuine shift toward greener growth, or simply become a means of looking for new growth possibilities that would deplete the natural capital in the long term) remained in question. There were also outstanding technical concerns about the comparability and reliability of local data (and the aggregation of data for the decision making purposes of higher authorities).

Nonetheless, it was quite plausible that the adoption of NCA in subnational China was to a large part galvanized by the central eco-civilization campaign that also played a part in motivating the revival of green GDP. To be sure, the top-down campaign was not just another state-led green movement that could be dismissed, nor was it simply a reiteration of the same idea of the Hu-Wen administration that had withered on the vine. The strong leadership and centralizing tendency of Xi Jinping and his associates signaled that the degree to which the campaign would be followed through and implemented by local governments was quintessentially a loyalty test for local cadres (Goodman and Parker, 2015). As such, despite the relatively short history of NCA research within China that had been begun in 2011 by researchers at the Bank of China, Fudan University, and the Chinese Academy of Social Sciences, both the notion and practice of NCA readily entered the official sustainable development discourse, and was recognized as a requisite repertoire in local environmental governance (Feng et al., 2015; Sun et al., 2016).

This trend was further fostered by discussions at the global level. In addition to SEEA2012, which provided the overarching accounting and operational framework, the development and applications of NCA promoted by the World Bank were equally critical. In 2010, the Bank inaugurated Wealth Accounting and the Valuation of Ecosystem Services (WAVES), a transnational multi-sectoral partnership platform that encouraged the use of ecosystem accounting. From inception, the global partnership identified three "resource accounts," including forests, land and water, for national and regional implementation. The three resource accounts were seen as the abundant natural capitals in developing economies and therefore it was imperative to thoroughly assess their stocks and flows, together with their change over time, in order for the authorities to prepare long term development strategies.

Although China was not among the seven core implementing countries of the WAVES initiative that formally endorsed and experimented with NCA at the national level, or a national supporter of the global partnership, the country's diverse local experience with NCA increasingly complemented the endeavors of WAVES, and contributed to ongoing projects refining accounting frameworks (WAVES Partnership, 2016).[4] Since 2015, China has been involved in a four-year global study of ecosystem services value by the Ecosystem Services Accounting for Development working group, coordinated by WAVES expert groups, and Swedish international development and environmental protection agencies. As in the other six participating countries of the study, China's officials and researchers concentrated on the development of methodologies and standards for the valuations of pollination, water quality amelioration, and green urban amenities. In the lattermost domain, Beijing and nine other cities tested various approaches appraising the economic values of urban green spaces in order to generate empirical data before the results were scaled up to the WAVES network for cross-national analysis (Environment for Development, 2016).[5]

Conclusion

Some form of environmental accounting tool is essential for assessing the real consequences of economic growth and, ultimately, for estimating the sustainability of an economy. Environmental accounting should be a component of ecological modernization discourse and discussion. In most countries, such national environmental accounts have been used only for particular sectors of the economy. There are many technical problems and challenges to producing an aggregated environmental cost account such as a green GDP, including the many unquantifiable elements of environmental impacts. Nevertheless, there are many precedents in other countries for such measures for particular sectors or localities.

However, none of these exercises were comparable to the expansive scale of China's green GDP accounting between 2004 and 2006 that sought to compute the ecological costs of three major sources of pollution and come up with green GDP figures for 42 industries in ten provinces and municipalities. This indicates how bold some of the central environmental officials were in bringing environmental impacts into the middle of policy discussions about sustainable development. Indeed, China's experiment has been arguably the most striking attempt at environmental accounting on a national level in either the developed or developing world for the past few decades. Domestically, it has also been an attempt to introduce environmental accounting into the career assessments of officials – attempting to force officials to pay attention to environmental degradation resulting from economic growth.

The ambitious attempts to formulate a green GDP, however, met strong resistance on both methodological and political grounds, leading to a suspension that embarrassed the environmental bureaucracy. Research endeavors by environmental scientists to address the technical challenges have borne fruit only after a decade of work, when China's new administration finally aligned sustainable development rhetoric with the long-term economic development mandate of the Chinese party-state. Despite an expected revival, the prime time for re-introducing the green GDP in China seemed to have passed as the MEP lost its exclusive say on environmental accounting matters. As Wang Jinnan conceded in 2016:

> Not only is the government insufficiently prepared, but the current capacity of concerned agencies to implement GDP accounting is inadequate. Therefore, we are also some way off

> from fully integrating green GDP into the performance evaluation system for party and government officials. There are significant inconsistencies and uncertainties in how application of research outcomes by can be incorporated . . .
>
> *(Wang et al., 2016b: 227)*

NBS, together with an array of bureaucratic counterparts, have been instrumental in promoting NCA, a different accounting approach that might compromise the relevance of green GDP, which rests on computation of pollution costs. With its emphasis on the stock-taking of natural resource assets, the NCA was actively endorsed and pursued by both Beijing and local governments in an effort to understand the full economic potential of their natural resources, and to strategize growth roadmaps that transcend existing industrial structures and constraints. These do not bode well for the fate of the green GDP exercise in China. Nevertheless, the orientation toward NCA has been in alignment with the latest greening of the state discourse and the interests of the party/state authorities, and thus will likely help facilitate China's transition "beyond GDP" – a movement championed by international financial institutions and advanced economies (Costanza et al., 2014a).

By examining the existing stocks of natural resources, the authorities will be in better shape to assess unrealized sources for the generation of income in the future that balance the political economic imperative of growth with its environmental sustainability. This might, hopefully, offer a modest dose of optimism to the prospect of China becoming a mature ecological civilization as Xi envisioned.

Acknowledgement

Parts of the chapter are drawn from Li and Lang (2010). Copyright © *Journal of Contemporary Asia*, reprinted by permission of Taylor & Francis Ltd, www.tandfonline.com on behalf of the *Journal of Contemporary Asia*.

Notes

1 The London Group on Environmental Accounting was established with a mandate from the Statistical Commission of the UN to review and develop a "System of Economic Environmental Accounting." The first meeting was in London (hence the name "London Group"). Statisticians attending the meetings are drawn from national statistical offices, and there are also representatives on the coordinating committee from the Statistical Office of the EU (Eurostat), the Organization of Economic Cooperation and Development, the UN Statistics Division, and the World Bank. The London Group has been widely recognized for the capacity to provide expert inputs to the UN and other organizations on environmental accounting systems. For details, see http://unstats.un.org/unsd/envaccounting/londongroup/.

2 Since 1968, SNA, jointly published by UN, European Commission, International Monetary Fund, Organisation for Economic Co-operation and Development and World Bank, has been an internationally accepted system of standards and practices for countries with a market economy to understand their economic performances. It has "an integrated set of macroeconomic accounts, balance sheets and tables based on internationally agreed concepts, definitions, classification and accounting rules." For details, see United Nations Statistics Division (1993). For a recent critical review of the green GDP accounting practices within China, see Gao (2016) and Wang et al. (2016b).

3 The three cities include Changsha, Xiangtan and Zhuzhou, respectively the provincial capital, the third and fourth largest cities in Hunan.

4 The seven "core implementing countries" include Botswana, Colombia, Costa Rica, Guatemala, Madagascar, and Rwanda, as well as Indonesia and the Philippines in Asia.

5 In addition to China, Costa Rica, Ethiopia, Kenya, Sweden, South Africa, and Tanzania are also part of the global research collaboration, representing economies of different levels of development and composition of natural resources.

References

Alfsen, K.H., et al (2006) *International Experiences with "Green GDP"* (Oslo: Statistics Norway).

Beijing Planning Office of Philosophy and Social Sciences (2003) "Yi EDP wei hexin zhibiao de guomin jingji hesuan tiji yanjiu" (A GDP study using EDP as the core indicator) (December 24). Available at www.bjpopss.gov.cn/xxgl/xmk/23.htm.

Biganzi (2006) "How the Green GDP Report was Greened," *China Digital Times* (September 17). Available at http://chinadigitaltimes.net/2006/09/how_the_green_gdp_report_was_greened.php.

Biganzi (2007) "Green GDP Praying for Hu's Help," *China Digital Times* (August 9). Available at http://chinadigitaltimes.net/2007/08/green_gdp_seeks_hus_help.php.

Chan, K.M. (2010) "Harmonious Society," In H.K. Anheier & S. Toepler (Eds.) *International Encyclopedia of Civil Society* (New York: Springer Science), 821–825.

Chan, Y., Seip, H.M., & Vennemo, H. (2001) "The Environmental Cost of Water Pollution in Chongqing, China," *Environmental and Development Economics*, 6(3), 313–333.

Chinese Academy of Sciences (2007) *China Modernization Report 2007 – A Study on the Ecological Modernization* (Beijing: Chinese Academy of Sciences).

Costanza, R. et al. (1997) "The Value of the World"s Ecosystem Services and Natural Capital," *Nature*, 387 (May 15), 253–260.

Costanza, R. et al. (2014a) "Time to Leave GDP Behind," *Nature*, 505 (January 16), 283–285.

Costanza, R. et al. (2014b) "Changes in the Global Value of Ecosystem Services," *Global Environmental Change*, 26, 152–158.

DeTao Institute of Green Investment (2015) "Sanya shi luse jueqi de dianjishi: ziran ziyuan zichan fuzhai biao bianzhi shuoming" (The foundation of the green ascent of Sanya: an illustration of natural capital balance sheet preparation) (April).

Environment for Development (2016) "Multi-country study seeks common valuation for urban parks," (April 21). Available at www.efdinitiative.org/news/archive/multi-country-study-seeks-common-valuation-urban-parks.

Feng, Z. et al. (2015) "National Balance Sheets and Implications for Natural Resources Balance Sheet," *Resources Science*, 37(9), 1685–1691.

Gao, M. (2016) "Green GDP Accounting in China: Controversies and Progress," In Y. Zheng (Ed.) *Chinese Research Perspectives on the Environment, Special Volume: Critical Essays on China's Environment and Development* (Leiden, NL: Brill), 230–244.

Goodman, M.P., & Parker, D.A. (2015) *Navigating Choppy Waters: China's Economic Decision-making at a Time of Transition* (New York and London: Rowman & Littlefield).

Green GDP Technical Working Group (2004) *Zonghe Huanjing yu Jingji HeSuan (Luse GDP) Yanjiu Jianbao* (Integrated Economic and Environmental Accounting (Green GDP) Research Brief), (March), no. 3.

Li, C. (2011) "Introduction," In A. Hu (Ed.), *China in 2020: A New Type of Superpower* (Washington, DC: Brookings Institution Press), xv–xl.

Li, V., & Lang, G. (2010) "Ecological Modernization or the "Treadmill of Production"? The Attempt to Implement 'Green GDP' Accounting in China," *Journal of Contemporary Asia*, 40(1), 44–62.

Li, W., & Higgins, P. (2013) "Controlling Local Environmental Performance: An Analysis of Three National Environmental Management Programs in the Context of Regional Disparities in China," *Journal of Contemporary China*, 22(81), 409–427.

MEP (2015) "Jiakuai tuijn shengtai wenming jianshe youxiao tuidong xin 'huanbao fa' luoshi Huanjing Baohu Bu chongqi luse GDP yanjiu" (MEP to restart green GDP research in order to accelerate the construction of ecological civilization and help implement the new Environmental Protection Law) (March 30). Available at www.mep.gov.cn/gkml/hbb/qt/201503/t20150330_298346.htm.

Narloch, U., Kozluk, T., & Lloyd, A. (2016) "Measuring Inclusive Green Growth at the Country Level," GGKP Research Committee on Measurement and Indicators. Available at www.greengrowthknowledge.org/sites/default/files/downloads/resource/Measuring_Inclusive_Green_Growth_at_the_Country_Level.pdf.

NBS (2016) "Xin yi lun "Zhongguo senlin ziyuan hesuan ji luse jingji pingjia tixi yanjiu" xiangmu qudong" (A new round of "Research of China"s Forest Resource Auditing and Green Economy Evaluation System" begins) (July 6). Available at www.stats.gov.cn/tjgz/tjdt/201607/t20160706_1374422.html.

NDRC (2007) "Guojia Fazhan Gaige Wei guanyu pizhun Wuhan chengshi quan he Zhang Zhu Tan chengshi qun wei quanguo ziyuan jieyue xing he huanjing youhao xing shehui jianshe zonghe peitao gaige shiyan qu de tongzhi" (NDRC approves the creation of experimental zones for building resource-conserving and environmentally friendly metropolises in Wuhan and the Changsha-Xiangtan-Zhuzhou area) (December 14).

Qiu, J. (2007) "China's Green Accounting System on Shaky Ground," *Nature*, 448 (2 August), 518–519.

Rauch, J.N., & Chi, Y.F. (2010) "The Plight of Green GDP in China," *Consilience: The Journal of Sustainable Development*, 3(1), 102–116.

SEPA (2004) "Guanyu zhengji kaizhan luse GDP hesuan he huanjing wuran jingji sunshi diaocha gongzuo shidian sheng shi de tongzhi" (Notice on soliciting provinces and cities participation in pilot green GDP audit and investigating economic costs of pollution) (October 20). Available at www.zhb.gov.cn/info/gw/bgth/200410/t20041020_62176.htm.

SEPA & NBS (2006) *China Green National Accounting Study Report 2004 (Public Version)* (Beijing: SEPA and NBS).

Shanghai Securities News (2007) "Luse GDP hesuan xiao zu cheng youxie shengfen GDP shiji ling zengzhang" (Green GDP Research Group says that some provinces have (after adjustment) zero growth in GDP), *Shanghai Securities News* (August 3).

State Council of China (2015a) "Zhonggong zhongyan guowuyuan guanyu jiakuai tuijin shengtai wenming jianshe de yijian" (Opinions of CPC Central Committee and State Council on accelerating the construction of ecological civilization) (April 25).

State Council of China (2015b) "Guowuyuan bangong ting guanyu yinfa bianzhì ziran ziyuan zichan fuzhai biao shidian fangan de tongzhi" (State Council Circular on the Pilot Initiative of Preparing Natural Capital Balance Sheet) (November 17). Available at www.gov.cn/zhengce/content/2015-11/17/content_10313.htm.

Steinhardt, H.C., & Jiang, Y. (2007) "The Politics of China's 'Green GDP'," *China Aktuell: Journal of Current Chinese Affairs*, 5, 27–39.

Sun, Z., et al. (2016) "Ziran ziyuan zichan fuzhai biao lilun jichu yu mubiao dingwei" (Theoretical Basis and Objectives of Natural Capital Balance Sheet), *Modern Accounting*, 85(1), 26–27.

Tong, Y. (2007) "Bureaucracy Meets the Environment: Elite Perceptions in Six Chinese Cities," *The China Quarterly*, 189, 100–121.

Tsui, K.-Y., & Wang, Y. (2004) "Between Separate Stoves and a Single Menu: Fiscal Decentralization in China," *The China Quarterly*, 177, 71–90.

UNCED (1993) *Agenda 21: Earth Summit – The United Nations Programme of Action from Rio* (New York: United Nations Department of Public Information).

UNEP (2016) *Green is Gold: The Strategy and Actions of China's Ecological Civilization* (Nairobi, Krnya: UNEP). Available at web.unep.org/greeneconomy/sites/unep.org.greeneconomy/files/publications/greenisgold_en_20160519.pdf.

UNEP & Tongji Institute of Environment for Sustainable Development (2008). "Green Accounting Practice in China (Draft Report)" (April).

United Nations, et al. (2003) *Integrated Environmental and Economic Accounting: Final Draft Circulated for Information Prior to Official Editing* (New York: United Nations).

United Nations, et al. (2014) *System of Environmental–Economic Accounting 2012 – Central Framework* (New York: United Nations).

United Nations Statistics Division (1993) *Integrated Environmental and Economic Accounting: An Interim Version* (New York: United Nations).

Wang, J., Jiang, H., & Yu, F. (2004) "Green GDP Accounting in China: Review and Outlook," Paper for the 9th Meeting of London Group of Environmental Accounting Meeting, Copenhagen (September 22–24).

Wang, J. et al. (2016a) "Revive China's Green GDP Programme," *Nature*, 534 (June 2), 37.

Wang, J. et al. (2016b) "Green GDP Accounting Research in China: Looking Back and Forward," In Y. Zheng (Ed.) *Chinese Research Perspectives on the Environment, Special Volume: Critical Essays on China's Environment and Development* (Leiden, NL: Brill), 213–229.

Wang, L., & Ren, Z. (2005) "An Elementary Discussion and Analysis of Green GDP Calculation Methods: A Case Study of Datong City in Shanxi Province," *Deli Kexeu Jinzhan* (Progress in Geography) 2, 100–105.

WAVES Partnership (2016) "From WAVES to WAVES+: Accounting for Natural Capital in Development" (June 1). Available at www.wavespartnership.org/sites/waves/files/images/WAVES%2B_APM%202016.pdf.

Wu, X. (2005) "Bie ba luse GDP tuishang shentan" (Do not put the Green GDP onto the altar), *Environmental Economy*, 8, 57.

Xinhua Net (2006) "2006, Zhejiang de jian luse GDP hesuan shidian zhilu" (In 2006, a pilot scheme of light-green GDP audit in Zhejiang) (December 21). Available at http://zj.xinhuanet.com/tail/2007-01/10/content_9009231.htm.

Xinhua Net (2015) "Xi Jinping tan zhiguo li zheng zhi ba: Jianshe shengtai wenming" (Xin Jinping on governance, no. 8: constructing ecological civilization) (August 7). Available at www.scio.gov.cn/ztk/dtzt/2015/33995/34002/34015/Document/1463039/1463039.htm.

Yang, Y., & Zhang, W. (2005) "Luse GDP yu kechixu fazhan shizheng yanjiu: yi Sichuan Yaan Shi Weili" (An empirical study of green GDP and sustainable development: an example of Yaan, Sichuan Province), *Nongcun Jingji* (Rural Economy), 7, 100–102.

Zhang, B. (2017) "China's New Environmental Protection Regulatory Regime: Effects and Gap," *Journal of Environmental Management*, 187, 464–469.

Zhang, L., Mol, A.P.J., & Sonnenfeld, D.A. (2007) "The Interpretation of Ecological Modernisation in China," *Environmental Politics*, 16(4), 659–668.

28
Legal solutions to air pollution control in Malaysia

Maizatun Mustafa

Introduction

The importance of protecting and enhancing the quality of air has been well documented and recognized by the United Nations General Assembly (2012) which supports the World Health Organization's (WHO) resolution that considers air pollution as one of the leading causes of disease and death globally. In its recent report, WHO (2012) estimated that air pollution killed about 7 million people across the globe in 2012, making it the world's largest single environmental health risk. The protection of air quality is now becoming of paramount importance for countries worldwide, requiring the setting up of policy and legal framework at the national level (International Law Commission 2015). However, for a developing country like Malaysia, the task of controlling air pollution can be a challenge, not only in understanding and dealing with complex interactions between emissions and resulting air quality, but in identifying and applying the most suitable pollution control strategies in order to achieve the overall targets of air quality enhancement and sustainable development. In Malaysia, most of the air pollution problems are associated with increased concentration of people and economic activities in urban and sub-urban areas, as well as growing numbers of agricultural areas and transportation. This chapter focuses on discussing the main sources of air pollution in Malaysia, and highlights existing environmental policy and law related to air pollution control. It also highlights present regional air pollution problems facing Malaysia and its neighboring countries, namely that of transboundary haze pollution, and discusses applicable laws toward haze pollution control.

Malaysia in general

Malaysia, which is located in Southeast Asia, is geographically divided into two parts, the Peninsula Malaysia or West Malaysia and the East Malaysia. The former shares common land borders with Thailand and Singapore, whereas the latter is situated in Borneo and shares a common land boundary with Brunei and Indonesia. The current population of Malaysia is around 31 million and consists of a multiracial society (Department of Statistics Malaysia 2016a). Malaysia has an equatorial monsoon climate with uniformly high temperatures from 21 to 36 degrees Celsius, and high humidity throughout the year. This tropical country has a varied topography ranging from mountainous regions, flat coastal plains, to coastal areas while its tropical rainforests are very rich in species with extremely complex ecosystems. According to the Ministry of Natural Resources and Environment (2016), in 2014, the total forested area for Malaysia was 18.27 million hectares from the total 32.86 million hectares land area. Since the 1980s, Malaysia, which is considered a developing economy by the World Bank (2016) has progressed rapidly in economic development and social transformation, and has become a leading exporter of electrical appliances, electronic parts and components, palm oil, and natural gas. For 2015, the gross domestic product (GDP) was 5.0 percent, as compared to a 6.0 percent growth rate for 2014. Data from the Department of Statistics Malaysia (2016b) shows that the main contributions to GDP for the year 2015 were from the services sector for around 54 percent of GDP. The manufacturing sector accounted for 25 percent of GDP and more than 60 percent of total exports, followed by mining and quarries (9 percent), and agriculture (9 percent).

Sources of air pollution

Until relatively recently, air pollution was not regarded as a significant environmental problem in Malaysia. However, since the quality of air is very much dependent on the level and pace of urban development, it is inevitable that the increasing number of transportation methods as well as industrial and agricultural activities have impacted the quality of air (Mustafa 2013, 59). For Malaysia, industrialization has becoming an important factor in the development of its economy through the establishment of plants and factories. However, the by-products discharged from industrial fuel burning and industrial production processes can contain various kinds of contaminants that pollute the air. The Department of Environment (2015b, 134–135) predicted that the problem of air pollution from industries and power plants is expected to grow both in complexity and extent, in view of the expanding manufacturing and power plant activities in Malaysia. Apart from industrial emissions, emissions from motor vehicles, produced from incomplete carbon reactions, unburned hydrocarbons or other elements present in the fuel or air during combustion, is another source of air pollution. Pollutants emitted from motor vehicles include carbon monoxide, soot, hydrocarbons, sulfur oxides, nitrogen oxides, as well as ash and lead. According to the Department of Road Transport (2016), there were over 25 million registered road vehicles in Malaysia in 2014, and of about 1 million numbers of new vehicles registered that year, passenger cars and motorcycles made up the highest number at over 90 percent, with the remaining vehicles consisting of goods transportation vehicles, taxis and buses. In terms of air pollutant emission loads from various sources, the DOE (2015b, 136–137) estimated that for 2014, the combined air pollutant emission load accumulated to over 1.9 metric tons of carbon monoxide, 836,708 metric tons of nitrogen oxides, 221,471 metric tons of sulfur dioxide, and 25,673 metric tons of particulate matter.

In addition to stationary and mobile sources pollution, open burning is another activity that contributes to the problem of air pollution. In Malaysia, open burning is considered to be the main cause of haze, which happens due to high concentration of particulate matters suspended in the atmosphere, resulting in diminished horizontal visibility. The occurrence of the haze phenomenon was first noted in the 1960s, and by the 1990s it has become a regular problem especially during the relatively dry months of February and March, and from June to September (DOE 2016a). The problem of uncontrolled open burning in Malaysia is compounded by the occurrence of the El Niño phenomenon that takes place every few years, causing drought and desiccation in addition to a reduction of rain, and an increase in temperature, which has contributed to the occurrence of forest fires that cause haze (Department of Meteorology 2016a). It has been reported by the Department of Environment (2015a, 108) that over 6,000 open burning cases were detected all over the country in 2014, which consisted of burning of garbage in residential areas or roadsides, burning of articles for religious purposes, and burning of bushes, forests and agriculture areas. Surveillance through satellites has detected the existence of over 4,000 hotspots in Malaysia throughout 2014.

Air quality standards and air pollution index

Malaysia Ambient Air Quality Standards (MAAQS) are air quality objectives for pollutant concentrations in outdoor air which might adversely affect the health and welfare of the general public. The MAAQS sets national standards for the six key air pollutants which are contaminants of most concern in Malaysia, namely carbon monoxide, ozone, sulfur dioxide, nitrogen dioxide, lead and particulate matter. Prior to the introduction of the MAAQS in 2013, Malaysia relied on the Ambient Air Quality Guideline which only contained five air pollutants including particulate matter with a size of less than 10 microns. However, the recent MAAQS have been improved through the addition of particulate matter with the size of less than 2.5 microns. At the same time, the MAAQS' air pollutants concentration limits are made more stringent and regulated in stages until the year 2020, through three interim targets as illustrated in Table 28.1.

The ambient air quality measurement in Malaysia is described in terms of Air Pollutant Index (API) based on ranges of values as a means of reporting the quality of air instead of using the actual concentration of air pollutants. This index is a color-coded tool which reflects its effect on human health, ranging from good to hazardous, with steps that can be taken by the public to reduce daily exposure to pollution. The Malaysian API system closely follows the Pollutant Standard Index (PSI) developed by the United States Environmental Protection Agency (US-EPA), which provides easily comprehensible information about the air pollution level (DOE 2016a). Generally, the API would integrate information for the different criteria pollutants into normalized values that range from 0 to 500, which represent the daily air quality status of a particular area. The air pollutants included in Malaysia's API are the five major air pollutants which could

Table 28.1 Ambient air quality standard targets

Pollutants	*Average measurement period*	*Ambient air quality standard*		
		Target 1 2015 (micrometer)	*Target 2 2018 (micrometer)*	*Target 3 2020 (micrometer)*
Particulate matter with	1 year	50	45	40
the size of less than 10 microns	24 hour	150	120	100
Particulate matter with the	1 year	35	25	15
size of less than 2.5 microns	24 hour	75	50	35
Sulfur Dioxide	1 year	350	300	250
	24 hour	105	90	80
Nitrogen Dioxide	1 year	320	300	280
	24 hour	75	75	70
Ground Level Ozone	1 year	200	200	180
	24 hour	120	120	100
Carbon Monoxide*	1 year	35	35	30
*(mg/m3)	24 hour	10	10	10

Source: Department of Environment Malaysia.

cause potential harm to human health should they reach unhealthy levels and which are generally comparable to the corresponding air quality standards recommended by the WHO and other countries. These pollutants are ozone, carbon monoxide, nitrogen dioxide, sulfur dioxide and particulate matter with a diameter of less than 10 microns.

Following the requirement of the MAAQS, the air pollutants are measured at varying averaging times in accordance with the WHO standard. To determine the API for a given time period, the sub-index values for all five air pollutants are calculated based on the average concentration calculated for the air quality data collected from air quality monitoring stations. Malaysia's air quality in the country is monitored continuously by the DOE (2015a, 39) through 52 stations strategically located throughout the country to detect any changes in the ambient air quality status that may cause harm to human health and the environment. This air quality monitoring network is complemented by manual air quality monitoring located at another 14 different sites. The API value reported for a given time period represents the highest API value among all the sub-APIs calculated during that particular time period. This time period varies from 1 to 24 hours depending on the pollutants, representing the period of time over which measurements are monitored and reported. Table 28.2 shows the API values and the level of pollution and the health measures applicable to Malaysia.

Apart from monitoring air pollution, the DOE also conducts an aerial surveillance program to detect air pollution due to activities such as open burning and industrial emissions (DOE 2015a, 109). Another form of management directly relevant to air pollution monitoring is the Fire Danger Rating System (FDRS) program conducted by the Department of Meteorology (2016b). The RDRS, which is based on the Canadian Forest Fire Danger Rating System, contains six standard components: the Fine Fuel Moisture Code; the Duff Moisture Code; the Drought Code; the Initial Spread Index; the Buildup Index; and the Fire Weather Index. These multiple index systems, which provide relative numerical ratings of fire potential for a standard fuel type based on weather inputs, are applied to monitor forest and vegetation fire risks and to give an early warning of the potential for large forest fires that can cause haze. This early warning system can be used to predict fire behavior and can be used as a guide for policymakers in developing actions to protect life, property and the environment, apart from assisting management in implementing operations to reduce fire before it becomes critical. At the regional level, Malaysia which is a member of the Association of Southeast Asian Nations (ASEAN) collaborates with other neighboring countries in the ASEAN Specialized Meteorological Centre (ASMC 2016). This Center provides a collaborative program between the national meteorological services of ASEAN

Table 28.2 API values and pollution and health measure for Malaysia

Air pollution index	*Status*	*Level of pollution*
Below 50	Good	Low pollution without any bad effects on health
51–100	Moderate	Moderate pollution that does not pose any bad effects on health
101–200	Unhealthy	Pollution that worsens the health condition of high risk people with heart and lung complications
201–300	Very Unhealthy	Pollution that worsens the health condition and low tolerance of physical exercises to people with heart and lung complications. Affects public health
More than 300	Hazardous	Hazardous to high risk people and to public health

Source: Department of Environment Malaysia.

member countries to manage regional air pollution problem. The Center's primary roles are to monitor and assess land and forest fires, as well as the occurrence of transboundary smoke haze for the ASEAN region; and to conduct seasonal and climate predictions for the ASEAN region. For Malaysia, input gathered from the Center, including the haze map showing hotspots and wind flow would help in evaluating the regional pollution index and climate conditions, monitoring the occurrences of local and cross-boundary haze, and preparing action plans and remedial measures to combat haze caused by open burning, forest fires and other sources of smoke.

Environmental governance and policy

Malaysia practices the federal system of government, in which the powers and responsibilities of the federal and state governments are clearly defined by the Federal Constitution. Nevertheless, most of the legal provisions relating to air pollution control are legislated by parliament, thus they are considered to be federal laws and applicable to all states in Malaysia uniformly. Environmental matters are administered by the Ministry of Natural Resource and Environment. Under this Ministry, the DOE is created to become the main body dealing with environmental protection and management, including the monitoring of pollution and enforcement of the law for the whole of Malaysia.

Until the early 1970s, environmental protection and management were never considered part of a formal agenda for Malaysia despite the fact that the country was already facing adverse environmental impacts due to economic development (Aiken 1982). However, pursuant to the participation in the United Nations Conference on the Human Environment in Stockholm in 1972, Malaysia began to plan for its national environmental protection agenda and set its environmental policy directives within the Malaysia Plans. As a member state of various United Nations (UN) environmental conventions, Malaysia is highly influenced by, and committed itself to, the UN's sustainability agenda (Mustafa 2013, 46). In 2002, the National Policy on the Environment Malaysia, which was introduced by the Ministry of Science, Technology and the Environment (2002), provided a framework for a comprehensive approach to natural resource development and aimed at promoting economic, social and cultural progress through environmentally sound and sustainable development. The Policy adopts broad-based strategic approaches in key areas such as prevention and control of pollution, which are used as a basis to implement environmental strategies, programs and directives within the legal and institutional framework. These policy directives are supported by the current 11th Malaysia Plan (2016–2020) which recognizes the importance of environmental sustainability as part of a comprehensive socio-economic development plan, both in order to raise Malaysians' quality of life, as well as for the purpose of environmental protection and climate change mitigation (Economic Planning Unit 2015). In essence, the National Policy on the Environment, together with the Malaysia Plans, guide the manner in which environmental law is to be formulated and enforced, including that pertaining to air quality enhancement and pollution control.

Air pollution control law

The most important legislation on air pollution control in Malaysia is the Environmental Quality Act of 1974 (EQA), which was enacted for the purposes of "prevention, abatement, controlling of pollution and enhancement, and for the purposes connected therewith." This Act, which is applicable throughout Malaysia, forms the basic legislation for achieving national environmental objectives and policies (Mustafa 2013, 32). The EQA has undergone continuous changes both in terms of its scope and its strategies, which are meant to provide long term solutions to environmental pollution problems. There are various strategies applied by the Act in controlling different sources of air pollution, as elaborated below.

Criminal sanctions and acceptable conditions

One of the earliest air pollution control strategies applied by the EQA is in the form of criminal sanctions through Section 22. There is a general presumption that the discharge of polluting matter into the atmosphere is illegal unless licensed. Section 22 states that "no person shall, unless licensed, emit or discharge any environmentally hazardous substances, pollutants or wastes into the atmosphere in contravention of the acceptable conditions specified under Section 21." The principle of air pollution offences under this section is formulated in terms of actions and intentions whereby any person who is found liable under the section, upon conviction, shall be fined for up to RM100,000 (USD25,500), or to imprisonment for a period up to five years, or to both. However, under this section, the restriction on emission of air pollution is not absolute but conditional upon the provision of acceptable conditions in Section 21. The term "acceptable conditions" refers to an environmental standard that sets the maximum allowable limit of concentration of a particular medium of the environment. To avoid contravention of this law, an authorization in the form of a license must be obtained from the DOE. Thus, the emission of pollutants exceeding the permitted limit is an offense unless the person who commits such emission is licensed to do so in accordance with the Environmental Quality (Licensing) Regulations of 1977. This administrative scheme licensing system is common-place in Malaysia's environmental management system in which a license may be granted subject to particular conditions, and can be revoked if conditions are not being fulfilled. In this way, the DOE as the enforcement agency can have close and continuous control over economic activities that are causing air pollution, and has the discretionary power to set any conditions taking into account various factors, including the effect of emissions on the environment (Mustafa 2013, 29–30). The main feature of the licensing system is therefore the ability of the DOE to take enforcement action against the emitter when the conditions of the license are breached. While the EQA provides for regulatory actions that involve using prosecution through the courts, the Act also contains mechanisms which allow for less severe action to be taken before recourse to criminal law sanctions is imposed. They include the issuance of a prohibition order to require the activity to stop before a legal action is taken, and the payment of compound. Generally, compounding is a settlement process allowing the accused to pay compounding charges instead of undergoing lengthy prosecution. Section 45 of the EQA empowers the enforcement officers to compound any compoundable offences by accepting from the person suspected of having committed the offence an amount not exceeding RM2000 (USD 510). The Act also provides the power to the DOE to require the emitter to submit a plan for improvement to a process or plant. Through the usage of end-of-pipe controls as the basic form of air pollution control, the protection of the environment is accomplished by controlling only what is emitted from a discharge point.

Control of stationary sources pollution

Previously, the combined administrative and criminal sanctions methods had been widely used to regulate emission of air pollutants from stationary sources. From 1978 up until 2014, these methods were applied to control air pollution from premises, such as industrial or trade premises used to burn waste, any facility that discharged air impurities into open air, and every chimney, industrial plant and fuel burning equipment. During that time, these stationary sources of air pollution were regulated based on the licensing system through the now-revoked Environmental

Quality (Clean Air) Regulations of 1978. The 1978 Regulations relied upon the application of acceptable conditions based on parameter limits to regulate emissions of dark smoke, air impurities and gaseous emissions from the said facilities or processes. When these emission standards came into effect in 1978, they were enforced as phased regulations over several stages. At the same time, emissions of dark smoke from facilities were controlled using the Ringelmann Chart. Another method adopted by the 1978 Regulations was the requirement of "best practical means" to prevent the emission of noxious or offensive substances and to render them harmless and inoffensive. The Regulations provided the list of items deemed to be "noxious and offensive substances" and defined the term "best practicable means" to include the following: size, design and inherent operation characteristics of the plant or processes; the provision and appropriate use of mist eliminators, dust arrestors, gas absorbers and control instrumentation; the use of suitable raw material or suitable fuel; the alternative processes within the capacity and design capability of the plant; the alternative manner of operation or procedures within the capacity and design capability of the plant or processes; the proper conduct and adequate supervision of operations; and regular and efficient maintenance of plant and control equipment. Through the concept of best practicable means, consideration was given to the premises' local conditions and circumstances, the current state of technical knowledge, and financial implications.

However, the continuous emergence of manufacturing and processing industries over the years that cause higher emissions of air pollutants have led Malaysia to revise its policy and strategy relating to air pollution control. For this reason, in 2014, the Environmental Quality (Clean Air) Regulations of 1978 was repealed and replaced by the Environmental Quality (Clean Air) Regulations of 2014. The 2014 Regulations' approach to air pollution control departs substantially from that of the previous ones by giving more focus to source reductions and planning, design modifications, taking into account available technologies, and well as economic and other factors. For these reasons, air pollution emitted from any premises are now regulated through management and operational changes by way of stringent standards and advanced strategies. The scope of the 2014 Regulations is also wider, including the following establishments or processes:

- premises that are used for any industrial or trade purposes, or on which matter is burnt in connection with any industrial or trade purposes, including burning of waste;
- any other premises or process that discharges or is capable of discharging air pollutants into the open air;
- any industrial plant; and
- any fuel burning equipment, which include any furnace, boiler, fireplace, oven, retort, internal combustion engine, vessel, or any other apparatus, device, mechanism, stack, chimney or structure used in connection with the burning of any combustible material.

The 2014 Regulations require new premises to comply with limitation values and technical standards specified therein, whereas existing premises must comply with such values within five years from the date of the Regulations. In addition, they are also required to notify the DOE before carrying out the following: any change in operation of the premises; any work on any premises that may create a source of emission; construction on any land, any building or premises designed or used for a purpose that may result in a new source of emissions; making, causing, or permitting any change to be made to any plant, machine, or equipment used or installed at the premises that causes a material change in the quantity or quality of emission from an existing source; or carrying out any changes or modifications to an existing air pollution control system.

One important feature of the 2014 Regulations is the mandatory self-regulation on the part of the premise known as "Best Available Techniques Economically Achievable" (BAT) which is considered a measure to prevent pollution and, where that is not practicable, generally to reduce emissions into the air from industrial activities and to reduce their impact on the environment as a whole. The BAT, which seek to demonstrate compliance with the optimization requirement through selections of best management practices is introduced within the 2014 Regulations to replace the previous requirement that employed best practicable means. The BAT's overall purpose is to reduce industrial discharges and ensure a high level of protection for the environment as a whole, taking into account different types of environmental impacts. Thus, during the operating processes, the premises involved must use BAT to prevent the release of the prescribed substances, or where it is not practicable, to minimize any release into the environment. In this regard, the term "Techniques" includes both the technology used and the way in which the facility is designed, built, maintained, operated and decommissioned. Whereas "Available Techniques" means those techniques that are accessible to the occupier and that are developed on a scale that allows implementation in the relevant industrial sector, under economically and technically viable conditions, taking into consideration the costs and advantages; and "Best" means effective in achieving a high general level of protection of the environment as a whole (Department of Environment 2016c).

Activities that are subjected to BAT include fuel burning, including heat and power generation in boilers, combustion turbines or generators; production and processing of ferrous and non-ferrous metals; oil and gas industries; non-metallic industry in cement production; all stationary asphalt mixing plants in the form of liquid, solid or gas; the pulp and paper industry; the chemical and petrochemical industry; production of pharmaceutical products, plant health products and biocides, and mixing and packaging of chemicals, pesticides, pharmaceutical products; solvent use in industry for dressing, printing, coating, degreasing, waterproofing, painting; and waste incinerators. There are various requirements imposed on these premises or processes, including compliance with specific parameters, concentrations or levels; equipping of air pollution control system in the premise; equipping the premises with relevant equipment and conducting performance monitoring of the air pollution control system, and maintaining records of performance monitoring of the air pollution control system. In addition, it is a requirement upon the premises to incorporate measures to reduce the emission of air pollutants in accordance with the BAT, including restrictions on opacity and black smoke. On the other hand, BAT does not constrain the development of cleaner techniques, nor does it restrict the premise's choice of means to achieve the specified standards. For the DOE, the application of BAT which allows for self-regulation on the part of premises or processes is also meant to assist them in planning and designing a more effective air pollution control system. Among the focuses are energy-efficiency, waste-minimization, process-minimization, the promotion of cleaner production concepts, and alternative processes that are more environmentally friendly. Through the BAT, the said premises or processes are regulated to restrict their emissions in a manner that emphasizes pollution prevention techniques rather than end-of-pipe treatment. The EQA also encourages the premises to develop and introduce new and innovative technologies and techniques which meet BAT criteria, and look for continuous improvement in their overall environmental performance as part of the sustainable development process.

Control of mobile source pollution

Most of the motor vehicles in Malaysia are powered by either petrol or diesel burning combustion systems which produce by-products in the form of air pollutants such as unburned hydrocarbons, nitrogen oxides, carbon monoxide and carbon dioxide. Presently, motor vehicles are considered to be the major source of mobile air pollution in Malaysia, and remain the highest contributor to the emission of carbon monoxide (DOE 2015b, 134–235). The amount of emissions attributable to the transport sector in Malaysia is influenced by several factors, such as the age of the vehicle fleet and the technology used within it, and the appropriate fuels used by the vehicles. Even as early as the 1970s, focus was given to the regulation of mobile sources pollution through the passing of the Motor Vehicles (Control of Smoke and Gas Emission) Rules of 1977 under the Road Traffic Ordinance of 1958. At that time, the Rules were considered to be a major piece of legislation for motor-vehicle emission which stipulates an emission standard of 50 Hatridge Smoke Units for exhaust smoke from diesel vehicles. The Rules also require that all new motor vehicles powered by a four stroke engine to be equipped with anti-blow-by devices to prevent the escape of gas from crankcases. Nevertheless, the main limitation of the Rules lies within the fact that their application is confined to diesel vehicles only, and does not cover emissions from petrol engines. In addition, the Rules are not applicable to car assemblers in relation to pollution control requirements associated with motor vehicle engines. By the 1980s, the EQA began to develop a coherent set of air pollution control strategies for mobile sources pollution that are technology-oriented, targeting the vehicles and fuels used, one of which is the enactment of the Environmental Quality (Control of Lead Concentration in Motor Gasoline) Regulations of 1985, which is meant to control high levels of atmospheric lead, frequently observed in the urban areas, due to their harmful effects to human health and the environment (Mustafa et al. 2012). The main objectives of the Regulations are to reduce and subsequently eliminate the use of lead additives in motor gasoline through the restriction of imports or manufactures, and the restriction of possession of motor gasoline lead or lead compounds in excess of 0.40 grams per liter. Due to Malaysia's phasing out policies of lead as well as the introduction of unleaded petrol in the market, lead concentration in the air has been reduced and continues to remain low (Hirota 2010, 145–162).

In 1996, the EQA passed two Regulations meant to regulate emissions from diesel and petrol engines through allowable emission limits for motor vehicles, which are in accordance with the UN's standards. They are the Environmental Quality (Control of Emissions and Diesel Engines) Regulations of 1996, and the Environmental Quality (Control of Emission from Petrol Engines) Regulations of 1996. The former applies to all motor vehicle registered after August 31, 1996 as well as to motor vehicles which are already registered but which have new engine systems to replace existing ones. The latter applies to a new motor vehicles registered after January 1, 1997 and to motor vehicles which are already registered but which have new engine systems to replace existing systems. These Regulations prescribed different gaseous pollutants emissions standards for diesel and petrol engines with different gross vehicle weight/total mass. The Regulations also impose emissions standards of pollution, such as carbon monoxide, hydrocarbons, and nitrogen oxides, on the relevant motor vehicles based on related Economic Commission for Europe standards. In addition, there are various other requirements imposed by the Regulations, including those on installation or replacement of engine systems and requirements on assemblers or manufacturers to conduct certain tests on the vehicles. The control of smoke emissions as well as on the density of smoke emitted from exhaust pipes are also applied to every motor vehicle irrespective of whether it is in use or stationary, or in any bus terminus, taxi stand or private premises or on any private road based on the Ringelmann Chart.

Another legal measure applied to reduce emissions from the transportation sector is the introduction of higher European Fuel Directive standards (EURO) for fuel used in any internal combustion engine (mobile and stationary applications) and in industrial plants through the Environmental Quality (Control of Petrol and Diesel Properties) Regulations of 2007. Under the Regulations, fuel which is produced, stored, distributed, transported, supplied, sold or offered for sale within Malaysia shall comply with specific standards of properties, namely the European emission standards of EURO 2 for both petrol and diesel. These new standards mean a reduction in the sulfur content from 3,000 parts per million (ppm) to 500 ppm for diesel, and from 1,500 ppm to 500 ppm for petrol. In order to determine the properties of the fuel prescribed by the Regulations, the fuel samples need to be collected and analyzed according to the American Society of Testing and Material (ASTM) standards. Malaysia is gradually adopting higher EURO standards for both diesel and petrol fuels, and upgraded to the EURO 3 standard in 2014, and the EURO 4 standard in 2015 (ACFA 2012).

One more form of mobile source pollution regulated by the EQA is the emission from motorcycles. In developing countries such as Malaysia, motorcycles are considered to be economically affordable and a flexible form of transportation (UNEP 2016). According to the Ministry of Transport (2014), the total number of motorcycles in 2013 was over 11 million, consisting mostly of small capacity, two or four stroke engine motorcycles. Previously, motorcycles emissions received less regulatory attention as compared to other types of motor vehicles, despite the fact that the less sophisticated engine technology of motorcycles has resulted in emissions of particulate matter, hydrocarbons, volatile organic compounds, nitrogen oxides, lead and carbon dioxide. The need to reduce emissions from motorcycles has prompted Malaysia to introduce emissions regulations that are more advanced in accordance with more stringent standards and technologies required by the market. Thus in 2003, the Environmental Quality (Control of Emission from Motorcycles) Regulations were enacted to be applicable to all motor vehicles registered as a motorcycle under the Road Transport Act of 1987. Similar to diesel and petrol engine emissions, gaseous emissions limits for motorcycle engines, as well as tests to be conducted by the manufacture, are also based on international standards including the EEC Council Directive 97/24/EC of June 17, 1997. For this purpose, the emission of carbon monoxide, hydrocarbons and nitrogen oxides is controlled according to specific categories of motorcycles, such as those that are imported or locally manufactured or assembled; new models or current models; and engine type. Since the two-stroke engine motorcycles emit more volatile organic compounds, hydrocarbons and particulate matter compared to four-stroke engines, the 2003 Regulations impose two different gaseous emissions limit for both 2 stroke and 4 stroke motorcycle engines respectively. Any manufacturer who fails to comply with these requirements, or fabricates the test results commits an offense and shall on convictions be liable to a fine not exceeding RM100,000 (USD 25,500), or to imprisonment not exceeding five years, or to both. On the part of the registered owner or rider of any motorcycle in use, there is also a requirement by the Regulations to ensure that such motorcycle does not emit gaseous pollutant exceeding the prescribed limit, as otherwise it would be an offense, and upon conviction would be liable to a fine up to RM5,000 (USD1,270). The idling gaseous emissions test for any motorcycle in use is conducted by an authorized officer in order to ensure that emissions control systems are effective when motorcycles are used as recommended. A penalty shall be imposed upon those who obstruct the authorized officer in exercising his power, and these individuals may be liable for a fine of up to RM10,000 (USD2,550), or to imprisonment for up to two years, or to both.

Haze pollution control

Previously, Malaysia did not have any specific laws to regulate open burning activities and relied upon Section 22 of the EQA, which was later found to be very inadequate to deal with open burning's consequential effects on the quality of air. Due to the seriousness and continuous emergence of haze, a well-defined law on open burning was therefore enacted in the form of Section 29A of the EQA that completely bans "open burning" and strictly prohibits any person from causing open burning on any premises, and land (Mustafa 2013, 66). The penalty imposed by this section is a fine of up to RM 500,000 (USD 127,500), or a jail term of five years, or both.

The application of Section 29A which is based on criminal law allows for the delegation of power to investigate open burning activities to related agencies such as the Fire and Rescue Department, the Ministry of Health, the local authority and even the police.

While Section 29A is meant to provide for a total prohibition on open burning, in practice such prohibition might not be practicable to Malaysia, considering that some activities that are normally practiced by the locals require wastes or residues to be burnt openly (Tiraieyari et al. 2014). For example, agricultural burning, which is one of the main sources of open burning in Malaysia, is commonly performed for post-harvest land clearing on various food crops as well as for removing unwanted insects and pests (Rosmiza et al. 2014, 30–43). Burning is also considered to be the cheapest and fastest way to clear land in preparation for planting. Thus a total prohibition on open burning would cause undue hardship or otherwise be unreasonable or infeasible under the circumstances, particularly when there is no practical alternate method to dispose of waste other than open burning. Taking into consideration farming requirements and other needs, another provision, Section 29AA, was subsequently introduced to provide for some exceptions to certain open burning activities in the form of "Declared Activities" as listed in the Environmental Quality (Declared Activities) (Open Burning) Order of 2003. Altogether, there are 15 instances which are deemed to be declared activities and exempted from the prohibition of Section 29A. They include the burning of residue from land cleared for cultivating food crops, rice stalks, and sugar cane leaves prior to harvesting in an area that does not exceed 20 hectares; residue from smallholdings cleared for planting or replanting crops in an area not exceeding two hectares per day; certain religious rites; and activities involving health and safety measures as required by certain laws. Under the EQA, there is no requirement of a written permit on any person to cause open burning of the declared activities. However, there are specific conditions imposed by the law on each of the declared activities before the burning takes place. They include the requirement to notify the Director General of the DOE in writing before the burning is carried out; with information on the potential content of the material to be burned; the circumstances of combustible material generation; the weather condition; and type of soil on which the open burning is to be carried out. The law prohibits any type of open burning to be done on peat soil as it can burn easily, tends to produce a lot of smoke, and is difficult to extinguish. While Section 29AA of the EQA allows for open burning practices, this permission is not absolute. In the event that the API reading has reached an unhealthy level, or where such activity would be hazardous to the environment, the exemption will be withdrawn. Thus, under that situation, any such fire, combustion or smoldering would not be permitted (DOE 2016d). In the event that the API level reaches 200, schools in the affected areas would be closed in accordance with the DOE's National Haze Action Plan, which provides for emergency response mechanisms applicable to the whole nation.

In Malaysia, haze pollution has previously been addressed as a local issue, thus requiring interventions only at the national level. However, for the past few years, the recurring haze problem has been attributed mainly to forest fires and open burning activities in the neighboring country Indonesia (Jayakumar et al. 2015), which has caused the API to reach the hazardous level of 500 (DOE 2016b). Unlike other types of air pollution, transboundary haze pollution poses a great challenge for Malaysia due to the fact that the haze is originating from abroad, beyond the national border. According to Siegert and Hoffmann (2000), in Indonesia, forest fires are used as means of large scale land clearing for palm oil plantations and other purposes. The occurrence of serious haze pollution has been recorded by the Department of Environment (2016e) starting in 1991, when Malaysia experienced very hazy weather condition due to the forest fires in various parts of Indonesia and has continued to recur almost every year until the present. The substantial health, economic and other costs of haze endured annually have raised a significant question about the position of law in Malaysia in dealing with transboundary haze pollution. While the application of domestic law on haze pollution is quite direct, such law is not applicable toward transboundary haze pollution. In the event that the source of haze is originated from abroad, Malaysia can only rely on the provisions of international law. At present, the only international legal document available relating to haze is the ASEAN Agreement on Transboundary Haze Pollution which has been ratified by all the ASEAN members including Malaysia. The objective of this Agreement is to prevent and monitor transboundary haze pollution through national efforts and regional and international cooperation, and mandates that the parties take precautionary measures by taking steps to anticipate, prevent and monitor transboundary haze pollution resulting from land and forest fires. The Agreement addresses crucial aspects of fire and haze pollution including prevention, monitoring and mitigation, and requires the parties to ensure that activities within their jurisdiction or control do not cause damage to the environment and harm to human health of other states or of areas beyond the limits of national jurisdiction. Nevertheless, it has been argued by scholars such as Tan (2014) and Jayakumar et al. (2015) that the content of this Agreement does not forbid certain types of conduct that cause open burning, nor does it include obligations for compensation. According to Article 27 of the Agreement, any dispute between the parties as to the interpretation or application of, or compliance with, the Agreement or any Protocol thereto, shall be settled amicably by consultation or negotiation. This provision is an indication that enforcement of the agreement remains a matter of diplomacy instead of a direct legal redress (Heilmann 2015). At the same time, there is no inclusion of enforcement measures or rule on state liability within the Agreement. It is argued by Varkkey (2015) that without such measures, it is not possible for Malaysia to hold Indonesia, or any corporation or individual responsible for haze. Thus, despite the Agreement's existence, there is still a huge need for improvement both in content and application, including concerted coordination and action at the regional level for parties to strengthen their capabilities to comply with its provisions.

Conclusion

Like many other developing countries in the Southeast Asia, Malaysia's high rate of economic development and industrialization, in addition to land clearing activities for agricultural, plantation, infrastructure and other purposes, have unavoidably caused considerable environmental quality issues, including that of air pollution. The main challenge for Malaysia is in finding the right strategies to control air pollution, taking into consideration factors such as the importance of energy consumption for transport and power generation as prerequisites to economic growth. Malaysia has taken various actions to address the problem of air pollution starting with the enactment of the EQA as the main legislation on pollution control. Various provisions have already been introduced by the Act to regulate emissions from specific sources. The EQA's application of limit value based on acceptable conditions often takes into account economic status of the premise concerned. It is argued that this type of strategy, while allows for administrative and legal measures to control air pollution, depends heavily on the enforcement capacity of the authority. In addition, such measures can be costly and time-consuming, apart from being less dynamic in the sense that they are not able to provide continuous incentives toward attaining the desired air quality standards (Mustafa 2013, 50–53). While criminal sanctions and licensing systems are the main approaches used in controlling air pollution, for less serious breaches, several possibilities for action are applicable, including the use of prohibition orders to stop the process, or revocation of licenses, while failure to take such action may lead to court proceedings. However, with the recent amendment of the EQA that introduces the concept of BAT, stationary source pollution control would now start at the beginning of the process to minimize effluent emissions in order to achieve the lowest impact on the environment from the process as a whole. With the emergence of new industries and processes that emit different types of pollutants, BAT is considered a change in the EQA's strategy by allowing for a self-regulation on the part of the premises and processes aiming at reducing regulatory and compliance costs in the interest of achieving the objective of environmental quality enhancement and pollution control. However, the introduction of BAT within the law, which is generally a single-medium approach, is still in its infancy, thus it is not yet possible to measure its effectiveness in the context of air pollution control. Another primary target of emission control is mobile air pollution, which has been recognized as one of the major contributors to air pollution. Recognizing the significant role mobile sources play in the overall air pollution problem, the DOE is given a broad authority under the EQA to regulate motor vehicle pollution, and the Act's standards on emission control have become progressively more stringent toward such emissions. In addition, rapid growth of motor-vehicle fleets in Malaysia also requires the law to impose the reduction of emissions through extensive interventions, maintenance and inspection programs imposed on manufacturers and assemblers. While Malaysia is persistent in addressing mobile emissions' effective technological controls and other legal means of emissions controls, there are other factors that contribute to motor vehicle pollution. The rising population and increased number of registered motor vehicles, apart from the increase in total number of miles traveled by each person, are factors that need to be considered by Malaysia in devising new approaches to mobile air pollution control.

While Malaysia is relying on legal measures in the form of enforcement and compliance to control various sources of air pollution, such measures need to be supported by administrative programs such as the air quality monitoring system that documents air pollution concentrations, and the adoption of National Ambient Air Quality Standards in light of current air quality guidelines of the WHO. The new ambient air quality standards for Malaysia that include ground-level ozone and particulate matter with the size less than 2.5 micron are expected to provide benefits to the quality of human health. The new standards are also pertinent in light of the seriousness of the haze pollution problem and the importance of regulating open burning activities that contribute to haze pollution. The application of a stringent law on open burning is also accompanied by air quality monitoring and surveillance with relevant agencies, apart from collaboration between the regulators and the likely polluters for the purpose of effective enforcement of the law. However, in practice, regulations aimed at controlling open burning activities are extremely difficult to enforce effectively due to various factors, including the nature of the offence itself. This difficulty is compounded by the fact that Malaysia is also facing another wide array of diffuse, difficult-to-control air pollution sources in the form of transboundary haze pollution. This is a great challenge for Malaysian officials, who desire to control emissions but do not have authority over the sources. At present, the available international effort toward transboundary haze pollution is only through the ASEAN Agreement on Transboundary Haze Pollution. This agreement bears witness to the concern and interest of Malaysia and other ASEAN countries in preventing the deterioration of regional air quality due to transboundary haze pollution. The potential damage from transboundary pollution, and Malaysia's economic capacity and technological know-how are compelling reasons for the nation to be deeply engaged in regional and international environmental affairs. Overall, Malaysia is playing a strong role in solving this regional environmental problem through the ratification of the Agreement. However, greater regional as well as international environmental challenges concerning air pollution, including that of climate change, are such that Malaysia's initiatives will continue to be essential in the years ahead.

From this discussion, it is clear that Malaysia's pollution control law is complex and evolving both at international as well as domestic levels. Malaysia's environmental law, including that relating to air pollution control have been changing and moving away from a reactive approach of command and control systems toward a preventive and quality-based concept of regulation. As a developing country that continues to face rapid industrialization and urbanization, Malaysia always refer to countries with more experience, in order to have advanced strategies and technologies in air pollution control for best practices. Over the years, Malaysia has begun to search for a new path of sustainable development through the promotion of new approaches to environmental problems, reflecting new concepts in policy. There are other potential legal and regulatory instruments which are available for air pollution prevention and control. However, their application by Malaysia must take into consideration factors such as Malaysia's financial ability and capability to deliver the end result based on achievable targets. At the same time, while environmental law, which is applicable to control environmental pollution, needs to be dynamic in order to cover various sources of air pollution, the law must also be prepared to deal with emerging regional and global air pollution issues affecting the country.

Acknowledgment

This work is funded by the Fundamental Research Grant Scheme, Ministry of Higher Education Malaysia.

References

ACFA, The Asian Clean Fuel Association. (2012) "Malaysia to Implement EURO 4M in 2015." www.acfa.org.sg/newsletterinfocus08_01.php.

Aiken, Robert. (1982) *Development and Environment in Peninsular Malaysia*. Singapore: McGraw-Hill International.

ASMC, ASEAN Specialized Meteorological Center. (2016) "Regional Haze Situation." http://asmc.asean.org/home/.

Department of Environment (DOE). (2015a) *Annual Report (2014)*. Putrajaya: Jabatan Alam Sekitar.

Department of Environment (DOE). (2015b) *Environmental Quality Report (2014)*. Putrajaya: Jabatan Alam Sekitar.

Department of Environment (DOE). (2016a) "Haze Air Pollution Phenomena." www.doe.gov.my/portalv1/en/info-umum/jerebu-fenomena-pencemaan-udara/128.

Department of Environment (DOE). (2016b) "Air Pollutant Index (API)." www.doe.gov.my/portalv1/en/info-umum/english-air-pollutant-index-api/100.

Department of Environment (DOE). (2016c) "Best Available Techniques Guidance Document on Oil and Gas Industry." www.doe.gov.my/portalv1/wp-content/uploads/2014/07/BEST-AVAILABLE-TECHNIQUES-GUIDANCE-DOCUMENT-ON-OIL-AND-GAS-INDUSTRY.pdf.

Department of Environment (DOE). (2016d) "Air Pollutant Index of Malaysia." http://apims.doe.gov.my/v2/information.html.

Department of Environment (DOE). (2016e) "Chronology of Haze Episodes in Malaysia." www.doe.gov.my/portalv1/en/info-umum/info-kualiti-udara/kronologi-episod-jerebu-di-malaysia/319123.

Department of Meteorology. (2016a) "Current Sea Surface Temperature and Outlook for June to December (2016)." www.met.gov.my/documents/10661/75396/enso_outlook.pdf.

Department of Meteorology. (2016b) "Malaysia Fire Danger Rating System (FDRS)." www.met.gov.my/web/metmalaysia/climate/fdrs/malaysia.

Department of Road Transport. (2016) *Annual Report (2014)*. Putrajaya: Jabatan Pengangkutan Jalan.

Department of Statistics Malaysia. (2016a) "Malaysia Population Clock." www.statistics.gov.my/.

Department of Statistics Malaysia. (2016b) "Gross Domestic Product Fourth Quarter (2015)." www.statistics.gov.my/index.php?r=column/cthemeByCat&cat=100&bul_id=QklmOEdsaXMra29vdHNjNFF1UFErdz09&menu_id=TE5CRUZCblh4ZTZMODZIbmk2aWRRQT09.

Economic Planning Unit. (2015) *Eleventh Malaysia Plan 2016–2020*. Kuala Lumpur: Percetakan Nasional Malaysia Berhad.

Heilmann, Daniel. (2015) "After Indonesia's Ratification: The ASEAN Agreement on Transboundary Haze Pollution and Its Effectiveness as a Regional Environmental Governance Tool." *Journal of Current Southeast Asian Affairs* 34: 3.

Hirota, K. (2010) "Comparative Studies on Vehicle Related Policies for Air Pollution Reduction in Ten Asian Countries." *Sustainability* 2: 145–162.

International Law Commission. (2015) "Annual Reports: Report on the Work of the Sixty-Seventh Session." http://legal.un.org/ilc/reports/2015/.

Jayakumar, S., T. Koh, R. Beckman, and H.D. Phan, eds. (2015) *Transboundary Pollution Evolving Issues of International Law and Policy*. Cheltenham: NUS Center for International Law, Edward Elgar Publishing.

Ministry of Natural Resources and Environment (2016) "Total Forested Areas in Malaysia (1990–2014)." www.nre.gov.my/en-my/Forestry/Pages/Statistics-Forest.aspx.

Ministry of Science, Technology and the Environment. (2002) *National Policy on the Environment*. Kuala Lumpur: Ministry of Science, Technology and the Environment, Malaysia.

Ministry of Transport. (2014) *Transport Statistics Malaysia*. Putrajaya: Ministry of Transport.

Mustafa, Maizatun. (2013) *Environmental Law in Malaysia*. The Netherlands: Kluwer Law International.

Mustafa, Maizatun, S.Z. Syed Abdul Kader, and A. Sufian. (2012) "Coping with Climate Change through Air Pollution Control: Some Legal Initiatives from Malaysia." *International Proceedings of Chemical, Biological & Environmental* 33: 101.

Rosmiza, M.Z., W.P. Davies, C.R. Rosniza Aznie, M. Mazdi, and M.J. Jabi. (2014) "Farmers' Knowledge on Potential Uses of Rice Straw: An Assessment in MADA and Sekinchan, Malaysia." *Geografia* 10 (5).

Siegert, F. and A.A. Hoffmann. (2000) "The 1998 Forest Fires in East Kalimantan (Indonesia): A Quantitative Evaluation Using High Resolution, Multitemporal ERS-2 SAR Images and NOAA-AVHRR Hotspot Data." *Remote Sensing of Environment* 72: 64–77.

Tan, A. (2014) "The Haze Crisis in Southeast Asia: Assessing Singapore Transboundary Haze Pollution Act (2014)." http://law.nus.edu.sg/wps/.

Tiraieyari, Neda, Neda, A. Hamzah, and B. Abu Samah. (2014) "Organic Farming and Sustainable Agriculture in Malaysia: Organic Farmers' Challenges towards Adoption." *Asian Social Science* 10 (4): 1–7.

UNEP, United Nations Environmental Program. (2016) "Cleaner Motorcycle. Promoting the Use of Four-Stroke Engines." www.unep.org/transport/pcfv/PDF/KGR_CleanerMotorcycles_new.pdf.

United Nations General Assembly. (2012) "The Future We Want." Resolution Adopted by the General Assembly on July 27 (2012) New York: UN. https://sustainabledevelopment.un.org/futurewewant.html.

Varkkey, H. (2015) *The Haze Problem in Southeast Asia: Palm Oil and Patronage*. Oxon: Routledge.

World Bank. (2016) "Overview: Malaysia." www.worldbank.org/en/country/malaysia/overview.

World Health Organization. (2012) "Sixty-eighth World Health Assembly." www.who.int/mediacentre/events/2015/wha68/en/.

29

Regulating trans-boundary haze in Southeast Asia

Lahiru S. Wijedasa, Zeehan Jaafar, Mary Rose C. Posa and Janice S.H. Lee

Global carbon cycle and emissions

Greenhouse gases in the Earth's atmosphere, particularly carbon dioxide (CO_2), have continued to increase despite overwhelming evidence of their destabilizing effects on the global climate (IPCC 2014). The release of carbon from anthropogenic sources has been unprecedented, averaging at approximately 10 gigatons of carbon (GtC) per year from 2005 to 2014 (Le Quéré et al. 2015). The average global atmospheric CO_2 concentration is estimated to be 403.57 $\pm$ 0.1 ppm (Dlugokencky and Tans 2014), having long transgressed the proposed safe threshold of 350 ppm (Rockström et al. 2009). Future average global atmospheric CO_2 concentration is predicted to remain above 400 ppm for the foreseeable future (Betts et al. 2016). Reducing the amount of carbon dioxide released to the atmosphere must be a critical international priority.

Land use and land cover change (LULCC) is the second largest anthropogenic source of carbon dioxide, contributing to 25 percent of total emissions. Most of the net carbon flux from LULCC activities is attributable to deforestation in the tropics (Houghton 2008; Houghton et al. 2012) where fire is a common means of land clearance (Van der Werf et al. 2010). Southeast Asia is a major source of carbon emissions (Calle et al. 2016) as conversion to cash crop plantations such as oil palm and pulpwood continues to drive natural habitat losses (Stibig et al. 2014). In particular, the tropical peat swamp forest ecosystem (TPSF) in Southeast Asia, covering over 200,000 km^2, represents a significant carbon pool (Page, Rieley, and Banks 2011). The organic peat soils on which TPSF establish are formed from un-decayed vegetation accumulated over thousands of years in waterlogged areas and can be tens of meters deep (Page et al. 2004; Dommain, Couwenberg, and Joosten 2011; Dommain et al. 2014). This below-ground carbon source is not accounted for in many carbon budget analyses, and may increase emission estimates by 25 percent (Harris et al. 2012; Houghton et al. 2012).

Over the past three decades, TPSF have been deforested at an alarming rate and converted to large and small-scale plantations (Miettinen et al. 2016). In Peninsular Malaysia, and the islands of Sumatra and Borneo where TPSF was once common, only 29 percent of forest cover remains (Miettinen, Shi, and Liew 2012, 2016). The loss of TPSF is strongly associated with fire, especially because anthropogenic disturbances adversely impact hydrological processes and make peat soils vulnerable to ignition (Van der Werf et al. 2008; Page and Hooijer 2016). Drained TPSFs tend to burn extensively and repeatedly, with deep peat undergoing a smoldering combustion that can persist for weeks or months (Turetsky et al. 2015). In addition to the globally significant amounts of carbon dioxide released, particulate matter from peat fires cause a persistent trans-boundary air pollution, also commonly referred to as 'haze' (Heil, Langmann, and Aldrian 2007; Van der Werf et al. 2008; Hooijer et al. 2010).

El-Niño and history of fires across Southeast Asia

Fires occurrences in Southeast Asia have intensified over the last century (Van der Werf et al. 2008). Undisturbed tropical rainforests are fire resistant, but these forests become vulnerable to fire events during periods of low rainfall or by anthropogenic land use changes (Siegert et al. 2001). Prolonged drought conditions induced by the El-Niño Southern Oscillation (ENSO), coupled with the positive phase of the Indian Ocean Dipole (IOD), intensify burning and smoke episodes as dry vegetation becomes susceptible to ignition (Hendon 2003; Wang, Field, and Roswintiarti 2004; Van der Werf et al. 2008). Southeast Asian fire and haze episodes between 1960 and 2006 have coincided with ENSO and/or IOD conditions (Field et al. 2009). Burnt peatlands areas in particular are prone to recurrent fires (Toriyama et al. 2014). These conditions lead to more land converted through burning, and more fires burning out of control.

Furthermore, forests will likely continue to remain vulnerable to fire events as projected climate trends indicate the increase of dry periods, droughts (Dai 2011), as well as frequent and prolonged El-Niño conditions (Cai et al. 2014). However, even in the absence of prolonged droughts, alteration of natural systems has made them fire prone as exemplified by the 2013 Southeast Asian fire and haze events, which occurred in a year with above average rainfall. This suggests that anthropogenic modification of peatlands in particular, have resulted in fire-prone conditions outside of the El-Niño dry period (Gaveau et al. 2014; Turetsky et al. 2015; Kettridge et al. 2015).

Fire distribution

Fires, and recurrence of fires, across Southeast Asia are not evenly distributed; over 50 percent of fire events occur on peat soils that make up only 21 percent of the land area. A review of the fire hotspots – areas identified by satellite borne sensors as fire when the temperature detected is above a specified threshold – indicate different patterns of density and recurrence in fires on mineral and peat soils. Unlike fires on mineral soils, those on peat soils tend to recur at the same location and in high-density clusters. These differences have been attributed to the dominant organic matter within the substrate that burns during fire events.

When fires occur on mineral soil, the above ground vegetation, and sometimes roots, are burnt. The duration of fire events is limited by the biomass available. Once the above ground biomass is burnt, recurrence of fire is conditional on the rate of vegetation regrowth to support subsequent fire events. If the land is converted to industrial plantations post fire, plantation management practice fire management by limiting biomass accumulation. The low availability of flammable biomass limits the duration in which a fire burns, the density of fires, and the recurrence of fires.

Peat swamp forests store the highest density of carbon among all terrestrial ecosystems (UNEP 2012). In addition to the above ground biomass similar to those found on mineral soils, peat soils confer supplementary biomass. Peat soils average 8 m deep, and can be as deep as 30 m. Southeast Asian peat soils are made up of 60 percent or more carbon, and store up to 70 Gt of carbon (Page, Rieley, and Banks 2011). Accumulation of such vast quantities of carbon in the soil resulted from the permanent inundation of water and constant biomass input from forest vegetation, processes that supersede carbon loss through soil erosion and microbial breakdown of organic matter. Conversion of peatlands requires draining of waterlogged peat soils to create an aerobic environment for agricultural crops such as oil palm and *Acacia* (Hooijer et al. 2012). The drying of carbon rich peat soils makes the disturbed ecosystem vulnerable to fires (Konecny et al. 2015; Cattau et al. 2016). Fires that burn the above ground biomass ignite the underlying peat, which in turn continue to smolder long after the above ground biomass has been exhaustively burnt. These fires can travel below ground, and ignite adjacent peat areas leading to high-density fires. As most of the carbon source in peatlands is stored below ground, of which only a fraction burns in each fire event, fire recurrence is not contingent on above ground biomass regrowth and tends to recur in the same location. The recurrence and density of fires on peatlands is the primary driver of haze events. With up to 39 percent (Miettinen and Liew 2010; Miettinen, Shi, and Liew 2012; Wijedasa et al. 2012) of original peat swamp forests now converted to agriculture, and a similar proportion under various stages of degradation, flammable peatland area has increased greatly. Consequently, high intensity, recurrent fires that cause significant atmospheric pollution are now frequent occurrences outside of El-Niño conditions.

Fire timing and the 2013 haze event

Over the past 15 years, Southeast Asian fires have been closely linked with the El-Niño conditions and lower rainfall. Low rainfall resulted in drier biomass prone to ignition, and caused uncontrolled fires and peak fire events. Distribution of fires in El-Niño years mirror peatland distribution. Water tables in peatlands under agriculture are kept low to permit agriculture. The low rainfall in El-Niño years further lowers the water table, exposing a greater volume of dry, flammable, and carbon-rich peat soil. Once ignited, accidental or otherwise, dry peatlands burn for long periods.

The 2013 fire and haze event was unusual because it occurred outside an El-Niño period (Gaveau et al. 2014). Fires of this particular event in Sumatra occurred in a small area, over a long duration, in a year that experienced higher than average rainfall. Most of the areas burnt were not forested, demonstrating the natural resistance of intact peat swamp forests to fire. Further, in 2013, a high number of peatland fires was localized to a small area in the province of Riau in Sumatra (Gaveau et al. 2014), although this phenomenon is yet to be studied.

What is 'trans-boundary haze'?

Unregulated trans-boundary atmospheric pollution has far-reaching consequences beyond the area of origin. In Southeast Asia, resultant smoke from the burning of plant biomass, especially on the islands of Borneo, Kalimantan, and Sumatra, adversely impacts the air quality of neighboring nations. Trans-boundary air pollution in this region has increased in frequency, intensity, and severity over the past five decades (Heil and Goldammer 2001). Yet, attempts to curb this phenomenon have met with little success (Putri 2014). Burning is cheap and convenient, and continues to be the choice method for land clearing by agri-industrial commercial oil palm and pulpwood companies, as well as smaller-scale plantation developers. Extant vegetation in ecosystems ranging from primary rainforests, to agricultural lands and plantations, to peatlands, are deliberately burnt to secure arable areas (Tacconi and Vayda 2006). Burning activities begin in May and end in November, and peak during the inter-monsoon dry season between the months of July and October (Heil and Goldammer 2001; Nichol 1998). Gaseous emissions and particulate matter from fire sources form smoke plumes that are transported by prevailing winds to other parts of

Indonesia, as well as neighboring Brunei, Cambodia, Malaysia, Philippines, Singapore, Thailand and Vietnam (Heil and Goldammer 2001; Aiken 2004). This trans-boundary air pollution is specifically referred to as 'trans-boundary haze' or in the regional context, simply as 'haze'.

Biomass burning, emissions and particulates

In 1996–1997, the region experienced the strongest ENSO and IOD in the twentieth century (Gaveau et al. 2014). This weather anomaly coincided with the largest fire event in the past two decades; a total of 97,000–117,000 km^2 of primary rainforests and peatlands were destroyed on the islands of Borneo and Sumatra (Murdiyarso and Adiningsih 2007; Tacconi, Moore, and Kaimowitz 2007). Carbon emissions were reported to be 0.81–2.57 Pg (Page et al. 2002) and the Pollutants Standard Index in Singapore peaked at 138.

Burning and haze events in Sumatra in June 2013 were unprecedented in the emission of atmospheric pollutants; carbon emissions were reported to be approximately 0.031 Pg (Gaveau et al. 2014). The Pollutants Standard Index (PSI) in Singapore and Indonesia reached hazardous levels, with values that spiked above 400 (average daily PSI from January to June 2013 has been 10–30), while in Malaysia, the Air Pollution Index values reached 750 (Jaafar and Loh 2014; Velasco and Rastan 2015). On June 24, 2013 alone, NOAA satellite 18 detected 437 discrete fire hotspots on Sumatra (Jaafar and Loh 2014). Yet, in 2013, there were no climate or weather anomalies; and the year was considered to experience mild to moderate ENSO with higher than average rainfall, except for a brief dry spell that preceded the fire event (Gaveau et al. 2014). Further, the 2013 burning episode was short-lived, and the area burned was a fraction of that in 1996–1997. The comparatively high carbon emission from the 2013 event was attributed to the disproportionately larger area of peatlands that was burned (Gaveau et al. 2014). This anomalous pattern, in which fire and haze events persist in non-ENSO years and cause severe atmospheric pollution, is hypothesized to continue with ongoing peatland developments in the Southeast Asian region (Gaveau et al. 2014).

The use of fire to clear vegetation in initial land use clearance, or as a widely used tool to dispose of organic matter, is common throughout all agriculture systems (Saharjo and Munoz 2005; Saharjo 2007). However, the modification of existing ecosystems and drying of peatlands by drainage for agriculture has increased the chances of these fires going out of control. It is widely accepted that most fire ignitions that result in trans-boundary smoke pollution are anthropogenic (Cattau et al. 2016; Gaveau et al. 2016). While dry weather does increase the occurrence of flammable conditions, the latter do not ignite fires.

The development of peatlands continues to drive forest fires. Fires in 2015 for example, were identified as the second worst burning event in the past two decades; 25 percent of the 26,100 km^2 burned were on peatlands (Tacconi 2016). The resultant emissions, estimated to be 1.75 GtCO_2e, were twice that of Germany's annual emission rates (Tacconi 2016).

There are two predominant types of fires, flaming and smoldering, that cause smoke plumes and haze (Cochrane 2003). Flaming fires release vast quantities of energy and are characterized by visible flames; these fires are detected from space. Smoldering fires are low temperature flameless fires that slowly burn over time, are hard to suppress, and can continue to burn underground for prolonged duration (Rein et al. 2008; Prat-Guitart et al. 2016; Wijedasa 2016). Often major fire fronts are flaming fires which are followed behind by smoldering fires (Lacaux, Delmas, and Jambert 1996; Wooster et al. 2011). While both fire types produce haze, the quantity and persistence of pollutants differ. Flaming fires produce large quantities of instantaneous haze, resulting in episodic peak PSI values, whereas smoldering fires produce similar haze quantities over a prolonged period while retaining the potential to cause high PSI values.

Impacts of biomass burning and haze events

Impacts of biomass burning and haze events are known, but most originate from reports based on anecdotal observations or studies that are qualitative in nature. When biomass, vegetation and peat in this instance, are burned, more than 100 compounds are released (Muraleedharan et al. 2000a, 2000b; Radojevic 2003; Reddington et al. 2014). Of these, pollutants such as CO, NO, NO_2, O_3, and SO_2 inform air quality indices. Other emissions include petroleum hydrocarbons, aldehydes, polynuclear aromatic hydrocarbons, acetic acid, phenol and trace metals (Radojevic 2003; He, Zielinska, and Balasubramanian 2010; Betha et al. 2013; Hayasaka et al. 2014). Impacts of biomass burning and haze events are pervasive, with repercussions on human health, regional economies, and the environment.

Impacts to natural ecosystems and the environment

Natural ecosystems in Southeast Asia are considered some of the most biologically diverse in the world, and support high levels of endemism (Myers et al. 2000; Sodhi et al. 2004; Barber 2009). Many of these ecosystems are already anthropogenically threatened, and are considered global conservation priorities (Carpenter and Springer 2005; Burke et al. 2011; Sodhi and Ehrlich 2010).

Studies on the detrimental effects of biomass burning and resultant haze have focused primarily on terrestrial and atmospheric systems. In particular, primary impacts to terrestrial ecosystems, especially in terms of habitat losses or burnt areas, remain the key criteria included in almost all studies reporting burning events. These fires destroy sessile and sedentary organisms, while displacing vagile ones. With most mineral soil forests cleared, peatlands bear the brunt of current conversion to palm oil and pulp plantations, often achieved through burning. Draining and subsequent burning of peatlands impact ecosystem functionality and affect hydrology of the area (Yule 2010; Evers et al. 2017; Wijedasa et al. 2016a, Wijedasa et al. 2016c). Large-scale losses in biodiversity within burnt areas have not been quantified, but primate behavior and abundance (Morrogh-Bernard et al. 2003; Cheyne 2008), avian fauna composition (Posa 2011; Koh et al. 2011; Posa and Marques 2012), and freshwater ichthyofauna composition (Giam et al. 2012), are adversely impacted by habitat degradation and conversion in affected areas.

In addition to area burnt, key emissions from the smoke haze as a result of burning events, are tracked to inform pollution indices in the region. Unsurprisingly, the atmospheric system is another aspect of this phenomenon that has had much attention, ranging from analyses of compounds being released to characterizing the smoke from burnt areas (He, Zielinska, and Balasubramanian 2010; Hayasaka et al. 2014; Behera, Cheng, and Balasubramanian 2014; Fujii et al. 2015). Smoke aerosol released from the fires in September 1997 reduced 63–75 percent of photosynthetically active radiation (PAR) in Sumatra and central Kalimantan, compromising the ability of photosynthetic activities of primary producers (Kobayashi et al. 2004).

Topsoil and ash runoff during burning episodes increase nutrient concentration in aquatic systems, with high likelihoods of contamination of groundwater and aquifers (Hammen 2007). In addition to runoffs, dry and wet atmospheric deposition of higher concentrations of nutrients in the atmosphere during haze episodes translate to increased nutrient enrichment in aquatic systems (Sundarambal et al. 2010). Elevated nutrient concentrations in aquatic systems cause algal blooms and eutrophication, and can trigger cascading impacts such as seagrass-bed losses (Jaafar and Loh 2014; Abrams et al. 2015; Unsworth, Jones, and Cullen-Unsworth 2016).

Impacts to human health

Hazardous air quality such as those experienced during haze episodes, are associated with increased mortality and incidences of respiratory morbidity (Sastry 2002; Kunii et al. 2002; Jayachandran

2006). In addition to chemical composition, particle sizes are relevant to air quality; particles with diameter less than 10 micrometers (PM_{10}) are able to enter the respiratory tract while those with diameter less than 2.5 micrometers ($PM_{2.5}$) are able to enter the bloodstream (McClellan 2002; Betha et al. 2013). Exposure to air with high particle concentration can cause inflammation of respiratory tracts, reduce lung function, and exacerbate coughs, bronchitis, and asthmatic attacks (Aditama 2000; Frankenberg, Mckee, and Thomas 2005). In Indonesia, 19 deaths were attributed to the fire events in 2015, and affected millions of people in the region, especially those with pre-existing conditions (Tacconi 2016).

Impacts to regional economies

Economies of countries affected by biomass burning and haze suffered during these episodes. The poor, and often hazardous air quality had social implications. In the fire episodes of 2013, states of emergency were declared in burnt areas in Indonesia, as well as in Muar and Ledang in Malaysia where air pollution was deemed hazardous. Consequently, hundreds of schools were closed and many flights were canceled in these areas (Carrasco 2013; Jaafar and Loh 2014). The 1997 haze was estimated to cause losses of USD $4.5 billion while the recent 2015 event has been estimated to cause losses of USD $16 billion. The hazardous air quality was estimated to cost USD $1 billion in tourism revenue (Park and Ng 2013).

Economic losses to regional economies from the 1997 and 2015 haze episodes were estimated at totals of approximately USD $4.5 billion (Glover and Jessup 1999; Tomich, Thomas, and Van Noordwijk 2004) and USD $16.5 billion (Chisholm, Wijedasa, and Swinfield 2016), respectively. Tourism and aviation sectors were most severely affected. Singapore suffered a substantial loss in the tourism sector in 1997, estimated at USD $136–210 million (Quah 2002). Similarly, Malaysia estimated a loss of USD $700 million in the aviation industry (Nichol 1998). Various industries in Indonesia likely suffered losses, but this was not reported.

Smoke and particulates generated during burning episodes can severely limit visibility, in some instances to almost 0 km (Wang, Field, and Roswintiarti 2004). News reports cite the smoke haze for several watercraft, and aircraft, collisions. For example, smoke haze was a contributing factor in the collision between two bulk carriers 6.6 km off eastern Singapore on July 1, 2013. In Singapore, air pollution from haze episodes partially blocks sunlight, and affects electric power generation of solar photovoltaic systems, with losses of up to 25 percent (Nobre et al. 2016).

Sustainable solutions

"Zero-burning" legislation does exist in Indonesia and there are nationwide prohibitions against starting fires in or developing peat areas that are more than 3 m deep (Tan 2015). An entity found guilty of setting an illegal forest fire could be imprisoned for 5–15 years and fined up to 5 billion Rupiah (USD $420,000) (Tan 2015). However, explicit allowances are made for local communities to use fires for land clearing (Tan 2015). The complexities of political governance, elite capture from land use, as well as entrenched economic interests in plantation development in Indonesia result in ineffective enforcement of, and compliance with, these national legislations (Varkkey 2012; Tan 2015).

Trans-boundary environmental problems are difficult to resolve due to disputes over territorial sovereignty and placing the onus of environmental protection on economically beneficial industries in the offending country. Self-interests and fear of challenging other nations' rights to economic development often result in little action toward addressing an international environmental problem. The Association of Southeast Asia Nations' (ASEAN) Agreement on Transboundary Haze Pollution is an example of a treaty which entails obligations for member states to co-operate on tackling the haze, but lacks state accountability and legally binding terms to hold offending countries responsible for the trans-boundary air pollution (Tan 2005). The Agreement came into force in 2003, with the ratification of Singapore, Malaysia, Myanmar, Brunei, Vietnam, Thailand, and the Lao People's Democratic Republic. Indonesia, where the majority of the haze originates from, only became a party to the Agreement in 2014, after the devastating 2013 haze event caused air quality indices in Malaysia and Singapore to reach hazardous levels. Although the Agreement has been a useful tool to encourage regional co-operation toward resolving the haze, the weak legislative framework and Indonesia's late entry into the Agreement has made it a less than effective tool in stemming the haze problem (Tan 2005; Yong and Peh 2014).

After the 2013 haze event, the Singapore Parliament passed the Transboundary Haze Pollution Act (THPA) which allows for imposition of fines on companies that cause or contribute to trans-boundary haze pollution in Singapore (Government of Singapore 2014; Lee et al. 2016). This trans-boundary legislation targets multinational palm oil and pulpwood companies that operate large plantation concessions in Sumatra and Kalimantan. By recognizing its own agribusiness sector as part of the problem and taking legal action against polluting companies in Indonesia, Singapore's THPA is making a regional environmental problem tractable by subjecting these companies to its judicial system (Lee et al. 2016). However, the THPA is also fraught with limitations. In reality, on the ground resistance from economic beneficiaries and supporters of plantation development will pose a challenge to the implementation of the THPA (Varkkey 2012). Additionally, prosecution of perpetrators responsible for fires hinges on accurately identifying these entities, a challenge introduced by land conflicts in Indonesia and unreliability of land-use maps (Gaveau et al. 2014, 2016).

At a bilateral level, Singapore and Malaysia coordinated fire mitigation efforts in various social and technical programs. In 2007, Singapore collaborated with the Jambi Provincial Government to supply meteorological equipment to monitor air and wind conditions, and developed alternative livelihood schemes in aquaculture so that farmers will not have to resort to burning to clear land for cultivation (Nazeer 2013). Despite initial uptake and enthusiasm from local communities, these programs have largely halted and the Singaporean government is awaiting a response from the Jambi Provincial Government for a renewal of the Memorandum of Understanding ("Lack of Progress on MOU to Combat Haze with Jambi 'Unfortunate': Masagos" 2016). Malaysia also had a similar partnership with the Riau Provincial Government which has come to a standstill (Quah and Varkkey 2013). More recently, Malaysia is working with Indonesia to develop a bilateral pact which looks into exchanging information on Malaysian palm oil companies operating in Indonesia, and establishing joint research focusing on fire prevention (Nazeer 2014). Several online platforms have been developed to monitor and respond to forest and land fires in ASEAN using near real-time satellite imagery and land use maps. Some examples include IndoFire, which is a collaborative effort between Australia and Indonesia (IndoFire, Indonesian Ministry of Forestry, The Insitute of Aeronautics and Space LAPAN, Indonesian Ministry of Environment, the Australian Government AusAID and the Western Australian Government Department Landgate 2016), the Haze Tracker, which is developed and maintained by the Singapore Institute of International Affairs (2016), and Global Forest Watch Fires, developed by the World Resources Institute (2016). In addition to monitoring fires real-time, an interactive map known as the Fire Risk Map on GFW-Fires shows where dry conditions increase fire risk in Indonesia and Malaysia and helps decision-makers take action to prevent fires before they ignite (Minnemeyer et al. 2016).

Of great importance and relevance to tackling the root of the haze is the issue of peatland protection and management (Page and Hooijer 2016). Satellite imagery of the June 2013 fires showed that burning of degraded peatlands accounted for more than 80 percent of the fires (Gaveau et al. 2014). The burning on peatlands also led to the catastrophic 2015 fires which had higher carbon emissions than the record breaking 1997/98 fires (Huijnen et al. 2016). In response to the ecological and humanitarian disaster from the 2015 haze, Indonesia's President Joko Widodo called for an end to licensing peatland concessions and pledged to restore peatlands through the Peatland Restoration Agency (Koswaraputra 2015; Indonesian President Joko Widodo Sets up Peatland Restoration Agency 2016; President of Indonesia 2016). The drainage of peatlands significantly damages peat ecosystems and reduces its resilience to fires (Page and Hooijer 2016). Therefore, 'sustainable' peatland development plans using any form of drainage, even with the best agricultural practices, cannot be considered to be sustainable (Evers et al. 2017). Peatland protection and supporting the long-term integrity of peatlands entails detailed attention to the hydrology of the system, as well as the restoration of native plant communities (Posa, Wijedasa, and Corlett 2011; Satura and Arumingtyas 2016; Wijedasa et al. 2016b). Resolving overlapping land ownership of peatlands is also crucial to developing the right policies for the long-term management of peat ecosystems (Page and Hooijer 2016).

On a local-scale, bottom-up initiatives can be encouraged through grassroots involvement to cultivate local ownership of fire prevention as well as sustainable land use development (Yong and Peh 2014). The Fire Free Village Program (FFVP) launched by a major pulp and paper company is an example of a community engagement program for local communities around their plantation concession in Riau ("A Step Closer towards National Movement, Fire-Free Village Program to Free Indonesia from Fire and Haze" 2016). The FFVP educates farmers on the importance of being prepared for fire disasters, and provides land clearing machinery to reduce land burning behavior by farmers. While this program is effective in reducing fire activity from land clearing, it has little effectiveness in reducing fire activity as a result of land tenure conflicts and retaliation against perceived unfair land allocation in Indonesia (Suvanto et al. 2004; Dennis et al. 2005). It is therefore highly crucial to gain a deeper understanding of the underlying social causes of fire activity in Indonesia (Dennis et al. 2005) and disentangle overlapping land claims on the ground (Gaveau et al. 2016) to develop appropriate local policies and hold relevant land owners accountable for burning activities.

The recurring social and economic consequences of the haze in Southeast Asia have spurred the enactment of various national and regional legislation, as well as bilateral partnerships with Indonesia to mitigate the haze. Remote sensing technologies have enabled the development of a range of online platforms which facilitate the monitoring of real-time fire activity. Recent spatial analyses show a large proportion of fires occurring over peatlands, which require stronger regulations for their protection and restoration. Hence, a framework of national and regional legislation, as well as real-time, monitoring capabilities do exist. However, the effectiveness of these legislations and technologies are hampered due to on-the-ground political and economic interests in unsustainable plantation development as well as unclear land tenure and mixed motivations from local communities on fire activity. At present, small wins against Southeast Asia's trans-boundary haze can be found in the penalization of companies for fire activity, consumer action to limit purchases from companies associated with burning and the successful engagement of local communities for fire prevention (Wijedasa, Posa, and Clements 2015; Jacobson 2016; "AStep Closer towards National Movement, Fire-Free Village Program to Free Indonesia from Fire and Haze" 2016). In the long term, clarifying land tenure procedures, ensuring peatland protection, and aligning agricultural development policies with ecosystem protection, hold the keys to a sustainable solution for the fire and haze problems in Southeast Asia.

Acknowledgements

LSW acknowledges funding from the Lady Yuen Peng McNeice Graduate Fellowship and support from the Center for Environmental Sensing and Modeling of the Singapore-MIT Alliance for Research and Technology. ZJ acknowledges funding from Herbert R. and Evelyn Axelrod Chair in Systematic Ichthyology in the Division of Fishes (USNM) and support from Department of Biological Sciences, National University of Singapore.

References

"A Step Closer towards National Movement, Fire-Free Village Program to Free Indonesia from Fire and Haze." (2016) *The Jakarta Post*, June 13. www.thejakartapost.com/adv/2016/06/13/a-step-closer-towards-national-movement-fire-free-village-program-to-free-indonesia-from-fire-and-haze.html.

Abrams, Jesse F., Sönke Hohn, Tim Rixen, Antje Baum, and Agostino Merico. (2015) "The Impact of Indonesian Peatland Degradation on Downstream Marine Ecosystems and the Global Carbon Cycle." *Global Change Biology* 22 (1), 325–337.

Aditama, Tjandra Y. (2000) "Impact of Haze from Forest Fire to Respiratory Health: Indonesian Experience." *Respirology* 5 (2): 169–174. doi: 10.1046/j.1440-1843.2000.00246.x.

Aiken, S. Robert. (2004) "Runaway Fires, Smoke-Aze Pollution and Unnatural Disasters in Indonesia." *The Geographical Review* 94 (1): 55–79.

Barber, Paul H. (2009) "The Challenge of Understanding the Coral Triangle Biodiversity Hotspot." *Journal of Biogeography* 36 (10): 1845–1846. doi: 10.1111/j.1365-2699.(2009)02198.x.

Behera, Sailesh N., Jinping Cheng, and Rajasekhar Balasubramanian. (2014) "In Situ Acidity and pH of Size-Fractionated Aerosols during a Recent Smoke-Haze Episode in Southeast Asia." *Environmental Geochemistry and Health* 37 (5): 843–859. doi: 10.1007/s10653-014-9660-1.

Betha, Raghu, Maharani Pradani, Puji Lestari, Umid Man Joshi, Jeffrey S. Reid, and Rajasekhar Balasubramanian. (2013) "Chemical Speciation of Trace Metals Emitted from Indonesian Peat Fires for Health Risk Assessment." *Atmospheric Research* 122 (May 1998): 571–578. doi:10.1016/j.atmosres.(2012)05.024.

Betts, Richard A., Chris D. Jones, Jeff R. Knight, Ralph F. Keeling, and John J. Kennedy. (2016) "El Nino and a record CO_2 rise." *Nature Climate Change* 6: 806–810. doi: 10.1038/nclimate3063.

Burke, Lauretta, Kathleen Reytar, Mark Spalding, and Allison Perry. (2011) "Reefs at Risk Revisited." *National Geographic*. Washington, DC: World Resources Institute. doi:10.1016/0022-0981(79)90136-9.

Cai, Wenju, Agus Santoso, Guojian Wang, Evan Weller, Lixin Wu, Karumuri Ashok, Yukio Masumoto, and Toshio Yamagata. (2014) "Increased Frequency of Extreme Indian Ocean Dipole Events due to Greenhouse Warming." *Nature* 510 (7504): 254–258. doi: 10.1038/nature13327.

Calle, Leonardo, Josep G. Canadell, Prabir Patra, Philippe Ciais, Kazuhito Ichii, Hanqin Tian, Masayuki Kondo, et al. (2016) "Regional Carbon Fluxes from Land Use and Land Cover Change in Asia, 1980–2009" *Environmental Research Letters* 11 (7): 74011. doi: 10.1088/1748-9326/11/7/074011.

Carpenter, Kent E., and Victor G. Springer. (2005) "The Center of the Center of Marine Shore Fish Biodiversity: The Philippine Islands." *Environmental Biology of Fishes* 72 (4): 467–480. doi: 10.1007/s10641-004-3154-4.

Carrasco, Luis R. (2013) "Silver Lining of Singapore's Haze." *Science* 341 (July): 342–343.

Cattau, Megan E., Mark E. Harrison, Iwan Shinyo, Sady Tungau, María Uriarte, and Ruth DeFries. (2016) "Sources of Anthropogenic Fire Ignitions on the Peat-Swamp Landscape in Kalimantan, Indonesia." *Global Environmental Change* 39: 205–219. doi: 10.1016/j.gloenvcha.(2016)05.005.

Cheyne, Susan M. (2008) "Effects of Meteorology, Astronomical Variables, Location and Human Disturbance on the Singing Apes: *Hylobates albibarbis*." *American Journal of Primatology* 70 (4): 386–392. doi: 10.1002/ajp.20502.

Chisholm, Ryan A., Lahiru S. Wijedasa, and Tom Swinfield. (2016) "The Need for Long-Term Remedies for Indonesia's Forest Fires." *Conservation Biology* 30 (1): 5–6. doi: 10.1111/cobi.12662.

Cochrane, Mark A. (2003) "Fire Science for Rainforests." *Nature* 421 (6926): 913–919. doi: 10.1038/nature01437.

Dai, Aiguo. (2011) "Drought under Global Warming: A Review." *Wiley Interdisciplinary Reviews: Climate Change* 2 (1): 45–65. doi: 10.1002/wcc.81.

Dennis, Rona A., Judith Mayer, Grahame Applegate, Unna Chokkalingam, Carol J. Pierce Colfer, Iwan Kurniawan, Henry Lachowski, et al. (2005) "Fire, People and Pixels: Linking Social Science and Remote Sensing to Understand Underlying Causes and Impacts of Fires in Indonesia." *Human Ecology* 33 (4): 465–504. doi: 10.1007/s10745-005-5156-z.

Dlugokencky, Edward J., and Pieter Tans. (2014) "Trends in Atmospheric Carbon Dioxide, National Oceanic & Atmospheric Administration, Earth System Research Laboratory (NOAA/ESRL)."

Dommain, René, John Couwenberg, Paul H. Glaser, Hans Joosten, I. Nyoman N. Suryadiputra. (2014) "Carbon Storage and Release in Indonesian Peatlands since the Last Deglaciation." *Quaternary Science Reviews* 97: 1–32. doi: 10.1016/j.quascirev.(2014)05.002.

Dommain, René, John Couwenberg, and Hans Joosten. (2011) "Development and Carbon Sequestration of Tropical Peat Domes in South-East Asia: Links to Post-Glacial Sea-Level Changes and Holocene Climate Variability." *Quaternary Science Reviews* 30 (7–8): 999–1010. doi: 10.1016/j.quascirev.(2011)01.018.

Evers, S., C.M. Yule, R. Padfield, R., P. O'Reilly, and H. Varkkey. (2017) "Keep Wetlands Wet: The Myth of Sustainable Development of Tropical Peatlands – Implications For Policies And Management." *Global Change Biology*, 23 (2): 534–549.

Field, Robert D., Guido R. Van Der Werf, and Samuel S.P. Shen. (2009) "Human Amplification of Drought-Induced Biomass Burning in Indonesia Since 1960." *Nature Geoscience* 2 (3): 185–188.

Frankenberg, Elizabeth, Douglas McKee, and Duncan Thomas. (2005) "Health Consequences of Forest Fires in Indonesia." *Demography* 42 (1): 109–129.

Fujii, Yusuke, Haruo Kawamoto, Susumu Tohno, Masafumi Oda, Windy Iriana, and Puji Lestari. (2015) "Characteristics of Carbonaceous Aerosols Emitted from Peatland Fire in Riau, Sumatra, Indonesia (2): Identification of Organic Compounds." *Atmospheric Environment* 110: 1–7. doi: 10.1016/j.atmosenv.(2015)03.042.

Gaveau, David L.A., Romain Pirard, Mohammad A. Salim, Prayoto Tonoto, Husna Yaen, Sean A. Parks, and Rachel Carmenta. (2016) "Overlapping Land Claims Limit the Use of Satellites to Monitor No-Deforestation Commitments and No-Burning Compliance." *Conservation Letters* 10 (2): 257–264.

Gaveau, David L. A., Mohammad A. Salim, Kristell Hergoualc'h, Bruno Locatelli, Sean Sloan, Martin Wooster, Miriam E. Marlier, et al. (2014) "Major Atmospheric Emissions from Peat Fires in Southeast Asia during Non-Drought Years: Evidence from the 2013 Sumatran Fires." *Scientific Reports* 4: 1–7. doi: 10.1038/srep06112.

Giam, Xingli, Lian P. Koh, Heok H. Tan, Jukka Miettinen, Hugh T.W. Tan, and Peter K.L. Ng. (2012) "Global Extinctions of Freshwater Fishes Follow Peatland Conversion in Sundaland." *Frontiers in Ecology and the Environment* 10 (9): 465–470. doi: 10.1890/110182.

Glover, David, and Timothy Jessup, eds. (1999) *Indonesia's Fires and Haze: The Cost of Catastrophe.* Singapore: Markono Print Media Pte Ltd.

Government of Singapore. (2014) *Transboundary Haze Pollution Act 2014 (No. 24 of 2014).* Vol. (2014). http://statutes.agc.gov.sg/aol/download/0/0/pdf/binaryFile/pdfFile.pdf?CompId:113ccc86-73fd-48c9-8570-650a8d1b7288.

Hammen, Volker C. (2007) "Long-Time Risk of Groundwater/drinking Water Pollution with Sulphuric Compounds Beneath Burned Peatlands in Indonesia." *Water Science and Technology* 56 (1): 253–258. doi: 10.2166/wst.(2007)459.

Harris, Nancy L., Sandra Brown, Stephen C. Hagen, Sassan S. Saatchi, Silvia Petrova, William Salas, Matthew C. Hansen, Peter V. Potapov, and Alexander Lotsch. (2012) "Baseline Map of Carbon Emissions from Deforestation in Tropical Regions." *Science* 336 (June): 1573–1576. doi:10.1126/science.1217962.

Hayasaka, Hiroshi, Izumi Noguchi, Erianto I. Putra, Nina Yulianti, and Krishna Vadrevu. (2014) "Peat-Fire-Related Air Pollution in Central Kalimantan, Indonesia." *Environmental Pollution* 195: 257–266. doi: 10.1016/j.envpol.(2014)06.031.

He, J., B. Zielinska, and R. Balasubramanian. (2010) "Composition of Semi-Volatile Organic Compounds in the Urban Atmosphere of Singapore: Influence of Biomass Burning." *Atmospheric Chemistry and Physics* 10 (23): 11401–11413. doi: 10.5194/acp-10-11401-(2010).

Heil, Angelika and Johan Goldammer. (2001) "Smoke-Haze Pollution: A Review of the 1997 Episode in Southeast Asia." *Regional Environmental Change* 2 (1): 24–37.

Heil, Angelika, Baerbel Langmann, and Edvin Aldrian. (2007) "Indonesian Peat and Vegetation Fire Emissions: Study on Factors Influencing Large-Scale Smoke Haze Pollution Using a Regional Atmospheric Chemistry Model." *Mitigation and Adaptation Strategies for Global Change* 12 (1): 113–133. doi: 10.1007/s11027-006-9045-6.

Hendon, Harry H. (2003) "Indonesian Rainfall Variability: Impacts of ENSO and Local Air-Sea Interaction." *Journal of Climate* 16 (11): 1775–1790. doi:10.1175/1520-0442(2003)016<1775:IRVIOE>2.0.CO;2.

Hooijer, Aljosja, Susan E. Page, J. G. Canadell, Marcus Silvius, J. Kwadijk, H. Wösten, and J. Jauhiainen. (2010) "Current and Future CO_2 Emissions from Drained Peatlands in Southeast Asia." *Biogeosciences* 7 (5): 1505–1514. doi: 10.5194/bg-7-1505-(2010).

Hooijer, Aljosja, Susan E. Page, J. Jauhiainen, W.A. Lee, X.X. Lu, A. Idris, and G. Anshari. (2012) "Subsidence and Carbon Loss in Drained Tropical Peatlands." *Biogeosciences* 9: 1053–1071. doi: 10.5194/bg-9-1053-(2012).

Houghton, Richard A. (2008) "Carbon Flux to the Atmosphere from Land-Use Changes: 1850–2005" Carbon Dioxide Information Analysis Center, Oak Ridge National Laboratory, US Department of Energy, Oak Ridge, TN: In *TRENDS: A Compendium of Data on Global Change*. http://cdiac.ornl.gov/trends/landuse/houghton/houghton.html.

Houghton, Richard A., Jo I. House, Julia Pongratz, Guido R. Van Der Werf, Ruth S. Defries, Mathew C. Hansen, Corinne Le Quéré, and Navin Ramankutty. (2012) "Carbon Emissions from Land Use and Land-Cover Change." *Biogeosciences* 9 (12): 5125–5142. doi: 10.5194/bg-9-5125-(2012).

Huijnen, Vincent, Martin J. Wooster, Johannes W. Kaiser, David L. A. Gaveau, Johannes Flemming, Mark Parrington, Antje Inness, Daniel Murdiyarso, B. Main, and Michiel van Weele. (2016) "Fire Carbon Emissions over Maritime Southeast Asia in 2015 Largest since 1997." *Scientific Reports* 6 (February): 26886. doi:10.1038/srep26886.

"IndoFire, Indonesian Ministry of Forestry, The Institute of Aeronautics and Space LAPAN,Indonesian Ministry of Environment, the Australian Government AusAID and the Western Australian Government Department Landgate." (2016) http://indofire.landgate.wa.gov.au/.

"Indonesian President Joko Widodo Sets up Peatland Restoration Agency." (2016) *The Straits Times*, January 13. www.straitstimes.com/asia/se-asia/indonesian-president-joko-widodo-sets-up-peatland-restoration-agency.

IPCC. (2014) *Climate Change 2014: Synthesis Report*. Contribution of Working Groups I, II and III to the Fifth Assessment Report of the Intergovernmental Panel on Climate, edited by The Core Writing Team, Rajendra K. Pachauri, and Leo A. Meyer. Geneva, Switzerland: IPCC. http://epic.awi.de/37530/1/IPCC_AR5_SYR_Final.pdf.

Jaafar, Zeehan, and Tse L. Loh. (2014) "Linking Land, Air and Sea: Potential Impacts of Biomass Burning and the Resultant Haze on Marine Ecosystems of Southeast Asia." *Global Change Biology* 20 (9): 2701–2707. doi: 10.1111/gcb.12539.

Jacobson, Philip. (2016) "Company Ordered to Pay Record $76m over Fires in Sumatra." *Mongabay*, August 12. https://news.mongabay.com/2016/08/company-ordered-to-pay-record-76m-over-fires-in-sumatra/.

Jayachandran, Seema. (2006) "Air Quality and Early-Life Mortality: Evidence from Indonesia's Wildfires." *UCLA*. doi:10.1353/jhr.(2009)0001.

Kettridge, Nicholas, Merrit R. Turetsky, James H. Sherwood, Dan K. Thompson, C.A. Miller, Brian W. Benscoter, Mike D. Flannigan, Mike B. Wotton, and James M. Waddington. (2015) "Moderate Drop in Water Table Increases Peatland Vulnerability to Post-Fire Regime Shift." *Scientific Reports* 5: 8063. doi: 10.1038/srep08063.

Kobayashi, Hideki, Tsuneo Matsunaga, Akira Hoyano, Masatoshi Aoki, Daisuke Komori, and Samakkee Boonyawat. (2004) "Satellite Estimation of Photosynthetically Active Radiation in Southeast Asia: Impacts of Smoke and Cloud Cover." *Journal of Geophysical Research* 109 (D4). doi:10.1029/2003JD003807.

Koh, Lian P., Jukka Miettinen, Soo C. Liew, and Jaboury Ghazoul. (2011) "Remotely Sensed Evidence of Tropical Peatland Conversion to Oil Palm." *Proceedings of the National Academy of Sciences of the United States of America* 108 (12): 5127–5132. doi: 10.1073/pnas.1018776108.

Konecny, Kristina, Uwe Ballhorn, Peter Navratil, Juilson Jubanski, Susan E. Page, Kevin Tansey, Aljosja Hooijer, Ronald Vernimmen, and Florian Siegert. (2015) "Variable Carbon Losses from Recurrent Fires in Drained Tropical Peatlands." *Global Change Biology* 22: 1469–1480. doi: 10.1111/gcb.13186.

Koswaraputra, Dandy. (2015) "Jokowi Calls for Peatland Moratorium after 10 Killed by Haze." *The Jakarta Post*, October 23. http://m.thejakartapost.com/news/2015/10/23/jokowi-calls-peatland-moratorium-after-10-killed-haze.html#sthash.RkjeJGQm.dpuf.

Kunii, Osamu, Shuzo Kanagawa, Iwao Yajima, Yoshiharu Hisamatsu, Sombo Yamamura, Takashi Amagai, and Ir T. Sachrul Ismail. (2002) "The 1997 Haze Disaster in Indonesia: Its Air Quality and Health Effects." *Archives of Environmental Health* 57 (1): 16–22. doi: 10.1080/00039890209602912.

Lacaux, J.P., R. Delmas, C. Jambert and T.A.J. Kuhlbusch. (1996) "NO x Emissions from African Savanna Fires." *Journal of Geophysical Research: Atmospheres* 101 (D19): 23585–23595.

"Lack of Progress on MOU to Combat Haze with Jambi 'Unfortunate': Masagos." (2016) *Channel News Asia*, April 12. www.channelnewsasia.com/news/singapore/lack?of?progress?on?mou/2688664.html.

Le Quéré, C., R. Moriarty, R.M. Andrew, J.G. Canadell, S. Sitch, J.I. Korsbakken, P. Friedlingstein, et al. (2015) "Global Carbon Budget (2015)." *Earth System Science Data* 7 (2): 349–396. doi: 10.5194/essd-7-349-(2015).

Lee, Janice Ser Huay, Zeehan Jaafar, Alan Khee Jin Tan, Luis R Carrasco, J. Jackson Ewing, David P. Bickford, Edward L. Webb, and Lian Pin Koh. (2016) "Toward Clearer Skies: Challenges in Regulating Transboundary Haze in Southeast Asia." *Environmental Science and Policy* 55: 87–95. doi: 10.1016/j.envsci.(2015)09.008.

McClellan, Roger O. (2002) "Setting Ambient Air Quality Standards for Particulate Matter." *Toxicology* 181–182: 329–347. doi: 10.1016/S0300-483X(02)00459-6.

Miettinen, J., and S.C. Liew. (2010) "Degradation and Development of Peatlands in Peninsular Malaysia and in the Islands of Sumatra and Borneo since 1990." *Land Degradation & Development* 21: 285–296. doi: 10.1002/ldr.976.

Miettinen, J., C. Shi, and S.C. Liew. (2012) "Two Decades of Destruction in Southeast Asia's Peat Swamp Forests." *Frontiers in Ecology and the Environment* 10 (April): 124–128. doi:10.1890/100236.

Miettinen, J., C. Shi, and S.C. Liew. (2016) "Land Cover Distribution in the Peatlands of Peninsular Malaysia, Sumatra and Borneo in 2015 with Changes since 1990." *Global Ecology and Conservation* 6: 67–78. doi: 10.1016/j.gecco.(2016)02.004.

Minnemeyer, Susan, Sarah Sargent, Karyn Tabor, and Greg Soter. (2016) "As Indonesia's Dry Season Looms, a New Tool Can Predict Daily Forest Fire Risk." *World Resource Institute*, July 7. www.wri.org/print/44254.

Morrogh-Bernard, H., S. Husson, Susan E. Page, and John O. Rieley. (2003) "Population Status of the Bornean Orang-Utan (Pongo pygmaeus) in the Sebangau Peat Swamp Forest, Central Kalimantan, Indonesia." *Biological Conservation* 110 (1): 141–152. doi: 10.1016/S0006-3207(02)00186-6.

Muraleedharan, T.R., Miroslav Radojevic, Allan Waugh, and Anthony Caruana. (2000a) "Chemical Characterisation of the Haze in Brunei Darussalam during the 1998 Episode." *Atmospheric Environment* 34: 2725–2731. doi: 10.1016/S1352-2310(99)00341-6.

Muraleedharan, T.R., Miroslav Radojevic, Allan Waugh, and Anthony Caruana. (2000b) "Emissions from the Combustion of Peat: An Experimental Study." *Atmospheric Environment* 34: 3033–3035. doi: 10.1016/S1352-2310(99)00512-9.

Murdiyarso, Daniel, and Erna S. Adiningsih. (2007) "Climate Anomalies, Indonesian Vegetation Fires and Terrestrial Carbon Emissions." *Mitigation and Adaptation Strategies for Global Change* 12 (1): 101–112. doi: 10.1007/s11027-006-9047-4.

Myers, Norman, Russell A. Mittermeier, Cristina G. Mittermeier, Gustavo A.B. da Fonseca, and Jennifer Kent. (2000) "Biodiversity Hotspots for Conservation Priorities." *Nature* 403 (6772): 853–858. doi: 10.1038/35002501.

Nazeer, Zubaidah. (2013) "Singapore-Funded Efforts to Fight Haze Face Challenges on Ground." *The Straits Times*, July 3.

Nazeer, Zubaidah. (2014) "Indonesia, Malaysia Drawing up Haze Agreement." *The Jakarta Post*, September 26. www.thejakartapost.com/news/2014/09/26/indonesia-malaysia-drawing-haze-agreement.html.

Nichol, Janet. (1998) "New Directions Smoke Haze in Southeast Asia: A Predictable Recurrence." *Atmospheric Environment* 32 (14–15): 2715–2716. doi: 10.1016/S1352-2310(98)00086-7.

Nobre, André M., Shravan Karthik, Haohui Liu, Dazhi Yang, Fernando R. Martins, Enio B. Pereira, Ricardo Rüther, Thomas Reindl, and Ian M. Peters. (2016) "On the Impact of Haze on the Yield of Photovoltaic Systems in Singapore." *Renewable Energy* 89: 389–400. doi: 10.1016/j.renene.(2015)11.079.

Page, Susan E., and A. Hooijer. (2016) "In the Line of Fire: The Peatlands of Southeast Asia." *Philosophical Transactions of the Royal Society of London. Series B, Biological Sciences* 371 (1696): 20150176.

Page, Susan E., John O. Rieley, and Christopher J. Banks. (2011) "Global and Regional Importance of the Tropical Peatland Carbon Pool." *Global Change Biology* 17: 798–818. doi: 10.1111/j.1365-2486.(2010)02279.x.

Page, Susan E., Florian Siegert, John O. Rieley, and Hans-dieter V. Boehm. (2002) "The Amount of Carbon Released from Peat and Forest Fires in Indonesia during 1997." *Nature* 1999 (1): 61–65. doi: 10.1038/nature01141.1.

Page, Susan E., R.A.J. Wüst, D. Weiss, John O. Rieley, W. Shotyk, and S.H. Limin. (2004) "A Record of Late Pleistocene and Holocene Carbon Accumulation and Climate Change from an Equatorial Peat bog

(Kalimantan, Indonesia): Implications for Past, Present and Future Carbon Dynamics." *Journal of Quaternary Science* 19 (7): 625–635. doi: 10.1002/jqs.884.

Park, K. and J. Ng. (2013) "Singapore Smog Reaches 'Hazardous' All-Time High on Fires." Bloomberg Businessweek (June 20, 2013); www.businessweek.com/news/2013-06-19/.

Posa, Mary R.C. (2011) "Peat Swamp Forest Avifauna of Central Kalimantan, Indonesia: Effects of Habitat Loss and Degradation." *Biological Conservation* 144 (10): 2548–2556. doi: 10.1016/j.biocon.(2011)07.015.

Posa, Mary R.C., and David A. Marques. (2012) "Peat Swamp Forest Birds of the Tuanan Research Station, Central Kalimantan, Indonesia, with Notes on Habitat Specialists." *Forktail* 28 (28): 29–37.

Posa, Mary R.C., Lahiru S. Wijedasa, and Richard T. Corlett. (2011) "Biodiversity and Conservation of Tropical Peat Swamp Forests." *BioScience* 61 (1): 49–57. doi: 10.1525/bio.(2011)61.1.10.

Prat-Guitart, Nuria, Guillermo Rein, Rory M. Hadden, Claire M. Belcher, and Jon M. Yearsley. (2016) "Propagation Probability and Spread Rates of Self-Sustained Smouldering Fires under Controlled Moisture Content and Bulk Density Conditions." *International Journal of Wildland Fire*, 25 (4): 456–465. doi: 10.1071/WF15103.

President of Indonesia. (2016) Presidential Regulation Number 1 of Year 2016 About Peat Restoration Agency. Indonesia.

Putri, Adelia A. (2014) "Indonesia Ratifies Haze Treaty After 12 Years of Stalling." *Jakarta Globe*. http://thejakartaglobe.beritasatu.com/news/indonesia-ratifies-haze-treaty-12-years-stalling/.

Quah, Euston. (2002) "Transboundary Pollution in Southeast Asia: The Indonesian Fires." *World Development* 30 (3): 429–441. doi: 10.1016/S0305-750X(01)00122-X.

Quah, Euston, and Helena M. Varkkey. (2013) "The Political Economy of Transboundary Pollution: Mitigation Forest Fires and Haze in Southeast Asia." In *The Asian Community: Its Concepts and Prospects*, edited by H. H. Sei, 323–358. Tokyo: Soso Sha.

Radojevic, Miroslav. (2003) "Chemistry of Forest Fires and Regional Haze with Emphasis on Southeast Asia." *Pure and Applied Geophysics* 160 (1–2): 157–187. doi: 10.1007/s00024-003-8771-x.

Reddington, C.L., M. Yoshioka, R. Balasubramanian, D. Ridley, Y.Y. Toh, S.R. Arnold, and D.V. Spracklen. (2014) "Contribution of Vegetation and Peat Fires to Particulate Air Pollution in Southeast Asia." *Environmental Research Letters* 9 (9): 094006. doi: 10.1088/1748-9326/9/9/094006.

Rein, Guillermo, Natalie Cleaver, Clare Ashton, Paolo Pironi, and Jose L. Torero. (2008) "The Severity of Smouldering Peat Fires and Damage to the Forest Soil." *Catena* 74 (3): 304–309. doi: 10.1016/j.catena.(2008)05.008.

Rockström, Johan, Will Steffen, Kevin Noone, Åsa Persson, F. Stuart Chapin, Eric Lambin, Timothy M. Lenton, et al. (2009) "Planetary Boundaries: Exploring the Safe Operating Space for Humanity." *Nature* 461: 472–475. doi: 10.1038/461472a.

Saharjo, Bambang H. (2007) "Shifting Cultivation in Peatlands." *Mitigation and Adaptation Strategies for Global Change* 12 (1): 135–146. doi: 10.1007/s11027-006-9048-3.

Saharjo, Bambang H., and Canesio P. Munoz. (2005) "Controlled Burning in Peat Lands Owned by Small Farmers: A Case Study in Land Preparation." *Wetlands Ecology and Management* 13 (1): 105–110. doi: 10.1007/s11273-003-5110-z.

Sastry, Narayan. (2002) "Forest Fires, Air Pollution, and Mortality in Southeast Asia." *Demography* 39 (1): 1–23.

Satura, Sapariah, and Lusia Arumingtyas. (2016) "Indonesia's Peat Restoration Chief Calls for Protection of All Peat Domes." *Mongabay*, August 18. https://news.mongabay.com/2016/08/indonesias-peat-restoration-chief-calls-for-protection-of-all-peat-domes/.

Siegert, F., G. Ruecker, A. Hinrichs, and A.A. Hoffmann. (2001) "Increased Damage from Fires in Logged Forests during Droughts Caused by El Niño." *Nature* 414 (6862): 437–440. doi: 10.1038/35106547.

Singapore Institute of International Affairs. (2016) *Haze Tracker*. www.hazetracker.org/.

Sodhi, Navjot S., and Paul R. Ehrlich. (2010) "Conservation Biology," in *Conservation Biology for All*. Vol. 1, edited by N.S. Sodhi and P.R. Ehrlich, 7–26. Oxford: Oxford University Press. doi:10.1093/acprof:oso/9780199554232.001.0001.

Sodhi, Navjot S., Lian P. Koh, Barry W. Brook, and Peter K.L. Ng. (2004) "Southeast Asian Biodiversity: An Impending Disaster." *Trends in Ecology & Evolution* 19 (12): 654–660. doi: 10.1016/j.tree.(2004)09.006.

Stibig, H.-J., F. Achard, S. Carboni, R. Raši, and J. Miettinen. (2014) "Change in Tropical Forest Cover of Southeast Asia from 1990 to 2010." *Biogeosciences* 11 (2): 247–258. doi: 10.5194/bg-11-247-(2014).

Sundarambal, Palani, Rajasekhar Balasubramanian, Pavel Tkalich, and J. He. (2010) "Impact of Biomass Burning on Ocean Water Quality in Southeast Asia through Atmospheric Deposition: Field Observations." *Atmospheric Chemistry and Physics* 10 (23): 11323–11336. doi: 10.5194/acp-10-11323-(2010).

Suvanto, S., Grahame Applegate, Rizki P. Permana, Noviana Khususiyah, and Iwan Kurniawan. (2004) "The Role of Fire in Changing Land Use and Livelihoods in Riau-Sumatra." *Ecology and Society* 9 (1). doi:Artn 15.

Tacconi, Luca. (2016) "Preventing Fires and Haze in Southeast Asia." *Nature Climate Change* 6 (7): 640–643. doi: 10.1038/nclimate3008.

Tacconi, Luca, Peter F. Moore, and Damien Kaimowitz. (2007) "Fires in Tropical Forests – What Is Really the Problem? Lessons from Indonesia." *Mitigation and Adaptation Strategies for Global Change* 12 (1): 55–66. doi: 10.1007/s11027-006-9040-y.

Tacconi, Luca, and Andrew P. Vayda. (2006) "Slash and Burn and Fires in Indonesia: A Comment." *Ecological Economics* 56 (1): 1–4. doi: 10.1016/j.ecolecon.(2005)03.034.

Tan, Alan K.-J. (2005) "The ASEAN Agreement on Transboundary Haze Pollution: Prospects for Compliance and Effectiveness in Post-Suharto Indonesia'." *New York University Environmental Law Journal* 13 (647).

Tan, Alan K.-J. (2015) "The 'Haze' Crisis in Southeast Asia: Assessing Singapore's Transboundary Haze Pollution Act (2014)" NUS Law Working Paper 2015/002. doi:10.2139/ssrn.2547379.

Tomich, Thomas P., David E. Thomas, and Meine Van Noordwijk. (2004) "Environmental Services and Land Use Change in Southeast Asia: From Recognition to Regulation or Reward?" *Agriculture, Ecosystems and Environment* 104 (1): 229–244. doi: 10.1016/j.agee.(2004)01.017.

Toriyama, Jumpei, Tomoaki Takahashi, Sen Nishimura, Tamotsu Sato, Yukako Monda, Hideki Saito, Yoshio Awaya, et al (2014) "Estimation of Fuel Mass and Its Loss during a Forest Fire in Peat Swamp Forests of Central Kalimantan, Indonesia." *Forest Ecology and Management* 314: 1–8. doi: 10.1016/j.foreco.(2013)11.034.

Turetsky, Merritt R., Brian Benscoter, Susan Page, Guillermo Rein, Guido R. Van der Werf, and Adam Watts. (2015) "Global Vulnerability of Peatlands to Fire and Carbon Loss." *Nature Geoscience* 8 (1): 11–14. doi: 10.1038/ngeo2325.

UNEP. (2012) *UNEP Year Book—Emerging Issues in Our Global Environment*. www.unep.org/yearbook/(2012).

Unsworth, Richard K. F., Benjamin L. Jones, and Leanne C. Cullen-Unsworth. (2016) "Seagrass Meadows Are Threatened by Expected Loss of Peatlands in Indonesia." *Global Change Biology*, 22: 2957–2958. doi: 10.1111/gcb.13392.

Van der Werf, Guido R., Jan Dempewolf, Simon N. Trigg, James T. Randerson, Prasad S. Kasibhatla, Louis Giglio, Daniel Murdiyarso, et al (2008) "Climate Regulation of Fire Emissions and Deforestation in Equatorial Asia." *Proceedings of the National Academy of Sciences of the United States of America* 105 (51): 20350–20355. doi: 10.1073/pnas.0803375105.

Van der Werf, Guido R., James T. Randerson, Louis Giglio, G. J. Collatz, M. Mu, Prasad S. Kasibhatla, Douglas C. Morton, R. S. Defries, Y. van Jin, and Thijs T. van Leeuwen. (2010) "Global Fire Emissions and the Contribution of Deforestation, Savanna, Forest, Agricultural, and Peat Fires (1997–2009)." *Atmospheric Chemistry and Physics* 10: 11707–11735. doi: 10.5194/acp-10-11707-(2010).

Varkkey, Helena M. (2012) "Patronage Politics as a Driver of Economic Regionalisation: The Indonesian Oil Palm Sector and Transboundary Haze." *Asia Pacific Viewpoint* 53 (3): 313–328. doi: 10.1111/j.14678373.(2012)01493.x/abstract.

Velasco, Erik, and Soheil Rastan. (2015) "Air Quality in Singapore during the 2013 Smoke-Haze Episode over the Strait of Malacca: Lessons Learned." *Sustainable Cities and Society* 17: 122–131. doi: 10.1016/j.scs.(2015)04.006.

Wang, Yonghe, Robert D. Field, and Orbita Roswintiarti. (2004) "Trends in Atmospheric Haze Induced by Peat Fires in Sumatra Island, Indonesia and El Niño Phenomenon from 1973 to 2003." *Geophysical Research Letters* 31 (4): 1–4. doi: 10.1029/2003GL018853.

Wijedasa, Lahiru S. (2016) "Peat Soil Bulk Density Important for Estimation of Peatland Fire Emissions." *Global Change Biology* 22 (9): 2959. doi: 10.1111/gcb.13364.

Wijedasa, Lahiru S., Jyrki Jauhiainen, Mari Könönen, Maija Lampela, Harri Vasander, Marie-Claire LeBlanc, Stephanie Evers, et al. (2016a) "Denial of Long-Term Issues with Agriculture on Tropical Peatlands Will Have Devastating Consequences." *Global Change Biology*. doi:10.1111/gcb.13516.

Wijedasa, Lahiru S., Matti A. Niissalo, Voradol Chamchumroom, Pachok Puudjaa, Thaveechock Jumruschay, and Peter C. Boyce. (2016b) "Hanguana thailandica (Hanguanaceae): A New Peat Swamp Forest Species from Thailand." *Phytotaxa* 280 (2): 195–199.

Wijedasa, Lahiru S., Susan E. Page, Christopher D. Evans, and Mitsuru Osaki. (2016c) "Time for Responsible Peatland Agriculture." *Science* 354 (6312): 561.

Wijedasa, Lahiru S., Mary R.C. Posa, and Gopalasamy R. Clements. (2015) "Peat Fires: Consumers to Help Beat Them out." *Nature* 527: 305.

Wijedasa, Lahiru S., Sean Sloan, Dimitrios G. Michelakis, and Gopalasamy R. Clements. (2012) "Overcoming Limitations with Landsat Imagery for Mapping of Peat Swamp Forests in Sundaland." *Remote Sensing* 4 (12): 2595–2618. doi: 10.3390/rs4092595.

Wooster, M.J., P.H. Freeborn, S. Archibald, C. Oppenheimer, G.J. Roberts, T.E.L. Smith, N. Govender, M. Burton, and I. Palumbo. (2011) "Field Determination of Biomass Burning Emission Ratios and Factors via Open-Path FTIR Spectroscopy and Fire Radiative Power Assessment: Headfire, Backfire and Residual Smouldering Combustion in African Savannahs." *Atmospheric Chemistry and Physics* 11 (22): 11591–11615. doi: 10.5194/acp-11-11591-(2011).

World Resources Institute. (2016) *Global Forest Watch Fires*. http://fires.globalforestwatch.org/home/.

Yong, Ding L., and Kelvin Peh. (2014) "South-East Asia's Forest Fires: Blazing the Policy Trail." *Oryx*, 50 (2): 207–212. doi: 10.1017/S003060531400088X.

Yule, Catherine M. (2010) "Loss of Biodiversity and Ecosystem Functioning in Indo-Malayan Peat Swamp Forests." *Biodiversity and Conservation* 19: 393–409. doi: 10.1007/s10531-008-9510-5.

30

Energy security performance in Japan: historical and scenario analysis

Ken'ichi Matsumoto

Introduction

Brief story of energy situation and recent energy policy in Japan

The self-sufficiency rate of energy was 6 percent in 2013 in Japan, including nuclear and renewable energy (Agency for Natural Resources and Energy, 2015). Japan highly depends on fossil fuels; these accounted for more than 80 percent of energy supply before the Fukushima Daiichi nuclear disaster and at present account for more than 90 percent (see Figure 30.1). These fossil fuels are mostly imported and are mainly sourced from the politically unstable Middle East. Because energy demands in emerging countries (e.g., China and India) are increasing and these countries are trying to secure their energy supply, it will be more difficult for Japan to rely on cheap imported fuels in the near future. Thus, producing its own energy sources and reducing dependence on energy import are essential for Japan.

Nuclear energy has been one of energy sources that can reduce dependence on fossil fuels. Also, in the Act on Promotion of Global Warming Countermeasures of 1998, nuclear energy is considered one of the important energy sources for reducing greenhouse gas emissions. However, the Fukushima nuclear disaster changed the situation,[1] highlighting the safety issues of using nuclear energy, such that at present, only one nuclear power plant (Sendai nuclear power plant in Kyushu) is in operation.

As an alternative energy source, renewable energy will be one of the most important elements in securing Japan's national energy supply and solving other environmental issues such as climate change and air pollution simultaneously. Although multiple national renewable-energy-related policies were introduced to diffuse renewable energy after the oil shocks in the 1970s, renewable energy other than hydropower accounted for only a small percentage of total primary energy supply.

As a policy to promote the use of renewable energy, the Renewable Portfolio Standard (RPS) was enacted in 2003. The net-metering scheme for photovoltaic power was then launched in 2009. Under this scheme, electricity companies were required to purchase any surplus electricity generated by customers' PV facilities. The cost of buying back surplus electricity is borne by electricity

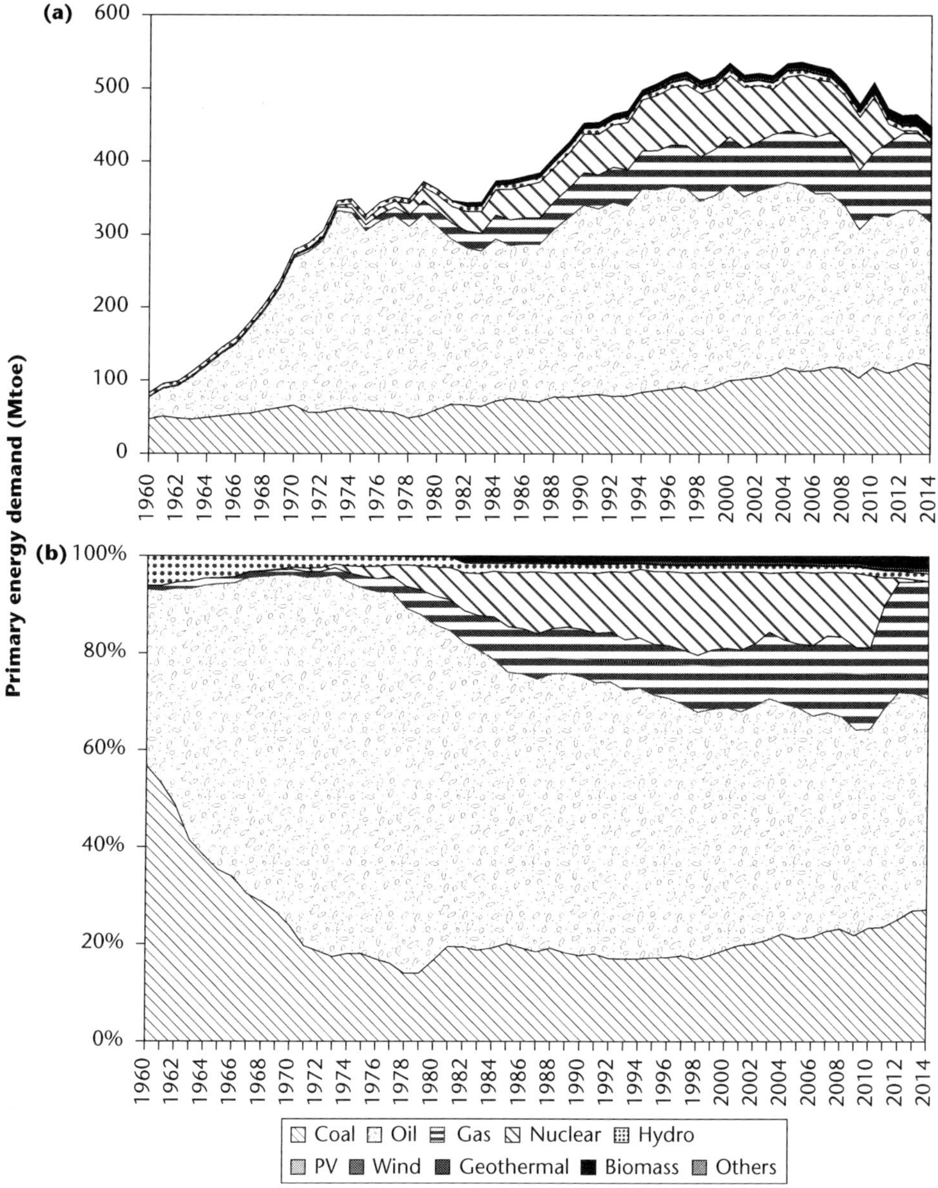

Figure 30.1 a and b: Primary energy demand (a) and the share of each energy source (b)

Note: "Others" means other renewable energy.

Source: IEA (2015b).

consumers in the form of a PV promotion surcharge (Ministry of Economy, Trade and Industry, 2012). This scheme has evolved into the Feed-in Tariff (FIT) scheme, launched in July 2012.

The RPS and net-metering schemes had some effects in increasing renewable energy. In particular, there was a large increase in PV after the net-metering scheme was introduced. However, the share of renewable energy was still small when the two schemes ended, suggesting that such previous schemes were not successful in significantly increasing the share of renewable energy. In addition, although the net-metering scheme has contributed to increasing the capacity of PV, it did not support other types of renewable energy, and electricity is purchased only from residential/non-residential PV installments, not from power generators. After the Fukushima nuclear disaster, a large part of the Japanese population wished to abandon nuclear power plants because of safety concerns, and to increase the share of renewable energy. Then-Prime Minister Naoto Kan and his cabinet decided that the share of renewable energy should be expanded. Consequently, in 2012, the net metering evolved into the FIT scheme.

The FIT scheme in Japan requires that electricity companies accept electricity supply contracts requested by producers of renewable-energy-based electricity at a long-term fixed purchase price that is guaranteed by the Government of Japan (the details of the FIT in Japan is explained in Morita and Matsumoto 2014). It covers PV, wind, small- and medium-scale hydro, geothermal, and biomass power. The FIT is expected to reduce uncertainty in investment recovery for renewable electricity facilities, and to encourage investment in order to increase the generation of renewable electricity (Kitamura, 2013). Because of the FIT, the introduction of renewable energy was greatly promoted in Japan.

On April 11, 2014, the latest version of the Basic Energy Plan, which was developed after the Fukushima nuclear disaster, was endorsed by the cabinet. Its purpose was to completely revise the energy strategy of Japan, particularly reducing dependency on nuclear power, considering the Fukushima nuclear disaster. The policy prioritizes energy security, but also considers economic efficiency and the conservation of the environment, all with a strong focus on safety (3E+S). However, to tackle energy-related issues and concerns regarding climate change, many different factors need to be taken into account, including supply- and demand-side technologies, energy storage, securing resources, the environment, and economic cost.

Under the Basic Energy Plan, coal-fired thermal, nuclear, conventional hydro, and geothermal power generation are considered to act as the 'baseload' power sources. Coal-fired thermal power, in particular, is considered to be a very important power source because of its low geopolitical risk among fossil fuels and its low cost. Nuclear power is still considered an important element in the energy mix because of its low operational costs and low CO_2 emissions. In addition, it is considered a semi-domestic energy source. Gas-fired thermal power is considered to be a 'middle' (flexible) power source. The percentage of natural gas-fired thermal power is expected to be increased because of natural gas' low CO_2 emissions among fossil fuels. Finally, oil-fired thermal, pumped hydro, and other renewable power generation is considered 'peak-load' power. Although the Basic Energy Plan emphasizes the importance of renewable energy and stresses that the introduction of renewable energy should be accelerated, it is treated as peak-load power. Furthermore, no specific targets for renewable energy capacity are given in the plan.

The Bill of the Basic Act on Global Warming Countermeasures included the target of raising the share of renewable energy to 10 percent of the total primary energy supply by 2020. In addition, since the shutdown of nuclear power plants across Japan after the Fukushima nuclear disaster, there has been a growing demand to increase the generation of renewable electricity. Furthermore, the Energy and Environmental Council of the Government of Japan decided in September 2012 to aim for zero nuclear power generation by the 2030s. The act and the decision by the council, however, were scrapped after the dissolution of the lower house. However, public awareness of the need for renewable energy has been raised, particularly after the Fukushima nuclear disaster.

In addition to the above policies, there are other schemes for promoting renewable energy, such as tax reductions, subsidies, and loans (Agency for Natural Resources and Energy, 2016). Furthermore, several voluntary schemes designed to enhance the use of renewable energy, such as the Green Power Certificate, exist (Ministry of the Environment, 2016). Since the FIT was launched in 2012, the Government of Japan has been trying to unite renewable-energy-related policies under it.

In transitioning toward a sustainable society, Japan faces many challenges. The main challenges of energy policies can be summarized as follows. In the Basic Energy Plan, no best energy mix is defined. To establish a sustainable society, the plan indicates that the share of renewable energy should be increased. However, no numerical targets exist for renewable energy and also coal-thermal power is still considered an important baseload power. Furthermore, the position of the government regarding nuclear power is not clearly stated. As mentioned above, the plan indicates that nuclear power is an 'important' baseload power source and, at the same time, that dependency on it should be reduced – it is why developing investment plans is difficult for electricity producers, particularly large electricity companies. The energy structure also closely relates to energy security. Since Japan imports most energy resources, energy costs and a stable energy supply may be at risk if Japan continues to rely on imported fossil fuels.

The FIT, which is the most recent renewable energy policy in Japan, has already successfully increased the share of electricity from renewable energy, and aims to accelerate the deployment of renewable energy further. However, it has also had negative impacts, such as large cost burdens to electricity consumers due to high purchasing prices, a biased introduction of renewable energy (most of introduced capacity is photovoltaics), and unstable power system connection (see Morita and Matsumoto (2014) for further information on the challenges of this scheme).

Literature review on energy security in Asia

Many types of research on energy security have been implemented in the literature, reviewing different countries and regions, different methods, and different periods. In particular, there are many studies focusing on Asian countries, but few for the case of Japan. Therefore, we examine the wider literature and methodologies used to analyze energy security in Asia.

Shin et al. (2013) analyzed energy security in the Korean gas sector using a model approach (quality function deployment and system dynamics) from the past to the future (1998–2015). Ren and Sovacool (2014, 2015), Wu (2014) and, Yao and Chang (2014) targeted China. Ren and Sovacool (2014) applied the DEMATEL method for analyzing energy security from availability, affordability, acceptability, and accessibility (4As). Ren and Sovacool (2015) applied Analytic Hierarchy Process to evaluate energy security with respect to low-carbon energy. Wu (2014) examined China's energy security strategies by focusing on overseas oil investment, strategic petroleum reserves, and unconventional gas development in the 11th and 12th Five-Year Program. Yao and Chang (2014) also used the 4As approach and evaluated the transition of energy security performance by areas of rhombus made by the 4As in the past (1980–2010). Chuang and Ma (2013) evaluated energy policy in Taiwan using energy security indicators composed of six indicators of four dimensions in the past (1990–2010) and also the future energy policy in terms of energy security using both a modeling approach and the indicators. Martchamadol and Kumar (2012) evaluated energy security in Thailand from the past to the future (1986–2030). The authors applied five-dimensional (19 indicators in total) indicators, using statistical data for the historical analysis and a scenario approach for the future analysis within the evaluation. Thangavelu et al. (2015) used an optimization model for exploring a long-term energy mix for society with high energy security and low carbon in the future in Indonesia. Ang et al. (2015a) evaluated historical energy security (1990–2010) in Singapore using 22 indicators of three dimensions. The authors also conducted scenario analysis for the future (until 2035) based on a business-as-usual projection. Sharifuddin (2014) evaluated energy security in five Southeast Asian countries (Malaysia, Indonesia, the Philippines,

Thailand, and Vietnam) using 35 indicators representing 13 elements grouped into five aspects of energy security in three periods (2002, 2005, and 2008). Selvakkumaran and Limmeechokchai (2013) evaluated the future energy security (until 2030) with respect to oil security, gas security, and sustainability in three Asian countries (Sri Lanka, Thailand, and Vietnam) using a model approach. Similarly, Matsumoto and Andriosopoulos (2016) used an economic model for evaluating the future energy security (until 2050) in three East Asian countries (Japan, China, and Korea) under climate mitigation scenarios. There is also a special issue on Asian energy security from Energy Policy (volume 39 issue 11) in 2011.

As shown in the above-mentioned literature, there are many studies on energy security focusing on Asian countries. However, the studies targeting Japan are few, although energy security is an important issue for Japan. Takase and Suzuki (2011), using the long-range energy alternatives planning software system, analyzed future energy pathways, which have impact on energy security, in Japan. The authors mainly focus on energy structures in the future under different nuclear power development and greenhouse gas emission abatement. Matsumoto and Andriosopoulos (2016), mentioned above, examined how energy security changes in the future when climate mitigation policy is implemented. The authors found that climate mitigation, which often showed economic loss compared with a business-as-usual scenario, contributed to improve energy security in Japan (and the other countries analyzed), and thus was able to contribute to economic activities in terms of securing energy supply.

In terms of methodology for evaluating energy security, most studies apply some sort of 'indicators' to statistical data or results of model or scenario analysis. However, different definitions, dimensions, or indexes have been used in each study (see for example Ang et al. (2015b) for a comprehensive review of energy security studies), meaning that there are no consistent definitions or evaluation methods for energy security performance. When evaluating energy security of countries, the most important point is the availability of energy as it is included in the indicators in most of the related studies (Ang et al., 2015b). Furthermore, considering that such indicators are used by policymakers to establish energy policy in a country, a simple and comprehensible methodology is appropriate.

The purpose of this chapter is to evaluate energy security performance in Japan from the past to the future, using comprehensive energy security indicators. For the past, statistical data are used, whereas for the future, energy scenarios from the government and a research institute are used. There have been no studies that analyze the past energy security for the long term in the literature. Such long-term analysis is important to understand what contributes for improving energy security. In addition, the scenario analysis for the future can show how energy mix that considered under energy policy or scenarios in Japan can contribute to improve energy security.

Methods

Energy security indicators

In order to analyze the historical transition of energy security performance and energy security performance in the future under energy scenarios in Japan, three energy security indicators are employed (Lehl, 2009). The proposed indicators enable the analysis of energy security data in the past and the future, and the presented results facilitate the formulation of energy policy recommendations. The first proposed indicator (S1, eq.(1)) evaluates the diversity of energy sources based on the Shannon–Wiener index, which is an indicator for evaluating diversity (Shannon, 1948). Diversity is important for maintaining energy security, because the probability of compensating for the loss of a primary energy source by other energy sources will increase, thus preserving energy security. However, concerning the energy security of countries, it is important to consider where the energy sources come from. In general, domestic energy is safe but a procurement risk exists for imported energy. In addition, similar to diversity of energy sources, diversity of the origin of imported energy contributes to energy security. The second indicator (S2, eq.(2)), then, considers the import dependence of each country on its energy sources, as well as its energy imports by origin. In this indicator, all of the energy exporters are treated equally. However, energy security will improve if energy sources are imported from politically and economically safer countries. Therefore, the third indicator (S3, eq.(5)) extends the second one by incorporating a country-risk factor associated with a country's energy imports origins. By definition, the values of three indicators will be S1 ≥ S2 ≥ S3, and they are not comparable.

$$S1 = -\sum_{i=1}^{N} p_i \ln(p_i) \tag{1}$$

$$S2 = -\sum_{i=1}^{N} c2_i p_i \ln(p_i) \tag{2}$$

$$c2_i = \left(1 - m_i\left(1 - \frac{S_{i2}^{m}}{S_{i2}^{max}}\right)\right) \tag{3}$$

$$S_{i2}^{m} = -\sum_{j=1}^{M} m_{ij} \ln(m_{ij}) \quad S_{i2}^{max} = -M\frac{1}{M}\ln\left(\frac{1}{M}\right) \tag{4}$$

$$S3 = -\sum_{i=1}^{N} c3_i p_i \ln(p_i) \tag{5}$$

$$c3_i = \left(1 - m_i\left(1 - \frac{S_{i3}^{m}}{S_{i3}^{max}}\right)\right) \tag{6}$$

$$S_{i3}^{m} = -\sum_{j=1}^{M} A_j m_{ij} \ln(m_{ij}) \quad S_{i3}^{max} = -M\frac{1}{M}\ln\left(\frac{1}{M}\right)$$
$$A_j = \frac{r_j}{\max\limits_{j} r_j} \tag{7}$$

where *i*: types of primary energy; *j*: origin of primary energy imports; *p*: share of primary energy; *m*: share of imports; *r*: risk indicator; *N*: the number of primary energy types; *M*: the number of the origin of primary energy imports

Historical data

To calculate the three indicators for the past from 1978 to 2014, we obtained the data from the following data sources. First, primary energy demand in each country (to calculate the share of primary energy p_i) is from the Energy Balances of OECD Countries (IEA, 2015b). Since the types of primary energy are broad in this database, they are aggregated into ten types of primary energy (coal, oil, gas, nuclear, hydro, PV, wind, geothermal, biomass, and other renewable energy).

Primary energy imports by origin (to calculate the share of imports m_{ij}) in each country are from the Coal Information, Oil Information, and Natural Gas Information (IEA, 2015a, 2015c, 2015d).

Finally, the risk indicator is obtained from the World Governance Indicators (World Bank, 2015). Since the original data range from approximately –2.5 to 2.5,[2] they are converted to the scale of 0 to 1. The smaller the values, the larger the country risks to secure energy supply.

Among these databases, natural gas imports by origin and risk indicators do not cover the data before 1992 and 1995, respectively. To cover a sufficient time span for the analysis, we complemented the missing data by using the data in the closest existing year (i.e., 1993 and 1996, respectively).

In Japan, total primary energy demand has largely increased from 1960 to the present (Figure 30.1). After its peak in early 2000s, the total demand tended to decline. The large increase in the total primary energy demand are mainly due to increases oil demand. However, after the oil shocks in the 1970s, oil demand did not increase, but rather tended to decrease. Until the early 1980s, coal and oil occupied the largest part of primary energy demand, but after that the shares of nuclear and natural gas increased. Hydropower, which is for power generation, was used constantly during the observed periods. The share of other renewable energy sources has increased recently, although these percentages are still small compared to traditional energy sources. After the Fukushima nuclear disaster in March 2011, the trend has tremendously changed. Because all nuclear power plants in Japan were shut down and most of them have not been resumed, the share of nuclear power was reduced to almost zero. Although total primary energy demand is getting smaller in recent years, such a decline in demand could not compensate for the shut-down of nuclear power plants. This decrease in primary energy supply is compensated for by increases in coal and natural gas. As a result, the share of fossil fuels rose to more than 90 percent. Although the introduction of renewable energy, particularly PV, has increased after the FIT was implemented in July 2012, the share is still very small.

Figure 30.2 shows how much Japan depends on external energy. During the observed period, almost 100 percent of oil was imported. Dependence on imported coal and natural gas was not great from the 1960s to the early-1970s. However, the dependence on imports is rising over time, increasing to almost 100 percent for these two fossil fuels, similar to oil.

Scenario analysis

For our scenario analysis, scenarios developed by two sources are employed. One is the Long-term Energy Supply–Demand Outlook (hereafter, Outlook) by the Government of Japan (Ministry of Economy, Trade and Industry, 2015), whereas the second one is an energy scenario developed by the Institute of Energy Economics, Japan (IEEJ; IEEJ, 2015a, 2015b). Both scenarios target the year 2030.

The Outlook is developed based on the Basic Energy Plan published in 2014, considering the situation after the Fukushima nuclear disaster (see the Introduction for a brief explanation of the Basic Energy Plan). It shows the energy supply demand structure in the future under a scenario of realized energy policy, assuming policy goals based on the 3E+S. Under this outlook, tremendous energy efficiency improvement comparable to that experienced after the oil shocks is assumed to be attained through energy saving, although energy demand is assumed to increase as a result of economic growth if any measures are taken. In the projection, economic growth of 1.7 percent per annum and the latest demographic shifts estimated by the National Institute of Population and Social Security Research are used. In addition, technologically feasible and realistic energy saving

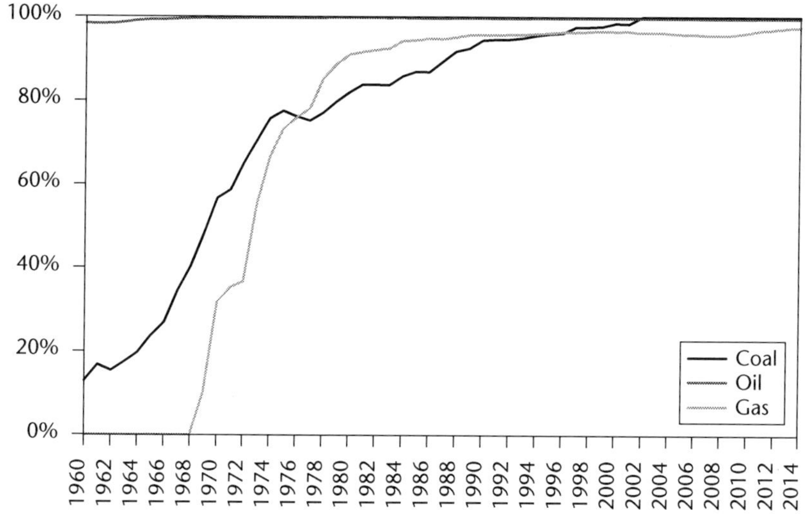

Figure 30.2 Dependence on import of fossil fuels

Source: IEA (2015b).

measures in industrial and service sectors, households, and transportation sectors are considered. For power generation, maximum introduction of renewable energy, efficiency improvement in thermal power generation, and decrease in dependence on nuclear power are taken into account as basic principles, as well as energy savings as explained above, under the 3E+S.

As a result, energy demand is estimated to be 293 Mtoe in 2030, which includes 45 Mtoe energy saving from business as usual. Primary energy supply is estimated to be 440 Mtoe (Figure 30.3). The rate of energy self-sufficiency will be around 24.3 percent in this scenario (Ministry of Economy, Trade and Industry, 2015).

IEEJ's energy scenarios were established using an econometric model considering future uncertainties. Four scenarios, hereafter called IEEJ 1–4 scenarios, were developed which particularly focus on the power generation mix (renewable energy and nuclear use). Table 30.1 shows the overview of IEEJ's scenarios. The IEEJ 1 scenario assumes to use more renewable energy and no nuclear power, whereas the IEEJ 4 scenario uses less renewable energy and more nuclear power. The IEEJ 2 and 3 scenarios are in-between. Nuclear power plants meeting the regulatory standards will operate for 40 years in the IEEJ 2 scenario, whereas power plants passing the special inspection extend their operating periods in the IEEJ 3 and 4 scenarios. Power generation by renewable energy will be 2.1 to 4.1 times higher than the current level. Since it is not possible to fully replace nuclear power plants, which comprise baseload power, with renewable energy, the share of thermal power is higher in the high-renewable-energy scenario. Consequently, IEEJ 4 shows lower CO_2 emissions and higher GDP than the other scenarios. Figure 30.4 shows the primary energy structure under the four scenarios.

Results and discussion

Historical trend of energy security performance

Figure 30.5 shows historical trends of energy security performance evaluated by three indicators.[3] In the early stage of the analysis (from 1978 to early 1980s), all of the three indicators have

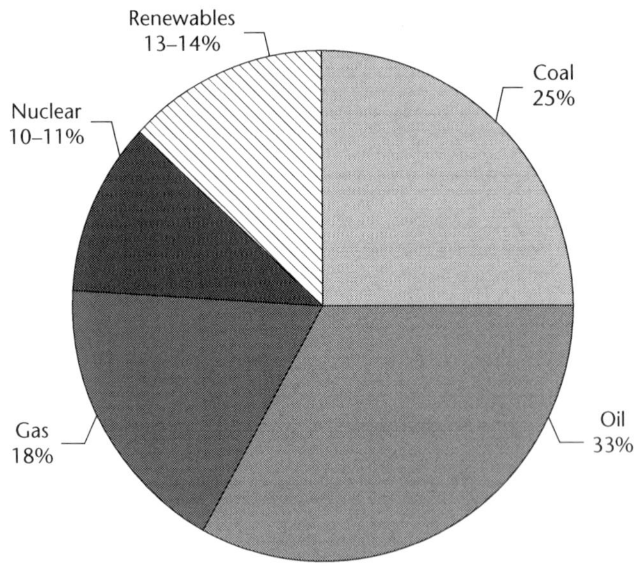

Figure 30.3 Primary energy structure in the Long-term Energy Supply–Demand Outlook

Note: Renewable energy includes hydropower: 5.2–5.5 percent, PV: 4.1 percent, wind: 1.0 percent, biomass: 2.2–2.7 percent, and geothermal: 0.6–0.7 percent.

Source: Ministry of Economy, Trade and Industry (2015).

Table 30.1 Overview of the IEEJ's energy scenarios

		IEEJ 1	*IEEJ 2*	*IEEJ 3*	*IEEJ 4*
Power generation mix	Renewable energy (%)	35	30	25	20
	Thermal (%)	65	55	50	50
	Nuclear (%)	0	15	25	30
	Power generation (PWh)	1.1	1.2	1.2	1.2
Economy	Power generation costs (JPY/kWh)	21.0	19.0	16.4	14.8
	Real GDP (trillion JPY)	684	690	693	694
Energy	Self-sufficiency ratio (%)	19	25	28	28
Environment	CO_2 emissions (percent change from 2005 level)	–20	–24	–26	–26

Source: IEEJ (2015a).

increased. This is due to a decrease in the share of oil and an increase in the share of natural gas and nuclear power in the primary energy structure in this period – this trend is brought about by the oil shocks (see also Figure 30.1). However, the trends are different in terms of various indicators after that. The S1 indicator has continuously increased until the early 2010s, whereas the S2 and S3 indicators (in which energy imports and country risks were applied) generally continued to be flat, or become even slightly worse, in the same period.

The S1 indicator purely measures diversity of primary energy. During the corresponding period, the share of oil continuously decreased, whereas the share of natural gas and nuclear power continuously increased. In addition, the share of renewable energy increased. These effects in total

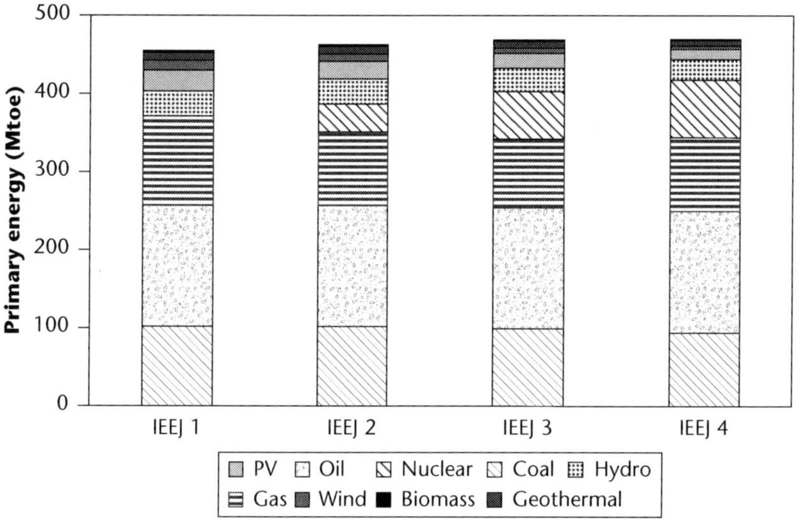

Figure 30.4 Primary energy structure under the IEEJ's scenarios

Source: IEEJ (2015b).

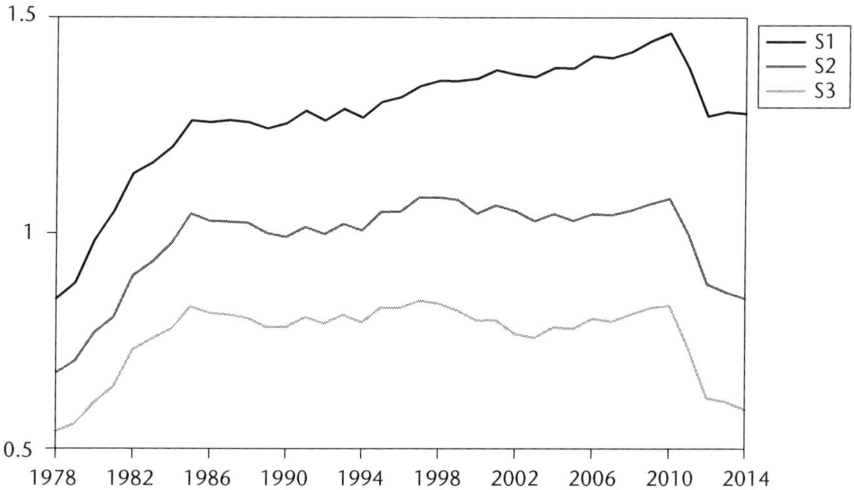

Figure 30.5 Historical energy security performance in Japan

increased the diversity of the primary energy structure. In the case of the S2 and S3 indicators, the dependence on imports cause the indicators to be flat from the 1980s to the 2000s. As shown in Figure 30.2, the import of natural gas sharply increased until 1980 and slowly but continuously increased after that. The import of coal also increased from 1978 to the present. Such increases in imports offset the increases in value by diversifying energy sources (i.e., through the S1 indicator). For the country risk indicator, because same data are used until 1996, country risk affects the energy security indicator when the share of import by origin changes. If more fossil fuels are imported from higher-risk countries, the energy security indicator synergistically declines. From 1996, the situation is similar to that of before 1996 since the country risk indicator does not change greatly. In the case of coal, imports from Australia and Indonesia increased from the mid-1990s to 2000s, whereas those from Canada and the US decreased. Australia, Canada, and the US are lower-risk countries, whereas Indonesia is a higher-risk country. With regard to oil, imports from Saudi Arabia, which is a higher-risk country, increased, whereas small decreases were observed in some countries in the same period. With regard to natural gas, imports from Australia, Qatar, and Russia increased, whereas those from Brunei and Indonesia decreased. Australia is a lower-risk country as indicated above, whereas Brunei and Qatar are in the middle, and Indonesia and Russia are higher-risk countries. Comparison between the S2 and S3 indicators suggests that import factor is more influential in determining the values than the country risk factor.

Finally, after 2010, all the indicators declined tremendously due to the shutdown of nuclear power plants after the Fukushima nuclear disaster in March 2011. During this period, the decrease in the use of nuclear power was compensated for by fossil fuels, particularly natural gas. This change caused a reduction in the diversity of the primary energy structure.

The above results suggest that the diversity of energy structure is the primary factor in determining the performance of energy security. In addition, imports (total imports and diversity of the origin of imports) are also an important factor. As the country risk indicator does not seem to affect the performance in this study, it might be due to the fact that the risk indicator changes only slightly over time. Therefore, if an incident, such as a war or a civil war, largely changes the situation of a country it can affect the energy security performance.

Comparison of scenarios

In analyzing the two scenario groups, primary energy sources in the original references were aggregated into the sources treated in the historical analysis, although both scenario groups do not include the "others" (other renewable energy). Since the share of "others" is very small, this difference does not affect the comparison between the historical and scenario analysis. Note that since only primary energy structure is available from the references, historical data are applied for energy imports and country risk indicators.

When calculating the S2 indicator, three assumptions are considered for $c2_i$: the minimum coefficient (MinC) the maximum coefficient (MaxC), and the coefficient of fossil fuel production in the latest year (ProC). The minimum coefficient makes use of the minimum values by energy for the last 10 years. Similarly, the maximum coefficient utilizes the maximum values by energy from the last 10 years. The third coefficient assumes that fossil fuel production does not change in 2030 from the current level (production of the 10-year average is used) and the fossil fuel demand that cannot be fulfilled by the production is imported. Similar to the S2 indicator, these three assumptions on the coefficient ($c3_i$) are also considered for calculating the S3 indicator. All three assumptions are applied for the scenario in the Outlook, whereas only the third assumption is applied for the IEEJ's energy scenarios.

In the Outlook, since the share of renewable energy and nuclear power are shown in the range (see Figure 30.3), but are not exact percentages, the mean values are used in the analysis. Figure 30.6 shows the results of the scenario analysis. Because the three assumptions are relevant to imports, they do not affect the S1 indicator. The S1 indicator is 1.71, which is higher than historical values in any given year. Comparing primary energy structure in the past and within the scenario, the share of oil and gas decreases in the scenario, whereas that of nuclear and renewable energy increases. The indicator reaches a peak when the share is even by primary energy source (i.e., around 11 percent in the case of nine energy types). Thus, such a transition contributes to diversifying the primary energy structure. With regard to the S2 and S3 indicators, the values are different under different assumptions. Naturally, the MaxC case is higher than the MinC case.

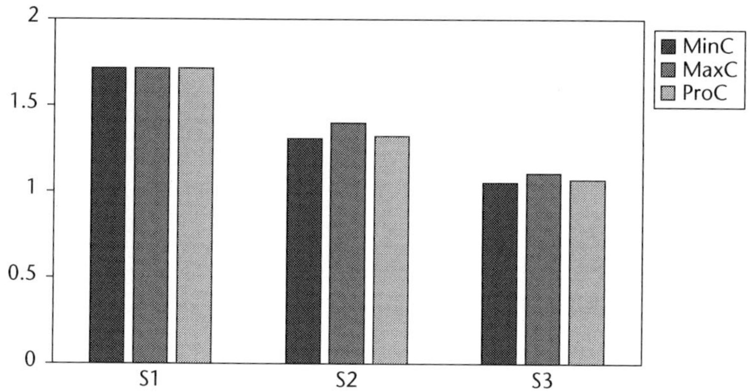

Figure 30.6 Future energy security performance under the Long-term Energy Supply–Demand Outlook scenario

Note: MinC: minimum coefficient, MaxC: maximum coefficient, and ProC: coefficient when fossil fuel production in the latest year is kept.

The ProC case is in between the two cases, but close to the MinC case. It is because the domestic production of fossil fuels is small and the production is decreasing in Japan (see Figure 30.2). As with the S1 indicator, the S2 and S3 indicators are also higher in the scenario than the historical values. Since the influence of imports is small due to the assumption, the change in energy structure is more greatly affected.

Figure 30.7 shows the results under the IEEJ's scenarios. In this analysis only the third assumption on the coefficients are applied for the S2 and S3 indicators, as the influence of three assumptions were shown in the above analysis. Thus, we here focus on the differences by scenario. Since the same assumption is applied for imports and country risk indicators for all the scenarios, the differences by scenario are similar for each indicator. The results suggest that IEEJ 2 and 3 scenarios are the highest (the second scenario is slightly higher than the third one for the S1 indicator, whereas the third one is slightly higher than the second one for the other two indicators), whereas the IEEJ 1 is the lowest. As Table 30.1 and Figure 30.4 showed, the IEEJ 1 is the extreme scenario, which uses no nuclear power at all. It means that the primary energy structure is biased toward fossil fuels, although the use of renewable energy is larger than in the other scenarios. The IEEJ 2 and 3 have more balanced primary energy structures, particularly for important energy sources (energy sources with larger shares), compared to the other two. IEEJ 4 also looks to have balanced energy structure, but the large share of nuclear power reduces the share of renewable energy that consists of several energy types. Consequently, the IEEJ 2 and 3 scenarios have more diversified primary energy structures. Observing the S2 and S3 indicators, because import and country risk factors affect evaluation against fossil fuels, the scenarios with higher shares of fossil fuels tend to be more greatly affected.

Comparing the above results with the historical analysis, the values in the four scenarios are higher than those in the historical analysis for all the indicators, meaning that the energy security performance improves in the given future scenarios. For the three scenarios using nuclear power (IEEJ 2–4), use of nuclear power as well as increase in renewable energy contributes to improving energy security performance. On the other hand, nuclear power is not used in the IEEJ 1 scenario. Comparing the primary energy structure in this scenario (Figure 30.4) with the historical one (Figure 30.1), the decrease in nuclear power is compensated for by greater use of

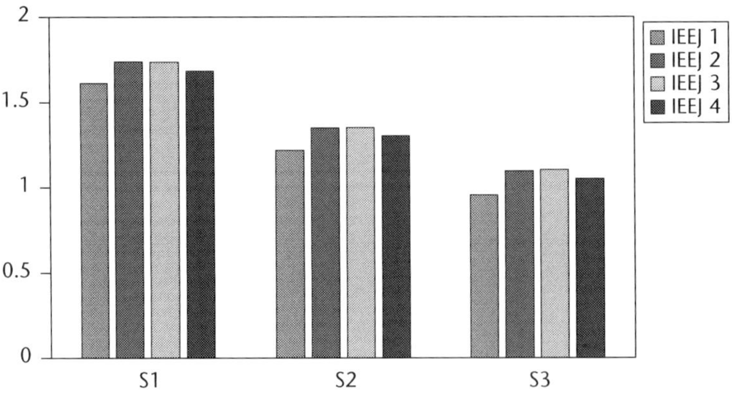

Figure 30.7 Future energy security performance under the IEEJ's scenarios

renewable energies. In addition, although the total share of fossil fuels remains almost the same, the structure is more balanced by using more natural gas and less oil.

Conclusion

Because Japan is poor in energy sources and because the energy situation in Japan will be tougher in the future, securing its energy supply will be a more important issue for Japan. In this chapter, we first evaluated changes in the historical energy security performance and then analyzed energy security in the future under several scenarios for Japan.

From the historical evaluation, it was shown that energy security performance evaluated by three energy security indicators improved over time, although the indicators S2 and S3 were almost flat from the late 1980s to the early 2010s. However, energy security declined from 2011 due to the Fukushima nuclear disaster. This means that diversity of primary energy sources, including nuclear power, is important for high energy security performance, as measured by the three indicators introduced in this study. From the scenario analysis, energy security will improve under the future scenarios used in this study. It is suggested that energy balances mentioned above and also energy saving can improve the energy security performance of Japan compared to the historical situation.

To further improve energy security, additional measures can be considered. First, an increase in the share of renewable energy is necessary to balance primary energy structure. This will also decrease dependence on imported fossil fuels. However, if the share of unstable renewable energy increases too much, power system stability will be affected. Therefore, increases of stable renewable sources (e.g., medium- and small-hydro, biomass, and geothermal power) are expected. In addition, introducing energy storage systems will reduce the influence of increasing unstable renewable energy, although such storage systems will generate an additional cost. Next, with regard to energy imports, balancing the origin of imported energy and reducing imports from high-risk countries will also contribute to improvements in energy security, although these affect only the indicators S2 (only the former) and S3. Last but not least, reducing energy demand (energy saving) is also an important factor for improving energy security performance. By reducing energy demand, energy supply from fossil fuels can be reduced. This will contribute to balancing primary energy sources (increasing the share of renewable energy sources), balancing the origin of energy import, and reducing energy imports from high-risk countries.

Acknowledgments

This research was supported by JSPS KAKENHI Grant Number 15K16161 and 15K00669, and MEXT KAKENHI Grant Number 25241030.

Notes

1 The Fukushima nuclear disaster is an accident at the Fukushima Daiichi Nuclear Power Plant, caused by the tsunami following the Great East Japan Earthquake on March 11, 2011. The insufficient cooling due to loss of the cooling system led to three nuclear meltdowns and the release of radioactive materials. It is the largest nuclear disaster since the Chernobyl disaster and the second disaster to be given the Level 7 event of the International Nuclear Event Scale.
2 http://info.worldbank.org/governance/wgi/index.aspx#doc-methodology.
3 If calculating the indicators before 1978 using the same method for complementing the missing data with 1978–1992 or –1995, during the period of rapid economic growth, indicators declined because the dependence on oil increased. After 1973, the indicators increased as shown in Figure 30.5.

References

Agency for Natural Resources and Energy. (2015) "Support System for Renewable Energy Introduction." Accessed April 21, 2016, www.enecho.meti.go.jp/category/saving_and_new/saiene/support/index.html (in Japanese).
Agency for Natural Resources and Energy. (2016) "Energy Whitepaper (2015)." Accessed March 18, 2016, www.enecho.meti.go.jp/about/whitepaper/2015html/2-1-1.html (in Japanese).
Ang, B.W., W.L. Choong, and T.S. Ng. (2015a) "A Framework for Evaluating Singapore's Energy Security." *Applied Energy* 148: 314–325.
Ang, B.W., W.L. Choong, and T.S. Ng. (2015b) "Energy Security: Definitions, Dimensions and Indexes." *Renewable and Sustainable Energy Reviews* 42: 1077–1093.
Chuang, M.C. and H.W. Ma. (2013) "An Assessment of Taiwan's Energy Policy Using Multi-Dimensional Energy Security Indicators." *Renewable and Sustainable Energy Reviews* 17: 301–311.
International Energy Agency (IEA). (2015a) *Coal Information*. Paris: International Energy Agency.
International Energy Agency (IEA). (2015b) *Energy Balances of OECD Countries*. Paris: International Energy Agency.
International Energy Agency (IEA). (2015c) *Natural Gas Information*. Paris: International Energy Agency.
International Energy Agency (IEA). (2015d) *Oil Information*. Paris: International Energy Agency.
Institute of Energy Economics, Japan (IEEJ). (2015a) "Toward Choosing Energy Mix (Summary)." Accessed April 21, 2016, https://eneken.ieej.or.jp/en/press/press150116c.pdf.
Institute of Energy Economics, Japan (IEEJ). (2015b) "Toward Choosing Energy Mix (Presentation Material)." Accessed April 21, 2016, https://eneken.ieej.or.jp/en/press/press150116d.pdf.
Kitamura, T. (2013) "Situation of the FIT Scheme and Challenge Toward Substantial Expansion of Renewable Energy." *Energy and Resources* 34: 129–133 (in Japanese).
Lehl, U. (2009) "More Baskets?: Renewable Energy and Energy Security." *GWS Discussion Paper* 2009/8.
Martchamadol, J. and S. Kumar. (2012) "Thailand's Energy Security Indicators." *Renewable and Sustainable Energy Reviews* 16: 6103–6122.
Matsumoto, K. and K. Andriosopoulos. (2016) "Energy Security in East Asia Under Climate Mitigation Scenarios in the 21st Century." *Omega* 59: 60–71.
Ministry of Economy, Trade and Industry. (2012) "Approval of Electricity Charges Followed by the Fixing of FY 2012 Photovoltaic Power Promotion Surcharge Rates." Accessed April 21, 2016, www.meti.go.jp/english/press/2012/0125_02.html.
Ministry of Economy, Trade and Industry. (2015) "Long-term Prospect of Supply and Demand of Energy." (in Japanese).
Ministry of the Environment. (2016) "What is a Green Electricity Certificate?" Accessed April 21, 2016, www.env.go.jp/earth/ondanka/greenenergy/ (in Japanese).
Morita, K. and K. Matsumoto. (2014) "Renewable Energy-Related Policies and Institutions in Japan: Before and After the Fukushima Nuclear Accident and the Feed-In Tariff introduction." In *Legal Issues*

of Renewable Energy in the Asia Region: Recent Development in a Post-Fukushima and Post-Kyoto Protocol Era, edited by Anton M.Z. Gao and C.T. Fan, 3–28. Alphen aan den Rijn: Kluwer Law International.

Ren, J. and B.K. Sovacool. (2014) "Quantifying, Measuring, and Strategizing Energy Security: Determining the Most Meaningful Dimensions and Metrics." *Energy* 76: 838–849.

Ren, J. and B.K. Sovacool. (2015) "Prioritizing Low-carbon Energy Sources to Enhance China's Energy Security." *Energy Conversion and Management* 92: 129–136.

Selvakkumaran, S. and B. Limmeechokchai. (2013) "Energy Security and Co-Benefits of Energy Efficiency Improvement in Three Asian Countries." *Renewable and Sustainable Energy Reviews* 20: 491–503.

Shannon, C.E. (1948) "A Mathematical Theory of Communication." *Bell System Technical Journal* 27: 379–423.

Sharifuddin, S. (2014) "Methodology for Quantitatively Assessing the Energy Security of Malaysia and Other Southeast Asian Countries." *Energy Policy* 65: 574–582.

Shin, J., W.-S. Shin, and C. Lee. (2013) "An Energy Security Management Model Using Quality Function Deployment and System Dynamics." *Energy Policy* 54: 72–86.

Takase, K. and T. Suzuki. (2011) "The Japanese Energy Sector: Current Situation, and Future Paths." *Energy Policy* 39: 6731–6744.

Thangavelu, S.R., A.M. Khambadkone, and I.A. Karimi. (2015) "Long-Term Optimal Energy Mix Planning Towards High Energy Security and Low GHG Emission." *Applied Energy* 154: 959–969.

World Bank. (2015) "World Governance Indicators." Accessed June 16, 2015, http://databank.worldbank.org/data/reports.aspx?source=worldwide-governance-indicators#.

Wu, Kang. (2014) "China's Energy Security: Oil and Gas." *Energy Policy* 73: 4–11.

Yao, L. and Y. Chang. (2014) "Energy Security in China: A Quantitative Analysis and Policy Implications." *Energy Policy* 67: 595–604.

31

Transformations for sustainable development in Asia and the Pacific[1]

Hitomi Rankine, Kareff Rafisura and José A. Puppim de Oliveira

The need for a transformation to sustainable development

The world is entering into a new era of discussions about development, what it means, how to promote it and how to evaluate progress. With the 2030 Agenda for Sustainable Development released in 2015 (UN, 2015), the world's leaders committed to unprecedented *transformation*. "Transformation" here is defined as a change in society that alters the "fundamental attributes of a system (including value systems; regulatory, legislative, or bureaucratic regimes; financial institutions; and technological or biological systems)" (IPCC, 2012, p. 3). The understanding that transformative rather than incremental changes are needed goes beyond the political realm – scientists also agree that "transformation" is an appropriate term to describe the extent of the changes needed, as in a recent IPCC report that states: "Actions that range from incremental steps to transformational changes are essential for reducing risk from climate extremes" (Field et al., 2012, p. 20).

The 2030 Agenda describes a better future in several dimensions, from poverty, hunger and want, where there is universal literacy, peace, security, and safe and healthy environments. A future in which all life can thrive, children are invested in and there is universal access to quality education and health care. And a future in which the rights of all are also respected, the use of all natural resources takes place at a sustainable rate, humanity lives in harmony with nature and critical ecosystems are protected.

The core of the Agenda proposes 17 Sustainable Development Goals (SDGs) to be achieved by 2030 (UN, 2015):

Goal 1. End poverty in all its forms everywhere
Goal 2. End hunger, achieve food security and improved nutrition and promote sustainable agriculture
Goal 3. Ensure healthy lives and promote well-being for all at all ages
Goal 4. Ensure inclusive and equitable quality education and promote lifelong learning opportunities for all

Goal 5. Achieve gender equality and empower all women and girls
Goal 6. Ensure availability and sustainable management of water and sanitation for all
Goal 7. Ensure access to affordable, reliable, sustainable and modern energy for all
Goal 8. Promote sustained, inclusive and sustainable economic growth, full and productive employment and decent work for all
Goal 9. Build resilient infrastructure, promote inclusive and sustainable industrialization and foster innovation
Goal 10. Reduce inequality within and among countries
Goal 11. Make cities and human settlements inclusive, safe, resilient and sustainable
Goal 12. Ensure sustainable consumption and production patterns
Goal 13. Take urgent action to combat climate change and its impacts
Goal 14. Conserve and sustainably use the oceans, seas and marine resources for sustainable development
Goal 15. Protect, restore and promote sustainable use of terrestrial ecosystems, sustainably manage forests, combat desertification, and halt and reverse land degradation and halt biodiversity loss
Goal 16. Promote peaceful and inclusive societies for sustainable development, provide access to justice for all and build effective, accountable and inclusive institutions at all levels
Goal 17. Strengthen the means of implementation and revitalize the global partnership for sustainable development.

The 2030 Agenda is an evolution in the discussions about development. Between 2000 and 2015, the Millennium Development Goals (MDGs) were the main guiding principles to measure development achievements and guide development policies, particularly at the international level. The commitments toward the MDGs were mostly applicable to developing countries, as the wealthier countries had achieved them already. The (new) 2030 Agenda proposes more ambitious goals, which are relevant for both developing and developed countries. The meaning of "developed countries" was also blurred, as no country can be considered fully developed in face of the SDGs.

Although people are now wealthier, better nourished and more educated than they were 15 years ago, the world remains far off a sustainable path. Commenting on the progress since the establishment of the MDGs in 2000, the United Nations Secretary-General's synthesis report on the post-2015 development agenda pointed out:

> "Amid great plenty for some, we witness pervasive poverty, gross inequalities, joblessness, disease and deprivation for billions . . . . The impacts of the global economic, food and energy crises are still being felt. The consequences of climate change have only just begun."
>
> *(UN, 2014)*

In that future, the 17 Sustainable Development Goals (SDGs) and targets that comprise the 2030 Agenda "are integrated and indivisible and balance the three dimensions of sustainable development." Through these ambitious goals, multiple co-benefits are expected across the economic, social and environmental dimensions of the development process (Puppim de Oliveira, 2013).

Until now, co-benefits across the three dimensions of sustainable development have been elusive. Nature and people are often treated as externalities in economic decision-making, for instance. Environmental resources are often given zero value and are believed to be infinite. Human rights are treated as negotiable or applicable on a case-by-case basis. As a result, both public and private investments can erode rather than build and sustain environmental, human and social well-being. Changes in economic structures do not always provide the best outcomes for people and the planet, and patterns of resource use do not reflect their finite nature.

The Asia-Pacific (AP) region is fundamental to the implementation of the 2030 Agenda and toward achieving the SDGs, as more than 50 percent of the world's population is concentrated in the region. Moreover, the region is responsible for a growing part of the economy and greenhouse gas emissions, which can set the pace for the future of sustainable development not only in the region, but worldwide.

Transformations for sustainable development must be based on the reform of the relationships between the environment, the economy and society in the AP region. New mindsets and behaviors, incentives and shared values must work toward a sustainable future. Thus, this chapter discusses the challenges and opportunities toward transformative change in the Asia-Pacific region, in line with the 2030 Agenda for Sustainable Development, in light of the regional megatrends, such as urbanization, rising incomes, changing consumption patterns and economic and trade integration.

Regional megatrends and sustainable development

The 2030 Agenda for Sustainable Development provides guidance and direction setting, but the responses need to be fine-tuned and adapted to the realities of the region and each country. The political consensus at the Paris Conference of Parties (COP) of the United Nations Framework Convention on Climate Change (UNFCCC) sets the stage for governments, markets, businesses and individuals to foster a transformation that was previously thought beyond reach. However, what kind of transformation and how to foster them need to be better understood. In the context of AP, there are many trends that are important to shaping the development path of the region. How we can better grasp those trends can help us to understand the transformation needed to compel the region toward a more sustainable path to achieve the SDGs.

The potential for this transformation to quickly take root in the region should not be underestimated. The region is now home to more than half of the global population and produces almost 40 percent of the world's gross domestic product (GDP) (UNESCAP, ADB and UNDP, 2017). This is a region of people on the move, who are better educated, have greater purchasing power, enjoy improved quality of life and have access to information and communications technology that has allowed the spread of new opportunities, social connections and ideas. Intraregional trade and investment flows now shape infrastructure development and spur private sector growth and economic structural changes in almost every sub-region. More inclusive forms of governance are beginning to address sustainability crises (Zusman et al., 2014; Berkhout et al., 2009).

But there remains a less positive side to this progress. The region's contributions to global CO_2 emissions more than doubled between 1990 and 2012 (Figure 31.1). Development paths across the region are characterized by high resource intensity, increasingly evident resource constraints, widening income and social inequalities and persistently unmet needs (UNESCAP, 2014b). The extraction of resources to meet the needs (and demands) of an expanding consuming class as well as to use in infrastructure development influences global resource-use trends.

Regional overviews of sustainable development have also highlighted the shared concern that the considerable economic potential will not benefit all – and that deepened social divisions as well as other dimensions of social and demographic change will lead to social and political conflicts (see for example, UNESCAP, 2014b).

Of the 56 countries in the Asia-Pacific region covered by this chapter (ESCAP members until end of 2015, see the complete list at www.unescap.org/about/member-states), 12 retain

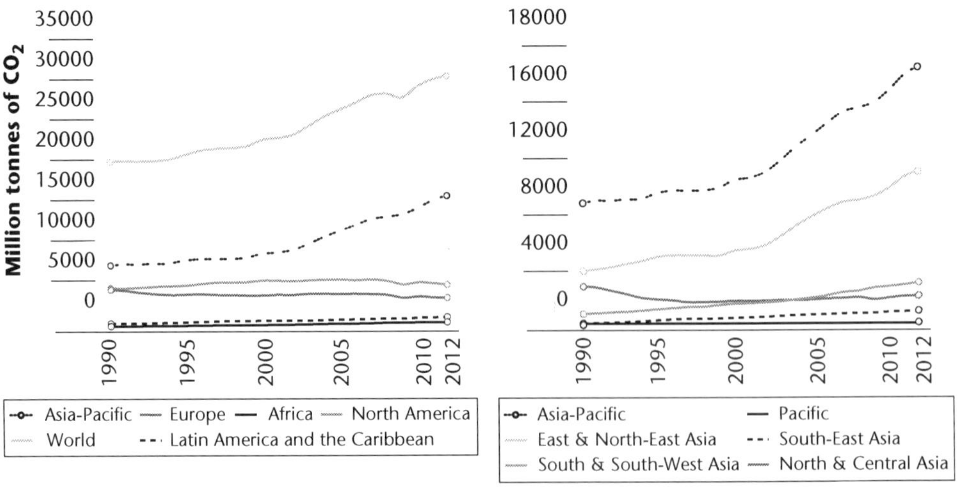

Figure 31.1 Asia and the Pacific's contributions to global CO emissions from fuel combustion, 1990–2012

Source: ESCAP Asia Pacific Energy Portal, based on data from the International Energy Agenda, CO emissions from fuel combustion statistics.

Box 31.1 The fate of the Aral Sea

In the summer of 2014, the eastern basin of the Aral Sea went completely dry – for the first time in 600 years – due to farmland irrigation. In 2005, a World Bank-funded dam and restoration project began in Kazakhstan with the goal of improving the health of the Aral Sea. Since then, the water level has risen and salinity has decreased. Yet, 2014 satellite images (below) indicate that the cyclical drying appears to continue, particularly in the eastern basin.

22 August 1964

20 August 2000

19 August 2014

Source: NASA Earth. Observatory, 2015.

least developed country status. Some 400 million people living in extreme income poverty ($1.90 per day, 2011 PPP) between 2010 and 2013 (UNESCAP, ADB, UNDP, 2017), 1.5 billion people are without access to sanitation, and approximately 277 million people are without access to an improved water supply in 2015 (UNESCAP, 2015b). Economic expansion has not benefited all – millions of workers are vulnerable, and the numbers of working poor are increasing. The vulnerable employment rate in Asia-Pacific was 54 percent, or 1 billion workers, in 2015 (UNESCAP, 2016).

The economic structures across the region are strongly resource dependent. The resources used within the region have tripled since 1990 (UNEP, 2015). Resource-efficiency improvements, where they exist (in energy and water use mostly), have not been enough to compensate for the increase in the consumption of these resources. In some countries that use the largest proportions of their water resources, water use per capita is quite low and can be expected to grow (UNESCAP, UNEP, UNU and IGES, 2016). Across the region are signs of resource use beyond capacity. The Aral Sea, for instance, remains a symbol of environmental catastrophe (Box 31.1).

There are still shortcomings in the capacity to deal with the most fundamental aspects of environmental quality, such as air pollution (Figure 31.2). Biodiversity loss is a direct impact of habitat loss related to resource use, in particular deforestation, which still impacts the region, especially South-East Asia (Figure 31.3).

Environmental constraints and ecosystem changes are part of a business-as-usual future that will impact everyone. Without urgent intervention, these environmental pressures and changes will have immediate impact on water supplies, with growing pressure due to population growth, rapid urbanization, industrialization and economic expansion; and rural livelihoods and food security, including through impacts on fish stocks (Box 31.2).

Future resource constraints will be a major concern for this region. Rising consumption, economic expansion and natural resource constraints are already aggravating geopolitical tensions in the region. Economic structures, investment patterns and resource constraints that affect the most vulnerable of populations are likely to lead to social tension and constrained economic growth and dynamism.

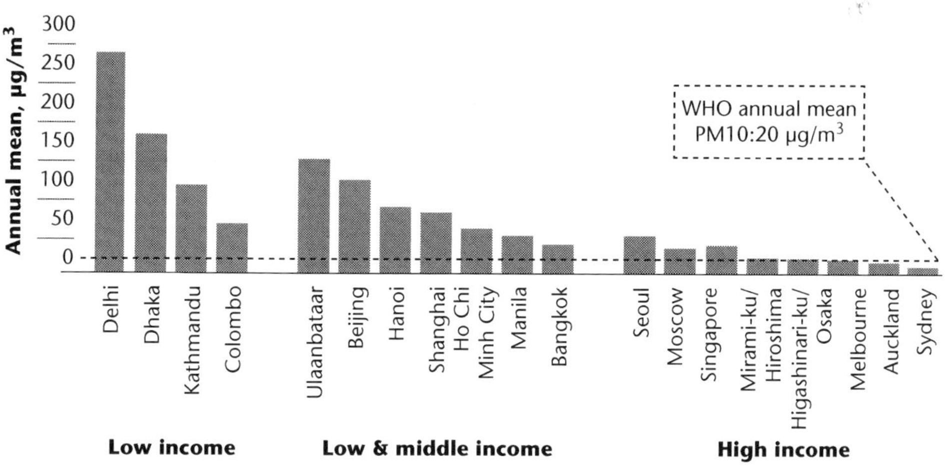

Figure 31.2 Ambient (outdoor) air pollution in selected cities, 2008–2013

Source: World Health Organization ambient (outdoor) air pollution data in cities, 2014. See www.who.int/phe/health_topics/outdoorair/databases/cities/en/.

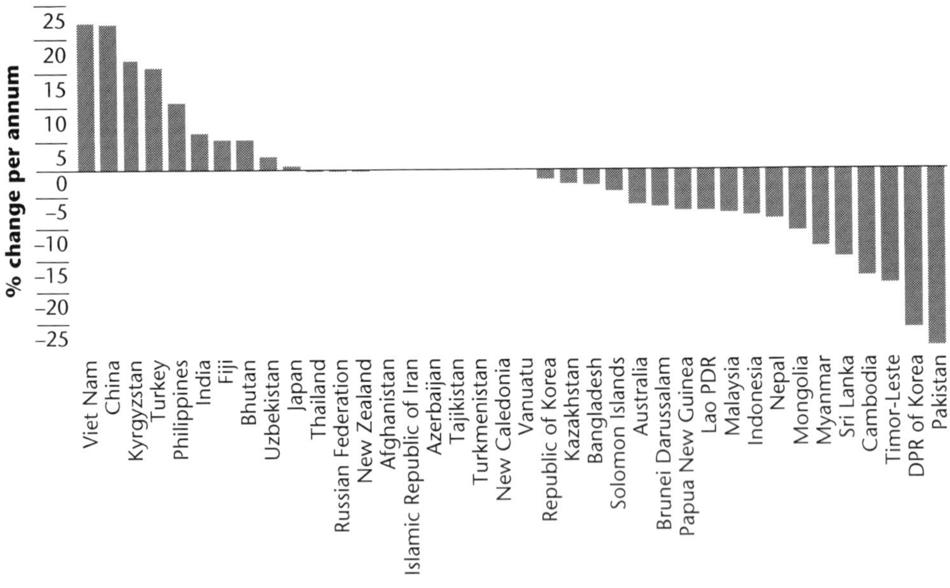

Figure 31.3 Percentage change in forest cover, 2000–2012

Source: ESCAP statistical database, based on FAOSTAT and Global Forest Resource Assessment 2010.

Box 31.2 Oceans: the region's coral reefs at risk

The region has vast areas of coastal and marine ecosystems, which are critical for livelihoods and food security. Major threats to coral reefs from climate change are the increase in sea surface temperature (such as coral bleaching) and ocean acidification.[a] Ocean acidification may increase by 170 percent by the end of the century, bringing significant ecosystem and economic losses. At this rate, coral reef erosion is likely to outpace reef building sometime this century.[b] These environmental changes particularly threaten the coastal communities and economies of Australia, New Zealand, the Pacific island countries and countries in East and North-East Asia.

Source: [a] UNEP, 2015; [b] International Council for Science, n.d.

Among the rapid changes in the region, there are four regional trends that have defined the development outcomes:

- rapid urbanization,
- economic structure change,
- trade and economic integration,
- rising income and changing consumption patterns.

These megatrends are transformative forces by nature, hence their power to either improve or undermine the prospects for achieving sustainable development.

Rapid urbanization

The Asia-Pacific region added nearly one billion people to the urban population between 1990 and 2014. Urban growth will continue to be significant, with half of the population expected to be urban by 2018. Seventeen of the world's 28 megacities are here; in 2030 the region may have 22 megacities (UN-Habitat and ESCAP, 2015).

Urbanization processes are instrumental in the transformation for sustainable development because of the dominant contribution of cities to economic and population growth and the pressure to deliver infrastructure and basic services (housing, services, transport and commercial space) in short periods of time. Besides the specific SDG 11, the way countries urbanize affects most of the SDGs, such as SDG 3 (health), SDG 6 (water) and SDG 13 (climate change).

For example, urbanization and associated lifestyle changes increase the demand for material consumption, drive land-use change and greenhouse gas emissions (Sethi and Puppim de Oliveira, 2015). Whether urbanization becomes a positive force for sustainable development depends on actions and investment decisions taken now to prevent the entrenchment of high-carbon, resource-intensive path dependencies and social divisions in cities and beyond (see Box 31.3).

A commitment to sustainable development is a commitment to shared prosperity and environmental protection. Asian and Pacific cities must become places in which environmental protection and an enhanced quality of life for all (with good access to services provided by high-quality, resource-efficient infrastructure and vibrant economies) are mutually supportive.

Economic structure change

With rapid urbanization, there has been rapid economic growth and structural change. How the economy grows have an important impact on 2030 Agenda. SDG 1 (end poverty) and SDG 3 (end hunger) depend heavily on how countries grow and how the material benefits are distributed.

Many countries in the region began transitioning from agriculture biomass-based economies to modern industrial and service economies in the 1970s. The share of agriculture as a percentage of regional GDP has halved, from 14 percent in 1970 to 7 percent in 2012, while the contribution of services rose from 46 percent to 59 percent. The share of industry declined during that time, from around 40 percent to 34 percent (UNESCAP, 2014c).

The economies of Japan, Hong Kong (China), the Republic of Korea, Singapore and Taiwan Province of China have completed the transition from developing to developed high income regions. While their experiences have been diverse, these economies have similar features: economic growth that outpaced the rest of the world; changing sectoral composition toward a diminished share of agriculture in GDP; and a dramatic increase in labor productivity.

On the other hand, the economic transition of the Asia-Pacific region has been accompanied by significant increases in the consumption of natural resources, making the region the largest user of materials since 2003, which can undermine the achievement of some of the SDGs, such as SDG 13 (climate change). The continuing transformation of the economies has long-term implications for the increasing resource use and the region's material footprint, depending on where investments are directed, the types of infrastructure that are built to support economic growth and the governance mechanisms used to manage the tension between the environmental risks and economic opportunities, especially those related to resource extraction.

Economic structural changes have been accompanied by labor productivity (output per person employed) increases. During 2000–2014, labor productivity increased more rapidly in Asia and the Pacific than in any other region in the world (3.2 percent per year relative to the global average of 1.1 percent). The average annual growth rate in labor productivity since 2000

Box 31.3 Urban–rural carbon disparities

Cities have been recognized as key to the governance of climate change.* As the world takes an unprecedented rural–urban population tilt, the twenty-first century poses a challenge for tackling disparities in access and allocation of carbon between urban and rural areas. Urbanization is historically correlated with the massive use of fossil fuel initiated by the Industrial Revolution. Some carbon accounts are strongly associated with production and consumption of energy within cities, indicating that more than 70 percent of the global greenhouse gases are produced within urban areas and consume 60–80 percent of final energy use globally.

In addition to the global North–South economic divide, there is a stronger component of urban–rural spatial disparity in the making. Evidence based on analyses of data from more than 200 countries over five decades shows that the rates of urbanization are more correlated with carbon emissions than with wealth (GDP per capita). Urbanized middle-income countries emit carbon per capita similarly to richer countries. This urban–rural divide is likely to further precipitate into a much local but complex dynamic, particularly relevant to the developing world, which faces the double challenge of rapid urbanization and environmental sustainability. This has implications for designing a fair global regime for tackling climate change and achieving the Sustainable Development Goals due to ethical, empirical and governance gaps related to the urban–rural carbon dynamic.

The issue is of serious concern for urban areas in the developing world. As these countries urbanize, the contributions of carbon emissions and greenhouse gases from their cities become disproportionately high in comparison with their population share and wealth. Most of the population growth for the remainder of this century reportedly will occur in urban areas of low- and middle-income nations. UN-Habitat and ESCAP's *State of Asian and Pacific Cities 2015* report has pointed out that Asia alone added one billion urban dwellers in 30 years (1980–2010), more than the population of Western Europe and the United States combined. And it is expected to add another billion by 2040.

Thus, a radical and urgent transformation in the way we build our cities is necessary to avoid a disproportional increase in carbon emissions and inequalities between rural and urban emissions. The inclusion of cities in Sustainable Development Goals 11 offers an opportunity to promote solutions for sustainable cities globally. It also hands leaders the responsibility to impose ecological limits that affect people and the environment beyond their borders.

There are immense barriers in changing urbanization paths, however. For example, India, the next large urbanization frontier, has many political, financial and institutional challenges to changing its urbanization patterns. There is an urgent need to catalyze and scale up innovations that provide adequate housing, energy access, transportation and economic opportunities for its growing urban population in a sustainable manner. The climate co-benefits would be immense from changes towards more sustainable urbanization patterns, but the institutions and capabilities in place need to be strengthened to lead the transformation.

Source: Sethi and Puppim de Oliveira (2015).

was greatest in Azerbaijan, followed by Armenia, Georgia, Kazakhstan and Timor-Leste (UNESCAP, 2016). Economies that experienced a high rate of labor productivity increases (Japan, the Republic of Korea and Taiwan Province of China) have also experienced a rapid increase of consumption and improvements in living standards. At the same time, however, labor participation rates have been higher for men than women in most countries.

Increases in labor productivity are important for growth, but are also linked with the phenomenon of jobless growth that is a regional concern. In many places, labor productivity improvements have been achieved due to increased inputs of energy and capital-intensive investment. Expansion of economic activity in new sectors as well as investments in labor-intensive, high-value "green" sectors (such as renewable energy) will help to increase an economy's capacity to create new jobs while increasing labor productivity, creating more employment and reducing environmental pressures (UNIDO, 2013).

Sustainable development requires that an economy's capacity to create decent jobs is increased and that economic activities and lifestyles become less resource intensive and more resource efficient.

Trade and economic integration

Global trade is characterized by increasing levels of integration, with Asia the fulcrum of the emerging trade architecture (Ernst & Young, 2014). Since the 1970s, the opening up of several economies has been a huge part of the region's economic transition story—China in the late 1970s, Vietnam in the late 1980s and, recently, Mongolia and Myanmar. Without exception, their transition toward market economies was followed by a period of increase in trade, rapid integration with the outside economy and economic growth. How the process of economic integration happens influences the achievement of the SDGs, such as SDG 8 (decent employment) and SDG 10 (reduction of inequality among countries).

Many countries are negotiating major trade agreements. A 2014 report from the Economic and Social Commission of Asia and the Pacific (UNESCAP, 2014a) described the region as "the most dynamic pole of the global economy," with around 60 percent of the 262 preferential trade agreements that were in force at that time (UNESCAP, 2015a). Intraregional foreign direct investment is also expanding in importance (UNESCAP, 2014a).

However, many of those agreements focus mostly on the economic benefits, and less on the social and environmental sustainability of an increase in trade. This could undermine the achievement of some goals, as SDG 12 (sustainable production and consumption). More regional cooperation on trade would beget both benefits (technology and information transfer and investments in green technologies) and risks to the environment (resource extraction and greater movement of goods and services). Trade integration will not automatically support sustainable development – it requires establishing the upward convergence of environmental standards (a race to the top rather than to the bottom) as an intrinsic feature of trade agreements.

Regional economic relationships must encourage a competitiveness that is defined by high levels of environmental quality and reduced environmental risk, shared prosperity and decent jobs for all so that markets deliver expanded opportunities.

Rising incomes and changing consumption patterns

Rapid economic growth has resulted in the expansion of the consuming class, which in turn has stimulated strong consumption growth (OECD, 2013). Although there is no agreed definition of what constitutes a consuming class, it is often understood to be associated with the middle class, whose numbers range from 500 million to 1 billion, according to Asian Development Bank (ADB) estimates (ADB, 2010, p. 48). Asia is expected to soon have a larger middle class than North America and Europe combined, has reportedly become the world's second-wealthiest region, and is projected to soon overtake North America. How the increase in consumption occurs can have implications for many SDGs, particularly SDG 12 (sustainable production and consumption) and SDG 13 (climate change).

The environmental consequences are not insignificant – the consuming class demand for energy, goods, metals and water will put considerable pressure on natural resources and the environment (ADB, 2010). Private demand will have implications for the demand of public services and infrastructure (more cars need expansion of roads and related infrastructure; larger houses increase demand for electricity and water).

With better education and awareness of environmental issues, the new consumers could become a driving force for sustainable development transformations via their purchasing and investment decisions. But this will require innovations in the provisions of services and goods and nudging social preferences toward sustainable choices.

Fostering transformations for sustainable development

The regional megatrends as they develop now will most likely benefit the region in the short term. However, without transformations in social justice, investment flows, economic structural change and resource use patterns, ultimately these megatrends will impede achievement of many the SDGs.

Resource efficiency transformations seek to bring together the objectives of environmental protection, economic growth and social progress to ensure that economic activity stays within the environmental limits and that all people have the potential to access the resources that they need (Daly, 2003). In the context of urbanization trends, such a transformation would call the attention of city governments to focus on infrastructure that uses energy, water and other resources efficiently and services that promote resource-efficient and low-waste lifestyles. In the context of trade and economic integration, resource efficiency transformation will foster a region less vulnerable to fluctuations in resource prices and constraints and environmental risks. As incomes rise and consumption patterns change, resource efficiency transformation will hopefully shift consumer preferences and producer behavior toward more sustainable choices and lifestyles.

Social justice transformation will move people from the periphery to the center of economic and other decisions, ensuring that all people have access to the services and resources they need. By ensuring that human rights are respected, that people have a voice in decisions that impact them and that they have access to information, countries in the Asia and the Pacific will become places that enhance the well-being of all in the transformation processes (Meadowcroft, 2011; Brand et al., 2013), and be able to achieve the SDGs. Regional trade and economic integration processes can be strengthened by human and social capital that are invested in rather than degraded; environmental protection and access to natural resources will be maintained for local populations who most need them. Rising incomes and changing consumption patterns can also enhance well-being for all rather than entrench social differences.

Transformations in investment flows have to ensure that investments in environmental protection and natural capital are given greater priority and promote a higher quality of economic growth. Through a reshaping of markets and other incentives, countries can attract investments to infrastructure and services that are more resource efficient and promote a higher quality of life while reducing environmental risks. The expanded investment flows that are expected to accompany regional trade and economic integration could be attracted to "greener" economic activities and practices, driving growth that is in greater alignment with sustainable development outcomes. Consumers should have ample access to choices that are more in line with sustainable development as well, so they can make better more sustainable decisions.

Economic structure transformations will boost the productive capacities of the AP region on the basis of sustainable consumption and production patterns and more equitable distribution of the benefits of economic growth. By changing the incentive frameworks and capacity of economies to diversify toward more resource-efficient products and services that need higher value-added employment, innovative business models that prioritize social capital and environmental protection can be scaled up as countries grow and as economies integrate and intraregional trade expands. Technological innovation can shift the balance of economic inputs so that human capital, skills development and a focus on resource efficiency can complement and strengthen ongoing sectoral shifts.

These transformations are mutually supportive and linked. They comprise essential requirements for achieving the 2030 Agenda for Sustainable Development and for much-needed policy coherence, which will reduce the potential for trade-offs between the SDGs.

Making the transformation: governance, capacities and regional action

The 2030 Agenda for Sustainable Development embodies the global consensus on the need to pursue a transformative development agenda. The *Transformations for Sustainable Development* underscores that successful transformations require vertical (top to bottom) and horizontal (across actors) alliances among governments, technology innovators, market actors and citizens. It recognizes that that there is not one not one regional solution, but there are common governance capacities that are needed to make the transformation to sustainable development.

Governments in the Asia and the Pacific need to take the lead and develop their capacities to set clear direction for transformation, implement structural changes and manage the transformation process.

The successful sustainability initiatives taking place already in the Asia-Pacific demonstrate the crucial role of an active government for catalyzing transformations in various economic, social and political contexts by envisioning, empowering and nurturing alternatives to business-as-usual development. Effective government leadership is needed to manage the politically complex nature of transformation. But a government acting alone will not succeed – transformations need a dynamic private sector, engaged citizens and active civil societies.

While the most critical actions to bring out transformations for sustainable development need to happen at the national and local level; the role of regional platforms and alliances will be also critical. The region's megatrends described in the previous sections, will have strong influence on the environment's health in the coming decades. Managing sustainable development requires pulling megatrends into alignment with the needed transformative shifts to achieve the SDGs. This begins with making existing regional integration efforts in trade, investment and infrastructure consistent with sustainable development. These integration efforts hold enormous potential once they are framed by the three dimensions (economic, social and environmental) of sustainable development.

Transformational alliances to implement the 2030 Agenda need to be forged beyond national boundaries – energy systems, transport systems and resource-exploitation regimes are all influenced by national and international norms and agreements. Hence, many policy and market changes will be more effective if implemented across national boundaries. For example, rules and instruments that are affected by regional trade and investment agreements (intellectual property rights, investment policies, resource pricing and supply chain regulations) need to be harmonized to facilitate a race to the top, or the upward convergence of environmental standards that impact positively on social standards. Trade integration should establish mechanisms to promote resource productivity and sustainability across the entire production and supply chains.

Regional action can also be an important support for countries that have technical capacity and resource constraints to fully implement the 2030 Agenda. In 2017, governments in the Asia-Pacific adopted road map for regional cooperation on implementing the 2030 Agenda for Sustainable

Development in this regard. The road map identifies priority areas for regional cooperation around social development, disaster risk reduction, climate change, management of natural resources, connectivity and energy. It also lays down implementation arrangements and a process to track progress on the Sustainable Development Goals (SDGs).

Good practices that can contribute to transformations are emerging and can be adopted across the region through peer learning. Finally, regional action can potentially facilitate convergence around norms and values that are critical to sustainable development – human rights; the centrality of human beings to sustainable development; the importance of the environment for current and future generations; and participation of all citizens.

Note

1 This chapter is based on chapter 1 of the report 'Transformations for sustainable development: Promoting environmental sustainability in Asia and the Pacific 2015' published in 2016 by the United Nations Economic and Social Commission for Asia and the Pacific (ESCAP), the United Nations Environment Programme (UNEP), the United Nations University (UNU), and the Institute for Global Environmental Strategies (IGES). The report can be downloaded at: www.unescap.org/publications/transformation-for-sdg/.

References

Asian Development Bank (ADB) (2010). The Rise of Asia's Middle Class: Key Indicators for Asia and the Pacific 2010. Manila, ADB. Available from www.adb.org/sites/. . ./ki2010-special-chapter.pdf.

Berkhout, F., D. Angel, and A.J. Wieczorek (2009). Asian development pathways and sustainable socio-technical regimes. Technological Forecasting and Social Change, vol. 76, No. 2, pp. 218–228.

Brand, U., et al. (2013). Debating transformation in multiple crises. In World Social Science Report 2013: Changing Global Environments. Paris, Organisation for Economic Co-operation and Development and UNESCO Publishing. Available from dx.doi.org/10.1787/9789264203419-90-en.

Daly, H.E. (2003). Ecological Economics: The Concept of Scale and its Relation to Allocation, Distribution, and Uneconomic Growth. Available from www.greeneconomics.net/2003HDaly.pdf.

Ernst & Young (2014). Rethinking private banking in Asia-Pacific. An EY Discussion Paper for Bank Executives. Available from www.ey.com/Publication/vwLUAssets/Rethinking_private_banking_in_Asia-Pacific/$File/Rethinking%20private%20banking%20in%20Asia-Pacific%20%20Web%20Version%20.pdf.

Field, C.B., et al. (2012). Managing the Risks of Extreme Events and Disasters to Advance Climate Change Adaptation. A Special Report of Working Groups I and II of the Intergovernmental Panel on Climate Change. Cambridge, UK and New York, Cambridge University Press.

Intergovernmental Panel on Climate Change (IPCC) (2012). Summary for policymakers. In Managing the Risks of Extreme Events and Disasters to Advance Climate Change Adaptation, C.B. Field, and others, eds. A Special Report of Working Groups I and II of the Intergovernmental Panel on Climate Change. Cambridge, UK and New York, Cambridge University Press, pp. 1–19.

Meadowcroft, J. (2011). Engaging with the politics of sustainability transitions. Environmental Innovation and Societal Transitions, vol. 1, No. 1, pp. 70–75.

Organisation for Economic Co-operation and Development (OECD) (2013). Southeast Asian Economic Outlook 2013: With Perspectives on China and India. Paris: OECD. Available from www.oecd.org/dev/asia-pacific/Pocket%20Edition%20SAEO2013.pdf.

Puppim de Oliveira, J.A. (2013). Learning how to align climate, environmental and development objectives in cities: Lessons from the implementation of climate co-benefits initiatives in urban Asia. Journal of Cleaner Production, vol. 58, pp. 7–14.

Sethi, M. and Puppim de Oliveira, Jose A. (2015). From global 'North–South' to local 'Urban–Rural': A shifting paradigm in climate governance? Urban Climate (Elsevier), vol. 14, No. 4, pp. 529–543.

United Nations (UN) (2014). The Road to Dignity by 2030: Ending Poverty, Transforming All Lives and Protecting the Planet. Synthesis Report of the Secretary-General on the Post-2015 Agenda. Sales No. A/69/700. Available from www.un.org/ga/search/view_doc.asp?symbol=A/69/700&Lang=E.

United Nations (UN) (2015). Resolution A/RES/70/1 adopted by the General Assembly at its Seventieth session on September 25, 2015. Transforming our world: the 2030 Agenda for Sustainable Development. Available from https://sustainabledevelopment.un.org/post2015/transformingourworld.

United Nations, Economic and Social Commission for Asia and the Pacific (UNESCAP) (2014a). Asia Pacific Trade and Investment Report 2014. Bangkok.

United Nations, Economic and Social Commission for Asia and the Pacific (UNESCAP) (2014b). Fostering Sustainable Development in Asia and the Pacific: Note by the Secretariat for the Asia-Pacific Forum on Sustainable Development. Sales No. E/ESCAP/FSD/1.

United Nations, Economic and Social Commission for Asia and the Pacific (UNESCAP) (2014c). Statistical Yearbook for Asia and the Pacific 2014. (ST/ESCAP/2704). Available from www.uis.unesco.org/Library/Documents/statistical-yearbook-asia-pacific-country-profiles-education-2014-en.pdf.

United Nations, Economic and Social Commission for Asia and the Pacific (UNESCAP) (2015a). Economic and Social Survey of Asia and the Pacific 2015 – Part II: Balancing the Three Dimensions of Sustainable Development: From Integration to Implementation. Available from www.unescap.org/sites/default/files/survey2015-pt2-cs71-theme-study.pdf.

United Nations, Economic and Social Commission for Asia and the Pacific (UNESCAP) (2015b). Statistical Yearbook for Asia and the Pacific 2015. Bangkok.

United Nations, Economic and Social Commission for Asia and the Pacific (UNESCAP) (2016). Economic and Social Survey of the Asia and the Pacific 2016. Bangkok: United Nations.

United Nations Environment Programme (UNEP) Inquiry (2015). Aligning the Financial Systems in the Asia Pacific Region to Sustainable Development. Jakarta: UNEP Inquiry. Available from www.switch-asia.eu/fileadmin/user_upload/Publications/2015/Unep-Inquiry_Asia_Finance_Final.pdf.

United Nations-Habitat and Economic and Social Commission for Asia and the Pacific (2015). The State of Asian and Pacific Cities 2015. Bangkok. Available from www.unescap.org/resources/state-asian-and-pacific-cities-2015-urban-transformations-shifting-quantity-quality.

UNESCAP, ADB and UNDP (2017). Eradicating Poverty and Promoting Prosperity in a Changing Asia-Pacific. Bangkok: United Nations.

UNESCAP, UNEP, UNU and IGES (2016). Transformations for Sustainable Development: Promoting Environmental Sustainability in Asia and the Pacific. Bangkok: United Nations. Available from www.unescap.org/publications/transformations-sustainable-development-promoting-environmental-sustainability-asia-and.

United Nations Industrial Development Organization (UNIDO) and Agence Francaise de Developpement (2013). Green Growth: From Labour to resource productivity, Best Practice Examples, Initiatives and Policy Options. Paris. Available from www.greengrowthknowledge.org/resource/green-growth-labour-resource-productivity-best-practice-examples-initiatives-and-policy.

Zusman, E., et al. (2014). Governing Sustainability Transitions in Asia: Cases from Japan, Indonesia and Thailand. ECO: The Korean Journal of Environmental Sociology, vol. 18. Available from http://pub.iges.or.jp/modules/envirolib/view.php?docid=5585.

Index